*Encyclopedia of*
# THE RENAISSANCE
# AND THE REFORMATION

REVISED EDITION

*Encyclopedia of*
# THE RENAISSANCE
# AND THE REFORMATION

## REVISED EDITION

Thomas G. Bergin, Consulting Editor (first edition)

Jennifer Speake, General Editor

☑®
Facts On File, Inc.

**Encyclopedia of the Renaissance and the Reformation, Revised Edition**

Copyright © 2004, 1987  Market House Books Ltd

Facts On File, Inc.
132 West 31st Street
New York NY 10001

**Library of Congress Cataloging-in-Publication Data**

Bergin, Thomas Goddard, 1904-
Encyclopedia of the Renaissance and the Reformation / Thomas G.
Bergin, consulting editor; Jennifer Speake, general editor. – Rev. ed.
p. cm.
Rev. ed. of Encyclopedia of the Renaissance / Thomas G. Bergin,
Jennifer Speake. c1987.
Includes bibliographical references (p.) and index.
ISBN 0-8160-5451-7
1. Renaissance–Encyclopedias. 2. Reformation–Encyclopedias.
I. Speake, Jennifer. II. Bergin, Thomas Goddard, 1904-   Encyclopedia
of the Renaissance. III. Title.
CB359.B47 2004
940.2'1'03–dc22
20030259974

Facts On File books are available at special discounts when purchased in
bulk quantities for businesses, associations, institutions, or sales
promotions. Please call our Special Sales Department in New York
at (212) 967-8800 or (800) 322-8755.

You can find Facts On File on the World Wide Web at htpp://www.factsonfile.com

Compiled and typeset by Market House Books Ltd, Aylesbury, UK

Printed in the United States of America

VB MH 10 9 8 7 6 5 4 3 2 1

This book is printed on acid-free paper

## GENERAL EDITOR

Jennifer Speake, MA, MPhil

## CONSULTING EDITOR (first edition)

Thomas G. Bergin, PhD, LHD, LittD, OBE (1904–1987)

## COORDINATING EDITOR

Jonathan Law, BA

## CONTRIBUTORS

D'Arcy Adrian-Vallance, BA
Evadne Adrian-Vallance, BA
Dr. Charles Avery, FSA
Daniel Bender, MA, PhD
Virginia Bonito, PhD
Paul Browne, MA
Andrew Connor, BA
Kevin De Ornellas, BA, MA, PhD
Graham Dixon, MA, BMus, PhD, FRCO
Ted Dumitrescu, DPhil
William E. Engel, PhD
Mark L. Evans, BA, PhD
Rosalind Fergusson, BA
David Ferraro, BA, MA
Stephen Freer, MA
Derek Gjertsen, BA
François-Xavier Gleyzon
Edward Gosselin, BA, MA, PhD
John Grace, MA, PhD

Dina Ickowicz, MA
Jonathan Law, BA
T. H. Long, MA
Arthur MacGregor, MA, MPhil, FSA
Chris Murray
Kate Murray, BA, MPhil
Andrew Pettegree, MA, DPhil
Andrew Pickering, BA, MA
David Pickering, MA
Sandra Raphael, BA, Dip Lib
Helen Rappaport, BA
Kenneth Scholes
J. B. Schultz, PhD
Mary Shields, PhD
Linda Proud Smith
Graham Speake, MA, DPhil
Jennifer Speake, MA, BPhil
David G. Wilkins, PhD
Edmund Wright, MA, DPhil

## PICTURE RESEARCH

Margaret Tuthill, BSc

## TYPESETTING

Anne Stibbs, BA

# CONTENTS

# PREFACE

The second edition of this encyclopedia, under its new title of *Encyclopedia of the Renaissance and the Reformation*, aims to capitalize on the strengths of its predecessor while also expanding its coverage of areas that have risen in prominence during the sixteen years since the first edition appeared. The first edition treated the controversies and course of the religious turmoil of the 16th century as background to the cultural developments, but with the inclusion of *Reformation* in the present title these have now become the subject of more focused examination. Over 200 entirely new entries have been written, and many existing ones enlarged, to take account of the widened scope.

Another aspect of which the new edition takes account is the recent upsurge of interest in women's history with a greatly increased coverage of this area and of social history generally. As the late Thomas G. Bergin implies in his Introduction to the first edition, all start and end limits for historical movements are necessarily porous. A slight relaxation of the previous end date—1620, or the Battle of the White Mountain—has enabled some useful threads to be further pursued, especially in the fields of music and science.

A short list of English-language Further Reading follows after many of the articles and a bibliography of more general works on the period has been supplied at the end of the book. However, information on the publishing history and reception of key Renaissance texts has been incorporated into the articles in line with the belief that the spread of both Renaissance and Reformation was, as far as we can reconstruct it, very largely a book-based dynamic. The flood of new ideas that the individual reader could tap into for him- or herself unleashed a potential that had hitherto been circumscribed by the authoritarian structures of the medieval Church or feudal society. In these movements lie the roots of the modern perception of the validity of the individual—which is what makes the study of them necessary and fruitful if we are to understand our own position in the continuum of Western civilization.

Jennifer Speake
October 2003

**Note:** The entries in this book are arranged alphabetically, with cross references to other relevant articles indicated by the use of SMALL CAPITALS. Although this arrangement is largely self-indexing, a separate index at the end of the book enables people mentioned in the text to be located. References to plate numbers are given in certain of the articles (e.g.: See Plate I). These refer to the section of color plates included at the center of the book.

# INTRODUCTION TO THE FIRST EDITION

The Renaissance, a vast cultural movement spanning some three centuries of European history, is so rich, so many-faceted, and so impressive in its achievements that it defies easy measurement or even accurate definition. An early aspect, and no doubt a determinant for the course of its development, was the rediscovery of the classics, studied without theological preconceptions for the first time since the dark ages. But, as Walter Pater (the nineteenth-century English critic) observed, the phenomenon of the Renaissance was of such complexity that humanism, as the cult of antiquity was styled, can be considered only one element or symptom. Indeed, even before the fourteenth century (the time of Petrarch, the pioneer of humanism) adumbrations of a new spirit were apparent in the culture of the Western world.

It is hard to imagine a figure more representative of what we have come to think of as "the Renaissance man" than the Emperor Frederick II—tolerant, inquisitive, and versatile—and born more than a century before Petrarch. The emergence of such a personality suggests that humanism was not spontaneously generated but had its roots in a combination of social, political and intellectual impulses that must have been at work in the collective subconscious of Europe, or at least of Italy, where the great movement had its beginnings.

Whatever may have been its genesis, the contributions of this dynamic age are manifold and spectacular. It was a period of exploration, inquiry, renovation, and renewal, characterized by a unique vitality. It is to the Renaissance that we owe the discovery of America and the Indies, the invention of printing, the Protestant Reformation, and in the field of arts and letters the unrivaled achievements of Michelangelo, Leonardo, Dante, Petrarch, and Boccacio; overflowing the boundaries of its Italian birthplace, its genius later appeared in Montaigne, Shakespeare, and Cervantes, to invigorate the arts throughout Europe.

Perhaps more important than any individual inspiration, the Renaissance brought a new sense of freedom and a new appreciation of man and his potential: a legacy that has been the precious patrimony of all succeeding generations. For historians the age of the Renaissance had an ending, as all human things must, but in a deeper and truer sense the Renaissance is still alive. The creations of its great artists are still contemplated with awe, its paladins in letters are still read and indeed are still "best sellers"; with no less devotion if perhaps less rapture, the nature and significance of these unique centuries are still studied and analyzed by scholars.

It may not be inappropriate, as we grope for an understanding of the nature of the great era, to let two of its most memorable figures come to our assistance. In Canto XXI of the Inferno Dante puts into the mouth of the doomed Ulysses the following exhortation to his shipmates:

> To this, the last brief vigil of your senses
> That yet remains to you, do not deny
> Experience of that unpeopled world
> Which lies beyond the sun, unknown to all.
> Reflect upon the seed from which you spring.
> You were not made to live the lives of brutes,
> But rather to seek virtue and to learn.

And from Shakespeare we need only one brief but luminous phrase:

> Oh brave new world...

It is the enduring lesson of the Renaissance that the search for knowledge is for mankind not only a right but also a duty —and above all that the study of our world is joyous and exhilarating. In seeking the old world, the Renaissance—like Columbus, who was nourished in its climate—discovered the new and found the discovery both exciting and rewarding.

Thomas G. Bergin

**Aachen, Hans von** (1552–1615) *German painter*
Despite his name, von Aachen was born at Cologne. Like Bartholomäus SPRANGER, whom he later joined in Prague, and other northern artists of his time, von Aachen spent a long period as a young man in Italy, modifying his own German style with an Italian grace and roundedness of form, as well as warmer colors. He lived in Venice between 1574 and 1588, visiting Rome and Florence. On his return to southern Germany he painted portraits and historical and religious scenes, gaining a wide reputation (his patrons included the FUGGER FAMILY, who commissioned portraits). In 1592 Emperor Rudolf II appointed him court painter at Prague, although von Aachen did not move there until 1597. Here he was commissioned to paint mythological and allegorical subjects, such as his *Liberation of Hungary* (1598; Budapest). He also made many designs for sculptors and engravers, for example, for Adriaen de VRIES's Hercules fountain in Augsburg.

**abacus** In early modern Europe, a system of parallel columns of lines representing successive powers of 10, on which the elementary operations of addition, subtraction, multiplication, and division, were performed with the aid of counters. The lines of this instrument, the line abacus or exchequer board, could be drawn in the dust, incised in wax, or carved on a board or table. In the absence of satisfactory algorithms for calculation such devices were used by officials, tradesmen, and schoolboys, but once satisfactory methods were developed, the abacus rapidly disappeared from general use. The system of pierced beads sliding along metal rods, though familiar today, originated in China and was little used in Renaissance Europe.
See also: ARITHMETIC

**Abarbanel, Isaac** (1437–1508) *Jewish statesman, philosopher, and scholar*
Born in Lisbon, he became a trusted state official under King AFONSO V of Portugal, but on the king's death (1481) he was forced to seek refuge in Spain. Here he was minister of state under FERDINAND II AND ISABELLA I and was an early patron of COLUMBUS. He endeavored to prevent the expulsion of the Jews from Spain (1492) by offering their Catholic Majesties a huge bribe, but was exiled with his coreligionists. He went to Italy and then Corfu before ending his days as a servant of state in Venice. Abarbanel published several books of biblical exegesis, much used by Christian scholars; these commentaries were particularly noteworthy for their attention to social and political structures in biblical times.

**Abarbanel, Judah** See LEONE EBREO

**Abbate, Niccolò dell'** (c. 1509–1571) *Italian painter*
He first studied sculpture in his native Modena but it was his frescoes, particularly the *Martyrdom of St. Peter and St. Paul* (1547) in the church of San Pietro, for which he became known. The influence of his contemporaries MANTEGNA, CORREGGIO, and PARMIGIANINO helped to form the mature style that followed his move to Bologna in 1548. The Palazzo dell' Università in Bologna contains some of his surviving mannerist landscapes.

In 1552 Abbate was invited to the court of Henry II of France at Fontainebleau. Here, working with PRIMATICCIO, he introduced Mannerism to France and helped to create the FONTAINEBLEAU style, the first completely secular movement in French painting. Few of his murals and easel paintings have escaped destruction;

those that have are mainly graceful landscapes with pagan themes.

### Abbot, George (1562–1633) *English divine*

Born at Guildford, the son of a clothworker, Abbot was educated at Guildford grammar school and Balliol College, Oxford. He helped prepare the Authorized Version of the Bible, first obtained a bishopric in 1609, and became archbishop of Canterbury in 1611. Abbot was a moderate Puritan, committed to Calvinistic principles and hostile to Rome and to the English Arminians (*see* ARMINIANISM) led by William Laud. In 1621 Laud availed himself of Abbot's accidental shooting of a gamekeeper to try to have him ejected from holy orders, but James I exercised his casting vote in Abbot's favor. A firm critic of Charles I's pro-Spanish and pro-Laudian policies, Abbot was suspended from his archiepiscopal functions for one year in 1627 after attacking a sermon defending Charles's arbitrary use of power. From then on Laud increasingly usurped Abbot's role as primate of England, before succeeding to the post on Abbot's death.

### Academia secretorum naturae (Accademia dei Segreti, Accademia degli Oziosi)

The first scientific academy, founded at Naples by Giambattista DELLA PORTA in 1560. Membership was open to those who had made some discovery in the natural sciences, which members presented at meetings held at della Porta's house. Its activities became the subject of ecclesiastical investigation (1580) and della Porta was ordered to close his academy.

### academies

In the Renaissance, associations of scholars, philosophers, writers, and (later) artists that more or less deliberately drew their inspiration from Plato's Academy in Athens in the fourth century BC. In the 15th century informal groups of scholars began to be referred to as "academies"; probably the earliest was the literary circle patronized by ALFONSO (I) the Magnanimous at Naples (*see* NEAPOLITAN ACADEMY), which later came to be known from its most eminent member as the Accademia Pontaniana (*see* PONTANO, GIOVANNI). Study and appreciation of the languages, literature, art, and thought of the classical world assumed different forms in different places. The intellectual world reflected in Plato's dialogues captured the imagination of Cosimo de' MEDICI and Marsilio FICINO, who founded the most famous of Renaissance academies, the Accademia Platonica (*see* PLATONIC ACADEMY) at Florence in the early 1460s. In Venice the NEAKADEMIA devoted itself to Greek studies, while the ROMAN ACADEMY concentrated on classical Rome. In the 16th and 17th centuries nearly every Italian city had its academy, which often amounted to little more than a gentlemen's debating club, though some, like the ACCADEMIA DELLA CRUSCA, set themselves a more serious aim.

Forerunner of later scientific academies was DELLA PORTA's short-lived Accademia dei Segreti (*see* ACADEMIA SECRETORUM NATURAE) at Naples in 1560. The ACCADEMIA DEI LINCEI lasted rather longer. In the fine arts, informal schools of teachers and pupils were often called "academies" from the 15th century onwards: for example, an engraving by AGOSTINO VENEZIANO, dated 1531 and showing BANDINELLI with a group of pupils studying statuettes by candlelight in Rome, is entitled "Academia." However, the first formally organized teaching academy was the ACCADEMIA DEL DISEGNO founded in Florence in 1562, followed by the Roman Accademia di San Luca (1593).

Elsewhere humanist academies were slower to emerge. The French Académie des Jeux Floraux derived from a 14th-century troubadour festival at Toulouse, and in the Netherlands CHAMBERS OF RHETORIC performed many of the functions of academies before the founding of the DUYTSCHE ACADEMIE in 1617. The Académie de la poésie et de la musique (1570–74) and the Académie du palais (1576–84) were less successful than the more haphazard grouping of the PLÉIADE in introducing classical standards into French poetics. In England Spenser's AREOPAGUS may have had only a fictional existence.

**Further reading:** Frances A. Yates, *The French Academies of the Sixteenth Century* (London: Warburg Institute, 1947; repr. Routledge, 1988).

### Acarie, Barbe Jeanne (1566–1618) *Founder in France of the Reformed (Discalced) Order of Carmelite nuns*

Born in Paris, Mme Acarie was the daughter of a royal councillor, Nicolas Avrillot. In 1582 she was married to Pierre Acarie by whom she had six children. A leading light in Parisian society, she became deeply involved in the Catholic reform movement and was a close friend of the Bérulle family (*see* BÉRULLE, PIERRE DE). In 1604 she introduced the Carmelite nuns into France and, after her husband's death (1613), entered their Amiens convent herself. On becoming a professed nun she adopted the name of Mary of the Incarnation (1615) and transferred to Pontoise (1616) where she remained until her death. She was beatified in 1791.

### Accademia dei Lincei

The scientific society founded in Rome in 1603 by Prince Federico Cesi. GALILEO and Giambattista DELLA PORTA were early members. It was revived in the 1870s to become the national academy of Italy, encompassing both literature and science among its concerns.

### Accademia del Disegno

The first true art academy, founded in Florence in 1562, mainly at the instigation of VASARI. Its founder was Duke COSIMO I DE' MEDICI, who was joint head of the new institution with MICHELANGELO. It had an elected membership of 36 artists; amateurs were also admitted. It gained enormous international prestige and enhanced the status of artists vis-à-vis the other Florentine guilds.

**Accademia della Crusca** The preeminent linguistic academy of Italy, founded in 1582 in Florence. Its object was the purification of the vernacular, symbolized in the academy's emblem of a sieve. It was the first academy to undertake the compilation of a standard dictionary; its *Vocabolario* (1612), which followed the linguistic principles advocated by BEMBO, exercised a powerful influence over the subsequent evolution of literary Italian.

See also: QUESTIONE DELLA LINGUA; SALVIATI, LEONARDO

**Accademia Platonica** See PLATONIC ACADEMY

**Accademia Pontaniana** See NEAPOLITAN ACADEMY; PONTANO, GIOVANNI

**Acciaiuoli family** Having migrated from Bergamo in the 12th century, the Acciaiuoli family became prominent Florentine businessmen and bankers and by the 1340s ran the third richest Italian bank. Niccolò Acciaiuoli (1310–65), who went to Naples (1331) to direct the family's interests there, became grand seneschal and virtual ruler of the kingdom under Queen Joanna I in 1348. He also founded (1342) the Certosa del Galluzzo, a monastery near Florence. His nephew, Ranieri (died 1394), established himself in Greece, conquering Athens in 1388. Meanwhile, the family bank had been bankrupted (1345) by the combination of high Florentine taxation, loss of business in Rome due to strained relations between Florence and the papacy, and (from 1341) the default of Edward III of England on his loan repayments. The Acciaiuoli continued to play a major role in Florentine politics; in 1434 Agnolo Acciaiuoli helped the MEDICI overcome their enemies the ALBIZZI, and the family's subsequent loyalty to the Medici brought them rewards in the form of important civil and ecclesiastical posts. Donato Acciaiuoli (1428–78), *gonfaloniere* of Florence in 1473, wrote commentaries on Aristotle and published a Latin translation of some of Plutarch's *Lives* (1478).

**Accolti family** A family from Arezzo that produced several distinguished churchmen, jurists, and authors in the 15th and 16th centuries. Benedetto Accolti (1415–64) taught jurisprudence at the university in Florence and in 1458 became chancellor of the Florentine republic, but he is chiefly remembered for his Latin history of the First Crusade, which was printed in 1532, translated into Italian in 1543, and furnished material for Tasso's GERUSALEMME LIBERATA. His brother Francesco (Francesco Aretino; 1416–c. 1484) was also a jurist and wrote a verse translation of Leonardo Bruni's *De bello italico adversus Gothos* (1528). Benedetto's son Bernardo (1465–1536),

generally known to his contemporaries as Unico Aretino, was a poet who acquired considerable renown at several Italian courts as a reciter of impromptu verse. His comedy *Virginia*, based on a story in the DECAMERON, was first performed in 1493 and published in 1535, and a collected edition of his works, *Opera nova*, was first published in 1513. Another of Benedetto's sons, Pietro (1455–1532), was made a cardinal by Julius II and became archbishop of Ravenna in 1524. Pietro's nephew, another Benedetto (1497–1549), continued the family tradition of learned churchmen, becoming a cardinal under Clement VII.

**Acosta, José de** (1539–1600) *Spanish naturalist and missionary*
Born at Medina del Campo, Acosta joined the Jesuits in 1551 and accompanied them in 1571 to Peru where he remained until his return to Spain in 1587. In 1598 he became rector of the Jesuit college at Salamanca. While in South America he published (1583) a Quechua catechism, the first book to be printed in Peru. His *Historia natural y moral de las Indias* (1590), an influential and much translated work, introduced many to the distinctive flora and fauna of Latin America. They had originated, he argued, in the Old World and had spread to the New World via an undiscovered land bridge. He also pointed out Aristotle's error in claiming equatorial lands to be uninhabitable.

*Adagia* A collection of proverbs and allusions gathered from classical authors by ERASMUS. The first version, entitled *Collectanea adagiorum*, appeared in Paris in 1500 with a dedication to Lord Mountjoy. By the time of the second edition, *Chiliades adagiorum* (1508), published by the ALDINE PRESS in Venice, Erasmus had expanded the collection from around 800 to over 3000, including a number of Greek sayings. The collection was accompanied by a commentary designed to inculcate an elegant Latin style, and the *Adagia* quickly became enormously successful, with numerous editions throughout the 16th century.

*Adoration of the Lamb* See GHENT ALTARPIECE

**Adrian VI** (1459–1523) *Pope (1522–23)*
Born Adrian Dedel in Utrecht, he served as boyhood tutor to CHARLES V and subsequently (1516) became inquisitor-general of Aragon. On becoming pope he was immediately beset by the menace of the Turks in the east, the continued war between Charles V and FRANCIS I of France, and the revolt of LUTHER in Germany. The significance of Adrian's pontificate lies in his aims rather than his achievements, notably his instruction (December 1522) to Father Chieregati, Rome's representative in Nuremberg, with its admission that reform in Christendom must be preceded by reform of the Curia itself. This broke the pattern established by the Renaissance popes and can be seen as the beginning of the COUNTER-REFORMATION.

**Adriano Fiorentino** (**Adriano di Giovanni de' Maestri**) (c. 1450/60–1499) *Italian sculptor and medalist*
Born in Florence, he was first recorded as a bronze founder in an inscription on the base of the *Bellerophon and Pegasus* (Vienna), a bronze statuette designed by BERTOLDO in Florence during the early 1480s. Adriano then moved to Naples, serving King Ferrante (Ferdinand I) and his commander-in-chief as military engineer and artillery founder, as well as producing medals of members of the house of Aragon and their court poet PONTANO. In 1495 Adriano was serving Elisabetta Gonzaga, Duchess of Urbino, and then her brother Gianfrancesco Gonzaga, Duke of Mantua. By 1498 he was in Germany, where he produced a bust in bell-metal of Elector FREDERICK (III) THE WISE in contemporary costume (Grünes Gewölbe, Dresden). A bronze statuette of *Venus* (Philadelphia) and one of a *Satyr* with pan-pipes (Vienna) are among Adriano's signed works on a small scale and herald the High Renaissance in sculpture.

**Aertsen, Pieter** (1509–1575) *Netherlands painter*
Aertsen was a student of the engraver Allaert Claesz in Amsterdam, before moving to Antwerp about 1530, whence he returned to his native city in 1557. He painted a number of altarpieces, many of which were destroyed in the ICONOCLASM that followed the arrival of Calvinism in the Netherlands. Aertsen was the creator of a new type of genre scene, featuring large figures of maids or cooks, surrounded by fruit, vegetables, and other provisions, in domestic interiors. Famous examples are the *Farmer's Wife* (1543; Lille) and *Market Woman at a Vegetable Stand* (1567; Berlin). The peasants, housewives, and domestic servants who populate these canvases have a grandeur and self-confidence prophetic of much later social realist works. Some of his paintings, such as the *Butcher's Shop with the Flight into Egypt* (1551; Uppsala) include well-known religious scenes in the background—a reversal of the customary order of priority. Aertsen's students included his sons Pieter ("Jonge Peer"; 1543–1603) and Aert Pietersz. (1550–1612), as well as his nephew Joachim Beuckelaer (c. 1533–c. 1573). His style stimulated imitation as far afield as Italy, as is evident from certain canvases by Vincenzo Campi (1536–91), Bartolommeo PASSAROTTI, and Annibale CARRACCI.

**Afonso V** (1432–1481) *King of Portugal (1438–81)*
Afonso was nicknamed "Africano" on account of his campaigns against the Moors in North Africa, during which he acquired Tangier for Portugal in 1471. In 1475 he invaded Castile, but in 1476 FERDINAND (II), husband of Isabella of Castile, defeated him at Toro and he was forced to abdicate in favor of his son John (later John II). During Afonso's reign his uncle, HENRY THE NAVIGATOR, laid the foundations of Portugal's sea-borne empire; the inclusion of what is believed to be Henry's posthumous portrait in GONÇALVES' San Vicente altarpiece (c. 1465) may be Afonso's acknowledgment of his uncle's role in Portugal's successes during his reign.

**Agostino di Duccio** (1418–1481) *Italian sculptor*
Agostino was born in Florence, but his training is unknown, and his first dated work was in 1442 in Modena. In 1449 and 1454 Agostino appears in documents at Rimini, where he carved many marble panels in the interior of the TEMPIO MALATESTIANO. Agostino's style is incisive and calligraphic; it was possibly inspired initially by DONATELLO's low reliefs, though not by their emotional content, of which Agostino was incapable. Between 1457 and 1462, Agostino was carving the façade of the oratory of San Bernardino in Perugia with reliefs of Christ in majesty, the Annunciation, and the saints in glory, surrounded by flying angels and statues in niches. After an unsuccessful year in Bologna, Agostino returned to Florence (1463), joined the guild of sculptors, and received (abortive) commissions for colossal statues on the cathedral (one of which eventually was carved by Michelangelo into his *David*). After carving several Madonna reliefs, one for the Medici (Louvre, Paris), he returned to Perugia, where he carved continuously until his death. His talents were better appreciated in this provincial city than in his native metropolis.

**Agostino Veneziano** (**Agostino de' Musi**) (c. 1490–c. 1536) *Italian engraver*
Originally active in his native Venice, Agostino was influenced by Giulio CAMPAGNOLA and by Jacopo de' BARBARI. In 1516 he left Venice for Rome, where he became the foremost pupil of Marcantonio RAIMONDI and, like his master, important in disseminating Italian Renaissance themes and motifs through the medium of engraving. Raphael and Giulio Romano were among the artists whose works were made more widely available through Agostino's prints.

**Agricola, Georgius** (**Georg Bauer**) (1494–1555) *German mineralogist and physician*
Agricola studied at Leipzig and several Italian universities before graduating in medicine. He was physician (1527–33) in the Bohemian mining town of Joachimsthal (now Jachymov in the Czech Republic) before returning to practice for the rest of his life at Chemnitz in his native Saxony. His first scientific publication was *Bermannus* (1530), a dialogue in which the main speaker is a celebrated miner and in which many minerals are first described under their German names (e.g. bismuth). He published numerous other geological and metallurgical works, notably *De natura fossilium* (1530) (*see* MINERALOGY). These culminated in *De re metallica* (1556), the first systematic textbook of the subject, issued, as all his scientific works had been, by the publishing house of FROBEN

at Basle. Agricola also wrote from practical experience on weights and measures (*De mesuribus et ponderibus*, 1533), subterranean fauna (*De animantibus subterraneis*, 1549), and the plague (*De peste*, 1554).

## Agricola, Johann (c. 1494–1566) *German Protestant reformer*

Agricola was born at Eisleben and became a student of LUTHER at Wittenberg. An early venture was his collection of German proverbs (1528). Agricola found himself opposed by Luther for his denial of the necessity of the preaching of Mosaic and moral law as well as the Gospel (the antinominian heresy), and Luther's growing intolerance of dissent obliged Agricola to leave Wittenberg (1540) in order to avoid being put on trial. He became court preacher to Joachim II of Brandenburg and in 1548 helped prepare the Interim of AUGSBURG. The resulting adiaphorist controversy, concerning whether or not certain actions or rites were matters of indifference to true Christian doctrine, became Agricola's main preoccupation as he unsuccessfully attempted to resolve it. He died during a plague epidemic.

## Agricola, Rudolf (Roelof Huysman) (1442–1495) *Dutch humanist philosopher and scholar*

Agricola was born near Groningen and became a pupil of Nicholas CUSANUS; he was, like him, one of the Brethren of the Common Life. From 1468 to 1479 he studied, though not continuously, at Padua and Ferrara and impressed Italian humanists with his fluency in Latin. He was also an accomplished Hebrew scholar who translated the Psalms into Latin. He had great enthusiasm for the works of Petrarch, whose biography he wrote. Unlike many Italian humanists Agricola remained a devout Christian, believing that though the study of the ancients was important it was not a substitute for the study of the Scriptures. He used the phrase "Philosophia Christi" to describe his teaching, the object of which was to mediate between the wisdom of the ancients and Christian belief. These ideas exercised considerable influence over ERASMUS, his most distinguished pupil.

## Agrippa von Nettesheim, (Henry) Cornelius (1486–1535) *German lawyer, theologian, and student of the occult*

Born near Cologne, of a family of minor nobility, he entered the service of the emperor and went to Paris (1506). There he studied the CABBALA and around 1510 wrote *De occulta philosophia* (1531). In 1510 Agrippa was sent to London where he met John COLET. In 1515 he was teaching occult science at Pavia. He then moved to Metz, but opposition forced him to leave and he settled in Geneva. He became a doctor in 1522 and was appointed physician to Louise of Savoy, queen mother of France, his duties

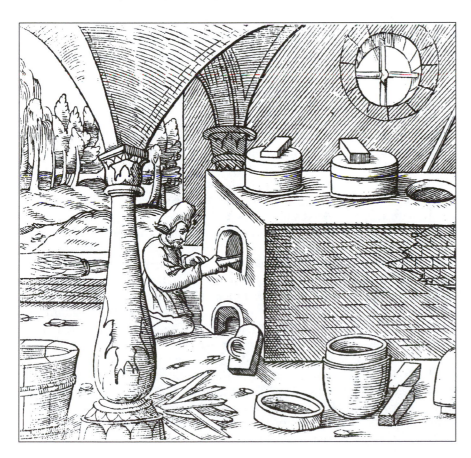

**Georgius Agricola** A woodcut from the first edition of his *De re metallica* (1556), the first systematic textbook on mining and metallurgy. The operator is seen riddling a smelting furnace.

consisting mainly of writing horoscopes. In 1530 Agrippa published his major work, *De vanitate et incertitudine scientiarum et artium*, a survey of the state of knowledge in which human learning is unfavorably compared with divine revelation. In 1528 he had been made historiographer to Charles V but hostility to his occult studies led to his disgrace. He was banished from Germany in 1535 and died at Grenoble. His major contribution to the Renaissance was his skepticism.

**Further reading:** Christopher I. Lehrich, *The Language of Demons and Angels: Cornelius Agrippa's Occult Philosophy* (Leyden, Netherlands: Brill, 2003).

**Ailly, Pierre d'** (1350–1420) *French geographer and theologian*
Born at Compiègne and educated at the university of Paris, d'Ailly pursued a clerical career, rising in 1411 to the rank of cardinal. Caught up in the GREAT SCHISM, he broke with Pope Benedict XIII in 1408 and argued in his *Tractatus super reformatione ecclesiae* (1416) for the supremacy of Church councils over popes. He was also the author of *Imago mundi* (c. 1410), one of the foremost geographical texts of the period. The inspiration for the work remained predominantly classical; d'Ailly took little notice of the growing travel literature. A related work, *Compendium cosmographiae* (1413), did little more than repeat the geography of Ptolemy (2nd century CE). Whereas, however, Ptolemy had assumed that both land and sea covered about 180° of longitude, d'Ailly extended the land mass to 225°. The implications of such a framework were not lost on Christopher COLUMBUS, a careful reader of d'Ailly.

**Alamanni, Luigi** (1495–1556) *Italian poet and humanist*
Alamanni was born in Florence and took part in the unsuccessful conspiracy of 1522 against Giulio de' Medici (later Pope CLEMENT VII) and was forced to flee to France. He returned and briefly served in the Florentine republican government of 1527–30, but thereafter lived in exile, enjoying the patronage of Francis I, Henry II, and Catherine de' Medici. As a protégé of the French court, he made many return journeys to Italy and maintained contacts with BEMBO, VARCHI, and other leading figures. In Florence he had been associated with the ORTI ORICELLARI, and from that time had been a close friend of MACHIAVELLI, who made Alamanni one of the speakers in *Arte della guerra*. Alamanni played an important role in the establishment of Italian cultural influence in 16th-century France. His works include *Flora* (1549), a comedy based on Roman models, *Antigone* (1556), a tragedy after Sophocles, *Avarchide* (1570), a minor epic imitative of the *Iliad*, and *Girone il cortese* (1548), which drew on medieval French material. Most influential, however, was *La coltivazione* (1546), a didactic blank-verse imitation of Virgil's *Georgics*.

**Alarcón y Mendoza, Juan Ruiz de** See RUIZ DE ALARCÓN Y MENDOZA, JUAN

**Alba, Fernando Alvarez de Toledo, 3rd Duke of** (1507–1582) *Spanish nobleman*
He served Charles I of Spain (who was also Emperor CHARLES V) and PHILIP II of Spain as military commander, political adviser, and administrator. In the service of Charles, Alba fought the French (1524), attacked Tunis (1535), helped lead the imperial forces to their important victory over the German Protestant princes at MÜHLBERG, and became commander-in-chief of the emperor's armies in Italy (1552). He was one of Philip II's leading ministers from 1559 until 1567, when he was ordered to the Netherlands to crush the Calvinist Dutch rebels and to reassert Spanish authority (*see also* NETHERLANDS, REVOLT OF THE). His harsh rule as governor-general of the Netherlands fueled Dutch hatred of Spain; worst hated was Alba's Council of Troubles (nicknamed the TRIBUNAL OF BLOOD by the Dutch) which set aside local laws, imposed heavy taxation, confiscated property, sent hundreds of Dutch to their deaths, and drove thousands more into exile. Lacking both money and sufficient naval resources, Alba lost control over parts of Holland. This failure, combined with the intrigues of his enemies at the Spanish court, led to his recall to Spain (1573) and house arrest (1579). Although Alba led the successful invasion of Portugal (1580), he never regained Philip II's favor.

**Further reading:** William S. Maltby, *Alba: A Biography of Fernando Alvaraz de Toled, Third Duke of Alba, 1507–1582* (Berkeley, Calif.: University of California Press, 1983).

**Alberti, Leon Battista** (1404–1472) *Italian architect and humanist*
A member of a prominent merchant-banking family exiled by political opponents from its native Florence in 1402, Alberti, who was illegitimate, was born in Genoa and brought up by his father and stepmother in Venice. He attended GUARINO DA VERONA's school in Padua and in the 1420s studied law at Bologna University. The Florentine ban against his family was lifted in 1428 and by 1432, when he was employed as a secretary in the papal chancery, Alberti had made his first visit to the city. There he became acquainted with such men as DONATELLO, GHIBERTI, and MASACCIO, and with BRUNELLESCHI, to whom he dedicated the preface of his treatise *Della pittura* (On Painting; 1435), a work that contains the first description of PERSPECTIVE construction.

Alberti's study of the Roman architectural writer VITRUVIUS resulted in *De re aedificatoria*, a treatise on architecture in 10 books dedicated to Pope Nicholas V (1452). The treatise was first published in 1485 at Florence, with a prefatory letter by POLITIAN addressed to Lorenzo de' Medici. This Latin edition was subsequently reprinted at

Paris (1512) and Strasbourg (1541); the first Italian translation appeared in Venice in 1546, and French (1553) and Spanish (1582) versions were also printed during the 16th century. Alberti was employed by the pope on a number of architectural projects in Rome but his most famous buildings are in Florence, Rimini, and Mantua. In Florence he designed the Palazzo Rucellai (c. 1445–51), the classical forms of its facade being influenced by the Roman Colosseum, and the main facade of Sta. Maria Novella (1456–70); in Rimini the famous TEMPIO MALATESTIANO; and in Mantua the churches of San Sebastiano (1460–70) and Sant' Andrea (c. 1470), in which the Tempio's triumphal-arch motif was again incorporated. Alberti's humanistic interests found expression in a number of prose works, notably *Della famiglia* (On the family; 1435–41), *De iciarchia* (On the ruler of his family; 1470), and the first Italian grammar. Also a poet, mathematician, and engineer, Alberti exemplified his own belief that "men can do all things." He died in Rome.

The first illustrated edition of *De re aedificatoria* (1550) was Cosimo Bartoli's Italian version that superseded the Venetian version of 1546. Giacomo Leoni (1686–1746), a Venetian architect living in England, published his English translation in 1726, with engravings based on his own drawings after the woodcuts of the 1550 Bartoli edition. Leoni's translation was twice reprinted in the 18th century (1739, 1755), and the 1755 edition was the basis of a photographic reprint edited by Joseph Rykwert (London, 1955; New York, 1966, 1986). Rykwert's own translation (with Neil Leach and Robert Tavernor) appeared under the title of *On the Art of Building in Ten Books* (Cambridge, Mass.: MIT Press, 1988).

**Further reading:** Franco Borsi, *Leon Battista Alberti: The Complete Works* (Oxford, U.K.: Phaidon, 1977); Anthony Grafton, *Leon Battista Alberti: Master Builder of the Renaissance* (New York: Hill & Wang, 2000); Liisa Kanerva, *Defining the Architect in Fifteenth-Century Italy: Exemplary Architects in L. B. Alberti's De re aedificatoria* (Helsinki: Suomamalainen Tiedeakatemia, 1998).

**Albertinelli, Mariotto** (1474–1515) *Italian painter*
Albertinelli was born in Florence, where he trained under Cosimo ROSSELLI. Through Rosselli he met Fra BARTOLOMMEO, with whom he collaborated for a number of years, for example on the altarpiece of Sta. Maria della Quercia, near Viterbo. Albertinelli also painted an *Annunciation* for the Duomo in Volterra (1497), another now in the Accademia, Florence (1510), and a *Visitation* (1503; Uffizi, Florence). His works show the influence of Perugino and Leonardo da Vinci, as well as that of Fra Bartolommeo.

**Albert of Austria** (**Albrecht von Hapsburg**) (1559–1621) *Archduke and coruler of the Spanish Netherlands (1598–1621)*
The youngest son of Emperor Maximilian II, Albert began his career in the Church, being appointed cardinal at age 18. However, he later renounced his orders so as to marry (1598) his cousin, the Infanta ISABELLA, to whom control of the Spanish Netherlands was to be ceded. Albert and Isabella became corulers. Continuing Spanish attempts to subdue the independent Dutch provinces to the north bedeviled the first decade of the Archdukes' reign, but in 1609 Albert prevailed upon the Spanish government to agree to a 12-year truce. During this period the Archdukes worked energetically to repair the ravages of war (although Protestants in their territories continued to be harassed). Patronage of artists and musicians was part of their program of reconstruction: Otto van VEEN and RUBENS were both close associates of Albert, Jan BRUEGHEL was his court artist from 1609, and Peter PHILIPS was his court organist from 1597.

**Albert of Prussia** (1490–1568) *Grand Master of the Teutonic Knights (1511–25) and first duke of Prussia (1525)*
Albert was the grandson of Elector Albert Achilles of Brandenburg and was chosen as grand master of the Teutonic Knights in the hope that his uncle, the king of Poland, would facilitate a settlement over east Prussia. These lands had been held by the Knights under Polish suzerainty

**Leon Battista Alberti** His architectural designs include the facade of the west front of Sta. Maria Novella, Florence (1456–70).
*Anthony Kersting, London*

since the Second Treaty of Thorn (1466). In 1522 he visited Nuremberg where he met the religious reformer Andreas OSIANDER under whose influence he became a Protestant. On the advice of Martin LUTHER, he secularized the dominions of the Teutonic Knights, thereby becoming duke of the hereditary duchy of Prussia. The early years of his rule were prosperous and he established a great number of schools, including Königsberg University (1544). However, his later years were marred by violent religious and political disputes revolving around Albert's support for Osiander's doctrine and ending in strict Lutheranism being imposed in his domains.

**Albizzi, Rinaldo (degli)** (1370–1442) *Italian statesman*
Rinaldo was a leading member of the Albizzi family, which dominated the government of Florence between the revolt of the CIOMPI (1378) and the MEDICI seizure of power (1434). After his cousin Maso Albizzi died (1417) Rinaldo took control of the oligarchic regime in Florence. He organized the unpopular and unsuccessful expedition against Lucca (1429–33), which was opposed by Cosimo de' MEDICI. Although Rinaldo had Cosimo exiled (1433), he returned to Florence in 1434, overthrew the Albizzi, and sent Rinaldo into exile.

**Albornoz, Egidio d'** (Gil Alvarez Carrillo d'Albornoz) (1310–1367) *Spanish churchman*
Albornoz was born at Cuenca, Castile. He fought bravely against the Moors, was a favorite of Alfonso XI, and became archbishop of Toledo (1338), but was exiled (1350) by Alfonso's son, Peter the Cruel. Albornoz was made a cardinal (1350) and appointed papal legate and vicar-general of Italy (1353–57, 1358–64) by Innocent VI to protect papal interests against Guelf Florence and to recover territory lost to the papacy (*see* AVIGNON, PAPACY AT). His long series of wars made some gains and facilitated a papal return to Rome, briefly in 1367 and permanently in 1377. Often he merely legitimized existing local tyrants as papal vicars in return for a recognition of papal authority, without breaking their power. Of more lasting importance was his work in administration and education. His codification of the laws of the Papal State (*Constitutiones egidianae*, 1357) provided the model for papal government until 1816. In 1365 he founded the Spanish college at Bologna.

**Albret, Jeanne d'** See JEANNE D'ALBRET

**Albuquerque, Afonso** (1453–1515) *Portuguese admiral, second viceroy of Portuguese India*
Born near Lisbon and educated at court, Albuquerque made his name during King AFONSO V's invasion of Spain (1476). His first eastern expedition (1503) was to befriend the king of Cochin and build a fort there. He succeeded, and in 1506 he assisted the Portuguese admiral Tristão da

Cunha during his massive expedition to India. Over the next few years Albuquerque carried out a series of attacks on Arab cities, establishing Portuguese trading routes and rights. His outstanding success was his recapture of Goa in 1510, where he established a senate and appointed native administrators. Albuquerque's enlightened administration was extended to other territories he conquered, notably Malacca and the Spice Islands. His success aroused jealousies in the Portuguese court, and Lope Suàrez, a personal enemy, was appointed in his stead. Albuquerque died at sea and was buried at Goa, where his tomb became a shrine for Indians oppressed by his successors.

**Alcalá (de Henares)** A town in central Spain on the River Henares, east of Madrid. Identified with the Roman settlement of Complutum, it was refounded by the Moors in 1083; its present name derives from the Moorish word for "castle." During the Renaissance it became a center of learning under the patronage of Cardinal XIMÉNES DE CISNEROS, to whom a handsome marble monument remains in the church of the Colegiata. He founded the university there in 1500 (opened 1508); the chief university building, the college of Sant' Ildefonso, dates from 1583. Many of the scholars whom Ximénes brought to Alcalá were engaged on the production of the great edition of the Bible known as the COMPLUTENSIAN POLYGLOT.

**alchemy** The pseudoscience that in the Renaissance period was inextricably linked with the beginnings of chemistry. Renaissance alchemists inherited from their medieval forebears two main quests: for the process or substance (the philosopher's stone) that would transmute base metals into gold and for the universal medicine (panacea). The elixir of life, the principal goal of Chinese alchemy, was of minor importance as being clearly contrary to Christian doctrine.

Alchemists in pursuit of the philosopher's stone, who beggared themselves buying materials for their experiments or poisoned themselves with their processes, were properly ridiculed. Nonetheless they frequently imposed upon the greedy and gullible; Ben JONSON's comedy *The Alchemist* (1610) is a comprehensive exposé of the tricks of this kind of alchemical trade. The Church regarded alchemy, along with other occult learning, with hostility, condemning alchemists with other "sorcerers" in its decrees. Gold-hungry Renaissance princes, with wars or other projects to finance, took a more pragmatic line. RUDOLF II attracted many occult practitioners from all over Europe to Prague, among them the alchemists DEE, DREBBEL, and SENDIVOGIUS.

Regarding the quest for the panacea, the theories of PARACELSUS greatly stimulated spagyrical medicine. (The Latin word *spagyricus* "alchemical" was apparently a Paracelsian coinage.) Some practitioners developed their researches in the direction of IATROCHEMISTRY, but others, notably the Rosicrucians, interpreted the quest in spiritual as well as alchemical terms (*see* ROSICRUCIANISM).

The terminology of alchemy, conspiring with the pathological secretiveness of its practitioners, thwarted any incipient usefulness it might have had to the embryonic science of chemistry. Renaissance alchemists continued to rely on such texts as the 13th-century Latin versions of the Arab Geber, the writings of Arnold of Villanova and Albertus Magnus, and such venerable classics of obfuscation as the *Turba philosophorum* and pseudo-Aristotle, in which metals were called after their astrological equivalents—Sol (gold), Luna (silver), Saturn (lead), etc.—and other materials were identified in fanciful metaphors; a powerful acid, for example, would be called "the stomach of the ostrich" in tribute to its digestive properties. To some, the whole alchemical enterprise itself became a metaphor for the purgation and salvation of the soul and the process became associated with the cosmic manipulations of the Renaissance MAGUS.

**Further reading:** Pamela H. Smith, *The Business of Alchemy* (Princeton, N.J.: Princeton University Press, 1994; repr. 1997).

## Alciati, Andrea (1492–1550) *Italian lawyer and humanist*

Alciati was a native of Milan and after legal studies at Pavia and Bologna he was professor of jurisprudence at Avignon (1518–22, 1527–29) and at Bourges. Alciati's main contribution was in the field of juristics; he published a number of treatises on the *Corpus Iuris Civilis*. However, his most famous book was *Emblemata* (1531), a repertory of allegorical images illustrated by woodcuts accompanied by Latin epigrams pointing up the interaction of the visual image and the ethical message (*see* EMBLEMS). This volume exercised a profound influence on the iconography of mannerist and baroque art. Alciati also published a volume of notes on the historian Tacitus.

One of the best-sellers of the 16th century, Alciati's *Emblemata* was first published at Augsburg in 1531 in an edition containing 103 emblems; an edition revised by the author and enlarged to 211 emblems appeared at Lyons in 1550. The work was rapidly disseminated throughout Europe, both in complete and abridged versions of the Latin original and in French (1536), German (1542), and Spanish (1549) rhyming translations. Many of the emblems are reproduced in the massive compilation of *Emblemata* by Arthur Henkel and Albrecht Schöne (Stuttgart, 1967), which also provides valuable comparative material from other emblem books. Peter M. Daly (ed.) in *Andreas Alciatus*, 2 vols (Toronto, 1985) prints the emblems in Latin and also supplies English translations, along with useful indexes.

**Further reading:** Peter M. Daly (ed.), *Andrea Alciati and the Emblem Tradition* (New York: AMS, 1989).

## Aldegrever, Heinrich (1502–55/61) *German print maker and painter*

Aldegrever who was born at Paderborn, probably studied in DÜRER's workshop. About 1527 he settled at Soest, where he died. He executed relatively few paintings, mostly portraits, which are notable for their characterization. Aldegrever is best known for his numerous engravings of religious subjects, events from classical antiquity, genre scenes, portraits, and decorative motifs. These reveal the influence of Dürer, but also of Italian engravers, including POLLAIUOLO. His delicate, slender figures have a mannerist elegance, and his meticulous engraving technique, reminiscent of Dürer's own, allowed him to depict effects of light and texture with considerable fidelity. He also designed woodcuts, and may be characterized as the most significant north German print maker of the 16th century.

## Aldine press

The press set up in Venice by Aldus MANUTIUS in 1494/95, specializing in scholarly texts of Greek and Latin classics. Until 1515 many of them were edited by Marcus Musurus (1470–1517), one of the Venetian community of exiled Greeks. A folio Aristotle (1495–98) is an early example of the press's high standards, though the HYPNEROTOMACHIA POLIFILI (1499), a fine illustrated book, is more famous. Italian classics were also printed, among them Petrarch (1501) and Dante (1502), both edited by BEMBO.

Francesco Griffo, who cut the Aldine Greek type, modeled on Musurus's script, also made the first italic types, which appeared in a 1501 Virgil. A series of compact little books followed, the small format and italic type setting a fashion that was soon copied, especially in Lyons. Griffo's roman type, commissioned by Aldus in 1495, influenced GARAMOND and other designers, though Nicolas JENSON's types and matrices had also been bought for the press. The Aldine device of a dolphin and anchor, found on coins of the Roman emperor Titus Vespasianus (39–81 CE), was used in a series of versions after 1502, as well as being copied by several French printers during the next century and many others thereafter (*see* illustration p. 200).

From 1515 to 1533 the press was run by the founder's brothers-in-law, the Asolani, who failed to maintain its scholarly editing. Aldus's youngest son, Paulus (Paolo) Manutius (1512–74) took over in 1533 and concentrated on Latin classics, especially Cicero.

**Further reading:** Martin Davies, *Aldus Manutius: Printer and Publisher of Renaissance Venice* (Oxford, U.K.: Oxford University Press, 1995); H. George Fletcher, *In Praise of Aldus Manutius: A Quincentenary Exhibition* (New York: Pierpont Morgan Library, 1995).

**Aldrovandi, Ulisse** (1522–1605) *Italian natural historian*
The son of a wealthy Bolognese notary, Aldrovandi was educated at the university of Bologna where he later became professor of natural history. Financially independent, he was free to pursue his interests through extensive European travel. In this manner he accumulated a good deal of information on European fauna, and preparation of this material for publication dominated the remainder of his life. By his death only the volumes on birds, *Ornithologiae* (1599–1634), and insects (1602) had begun to appear. Ten further volumes, dealing with almost every aspect of the animal kingdom, were edited by pupils and appeared before 1668. Despite his considerable first-hand experience, Aldrovandi continued to operate mainly in a literary tradition, giving fanciful tales from the classical writers Strabo and Pliny the same authority as his own observations. Consequently, while there was a place for the hydra and basilisk in Aldrovandi's bestiary, fossils were dismissed in his *Musaeum metallicum* (1648) as of little importance.

**Aldus Manutius** See MANUTIUS, ALDUS

**Aleandro, Girolamo** (1480–1542) *Italian humanist and diplomat*
Born at Treviso, he studied at Padua and then Venice, where he met Aldus MANUTIUS. In 1508 he went to Paris on the advice of and with an introduction from Erasmus. BUDÉ was among his first private pupils. In 1509 he gave a course of lectures in Hebrew, Greek, and Latin at Paris and taught there intermittently until 1513. His *Lexicon Graeco-Latinum* appeared in 1512. After ill health forced him to give up teaching he was employed as a papal envoy, having a notorious confrontation with LUTHER in Germany in 1520–21. He became Vatican librarian (1519) under Leo X and later cardinal (1536). Aleandro was an influential teacher. Sometimes his classes numbered 1500 students and he was largely responsible for introducing GREEK STUDIES to Paris.

**Alemán, Mateo** (1547–1615) *Spanish novelist*
Descended from Jews who had been forcibly converted to Catholicism, Alemán, who was born the son of a prison doctor in Seville, studied medicine in Salamanca and Alcalá but abandoned his studies before completion. His most important literary work, GUZMÁN DE ALFARACHE (1599), is one of the earliest PICARESQUE NOVELS. Such was its popularity throughout Europe that there were several pirated editions, as well as a spurious sequel, which appeared even before Alemán could complete the second part of his own work (1604).

Success however did not alleviate his constant financial difficulties; he had supported himself in a series of insignificant administrative jobs, but in 1601 he was imprisoned for debt for the third time. Alemán's fortunes prospered only after he emigrated to Mexico (1608) with his patron Archbishop García Guerra, whose biography he published in 1613. His other minor works include a biography of St. Anthony of Padua (1603) and *Ortografía Castellana* (1609), the latter containing some sensible proposals for the reform of Spanish spelling.

**Alençon, Francis, Duke of** See FRANCIS, DUKE OF ALENÇON

**Alesius, Alexander** (Alexander Alane, Alexander Ales(s)) (1500–1565) *Scottish-born Lutheran theologian*
He was born in Edinburgh and graduated at the University of St. Andrews (1515) and became a canon there. In 1527 he was chosen to refute the Lutheran doctrines of Patrick HAMILTON, but ended up converting to them himself. Following a spell in prison, he escaped abroad (1532), meeting Luther and other leaders of the German Reformation, while maintaining his attack on ecclesiastical abuses in Scotland, as the result of which he was excommunicated (1534). After carrying a letter from Philipp MELANCHTHON to HENRY VIII of England in 1535, he became a lecturer at Cambridge University, under the patronage of Thomas CROMWELL. However, his lectures on the Psalms so enraged the Cambridge Catholics that he had to retreat to London. Fearing further harassment, he returned to Germany (1539), where he was again involved in controversy, and eventually settled in Leipzig, where he died. He wrote exegetical works on the Psalms and Epistles and a defense of the view that there is biblical authority for just two sacraments. His translation of parts of the BOOK OF COMMON PRAYER into Latin was published in 1551.

**Alessi, Galeazzo** (1512–1572) *Italian architect*
Alessi was born in Perugia and later (1568) designed the principal doorway for the cathedral there. He visited Rome in the late 1530s and his style was formed by his enthusiasm for classical architecture, especially as mediated by MICHELANGELO. His most distinguished work combines the dignity of the classical orders with sumptuous detail, as exemplified in the courtyard of the Palazzo Marino, Milan (1553–58). From 1549 onward he designed a number of notable buildings in Genoa, among them the church of Sta. Maria Assunta di Carignano (begun 1552) and some fine villas and palaces in the Strada Nuova (now the Via Garibaldi), which he himself may have laid out. Other examples of his work appear in the Certosa di Pavia (sarcophagus of Giangaleazzo Visconti), at Brescia (the upper part of the Loggia), and Bologna (gateway to the Palazzo Communale; c. 1555). His style was much admired and influenced buildings as far afield as Spain and Germany, especially after RUBENS published *Palazzi di Genova* (1622), a study in which Alessi's Genoese work features prominently.

## Alexander VI (Rodrigo Borgia) (1431–1503) *Pope (1492–1503)*

He was born at Xativa, Spain, studied law at Bologna, and was first advanced in the papal service by his uncle Alfonso Borgia, Pope Calixtus III, under whom he became head of papal administration, a post which he held ably for 35 years (1457–92). Political corruption and immorality in the Vatican reached their height under Alexander, deeply involved as he was in the struggle between the leading Italian families for power and wealth (*see* BORGIA FAMILY). His contribution to the secularization of the Curia probably enhanced the spreading popularity throughout Italy of preaching friars who condemned the papacy and called upon clergy and laity to repent.

Alexander's pontificate was set against the background of the Wars of ITALY. When CHARLES VIII of France invaded Italy (1494), seizing Rome and Naples, Alexander helped organize the League of Venice, an alliance between Milan, Venice, Spain, and the Holy Roman Empire, which was successful in forcing Charles to leave Italy. However, in the interests of the Borgias, particularly of his son Cesare, he later adopted a pro-French policy and aided the French invasion that led to their occupation of Milan in 1499. Monies from the jubilee year, proclaimed by Alexander in 1500, were diverted to Cesare to help him finally crush the Orsini and Colonna families. The marriages of Alexander's daughter Lucrezia BORGIA were also directed towards political ends.

During Alexander's pontificate Spain laid claim to the New World, following the discoveries of COLUMBUS, and it was Alexander who determined the Spanish and Portuguese spheres of influence there (*see* TORDESILLAS, TREATY OF). He is also remembered as a patron of artists and architects, including BRAMANTE and PINTURICCHIO. The diary of Johann Burchard (died 1506), Alexander's master of ceremonies, gives an intimate account of life close to this most notorious pope; it was published under the title *Historia arcana* (1597) and in an English version as *At the Court of the Borgia* (1963).

## Alfonsine Tables See ASTRONOMY

## Alfonso I (1395–1458) *King of Naples (1442–58) and (as Alfonso V) king of Aragon (1416–58)*

Known as Alfonso the Magnanimous, he was admired as a model prince and a devout Christian. The son of a Castilian prince, who became Ferdinand I of Aragon in 1412, and of Leonor of Albuquerque, he was brought up in Castile and moved to Aragon in 1412. In 1415 he married Maria of Castile; their marriage was unhappy and childless. After succeeding to Aragon in 1416 Alfonso angered his subjects by relying on Castilian advisers, but he did follow the Aragonese tradition of expansion in the Mediterranean. In 1420 he set out to pacify his Sicilian and Sardinian subjects and to attack the Genoese in Cor-

sica. He arrived in Naples in 1421 and persuaded Queen Joanna (Giovanna) II to adopt him as her son and heir in exchange for his help against the Angevin claimant to the throne of Naples. After quarreling with Joanna in 1423 he returned to Spain and busied himself with Spanish problems until her death in 1435. Alfonso then returned to Naples to claim his throne and succeeded in driving out his main rival, RENÉ OF ANJOU, after seven years of struggle. He left the government of his other territories to viceroys and settled permanently in Naples from 1443. He reorganized its finances and administration and made his court at Naples a brilliant center of learning and the arts. Understanding the importance of presenting himself as a Renaissance prince, Alfonso employed some major humanist figures about his court: Lorenzo VALLA wrote several of his most significant works during his decade in Naples, while Antonio BECCADELLI and Bartolomeo Facio (or Fazio; c. 1400–47) combined work in Alfonso's secretariat with writing accounts of his reign. The triumphal arch at the Castel Nuovo in Naples (built 1453–66) commemorates Alfonso's grand entry into the city in 1443. He died in battle against Genoa, leaving Naples to his illegitimate son, Ferrante (FERDINAND I); his other domains passed to his brother John.

## Alfonso II (1448–1495) *King of Naples (1494–95)*

The son of FERDINAND I (Ferrante) and Isabella of Naples, Alfonso, who was cowardly and cruel, was very unpopular. Before succeeding his father, he was associated with and blamed for much of his father's misrule. Through his marriage to Lodovico Sforza's sister, Ippolita, and through his sister's marriage to Ercole d'Este of Ferrara, Alfonso was involved in various Italian conflicts. He defeated Florence at Poggio (1479) and the Turks at Otranto (1481). When CHARLES VIII of France was advancing on Naples early in 1495 Alfonso abdicated in favor of his son, Ferdinand II (Ferrantino), and died later the same year.

**Further reading:** George L. Hersey, *Alfonso II and the Artistic Renewal of Naples, 1485–95* (New Haven, Conn.: Yale University Press, 1969).

**algebra** While ancient mathematicians made enormous contributions to GEOMETRY and ARITHMETIC, their achievements in algebra were less impressive. A tendency to solve problems geometrically, and the failure to develop a convenient symbolism, had led the Greeks in a different direction, but the subject was developed by Indian and Muslim mathematicians, who bequeathed to the Renaissance a number of simple rules for the solution of equations. While Renaissance mathematicians made significant advances in the theory of equations, they proved less successful in developing an adequate symbolism. There was little uniformity of symbolism, and notation was cumbersome and unhelpful. The simple equation

$$ax^2 + bx + c = 0$$

where $x$ is the unknown, and $a,b,c$, stand for given numbers could not have been written before 1637. The equality sign ($=$) was introduced by Robert Recorde in 1537, and the custom of equating the function to zero was established by René Descartes in 1637.

Exponents proved more troublesome. In his *In artem analyticam isagoge* (1591) François VIÈTE had, following the Greek custom, written $A^2$, $A^3$, as AQ, and AC, where the Q and C stood for "quadratus" and "cubus" respectively. The modern convention of $A^2$ and $A^3$ dates, once more, from Descartes, as does the use of letters of the alphabet to stand systematically for the unknowns. The 16th-century Italian mathematicians TARTAGLIA and CARDANO would have written the equation

$$x^3 + 6x = 12$$

as

cubus p: 6 rebus aequilis 12

which translates as

a cube plus 6 things equals 12.

Despite the opacity of their notation, Tartaglia and Cardano still managed to make the first major breakthrough in modern algebra. Neither Greek nor medieval mathematicians had worked out a suitable algorithm for the solution of cubic or higher equations. Algebra seemed stuck at the level of quadratics. In this latter field BOMBELLI had shown how quadratics could be solved by completing the square, while solution by factorization was first worked out by Thomas HARRIOT. Linear equations, by contrast, tended to be solved by a number of traditional rules. Known by such names as "the rule of false position" and "the method of scales," they could be applied quite mechanically.

There remained the cubic equation. In 1535 Tartaglia publicly solved 30 cubics in a competition with the Italian mathematician Scipione del Ferro. Four years later he revealed his algorithm to Cardano, who unhesitatingly published his own variant of the solution in *Ars magna* (1545). Cardano also reported on the solution of the biquadratic or quartic discovered by his pupil Ludovico Ferrari (1522–c. 1560). To advance further, however, required the possession of techniques unknown to Renaissance mathematicians.

**Allen, William** (1532–1594) *English Roman Catholic scholar and cardinal (1587)*
Refusal to comply with the conditions of the Protestant settlement under Elizabeth I obliged him to relinquish his academic post at Oxford and in 1565 to go into permanent exile. He devoted his life to the training of priests for missions to England to reclaim the country for the Roman Catholic Church, establishing colleges for that purpose at DOUAI (1568), Rome (1575), and Valladolid (1589), and instigating the Douai–Reims translation of the Bible into English. However, his backing for the attempted Spanish invasion of England in 1588 alienated many English Catholics. He died at the ENGLISH COLLEGE, his foundation in Rome.

**Alleyn, Edward** (1566–1626) *English tragic actor and theatrical impresario*
Having made his reputation on the London stage in the 1590s, he went into partnership with Philip Henslowe (died 1616) to build the Fortune Theatre (1600). In 1604 they became joint masters of the royal bear-baiting establishment. Alleyn's performances in roles such as MARLOWE's Faustus earned him comparisons with the classical Roman actor Roscius. A shrewd businessman, he amassed a considerable fortune from his theatrical and other properties, using it to buy up the manor of Dulwich, southeast of London, where he founded (1616–19) "the College of God's Gift," now the public school Dulwich College.

**Allori, Alessandro** (c. 1535–1607) *Italian painter*
Allori was active in Florence, where he studied under his uncle BRONZINO, of whom he was a close follower. A visit to Rome (1554–56) also brought him under the influence of MICHELANGELO, which is visible in his frescoes from the early 1560s in SS. Annunziata, Florence. He was patronized by Francesco I de' Medici and contributed paintings in the manner of Bronzino to the duke's Studiolo in the Palazzo Vecchio. Other work for the Medici includes decoration in the Salone of their villa at Poggio a Caiano. His later works, among them a *Birth of the Virgin* (1602; SS. Annunziata, Florence) and an *Ascension* (1603; San Michele, Prato), are in a softer, more relaxed style. His son Cristofano (1577–1621) followed the emerging baroque tendency in Florentine art. Cristofano's best-known picture, *Judith* (Palazzo Pitti, Florence), incorporates portraits of the artist and his wife.

**Altdorfer, Albrecht** (c. 1480–1538) *German painter, print maker, and architect*
The son of an illuminator, Altdorfer became a citizen of his home town of Regensburg in 1505. A member of Regensburg city council since 1519, he was appointed surveyor of public buildings in 1526. In 1535 he was chosen as an ambassador to Vienna, possibly because of his knowledge of the region.

Together with Wolf HUBER and the young CRANACH, Altdorfer was a chief exponent of the socalled "Danube style". Possibly influenced by the pastoral poetry of Konrad CELTIS, these painters delighted in portraying the lush vegetation and dreamy enchantment of the German woods. This fascination with the luxuriance of nature is strongly apparent in Altdorfer's tiny Berlin *Satyr Family* (1507). Despite the emphatically Germanic location of this scene, the figures are Italian in derivation; the artist copied engravings after MANTEGNA from as early as 1506. In the Berlin *Nativity* (c. 1512) Altdorfer utilized dramatic lighting effects and one-point perspective with brilliant effect. This fundamental bent towards Mannerism developed still further in the eerie viewpoints and stunning colors of the now dismantled altarpiece (1517) for St. Florian near Linz. The high point of Altdorfer's career is his Munich *Battle of the Issus* (1529), one of the great visionary paintings of all time. Depicted from an almost astral viewpoint, the forces of Alexander the Great pursue the hordes of Darius into Asia. The background landscape curves to reveal the rim of a spherical earth upon which Cyprus and the North African coast may be plainly seen, upside down, as though viewed from the north and an immense height. Altdorfer was also outstanding as a draftsman of *chiaroscuro* drawings and a designer of woodcuts. He was arguably the most individual genius in German painting of the 16th century.

**Further reading:** Christopher S. Wood, *Albrecht Altdorfer and the Origins of Landscape* (London: Reaktion Books, 2003).

**Altichiero** (1320/30–1395) *Italian painter*
Altichiero was born at Zevio, near Verona, and was mainly active in Verona and Padua. His style was influenced by GIOTTO and he himself had numerous followers. Frescoes by him can be seen in San Stefano and Sant' Anastasia in Verona and in the Santo and Oratorio di San Giorgio in Padua.

**Alva, Duke of** See ALBA, FERNANDO ALVAREZ DE TOLEDO, 3RD DUKE OF

**Amadeo, Giovanni Antonio** (1447–1522) *Italian marble sculptor*
He was born in Pavia and is documented from 1466 working on sculpture for the magnificent new Certosa (Carthusian monastery) in his native town; in 1474 he was made jointly responsible with the brothers Mantegazza for its huge polychrome marble façade. Between 1470 and 1476 he carved the monuments and reliefs of the Colleoni chapel in Bergamo and in 1490 was employed on Milan cathedral. Apart from portraits, in which his work was influenced by classical prototypes, his sculpture was mostly carved in relief, with religious themes predominating.

**Amberger, Christoph** (c. 1500–61/62) *German painter*
Amberger was born at Augsburg and probably trained there under Hans BURGKMAIR and Leonhard BECK. In 1548 he met TITIAN, then visiting Augsburg. Amberger's Berlin portrait of Charles V (c. 1532) was influenced by the Netherlandish court painter Jan VERMEYEN, who was at Augsburg in 1530. References to the Venetian painters PALMA VECCHIO and Paris BORDONE appear in Amberger's

Vienna portraits of a man and a woman (1539) and his Munich *Christoph Fugger* (1541). In the Berlin portrait of Sebastian MÜNSTER (c. 1552), Amberger eschewed this international mannerist style in favor of a more traditional German approach. His altar for Augsburg cathedral (1554) is similarly conservative, translating the late Gothic architectual motifs of HOLBEIN THE ELDER into a contemporary Italianate idiom.

**Ambrose of Camaldoli** See TRAVERSARI, AMBROGIO

**Ambrosiana, Bibliotheca** The chief LIBRARY of MILAN, founded by the bishop of Milan, Cardinal Federico Borromeo (1564–1631), who named it after St. Ambrose, patron saint of the city. It was the first public library in Italy and opened on December 8, 1609, with a collection of over 30,000 books and 12,000 manuscripts housed in the palace built by Borromeo between 1603 and 1609 on the site of the Scuole Taverna. The library was enriched by many private donations and bequests, as well as by the acquisitions of its agents traveling abroad.

**Ambrosian Republic** (1447–50) A Milanese regime established immediately after Duke Filippo Maria Visconti (*see* VISCONTI FAMILY) died without an heir. Twenty-four local notables—"captains and defenders of liberty"—named the republic in honor of St. Ambrose, Milan's patron. Divisions within the ruling group, discontent from the lesser bourgeoisie, rebellion in subject cities, and the hostility of Venice brought the republic close to collapse. In autumn 1449 Francesco SFORZA, a condottiere formerly in Duke Filippo Maria's employ and married to the duke's illegitimate daughter, besieged the city; in March 1450 the republic surrendered and Sforza was installed as duke of Milan.

**Amerbach, Johannes** (1443–1513) *Swiss printer and publisher*
He studied in Paris and then returned to Basle to set up a printing house (1475) with the principal aim of producing good texts of the works of the Church Fathers (*see also* PATRISTIC STUDIES). He gathered round him a circle of scholars that included REUCHLIN, and in 1511 employed a Dominican, Johannes Cono of Nuremberg (1463–1513), to instruct his sons and any other interested parties in Greek and Hebrew in his own house, which became a virtual academy for northern European scholars. This intellectual tradition was continued by Amerbach's successor, FROBEN.

**Ames, William** (Amesius) (1576–1633) *English Puritan divine*
Ames was born at Ipswich. Having gained a reputation as a controversialist while at Cambridge, he left England for the Netherlands after being forbidden to preach at Col-

chester by the bishop of London. Here he soon made a name for himself as the champion of Calvinism in his debate with the minister of the Arminians (*see* ARMINIANISM) at Rotterdam in 1613. Between 1622 and 1633 he was professor of theology at Franeker university in Friesland, where his reputation was such that he attracted students from all over Europe. Ill health led to his resignation and he died at Rotterdam a few months later.

**Amman, Jobst** (1539–1591) *Swiss-born print maker and designer of stained glass*
The son of a choirmaster and teacher of rhetoric, Amman worked first as a stained-glass designer in his native Zürich before moving, successively, to Schaffhausen, Basle, and Nuremberg. Although he is not documented as an assistant of Virgil SOLIS, he was effectively the latter's successor as the leading book illustrator in Nuremberg. His voluminous output included numerous ornamental and heraldic prints and title-pages, as well as narrative illustrations. He received numerous commissions from humanists and editors, such as Sigmund Feyerabend of Frankfurt. In 1574 he married the widow of a Nuremberg goldsmith and became a citizen of his adopted city. On account of his commissions he traveled widely: to Augsburg (1578), Frankfurt and Heidelberg (1583), Würzburg (1586–87), and Altdorf (1590). Amman's penetrating portraits, such as *Hans Sachs* and *Wenzel Jamnitzer*, and his genre works and studies, such as the *Series of Animals*, constitute his finest work.

**Ammanati, Bartolommeo** (1511–1592) *Italian sculptor*
Born near Florence, Ammanati trained in the workshop of Pisa cathedral, where his first independent work is found (1536). In 1540 he tried to make his mark in Florence with a private commission for the tomb of Jacopo Nari, but it was sabotaged by the jealous BANDINELLI, leaving only the effigy and a good allegorical group of *Victory* (both Bargello, Florence). Ammanati left for Venice, where he was helped and influenced by his fellow-countryman Jacopo SANSOVINO. His principal sculptures in north Italy were Michelangelesque allegories for the palace and the tomb of the humanist Marco Benavides (1489–1582) in the Eremitani church in Padua.

After Pope Julius III was elected (1550) Ammanati moved to Rome, where he executed all the sculpture on the monuments to members of the pope's family in San Pietro in Montorio. The portrait effigies and allegories are among Ammanati's masterpieces. Moving with VASARI to Florence, he entered the service of the Medici dukes. His spectacular fountain of Juno has six over-life-size marble figures mounted on a rainbow (components now in the Bargello). Ammanati's best-known sculpture is the fountain of Neptune in the Piazza della Signoria, Florence (c. 1560–75). The central figure was carved out of a colossal block of marble already begun by Bandinelli before his death (1560); this inhibited Ammanati's treatment. More successful are the surrounding bronze figures of marine deities, fauns, and satyrs, modeled and cast under his supervision. These figures and his *Ops*, a female nude statuette that Ammanati contributed (1572–73) to the Studiolo of Francesco de' Medici, epitomize his style, which concentrates on grace of form at the expense of emotion. Ammanati rivalled Vasari as a mannerist architect, with his amazingly bold but capricious rustication in the courtyard of the Palazzo Pitti (1558–70) and his graceful bridge of Sta. Trinità (1567–70). By 1582 the COUNTER-REFORMATION had so strongly influenced the sculptor that he denounced on moral grounds the public display of nude sculpture.

**Amorbach, Johannes** See AMERBACH, JOHANNES

**Amsdorf, Nikolaus von** (1483–1565) *German Lutheran theologian*
Probably born at Torgau on the Elbe, Amsdorf studied at Wittenberg, where he later met LUTHER. He soon became a close friend and one of Luther's most determined supporters. Amsdorf assisted in the translation of the Bible and accompanied Luther to the Leipzig conference (1519) and the Diet of WORMS (1521). He became an evangelical preacher, spreading word of the Reformation at Magdeburg (1524), Goslar (1531), Einbeck (1534), and Schmalkald (1537). John Frederick, Elector of Saxony, appointed him bishop of Naumburg-Zeitz in 1542, a post he held until 1547. In 1548 he helped found the university of Jena, and, in the same year actively opposed the Interim of AUGSBURG. From 1552 until his death he lived at Eisenach, remaining a conservative and influential Lutheran.

**Amsterdam** A Netherlands city and port on the Ijsselmeer, an inlet of the North Sea. As a small fishing village Amsterdam gained toll privileges from Count Floris V of Holland in 1275 and prospered during the Renaissance to become Holland's largest commercial center by the late 15th century. Political developments, combined with the expansion of trade, fishing, and shipbuilding, made 16th-century Amsterdam one of the greatest European financial and commercial centers. Its citizens rejected Spanish rule and adopted the Calvinist cause under the leadership of WILLIAM THE SILENT (1578); they profited from the Spanish recapture of Antwerp (1585) and the subsequent closure of the River Scheldt to trade. By the early 17th century Amsterdam had close to 100,000 inhabitants and could claim to be not only Europe's financial capital but also a center of world trade, especially the tea and spice trades. Its institutions included the Dutch East India Company (founded 1602), the Amsterdam exchange bank (founded 1609), and the Amsterdam stock exchange. The Nieuwe Kerk is the city's most notable surviving Renaissance building.

**Amyot, Jacques** (1513–1593) *French bishop and classical scholar*
Born at Melun and educated at Paris university, he became professor of Latin and Greek at Bourges, where he began his work of translating classical authors: Heliodorus (*L'Histoire éthiopique*, 1548), Longus (*Daphnis et Chloé*, 1559), and, above all, PLUTARCH. His translation of Plutarch's *Lives*, finally completed under the patronage of Francis I in 1559, supplied the writers and playwrights of several generations with characters and situations. Retranslated into English by Thomas NORTH (1579), this was Shakespeare's major source for his Roman plays. Amyot's version of Plutarch's *Moralia* appeared in 1572, completing a task that made him deservedly hailed by his contemporaries as "le prince des traducteurs." Favored by four successive French kings and tutor to two of them, Amyot was finally made bishop of Auxerre in 1570, where he spent the rest of his life.

**Anabaptists** A variety of separate religious movements on the radical wing of the REFORMATION. The Anabaptists emerged from the underprivileged layers of society, often with exceptionally radical social, economic, and religious programs. Features common to all included the practice of adult baptism (hence the term "Anabaptists," coined by their enemies), a belief in continual revelation, and a doctrine of separation from the unconverted. Consequently they gained a reputation as dangerous revolutionaries, intent on the destruction of the established social and religious order.

Anabaptist activity in Münster (1532–35) marks the peak of their political influence. Religious radicals such as the preacher Bernhard Rothmann (c. 1495–c. 1535) and the merchant Bernhard Knipperdollinck (c. 1490–1536) combined to turn Münster into an Anabaptist city, a situation temporarily condoned by Landgrave PHILIP OF HESSE. The existing order in Münster was overthrown in 1534 by Dutch Anabaptists led by Jan Matthysz., a baker of Haarlem, and John of Leyden (Jan Leyden) who hoped to turn the city into a New Jerusalem from which the spiritual conquest of the world could be directed. Matthysz. ordered the confiscation of all property and destruction of all books except the Bible. His followers' iconoclasm brought about the destruction of much of Münster's heritage of religious art. The prince-bishop besieged the city, and Matthysz. was killed during a sortie (April 1534). John of Leyden then proclaimed himself "king" and introduced polygamy. The prince-bishop captured the city in June 1535, and the following January the surviving Anabaptist leaders were tortured and executed. The end of the Anabaptist "kingdom" of Münster was not the end of Anabaptism, which had extended into other parts of northern and central Europe. The chief centers of activity were Saxony, Zürich, Augsburg and the upper Danube, Austria, Moravia, the Tyrol, Poland, Lithuania, Italy, the lower Rhine, and the Netherlands. Groups in these places often held differing doctrinal views, although united in their rejection of infant baptism. Menno Simons (*see* MENNONITES) was the leader of one such group. Others were the Melchiorites or Hoffmanites (called after their leader Melchior Hoffman) in the Netherlands; the Hutterites (after their leader Jakob Hutter) in Moravia; the socalled Zwickau Prophets in Saxony; and the Swiss Brethren. All were liable to often savage persecution from their Catholic and Protestant neighbors.

See also: MILLENARIANISM

Further reading: James M. Stayer, *The German Peasants' War and Anabaptist Community of Goods* (Montreal, Canada and London: McGill-Queen's University Press, 1991).

**anamorphosis** In art, an image distorted in such a way that it only becomes recognizable when viewed from a particular angle or under certain other conditions. The transliteration of the Greek word (meaning "transformation") did not appear until the 18th century, but is generally used to refer to earlier compositions. Plato (*Sophist*, 236) was the first to make mention of the idea. It was reintroduced explicitly by Daniele BARBARO in his *Pratica della perspettiva*, published in Venice in 1568/69, with the following definition: "Often, and with no less pleasure than amazement, one may gaze on some of those pictures or cards showing perspectives in which, if the eye of s/he who looks at them be not placed at a particular point, something totally different from what is depicted appears, but, contemplated afterwards from its correct angle, the subject is revealed according to the painter's original intention."

For the painter, anamorphosis is a special application of the laws of perspective. Shapes are projected outside themselves and dislocated in such a way that they re-form when they are seen from another viewpoint. The practice of anamorphosis shows that artistic technique could have other aims than that of restoring a third dimension (the sole aim recognized in ALBERTI's treatises). The "curious" perspective of anamorphosis is, rather, a stimulus to fantasy and an illustration of the fleeting, oblique nature of pictorial truth. The earliest examples of the technique in the Renaissance are met with in the notebooks of LEONARDO DA VINCI. The two best-known examples of anamorphosis in painting are the skull in HOLBEIN's *Ambassadors* (1533; National Gallery, London) and Guilim (William) Scrots's portrait of the future King EDWARD VI (1546; National Portrait Gallery, London). The latter, displayed at Whitehall Palace, apparently had some special viewing device attached to it to enable the head to be seen in correct perspective.

Further reading: Jurgis Baltrusaitis, *Anamorphic Art*, transl. W. J. Strachan (New York: Harry N. Abrams, 1977); Ernest B. Gilman, *The Curious Perspective: Literary and*

*Pictorial Wit in the Seventeenth Century* (New Haven, Conn. and London: Yale University Press, 1978).

**anatomy** Renaissance anatomists worked almost exclusively in the tradition established by the 2nd-century Greek physician Galen (*see* GALENISM, RENAISSANCE). The tradition is clearly seen in the *Anathomia* (1316) of Mondino de' Luzzi, the leading textbook of the early Renaissance. It suffered from two basic weaknesses. In the first place, because of constraints on human DISSECTION, anatomists had often been forced to work with Barbary apes and domestic animals. For this reason they readily followed Galen in describing the *rete mirabile*, a vascular structure they had all supposedly seen at the base of the human brain, despite the fact that it is found in the ox and the sheep but not in man. Once such fictions as the *rete mirabile* and the five-lobed liver entered the literature, they seemed impossible to eliminate. Secondly, anatomy was made to serve the misguided Galenic physiology. If Galen's system needed septal pores to allow blood to pass directly from the right to the left side of the heart, they were conveniently "seen" and reported. To overcome these difficulties it would be necessary to prefer the evidence of nature to the authority of an ancient textbook.

The first real signs of such a transfer of allegiance can be seen in the early 16th century. Monographs revealing this tendency were produced by LEONARDO DA VINCI, Berengar of Carpi (died 1530), Charles ESTIENNE, Gunther of Andernach (1487–1584), Jacobus Sylvius (1478–1555), and, above all, VESALIUS. The new-style monograph used the full resources of Renaissance artists and printers to provide, for the first time, detailed realistic illustrations, whereas earlier works had provided no more than extremely crude stylized diagrams. Moreover, anatomy was becoming a subject of serious artistic study in its own right, with Leonardo and Antonio del POLLAIUOLO leading the way, followed closely by MICHELANGELO. A detailed account of the fruits of anatomical studies for artists appears in LOMAZZO's *Trattato* (1584). The first printed anatomical figures appeared in the *Fasciculo de medicina* (1493); 50 years later the *De fabrica* of Vesalius contained some 250 detailed blocks by Jan Steven van CALCAR. At last anatomists had something objective against which to judge their own observations. They soon came to realize that items such as septal pores and five-lobed livers could not be found in the human body.

Once having seen that the traditional account of human anatomy was questionable, anatomists could begin the serious task of restructuring their discipline. Part of this task involved the construction of a new vocabulary. Many terms such as "pancreas" and "thyroid" came from Galen himself; others came from Arabic and Hebrew sources; the bulk, however, came from Renaissance anatomists. The Renaissance also saw the emergence of the new discipline of comparative anatomy. BELON in 1551

had written on the anatomy of marine animals, while Carlo Ruini in his *Anatomia del cavallo* (1599) tackled the anatomy of the horse. On the basis of such detailed monographs Giulio Casserio (1561–1616) could at last present genuinely comparative material in his *De vocis auditusque organis* (1601), a study of the vocal and auditory organs of man, cow, horse, dog, hare, cat, goose, mouse, and pig.

**Further reading:** Andrea Carlino, *Books of the Body: Anatomical Ritual and Renaissance Learning* (Chicago, Ill.: University of Chicago Press, 1999); Jonathan Sawday, *The Body Emblazoned: Dissection and the Human Body in Renaissance Culture* (London and New York: Routledge, 1997).

**Andrea da Milano** See BREGNO, ANDREA

**Andrea del Castagno** (1417/19–1457) *Italian painter*
Castagno, so named after his birthplace, was an important innovator like MASACCIO before him; he introduced a rugged vitality into Florentine painting. Most of Castagno's few surviving paintings and documented lost works are frescoes, including his earliest known commission, the effigies of hanged criminals for the façade of the Bargello (then the communal prison) in Florence in 1440 (now lost). Castagno's serious and heroic figures and interest in movement are already apparent in his earliest frescoes at the chapel of San Tarasio at San Zaccaria, Venice (1442, in collaboration with the little-known Francesco da Faenza). His *Last Supper with Scenes of the Passion*, which fills the end wall of the refectory at Sant' Apollonia, Florence (1440s), is painted in an unusually dark and rich palette and reveals his skill in difficult perspective effects (for which he was praised by Cristoforo LANDINO in 1481), his taste for moments of intense drama, and his involvement in the antiquarianism of the early Renaissance in Florence. *The Trinity Adored by St. Jerome and Two Female Saints* (c. 1454; SS. Annunziata, Florence), a penitential subject, combines a mood of grave intensity with dramatic foreshortening, qualities also noted in Castagno's moving and tragic *Lamentation*, a design for a stained glass rondel in the drum of the dome of Florence cathedral (1440), in a program that includes designs by DONATELLO, GHIBERTI, and UCCELLO.

Castagno's work in Rome for Pope Nicholas V in 1454 has been identified as a much restored architectural decoration in the Biblioteca Graeca of the Vatican palace. Landino also praised Castagno for a technique full of spontaneity and liveliness and his ability to create figures which express movement; these traits are best seen in the *Victorious David* (c. 1450; National Gallery, Washington), one of the few surviving Quattrocento parade shields, and the EQUESTRIAN MONUMENT for Niccolò da Tolentino (fresco, 1455–56; Florence cathedral), which is a pendant and a foil for Uccello's *Sir John Hawkwood*. The *Famous Men and Women* frescoes from the Villa Carducci (c. 1450;

now Uffizi, with fragments *in situ*) are among the most important surviving Quattrocento secular decorations; Castagno and his patron abandoned well-established iconographic prototypes to introduce Florentine literary figures (Dante, Petrarch, and Boccaccio) and Florentine military leaders (Niccola Acciaiuoli, Farinata degli Uberti, and Pippo Spano) into the company of heroic women from antiquity (Esther, the Cumaean Sybil, and Queen Tomyris). These impressive sculpturesque figures in illusionistic niches reveal Castagno's sources, for in monumentality and boldly massed drapery they recall Masaccio, while in the lucid, sharp outlines, vigorous drapery patterns, and even in pose they convey the impact of the sculpture of Donatello. They offer an appreciation of human dignity and accomplishment that is central to an understanding of Renaissance attitudes.

**Further reading:** Marita Horster, *Andrea del Castagno* (Oxford, U.K.: Phaidon, 1980); John R. Spencer, *Andrea del Castagno and his Patrons* (Durham, N.C. and London: Duke University Press, 1991).

### Andrea del Sarto (1486–1530) *Italian painter*

Andrea d'Agnolo di Francesco was born in Florence, the son of a tailor (hence "del Sarto"). At the age of seven he was apprenticed to a goldsmith, shortly thereafter to a Florentine painter Gian Barile (otherwise unknown), and finally to the eccentric but technically brilliant master PIERO DI COSIMO. Internal stylistic evidence suggests that he may have spent time with Raffaellino del Garbo (c. 1466–c. 1524), a painter also known for technical proficiency, although not for innovation. VASARI reports that like many young artists Andrea drew from cartoons by Leonardo da Vinci and Michelangelo, thus absorbing the achievements of the leading artists of the High Renaissance. In style and temperament his leaning was to Leonardo. By about 1506 he had taken a studio near the Piazza del Grano with FRANCIABIGIO, a pupil of ALBERTINELLI, the latter a partner of Fra Bartolommeo. The early interest in Leonardo and the connection to Fra Bartolommeo through Franciabigio reinforced Andrea's interest in classic compositional solutions, modulated tonal harmonies, and SFUMATO, as shown in *The Marriage of St. Catherine* (1512–13; Dresden). He befriended the young sculptor Jacopo SANSOVINO, pupil of Andrea Contucci (called Sansovino), and he and Franciabigio moved into a new studio near the SS. Annunziata which they shared with Jacopo. The two painters soon received commissions for frescoes for the entrance courtyard of the Annunziata (1509–14; *Birth of the Virgin, Arrival of the Magi*, scenes from the life of St. Filippo Benizzi) and for the little cloister of the Confraternity of the Scalzo (1511–26; scenes from the life of John the Baptist).

Andrea was influenced as much by the sculpture of the two Sansovinos as by the painters of his generation. The figures of Christ and John the Baptist and of Justice in the Scalzo grisaille murals are quoted directly from identical figures by Andrea Sansovino; Jacopo Sansovino made models for figures which appeared in Andrea del Sarto's paintings, for instance, the Madonna and the St. John in the *Madonna of the Harpies* (1517; Uffizi, Florence). The painter collaborated with Jacopo on the design and decoration of the mock façade for the Florentine Duomo, one of the elaborate temporary ornaments commissioned for the state visit of Pope Leo X to Florence in 1515. He also worked on stage sets with one of his assistants, Bastiano (Aristotile) da SANGALLO, a member of the prominent family of architects. These contacts with sculptors and architects help to explain Andrea's highly developed sense of volume and perspective in his figures and architecture. His figures display an earthbound naturalism in their breadth and volume, yet they exude grace and sensitivity. In 1516 he married the widow Lucrezia, whose features served as the model for his broad-faced Madonnas.

By 1509, with Leonardo in Milan, Michelangelo and Raphael in Rome, and Fra Bartolommeo visiting Venice, Andrea took his place as the premier painter in Florence. Gestures, poses, and compositional groupings in his paintings represent a continual dialogue with his distinguished contemporaries, translated into a pictorial language distinctly his own. Tender blues, delicate violets, and rose tints applied in soft brushwork but with a supreme understanding of form are the pictorial counterpart of the psychological balance between emotion and restraint in his figures (see Plate I).

Andrea worked almost his entire career in Florence. He traveled to France by invitation of Francis I in spring 1518, returning to Florence by summer the following year. His interest in Leonardo was renewed by the presence of that great master at the French court, while two new paintings that he saw there, the *St. Michael* and the *Holy Family of Francis I* (both Louvre, Paris), presented a point of contact with Raphael's mature Roman style, as witness Andrea's *Caritas* (1518; Louvre) and *Pietà* (1524; Palazzo Pitti, Florence). Among Andrea's pupils and assistants are to be counted the leaders of the next generation of Florentine artists. His use of unconventional effects of color and light were signals picked up by these young painters, particularly the great "mannerists" PONTORMO and ROSSO FIORENTINO, as well as Vasari and SALVIATI. Andrea weathered the siege of Florence (1529–30) but died at the end of September 1530 in the plague that followed it.

**Further reading:** Antonio Natali, *Andrea del Sarto* (New York: Abbeville, 1999); John K. G. Shearman, *Andrea del Sarto*, 2 vols (Oxford, U.K.: Clarendon Press, 1965).

### Andreoli, Giorgio (Maestro Giorgio) (c. 1470–1553) *Italian potter*

He was born at Intra on Lake Maggiore into a family

from Pavia, but is famous for his association with the MAJOLICA works of Gubbio, where he was based from 1498. He held a monopoly in a distinctive ruby glaze, which is one of the most characteristic products of the Gubbio potteries.

## Andrewes, Lancelot (1555–1626) *English preacher and theologian*

The son of a London merchant, Andrewes received an academic education. After taking holy orders (1580) he rose steadily in the Church through his learning (he is reported to have mastered 15 languages) and his exceptional qualities as a preacher. Under James I, at whose court he regularly preached on Church feast days, he became succesively bishop of Chichester (1605), of Ely (1609), and of Winchester (1619). He played a prominent role in the Hampton Court Conference (1604) at which it was decided to produce a new English version of the Bible; when the Authorized (King James) Version was published (1611), Andrewes's name headed the list of translators. Apart from a controversy with Cardinal ROBERT BELLARMINE concerning the oath of allegiance imposed after the Gunpowder Plot (1605), Andrewes published little in his lifetime, and his two most famous works, *Ninety-six Sermons* (1629) and *Preces Privatae* ("Private Prayers"; 1648), were collected posthumously. Nonetheless, he had a formative influence upon Anglican theology and was renowned for his personal integrity as much as for his theological scholarship.

**Further reading:** Nicholas Lossky, *Lancelot Andrewes the Preacher (1555–1626): The Origins of the Mystical Theology of the Church of England*, transl. Andrew Louth (Oxford, U.K.: Clarendon Press, 1991).

## Anerio, Felice (c. 1560–1614) *Italian composer*

As a boy Anerio sang in the choirs of several major Roman institutions, and his first known composition is music for a Passion play (1582). He was *maestro di cappella* of the English College in Rome (1584–85) and *maestro* of the Vertuosa Compagnia dei Musici di Roma, a society founded (1584) by leading Roman musicians. In 1594 Anerio succeeded PALESTRINA as composer to the papal choir. He was also appointed *maestro di cappella* to Duke Altaemps.

Most of Anerio's earlier works are secular (madrigals and canzonettes); his sacred works were written largely during his period as papal composer. His Masses, psalms, responsories, and motets are strongly influenced by Palestrina's style, but use some more progressive devices such as frequent word repetitions to stress parts of the text. While Felice Anerio's roots lay firmly in the Palestrina tradition, his brother, Giovanni Francesco (1567–1630), wrote in a distinctly baroque style and concentrated on the small-scale motet with continuo.

## Angela Merici, St. (1474–1540) *Italian religious, founder of the Ursulines*

She spent most of her life at Brescia, where she taught young girls and cared for ill and needy women. On a pilgrimage to the Holy Land (1524–25) she was smitten with temporary blindness. Urged by visions, she founded (1535) a religious community for women at Brescia which she called after St. Ursula (*see* URSULINES) and of which she became superior in 1537. She was canonized in 1807.

## Angeli, Pietro Angelo (Pier Angelo Bargeo) (1517–1596) *Italian humanist poet*

His alternative name derives from his birthplace of Barga, near Lucca. *Siriade* (1591), a Latin epic on the crusader conquest of Jerusalem, was drawn upon by TASSO for the *Gerusalemme conquistata* (*see* GERUSALEMME LIBERATA). Besides his Latin verse, Angeli also wrote pastoral poetry in Italian (*Poesie amorose*, 1589) and translated Sophocles' *Oedipus Rex* into the vernacular.

## Angelico, Fra (c. 1395/1400–1455) *Italian painter*

Fra Angelico, who was born at Vicchio di Mugello, northeast of Florence, was known to his contemporaries by the secular name Guido di Piero and by the religious name Fra Giovanni da Fiesole. Vasari placed his birth about 1387, but reconsideration of documents points to a more likely date of about 1395/1400. The difference of a decade helps correct the older view of Fra Angelico as a painter in the TRECENTO tradition, and instead places him in the vanguard of artists working in the third and fourth decades of the QUATTROCENTO.

He may have been trained by the miniaturist Battista di Biagio Sanguigni and by the painter Ambrogio di Baldese. A payment recorded to "Guido di Piero" in 1418 is evidence that the young artist was then still a layman; in 1423 his name appears as "Frate Giovanni di San Domenico di Fiesole". Thus he joined the Dominican Order at its house of San Domenico in Fiesole between 1418 and 1423, perhaps inspired by the preaching of the Dominican Fra Manfredi da Vercelli.

As a friar Angelico continued painting, operating a workshop at San Domenico until about 1440, then transferring it to San Marco in Florence, as fresco decoration of that convent was under way. Historical evidence indicates that Angelico was highly regarded in his lifetime both as an intellect and as a painter. Administrative capabilities led to his appointment as substitute *vicario* at San Domenico in 1435, and as *sindicho* at San Marco in 1443. Tradition has it that Pope Eugenius IV, rejecting a number of distinguished candidates for the vacant archbishopric of Florence, offered it to Angelico, but that the artist was instrumental in securing the appointment of Fra (later St) ANTONINO to that position in 1446. In a lost epitaph for his tomb in Sta. Maria sopra Minerva, Rome, Angelico was celebrated as "…consummate painter, who had no equal in his art"; in a poem by the 16th-century painter Giovanni Santi, the father of Raphael, he is mentioned alongside Fra Filippo Lippi and Domenico Veneziano as "Giovan da Fiesole frate al ben ardente."

Establishing a chronology for Angelico's oeuvre poses problems of connoisseurship and dating, particularly for his earliest period. Notable among the early works are the *Annunciation* (1428–32; Museo Diocesano, Cortona) and the Linaiuoli tabernacle (1433–35; Museo di San Marco, Florence), in which Angelico demonstrated an interest in the new manner of Masaccio and Ghiberti. He employed skillful perspective and spatial continuity and contributed advances in the depiction of natural phenomena. The period 1438–45 is dominated by a commission from the church and convent of San Marco for the altarpiece of the *cappella maggiore* and for the fresco decoration of the public quarters and private cells of the convent. The design and concept, linking the group of 54 frescoes, are Angelico's, though the work is largely that of assistants. The meditative clarity, simplicity, and order reflect MICHELOZZO's architectural schemes, emphasizing, through economy of detail, the didactic and doctrinal gestures of the saints and biblical figures represented. In contrast, the San Marco altarpiece is rich in sumptuous textiles and architectural devices used to project and delimit an original perspective scheme. In the *Deposition* (Museo di San Marco), a frieze of foreground figures gives way to a panoramic landscape, bathed in a light which renders spatial coherence to the composition.

Angelico was called to Rome in 1445. It was during this Roman sojourn that he probably frescoed the private chapel of Pope Nicholas V in the Vatican with scenes from the lives of St. Stephen and St. Lawrence; in these the figures and architecture take on a new volume and gravity. In 1449 he was elected prior of his convent.

Angelico's reputation and (certainly) his nickname depend on the appeal of precious images of the Madonna and Child framed in a glory of angels, delicately painted in enamel-like colors on a gold ground. But it is the power to translate the quality of the miniaturist's art into the scale and vocabulary of the modern mode which distinguishes him. The result is an edifying and pious pictorial language, brilliant in the balance struck between celestial vision and the laws of nature.

**Further reading:** Luciano Berti, *Fra Angelico: The Life and Work of the Artist* (London: Thames & Hudson, 1968); Georges Didi-Huberman, *Fra Angelico: Dissemblance and Figuration*, transl. Jane Marie Todd (Chicago, Ill.: University of Chicago Press, 1995); William Hood, *Fra Angelico at San Marco* (New Haven, Conn. and London: Yale University Press, 1993).

**Anghiera, Pietro Martire d'** See PETER MARTYR (Pietro Martire d'Anghiera)

**Anglican Church** See BOOK OF COMMON PRAYER; ELIZABETHAN SETTLEMENT; THIRTY-NINE ARTICLES

**Anguisciola, Sophonisba** (1527–c. 1623) *Italian painter*
A native of Cremona, Sophonisba was the daughter of a Piedmontese nobleman and one of the first Italian women to become an artist. She was a pupil of Bernardino CAMPI and became a noted portrait painter in the mannerist style, executing several self-portraits and depictions of prominent figures in society. Her best works include a family group portrait of her sisters playing chess (Museum Narodowe, Pozna[, Poland). She moved to Madrid in 1559 and also worked in Sicily, only returning to Italy late in her life.

**Anjou, Francis, Duke of Alençon-** See FRANCIS, DUKE OF ALENÇON

**Anjou, houses of** Three French dynasties whose power was initially based on the lower Loire region of France. The first house of Anjou lasted from the ninth century until it lost its territories to the French crown in the early 13th century; it also ruled England from 1154 to 1157. The second was founded in 1246 by Charles, brother of Louis IX of France and later king of Naples and Sicily. One line of his descendants ruled Naples, another Hungary. When Philip of Valois succeeded to the French throne in 1328, Anjou, which he had inherited from his mother, was reunited to the French crown. In 1351 the third house of Anjou was founded when John II of France invested his younger son Louis with Anjou. Joanna I of Naples promised Naples to Louis in 1379 and in the 15th century the later Angevins spent much of their time fruitlessly pursuing their claim to Naples. In 1480 RENÉ I, the last male heir, died, and Angevin claims to Naples, Sicily, Hungary, and Jerusalem passed to the French crown. See family tree overleaf.

**Antico (Pier Jacopo di Antonio Alari Bonacolsi)** (c. 1460–1528) *Italian sculptor, bronze-founder, and medalist*
Born in Mantua and trained as a goldsmith, he had received his nickname by 1479 (when he used it to sign two medals) owing to his knowledge of antiquity, interest in archaeology, and brilliance at recreating in bronze statuettes some of the fragmentary masterpieces of Greco-Roman sculpture (e.g. the *Apollo Belvedere*, *Venus*, *Meleager*, and *Hercules and Antaeus*). He worked for various members of the GONZAGA FAMILY in and around Mantua, notably for Isabella d'Este, and visited Rome twice in the 1490s. His style is a sculptural counterpart to MANTEGNA's in painting, emphasizing the smooth, rotund forms of the human body and contrasting their polished surfaces with intricately chiseled details in the hair, drapery, and accoutrements, which are often gilded, while the

eyes are sometimes inlaid in silver, as in the bronze bust of a young man in the J. Paul Getty Museum (c. 1520).

**antiquarianism** Although springing initially from a desire to recover the MANUSCRIPTS of classical texts, the antiquarian impulse that spread throughout Europe during the Renaissance came to include the collection and study of coins (*see* NUMISMATICS), architectural fragments, and many other artefacts from the past. Discovering what these objects meant to collectors provides an insight into their views of history and time, art and humanity. When Pliny the Elder (23–79 CE) commented on ancient marvels he paid most attention to those that were especially large, costly, or created by famous men. By contrast, Renaissance HISTORIOGRAPHY led scholars to look systematically at the achievements of past civilizations, and to compare them with those of their own era. PETRARCH, one of the earliest collectors of manuscripts and coins, saw the

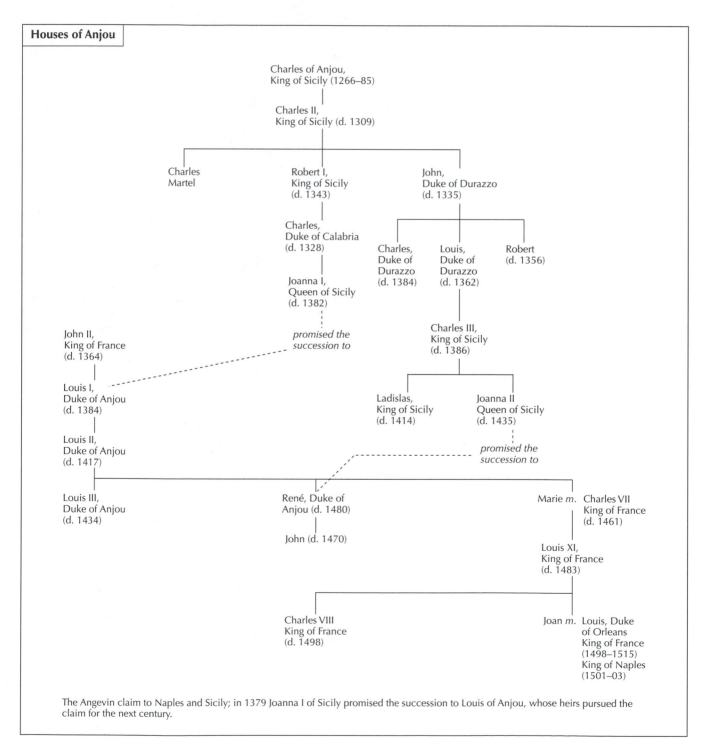

**Houses of Anjou**

The Angevin claim to Naples and Sicily; in 1379 Joanna I of Sicily promised the succession to Louis of Anjou, whose heirs pursued the claim for the next century.

classical age as the highest point of civilization, followed by a thousand-year downward spiral until the beginnings of a revival in his own day. In the 15th century GHIBERTI adapted this model to accord with the emerging ideology of humanism, in which man is the measure of all things. VASARI likewise drew close parallels between the flowering of antiquity and his own day. His *The Lives of the Artists* (1550, 1568) also called for careful judgments to be made in the attribution of works to individuals.

A concern for historical accuracy was one factor that marked Renaissance antiquarianism as different from earlier approaches. However, this was complicated by the fact that, during the Latin Middle Ages, once a manuscript had been copied, it was then used for some other purpose; thus the texts that formed the basis of any later study were tantalizingly one step removed from the originals. By the end of the 14th century manuscripts were being more carefully preserved, catalogued, and classified. As knowledge of classical art and literature became more accurate and more widespread, some legendary or bogus works were debunked. But such knowledge could be put to other uses: the Dominican scholar Giovanni Nanni (Annius) of Viterbo (1432–1502) skillfully forged histories by ancient authors, which drove real histories from the marketplace for almost a century. A return to historical accuracy came with the work of Joseph SCALIGER, editor of a long series of Greek and Latin texts in the later 16th century. Using philological and astronomical techniques, Scaliger reconstructed the whole framework of dates that underpinned ancient and medieval, Near Eastern and Western history.

In the Mediterranean area, remains from the classical world were abundant and trade in antiquities was brisk. CYRIAC OF ANCONA is an early example of an antiquarian in the field. From the 1410s Francesco SQUARCIONE collected antiquities that would subsequently feature in his paintings. The often chance unearthing of classical artefacts, such as the discovery of the Laocoön statue group in Rome in 1506, encouraged antiquarian speculation. Beyond the boundaries of the Mediterranean world, emerging nation states sought to validate their identities by looking to the remains of their own past and linking them to the chronologies of classical antiquity. Without a timeframe in which to accommodate prehistoric artefacts, scholars believed that the megalithic monuments of northern Europe, such as Stonehenge in England, were the work of the Druids mentioned in Latin texts. Pierre BELON and later Pietro DELLA VALLE carried their antiquarianizing interests to Egypt and beyond.

In England, beginning in 1536, Henry VIII dissolved the monasteries and the Crown took possession of their libraries and treasuries (*see* DISSOLUTION OF THE MONASTERIES). The preservation of the historically valuable contents fell to private individuals since nothing came of the plan to create a national library. The largest collection of Anglo-Saxon manuscripts, for example, was that of Matthew

PARKER, archbishop of Canterbury under Elizabeth I. He contended that these documents would prove that the early English Church was not under Rome's authority. Indeed, antiquities rarely were studied for their own sake but put in the service of validating or refuting claims about origins—whether local, dynastic, national, or cultural.

Another side of antiquarianism, the sincere desire to further knowledge no matter where it led, is exemplified by Sir Robert Bruce COTTON, who made his collection available to a range of people that included Francis BACON, William CAMDEN, John Selden (1584–1654), and Bishop James Ussher (1581–1656). Bacon wrote voluminously about history's scope and purpose; he was careful not to equate philological scholarship or antiquarianism with history. Camden, writing in Latin, won international repute for his *Britannia* (1586), a survey of the antiquities of England and Wales, especially the Roman remains. Selden was employed by Cotton to copy records, and went on to write *England's Epinomis* and *Janus Anglorum* (1610), which subsequently led to his being accounted the father of legal antiquarianism. His *De diis Syriis* (1617) was similarly pioneering in the method it brought to bear on ancient Near Eastern mythology. Ussher, an Irish theologian, at one time possessed what was probably the largest collection of books in western Europe, but is best known today for pinpointing the moment when the universe was created (October 23, 4004 BCE).

In summary, Renaissance antiquarianism took many forms and served a host of objectives; by studying these, we can recover some of the ways in which people of the time sought to understand themselves and their world using the past as a mirror.

**See also:** CABINETS; CRITICISM, TEXTUAL; EGYPTIAN STUDIES

**Further reading:** Anthony Grafton, *Forgers and Critics: Creativity and Duplicity in Western Scholarship* (Princeton, N.J.: Princeton University Press, 1990); Graham Parry, *The Trophies of Time: English Antiquarians of the Seventeenth Century* (Oxford, U.K.: Oxford University Press, 1995).

**Antiquaries, Society of** A British society dedicated to the preservation of the national historic heritage. In its original form it was founded in 1572 by Archbishop Matthew PARKER with the collaboration of William CAMDEN and other scholars. Its early proceedings were preserved among Sir Robert COTTON's papers and were published in 1720 as *A Collection of Curious Discourses*. James I suppressed the society in 1604, on suspicion of political intrigue, but it was formally revived in 1717.

**antisemitism** Contempt and hatred for JEWS has been expressed by many religious and other groups worldwide, but the focus here is on early modern Christian antisemitism. Gavin I. Langmuir's definition of the term is derogatory, as is usual in the West today: "by 'anti-semitism' we mean all instances in which people, because they are labeled Jews, are feared as symbols of subhumanity and hated for threatening characteristics they do not in fact possess." Although the term was invented to express approval for an anti-Jewish manifesto (by Wilhelm Marr) in 1873, it is not anachronistic to call Renaissance attitudes towards Jews "antisemitic." As Lionel B. Steiman writes, "the ideas and attitudes to which it refers have belonged to Western history for two thousand years…There is an inherent consistency in Western attitudes towards Jews which justifies use of the term antisemitism" for all periods of Christianity.

After 1500 there was little direct physical aggression toward European Jews: most Jews had already been contained or removed by medieval suppression. Judean people had been attacked within and without Europe, suffering through crusading voyages and local, hardship-motivated riots: Jews were easy targets for aggrieved mobs. The Fourth Lateran Council (1215) imposed sumptuary laws to force Jews to dress distinctly from Christians. States began to expel them by force: England shipped out most of its Jews in 1290, as did France (1392), Spain (1492), and Portugal (1496). Similar Italian actions came later, with Pope Paul IV ghettoizing Jews in Rome in 1555, practically and psychologically marginalizing them.

Despite their reduced numbers, Jews remained a focus for vitriolic detestation throughout the Renaissance and Reformation. Each branch of Christianity had its own sort of Jew-hatred. For Catholics, Jews were despised members of a sinning creed: by definition, Jews were opposed to the redeeming work of the Son of God, Jesus Christ. Frequently accused of ritual murder, poisoning water supplies, and excessive wealth accumulation, Jews were to be kept alive as an example of the depravity of those who reject Christ. It was patronizingly believed that Christ would redeem the mistaken Jews at his Second Coming, although great energy and sometimes coercion (particularly in 16th-century Spain) was expended to convert Europe's remaining Jews. ERASMUS remarked in a letter (August 11, 1519) that "If hate of the Jews is the proof of genuine Christians, then we are all excellent Christians." LUTHER's attitude to Jews was initially conciliatory but became more hostile: his growing antisemitism can be acknowledged simply by comparing the titles of two of his works: *That Jesus Christ Was Born a Jew* (1523) and *On The Jews and Their Lies* (1543). Calvinism tends to be associated much less with antisemitism than Catholicism or Lutheranism, but this reflects John Calvin's general silence on Jewry rather than any affection or tolerance for Judaism.

Despite or because of the low numbers of Jews in Europe, Jewish characters feature prominently in the literature of Renaissance Europe. Superficially at least, these characters are uniformly typecast: they lend money at extortionate rates, they have large noses, they are scheming

and untrustworthy, they revere circumcision, and they are murderous in intent. The hateful Jew was particularly common on the Elizabethan English stage. In Shakespeare's play *The Merchant of Venice* only the happy ending required by the comic genre prevents Shylock from spitefully killing a Christian merchant who cannot pay a debt. Critics will forever argue about whether or not such representations of Jews are innately antisemitic, or whether the dramas tend rather to show that Christians have similar characteristics to the Jews to whom they wrongly feel morally superior. This ambiguity is troublingly apparent in Christopher MARLOWE's tragedy *The Jew of Malta*. The title character embarks upon a gleeful killing spree, murdering Christians with supposedly traditional Jewish methods of poisoning and expertly choreographed trickery. But he is provoked into this campaign by Christians who exploit his money and eventually brutalize him when he no longer serves any economic end. Are the Jew's actions any worse than the Christians'?

Less ambiguous is the tale of the "Wandering Jew," a 13th-century myth about a Jew who taunted the cross-bearing Christ that resurfaced during the 1500s. For this mockery, the Wandering Jew was condemned to roam the earth until Judgment Day. A pamphlet promoting this legend was printed in 1602, supposedly at Leyden: within two decades, the text had become assimilated and appreciated all over Europe. As the influence of this myth indicates, late-Renaissance antisemitism had international appeal.

The Holocaust of the mid-20th century was, in part, made possible by the two-millennium-old hatred of Jewry. Renaissance and Reformation thinkers and nonthinkers have an assured place in this grim legacy, one that remains politically hypersensitive to this day.

**Further reading:** Gavin I. Langmuir, *Toward a Definition of Antisemitism* (Berkeley, Calif. and London: University of California Press, 1996); Albert S. Lindemann, *Esau's Tears: Modern Anti-Semitism and the Rise of the Jews* (Cambridge, U.K.: Cambridge University Press, 1997), esp. pp. 3–35; Lionel B. Steiman, *Paths to Genocide: Antisemitism in Western History* (Basingstoke, U.K.: Macmillan and New York: St. Martin's Press, 1998), esp. pp. xi–xv, 52–70.

## Antonello da Messina (c. 1430–1479) *Sicilian-born Italian painter*

Antonello probably trained initially with COLANTONIO in Naples. His earliest surviving pictures, such as the London *Salting Madonna*, are however more profoundly conditioned by Netherlandish works than anything which Colantonio is known to have painted, so it seems likely that Antonello also received tuition from a Netherlandish painter, probably Petrus CHRISTUS or a close follower. Antonello's *St. Jerome in Penitence* and *Visit of the Three Angels to Abraham* and his London *Salvator Mundi* (1465) show the distinct influence of van EYCK. His slightly later London *St. Jerome in his Study* incorporates compositional motifs derived from van Eyck and Rogier van der WEYDEN. It is plausible that this picture was executed during an undocumented visit to Venice (c. 1465–70), for Antonello's *St. Gregory* polyptych (Messina; 1473) and *Fathers of the Church* altarpiece (Palermo) indicate a knowledge of both the figure style of PIERO DELLA FRANCESCA and the altarpieces of Giovanni BELLINI. His Syracuse *Annunciation* (1474) revolutionalizes a typical Netherlandish interior by the addition of a monumental figures and architectural motifs derived from Piero and the rigorous application of one-point perspective.

In 1475–76 Antonello was in Venice, where he painted the now fragmentary San Cassiano alterpiece (Vienna), partly modeled on Giovanni Bellini's lost altarpiece at the Venetian church of SS. Giovanni e Paolo. In its turn, it was influential upon Venetian altarpieces to the end of the 15th century. Antonello's last major work, the Dresden *St. Sebastian*, was also painted in Venice. In addition to religious works, Antonello painted a number of portraits which forcefully reinterpret a format initiated by Jan van Eyck.

By far the most significant south Italian painter of the 15th century, Antonello's importance is far from merely local. He was the first Italian artist to be thoroughly conversant with the Netherlandish glazed oil technique and was a major influence upon the course of Venetian Renaissance painting.

**Antoniazzo Romano** (c. 1460–1508) *Italian painter*
Trained under the Umbrian followers of Fra ANGELICO and Benozzo GOZZOLI, Antoniazzo was also influenced by MELOZZO DA FORLÌ, PERUGINO, BOTTICELLI, and GHIRLANDAIO. He executed numerous frescoes in Rome and elsewhere and paintings by him of Madonnas and other religious subjects survive in several northern Italian galleries. During the second half of the 15th century he was the most significant painter working in Rome.

**Antonino, St.** (Antonio Pierozzi) (1389–1459) *Italian theologian, historian, and economist*
Inspired by the preaching of John Dominici, Antonino joined the Dominican Order in 1405 at Cortona. From an early age he was greatly troubled by corruption in Church and society, and much of his life was spent in fighting this corruption. He became prior of the Dominican house in Fiesole in 1425. In 1436 or 1437, with the aid of Cosimo de' MEDICI, he established the convent of San Marco in his native Florence. Between 1439 and 1445 he attended the Council of Florence (*see* FLORENCE, COUNCIL OF) and secured the lasting respect of the papacy. He received the archbishopric of Florence in 1446 but continued to live as a humble friar, spending what he could of the see's revenues on the poor. At the same time he appreciated the value of trade in relation to ecclesiastical wealth and was influential in lessening the Church's medieval distrust of

commerce. Antonino was canonized in 1523, and his works continued to be widely published throughout the 16th century.

**Antwerp** A Netherlands (now Belgian) city and port on the River Scheldt, 55 miles from the North Sea. Antwerp was a Gallo-Roman foundation (about 200 CE), which was ruled by Franks or Frisians after the fall of Rome. By the early 14th century it was ruled by the dukes of Brabant and known for its flourishing trade with England, Venice, and Genoa and for its trade fairs. Antwerp's population grew rapidly from 20,000 in 1400 to 100,000 in 1550, overtaking Bruges as the leading mercantile center in the Netherlands. In the first half of the 16th century Antwerp received its first cargo of pepper from Lisbon (1501) and became a center for the spice trade; Antwerp at first prospered under HAPSBURG rule (from 1477), pioneering the extension of credit and making the first public loan to the Netherlands government (1511). The Antwerp stock exchange is one of the oldest in Europe (established 1531).

Later in the 16th century Antwerp's prosperity was destroyed by religious and political disputes. As an important Calvinist center by 1560, Antwerp suffered severely during the revolt of the NETHERLANDS; a savage Spanish attack, the "Spanish fury" (1576), destroyed about a third of the town and killed about 7000 citizens. Later (1583), in the "French fury", the town was attacked by French troops under FRANCIS, DUKE OF ALENÇON. After Spain recaptured Antwerp (1585) its power and wealth declined, crippled by the war and the closure of the River Scheldt to trade. During the Renaissance Antwerp was an important center for arts and scholarship with its own school of painting in the late 15th century and numerous printing presses after the arrival of PLANTIN (1548). It was also a center for humanist scholarship. Antwerp's most notable building from the Renaissance period is the town hall (1561–66).

**Antwerp Polyglot Bible** See ARIAS (Y) MONTANO, BENITO; HEBREW STUDIES; PLANTIN PRESS

**Aphrodite** See VENUS

**Apian, Peter** (Peter Bienewitz) (1495–1552) *German astronomer, mathematician, and geographer*
Educated at the universities of Leipzig and Vienna, Apian was later appointed to the chair of mathematics at Ingolstadt university. He established his reputation with the issue of a world map in 1520, and the subsequent publication of his *Cosmographia* (1524), a work of geography. He later published an arithmetical textbook, *Rechnung* (1527), which contained the first printed account of Pascal's triangle. In astronomy Apian's most important work was his *Astronomicum caesareum* (1540), containing a detailed description of five comets, one of which was the

Corus Weftnoort    Circius Noortweft    SEPTEN Boreas Noorden TRIO    Aquilo Noordt ooft    Hellefpontus Ooftnoorden

OCCI DENS    Fauonius weft    Africus weftfluyt

ORI ENS    Subfolanus Ooft    Vulturnus Ooftenfuyden

Auſter Africus Suyd weſt    MERI Notus Suyden DIES    Euro Auſter Suyd ooft

REGIONVM LONGITVDO AD ORTVM

**Peter Apian** A map of the world from the first French translation (1544) of his *Cosmographia* (1524). The maps in this work were among the first to name (South) America and to show it as a separate continent.

1531 appearance of Halley's comet. Apian was also the first to note that the tails of comets invariably point away from the sun. His son, Philipp Apian, also made an important contribution to CARTOGRAPHY.

**Apollo** The classical sun-god, who was adopted into Renaissance iconography as the embodiment of reason and order, and thus particularly associated with philosophy. He was also closely associated with artistic creativity, and he appears as patron of the MUSES and GRACES in music, art, and literature. This concept is epitomized in the crude woodcut illustrating GAFFURIO's *Practica musicae* (1496), showing a whole range of musical correspondences, with Apollo, crowned and holding a musical instrument, at the head of the picture, three dumpy Graces on his right, and below them medallions depicting the Muses.

Apollo's role as the creator of universal order through music is also celebrated in the myth of his victory in a musical contest with the satyr Marsyas (symbol of the irrational and uncontrollable), a subject treated by RAPHAEL in a fresco for the Stanza della Segnatura, as well as by Pietro PERUGINO, GIULIO ROMANO, TITIAN, and Guido RENI. An al-

legory of the pursuit of artistic excellence was perceived in the story, taken from Ovid's *Metamorphoses*, of Apollo's pursuit of the nymph Daphne, who was transformed into a laurel tree at the instant that he caught her; the scene is depicted in a painting attributed to Antonio Pollaiuolo (National Gallery, London).

**Aquaviva, Claudius** (1543–1615) *Italian theologian, fifth general of the Society of Jesus*
Having joined the JESUITS in 1567, Aquaviva was elected general in 1581, the youngest in the history of the society. He was faced with a variety of internal disputes, most importantly the claims of the Spanish Jesuits for special privileges; these he successfully opposed by defeating Spanish demands for an additional commissary-general for Spain. Aquaviva's writings include his *Directorium* (1591), a guide to IGNATIUS LOYOLA's *Spiritual Exercises*, and his *Ratio studiorum* (Method of studies; 1586), a system of education for Jesuit schools that remained unchallenged until the 20th century. His introduction of *Litterae Annuae* helped improve the society's efficiency, and during his time in office its membership increased from around 5000

to over 13,000. Aquaviva is honored for his work in helping to preserve the society's Ignatian tradition during a time when Loyola's principles were seriously threatened.

**Aragon, house of** The royal family descended from Ramiro of Navarre who inherited the Pyrenean territory of Aragon in 1035. Succeeding generations enlarged the family's inheritance by judicious marriages and by conquest. By the end of the 13th century they had driven the Moors out of northern Spain and ruled Aragon, Catalonia, Valencia, and the Balearic Islands. Peter III's acquisition of Sicily after the ejection of the island's Angevin rulers following the Sicilian Vespers (1282) enabled the house of Aragon to become a major Mediterranean power, ruling over Sardinia, Naples, Sicily, and Athens, and enjoying the benefits of a flourishing maritime trade. Alfonso V, who had conquered Naples in 1442 (*see* ALFONSO I), left Naples to his illegitimate son, Ferrante (FERDINAND I), in 1458; his other domains passed to his brother. The last male heir, FERDINAND II, whose marriage to Isabella of Castile prepared the way for the union of Spain, reunited Naples with the crown of Aragon in 1504.

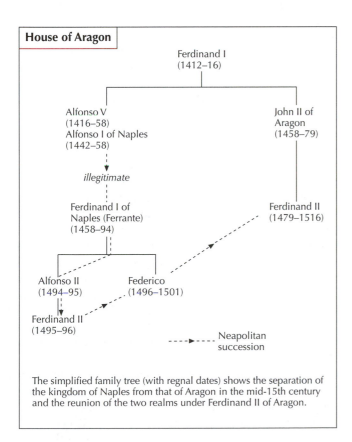

**House of Aragon**

Ferdinand I
(1412–16)

Alfonso V
(1416–58)
Alfonso I of Naples
(1442–58)

John II of Aragon
(1458–79)

*illegitimate*

Ferdinand I of Naples (Ferrante)
(1458–94)

Ferdinand II
(1479–1516)

Alfonso II
(1494–95)

Federico
(1496–1501)

Ferdinand II
(1495–96)

------▶------ Neapolitan succession

The simplified family tree (with regnal dates) shows the separation of the kingdom of Naples from that of Aragon in the mid-15th century and the reunion of the two realms under Ferdinand II of Aragon.

**Aragona, Tullia d'** (1508–1556) *Italian poet and courtesan*
The daughter of a courtesan and possibly of Luigi, cardinal of Aragon, Tullia attracted numerous aristocratic and

scholarly admirers, including the Florentine historians Jacopo NARDI and Benedetto VARCHI and the Paduan poet Girolamo MUZIANO. She published poems, mainly imitating Petrarch, in *Rime* (1547), dedicated to Eleonora, wife of Cosimo I de' MEDICI. Her *Dialogo dell'infinità d'amore* (1547) is a fashionable Neoplatonic essay on love.

**Arca, Niccolò dell'** See NICCOLÒ DELL'ARCA

**Arcadelt, Jacques** (c. 1505–1568) *French or Flemish composer*
Though little is known about his early life, there is evidence he may have spent time in Florence after 1532, when the Medici regained control there. On the assassination of Alessandro de' Medici (1537), Arcadelt probably moved to Venice and from 1540 he was in papal service in Rome. In 1544 he entered the employ of Charles of Lorraine, later archbishop of Reims, and settled in Reims until at least 1562. He may have belonged to the French court chapel and died in retirement in Paris.

Arcadelt almost certainly studied with Josquin DES PRÉS; his Masses in particular show Josquin's influence. Arcadelt began by composing sacred music, but his secular works are better known. There are extant 126 chansons and over 200 madrigals. The chansons were very popular, the earlier ones reflecting the influence of Josquin and the later ones written in Arcadelt's characteristic homophonic style, shifting between triple and duple time. All are of a sentimental nature and eschew licentious texts. In the madrigals, the text is of paramount importance, and musical effects are not permitted to interfere with its rhythmic requirements. One such madrigal, "Il bianco e dolce cigno" was consistently popular.

**Arcadia** The remote, mountainous area of southern Greece to which Virgil referred in his *Eclogues* and which thus passed into literary convention as the setting for the idealized world of the PASTORAL. When writers revived the pastoral as a literary form in the Renaissance, it was the idealized landscape of Arcadia, not the reality, which dominated their works, and "Arcadia" became the title of more than one book. In 1504 a sequence of verse eclogues linked by prose narrative was published by the Neapolitan poet Jacopo SANNAZARO. The first pastoral romance, it concerns the unrequited love of the hero Sincero who retires into Arcadia to share the rustic life of the shepherds. Written in Italian, rather than Latin, it was a very popular and influential work. The *Arcadia* of Sir Philip SIDNEY, a pastoral romance in prose, interspersed with lyrics, exists in two versions. The first was written between 1577 and 1580, but during the years 1580–84 Sidney undertook a radical revision of the work and added a third book. This version was published posthumously as *The Countesse of Pembroke's Arcadia* (1590). Common to both is the golden world of Arcadia itself and the trials and exploits of the two princes Musidorus and Pyrocles as they struggle to win their loves.

**Further reading:** Reinhold Grimm and Jost Hermand (eds), *From the Greeks to the Greens: Images of the Simple Life* (Madison, Wis.: University of Wisconsin Press, 1990); Simon Schama, *Landscape and Memory* (New York and London: HarperCollins, 1995), esp. pp. 516–38.

**archeus** A word introduced by PARACELSUS to denote the vital power of an organism to respond appropriately to various stimuli. Thus, the role of the archeus of the stomach was to extract the digestible parts of food and dispose of the remainder. A failure of the archeus would lead to poisoning and sickness. The notion persisted throughout the 17th century but finally disappeared before the growing acceptance of the mechanical philosophy.

**architecture** Humanist scholarship of the early 15th century, characterized by a nostalgic yearning for the bygone age of Roman splendor, had far-reaching repercussions within the visual arts. Both classical literature and the antique monuments that survived throughout Italy acted as testimonials to the glories of Rome before the influx of the barbarians and their foreign (Gothic) culture. Not surprisingly, architects were quick to translate the humanists' literary attempts to emulate antiquity into "the ancient manner of building." VITRUVIUS, whose architectural treatise, *De architectura*, survived from antiquity, was known throughout the Middle Ages in Italy, but Poggio BRACCIOLINI's discovery (1414) of a superior manuscript of *De architectura* coincided with a surging interest in the principles of ancient building. The *editio princeps*, without illustrations, appeared at Rome (c. 1486); Fra GIOCONDO published an illustrated edition at Venice in 1511; Cesariano's Italian translation followed in 1521, and Daniele BARBARO's version came out in 1556, with illustrations by PALLADIO.

Vitruvian theory centered upon three elements: utility, strength, and beauty. The concept of beauty was to preoccupy Renaissance architects from BRUNELLESCHI to Inigo JONES. Vitruvius' notion of beauty derived from the modular interrelationship of every part of the whole, creating a harmonious and symmetrical unit. ALBERTI, in his widely disseminated treatise *De re aedificatoria* (*editio princeps* 1485), defined beauty as "the harmony of all the parts … fitted together with such proportion and connection that nothing could be added, diminished, or altered but for the worse...." This summarized the underlying principles of Renaissance architecture. Thus Alberti introduced large volutes on the upper story of Sta. Maria Novella (1456–70) in Florence in order to unify visually the nave and aisles, and Brunelleschi, in designing the Ospedale degli Innocenti (1421), also in Florence, laid out the plan on a grid system and ensured that the placement of the exterior doors mirrored the disposition of the interior spaces.

Vitruvius regarded architecture as an imitation of nature. For instance, he distinguished three column types, Doric, Ionic, and Corinthian, whose proportions and symbolism derived, respectively, from a man, matron, and young girl. This anthropomorphic view of architecture had a profound influence on Renaissance architects who were working in an age that celebrated man's individuality. However, the correct use of the vocabulary of orders was a High Renaissance phenomenon. BRAMANTE employed the Tuscan Doric order in the Tempietto in San Pietro in Montorio, Rome, as befitting a martyrium commemorating St. Peter but FRANCESCO DI GIORGIO MARTINI, the early Renaissance theorist, took anthropomorphism to fanciful extremes in his sketches of young girls trapped within the confines of a column shaft.

Nineteenth-century art historians castigated the Renaissance masters for their imitation of pagan antiquity, but the Renaissance was not about imitation, rather the application of the antique to provide a new architectural vocabulary employed in a creative manner. Brunelleschi's Pazzi chapel in Florence, begun in 1429, has a portico carried on columns and pilasters on the interior walls which look as if they support an entablature, creating a visual harmony of forms and colors which derive from, but do not plagiarize, antique motifs. Alberti imposed a pedimented triumphal arch on the façade of the Mantuan church of Sant' Andrea (c. 1470) and placed sarcophagi in arches along the side of the TEMPIO MALATESTIANO in Rimini in emulation of the antique. Pagan temples, such as that of Minerva Medica in Rome, were to inspire a fascination with the circular form. Brunelleschi, Alberti, LEONARDO DA VINCI, MICHELOZZO and Bramante all experimented with circular forms in relation to church design. Its association with pagan worship lent the circular plan an air of controversy, although Alberti maintained that the circle, according to Neoplatonic theory, was appropriate to Christian piety, for it was the basis of divine harmony in nature. The problem remained, however, that a centrally planned church did not accommodate the need to separate clergy and laity according to Roman liturgy. Thus, although Bramante designed St. Peter's, Rome, in the form of a Greek cross, it was built in the traditional basilica shape.

Secular architecture gave Renaissance architects far more scope in the use of antique vocabulary. Designs for THEATERS show the gradual adaptation of classical plans to the different dramatic circumstances of the Renaissance. The urban *palazzo* emerged quite naturally from the classical *insula*, with its shops on the ground floor and living quarters on the *piano nobile*. Michelozzo's Palazzo Medici Riccardi (1444), with its rusticated basement and airy courtyard, has a massive classical cornice, and Alberti's Palazzo Rucellai (c. 1445–51) exhibits a network of superimposed pilasters on its façade. These examples of early Renaissance architecture are characterized by a superficial application of classical motifs. RAPHAEL's design for the Villa Madama (c. 1518) in Rome was a reinterpretation of an antique villa based upon the writings of Pliny the Younger (c. 61–c. 113 CE).

Pope JULIUS II's ambitious building program, which included the reconstruction of St. Peter's and the Vatican palace, as well as the development of new streets, moved the focus of Renaissance art from Florence to Rome. Working in the shadow of majestic classical monuments, architects were compelled towards a new and archaeologically pure interpretation of the antique. In 1515 Raphael was appointed superintendent of Roman antiquities, which prompted his scheme to measure and draw Roman remains. The newly uncovered Domus Aurea (Golden House) of Nero, with its rich GROTESQUE interior decoration, inspired the all'antiqua decoration of Raphael's Vatican Loggie (1518–19) and the facade of the Palazzo dell' Aquila (now destroyed). An increasing desire for a "Roman" quality in architecture, led to a greater monumentality in the handling of space and a greater plasticity in ornamentation. Bramante's design for the internal spaces of St. Peter's shows apses and chapels scooped out of the heavy wall mass. The Roman Palazzo Vidoni Cafarelli, perhaps by Raphael (c. 1525), has a grandly sculpted façade with windows on the piano nobile set between paired columns. This rich and rhythmical façade contrasts with the flat surface of the Palazzo Rucellai, where the ornamentation is applied rather than organic. The Palazzo FARNESE, begun in 1517 to designs by Antonio da SANGALLO and modified by MICHELANGELO, VIGNOLA, and Giacomo DELLA PORTA, was the last great Roman monument of the High Renaissance. The huge wall expanse, enlivened by perfectly proportioned aedicules and bold quoins, and the imposing central doorway create a gravity and elegance that summarized the architectural aims of the period. Henceforth the High Renaissance buildings of Rome would combine with classical remains as a source for architects such as Palladio, who would spread the new architectural vocabulary to northern Italy and beyond.

The Italian Renaissance was exported to the north in the wake of the French invasions of Italy, beginning in 1494 when the armies of Charles VIII marched into Lombardy. The spread of Renaissance values depended upon political and economic circumstances; after 1620, for instance, the Thirty Years' War precluded building on any scale in Germany and Austria during the first half of the 17th century, and abruptly curtailed the output of those architects, like Elias HOLL, who had transplanted the Italian ideals.

Without first-hand knowledge of remains of classical antiquity, the northern architects' response to Renaissance principles was fundamentally derivative. In France and England the Italian style of building was applied merely to surface decoration. The 16th-century French châteaux of CHAMBORD and CHENONCEAUX were sophisticated pastiches of Italian palazzi, with antique motifs superimposed upon the medieval French fortress plan. In England an extravagant expression of mainly medieval splendor emerged during the Elizabethan age (see ELIZABETHAN STYLE), 150 years after Brunelleschi initiated the Renaissance in Florence. The only country to employ a pure Italian style in the 16th century was Spain, although the exuberant PLATERESQUE idiom was also in evidence at least until mid-century. The ESCORIAL, built for Philip II, displays an austere classicism, the centralized plan of its church recalling Bramante. However, by the 17th century this Italianate style was eclipsed by the excesses of the BAROQUE. Elsewhere the deeply rooted Gothic traditions continued until the advent of Inigo Jones in England and François Mansart and Louis Le Vau in France in the 17th century.

**Further reading:** Peter Murray, *Renaissance Architecture* (London: Faber, 1986); Christine Smith, *Architecture in the Culture of Early Humanism: Ethics, Aesthetics and Eloquence, 1400–1470* (Oxford, U.K.: Oxford University Press, 1992); Rudolf Wittkower, *Architectural Principles in the Age of Humanism* (Chichester, U.K.: Academy Editions, 5th ed. 1998) ENGLAND: Malcolm Airs, *The Making of the English Country House, 1500–1640* (London: Architectural Press, 1975) FRANCE: Ian Dunlop, *Royal Palaces of France* (London: Hamilton, 1985); Christiane de Nicolay-Mazery and Jean-Bernard Naudin, *The French Chateau: Life—Style—Tradition* (London: Thames & Hudson, 1991) GERMANY: Henry R. Hitchcock, *German Renaissance Architecture* (Princeton, N.J.: Princeton University Press, 1981) ITALY: Ludwig H. Heydenrich, *Architecture in Italy, 1400–1500* (New Haven, Conn. and London: Yale University Press, rev. ed. 1996); Ludwig H. Heydenrich and Wolfgang Lotz, *Architecture in Italy: 1400–1600* (Harmondsworth, U.K.: Penguin, 1974; rev. ed. 1995); Andrew Hopkins, *Italian Architecture: From Michelangelo to Borromini* (London: Thames & Hudson, 2002); Wolfgang Lotz, *Studies in Italian Renaissance Architecture* (Cambridge, Mass. and London: MIT Press, 1977); Peter Murray, *The Architecture of the Italian Renaissance* (New York: Schocken, 1986).

**Arcimboldo, Giuseppe** (c. 1527–1593) *Italian painter*
His early designs for stained-glass windows (1549–58) for the cathedral in his native Milan gave little hint of the bizarre later paintings for which he is best known. In 1562 he moved to the Hapsburg court in Prague, where he designed court entertainments and ceremonies and painted settings for the imperial theater. The volume of drawings of designs for Hapsburg court festivities that Arcimboldo presented to Emperor Rudolf II in 1585 (now in the Uffizi, Florence) displayed to his patron the artist's technical

mastery and inventive talent. His grotesque oil paintings of symbolic figures composed of such objects as pieces of fruit, vegetables, and birds are said to have influenced 20th-century surrealist painters; his depictions of *Summer* and *Winter* (1563, Kunsthistorisches Museum, Vienna) are typical examples, as is his famous portrait of Rudolf as *Vertemnus* (c. 1591; Skoklosters Slott, Sweden). He was made a count palatine by Rudolf in 1592, a year before his death in Milan.

Further reading: Giancarlo Maiorino, *The Portrait of Eccentricity: Arcimboldo and the Mannerist Grotesque* (University Park, Pa: Pennsylvania State University Press, 1991).

**Arena Chapel** (Scrovegni Chapel) The chapel built (1303–05) for Enrico Scrovegni on the site of a first-century Roman amphitheater (arena) in Padua. The interior is decorated with frescoes by GIOTTO and his followers. The main decorative scheme, in three zones along the side walls, depicts the history of the Redemption in scenes from the lives of Mary and Jesus Christ. A fourth zone, below these, has monochrome allegorical figures of the virtues and vices. The Arena frescoes are a significant move away from the Byzantine style that then dominated Italian art, but not yet a definitive break with it. In the depiction of the Kiss of Judas, for example, there is an intense stillness in the central figure of Christ amid a throng of agitated figures and brandished weapons as the hunched figure of Judas approaches him; the drama and emotion of this scene are quite alien to the hieratic, essentially static forms of the Byzantine tradition.

Further reading: Bruce Cole, *Giotto: The Scrovegni Chapel, Padua* (New York: George Braziller, 1993).

**Areopagus** A shadowy, perhaps fictitious, literary society of poets who aimed to reform English poetry along classical lines in the late 1570s. Chief among them were SPENSER, SIDNEY, and Sir Edward Dyer (1543–1607), all protégés of the earl of Leicester, at whose house they could have met. The name derives from the hill northwest of the Athenian Acropolis, on which the tribunal of the ancient city used to meet.

**Aretino, Francesco** See ACCOLTI FAMILY

**Aretino, Leonardo** See BRUNI, LEONARDO

**Aretino, Pietro** (1492–1556) *Italian poet and dramatist*
The son of a shoemaker in Arezzo (the town from which he took his name), Aretino probably received little formal education. However, in 1510 he went to Perugia where he was soon welcomed into the company of cultivated men and was able to develop his interest in painting and poetry. In 1517 he moved to Rome, eventually joining the literary circle around Pope LEO X. Here his lifelong love of politi-

cal and ecclesiastical gossip surfaced in a series of vicious pasquinades that found favor with Cardinal Giulio de' Medici, whose rivals for the papacy Aretino lampooned (see CLEMENT VII). Predictably, Aretino soon went too far with his pornographic illustrated collection of *Sonnetti lussuriosi* (Lewd Sonnets; 1524); he was eventually forced to retreat to Venice (1527) where he lived out his life in grand, if dissolute, style, surrounded by many of the great artists of the day.

Aretino continued his satirical campaigns, transforming Venice's somewhat unsophisticated broadsheets by his acute political comments. His six volumes of letters (1537–57) also demonstrate the great force and versatility of his writing. Known, in a phrase of ARIOSTO's, as "il flagello dei principe" (the scourge of princes), Aretino never moderated his attacks on the powerful, many of whom placated him with gifts which became the chief source of his income. *Ragionamenti* (1534–36), in which Roman prostitutes discuss their eminent clients, shows him at his most venomous in his condemnation of moral and political corruption in Rome. His plays, on the other hand, lack the obsessively satirical intent of his prose works. The tragedy *Orazia* (1546) and his five comedies written between 1524 and 1544 are often considered to be some of the greatest works of the period. The comedies, which deal mainly with lower-middle-class life, are noticeably free from the conventions that dogged most other dramas of the time. Best known among them is *La cortigiana* (Life at court), which was first performed in 1537. Aretino, who also tried his hand at the genres of poetry, devotional writing, and romantic epic, was one of the most vigorous and inventive writers of the 16th century.

**Aretino, Unico** See ACCOLTI FAMILY

**Argyropoulos, John** (c. 1415–1487) *Byzantine scholar*
He was born into a noble family in Constantinople, where he became a priest. His first visit to Italy was before 1434; in that year he was lecturing at Padua on the works of Aristotle. In 1439 he attended Emperor John Palaeologus at the Council of FLORENCE. By 1441 he was back in Constantinople, but he returned to Italy in 1442, when he became rector of Padua university. Cosimo de' MEDICI was one of his patrons and he was tutor to Piero, Cosimo's son, and to Lorenzo de' MEDICI. When Lorenzo assumed power in Florence, Argyropoulos became a leading member of his PLATONIC ACADEMY, where he taught POLITIAN and other humanists. In 1456 he visited France, then returned to Florence, and eventually settled in Rome some time before 1471. He continued to expound the works of Aristotle and other Greek authors. The German scholar REUCHLIN was among his pupils. He wrote many original commentaries on Aristotle and translated a number of his works into Latin; much of Argyropoulos' original work remains unprinted. He was an important member of the first

generation of Greek teachers in the West who helped to encourage the revival of classical learning.

**Arias (y) Montano, Benito** (1527–1598) *Spanish priest and writer*
Arias Montano was born at Fregenal de la Sierra, near Badajoz, and studied oriental languages at Seville, Alcalá, and Leon. He accompanied the bishop of Segovia to the Council of TRENT, and was noted for his ability and erudition. He returned to a hermitage at Aracena, near Seville, and later was appointed professor of oriental languages and librarian at the ESCORIAL. As editor of the Antwerp Polyglot Bible (1568–73) he was denounced to the Inquisition for attaching too much importance to the Hebrew and Aramaic texts; tried and acquitted, he afterwards retired to Seville. He was the author of theological and historical works, including one on Jewish antiquities (1593), and a poetic paraphrase of the Song of Solomon.

**Ariosto, Ludovico** (1474–1533) *Italian poet*
Ariosto was born at Reggio, in Emilia. He studied law by necessity and literature by inclination at Ferrara, then joined the household of Cardinal Ippolito d' Este, whom he served from 1503 to 1517. After this he entered the service of the cardinal's brother, Duke Alfonso I, who appointed him ducal commissioner at Garfagnana (1522). Ariosto spent three testing years there, after which he retired (1527) to Ferrara where he devoted his remaining days to meditation and the revising of his masterpiece OR-LANDO FURIOSO, which he had started in 1502 and completed only a few months before he died.

Ariosto's other major work belongs to the period 1517–25, a set of seven *Satires* or verse epistles in the Horatian manner, written in *terza rima* and depicting Ferrarese court life. Ariosto has also been seen as a pioneer dramatist, since his verse comedies, such as *I suppositi* (1509), though minor works in themselves, were the earliest vernacular plays based closely on Latin models which were to be a feature of European domestic comedy. He also supervised the building of a theater at Ferrara in which his plays were performed. He died in Ferrara, having achieved recognition during his last years as Italy's greatest contemporary poet.

**Further reading:** Albert Russell Ascoli, *Ariosto's Bitter Harmony: Crisis and Evasion in the Italian Renaissance* (Princeton, N.J.: Princeton University Press, 1987).

**Aristotelianism, Renaissance** The first printed edition of ARISTOTLE's *Opera omnia* appeared in Padua in 1472–74; it was followed in the period 1495–98 by the publication of the Greek *princeps*. Thereafter the continuing importance of Aristotle to the Renaissance scholar is revealed by the publication of 13 further editions of his collected works during the 16th century. For some, the Aristotelian canon was both comprehensive and authoritative. So

much so, according to a well-publicized minority, that anything unrecorded by Aristotle was obviously fictitious. Such obtuseness was shown, for example, by the Paduan philosopher Cesare Cremonini in 1610 in response to Galileo's reported discovery of the moons of Jupiter. As they were unrecorded by Aristotle, Cremonini objected, they could not possibly exist. Equally dogmatic positions were adopted by RAMUS and BACON in opposition to Aristotle. Ramus had reportedly argued in Paris in 1536 that everything taught by Aristotle was false. More reasonably, Bacon had warned his contemporaries to apply themselves to "the study of things themselves. Be not for ever the property of one man."

The majority of scholars, however, adopted neither extreme position. For them Aristotle offered a comprehensive account of the universe, together with detailed textbooks on virtually all branches of knowledge. Consequently most scholars worked unthinkingly within the confines of Aristotelianism, and even those wishing to break free often found they could do no more than modify its basic structure. In many areas Aristotelian principles emerged from the Renaissance unscathed. When, for example, Isaac Newton entered Cambridge in 1661 he studied as an undergraduate Aristotelian physics, logic, rhetoric, ethics, and metaphysics. Missing from the list are astronomy and cosmology, the first disciplines, under the influence of COPERNICUS, GALILEO, and KEPLER, to break away from their classical assumptions.

With regard to the more basic concepts of matter, motion, and change, less progress was apparent. Aristotle had rejected the atomism and the monism of his predecessors and argued that matter was formed from four basic elements: earth, air, fire, and water. While many Renaissance scientists quarrelled with details of this account, none could break away completely. The names of the elements might be changed and the numbers decreased to three, or increased to five or more, but the theory remained in essence Aristotelian. Equally, while all agreed that Aristotle's account of motion was inadequate, it was less easy to find an acceptable replacement. The problem lay with the motion of projectiles, falling bodies, and the planets. What kept them in motion? Aristotle's answer in terms of "natural" motion, or the action of the medium, had never proved popular, not even to otherwise committed Aristotelians. No significant advance could be made, however, until the concept of inertia was introduced into physics, and this was a post-Renaissance development. At a more fundamental level Aristotle had insisted that change of all kind must be explained in terms of his four causes: material, efficient, formal, and final. Thus, for Aristotle, a statue would have been caused by the material it was made from, the sculptor who made it (efficient cause), the object it represented (formal cause), and its final cause or purpose. While much of the Aristotelian vocabulary survived the Renaissance, some scholars began to question the value assigned to final causes. "Research into final causes," Bacon asserted, "like a virgin dedicated to God is barren and produces nothing."

Although Bacon's strictures found wide support among a later generation of physicists, Renaissance biologists remained uncompromisingly Aristotelian. Consequently, Aristotle's classification of animals on the basis of their modes of reproduction and development remained without serious challenge until the 18th century. In the field of generation, using concepts derived from his metaphysics, Aristotle argued that the female parent contributed the matter of the embryo and the male parent its form. It was precisely this view that William HARVEY began to consider in the opening chapter of his *De generatione animalium* (1651).

As a final area of intellectual domination there remains Aristotelian logic. Despite the objections of Ramus and Bacon, the bulk of Renaissance logic textbooks worked exclusively within the parameters set out by Aristotle in the *Organon*, as indeed did the textbooks of the 17th and 18th centuries. It should, however, be remembered that traditions other than Aristotelianism were present during the Renaissance, and that, in their own way, NEOPLATONISM, skepticism, and atomism exercised a comparable influence.

**See also:** CRITICISM, LITERARY

**Further reading:** David A. Lines, *Aristotle's* Ethics *in the Italian Renaissance (1300–1600): The Universities and the Problem of Moral Education* (Leyden, Netherlands: Brill, 2002); Charles B. Schmitt, *Aristotle and the Renaissance* (Cambridge, Mass.: Harvard University Press, 1983).

**Aristotle** (384–322 BC) *Greek philosopher*
He was born at Stagira (hence allusions to him as "the Stagirite") and studied philosophy at Athens under PLATO for 20 years from 367. After short spells teaching at Assos in the Troad and Mytilene he became (342) tutor to Alexander the Great. In 335 he returned to Athens to found his own philosophical school, the disciples of which were known as Peripatetics on account of the master's habit of walking to and fro while teaching.

The huge quantity of Aristotle's surviving works cover a vast range of subjects: logic, physics, biology, psychology, metaphysics, politics, ethics, rhetoric, and poetry. Many of the treatises were known to medieval scholars in the West only through Latin translations of Arabic versions. Nonetheless his works were the basis of the predominant scholastic philosophy, and although there was some reaction against him in the Renaissance, especially in favor of PLATO, he continued to dominate philosophical and scientific discourse well into the 17th century (*see* ARISTOTELIANISM, RENAISSANCE). In the 16th century his rediscovered *Poetics* became the basis of Renaissance literary theory (*see* CRITICISM, LITERARY), affecting the status and composition of both EPIC and TRAGEDY.

**arithmetic** Both the Greeks and the Romans had represented numbers with letters of their alphabets, a custom that mattered little as long as problems were presented geometrically, and as long as calculations were performed on an ABACUS. A more sophisticated arithmetic required a more lucid symbolism, which was first provided by the mathematicians of the Renaissance. Hindu numerals entered Europe through Islam. They were picked up by Gerbert in 10th-century Spain and later used by Leonardo of Pisa in his influential *Liber abaci* (1202). Consequently, by the time of the Renaissance, there was a growing need to develop appropriate algorithms in the new symbolism for the basic arithmetical operations of multiplication, division, subtraction, addition, exponentiation, and the extraction of roots. The result was a number of elementary textbooks appearing throughout Europe, all designed to convey the secrets of the new arithmetic to a public becoming increasingly concerned with numerical problems arising in commerce. Such works as PACIOLI's *Somma* (1494), Robert Recorde's *Grounde of Artes* (1540), and Michael Stifel's *Arithmetica integra* (1544) performed this task in France, Italy, England, and Germany respectively. A bewildering variety of methods was presented, sufficiently complex to engender the belief that long division could be performed only by a professional mathematician.

The Renaissance also saw extensions to the concept of number. CARDANO, for example, in his *Ars magna* (1545), accepted into mathematics the long-suspected negative and complex numbers. Later in the century decimals were introduced by Simon STEVIN, and in 1614 John NAPIER successfully introduced the notion of a logarithm. He had not, however, expressed his logarithms in terms of a decimal base. This latter innovation was carried through by Henry BRIGGS who published in 1617 a table of logarithms to the base 10 of the numbers 1 to 1000.

**Armada** See SPANISH ARMADA

**armillary spheres** Astronomical instruments consisting of linked adjustable rings (the name derives from Latin *armilla*: bracelet) representing the circles of the celestial sphere such as the ecliptic and equator. A sphere in the center represents the earth. Used by Hipparchus (second century BCE) they were described by Ptolemy in his *Almagest* (*see* PTOLEMAIC SYSTEM) and later became an indispensable tool of Renaissance astronomers. Fitted with sights (alidades), they could be used to make quite precise measurements. One of the most accurate of such instruments, with a diameter of nearly nine feet, was built by Tycho BRAHE at his Uraniborg observatory.

**Arminianism** A moderate reformed theology named after the Dutch theologian Jacob Arminius (1560–1609). With its insistence upon free will and the denial of the concepts of PREDESTINATION and irresistible grace, Arminianism was anti-Calvinistic and in Holland found expression in the sect of REMONSTRANTS, whose doctrines were set out in the Remonstrance of 1610. Suspected of pro-Spanish sympathies, the Dutch Arminians suffered bitter persecution after the Calvinists' triumph at the Synod of DORT (1618–19).

"Arminianism" was also the name used by English Puritans to describe the doctrines of William Laud who, like the Dutch Arminians, adopted an explicitly anti-Calvinistic policy. As bishop of London (1628–33) and, from 1633, archbishop of Canterbury, Laud dominated religious affairs in England throughout Charles I's reign. "Laudianism," as it is more accurately described, emphasized the importance of vestments, ceremony, and decoration in church, and ruled that the communion table should be transferred to the east end; it also enhanced the authority of the clergy over the laity.

**Further reading:** Hugh Trevor-Roper, *Catholics, Anglicans and Puritans* (London: Secker & Warburg, 1987).

**armor** Body protection for soldiers in the 14th century saw a general trend away from the use of mail and towards the use of plate. In Scandinavia and eastern Europe lamellar armor composed of small plates laced or riveted together became widespread; it was worn under a leather jerkin. Elsewhere soldiers increasingly wore pieces of solid plate strapped onto their mail hauberks or attached to the inside of a leather jerkin to protect vulnerable joints and limbs. For mounted soldiers, whose legs were an easy target for foot soldiers, plate leg protection was evolved, comprising sabaton (foot), greave (shin), poleyn (knee), and cuisse (thigh) sections. By the end of the century armorers were attaching the pieces of limb protection to each other by metal strips known as lames, rather than to another garment. Leather straps and loose riveting provided the necessary flexibility. Armorers also began to demonstrate their skill in designing surfaces curved in such a way as to deflect an enemy's weapon point away from vulnerable body areas.

Two distinct styles in western European armor emerged during the 15th century—the Italian and the German. Italian armor is characterized by smoothness and roundness in the modeling of the individual pieces. Milan was an important center of manufacture (*see* MISSAGLIA FAMILY). The German style, more angular and spiky, is often referred to as "Gothic"; its main centers of manufacture were Innsbruck, Nuremberg, and Augsburg. These differences are exemplified in two common forms of head protection: the smooth cylindrical shape of the Italian barbut, based on ancient Greek helmet designs, and the prominent projections of the German sallet with its

pointed neck guard. However, as both countries exported armor and armorers (HENRY VIII employed first Italians and then, from 1515, Germans in his Greenwich workshops) elements from both soon blended in European armor.

In Germany in the early 16th century the armorers' craft received strong encouragement from the informed patronage of Emperor MAXIMILIAN I. Among the famous makers who worked for Maximilian and his successors were the SEUSENHOFER FAMILY of Innsbruck and the HELMSCHMIED FAMILY of Augsburg. Maximilian's name is associated with the type of ridged plate that represented the most advanced scientific design attained in European armor, combining strength and flexibility to a marked extent. A curious vagary in this period was the attempt to re-

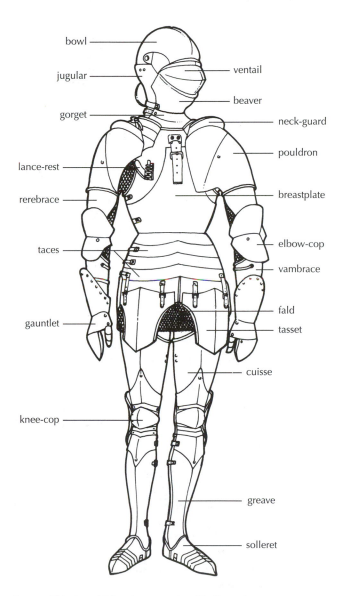

**Armor** This late 15th-century suit of Italian plate armor covers the entire body. During the late 15th century and the early 16th century the art of the armorer reached its peak.

produce in metal the puffed and slashed garments of contemporary civilian fashion, even down to simulation of the stitching. From the mid-16th century changes in military strategy and increasing deployment of firearms made mobility more desirable than all-over body protection; plainer suits, often without the lower leg protection, became more common for practical purposes, while the parade or ceremonial armor of princes became increasingly ornate. The use of etching (in northern Europe) or embossing (predominantly an Italian fashion) for decoration naturally negated one of the primary functions of plate armor—to present a smooth surface off which a weapon point would glance.

Besides suits of armor for the battlefield, armorers also evolved specialist equipment to meet the rather different demands of the tournament. Heavily reinforced pieces protected the knight's left shoulder and arm, as the side that would take the brunt of his opponent's attack. A premium was placed on helmet design that protected the wearer against an opponent's lance; the English great helm and German frog-mouth helm are examples of this specialist type. For foot combat this kind of helmet restricted visibility to an impractical degree, so a helmet with a visor was used instead. The need to adapt armor for different purposes led to the evolution of the garniture, in which the basic suit of armor is provided with additional matching pieces for special applications, such as a tournament or a parade. Garnitures such as those made for Henry VIII of England and Emperor Charles V and preserved in such collections as the Tower of London or the Armería Real, Madrid, exhibit the armorers' ingenuity in the design and decoration of these sets, which of course only the rich and powerful could afford or needed. Sometimes matching sets of horse armor were provided as well; one such set was the ceremonial armor made for Eric XIV of Sweden in 1563.

**Further reading:** David Edge and John Miles Paddock, *Arms and Armor of the Medieval Knight: An Illustrated History of Weaponry in the Middle Ages* (New York: Crescent Books, 1988); Alan Williams, *The Knight and the Blast Furnace: A History of the Metallurgy of Armour in the Middle Ages and the Early Modern Period* (Leyden, Netherlands: Brill, 2003).

**Arrabbiati** (Italian, the "Enraged") The Florentine faction most hostile to SAVONAROLA. Its leaders were men of wealth, who, while they did not hanker after Medici rule, detested Savonarola's property tax and other measures against luxury and inequality. See PIAGNONI.

*ars nova* (Latin, "new art") A movement in French and Italian music named after *Ars nova musicae* (c. 1320), a treatise by Philippe de VITRY. It marked a sharp break with the older music, the *ars antiqua*, which had practically ignored rhythm and from which the *ars nova* is distin-

guished by its rhythmical and contrapuntal innovations. Musical parts became more independent, and a greater use was made of instruments (the rebec, shawm, recorder, viol, lute, and portative organ). Originating in France, the *ars nova* was soon taken up in Florence, Bologna, Pisa, and elsewhere in northern Italy. Building upon the tradition of the troubadours and trouvères, the new art took a more casual approach to musical composition. More secular texts were set, and the Italian MADRIGAL was born, and the French *ballade* and *chace*—and the related Italian *ballata* and *caccia*—flourished. The Church was initially hostile to the *ars nova*; in 1324/25 Pope John XXII condemned the "lascivious wantonness" of de Vitry and others who practiced the new art. Nevertheless, it entered the church in the form of the isorhythmic motet, in which the plainchant basis of liturgical compositions was broken into sections, each having the same set of internal time values. The leading exponents of the *ars nova*, besides de Vitry, were Guillaume de MACHAUT and Francesco LANDINI. In the later stages of the movement, the work of CICONIA, a Walloon resident in Italy, is notable. His music foreshadows that of DUFAY and the Burgundian school of composers.

**Further reading:** John D. Gray, *The Ars Nova Treatises Attributed to Philippe de Vitry: Translations and Commentaries* (Ann Arbor, Mich.: UMI Press, 1997).

*arte mayor* In Iberian poetry, a verse line usually of 11 or 12 syllables with a strong caesura dividing the line into half-lines, each having two major stresses, giving an anapaestic rhythm. Towards the end of the 14th century, this metre gradually superseded the earlier *cuaderna vía* ("fourfold way"), a narrative stanza used by clerical poets (a 14-syllable line with strong caesura, arranged in four-line stanzas having a single rhyme, aaaa, bbbb, ...). Alfonso Álvarez de Villasandino (c. 1345–c. 1425) was especially influential in establishing *arte mayor* verse, and it was popularized by humanists like Juan de MENA. The beginning of the *Siglo de Oro* is dated from a further metrical reform, inspired by Italian verse, introduced in the works (1543) of Juan BOSCÁN and GARCILASO DE LA VEGA. However, *arte mayor* continued to be used in some courtly verse until the 18th century.

**Artemis** See DIANA

**Arthur, legend of** The cycle of stories, also known as "the matter of Britain", surrounding King Arthur and the Round Table. It grew from a tiny germ in medieval chronicles concerning a fifth- or sixth-century British general or chieftain who defied the Saxon invaders, was embroidered in the 12th century, and then expanded into prose and verse romances by English, French, and German authors. The English writer Sir Thomas Malory (c. 1400–71) stands at the intersection of medieval and Renaissance treatments of Arthurian legend with his prose *Morte Darthur*, written in the mid-15th century, when the age of chivalry (if it had ever existed) was long past. It kept alive the ideals of love and war as the twin poles of a world populated almost exclusively by knights and ladies.

Perception of Arthur as a national hero was fueled by the story that, like CHARLEMAGNE, he would one day return and lead his people to great victories; 12th-century writers had reported that on his tomb in Glastonbury were the words "Rex quondam et rexque futurus" (the once and future king). The quasi historical aspect of Arthurian legend was first exploited by the Tudors. Henry VII had his genealogy traced back to Arthur and christened his first-born son Arthur (1486–1502) in his honor. The Round Table in Winchester castle predates the Tudors but was repainted by Henry VIII with the Tudor rose for the visit of Emperor Charles V in 1522, and the names and motifs of Arthurian legend provided a framework for the neo-medieval tournaments laid on by Elizabeth I. As late as 1610 James I's eldest son Henry (1594–1612) was presented by "King Arthur" with a sword to restore chivalry in an entertainment scripted by Ben JONSON.

By enrolling Arthur as one of the Nine Worthies of the World (preface to *Morte Darthur*, 1485), the printer Caxton guaranteed his place in innumerable pageants, but on a more serious literary level it was felt that Arthur ought to be the subject of a British national epic. Edmund Spenser's plan for THE FAERIE QUEENE, set out in the letter to RALEIGH appended to the first edition (1590), seems to take this into account, but the completed part of the poem does not place Arthur in the center of the action as might have been expected. Nonetheless, as the embodiment of the peculiarly Renaissance virtue of "Magnificence," he makes significant interventions in the affairs of the poem. As late as the 1640s John Milton was still planning an Arthuriad, a national epic with Arthur as its hero.

**Further reading:** Jonathan Hughes, *Arthurian Myths and Alchemy: The Kingship of Edward IV* (Stroud, U.K.: Sutton, 2003); James D. Merriman, *The Flower of Kings: A Study of the Arthurian Legend in England Between 1485 and 1835* (Wichita: University Press of Kansas, 1973).

**artillery** In the medieval period, any missile-throwing device, including the javelin-launching ballista and stone-hurling trebuchet. Introduced first by Greek and Roman engineers, their effectiveness against the increasingly massive castles of the late medieval period had become much reduced. Conditions changed in the 14th century with the introduction of the CANNON. Although the first certain reference to the cannon dates from 1326, it took time before the early primitive models could be adapted to the demands of field artillery officers. To begin with, GUNPOWDER needed to be improved. Made from saltpeter, sulfur, and charcoal, and ground into a fine powder known as serpentine, early samples tended to separate when transported over rough European roads, with unpredictable results. The solution came with the invention (c. 1425) of corned powder, in which the ingredients were first mixed into a wet paste before being allowed to dry.

Further problems arose over the question of mobility. Although never really solved, the introduction in the late 1300s of light two-wheeled carts known as ribauldequins gave artillery officers greater access to the battlefield. Such factors, together with improved cannon design, began to shift the balance of military power. Even the mighty fortress of Constantinople was unable to withstand such pressure and fell in 1453 to the artillery of Mehmet II (ironically, the technology was imported from the West). The power of artillery was again demonstrated when CHARLES VIII of France invaded Italy in 1494 and managed without undue difficulty to destroy any town offering resistance.

It took longer, however, to adapt artillery to naval use. Although known to have been in use as early as 1338, guns were at first mounted only on the upper decks and it was not until the early 16th century that ports were cut in ships' hulls enabling cannon to be sited on the main deck. Thereafter the fire-power of ships continued to grow and, as at the battle of Lepanto in 1571, would henceforth be decisive in determining naval supremacy.

**See also:** FORTIFICATION

**Ascensius, Jodocus Badius** See BADIUS ASCENSIUS, JODOCUS

**Ascham, Roger** (c. 1515–1568) *English humanist and writer*
He was born near York and educated at Cambridge where he became a fellow of St. John's (1534) and a reader in Greek. He attracted HENRY VIII's attention with his *Toxophilus* (1545), a treatise on archery, written (unusually for the time) in English. Between 1548 and 1550 he was tutor to the future ELIZABETH I, and then served Sir Richard Moryson, England's ambassador to CHARLES V, for several years, during which he traveled widely on the Continent. A noted penman, he was appointed Latin secretary (1553) to MARY I, which post he subsequently also held under Elizabeth. One of the leading English humanists of his day, Ascham strove to make the vernacular a vehicle of true eloquence; to facilitate this, he urged the adoption of Senecan and Ciceronian models, while abhorring excessive pedantry and affectation (see CICERO; SENECA). He himself wrote simple, lively, lucid prose, often enhanced by vivid and humane observations. His best-known book, *The Scholemaster* (1570), was a landmark in educational theory, concerned not only with the teaching of Latin prose composition, but also with the nature and proper scope of education.

**Askew, Anne** (Anne Kyme) (1520–1546) *English Protestant writer and martyr*
Daughter of a wealthy Lincolnshire landowner, she was well educated in the Scriptures and interested in theological debate. She was forced into an unhappy marriage to a Catholic landowner, Thomas Kyme, but became alienated from him as she embraced Protestantism. In about 1544 he renounced her as a heretic. Now the mother of two children, Askew tried and failed to obtain a divorce. She moved to London, associating with Protestants in the circle of Queen Catherine PARR. In 1545 she was arrested, examined for heresy, and released. Arrested again (June 1546), she was crippled by torture on the rack (unprecedented in view of her status as a gentlewoman), possibly in an attempt to obtain incriminating evidence of the queen's reformist activities. During her incarceration in the Tower of London Askew wrote *The First Examynacyon of Anne Askew* (1546) and *The Lattre Examynacyon of Anne Askew* (1547). In July 1546 she was burned at the stake at Smithfield. The autobiographical *Examynacyon*s, one of the first such examples of women's writing, featured in John FOXE's *Book of Martyrs* (1563).

**Aspertini, Amico** (c. 1475–1552) *Italian painter and sculptor*
A native of Bologna, Aspertini was a pupil of ERCOLE DE' ROBERTI of Ferrara and assistant to both COSTA and FRANCIA, with whom he worked on the frescoes of the oratory of Sta. Cecilia in San Giacomo Maggiore, Bologna (1506). Aspertini also visited Rome and Florence and absorbed features of the styles of such painters as SIGNORELLI, PINTURICCHIO, RAPHAEL, and Filippino LIPPI, whose works he studied in detail. Notable works include a series of reredoses and a cycle of frescoes (1508–09) in the church of San Frediano, Lucca. Other paintings are remarkable for their elements of fantasy. As a sculptor he collaborated on the portals of San Petronio, Bologna. His sketchbook in the British Museum shows his interest in antique models.

**astrolabes** Astronomical instruments formerly used to determine time, latitude, and the altitude of various celestial bodies above the horizon. The name means literally "a star-taking" (Greek *astrolabos*). An astrolabe consists of a flat circular plate (mater), usually made of brass, on which is engraved a stereographic projection of the heavens. Centered on one of the celestial poles, this normally shows the tropics, celestial equator, ecliptic, and the observer's zenith and horizon. Subsidiary plates which can be placed over the mater are often provided for use in different latitudes. Over the mater is fixed an adjustable rete, or fretted plate, showing the positions of the brightest stars. A sighting arm (alidade) is also attached. A simplified version of the instrument, known as the mariner's astrolabe, was available for use at sea. There was also a rare spherical form.

Although the planispheric astrolabe described above is not mentioned by Ptolemy (*see* PTOLEMAIC SYSTEM), the principles behind its design were familiar to him, and through the influence of Islamic astronomers, particularly Masha'allah (eighth century CE), knowledge of the instrument passed to the West. Among early works on the subject to draw upon Masha'allah is Chaucer's *Treatise on the Astrolabe* (1391–92). Renaissance refinements of the astrolabe include two forms of the socalled "universal" astrolabe, suitable for use in any latitude: the *astrolabium catholicum* of GEMMA FRISIUS and the Rojas astrolabe, based on an orthographic projection first described by the Frisian Hugo Helt in Juan de Rojas's *Commentarii* (1550).

**astrology** The study of movements of stars and planets, traditionally divided into two distinct types: natural astrology, which simply predicted the motions of heavenly bodies and is now part of astronomy, and judicial astrology, which foretold future terrestrial events on the basis of celestial signs. The most significant branch of judicial astrology, genethliacal astrology, purported to throw light on human destiny by constructing natal horoscopes (i.e. horoscopes based on the aspect of the heavens at the exact time and place of the subject's birth).

Although the origins of astrology can be traced to Babylonian times, with the earliest known horoscopes dating back to 409 BCE, the fullest exposition of astrology in antiquity occurs in the *Tetrabiblos* of Ptolemy (fl. 127–48 CE), a work from which much of Renaissance, and indeed modern, astrology ultimately derives (*see* PTOLEMAIC SYSTEM). This, in turn, was based largely on the prevailing assumptions of Hellenistic science. It was, at that time, reasonable to suppose that celestial events influenced human affairs; if ignorant sailors, Ptolemy argued, could predict the weather from the sky, how much more capable would learned scholars be to foresee its influence on man. The precise links between the heavens and earth were forged in terms of the traditional four elements. Planets were assigned properties on the basis of their supposed composition with, for example, the moon being classed as hot and moist, and SATURN as cold and dry. As a moist heat was deemed beneficial, and a cold dryness damaging, it followed that the moon exercised a benign influence on man and Saturn a harmful one. Greater complexity was introduced by allowing celestial influences to be modified by a planet's position, both along the ecliptic (zodiac) and relative to other planets (aspects). The rules derived from these assumptions proved sufficiently comprehensive to allow astrologers to deal with almost any situation.

Opposition to astrology first arose within the Church; both St. Augustine and St. Thomas Aquinas set their great authority against it. Something of an astrological revival nonetheless occurred in the 13th century, through the writings of such figures as Arnold of Villanova, Pietro d'Abano, and, more significantly, Guido Bonatti whose

*Liber astronomicus* served as the leading textbook of the early Renaissance. It was in fact Bonatti who was chosen by DANTE to represent astrology in the eighth circle of the Inferno, where he was depicted with his head on backwards and no ability to see ahead.

Interest in astrology continued to grow and was well served by the newly developed printing press. Almanacs had appeared before GUTENBERG but after he issued the first printed copy in 1448 they emerged with much greater frequency, variety, and number. However, they often provoked the hostility of an officialdom prone to suspect partisan motives behind political predictions. For this reason Pope Sixtus V issued a bull in 1586 condemning judicial astrology. In England the lucrative trade of almanac publishing was made the monopoly of the Stationers' Company, through which the state was able to exercise control over the content of the publications.

Scientific opinion appeared divided: such early Renaissance scholars as Nicholas CUSANUS and PICO DELLA MIRANDOLA were critical, but astronomers of the standing of RHETICUS, KEPLER, and BRAHE openly practiced as astrologers. It may have been, however, that in some cases their intellectual commitment was less urgent than their need to subsidize their astronomical researches. Astrology as a scientific discipline barely outlived the Renaissance. By the time of Isaac Newton, at the end of the 17th century, astronomers had begun already to rewrite their history and to dismiss much of their past, although Newton himself had an interest in the occult, including astrology.

**Further reading:** Anthony Grafton, *Cardano's Cosmos: The Worlds and Works of a Renaissance Astrologer* (Cambridge, Mass.: Harvard University Press, 2000).

**astronomy** The scientific study of celestial bodies (*compare* ASTROLOGY). At the beginning of the Renaissance, scholars accepted unquestioningly the COSMOLOGY of Aristotle and the astronomy of Ptolemy (*see* PTOLEMAIC SYSTEM). These views formed the background to DANTE's *Divine Comedy* and, more prosaically, were found expressed in the numerous editions of the popular 13th-century text, the *De sphaera* of Sacrobosco.

The first tasks facing the astronomers of the Renaissance were to acquaint themselves with the details of ancient astronomy and to develop new mathematical techniques to describe better the complexities of planetary motion. To this end such scholars as PEURBACH, REGIOMONTANUS, and RHETICUS sought to establish accurate texts of Ptolemy's *Almagest* and related works, and to master and deploy the new language of TRIGONOMETRY, to astronomical observations. There followed developments which, by the time of the death of GALILEO (1642), had completely transformed man's view of the heavens. The traditional view that they were immutable and incorruptible was called into question by the discovery in 1572 by Tycho BRAHE of a NEW STAR. Even more damaging were the

observations in 1610 by Galileo of the formerly unsuspected satellites of Jupiter, and the presence of mountains and craters on the moon. Further evidence of celestial corruptibility came in 1611 with Christoph SCHEINER's observations of sunspots. Additional difficulties were presented by the comet of 1577. Careful observation by Brahe revealed it to be a genuine feature of the heavens and not, as Aristotle had supposed, a transitory atmospheric phenomenon.

Behind much of this success there lay an enormous improvement in the instruments available to astronomers. Brahe at his Uraniborg observatory developed such traditional instruments as ARMILLARY SPHERES and QUADRANTS to the limits inherent in naked-eye observation. The greatest advance, however, came with the invention of the TELESCOPE early in the 17th century. First applied to the heavens in 1610 by Galileo, it rapidly became the most fundamental tool of astronomy. Equally significant was the increasing accuracy of astronomical observations. Early Renaissance astronomers had relied upon the Alfonsine Tables (1252). When COPERNICUS came to apply them in 1504 to an expected conjunction of Mars and Saturn he found the tables to be as much as 10 days adrift. They continued in use, however, until 1551 when they were replaced by the Prutenic Tables compiled by Erasmus REINHOLD, the first tables to be based on the Copernican hypothesis. These, in turn, were superseded by the Rudolfine Tables (1627) which were prepared by Brahe and KEPLER and were to remain in use for the rest of the 17th century.

The period also saw an advance in the system of stellar nomenclature. Copernicus and his colleagues had, in the manner of Ptolemy, referred to stars as being located in the head, tail, or foot of a particular constellation. The modern system of identifying stars alphabetically by their brightness was introduced by Johann BAYER in *Uranometria* (1603) and found quick support.

Equally significant were the more theoretical innovations associated with Copernicus and his successors. Since antiquity planetary orbits were taken as unquestionably circular, with the planets themselves, and all other heavenly bodies, moving with a pleasingly simple uniform motion around a central, stationary earth. In 1543 Copernicus initiated the first great astronomical revolution of modern science by replacing the central earth of antiquity with an equally stationary sun. The resulting heliocentric system remained dependent upon the traditional circular orbits of antiquity. Nor were they questioned by Brahe or Galileo. The break eventually came with Kepler. After spending several years trying to establish the orbit of Mars he finally saw that by assuming planets to move in elliptical orbits he would finally be able to make sense of the available data. He went on to propose in 1609 his first law: planets move in elliptical orbits, with the sun occupying one focus. Two other laws were formulated by Kepler. The second law tackled the problem of why planets move around the sun with varying speed by declaring that a radius vector joining the sun and planet would sweep out equal areas in equal times. In his third law Kepler noted the basic relationship between a planet's distance from the sun and its orbital period by noting that the square of the period varied as the cube of the distance. The harmonic law, as it became known, would later prove to be the key with which astronomers would work out the scale of the solar system. Kepler's laws also posed the problem of what held the system together, and why there seemed to be such a close relationship between the orbit and velocity of a planet and the sun. Kepler himself could do little more than talk unconvincingly of a magnetic attraction emanating from the sun. It remained for Isaac Newton, later in the century, to provide a firm dynamical basis for Kepler's laws with his introduction into astronomy of universal gravitation.

**Further reading:** Howard Margolis, *It Started With Copernicus: How Turning the World Inside Out Led to the Scientific Revolution* (New York: McGraw–Hill, 2002); Richard Parek, *Seeing and Believing: How the Telescope Opened Our Eyes to the Heavens* (New York: Penguin Viking, 1998).

**Athene** See MINERVA

**Aubigné, Theodore d'Agrippa d'** (1551–1630) *French poet, soldier, polemicist, and historian of his own times*
After a studious youth at several European universities, Aubigné, an ardent Protestant, joined the Huguenot forces and served throughout the French religious wars, latterly as master of horse to Henry of Navarre. After Henry's accession (1589) as HENRY IV and conversion to Catholicism, Aubigné withdrew to his estates in Poitou, where he did much of his writing and became gradually estranged from his fellow Protestants. Haunted perhaps by his king's abjuration, he frequently depicts in his work the conflict between truth and outward show and celebrates the justice of an avenging deity, as in his epic poem, *Les Tragiques* (1616). His most interesting work is probably his *Histoire universelle* (1616–20), which deals with the years 1553–1602 and contains many lively eyewitness accounts of the events in which he played a part. Publication of the final volume of the history caused Aubigné to be proscribed, after which he lived in Geneva until his death.

**Auerbach, Johannes** See AMERBACH, JOHANNES

**Augsburg** A south German city on the junction of the Wertach and Lech rivers. Founded as a Roman colony (15 BCE), Augsburg became the seat of a bishopric (759), an imperial free city (1276), and a member of the Swabian League (1331). Close to rich silver mines and situated on the principal trade route from the Mediterranean to north-

ern and western Europe, Augsburg developed as a major banking and commercial center in the 15th and 16th centuries. The FUGGER FAMILY, its leading merchants, became Europe's greatest bankers and lent large sums to the HAPSBURGS and other princes. Augsburg was one of the first important centers of Renaissance arts and scholarship outside Italy. It was a center for humanist scholars and the artists Hans HOLBEIN, Elder and Younger, were natives of the city. The oldest European settlement for the poor, the Fuggerei, was built in Augsburg in 1519. Notable buildings from the Renaissance period include the Gothic additions (1331–1432) to the 11th-century cathedral, the church of SS. Ulrich and Afra (1474–1604), and the town hall (1615–20).

**Augsburg, Confession of** The classic statement of Lutheran doctrine submitted to the Diet of Augsburg on June 25, 1530, and originally called the Articles of Schwabach. The diet had been called by CHARLES V in his search for German unity at a time when the empire was threatened by Turkish invasion. The confession was compiled by MELANCHTHON and approved by LUTHER prior to its presentation to the diet. It was divided into two parts, the first comprising 21 articles conciliatory and comparatively inoffensive to the Roman Church. The second part, however, consisted of seven articles attacking what the Lutherans considered its main abuses; these included aspects of Roman ceremony, certain clerical vows, and the secular authority exercised by its bishops. In response the Roman Catholics drew up the Confutatio presented in August 1530, rejecting any settlement based on the confession.

**Augsburg, Interim of** (1548) A peacetime agreement drawn up under the direction of Emperor CHARLES V, designed to satisfy Lutherans without greatly offending Catholics. It admitted the universality and indivisibility of the Church, the seven sacraments, and the doctrine of TRANSUBSTANTIATION, while allowing to the Protestant side the legality of clerical marriages and, to some extent, the doctrine of JUSTIFICATION BY FAITH.
**See also:** LEIPZIG, INTERIM OF

**Augsburg, Peace of** The treaty concluded on September 25, 1555 that ended the religious wars in Germany during the Reformation period. It was the product of the Diet of Augsburg, held between February and September that year. For the first time in the Christian West two confessions, Roman Catholicism and Lutheranism, were accorded equal legal recognition. This and the freedom it gave individual princes to choose their own and their subjects' religion marked the ultimate defeat of CHARLES V's endeavors to create a unified Germany. In addition, Lutheran or Roman Catholic dissenters were to be allowed freedom to emigrate, Lutheran knights and towns within

Roman Catholic states were to be allowed to maintain their form of worship, and all ecclesiastical lands secularized by the Lutherans before the treaty of Passau (1552) were to remain Lutheran. Although the exclusion of any concessions to other sects, most importantly the Calvinists, was to have serious repercussions, the Peace of Augsburg lasted for 63 years.

**Aulic Council** (German *Reichshofrat*) The court council of the Holy Roman Empire from 1498 until the empire's dissolution in 1806. Attempting to make his government more effective, Emperor MAXIMILIAN I established the council as his supreme executive and judicial body with responsibility for everything except finance and drafting documents. He appointed and paid the members who followed his court until settling permanently in Vienna. In 1559 Ferdinand I strengthened the council, especially in the exercise of the emperor's judicial powers. During the 18th century the Aulic Council grew stronger as its rival body, the *Reichskammergericht*, declined.

**Aurispa, Giovanni** (**Giovanni Pichumerio**) (c. 1370–1459) *Sicilian-born teacher of Greek and collector of manuscripts*
He made two trips to the East (1405–13, 1421–23), principally to look for texts of Greek authors but also to take Greek lessons from Manuel CHRYSOLORAS. Aurispa recovered over 300 manuscripts, including the Venetian manuscript of the *Iliad* (MS. Venetus A), the Laurentian manuscript of Aeschylus, Sophocles, and Apollonius of Rhodes, and manuscripts of the Homeric Hymns and the Greek Anthology. In 1438 Aurispa was made a papal secretary by Eugenius IV. He died at Ferrara. Aurispa produced few works; he translated the commentary of Hierocles on the Golden Verses of Pythagoras (1474) and may have translated the works of Archimedes. His main importance lies in his efforts to copy and encourage the copying of Greek texts and to distribute them. He also drew attention in his teaching while professor of Greek at Florence to literary rather than philosophical values in Greek literature.

**autobiography** The narrative re-creation of the writer's own life, which only emerged as a distinct literary genre in the Renaissance. There are very occasional examples of autobiography in antiquity and in the Middle Ages; the *Confessions* (c. 400) of St. Augustine of Hippo contains a celebrated account of his early life and spiritual quest, but no one else was to approach its degree of introspection for over a thousand years. DANTE's *Vita nuova* (c. 1292–1300) and PETRARCH's *Secretum* (1342–43) are autobiographical without being in the strict sense autobiographies. Rather, for the beginnings of secular autobiography, it is necessary to look to the personal records kept by Italian merchants

from the late 13th century onwards. Some are merely accounts of business negotiations, but others, like the *Zibaldone quaresimale* (1457–85) of the Florentine Giovanni Rucellai, also contain passages of self-questioning. The first full-scale autobiography is arguably the *Commentarii* (1458–64) of Aenea Silvio Piccolomini, who became Pope PIUS II. While focusing on external events, and on the characters and politics of the period, it does contain an implicit portrait of the man himself. Perhaps the two most interesting and revealing Renaissance autobiographies, however, are the famous *Life* (or *Autobiography*) of Benvenuto CELLINI and *De vita propria liber* (*The Book of My Life*) of Girolamo CARDANO. Remarkable for its profound self-scrutiny, Cardano's document was written in his old age and not published until 1643. To find such an essay in the genre in England it is necessary to wait until the early 17th century and the *Life* of Edward, Lord Herbert of Cherbury (1582–1648), which traces his adventures from birth to 1624, and is a splendidly unabashed account of the author's own abundant virtues.

See also: BIOGRAPHY

*auto sacramental* (Spanish, "sacramental act") A dramatic genre in Spain that reached its height in the 17th century with the *autos* of Pedro Calderón de la Barca (1600–81). The *auto* was a one-act allegorical play in verse, originally dealing with an aspect of the Holy Eucharist; it derived from the tableaux, which had traditionally been part of the procession accompanying the Eucharist as it was carried through the streets during the festival of Corpus Christi. These tableaux had developed into a dramatic form similar to that of the miracle and mystery plays in England and the Netherlands in the Middle Ages, and, like them, were mounted on carts and performed out-of-doors. The *autos* began to appear in Spain in the 16th century and were transformed by Calderón from a simple form of pious entertainment into a significant new dramatic form. He exploited the allegorical elements of the *auto* and extended its range in the process, but after his death, it degenerated into farce until performances were finally prohibited by royal decree in 1765.

**Averlino Antonio** See FILARETE

**Avignon, papacy at** The period of papal exile from Rome when Avignon was the seat of seven popes (1309–78) and also of four who claimed the title during the Great Schism (1378–c. 1430). Following the bankruptcy of the papacy, the Frenchman Clement V (pope 1305–14) chose Avignon as his residence in 1309. During this socalled BABYLONIAN CAPTIVITY, all seven Avignon popes were0French, as were most of the cardinals they appointed. All except Clement VI (pope 1342–52) were university trained and demonstrated considerable skill in handling papal business. The Avignon popes, particularly John XXII (pope 1316–34), were highly effective in reorganizing their finances, exploiting every possible means of extracting money from religious foundations and their subjects. These included the introduction of the annate (payment of a newly appointed bishop's first year's income) and the payment to the papacy of all incomes derived from vacant sees. Most importantly they helped prepare the way for LUTHER's conflict with Johann Tetzel by their increased reliance on the sale of INDULGENCES. Using such methods the Avignon popes eventually succeeded in collecting an income three times greater than that of the king of France.

In 1348 Clement VI bought the city of Avignon from Queen Joanna I of Naples. The papal palace (built 1316–70) and fortified walls remain there as witness to the popes' presence. Several Italian artists were attracted to Avignon to work on the papal palace; they include Simone MARTINI and Matteo Giovanetti, who was responsible for the beautiful frescoes in the Chambre du Cerf and Grande Audience.

The new tradition of an Avignon-based papal seat was fundamental to the development of the Great Schism following the departure of Gregory XI (pope 1370–78) for Rome (1377) to restore order in the Italian Papal States. After the election of Urban VI (pope 1378–89) to the Roman seat in April 1378, the majority of Frenchmen among the cardinals (11 out of 16), all chose to share in the election of the antipope, Clement VII, at Avignon in August of the same year. Although the schism was effectively ended by the abdication of the Avignon candidate, Benedict XIII, in 1417, Avignon continued to put up rival claimants until about 1430.

# B

**Babylonian Captivity** The phrase adopted to describe the period 1305–78 when the papal seat was at Avignon instead of Rome. The allusion is to the biblical captivity of the Jews in Babylon that lasted for 70 years. The Babylonian Captivity followed the bankruptcy of the papacy and comprised seven pontificates before the return to Rome and the ensuing Great Schism.

**See also:** AVIGNON, PAPACY AT

**Bacchus** The Roman god of wine, identified with the Greek god Dionysus, many of whose attributes he adopted. In classical mythology Dionysus was the son of Zeus (Roman Jupiter) and Semele, who was brought up by nymphs after his mother was destroyed by his father's thunderbolts. As the god associated with the intoxicating power of wine, he is accompanied by a train of creatures under its influence: the ecstatic women known as bacchantes or maenads, sileni, satyrs, and centaurs. The god himself often rides upon a panther or leopard. It is a train like this that comes upon Ariadne (whom, the legend says, Theseus abandoned on the island of Naxos) in the painting by TITIAN (National Gallery, London), and other artists too were drawn to the pictorial qualities of the Bacchic entourage. The love of Bacchus and the mortal Ariadne, too, was susceptible to allegorical interpretation as the union of the soul with the divine being.

MICHELANGELO's statue of the drunken Bacchus with vine leaves in his hair and accompanied by a young satyr (Bargello, Florence) epitomizes the Renaissance impulse to imitate pagan antiquity—in this case so successfully that many contemporaries looked on it as a genuine classical piece, as Francisco da Hollanda records in his treatise on painting.

**Bachelier, Nicolas** (c. 1500–1556) *French architect and sculptor*
Bachelier was a native of Toulouse, the scene of his principal works. He was primarily influenced by SERLIO. Among the buildings ascribed to Bachelier is the elegant Hôtel d'Assézat (1555) in Toulouse, to which he also contributed the sculptural embellishments.

**backstaffs** Navigational instruments, also known as Davis's quadrants, for measuring the altitude of a celestial body. The ancestor of the backstaff, the cross-staff or Jacob's staff, was reputedly invented by a Jew from the Languedoc, Levi ben Gerson (1288–1324). It consisted of no more than a graduated staff and movable cross-piece(s) or transom(s). If the staff was pointed towards a celestial object and the transom suitably adjusted, the object's altitude above the horizon could be read off the staff. The instrument was used by surveyors and navigators, but it suffered from the disadvantage that the operator had to face the sun's glare whenever a measurement of solar altitude was required. The obvious solution was introduced by the English seaman John DAVIS in his *Seamans Secrets* (1594). His backstaff allowed the observer to stand with his back towards the sun and gain his reading by noting the position of the sun's shadow. The backstaff was the lineal ancestor of the sextant, which appeared in the late 18th century. It was also yet one more discovery described in the unpublished manuscripts of Thomas HARRIOT.

**Bacon, Francis, 1st Baron Verulam, Viscount St. Albans** (1561–1626) *English philosopher, lawyer, and politician*
Bacon was born in London, the son of Sir Nicholas Bacon

and the nephew of Lord Burghley, both political advisers to Elizabeth I. After studying law at Cambridge Bacon began his own political career by entering parliament in 1584. His career flourished under JAMES I, whom he served successively as solicitor-general, attorney-general, and, after 1618, lord chancellor. It ended abruptly in 1621 when, found guilty of corruption, he was fined £40,000 and imprisoned briefly in the Tower of London.

Bacon had earlier, in his *Advancement of Learning* (1605), begun the ambitious program of working out the methodology of and laying the foundations for the newly emerging science of his day. Dismissive of traditional Aristotelian procedures (*see* ARISTOTELIANISM, RENAISSANCE), he sought to develop new inductive methods, the exercise of which would lead more readily to scientific discovery. His *Instauratio magna* (The Great Renewal), an encyclopedic survey of all knowledge, was to have been his crowning achievement, but only a fragment, the *Novum organum* (1620), was completed before his death. Following his banishment from court in 1621, Bacon did, however, manage to revise much of his earlier work in his *De augmentis scientiarum* (1623). In a further work, published posthumously as *The New Atlantis* (1626), Bacon described a utopian society which contained an institution called Solomon's House, charged with the organized study of nature. The suggestion was partially realized later in the century by the foundation of the Royal Society.

Bacon is also known as a polished and epigrammatic essayist. Ten essays were published in 1597 while the third edition of the *Essays* (1625) contained an additional 48 pieces. He died from a chill contracted while attempting to see "why [chicken] flesh might not be preserved in snow, as in salt," leaving debts of £22,000.

**Further reading:** Lisa Jardine and Alan Stewart, *Hostage to Fortune; The Troubled Life of Francis Bacon* (New York: Farrar, Straus & Giroux, 1999); Julian Martin, *Francis Bacon, the State, and the Reform of Natural Philosophy* (Cambridge, U.K. and New York: Cambridge University Press, 1992); Paolo Rossi, *Francis Bacon: From Magic to Science* (London: Routledge & Kegan Paul and Chicago, Ill.: University of Chicago Press, 1968).

**Badius Ascensius, Jodocus (Josse Bade) (1462–1535)**
*Flemish scholar and printer*
Badius was born at Aasche, near Ghent, and after studying in Louvain and Bologna settled in Lyons (1492), where he taught classics. There he married the daughter of the printer Jean (Johann) Trechsel (died 1498) and became his editor, responsible for the first Lyons book printed in roman type ("Italian types"), a 1492 edition of the orations of Philippus Beroaldus. His illustrated edition of Terence, first published in 1493, was reprinted many times. In 1499 he moved to Paris, working there in association with Jean Petit before starting on his own in 1503. In the next 30 years he produced about 800 books, among them

ERASMUS's early works. The designs of Badius's books sometimes used title-page borders modeled on manuscript borders, for example his 1511 Cicero. His Thucydides translation of 1528 was printed with type bought from FROBEN of Basle.

Badius was succeeded by his son-in-law, Robert ESTIENNE, and a subsequent dynasty of scholar-printers.

**Baena, Juan Alfonso de (early 15th century)** *Spanish poet*
A minor CONVERSO poet, Baena is remembered as the compiler of the *Cancionero de Baena*, a collection of 612 poems by 54 poets which was prepared for King John II of Castile in 1445. The anthology contains *canciones* (lyrics) and *decires* (narratives, satires, and panegyrics) dating from the reign of John I (1379–90) and extending into the 15th century. The lyrics are in octosyllabic lines, often varied with half-lines (*pie quebrado*); the narratives and satires are written either in octosyllabic lines or in 12-syllable ARTE MAYOR. Linguistically, the anthology shows the change from the Gallego-Portuguese (or Galician-Portuguese) dialect used by Castilian poets in the 13th and 14th centuries to the Castilian Spanish adopted towards the end of the 14th century. LÓPEZ DE AYALA is the earliest poet represented. Baena gives highest praise to the *trovador* Alfonso Álvarez de Villasandino (c. 1345–c. 1425). The collection as a whole reflects the Provençal and Galician troubadour tradition of courtly poetry.

**See also:** CANCIONERO

**Baffin, William (c. 1584–1622)** *English explorer, who attempted to solve some of the major navigational challenges of his day*
Little is known of Baffin's early life, which was probably passed in learning his trade as a seaman. In 1612 he explored the west coast of Greenland, and the following two years led expeditions engaging in whaling to Spitzbergen and Greenland under the sponsorship of the MUSCOVY COMPANY. In 1615 and 1616 he took up the quest for the NORTHWEST PASSAGE, on the latter voyage discovering and exploring much of Baffin Bay. Ironically, although Baffin became convinced that a northwest passage did not exist, he did in fact discover the opening leading to it at the entrance to Lancaster Sound. Two later voyages (1617–19, 1620–22) took him to the East under the auspices of the EAST INDIA COMPANY. He died while joining the Persian army in an attack on the Portuguese-held town of Kishm.

His accounts of four of his Arctic voyages (1612, 1613, 1615, 1616) were published by Samuel PURCHAS. They are remarkable for the scientific observations they contain, including Baffin's attempts to find a means of calculating longitude and to deal with the problem of the sun's refraction.

**Baglioni family** A powerful and wealthy Umbrian family, notorious in the Renaissance for its crimes. The Baglioni gained their wealth from employment as CONDOTTIERI in the 13th century and political power from Malatesta Baglioni (1389–1427), who was awarded territories by Pope Martin V and who virtually ruled Perugia. From 1488, after massacring or exiling their rivals, the Baglioni ruled Perugia through a council of 10 family members. Giampaolo Baglioni (1470–1520) seized power after the murder of several leading Baglioni (1500) in family disputes. He tried to murder Pope JULIUS II (1506) and was himself murdered on Pope LEO X's orders. Ridolfo Baglioni (1518–54) was exiled by Pope PAUL III after the SALT WAR of 1540 brought an end to Perugia's privileges as an autonomous city.

**Baianism** The doctrine of Michel de Bay (1514–89), a Louvain theologian more generally known as Baius. His writings on free will, righteousness, and justification (1563–64) were openly condemned by Pope Pius V in his bull *Ex omnibus afflictionibus* (1567) as false and heretical. Baianism, inspired by Augustinian doctrine, insisted upon man's total depravity and moral incapacity. In so doing it rejected the doctrine recognized at the Council of TRENT (1551) that rested upon the concept of man's preternatural innocence. Baius launched the first attack on man's freedom of will and denied the possibility of achieving spiritual and moral perfection in this life. His arguments were offensive to the Jesuits and were countered by their spokesman ROBERT BELLARMINE. The conflict between Baianism and the Jesuits during the 16th century anticipated that of the Jansenists and Jesuits during the 17th.

**Baïf, Jean-Antoine de** (1532–1589) *French poet and most learned member of the Pléiade*
Born in Venice, the natural son of the humanist Lazare de Baïf (c. 1496–1547), he received a classical education. He studied in Paris (1547) with RONSARD under Jean DAURAT, and together with Joachim DU BELLAY, they formulated plans to transform French poetry by employing classical and neoclassical models (*see* PLÉIADE). Baïf produced two collections of poetry, *Les Amours de Méline* (1552) and *L'Amour de Francine* (1555), in accordance with the principles they had laid down, followed by *Le Brave* in 1567, adapted from Plautus' *Miles gloriosus*. But his poetic gifts were inferior to his great learning, which is best displayed in his *Mimes* (1581) and in his many translations, including Terence's *Eunuchus* and Sophocles' *Antigone*. His interest in Platonic theories of the relation between music and poetry led him to set up (1567) a short-lived academy of the two arts with the musician Thibault de Courville.

Baïf is also remembered as an innovator in matters of language and versification, inventing a system of phonetic spelling and a new metrical form, the 15-syllable *vers baïfin*. His theories are expounded in *Etrènes de poesie francoêze en vers mezurés* (1574). Having received various marks of favor from Charles IX and Henry III during his last years, he died peacefully in Paris.

**Bakfark, Valentine** (c. 1507–1576) *Hungarian composer*
Bakfark was one of the most famous and celebrated lutenists of his time but very little is known about his life. He traveled throughout Europe, particularly Italy, France, and Germany and he served (1549–66) at the court of the Polish king, Sigismund II Augustus. His surviving works, some of which are featured in the *Thesaurus musicus* (1574) of the Netherlandish publisher Pierre Phalèse, include a small number of highly elaborate fantasias and some transcriptions of vocal music. However, Bakfark destroyed much of his work before dying of the plague in Padua, Italy.

**Balassi, Bálint** (Bálint Balassa) (1554–1594) *Hungarian poet*
Balassi was born into an aristocratic family and educated by his mother, the ardently Protestant Anna Sulyok, and the religious reformer Peter Bornemissza. He is widely regarded as Hungary's first great vernacular poet. After joining the army he served at the fortress of Eger, defending the border lands against the Turks. Here he fell in love with Anna Losonczi, the heroine of his cycle of "Julia Poems." Balassi's poetry consists of patriotic and martial songs, erotic poems, and adaptations from Latin and German verse. He led a troubled, litigious and often itinerant life and was expelled from Hungary (1589) after divorcing his wife, Krisztina Dobó, and converting to Catholicism. He returned to Hungary to fight in the Turkish war (1594) and died at the siege of Esztergom that year. Balassi also invented a verse form, the nine-line "Balassi stanza," with the rhyme scheme *aabccbddb*. His best works, his erotic poems, were known in manuscript form but not published until 1874.

**Balbi, Gerolamo** (c. 1450–1535) *Italian bishop and humanist*
Little is known of Balbi's early life although it is likely that he studied in Rome. By 1485 he was in Paris where he obtained a university chair (1489). Faced with accusations of sodomy and heresy he took refuge first in England (1491) and then Vienna (1493), after which he moved on to the court of King Ladislas of Bohemia in Prague. Following new allegations of sodomy he fled to Hungary, where he was ordained to the priesthood and became bishop of Gurk (1523). Balbi's main achievement was the dissemination of humanism in eastern Europe, and his poetry, philosophical writing, and letters reveal a man of great learning. He was acquainted with many leading international humanists including Pomponio LETO (his teacher), Konrad CELTIS, and King MATTHIAS CORVINUS. However, Balbi was a controversial figure, which is wit-

nessed by his authorship of *Opusculum epigrammatum* (1494), a collection of inflammatory epigrams.

**Balboa, Vasco Nuñes de** (c. 1475–1517) *Spanish explorer*
Balboa was born into a good Estremaduran family and went to the West Indies in 1501. In 1510 he assumed command of an expedition to Darien, and, making friends with the native peoples, he heard rumors about the great ocean beyond the mountains west of the gulf of Darien. While at Darien Balboa heard that his enemies had complained of him to King Ferdinand II, so, endeavoring to recover the king's favor, he set out on an expedition over the mountains, from which he caught his first sight of the Pacific Ocean (September 1513). A few days later he took possession of the new sea for the Spanish crown. He returned to Darien with considerable booty and when news of his exploits reached Spain the king rewarded him with the title of admiral. Nonetheless his enemies managed to frustrate his intended search for the gold of Peru and finally managed to have him executed for alleged treason at Acla, near Darien.

**Baldovinetti, Alesso** (c. 1426–1499) *Italian painter and mosaicist*
His work, which was mainly in and around Florence, is documented by his diary recording his commissions. Some of his paintings, such as the *Madonna and Child* in the Louvre, Paris, and the damaged *Nativity* fresco in SS. Annunziata, Florence, have attractive, if unsophisticated, landscape views of the Val d'Arno in the background. Among his mosaics are decorations in the baptistery, Florence, and the tympanum over the south door of Pisa cathedral. The main influences visible upon his work are those of DOMENICO VENEZIANO and ANDREA DEL CASTAGNO.

**Baldung Grien, Hans** (Hans Baldung Grün) (1484/85–1545) *German painter and print maker*
While he was still a child, Baldung's family moved from his native Schwäbisch-Gmünd to Strasbourg, where he probably received his initial training. By about 1500 he was in DÜRER's Nuremberg workshop, where he remained until 1508, when he returned to Strasbourg. There he remained for the rest of his career, save for the years 1512–17, when he was based at Fribourg. At Nuremberg, Baldung contributed numerous woodcuts to the books *Beschlossen Gart* (1505) and *Speculum Passionis* (1507) by Ulrich Pinder and painted two altarpieces for the city of Halle. The latter's remarkably lustrous coloristic effects imply knowledge of the early works of CRANACH. Baldung's key early work is the huge high altar of Fribourg minster. Although related to earlier compositions by Dürer, its central panel of the *Coronation of the Virgin* has a flamboyance of form and color quite distinct from Dürer's disciplined style. Baldung's woodcuts of the same period, notably the famous *Witches* (1513), reveal a growing interest in the demonic. This tendency reached a high point of mingled horror and eroticism in the *Woman Embraced by Death* at Basle, painted in about 1517. With the coming of the Reformation to Strasbourg, Baldung's subject matter shifts away from religious themes, towards secular ones. These include portraits, such as the woodcut likeness of Luther (1521) and the oil painting of a young man in Nuremberg (1526). Baldung also painted genre scenes, such as the moralizing *Ill-Matched Couple* (1527) in Liverpool, and classical legends, such as *Pyramus and Thisbe* (1530) in Berlin. A highly intellectual artist, Baldung was far more than merely Dürer's greatest pupil. His style was always quite distinct from that of his master or any other painter, culminating in a highly personal contribution to European MANNERISM.

**Bale, John** (1495–1563) *English bishop, controversialist, and dramatist*
Born at Cove, Suffolk, Bale was a convert to Protestantism whose uncompromising views provoked great hostility (he was known as "Bilious Bale"). He was twice forced into exile—to Germany in 1540–47 and to Basle during the reign (1553–58) of Mary I. However, Edward VI made him bishop of Ossory (1552) and under Elizabeth I he ended his days in peace as a prebendary of Canterbury. He produced numerous polemical writings, a history of English literature, and several dramas, the most notable of which is *King John* (1548), often seen as the first English historical play.

**balìa** A committee with special powers, set up in an Italian city to handle particular constitutional situations. While overtly a republican institution, the Florentine *balìa* fell inexorably under the control of the MEDICI during the 15th century.

**ballade** A French medieval metrical form, not to be confused with the English "ballad." It consists of a poem of fixed form and strict rhyme scheme with three stanzas of either 10 lines (*dizains*) or eight lines (*huitains*) each, the lines being most commonly of six or eight syllables; there is a concluding four-line *envoi*, in which the poet usually addresses his patron. All four parts end with the same line, constituting the refrain, though departures from the regular forms exist. The greatest exponent of the *ballade* was François Villon (1431–??), who included a number of them in his *Testament* (1461).

**ballet de cour** A form of entertainment combining DANCE, spectacle, music, song, and drama, which evolved at the French court in the mid-16th century. CATHERINE DE' MEDICI, who would have encountered similar entertainments at the Florentine court in her youth, laid on the sumptuous *Balet comique de la Reine* in 1581 to celebrate the marriage of her daughter, and the fashion for hugely expensive and spectacular shows of this nature continued in the reigns of Henry IV (1589–1610) and Louis XIII (1610–43). Costume designs surviving from the early 17th century, especially those by Daniel Rabel (1578–1637), indicate the grotesque and humorous, as well as the opulent, aspects of these *ballets*. The *ballet de cour* had developed into the ballet as we know it by the end of the 17th century.

See also: MASQUE

**Bandello, Matteo** (1485–1561) *Italian writer, cleric, diplomat, and soldier*
Bandello was born at Castelnuovo Scrivia, near Tortona, and educated in Milan and at Pavia university. Among other appointments in Lombardy, he was tutor to Lucrezia GONZAGA. After the Spanish attack on Milan following the battle of PAVIA (1525), in which he lost his house and many documents, he fled to France. In 1550 he was made bishop of Agen, where he spent the rest of his life.

His works include a collection of Petrarchan verse (*Il Canzoniere*, 1544) and an Italian version of Euripides' *Hecuba*, but it was his prose *Novelle* (1554, 1573) containing 214 stories, which made him famous and initiated a new phase in narrative literature. Bandello did not aim at classical dignity in his writing, but he did help promote the vernacular as the literary language of Italy. Containing a extraordinary variety of tales, the collection was also an important source for later Renaissance playwrights who drew on it either directly or in translation (SHAKESPEARE, for instance, utilized Bandello's "Giulietta e Romeo").

**Bandinelli, Baccio** (Bartolommeo Bandinelli) (1488–1560) *Italian sculptor in marble and bronze*
He was born in Florence and after training under his goldsmith father, worked with RUSTICI, the sculptural associate of LEONARDO DA VINCI. His career was dedicated to trying in vain to equal the sculpture of MICHELANGELO, in a series of commissions from the MEDICI FAMILY, both in Florence and Rome; many of these remained unfinished. Much of his original monumental statuary can be criticized: for example, the *Hercules and Cacus* (1534; Piazza della Signoria, Florence), which he pretentiously carved as a pair of Michelangelo's *David*. His best work is either closely based on classical statuary, like the *Laocöon* in the Uffizi, Florence (1525), or is in low relief, like the *Prophets* in the choir of Florence cathedral (1555). As court sculptor to Duke Cosimo I, he was a rival of CELLINI, who attacked him in his autobiography. He also produced portraits, bronze statuettes, paintings, and drawings, most of which are still in Florence.

**banking** Renaissance banking was basically the same as medieval banking, with a few great houses offering merchant banking services (particularly long-distance money transfer and the provision of loans). The first such organization was that of the KNIGHTS TEMPLAR, who by 1200 were in effect bankers to the kings of England and France. The 13th century saw the rise of the great Italian houses—the ACCIAIUOLI, BARDI, and Peruzzi of Florence, the Frescobaldi of Lucca, and others—who used the capital amassed in trade to move into banking. With kings always short of cash for major enterprises, especially wars, these bankers quickly became immensely wealthy and influential. However, this had its risks: the default of Edward III of England (1341) bankrupted the Peruzzi (1343), Acciaiuoli (1345), and Bardi (1346). Later bankers, such as the MEDICI and Spinelli, adopted a more decentralized organization, so the failure of one branch could not ruin the whole company, and in general took fewer risks.

Italian dominance continued until the end of the 15th century, when economic and political changes shifted the focus northwards. After 1494, when Charles VIII of France captured Florence, the Medici bank ceased to function. The great bankers of the 16th century were the FUG-

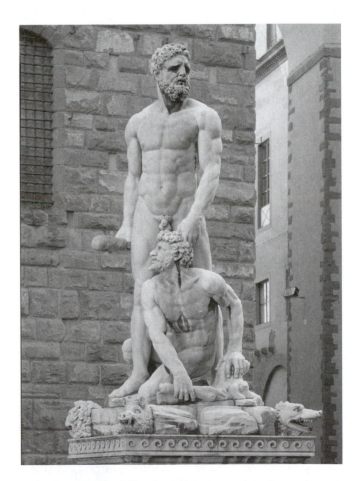

**Baccio Bandinelli** *Hercules and Cacus* (1534). The sculpture records the exploit of Hercules in which he killed the giant Cacus, who had stolen some of the hero's cattle. It stands in the Piazza della Signoria, Florence.
*The Bridgeman Art Library*

GER FAMILY of Augsburg, who had built their fortune in the silver and copper mines of Slovakia, the Welsers, also of Augsburg, and the Höchstetters. The commercial and financial capital of Europe was then Antwerp. However, the opening up of the world beyond Europe occasioned further changes; by the early 17th century the lead had passed to the Dutch, backed by the wealth from their East Indian empire.

What distinguished these firms were their international connections and the scale of their operations. Almost anybody with capital could, and did, lend money. For example, the English kings of the late 14th and early 15th centuries preferred to deal with syndicates of English merchants rather than the Italian houses. At a lower level, money-lenders and pawnbrokers abounded. The taking of interest—usury—was technically against canon law, but was generally practiced, especially by the JEWS upon whom, of course, canon law was not binding.

In the late 16th century there began to emerge a major change in banking: the provision of capital for loans by accepting deposits, on which interest was paid. This led to the establishment of firms that concentrated solely on banking, without a base in trade, commerce, or other industry. Such a "public bank," the Banco della Piazza di Rialto, was established in Venice in 1587, and in 1609 the Dutch launched the great Bank of Amsterdam.

**Further reading:** Fernand Braudel, *The Wheels of Commerce* (New York: Harper & Row, 1985; new ed. Berkeley, Calif.: University of California Press, 1992); Frederic Chapin Lane and Reinhold C. Mueller, *Money and Banking in Medieval and Renaissance Venice*, 2 vols (Baltimore, Md. and London: Johns Hopkins University Press, 1985, 97); Raymond de Roover, *The Rise and Decline of the Medici Bank 1397–1494* (Cambridge, Mass.: Harvard University Press, 1963); Richard Fremantle, *God and Money; Florence and the Medici in the Renaissance* (Florence, Italy: Olschki, 1992).

**Barbari, Jacopo de'** (c. 1450–c. 1515) *Italian painter and engraver*
Barbari was a native of Venice and may have met DÜRER on the latter's visit to Italy in 1495, but little is known of his early career. He produced a grand woodcut panorama of Venice in 12 sheets, and the same year (1500) he moved to Nuremberg as painter to Emperor Maximilian I. During his peripatetic career in northern Europe he was immensely important in propagating Italian Renaissance motifs and style among northern artists. After a period (1503–05) serving Frederick (III) the Wise of Saxony, he moved to the Netherlands (c. 1508), working first for Philip of Burgundy and later for the Hapsburg regent Margaret of Austria. His still life of a dead bird (1504; Munich) is a very early example of the genre. Among the artists who were deeply influenced by him were Jan GOSSAERT and Bernard van ORLEY.

**Barbaro, Daniele** (1513–1570) *Italian nobleman and polymath*
Barbaro belonged to a landed Venetian family and studied science, philosophy, mathematics, and literature in Padua. In 1545 he founded and became curator of the botanic garden there. In 1548 he was sent to England as ambassador and on his return (1550) was appointed patriarch of Aquileia, in which role he attended the Council of TRENT. He commissioned the Villa Barbaro (1560–68) at Maser from PALLADIO, who had earlier provided the illustrations to Barbaro's edition of VITRUVIUS (1556), and engaged VERONESE to decorate the interior. Barbaro's *Pratica della perspettiva* (1568/69), giving an interesting account of the camera obscura, has some illustrative material borrowed from the 1566 edition of SERLIO's architectural treatise; the fact that this edition had been dedicated to Barbaro is still further evidence of his informed patronage.

**Barbaro, Ermolao (Almoro di Zaccaria)** (1453–c. 1493) *Italian poet and scholar*
He was born at Venice and studied at Rome under Pomponio LETO, was crowned laureate at 14, and appointed professor of philosophy at Padua in 1477. There he corresponded with POLITIAN and PICO DELLA MIRANDOLA and lectured on Aristotle. He went on a number of diplomatic missions for the city and was made patriarch of Aquileia by Pope Innocent VIII (1491). Unfortunately he failed to obtain the permission of the Venetian senate for this post and he was banished to Rome, where he died, probably of plague. His major scholarly activity was textual criticism (his *Castigationes Pliniae* (1492) emended over 5000 passages in Pliny the Elder's *Natural History*). He also edited Pomponius Mela (1493) and translated Themistius's Greek commentary on Aristotle (1480). His translation of Aristotle's *Rhetorica* into Latin was not printed until 1544.

**Barbarossa** (Italian, "Redbeard," **Khair ed-Din**) (c. 1465–1546) *Barbary pirate and admiral of the Ottoman fleet*
Raised on Lesbos, he moved to Djerba with his three brothers when their father died. Scorning both the weakness of the Muslim rulers and the presence of Iberian invaders in North Africa, the brothers undertook a campaign of brutal piracy. They formed a principality on Djidjelli, but Spain captured their land in 1518. Barbarossa, now the head of the family, was saved from annihilation by the sultan of Turkey, and for the rest of his life he worked for the sultan. He conquered Tunis for the Ottomans (1534) and permanently loosened Spain's grip on North Africa.

**Bardi, Count Giovanni de'** (1534–1612) *Italian composer and writer*
Bardi was the founder of the Florentine Camerata, a group of scholars who sought to rediscover the music and drama of ancient Greece. They believed that the Greek tragedies

were recited to a musical accompaniment and their attempts to recreate these conditions resulted in the first operas. Notable members of the Camerata included the poet Ottavio Rinuccini, Giulio CACCINI, Vincenzo GALILEI, the father of Galileo, and, probably, Jacopo PERI. Bardi's *Discorso mandato a Caccini sopra la musica antica* (Discourse to Caccini on ancient music; 1580) is a theoretical work advocating the abandonment of counterpoint in favor of a monodic form, a single vocal line with only light accompaniment. His only surviving musical compositions, ironically, are two highly contrapuntal madrigals.

See also: MUSIC THEORY

**Bardi family** The Florentine family of Bardi won a large fortune and European influence through international BANKING. By 1310 they were the wealthiest family in Florence and used their position to secure political dominance. However, as part of Edward III of England's manoeuvres to finance the Hundred Years' War, they participated from 1338 in schemes to exploit the English wool trade though monopolistic syndicates, intended to repay the large loans they made to the king. These did not work, and Edward defaulted on his repayments (1341); by 1345 the Bardi were owed at least £103,000. This, combined with the burden of supporting Florence's war against Lucca, forced them into bankruptcy (1346), and they also lost their political power. The sole surviving evidence of the Bardi fortune can be seen in their gifts to the church of Sta. Croce, Florence. Count Giovanni BARDI was an intellectual leader in late 16th-century Florence, the patron of musicians, scholars, and poets, as well as being a composer himself.

**Barends, Dirk** (1534–1592) *Netherlands painter*
He was born in Amsterdam and around 1555 traveled to Venice where he worked in the studio of TITIAN. Back in Amsterdam by 1562, he became known as a portrait painter and one of the earliest to produce a group portrait (*schuttersstuk*) of the kind made famous in the 17th century by such masterpieces as Rembrandt's *The Night Watch*. His style is characteristic of the MANNERISM prevalent in the northern Netherlands during this period.

**Barents, Willem** (died 1597) *Dutch navigator, after whom the Barents Sea was named*
Barents pioneered the NORTHEAST PASSAGE to Asia. In 1594 his first attempt to find a route was defeated by the harsh climate of Novaya Zemlya, where he was following the western coastline. The following year a seven-ship convoy attempted to penetrate the strait between Vaigach Island and the continental coast. His third expedition, under Jakob van Heemskerck (died 1607), discovered Spitzbergen, but was aborted during the winter of 1596/97, when ice trapped their ship north of Novaya Zemlya, and the crew became the first Europeans to winter so far north.

They only escaped in two home-built open boats in June 1597. Barents died later that month, en route for the Kola Peninsula where most of his shipmates eventually reached safety.

See also: VEER, GERRIT DE

**Bargeo, Pier Angelo** See ANGELI, PIETRO ANGELO

**Bari, Niccolò di** See NICCOLÒ DELL'ARCA

**Baro, Peter** (1534–1599) *French divine*
Baro was born at Étampes and admitted to the ministry by John Calvin himself at Geneva in 1560. He fled persecution in France a year later and settled in England. Here, under the patronage of William Cecil, Lord Burghley, he was appointed to a chair of divinity at Cambridge (1574). By 1581 his increasing toleration of the tenets of Rome was apparent and he aroused considerable hostility, including that of Elizabeth I. He left Cambridge in 1596 and passed his remaining years in London. Baro was the first divine in England to interpret the creed of the Church of England upon definite anti-Calvinistic principles and so anticipated the work of Richard Bancroft and William Laud in the next century.

**Barocci, Federico** (**Il Baroccio**) (c. 1535–1612) *Italian painter*
Born and trained in Urbino, Barocci was also known as Fiori da Urbino and became celebrated for his innovative emotional style strongly influenced by the works of CORREGGIO. He visited Rome twice (1550, 1560) to study Raphael's works and was probably encouraged there by Michelangelo. On his second visit he worked with Federico ZUCCARO on the decoration of the ceiling of the Casino of Pius IV in the Vatican gardens (1561–63), which established his reputation as a leading Italian artist. Barocci spent the rest of his career in Urbino, where he enjoyed ducal patronage; he painted mainly religious subjects, aspects of which anticipated the BAROQUE. Later works included the *Madonna del Popolo* (1575–79; Uffizi, Florence), the *Vision of St. Sebastian* (1595; Genoa cathedral), the *Nativity* (1597; Prado, Madrid), and a number of sensitive drawings. He was also a pioneer of the use of pastel chalks and often employed mannerist devices in his compositions.

**Baronius, Cesare** (**Cesare Baronio**) (1538–1607) *Italian historian of the Roman Catholic Church*
Baronius was born at Sora, educated at Naples, joined the Oratory in Rome in 1557, and eventually (1593) succeeded St. PHILIP NERI as its head. He became confessor to Pope CLEMENT VIII, who made him a cardinal and librarian of the Vatican. He is best remembered for his 12-volume *Annales ecclesiastici* (1588–1607), a justification of his faith by the history of the Church to 1199 CE, designed to

counter the claims of the Lutheran CENTURIATORS OF MAGDEBURG. Although poorly arranged, dull, and inaccurate, this work has long been praised as a pioneering accumulation of historical sources drawn from the Vatican and leading Italian libraries. Baronius's support, on the basis of his studies, for the papal claim to Sicily against that of Spain reputedly lost him the papacy, due to Spanish opposition. He also revised and corrected the Roman Martyrology (1586, 1589).

**Baroque** A movement in the arts that began in Rome at the end of the Renaissance and later spread throughout Europe and the colonies. Possibly deriving its name from the Spanish word *barrueco* (meaning an irregularly shaped pearl) and used at first as a term of abuse, the Baroque prospered chiefly in Roman Catholic countries, where it was employed as a medium for propaganda during the COUNTER-REFORMATION and reached its climax in the mid-17th century (the High Baroque). The Baroque saw a new emphasis upon naturalism and emotionalism and a new boldness in combining different art forms to achieve a complete balanced work of art. In architecture and sculpture, the principal exponent of the style was Giovanni Lorenzo Bernini (1598–1680), who invested his works with a sense of movement and emotional urgency, encouraging the spread of such ideas during his travels around Europe. Other notable architects active mainly in Rome included Francesco Castelli Borromini (1599–1667).

The artists of the Baroque inherited an interest in the classical tradition via MANNERISM and were deeply influenced by such masters as Michelangelo, Titian, and Raphael. Among the early exponents were CARAVAGGIO, whose command of such techniques as *chiaroscuro* contributed to the revolutionary atmosphere of realism and emotional seriousness; Annibale CARRACCI, who broke new ground in rejecting some of the excesses of the mannerists; Pietro da Cortona (1596–1669), who specialized in overwhelming illusionistic ceilings (for example, those in the Palazzo Pitti, Florence); and later RUBENS, who became acquainted with the Baroque in Rome between 1600 and 1608, before establishing himself as the greatest of the northern Baroque artists.

The movement outside Italy subsequently produced a number of other important artists and architects, who combined Italian ideals with their own national characteristics, notably Jan Vermeer and Rembrandt in the Netherlands, Velázquez in Spain, Balthasar Neumann in Germany, Nicolas Poussin in France, and van Dyck, Inigo JONES, Christopher Wren, and Sir John Vanbrugh in England. The baroque taste for ornate decoration ultimately achieved an extreme form in the highly decorated rococo style of the early 18th century.

In music, the term Baroque is used to denote a period (approximately 1600–1750) rather than a particular style

or movement; the term therefore covers developments in European music from the time of MONTEVERDI to that of J. S. Bach and Handel over a century later. The music of the Baroque is most clearly distinguished from that of the late Renaissance in its use of *basso continuo* and its introduction of major and minor tonality in place of the earlier system of modes. However, the period's emphasis on emotional affect and the expressive setting of texts is continuous with trends in the music of the late Renaissance. Major forms to emerge during the period include opera, oratorio, and the instrumental concerto.

**Further reading:** Giovanni Careri and Ferrante Ferranti, *Baroques* (Princeton, N.J.: Princeton University Press, 2003); Rolf Toman and Achim Bednorz, *The Baroque: Architecture, Sculpture, Painting* (Cologne, Germany and New York: Konemann, 1998); Rudolf Wittkower, *Bernini: The Sculptor of the European Baroque* (London: Phaidon, 1997).

**Barricades, Journée des** See JOURNÉE DES BARRICADES

**Barros, João de** (1496–1570) *Portuguese historian and administrator*
Barros was born at Vizeu and brought up at the court of King Manuel I of Portugal, where he was a favorite of the king and also of Prince John, later King John III. In 1532 he was appointed head of the overseas administration, dealing with Portuguese trade with the East and colonial expansionism. Barros's own venture in colonialism, his 1539 expedition to Brazil, was a disaster and he suffered severe financial loss when his fleet was shipwrecked.

A chivalric romance, the *Crónica do Emperador Clarimundo* (1522), was his first published work. Later works include the humanist dialogue *Rópica pnefma* (1532) and one of the earliest Portuguese grammars (1539), but his crowning achievement is his history of Portuguese ventures in the East. This work, the *Asia*, appeared in four "Décadas" (1552, 1553, 1563, 1615); it was continued after his death by Diogo do COUTO. Barros, who modeled his style on that of the Roman historian Livy, celebrated his country's overseas discoveries and conquests from the vantage-point of his own position in the colonial administration; the *Asia* is still a valuable record of the great years of Portuguese expansionism.

**Barthélemy, Nicolas** (1478–c. 1540) *French Benedictine monk and writer*
Barthélemy was born at Loches, near Tours, and became prior of Fréteval, near Vendôme, and later of Notre-Dame-de-Bonne-Nouvelle, Orleans. He studied law at Orleans university and was a friend of BUDÉ. Among his poems in Latin were *Epigrammata et eydillia* (1532), and his drama *Christus Xylonicus* (1529) combined elements of the humanist approach to tragedy with aspects of the vernacular mystery plays. He is also known for having influenced RA-

BELAIS. His biographies of two dukes of Orleans, Charles the poet (1394–1465) and his son, later King LOUIS XII, have survived in manuscript.

**Bartholomew('s Day), Massacre of St.** See MASSACRE OF ST. BARTHOLOMEW

**Bartolommeo, Fra** (Baccio della Porta) (1472–1517)
*Italian painter and draftsman*
Born in Florence, Bartolommeo trained as an artist under Cosimo ROSSELLI before joining the convent of San Marco and coming under the influence of its prior SAVONAROLA. Early works from this period include the *Annunciation* (1497; Volterra cathedral) and the *Last Judgment* (1499; Museo di San Marco). After Savonarola's death Bartolommeo joined the Dominican Order (1500) and gave up painting until 1504, when he became head of the monastery workshop at San Marco. Works from this period, such as *Vision of St. Bernard* (1507; Accademia, Florence) and *God the Father with SS. Catherine of Siena and Mary Magdalene* (1509; Pinacoteca Civica, Lucca), show the influences of Giovanni Bellini and Leonardo da Vinci and served to establish Bartolommeo as the foremost painter in Florence by 1510. His control of color and composition is evident in many of his subsequent works, including *The Mystic Marriage of St. Catherine* (1511; versions in Louvre, Paris and Uffizi, Florence) and his *Pietà* (1515; Palazzo Pitti, Florence). His later paintings were also influenced by the works of Raphael and Michelangelo. He also executed many notable drawings, for instance in his sketchbook, now in Rotterdam.

**Basle** (Basel, French Bâle) A Swiss city on the Rhine, close to the French and German borders. First mentioned in 374, Basle became the seat of a bishopric in the fifth century and was the venue of the ecumenical council (1431–49) (*see* BASLE, COUNCIL OF). ERASMUS taught at Basle university (1521–29) and is buried in the city. During the first half of the 16th century Basle, which from at least as early as 1468 had boasted a printing press, became a focus for humanist learning and the Reformation. In 1522 OECOLAMPADIUS persuaded the Basle magistrates that the Church should be reformed. After a popular rising, government of the city passed from the bishop to the magistrates and the Mass was abolished. Basle became an important center of Protestantism, welcoming CALVIN in the 1530s. Notable buildings from the Renaissance period include the 15th-century St. Paul's Gate, the Münster (1019–1528), the town hall (1504–21), and the church of St. Martin.

**Basle, Confessions of** The earliest reformed confessions of faith, comprising the Basle Confession of 1534 (sometimes called the Confession of Mühlhausen) and the First Helvetic Confession of 1536 (sometimes called the Second Confession of BASLE). In 1529, under the guidance of the Zwinglian reformer, OECOLAMPADIUS, Basle broke with Rome and joined ZWINGLI's Christian Civic Alliance. The (first) Basle Confession was written by Oswald Myconius (1488–1552) but based on the work of Oecolampadius, and is a confession of moderate Zwinglianism, fully endorsing Zwingli's view of Scripture. It held its place in the Church of Basle until 1872. The First Helvetic Confession was compiled by Heinrich BULLINGER and, though also essentially Zwinglian, a Lutheran influence can be detected.

**Basle, Council of** A council of the Church that sat intermittently between 1431 and 1449. The calling of this council was urged upon Pope Martin V by Emperor Sigismund in the hope of making some kind of settlement with the HUSSITES. This resulted in the drawing up in July 1436 of the Compacts of Prague, by the terms of which the Bohemians and Moravians were granted a considerable amount of ecclesiastical independence in return for oaths of fealty to Sigismund. With their legal recognition of divergent practices within Christendom, the Compacts marked a significant change in the Church's policy.

Even before the Compacts were drawn up, relations between the papacy and the council were not good. To thwart the council's attempts to restrict papal authority, Pope EUGENIUS IV ordered the transfer of the council from Basle to first (1437) Ferrara, then Florence, and finally (1443) Rome (*see* FLORENCE, COUNCIL OF). Only a small minority of those sitting on the council at Basle accepted this; the majority, declaring the Council's authority superior to that of the pope, remained at Basle and began the proceedings that led to Eugenius's socalled excommunication and deposition and the election of an antipope, Felix V, in 1439. These moves lost the council many supporters, and a lasting schism was avoided when the council submitted to Rome by securing the abdication of Felix, following the death of Eugenius (1447) and the election of NICHOLAS V. The dissolution of the council in 1449 marked the end of the "conciliar period," which left a lasting papal suspicion of Church councils.

**Bassano, Jacopo da Ponte** (1510/19–92) *Italian painter*
The son of Francesco da Ponte the Elder (c. 1475–1539), Jacopo was born in Bassano and studied first under his father and then under Bonifacio Veneziano (de' Pitati) in nearby Venice. There contact with the paintings of TITIAN stimulated in him the feeling for color and light that is characteristic of much of his work. From the 1530s he worked mainly in Bassano. His style changed continually according to changing influences and around 1540 he adopted a mannerist style with graceful attenuation of figures, as in his *Adoration of the Magi* (Kunsthistorisches Museum, Vienna). This painting was one of a number which included peasants and animals; Bassano was one of the first painters of religious scenes to do this. The

large rustic genre scenes that he produced after 1565 were also innovatory. Bassano's four sons included the painters Francesco the Younger (1549–92) and Leandro (1557–1622).

**Batalha** (Portuguese, "Battle") The usual name of the Dominican abbey of Sta. Maria da Vitória about 100 miles north of Lisbon. It was founded in 1388 to commemorate the victory of the Portuguese under John I over the Castilians at nearby Aljubarrota (1385), a victory that secured Portugal's independence from Spain. Built over a 150-year period, Batalha in its earliest parts is Gothic in style, the work of one Master Huguet, who was possibly an English architect brought to Portugal by John I's English wife Philippa of Lancaster. Its socalled "Unfinished Chapels" are dazzling 16th-century masterpieces in the MANUELINE STYLE.

**Báthory, Elisabeth** (**Countess Nadasdy**) (1560–1614) *Hungarian murderess and vampire*
Beautiful and rich, Báthory married Count Ferenc Nadasdy at age 15. At her castle of Csejthe in the Carpathian Mountains, she was bored during his absences on military campaigns and began indulging her sexual and sadistic fantasies, dabbling in black magic and alchemy. After her husband's death (1604), and fearful that her famous beauty was fading, the countess sought an elixir of youth by drinking and bathing in the blood of young peasant women, procured by her acolyte Dorotta Szentes. By 1609 seeking higher-born victims, she established an academy for daughters of the nobility. When four of these girls were found murdered in 1610, Emperor Matthias had Szentes burnt at the stake. As an aristocrat Báthory could not be tried, but was condemned to be walled up in her castle, fed on scraps passed through a hatch. She died four years later. All public accounts of her crimes were banned until Michael Wagener's *Beiträge zur philosophischen Anthropologie* (1796).

**Baudart, Willem** (1565–1640) *Dutch scholar and reformed minister*
Baudart was born at Deinze, near Ghent, but his parents fled from religious persecution to England, and he was educated at Sandwich and Canterbury. In 1577 the family returned to Flanders. Baudart studied at Leyden, Franeker in Friesland, Heidelberg, and Bremen, and became proficient in Hebrew and Greek. He returned to his native country in 1593 and filled posts at Kampen and Zutphen. In 1619 he was chosen as one of the translators of the Old Testament for the Dutch Bible commissioned by the Synod of DORT. He retired to Leyden in 1626. Among his works were an index to the Hebrew, Greek, and Latin Bibles (1596) and a history of the Dutch war of liberation. His *Morgenwecker* (1610) was one of the most eloquent tracts written against the truce with Spain negotiated by OLDEN-BARNEVELDT in 1609.

**Bauhin, Gaspard** (1560–1624) *Swiss-born botanist and anatomist*
His father, a doctor, had become a Protestant and been forced by religious persecution to leave his native Amiens. Bauhin's textbooks of anatomy (1588–1605) supplemented VESALIUS's illustrations, but in spite of his nomenclature of muscles, which is still used, his botanical books, *Phytopinax* (1596), *Prodromos theatri botanici* (1620), and *Pinax* (1623) are better known. The last, a concordance of the various names of about 6000 plants, remained an essential tool for at least 150 years. His descriptions classified related plants into genera and species, although his *Theatrum botanicum* remained unpublished, except for a first instalment edited by his son in 1658. His elder brother, Jean Bauhin (1541–1613), was also a physician and a botanist and one of the pupils of Konrad GESNER. *Historia plantarum universalis*, posthumously published (1650–51) by his son-in-law, Jean-Henri Cherler, attempted to reconstruct Gesner's unfinished *Historia plantarum*. The book includes concise descriptions of over 5000 plants, mostly European, with a few from the Far East or America, and reflects Jean Bauhin's visits to BOTANIC GARDENS at Padua and Bologna, as well as his connection with a similar garden at Lyons.

**Bayer, Johann** (1572–1625) *German astronomer*
A Protestant lawyer from Augsburg, Bayer made a lasting contribution to ASTRONOMY in his *Uranometria* (1603), in which he identified stars by assigning letters of the Greek alphabet to them, in order of brightness. Under this system Aldebaran, previously described as the star in the southern eye of Taurus, became $\alpha$ Tauri. He was, however, less successful with his attempts to reform the names of constellations. His posthumously published *Coelum stellatum christianum* (1627) proposed replacing their heathen names with biblical ones, but scholars continued to prefer such traditional names as Cassiopeia and Argo to his suggested Mary Magdalen and Noah's Ark.

**Beaufort, Lady Margaret** (1443–1509) *Countess of Richmond and Derby; English noblewoman, translator, and patron of printers*
Herself descended from Edward III, she was, by her first marriage (to Edmund Tudor), mother of Henry VII of England, to whom she gave birth at age 14. After Henry, with her support, obtained the throne in 1485, Lady Margaret retired to a life of study and charitable work. She established the Lady Margaret professorships of divinity at Oxford and Cambridge universities (1501), supported the foundation of Christ's College, Cambridge (begun 1505), and left an endowment to the newly founded St. John's College. Highly intelligent and an avid reader, she studied

medicine, theology, and literature. She translated various religious texts from French, including *The Mirroure of Golde for the Sinfull Soule* (1522), and book four of Thomas à Kempis's *Imitatio Christi* (1504); she also commissioned other translations from Latin, publishing them at her own expense. In so doing, she promoted the work of the printers William CAXTON, Wynkyn de Worde, and Richard Pynson.

**Beaumont, Francis** (c. 1584–1616) *English dramatist*
Born into an old established Leicestershire family, Francis was the younger brother of the poet Sir John Beaumont (1583–1627), who is remembered chiefly as an early exponent of the heroic couplet in English in such poems as the mock-heroic *Metamorphosis of Tobacco* (1602) and the narrative *Bosworth-Field* (1629). Francis followed John to Oxford (1597) and the Inner Temple (1600). In London he met and became the disciple of Ben JONSON; it may have been through Jonson that Beaumont met John FLETCHER, who became his close friend and with whom he collaborated in the writing of plays from about 1606. Beaumont's best-known independent poem is the Ovidian *Salmacis and Hermaphroditus* (1602).

The first collected edition of the works of Beaumont and Fletcher appeared in 1647 and contained 34 plays and a masque; the 1679 edition raises the number to 52 plays and the masque. Scholars have disentangled the style of each dramatist so that it is possible to say with some confidence which works are truly collaborative efforts, which solely or mainly by Beaumont, and which by Fletcher alone or with a third party. Among the plays generally thought to be by Beaumont is *The Knight of the Burning Pestle*, a burlesque of knight-errantry written about 1609 and published in 1613; *The Maid's Tragedy*, written in 1611 and first printed in 1619, and *Philaster*, written in 1611 and printed in 1620, are two of the most successful products of the collaboration. Beaumont alone is thought to have written (1613) *The Masque of the Inner Temple*.

**Beccadelli, Antonio** (1394–1471) *Italian poet*
Born in Palermo (Latin: Panormus), the town from which he took his nom-de-plume, "Il Panormita," Beccadelli studied law and classical poetry in several northern Italian cities (1420–34). In 1425 he published a Latin poem that brought him immediate notoriety: *Hermaphroditus*, explicitly extolling homosexual love with a scandalous nonchalance. Copies of the poem, together with portraits of Beccadelli, were publicly burned. However, others hailed it as a masterpiece, Cosimo de' Medici accepted the dedication of the poem, and Beccadelli's undoubted scholarship and skill gained him the post of court poet at Pavia, which he held until he returned to Naples. There he founded (1442) the Academia Pontaniana (*see* NEAPOLITAN ACADEMY). He spent the rest of his life as a respected servant of ALFONSO I ("the Magnanimous"), for whom he composed *De dictis et de factis Alphonsi regis* (1455), later to become the chief source of the legend of that monarch's magnanimity.

**Beccafumi, Domenico** (c. 1486–1551) *Italian painter*
Born near Siena, the son of a peasant named di Pace, Domenico took the name of his patron, Lorenzo Beccafumi. His studies took place in Siena and Rome. Returning to Siena in 1512, he worked on the decoration of the facade of the Palazzo Borghese and produced a mosaic for the church of San Bernardino (1517) and 35 biblical scenes for the marble pavement of the cathedral. In 1541 he went to Genoa where he painted a fresco, now lost, for Andrea DORIA, but he then spent the rest of his life in Siena, where he was the most important mannerist painter. His *Birth of the Virgin* (1543; Pinacoteca, Siena) is a characteristic example of his mannerist style, with its elongated and foreshortened forms and its contrasts of light and dark. He also produced some sculpture, such as the bronze angels for the cathedral (c. 1548). His decoration of the ceiling of the Palazzo Bindi Sergardi anticipated the erotic tendencies of 16th-century MANNERISM.

**Beck, Leonhard** (c. 1480–1542) *German painter and woodcut designer*
The son of an Augsburg manuscript illuminator, Beck was apprenticed to HOLBEIN THE ELDER in 1495, became his assistant, and was registered as an independent master in 1503. His early style was close to that of his master, although he was subsequently influenced by Hans BURGKMAIR and Jörg Breu. Beck was involved with Hans Schäufelein, Breu, and Burgkmair on the large cycles of woodcuts known as the *Theuerdank* and *Weisskunig*, commissioned by Emperor Maximilian I. Unaided, he designed the 123 woodcuts of saints in another of Maximilian's commissions, the *Sipp-, Mag-, und Schwägerschaften*. A series of chalk drawings of considerable force, portraying Augsburg artists and dated 1502–15, has also been attributed to Beck. His later portraits are often confused with those of his son-in-law and pupil, Christoph AMBERGER.

**Behmen, Jakob** See BOEHME, JAKOB

**Belgic Confession** (1561) Articles of faith drawn up in French by Guy de Brès, aided by Hadrian à SARAVIA, for the Walloon and Flemish reformed churches. It was based on the GALLICAN CONFESSION of 1559. Dutch, German, and Latin translations were made; between 1566 and 1581 it was accepted by synods at Antwerp, Wesel, Emden, Dort, and Middelburg, and again by the major Synod of DORT in 1619. Less polemical than its predecessor, it was the best statement of Continental Calvinist doctrine; an English version was adopted by the reformed church of America.

**Bellano, Bartolommeo** (c. 1440–96/97) *Italian sculptor*
Born at Padua, the son of a goldsmith, Bellano is first documented in 1456 as an assistant to DONATELLO in Florence. By 1463 he was probably assisting Donatello with the bronze reliefs for the pulpits of San Lorenzo as his style is discernible in the angular chiseling of several panels. In 1467 he was in Perugia, making a statue of Pope Paul II, and VASARI claims that he served the pope in Rome too; nevertheless, by 1468 Bellano had settled again in Padua. He executed a marble revetment for the reliquary chest of St. Anthony of Padua in the sacristy of the basilica (1469–72): the panel of the *Miracle of the Mule* is characteristic of his angular and linear style of marble carving. Between 1484 and 1488 he produced his masterpiece, a cycle of 10 bronze reliefs of Old Testament stories for the interior of the basilica choir enclosure.

**Bellarmine, St. Robert** See ROBERT BELLARMINE, ST

**Belleau, Rémy** (1528–1577) *French scholar and poet*
Belleau, who was born at Nogent-le-Rotrou, gained first the patronage of the Abbé de Choiseul and later that of Charles IX and Henry III. After taking part in the French campaign against Naples (1557), he settled at Joinville as tutor and counsellor to the GUISE FAMILY. There he found inspiration for his popular pastoral in verse and prose, *La Bergerie* (1565–72). Described as a "painter of nature" by RONSARD, his erstwhile associate at the Collège de Coqueret, Belleau was renowned for detailed descriptions that won him the reputation of a poetic miniaturist. He also wrote some didactic verse, a commentary on precious stones and their virtues, and *La Reconnue* (1557), an unfinished comedy in verse, but it was his translation of Anacreon's *Odes* (1556) that won him membership of the PLÉIADE. He died in Paris.

**Bellegambe, Jean** (c. 1470–c. 1535) *Flemish painter*
Probably a native of Douai, then in the Spanish Netherlands, Bellegambe was a follower of Simon Marmion (active 1449–89) and became the foremost history painter in Flanders at that time, combining elements of Flemish and French art in his own work. He may also have been influenced by several other artists of northern Europe, notably Quentin METSYS. Bellegambe's works include a polyptych (c. 1511; Notre Dame, Douai), two altar wings depicting the glorification of the Virgin (1526; Notre Dame, Douai), and an *Adoration of Infant Christ* (1528). Also the designer of buildings, furniture, frames, and embroidery, Bellegambe was idolized in Douai.

**Belli, Valerio** (c. 1486–1546) *Italian gem engraver, medalist, and goldsmith*
Belli was born in Vicenza but spent much of his career in Rome where he worked for Pope Clement VII and his successor Paul III. He produced around 50 medals portraying idealized figures from antiquity. He was a member of artistic and literary circles which included Michelangelo and the humanist Pietro Bembo.

**Bellini, Giovanni** (c. 1430–1516) *Italian painter*
The son of the artist Jacopo BELLINI, Giovanni trained in his father's workshop alongside his brother Gentile Bellini (c. 1429–1507) and was the brother-in-law of MANTEGNA, whose influence is clear on Giovanni's early works. He worked with Gentile on several large narrative cycles and at an early stage showed his skill as a draftsman in a number of small devotional pieces, notably in his versions of the *Pietà*. Many of these early paintings, such as the *Agony in the Garden* (1465; National Gallery, London), use settings of natural landscapes and demonstrate Giovanni's masterly handling of light and color. In 1483 he became state painter to the Venetian republic, a post he retained until his death. In this capacity he executed paintings in the doge's palace (destroyed by fire in 1577) and was commissioned for several major portraits, including the *Doge Leonardo Loredan* (1501; National Gallery, London).

Important altarpieces by Giovanni include that for the church of SS. Giovanni e Paolo in Venice, influenced by ANTONELLO DA MESSINA, from which stemmed the *sacre conversazioni* for San Giobbe (c. 1483–85) and San Zaccaria (1505). His later works include the secular paintings the *Feast of the Gods* (c. 1514; National Gallery, Washington), painted for Alfonso d'Este, and his only known female nude, the *Toilet of Venus* (1515; Kunsthistorisches Museum, Vienna). Other works include many versions of the Virgin and Child, a *Transfiguration* (c. 1480; Frick College, New York), and the *Sacred Allegory* (c. 1500; Uffizi, Florence; see Plate II).

Giovanni established Venice as an artistic center on a level with Florence and Rome and was the teacher of such pupils as GIORGIONE, TITIAN, PALMA VECCHIO, and SEBASTIANO DEL PIOMBO. He also exerted considerable influence over succeeding artistic schools through his development of the use of pure oil color as opposed to the use of tempera.

**Further reading:** Rona Goffen, *Giovanni Bellini* (New Haven, Con.: Yale University Press, 1989); Peter Humfrey (ed.), *The Cambridge Companion to Giovanni Bellini* (Cambridge, U.K.: Cambridge University Press, 2003).

**Bellini, Jacopo** (c. 1400–c. 1471) *Italian painter*
The father of the artists Gentile Bellini (c. 1429–1507) and Giovanni BELLINI and the father-in-law of Andrea MANTEGNA, Jacopo was born in Venice and was a pupil of GENTILE DE FABRIANO. After visiting Florence and being exposed to the works of other leading Italian artists, Jacopo returned to Venice and by 1429 was established as the pre-eminent painter there. Very few paintings certainly by him survive and are all executed in a stiff Venetian Gothic style; those that are signed include *Virgin and Child*

(Accademia, Venice), *Christ on the Cross* (Museo Civico, Verona), and two *Madonnas* (Lovere and Brera, Milan). Jacopo is best known, however, for his two surviving sketchbooks (Louvre, Paris and British Museum, London) containing many experimental drawings and designs that were later adapted by his sons in their own works. He received many commissions for religious works in Venice and Padua and in 1441 he triumphed over PISANELLO in a competition to execute the portrait (now lost) of the ruler of Ferrara, Leonello d'Este. The master of a flourishing workshop, he died in Venice.

## Belon, Pierre (1517–1564) *French zoologist*
Although born into a poor family at Le Mans, Belon was allowed to pursue his education at the university of Paris through the support of his local bishop. He was further enabled to develop his interests in natural history by the patronage of the wealthy Cardinal Tournon and the later backing of FRANCIS I, with whose financial support he traveled through much of Europe and the Near East. He revealed the results of his researches in two works. In the first, *La nature et diversité des poissons* (1551), he described 110 species of marine animals. Like Guillaume RONDELET, Belon used the term fish to cover virtually all

**Pierre Belon** A woodcut of a wading bird made by Pierre Goudet (Gourdelle) for Belon's *L'Histoire de la nature de la oyseaux* (1555).

animals found in the sea; it was even allowed to include the hyena! Belon also published an early ornithological work, *L'Histoire de la nature des oyseaux* (1555). He died at the hands of a highwayman in the Bois de Boulogne.

See also: ZOOLOGY

**Bembine Table** An inscribed bronze table-top made in Rome in the first century AD and excavated in the 1520s from the ruins of the temple of Isis (hence its other name of "Isiac Table"). In 1527 it came into the possession of Cardinal BEMBO. Its hieroglyphs made it an intriguing object to Renaissance scholars (*see* EGYPTIAN STUDIES). An accurate engraving of it was made by Enea Vico (1559) and it was published in 1605 by Lorenzo Pignorio in his *Vetustissimae tabulae aenaea sacris Aegyptiorum simulachris coelatae accurata explicatio* (An accurate account of a most ancient bronze tablet engraved with sacred symbols of the Egyptians).

## Bembo, Pietro (1470–1547) *Italian scholar, poet, and humanist*
Born at Venice, he was educated by Ermolao BARBARO among others. He met the great scholar POLITIAN in 1491 and in the same year traveled to Messina to learn Greek from Constantine Lascaris. In 1493 he returned to Venice and edited Lascaris's Greek grammar for the printer MANUTIUS, who also issued Bembo's editions of Petrarch (1501) and Dante (1502). *Gli Asolani* (1505), dialogues on love dedicated to Lucrezia BORGIA, brought Bembo to Urbino where he is depicted as the advocate of platonic love in Castiglione's COURTIER. In 1513 in Rome Bembo published *De imitatione*, which championed Ciceronianism (*see* CICERO) and led to his appointment as secretary (1513–21) to Pope LEO X, after which he went to Padua. In 1530 he published *Rime*, a collection of his Italian poetry, and was nominated historian and librarian of the Venetian republic. In 1539 he became a cardinal and moved back to Rome, where he died.

Bembo was an important member of the skeptical group which flourished around Leo X, and was patron of the freethinking POMPONAZZI. He was also an important figure in the revival of interest in vernacular poetry, starting a vogue for imitations of Petrarch. He showed a much greater sensitivity to form than did those humanists who concentrated on classical literature; his *Prose della volgar lingua* (1525), the first critical history of Italian literature since Dante, used Petrarch and Boccaccio as models for a vernacular which would be natural as well as artistic.

See also: BEMBINE TABLE

Further reading: Christine Raffini, *Marsilio Ficino, Pietro Bembo, Baldassare Castiglione: Philosophical, Aesthetic, and Political Approaches in Renaissance Platonism* (New York: Peter Lang, 1998).

**Benedetto da Maiano** (1442–1497) *Italian sculptor*
A member of a notable artistic family of Florence, Benedetto trained as a stone carver and developed a style of decorative realism that reflected the influence of his master Antonio ROSSELLINO. His earliest surviving work was the shrine of San Savino (1472; Faenza cathedral), upon which he worked with his brother, the architect GIULIANO DA MAIANO. His best-known work, however, was his series of marble reliefs on the pulpit in Sta. Croce, Florence (1472–75), sketches of which survive in the Victoria and Albert Museum in London; this shows the influence of DESIDERIO DA SETTIGNANO, DONATELLO, Lorenzo GHIBERTI, and antique pieces. At about the same time he also worked on an altar for Sta. Fina in the Collegiata at San Gimignano where he became familiar with the naturalistic style of Ghirlandaio. Benedetto's other works included a number of portrait busts, including one of Pietro Mellini (1474; Bargello, Florence), who commissioned the marble reliefs in Sta. Croce, contributions to churches in Naples, the tomb of Mary of Aragon, a portrait bust of Filippo STROZZI (Louvre, Paris), and the altar of San Bartolo in Sant' Agostino at San Gimignano (1494). His architectural pieces included the Palazzo Strozzi (begun c. 1490) in Florence.

**Benivieni, Girolamo** (1453–1542) *Italian poet and humanist*
A Florentine by birth, he joined the scholarly circle under the patronage of Lorenzo de' Medici. He is mainly remembered for his *Canzone d'amore* ("Ode to love"; c. 1487), a versification of FICINO's translation of Plato's *Symposium*. When PICO DELLA MIRANDOLA produced an extensive commentary on the poem, Benivieni's fame was assured. The poem greatly assisted the spread of NEOPLATONISM and had an enormous influence on many other writers. After becoming a follower of SAVONAROLA, Benivieni wrote some religious poetry, undertook a study of Dante's *Inferno*, and translated one of Savonarola's treatises. He died in Florence and lies buried next to his friend Pico in the church of San Marco.

**Bentivoglio family** A powerful family in 15th-century Bologna. Giovanni I ruled for a short time (1401–02) before the VISCONTI overthrew him. His son, Antongaleazzo, held power briefly in 1420 before Pope Martin V expelled him. Annibale (died 1445) successfully ejected the papal forces, and after his assassination his cousin, Sante, controlled Bologna (1445–63). Sante established a close relationship with the SFORZA and defined the extent of Bologna's independence from the papacy (1447). Giovanni II then governed Bologna, improving buildings and waterways, encouraging the arts and learning, and strengthening the army until he was forced into exile in

Ferrara by Pope JULIUS II (1506). Giovanni's son, Annibale II, was temporarily restored by the French (1511–12).

**Bermejo, Bartolomé** (died 1498) *Spanish painter and designer of stained glass*
He came from Cordova but is documented as being active in Barcelona from 1486. His *Pietà* (1490), commissioned for the cathedral there, is his masterpiece and shows both Flemish and Italian influence.

**Bernardines** See FEUILLANTS

**Bernardino of Siena, St.** (1380–1444) *Italian Franciscan reformer*
Born at Massa di Carrara, between La Spezia and Pisa, Bernardino took charge of a hospital at Siena during an epidemic there. In 1402 he entered the Franciscan Order and became a popular preacher, exhorting his brethren to a stricter observance of their rule and condemning the evils of his time, especially usury and party strife. His devotion to the Holy Name of Jesus gave rise to the sobriquet "Apostle of the Holy Name." Suspected of heresy by the theologians of Bologna university, he was eventually exonerated. In 1439 he was present at the Council of FLORENCE, at which he played an active part. His simplicity led him to accept conventional notions about the guilt of the JEWS and the power of WITCHCRAFT. He died at Aquila degli Abruzzi, on his way to preach at Naples.

Further reading: Franco Mormando, *The Preacher's Demons: Bernardino of Siena and the Social Underworld of Renaissance Italy* (Chicago, Ill.: University of Chicago Press, 1999); Cynthia L. Polecritti, *Preaching Peace in Renaissance Italy: Bernardino of Siena and His Audience* (Washington, D.C.: Catholic University of America Press, 2000).

**bernesco** A type of lyric burlesque named after the Florentine poet Francesco BERNI. It was anti-Petrarchan in spirit and consisted of a caricature of manners marked by grotesque details, outrageous comparisons, and bold paradox. Berni drew on a long tradition of humorous vernacular poetry and also on his immediate literary forebears Domenico di Giovanni (1404–49) and Luigi PULCI. No character, however exalted, was safe from his biting satire. His best-known successor in the mode was Charles de Sygognes (1560–1611).

**Berni, Francesco** (c. 1497–1535) *Italian poet*
Born at Lamporrechio, Berni became a canon in Florence (c. 1530). It is said that his death there was occasioned by his being poisoned by Duke Alessandro de' Medici when he refused that worthy's order to poison a cousin of the duke's. Berni's poems are mainly satirical and jocose, often on occasional topics (*see* BERNESCO). He was also famous for his *Rifacimento* (recasting) of BOIARDO's *Orlando innamorato* into his own Tuscan dialect. The *Rifacimento*,

published posthumously in 1541, contains interpolated stanzas of Berni's own. Although much lauded by contemporaries, Berni's version is now rejected in favor of Boiardo's original.

## Berruguete, Alonso Gonzales (c. 1488–1561) *Spanish sculptor*

Born at Paredes de Nava and may have studied in Naples, the son of Pedro BERRUGUETE, Alonso followed his father's footsteps in visiting Italy (c. 1504–17). In Florence he was highly impressed by MICHELANGELO's sculptural style, as is evident from his alabaster *Resurrection* in Valencia. Although Berruguete was appointed a court artist to CHARLES V in 1518, he did not accompany the emperor when he moved to Germany in 1520, but remained in Valladolid where he enjoyed considerable patronage. His numerous large sculptured altarpieces, such as those for the monastery of La Mejorada (1526) and for San Benito at Valladolid (1527–32), reveal a debt to DONATELLO. Although Berruguete's stylistic vocabulary was distinctly Italianate, the format of the large Spanish altarpiece with numerous subdivisions, bright colors, and ornate decoration was essentially late Gothic. The exaggerated, contorted style of his figures is decidedly anticlassical and reminiscent both of 15th-century wood carving and contemporary Italian MANNERISM. Berruguete had numerous pupils but his style defied imitation.

## Berruguete, Pedro (active 1483–1504) *Spanish painter*

Documents indicate that Berruguete, who was born at Paredes de Nava and may have studied in Naples, was employed at the cathedrals of Toledo and Avila between 1483 and 1500 and that in 1502 he became a court painter to Philip the Handsome, later king of Spain. He specialized in large painted altarpieces of many panels, some of which were painted in collaboration with other artists. He was responsible for the massive altarpiece in Ávila cathedral, its three registers depicting (from the top) the Passion, scenes from the life of Christ, and saints, all set in richly decorated golden frames. His altarpiece for the monastery of San Tomás in Ávila (1499–1503; Prado, Madrid) is considered his masterpiece. Berruguete's attributed works indicate points of contact with the painted decorations of the studies of Federico da Montefeltro in Urbino and Gubbio in Italy (1473–80); he is recorded as being at work in the ducal palace of Urbino in 1477. However, Berruguete's Spanish oeuvre is not of such high quality as these decorations, which should more properly be ascribed to JUSTUS OF GHENT, as whose assistant Berruguete probably worked in Spain. Berruguete's hybrid Italo-Flemish style is an important pointer to the early 16th-century reorientation of Spanish painting, away from Netherlandish and towards Italian models. His son, Alonso Gonzales BERRUGUETE, was an important sculptor.

## Bersuire, Pierre (c. 1290–1362) *French biblical scholar*

He was born at St.-Pierre-du-Chemin, but little else is known about his life. A friend of PETRARCH, whom he met at Avignon, Bersuire was probably a Franciscan monk and was apparently imprisoned for heresy at one time, before becoming prior of St.-Éloi in Paris. He is remembered as the author of a widely influential translation of the Roman historian Livy, made in the 1350s, and also as one of the first scholars to use a classical model to dignify the vernacular. His biblical guide, the *Reductorium repertorium et dictionarium moral utriusque testament* (c. 1340) enjoyed considerable success, being issued 12 times by 1526.

## Bertaut, Jean (1552–1611) *French poet*

He was born near Caen and, as tutor to the children of a noble family, was introduced to court life as a young man. Soon he was writing lyric and elegiac poetry strongly influenced by RONSARD and DESPORTES. He was appointed official court poet under Henry III, and again under Henry IV, and composed many occasional poems admired for their polished, graceful style. Later he turned to religious subjects and paraphrases of the psalms. Bertaut published two collections: *Recueil des œuvres poétiques* (1601) and *Recueil de quelques vers amoureux* (1602). He also held various positions at court and was eventually made bishop of Sées (1606) in Normandy, where he spent his last years.

## Bertoldo di Giovanni (c. 1440–1491) *Italian maker of bronze statuettes and medals*

Of obscure origin, perhaps born in Florence as an illegitimate son of Giovanni di Cosimo de' Medici, Bertoldo worked mainly in the circle of the MEDICI, especially of Lorenzo the Magnificent, and was influenced by the elderly Donatello. His earliest dated piece is a medal of 1469 showing Emperor Frederick III, while his most original one shows the scene in Florence cathedral of the PAZZI CONSPIRACY (1478) when Giuliano de' Medici was assassinated. His most famous work is a bronze panel showing a *Cavalry Battle* (Bargello), based on a fragmentary Roman sarcophagus in Pisa; it once decorated a mantelpiece in the Medici palace. His finest bronze group, cast by ADRIANO FIORENTINO, is *Bellerophon and Pegasus* (Vienna), which is indebted to the *Horse-tamers* of the Quirinal Hill, Rome. Bertoldo's several statuettes of Hercules show his firm grasp of the masculine anatomy in action. He was curator of the Medici sculpture collection.

## Bérulle, Pierre de (1575–1629) *French cardinal and statesman*

He was born at Serilly, near Troyes, and educated by the Jesuits at the university of Paris. Bérulle later emerged as one of the leading lights of the COUNTER-REFORMATION. In 1611 he established the Congregation of the French Oratory, an institution for the study of church history, Hebrew, and biblical criticism. As statesman he helped arrange

Henrietta Maria's marriage (1625) to Charles I of England, concluded the treaty of Monzon (1626), and was instrumental in the reconciliation of Louis XIII with his mother Marie de' Medici. He was created cardinal in 1627 and a councillor of state; the latter post he soon relinquished as a result of Cardinal Richelieu's opposition to his Austrian policy. His writings, including *Grandeurs de Jésus* (1623), were popular among the French Jansenists.

**Bessarion, Cardinal John** (c. 1395–1472) *Greek-born humanist scholar, churchman, philosopher, and collector of manuscripts*

Born at Trebizond, he was educated in Constantinople. In 1423 he heard PLETHON lecture on Plato and was attracted to his ideas. Unlike Plethon however, he was a Platonist who could recognize the value in contemporary Aristotelianism and he endeavored to reconcile the two systems. By substituting the original works of Greek genius for an outworn scholasticism, thus bringing men's minds back to the pristine sources of antiquity, Bessarion was the principal author of the philosophical Renaissance. Created archbishop of Nicaea (1437), he visited Italy with Emperor John VIII Palaeologus to join in discussions intended to bring about unity between the Eastern and Western Churches. His support for the Roman Church at the councils of Ferrara and FLORENCE recommended him to Pope Eugenius IV, who made him a cardinal (1439).

From then on Bessarion lived in Italy, encouraging the spread of Greek studies. He received the archbishopric of Sipunto and the bishoprics of Sabina and Frascati, and his palace in Rome was a meeting-place for philosophers; refugee Greeks were especially welcome and he thus made a major contribution to the diffusion of Hellenism. He translated Aristotle's *Metaphysics* and also wrote Platonic treatises *De natura et arte* and *In calumniatorem Platonis*, the latter being an attack on GEORGE OF TREBIZOND. Despite this, he was not an uncompromising Platonist and his works made Platonism more hospitable to orthodox theology and encouraged theology to be more speculative. Bessarion's collection of 800 manuscripts, nearly 500 of them Greek, was presented (1468) to the Venetian senate and became the nucleus of the Bibliotheca MARCIANA.

See also: PLATONISM, RENAISSANCE

**Bess of Hardwick** See HARDWICK, ELIZABETH

**Beza** (Théodore de Bèze) (1519–1605) *French theologian and scholar*

Born in Vézelay and educated at Orleans and Bourges as a Protestant, he practiced law in Paris (1539), where his life was marked by worldliness and frivolity. In 1548 a serious illness effected a change in his outlook. He became a Calvinist and in November 1549 was appointed professor of Greek at Lausanne. There he helped CALVIN with a number of works, including the *De haereticis a civili mag-*

*istratu puniendis* (1554), which justified the persecution of those who refused to accept Calvin's teaching. In 1558 he moved to Geneva. On Calvin's death (1564) Beza became his successor and wrote his biography. His main contribution to scholarship was his work on the New Testament; his editions influenced the Genevan English versions (1557, 1560) and the Authorized Version (1611). In 1581 he presented D (the Codex Bezae), one of the primary manuscripts for the text of the New Testament, to Cambridge University, but little attention was then paid to it. His play *Abraham sacrifiant* (1550) is claimed to be the first French tragedy; it was translated into English by Arthur Golding in 1575. Beza's inaccuracies as a historian originated many errors made by later writers. His lasting importance lies in the modifications he made to the rigors of Calvin's rule. He broadened the appeal of Protestantism by adopting a more tolerant approach to the details of administration, though he remained firm on the central points of Calvin's doctrine.

**Bibbiena, Bernardo Dovizi, Il** (1470–1520) *Italian churchman, diplomat, and author*

Called after his birthplace of Bibbiena, near Florence, Bibbiena was a protégé of Cardinal Giovanni de' Medici, whom he followed into exile in 1494. Bibbiena worked assiduously on his patron's behalf and when Giovanni became Pope LEO X (1513) he was rewarded by being made a cardinal and Leo's treasurer-general. He also undertook several important diplomatic missions. Bibbiena was a friend of RAPHAEL, who painted his portrait, and his character is favorably depicted in Castiglione's THE COURTIER. Apart from his letters, Bibbiena is mainly remembered as the author of *La calandria*, a *commedia erudita* first performed at Urbino in 1513, which had many revivals and imitators during the Renaissance.

**Bible, editions of** Throughout the Middle Ages the Latin translation of the Bible made by St. Jerome in the fourth century AD (the Vulgate) remained the basis of Bible texts. It was some time before the new approaches to textual criticism made an impact on biblical scholarship. Conservative scholastic exegetes, exemplified by the theological faculty of the Sorbonne, branded as heresy the subjecting of Scripture to the same kinds of critical test as secular literature. Moreover the Hebrew text of the Old Testament could not be studied without the help of Jewish scholars and this too aroused hostility (*see* HEBREW STUDIES).

Hebrew printing began in Italy around 1475, and the first important editions of biblical texts were printed at Soncino, east of Milan (1485–86). The whole of the Hebrew Old Testament was printed in 1488. The next stage was the printing of the COMPLUTENSIAN POLYGLOT at Alcalá (1514–17), though the edition was not published till 1522. In 1516 the first edition of the rabbinical Bible was published. The only other important edition of the Hebrew Bible in this period was the Antwerp Polyglot (1568–73) printed by PLANTIN.

The edition of ERASMUS (1516), with a parallel Latin translation by the editor, was the first published Greek text of the New Testament. Subsequent editions (1519, 1522) made considerable improvements and were used as the bases of LUTHER's and TYNDALE's translations respectively. The first attempt at a really critical text of the New Testament appeared in 1534, but it was not until the Stephanus folio New Testament (1550) (*see* ESTIENNE PRESS) that a text appeared based on the collation of a large number of manuscripts.

Scholars also addressed the problem of a reliable text of the Vulgate. The Stephanus editions from 1528 onwards represented a major advance but were rejected by the Catholic authorities. The text finally accepted by the Church was the Sistine-Clementine version, first published (1590) under Pope SIXTUS V and reissued (1592) with extensive correction under CLEMENT VIII.

**Further reading:** Jerry H. Bentley, *Humanists and Holy Writ: New Testament Scholarship in the Renaissance* (Princeton, N.J.: Princeton University Press, 1983).

**Bible, translations of** Translations of the Scriptures go back to the third century BCE when the Septuagint was produced to satisfy the needs of Greek-speaking Jews in Alexandria. St. Jerome in the fourth century CE produced, in the Vulgate, a Latin translation which catered for the Western Church and became the Bible of the Middle Ages.

The impetus to translate the Bible into vernacular languages was part of the general reform movement that spread through northern Europe in the 15th and 16th centuries, and these translations were often made with a polemical purpose. For English speakers the first important name is that of John WYCLIF, whose translation, based on the Vulgate, first appeared in the 1380s; the fact that nearly 200 manuscripts survive, containing all or a substantial part of the Scriptures, shows the wide diffusion of this work. Wyclif's translation was used to support a challenge to Church authority (*see* LOLLARDS) and Archbishop Thomas Arundel tried to suppress it. A similar series of events led LUTHER to the production of his German Bible (New Testament 1522, Old Testament 1523–32, complete text 1534), which had an immense impact not only upon the religious debate but also upon the GERMAN LANGUAGE. (Although by far the most famous, Luther's was certainly not the first German translation of the Bible; there had been no fewer than 18 earlier versions, with the earliest printed version appearing in 1466.)

Wyclif's work circulated in England in manuscript; even so it reached a wide audience and traveled as far as Bohemia where it influenced the HUSSITE movement. The invention of printing had a profound impact on Bible translation, enabling new versions to gain currency with unprecedented speed. The study of Greek, encouraged by

Florentine humanism, led to the study of the New Testament in the original language and eventually to translations from Greek rather than from Jerome's Latin version. William TYNDALE was the first to produce an English translation from Greek (1525). Religious pressures forced Tyndale out of England and the work was printed at Cologne. It received hostile treatment from the government, Sir Thomas MORE being particularly opposed to it. Tyndale's work was the basis for the translation (1535) by Miles Coverdale (1488–1568), a version that circulated in England with government approval as a consequence of the changed political climate. The edition known as Matthew's Bible (1537) combines the work of Tyndale and Coverdale. Coverdale also edited the large format Great Bible (1539), designed to be read aloud from church lecterns. The Geneva Bible (1560) was the work of Protestant exiles on the Continent during the reign of Mary I, but its extreme Puritan marginalia made it unacceptable to the moderate Elizabethan Church, which countered with the Bishops' Bible (1568). English Protestant translations of the Bible in this period culminated in the Authorized Version of 1611 (also known as the King James Bible), which became the standard English Bible until the Revised Version of 1885.

The Reformation forced the Roman Church to produce its own vernacular translations of the Scriptures. One of the earliest was the German version by Hieronymus EMSER (1527). An English Bible was published at Reims (New Testament 1582) and Douai (Old Testament 1609). The Douai-Reims text, with its strongly Latinate language, followed the Vulgate minutely, even to the point of reproducing nonsense, but nonetheless became the accepted version for the English Catholic community. The Polish Catholic Bible (1599) of the Jesuit scholar Bishop Jakub Wiyek (1541–97) has greatly influenced the Polish vernacular.

Following Luther's example, Protestant scholars all over Europe translated the Scriptures into their native tongues. An early Lutheran New Testament was published in Sweden in 1526; it was associated with Olaus PETRI, who also worked on the complete Gustavus Vasa Bible of 1541. Another Lutheran New Testament was that published in 1529 by the Dane Christiern Pedersen (c. 1480–1554), who later collaborated on the socalled Christian III Bible (1550). In France LEFÈVRE D'ÉTAPLES made a translation of the New Testament from the Vulgate (1523); his French Old Testament appeared five years later. OLIVETAN, whose Bible was published in 1535, made the first French translation of the Old Testament direct from the Hebrew, but his New Testament is merely a revision of Lefèvre's. ENZINAS (Dryander) published *El Nuevo Testamento* in Antwerp in 1543, and a complete Spanish version by the friar turned Protestant, Casiodoro de Reina (died c. 1581), appeared at Basle in 1569. A Bible in Latin was produced by CASTELLIO in the late 1540s to save learned Protestants from the necessity of using the Vulgate.

**Further reading:** Benson Bobrick, *Wide as the Waters: The Story of the English Bible and the Revolution It Inspired* (New York, Simon & Schuster, 2001); Stefan Füssel (ed.), *The Luther Bible of 1534*, facsimile, 2 vols and booklet (Cologne, Germany: Taschen, 2003); Alister E. McGrath, *In the Beginning: The Story of the King James Bible and How it Changed a Nation, a Language, and a Culture* (New York: Doubleday, 2001); Adam Nicolson, *God's Secretaries: The Making of the King James Bible* (New York and London: HarperCollins, 2003).

**Bicci, Neri di** See NERI DI BICCI

**Bidermann, Jakob** (1578–1639) *German Jesuit dramatist*
Born at Ehingen, near Ulm, and educated at Augsburg, Bidermann entered the Society of Jesus in 1594. For eight years he was in charge of dramatic activities in the Jesuit school in Munich, before being sent to Dillingen university and finally to Rome, where he died. Bidermann was probably the greatest exponent of *Jesuitendrama*, plays written in Latin which were predominantly educational and propagandist in intent, but which nevertheless exerted a powerful influence not just in Germany, but throughout Europe. His most famous plays were *Cenodoxus* (1609) and *Belisarius* (1607). Most of his work draws on the Old Testament and legends of the saints.

**Bigi** (Italian, "Greys") The party that intrigued for the restoration of the MEDICI during their period of exile from Florence (1494–1512), following the ousting of Lorenzo the Magnificent's son Piero Medici. The Bigi triumphed in 1512 after the threat of invasion by Spanish troops had effectively wrecked the Florentine republic.

**Bijns, Anna** (1493–1575) *Dutch poet*
As one of the first secular women writers, she is often referred to as "the Sappho of Brabant". Born in Antwerp, she taught in a school, possibly as a lay nun, and eventually founded her own school when she was in her forties. She associated with the Antwerp Minorites and strongly opposed the Reformation, attacking the teachings of Martin Luther in her writings. She published lyric verse in the form of lamentations on the state of the Catholic Church, as well as verse satires in the style of the rhetoricians (*see* CHAMBERS OF RHETORIC), in which she commented on the decline in morality. Three volumes of her verse (*Refereynen*) appeared in 1528, 1548, and 1567, and her work is regarded as an important step in the evolution of the Dutch language (Nederlands) into a literary medium.

**Binchois, Gilles de** (c. 1400–1460) *Franco-Flemish composer*
Binchois was probably born in Binche, near Mons, and from 1419 to 1423 was organist at the church of Ste. Waldetrude, Mons. He was possibly in the service of the duke of Suffolk in the early 1420s but from at least 1431 served PHILIP THE GOOD at the Burgundian court chapel, remaining there until 1453. On retirement he moved to Soignies, where he became provost at the church of St. Vincent. Binchois is generally regarded as a major figure in 15th-century music along with DUFAY (whom he knew) and DUNSTABLE. Binchois's sacred music is simple in style; he wrote 28 Mass sections, six Magnificats, and around 30 smaller works (motets and hymns). He is chiefly remembered for his secular compositions; he wrote around 55 chansons, mostly in the rondeau form, with texts dealing with courtly love. Nearly all are set for one voice and two instruments, with graceful melodies; they are symmetrical and pay great attention to the form of the poetic text.

**biography** The narrative re-creation of another person's life. Secular biography in the modern sense was very much a Renaissance invention. Saints' lives had been very popular reading in the Middle Ages, but nondevotional biography had tended to take the form of extended panegyrics of princely patrons; BECCADELLI's life of ALFONSO I of Naples (1455) falls into this category. Another use to which biographical materials was often put was to demonstrate the futility of human affairs and in works of this kind the subject's motives and personality are strictly subordinated to the moral lesson; BOCCACCIO's *De casibus virorum illustrium* was a leader in the genre, starting a tradition that survived well into the Renaissance with such works as the English verse biographies in the multi-author *Mirror for Magistrates* (1559).

The prime classical inspiration for early biographers was Plutarch, whose *Parallel Lives* of Greek and Roman dignitaries was very widely read. In Italy in the 15th century Aenea Silvio Piccolomini (*see* PIUS II) and Vespasiano da BISTICCI led the way in writing biographical accounts of their important contemporaries, often on the basis of personal knowledge. The culmination of the Italian biographical effort is reached in the following century with VASARI's *Vite dei più eccellenti pittori, scultori, e architetti* (1550; revised and expanded edition 1568).

Before the 17th century, however, biography remained a comparatively underexploited genre in most countries, although biographical material is of course embedded in letters and memoirs (as in the *Memoirs* of Pierre de BRANTÔME). In England Sir Thomas MORE's controversial *History of Richard III* (1543), written, though never finished, in both English and Latin around 1513, is a landmark in the evolution of biography, notable for the strikingly dramatic quality of the scenes and its insights into human motivation. The life of More himself was written (c. 1535) by his son-in-law William Roper (1496–1578) and between 1554 and 1557 George Cavendish (c. 1500–c. 1561) wrote his *Life and Death of Cardinal Wolsey*, both of them accounts of great and complex public figures by men who knew them intimately; neither biography was published until the following century.

See also: AUTOBIOGRAPHY

**Biondo, Flavio** (1392–1463) *Italian historian and archeologist*
Born at Forlì and educated at Cremona, he was caught up in the politics of the time and lived in exile in Imola, Ferrara, and Venice until Pope Eugenius IV employed him in the papal Curia in 1433. Though he had little interest in the speculative side of the Renaissance he was the first historian who showed awareness of the gap separating the classical from the medieval world. He published three volumes which collected the antiquities of Italy as far as they were then known: *Roma instaurata* (1440–63), *Roma triumphans* (1456–60), and *Italia instaurata* (1456–60). The effect of these books was to stimulate topographical research and encourage the development of chorography, the study of local history from surviving remains. They also influenced artists, particularly MANTEGNA. Biondo's last work, left incomplete at his death, was his *Historiarum ab inclinatione Romane imperii decades* in 42 books, dealing with the period 410–1441.

**Biringuccio, Vannoccio** (1480–c. 1539) *Italian metallurgist*
The son of a Sienese official, Biringuccio began his career in the arsenal of Pandolfo Petrucci, ruler of Siena. After a period of exile during which he worked in Parma, Ferrara, and Venice, he returned to Siena in 1530. In 1538, shortly before his death, he entered the service of Pope Paul III in Rome as superintendent of the papal arsenal. Biringuccio's observations on his lifetime's trade were published posthumously in his *Pirotechnia* (1540). Lavishly illustrated, it contained detailed accounts of the mining and extraction of ores, the blast furnace, the manufacture of cannon and gunpowder, and the production of glassware. There were 10 editions of the work before 1678, including translations into English and French, keeping Biringuccio's work in wide use as a practical text well into the 18th century.

**Bisticci, Vespasiano da** (1421–1498) *Florentine bookseller, scholar, and biographer*
He was agent for the three greatest collectors of MANUSCRIPTS of the early Renaissance: Cosimo de' MEDICI, Pope NICHOLAS V, and Federico da MONTEFELTRO, duke of Urbino. Manuscripts from his workshops were exported all over Europe, even to England and Hungary. He was the largest employer of copyists in Europe and his reputation for craftsmanship maintained the market for manuscripts

for some time after the invention of printing. On one occasion he and a team of 45 copyists produced 200 volumes in 22 months for Cosimo's library in the Badia, Fiesole. He took a scholarly interest in the books his workmen produced and guaranteed the accuracy of the texts as well as the beauty of the execution. This interest helped him to make the contacts with scholars and humanists which he used in his *Vite d'uomini illustri del secolo XV* (Lives of famous men of the 15th century; written after 1480), which gives many biographical details not available elsewhere and is notable for its lack of malice.

**Black Death** See PLAGUE

**Blaeu, Willem Jansz.** (1571–1638) *Dutch cartographer and astronomer*
Born at Alkmaar, Blaeu served a two-year apprenticeship in Amsterdam, then developed his geographical and astronomical skills under the guidance of Tycho BRAHE. In 1596 he returned to Amsterdam, and established himself as a maker of both globes and scientific instruments. He also founded a publishing house (1599), specializing in cartography. Blaeu enjoyed universal acclaim for the quality of his work; his instruments and globes featured unprecedented precision, and he developed a new type of press for mapmaking. His most famous works are a world map issued in 1605, *Het Licht der Zeevaerdt* (*The Light of Navigation;* a three-volume sea atlas, 1608–21), and a magnificent series of atlases, beginning in 1638 and ongoing at the time of Blaeu's death. After Blaeu died, his son Jan Blaeu (died 1673) continued his work, the 11-volume *Atlas Major* (1662) being the firm's greatest achievement.

**Blahoslav, Jan** (1523–1571) *Czech humanist scholar and theologian*
Blahoslav was born in P&rbreve;erov, northeast of Brno, and was a leading member of the CZECH BRETHREN, whose bishop he became in 1557. Under his leadership the brethren became a significant force on the Czech cultural scene. Blahoslav translated the New Testament into Czech (1564), and his version was incorporated virtually unaltered into the Kralice Bible (1588). His Czech grammar was influential in establishing Czech as a literary language, and he also contributed to musicology, producing the first theoretical treatise in the vernacular under the title *Musica* (1558) and a hymn book (1561) with well over 700 tunes.

**block-books** See BOOK ILLUSTRATION

**Bloemaert, Abraham** (1564–1651) *Dutch painter*
Bloemaert was born in Gorinchem, the son of the architect Cornelis Bloemaert (c. 1540–95). Abraham trained in Utrecht, visited France (1580–83), and then settled in Utrecht, where he ran a school that attracted many pupils,

including his own four sons. Apart from a brief sojourn in Amsterdam (1591–93), when his father was appointed city architect there, Abraham remained in Utrecht for the rest of his long life. A versatile artist, he painted biblical and mythological subjects in the mannerist mode made current in northern Europe by Frans FLORIS and SPRANGER. Bloemaert later came under the influence of CARAVAGGIO, as mediated by his pupil Gerard Honthorst (1590–1656) who studied in Italy between 1610 and 1620, and later still he adopted a more classical style. He was also a portraitist and a prolific and accomplished draftsman, particularly notable for his landscape drawings.

**Blois** A French city on the River Loire. First mentioned in the sixth century, it was the seat of the powerful counts of Blois in the Middle Ages. The city was acquired by Louis of Orleans late in the 14th century and passed to the French crown when his grandson became LOUIS XII of France (1498). In the 16th century Blois was an important administrative and royal center. Its many Gothic and Renaissance buildings include the château with its famous FRANCIS I facade (1515–24). The château was the scene of the murder (1588) of the duke of GUISE by order of HENRY III.

**Blondeel, Lancelot** (1496–1561) *Flemish painter, architect, designer, and engraver*
He was born at Poperinghe, but became a master painter in the guild at Bruges in 1519. The chimneypiece (1530) for the Greffe du Franc, Bruges, is an example of his architectural work in the early Renaissance style, and Renaissance elements also appear in his triptych of *SS Cosmas and Damian* (1523; St. Jacques, Bruges). In 1550 he and Jan van SCOREL were commissioned to restore the GHENT ALTARPIECE.

**Blood, Tribunal** or **Council of** See TRIBUNAL OF BLOOD.

**Blundeville, Thomas** (1522–1606) *English polymath and autodidact*
Blundeville spent most of his life near the English city of Norwich, with occasional trips to London to present publishers with the fruits of his liberal studies—in historiography, moral philosophy, politics, and logic. He also published books on the training of horses, on astronomy, and celestial navigation. He is perhaps best remembered as the author of *Exercises* for "young gentlemen" on astronomy, navigation, and other topics (1594, with several later editions), and as the earliest translator into English of Federico Grisone's popular Italian text on horsemanship, *Gli ordini di cavalcare* (1550) as *A newe booke containing the arte of ryding, and breakinge great Horses…*(1560; *see* EQUITATION). His career is notable for its confidence in self-directed learning: in *The Art of Logike* (1599), he stated his credo that "Everie man [may] by his own industrie attaine unto right good knowledge & be made thereby the more able to glorify God & to profit his country."

**Boccaccino, Boccaccio** (c. 1466–1525) *Italian painter*
Boccaccino came from Ferrara and was influenced by the Ferrarese master ERCOLE DE' ROBERTI. He also adopted elements of the Venetian style. His best work was the frescoes he executed in the cathedral at Cremona between 1506 and 1519. Other works on religious subjects are preserved in the Accademia and Museo Correr, Venice. Galeazzo CAMPI was among his Cremonese followers, and Boccaccino's son Camillo (1501–46) was among those who worked, like the Campi brothers, on the frescoes in San Sigismondo, Cremona.

**Boccaccio, Giovanni** (1313–1375) *Italian poet and scholar*
He is one of the greatest figures in the history of European literature. The recovery and study of classical texts, which was the driving force behind Renaissance HUMANISM, can justly be claimed to have originated with Boccaccio and his older contemporary PETRARCH. Their determination that the classical ideal should permeate every aspect of life led to what has been called the "humanism of the vernacular": the ennobling not only of their native tongue, but also of everyday experience, under the influence of classical models.

Boccaccio's birthplace is uncertain, but was probably either Certaldo or Florence. He spent his early years in Florence before being sent to Naples (c. 1328) to learn business in the service of the wealthy BARDI FAMILY: his merchant father had apparently little sympathy with his son's literary aspirations. The dozen or so years Boccaccio spent in Naples were decisive for him, since it was there that he gained the support of King ROBERT OF ANJOU, was introduced into the circle of humanists around the king, and began to write. It was also during this period that he fell in love with the mysterious "Fiammetta" (possibly Maria d'Aquino, the king's illegitimate daughter), who, like Dante's Beatrice or Petrarch's Laura, was to be the inspiration for his writing for many years. Among the works he produced at this time are the prose *Il filocolo* (c. 1336) and the verse *Il filostrato* (c. 1338); the latter was to be a major influence on CHAUCER's *Troilus and Criseyde* (c. 1380–85). In 1341 he also finished *Teseida*, an epic in *ottava rima*, the verse meter which was to become the characteristic vehicle for Italian epic or narrative poetry. The following year he completed his *Ameto* (*see* PASTORAL).

In all his early writings Boccaccio is an innovator, but it was the decade following his return to Florence (c. 1340) that saw him at the height of his powers, culminating in the composition of the DECAMERON (1348–53).

During the period of the *Decameron's* composition Boccaccio received a series of appointments as ambassador, and in 1351 he was sent to recall the exiled Petrarch to Florence. His friendship with Petrarch was very significant; under his influence Boccaccio turned more and more towards scholarship, and together they traced the paths along which humanism was to develop. One result of these interests was that Boccaccio worked until the end of his life on a huge encyclopedia of ancient mythologies, the *De genealogiis deorum*. His biographical compilations, *De casibus virorum illustrium* ("On the fates of famous men") and *De claris mulieribus* ("On famous women") were mines of material for later writers. He wrote a biography of Dante (c. 1355) and in 1373 lectured in Florence on the *Divina commedia*. Later that year illness forced him to retire to Certaldo, where he died. When he died, within 18 months of Petrarch, Franco SACCHETTI expressed the feelings of many when he said that all poetry was now extinct.

Individual stories from the *Decameron* circulated throughout Europe in the Middle Ages and there have been numerous modern editions. Henry Parker, Lord Morley (1476–1556) translated into English 46 of the lives in *De claris mulieribus*, probably using the text of the Latin edition published at Louvain in 1487 (manuscript at Chatsworth House, England; printed Early English Text Society, 1970). A new translation by Virginia Brown was published by Harvard University Press in 2003.

**Further reading:** Corradina Caporello Szykman, *The Boccaccian Novella: Creation and Waning of a Genre* (New York: Peter Lang, 1990).

**Boccador, Le** See DOMENICO DA CORTONA

**Boccanegra, Simone** (c. 1301–1363) *Doge of Genoa (1339–44, 1356–63)*
Born into a prominent Genoese family, Boccanegra was first appointed doge in the Guelf–Ghibelline crisis of 1339, the Genoese hoping that he would show leadership qualities similar to those of his great-uncle, Guglielmo (captain of the people, 1257–62). However, he failed to end the conflict, and his greed and heavy tax exactions led to his exile to Pisa (1344). He later participated in Genoa's revolt (1355) against the Visconti of Milan, who had taken control of the city in 1353, and was reappointed doge the next year. He remained in office until his sudden death, traditionally explained as the result of poisoning at a banquet. The composer Verdi made him the hero of an idealized opera (1857).

**Bodin, Jean** (1530–1596) *French lawyer and political philosopher*
Born at Angers, he became professor of Roman law at Toulouse until he entered the service of the French Crown (1567). In 1581 he was involved in negotiations for the projected marriage of Elizabeth I of England and FRANCIS, DUKE OF ALENÇON. His reputation rests on his political writings, in particular, *Six livres de la république* (1576), which he himself translated into Latin (1586). The work expounds his theories of an ideal government based on a powerful hereditary monarchy kept in check by certain political institutions. It established Bodin as the founder of political science in France and was to exert a great influence on later thinkers such as Hobbes, Montesquieu, and Rousseau. His wide-ranging works include *De la démonomanie* (1580), a denunciation of witchcraft, and a comparative study of religions, the *Colloquium Heptaplomeres*, written in 1588 but not published until the 19th century. He died in Laôn of the plague.

**Bodleian Library** The main library of Oxford University and one of the oldest and most important non-lending reference libraries in Great Britain. Founded originally in the 14th century, its first major benefactor was Humfrey, duke of Gloucester (1391–1447), but by the mid-16th century his collection of rare manuscripts had been dispersed. The library was refounded in 1598 by Thomas Bodley (1545–1613), diplomat and scholar. Originally designed as a fortress of Protestant learning, the library soon became a storehouse of valuable books and manuscripts. This was largely owing to Bodley's arrangement (1610) with the Stationers' Company of London, in which they undertook to give the library a copy of every book they printed, but also to a series of important acquisitions since Bodley's time; these included the library of the antiquarian John Selden in 1659, and the Tanner, Rawlinson, Malone, and Douce collections.

**Boehme, Jakob** (Jakob Behmen) (1575–1624) *German mystic*
The son of a farmer at Altseidenberg in Upper Lusatia, Boehme became a shoemaker in 1589. He moved to Görlitz in Silesia where he published his first work *Aurora, oder die Morgenröte im Aufgang* (1612). This mystical work aroused the wrath of the Lutheran pastor, Gregory Richter, who persuaded the municipal council to suppress Boehme's works. Boehme, however, continued writing; several more treatises, some of them published posthumously, were completed before his death at Görlitz. These include the devotional work *Der Weg zu Christo* (1623), *De signatura rerum* (1623) on cosmology (*see* SIGNATURES, THEORY OF), and *Mysterium Magnum* (1623), a mystical interpretation of Genesis. Although obscure (especially in their use of Paracelsian terminology) and open to dualist and pantheistic interpretations, his works had a lasting influence on people as diverse as the Quaker George Fox, the Cambridge Platonists, and the great German Romantics.

**Bohemian Brethren** See CZECH BRETHREN

**Boiardo, Matteo Maria** (1441–1494) *Italian poet and courtier*
Born at Scandiano, of which he became count, member of a prominent Ferrarese family, Boiardo received a classical education in Latin and Greek, law and philosophy. As a courtier he served the dukes of Ferrara—Borso, Ercole, and Sigismondo d'ESTE—and was appointed governor of Modena and later of Reggio.

Boiardo's works reflect the polished manners and the brilliant literary culture of the Este court. Among his earlier works are eclogues written in imitation of Virgil and translations of Herodotus and Apuleius. His reputation as one of the finest lyric poets of the 15th century rests on three *Amorum libri* (1499), comprising 180 poems, Petrarchan in style though not excessively so, which commemorate his love of Antonia Caprara. Boiardo's major work is the epic *Orlando innamorato*, of which he completed two books (1483) and left unfinished a third (1495). Drawing on French romances, which were in vogue at Ferrara, Boiardo combined heroic legends of CHARLEMAGNE and his knights (as in the *Chanson de Roland*) with the romantic and fantastic matter of Britain (*see* ARTHUR, LEGEND OF); he also imposed courtly ideals of love and courtesy on cruder sources of popular origin. These innovations were carried further and refined by ARIOSTO in ORLANDO FURIOSO. Boiardo's text, which had regional features in its language, was Tuscanized by Francesco BERNI in 1541, and the original text was not recovered until the 19th century.

**Boleyn, Anne** (1507–1536) *English queen, second wife of Henry VIII*
She spent her youth in France and received an excellent education during her attendance at the French court, developing talents as a poet and letter-writer. Her elder sister, Mary, became HENRY VIII's mistress in 1522; around 1526 Henry became infatuated with Anne. She refused for several years to enter into sexual relations with him, insisting on marriage. After protracted negotiations to divorce his first wife, CATHERINE OF ARAGON, Henry broke with the Church of Rome and married Anne in secret (1533), by which time she was pregnant. Her child, the future ELIZABETH I, was born in September that year. However Henry rapidly lost interest in Anne after her only son was miscarried, and Jane Seymour supplanted Anne in his affections. To get rid of Anne, Henry used the pretext of her indiscreet behavior at court to accuse her of adultery, as well as incest with her brother. Tried on May 15, 1536, she was beheaded four days later on Tower Green, London.

**Bologna** A north Italian city at the foot of the Apennines. Originally the Etruscan town of Felsina, Bologna prospered on account both of its position on an important trade route to Florence and of its textile industry, especially silk. Claimed by the papacy in 1278, the city suffered from the region's political turmoil and rivalries; it was dominated by a series of lords, notably the BENTIVOGLIO FAMILY during the 15th century. Pope JULIUS II finally established papal authority over Bologna in 1506. The old and famous university of Bologna (founded in the 11th century) attracted scholars from all over Europe during the period of the Renaissance; from the 12th century its faculty of law led legal studies in Europe. The late 16th and early 17th century Bolognese school of artists included the CARRACCI, Guido RENI, Domenichino, and Francesco Albani. Notable palaces and churches from the Renaissance period include San Petronio and SANMICHELI's Palazzo Bevilacqua (1477–82). The university was housed (1562–1800) in the Archiginnasio, remodeled for it by Antonio Morandi.

**Bologna, Concord(at) of** (1516) An agreement between Pope Leo X and Francis I of France, which revoked the Pragmatic Sanction of BOURGES and restored papal authority over the Gallican (French) Church. Nonetheless, Francis maintained a significant degree of control over ecclesiastical affairs in France under those clauses that stated that the king was to appoint archbishops, bishops, abbots, and conventual priors, and, subject to certain rules, the pope was to confirm the nominations. If two successive royal nominations were found to be invalid, the appointment lapsed to the pope.

**Bologna, Giovanni (da)** See GIAMBOLOGNA

**Bologna, Niccolò da** See NICCOLÒ DELL'ARCA

**Bombelli, Raffaele** (c. 1526–1573) *Italian mathematician and engineer*
Little is known of Bombelli's life other than that he was born at Bologna, became an engineer in the service of the bishop of Melfi, and was the author of *L'algebra* (1572). This was the first Italian text to be so called and contained notable advances in the history of equations, and in the development of an adequate algebraic symbolism. The analysis of the cubic equation proposed by Niccolò TARTAGLIA had led to a number of cases involving roots of negative numbers. Unsure of how to deal with such items, Renaissance mathematicians had classified them as irreducible cases and ignored them. Bombelli, however, made the first significant advance in the handling of such problems. In the field of symbolism he took the step of representing unknown quantities and exponents by special symbols. Though other systems came to be preferred, Bombelli had nonetheless shown the need for such expressions.

**Bon, Bartolommeo** See BUON, BARTOLOMMEO

**Bontemps, Pierre** (c. 1507–1568) *French sculptor*
Assistant to PRIMATICCIO at FONTAINEBLEAU, Bontemps is best known for his work on the tomb of Francis I and Claude de France and their children (1547–58) at the church of St. Denis. The monument was designed by Philibert DELORME; Bontemps worked on it alongside François Marchand. Bontemps also worked on a monument for the heart of Francis I in the same church, incorporating a number of features from the outdated Gothic tradition. As a Huguenot, he became a religious fugitive after 1562.

**book illustration** The earliest illustrated books inevitably suffered by comparison with illuminated MANUSCRIPTS. Some copies of early printed books have however been decorated as though they were manuscripts, for example, the Bodleian Library copy of Jenson's 1476 edition of Pliny's *Natural History*, enriched with splendid Florentine illumination. Printing was slow to kill the earlier craft in most of Europe, especially Italy.

Block-books, mostly German, with text and picture cut on the same block, began to be produced about 1430. The oldest surviving single woodcut is a St. Christopher of 1423. Although WOODCUTS and text were formed into books soon afterwards, no extant block-book bears a date before 1470, and by 1480 they were ousted by the spread of printing with movable type. Most block-books were intended for those who preferred stories in pictures, with as few words as possible, so the *Biblia pauperum* and other religious writings provided most of the material.

Ornamental initials, sometimes printed in color, and woodcuts soon appeared, to such an extent that about a third of all INCUNABULA are thus illustrated. Albrecht Pfister of Bamberg added woodcuts to his popular books in the 1460s, though the pictures were printed after the text. The quality of book illustration in Italy was soon the best in Europe, culminating in the HYPNEROTOMACHIA POLIFILI (1499). Engraving on metal was first used in Florence in 1477, though the process was not taken up on a significant scale until the middle of the next century. The use of roman or italic type in Italy led to smaller books with a lighter appearance than black-letter printing, an effect echoed in the illustrations (*see* TYPOGRAPHY).

In Germany the printers of Augsburg specialized in illustrated books, and Günther Zainer's *Golden Legend* (1471) has historiated initials echoing manuscript ones. A little later his brother Johann, working in Ulm, printed an edition of Aesop the illustrations of which were subsequently used in CAXTON's 1484 London edition, the first known example of a sort of borrowing that later became widespread. The *Liber chronicarum* (*Nuremberg Chronicle*), was printed in Nuremberg by Anton Koberger in 1493, with nearly 2000 pictures from only 645 blocks, an economy allowed by using illustrations as decoration rather than an integrated complement to the text.

The first named illustrator was Erhard Reuwich, whose pictures for *Peregrinationes in terram sanctam* (Mainz, 1486) are an essential part of the book. Later, professional illustrators like Hans (II) WEIDITZ, who designed woodcuts for BRUNFELS's herbal, were also given credit in print for their work.

In the 1530s and 1540s Basle became a famous center for illustrated books. Dürer may have worked there in the 1490s, and his influence certainly refined the local style. The HOLBEIN family lived there, though the books they illustrated were often printed in France, like the *Dance of Death* (Lyons, 1538). Leonhart FUCHS's herbal (1542) and VESALIUS's textbook of human anatomy (1548) were two famous Basle productions of this period.

EMBLEM books were another development of the 1530s. Soon afterwards topographical books, illustrated by engravings, began to be published in Italy; the first, *Speculum Romanae magnificentiae* (Rome, 1548–68), has nearly 150 plates of monuments in the city. Some printers became specialists in engraving on metal, like the DE BRY FAMILY in Frankfurt and the Dutch printers of cartographic works like ORTELIUS's *Theatrum orbis terrarum* (1570) and MERCATOR's *Atlas* (1595).

PLANTIN's Antwerp Polyglot Bible (1568–73) features both woodcuts and copper engravings. This printer, who encouraged the use of pictures, organized his illustrators on a grand scale, so that blocks from his store were often borrowed and used elsewhere. By the end of the 16th century, engravings, which allowed greater delicacy, were overtaking woodcuts for book illustration. The products of both methods were still colored by hand, sometimes in the printers' own workshops, if colored copies were required. The quality of the engraving, as in flower books like Crispin de Passe's *Hortus floridus* (Utrecht, 1614) is sometimes so fine that the addition of color is the reverse of improvement.

**Further reading:** Jonathan J. G. Alexander (ed.), *The Painted Page: Italian Renaissance Book Illumination 1450–1550* (Munich, Germany: Prestel, 1994); Lilian Armstrong *Studies of Renaissance Miniaturists in Venice* (London: Pindar Press, 2003).

**Book of Common Prayer** The official service book of the Church of England, containing offices of morning and evening prayer, guides on how to administer the sacraments and other rites, Psalms, and (since 1552) the Ordinal (rules for appointing clergy). The Prayer Book is an essential record of 16th-century Protestantism. During the 1530s, Thomas CRANMER and other English reformers endeavored to amend, simplify, and standardize liturgical instructions for priests and worshipers. The first Prayer Book was eventually printed by EDWARD VI's Parliament of 1549, and a Uniformity Act enforced its exclusive use. Typically for a Tudor Anglican document, the book displeased both Catholic traditionalists and Protestant innovators.

The second edition of 1552 went further towards Protestantism, dropping the word "Mass," for example. But in 1553 the Catholic Mary I abolished the Prayer Book altogether, restoring Latin Masses. It returned in 1559, under Elizabeth I's Protestant regime (*see* ELIZABETHAN SETTLEMENT). This version effectively reproduced the 1552 text, although its Edwardian antipapism was moderated. Although banned during the Puritan-dominated years of 1645–60, subjected to numerous later changes (the last major revision was executed in 1662), and largely replaced by modern-language services in the 1970s, the Book of Common Prayer remains a permanent reflection of Anglican principles and practices. Superb reprints of every major edition are accessible on the Internet.

**Book of Concord** See CONCORD, BOOK OF

**book trade** The distribution of printed books was able to follow patterns established by the commercial production and sale of multiple manuscript copies of texts in demand. Trade fairs, such as those of Frankfurt (originally two a year) and Lyons (four a year) existed before printing, but they were developed as useful centers for printers, publishers, and booksellers to meet. In 1498, for example, Anton Koberger of Nuremberg was already ordering 100 copies of a book from Milan to be delivered to his representative at Frankfurt. For two centuries Frankfurt was the major market-place for book dealers from Holland, Switzerland, France, and Italy, as well as Germany, though the censorship imposed there in 1576 sent Protestant publishers off to establish an alternative center in Leipzig.

Printed catalogues helped to publicize books available at the fairs; individual publishers or printers issued them from the 1560s and joint ones were compiled by the fair organizers from 1590 in Frankfurt and 1594 in Leipzig. Hopeful predictions of publication dates were as common then as now, for in 1653 James Allestrye, an Englishman, complained that "it is a very usual thing for the booksellers of Germany to send the titles of their books to be put in the catalogue before they are printed, so that at present they are not to be had." Even so, the choice was wide, for 22,000 books were listed between 1564 and 1600. The fairs were also appropriate places to buy and sell type or engage illustrators, translators, editors, or even authors.

Latin remained the predominant language of the printed book until at least 1500, so the market for books was effectively an international one from the start, and the size of editions printed in trading centers like Venice grew to reflect the demand for them. As German craftsmen became printers in other countries, they naturally turned to German merchants to sell their products elsewhere. Barrels of books packed in sheets followed trade routes all over Europe, with the reputations of the greatest printing houses, like those of ESTIENNE, FROBEN, or PLANTIN, being just as widespread. The growth of vernacular printing inevitably restricted the distribution of the books concerned, although, in the hands of publishers such as the ELZEVIR family, books in the main European languages were not necessarily printed in their native countries. Even CAXTON's first book in English was actually printed in Bruges.

See also: PRINTING

**Further reading:** Lisa Jardine, *Worldly Goods: A New History of the Renaissance* (New York: W. W. Norton, 1998).

**Bordone, Paris** (1500–1571) *Italian painter*
Bordone came from a noble family at Treviso and was probably a pupil of TITIAN and of GIORGIONE in Venice. Although there is very little originality in his pictures Bordone had a very successful career and was regarded as highly as Titian for the quality of his work and its rich coloring and chiaroscuro. An excellent portraitist, he received commissions from many parts of Europe, including the royal houses of Poland, Austria, and France, and he was knighted by King Francis II of France. He also painted mythological pictures such as his *Daphnis and Chloe* (National Gallery, London) and religious works, which included frescoes and numerous easel paintings, many still in Treviso. His *Fisherman presenting St. Mark's Ring to the Doge* (Accademia, Venice) features a characteristically attractive architectural backdrop.

**Borgia, Cesare** (1475/76–1507) *Italian soldier and nobleman*
The second son of Rodrigo Borgia (Pope ALEXANDER VI) and Vanozza Catanei, Cesare was carefully educated and destined for the Church. His father made him archbishop of Valencia (1492) and cardinal (1493), but Cesare renounced holy orders after his brother's death. As part of a deal made between Alexander VI and LOUIS XII of France, Cesare became duke of Valentinois and married (1499) Charlotte d'Albret, a sister of the king of Navarre. With his father's support Cesare began to conquer a state for himself in central Italy (1499–1503), making rapid advances in a successful military campaign and winning the title of duke of Romagna (1501). The model state he established was admired by many, and Cesare partly inspired MACHIAVELLI's concept of the prince. Alexander's death (1503) ruined Cesare. He was imprisoned by Pope JULIUS II, released, and imprisoned again in Spain. In 1506 he escaped to Navarre and died at the siege of Viana, fighting for his brother-in-law.

**Further reading:** Sarah Bradford, *Cesare Borgia: His Life and Times* (London: Weidenfeld, 1976; new ed. Phoenix, 2001).

**Borgia, Lucrezia** (1480–1519) *Italian noblewoman*
The daughter of Rodrigo Borgia (Pope ALEXANDER VI) and Vanozza Catanei, Lucrezia seems to have been a pawn in her family's intrigues, and accusations against her of poisoning and incest appear unfounded. Her marriage (1493) to Giovanni Sforza, lord of Pesaro, was annulled (1497) after her father quarreled with the Sforza clan. Furthering his plan to strengthen the Neapolitan alliance, Alexander then married her to Alfonso of Aragon (1498), an illegitimate son of ALFONSO II of Naples. When this alliance collapsed Alfonso was murdered (1500), probably at Cesare's command. Lucrezia then married Alfonso d'Este, the duke of Ferrara's heir (1502). This apparently happy marriage produced seven children. Lucrezia devoted herself to charitable works and her children's education; after becoming duchess of Ferrara (1505) she made the court a center for artists, poets, and scholars, among them TITIAN and ARIOSTO.

Further reading: Maria Bellonci, *The Life and Times of Lucrezia Borgia*, transl. B. and B. Wall (London: Phoenix, 2000).

**Borgia family** A Spanish-Italian family of great power and influence during the late 15th and the 16th centuries, which has earned an unsavory reputation for immorality, treachery, nepotism, and greed. Alfonso Borgia (1378–1458), the founder of the family fortunes, became Calixtus III (pope 1455–58). He was known not only for his enthusiasm for a crusade against the Turks but also for his nepotism, which led him to make his nephew, Rodrigo, a cardinal in his mid-twenties. As Pope ALEXANDER VI, Rodrigo schemed to advance the fortunes of his illegitimate children, Cesare and Lucrezia. The family also included a number of cardinals, a viceroy of Sardinia, a viceroy of Portugal, a general in Flanders, and a saint. St. Francis Borgia (1510–72), great-grandson of Alexander VI, was third general of the Jesuits (1565–72) and did much to redeem his family's reputation: he founded the university of Gandia and his generosity led to the foundation of the GREGORIANA at Rome.

Further reading: Michael Mallett, *The Borgias: The Rise and Fall of a Renaissance Dynasty* (London: Bodley Head, 1969; new ed. Academy Chicago, 1987).

**Borromeo, St. Charles** See CHARLES BORROMEO, ST

**Borromeo family** An Italian family of Tuscan origin which from the 12th century held land near Lake Maggiore. In the 15th century the family amassed great wealth from banking in Milan and acquired the title of counts of Arona. Notable members of the family include St. CHARLES BORROMEO, a leading COUNTER-REFORMATION figure, and Cardinal Federico Borromeo (1564–1631), archbishop of Milan from 1595 and founder of the Bibliotheca AMBROSIANA, for which he collected 9000 manuscripts. The family built beautiful gardens on the Borromean islands in Lake Maggiore.

**Bos, Cornelis** (c. 1506–1556) *Netherlands engraver*
Bos was born at 's-Hertogenbosch, but many other details of his biography are uncertain. As a young man he seems to have studied in Rome under RAIMONDI. By 1540 he was in Antwerp, but was forced to leave for religious reasons in 1544. He died in Groningen. Bos was particularly influential in his engravings after Italian or Flemish-influenced Italian paintings of his day, but he was also significant in his own original designs. His brother Balthasar Bos (1518–80) was also a Raimondi-trained engraver.

**Boscán de Almogáver, Juan** (Juan Boscà Almugáver) (c. 1492–1542) *Spanish poet*
Born at Barcelona into an aristocratic Catalan family, but brought up in Castile, Boscán was tutor to the future duke of ALBA and an attendant at the court of Charles V. There he met and became a friend of his younger fellow-poet, GARCILASO DE LA VEGA. In Granada in 1526 Boscán met the Venetian ambassador, Andrea NAVAGIERO, who suggested that Boscán try his hand at writing sonnets and other types of verse practiced by Italian poets. Boscán, who was already acquainted with the hendecasyllabic line of Provençal and Catalan lyric poetry, rapidly mastered the Italian forms and introduced into Spanish the 11-syllable meters that effected a transformation of Spanish poetry. He wrote OTTAVA RIMA in imitation of Ariosto, sonnets, tercets (TERZA RIMA), and blank verse (*verso suelto*). Although the quality of his poetry cannot match that of Garcilaso, who also started to write in the Italian mode, the impact of his metrical innovations was enormous.

Published posthumously by Boscán's widow, *Las obras de Boscán y algunas de Garcilaso de la Vega repartidas en quatro libros* (*The Works…in Four Books*; Barcelona, 1543) is customarily taken as initiating the Golden Age (SIGLO DE ORO) of Spanish literature. At Garcilaso's urging, Boscán also translated Castiglione's THE COURTIER (*El Cortesano*; 1534).

**Bosch, Hieronymus** (c. 1453–1516) *Netherlands painter*
Bosch's grandfather and father were both painters and he probably trained in the family workshop. In 1486/87 he joined the Brotherhood of Our Lady at the church of St. Jan in his native town of 's-Hertogenbosch; to this he apparently belonged for the remainder of his life. He executed works for Philip the Handsome and MARGARET OF AUSTRIA, and after his death his paintings were avidly collected by PHILIP II; thus, the better part of his oeuvre is now in Spain. None of Bosch's paintings is precisely dated and, as his style changed relatively little, the course of his development remains elusive.

Bosch's pictures are primarily important for their subject matter. The *Seven Deadly Sins* (Madrid), originally a pair with a lost *Seven Sacraments*, depicts the Sins in a circular narrative strip with a circular painting of the Man of Sorrows in the center and four roundels of the Four Last Things (Death, Judgment, Heaven, and Hell) around the main composition. The meaning of the picture is elucidated by a text scroll: "Beware, beware, God is watching." Other presumably early works include the Berlin *St. John on Patmos* and the Washington *Death of the Miser;* both reveal a growing taste for the fantastic in the inclusion of tiny demonic figures. Demons appear in force in Bosch's extraordinary triptych *The Haywain* (Madrid). The shutters depict the fall of man, with the fall of Lucifer in the background, and, while in the center panel men and women of every estate crowd around a haywain, drawn by devils towards hell, ignoring an apparition of Christ as the Man of Sorrows. Bosch's iconography probably relates to Isaiah's text, "All flesh is grass," and is evidently a denunciation of pride leading to materialism and sinfulness.

Temptation is the central theme of Bosch's *Temptation of St. Anthony* triptych (Lisbon). In this painting the dilemma of the saint is almost lost in an extensive, stricken landscape, peopled by all manner of demons, some part animal or vegetable, of every conceivable shape and size. In Bosch's most famous work, *The Garden of Earthly Delights* (Madrid), three fantastic landscapes are presented. One shutter depicts the creation of man in a beautiful Eden filled with wonderful animals and flowers, and the other a black hell, lit by burning buildings, in which sinners are tormented by swarming devils, utilizing enormous musical instruments as instruments of torture. The central panel portrays an alien landscape filled to capacity with nude men and women, animals, and colossal fruits. While the subject matter is presumably a denunciation of hedonism, the painting is primarily memorable for its superb decorative patterns, glowing colors, and boundless inventiveness.

Over the centuries innumerable theories, many of them as fantastic as the painter's imagery, have grown up around Bosch's work. His membership of a religious confraternity and his aristocratic patrons and collectors indicate that his own religious ideas and those embodied in his work were considered entirely respectable. The roots of his personal iconography lie so deep in popular belief that it is unlikely ever to be entirely understood. In a sense, his pictures are the ultimate exotic fruit of the taste for concealed religious symbolism that so proccupied 15th-century Netherlands artists.

**Further reading:** Ludwig von Baldass, *Hieronymus Bosch* (London: Thames & Hudson, 1960); Laurinda Dixon, *Bosch, Art and Ideas* (London: Phaidon, 2003); Jos Koldeweij *et al, Hieronymus Bosch: The Complete Paintings and Drawings* (New York: Harry N. Abrams, 2001).

**Bosio, Antonio** (c. 1576–1629) *Maltese-born Italian archaeologist*
The nephew of Giacomo Bosio, he succeeded his uncle as agent for the Knights of Malta in Rome. From 1593 he used his leisure time to explore the underground areas of ancient Rome, particularly the catacombs. These researches formed the basis for *Roma sotteranea*, which his executor published in 1634. The volume, often reprinted, was the first, and until the 19th century the fullest, work on the subject.

**botanic gardens** (**physic gardens**) Collections of growing plants designed originally to teach student physicians to recognize the sources of most of the medicines they used. The earliest were established in Italy in the 16th century, first at Pisa (c. 1543) and Padua (1545) and soon in many other university towns, including Leipzig (1579), Leyden (1587), Montpellier (1592), Oxford (1621), and Paris (as the Jardin du Roi; 1635). Under the direction of Carolus CLUSIUS from 1594, the Leyden Hortus Academicus became the center to which numerous plants new to Europe were sent and from which they were disseminated to other gardens. From plants with known benefits, the scope of physic gardens thus grew to include plants newly introduced to Europe from the Americas and elsewhere, whose possible virtues had still to be discovered; this innovation soon made the gardens attractive to visitors other than students. Herbaria (reference collections of dried plants) were added to the living ones, and CABINETS of natural history curiosities were often situated in botanic gardens too, as in Bologna, where Ulisse ALDROVANDI was professor of natural history and first director of the garden. A few private botanic gardens, like Cardinal Odoardo Farnese's in Rome and the short-lived one at Eichstätt, near Nuremberg, belonging to the Prince Bishop Johann Konrad von Gemmingen, had their contents described in print, as did many of the academic gardens.

**Further reading:** John Prest, *The Garden of Eden: The Botanic Garden and the Re-creation of Paradise* (New Haven, Conn. and London: Yale University Press, 1981).

**botany** Perhaps the most obvious feature of botany during the Renaissance is an increasing concern with the accurate identification of plants, including new ones brought to Europe by explorers of distant lands, and the emergence of schemes of classification to reduce the plant kingdom to an orderly pattern. Aristotelian botany, transmitted through the work of his pupil Theophrastus (first printed in 1483), divided plants into herbs, sub-shrubs, shrubs, and trees and gave some account of plant structure as well as descriptions of individual plants. HERBALS, practical handbooks of medical advice based on remedies from plants and other sources, which had a much wider audience, mainly relied on the work of the first-century Greek physician Dioscorides. The famous Byzantine illustrated manuscript of the latter's *De materia medica*, made about 512, was rediscovered in Constantinople in the mid-16th century and sold to the Holy Roman Emperor. This so-called Codex Vindobonensis is still in Vienna. Other manuscripts of Dioscorides had been copied and then printed, but this one remains a landmark for the quality of its illustrations, obviously made from live plants. Elsewhere naturalism was rarely seen in manuscript herbals until late in the 14th century, when, for example, the artist of the Carrara Herbal (British Library, MS. Egerton 2020) was certainly drawing from life rather than copying his illustrations from increasingly stylized ones in earlier manuscripts. Herbals spread some knowledge of plants among a wide public, for demand placed them among the earliest scientific books to be written and then printed in vernacular languages.

Accurate illustrations were needed as one route to accurate identification, and the great herbals of the 16th century, foremost among them those of BRUNFELS, FUCHS, and MATTIOLI, are distinguished by the quality of their pictures. The texts, in general, still dwell in the shadow of Dioscorides, though descriptions of local plants from northern Europe began to be added to those he had known. Mattioli's book, like some earlier herbals, included instructions on distillation in some editions, a skill considered necessary in the preparation of effective remedies. Even the 16th-century doctrine of SIGNATURES, by which plants were said to help the parts of the body they resembled, necessitated reliable identification of the plants concerned.

Practical instruction in the study of plants was made easier by the establishment of BOTANIC GARDENS to teach medical students about the sources of their remedies. From the 1540s these gardens spread from Italy to most other parts of Europe, often in association with newly established professorships of botany. Herbaria (reference collections of dried plants, both wild and cultivated) began to be made about the same time. The gardens soon became centers for the introduction of new plants as they were discovered, for it was assumed that anything new might have useful properties. Travelers imported new plants from the East and West Indies, Asia, and North and South America, among them cocoa, tobacco, and the potato. Francisco Hernández (c. 1514–87), physician to Philip II of Spain and the earliest traveler in the New World to focus on plants, wrote up the results of his 1571–77 expedition to Mexico for the king in his massive manuscript "Rerum medicarum novae Hispaniae thesaurus" (Treasury of the medical things of New Spain); much of this manuscript was unfortunately lost in a fire in the Escorial in 1671, by which time it had been published only partially and long after the author's death (Mexico, 1615; illustrated edition Rome, 1651). More fortunate was the *Coloquios dos Simples, e Drogas he Cousas Mediçinais da India*, by the Portuguese doctor Garcia da Orta (or Da Horta;

died 1570), who spent the last 36 years of his life in Goa, where his book was published in 1563; the Flemish botanist Carolus CLUSIUS made a Latin abridgment of it (1567, and several times reprinted), and the abridgment was itself retranslated into English (1577), Italian (1582), and French (1619). Betel nut and several kinds of spices (cloves, nutmeg, mace) are among the plants discussed by da Orta. A little later the *Tractado de las drogas y medicinas de las Indias Orientales*, which although written in Spanish was the work of another Portuguese doctor who visited Goa, Cristoval Acosta (died 1580), was published at Burgos in 1578, illustrated with woodcuts drawn from nature.

The greater the number of plants known, the greater the need to classify them by a more sophisticated method than by grouping those with similar uses or effects. The important herbal compiled by Hieronymus Bock (1539) echoed Theophrastus in its suggested divisions of the plant kingdom, adding observations of his own to support the arrangement. Other botanists proposed the form of leaves or other parts of plants as a basis for classification, but CESALPINO's scheme, using the characters of seeds and fruit as criteria for subdividing the larger groups of trees, shrubs, and herbs, was the outstanding one of its period. Gaspard BAUHIN, in his *Pinax* (1623), grouped plants with common properties, and made divisions that roughly resemble genera and species, giving them distinctive names that foreshadow the standard binomial nomenclature developed in the 18th century by Linnaeus. Bauhin's system started with relatively simple plants like grasses and ended with more complex ones like trees, though he seems to have been puzzled by the question of an appropriate niche for the cryptogams. His classification seems a recognizable precursor of those of John Ray and Joseph Tournefort later in the century, and even that of Linnaeus. The Swiss naturalist Konrad GESNER also distinguished genera and species, but most of his botanical work remained unpublished until the 18th century.

As early as 1592, in his *Methodi herbariae*, Adam ZALUZANSKÝ argued for the separation of botany from medicine, although this independence was not achieved until much later. Even so, the progression from early herbals, mixing plant descriptions with folklore and stylized illustrations, to more rigorous ones with accurate drawings from live specimens and accounts of new plants, shows the development of the science. The systematic recording and classification of all known plants established a base for the growth of botanical studies, as more material became available through exploration within Europe and beyond.

**Further reading:** Mauro Ambrosoli, *The Wild and the Sown: Botany and Agriculture in Western Europe, 1350–1850* (Cambridge, U.K. and New York: Cambridge University Press, 1997); Edward Lee Greene, *Landmarks of Botanical History*, 2 vols (Stanford, Calif.: Stanford University Press, 1983).

**Botero, Giovanni** (1544–1617) *Italian political theorist*
Botero was born in Cuneo, Piedmont, and was sent to a Jesuit seminary in Palermo, from which he joined the order. While a Jesuit he pursued his studies in a number of centers, including Paris, but in 1580 he left the order to take service with Cardinal (later St) CHARLES BORROMEO. After the latter's death (1584), Botero was secretary to Cardinal Federico Borromeo, but from 1599 he was tutor and adviser at the Turin court of Carlo Emanuele I, duke of Savoy.

Botero's reputation as a political consultant was made by the publication of two works: *Cause della grandezza... delle città* (1588) and *Della ragion di stato* (1589). The former broke new ground with its analysis of factors determining the growth and prosperity of cities, and the latter argues, against MACHIAVELLI, for Christian ethics as a viable component in political life. *Relazioni universali* (1596) expands his views on population studies, a field in which he often anticipates the English theorist Thomas Malthus.

**Botticelli, Alessandro di Mariano Filipepi** (1444–1510) *Italian painter*
Botticelli was born into the family of a poor Florentine tanner and was apprenticed first to a goldsmith before becoming (1458/59) the pupil of Filippo LIPPI, whose assistant he seems to have remained until 1467. The influence of VERROCCHIO, who also ran an important workshop in Florence at this time, is less definite but is perhaps visible in the earliest dated work by Botticelli, the figure of *Fortitude* from a series representing the Virtues (1470; Uffizi, Florence). The socalled *Madonna of the Rose-bush* (Uffizi) also dates from this early period.

In the 1470s Botticelli attracted the patronage of the Medici; portraits of family members and their adherents (with Botticelli himself on the extreme right) feature prominently in the Uffizi *Adoration of the Magi* (c. 1477). Moving in the circles surrounding Lorenzo de' MEDICI ("the Magnificent"), Botticelli became imbued with their brand of PLATONISM and created for the first time in Renaissance art a series of paintings in which pagan mythological subjects embody profound philosophical and even spiritual truths. There is doubt about the exact dates of these allegories, but at least two—LA PRIMAVERA and *The Birth of Venus* (both Uffizi; see Plate III)—were painted for the Villa di Castello on the outskirts of Florence, which was acquired by Lorenzo the Magnificent in 1477; the man who commissioned them was probably Lorenzo di Pierfrancesco de' Medici, a second cousin and ward of Lorenzo the Magnificent, for whom Botticelli certainly executed in the early 1490s a famous set of drawings illustrating Dante's *Divine Comedy*. *Minerva and the Centaur* (Uffizi) and *Mars and Venus* (National Gallery, London) are the other two mythological paintings in which decorative and allegorical elements perfectly combine to epitomize Platonic theory on the ideal relationship between beauty of form and truth.

Botticelli also continued a steady output of religious subjects, notable among which is the powerful fresco of St. Augustine in his study (1480; Ognissanti, Florence). In 1481–82 he was in Rome, his only significant sojourn away from Florence; while there he was employed on the frescoes of the Sistine Chapel. Another venture at this time was the series of small illustrations to LANDINO's edition of the *Divine Comedy* (1481). In the later 1480s he executed several altarpieces and the tondi known as the *Madonna of the Magnificat* and the *Madonna with a Pomegranate* (both Uffizi). The *Calumny of Apelles* (Uffizi), which tells a story taken from Lucian, is a conscious exercise in the revival of the antique. He also painted frescoes in the Villa Lemmi (1486; Louvre, Paris) and a number of accomplished portraits.

According to VASARI, Botticelli was profoundly influenced by SAVONAROLA; certainly Botticelli's brother Simone, who shared the artist's house from 1493, was one of the friar's most devout disciples. After 1498 there is no further record of any relationship between Botticelli and the Medici, and his latest works are all religious in character. Ecstatic religious feeling informs such works as the Munich *Pietà* and the London *Mystic Nativity* (1500). Later records show him on the committee of artists convened (1503–04) to decide the placing of Michelangelo's colossal *David* and finally note his burial in the garden of Ognissanti, Florence.

**Further reading:** R. W. Lightbown, *Sandro Botticelli, Life and Work* (New York: Abbeville, 1989); Leopold D. and Helen S. Ettlinger, *Botticelli* (London: Thames & Hudson and New York: W. W. Norton, 1977).

**Bourgeois, Louyse** (1563–1636) *French midwife*
Her barber-surgeon husband trained her in obstetric techniques. Dispossessed after the siege of Paris in 1590, the couple lived in poverty, but their fortunes changed in 1601 when Bourgeois, now a member of the Guild of Midwives, was summoned to deliver the first child of Queen Marie de' Medici. Royal patronage brought her status and rich clients, until the duchesse d'Orléans died from puerperal fever, after which Bourgeois came under attack. She defended her methods, in 1609 publishing a treatise on midwifery, in which she criticized the manhandling of women in labor by incompetent practitioners and emphasized the importance of cleanliness. With diagrams and detailed observations based on some 2,000 deliveries, *Observations diverses sur la stérilité, perte de fruict, fécondité, accouchements et maladies des femmes et enfants nouveaux naîz* proved a landmark study. Translated into Dutch, English, French, German, and Latin, it was influential on practitioners throughout Europe. Despite her accomplishments, Bourgeois was forced to abandon her practice in 1630. She also published *Recit véritable de la naissance des*

*enfants en France* (1625) and *Receuil des secrets de Louise Bourgeois* (1635).

## Bourgeois, Loys (c. 1510/15–c. 1560) *French composer and theorist*
Bourgeois, as a singer at the churches of St. Pierre and St. Gervais in Geneva, taught the choristers to lead congregational singing according to the monophonic Calvinistic Psalter. His book of psalm tunes (1551) proved highly unpopular with the Geneva council, who claimed that the new melodies confused congregations. Bourgeois was imprisoned, but was released the next day on the intercession of CALVIN. In August 1552 he took leave to visit Lyons and did not return. By 1560 he had moved to Paris. Bourgeois is chiefly known for his Calvinistic psalm settings, in which he adapted popular chansons and Latin hymns as well as composing new melodies for translations by Clément MAROT and BEZA. He also wrote *Le droict chemin de musique* (1550), the first didactic manual in French dealing with singing and sight reading. In this he introduced the concept of solfège and advocated a simplified system of music theory and practice.

## Bourges, Pragmatic Sanction of (1438)
A decree of Charles VII, in response to a resolution of an assembly of prelates and delegates, named by the king, to regulate the affairs of the Church in France. It was designed to limit papal power in France, especially concerning nomination to bishoprics and other benefices, and to protect the liberties of the Gallican (French) Church. It was terminated by the Concord(at) of BOLOGNA (1516).

## Bouts, Dirk (c. 1415–1475) *Netherlands painter*
Bouts was born in Haarlem, but from 1445/48 until his death was based in Louvain. His key work is the *Last Supper* triptych (1464–67) for the Brotherhood of the Holy Sacrament at the church of St. Peter's, Louvain. Its central panel reveals the early use of one-point perspective. For the municipal authorities of his home town Bouts painted a *Last Judgment* triptych, of which the wings survive in Lille, and a diptych of *The Justice of the Emperor Otto*, now in Brussels, which was unfinished on his death. His London *Portrait of Man* (1462) may be a self-portrait. Bouts's angular and undemonstrative style is derived from Rogier van der WEYDEN but has a peculiar intensity of its own. He had a number of followers, including his sons Dirk (died 1490/91) and Aelbrecht (died 1548).

## Bracciolini, Poggio (1380–1459) *Italian humanist scholar and collector of manuscripts*
Born at Terra Nuova d'Arezzo and educated at Florence under John of Ravenna and Manuel CHRYSOLORAS, he attracted the attention of Coluccio SALUTATI, who found work for him (1403) in the Curia, which he served for 50 years. In his capacity as secretary Poggio attended the Council of CONSTANCE (1414–18); this gave him the opportunity to make four journeys to French and German monasteries in search of manuscripts. He discovered numerous manuscripts of classical authors, including hitherto unknown speeches of CICERO with the commentaries of the first century CE scholar Asconius, and important texts of works by QUINTILIAN, Valerius Flaccus, LUCRETIUS, Silius Italicus, VITRUVIUS (*see also* ARCHITECTURE), and Statius. His Ciceronian discoveries in particular caused a sensation when they reached Italy. In 1418 Poggio accompanied Cardinal Henry Beaufort to England where he remained four years, occupying himself with PATRISTIC STUDIES and looking unsuccessfully for manuscripts. On his return to Rome he continued his textual studies and added archaeology to his interests. In 1453 he retired to Florence as chancellor and composed a history of the city covering the previous century.

Poggio was also famous as a story-teller and his *Liber facetiarum*, anecdotes often of a salacious and scandalous nature, became very popular (*see* FACETIAE). He was a great letter-writer, corresponding with most leading scholars of the day, and his letters are a valuable source of information; they include, for instance, an eyewitness account of the trial and execution of Jerome of Prague (1416). Poggio's last years were clouded by a furious quarrel with Lorenzo VALLA; he actually tried to have Valla murdered. The quarrel arose from Valla's insistence that Latin should be written according to classical models, while Poggio wrote Latin as if it were a living language. The feud marked a turning point in the resurrection of ancient literature: the stylistically naive approach of the first-generation humanists was replaced by a more self-consciously artistic observance of Ciceronian canons, which in turn led to the kind of extravagances later parodied by ERASMUS.

## Brahe, Sophie (1556–1643) *Danish astronomer*
The younger sister of Tycho BRAHE, Sophie was unable, as a woman, to enter university, but studied mathematics, music, astrology, medicine, and alchemy with tutors at home. She learned astronomy at her brother's observatory on Hven, assisting him in the study of eclipses and translating Latin texts on astrology into Danish. After her arranged marriage to a much older man, she took up chemistry, biology, and horticulture, and designed her garden at Eriksholm, in Scania. Following her husband's death she worked again with her brother, tracing the orbit of planets and their position relative to the stars. Her impecunious second husband brought debts upon the family, which she paid off by casting horoscopes and working as a herbalist and healer. Sophie's contribution to astronomy is frequently subsumed within her brother's groundbreaking work.

**Brahe, Tycho** (1546–1601) *Danish astronomer*
The first important observational astronomer of modern times, Brahe was born at Knudstrup, the son of a nobleman, and educated at Leipzig university. After a tour of Europe, in the course of which he lost the tip of his nose in a duel, Brahe returned to Denmark and established his international reputation with his observation in 1572 of the first ever NEW STAR to be recorded in the West. His report, *De nova...stella* (1573), was taken by many as proof of the inadequacy of the traditional Aristotelian COSMOLOGY. With the financial support of the Danish king, Frederick II (1534–88), Brahe began to build at Uraniborg on the island of Hven the finest observatory of his day. Using a nine-foot ARMILLARY SPHERE and a 14-foot mural QUADRANT, Brahe undertook a major survey of the heavens, often working in collaboration with his sister, Sophie (*see*

BRAHE, SOPHIE). Within a decade he had calculated the position of nearly 800 stars with an unparalleled accuracy. Whereas earlier astronomers had worked within a margin of error of 10′, Brahe reduced this to the 4′ recognized to be fairly close to the limits of naked-eye observation.

Although anxious to replace the unsatisfactory Prutenic Tables (*see* ASTRONOMY) with his own observations, Brahe proved to be the victim of his own imperious temperament. A quarrel with Frederick's successor, Christian IV (1577–1648), led to a withdrawal of patronage and forced Brahe to abandon Hven (1596). After several years' travel he settled finally in 1599 at the court of Emperor RUDOLF II in Prague. Appointed imperial mathematician, he set up his new observatory at Benatek outside Prague where, with the assistance of the young KEPLER, he began to prepare his observations for publication. Although

**Tycho Brahe** A portrait of the author in the posthumously published *Astronomiae instauratae progymnasmata* (1610), which was seen through the press by Johannes Kepler. The book contains a detailed description of the nova of 1572.

Brahe died long before the work could be completed, it was finally published in 1627 by Kepler as the Rudolfine Tables.

At a more theoretical level Brahe was led, following his observation of the nova of 1572, and the comet of 1577, to reject the crystalline spheres of classical cosmology. He did not, however, as might have been expected, embrace the heliocentric system of COPERNICUS, but instead proposed in his *De mundi aetherei recentioribus phaenominis* (On recent phenomena of the aetherial world; 1588) his alternative TYCHONIC SYSTEM.

**Further reading:** Kitty Ferguson, *Tycho and Kepler* (New York: Walker, 2002); R. Taton and C. Wilson, *The General History of Astronomy, Vol. 2A: Tycho Brahe to Newton* (Cambridge, U.K. and New York: Cambridge University Press, 1989); Victor Thoren, *The Lord of Uraniborg* (Cambridge, U.K. and New York: Cambridge University Press, 1990).

**Bramante, Donato** (c. 1444–1514) *Italian architect*
Born near Urbino, Bramante began his career as a painter, allegedly a pupil of PIERO DELLA FRANCESCA and MANTEGNA who instilled in him an appreciation of classical antiquity as mirrored in the architecture of the Palazzo Ducale, Urbino. Little is known of him until 1497 when he entered the service of Duke Lodovico Sforza "il Moro" of Milan, who also patronized LEONARDO DA VINCI. Leonardo's fascination with centrally planned forms and his understanding of BRUNELLESCHI's concept of perspective profoundly influenced Bramante, whose design for Sta. Maria presso San Satiro, Milan (1482–86), displays an awareness of Brunelleschi's Pazzi chapel in Florence (1429–69) in its oblong plan with niches carved out of the wall mass; the coffered dome is evidence of an impressive implementation of antique style and techniques. Bramante's concern with harmonious spatial effects led him to create an illusionistic east end for this church—necessary because a street ran across the end of the building. His manipulation of real and illusionistic space also manifested itself in Sta. Maria delle Grazie, Milan, begun in 1493; there the fictive roundels of the dome and fake pedimented windows in its base create an impression of clarity and light. The spatial solutions of the centrally planned east end reflect Leonardo's handling of volume in the LAST SUPPER in the refectory of the same church. The cloisters of Sant' Ambrogio (1497–98) demonstrate Bramante's increasing understanding of the classical language of orders. His use of basket capitals and tree-trunk columns in the Corinthian cloister shows a radical interpretation of VITRUVIUS.

In 1499 Bramante moved to Rome. First-hand contact with Roman antique architecture introduced a new and weighty classicism to his designs. The cloister of Sta. Maria della Pace, begun in 1500, has sturdy piers and attached Ionic columns on the ground floor, deriving from

the Colosseum. This air of majestic gravity reached its apogee in the Tempietto (1502) at San Pietro in Montorio, Rome. The small circular structure, erected as a martyrium to St. Peter, is reminiscent of the temple of Sibyl at Tivoli, with its classical entablature carried on a Tuscan Doric colonnade and rich frieze of metopes and triglyphs. It is the first monument of the High Renaissance and established a prototype for 16th-century church design. Bramante's Palazzo Caprini (1510, now destroyed) did the same for palace design in its symmetrical plan and repetitive use of simple but elegant elements.

Bramante's last years were spent in the service of POPE JULIUS II for whom he remodeled part of the Vatican palace. The Cortile di San Damaso was built as a series of open arcades and the Belvedere was linked to the palace by a classically inspired amphitheater on three levels. His most important project was that of ST. PETER'S, which, taking its cue from the Tempietto, was envisaged as a martyrium on a heroic scale. His plan—a Greek cross with four smaller Greek crosses in the angles—was to have been crowned by a huge cupola reminiscent of the Pantheon. Although only the central crossing was built according to his plan, Bramante's ideas were the starting point for all subsequent designs, and his work in Rome was the foundation of Roman High Renaissance architecture.

**Further reading:** Arnaldo Bruschi, *Bramante* (London: Thames & Hudson and New York: W. W. Norton, 1977).

**Brant, Sebastian** (1457/8–1521) *German humanist and poet*
Famed in his time both as a poet and as a legal authority, Brant is remembered now as a major influence on German literature. Born at Strasbourg, he was introduced to humanism at Basle university, where from 1475 he studied law and then taught it. In Basle he also practiced as a lawyer and selected and edited books for the city's printers. In 1501 he returned to Strasbourg, where he became municipal secretary and co-founded a literary society. Throughout his life he corresponded with other eminent humanists. His wide-ranging interests expressed themselves in poetry (composed initially in Latin but increasingly in German), translations from Latin and medieval German, legal and historical works, and secular pamphlets and broadsheets. It was, however, his satirical poem *Das Narrenschyff* (1494; translated as *The Ship of Fools*) that proved most influential. It describes every imaginable type of fool, such as the complacent priest and deceitful cook, with the didactic aim of bringing the reader to recognize his own folly. An immediate popular success—not least because of its outstanding woodcuts—it went into numerous editions and was quickly translated into Latin, French, English, and Dutch. See illustration overleaf.

**Sebastian Brant** Ships laden with fools wearing jesters' caps and armed with the tools of their trade adorn the opening page of the 1509 Latin translation of *Das Narrenschyff*.

**Brantôme, Pierre de Bourdeille, Abbé et Seigneur de** (c. 1540–1614) *French chronicler, soldier, and courtier*
Brantôme was born at Bourdeille (now Bourdeilles) and spent his early years at the court of MARGUERITE DE NAVARRE. He then studied in Paris and at the university of Poitiers before embarking on a military career. He fought in Italy, Spain, and Portugal, in Africa against the Turks, and supported the GUISE faction in the Wars of RELIGION. Forced to retire through injury, after falling from his horse, he began to write his memoirs: these were published posthumously (1665–66) and include *Les Vies des hommes illustres et des grands capitaines*, an informative account of military life in the 16th century, *Les Vies des dames galantes*, an anecdotal exposé of the scandals of the French court, and *Discours sur les duels*.

**Breda, Compromise of** (1566) A petition by Dutch noblemen and burghers to the Hapsburg regent, MARGARET OF PARMA, against the attempts of PHILIP II of Spain to force

Catholicism on the Netherlands. The scornful rejection of the petitioners as "beggars" and Philip's refusal to modify his religious policy were followed by an uprising (*see* NETHERLANDS, REVOLT OF THE).

**Bregno, Andrea** (**Andrea da Milano**) (1421–1506) *Italian sculptor*
He was born at Osteno, near Lugano, and was active in Rome from 1465, producing monumental decorative sculptures, tombs, and altars in marble. Gian Cristoforo ROMANO was one of the pupils in this thriving workshop. In Rome he is principally noted for his work in Sta. Maria del Popolo, while outside Rome he made the Piccolomini altar in Siena cathedral (1485), which has statues of saints by Michelangelo, and the tabernacle in Sta. Maria della Quercia outside Viterbo (1490).

**Briggs, Henry** (1561–1631) *English mathematician*
Born at Warley Wood, near Halifax, and educated at Cambridge, Briggs served as professor of geometry at Gresham College, London (1596–1619), and as Savilian professor of geometry at Oxford from 1620 until his death. In 1615 he visited John NAPIER, the inventor of logarithms, and they agreed to develop a system of decimal logarithms in which log. 1 = 0, and log. 10 = 1. Napier, however, was too old to undertake the prolonged labours involved in constructing the necessary tables, so the task fell to Briggs. In 1617 he published his *Logarithmorum chilias prima* in which the logarithms of the numbers 1 to 1000 were listed to 14 decimal places. The tables were extended in his *Arithmetica logarithmica* (1624) to include the numbers up to 20,000 and from 90,000 to 100,000. The gap between 20,000 and 90,000 was filled by Adrien Vlacq (1600–66) in 1628. Briggs was also keen to see science applied in other areas. Consequently he worked with, among others, William GILBERT on magnetism, merchants on the application of mathematics to navigation, and surveyors wishing to master the use of logarithms.

**Briosco, Il** See RICCIO, ANDREA DI AMBROGIO BRIOSCO

**Briot, François** (c. 1550–1616) *French metalworker*
Briot was born in Damblain, but was active from 1579 in Montbeliard, in the county of Württemberg. He was celebrated as a master of pewter relief work, especially for his masterpiece, the Temperantia Dish (1585–90; Louvre, Paris), with its central allegorical figure of Temperance. Other works included the Mars Dish and, probably, the Suzannah Dish both of which were later imitated by Gaspar ENDERLEIN and other notable metalworkers at Nuremberg.

**Brito, Bernardo de** (1568–1617) *Portuguese Cistercian monk and historian, born at Almeida*

His *magnum opus* on Portuguese history, *Monarchia Lusitania* (two parts, 1597, 1609) begins with the creation of Adam and includes more fabulous material than sober historical data. Despite its shortcomings it was continued by four other hands. His *Primeira parte da Chronica de Cister* appeared in 1602.

**Broeck(e), Willem van den** See PALUDANUS, GUILIELMUS

**Bronzino, Il** (**Agnolo Allori di Cosimo di Mariano**) (1503–1572) *Italian painter*

Born at Monticelli, near Florence, he was the pupil and adopted son of PONTORMO, whom he assisted in a number of works that included the decorations, now destroyed, in the chapel of San Lorenzo, Florence. Bronzino's first paintings are in the early mannerist style of Pontormo but they quickly developed away from the sensitivity of Pontormo towards the cold, courtly, artificial, and technically superb style of portraiture for which Bronzino is best known. As court painter to COSIMO I DE' MEDICI, he undertook portraits of the Medici and of eminent figures from the past like BOCCACCIO, DANTE, and PETRARCH. The sitters appeared stiff, elegant, and reserved, set apart from the rest of humanity. Fine rich colors were used and, unlike most portraits of the day, dark forms were set against a light background. The development of European court portraiture was strongly influenced by these works. Bronzino also produced rather feelingless religious paintings, whose grandeur of design reflects his study of Michelangelo, and equally cold allegorical works such as *Venus, Cupid, Folly, and Time* (1546; National Gallery, London). Mannerist figure elongation is evident in both these categories (*see* MANNERISM). He also wrote poetry.

**Further reading:** Charles McCorquodale, *Bronzino* (London: Jupiter Books, 1981).

**Brownism** A separatist movement within the Church of England, out of which the Independent or Congregationalist churches developed. Robert Browne (c. 1550–1633) maintained that local gathered churches should reform their doctrines and practices without waiting for authority from the civil power. He established congregations at Norwich and elsewhere but on suffering harassment from the Church authorities, he and some of his disciples moved (1581) to Middelburg in the Netherlands. Browne soon returned and submitted to the Anglican authorities in the late 1580s; he was ordained in 1591 and from then until his death held the living of Achurch, Northamptonshire. In 1593 some of his principal followers were hanged. Later many emigrated to America; others became the predominant element in Oliver Cromwell's army.

**Brueghel, Jan** ("Velvet" Brueghel or Breughel) (1568–1625) *Netherlands painter*

Born in Brussels, Jan lost his famous father, Pieter, when he was only one year old. He received his initial training from his grandmother, Maria Bessemers, a miniaturist. Between 1590 and 1595 he was in Naples, Rome, and Milan under the patronage of Cardinal Federico Borromeo. In 1596 he returned to Antwerp where, a year later, he entered the artists' guild, of which he became dean (1602). In 1604 he visited Prague and in 1606 Nuremberg. Appointed court artist to Archduke Albert of Austria at Brussels in 1609, he also worked for Emperor RUDOLF II and King Sigismund of Poland. His collaborators included RUBENS, Frans Francken II, Hans Rottenhammer, and Joos de Momper; the Flemish flower painter Daniel Seghers was his pupil. Breughel was famous for his brightly colored historical subjects, filled with tiny figures, and for his landscapes and flower paintings.

**Brueghel, Pieter** (**Pieter Bruegel** or **Breughel**) (c. 1525–1569) *Netherlands painter and print designer*

Brueghel was possibly born near Breda and apparently trained in Brussels under Pieter COECKE VAN AELST, whose daughter he married. After Coecke's death, he visited Rome (1552–53), where he became acquainted with the miniaturist Giulio CLOVIO. From Rome he returned to Antwerp, where he remained until 1563; he then moved to Brussels, where he subsequently died.

As a young artist, Brueghel was principally a designer of prints for the engraver and publisher Hieronymus Cock in Antwerp. Such famous works as the *Big Fish Eat Little Fish*, published in 1557, and the cycles of the *Seven Deadly Sins* and the *Seven Virtues* reveal a perceptive study of the paintings of Hieronymus BOSCH, whose work remained internationally famous decades after his death. The moralizing subject matter of Brueghel's early designs for engravings conditioned the outlook of much of his subsequent painting. For example, the *Fall of Icarus* (c. 1555; Brussels) is essentially a condemnation of pride. In the Berlin *Netherlandish Proverbs* (1559), sometimes misunderstood as a compendium of folk customs, mankind's foolishness is expressed through illustrations of popular sayings. The *Combat Between Carnival and Lent* (also 1559; Vienna) is an ironic condemnation of the hypocrisy of both Protestants and Catholics, which inclines only slightly towards the latter, the artist's own coreligionists. An extremely important illustration of intellectual attitudes towards the religious strife in the Netherlands on the eve of the Dutch revolt, this painting reflects Brueghel's connections with the liberal humanistic circle of the geographer Abraham ORTELIUS. References to the uneasy political situation in the Netherlands have also been divined in his *Road to Calvary* (1564; Vienna) and his *John the Baptist Preaching in the Wilderness* (1566; Budapest). There is a resurgence of Bosch's influence in

**Pieter Brueghel** *The Beekeepers,* one of Brueghel's many scenes of rural peasant life, engraved in the 1560s. *Photo AKG London*

Brueghel's paintings of 1562: the Brussels *Fall of the Rebel Angels,* the Antwerp *Dulle Griet,* and the Madrid *Triumph of Death.* However, naturalism reigns supreme in the five paintings of the *Months,* dated 1565 and currently divided between Vienna, Prague, and New York. Although the subject matter of these works derives from 15th-century manuscript illuminations, they are fundamentally innovatory as depictions not only of seasons but also of specific effects of weather.

For most of his career Brueghel was primarily concerned with the depiction of landscapes peopled with multitudes of tiny figures. Larger figures predominate in his *Peasant Dance* and *Peasant Wedding* (1566–67; Vienna). This development culminates in the Vienna *Parable of the Bird's Nest,* executed the year before his death. Brueghel was certainly the most accomplished landscape painter of the 16th century. On account of his penchant for peasant scenes, he is often considered as the originator of the genre scene popularized by 17th-century Dutch artists. However, the thrust of Brueghel's own peasant paintings was directed principally at questions of morality and the human condition. Historically, he may be considered as the artist who concluded the great chapter of northern painting initiated more than a century earlier by Jan van EYCK.

**Further reading:** Nadine M. Orenstein (ed.), *Pieter Bruegel the Elder: Prints and Drawings* (New Haven, Conn.: Yale University Press, 2001); Philippe Roberts-Jones, *Pieter Bruegel* (New York: Harry N. Abrams, 2002).

**Bruges** (Flemish **Brugge**) A city in the province of West Flanders, Belgium, situated a few miles from the coast, to which it is now linked by canals. The Flemish name, Brugge (bridge), is of Norse origin. The town was a trading center by 1000, the capital of Flanders, and chief residence of its counts. Although the capital moved to Ghent in the late 12th century, Bruges continued as a major mercantile center, especially for the wool trade with England,

under the auspices of the HANSEATIC LEAGUE; during the 14th century its bourse governed the rates of exchange in northern Europe. Like the burghers of the other rich Flemish cities, the merchants of Bruges stubbornly resisted any attempts by princes to encroach upon their privileges. In 1440 Bruges's defiance of its Burgundian overlord, PHILIP THE GOOD, brought upon it severe punishment, but generally it continued to thrive under Burgundian rule and under the early Hapsburgs, and some fine buildings remain from this period. The silting up of the Zwyn, total by 1490, however, ended Bruges's position as a maritime trading center and in the late 16th century it suffered depopulation and depression as a result of the Netherlanders' uprising against their Spanish Catholic rulers (*see* NETHERLANDS, REVOLT OF THE).

Bruges was a significant cultural center during its 14th- and 15th-century heyday. Jan van EYCK and Petrus CHRISTUS worked there, and later Hans MEMLING. It was home to perhaps the most famous of the CHAMBERS OF RHETORIC, De Drie Santinnen, one of whose stars was the poet and comic playwright Cornelis Everaert (c. 1480–1556). The city's first printing press was set up in 1474/75 by CAXTON.

**Brunelleschi, Filippo** (1377–1446) *Italian architect*
He trained first as a goldsmith, but at some time (c. 1401) appears to have gone to Rome where his studies of antique monuments led him to formulate the law of perspective (developed by ALBERTI in his treatise *Della pittura*) and provided him with structural solutions to technical building problems. His execution of the dome (1420) for the cathedral of his native Florence was an achievement of constructional engineering which looked to the Pantheon for inspiration and inaugurated the Renaissance in Italy. The lantern (1445–67) exemplifies Brunelleschi's experimental approach to the antique with the employment of inverted classical consoles, in place of flying buttresses.

The Ospedale degli Innocenti in Florence (1421–44) was hailed as the first Renaissance building, despite being influenced by Tuscan Romanesque form. The implementation of a strict modular system, based on the square and circle, to provide a regularized plan had a profound impact on town palace architecture. *All' antiqua* quotations are evident in the symmetrically aligned facade with arches carried on Corinthian columns, forming a loggia of pendentive vaults, which established a new canon of architectural beauty. Brunelleschi's preoccupation with the classically inspired values of harmony and geometric proportion is demonstrated in the basilica of San Lorenzo, begun in 1419. Using the square of the crossing as his module, Brunelleschi established a visual rapport between the semicircular arches of the nave arcade and the transverse arches of the side aisles. The combination of pietra serena and white plaster became Brunelleschi's decorative leitmotif, used to great effect in the old sacristy of the same church (1421–28). Once again, the design centered upon the interplay of a square, that of the main cella, and a circle, the umbrella dome. The transition of one shape into another was effected by the pendentives of the dome. A more sophisticated version of this design was realized in the Pazzi chapel (1429–69: Sta. Croce, Florence), where a combination of grey Corinthian pilasters and arches incised onto the white plaster walls, with glazed terracotta reliefs in the spandrels, subtly emphasized the harmonious proportions of the interior. Although the Spanish chapel (Sta. Maria Novella, Florence), a Tuscan Romanesque design, exerted a certain influence on the Pazzi chapel, Brunelleschi's stress on logical spatial organization is a typically Renaissance feature.

Brunelleschi's later designs are characterized by a more sculptural approach to the treatment of wall mass, suggesting a renewed study of antiquity. The incomplete Florentine church of Sta. Maria degli Angeli (1434–37), with its alternating concave and convex niches scooped from the outer walls, is the first centrally planned church of the Renaissance, reflecting the temple of Minerva Medica, Rome. The radiating chapels of Sta. Maria degli Angeli were adapted to the basilica of San Spirito (1434–82; Florence), the foundations of which were laid on a chequerboard grid. The flat pilasters of San Lorenzo were replaced by half-columns giving a richly plastic spatial rhythm. All of Brunelleschi's important works are in Florence, yet his fame spread to Milan and Urbino, influencing BRAMANTE and underlying the emergence of the High Renaissance in Rome. His claim to be considered the first Renaissance architect was acknowledged and established by his pupil and biographer, Antonio Manetti (1423–97).

**Further reading:** Eugenio Battisti, *Brunelleschi: The Complete Work* (London: Thames & Hudson, 1981); Ross King: *Brunelleschi's Dome: The Story of the Great Church in Florence* (New York: Walker, 2000); Heinrich Klotz, *Filippo Brunelleschi: The Early Works and the Medieval Tradition* (London: Academy Editions and Milan, Italy: Rizzoli, 1990); Howard Saalman, *Filippo Brunelleschi: The Buildings* (London: Zwemmer, 1993).

**Brunfels, Otto** (1489–1534) *German physician and botanist*
His *Herbarum vivae eicones* (1530–36), the first of the great printed HERBALS, was illustrated with plants drawn from nature by Hans (II) WEIDITZ, using live models rather than earlier drawings. In spite of his artist's originality, Brunfels' text still concentrated on the plants known to the first-century authority Greek Dioscorides, instead of those of northern Europe.

**Bruni, Leonardo** (Leonardo Aretino) (c. 1370–1444) *Italian humanist scholar and translator*
His other name, "Aretino," derives from his native Arezzo. Bruni was a pupil of Coluccio SALUTATI and learned Greek from Manuel CHRYSOLORAS in Florence. His thorough knowledge of the language enabled him to make the first idiomatic translations of Greek literature. He spent most of his mature years as a papal secretary but in 1415 returned to Florence, where, like his master Salutati, he became secretary to the republic (1427–44).

Most of Bruni's translations were of prose works, although he also translated some passages of Homer and Aristophanes. In 1406 he produced a translation of Demosthenes' *De corona* and *De falsa legatione*. By 1414 he had begun to translate Aristotle's *Ethics*. Between 1414 and 1437 he translated six of Plato's dialogues, including the *Phaedo* and *Apology*, and he sought to reconcile Platonism with Christian doctrine. These translations were the means by which the political thought of Greece entered into the life of 15th-century Italy. Bruni also translated PLUTARCH's *Lives*—his Latin was the basis of all early vernacular translations—and works by the Greek historian Xenophon. In 1437, at the request of Humfrey, Duke of Gloucester, he translated Aristotle's *Politics*. He wrote *De interpretatione recta* to defend his theory of translation and also discoursed on Ciceronian prose rhythm.

As early as 1404 Bruni had begun work on his history of Florence, the 12-book *Historiarum Florentini populi libri*; this remained unfinished at his death. The work represented a new departure in HISTORIOGRAPHY, showing the influence of PETRARCH and Salutati as well as classical models. It was translated into Tuscan and published by Donato ACCIAIUOLI at Venice (1476). The estimate Bruni made of his own Latin scholarship can be gauged by the fact that he "restored" the lost second decade of the Roman historian Livy in his work *De bello punico primo*. Bruni was buried in Sta. Croce, Florence, at public expense. With his friends Salutati and NICCOLI, he was one of the first to use "Humanitas" as a term for literary studies.

**Bruno, Giordano** (1548–1600) *Italian philosopher*
The son of a soldier, Bruno was born at Nola, near Naples, and joined the Dominican Order in 1563. For unknown reasons he was forced in 1576 to flee both Naples and his order. By this time he had already established his reputation as a teacher of the then fashionable discipline of mnemonics (*see* MEMORY, ART OF) and was probably already committed to the hermetic neoplatonic views that he later expounded throughout his extensive European travels. After visiting Italy and Switzerland, he appeared at the court of HENRY III in Paris in 1581, and in 1585 he discussed his system with the scholars of Oxford. In 1591 he was arrested in Venice, extradited to Rome, and later tried and burnt at the stake as a heretic. Unfortunately, the precise nature of Bruno's offense remains a matter of speculation as the trial papers were not preserved. It is known, however, from his *Cena de le ceneri* (The Ash Wednesday supper; 1584) that he supported the COPERNICAN SYSTEM. More likely to have sent him to the stake were the claims, expressed in his *De l'infinito universo e mondi* (1584), that "there are innumerable suns, and an infinite number of earths revolve around these suns, just as the seven we can see revolve around the sun close to us."

**Further reading:** Frances Yates, *Giordano Bruno and the Hermetic Tradition* (London: Routledge & Kegan Paul, 1964; new ed. 2002).

**Brussels** A city in the Netherlands (now Belgium). By the late Middle Ages Brussels had developed from an island fort into a thriving market community at a road–river junction in the duchy of Brabant. Thousands of workers employed in the manufacture of luxury fabrics made a few merchant families very rich. These families abused their considerable political power and provoked a number of workers' revolts (1280, 1303, 1421); after the 1421 revolt the guilds of workers and craftsmen gained some political influence. The count of Flanders occupied Brussels briefly; his expulsion from the city (1357) was followed by the construction of strong city walls.

Under Burgundian rule Brussels prospered as a center of art, learning, and administration. Its most distinguished artist at this time was Rogier van der WEYDEN. Under Hapsburg rule (from 1477) the guilds were excluded from the administration of the city by CHARLES V (1528), but Brussels remained the administrative center of the Netherlands. In 1577 radical supporters of the Calvinist cause seized power in Brussels, but the Spanish Hapsburgs regained control in 1585. Notable buildings from the Renaissance period include the Coudenberg palace, the Hôtel de Ville (1402–54), and fine early 17th-century baroque buildings. Otto van VEEN and RUBENS were attached to the court of the Hapsburg Archdukes in Brussels in the early 17th century.

**Bry family** See DE BRY FAMILY

**Bucer, Martin** (Martin Butzer, 1491–1551) *German reformer and theologian*
Born at Schlettstadt (now Sélestat in France), Bucer became a Dominican monk, but was won to the side of Reformation by Martin LUTHER at the Heidelberg Disputation (1518), and embarked on a career as a Lutheran preacher. In 1523 he settled in Strasbourg where he remained for 25 years, emerging in this period as a leading figure among the reformers. He attempted to mediate in the Eucharistic controversy between Luther and ZWINGLI and later took a leading role in the conferences with leading Catholic theologians at Worms and Regensburg (1540–41) aimed at reuniting the Church. His organizational work at Strasbourg also had a profound influence, particularly on John CALVIN, who spent three formative years there.

Forced to leave Strasbourg in 1549 by the imposition of the AUGSBURG Interim, Bucer settled in England, where CRANMER secured for him the post of regius professor of divinity at Cambridge. Although he died less than two years later, he exercised a major influence on the English Reformation, submitting at Cranmer's request detailed suggestions for the revision of the 1549 Prayer Book (known as the *Censura* of 1550; *see* BOOK OF COMMON PRAYER). His last work, *De regno Christi*, a blueprint for a godly commonwealth dedicated to King Edward VI, was published posthumously (c. 1557). It is available in English translation, together with Philipp Melanchthon's *Loci communes*, in *Melanchthon and Bucer* (London: SCM Press, 1969). Brill of Leyden began to issue an edition of Bucer's correspondence (in Latin with French or German commentary), edited by Jean Rott *et al*, in 1979. His *Censura* was republished in Latin with English text by the Alcuin Club in 1974.

**Further reading:** Constantin Hopf, *Martin Bucer and the English Reformation* (Oxford, U.K.: Blackwell, 1946); Christian Krieger and Marc Lienhard (eds), *Martin Bucer and Sixteenth-Century Europe* (Leyden, Netherlands: Brill, 1993).

**Buchanan, George** (1506–1582) *Scottish humanist scholar*
Buchanan was born at Killearn and attended St. Andrews university (1524). In 1526 he moved to Paris, where he subsequently taught. Back in Scotland (1536) he became tutor to an illegitimate son of James V, but the furore caused by his verse satires against the friars forced him to flee back to France. There he established his reputation for scholarship and wrote some highly admired Latin poetry and four tragedies on classical models, including *Baptistes* (1554); MONTAIGNE was among his pupils who acted in these plays. Invited to Coimbra (1547), he fell foul of the Inquisition and was imprisoned (1549–51). He held several more teaching posts in Europe before returning to Scotland (c. 1560) where, although now openly a Protestant, he was tutor to MARY, Queen of Scots, and active in

state affairs. After her downfall, in which Buchanan played a role by identifying her handwriting in the casket letters, incriminating her in Darnley's murder, he was tutor (1570–78) to young James VI, later JAMES I of England. Buchanan's major prose works were *De jure regni* (1579), which influenced 17th-century writers on the theory of kingship, and a Scottish history, *Rerum Scoticarum historia* (1582).

***bucintoro*** The state barge of the doge of Venice. The name derives from Italian *buzino d'oro* (golden barque). It headed the procession of boats in the Ascension Day ceremony of the *sposalizio del mar* (marriage of the sea), in which the doge sailed to the Porto del Lido and threw a consecrated ring into the Adriatic. The custom commemorated Venice's conquest of Dalmatia in 1000 CE. Remains of the last *bucintoro*, destroyed by the French in 1798 for the sake of its gold ornamentation, survive in the Museo Correr, Venice.

**Budé, Guillaume** (Budaeus) (1468–1540) *French scholar and humanist*
He was born in Paris and studied law at Orleans, before learning Greek with John Lascaris and Jerome of Sparta. He was employed as secretary and ambassador by LOUIS XII and as court librarian by FRANCIS I, and helped the latter develop his idea of a university (the Collège Royal, later the Collège de France) to provide an alternative to the scholasticism of the Sorbonne. By his influence on Francis I he shaped the curriculum of the new institution to include the new learning that he had met on his diplomatic missions to Rome in 1503 and 1515, although he rejected the secular emphasis of the Italian scholars. Budé wrote on Roman law (*Annotationes ad Pandectas*, 1508), Roman coinage (*De asse eiusque partibus*, 1514), and the Greek language (*Commentarii linguae Graecae*, 1529). In 1532 he published *De philologia*, a general account of classical scholarship. J. C. SCALIGER called him the greatest Grecian in Europe. Budé brought the critical approach of humanism to the study of Christian texts and set an early example of that personal interpretation of the Scriptures that led to the Reformation.

**Bugenhagen, Johannes** (1485–1558) *German Lutheran theologian*
After a career as a Premonstratensian canon at Treptow in his native Pomerania, Bugenhagen became, through a reading of LUTHER's *De captivitate Babylonica ecclesiae*, an early convert to the Reformation. In 1521 he abandoned his post as rector of the city school in Treptow and enrolled as a theology student in Wittenberg, where he was appointed minister of the town church in 1523 and professor in 1535. He became one of Luther's closest friends and associates, serving as his confessor and assisting him in his New Testament translations. Although Bugenhagen

remained in Wittenberg until his death, his most important work was undertaken in missions away from the city, particularly in northern Germany and Denmark. As the architect of numerous church orders (for Hamburg in 1529, Lübeck in 1531, and Denmark in 1537) Bugenhagen played an essential role in the establishment of the Reformation in these northern lands. His contribution to the Danish Reformation, during an extended stay of two years (1537–39), was particularly important. He translated several of Luther's works and was responsible for the production of a Lower German edition of Luther's Bible. He was one of the signatories of the SAXON CONFESSION.

**Bull, John** (c. 1562/63–1628) *English composer, organist, and virginalist*
As a boy chorister Bull sang at Hereford cathedral and the Chapel Royal. In 1583 he was appointed organist and master of the choristers at Hereford; on his dismissal from Hereford, he became a gentleman of the Chapel Royal (1586). Bull gained doctorates in music at both Oxford and Cambridge and in March 1597 was elected first public reader in music at Gresham College, London, on Elizabeth I's recommendation; this post he was obliged to resign in 1607 on account of his marriage. Throughout this period he continued his duties at the Chapel Royal. By 1610 he had probably entered the service of James I's heir, Prince Henry, to whose sister, Princess Elizabeth, he dedicated the first printed volume of virginal music: *Parthenia* (1613). In 1613 Bull was charged with adultery and fled to the Netherlands, never to return. Archduke Albert employed him at Brussels but he was dismissed the following year at the request of James I, displeased at the flight of his organist. In 1617 Bull was appointed cathedral organist at Antwerp, where he died.

Bull was a keyboard virtuoso and is chiefly remembered for his keyboard music, which makes unprecedented technical demands on the player. Among his most astounding works are the hexachord fantasias, most suitable for organ. Bull's virginal music mainly comprises settings of pavans, galliards, and other dance tunes, employing brilliant technical and rhythmical devices. His canons, of which 200 survive, are extraordinary in their complexity and ingenuity.

**Bullant, Jean** (1520/25–1578) *French architect*
Born at Amiens, Bullant studied in Italy where he was influenced by the classical style. He returned to France in 1540 to enter the service of Constable Anne de MONTMORENCY, for whom he worked on the Château d'Écouen (c. 1555), and became the first French architect to make use of the colossal order by modelling his work on the Pantheon in Rome. Subsequent works included the Petit Château (Capitainerie) at Chantilly (c. 1561) and a bridge and gallery combining ancient Roman and mannerist ideals at Fére-en-Tardenois (1552–62). In 1570 Bullant

succeeded DELORME as architect to CATHERINE DE' MEDICI, for whom he executed work at the Chapelle des Valois and the TUILERIES and drew up plans for the enlargement of the châteaux of St.-Maur and CHENONCEAUX and for the Hôtel de Soissons. He was also the author of a treatise on architecture, *La Règle générale d'architecture, étude des cinq ordres de colonnes* (1564), which became a textbook for French architects.

**Bullinger, Johann Heinrich** (1504–1575) *Swiss reformer and theologian*
The son of a parish priest, Bullinger studied in Germany before returning to take up his father's post in his native Bremgarten. In 1531 Bullinger was appointed minister in Zürich in succession to ZWINGLI; his resolute defence of the church there preserved it through the many difficulties that followed Zwingli's death. In the Eucharistic controversy Bullinger defended the Zwinglian position, but he also associated himself with BUCER in attempts to reconcile the German and Swiss churches. In 1549 he and CALVIN made the important ZÜRICH AGREEMENT (Consensus Tigurinus), which defined a common sacramental doctrine for the Zürich and Geneva churches. By this time Bullinger enjoyed a considerable international influence, largely through his enormous correspondence (12,000 surviving pieces). A prolific writer, he wrote sermons (published as the *Sermonorum decades quinque)* that had an enduring popularity, particularly in England where his reputation rivaled that of Calvin. Bullinger was also the architect of the Second HELVETIC CONFESSION (1566) and the author of a history of the Reformation down to 1532.

**Buon, Bartolommeo** (Bartolommeo Bon) (c. 1374–c. 1467) *Italian architectural sculptor*
Trained by his father Giovanni Buon, Bartolommeo is first recorded collaborating with him on the facade of Sta. Maria dell' Orto in his native Venice (1392). They next appear in 1422 working, with others, on the Ca d'Oro (until 1437); the large well-head in its courtyard, adorned with allegorical figures, is documented to Bartolommeo in 1427. From the late 1430s date a lunette over the entrance to the Scuola di San Marco and the Porta della Carta of the ducal palace, with its *Lion of St. Mark*, statue of *Justice* and several *Virtues*, and many subsidiary ornaments. This is Buon's masterpiece. An important carving is the lunette of the *Madonna of Mercy* (now Victoria and Albert Museum, London) from the facade of the Misericordia, a charitable brotherhood. Buon's style, with its emphasis on luxuriant foliage and heraldry, is still basically Gothic and has an attractive boldness, owing to the relatively hard local stones he used: Verona red marble and Istrian limestone.

**Buonarroti, Michelangelo** See MICHELANGELO BUONARROTI

**Buondelmonti, Cristoforo** (c. 1385–1430) *Italian traveler and monk*
Buondelmonti received a sound humanist education, learning Greek from GUARINO DA VERONA. After 1414, when he abandoned his church duties in Florence, he spent much of the rest of his life traveling in the Levant, indulging his enthusiasm for the Greek classics, and collecting books for Florentine friends and patrons. At least one book he obtained in Crete is still in Florence's Bibliotheca Laurenziana. Basing himself on Rhodes, he crisscrossed the eastern Mediterranean from Crete to Constantinople. His manuscript *Librum insularum archipelagi*, sent to Cardinal Giordano Orsini in 1422, is known from later copies but remained unpublished until 1824. His description of Mount Athos is the earliest Western account to describe details of the monastic routine there.

**Buoninsegna, Duccio di** See DUCCIO DI BUONINSEGNA

**Buontalenti, Bernardo** (c. 1536–1603) *Italian architect, engineer, painter, and sculptor*
Buontalenti was born in Florence and when he was 11 years old, his parents were ruined as a result of flooding and he was taken under the protection of COSIMO I DE' MEDICI. The duke had Buontalenti trained in architecture, painting, and sculpture and from 1567 employed him as a river engineer. Buontalenti built the Casino Mediceo in Rome in the early 1570s and the Casino di San Marco, now the Palazzo dei Tribunali, in Florence in 1574 in an exuberantly mannerist style (*see* MANNERISM). Parts of the Uffizi and Palazzo Vecchio are his, built in the 1580s. As a theater architect and technician he was responsible for spectacular court productions and created special effects, costumes, and firework displays of a kind never seen before. He designed automata and waterworks for villa gardens and he even arranged a naval battle inside the Palazzo Pitti. He also worked on fortifications and wrote two books on military engineering. His best-known paintings are the miniatures he did for Francesco, son of Cosimo I, and his self-portrait in the Uffizi.

**Bürgi, Jost** (1552–1632) *Swiss-born horologist and mathematician*
After serving as court clockmaker to WILLIAM IV of Hesse-Kassel (from 1579), Bürgi moved in 1603 to a similar post at the Prague court of Emperor RUDOLF II. One of the first clockmakers to use second hands, Bürgi also introduced into his designs the cross-beat escapement and the remontoire, an ingenious device providing the escapement with a constant driving force. In mathematics Bürgi took the fundamental step in the 1580s of working out a comprehensive system of logarithms, a quarter-century before NAPIER published his own system. Bürgi's work remained unknown until 1620 when he published his *Arithmetische und Geometrische Progress-Tabulen*. By this time the glory

had gone to Napier, and Bürgi's own role remained unrecognized until relatively recent times.

## Burgkmair, Hans (1473–1531) *German painter and print maker*

Born at Augsburg, Burgkmair received his initial training from his father, and between 1488 and 1490 studied with Martin SCHONGAUER in Colmar. On his return to Augsburg (1490) he designed woodcuts for the printer RATDOLT and assisted HOLBEIN THE ELDER with portraits and altarpieces. In 1498 he was admitted to the Augsburg guild. Burgkmair traveled to Cologne in 1503 and in about 1507 visited northern Italy, including Venice and Lucca. His portraits, such as the *Sebastian Brant* in Karlsruhe, are remarkable for their realism and psychological intensity. Classicizing architectural motifs of Italian derivation appear in his altarpieces, such as the Nuremberg *Virgin and Child* (1509). Burgkmair was a prolific designer of woodcuts, executing the largest part of the *Triumphal Procession of the Emperor Maximilian* and the *Weisskunig*. As a print maker he is important as a pioneer of the multicolored *chiaroscuro* woodcut.

## Busbecq, Ogier Ghislain de (c. 1520–1591) *Flemish diplomat*

Born at Comines (Komen) in the Spanish Netherlands (now on the Franco-Belgian border), he studied at the University of Leuven in the 1530s, then at Paris, Venice, Bologna, and Padua. He began his diplomatic career by acompanying the representative of Ferdinand of Austria (later Holy Roman Emperor FERDINAND I) to England for the marriage of Mary I to Philip II of Spain (1554). The same year Ferdinand appointed him his ambassador to Sultan Suleiman the Magnificent at the Ottoman Porte, where he remained nearly seven years (1555–62); his efforts to check Ottoman expansionism by means of diplomacy eventually resulted in a satisfactory treaty. He was knighted for his achievements and spent the remainder of his life in the imperial diplomatic service, dying in France while personal representative of RUDOLF II at the French court.

Busbecq wrote four letters about his Turkish mission which, despite their purported dates (1554, 1555, 1560, 1562), were probably composed after 1579. The first edition was published under the title *Itinera Constantinopolitanum et Amasianum* (Travels to Constantinople and Amasya) by Christopher Plantin of Antwerp (1581); this contained only the first letter and Busbecq's small treatise *Exclamatio, sive de re militari contra Turcam instituenda consilium* (Appeal, or plan for waging war on the Turks), written in 1576. Plantin added the second letter to the second edition of 1582; letters three and four first appeared in the 1589 Paris edition. Busbecq was an open admirer of many aspects of Ottoman military and administrative organization. An accomplished linguist, he wrote elegant Latin and took an interest in a wide range of topics: antiquities, numismatics, flora and fauna, and the now extinct East Germanic language of Crimean Gothic. He is popularly, but wrongly, credited with having introduced the tulip, a flower much admired at the Ottoman court, into western Europe.

**Further reading:** *The Turkish Letters of Ogier Ghiselin de Busbecq, Imperial Ambassador at Constantinople 1554–1562*, transl. and abridged by Edward Seymour Forster (Oxford, U.K.: Clarendon Press, 1927; new ed. London: Sickle Moon Books, 2001).

## Butinone, Bernardino See ZENALE, BERNARD(IN)O

## Buxtorf, Johannes (I) (1564–1629) *German Hebrew scholar*

The son of a Protestant minister, Buxtorf was born at and studied at Marburg and later at Geneva and Basle under BEZA. For 38 years from 1591 he occupied the chair of Hebrew at Basle, rejecting attractive offers from Saumur and Leyden. To the study of Hebrew Buxtorf brought rabbinical learning acquired from the many scholarly Jews whom he befriended. His main works had an educational purpose: a number of elementary grammars and readers, a Hebrew-Chaldee *Lexicon* (1607), and a Hebrew reference grammar (1609). He also produced an edition of the Bible with rabbinic commentary and the Chaldean paraphrases (1618–19). His son, Johannes II (1599–1664), followed him as professor of Hebrew at Basle and completed his father's *Lexicon Chaldaicum Talmudicum et rabbinicum* (1639), which provided a scientific basis for the study of postbiblical Jewish writings.

## Byrd, William (1543–1623) *English composer*

Although possibly born in Lincoln, Byrd at an early age became a pupil of TALLIS in London. He was organist and master of the choristers at Lincoln cathedral (1563–72) and became a gentleman of the Chapel Royal in 1570. In London Byrd's patrons included the earls of Worcester and Northumberland. With Tallis, Byrd was granted a crown patent for the printing and selling of part music and lined music paper; together they issued *Cantiones, quae ab argumento sacrae vocantur* (1575), which comprised Latin motets by both composers and was dedicated to the queen. In the 1580s, as a known recusant (*see* RECUSANCY), Byrd suffered considerable yearly fines, though he was granted certain concessions, probably because the queen favored his music. In 1587, after the death of Tallis, Byrd was left in sole possession of their patent, and with the printer Thomas East dominated English music printing until the expiration of the patent nine years later. Among Byrd's publications at this time were *Psalmes, Sonets and Songs* (1588), *Songs of Sundrie Natures* (1589), and *Cantiones sacrae* (1589). In the 1590s and 1600s Byrd wrote music for Catholic services; notable from this period are his three MASS settings and the two-volume *Gradualia* (1605, 1607). He died at Stondon Massey, Essex, where he had spent the last 30 years of his life.

Byrd is chiefly remembered for his church music, notably his verse anthems (a form that he may have invented) and music for the Anglican service. Byrd's Latin motets, frequently with words lamenting a captive people, may have been composed as a solace to the persecuted Catholic community. The three-, four-, and five-part Masses are in a simple style with little word repetition and a restricted use of polyphony. Byrd was also well regarded for his keyboard music, including grounds, descriptive pieces, variations, pavans, and galliards. His best-known collection is the manuscript "My Ladye Nevells Booke" (1591).

**Further reading:** Gustave Reese, *The New Grove High Renaissance Masters: Josquin, Palestrina, Lassus, Byrd, Victoria* (London: Macmillan, 1984).

**Byzantium** See CONSTANTINOPLE

# C

**Cabbala** A body of Jewish mystical literature, the name of which derives from the Hebrew *kabbalah*, with the literal meaning "that which is received by tradition." Originally an esoteric doctrine, it spread throughout Europe with the expulsion (1492) of the JEWS from Spain.

The Cabbala is based on a number of texts, the two most important being the *Sefer yetzirah* (Book of creation; third–sixth centuries CE) and the *Zohar* (Splendor; c. 1300) of Moses de Leon of Granada. Though ignored by Marsilio FICINO, the Cabbala was introduced to Renaissance Italy by PICO DELLA MIRANDOLA in his 72 *Conclusiones cabalisticae* (1486). Cabbalistic ideas were further expounded by Johann REUCHLIN in his *De verbo mirifico* (1494) and the *De arte cabalistica* (1517), the first full-length work on the subject by a non-Jew. Thereafter the ideas became part of the general Neoplatonic intellectual background of the more scholarly Renaissance MAGUS.

At the heart of the system are the 10 *sephiroth*, the divine attributes extending from *kether* to *malkuth* and relating God to the universe. Each of these is linked with one of the 10 spheres of the heavens and, in an ever-widening system of correspondences, with all other aspects of nature. The divine names, suitably expressed in the 22 letters of the Hebrew alphabet, yielded power over their appropriate sphere of influence. At its crudest the Cabbala involved no more than the attempt to gain power over angels and demons through possession of their names, and was the camouflage adopted by the charlatan to impose on the gullible. To the Neoplatonist, however, it offered the means to apprehend a transcendent God and to understand the harmonies which so clearly existed in nature. As such, it ceased to exercise any serious influence in Western thought after the rise of the mechanistic philosophy in the 17th century.

**See also:** MAGIC

**Further reading:** Léo Bronstein, *Kabbalah and Art* (Hanover, N.H.: Brandeis University Press, 1980; 2nd ed. New Brunswick, N.J. and London: Transaction, 1997).

**Cabezón, Antonio de** (1510–1566) *Spanish composer*
Cabezón was born in Castrillo de Matajudios, near Burgos, and he was blind from a young age. He studied organ music at Palencia with Garcia de Breza before becoming (1526) organist and clavichordist to the empress Isabella of Portugal, wife of Charles V. After her death (1539) he worked for her children, mainly Prince Philip who later became King PHILIP II and who was Cabezón's sole employer after 1548. At the royal court he met the composer Thomás de Santa Maria and the vihuelist Luis de Narváez. He traveled with the choir of the royal chapel to Italy, the Netherlands, and Germany (1548–51) and to England and the Netherlands (1554–56), where he influenced the English virginal composers as well as the organ music of the Low Countries, including, later, the work of Jan Pietersz. SWEELINCK.

Some of Cabezón's extant music was published in Luis Venegas de Henestrosa's *Libro de cifira nueva* (Book of new tablature; 1557), which includes works by other composers. Far more of his compositions were published posthumously by his son Hernando in *Obras de nuisica-para tecla, arpa y vihuela de Antonio de Cabezón* (1578), which includes instructions on keyboard playing. Cabezón was one of the first composers to write instrumental music specifically for the keyboard, although his compositions can also be played on the vihuela and the harp. His large output of works for organ and stringed keyboard instruments includes *diferencias* (sets of variations on secular melodies and popular dances), *glosas* (compositions based on works by other, usually non-Spanish, composers), *tientos* (fantasias), and *fabordones* (embellishments of hymns and plainsong). Among his best-known works are the variations on the song "Canto del caballero." Cabezón's works were highly influential in the development of keyboard music throughout Europe.

**cabinets** (Italian *studioli*, German *Wunderkammern*, French *cabinets de curiosités*) Collections of rarities of art and nature through which the Renaissance originated the idea of the museum. The term "cabinets," it should be noted, refers to the collections themselves or to the rooms housing them, not to the cupboards in which they might be stored or displayed. Several present-day European museums can indeed trace their origins directly to such collections.

During the 16th and 17th centuries the European's conception of the world he or she lived in was constantly assailed. New territories populated by undreamt-of peoples, animals, and plants were discovered; scientific advances inconceivable in the medieval period were made at an ever-increasing rate. Cabinets encapsulated the products and apparatus of these discoveries, making them at once more tangible and more comprehensible. Within his or her cabinet the collector confronted the mysteries of the universe.

Universality was the theme common to almost all such collections: their ambitious aim was no less than the re-creation of the world in microcosm. Although this quest could result in an amazingly heterogeneous range of material, both natural and man made, most collectors were content to seek a purely symbolic completeness, in which certain items or categories of exhibit stood emblematically for each of the continents, for each of the elements, or for scientific, historical, mythological, or magical themes.

To the Renaissance grandee a cabinet was as indispensable as a LIBRARY: the two served complementary philosophical purposes and frequently occupied adjacent chambers. In Italy almost every princely household had its *studio*, that of Francesco I de' Medici (1541–87) being the most perfectly realized. Further north the Hapsburgs and other noble dynasties populated Austria and Germany with numerous *Kunst-und Wunderkammern*: the collection of Archduke Ferdinand of Tyrol still exists at Schloss Ambras, near Innsbruck, and elements of other princely cabinets survive in Stuttgart, Munich, Berlin, Dresden, and elsewhere. Frederick III established one *Kunstkammer* in Denmark and Gustavus Adolphus another in Sweden. In France the ducal collections of Montmorency (1493–1567) and Orleans (1608–60) preceded the founding of the *cabinet du roi* in the 17th century. Their invariable purpose was for the personal recreation of their owners.

Cabinets were not solely the prerogative of noble households; many of the most influential were developed by scholars as resources for scientific study rather than for philosophical diversion. Such purposefulness can be detected in the cabinets of men like Ulisse ALDROVANDI and Ferrante Imperato (1550–1631) in Italy, of Konrad GESNER (1516–65) in Zürich, of Bernard Paludanus (1550–1633) in the Netherlands, and Olaus Worm (1588–1654) in Denmark. Men like these systemized and classified the wonders of the world, while their publications described not only the contents of their cabinets but also the greater world which they represented. An indication of how widespread the practice of assembling a cabinet of curiosities had become by the mid-16th century can be seen in the list of nearly 1000 names compiled by the Flemish printmaker and collector Hubert Goltz (or Goltzius; 1526–83), who between 1556 and 1560 journeyed around the Netherlands, Germany, Austria, Switzerland, Italy, and France visiting every place at which such a collection existed; among the collectors named by Goltz were lawyers, doctors, monks, poets, and artists, as well as the more predictable grandees such as the pope, the emperor, and other princes.

From the early 17th century the numbers of private citizens of lesser means who founded collections began to increase. Some bourgeois collectors, such as Pierre Borel (1620–71) of Castres, emulated their social superiors in forming cabinets as a basis for romantic contemplation. Others, such as Manfredo Settala (1600–80) of Milan, pursued more scientific goals. The John Tradescants at Lambeth, London (the elder died 1638; the younger 1608–62) were of a more practical bent, opening their collection to the public and deriving income from it. As the numbers of collectors increased, the universal nature of the prototype cabinets was abandoned in favor of collections specializing in specific aspects of natural history, art, or antiquity.

Academic institutions also began to recognize the practical value of cabinets. That of the anatomy school at Leyden was perhaps the most famous, having opened its doors to the public from the early 1600s. At Oxford several smaller collections within the university were overshadowed by the founding (1683) of the Ashmolean Museum. Within the Royal Society in London, which received its charter in 1662, the aim of founding a museum with a precisely defined collecting program, designed to produce comprehensive and systematic collections (particularly of natural history specimens), clearly demonstrates the extent to which the original concept of the cabinet of curiosities had become outmoded.

**See also:** BOTANIC GARDENS; ZOOLOGICAL COLLECTIONS
**Further reading:** Patrick Mauriès, *Cabinets of Curiosities* (London: Thames & Hudson, 2002); Krzysztof Pomian, *Collectors and Curiosities: Paris and Venice*

*1500–1800*, transl. Elizabeth Wiles-Portier (Cambridge, U.K.: Polity, 1990).

## Cabot, John (Giovanni Caboto) (1450–1498) *Italian navigator and explorer*

Born in Genoa, Cabot moved to Venice in 1461. His trading voyages around the Mediterranean made him an expert navigator. In 1484 he moved to London, and then on to Bristol. The move was probably inspired by Britain's Atlantic position and status as a trading nation, encouraging Cabot's vision of a NORTHWEST PASSAGE to Asia.

In 1496 Henry VII commissioned Cabot and his sons to colonize any territories they discovered for England; in return Cabot was to enjoy trading rights. On May 2, 1497 the *Matthew* sailed west for Asia with Cabot and 18 sailors aboard. He landed on Cape Breton Island off the coast of Canada on June 24 and claimed it for England. Convinced he had discovered Asia, Cabot returned to Bristol, where he easily found backing for a five-ship expedition. This sailed in May 1498. Cabot hugged the east coast of Greenland at first but later may have gone south along the east coast of America as far as Chesapeake Bay. Lack of supplies caused a mutiny, and Cabot was forced to return to England, where he died in obscure circumstances.

**Further reading:** James A. Williamson, *The Cabot Voyages and Bristol Discovery under Henry VII* (Cambridge, U.K.: Cambridge University Press for the Hakluyt Society, 1962).

## Cabot, Sebastian (1476–1557) *Italian navigator*

Probably born in Venice, then raised in England, Cabot was the son of John CABOT, on whose northwestern voyages he began his career. In 1512 HENRY VIII employed him as cartographer, an occupation he continued for King Ferdinand II of Aragon. Ferdinand's successor, Charles V, promoted Cabot to pilot major (1519). In 1525 he was sent to develop commercial relations with the Orient, but was distracted by fabulous tales of South America's wealth. For five years he explored the navigable rivers of the continent, before returning to a furious Charles V who banished him to Africa. In 1533 he was pardoned and reappointed pilot major. In 1548 Cabot returned to England where he ended his days as governor of the Merchant Adventurers. His 1544 world map shows details of his own and his father's American discoveries.

## Cabral, Pedro Alvares (c. 1467–c. 1520) *Portuguese explorer*

Born in Belmonte of the lesser nobility, Cabral was appointed by King Manuel I to command a fleet of 13 ships and 1200 men bound for the East Indies. He set sail on March 9, 1500. He soon drifted westwards a long way off course, a mistake which some authorities suspect was premeditated. He became caught in the Atlantic's westerly currents, and made landfall in Brazil, which he claimed for Portugal. After 10 days in Brazil, Cabral sent one ship home with news of his discovery, and sailed east for India with the rest. During the voyage seven vessels sank. Bartholomeu DIAZ was among the dead. After founding a factory at Calicut, Cabral returned to Portugal and retired.

## Caccini, Francesca (1587–after 1641) *Italian composer and court singer*

The daughter of Giulio CACCINI, she was born into a talented family of professional musicians; her sister Settimia Caccini was also a singer. At home, she learned to play the guitar, harp, and keyboard and also wrote poetry. She was a singer at the wedding of Marie de' Medici and Henry VI of France in Florence in 1600. In 1607, the year she married court singer Giovanni Battista Signorini, she herself entered Medici service as singer (of both sacred and secular works), singing teacher to the duke's daughters, and composer. Her first publicly performed work was music for a carnival in 1607; during her 20 years at the Medici court she became its highest paid musician, contributing compositions to 13 musical entertainments, as well as writing operas. Only one of these, *La liberazione di Ruggiero,* first performed in 1625 to honor the visit of a Polish prince, has survived. She toured Italy, performing with her husband in 1617. An anthology of her songs, *Il primo libro delle musiche* (1618), includes duets, arias, motets, and hymns, many from Latin sacred texts.

## Caccini, Giulio (c. 1545–1618) *Italian composer and singer*

Probably born in Tivoli or Rome, Caccini was taken to Florence by COSIMO I DE' MEDICI around 1565; his singing made a great impression there, and his fame spread throughout Italy. Caccini was among the musicians and intellectuals who frequented Count Giovanni BARDI's salon in Florence, and was acclaimed as the inventor of a new style of song, the *stile recitativo*, which was evolved there. Caccini's first mention as a composer was in 1589 when he contributed music for the marriage of Grand Duke Ferdinando I. In 1600 he was made musical director at the Medici court, remaining in the family's service until his death. His *Euridice* (1600) was the first published opera; it was written to rival Jacopo Peri's opera of the same name. His two songbooks, *Le nuove musiche* (1602, 1614), are collections for solo voice and figured bass. In the first there is a preface on the new style of singing and composition that Caccini had adopted; in the actual music, embellishments, which were normally improvised, are written out in full. Caccini's declamatory monody sought to capture the spirit of ancient Greek music, but is not noted for its lyricism.

**Ca' da Mosto, Alvise da** (c. 1430–1483) *Venetian nobleman and traveler*
Sailing for England in 1454, he put in by chance at Cape St. Vincent, Portugal, and gained permission to accompany one of HENRY THE NAVIGATOR's expeditions down the west coast of Africa. On a second voyage (1456) he possibly reached the Cape Verde Islands. After returning to Venice (1464) he held various official positions in the Venetian state, but his fame rests on his accounts of his two West African voyages, two manuscript versions of which (neither Ca' da Mosto's own) survive in Venice's Marciana Library. The first printed edition was in Fracanzano Montalboddo's collection *Paesi nouamente retrovati* (1507), which was soon translated into several languages (Latin and German in 1508, French in 1515).

**Cádiz, Raid on** (April 1587) The naval raid by Sir Francis DRAKE on Cádiz, where PHILIP II of Spain was gathering a fleet for the invasion of England. Taking advantage of ambiguous instructions from ELIZABETH I, Drake forced his way into the harbor, destroyed over 30 ships, and captured four vessels loaded with provisions. This raid cost Spain over 300,000 crowns and 13,000 tons of shipping, forcing Philip to delay the SPANISH ARMADA until summer 1588.

**Cádiz, Sack of** (June 1596) An attack on Cádiz led by Robert Devereux, earl of ESSEX, Lord Howard of Effingham, and Sir Walter RALEIGH. After defeating the Spanish fleet, Essex took 3000 men ashore and fought his way into the town, which surrendered. On his return to England with considerable booty he was greeted as a popular hero.

**Caius, John** (1510–1573) *English physician and humanist*
He was born at Norwich and educated at Gonville Hall, Cambridge, and Padua University, where he studied under VESALIUS. Caius returned to Cambridge in the 1540s. In 1557 he received permission to renovate his old college; he became master in 1559, and ever since the college has been known as Gonville and Caius. Despite his munificence, his tenure was unhappy; suspected of wishing to introduce Catholicism into the college, Caius found himself involved in lawsuits, with dissension and expulsions being the order of the day. Much of his own time was spent editing a number of Hippocratic and Galenic texts (*see* GALENISM, RENAISSANCE). He also produced *A Boke or Counseill against…the Sweatyng Sicknesse* (1552), a prime account of the mysterious epidemic which swept through 16th-century Britain, and involved himself with controversies over the pronunciation of Greek and the relative antiquity of Oxford and Cambridge.

**Cajetan, Thomas de Vio** (Gaetano) (1469–1534) *Italian theologian*
His name derived from his birthplace of Gaeta. Cajetan entered the Dominican Order in 1484 and taught philoso-phy and theology at Padua, Paris, and Rome. He was general of the order (1508–18), and was appointed a cardinal in 1517 and bishop of Gaeta in 1518. He spoke for reform at the Lateran Council of 1512–17 and disputed with LUTHER in 1518. The elections of Charles V as king in Germany (1519) and of Pope Adrian VI (1522) were partly his doing. He opposed the divorce of HENRY VIII from Catherine of Aragon. Cajetan was a prolific writer, and his commentary (1507–22) on the *Summa theologica* of St. Thomas Aquinas remains an important contribution to Thomist philosophy. Although he was antagonistic toward humanism and Protestantism, his approach to critical problems was remarkably modern.

**Calcar, Jan Steven van** (1499–1546/50) *German painter and woodcut designer*
Jan Steven was born at Kalkar and probably trained in the northern Netherlands. By 1536/37 he had moved to Venice, where he fell deeply under the influence of TITIAN. In 1545 VASARI met him in Naples, where he died. His oeuvre is much confused with that of Titian and his workshop, but one of the best documented examples of his style is the portrait of Melchior von Brauweiler of Cologne, dated 1540, in the Louvre, Paris. Steven's chief claim to fame is his woodcut illustrations to VESALIUS's *De humani corporis fabrica* (1543). This remarkable anatomical textbook, of considerable significance for the development of both medical science and figure painting, includes prints of dissected cadavers in dramatic action, reproducing the gestures and poses of living beings (see illustration p. 491).

**calendar** A system for structuring years, determining their beginnings, and ordering their subdivisions. Julius Caesar, aided by Sosigenes, an Alexandrian astronomer, restructured the 355-day calendar of republican Rome. Ten days were added, together with, every fourth year, an extra day. The Julian year thus averaged 365.25 days, a close approximation to the 365.243 days of the tropical year. Though undetectable over short periods of time the discrepancy became evident with the passage of centuries. For example, by the 16th century, the vernal equinox, crucial to the calculation of Easter, had slipped from March 21 to March 11. The slippage had begun to be the subject of proposals for reform in the 13th century, and by the 15th century ways to remedy it were being actively discussed, with REGIOMONTANUS among those to put forward ideas. LUTHER remarked on the discrepancy but considered it to be a matter for secular rather than ecclesiastical intervention (*see also* CALENDAR, CHURCH). However, it was the papacy that ultimately proved to have the resources and determination to carry through the necessary adjustments. To tackle the problem, Pope GREGORY XIII in 1578 summoned to Rome astronomers, mathematicians, and theologians to advise him on calendrical reform. It was decided to cancel 10 days: that October 4, 1582 would be followed by October 15, 1582. In addition, only centurial years exactly divisible by 400 (1600 and 2000 for example) would be leap years. The effect would be to shorten the calendar year to 365.2425 days and so keep the vernal equinox tied much more closely to March 21. The architect of the reform was Aloisio Lillo (1510–76), a physician at Perugia university. Though accepted immediately by Catholic states, the Gregorian calendar was ignored by most Protestant countries, and it was not until 1752 that Britain belatedly adopted the new system.

**Further reading:** David Ewing Duncan, *The Calendar* (London: Fourth Estate, 1998).

**calendar, Church** The annual cycle of feasts and fasts that begins in the Western Church with Advent Sunday. In both Roman Catholic and reformed Churches there are two preeminent feasts in the Church calendar to which most of the rest are related: Christmas, which is based on the solar calendar, and Easter, determined by the lunar. Advent and Lent are the seasons of fasting before Christmas and Easter respectively. During the Middle Ages, in addition to these major events and those linked to them, the Church observed a large number of other feasts, very often on saints' days. These in turn were often linked with traditional calendar lore, for example in the English saying about the weather on Candlemas Day (the feast of the Purification of the Virgin Mary; February 2), which is now adapted to American Groundhog Day: "If Candlemas Day be sunny and bright, winter will have another flight; if Candlemas day be cloudy with rain, winter has gone and will not come again."

It was a widespread practice to date events by the nearest festival of the Church: hence, in England, Christmas (December 25), the Annunciation (otherwise called Lady Day; March 25), the Nativity of St. John the Baptist (June 24), and Michaelmas (September 29) were the days designated as quarter days, when charges such as rents fell due. Some saints' days were recognized throughout Christendom; others were purely of local or regional significance. To say that an event happened "in vigilia Sanctae Luciae" (on the vigil of St. Lucy, i.e. St. Lucy's Eve) would have been widely understood as referring to December 12. Both feast days and ordinary Sundays were often referred to in the Middle Ages by the opening words of the Latin introit sung at Mass, a practice partially retained by the Lutheran Church.

The pre-Reformation Church calendar thus impinged upon ordinary people's consciousnesses to a far greater extent than it does in modern times—with some exceptions. Roman Catholic countries, particularly in southern Europe, maintain some practices, such as the revelries of Carnival (literally, "farewell to meat") in the pre-Lenten period, that either never really took hold in England or were condemned by the reformers. In pre-Reformation times, virtually every day of the year was dedicated to one or more saints, but in line with their objections to relics and "superstition," the reformers jettisoned commemoration of saints' days from their ecclesiastical year. The process is exemplified in England, where the pruning of traditional elements of the Roman Catholic year began in 1536; by the time the BOOK OF COMMON PRAYER appeared in 1549 only Christmas, Easter, and Whitsun remained of the feasts, plus a few biblical saints' days (St. Mary Magdalene, St. John the Baptist, the Apostles, and the Evangelists). The Reformation was thus responsible for setting in train a radical secularization of the calendar.

**Further reading:** Ronald Hutton, *The Stations of the Sun: A History of the Ritual Year in Britain* (Oxford, U.K.: Oxford University Press, 1996).

**Caliari, Paolo** See VERONESE, PAOLO

**Calixtus III, Pope** See BORGIA FAMILY

**calligraphy** The gothic, or black-letter, style of writing was used throughout western Europe in the later Middle Ages. There were local variations in the form of the letters, and Italian writing (*littera rotunda*) was less angular than that of northern Europe. In the 14th century, PETRARCH led the revival of interest in the classical Roman style. He was the chief of a group of humanists at Florence, who studied manuscripts of ancient authors and inscriptions on coins and monuments. The early manuscripts available to them mostly dated from the 10th and 11th centuries, with text in Carolingian minuscule script and display lines in monumental capitals. These became the basis of the Renaissance *littera antica*, which differs little from modern roman type.

Petrarch was followed by Coluccio SALUTATI, chancellor of Florence, two of whose followers, Poggio BRACCIOLINI and Niccolò NICCOLI, developed their styles on divergent lines. Poggio continued the formal Roman tradition; in 1403 he went to Rome and became secretary to the pope, and his hand influenced a number of scholars and artists from Verona and Padua, including Andrea Mantegna. Niccoli produced a more cursive script, with taller and narrower letters, differing less from the current gothic. This was the origin of the italic hand, which was used for less formal writing and for the more popular, small-format books. One form of italic, the *cancellaresca*, was developed for more rapid writing in government offices and for commercial and private use.

From the mid-16th century the italic style spread over the rest of western Europe, aided by popular copybooks, of which that by the papal scribe Lodovico degli Arrighi was the first (1523). In Italy and Spain and to some extent in France and in England, italic was used for the vernacular languages as well as Latin. In Germany and Scandinavia its use was more or less confined to Latin. In

England the bastard running secretary hand (a mixture of gothic and italic, with many variant forms of letters), was in common use till the early 17th century, but thereafter the italic prevailed and was the origin of the copperplate style from which modern handwriting is derived.

Greek texts began to be copied in Italy in about 1400. At first a clear simple style, introduced by Manuel CHRYSOLORAS, was used. Later, a formal script, favored by Cretan scribes, was employed for liturgical texts, while a more mannered style, with extensive use of ligatures employed for the classics, influenced the printing of Aldus MANUTIUS. In the reign of Francis I some Cretans at Fontainebleau cultivated a simpler style, which is the basis of the Greek type used today.

See also: MANUSCRIPTS; TYPOGRAPHY

Further reading: Albinia de la Mare, *The Handwriting of the Italian Humanists* (Oxford, U.K.: Oxford University Press for the Association internationale de bibliophilie, 1973– ); Alfred Fairbank and Richard W. Hunt, *Humanistic Script of the Fifteenth and Sixteenth Centuries* (Oxford, U.K.: Bodleian Library, 1960; rev. ed. 1993); Berthold L. Ullman, *The Origin and Development of Humanistic Script* (Rome: Edizioni di storia e letteratura, 1960); James Wardrop, *The Script of Humanism: Some Aspects of Humanistic Script, 1460–1560* (Oxford, U.K.: Clarendon Press, 1963).

## Calvaert, Denys (Dionisio Fiammingo) (1540–1619)
*Flemish-born painter*
Calvaert emigrated from his native Antwerp as a young man and around 1560 he was studying in Bologna under Prospero Fontana. After a short spell in Rome in the early 1570s, working on the Vatican, Calvaert returned to spend the rest of his life in Bologna, where he opened a very influential painting academy. Guido RENI was among his numerous pupils.

## Calvin, John (1509–1564) *French reformer*
Calvin was born at Noyon, Picardy, and was intended from an early age for a career in the Church. He spent six years studying in Paris (1523–28), mostly at the ultra-orthodox Collège de Montaigu, before moving to the more liberal atmosphere of the university of Orleans. In 1532 he published his first book, a commentary on Seneca's *De clementia*, a choice of subject which demonstrates the extent of his early interest in humanism and classical scholarship. His conversion to Protestantism occurred suddenly, probably in 1533; the following year he left France and settled in Basle in Switzerland. In 1536 he published *Christianae religionis institutio* (*The Institutes of the Christian Religion*, popularly known as THE INSTITUTES), a book which immediately established his own reputation among the reformers. A visit to Geneva this same year resulted in an invitation to remain and assist the local reformer, Guillaume FAREL, in his work; but Calvin and Farel soon alien-

ated the local populace, and in 1538 they were expelled from the city. Calvin settled in Strasbourg, where he acted as minister to the small French church in exile and observed with approval Martin BUCER's work in the city; he was able to put this experience to good use, when, in 1541, he was asked to return to Geneva.

Calvin acted quickly to assert his authority. His Ecclesiastical Ordinances (1541) defined the powers of the pastors and established the authority of the consistory, the assembly of pastors and laymen (elders) which exercised control over morals and doctrine within the city. Calvin's austere discipline inevitably aroused opposition, which reached its climax with the trial of Michael SERVETUS (1553) and the exiling of the leading "Libertines" in 1555. Thereafter Calvin's authority in Geneva was unchallenged, and he enjoyed a steadily growing international influence. A tireless writer, Calvin published numerous biblical commentaries and smaller dogmatic works. He also re-edited the *Institutes*, which became by the time of the definitive 1559 edition a complete systematic theology of the Calvinist Reformation. His treatise on PREDESTINATION, regarded as his characteristic doctrine, was published in 1552.

Further reading: William J. Bouwsma, *John Calvin: A Sixteenth-century Portrait* (Oxford, U.K.: Oxford University Press, 1988); Bernard Cottret, *Calvin: A Biography* (Grand Rapids, Mich.: Eerdmans, 2000); Harro Höpfl, *The Christian Polity of John Calvin* (Cambridge, U.K.: Cambridge University Press, 1982); Richard A. Muller, *The Unaccomodated Calvin* (Oxford, U.K. and New York: Oxford University Press, 2000).

## Calvinism
The system of theology based on the teachings of John CALVIN, the reformer of Geneva. Calvin shared with LUTHER a belief in the centrality of the Bible, the denial of human free will, and the doctrine of JUSTIFICATION BY FAITH alone. To these Calvin added double PREDESTINATION, the notion that God had predestined some to salvation and others to damnation. This doctrine, given greater emphasis still in the teaching of Calvin's successor BEZA, came in time to be the touchstone of Calvinist orthodoxy. On Eucharistic doctrine Calvin took a middle position between the symbolism of ZWINGLI and the more conservative teaching of Luther, gaining the support of the other leading Swiss churches in the important ZÜRICH AGREEMENT (1549). Calvin favored a strongly theocratic church polity, and his model of church government for Geneva (the Ecclesiastical Ordinances, 1541) proved extremely influential as Calvinism spread through Europe in the later part of the 16th century.

Important Calvinist churches were established in France (where the HUGUENOTS were of this persuasion), in the Netherlands (where Calvinism became the official state religion of the United Provinces in 1622), in Scotland, and in Eastern Europe. In England Calvinist theology exercised a significant influence on the doctrinal development of the Anglican Church (in the THIRTY-NINE ARTICLES). It also took a firm hold among the early nonconformist groups, who carried it with them to North America.

**Further reading:** R. T. Kendall, *Calvin and English Calvinism to 1649* (Oxford, U.K.: Oxford University Press, 1979; new ed. Carlisle, U.K.: Paternoster, 1997); Diarmuid MacCulloch, *Reformation: Europe's House Divided 1490–1700* (London: Allen Lane, 2003), as *The Reformation: A History* (New York: Penguin Viking, 2004); E. William Monter, *Calvin's Geneva* (New York: Wiley, 1967); Richard A. Muller, *After Calvin: Studies in the Development of a Theological Tradition* (New York: Oxford University Press, 2003); Bodo Nischan, *Lutherans and Calvinists in the Age of Confessionalism* (Aldershot, U.K.: Ashgate, 1999); M. Prestwich, *International Calvinism, 1541–1715* (Oxford, U.K.: Clarendon Press and New York: Oxford University Press, 1986).

**Camaldolese Chart** A world map commissioned in 1457 by King Afonso V of Portugal from the Italian cartographer Fra Mauro (died 1460). It was produced in the Camaldolese monastery on the island of Murano, Venice, and incorporates information drawn from the voyages of Marco Polo and the exploration sponsored by HENRY THE NAVIGATOR within the circular format of the ancient *mappa mundi*. Completed in 1459, it measures 6 feet 4 inches (190 cm) in diameter and is housed in the Marciana library, Venice.

**Cambiaso, Luca** (1527–1585) *Italian painter*
The son of the painter Giovanni Cambiaso, Luca was born at Moneglia, near Genoa. He became the first, and most important, master of a native Genoese school of painters. The vivacity of his early pictures reflects the speed and impetuosity with which he is said to have worked, without the usual preparatory drawing and even painting large areas with both hands at once. The frescoes and oils painted in his maturity show greater moderation and are more graceful in style, but he continued to develop a simplification of form, which in his drawings almost resembles cubism. Like Beccafumi, he often used light to dramatize his subjects, as in *The Virgin with a Candle* (c. 1570; Palazzo Bianco, Genoa). Cambiaso spent the last two years of his life decorating the ESCORIAL with large frescoes at the invitation of Philip II of Spain; he died in Madrid.

**Cambrai, League of** (1508) An alliance formed at Cambrai in northeast France by Emperor MAXIMILIAN I, LOUIS XII of France, and FERDINAND II of Aragon, nominally against the Turks, but really in order to dismember the Venetian empire. It was joined by the pope and the dukes of Mantua and Ferrara, all of whom had territorial disputes with Venice. After some initial successes, beginning at Agnadello (1509), the league began to collapse in 1510, owing to the defection of the pope and Ferdinand, and by 1517 Venice had won back virtually all the territory it had lost.

**Camden, William** (1551–1623) *English antiquarian and educationist*
Born into a London painter's family, Camden attended St. Paul's School before going to Oxford (1566–71). Patrons in London then supported his antiquarian researches until his appointment as second master at Westminster School (1575). This post, and his subsequent headmastership (1593–97) left him free time for extensive journeys researching his monumental topographical work *Britannia* (1586; 6th edition, much enlarged, 1607). This county-by-county survey was written in Latin and translated by Philemon Holland into English in 1610. In 1597 Camden was made Clarenceux King of Arms. He died at Chislehurst after a long illness. Besides *Britannia*, his life's work, he also published *Annales* (1615).

**Camerarius, Joachim** (1500–1574) *German scholar*
Camerarius, who was born in Bamberg, was a child prodigy. He studied Greek at Leipzig, then went to Wittenberg, attracted by the reputations of Luther and Philipp MELANCHTHON; he became the latter's close friend and biographer. In 1524 he published a Latin translation of Demosthenes' first *Olynthiac Oration*; the next year his commentary on Cicero's *Tusculan Disputations* brought him into contact with ERASMUS. The wars of religion then forced him to leave Wittenberg and in 1526 Melanchthon made him professor of Greek and Latin at the new Protestant college in Nuremberg. In 1530 he attended the Diet of Augsburg and collaborated on the formulation of the AUGSBURG Confession. A moderate voice in Lutheranism, even as late as 1568 he was discussing with Emperor MAXIMILIAN II the possibility of a Catholic–Protestant rapprochement. He moved subsequently to Tübingen (1535) and to Leipzig (1541), where he died.

Camerarius was one of the leaders of the Renaissance in Germany, combining the roles of scholar, theologian, and diplomat. He made a significant contribution in many areas but his most lasting work was the many editions and translations of Greek and Latin authors he produced throughout a long working life; notable among these are his Greek editions of Ptolemy's *Tetrabiblos* (1535) and *Almagest* (1538; with Simon Grynaeus) and the first complete modern edition of the works of the Roman playwright Plautus (1552).

**Camerata, Florentine** See BARDI, COUNT GIOVANNI; FLORENCE

**Camillus of Lellis, St.** (1550–1614) *Italian priest, founder of the Servants of the Sick (Camillians)*
Born in Abruzzi, he served in the Venetian army against the Turks, lost his fortune by gambling, and was employed (1574) as a laborer by the Capuchins. He tried to join their order and the Franciscan Recollects, but was rejected owing to ill health. He became bursar of a hospital in Rome, and, under the spiritual guidance of St. PHILIP NERI, became a priest in 1584 and established a congregation of priests and lay brothers, dedicated to nursing. As superior-general of this congregation until 1607, he did much to improve hospital methods and hygiene and to provide proper nursing and spiritual care for the dying. The Camillians won papal approval in 1586, and Camillus himself was canonized in 1746.

**Caminha, Pero Vaz de** (c. 1449–1500) *Portuguese traveler*
Caminha was born and lived most of his life in Oporto, where from 1476 he held the post of master of the mint. In 1500 he sailed with CABRAL's fleet for India in the capacity of a writer. His letter (*Carta*) reporting to King Manuel I on the Tupinamba Indians of "Vera Cruz" (Brazil) is an accomplished and classic piece of encounter literature. The discovery was considered so significant that Cabral dispatched a ship back to Portugal with it, though it remained unpublished until 1817. Caminha died at Calicut, on the Malabar coast of India, in December 1500.

**Camões, Luís Vaz de** (1524–1580) *Portuguese poet*
Many details of Camões's life are based on guesswork. Born in Lisbon, he appears to have been one of the old Galician aristocracy, impoverished but with prominent connections. He may have been educated at Coimbra: his work indicates a thorough classical education. He was at the court of John III in Lisbon in 1544. His love for a lady-in-waiting, Caterina de Ataide (called "Natercia" in his lyrics), was opposed by her family, who forced his withdrawal from the court. About this time he was writing lyrics and three plays, two in the native tradition of Gil VICENTE (*El Rei Seleuco, Filodemo*) and a comedy in the manner of the Roman playwright Plautus (*Enfatriões*). After taking part in an expedition to Morocco, where he lost an eye in battle, he returned to Lisbon in an unsuccessful attempt to regain royal favor. In 1553 John III pardoned him for being involved in a street brawl in which a minor palace official died; the pardon contains hints that Camões was to go to India in the service of the Crown. He was in the East until 1570, where he experienced shipwreck and the other common dangers faced by Portuguese adventurers of the time. He completed his masterpiece, *Os Lusíadas* (THE LUSIAD; 1572), soon after returning to Lisbon and was granted a small pension by King Sebastian for

his services in India. He died in poverty in an epidemic in Lisbon.

Although Camões was perhaps the greatest lyric poet of the Iberian peninsula and a master of the main Renaissance lyric forms (sonnets, odes, *canzone* [*canções*], eclogues, and elegies), virtually all of his non-epic poetry was published posthumously (1595; an expanded edition, *Rimas*, appeared in 1598). These early editions contained a number of unauthentic poems and only since the 1930s have there been attempts at critical editions of his complete works.

**Campagnola, Giulio** (c. 1482–c. 1518) *Italian engraver*
Born in Padua, Campagnola trained under Andrea MANTEGNA and by 1499 was executing work for the Ferrarese ducal court. His copies of works by DÜRER popularized the latter throughout Italy, while his own technique anticipated later schools of engraving. He was also much influenced by GIORGIONE and engraved several prints after his paintings. By 1509 Campagnola was working in Venice; his pupils included his adopted son Domenico Campagnola (c. 1484–c. 1563), also an engraver, who painted frescoes in the Sinola del Carmine, Padua (1520) and produced fine drawings of landscapes.

**Campana, Pedro de** (Pieter de Kempeneer) (1503–1580) *Flemish artist*
Although he was born in Brussels, Campana spent considerable time in Italy, where he worked at Bologna, Venice, and elsewhere. By 1537 he had moved to Seville. There he executed religious paintings for the cathedral, notably the *Descent from the Cross* (1547) and the *Group of Donors* (1555), which were typical of his many religious works in a broadly mannerist style (*see* MANNERISM). Having done much to popularize Italian ideals in Andalusia, Campana returned to Brussels where he ran a tapestry factory and was also active as a tapestry designer.

**Campanella, Tommaso** (1568–1639) *Italian philosopher*
Campanella was born at Silo, Calabria. Like BRUNO, he began his career by joining the Dominican Order (1582). After various quarrels with the authorities in Naples, Padua, and Rome, Campanella returned to his native Calabria to play a leading role in the revolt against Spanish rule. The revolt quickly collapsed and in 1599 Campanella found himself imprisoned in Naples. After undergoing repeated torture he was finally released in 1626. He spent the rest of his life based in Rome and, from 1634, Paris. During his prolonged imprisonment Campanella produced many books and poems. Best known is his utopian fantasy, *La città del sole* (The City of the Sun), written about 1602 but first published at Frankfurt in a Latin version, *Civitas solis*, in 1623. In the City of the Sun the "Solarians" regulate their lives by astrological principles; hermetic influences are also identifiable among them, and

they admire COPERNICUS and consider Aristotle to be a pedant. Campanella also wrote an *Apologia pro Galileo* (1622) and *De sensu rerum et magia* (1620), both of which had also to be published by his disciple Tobias Adami at Frankfurt.

**Further reading:** John M. Headley, *Tommaso Campanella and the Transformation of the World* (Princeton, N.J.: Princeton University Press, 1997).

*campanilismo* The sense of civic pride and identity felt by the citizens of the Italian city-states. The term derives from *campanile* (bell tower), a prominent feature of every town, however small, the bell of which would mark ordinary daily events or summon or warn the citizens in times of crisis.

**Campi family** *Italian painters from Cremona*
Galeazzo Campi (c. 1477–1536) was strongly influenced by BOCCACCINO, and examples of his work survive in the Cremonese churches of San Sigismondo and Sant' Agostino. Galeazzo's son Giulio (c. 1500–72) was influenced by GIULIO ROMANO and by PORDENONE and worked with his brother Antonio (c. 1535–c. 1591) on the frescoes in San Sigismondo, in which is preserved the most important of his works, *The Madonna appearing to Francesco and Bianca Sforza* (1540); it was in honor of their marriage (1441) that the present church of San Sigismondo was begun in 1463. Giulio also painted frescoes of the life of St. Agatha for the church of Sant' Agata, Cremona. A *Pietà with Saints* (1566) by Antonio is in the cathedral at Cremona and both Giulio and Antonio are represented by works in San Paolo Converso, Milan. Antonio also wrote a history of Cremona (1585), which he illustrated with his own engravings. The third of Galeazzo's sons, Vincenzo (1536–91), specialized in portraits with still lifes; typical of his output is the realistic *Woman with Fruit* (Brera, Milan). A cousin, Bernardino (c. 1522–c. 1592), also worked on San Sigismondo (1570); his works hint at the elegant manneristic style of CORREGGIO. A *Pietà* by Bernardino is in the Louvre, Paris.

**Campin, Robert** (1379–1444) *Netherlands painter*
Campin is now generally thought to be identical with the socalled Master of Flémalle, the painter of panels depicting St. Veronica and the Virgin (1430–35; Städelesches Kunstinstitut, Frankfurt) that were thought to come from Flémalle, near Liège. He was born at Valenciennes and is recorded as a master at Tournai (now in Belgium) in 1406, becoming a citizen of the town in 1410. There his most famous pupil was Rogier van der WEYDEN in the late 1420s.

Campin is considered one of the great innovators of the early Netherlandish school as he moved from the decorative but flat stylization of International Gothic to a mode in which realism and perspective played a more significant role. The triptych known as the Mérode altarpiece

(c. 1428; Metropolitan Museum, New York) shows the Annunciation taking place in a pleasantly furnished bourgeois room; the townscape visible through the window behind St. Joseph on the right wing has a faltering approach to perspective, which is more deftly handled in the *Nativity* (c. 1430; Dijon). A *Virgin in Glory with Saints* (1430–35; Musée Granet, Aix-en-Provence), the Werl altarpiece wings (1438; Prado, Madrid), and portraits of a man and a woman (1430–35; National Gallery, London) are among his later works. He is often compared with his greater contemporary, Jan van EYCK.

**Campion, Edmund** (1540–1581) *English Jesuit*
Born in London, the son of a bookseller, Campion went to Oxford where he enjoyed a distinguished career. He was ordained a deacon in the Church of England (1569) but his sympathies already lay with Roman Catholicism and he left Oxford for Dublin. In 1571 he went to DOUAI where he was received into the Catholic Church, before moving on to Rome, where he joined the JESUITS (1573). After his ordination (1578) he spent time in Bohemia before joining forces with Robert PARSONS to undertake the mission to reconvert England. His preaching in London and the recusant stronghold of Lancashire (*see* RECUSANCY) was enthusiastically received, and in 1581 he wrote *Decem rationes* (1581) challenging a Protestant–Catholic debate. The same year he was arrested, charged with conspiracy, tortured, and executed at Tyburn. He was canonized in 1970.

*cancionero* (Portuguese *cancioneiro*) In Iberian poetry, a verse anthology of songs and lyrics, usually of a particular era or school of poets, but also of individuals (those of Jorge MANRIQUE and Juan del ENCINA, for example). The earliest anthologies are 13th century, the oldest being *El cancioneiro de Ajuda* of King Dinis of Portugal (1259–1325), a collection of Portuguese verse in the troubadour tradition of Provence. Other Gallego-Portuguese anthologies contain written versions of Galician folksongs. Major *cancioneros* are those of Juan Alfonso de BAENA (1445) and the *Cancionero de Stúñiga* (named after the first poet to appear in it, Lope de Stúñiga (c. 1407–c. 1477)), which contains works chiefly from the court of Alfonso I of Naples (1443–58). The largest, the *Cancionero general* (1511), compiled by Hernando del Castillo, contains about 1000 poems by over 100 poets living from the reign of John II (1406–54) onwards. A similar Portuguese anthology is the *Cancioneiro geral de Resende* (1516), containing verses by 286 courtly poets of the late 15th and early 16th centuries writing in Spanish as well as Portuguese.

**Candia** The Venetian name for the largest city on the island of Crete, and, by extension, the name by which the whole island was commonly known in the Middle Ages. The word is a corruption of the Arabic name "Khandak," which refers to the great ditch that encompasses the ancient town. The Venetians took control of Crete in 1210 and subsequently made the town of Candia their capital and one of the major seaports in the eastern Mediterranean, fortifying it with walls, bastions, and gates. The military architect SANMICHELI was put in charge of the work there in 1538. After a great siege (1648–69) the town fell to the Turks. It was renamed Herakleion in 1898.

**Candida, Giovanni** (active c. 1475–c. 1504) *Italian medalist, diplomat, and author*
Candida was possibly born at Naples, but by 1475 was a secretary at the Burgundian court. In 1477 he was resident at Bruges, and between 1482 and 1483 he entered the service of Louis XI of France. He wrote a short Latin history of France for Louis' successor, Charles VIII, and by 1491 was a royal counselor on the first of several diplomatic missions to Italy. Candida's style is Italianate and was probably learned in his youth from Mantuan and Florentine medalists. His portrait medals include likenesses of Maximilian of Austria and Mary of Burgundy, the young Francis I of France, and numerous French and Italian statesmen. A fine medalist, Candida had a delicate style and considerable powers of characterization, but his primary art-historical significance is as a forerunner of the Italian artists who worked in France during the early 16th century (*see* FONTAINEBLEAU).

**Candido, Pietro** See WITTE, PIETER DE

**Cane, Facino** (c. 1350–1412) *Italian mercenary soldier*
A Piedmontese by birth, Cane led mercenary forces there and in Savoy from his youth up and established a reputation as a ruthless and efficient condottiere. The Genoese gave him a major command in 1394, and in 1397 he entered the employ of the VISCONTI FAMILY of Milan. By the death of Giangaleazzo (1402) he had become such a powerful figure in Milanese affairs that the new duke, the incompetent Giovanni Maria, relied for his position upon Cane's continuing support. Had it not been for his death, it is probable that Cane would have ousted the Visconti line from Milan. One of Duke Filippo Maria's first acts on succeeding his brother in 1412 was to establish his position by marrying Cane's widow, Beatrice, whom he later had put to death on a trumped-up charge of adultery (1418).

**Cangrande** See DANTE ALIGHIERI; DELLA SCALA FAMILY

**cannon** A large gun fired from a carriage or fixed platform. The first undisputed references to cannon date from the early 14th century. Using skills gained in the manufacture of bells, the earliest cannon were cast from bronze and muzzle-loaded. Such weapons, however, proved to be too expensive, too difficult to make, and too easily worn away, to be completely successful. Consequently, they were soon superseded by larger, more durable, wrought-iron models, forged from strips of iron and secured with hooped rings. These were replaced by cast-iron cannon which began to appear in the early 16th century. Although normally quite small, weighing no more than a few hundred pounds, giants like the 15th-century 12-ton Mons Meg (Edinburgh Castle) were occasionally constructed. Technology imported from the West was used to devastating effect by the Ottoman Turks in the final assault on the land walls of Constantinople in 1453 and later deployed by the Turks against the cities and castles of southeastern Europe, as in the 1529 siege of Vienna. Light artillery mounted on wagons became a feature of warfare all over Europe.from the mid-15th century, used both to batter enemy fortifications and against enemy troops in the field.

See also: ARTILLERY; FORTIFICATION

**Cano, Juan Sebastián del** (died 1526) *Spanish navigator*
Born at Guetaria, on the Bay of Biscay, Cano commanded the *Vittoria*, one of the five ships that participated in MAGELLAN's celebrated voyage. The expedition set sail in 1519, and when Magellan was killed (1521), Cano became commander of the fleet. After visiting the Moluccas, Cano returned to Spain, landing at Seville on September 8, 1522. He was accordingly heralded as the first circumnavigator of the world, and was rewarded by the king with an engraved globe and a pension. In 1526 Cano left on another expedition to the Moluccas, but died at sea on August 4.

**Cano, Melchior** (1509–1560) *Spanish theologian*
In 1523 he became a Dominican friar at Salamanca. He taught at Valladolid from 1533, and in 1543 became the first professor of theology at Alcalá. He defended Philip II in his political conflict with the papacy, and when in 1557 he was chosen as provincial of his order papal conformation of his appointment was long delayed. His doctrine of marriage, that the priestly blessing was the essential form of the sacrament, was controversial. His *De locis theologicis*, his principal work, was published in 1563.

**Capnion** See REUCHLIN, JOHANN

**Capponi family** A wealthy and influential Florentine family, established in the city from 1210. Although Gino (1350–1421) supported the ALBIZZI, Neri (1388–1475) was a prominent supporter of the MEDICI. Piero (1447–96) was employed as an ambassador by Lorenzo the Magnificent, but after the latter's death (1492) joined the anti-Medicean party, becoming head of the republic set up in Florence on the expulsion of Piero de' Medici in 1494. His defiance of CHARLES VIII of France in 1494 is famous; the French king, backed by 12,000 troops, issued an ultimatum which Capponi tore up in his face, and when Charles said menacingly, "Then we shall sound our trumpets," Capponi retorted, "And we shall ring our bells" (i.e. summon the citizens to fight in the streets). The king backed off. Unluckily for the Florentine republic, Capponi was soon afterwards killed fighting in the ill-starred war against the Pisans.

During the second Medicean expulsion, Niccolò di Piero (died 1529) was twice elected *gonfaloniere* (1527, 1528) but he was forced to resign when his attempts to make peace with the Medicean pope Clement VII were construed as high treason. After the restoration of the Medici (1530) many of the family were forced into exile.

**Capra, Villa** See ROTONDA, VILLA

**Capuchins** A branch of the Franciscans founded in the 1520s by Matteo di Bassi of Urbino, who wished to return to the original austerity of the Franciscan rule. The habit, based on St. Francis's own garb, includes the pointed cowl (*capuche*) that gives the order its name. Despite initial disapproval from other Franciscans, the Capuchin rule was established in 1529 and their preaching and missionary zeal made them valued agents of the COUNTER-REFORMATION. In 1619 they were recognized as an independent order, by which time they had spread all over Europe.

**Caravaggio, Michelangelo Merisi da** (1573–1610)
*Italian painter*
Born at Caravaggio, near Bergamo, he was trained in Milan by an undistinguished mannerist and was influenced by contact with the works of Venetian painters. He was in Rome by 1592, where his tempestuous nature led to trouble with the police, and his refusal to adopt the method favored in central Italy of careful preparation prior to painting caused controversy. Until his fortunes improved in 1597 he or she lived in poverty, painting still lifes and portraits and working for other painters; in that year the influence of Cardinal del Monte, who admired and bought his work, lead to a commission to decorate the chapel of San Luigi dei Francesi. Much of this work was subsequently rejected by the clergy on grounds of indecorum or theological error before it was finally finished in 1602. The same difficulties arose with his work in Sta. Maria del Popolo (1600–01). In fact opinion about his work was sharply divided: paintings that were angrily rejected by some clergy were eagerly bought by cardinals and noblemen who admired them. The reason was Caravaggio's scorn for traditional idealized representations of religious subjects and his insistence on naturalism together with dramatic use of chiaroscuro. Paintings such as the *Madonna di Loreto* (Sant' Agostino, Rome) and the *Death of the Virgin* (Louvre, Paris) introduced sweat and dirt into religious art, and the bloated corpse of the dead Virgin is said to have been painted from that of a drowned prostitute.

Caravaggio's personal life also remained stormy: in 1603 he was involved in a libel action by Giovanni Baglioni, who later became his biographer, and in 1606 he had to leave Rome after stabbing his opponent during a game of tennis. He fled to Naples and in 1607 to Malta where he was made a knight by the grand master of the KNIGHTS HOSPITALER, whose portrait he painted. However, after assaulting a judiciary he was imprisoned in 1608 but escaped to Sicily, pursued by agents of the knights. In 1609 he was wounded in a tavern brawl in Naples and he died of malaria the following year at age 37 while on his way back to Rome where friends were attempting to arrange a pardon for him. The paintings produced in Naples, Malta, and Sicily showed an even greater economy of style than those of his Rome period. They were dark pictures with little color and had an intense stillness new to his work. Caravaggio's work, produced in such a short time, inspired the Caravaggisti school in Spain and had a strong influence on the development of baroque painting.

**Further reading:** Howard Hibbard, *Caravaggio* (New York: Harper & Row and London: Thames & Hudson, 1983); John T. Spike *et al*, *Caravaggio* (New York: Abbeville, 2001).

**Caravaggio, Polidoro Caldara da** See POLIDORO CALDARA DA CARAVAGGIO

**caravel** (*carvel*, Portuguese *caravela*) A type of small, lateen-rigged, two- or three-masted sailing ship developed in southern Europe and used on the epic voyages of discovery in the 15th and 16th centuries. The name is asso-

**Caravel** A Portuguese caravel (c. 1450). This little ship took part in many of the voyages of exploration in the 15th century. Its lateen sails, based on Arab nautical prowess, enabled it to sail against the wind.

ciated with the method of construction, in which the ship-builder first sets up the frame of the ship and then attaches the planking to the frame (as opposed to the northern technique of clinker-building, in which ships have their planking nailed together first and the frame inserted afterward). The caravel as developed by the Portuguese from around 1430 had a high degree of maneuverability.

**Girolamo Cardano** A woodcut from his *Practica arithmetica et mensurandi singularis* (1539), one of the most influential 16th-century studies of arithmetic.

## Cardano, Girolamo (1501–1576) *Italian physician and mathematician*

Born at Pavia, the illegitimate son of a Milanese lawyer, Cardano was educated at the universities of Pavia and Padua. After practicing and teaching medicine in Milan and Pavia (1524–50), he spent some time traveling in France and Britain. While in London in 1552 he demonstrated his astrological skill by predicting that the ailing EDWARD VI would have a long life (he actually died in 1553 at the age of 16). On his return to Italy he held chairs of medicine in Milan, Pavia, Bologna, and Rome. Despite his conflict with TARTAGLIA, Cardano was a mathematician of considerable originality. His *Ars magna* (1545) is recognized as the first modern algebra text, while he was also one of the earliest writers to tackle problems in probability theory. Among his many books, the best known are the encyclopedic *De subtilitate* (1550) on the natural sciences,

augmented and supplemented by *De varietate rerum* (1557), and the dramatic and revealing account of his life, *De vita propria liber* (1643; translated as *The Book of My Life*, 1931).

## Cariani, Giovanni Busi (1485/90–c. 1547) *Italian painter*

Cariani was born near Bergamo and became a pupil of Gentile Bellini. He worked mainly in Venice, initially in the style of his teacher and those of the great Venetian masters GIORGIONE, TITIAN, and PALMA VECCHIO, with the result that a number of pictures attributed to these masters are now thought by some to be his work. An example is the two heads in the Louvre, Paris, supposedly by Bellini. Cariani's first and last recorded paintings (1514 and 1541) are both lost, but some of his portraits and religious paintings have survived, as well as fragments of frescoes in Bergamo.

## Carlo Emanuele I (1562–1630) *Duke of Savoy (1580–1630)*

The son of Emanuel Philibert (*see* SAVOY, HOUSE OF), Carlo Emanuele pursued his father's ambitions to make Savoy a major Italian power and involved the duchy in frequent wars. He annexed some territory, but constant warfare strained the duchy's finances; among other enterprises, he took advantage of the conflict between France and Spain to make some gains for Savoy, but then failed in his attack on Geneva (1602). Carlo Emanuele promoted commercial development and made his court at Turin a center of culture.

## Carlstadt, Andreas (Andreas von Bodenstein) (c. 1480–1541) *Academic, preacher, and radical reformist, born in Carlstadt, Bavaria*

He was awarded a theology doctorate at WITTENBERG in 1510 but excommunicated in 1520. His reputation for innovation was sealed on Christmas Day 1521, when he celebrated a vernacular Mass. He pressed for greater reform than that favored by his sometimes friend, sometimes opponent, LUTHER, campaigning against traditional Catholic predilections for iconography, infant baptism, ostentatious vestments, the existence of Purgatory, and priestly celibacy. For Carlstadt, the communion rite was merely a symbolic remembrance. Frequently harassed by political authorities, he spent his last years in effective asylum in Switzerland.

## Carmelites, Reform of the

The movement, originating in Spain, to restore the "primitive rule" in the houses of the Order of Our Lady of Mount Carmel. By the mid-16th century, the Carmelite friars and sisters had largely departed from the original austerity prescribed for the order in 1209, some 50 years after its foundation. In 1562 St. TERESA founded a small enclosed community of nuns at

Ávila, dedicated to a stricter observance of the rule of the order. In 1568 St. JOHN OF THE CROSS founded the first community of reformed Carmelite friars at Duruelo, and the movement gradually spread. The Discalced Carmelites (as they were called because they wore sandals instead of shoes to symbolize the austerity of their regime) were poor, held no property as individuals, had no contact with the secular world, and led ascetic lives of prayer and contemplation. They encountered much opposition, particularly from those within the order who continued to follow the "mitigated rule," but in 1579 a separate province of the reformed Carmelites was constituted, and in 1593 they were confirmed as a distinct order by papal ordinance.

## Caro, Annibale (1507–1566) Italian scholar, poet, and translator

Caro was born at Civitanova Marche, near Ancona, and studied in Florence, where he was a friend of Benedetto VARCHI. After living for a time at the court of Naples, he became secretary to Duke Pierluigi Farnese and, after Pierluigi's murder (1547), to Cardinal Alessandro Farnese. A thoroughly professional man of letters, Caro wrote a comedy in prose, *Gli straccioni* (The ragamuffins; 1554), which combined classical influence with characters based on real persons in the Rome of Caro's day, a collection of Petrarchan poems entitled *Rime* (1557), and satirical sonnets. His quarrel with Ludovico CASTELVETRO, who had criticized one of his poems, resulted in Castelvetro's fleeing into exile after Caro had accused him of having Lutheran sympathies. Two works, published posthumously, firmly established Caro's reputation among future generations: *Lettere familiari* (1573, 1575), a collection of 1000 letters, rhetorical in style and modeled on PETRARCH's; and the *Eneide* (1581), a blank-verse translation of Virgil's *Aeneid* which exercised an influence on Italian verse up to the 19th century.

## Carpaccio, Vittore (c. 1457–c. 1526) Italian painter

A native of Venice, Carpaccio was probably taught by Lazzaro Bastiano (c. 1425–1512), by whom he was profoundly influenced, and also absorbed many features of the works of Gentile BELLINI and ANTONELLO DA MESSINA. Although his career is poorly documented, Carpaccio was noted for his narrative skill and psychological insight and was commissioned by the Venetian confraternities (*scuole*) to execute several major cycles of large paintings, notably the nine pictures in *The Legend of St. Ursula* (1490–95; Accademia, Venice), which was commissioned by the Scuola di Sant'Orsola. His cycle of nine *Scenes from the Lives of St. George and Other Saints* (1502–07; also Accademia, Venice), painted for the Scuola di San Giorgio degli Schiavone, represents his mature style and accurate observation of naturalistic detail. Subsequent cycles of scenes from the lives of the Virgin (c. 1504) and St. Stephen (1511–20) are now scattered. Other works include an un-

dated painting of *Courtesans* (Museo Correr, Venice), the altarpiece of the *Presentation of Christ in the Temple* (1510; Accademia, Venice), and his last dated works, the two organ shutters for the Duomo at Capodistria (1523). Much admired in the 19th century by John Ruskin and others, Carpaccio was also one of the first artists to execute notable townscapes, which have documentary value in depicting the life of contemporary Venice.

## Carpi, Girolamo da (1501–1556) Italian painter

A pupil of Benvenuto Garofolo in his native Ferrara, Carpi also visited Parma and Modena where he studied and made copies of the works of CORREGGIO and PARMIGIANINO. He undertook commissions for portraits and produced original compositions for churches in Bologna and Ferrara, including three pictures in the cathedral in Ferrara. He painted for a time in Rome and some of his work, for example the *Adoration of the Magi* for San Martino Maggiore in Bologna, shows the influence of the Roman style. His Roman sketchbook shows his interest in antique decorative motifs. He died in Ferrara.

## Carracci, Annibale (1560–1609) Italian painter

The most gifted member of the Carracci family of Bologna, he trained as a fresco painter with his brother Agostino (1557–1602) and his cousin Lodovico in his native city. On study trips to Parma and Venice he admired the works of CORREGGIO and TITIAN. His earliest surviving pictures are genre paintings, such as *The Butcher's Shop* (c. 1582; Christ Church, Oxford) and caricature drawings. Monumental compositions were what he came to excel at, and he painted a number of large altarpieces. In 1585 the Carracci founded an academy called the Incamminati in Bologna, the teaching at which aimed to revive the canons of classical art; it played an important part in the development of a classical baroque style.

In 1595 Carracci was invited to Rome by Cardinal Odoardo Farnese to decorate the ceiling of the Camerino in the Palazzo Farnese with frescoes on classical themes. Two years later he began a larger work, which is considered to rank with MICHELANGELO's Sistine ceiling and RAPHAEL's decorations in the Vatican and Farnesina, from both of which Carracci drew inspiration. This was the decoration of the ceiling of the Galleria Farnese in the Palazzo Farnese on the theme of *The Loves of the Gods*, a series of pictures within an illusionistic framework of architecture and gilt frames that required over 1000 preparatory drawings. It was completed in 1604. His easel paintings at this time consisted of landscapes and history paintings such as *Domine, Quo Vadis?* (c. 1602; National Gallery, London). This, like many of his pictures, in notable for its powerful use of gesture. The language of gesture in painting owes much to Carracci, as does the ideal classical landscape used by later artists such as Nicolas Poussin. In 1605 Carracci became ill with what was described as MELANCHOLIA and he painted very little during the last five years of his life.

## Carracci, Lodovico (1555–1619) *Italian painter*
Though less gifted than his younger cousin Annibale CARRACCI, Lodovico was the dominant figure during their early partnership in their native Bologna. With the brothers Annibale and Agostino, Lodovico decorated the Fava, Magnani, and Sampieri palaces in Bologna in the 1580s and early 1590s, and with them founded a teaching academy there in 1585. This academy was run by him alone after his cousins left for Rome (1595) and was responsible for training most of the next generation of Bolognese painters including Domenichino, Il Guercino, and Guido Reni. Lodovico's best paintings were produced during the 10 years before he and his cousins parted company. They are remarkable for their forceful emotional expression.

## Cartier, Jacques (1491–1557) *French navigator, discoverer of the St. Lawrence River*
Born at St.-Malo, Cartier was commissioned by King Francis I to find a NORTHWEST PASSAGE to the Orient, and in 1534 he sailed with two ships and 61 men. He followed the coast of Newfoundland and established friendly relations with the Huron-Iroquois, by whose word for village, "Canada," he named the territory. Cartier returned to France for the winter, but went back to Canada in 1535. He landed at the bay of St. Lawrence on August 9, then navigated the river as far as the site of Montreal. Inspired by tales of an enchanted land north of Mexico, Cartier then decided to explore the Ottawa River, but before doing this he returned to France with 12 native American elders to convince a skeptical Francis I. In spring 1541 Cartier left St.-Malo with five vessels, and from his camp at Cap Rouge, he navigated the Ottawa. He returned to France with many mineral samples but these were found to be worthless. Consequently, Cartier fell from royal favor, and the French lost interest in Canada. The true value of Cartier's work was not realized until the French opted to develop their Canadian territory.

## cartography
The science of maps, charts, and globes. As the golden age of discovery, the Renaissance is the period in which cartography became established and flourished. New discoveries led to maps becoming more detailed and accurate; consequently, cartography became of greater use to EXPLORATION, and mutual development was promoted. Early Renaissance cartography was based on the work of the second-century Greek geographer Ptolemy, whose *Geographica* (first printed edition with maps, 1477) was the first-ever atlas (although the term "atlas" was not widely used until MERCATOR popularized it). The so-called T-O world maps of the medieval period persisted in early Renaissance publications. In 1492 the Nuremberg merchant Martin Behaim made a globe that still survives and so introduced a new dimension into cartography. Fra Mauro had portrayed the world in circular form as early as 1459 (*see* CAMALDOLESE CHART).

In the late 15th and early 16th centuries, the Portuguese made best practical use of the development of cartography. Their Casa du India provided information for many explorers and merchants, and the maps (1520) of Garcia de Toreno were vital to MAGELLAN's circumnavigation of the world. The Portuguese had enough confidence in their cartographers deliberately to misplace certain territories within areas granted to them under the Treaty of TORDESILLAS. The Italians and Germans continued to develop Ptolemy's ideas. In 1507 Martin Waldseemüller showed America as a separate continent for the first time (*see* VESPUCCI, AMERIGO). Some years later Johann Schöner popularized globes.

Between 1460 and 1540 German cartographers, such as Sebastian MÜNSTER and Philipp APIAN, revolutionized the instruments of the trade and cartography developed as a science. GEMMA FRISIUS used a planimetrum, Waldsmeemüller developed the polymetrum (an early form of theodolite), and Philipp Apian's map of Bavaria (1579) introduced grid references. The most important individual was Gerardus Mercator, inventor of the Mercator projection; this rectangular format for maps is still in common use. Using copperplate printing, which began to supersede the old woodcut technique around 1550, Mercator combined Ptolemy's data with technological developments to produce maps of unprecedented accuracy and proportion. Mercator's world map (1569) is the first example of his projection.

In 1579 Christopher SAXTON produced an atlas of England, the first ever national atlas. Maurice Bouguereau published the French counterpart, *Le Theatre Françoys*, in 1594. By 1620 most leading European nations boasted comprehensive geographies and atlases.

**Further reading:** Leo Bagrow and Robert W. Karrow Jr, *Mapmakers of the Sixteenth Century and Their Maps* (Chicago, Ill.: Speculum Orbis Press, 1993); Jerry Brotton, *Trading Territories: Mapping the Early Modern World* (Ithaca, N.Y.: Cornell University Press, 1998); David Buisseret, *The Mapmakers' Quest: Depicting New Worlds in Renaissance Europe* (Oxford, U.K.: Oxford University Press, 2003); Francesc Relaño, *The Shaping of Africa: Cosmographic Discourse and Cartographic Science in Late Medieval and Early Modern Europe* (Aldershot, U.K.: Ashgate, 2001); Kees Zandvliet, *Mapping for Money: Maps, Plans and Topographic Paintings and Their Role in Dutch Overseas Expansion in the 16th and 17th Centuries* (Amsterdam, Netherlands: Batavian Lion International, 1998).

## Casa, Giovanni della See DELLA CASA, GIOVANNI

## Casaubon, Isaac (1559–1614) *French classical scholar*
His Protestant family were refugees from the French reli-

gious wars, and Casaubon was born in Geneva. He was taught by his father until at age 20 he began intensive Greek studies in Geneva. His second wife was one of the printer Henry ESTIENNE's daughters. After lecturing in Geneva and Montpellier he was invited (1599) by HENRY IV to Paris, where his first official position was sub-librarian in the royal library. After Henry's murder (1610) Casaubon, declining to become a Catholic, came to England at the invitation of Richard Bancroft, Archbishop of Canterbury. He was enthusiastically received and at his death was buried in Westminster Abbey. Casaubon lacked extraordinary critical insight or linguistic knowledge but he had an enormous capacity for work and a desire to gain exhaustive understanding of the ancient world. The classical texts on which he wrote commentaries were well off the beaten track of scholarship, for example, Athenaeus (1600) and Strabo (1587). His massive commentary on Persius's *Satires* (1605) was prefaced by a study of Greek and Roman satirical poetry which was the first specialized work on a problem of ancient literary history.

**Cassander, Georg** (1513–1566) *Netherlands theologian and humanist*
After early study in his native Bruges and at Ghent, Cassander went to Cologne with the intention of finding some means of reconciling the orthodox Catholic and reforming positions. In 1561 he published anonymously *De officio pii ac publicae tranquillitatis…in hoc religionis dissidio* (On the duty of pious and public peace…in the present dispute of religion). This volume involved him in fierce controversy; he found his moderate line attacked by the extremists on both sides, but he gained support from those who saw the importance of compromise as a means to unity. As well as his voluminous theological writings Cassander produced treatises on antiquarian subjects. His eagerness for unity sometimes led him to adopt views that were doctrinally suspect but he remained faithful to the authority of the Church. He died at Cologne.

*cassoni* Wooden chests used in Italy in the Renaissance period for domestic storage of garments, documents, and valuables. Pairs of *cassoni* were made for bridal trousseaux, with one bearing the husband's armorial and the other that of the bride. Early examples have painted panels depicting Roman triumphs and battles, and, in northern Italy, religious subjects. Others had gilded carving and intarsia decoration. Mannerist influences later introduced carved and polished wood versions of antique sarcophagi on lion-paw supports. A variant on the *cassone* was the *casapanca*, to which a back and arms were added, enabling the piece to double as a storage chest and a seat. Being heirlooms, many *cassoni* survive.

**Castagno, Andrea del** See ANDREA DEL CASTAGNO

**Castellio, Sebastian** (Sebastien Châteillon) (1515–1563) *Savoyard teacher and translator*
Born at St.-Martin de Fresne, near Nantua, Castellio was educated at Lyons and kept a school for young gentlemen there. After reading CALVIN's *Institutio* he went to Strasbourg in 1540, met the author, and was converted to the reformed religion. He was appointed rector of the college at Geneva, but his humanism later brought him into conflict with Calvin. In 1552 he was appointed professor of Greek at Basle. He deplored Calvin's execution of SERVETUS for heresy (1553) and broke entirely with Calvin and BEZA after the publication of his tolerant tract concerning heretics in 1554. Castellio's Latin Bible, a version noted for its classical elegance, appeared between 1546 and 1551, and a French version came out in 1555. He was also a translator of Greek and Latin classics. His work on PREDESTINATION was not published until 1578 and his answer to Calvin's criticisms only appeared in 1612.

**Castelvetro, Lodovico** (1505–1571) *Italian scholar and critic*
Born in Modena, Castelvetro became one of the leading linguists of his day. His grasp of the historical evolution of Italian is demonstrated in his *Giunta fatta al Ragionamento di Messer Pietro Bembo* (1563) and in his commentaries on Petrarch's *Rime* and on the first part of Dante's *Inferno*. He also translated and wrote an influential commentary (1570) on Aristotle's *Poetics*. From 1560 he spent some years in exile after the Inquisition had condemned him for doctrinal irregularities, and he died at Chiavenna, north of Lake Como.

**Castiglione, Baldassare** (1478–1529) *Italian writer and courtier*
Born at Casatico, near Mantua, to minor landed gentry traditionally serving the dukes of Mantua, Castiglione was sent to Milan, where he acquired a fundamental education in the skills of a courtier under Duke Lodovico Sforza, "il Moro." After a brief stay at Mantua (1500–04), he entered the service of Guidobaldo da Montefeltro, Duke of Urbino, and his successor Francesco Maria DELLA ROVERE.

Guidobaldo, a distinguished soldier and statesman, scholar, patron of humanists and artists, collector, and connoisseur, epitomized the ideal ruler, and Castiglione's years at Urbino, the setting of his major work THE COURTIER, were the happiest of his life. As Urbino's representative in Rome, Castiglione met leading humanists and formed a friendship with Raphael. After the fall of Francesco della Rovere in 1515, Castiglione returned to Mantua. Following the death of his wife in 1520 he was ordained and in 1524 he was appointed papal nuncio to the court of Charles V in Spain. His final years were apparently lonely and especially troubled by the imperial sack of Rome (1527). He was made bishop of Ávila in

1528, the year *The Courtier* was published, and died in Toledo.

**Further reading:** Robert W. Hanning and David Rosand (eds), *Castiglione: The Ideal and the Real in Renaissance Culture* (New Haven, Conn.: Yale University Press, 1983); Christine Raffini, *Marsilio Ficino, Pietro Bembo, Baldassare Castiglione: Philosophical, Aesthetic, and Political Approaches in Renaissance Platonism* (New York: Peter Lang, 1998).

**Catalan Atlas** A set of manuscript charts created in 1375 in Majorca by Abraham Cresques for Charles V of France. The collection of beautifully decorated charts is in the PORTOLAN style and contains the first major portolan of an area outside Europe. The Catalan Atlas is distinguished by the first fairly accurate maps of China, India, and Africa, and contains a large quantity of information about inland Europe and its navigable waterways.

**Cateau-Cambrésis, Peace of** (April 3, 1559) A treaty principally between HENRY II of France and PHILIP II of Spain, ending more than 60 years of conflict between France and Spain. France restored Savoy-Piedmont to Emanuel Philibert of Savoy and Corsica to Genoa. Henry II renounced his claim to Milan and accepted Spanish domination of Italy. France gained some fortresses and the bishoprics of Toul, Metz, and Verdun. England had to accept the French reconquest of Calais. The treaty marked the end of dynastic struggles and paved the way for religious wars.

**Catena, Vincenzo di Biagio** (c. 1470–1531) *Italian painter*
Catena was born into a patrician Venetian family and was influenced by fellow-members of the VENETIAN SCHOOL, at first CIMA DA CONEGLIANO and Giovanni BELLINI and later TITIAN and GIORGIONE. Many of Catena's paintings are *sacre conversazioni*. He was a friend of Giorgione, whose influence can particularly be seen in the delightful *Holy Family with a Kneeling Knight* (National Gallery, London) and *The Vision of St. Christina* (1520; Sta. Maria Mater Domini, Venice). Among the eminent people who sat to him for a portrait was the poet Giangiorgio Trissino.

**Catherine de' Medici** (Catherine de Médicis) (1519–1589) *Queen consort of France*
The daughter of Lorenzo de' Medici (died 1519), duke of Urbino, she married the future HENRY II in 1533. Artistic and energetic, Catherine designed the TUILERIES in Paris and the Château de CHENONCEAUX; she made a great impression on the French court, despite Henry's attachment to DIANE DE POITIERS. After the death of her son Francis II (king 1559–60), she triumphed over the extremist GUISE faction, obtaining the regency of her next son, Charles IX (king 1560–74). The failure of initial attempts to reach a

religious compromise increasingly involved Catherine in the Wars of RELIGION. Alarmed at the Huguenot threat to Church and State, she approved the murder of leading Huguenots in the MASSACRE OF ST. BARTHOLOMEW (1572). The reign of her third son, HENRY III (1574–89), brought increasing disorder to France, but Catherine's efforts helped hold France together until the accession of HENRY IV (1589).

**Further reading:** Robert J. Knecht, *Catherine de' Medici* (London: Longman, 1998).

**Catherine of Aragon** (1485–1536) *First wife of Henry VIII of England, patron of the arts and scholarship*
As the daughter of FERDINAND II AND ISABELLA I of Spain she received an exceptional education, studying Latin and also being tutored by ERASMUS. In 1501 she came to England as the bride of Henry's elder brother, Arthur, but he died of consumption a year later. When he became king (1509), Henry married Catherine by papal dispensation. During the first, happy years of her marriage, Catherine was a notable patron of the arts at court. Her first six babies, including two sons, all died soon after birth; it was not until 1516 that she gave birth to the future Queen MARY. Henry viewed Catherine's failure to produce a son as divine vengeance for marrying his brother's widow, and cast her aside in 1527 for Anne BOLEYN, seeking an annulment from the pope. After his final separation from Catherine in 1531, she was forced to live out the rest of her life in poverty and seclusion and denied access to her daughter.

See also: HENRY VIII

**Catherine of Bologna, St.** (Caterina de' Vigri) (1413–1463) *Italian nun*
As a child Catherine received a humanistic education at the Este court at Ferrara. She then joined the Franciscan tertiaries (later Poor Clare nuns), becoming abbess of their convent in her native Bologna (1456), where she was famed for her visionary experiences and, after her death, for her uncorrupted corpse. A breviary copied out by her attests her skills in calligraphy and miniature painting. She also wrote a devotional treatise and other compositions in prose and verse.

**Catherine of Genoa, St.** (Caterina Fieschi) (1447–1510) *Italian mystic*
Born in Genoa, at 16 she was married to Giuliano Adorno, who was rich, dissipated, and unfaithful. She found no consolation in a frivolous social life, and in 1473 experienced a religious conversion; some years later, she influenced her husband to change his way of life. They devoted themselves to nursing, and she became matron of a hospital in Genoa. Her prayer life was intense, she fasted rigorously, and received communion daily; the quality of her

spiritual experiences can be gauged from the compilation *Vita e dottrina* (1551).

**Catherine of Siena, St.** (**Caterina Benincasa**) (1347–1380) *Italian mystic*
The daughter of a prosperous Sienese dyer, Catherine rejected proposals of marriage to become a Dominican tertiary (1363). She traveled widely in Italy, accompanied by a band of disciples, including priests and nobles. Her spiritual experiences were remarkable, including receiving the stigmata (1375). Drawn into a public role by her fame, she attempted to mediate in an armed conflict between the papacy and some of the Italian cities led by Florence, and to unite the Christian powers in a crusade against the Turks. She also went to Avignon and helped to persuade Pope Gregory XI to return to Rome (1377). From 1378 she supported Urban VI against the antipope Clement (VII) and attempted to win Queen Joanna I of Naples over to Urban's side.

**Catholic Majesties** The title accorded to FERDINAND II AND ISABELLA I of Castile, and subsequently to other kings and queens of Spain. It is said to have been bestowed upon Ferdinand by Pope Alexander VI in recognition of his having completed the reconquest of Spain from the Moors by the taking of Granada in 1492.

**Cattamelata, Il** See GATTAMELATA, IL

**Caus, Salomon de** (**Salomon de Caux**) (1576–1626) *French hydraulic engineer and garden designer*
Born into a Huguenot family in Normandy, de Caus visited Italy in the mid-1590s, observing the great Italian gardens such as those of the Villa d'Este and the Medici villa at Pratolino. He was in England in 1598 but later worked for the Archdukes in Brussels (c. 1603–05) before returning to England around 1607 to work for James I's queen, Anne of Denmark, and to tutor their son Henry, Prince of Wales, in perspective. In 1610 he was appointed Henry's architect and advised on a never-completed garden project at Richmond Palace. De Caus's *La Perspective, avec les raisons des ombres et miroirs* (1612) is dedicated to Henry. After the prince's untimely death he accompanied Henry's sister Elizabeth to Heidelberg in 1613 where he designed a garden for her and her husband, Elector Palatine Frederick V (*see* WINTER KING); a bird's-eye view of this complex garden appears in an engraving by Matthäus Merian for de Caus's *Hortus Palatinus* (1620), published by Johann Theodor DE BRY. Grottoes and hydraulic devices featured in this garden are illustrated in De Caus's *Les raisons des forces mouvantes* (1615; enlarged second edition, 1624), dedicated to Elizabeth. De Caus was also an authority on organs and published his theory of music in *Institution*

*harmonique* (1615). He later worked for Louis XIII and died in Paris.
**Further reading:** Roy Strong, *The Renaissance Garden in England* (London: Thames & Hudson, 1979).

**Cavalcanti, Guido** (c. 1250–1300) *Italian poet*
Born in Florence some time prior to 1257, Cavalcanti belonged to a prominent Guelph family. In 1267 he was betrothed to the daughter of a Ghibelline in one of several such engagements arranged to end the continual strife between the GUELPH AND GHIBELLINE parties. He represented the Guelphs in 1280 as a guarantor of peace and later served on the general council of the commune. Accused of being a leader of the Guelph faction, on June 24, 1300 he was condemned to exile. Although the ban was soon lifted, Cavalcanti died in Sarzana on August 29. DANTE dedicated the *Vita nuova* to him and they exchanged sonnets, but the friendship may not have lasted; in the *Divine Comedy* Dante only refers briefly to his "disdain" (*Inferno* X 63). The principal Florentine contributor to the DOLCE STIL NUOVO, Cavalcanti wrote sonnets, ballads, and *canzoni*, 52 of which are extant.

**Cavendish, Thomas** (1560–1592) *English navigator*
Cavendish, son of a wealthy Suffolk family, took part in RALEIGH's first Virginian expedition (1585). In 1586 he set sail in the *Desire* to circumnavigate the globe, the first person to set out with this express intention. He returned triumphant in 1588, hugely enriched by the capture of a Spanish treasure ship. In 1591 he embarked on a more ambitious expedition, aiming to establish trading relations with Japan and China, but after failing to pass the Straits of Magellan, he turned back and died in mid-Atlantic. Cavendish's journal of this disastrous voyage was published by HAKLUYT.

**Caxton, William** (c. 1420–1492) *English merchant and printer*
Caxton was born in Kent and after a career as a cloth merchant in Bruges, he learned to print in Cologne, probably with Johann Veldener. In partnership with Colard Mansion he then set up a printing press in Bruges, where the first book printed in English, his own translation of Raoul le Fèvre's *Recuyell of the Historyes of Troye*, was finished in 1474 or early 1475. In 1476, leaving Mansion to go on printing in Bruges, he brought the first English press to a shop by the chapterhouse of Westminster Abbey, where he printed about 100 books, 73 in English. The first dated publication was Earl Rivers's translation of *Dictes or Sayengis of the Philosophes* (1477), the first illustrated one *Myrrour of the Worlde* (1481). About 1478 he printed Chaucer's *Canterbury Tales*, with an illustrated edition five years later, followed by Sir Thomas Malory's *Le Morte Darthur* in 1485. As well as printing, Caxton imported and

**William Caxton** A manuscript illustration showing Earl Rivers presenting Edward IV of England with a copy of his *Dictes or Sayengis of the Philosophres* (1477) printed by Caxton, who is in attendance (Library of Lambeth Palace, London). *The Fotomas Index UK*

exported books and manuscripts. His successor, Wynkyn de Worde, had been his foreman from 1479.

**Further reading:** N. F. Blake, *William Caxton and English Literary Culture* (London: Hambledon, 2003).

**Cecchino, Il** See SALVIATI, FRANCESCO

**celestial spheres** (**celestial globes**) The representation of constellations and planets on the surface of a globe. The concept goes back at least to Eudoxus (fourth century BCE), but the earliest surviving globe is the Farnese marble (c. 200 BCE) in the Naples museum. The tradition persisted among Islamic astronomers and returned to the West in the 13th century through the Sicilian court of Frederick II. Islamic examples were generally made of engraved brass, but by the late 15th century printed paper gores were produced, which when cut out could be pasted onto a *papier mâché* or lath and plaster sphere. Elaborate and highly decorated globes were made during the Renaissance by such figures as APIAN, MERCATOR, and BLAEU. One with a diameter of five feet and on which 1000 stars were plotted was to be found at the Uraniborg observatory of Tycho BRAHE.

*Celestina, La* A novel in dramatic form by Fernando de ROJAS, first published anonymously in a 16-act version (1499) and later in a 21-act version. Originally entitled *La (tragi)comedia de Calisto y Melibea*, the story concerns a noble youth, Calisto, who falls in love with Melibea, the daughter of the Jew Pleberio. Calisto is persuaded to seek the help of the procuress or gobetween Celestina, who succeeds in overcoming Melibea's resistance by appealing to her compassion. Celestina is killed in a quarrel over money with Calisto's corrupt servants. Calisto seduces Melibea but falls to his death when leaving her; Melibea commits suicide. The expanded version introduces Centurio, a braggart soldier, in the final acts, but the ending is the same. The book was enormously popular, with 60 reprints in the 16th century. Despite its sexual subject and outspoken language, the characters pay dearly for their sins and so the novel never attracted the censure of the Inquisition.

**Cellini, Benvenuto** (1500–1571) *Italian goldsmith, die-engraver, sculptor, and writer*
From two books written toward the end of Cellini's life, his *Autobiography* (1558–62) and *Treatises on Goldsmithing and Sculpture* (1565), we are better informed about his career and attitude to his patrons than about any other Renaissance artist. Born in Florence and originally trained as a goldsmith, Cellini moved from city to city to make his fortune and to escape punishment for his misdemeanors: from 1519 until 1540 he worked in and around the papal court and mint in Rome; from 1540 until 1545 he served Francis I of France at Paris and Fontainebleau, alongside ROSSO FIORENTINO and PRIMATICCIO; back again in Florence, he turned his hand to major sculpture in bronze and marble for Duke COSIMO I DE' MEDICI. By 1560 his popularity as a court artist had declined and he resorted to writing.

The majority of Cellini's goldsmith work and jewelry, described with loving detail in both *Autobiography* and *Treatises*, has been lost; his activities on a small scale may be judged only from seals, coins, and medals, of which several examples survive. Some drawings by him, or of lost works (e.g. the fabulous cope-clasp for Pope Clement VII), also exist, and he influenced most of the jewelry and precious metalwork of Italy, France, and Germany during the second half of the 16th century. Fortunately, Cellini's masterpiece of miniature sculpture does survive, in Vienna: the salt-cellar in gold and enamel which he had begun in Italy and finished for Francis I. It is a typically mannerist artefact—intellectual, ingenious, colorful, and a technical *tour de force*. Anatomical forms are distorted for grace of line, as in a modern fashion plate. Cellini's most ambitious project for the French king, a series of 12 over-life-size statues of classical deities in silver, was never completed, though his designs are probably reflected on a reduced scale in some of his later bronze statuettes. However, a great bronze lunette for a portal at Fontainebleau, showing the nymph of the fountain surrounded by the animals of the hunt, survives in the Louvre, Paris, and there is a drawing of one of the satyrs that flanked the portal as caryatids.

In 1545 Cellini, suspected of embezzling precious metal and gemstones, fled from France back to Florence. There he persuaded Cosimo I to commission a group of two over-life-size bronze figures—*Perseus and Medusa* (1545–54)—to match Donatello's *Judith and Holofernes* of a century earlier under the arches of the Loggia dei Lanzi. Cellini's original wax and bronze models are in the Bargello; they are much more elongated than the finished work. A bronze study for the head of Medusa is in the Victoria and Albert Museum, London. The *Perseus and Medusa* is the most obviously mannerist sculpture in Florence (*see* MANNERISM). Its decorative marble pedestal comprises a repertory of mannerist motifs and contains four bronze statuettes of the ancestors of Perseus, as well as a narrative relief in bronze of Perseus rescuing Andromeda. Challenged by BANDINELLI to prove his worth as a sculptor by carving marble, Cellini produced several statues on classical themes, but his masterpiece in the medium is the *Crucifixion*, now in the Escorial.

Cellini's *Vita* was first published in Naples in 1728. The original manuscript then vanished for many years before being rediscovered in the early 19th century; it is now housed in the Laurenziana library in Florence. English versions have been variously titled *Life*, *Memoirs*, or *Autobiography*. The first English translation, made by Thomas Nugent (1771), has often been reprinted, as has the later version by John Addington Symonds (2 vols, 1888); an abridgment of the latter by Charles Hope and Alessandro Nova appeared in 1983. The version of the *Autobiography* for the Penguin Classics series (1956, rev. ed. 1999) was made by George Bull. A more recent translation is that by Julia Conaway Bondanella (Oxford World's Classics: 2002).

**Further reading:** John Pope-Hennessy, *Cellini* (London: Macmillan and New York: Abbeville, 1985).

**Celtis, Konrad** (1459–1508) *German humanist and poet*
Born a peasant near Würzburg, Celtis ran away at age 18 to study. He spent the next 20 years studying and teaching at a succession of universities—Cologne, Heidelberg, Erfurt, Rostock, Leipzig, Cracow, Nuremberg, Ingolstadt—before settling at Vienna university to teach poetry and rhetoric (1497). His travels included two years in Italy (1487–89), where he met many Italian humanists. Although generally disillusioned by Italy, he was inspired by LETO's academy in Rome to start similar societies in Germany where humanists could meet and work together—most notably the "Sodalitas danubiana" in Vienna. PEUTINGER and PIRCKHEIMER were among his friends and correspondents.

Celtis's own studies of Greek and Hebrew, his editions of Latin authors, and his Latin dramas were important in the humanist movement, as were his introduction of literary studies to various universities and his ideas on education. Resenting Italian cultural domination, he pas-

sionately wanted to revive German culture; significant here was his discovery (1492/93) at Regensburg of six Latin dramas by Hrosvitha von Gandersheim, a 10th-century nun, and his edition (1500) of the *Germania* of the Roman historian Tacitus. His great ambition was to write the first comprehensive geographical and historical survey of Germany, although only a few preparatory studies were completed. The first German to be crowned poet laureate by the emperor (1487), he was a gifted poet, as seen especially from his *Quattuor libri amorum* (1502). This is a semiautobiographical verse narrative of four love affairs, highly entertaining, with an amoral sensuality. Celtis died in Vienna of syphilis.

**Further reading:** Lewis W. Spitz, *Conrad Celtis: The German Arch-Humanist* (Cambridge, Mass.: Harvard University Press, 1957).

**Cenacolo** See LAST SUPPER

**Cenci, Beatrice** (1577–1599) *Roman noblewoman*
Her controversial execution under Pope CLEMENT VIII aroused great public interest and became the subject of numerous poems, dramas, and novels, notably Shelley's *The Cenci* (1819) and Alberto Moravia's *Beatrice Cenci* (1958). Treated with extraordinary cruelty by her father Francesco Cenci, Beatrice finally murdered him with the help of servants and other members of her family. They were all brought to trial, tortured, and sentenced to death, despite pleas for leniency on their behalf. The subsequent confiscation of the Cenci property was rumored to have been the pope's real object in the prosecution.

**Cenni di Peppi** See CIMABUE

**censorship** The invention of PRINTING was quickly perceived by both secular and religious authorities in the Renaissance to be a massive threat to their ability to control the spread of subversive ideas. The idea of censorship was not new, but the laborious production of manuscripts by scribes could relatively easily be dealt with by seizure and destruction of the finished product—as authorized, for instance, in the case of LOLLARD texts in England by the Merciless Parliament of 1388. The rapid multiplication of copies by printing made it expedient to introduce mechanisms of control at an earlier stage of production. One widely employed method was to require printers to submit material they proposed to publish to be licensed by an official censor or other competent body before it could legally be printed.

As European exploration in pursuit of trade routes gathered pace, there is evidence that some polities endeavored to suppress the dissemination of commercially sensitive information. For instance, a chart of Vasco da GAMA's voyage to India had to be smuggled out of Lisbon in 1502 by the agent of the duke of Ferrara, and PETER

MARTYR d'Anghiera caused some consternation to the Spanish authorities with the extent and accuracy of his disclosures about Spain's exploration of the New World in his *Decades de orbe novo* (1511–30). Fear on the part of English merchants involved in the Baltic trade that the Russians would take offense at Giles FLETCHER the Elder's observations in *The Russe Commonwealth* (1591) led to them to persuade Elizabeth I's chief minister, Lord Burghley, to suppress the book. However, by far the largest area of concern for the censors was writings suspected of posing a threat to religious orthodoxy, public order, or private morality—or often all three together.

The writings of the religious reformers were an obvious target for censorship (*see* COUNTER-REFORMATION). The Milanese senate issued an index of banned books in 1538 and other Italian cities soon followed suit. The INDEX LIBRORUM PROHIBITORUM issued in 1557 and 1559 under Pope PAUL IV was the forerunner of all subsequent lists of publications forbidden to Roman Catholics by reason either of heterodoxy or immorality. It became usual for printers to cite on their title-pages their authority to print, a practice ridiculed by John Milton in his great attack on licensing for the press, *Areopagitica* (1644): "Sometimes 5 *Imprimaturs* are seen together dialoguewise in the Piatza of one Title page, complementing and ducking each to other with their shav'n reverences..." Secular works also suffered the attentions of censor and expurgator; for instance, the writings of ARETINO and MACHIAVELLI were banned, Cinthio Fabrizi's collection of obscene proverbs, *Libro della origine delli volgari proverbi* (1526) provoked the initiation of censorship in Venice in 1527, and Boccaccio's DECAMERON suffered the indignity of expurgated editions in 1573 and 1582.

In England licensing for the press by the privy council was introduced in 1538. From 1557 the Stationers' Company was held responsible for the regulation of the book trade, and later decrees nominated various dignitaries as licensers. In 1586 the number of presses allowed per printer was strictly curtailed and their whereabouts limited to London, apart from one press each for the university cities of Oxford and Cambridge; unauthorized presses, such as those used to print the pamphlets in the MARPRELATE CONTROVERSY were rigorously pursued, and if found were destroyed. Furthermore, authors were liable to penalties of imprisonment, mutilation, or death for producing obnoxious material, and books themselves could be seized and burnt, as befell the satirical works of Thomas NASHE and Gabriel HARVEY under an edict of 1599.

As the Counter-Reformation advanced in Europe, censorship of the visual arts was also attempted. The most notorious incidence of this is probably the employment of a number of artists, among them El Greco, to paint draperies over the naked figures in Michelangelo's *Last Judgment* in the Sistine Chapel. A similar trend was manifested in music when Philip II of Spain insisted that plainsong only was to be used for the religious services in the Escorial, as the polyphonic church music hitherto popular in Spain had secular tunes worked into it.

**Centuriators of Magdeburg** The collective name for the authors of *Historia ecclesiae Christi*, a history of the Church century by century until 1400, published at Basle from 1559 to 1574. Among the Centuriators were Matthias Flacius (Vlacic), Nicolaus von Amsdorf, Johann Wigand, Nicolaus Gallus (Hahn), and Matthäus Judex (Richter). The work was begun about 1550 at Magdeburg and continued from 1562 at Regensburg (Ratisbon). It is broad in conception, but often inaccurate in detail, and was cogently attacked by the Catholic historian BARONIUS.

**ceramics** The technique of producing objects made of fired clay, which in the European Middle Ages and Renaissance could range from the purely practical (e.g. roof tiles) through decorative floor tiles and vessels to high art (e.g. the enameled terracotta sculptures of Luca DELLA ROBBIA). At the merely functional level, pottery was practiced wherever suitable clay could be found not too far from a source of water and sufficient wood for fuel; local production had the advantage of minimizing the expense and hazards of transporting the heavy but fragile finished products. For major building projects, such as palaces or monasteries, kilns would be set up on site to make the necessary tiles. Stamps were used to make the patterns on two-color floor tiles, with a (usually) white slip poured into the impressed areas of the design before firing.

The major Renaissance development in the field of decorative ceramics was the type of tin-glazed pottery known as MAJOLICA. In the 15th century Valencia was a major exporter of majolica wares. Elaborately decorated and colorful Italian majolica was exported all over Europe from such centers as the Montelupo potteries in Tuscany or Faenza, near Bologna. ("Faience," the generic name by which such tin-glazed wares were known in most of northern Europe, derives from the latter.) The technique was imported into England in 1567 by potters from Antwerp. An indigenous German type of pottery was salt-glazed stoneware (German: *Steinzeug*), manufactured in the Rhineland from the 12th century onward; clay and a fusible stone were fired at a high enough temperature to vitrify the stone to make nonporous vessels.

**Further reading:** Timothy Wilson, *Ceramic Art of the Italian Renaissance* (London: British Museum, 1987).

**Cereta, Laura** (1469–1499) *Italian humanist, feminist, and scholar*
From an aristocratic family in Brescia, she was educated at home by her father, who encouraged her interest in mathematics and taught her Latin and Greek. She also engaged in self-education, taking up astronomy, philosophy, theol-

ogy, and the study of literature, her great favorite being PETRARCH. She was widowed within 18 months of being married off when she was 15, by which time she had begun corresponding in Latin with humanist scholars in Brescia and the Veneto, as well as with Casandra FEDELE. Her scholarly activities attracted attention, and criticism, in Brescia, to which she responded with passion, defending the right of women to be educated. In 1488 she brought out a volume of her letters, but such was the hostility to female scholarship that she published no more, although she resisted the exhortations of her male critics to retire, as they deemed fit, to the contemplative life of a nunnery.

## Cervantes Saavedra, Miguel de (1547–1616) *Spanish novelist, poet, and dramatist*
One of the large family of a poor and unsuccessful doctor at Alcalá de Henares, Cervantes had little formal education apart from a period at a Madrid school run by a follower of Erasmus. In 1569 he went to Italy, joined the Spanish army there, and was wounded in the naval battle of Lepanto (1571), losing the use of his left hand. After completing military service, he boarded a ship for Spain in 1575 with a written commendation by Don John of Austria, but was seized by Algerian pirates and held captive by the Turks in Algiers for five years while he vainly tried to raise the necessary ransom. When it was finally paid by the Trinitarian Friars in 1580 and he returned to Spain, he hoped for some reward for past services but was ignored. His marriage in 1584 was an unhappy one and his first attempt to earn a living by writing, the pastoral romance *La Galatea* (1585), was hardly successful. He had a somewhat better return on his early plays for the Madrid theater, but his circumstances did not improve. In 1587 he was forced to leave Madrid to work in Andalusia as a tax collector. He was imprisoned two or perhaps three times for debt or trouble with his bookkeeping and spent a number of years living in Seville. After Part I of his great masterpiece DON QUIXOTE appeared (1605), he spent the final and most productive years of his life in Madrid. Despite his fame and the immense success of *Don Quixote*, his grave in Madrid was unmarked.

Though Cervantes wrote verse and included many poetic passages in his prose works, he acknowledged that he had little talent for it. Early lack of success in the theater did not discourage him from making a second attempt, and he collected his later plays in *Ocho comedias y ocho entremeses* (1615). The *entremeses*, one-act prose farces, proved especially congenial to his gift for comic dialogue and social satire. The 12 short stories collected in *Novelas ejemplares* (*Exemplary Novels*; 1613) contain his most interesting work after *Don Quixote*. A long romance, *Persiles y Sigismunda*, was published posthumously (1617) and translated into English two years later.

**Further reading:** P. E. Russell, *Cervantes* (Oxford, U.K.: Oxford University Press, 1985).

## Cesalpino, Andrea (1519–1603) *Italian physician and botanist*
Cesalpino was born at Arezzo, studied at Pisa, and in 1555 succeeded Luca Ghini as director of the Pisan BOTANIC GARDEN. He moved to the Sapienza in Rome in 1592. *De plantis libri XVI* (1583) starts with botanical principles; following Aristotle's division of plants into trees, shrubs, shrubby herbs, and herbs, Cesalpino's pioneering classification concentrated on fruits and seeds, neglecting broader affinities. The greater part of his book contains descriptions of about 1500 plants, but with less advice on their uses than the herbalists provided.

## Cesarini, Julian (1398–1444) *Italian churchman*
Cesarini was born in Rome and studied at Perugia and Padua, where he was a friend of NICHOLAS OF CUSA. He occupied several posts in the papal Curia, and in 1425 was sent on a diplomatic mission to John, Duke of Bedford, regent of France for Henry VI. In 1426 he was made a cardinal and transferred to England, where he met Cardinal Beaufort and the humanists patronized by Duke Humfrey of Gloucester. In 1431 he was appointed papal legate in Bohemia, Germany, Hungary, and Poland, to direct a crusade against the HUSSITES. He presided at the Council of BASLE, which opposed the policy of Pope Eugenius IV and attempted to limit the papal power. Later, at the Council of Ferrara, which transferred to Florence, he negotiated a settlement with the Greek Orthodox Church. In 1442 he went to Hungary to preach a crusade against the Turks, and was killed during the flight after the defeat of the Christian forces at Varna, Bulgaria.

## chain of being
The doctrine that all natural entities, whether mineral, vegetable, or animal, are linked in a single, continuous, unbroken sequence. It originated with Plato and began to lose its appeal only with the geological revolution of the late 18th century. The animal and vegetable kingdoms, it was claimed, are so connected that it was impossible to distinguish between the highest plant and the lowest animal—and so on throughout all parts of the natural world. Considered hierarchically the chain (or ladder) of being joined the lowest natural form in a continuous sequence ultimately to God himself. Further, according to the related principle of plenitude, the chain extended throughout the whole of nature. This latter view was apparently dramatically confirmed during the late Renaissance period by observations made through the newly invented MICROSCOPE. Every green leaf was shown to be swarming with animal life, while the animals themselves were also shown to be similarly inhabited.

**Further reading:** Arthur O. Lovejoy, *The Great Chain of Being: A Study of the History of an Idea* (Cambridge,

Mass.: Harvard University Press, 1936; repr. 1970); E. M. W. Tillyard, *The Elizabethan World Picture* (London: Chatto & Windus, 1960).

**chambers of rhetoric** Amateur literary societies in France and, more significantly, the Netherlands, active from about 1400. The *rhétoriqueurs* (French) or *rederijkers* (Dutch) were mainly middle-class townspeople who formed associations similar to guilds in order to promote their love of poetry and drama. They were mostly encouraged by the civic authorities and they reciprocated by organizing public celebrations, but the religious upheavals of the 16th century caused many of the chambers to fall under suspicion of heresy, and by 1600 their heyday was generally over.

Like the MEISTERGESANG guilds in Germany, the chambers of rhetoric were not usually innovative in their literary enterprises or particularly quick to respond to Renaissance ideas; they were however associated with the rise of secular drama in northern Europe, and the Dutch *Elckerlijk* (c. 1495) is probably the source for the English morality play *Everyman*. Significant Dutch writers associated with the *rederijker* tradition include: Cornelis Everaert (c. 1480–1556), playwright and member of De Drie Santinnen at Bruges; Matthijs de Castelein (1485–1550), author of the first Dutch treatise on poetry, *De Const van Rhetoriken* (1548); Colijn van Rijssele, the 15th-century author of the bourgeois drama cycle *De Spiegel der Minnen* (The Mirror of Love); Anna BIJNS, a schoolmistress at Antwerp; Dirck COORNHEERT; and Henrick SPIEGEL. The fanciful names adopted by the chambers were expressed in mottoes and emblems: they included De Egelantier and 't Wit Lavendel at Amsterdam, Het Bloemken Jesse at Middelburg, Trou moet Blijcken at Haarlem, De Fonteine at Ghent, and De Violieren at Antwerp.

See also: DUYTSCHE ACADEMIE

**Chambord, Château de** A château in central France, on the left bank of the River Cosson, a tributary of the Loire, east of Blois. Erected on the site of a hunting lodge and surrounded by forest, the château was mainly built (1519–47) during the reigns of Francis I and Henry II and incorporated many Renaissance features. The design was by the Italian architect DOMENICO DA CORTONA and was executed by Jacques Sourdeau, Pierre Neveu, and Denis Sourdeau. Although the château was laid out in a medieval Gothic style, its 440 rooms were decorated in a classical manner typical of the Renaissance; other details include a double spiral open staircase. See Plate IV.

**Champlain, Samuel de** (1567–1635) *French navigator, founder of Quebec, and governor of Canada*
Hailed as the key figure in the establishment of French interests in North America, Champlain was born at Brouage, his father a sea captain. Champlain fought for Henry IV in the religious wars as a youth and sailed to the West Indies for Spain in 1599, before his first visit to Canada in 1603. For the next five years he explored extensively, before founding Quebec in 1608. He then devoted himself to the welfare of this community, developing the fur trade and making frequent sorties into the hinterland. He became lieutenant of Canada in 1612, but was captured by an English expedition against Quebec in 1629 and taken to England. France regained Quebec in 1632, and Champlain returned the following year to end his days there.

**Chancellor, Richard** (died 1556) *English navigator and mathematician*
In his early years he lived in the household of Sir Henry Sidney, where his tutor was John DEE. Chancellor applied his mathematical abilities, which Dee rated very highly, to improving navigational techniques, but apparently his first practical experience of seamanship was on a voyage to Chios in 1550. In 1553 he joined the three-ship MUSCOVY COMPANY expedition searching for the NORTHEAST PASSAGE. Although his ship was only one to reach Russia, he completed the hazardous winter journey overland from Archangel to Moscow to negotiate trade terms with Tsar Ivan IV. He consolidated Anglo–Muscovite links on subsequent visits in 1555 and 1556, but died in a shipwreck off Scotland while returning from his final journey. His interesting account of Russia was published by HAKLUYT.

**chanson** A French polyphonic song of the medieval and Renaissance periods. A generic term, "chanson" encompasses rondeaux, *ballades*, and virelais. MACHAUT can be regarded as the first major chanson composer. In the second half of the 14th century composers regularly set poems polyphonically, usually in three parts, in a rhythmically complex manner. The chansons of DUFAY were refined, with a rich texture, inventive melodies, and rhythmic variety. Chanson style changed radically around 1500; Josquin DES PRÉS and his contemporaries treated each voice independently, and the new technique of imitative counterpoint was used with repetition of phrases. In Paris in the 1530s and 1540s the music printer Pierre Attaignant published many chansons, notably those by SERMISY and JANEQUIN; the Parisian chanson was much simpler in style and more chordal. In the 1550s and 1560s composers used more word-painting, with more variety of texture, though the genre never attained the scope of the MADRIGAL.

**Chantal, Jeanne Françoise de, St.** See JEANNE FRANÇOISE DE CHANTAL, ST.

**Chapman, George** (c. 1559–1634) *English poet, playwright, and translator*
Little is known for certain about Chapman's life; he may have been born near Hitchin in southeast England and

have attended both Oxford and Cambridge universities without taking a degree. His earliest published poems, *The Shadow of Night* (1594) and *Ovid's Banquet of Sence* (1595), are remarkable mainly for their obscurity; Chapman was never one to wear his learning lightly, a failing also apparent in his continuation of MARLOWE's *Hero and Leander* (1598). He probably began writing for the stage in the mid-1590s, producing such comedies as *An Humorous Day's Mirth* (1599) and *All Fools* (1605). Satirical allusions to the Scots in *Eastward Ho!* (1605) incurred the displeasure of King James I, causing Chapman and his coauthors Ben JONSON and John Marston to be briefly imprisoned. Chapman's best play is his tragedy *Bussy d'Ambois* (1607), the hero of which is his finest dramatic creation. Chapman's greatest achievement, however, was his translation of the whole Homeric corpus: the complete *Iliad* in rhymed 14-syllable lines appeared in 1611, followed by the *Odyssey* in rhymed decasyllables (1614–15) and the Homeric hymns (1616).

**Charlemagne, legend of** The cycle of narratives, also known as "the matter of France," that accumulated during the Middle Ages around the Frankish king Charlemagne (c. 742–814; emperor 800–814) and his knights (paladins). Much of the earliest material focuses on Charlemagne himself as the divinely appointed champion of Christianity against Islam, but the part of the Charlemagne cycle that really kindled the medieval imagination was the incident in 778 when the rearguard of the Frankish army was ambushed by Basques while returning from an abortive campaign in Spain and was annihilated at Roncesvaux in the Pyrenees. This historical kernel grew into the Old French *Chanson de Roland* (c. 1100), the epic tale of the rearguard's last stand under its commander Roland against overwhelming hordes of Saracens. The poem was translated into German as the *Rolandslied* (mid-12th century), and further material was added to the Roland theme in Spanish and Italian poems on the hero's exploits prior to Roncesvaux and in laments for the slaughtered knights. Grotesque, magic, and erotic elements were also attached to the Roland story, particularly in Italy, and PULCI's *Morgante* attempts to blend these with the story of Roncesvaux. Roland, Italianized as Orlando, also appears as the hero of the two greatest Italian romantic epics, BOIARDO's *Orlando innamorato* and ARIOSTO's *Orlando furioso*, in which the *materia cavalleresca* of Charlemagne's wars against the pagans provides the general narrative framework.

**Charles V** (1500–1558) *Holy Roman Emperor (1519–56); also Charles I of Spain (1516–56), archduke of Austria, and duke of Burgundy*
A HAPSBURG prince, the son of Philip (the Handsome) of Burgundy and Joanna (the Mad) of Castile, Charles inherited vast territories from each of his four grandparents. He

succeeded MAXIMILIAN I as Holy Roman Emperor, inheriting from him Austrian and other German territories. From Mary, heiress of Burgundy, Charles inherited the Netherlands, Franche-Comté, and other territories near the Rhine. From FERDINAND II AND ISABELLA I came Spain, Spanish territory in North Africa and the New World, and various Italian territories and claims. By his wife, Isabella of Portugal (1503–39), Charles begot the future PHILIP II of Spain; two of his illegitimate children—MARGARET OF PARMA and Don JOHN OF AUSTRIA—also played prominent roles in the late 16th century.

Charles was an earnest, but not particularly intellectual, man. His favorite painter was TITIAN. A devout, if rather unimaginative Catholic, he took his great responsibilities seriously and was determined to protect his faith both against the attacks of the OTTOMAN TURKS, who reached the gates of Vienna in 1529, and against the Protestants.

Charles was born in Ghent and educated in the Netherlands, where he succeeded his father in 1506 and assumed personal rule in 1515. He was later faced with serious revolts in some Netherlands cities, notably the revolt of Ghent, which was ruthlessly suppressed in 1540. In Spain too there were rebellions early in his reign (*see* COMUNEROS, REVOLT OF THE), but order was restored by 1522. Charles worked hard to reach an understanding with his Spanish subjects in the 1520s; during his reign Spanish power in the New World was developed and the monarchy in Spain became more unified and centralized.

In Germany, despite some attempts to reach a compromise, as for instance at the colloquy of REGENSBURG, Charles had to confront the Protestant challenge and years of sectarian warfare until the Peace of AUGSBURG (1555) suspended the religious struggle. In Italy, as Maximilian I had done, Charles continued to dispute French claims. The Wars of ITALY were the most obvious expression of Hapsburg–Valois rivalry for mastery in Europe.

In 1556, exhausted by the burdens of his inheritance, Charles retired to the Spanish monastery of Yuste. His inheritance was divided; Spain, the Netherlands, and other Spanish territories went to his son, Philip II of Spain. Austria, other German territories, and the Holy Roman Empire passed to his brother, FERDINAND I.

**Further reading:** Willem Pieter Blockmans, *Emperor Charles V: 1550–1558*, transl. Isola van den Haven-Varden (London: Edward Arnold, 2002); William D. Maltby, *The Reign of Charles V* (New York: Palgrave Macmillan, 2002).

**Charles VIII** (1470–1498) *King of France (1483–98)*
The only son of Louis XI and Charlotte of Savoy, Charles was frail and not very intelligent. During his minority (1483–91), Anne de Beaujeu, his sister, and her husband were regents. They administered France soundly and by arranging Charles's marriage (1491) to Anne, heiress of

Brittany, eventually secured Brittany for the French royal domain. This marriage infuriated Anne's erstwhile fiancé, MAXIMILIAN I, and presaged the long Hapsburg–Valois conflict. On attaining his majority Charles was able to pursue his dreams of conquest, chivalry, and a crusade against the Turks. His first step was to assert French claims in Italy. After making costly treaties to buy off possible enemies, Charles invaded Italy (1494). He met little opposition; SAVONAROLA welcomed him as a liberator to Florence, the pope opened the gates of Rome, and Naples surrendered without a fight. Charles was crowned king of Naples (May 1495), but France's enemies formed a league against her. Charles abandoned Naples to the Aragonese and fought his way back to France, where he died while preparing another Italian invasion.

## Charles Borromeo, St. (1538–1584) *Italian churchman*

Born at Arona, Borromeo was destined from childhood for the Church and in 1560 was appointed cardinal archbishop of Milan by his maternal uncle, Pope Pius IV. Until Pius IV died (1565) Cardinal Borromeo served in the Curia, playing an important part in the later sessions of the Council of TRENT and drafting the Roman catechism. After 1566 he devoted himself to the archdiocese of Milan. He reformed its administration, improved the morals of clergy and laity, supported the Jesuits, helped establish seminaries and religious schools, and aided the poor and sick. His heroic efforts during an outbreak of plague (1576–78) were much admired. A leading figure in the COUNTER-REFORMATION, he was canonized in 1610.

## Charles the Bold (1433–1477) *Duke of Burgundy (1467–77)*

The son of PHILIP THE GOOD, Charles was a rash man, who inherited extensive territories. His great ambitions were to gain a royal title and to win Alsace and Lorraine, the lands dividing his domains in the Netherlands from those in the Franche-Comté. He came close to realizing his first ambition, when Emperor Frederick III was on the brink of making Burgundy a kingdom. In pursuit of his second ambition he acquired power in Alsace and attacked Lorraine (1475). Alarmed at the prospect of a Burgundian kingdom stretching from the North Sea to the Alps, his neighbors combined against him. He died fighting the Swiss at Nancy and left his daughter Mary as his heiress. Her marriage to MAXIMILIAN I conveyed most of the Burgundian inheritance to the house of HAPSBURG.

**Further reading:** Richard Vaughan, *Charles the Bold: The Last Valois Duke of Burgundy* (London: Longman, 1973; new ed. Woodbridge, U.K.: Boydell & Brewer, 2002).

## Charonton, Enguerrand See QUARTON, ENGUERRAND

## Charron, Pierre (1541–1603) *French writer and moralist*

Born in Paris, he was one of a family of 25 children. After studying law at Orleans and Bourges he practiced as an advocate but became disenchanted with the profession. He turned to the Church and enjoyed a distinguished career as a preacher, becoming chaplain-in-ordinary to Margaret of Valois, first wife of Henry of Navarre. In 1588 he returned to Paris determined to join a religious order, but, when none would accept him because of his age, he retired to Bordeaux where he became close friends with MONTAIGNE. Charron published anonymously a treatise on *Les Trois Vérités* (The Three Truths; 1593), which combined an apology for Catholicism with an attack on DU PLESSIS-MORNAY. He died in Paris of a stroke.

Charron's most important work was *De la sagesse* (On Wisdom; 1601). The main thesis of this work was the incapacity of reason to discover truth and the need for tolerance on religious questions. The work was severely censured by the Sorbonne and was a forerunner of 17th-century deism.

## Charton, Enguerrand See QUARTON, ENGUERRAND

## Chaucer, Geoffrey (c. 1343–1400) *English poet*

Born the son of a rich London wine merchant, Chaucer was brought up in the household of the earl of Ulster. Captured by the French near Reims while serving with the English army, he was ransomed by Edward III (1360). He then visited Spain (1366) before joining the royal household in 1367. In 1369 or 1370 he produced his first important poem, *The Book of the Duchess*, commemorating the recently dead Blanche of Lancaster. He made two visits to Italy, the first on business with the Genoese (1372–73), the second (1378) negotiating with Bernabò Visconti of Milan. From 1374 to 1386 he was a customs controller in the port of London. Poems of the early 1380s include *The House of Fame*, *The Parliament of Fowls*, and *Troilus and Criseyde*. Around 1387 he began work on *The Canterbury Tales*. From 1385 he was associated with the county of Kent in some of his many official capacities and probably lived there until he moved to a house near Westminster Abbey in 1399. He was interred in the abbey the following year.

Acknowledged by his Renaissance successors as the greatest of earlier English writers, Chaucer was an important figure to them on several counts, despite what seems to us the thoroughly medieval nature of his poetry. First, his learning was singled out for special admiration, for instance in the dedication to the first complete edition of his works, published in 1532. The moral lessons implicit in his poetry particularly appealed to an age which held that "wholesome counsel and sage advice" (William Webbe, *Discourse of English Poetry*, 1586) should be mingled with "delight."

**Geoffrey Chaucer** An engraving based on an illumination in the Ellesmere manuscript (c. 1410) of Chaucer's *Canterbury Tales*. This is the earliest known likeness of the poet. *Mary Evans Picture Library*

However, it was in his role of "Dan Chaucer, well of English undefyled" (Spenser, THE FAERIE QUEENE IV ii 32) that he most influenced the literature of the English Renaissance. CAXTON's proem to his second edition of *The Canterbury Tales* (1484) praises Chaucer as "that noble and grete philosopher" who "enbelysshed, ornated, and made faire our Englisshe," and the theme was taken up by several subsequent writers on the development of the vernacular, although SIDNEY in his *Defence of Poesie* was more guarded: "I knowe not whether to mervail more, either that hee [Chaucer] in that mistie time could see so clearly, or that wee in this cleare age, goe so stumblingly after him. Yet had hee great wants, fit to be forgiven in so reverent an Antiquitie."

See also: DESCHAMPS, EUSTACHE

**Cheke, Sir John** (1514–1557) *English humanist*
Cheke was born in Cambridge, where he became a fellow of St. John's College (1529) and took his MA in 1533. He became first Regius Professor of Greek at Cambridge (1540), a canon of Christ Church, Oxford (1544), and tutor in Latin and Greek to King Edward VI. He was knighted in 1552, but, as a Protestant, he was imprisoned and then driven into exile (1554) on the accession of the Catholic Mary I. English agents captured him near Brussels (1556), and he was brought back to England where he was forced to make a humiliating public abjuration of his faith. Consumed with remorse for his recantation, he died in London the following year. A renowned scholar, Cheke made a number of translations of Greek texts into Latin. He also took part in the controversy surrounding the pronunciation of Greek (*see* GREEK STUDIES), his letters opposing Stephen GARDINER on the subject being published in Basle in 1555. This study of phonetics led him to evolve a reformed spelling for English which he used in gospel translations that he made around 1550 and in his letter to Sir Thomas HOBY, published in the latter's translation of Castiglione (1561).

**Chenonceaux, Château de** A château in central France, southwest of Paris, bridging the River Cher. Incorporating a single tower from an earlier building of the 15th century, the château was begun in 1513 by Thomas Bohier, the financial minister of Normandy, but was subsequently confiscated by Francis I and became a royal residence (1535). Noted for its combination of Gothic and Renaissance features, the château was inherited by Henry II who presented it to his mistress DIANE DE POITIERS. She added an arched bridge spanning the Cher, designed by Philibert DELORME. When the château passed to Catherine de' Medici this wing was enlarged (1570–78) by Jean BULLANT as the Grande Galerie.

**chiaroscuro** A term describing the handling of light and dark in the visual arts, particularly with regard to painting. Derived from the Italian words *chiaro* (lightness) and *oscuro* (darkness), chiaroscuro was first developed by artists during the 14th century as a means of heightening atmospheric qualities and achieving three-dimensional effects. The use of contrast of light and dark was also applied to manuscript illustration and, by UGO DA CARPI and PARMIGIANINO, to woodcuts. Also referred to as *tenebrismo*, the effect was employed by numerous artists of the Renaissance, such as CARAVAGGIO (whose followers were sometimes called "tenebristi"), and reached its greatest heights in the 17th-century works of Rembrandt.

**Chigi, Agostino** (1465–1520) *Italian banker and patron of the arts*
Also known as "Il Magnifico," Chigi was a member of a noted Sienese family and the founder of a major banking house in Rome (1485). As leasor (1500) of the papal alum mines and treasurer to the Church he exerted financial influence in several European countries and was in an ideal position to become acquainted with the foremost artists of his day. Peruzzi's masterpiece, the Villa FARNESINA, was built for Chigi near Rome and decorated by RAPHAEL, the

most distinguished of the many artists who enjoyed his patronage. He was also a patron of scholarship and literature, under whose auspices the Cretan Zacharias Calliergis (c. 1473–c. 1524) set up the first Greek press in Rome and published an important edition of Pindar (1515).

## Christian IV (1577–1648) *King of Denmark and Norway (1596–1648)*

Despite his ambitious endeavors to broaden the influence of his country, the status of Denmark as a great power in Europe was weakened during his reign. He embarked upon a series of wars against Sweden including the Kalmar War (1611–13), which Denmark won, and the Torstensson Feud (1643–49), which it lost and as a result of which parts of the kingdom were ceded to Sweden. His intervention in the Thirty Years' War from 1625 to 1629 against Emperor Ferdinand II resulted in the occupation of Jutland by German troops from 1627 to 1629. He erected a number of buildings in Copenhagen, including the Gothic-style Rosenborg Palace (1608–17).

## Christian Majesty, His Most (Latin *Rex Christianissimus*)

A title accorded to the kings of France, especially in papal correspondence of the 15th century onward.

## Christine de Pisan (c. 1364–c. 1430) *Venetian-born French poet and prose writer*

Christine de Pisan grew up at the court of Charles V of France, where her father was astrologer and physician to the king. Widowed with three children at age 25, she began to write poetry to support her family: the success of her early love ballads encouraged her to embark on more serious works in defence of women, such as *Épître au dieu d'amour* (1399), *Cité des dames* (1405; translated as *The Book of the City of Ladies*, 1982), and *Livre des trois vertus* (1406). She vigorously countered the prevalent view (based on Aristotle's *De generatione animalium*) that women were intrinsically inferior to men, illustrating her argument with examples of outstanding women from antiquity to more recent times. Socially conservative, she supported the institution of marriage and a hierarchical society, but argued that women by exercising virtue and moral responsibility were as important as men in maintaining the fabric of society and that they should be educated and respected accordingly. Her treatise on the education of princes, *Le Livre du Corps de Policie* (1407) was translated into Middle English as *The Bodye of Polycye*. Her other writings include a biography of Charles V, *Livre des faits et bonnes moeurs du roi Charles V* (1404), and a number of patriotic stories, notably *Ditié de Jeanne d'Arc*. After the French defeat at Agincourt (1415) Christine took refuge in a convent, where she spent the latter years of her life.

**Further reading:** Charity Cannon Willard, *Christine de Pisan: Her Life and Works* (New York: Persea Books, 1984); Kate Langdon Forham, *The Political Theory of Christine de Pisan* (Aldershot, U.K.: Ashgate, 2002).

## Christus, Petrus (c. 1410–72/73) *Netherlands painter*

Born in Baerle, Christus became in 1444 a citizen of Bruges, which remained his base for the rest of his life. His style was directly conditioned by that of Jan van EYCK, who was probably his master, and his early works such as the *Exeter Madonna* (Berlin) and a pair of triptych wings of 1452 (Berlin) are derived from Eyckian compositions. Christus's Frankfurt *Madonna and Child* (1457) reveals an early mastery of one-point perspective, which may have been learned in Italy. The latter hypothesis remains unproven, although Christus's work was appreciated in Italy shortly after his death and it seems likely that he influenced ANTONELLO DA MESSINA. Christus's style was essentially a simplification and systemization of Jan van Eyck's, which nevertheless perpetuated his mentor's influence during a period when most Netherlands painters sought inspiration in the work of Rogier van der WEYDEN.

## chronicles See HISTORIOGRAPHY

## Chrysoloras, Manuel (1350–1415) *Greek diplomat and teacher of Greek*

Chrysoloras was born in Constantinople and was a pupil of PLETHON. In 1393 he was sent by Emperor Manuel Palaeologus to seek aid from the Italian states against the Turks. He returned to Constantinople but was invited in 1395 to Florence, where he became professor of Greek; his pupils included Poggio BRACCIOLINI, Leonardo BRUNI, and Francesco Barbaro; he also translated Homer and Plato into Latin during his stay there. Chrysoloras then (1400) moved to Milan, Pavia, and Venice, remaining in the last for several years. He then went to Rome and in 1408 was sent to Paris as the Greek emperor's representative. In 1413 he served on the embassy that prepared the way for the Council of CONSTANCE. He died en route for the council to represent the Greek Church. His *Erotemata* (printed 1484) was the first Greek grammar used in the West. His influence was important in introducing a more critical approach to literature based on a close study of language.

## Cicero, Marcus Tullius (106–43 BCE) *Roman statesman and orator*

Cicero was important to the Renaissance on two grounds: the morals that could be drawn from his writings and his private and public life and the example set by his prose style. The former first made him an object of interest to PETRARCH, who as a philosopher and moralist himself was struggling to reconcile the counterclaims of the active and the contemplative life. Coluccio SALUTATI was more swayed by admiration for Cicero's important career in public life, and his view of the Roman statesman generally prevailed among the Florentine humanists and was transmitted through them to later Renaissance moralists. It was Petrarch and a little later Poggio BRACCIOLINI who were responsible for discovering and preserving almost half the writings of Cicero that we still possess, including the letters to Atticus and a number of his most famous orations.

Cicero's status as a model for humanist prose writers struggling to free themselves from medieval Latin style likewise stemmed from Petrarch and grew virtually unchecked, with the backing of men such as Lorenzo VALLA and the educationist GUARINO DA VERONA, for over a century. The powerful rhetoric of his orations, the easy familiarity of his letters, the lucid Latin of his philosophical treatises were all enthusiastically imitated. Inevitably there was a reaction; writers such as POLITIAN, rebuked for using un-Ciceronian vocabulary, defended their right to go beyond its limits in pursuit of self-expression, and ERASMUS wrote his *Ciceronianus* (1528) as a withering attack on the pedants who carried Ciceronianism to absurd extremes. Nevertheless, Cicero continued to be a major influence on Renaissance prose, not only in terms of style but also on account of his philosophy, since many writers found his Stoicism comparatively easy to reconcile with their Christianity. His dialogues on friendship (*De amicitia*) and old age (*De senectute*) were often imitated, and the dialogue form was also carried over into philosophical or didactic works in the vernacular.

## Ciconia, Johannes (c. 1373–1411) *Franco-Flemish composer*

He received his earliest musical education as a choirboy at St. Jean l'Evangeliste, Liège, around 1385. Before 1400 he went to Padua where he became *magister* and a canon at the cathedral, posts which he retained until his death. Mass sections, motets, and secular works, including *ballate*, survive. An advanced approach to imitation is evident in his motets, some of which are ceremonial, occasional works. These date largely from his time in Padua, and include two isorhythmic pieces in honor of the city's bishop.

## Cieco d'Adria, Il See GROTO, LUIGI

## Cieza de León, Pedro (c. 1529–1554) *Spanish conquistador and chronicler of the conquest of Peru*

Born in Extremadura, he spent the years 1535–50 in the New World taking part in the conquest of the northern Andes area (modern Colombia, Ecuador, Peru, and Bolivia). This personal experience, augmented by interviews with Indians and Spaniards, formed the basis of his ambitious *Crónica del Perú* describing the encounter between the *conquistadores* and the Incas. Only the first part, a geographical and ethnographical survey of the Andean provinces, which he presented to Philip II in 1552, was published in Cieza's lifetime (1553).

## Cigoli, Lodovico Cardi da (1559–1613) *Italian painter*

Born at Cigoli in Tuscany and brought up in the tradition of Florentine MANNERISM, he was a pupil of Alessandro ALLORI and SANTI DI TITO but was more influenced by the works of MICHELANGELO, PONTORMO, and ANDREA DEL SARTO. After traveling in Lombardy he returned to Florence, where he painted a series of works for the Palazzo Pitti at the request of the grand duke and frescoes for the church of Sta. Maria Novella (1581–84); the latter mark the transition from Mannerism to the BAROQUE. His best-known work is the very fine painting for St. Peter's in Rome, *St. Peter Healing the Lame Man at the Beautiful Gate of the Temple*. His pictures all comprise fervent ascetic treatments of religious subjects, especially saints. Cigoli died in Rome.

## Cimabue (Cenni di Peppi) (c. 1240–c. 1302) *Italian artist and mosaicist*

Known by his nickname (meaning "bullheaded"), Cimabue was trained in the Byzantine style but was recognized by later scholars, including GHIBERTI and VASARI—the latter began his *Lives* with an account of Cimabue's career—as marking the divide between the art of the Middle Ages and that of the Renaissance.

Although little is known of his life, Cimabue was in Rome in 1272, where he may have been influenced by the developing realism of sculptural art, and in Pisa in 1302. The only surviving work certainly attributed to Cimabue is *Christ in Glory*, part of a large mosaic of St. John in the apse of Pisa cathedral (c. 1302); other works probably by him include the badly deteriorated frescoes in the upper basilica at Assisi (c. 1290), the *Sta. Trinità Madonna* (c. 1290; Uffizi, Florence), and the *Madonna with Angels* (c. 1290–95; Louvre, Paris). These pieces are notable for their combination of traditional Byzantine forms and a new naturalism, seen particularly in his handling of human figures. Another work, the *Crucifix* (c. 1290; Sta. Croce, Florence), was badly damaged in the floods of 1966. Cimabue's approach was subsequently reflected in and indeed eclipsed by the revolutionary paintings of GIOTTO, who may have been Cimabue's pupil, as evidenced by DANTE in his *Divine Comedy*, in which the writer berates Cimabue for his pride and comments that "now Giotto hath the cry." Nonetheless, Cimabue is now generally recognized as the first herald of the ideals of the Renaissance and the most important artist in Italy before Giotto.

## Cima da Conegliano, Giovanni Battista (c. 1460–1518) *Italian painter*

Born at Conegliano near Venice, Cima probably trained under Bartolommeo MONTAGNA and later came under the influence of the style of Giovanni BELLINI. His earliest authenticated picture, an altarpiece now in the museum at Vicenza (1489), demonstrates his control of color and landscape; later works include paintings of the Madonna, the *Incredulity of St. Thomas* (1504; National Gallery, London), and an altarpiece (1493) for the cathedral of Conegliano. Typical of his contemplative paintings is the *Madonna with Six Saints* (c. 1496–99; Accademia, Venice).

**Cinquecento** (Italian, "five hundred") The period of artistic and cultural development in Italy during the 16th century. This period witnessed the culmination of the humanist movement in Renaissance Italy and the spread of mannerist ideals (*see* MANNERISM) from such cultural centers as Venice, Ferrara, Mantua, and Rome under the patronage of the MEDICI, ESTE, GONZAGA, and FARNESE FAMILIES, among others. Leading Italian figures of the century included ARIOSTO, MACHIAVELLI, and CASTIGLIONE in literature, LEONARDO DA VINCI, RAPHAEL, MICHELANGELO, GIORGIONE, TITIAN, and CORREGGIO in painting, Michelangelo in sculpture, PALESTRINA in music, and Michelangelo, Raphael, PALLADIO, VASARI, BRAMANTE, and PERUZZI in architecture.

**Cinthio** (Giambattista Giraldi) (1504–1573) *Italian dramatist, critic, and writer*
Cinthio (an epithet adopted in some of his verses) received a humanist education and taught rhetoric at the university of his native Ferrara (1541–62) until he fell from favor with Ferrara's Este rulers after a lengthy literary feud. He then taught in Pavia, returning to Ferrara shortly before his death. His *Orbecche* (1541), the first performance of tragedy in Italian, is important for introducing the Senecan model (*see* SENECA) in the Renaissance: its main features are a five-act structure, emphasis on the horror of events, and a moralizing style. Three further tragedies, *Didone*, *Cleopatra*, and *Altile* (c. 1543), were followed by the pastoral *Egle* (1545). Later plays look forward to the genre of tragicomedy. Cinthio's collection of *novelle*, *Hecatommithi* (*One Hundred Tales*; 1565) provided plots for his own plays and those of other dramatists, including Shakespeare (*Measure for Measure* and *Othello*). The theory of his dramatic practice was expounded in the discourse *Intorno al comporre delle commedie e delle tragedie* (1543) and a defense of the romance epic, such as ARIOSTO's *Orlando furioso*, was argued in *Intorno al comporre dei romanzi* (1548).

**ciompi** The low-paid day-laborers in Florence's wool industry. In July 1378 the ciompi rebelled against their low wages and their subjection to their employers and the wool guild. They armed themselves and seized power with the help of artisans and shopkeepers. Having overthrown the oligarchy, they then forced through radical and democratic legislation. Their extremism and the worsening economic situation alarmed their allies, many of whom deserted them. The guilds were able to regain control late in August 1378 and to restore oligarchy to Florence.

**Cisneros, Cardinal Francisco Ximénes de** See XIMÉNES DE CISNEROS, CARDINAL FRANCISCO

**Civitali, Matteo** (1436–1501) *Italian architect and sculptor in marble*
Civitali was born and died in Lucca, and most of his work remains in the city or its environs. The cathedral at Lucca contains tombs by Civitali, a pulpit (1494–98), and the Tempietto del Volto Santo (1484), an octagonal marble shrine housing a wooden image of Christ believed to have been the work of Nicodemus. Civitali was the original architect of Lucca's Palazzo Pretorio (1492) and his statue stands in the portico there. Outside Lucca, Civitali has a lectern and candelabra in the cathedral at Pisa and statues of Old Testament figures in Genoa cathedral.

**classics, study of** See CRITICISM, LITERARY; CRITICISM, TEXTUAL; GREEK STUDIES; HUMANISM; LATIN STUDIES

**Claudin** See SERMISY, CLAUDIN DE

**Clavius, Christopher** (Christoph Klau) (1537–1612) *German mathematician and astronomer*
Born at Bamberg, Clavius became a leading Jesuit and professor of mathematics at the Collegio Romano. His views were often sought by the Vatican on controversial scientific matters; thus, between 1588 and 1603, he wrote no fewer than five separate works defending the calendrical reforms of Pope GREGORY XIII in 1582. Clavius was again called upon in 1611 to advise the Vatican authorities upon the reliability and seriousness of GALILEO's telescopic observations. While responding sympathetically to Galileo's work, he advised, nonetheless, that the observations did not constitute a convincing proof of the COPERNICAN SYSTEM. The lunar mountains described by Galileo were covered, Clavius said, with a smooth but transparent crystalline surface. As a mathematician Clavius was known as the author of *Epitome arithmeticae* (1583) and *Algebra* (1608), widely used textbooks of arithmetic and algebra, and he also wrote a major treatise on gnomonics (1581).

Further reading: James M. Lattis, *Between Copernicus and Galileo: Christoph Clavius and the Collapse of Ptolemaic Cosmology* (Chicago, Ill.: University of Chicago Press, 1994).

**Clemens (non Papa), Jacobus** (c. 1510–55/56) *Franco-Flemish composer*
Clemens was succentor at Bruges cathedral (1544–45), and in late 1550 was at 's-Hertogenbosch. It is known that he spent some time in Ypres, but he also had links with Leyden and Dort. The reason for the "non Papa" (not the pope) in his name is uncertain, though it was probably coined as a joke, for Pope Clement VII died in 1534, and the name was not used in a publication until 1545. Clemens was a prolific composer known chiefly for his sa-

cred works. He also wrote many chansons, and his Mass settings are, with one exception, parody settings on chansons and motets by contemporary composers. He is most remembered for his settings of *souterliedekens*, the Dutch psalms. These three-voice pieces were the first polyphonic settings of the psalms in Dutch, with the use of popular song melodies as *cantus firmi*.

## Clement VII (1478–1534) *Pope (1523–34)*

Clement was born Giulio de' Medici at Florence, a bastard nephew of Lorenzo the Magnificent. During the Medici exile from Florence (1494–1512) he traveled extensively in Europe, gaining valuable experience. He took an active part in the Lateran Council of 1512–17, being made archbishop of Florence and a cardinal in 1513, and became political counselor to his cousin, Pope Leo X. He was a candidate for the papacy in 1521 and was elected pope in 1523. His policy was shifty and weak. He attempted to control Italy by supporting alternately Emperor CHARLES V and Francis I of France. After the Sack of Rome in 1527 by imperial troops, he was imprisoned in the Castel Sant' Angelo for several months. In 1530 he crowned Charles (already German king) as Holy Roman Emperor at Bologna. In 1533 he officiated at the wedding of his niece CATHERINE DE' MEDICI to the future Henry II of France. Clement's vacillations over HENRY VIII's petition for a divorce from Catherine of Aragon were one of the causes of the king's repudiation of papal authority. His attempts to deal with LUTHER's revolt were also unsuccessful, and he failed to effect any reforms within the Roman Church. Clement VII was a worldly figure, concerned for the advancement of his family and his own posthumous fame. He was a patron of such eminent artists as Raphael, Michelangelo, Benvenuto Cellini, and Sebastiano del Piombo (see Plate XIV), and of Machiavelli and Copernicus.

## Clement VIII (1536–1605) *Pope (1592–1605)*

He was born Ippolito Aldobrandini at Fano, near Pesaro, and studied law at Padua, Perugia, and Bologna. He held numerous offices in the Roman Curia, became a cardinal in 1585, and was elected pope in 1592. Clement reduced Spanish influence in the college of cardinals, and recognized Henry IV as king of France in 1593. In 1598 he annexed Ferrara to the Papal States, after the death of the last duke without legitimate heirs. He arranged the Treaty of Vervins between France and Spain in 1598, and tried to resolve the controversy between the Jesuits and Dominicans concerning grace and free will. He was responsible for a new standard edition of the Vulgate Bible (the Sistine-Clementine version) and for revisions of the missal, breviary, and pontifical.

## Clitherow, Margaret (c. 1556–1586) *English Roman Catholic martyr*

She married (1571) John Clitherow, a butcher, in her native city of York, whose family had Catholic connections, and in 1574 she converted to Catholicism. Her active zeal in her new faith caused her to undergo a lengthy period of imprisonment, during which time she learnt to read. On her release she set up a school in her house. In 1586 she was charged with harbouring Catholic priests and attending Mass. She refused to plead, and, despite the objections lodged on her behalf by a Puritan divine who had been sent to talk with her in prison, she was sentenced to die by *peine forte et dure*, that is, being crushed to death. She is one of the Forty Martyrs of England and Wales canonized in 1970.

## clocks

Although the clock has been described by Lewis Mumford (*Technics and Civilization*) as "the key-machine of the modern industrial age," little of this significance can have been apparent in the turret clocks which first began to appear in the early 14th century. Driven by falling weights, located in towers, controlled by a verge and foliot escapement, and without hands, they served more as planetaria than clocks. In addition, however, to displaying such phenomena as the phases of the moon, and the motions of planets, they rang bells and, in this manner, marked out the liturgical day for monks and other clerics. Clocks soon, also, came to regulate the working day of many residents of the rapidly growing towns. Such early instruments were too massive and too expensive to make and maintain to be anything other than the property of princes or corporations.

After 1450 the turret clocks were joined by chamber clocks. A common early design was the drum clock, a squat cylinder with the dial on its uppermost surface. This advance was made possible by the invention of the spring drive. Springs, though portable, fail to deliver constant power as they unwind. The solution consisted of attaching the spring by a chain to a conically shaped fusee which acted as an equalizing force as the spring unwound. Improvements in this basic design, together with the use of more accurately produced parts, allowed clockmakers to introduce the minute hand sometime in the 1470s. The second hand followed almost a century later in the decade 1560–70. A more fundamental advance came with the pendulum clock; conceived by GALILEO in 1637, the first such clock actually constructed was the work of Christian Huygens in 1653. The improvement in time-keeping was astonishing: the best clocks had previously varied by about 15 minutes a day, but early pendulum clocks reduced this to no more than 15 seconds.

**See also:** HOROLOGY; WATCHES

**Further reading:** Gerhard Horn-van Rossum, *History of the Hour: Clocks and Modern Temporal Orders*, transl. Thomas Dunlap (Chicago. Ill.: University of Chicago

Press, 1996); David S. Landes, *Revolution in Time: Clocks and the Making of the Modern World* (Cambridge, Mass. and London: Belknap Press of Harvard University Press, 1983).

## Clouet, François (c. 1510–1572) *French artist*
Born at Tours, the son of the Flemish-born painter Jean (or Janet) Clouet (c. 1485–1541), François Clouet inherited his father's position as official painter to Francis I of France. Subsequently painter to Henry II and Charles IX, Clouet continued in the tradition established by his father, executing notable portraits of the Valois court and a number of genre paintings. His portraits include those of Diane de Poitiers (National Gallery, Washington), Pierre Quthe (1562; Louvre, Paris), Charles IX (1570; Kunsthistorisches Museum, Vienna), and *Lady in her Bath* (c. 1570; National Gallery, Washington), which was probably modeled on Marie Touchet, mistress of Charles IX. Although his formal portraits were influenced by the works of his father, his more informal works bore the mark of Italian artists, while his genre paintings followed the style of the Netherlandish school. Clouet was also noted as a brilliant draftsman and many of his drawings survive in the Musée Condé in Chantilly.

## Clovio, Giulio (Jure Clovi1) (1498–1578) *Croatian-born painter*
Clovio was born in Grizane, but lived in Italy after 1516 and probably studied under GIULIO ROMANO in Rome. After the sack of Rome (1527), in which he was captured, Clovio escaped and took holy orders. He was renowned as a miniaturist, demonstrating his pre-eminence in this field in such sequences as his illustrations of the victories of Emperor Charles V (British Library, London) and those in the manuscript life of Federico, Duke of Urbino (Vatican Library). Other commissions included decorations in the Palazzo FARNESE and a *Pietà* (1553; Uffizi, Florence). Clovio also helped and encouraged the young El GRECO on his arrival in Rome.

## Clusius, Carolus (Charles de l'Ecluse) (1526–1609) *Franco-Flemish physician and botanist*
Clusius was born into a Lutheran family in Arras. From his travels in Spain, Portugal, France, Hungary, and Austria he introduced many new garden plants, especially bulbs, to western Europe. The imperial garden in Vienna, which he controlled from 1573 to 1587, was a source of plants from the East, including tulips from Turkey. Clusius was soon acknowledged by his contemporaries as the leading botanical authority of his day, and in addition to personal contacts made on his travels he had a network of correspondents throughout Europe. A number of the New World plants that he obtained were collected with the assistance of Sir Francis DRAKE. He was an accomplished linguist and aided the circulation of fellow botanists' vernacular works by publishing Latin translations or abridgments of them. Among texts to receive this treatment were two on Indian plants and spices: Garcia da Orta's Portuguese *Coloquios dos Simples, e Drogas he Cousas Mediçinais da India* (1563) and Cristoval Acosta's Spanish *Tractado de las Drogas y Medicinas de las Indias Orientales* (1578), of which Clusius published abridgments in 1567 and 1582 respectively. He performed the same service in 1574 for a book on plants of the New World, Nicolas Monardes' *Dos Libros...de nuestras Indas Occidentales* (two parts, 1569, 1571). His own first original work to be published was *Rariorum aliquot stirpium per Hispanias observatarum historia* (1576), the fruit of a botanizing expedition he had made to Spain and Portugal. His magnum opus, *Rariorum plantarum historia*, was prepared during his years as professor at Leyden, where he replanned the university's BOTANIC GARDEN (Hortus Academicus) in 1594; it was published, as many of his books had been, by the Plantin press in 1601.

## Cochanovius, Joannes See KOCHANOWSKI, JAN

## Cochlaeus, Johannes (Johann Dobneck) (1479–1552) *German humanist and Roman Catholic controversialist*
He was born at Wendelstein, near Schwabach, and studied philosophy at Nuremberg (where he was a protégé of PIRCKHEIMER) and Cologne. He was a Platonist and critical of the scholastics. About 1518 he was ordained priest in Rome, and from 1521 he was a bitter opponent of LUTHER. In 1525 he strenuously opposed the printing of TYNDALE's New Testament at Cologne. From 1526 he was a canon of Mainz, transferring to Meissen around 1535 and thence to Breslau (Wrocław, now in Poland) in 1539. His history of the HUSSITES in 12 books and his commentary on the words and deeds of Luther in the period 1517–46, both appeared in 1549.

## Codussi, Mauro (Mauro Coducci) (c. 1440–1504) *Italian architect*
Although he was born near Bergamo, Codussi was active from 1469 in Venice, where he developed a distinctive style based upon the classical architecture of Florence and central Italy. Early buildings included the church of San Michele in Isola (1469–79), which was the first Renaissance church in Venice. San Zaccaria (1483) and the Scuola Grande di San Marco (1485–95) are notable for their facades. The influence of ALBERTI's principles of architecture is evident in many of Codussi's buildings, including his best-known edifices, the Torre dell' Orologio (1496–99) and the Procurazie Vecchie (begun 1496) on the Piazza San Marco. Other major projects undertaken by Codussi were the churches of Sta. Maria Formosa (rebuilt 1492–1502) and San Giovanni Crisostomo (c. 1500), the latter being the first centrally planned Venetian church, the Scuola Grande di San Giovanni Evangelista (1498),

with its famous double staircase, and the Palazzo Corner-Spinelli (c. 1490) and Palazzo Vendramin-Calerghi (1501–09), both Lombardesque in style, but incorporating innovatory features, such as the free-standing classical orders on the facade of the latter palace.

### Coecke van Aelst, Pieter (1502–1550) *Netherlands painter, print maker, and author*

Coecke, who was born in Aelst, is believed to have studied under Bernard van ORLEY and is recorded as a master at Antwerp in 1527. He visited Italy (c. 1530) and Istanbul (1533) and in 1535 may have accompanied Emperor Charles V on his Tunis campaign. He was still at Antwerp in 1544, but subsequently moved to Brussels, where he died. He had a large workshop with many pupils, including the young Pieter BRUEGHEL. His wife, Meyken Verhulst, was also an artist. No surviving paintings of Coecke's can be identified with absolute certainty. His most famous composition, the *Last Supper* (c. 1527), is loosely based upon LEONARDO DA VINCI's famous fresco; it exists in several versions, all possibly replicas of a lost original. Coecke's numerous prints were highly influential and he also designed tapestries and stained glass. The drawings that he made in CONSTANTINOPLE of the exotic costumes, rituals, and topography of the Ottoman capital may have been made with the idea of producing Flemish tapestries with Turkish subjects for the Ottoman market; his widow published them in the form of a much-reproduced series of woodcuts in 1553 (see illustration on p. 116). His most important work, however, was his summary of VITRUVIUS's book on architecture and his translation of the first part of SERLIO's *Tutte l'opere d'architettura e prospettiva* (1539).

### Coelho, Alonso Sánchez (Alonso Sánchez Coello) (c. 1531–1588) *Spanish painter of Portuguese extraction*

Born at Benifayó near Valencia, Sánchez Coelho was educated in Flanders and Portugal and later studied in Brussels, where he became a pupil of Antonio MORO. In 1571 he succeeded his master as court painter to PHILIP II of Spain and established himself as a leading portraitist and royal favorite. Also influenced by Titian, he portrayed members of the Spanish court with great dignity and formality, as in his portraits of Elizabeth of Valois (c. 1560; Kunsthistorisches Museum, Vienna), Philip II (c. 1575; Prado, Madrid), and their daughter Infanta Isabella Clara Eugenia (1579; Prado, Madrid), later ruler of the Netherlands. Besides these portraits, which laid the foundation of the Spanish tradition of portraiture, Sánchez Coelho also produced a number of religious paintings for the Escorial, most of which were conventional and unremarkable. A portrait of St. Ignatius Loyola (1585) is now lost.

### Cognac, League of See ITALY, WARS OF

**coins** See NUMISMATICS

### Colantonio (mid-15th century) *Italian painter*

Active in Naples from about 1440 to 1470, Colantonio was notable chiefly for his fusion of Flemish and Italian artistic styles. Colantonio was apparently familiar with the works of van EYCK, among others, and employed many features of Flemish style in the extant paintings *St. Vincent* (c. 1456), painted for San Pietro Martire, and *St. Jerome* (Museo Nazionale, Naples), painted as part of an altarpiece for the church of San Lorenzo. A notable polyptych for San Severino is now lost. Colantonio's successful blend of Flemish and Italian was subsequently imitated by his own pupil ANTONELLO DA MESSINA.

### Colet, John (c. 1467–1519) *English humanist and educator*

Born in London and educated at Oxford (1483–90), he went in 1493 to France and Italy to complete his studies; in Paris he met BUDÉ and in Florence he studied Plato and Plotinus. He also applied the newly discovered principles

**John Colet,** dean of St. Paul's Cathedral, London. A 16th-century cast of the bust made for the cathedral by Pietro Torrigiano (1520s). This cast, which can be seen in St. Paul's School, London, has stood in successive school buildings since before 1550.

of textual criticism to the Church Fathers. In 1496 he returned to Magdalen College, Oxford, where he introduced the study of Greek. In 1499 he met ERASMUS at Oxford, subsequently exercising considerable influence on the latter's approach to the study of the Bible. In 1505 Henry VII made him dean of St. Paul's Cathedral, London, and in 1509 he established St. Paul's School, the largest Renaissance school to be founded in England. In his foundation statutes Colet decreed that "There shall be taught in the scole children of all nacions and contres indifferently..." Such racial and religious tolerance was remarkable in 16th-century England. Colet's approach to the Scriptures was to interpret them as living literature, going directly to the text rather than engaging in the mystical allegorization characteristic of Florentine Platonism.

Further reading: Sears Jayne, *John Colet and Marsilio Ficino* (Oxford, U.K.: Oxford University Press, 1963).

## Coligny, Admiral Gaspard de Châtillon (1519–1572)
*French Huguenot leader in the Wars of Religion*
He served in Italy and was colonel-general of the infantry before his appointment as admiral of France (1552). While a prisoner of war of Spain (1557–59), after the French defeat at ST-QUENTIN, Coligny converted to Calvinism. He endeavored to reach a compromise with the French monarchy, but after 1569 became the most important HUGUENOT military leader. Although defeated by the Catholic forces at the battle of Poitou in August 1570, Coligny managed to secure a reasonable compromise settlement under the treaty of St.-Germain the following year. He obtained considerable influence over the young king Charles IX, displacing the Catholic Guise faction at court, but his attempts to persuade Charles to send troops to the aid of the Dutch Protestants in their struggle against Spain alienated Charles's mother and former regent CATHERINE DE' MEDICI. The GUISE FAMILY, who blamed Coligny for the assassination of Francis, Duke of Guise in 1563, made a botched assassination attempt on Coligny on August 22, 1572 and two days later ensured that he was one of the first Huguenots to die in the MASSACRE OF ST. BARTHOLOMEW.

## Colleoni, Bartolommeo (1400–1475) *Italian condottiere*
Born near Bergamo, Colleoni first fought (1419) as a condottiere in southern Italy under the leadership of Braccio da Montone and then Muzio Attendolo (*see* SFORZA FAMILY). Colleoni served Venice on several occasions after 1431 and was highly esteemed for his skillful use of light field artillery. Anxious to retain the loyalty of such an able soldier, Venice made Colleoni its commander-in-chief (1454) and paid him lavishly. Colleoni lived luxuriously in his castle of Malpaga near Bergamo, where he received condottieri and also extended to artists and men of letters a cordial welcome that earned him a reputation as a patron

of the arts. The famous bronze EQUESTRIAN MONUMENT of Colleoni in Venice was created by VERROCCHIO in 1485–88.

## Colman family *See* HELMSCHMIED FAMILY

## Colocci, Angelo (1474–1547) *Italian humanist*
Colocci was born at Iesi and from 1497 was a papal secretary, first to Leo X and then to Clement VII. According to Pomponius LETO, Colocci was the true inspiration of Roman humanism. In 1537 he was made bishop of Nocera Umbra. He combined an interest in classical literature with a lively involvement in vernacular poetry, particularly the study of the origins of Italian poetry in Provence. He was himself a poet in both Latin and Italian and his house in Rome was a center for the discussion of literary theory and scholarship. He collected manuscripts and inscriptions but his collections suffered in the sack of Rome (1527). The surviving manuscripts are now in the Vatican library but the collection of inscriptions was dispersed. Colocci is a good example of the humanists' ability to reconcile the demands of religious orthodoxy with allegiance to the values of the classical world.

## Colombe, Michel (1430/35–c. 1515) *French sculptor*
Born in Brittany, Colombe was a member of a family of artists and brother of the miniaturist Jean Colombe (died 1529), who is associated with the Apocalypse manuscript in the Escorial (1482) and the completion of *Les Très Riches Heures du duc de Berry* (1485; Chantilly). Little is known of his early years, from which no works survive, and he is celebrated chiefly for just two sculptures. His masterpiece is the tomb (1502–07) of Francis II of Brittany and Marguerite de Foix in Nantes, with allegorical figures; his other work is the marble relief of St. George and the dragon (1508–09; Louvre, Paris) for the altarpiece of the château de Gaillon. The former of these works was designed by the sculptor Jean Perréal and also worked on by Girolamo da Fiesole; both works demonstrate Colombe's successful combination of the French Gothic style with the artistic ideals of the Italians.

## Colonia, Simón de (died c. 1511) *Spanish architect of German extraction*
His father Juan (died 1481) came to Burgos in the 1440s and built the spires at the western end of the cathedral, and Simón succeeded his father in the post of master of the works there. His two chief monuments are the octagonal Capilla del Condestable (1482–94) at Burgos and the facade of the church of San Pablo, Valladolid (1490–1504), both in the early PLATERESQUE style. Simón's son Francisco (died c. 1542) collaborated with him at Valladolid and succeeded him as master of works at Burgos (1511).

## Colonna, Francesco *See* HYPNEROTOMACHIA POLIFILI

## Colonna, Vittoria (1492–1547) *Italian poet*

A member of an illustrious Roman Ghibelline family, she was betrothed at the age of four and at 19 married to Ferdinando d'Avalos, Marquis of Pescara, to whom she was devoted. After his untimely death (1525) she lived mainly in convents, eventually settling in Rome; she became associated with religious reformers, though she remained within the Church through the influence of her adviser, Cardinal Reginald POLE. Her many literary friendships and correspondents included Aretino, Bembo, Castiglione, Sannazaro, and particularly MICHELANGELO, who addressed a number of poems and letters to her. Her own poems, *Rime* (published several times between 1538 and 1544), are mainly Petrarchan sonnets influenced by Bembo and are concerned with the memory of her husband and with Neoplatonic and religious subjects.

## Colonna family

A noble Roman family, whose members were senators and cardinals from the 13th century. During the 14th century the Colonna's bitterest rivals for power were the Caetani and Orsini families. As Pope Martin V (1417–31), Oddone Colonna increased his family's wealth and power with generous grants of land in the Papal States. The next pope, EUGENIUS IV (1431–47), tried unsuccessfully to force the family to return its estates, and over a century of bitter conflict with the papacy followed, especially when the BORGIA FAMILY was in the ascendancy. The power of the Colonna was eventually brought under control and the family was reconciled with the papacy in the later 16th century.

## colossal order (giant order)

An architectural device in which columns or pilasters rise for more than one story in a facade. Originally devised by the Romans and used on such edifices as triumphal arches, the style was revived during the Renaissance, being reintroduced by Michelangelo who first incorporated it into the Capitol at Rome. After the Renaissance the colossal order was taken up by the Baroque movement and, later, by such 18th-century architects as Sir John Vanbrugh and Nicholas Hawksmoor.

## Columbus, Christopher (Cristoforo Colombo, Cristóbal Colón) (1451–1506) *Italian explorer, credited with the discovery of the Americas*

Columbus was born in Genoa and initially joined the family wool-weaving business, having received little education. At 14 he went to sea, and by 1477 had been to the Levant, Iceland, Ireland, Portugal, and England. After settling in Lisbon, he married in 1479 and solicited patronage for an Atlantic expedition in search of a route to Asia. The king of Portugal refused, and Columbus left for Spain (1484). Through the aid of influential churchmen, Columbus eventually convinced Queen Isabella of the validity of his ideas; in turn, she persuaded King Ferdinand. On August 3, 1492 Columbus sailed from Saltes, an island near Palos, with 120 men and three small ships, led by the *Santa Maria*. He went first to the Canary Islands, then sailed westwards. In October he reached the Bahamas, much to the relief of his terrified crew. He proceeded to Cuba and Haiti (Hispaniola), where he founded the first Spanish settlement in the New World. On his return to Spain with gold, plants, birds, and six Indians, he was immediately made a grandee.

On September 24, 1493 Columbus set sail again. During the next three years he refounded the Hispaniola colony at Isabella and thoroughly explored and attempted to chart the West Indies. His third voyage in 1498 achieved landfall on the South American mainland, but mischief-makers persuaded Ferdinand to supplant Columbus as governor of Hispaniola, and Francisco de Bobadilla, the new governor, sent Columbus back to Spain in chains (1500). On his arrival, however, he was triumphantly vindicated, and in 1502 he set off to search for a route to Asia between Cuba and South America. This failed for obvious reasons, and Columbus returned (1504) to Spain much weakened in health. He died at Valladolid, but in 1542 his remains were transferred to Hispaniola.

Columbus's own log of his first journey, or the paraphrase of it by Bartolomé de LAS CASAS—opinions differ as to the status of the text—was edited and translated by J. H. Cohen along with other documents in *The Four Voyages of Christopher Columbus* (1969). Columbus's son Ferdinand (Fernando Colón) wrote the earliest biography of his father, translated into English by Benjamin Keen as *The Life of the Admiral Christopher Columbus, by His Son Ferdinand* (1959; 2nd ed., with new introduction, 1992). Since the 500th anniversary of Columbus's first voyage his achievements have often been negatively reassessed; it has been pointed out that he was not the first European to reach the Americas and, irrationally, he is held responsible for the genocidal impact of the Spanish conquest upon the native Americans.

**Further reading:** Miles H. Davidson, *Columbus Then and Now: A Life Reexamined* (Norman, Okla.: University of Oklahoma Press, 1997); Mary Ellen Jones (ed.), *Christopher Columbus and His Legacy: Opposing Viewpoints* (San Diego, Calif.: Greenhaven Press, 1992); Samuel E. Morison, *Christopher Columbus: Admiral of the Ocean Sea* (London: Oxford University Press, 1942), as *Admiral of the Ocean Sea: A Life of Christopher Columbus* (Boston, Mass.: Little Brown, 1942).

## comedy

There is little evidence of any significant staged comedy between the death of the Roman playwright TERENCE (159 BCE) and the late Middle Ages, when comic elements reemerged in the rough clowning that formed part of the mystery play and in the comic Vice of the morality play and the later INTERLUDE. In these, comic passages ridiculed everyday foibles, favorite subjects being love and money—that is, infidelity and financial chicanery. In France, the Feast of Fools was introduced in cathedral liturgies between Christmas and the Octave of the Epiphany (January 13) and gave an opportunity to the lower clergy to poke fun at their superiors with a parody sermon (*sermon joyeux*), an ass led into the church to add its bray to the responses, and other farcical proceedings. Secular farces, of which some 150 examples (each about 500 lines of octosyllabic verse) survive, evolved from these origins in France. Although there were doubtless many comic performances of some kind in the 14th and 15th centuries, they were apparently not considered worth preserving and documentation is therefore scarce. Under the auspices of the CHAMBERS OF RHETORIC medieval farce persisted well into the 16th century in the Netherlands; several such farces, known as *esbattements*, in a collection from this period made in Haarlem are representative of the genre. Furthermore, as with TRAGEDY, comedy was not in the medieval view conceived of as a dramatic production. The statement by Vincent of Beauvais (c. 1190–c. 1264) in the *Speculum maius*, that a comedy is a poem which begins in misfortune and concludes happily, is the same general conception echoed by Dante in explaining the purpose of the *Divine Comedy* (Epistle to Cangrande). Chaucer's one use of the word, at the end of *Troilus and Criseyde* (V 1788), reflects a similar understanding.

The revival of theatrical comedy in the Renaissance can be traced to the production in Ferrara in 1486 by Duke Ercole d'Este of PLAUTUS's *Menaechmi*. ARIOSTO, who was taken to this performance by his father, subsequently supervised theatricals at the Este court and took Roman comedy as his model, first in *La cassaria* (1508). The COMMEDIA ERUDITA was soon well established in Italy and with the rise of the COMMEDIA DELL'ARTE a rich and varied theatrical tradition emerged, with fruitful interaction between the two types of comedy. Productions in Latin or translations or adaptations of Plautus and Terence were common elsewhere as well in the early 16th century. In England HENRY VIII ordered two performances of Plautus in 1526 as part of an entertainment for the French ambassador, and the boys of St. Paul's School acted Terence's *Phormio* before Cardinal Wolsey. In France RONSARD translated Aristophanes' *Plutus* and Étienne JODELLE is credited with the first French comedy, *Eugène* (1552). Jacques GRÉVIN, Jean de LA TAILLE, Rémy BELLEAU, and Jean-Antoine de BAÏF also adapted Plautus and Terence directly or were influenced by them via Italian works. Other early translators or adapters include Jean Meschinot (c. 1420–91), Octavien Saint-Gelais (1468–1502), and Charles Estienne (1504–64). Most French comedy before Molière was written in octosyllabic verse, but the prose comedies of La Taille, Pierre de LARIVEY, and Adrien TOURNÈBE are notable exceptions.

In Spain, Bartolomé de TORRES NAHARRO distinguished (in *Propalladia*, 1517) two types of play: the *comedia a noticia* (comedy of wit, emphasizing plot and intrigue) and the *comedia de apariencia* (or *de tramoya* or *de ruido*), the comedy of spectacle depending on stage machinery, scene changes, etc. The former type flourished in the voluminous work of Lope de VEGA, whose thoroughly anti-classical recommendations in *Arte nuevo de hacer comedias* (c. 1607) include mixing comic and tragic elements and ignoring the unities.

In England the earliest important works are Nicholas UDALL's classical academic comedy *Ralph Roister Doister* (written c. 1553), *Gammer Gurton's Needle* (performed 1566), and George Gascoigne's *Supposes* (performed 1566), the first surviving prose comedy, which Gascoigne adapted from Ariosto's *I suppositi*. All three were first produced in an academic setting: in a London school, at Christ's College, Cambridge, and at Gray's Inn, respectively. Otherwise the works of SHAKESPEARE and Ben JONSON, written for the public theater or court performance, overshadow other English comedies. It has been noted that Shakespeare wrote every type of comedy—Plautine, romantic, pastoral, farce and the "dark" comedies—except satirical. This gap was filled by Jonson, whose plays are perhaps the best illustrations of the most common Renaissance view of comedy: a strong emphasis on its reformatory function in mercilessly exposing and ridiculing the vices and follies of man. Not only did Jonson observe the rules of classical construction, but he also developed a theoretical framework for his satire in the early comedies of humors and went on to write two of the comic masterpieces of the English theater, *Volpone* (performed 1606; printed 1607) and *The Alchemist* (performed 1610; printed 1612).

## Comes, Juan Bautista (1568–1643) *Spanish composer*

Comes began his musical education at the cathedral of Valencia where he was a chorister and a pupil of Gines Pérez. In 1605 he was appointed choirmaster at the cathedral of Lérida and in 1613 he became the choirmaster of Valencia cathedral. In 1619 he entered the service of Philip III in Madrid, returning to Valencia after 10 years when he resumed his post as choirmaster. The most notable of Comes's surviving compositions, which amount to around 250 pieces, are his *villancicos*, sacred songs based on secular polychoral arrangements.

## Commandino, Federico (1509–1575) *Italian humanist and mathematician*

Born into a noble family at Urbino, Commandino, after studying philosophy and medicine at Padua university, returned to his native land as tutor and physician at the court of the duke of Urbino. More importantly, Commandino began to collect and to translate into Latin the major surviving texts of Greek MATHEMATICS. Beginning in 1558 with an edition of Archimedes, Commandino went on to issue Latin translations of the *Conics* of Apollonius (1566), the *Elements* of Euclid (1572), and the *Pneumatics* of Hero (1575). He also wrote an original treatise on the center of gravity of solid bodies (1565). At his death Commandino was working on an Italian translation of Euclid's *Elements*.

*Commedia, Divina* See DIVINE COMEDY

*commedia dell'arte* (Italian, "comedy of the craft") The improvisational comedy that takes its name from the actor's craft, in the sense of both his technique and the guild of actors. Created by Italian theatrical troups, it flourished from the mid-16th to the end of the 18th centuries. A number of stereotyped characters were played by actors who specialized in particular roles and performed extempore from a three-act scenario that provided a mere outline of the proceedings. The emphasis was on broad comic action with all manner of theatrical business, including acrobatics, and a traditional stock of verbal and visual jests (*lazzi*). The characters were readily identifiable: Pantalone, the grasping Venetian merchant; Graziano, the pedantic Bolognese lawyer; the *miles gloriosus*, or braggart soldier, often a Spaniard (Captain Matamoros); lovers whose language was Petrarchan and Tuscan; comically coarse female servants (Franceschina); and a number of *zanni* (zanies, buffoons). The Bergamask Arlecchino and Neapolitan Pulcinella survive as Harlequin and Punch. The masked actors drew on a variety of sources and traditions and developed an enormous repertoire of dialogue and gesture. Since actors also performed in the COMMEDIA ERUDITA, literary theater was both enriched by and was a source for the *commedia dell'arte*. Guilds—for example, the Gelosi, Desiosi, Confidenti, Uniti, Accesi—were formed in the mid-16th century (the first recorded in 1545) and they spread the influence of the *commedia dell'arte* throughout Europe. Distinguished, highly respected, and academically honored actors and families of actors—for example, Francesco and Isabella Andreini and the nobleman Flaminio Scala—directed some of the *commedia dell'arte* companies.

Further reading: Robert Henke, *Performance and Literature in the Commedia dell'Arte* (Cambridge, U.K.: Cambridge University Press, 2003).

*commedia erudita* (Italian, "erudite comedy") Italian vernacular comedy of the 16th century that imitated the Latin comedies of Plautus and Terence. While the action, construction, and certain stock characters were derived from the Roman models, and the unities of time (a single day) and place were observed, the settings were contemporary Italian urban ones; the actions involved more than one plot and these drew on a wealth of postclassical stories and novellas as well as on the Latin sources. Typically the problems faced by lovers are finally resolved in marriage after much intrigue and trickery involving mistaken identities and disguises, conniving servants and other

clever, shady, or gullible comic types. Major examples of the *commedia erudita* are *La cassaria* (*The Coffer*; 1508) by ARIOSTO, *La calandria* (*The Follies of Calandro*; 1513) by BIBBIENA, and *La mandragola* (*The Mandrake Root*; 1518) by MACHIAVELLI. *La calandria* and Plautus's *Menaechmi* respectively provided inspiration for FIRENZUOLA's *La triunizia* and *I lucidi* (both 1549). Later examples tend to have more intricate plots, to develop moral and romantic elements, and to show the increasing influence of the COMMEDIA DELL'ARTE. Among the many writers of the type are Francesco d'Ambra (1499–1558), who wrote the prose play *Il Furto* (acted 1544) and *I Bernardi* and *La cofanaria* (acted 1547/65) in verse, Anton Francesco GRAZZINI, Giovanni Maria Cecchi (1518–87), Pietro ARETINO, Annibale CARO, and Giambattista DELLA PORTA.

**Common Life, Brothers and Sisters of the** The name adopted by the followers of Gerard (Geert) Groote (1340–84) of Deventer, a widely traveled Carthusian monk and mystic based in Holland. The Brethren of the Common Life were a quasi monastic association of laity and secular clergy dedicated to the cultivation of inner spirituality and good works. Their classic statement of belief is encapsulated in the *Imitatio Christi* (*Imitation of Christ*; c. 1418), attributed to Thomas à Kempis (c. 1380–1471), the most celebrated Christian mystical work ever written and widely read during his lifetime. Although essentially medieval and conservative, the book was to have lasting significance in its tendency to personalize religion and minimize the importance of formal Christianity. Another influential book that had its origins in the movement was the *Spieghel der Volcomenheit*, a treatise on mystical theology by Henricus Herp (died 1477), who later joined the Franciscans; it was translated into Latin and thence into several European languages. The brethren's emphasis on inner spirituality greatly influenced Christian humanists and some of the reformers; Nicholas CUSANUS and Rudolf AGRICOLA were among the influential figures in the first wave of northern European humanists who were members. Both ERASMUS and LUTHER were educated by members of the movement, which was at its peak during the second half of the 15th century.

See also: DEVOTIO MODERNA

**communications** The improvement in trade and transport during the Renaissance was modest compared to that of later centuries. Travel by land and sea was still slow and dangerous. At sea most ships hugged the Mediterranean or northern coasts, but improved NAVIGATION and ship design in the 15th century made sailors bolder. The development of the sea-going CARAVEL by Portugal (from about 1430) opened the way for the exploration of the world's oceans. By the late 16th century Europe was part of a global network of maritime communications.

Major rivers like the Po, Adige, Ebro, and Rhine were still prime routes for travel and trade, but were becoming unpopular because of frequent tolls, marked by chains stretched across the river. Canals existed but were used mainly for local drainage or irrigation, and their usefulness for transportation was limited; not only was upkeep on them very expensive, but until the invention of the lock to raise and lower boats they could only run over level areas. Although such devices possibly existed in the Netherlands in the 14th century, there is an early documented instance of a lock in 1438–39 in northern Italy, and one of LEONARDO DA VINCI's engineering feats was to construct six locks linking the canals of Milan.

Travel by land was slow; at best a traveler covered 60 miles in 24 hours. A third of that distance was more normal. Speediest of all were the professional courier services which were developed where more settled conditions allowed, mainly from the mid-15th century. These relied on regular changes of horse at establishments set up for the purpose ("post houses"). Such a service was beyond the means of most individuals and was the prerogative of governments or wealthy trading companies. Most travellers were pedestrians, sometimes with pack animals. Some roads were improved by paving, especially near big cities, and with adequate hostelries and policing roads could be tolerably pleasant, but most were muddy tracks, full of potholes and vulnerable to brigands. Vehicles were improved by movable front axles in the late 15th century and the first coaches appeared in the late 16th century.

**See also:** TRAVEL

**Further reading:** Margaret Wade Labarge, *Medieval Travellers* (London: Hamish Hamilton, 1982; New York: W. W. Norton, 1983); Antoni Mączak, *Travels in Early Modern Europe*, transl. Ursula Phillips (Cambridge, U.K.: Polity Press and Cambridge, Mass: Blackwell, 1995).

**Complutensian Polyglot** (1522) A six-volume Spanish edition of the Bible that made the text available for the first time in parallel columns of Greek, Latin, and Hebrew. Begun in 1502, it was edited and financed by Cardinal Francisco XIMÉNES DE CISNEROS, who was Queen Isabella's confessor and the founder of the university of Alcalá (Latin name: Complutum), the town after which this Bible is known. The Complutensian Polyglot is an outstanding early example of humanist scholarship employed in the service of religious reform within the Catholic Church.

**Compromise of Breda** See BREDA, COMPROMISE OF

**Comuneros, Revolt of the** (1520–21) The rebellion of the Spanish nobility and commoners against their Flemish-born king, Charles I (Emperor CHARLES V). On his first visit to Spain (1517), the new king enraged the nobles by his partiality for his Flemish advisers, upset the commoners by making heavy financial demands, and

united the two parties against him by his manifest intention of ruling Spain as an absentee while pursuing his European ambitions. Open disaffection broke out in 1520, and for a time Charles's position seemed seriously threatened. The king however managed to win round part of the malcontent aristocracy, certain towns, notably Seville, remained loyal, and after a defeat was inflicted on the rebels at Villalar in April 1521, the revolt collapsed, leaving Charles with enhanced power and prestige.

*conceptismo* See GÓNGORA Y ARGOTE, LUIS DE; QUEVEDO Y VILLEGAS, FRANCISCO GÓMEZ DE.

*concetto* (Italian, literally, "concept" or "idea") From the 17th century a term also having the specialized meaning "literary conceit," essentially an elaborate and striking metaphor drawing a parallel between two very unlike objects, qualities, or experiences. Two types are usually distinguished: the Petrarchan conceit, as employed by PETRARCH in his love poems, by his imitators (for example, the French and Elizabethan sonneteers), and by TASSO; and the metaphysical conceit, especially associated with the verse of John Donne and the English Metaphysical poets. The Petrarchan figure typically compares the beloved's beauty (or the lover's emotions) to very dissimilar concrete objects, often with hyperbolic exaggeration. In many of Petrarch's imitators, this amounts to nothing more than the trite and conventional love imagery which SHAKESPEARE deflates in his sonnet beginning "My mistress' eyes are nothing like the sun."

**Concord, Book of** (1580) The publication comprising the Lutheran statement of doctrine known as the Formula of CONCORD, the three ecumenical creeds, Luther's two catechisms, the Confession of AUGSBURG, the Apology for the Confession of Augsburg, and the SCHMALKALDIC ARTICLES. The book was accepted by 86 rulers, princes, and imperial cities, but rejected by many others, including the king of Denmark who threw his copy into the fire. It was first published in German at Dresden, and a Latin edition appeared in 1584.

**Concord, Formula of** (March 1577) A formulation of Lutheran faith. Its original inspiration lay in a series of articles by Jakob Andreae (1528–90) that had resulted in the Swabian-Saxon Formula of Concord (1575) and the Torgau Book (1576). The Formula of Concord clarified the Lutheran position concerning doctrines associated with MELANCHTHON and CALVIN by rejecting the former's doctrine of the Eucharist and the Calvinist doctrine of double PREDESTINATION. It proved to be only a partial settlement of Lutheran debates since many Lutherans, especially those outside Germany, rejected its conclusions, including the king of Denmark and several important cities. For this reason the Formula never possessed the authority of the Confession of AUGSBURG.

**condottieri** Mercenaries employed by Italian states under the system of *condotte* ("contracts"). Initially they were mainly foreigners, but condottieri of Italian origin grew in number as men like Niccolò PICCININO, Francesco Sforza (*see* SFORZA FAMILY), and Bartolommeo COLLEONI realized the financial and social opportunities afforded by mercenary activity. Facino CANE in Milan during the rule (1402–12) of the weak Giovanni Maria Visconti is a prime example of the over-powerful condottiere. Condottieri came from all classes. They were regarded, in MACHIAVELLI's venomous criticism of the system, as treacherous and dedicated to the perpetuation of strife. They studied war as an art, relying mainly on cavalry armed with lances, and their heyday passed with the development of infantry and artillery in warfare.

**confession** The Christian Church has always insisted that sins must be both acknowledged and denounced by the sinner who seeks reconciliation with God. By the early Renaissance period, it was standard practice to confess sins in private to a priest. The priest, having been given powers of distributing forgiveness (absolution) at ordination, stipulated a penalty (penance) for the sinner, and formally announced that the sinner's transgressions had been forgiven. Absolved sinners were properly and demonstrably to quash their ungodly habits (repentance).

Protestant reformers did not credit the ritual of confession with sacramental power and criticized it as a sideshow that distracted believers from communicating directly with an always accessible God. LUTHER complained that the process increased communities' awe for and reliance on a priesthood that was arrogantly usurping a forgiving role that only Christ could rightly exercise. The Protestants ultimately rejected formal private confession, believing that public, collective liturgies at religious ceremonies were adequate to demonstrate believers' shame at their sins.

*conquistadores* (Spanish, "conquerors") Spanish soldiers of fortune who overthrew the native American Indian civilizations of Central and South America in the 16th century and claimed their lands for Spain. Their exploits are recounted in the Spanish NEW WORLD CHRONICLES. Preeminent among them were Hernán CORTÉS, who conquered Mexico, and Francisco PIZARRO, conqueror of Peru.

**Consensus Tigurinus** See ZÜRICH AGREEMENT

**Constance, Council of** (1414–17) The Church council convoked at Constance in southern Germany by Pope John XXIII, at the insistence of Emperor Sigismund. It is an important landmark in the history of the movement for conciliar government of the Church, and in 1415 it declared itself a "general council," that is the supreme authority within Christendom, over and above that of popes. When the council convened in 1414 there were three cardinally elected popes, one in Rome, one at Avignon, and one at Pisa. The council was successful in ending this state of affairs, the GREAT SCHISM (*see* AVIGNON, PAPACY AT), by deposing two of the contending popes and ensuring the abdication of the third. In their place the council promoted Oddone Colonna as Martin V (pope 1417–31).

In accordance with the wishes of Sigismund, the council took action against the potentially heretical and revolutionary Bohemian HUSSITES. Employing its newfound authority the council condemned and executed the movement's leaders, Jan HUSS and Jerome of Prague. When the council dissolved itself (1417) it left as its legacy legislation that made possible the claims of supremacy made by Church councils during the next 50 years. Although power was restored in full to the papacy by the end of the century, the Council of Constance had demonstrated papal fallibility, and support for representative conciliar government remained.

**Constantinople** (formerly **Byzantium**, now **Istanbul**) The city on the European shores of the Bosphorus straits, now in Turkey. Its commanding position at the entrance to the Black Sea ensured its commercial and strategic significance ever since its foundation as the Greek colony of Byzantium in 667 BCE. It was refounded by Constantine the Great in 330 AD as Constantinopolis, the New Rome in the East. When the Roman empire split in 395 CE, Constantinople became the capital of the eastern part. Theological differences and rivalry between the patriarchate in Constantinople and the papacy in Rome led to schism in 1054. In 1204 forces of the Fourth Crusade, under Venetian leadership, sacked Constantinople. Attempts were made to heal the breach at the councils of Lyons (1276) and Florence (1439), but Western Christendom lacked the will to come to the aid of the Byzantine emperor in the face of the growing threat from the OTTOMAN TURKS. In 1453 Constantinople fell to the forces of Sultan Mehmet II ("the Conqueror").

Diplomatic contacts between Constantinople and the West in the 14th and early 15th centuries first alerted Western scholars to the treasures of classical Greek literature that had been preserved by Byzantine copyists; envoys from the East tarried in Italy to teach Greek to local scholars and these scholars sometimes visited Constantinople and returned home laden with Greek manuscripts (*see* AURISPA, GIOVANNI; FILELFO, FRANCESCO). As the Turks advanced, learned refugees from former Byzantine lands fled westwards, bringing with them their knowledge of Greek.

**Constantinople** This panorama by Pieter Coecke van Aelst, based on a drawing made during his visit in 1533, shows the western European's interest in the antiquities and buildings of the great city and the exotic appearance of its inhabitants.

Once Constantinople was under Turkish rule few westerners were enthusiastic about attempting to regain it for Christendom, despite some papal efforts to muster a crusade in the 1450s and 1460s; most people were much more concerned about the threat nearer home, as the Ottomans menaced the heartland of Europe. Nonetheless, there was some limited contact between Constantinople and the West during the 16th century. The mercantile nations such as England saw it as a promising destination for trading missions, while other visitors, such as Pieter COECKE VAN AELST, who went there in 1533, were interested in observing the exotic dress and rituals of the sultan's court. Diplomats who wrote of their experiences all remarked on the elaborate protocol that governed reception at the SUBLIME PORTE. Merchants from the West were keen to establish trading privileges that would enable them to obtain the luxury items for which the Ottoman capital was famous in the 16th century: textiles, carpets, and ceramics. The Turks' liking for sophisticated automata, often incorporating clocks, meant in turn that there was a ready outlet for items from European workshops such as a clockwork model of a Turkish ship made in Augsburg around 1585; it had two rowers, a monkey on the prow, and an admiral pasha standing on top of the cabin (the actual clock), all of which moved on the hour or quarter-hour. As a diplomatic overture from England in 1599 Queen Elizabeth dispatched the organ-builder Thomas Dallam with one of his instruments as a gift for the sultan. Artistic contacts date from near the start of the Ottoman period when Mehmet II invited the Venetian Gentile Bellini (c. 1429–1507) to live at his court (1479–81); Bellini's portrait of the sultan is in the National Gallery, London. However, it was artists in the entourages of ambassadors who were the prime means by which images of Ottoman Constantinople were transmitted to the West. One such was Nicolas de Nicolay, who visited in 1551 as part of Henry II of France's embassy to the sultan; he wrote a successful and much-translated book about his stay in Constantinople, illustrated with engravings that formed the stock images of Turks in the Western imagination for many years. Melchior Lorichs, who probably accompanied Ogier Ghislain de BUSBECQ in 1555, drew the architectural monuments of the city as well as producing figure studies and a portrait of Sultan Suleiman the Magnificent.

**Further reading:** Deno John Geanakoplos, *Constantinople and the West* (Madison, Wis.: University of Wisconsin Press, 1989); Stanley Mayes, *An Organ for the*

*Sultan* (London: Putnam, 1956); Gülru Necipolglu, *Architecture, Ceremonial, and Power: The Topkapi Palace in the Fifteenth and Sixteenth Centuries* (Cambridge, Mass.: MIT Press, 1992).

**contado** The territory adjoining an Italian city that was subject to the laws and taxes of that city.

**Contarini, Cardinal Gasparo** (1483–1542) *Italian Catholic reformer*
Born into a leading Venetian family, Contarini studied philosophy and natural science at Padua before turning to theology. He experienced a spiritual conversion in 1511 and remained throughout his life sympathetic to Erasmian doctrine and humanist principles. In 1518 he became an ambassador and developed a profound knowledge of Rome and the imperial court. Having been made a cardinal (1535) by PAUL III, in 1536 he was appointed head of a commission designed to initiate reform of the Church. In his work as commissioner and as papal legate at REGENSBURG (1541) it is evident that Contarini failed fully to appreciate the fundamental spiritual conflict between Protestant and Catholic in his assumption that formal reorganization of the Church, coupled with certain concessions to the Lutheran doctrine of JUSTIFICATION BY FAITH, would achieve reconciliation. Criticized on account of his *Epistola de justificatione* (1541) as a "crypto-Lutheran" and embittered by his failure at Regensburg, Contarini died the following year. Although he never shared in the true spirit of the coming COUNTER-REFORMATION, Contarini played a part through his keen support of IGNATIUS LOYOLA during the early 1540s. Besides works on theological topics and ecclesiastical reform, Contarini wrote (1523/24) a renowned book on Venetian statecraft, *De magistratibus et republica Venetorum* (1543); it was translated into English in 1599 and became a key text in debates on the optimum form of political constitution.

Further reading: Peter Matheson, *Cardinal Contarini at Regensburg* (Oxford, U.K.: Clarendon Press, 1972).

**Conti, Niccolò dei** (c. 1395–1469) *Italian traveler*
Born in Chioggia, in Venetian territory, he spent the years between 1415 and c. 1439 traveling in the Middle East, India, and Southeast Asia. Forced at one point to convert to Islam to save his life, he applied on his return to Italy for absolution from the pope and was interrrogated at length by the pope's secretary Poggio BRACCIOLINI, who wrote down his story and published it as an illustration of the fickleness of fortune in his *Historia de varietate fortunae* (1448). In later life Conti held various official posts in the Venetian state. The first printed edition of his narrative appeared in Milan in 1492; translations into Portuguese (1502) and Spanish (1503) followed. The Italian version in RAMUSIO's collection (1550) was widely circulated but has many errors.

*contrapposto* A pose, used especially in sculpture in the round, in which the torso of a sculpted figure is twisted and its weight thrown onto one leg. This device was developed originally by the ancient Greeks in the fifth century BCE and later revived in Renaissance Italy by LEONARDO DA VINCI and others, being employed to great effect in MICHELANGELO's *David* (Accademia, Florence). The pose was equally adapted to draped or nude figures and introduced both tension and realism, with an aesthetically interesting play of light on the different angles and masses of the sculpture. It was used at an early date by DONATELLO and VERROCCHIO, and exaggerated *contrapposto* (*figura serpentinata*) became a favorite device of the mannerist sculptors such as CELLINI and GIAMBOLOGNA.

**Contucci, Andrea** See SANSOVINO, ANDREA

*conversos* In Spain, Jews who had converted to Christianity. Although *conversos* and descendants of *conversos*, such as Álvaro de LUNA, rose to high office in 14th- and 15th-century Spain, ANTISEMITISM was a constant factor and was institutionalized in the persecutions conducted by the SPANISH INQUISITION. Curiously, some of the most zealous persecutors of the Jews were themselves of *converso* stock—the antipope Benedict XIII (Pedro de Luna; died 1423) and TORQUEMADA, to name but two. Particularly at risk were the *marranos*, professed converts, either Jews or Moors, who continued to practice their ancestral religion in secret.

See also: MENDES, GRACIA; MORISCOS

**cookery** See FOOD AND COOKING

**Coornheert, Dirck Volckertsz.** (1522–1590) *Dutch humanist and scholar*
As a young man Coornheert, who was born in Amsterdam, read widely on religious matters, eventually adopting a brand of evangelical humanism which brought him into conflict with both Catholics and reformers. From 1566 he was also associated with WILLIAM THE SILENT in the political struggle against Spain, an involvement which forced him to withdraw into exile in 1568, where he acted as the prince's political agent in Cleves. Returning to Holland in 1572, Coornheert became embroiled in a serious theological controversy with orthodox Calvinists, defending his views on free will. His writings influenced the young Arminius (appointed to refute Coornheert but in large measure persuaded by him), and he is consequently seen as one of the forebears of ARMINIANISM.

A truly versatile figure, Coornheert was also an engraver and book illustrator, illustrating NOOT's *Das Buch Extasis* (1576). From 1577 he was a notary at Haarlem, but moved to Delft and finally Gouda in 1588. He translated works by Cicero, Boethius, and Seneca, the *Odyssey*, and various tales from Boccaccio's DECAMERON. He also wrote poetry and plays and in his prose works, many of them polemics against the Calvinists, he strove to improve the quality of his native language. *Zedekunst* (1586) is modeled on the ethical treatises of the ancient Stoics. He also began, but left incomplete, a Dutch version of the New Testament.

**Copernican system** The cosmological scheme advanced in COPERNICUS's *De revolutionibus* (1543), contrary to the traditional geocentric astronomy of Ptolemy (*see* PTOLE-MAIC SYSTEM). In the Copernican system the universe is centered upon the sun, around which the earth and all other celestial bodies revolve with uniform motion in perfectly circular orbits; in addition the earth rotates daily around its own axis (see illustration p. 121). In this simple manner Copernicus accounted for the observed rotation of the heavens by the daily movement of just one body. Many, however, considered it most implausible to suppose that the earth could move in such a manner. Buildings would collapse, it was objected, and stones dropped from a hand would not fall directly to the ground. Cavils of this kind continued to be raised for some time; until, in fact, they were only dispeled by the better analysis of the nature of motion offered by GALILEO and his successors.

On the matter of planetary orbits, however, Copernicus appears less innovatory. Like Ptolemy, he assumed without question that planets moved in circular orbits with a uniform velocity. Such a theory is far too simple to describe the planets' paths as they move in their elliptical orbits with their varying velocities. Thus, to account, for example, for their variable velocities and their constantly changing distances from the sun, Copernicus found it necessary to locate each of the planets on its own epicycle. In this way he found himself as dependent upon eccentrics and epicycles as any Ptolemaic astronomer. It has been calculated that he actually increased the number of such constructions from the 40 of the *Almagest* to the 48 found in *De revolutionibus*. Complications of this kind persisted in ASTRONOMY until the time of KEPLER and his realization that planets moved in elliptical orbits.

Damaging theological objections remained. In the Bible Joshua, for instance, had commanded the sun, not the earth, to stand still (Joshua 10:12–13). Consequently, in 1616 the Holy Office placed *De revolutionibus* on the INDEX LIBRORUM PROHIBITORUM, where it remained until 1822. Kepler's *Epitome astronomiae Copernicanae* met a similar fate in 1619.

**Further reading:** Owen Gingerich, *The Eye of Heaven: Ptolemy, Copernicus, Kepler* (Berlin: Springer Verlag, 1993); Thomas S. Kuhn, *The Copernican Revolution* (Cambridge, Mass.: Harvard University Press, 1966; repr. 1992).

**Copernicus, Nicolaus** (1473–1543) *Polish astronomer*
The son of a merchant, Copernicus was born at Torun and educated at Cracow university and at various Italian universities where he studied medicine and law. On his return to Poland in 1506 he served as physician and secretary to his uncle Lucas, Bishop of Ermland. On his uncle's death (1512), Copernicus took up the post of canon of Frauenburg cathedral to which he had been appointed in 1499. By this time he had already abandoned the traditional astronomy of antiquity (*see* PTOLEMAIC SYSTEM) and had begun to formulate the revolutionary system with which his name has been associated (*see* COPERNICAN SYSTEM). The new system was first described in his *Commentariolus*, a brief tract completed sometime before 1514 and circulated in manuscript to interested scholars. Thereafter he worked out the details of the new system in an exact and comprehensive manner in his *De revolutionibus orbium coelestium* (1543; translated as *Concerning the Revolutions of the Heavenly Spheres*, 1952). Although it was complete in manuscript by 1530 Copernicus seemed, for no very clear reason, reluctant to publish his work. It was not, in fact, until RHETICUS arrived in Frauenburg in 1539 and intervened that Copernicus reluctantly allowed its publication. The work finally appeared just in time, according to popular legend, for it to be shown to Copernicus on his deathbed.

There were several other dimensions to the career of Copernicus. For much of his life Poland was under threat from the TEUTONIC KNIGHTS and Copernicus found himself on more than one occasion besieged by them and called upon to negotiate with them. He also, in his *De monete* (1522), wrote on the topic of Poland's debased currency, and, according to some scholars, is to be credited with the first formulation of the principle, later known as Gresham's law, that "bad money drives out good" (*see* GRESHAM, SIR THOMAS).

*De revolutionibus orbium coelestium* was first printed at Nuremberg in 1543 and republished during the Renaissance at Basle (1566) and Amsterdam (1611). There are facsimiles of the 1543 edition (Amsterdam, 1943) and of the 1566 Basle edition (Prague, 1971); the latter is edited by Z. Horský and contains Tycho Brahe's commentary on Copernicus's work, as well as an introduction and notes in Czech, English, French, German, and Russian. There is an annotated English translation by A. M. Duncan, *On the Revolutions of the Heavenly Spheres* (Newton Abbot, U.K., 1976). A more recent translation is that by Charles G. Wallis, published in the Great Minds series by Prometheus Books (1995).

**Further reading:** Owen Gingerich and Robert S. Westman, *The Wittich Connection: Conflict and Priority in Late Sixteenth-century Cosmology* (Philadelphia, Penn.: American Philosophical Society, 1988); Fred Hoyle, *Nicolaus Copernicus: An Essay on His Life and Work* (London: Heinemann, 1973).

**Cornaro, Caterina** (1454–1510) *Queen of Cyprus (1472–89)*
A Venetian noblewoman, she married James II of Cyprus by proxy in 1468 in order to ally Cyprus with Venice. James died (1473), leaving Cyprus to Caterina and her unborn child (James III). After the infant James III also died (1474) Caterina needed Venetian support in order to deal with numerous conspiracies against her and the threat of Ottoman attack, but Venice gradually usurped her power and forced her abdication (1489). Retiring to Asolo, near Treviso, she entertained literary figures, including Pietro BEMBO who entitled his dialogue on love *Gli Asolani* (1505).

**Cornaro, Luigi** (1467–1566) *Italian dietician*
A member of the powerful Cornaro family of Venice, he spent the first 40 years of his life indulging his passion for food and drink. Threatened by his physician with imminent death if he continued to indulge himself, Cornaro resolved to restrict his diet drastically. Initially it was reduced to a daily intake of 12 ounces of food and 14 ounces of wine. Eventually, however, it was reduced to a single egg a day. Details of Cornaro's austere regime were revealed in his *Discorsi della vita sobria* (1558). Assuming the accuracy of his birth date, Cornaro lived to be 98.

See also: FOOD AND COOKING

**Cornelisz., Cornelis** (**Cornelisz. van Haarlem**) (1562–1638) *Dutch painter*
Cornelisz. studied under Pieter Pietersz. (Jonge Peer) in his native Haarlem before visiting Rouen and Antwerp. Back in Haarlem (1583) he collaborated with GOLTZIUS and Carel van MANDER in their academy. Cornelisz., who specialized in history and portrait painting, retained a strong mannerist influence (*see* MANNERISM) throughout his working life. His bravura approach to figure drawing and foreshortening is exemplified in *The Massacre of the Innocents* (1591; Haarlem).

**Coronado, Francisco Vásquez de** (c. 1510–1554) *Spanish explorer*
Born in Salamanca, Coronado went to the West Indies and then Mexico, becoming governor of New Galicia (1538). He organized an expedition of several hundred Spaniards and Indians to find Cíbola, site of the fabled "Seven Cities of Gold" reported by Fray Marcos de NIZA, but found only the pueblos of present-day New Mexico and Arizona (1540). Back in New Galicia (1542) he lost his governorship and was unsuccessfully indicted (1546) for his conduct on the expedition. He died in Mexico City.

**Corpus Hermeticum** See HERMETICISM

**Correggio, Antonio Allegri** (c. 1489–1534) *Italian painter*
He took his name from his birthplace, Correggio, east of Parma, but otherwise little is known of Correggio's life. The obvious influence of MANTEGNA on his work suggests that he may have studied in Mantua. Another influence was that of LEONARDO DA VINCI, seen in the softness that is characteristic of all but his earliest work; Correggio's figures are however more sensual and fleshy than Leonardo's. In about 1518 he went to Parma, where the following year he decorated a ceiling in the convent of San Paolo, before working on the dome of the church of San Giovanni Evangelista (1520–23). The resulting fresco depicted the 12 apostles on clouds around the figure of Christ ascending into heaven, sharply foreshortened as if seen from below. The same technique (known as *sotto in su*) was used with more daring foreshortening in his *Assumption of the Virgin* in the dome of Parma cathedral (1526–30), which again presents to the spectator standing beneath it a visually convincing ascent into heaven. Although the work was described by one contemporary as "a hash of frogs' legs," this masterly illusionism of Correggio's, a development of that first used by Mantegna, set the style for almost all future ceiling decorations.

Correggio's oil paintings were equally bold in their composition, particularly his altar paintings, in which he also experimented with artificial effects of light. As well as religious paintings he painted a number of voluptuous mythologies, such as *The Loves of Jupiter* for Federico Gonzaga (1530 onward; various locations). He died in Correggio, having produced work that was to influence both baroque and rococo artists.

Further reading: David Ekserdjian, *Correggio* (New Haven, Conn. and London: Yale University Press, 1997).

**Corteccia, Francesco** (1502–1571) *Italian composer and organist*
From 1515 he served the church of San Giovanni Battista, Florence, in various capacities and was organist there from 1535 to 1539. In 1540 Corteccia was appointed *maestro di cappella* at San Giovanni Battista, at the cathedral, and at the Medici court. Corteccia made a substantial contribution to the early madrigal; he wrote many for particular occasions, the most famous being those composed for the wedding of Duke COSIMO I to Eleonora of Toledo (1539). Corteccia also wrote a prologue, five INTERMEDII, and an epilogue for the comedy, *Il comodo*, by Antonio Landi, which was performed at the wedding banquet. The *intermedii* were written for solo singers, ensemble, and varying combinations of instruments to depict different times of the day; these were published in Corteccia's madrigal collection of 1547. His considerable output of liturgical music is less progressive than his secular compositions.

*cortegiano, Il* See COURTIER, THE

## Cortés, Hernán (1485–1547) *Spanish soldier, conqueror of Mexico*

Born at Medellin, Estremadura, Cortés studied law at Salamanca before emigrating to Hispaniola (1504). He married and farmed there until 1511, when he sailed with Diego Velázquez to Cuba, where he became chief magistrate of Santiago.

His 11-ship expedition to Yucatan made landfall early in 1519. He founded a settlement at Vera Cruz and made contact with the native Indians, who were awestruck by the white men with their guns, ships, and horses. After burning his ships to discourage desertion, Cortés marched to Tenochtitlán, the Aztec capital (now Mexico City). Montezuma, the Aztec emperor, greeted Cortés as a representative of the gods, but an Aztec attack on the Spaniards at Vera Cruz soon shattered the myth of the Spaniards' divine invulnerability. Cortés went on the offensive, threw Montezuma into chains, and forced him to acknowledge Spanish sovereignty. Having drawn off some of his troops to defeat an expedition sent by Velázquez to supplant him, Cortés returned to Tenochtitlán to find fighting between the Spanish garrison in the city and the Aztecs. Montezuma was killed by his subjects while appealing for peace. The Spaniards fought their way out with heavy losses, but in July 1520 decisively defeated the Aztecs in the plain of Otumba. In August 1521 Cortés recaptured and destroyed Tenochtitlán.

Cortés's account of the conquest, in five letters to CHARLES V, was published, together with the first map of Mexico, in 1524. A full account, the *Historia de la conquista de México*, was written up by Cortés' secretary and published in 1552. The fall of the Aztec empire allowed Cortés to develop Mexico as a Spanish colony. He also made expeditions into Honduras (1524–26) and lower California (1536). However, Charles never entirely trusted Cortés and, despite receiving the title of marquis of Oaxaca (1529), Cortés found his authority was curtailed and he was passed over for viceroy (1535). Disillusioned, he returned to Spain around 1540 but still failed to win Charles's confidence. He eventually retired to die on his estate near Seville.

**Further reading:** Francisco López de Gómara, *Cortés: The Life of the Conqueror by His Secretary*, transl. and ed. Lesley Byrd Simpson (Berkeley, Calif.: University of California Press, 1964); Hugh Thomas, *The Conquest of Mexico* (London: Hutchinson, 1993), as *Conquest: Montezuma, Cortés, and the Fall of Old Mexico* (New York: Simon and Schuster, 1993).

## Coryate, Thomas (c. 1577–1617) *English traveler and writer*

Born at Odcombe, Somerset, Coryate studied at Winchester and Oxford, but failed to graduate. As a young man he lived in the court of James I, earning his keep as an unofficial court jester and by exploiting his opportunistic talents to the full. In 1608 he traveled through France, Switzerland, and Italy, covering 2000 miles in five months. Styling himself the "Odcombian Legstretcher" (although he used other means of transport besides walking), Coryate on his return marketed himself with considerable success as a celebrity traveler. His quirky, anecdote-packed account of the journey was published as *Coryate's Crudities* (1611). The following year he set out for the East, sending home reports of his experiences. From Constantinople he went to the Holy Land, then, attaching himself to long-distance caravans, walked through Turkey, Persia, and India, stopping at the Moghul emperor's court at Ajmer, Gujarat, in 1615, before continuing to explore northern India. Still traveling, he died in Surat, but not before he had achieved his ambition of having a picture drawn of himself riding an elephant. Coryate's five letters from India were published in pamphlet form (1616 and 1618), and PURCHAS published an abbreviated text of the notes and diary Coryate had sent back from Aleppo in 1614.

**Further reading:** Michael Strachan, *The Life and Adventures of Thomas Coryate* (Oxford, U.K.: Oxford University Press, 1962).

## Cosimo I de' Medici (1519–1574) *Duke of Florence (1537–74), first grand duke of Tuscany (1569–74)*

Cosimo assumed power as a youth of 18, after the assassination of his distant cousin Alessandro. With initial support from Emperor CHARLES V, Cosimo extended the Medici domains throughout Tuscany and in 1557 acquired Siena from the Spaniards, despite the efforts of FRANCIS I's soldiers.

Cosimo and his officials established an efficient modern despotism. Tuscan government was integrated and public services were centered on the UFFIZI, designed by Cosimo's superintendent of buildings, Giorgio VASARI. Other public works included road building, the completion of the Palazzo Pitti for Cosimo by Bartolommeo AMMANATI, the refurbishing of the Palazzo Vecchio, and the Boboli Gardens. Cosimo supported the ACCADEMIA DELLA CRUSCA, Etruscan archaeology and such artists as MICHELANGELO, PONTORMO, and BRONZINO. In 1564 he resigned active government to his son Francesco.

**Further reading:** Konrad Eisenbichler (ed.), *The Cultural Politics of Duke Cosimo I de' Medici* (Aldershot, U.K.: Ashgate, 2001).

**cosmology** The study of the nature of the universe. Traditional Renaissance cosmology derived ultimately from the metaphysics of Aristotle and the astronomy of Ptolemy (*see* PTOLEMAIC SYSTEM). The universe was divided into two fundamentally distinct parts. In the heavens celestial objects, composed from an incorruptible, quintessential

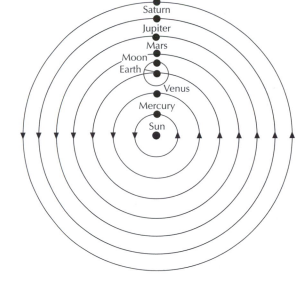

Fig. 1. Ptolemaic system

Fig. 2. Copernican system

## Cosmology

matter, were carried around the earth by solid crystalline spheres. All such bodies moved in circular orbits with a perfectly uniform motion (Fig. 1). In contrast, below the sphere of the moon a more degenerate matter, subject to change and composed from the four elements (earth, air, fire, and water), moved in more complex and varied ways. Superimposed upon this basically rational scheme there emerged a number of less realistic correspondences of which ASTROLOGY is the best known. By the 16th century traditional cosmology was under threat. COPERNICUS had shown that alternatives to Ptolemy could be plausibly developed (Fig. 2), while observations by BRAHE of comets revealed the nonexistence of crystalline spheres. Work by GALILEO demonstrated that the heavens were no less corruptible than the earth. The final rejection of the traditional cosmology came with René Descartes' presentation of a more viable mechanical system in the 1640s.

**Further reading:** Ernst Cassirer, *The Individual and the Cosmos in Renaissance Philosophy* (Oxford, U.K.: Blackwell, 1963; new ed. New York: Dover, 2000); S. K. Heninger Jr, *The Cosmographical Glass: Renaissance Diagrams of the Universe* (San Marino, Calif.: Huntington Library, 1977).

## Cossa, Francesco del (1436–c. 1478) *Italian painter*

Born in Ferrara, Cossa was possibly a pupil, and later a rival, of Cosimo TURA in that city. He also absorbed the influence of MANTEGNA and the Florentine painters, while his best-known work, the fresco series the *Months* (completed 1470) in the Palazzo di Schifanoia in Ferrara, clearly draws on parallel works by PIERO DELLA

FRANCESCA. Painted for the Este family, the series combines astrological themes with scenes of the daily life of the court and includes contributions by several of Cossa's pupils. Cossa then spent seven years in Bologna, where he executed a notable polyptych for the altar of San Petronio (c. 1474), which included a *Crucifixion* (National Gallery, Washington) painted in the style of ANDREA DEL CASTAGNO.

## Costa, Lorenzo di Ottavio (c. 1460–1535) *Italian painter*

Born in Ferrara, Costa probably trained under TURA and was also influenced at an early stage by the works of ERCOLE DE' ROBERTI and Francesco del COSSA. Paintings from this period include *The Concert* (National Gallery, London). In 1483 he went to Bologna where he executed work for the Bentivoglio court, decorating the Bentivoglio palace and going into partnership with the Bolognese artist Francesco FRANCIA. After succeeding MANTEGNA as court painter at Mantua (1506) his style became softer and more atmospheric in quality. Later works, which had a profound influence upon GIORGIONE, include two *Allegories* (Louvre, Paris) painted for Isabella d'Este. In his last years his reputation in Mantua was somewhat eclipsed by that of GIULIO ROMANO.

## Coster, Samuel (1579–1665) *Dutch dramatist and surgeon*

Coster is important as the founder of the DUYTSCHE ACADEMIE in his native Amsterdam and for his tragedies, which are in the tradition of SENECA. His *Iphigenia* (1617) was one of the anti-Calvinist satires that brought the academy into disfavor with the authorities; in other respects the tragedies, which also include *Ithys* (1615) and *Polyxena* (1619), exhibit the usual Senecan bias towards bloodcurdling horrors. Coster's farces, including *Teeuwis de Boer* (performed 1612), are written in the old *rederijker* mode (*see* CHAMBERS OF RHETORIC) and show little awareness of Renaissance trends.

**Coster's Academie** See DUYTSCHE ACADEMIE

**costume** With the disappearance of ancient Roman dress, even in Italy, the standard differentiation between male and female clothing was established in the early Middle Ages throughout Europe: men in trousers (or hose) and women in skirts. In the later Middle Ages clothing became one of the principal indicators of social class, and sumptuary laws were in force in most countries to ensure that the distinctions were observed. These laws also operated to protect home-produced textiles against encroachments by foreign goods. Another area with which sumptuary laws were often concerned was the banning of fashions that might encourage sexual license: low-cut dresses for women, exaggerated codpieces for men.

Sheep for wool and flax for linen had been familiar in Europe since prehistoric times. Silk came from the East as a luxury import until silkworm eggs were brought to Constantinople around 550 CE, and from there spread around the Mediterranean shores. Genoa, Venice, Florence, Lucca, and Milan were famous silk-manufacturing centers in the Middle Ages, and in 1480 Louis XI of France set up silk weaving at Tours, an initiative followed in 1520 by Francis I, who started the Rhône valley silk industry, based on Lyons and staffed by Genoese and Florentine weavers. Furs, mainly from central and northern Europe, were worn both as necessities and luxuries; as an item of male attire the wearing of certain prestigious furs was restricted to those of royal blood, and sumptuary laws often regulated very minutely the type and quantity of fur allowable to any particular social class.

By the late 14th century international vagaries of fashion can be discerned. Peasant dress varied according to locality and was more dependent upon local products, but the clothes of the prosperous merchant classes and of the aristocracy show pronounced and well-documented trends. Ostentatious impracticality in dress displayed the leisured status of well-born ladies, who wore trailing skirts, long sleeves, and elaborately horned or pinnacled headdresses, which reached a (literal) peak of extravagance in 15th-century France and Burgundy. At the same time courtiers affected the poulaine, an extremely long and tapering toe to the shoe; such shoes were known as "crakows," a word which, like "poulaine," indicates the Polish origin of the fashion. An English statute of 1464 banned any cobbler or leatherworker from making poulaines more than two inches long. By the end of the century abruptly squared-off toes became the rage.

In the 16th century men's outer clothes were frequently "slashed," that is decorated with numerous parallel cuts to show off the garment underneath; this fashion was even imitated in ARMOR. Later they also practiced "bombasting" or stuffing their garments with cottonwool or similar padding. A corresponding move away from the natural line of the body is seen in women's use of the farthingale or hooped petticoat in the same period. Costume became a major form of display in Renaissance courts, particularly on such state occasions as the FIELD OF THE CLOTH OF GOLD. JEWELRY was attached to it in profusion, modest lace collars or frills swelled to huge ruffs, and the art of the embroiderer in gold and silken threads was lavishly employed. At a slightly lower social level the law of the land still tried to tie the wearing of certain garments to social or military obligations; thus a Tudor gentleman whose wife wore silk petticoats and velvet kirtles, the cloth for which was an imported luxury, would be expected to provide one light cavalry horse with its accoutrements in time of war.

**Further reading:** Janet Arnold, *Queen Elizabeth's Wardrobe Unlock'd* (Leeds, U.K.: Maney, 1988); Carole Collier Frick, *Dressing Renaissance Florence* (Baltimore, Md.: Johns Hopkins University Press, 2002): Ann Rosalind Jones and Peter Stallybrass, *Renaissance Clothing and the Materials of Memory* (Cambridge, U.K.: Cambridge University Press, 2000).

**Cotton, Sir Robert Bruce** (1571–1631) *English politician and bibliophile*
Born in Denton, Huntingdonshire, the son of a wealthy landowner, Cotton was educated at Cambridge University, and then moved to London where he began his political career in 1601 as member of parliament for Newtown. By this time he had begun to assemble one of the finest collections of books and manuscripts ever seen in private hands. Used by many contemporary scholars, such as BACON, CAMDEN, and SPEED, it contained such items as the Lindisfarne Gospels and the manuscript of *Beowulf*. Although initially on good terms with JAMES I, Cotton was arrested in 1615 for involvement in the poisoning of Sir Thomas OVERBURY (1613). Released soon afterwards, he was later suspected by Charles I of sedition and arrested once more in 1629. Although released in the general amnesty of 1630 he was denied access to his own library. The collection itself was placed in the British Museum in 1753 where it remains today.

**Council of Ten** The Venetian body mainly responsible for state security. Its establishment dates from the investigation into Baiamonte Tiepolo's conspiracy (1310). Members were chosen for one year and could not serve consecutive terms of office. The numbers on the council varied and included the DOGE and his six councillors. The council employed spies, received reports, conducted secret diplomacy, and sometimes ordered assassinations. It supervised the manufacture and distribution of artillery and munitions until 1582. After the appointment of three inquisitors of state (1539) for the secret investigation and punishment of crimes, the council was widely perceived as a sinister organization.

**Counter-Reformation** The reform of ecclesiastical abuses and the vitalization of spirituality were lively concerns in the decades before LUTHER's posting of the Ninety-five Theses and the beginning of the Protestant REFORMATION. The early 16th-century Catholic Reformation continued after 1517 until, by the 1530s, it had become a vast movement of spiritual and moral renewal (*see* SPIRITUALI). The Catholic Reformation (meaning originally the reformist movement within the unitary pre-1517 Church) was therefore independent of the Protestant Reformation (meaning the reformation led by those who either removed themselves from the Roman communion or were excommunicated from that communion) and was not necessarily directed against it. Intellectuals such as Jacques LEFÈVRE D'ÉTAPLES, Desiderius ERASMUS, Francisco de QUIÑONES, and Juan de VALDÉS (to name but a few) were all representatives of this movement. To the degree that the Council of TRENT disciplined and revitalized the ecclesiastical offices of the Church, it too was part of the Catholic Reformation. However, after 1540 there was also a desire to combat Protestantism, to counterattack, and to regain lost ground. This movement is called the Counter-Reformation. It was destructive of some of the most liberal trends of the earlier 16th-century Church, and it created the psychology and worship of Roman Catholicism until Vatican II in the 1960s.

The Counter-Reformation can best be discussed under the headings of theology, psychology, triumphalism, and mysticism. First, theology. Since Protestant ideas and Catholic spiritualist notions (understood to their disadvantage in the context of the Counter-Reformation) had been spread largely by preachers and the new printing press (for example, between 1517 and 1526 there were over 2000 editions of works by Luther), ecclesiastical and temporal authorities deemed it necessary to "protect" their flocks against dangerous proselytizing. Kings, princes, and civic authorities strengthened CENSORSHIP. In 1520 the first index of prohibited books was issued by HENRY VIII who sought to protect England from Lutheran ideas. To guide civil authorities, the papacy finally (1559) issued its more famous INDEX LIBRORUM PROHIBITORUM. Local inquisitions and courts also took action against heretical theology. The Roman Inquisition was reestablished in 1542 to rid Italy of heresy. French provincial *parlements* actively tried heretics. Temporal lords began requiring printers to acquire royal "licences" before allow-

ing them to publish books. Should unwelcome books be published, the presses could then be shut down by revoking its licence. The Roman Catholic Church organized an elaborate censorship system by which texts had to obtain a *nihil obstat* ("there is nothing objectionable") and an *imprimatur* ("it may be printed") before the presses could run. It is paradoxical that the same invention, the printing press, could lead to the expansion of scholarship and the dissemination of ideas as well as to modern censorship.

The Counter-Reformation period also saw the foundation of new religious orders such as the Society of Jesus (JESUITS). Founded by IGNATIUS LOYOLA and a handful of companions in 1534, the order quickly grew in numbers and spread throughout western Europe. Ignatius was a soldier-mystic and, at one point, a near heretic. His *Constitutions* (first drawn up between 1547 and 1550) laid down a strict organization for the Jesuits. His *Spiritual Exercises*, setting out the method of prayer and meditation followed by the first generation of Jesuits, exemplify the commitment, ardor, and discipline of the Counter-Reformation "Christian soldier," very different from the early 16th-century Catholic-Reformation model offered in Erasmus's *Enchiridion militis christiani* (1504; *Handbook of the Christian Soldier*). The single-minded passion of the Counter-Reformation is reflected in Ignatius's words: "To arrive at complete certainty, this is the mental attitude we should maintain: I will believe that the white object I see is black if that should be the decision of the hierarchical church."

The Council of Trent (1542–65) solidified the theological armamentum of the Counter-Reformation Church. Taken as a whole, the council was as dogmatic and militant as Ignatius Loyola for the Catholic camp and John CALVIN for the Protestant side. The council, a long time in coming into being and sometimes precarious in its existence, managed to define Roman Catholic doctrine for the next 400 years. It countered Protestant doctrines, issue by issue, and in this way it set forth a basically systematic ordering of Roman Catholic doctrine, thus making crystal clear who was a Catholic and who a Protestant. As one historian has noted, the medieval Church was generally more ecumenical and permissive theologically than was the post-Tridentine religious world. Peaceful coexistence of competing theological ideas was no longer possible during the Counter-Reformation era.

While there was a clear doctrinal gap between the Counter-Reformation Church and the various Protestant churches after 1560, there was also a growing psychological gap in terms of devotional practice and style of piety. Counter-Reformation piety was characterized by a heated emotionalism, especially for the laity. The religious paintings of the late 16th and 17th centuries aimed at suggesting ideal worship practices: weeping, distorted figures, exaggerated gestures, and eyes turned piously toward heaven. Artistic examples of tearful repentance and contrition abounded: St. Peter shedding tears after having denied Jesus; St. Mary Magdalene's remorse for her earlier life. To encourage the Catholic viewer to share the tears and agonies of Christ on the cross as well as the martyrdoms of the saints, these scenes were pictured in gruesome detail: St. Agatha having her breasts torn away; St. Edward with his throat cut. Death became as much a preoccupation as it had been in the 14th-century plague years and quite unlike the halcyon days of the Renaissance when the epitaph on a cardinal's tomb (1541) read, "Why fear death, which brings us rest?" Now, the typical Counter-Reformation tombstone might read, "Ashes, ashes, nothing but ashes."

Triumphalism was an aspect, one could argue, of the psychology of the Counter-Reformation. However, it is distinct enough to be discussed separately. The Counter-Reformation Church was on the march in several regards. First, every attempt was made to enrich the ceremonial and feasts of the Catholic Church. The consecrated Host was displayed on feasts, proclaiming the Catholic doctrine of TRANSUBSTANTIATION, as opposed to the Protestant denials of this doctrine by ZWINGLI and others. The feast of Corpus Christi (the Body of Christ), although observed from the late 13th century, usually with public processions, was in its most developed form a child of the Counter-Reformation and served triumphantly to underline the Eucharistic doctrine of the Roman Catholic Church. Frescoes in St. Peter's, Rome, showed Peter walking on water and healing the sick, asserting artistically the primacy of Peter and his successors against the Protestant denials of the authority of the pope. In New Spain the Church adopted an assertive posture, trying to make up for the falling away of Protestants from the Catholic fold in Europe by bringing new, native American members into the Roman communion. And the churches of the New World were decorated just as lavishly as in Europe. In sum, the Counter-Reformation had succeeded in halting the victories of Protestantism and had begun to turn them back. The observer in 1540 might well have thought all of Europe would soon become Protestant. However, a few decades later, the same observer attending the triumphant polyphonies of PALESTRINA in the Jesuit church of Gesù in Rome would see the Church once more sure of itself doctrinally and psychologically.

Mysticism was at the heart of Counter-Reformation religious emotion. In few other periods have there been such attractive mystics as at this time. Of these the two most prominent were St. TERESA OF ÁVILA and St. JOHN OF THE CROSS. As individual as these two visionaries and reformers were, they are completely in harmony with the general qualities of Counter-Reform and the Council of Trent. One reason for their appeal is the harmony between the Tridentine doctrinal decrees and the assumptions of mysticism. Mystics such as Teresa and John believed that men and women, with the help of God's grace, could grad-

ually perfect themselves and briefly unite with God. Mysticism is totally unlike the assumptions of classical Protestantism (as exemplified by Luther and Calvin), for it is optimistic about man and God. In the mystics' planned and ordered meditations, spiritual exercises, and rigorous training of the will, 16th-century Roman Catholic mysticism complemented a theology which affirmed the freedom of the will, man's ability to cooperate in his own salvation, and the efficacy of good works and charity.

**See also:** PILGRIMAGE AND PILGRIMAGE SHRINES

**Further reading:** Robert Birely, *The Refashioning of Catholicism, 1450–1700: A Reassessment of the Counter-Reformation* (Washington, D.C.: Catholic University of America Press, 1999); Nicholas S. Davidson, *The Counter-Reformation* (Oxford, U.K.: Blackwell, 1987); Henry Outram Evennett, *The Spirit of the Counter-Reformation* (Cambridge, U.K.: Cambridge University Press, 1968; Notre Dame, Ind. and London: University of Notre Dame Press, 1970); Michael Mullett, *The Catholic Reformation* (London: Routledge, 1999).

*Courtier, The* (Italian *Il cortegiano*; 1528) The book by Baldassare CASTIGLIONE, describing the accomplishments of the ideal courtier and portraying the court of Urbino shortly before the death of Duke Guidobaldo da Montefeltro in 1508. Written and gradually expanded between 1508 and 1524, the work, following Plato and Cicero's *De oratore*, is cast in dialogue form as the lively informal conversations of a group of courtiers and ladies. Popularizing humanist (Aristotelian and Ciceronian) ideals of the model citizen, Castiglione depicts the courtier, though necessarily of noble birth and trained in arms, as a gentleman, learned, a connoisseur, of cultivated tastes and sensibility, excelling at a variety of civilized pursuits but always with effortless grace (SPREZZATURA).

Following its first publication in 1528, *Il cortegiano* very rapidly reached an audience all over Europe through versions in Spanish (1534), English (1561), Polish (1566), and Latin (1571). The English translation by Sir Thomas HOBY, entitled *The Book of the Courtier*, struck a chord with the aspirational gentry of Elizabethan England and was the forerunner of a whole genre of "courtesy" books explaining how to behave like a gentleman; a recent appearance of Hoby's text is in an edition by Virginia Cox (London and Rutland, Vt., 1994). George Bull, retaining Hoby's title, made a 20th-century version for the Penguin Classics series (Harmondsworth, U.K., rev. ed., 1976).

**Further reading:** Peter Burke, *The Fortunes of* The Courtier: *The European Reception of Castiglione's Cortegiano* (University Park, Pa: Pennsylvania State University Press, 1996).

**Couto, Diogo do** (1542–1616) *Portuguese historian*
Born in Lisbon and educated at the Jesuit college there, do Couto sailed to India (1559), where he spent virtually all

of his adult life. Philip II appointed him as royal historiographer, a position he used to expose the decadence of Portuguese affairs in the subcontinent, most notably in *Dialogo do soldado prático*. From 1602 do Couto also continued BARROS's *Décadas da Asia* on the Portuguese imperial adventure in the East. He died in Goa.

## Covarrubias, Alonso de (c. 1488–1564) *Spanish architect and sculptor*
Covarrubias was evidently trained in the Gothic tradition and, as one of the nine consultants on Salamanca cathedral, had an opportunity at an early age to practice in an essentially Gothic style. However, his subsequent works were executed in a manner influenced by contemporary Italian trends and became good examples of the PLATERESQUE style in Spain. Many of his most important works were executed in Toledo, where from 1504 he worked on the hospital of Sta. Cruz with the late Gothic architect Enrique EGAS; on Egas's death (1534) Covarrubias succeeded him as master mason at Toledo cathedral. Of his work there, the chapel of the New Kings (1531–34) survives as a testament to his skill. Other works included the church of the Piedad at Guadalajara (1526), a fine staircase at the archbishop's palace at Alcalá (c. 1530), and the rebuilding of the Bisagra Neuva gate at Toledo (1559). As architect to the royal castles he also oversaw the rebuilding of the Alcázar at Toledo (1537–53) for Charles V.

## Covilhã, Pero da (died 1525) *Portuguese explorer*
Covilhã, who was called after his birthplace in Beira, served at both the Castilian and Portuguese courts before being dispatched (1487) to explore the overland trade routes to the East and to discover the country of the legendary priest-king Prester John (i.e. Ethiopia). At the same time Bartolomeu DIAZ was sent to look for the southern sea route round Africa. From Barcelona Covilhã went via Naples to Rhodes and Egypt, and then to the Arabian peninsula and India. On his way back to Cairo he made a detour down the East African coast. From Cairo he sent back to Portugal a report on the feasibility of his route for the spice trade and then set out via Arabia for Ethiopia. There he was detained as an honored prisoner of state for the remainder of his life.

## Cracow
A city in Poland on a strategic site on the left bank of the Vistula. Traditionally said to have been founded about 700 CE by a mythical Prince Krak, Cracow was nearly destroyed by the Tatars in 1241, but the rebuilt town prospered and in 1305 became the capital of the Polish kings, who continued to be crowned and buried in Cracow's cathedral of St. Stanislas until 1764. Cracow university was founded in 1364 and played a leading role in strengthening the ties of the Polish Church with the West; the university library is housed in the fine 15th-century university buildings. Besides being famous as an intellectual center in the 15th and 16th centuries, Cracow is famous for the number and beauty of its churches; the cathedral, which was substantially rebuilt in the 14th century, houses masterpieces by Veit STOSS, Pieter VISCHER, Guido RENI, and others, and the Marienkirche contains Stoss's great altarpiece of the Virgin. The former royal castle on the rocky outcrop known as the Wawel was rebuilt in the Italian Renaissance style under King Sigismund I (reigned 1506–48), who married (1518) Bona Sforza of Milan, under whose influence the court at Cracow became a major northern center of Renaissance culture. The Sigismund chapel in the cathedral (1519–30) is an outstanding example of pure Italian Renaissance style.

## Cranach, Lucas (1472–1553) *German painter and print maker*
Born at Kronach and initially trained by his painter father Hans, Cranach had become established at Coburg by 1501. Subsequently he traveled through the Danube area to Vienna, where he stayed until 1504 and established contact with humanists at the university. His Winterthur portraits of Dr Johannes Cuspinian and his wife, his Berlin/Nuremberg portraits of Stephan Reuss and his wife, and his Berlin *Rest on the Flight into Egypt* all date from this period. Distinguished by vibrant warm colors and lush landscape backgrounds, these are key early works of the socalled DANUBE SCHOOL.

In 1505 Cranach was appointed court painter to Elector Frederick the Wise at Wittenberg, succeeding the itinerant Venetian Jacopo de' BARBARI. Shortly after this, Cranach's style began to change. His *Martyrdom of St. Catherine* (1506; Dresden) has a strongly decorative surface design and a light, transparent coloring reminiscent of DÜRER. Around 1506 Cranach began to produce woodcuts. Like BURGKMAIR, he pioneered the two-tone *chiaroscuro* print, of which his 1507 *St. George* is an early example. In 1509 Cranach visited the Netherlands. His Frankfurt *Holy Kinship* triptych (1509) revels the influence of METSYS in its subject matter and perspectively deep architectural setting, but the shallow surface linearity of its figure grouping indicates Cranach's own future development. These decorative qualities are manifest in the full-size, full-length portraits of Duke Henry the Pious and Duchess Catherine (1514; Dresden). Both figures are portrayed in brightly colored court dress against a flat black background, the effect emphasizing both silhouette and detail in a "heraldic" manner, reminiscent of a playing card.

At Wittenberg Cranach became closely associated with Martin LUTHER, who became godfather to one of the painter's children. Cranach's woodcut *Luther as Junker Jörg* (1521–22) is the first of a long series of portraits of the reformer. After the coming of Lutheranism to Saxony, Cranach concentrated increasingly upon portraits, secular themes from classical antiquity, and small religious pictures. With his Frankfurt *Venus* (1532) he perfected a particular type of slender, palid female nude which he and his workshop repeated in numerous variants until the mid-century, usually in pictures with titles such as *Venus and Cupid*, *Lucretia*, *The Nymph of the Fountain*, *Adam and Eve*, and *The Judgment of Paris*. Iconographically, an interesting departure in his later career is a series of religious pictures on novel themes acceptable to Protestant theology, such as *Christ and the Children* and *Allegory of the Old and New Testaments*. He also painted a small number of large, multifigure compositions set against landscape backgrounds, such as the Madrid *Stag Hunt* (1545) and the Berlin *Fountain of Youth* (1546). In 1550 Cranach followed his master, Elector John Frederick, to Augsburg and in 1552 to Weimar. He died there the following year while engaged upon a large triptych, the *Allegory of Redemption*, subsequently completed by his son, Lucas Cranach the Younger (1515–86). By then Cranach was the most influential and sought-after painter in northern Germany. The author of an unique and particularly successful form of German MANNERISM, he was also the principal visual apologist of the Reformation.

**Further reading:** Alexander Stepanov, *Lucas Cranach the Elder, 1472–1553* (Bournemouth, U.K.: Parkstone, 1997).

## Cranmer, Thomas (1489–1556) *Archbishop of Canterbury (1533–56)*

A learned theologian and an early admirer of LUTHER, in 1532 he visited leading Lutherans in Germany, where he married the niece of Andreas OSIANDER. He already enjoyed royal favor for supporting HENRY VIII's first divorce, and despite his marriage, which was in contravention of his clerical vows, he became the first Protestant archbishop of Canterbury in 1533; subsequently he aided the king in his three later divorces. During EDWARD VI's reign (1547–53) Cranmer worked to make the Church of England a truly Protestant Church. He encouraged publication of a new Bible in English and wrote much of the 1549 and 1552 BOOKS OF COMMON PRAYER. On her accession the Catholic MARY I stripped him of his office. Condemned as a heretic, Cranmer died bravely at the stake.

**Further reading:** Diarmaid MacCulloch, *Thomas Cranmer: A Life* (New Haven, Conn.: Yale University Press, 1998).

## Credi, Lorenzo di (Lorenzo d'Andrea d'Oerigo) (1459–1537) *Italian painter, sculptor, and goldsmith*

Credi was born in Florence and became a pupil with Perugino and Leonardo da Vinci in the workshop of Andrea del VERROCCHIO. He exhibited considerable skill as a draftsman and after Verrocchio's death he became the head of the most flourishing artistic workshop in Florence. He himself produced numerous pictures of seated Madonnas, including the *Madonna and Saints* altarpiece in Pistoia

(1510). Other works were highly imitative of Leonardo's early paintings. Among his best drawings is his *Self-Portrait* (c. 1490; National Gallery, Washington).

**Crete** See CANDIA

**criticism, literary** Theoretical discussion of the nature, kinds, and purpose of literature (as opposed to "practical" or applied criticism or guides to technique) originated and attained most sophistication in Italy. The common assumption in Renaissance criticism, as in the neoclassicism which succeeded it, was that literature imparted knowledge or truths. This view was usually stated in the Horatian formulation, that poetry combined delight and instruction, *dulce et utile*, these functions being taken rather simply and distinctly, with scant attention to their possible interactions.

In the first part of the 15th century in Italy, the recovery of classical authors, the cultivation of Latin style, and the role of classical rhetoric in the humanist conception of the active, public life produced the ideal of a poet-orator, emulating the ancients and bringing honor to his city and himself. By the end of the century, vernacular literature was thriving and soon reached full maturity. Systematic criticism developed in the course of the 16th century, stimulated by the publication of ARISTOTLE's *Poetics* (the Aldine press edition of the Greek text appeared in 1508). The commentaries and poetic treatises that followed were mainly concerned with the theory of imitation, with the genres, and with related matters arising from the interpretation of Aristotelian ideas. The *Poetics*, transmitted in the Middle Ages through Averroes' commentary, was freshly translated into Latin (by Giorgio Valla, 1498, and Alessandro Pazzi, 1536) and Italian (Bernardo Segni, 1549). Commentaries on it were written by Francesco Robortello (1548), Vincenzo Maggi (1550), and Lodovico CASTELVETRO (1570). While admitting imitation (of anything, not merely human actions and emotions) as an object of the literary work, Robortello is concerned with rhetorical persuasion rather than Aristotelian description and maintains the emphasis on the Horatian goals of moral instruction and aesthetic pleasure (one source of which is the marvelous). Castelvetro strays further from Aristotle's descriptive intention by reducing formal analysis, stressing rhetorical effect, and admitting only pleasure as the purpose of the literary work.

The imitation of models—specifically of Virgil and Cicero for Latin verse and prose, with Petrarch and Boccaccio as the vernacular equivalents—was central in Pietro BEMBO's arguments (*De imitatione*, 1512; *Prose della volgar lingua*, 1525) and decisive in resolving the QUESTIONE DELLA LINGUA. Marco Giralomo VIDA's *De arte poetica* (1527), a verse treatise in the Horatian style which continued to influence 18th-century neoclassicism, accepted imitation as the goal of poetry, Virgil as the ideal model, and epic as the supreme genre. Giangiorgio TRISSINO's *Poetica* (parts 1–4, 1529; 5–6, essentially a translation of the *Poetics*, 1563) is perhaps the most important early vernacular treatise, with extensive treatment of prosody and rhyme and examples drawn from Italian poetry to illustrate points. *La poetica* (1536) by Bernardino Daniello of Lucca (c. 1500–65), a disciple of Bembo, is the earliest work to take up the question of verisimilitude. CINTHIO's two theoretical discourses on drama and romance comment on many critical issues and are notable for a certain originality. Though influenced by Aristotle, he prefers the Roman and Senecan to the Greek model in tragedy and defends Ariosto and the romance (as a legitimate and distinct type of narrative). The dialogue *Naugerius* (1555) by Girolamo Fracastoro (1498–1553) takes into account the theories of Plato, Aristotle, and Horace. Julius Caesar SCALIGER (*Poetices libri septem*, 1561) emphasizes the didactic and moral purpose of art, which is held to be superior to nature, ranks Virgil above Homer, and gives clear definition to the genres. The work of Minturno (*De poeta*, 1559; *Arte poetica*, 1563) is the most comprehensive of Renaissance poetics in its coverage of mimetic theory, the rules of decorum, and the definition of genres (adding lyric to the traditional ones of drama and narrative); as such, it influenced TASSO, RONSARD, Sir Philip SIDNEY, and later neoclassicism. The *Della rhetorica* (1562) of Francesco PATRIZI presents a Platonic view opposed to the dominant Aristotelianism.

In France critical theorizing began with the poets of the PLÉIADE, whose ideals were definitively stated in DU BELLAY's *Défense et illustration de la langue française* (1549). It was much indebted to SPERONI's *Delle lingue* (1542), which followed Bembo in arguing for the imitation of classical models as a means of improving the vernacular. De Bellay's manifesto greatly enhanced the prestige of French—a suitable vehicle, he argued, for the most exalted subjects—and promoted the influence of Greek, Latin, and Italian forms of French verse. The excesses (especially in diction) and artificiality that eventually resulted were successfully countered by François de MALHERBE, who laid the foundations for French neoclassicism.

Although BACON and ASCHAM in England expressed misgivings about the use of the vernacular in preference to Latin, the ENGLISH LANGUAGE was both unified and solidly established in literary use in the 16th century and consequently one dimension of critical debate, so important in Italy and France, was minimized. More common than critical treatises in Elizabethan England were practical guides to writing or versifying, such as, for example, George Gascoigne's *Certayne Notes of Instruction Concerning the Making of Verse or Rhyme in English* (1575) and Thomas Puttenham's *Arte of English Poesie* (1589). The outstanding work of apologetics, reflecting a number of the principal themes of Renaissance criticism, was Sidney's *Defence*

*of Poesie* (1595). Probably written in the early 1580s, this treatise contains a list, significant in its brevity, of English literary works considered by Sidney as worthy of critical attention in that they possessed "poeticall sinnewes": Chaucer's *Troilus and Criseyde*, *The Mirror for Magistrates*, SURREY's lyrics, and SPENSER's *Shepheardes Calender*.

**Further reading:** Paul Oskar Kristeller, *Renaissance Thought and the Arts* (Princeton, N.J.: Princeton University Press, 1980).

**criticism, textual** As defined by the scholar poet A. E. Housman, "the science of discovering error in texts and the art of removing it." In as much as it is a matter of the application of common sense to emend slips of the keyboard, we practice it every day when we try to read a newspaper or email. In as much as it is a matter of the application of a set of rules (all of which are firmly based on common sense) to facilitate the restoration of a classical or biblical text, it is the product of a gradual but erratic development at the hands of scholars from the time of the Alexandrians (third century BCE) to the present.

The Alexandrians, notably Callimachus, Aristophanes of Byzantium, and Aristarchus, were concerned to ensure the survival of all extant Greek literature in its purest (i.e. most accurate) form. This involved the acquisition and collation (comparison) of the oldest and best manuscripts by means of which a "critical" edition, approximating as closely as possible to the author's own words, could be produced for the benefit of future readers. Their prime legacy to subsequent generations of textual critics was fidelity to tradition, and this remained the aim of the best scriptoria (centers of copying) throughout antiquity and for most of the Middle Ages.

During the 14th century scribal practices began to change. Less attention was given to the tradition, far more to the exercise of subjective "correction" of texts to make them conform with arbitrary notions of authenticity or readability. Motives varied from bowdlerization to meddling for its own sake, but most alterations that were deliberately introduced were the result of downright stupidity.

Happily there were exceptions. Demetrius Triclinius, for example, a schoolmaster in Thessalonica in the first quarter of the 14th century, made a notable contribution to the transmission of Greek tragedy and was personally responsible for the survival of about half of the plays of Euripides that we know today. In the West the Italian scholar and poet PETRARCH made similar contributions to the transmissions of Livy and Propertius.

In the 15th century, as the humanist tradition grew, and with it the fashion for collecting books and in particular the literature of the ancients, the pressure mounted on scribes to make more and more copies. The sudden proliferation of poor-quality texts was inevitable, but scholarly standards continued to be upheld in some quarters. Lorenzo VALLA, who went so far as to emend the Vulgate itself, exposed the socalled Donation of Constantine, purportedly a fourth-century document, as a later medieval forgery on historical and linguistic grounds. Angelo POLITIAN, probably the first Italian to be equally at home in Latin and Greek, saw his way through the welter of humanist copies to establish principles about the earliest recoverable stage of a textual tradition that were not to be superseded for three centuries.

Coincident with the proliferation of ancient texts was the invention of PRINTING. Most of the principal classical Latin authors had found their way into print by the end of the 15th century. Typographical difficulties held up the printing of Greek texts, but by the time of his death in 1515 Aldus MANUTIUS had overseen the first printing of most of the major authors. The survival of ancient literature was finally ensured, but the price was the quality of the text. In their haste to publish printed versions the early printers had often seized the first manuscript that came to hand, giving it at best a veneer of critical attention. For the next 300 years the activity of textual critics was to be dominated by the need to unpick the tangled web created by these first editions.

See also: ANTIQUARIANISM; GREEK STUDIES; LATIN STUDIES; MANUSCRIPTS

### Crivelli, Carlo (c. 1435–c. 1495) *Italian painter*

Born in Venice, Crivelli probably trained in the VIVARINI FAMILY workshop and was later influenced by the painters of Padua, including SCHIAVONE and MANTEGNA. After being imprisoned for adultery Crivelli left Venice and settled in Ascoli Piceno in the Marches (1468), developing a contemplative and highly ornamental style and concentrating upon executing religious scenes. Major paintings include the *Madonna della Passione* (c. 1457; Museo di Castelvecchio, Verona), a *Pietà* (1485; Museum of Fine Arts, Boston), and the *Madonna della Candellata* (c. 1490; Brera, Milan), but he is best known for the *Annunciation* (1486; National Gallery, London), an exotic and eccentric masterpiece.

### Croce, Giovanni (c. 1557–1609) *Italian composer*

A native of Chioggia, near Venice, and pupil of Gioseffo ZARLINO, Croce sang in the choir of St. Mark's as a boy. He took holy orders before 1585 and was employed for much of his life at the church of Sta. Maria Formosa. In 1603 he became *maestro di cappella* at St. Mark's. Croce wrote in an essentially conservative style; his madrigals and canzonettes are lightly textured with attractive melodies, and his sacred compositions are generally small-scale, with simple melodies and straightforward harmonies. The posthumously published *Sacre cantilene concertate* (1610) shows the adoption of the more modern *concertato* style. Croce's main influence outside Italy was as a madrigalist,

and his contribution to *Il trionfo di Dori* (1592) probably inspired MORLEY to compile *The Triumphs of Oriana*.

### Crocus, Cornelius (c. 1500–1550) *Dutch educationist and playwright*

Crocus was born in Amsterdam and after studying at Louvain was ordained a priest. He then became (1528) headmaster in Amsterdam, a post which he held until the year before his death, when he resigned it in order to travel on foot to Rome, where he was received by IGNATIUS LOYOLA into the Jesuit Order. He engaged in religious controversy against LUTHER and the ANABAPTISTS, wrote a popular textbook to assist children to form a correct Latin style (1536), and composed several Latin dramas for performance in schools. Of these the *Coemedia sacra Joseph* (1535) was the most successful, achieving over 20 editions and being imitated as far afield as Poland (*see* REJ, MIKOŁAJ).

### Croll, Oswald (c. 1560–1609) *German chemist and physician*

The son of the mayor of Wetter, near Marburg, Croll studied at a number of German universities, then spent several years traveling throughout Europe. Thereafter he practiced medicine and in about 1602 entered the service of Prince Christian of Anhalt-Bernberg. He is also reported to have served subsequently as a councilor to Emperor RUDOLF II. As a scientist Croll is best known for his *Basilica chymica* (Royal Chemistry; 1609), a highly influential text which did much to spread the ideas of PARACELSUS throughout Europe. The work also contained his *De signaturis*, an account of the widely held doctrine of SIGNATURES.

### Cromwell, Thomas (c. 1485–1540) *English statesman*

The son of a blacksmith at Putney, near London, Cromwell fought for the French in Italy before qualifying as a lawyer. In 1514 Thomas WOLSEY appointed him collector of the see of York's revenues. Cromwell entered parliament in 1523 and was made a privy councilor in 1531. As HENRY VIII's most trusted servant in the 1530s, Cromwell became chancellor of the exchequer (1533), lord privy seal (1536), lord high chamberlain (1539), and earl of Essex (1540). From 1535, as Henry's vicar-general, Cromwell carried out the English Reformation, dissolving the monasteries and confiscating their property (1536–39). He arranged the king's fourth marriage to Anne of Cleves, but when the marriage failed Cromwell fell from favor and was executed.

### Cronaca, Simone, Il (Simone del Pollaiuolo) (1457–1508) *Italian architect*

Cronaca was born in Florence and mainly worked there, apart from a period in Rome (1475–85), where he gained an understanding of classical architecture. In 1495 he built the Sala del Consiglio (now Sala dei Cinquecento) of the Palazzo Vecchio to accommodate the council instituted by SAVONAROLA on the lines of the Venetian MAGGIOR CONSIGLIO. He carried on BENEDETTO DA MAIANO's work on the Palazzo Strozzi, probably designed the Palazzo Guadagni, and also executed Giuliano da SANGALLO's design for the vestibule and sacristy of San Spirito. The church of San Salvatore al Monte, near Florence, which Cronaca built at the end of his life, is a model of classical simplicity and restraint, and was praised by Michelangelo.

**cross-staffs** See BACKSTAFFS

**cryptography** The science of devising and deciphering codes and ciphers. Simple ciphers were well known in antiquity. Like the basic Caesar alphabet, in which plaintext letters were replaced by letters three places further along the alphabet, they were invariably simple substitution ciphers. Such methods were readily employed in the Renaissance, for example, in the correspondence of the Avignon popes during the GREAT SCHISM. Before long, however, skilled cryptographers such as François VIÈTE could be found attached to most courts, happily reading the encoded correspondence of their enemies.

The obvious step of complicating the cipher by using different alphabets to encode different parts of the plaintext was first proposed by ALBERTI. Later generations of Renaissance cryptographers were left to work out precisely how polyalphabetic substitution could be deployed in practice. Alberti himself attempted to introduce polyalphabeticity by the use of two cipher discs, the setting of which could be changed for the encoding of each letter. A further step was taken by TRITHEMIUS in his *Polygraphia* (1518), in which he replaced the cipher discs of Alberti with the more familiar and useful rectangular tableau of alphabets. Precisely how such complicated ciphers could be made to operate with easily remembered and easily changed keys was shown by Giovanni Belaso in *La cifra* (1553).

The various innovations of Alberti, Trithemius, and Belaso were assembled and presented in a more convenient form by Blaise de VIGENÈRE in his *Traicté des chiffres* (1586). To their work he added the important notion of an autokey which, by using the plaintext as the key, endowed such ciphers with considerable security. So successful did Vigenère ciphers prove to be that they remained, when carefully constructed, indecipherable until the work of the great cryptanalyst Friedrich Kasiski in the mid-19th century.

**Cueva, Juan de la** (1543–1610) *Spanish dramatist*
On returning from Mexico (1577), where he had gone with his brother in 1574, Cueva wrote plays for the public theater in his native Seville. These were produced between 1579 and 1581, after which he devoted himself to verse and other writing, none of which is significant. *Exemplar poético*, a verse treatise on poetics, appeared in 1609. *La Conquista de Bética* (1603), his attempt at epic on a patriotic subject, has more historical than literary interest. His 14 surviving verse plays, 10 comedies and four tragedies, were published as *Comedias y tragedias* (1584). Three are based on classical subjects (for example, a tragedy on the death of Virginia, taken from the Roman historian Livy) and three on fictional sources. His important contribution, however, was introducing material drawn from Spanish historical chronicles and ballads. Examples of these are *La muerte del rey Don Sancho* (*The Death of King Sancho*) and *Los siete infantes de Lara* (*The Seven Infantes of Lara*). His allegorical play, *El infamador*, has similarities to the Don Juan legend and influenced TIRSO DE MOLINA's *Burlador de Sevilla* (1630). Cueva's mediocre work is rhetorical, Senecan, and scarcely dramatic at all, but in adapting national themes for the stage he anticipated the truly Spanish drama of great playwrights of the Golden Age like Lope de VEGA.

*culteranismo* See GÓNGORA Y ARGOTE, LUIS DE

**Cupid** (**Amor**) The god of love, usually depicted as a young winged boy with bow and arrows and flaming torches. He is the Roman equivalent of the Greek Eros, and is generally shown in the company of his mother VENUS (Greek Aphrodite). Another characteristic feature is that Cupid is often depicted as blind, or at least blindfolded, as in Botticelli's PRIMAVERA and TITIAN's *The Blindfolding of Amor* (Galleria Borghese, Rome); the Renaissance Neoplatonic interpretation of the blindness of love rejected the original notion that it symbolized uncomprehending animal passion and exalted it into a symbol of love's superiority to both body and intellect. Cupid also features in two other scenes that were vehicles of Neoplatonic allegories: Mercury teaching Cupid to read (an allegory of intellectual love), exemplified by CORREGGIO's picture of the subject in the National Gallery, London, and the love of Cupid and PSYCHE (the desire of the soul for divine love and their eventual union).

Following the Hellenistic tradition that there was not just one Eros, but a number of Erotes, Renaissance painters often depict several Cupids attending on Venus. These have a decorative function indistinguishable from that of the *putti* (Italian: young boys) found in both sacred and profane art.

**Cusanus, Nicholas** (**Nicholas of Cusa, Nicholas of Kues**) (1401–1464) *German philosopher and theologian*
Born at Kues on the Moselle, the son of a poor family, he entered the service of Ulrich, Count of Manderscheid, who supported him first while he studied at Deventer with the Brethren of the COMMON LIFE, then at Padua where he became a doctor of law (1423). He entered the Church

and was entrusted with several important diplomatic missions, eventually becoming papal legate in Germany (1440–47). Nicholas V made him a cardinal (1448) and bishop of Brixen (1450). In 1451 he was sent to Germany to reform the monasteries but came into conflict with his secular lord, Archduke Sigismund, and was for a time imprisoned. He retired to Umbria where he died. His valuable library was left to the hospital he founded in Kues.

Cusanus was important both as a philosopher and as a Church reformer. He rejected scholasticism and in *De docta ignorantia* (1440) he maintained that humans could gain no certain knowledge and that God can only be apprehended by intuition. This idea was basic to the mysticism of Giordano BRUNO. Cusanus was also a scientist and mathematician. He proposed reforms of the CALENDAR similar to those later undertaken by Pope GREGORY XIII, anticipated part of the Copernican theory by claiming that the earth rotated and was not the center of the universe, and professed in *De quadratura circuli* to have squared the circle.

## Cyriac of Ancona (Ciriaco de' Pizzicolli) (1391–1452)
*Italian merchant and antiquarian with a particular interest in classical Greece*

He traveled in Italy, Egypt, Greece, and the Near East, drawing monuments, copying inscriptions, and collecting manuscripts, statuettes, and medallions. His notebooks (Commentaries) and collection, although not published until the mid-18th century, have proved of immense value to archaeologists and classical scholars, particularly in the case of important monuments that have been destroyed since his day and to which his description is the only surviving witness.

## Czech Brethren (Bohemian Brethren)
A group representing a radical but pacific tendency within the HUSSITE movement of Bohemia. After the suppression of the militant Taborites in 1434, the Czech Brethren became the group most closely associated with the evangelical and social views of the early Hussites. Although possessing a sectarian tendency in their discipline and organization, they did demonstrate a desire for Protestant unity. Connections were established with LUTHER's Wittenberg and it was for them that Luther wrote his *Adoration of the Sacrament* (1523). Under the leadership of Jan Augusta, they endeavored (1532) to create greater unity through negotiation with Luther, Calvin, and Bucer, but this bore little fruit. The Brethren suffered persecution between 1548 and 1552 and many fled to Poland and Prussia. MAXIMILIAN II granted the Czech Brethren freedom to practice their religion (1575), and under RUDOLF II they played a leading role in education; however, after the battle of the WHITE MOUNTAIN (1620) they were dispersed and eventually merged with other groups.

**See also:** BLAHOSLAV, JAN

# D

**Daddi, Bernardo** (active 1290–c. 1349) *Italian painter*
A gifted pupil of GIOTTO, Daddi absorbed the seriousness of his master and combined it with the lyrical grace of the painters of Siena, becoming the leading artist in Florence during the 1340s. His earliest dated work was the *Madonna* triptych (1328; Uffizi, Florence), which was based upon Giotto's *Madonna Enthroned*, originally in the same church. The influence of the Sienese school is evident in Daddi's *Enthroned Madonna* (c. 1340; Uffizi), which reflects the style of the LORENZETTI brothers and Simone MARTINI in particular. Daddi also painted a number of notable smaller panels, such as *The Story of St. Cecilia* (Museo Civico, Pisa), which demonstrate his skill in the handling of color. Other works still in Florence include a *Madonna* (1347; Orsanmichele) and two frescoes showing the martyrdoms of SS. Lawrence and Stephen (Sta. Croce). Daddi's influence remained profound throughout the 14th century.

**Dalmau, Luís** (fl. 1428–1461) *Spanish artist*
A native of Valencia, Dalmau visited Bruges (1431) and Flanders before returning to Spain by 1437. There he worked as court painter to Alfonso V of Aragon (ALFONSO I of Naples). An admirer of van EYCK, he imitated the approach of the Flemish school in his own *Virgin of the Councillors* (1445; Barcelona museum), which was painted in the already outdated International Gothic style and is his only surviving documented work.

**dance** The Renaissance was perhaps more conscious of dance and dancing than any other period in Western history. As in the Middle Ages, dancing was a widely enjoyed physical pastime that also had an important role in courtship, social celebration, and the ritual of the courts. From the 15th century, however, dancing was discussed, analyzed, and celebrated as never before, and came to embody some of the most cherished ideals of the age. To the poet and philosopher, dance was a symbol of social order and cosmic harmony; to the humanist, it suggested the possibility of a perfect balance between mind and body, art and nature. The Renaissance saw the first theoretical writings about dance and the advent of the first professional dance teachers. It also saw the emergence of the distinction, unknown in the Middle Ages, between dance as a social activity and dance as a formal artistic spectacle.

The new attitudes to dance are first apparent in Italy, where dancing became an increasingly important part of court life from the late 14th century. The ability to dance with grace and vigor became an essential social accomplishment, indispensable to the aspiring courtier or the marriageable young lady. Dance was also the main element in the spectacular court festivities that arose at this time. These combined music and dancing with feasting, visual spectacle, and elements of pantomime or spoken drama to pay tribute to the reigning prince or duke. The usual mode was allegory or pastoral, and the performers the men and women of the court in elaborate costumes and masks (*see* MASQUE). A well-documented example is the lavish banquet given for the wedding of Giangaleazzo Sforza, duke of Milan, in 1489, in which the dancers assumed roles from Greek mythology.

Such spectacles clearly required a high degree of choreography, and to provide it a new profession arose— that of the dancing master. The role was a complex one, involving not only the organization of lavish pageantry but also the teaching of dance steps to the nobility and ad-

**Dance** *Dancing Peasant Couple* (1514), an engraving on copper by Albrecht Dürer.
*Photo AKG London*

vising in all matters of posture, deportment, and etiquette. The dancing masters published the first scholarly treatises on dance, and it is mainly owing to these works that we have any technical knowledge of the dances of the period. The earliest of the masters to be known by name is Domenico da Piacenza, whose *De arte saltandi et choreas ducendi* (On the art of dancing and directing choruses) was published in 1416. Domenico's book includes the earliest known classification of dance steps and the first attempt to analyse dances in technical language. It also lists the chief courtly dances of the era as (in ascending order of speed) the *bassedanza*, a slow processional dance with gliding steps, the more animated *quaternaria*, the *saltorella*, an exuberant dance that involved little jumps, and the *piva*, or hornpipe. The high social status enjoyed by the dancing master is best illustrated by the career of Domenico's disciple Antonio Cornazano (1431–c. 1500), who became an important official at the court of the SFORZA FAMILY in Milan. He was also apparently the first to use the word *balletto* (from Italian *ballare*, to dance) for the elaborate dance pageants of the day.

When Charles VIII of France invaded Italy in 1494, he and his courtiers were astonished by the *balleti* of the Italian courts, having seen nothing like them at home. However, it was France and not Italy that would see the development of dance into a formal theatrical art during the following century. The *balletto* was first introduced to the French court by CATHERINE DE' MEDICI, who married the future Henry II in 1533 and enticed the dancing master Baltazarini di Belgiosio (Balthasar de Beaujoyeulx; died c. 1587) to follow her. The first important BALLET DE COUR, as the form became known in France, was the *Ballet comique de la Reine*, devised for Catherine by Baltazarini in 1581. This spectacular five-hour entertainment, which combined dance with singing, recitations, and elaborate sets, was staged in front of some 10,000 people at the Louvre and is considered a milestone in the development of the ballet proper. Another factor was the publication in 1588 of the century's most important work on dance, the *Orchésographie* of Thoinot Arbeau (Jehan Tabouret; 1519–95). In this wide-ranging work Arbeau gave detailed descriptions of the era's most popular dances (notably the pavane, the galliard, and the gavotte) and introduced an early system of dance notation. He also described for the first time the five basic foot positions that would become the basis of classical ballet a century later. The development of the *ballet de cour* into the ballet as we know it was completed during the reigns of Louis XIII (1610–43) and Louis XIV (1643–1715), as the narrative element grew more important, courtiers were replaced by professional performers, and a paying public was admitted.

Although the establishment of dance as a theatrical art was largely a process of refinement and formalization, the history of social dance in the same period shows, in some respects, an opposite tendency. During the Renaissance courtly forms of dance were constantly revitalized by the influence of folk styles. In this there is a sharp contrast with the Middle Ages, which made a fairly rigid distinction between the gravely formal couple dances thought suitable for knights and their ladies and the boisterous ring and chain dances of the peasantry. The influence of popular on courtly dance becomes most evident in the later 16th century. In France, for example, many court dances developed from the *burla* or *branle*, a peasant round dance so vigorous that it is thought to be the origin of the English word "brawl." Similarly, the most frequently mentioned dance of the century, the *morisca*, developed from a folk dance of Moorish Spain. In England, a particularly lively style of dance predominated at the court of ELIZABETH I, where courtiers vied to show off their strength and agility in the jig. Elizabeth herself was a lover of country dances and, in her youth, a keen exponent of the *volta*, an energetic leaping dance of French peasant origin. In Spain there was a particularly wide range of regional folk styles, and these greatly influenced the formal and theatrical styles that developed during the SIGLO DE ORO. Another important influence on Spanish styles was the indigenous dances of the New World; the fandango, for example, is thought to be of Afro-Cuban origin, while the sarabande and the chaconne may also have Central American roots. Whether courtly styles had a comparable influence on popular forms is hard to say; to judge by the visual evidence, the peasant dances depicted by BRUEGHEL in the mid-16th century appear little changed from those in the manuscript illuminations of the late Middle Ages.

Further reading: Jack Anderson, *Ballet and Modern Dance: A Concise History* (Chicago, Ill.: Independent Publishers Group, 2nd ed. 1992); Susan Au, *Ballet and Modern Dance* (London: Thames & Hudson, 2nd ed. 2002); Joan Cass, *Dancing Through History* (Memlo Park, Calif.: Benjamin/Cummings, 1993); Curt Sachs, *A World History of Dance* (New York: W. W. Norton, 1963).

**dance of Death** (French *danse macabre*, German *Totentanz*) A pictorial and literary theme originating in the late Middle Ages, in which Death, usually in the form of a skeletal musician, leads away representatives of every class of society, from pope to beggar, from emperor to peasant. The dance of Death appeared first in the form of murals in churches, the earliest being recorded in Paris, dating from the mid-1420s (now destroyed). Other early examples of dance of Death murals were to be found elsewhere in France, in England, Switzerland, Germany, and Italy. It was also treated in other media—stained glass, tapestry, embroidery, and sculpture.

The first printed edition of a dance of Death cycle combining verses and woodcuts issued from the Parisian press ofGuyot Marchant in 1485. Prior to that, manuscript versions of the dance of Death texts had appeared in both Spain (*Dança general de la muerte*, c. 1400) and Germany (the Lübeck *Totentanz*, 1463). The most famous treatment of the theme was by Hans HOLBEIN THE YOUNGER in a series of 50 woodcuts designed about 1523/24 and printed at Lyons in 1538.

**d'Anghiera, Pietro Martire** See PETER MARTYR (d'Anghiera)

**Daniel, Samuel** (1562–1619) *English poet*
Daniel was probably born near Taunton, went to Oxford in 1579, and then may have visited Italy. In the 1590s Mary HERBERT, Countess of Pembroke appointed him as tutor to her son William, and from this congenial literary milieu he published his first poems, the sonnet sequence *Delia* and the *Complaynt of Rosamond* (both 1592). His Senecan tragedy *Cleopatra* was published in 1594. The first edition of his major work, a long poem in eight-line

stanzas on the *Civil Wars* (i.e. the Wars of the Roses), appeared in 1595; a considerably revised and enlarged version came out in 1609, showing Daniel's subtle and thoughtful approach to political philosophy. His *Defence of Rhyme* (1602) is a refutation of Thomas Campion's tract on the unsuitability of rhyme in English verse. He wrote a number of court masques and was eventually put in charge of a troupe of boy actors, the Children of the Queen's Revels (1615–18). He was a friend and brother-in-law of John FLORIO.

**Daniele (Ricciarelli) da Volterra** (1509–1566) *Italian painter and sculptor*
Trained under Sodoma, Daniele is best known as a close associate of MICHELANGELO. After moving to Rome in about 1541, he executed several notable frescoes, the most celebrated being the *Deposition* (1541) in the Orsini chapel in Sta. Trinita dei Monti, in which his skill as a draftsman is evident. Daniele is, however, usually remembered as the artist who was commissioned to paint loincloths on the nude figures in Michelangelo's *Last Judgment* in the Sistine Chapel—for which he acquired the nickname "Il Braghettone" (the breeches maker). He also produced a bronze portrait bust (c. 1564; Bargello, Florence, and Louvre, Paris) of Michelangelo and was present at the latter's deathbed.

*danse macabre* See DANCE OF DEATH

**Dante Alighieri** (1265–1321) *Italian poet*
Alighiero d'Alighiero, Dante's father, was a Florentine Guelph belonging to the lower nobility. His mother died while he was a child; his father remarried and had nine children by his second wife. Dante received a sound education though little is known of it in detail; he studied rhetoric under Brunetto Latini and in his youthful verse came under the influence of CAVALCANTI. His marriage, to Gemma di Manetto Donati, was arranged, taking place soon after his father's death in 1283; there were two sons (Pietro and Jacopo) and perhaps daughters by the marriage.

Dante fought in the battle of Campaldino (1289) and for several years took part in public life. He was one of the six priors (chief officials of the council) of Florence in 1300 when strife between the Black and White factions of the Guelph party led to the exile of Cavalcanti, among others. The following year Dante, who opposed papal policies, was taking part in a delegation to Boniface VIII when the Blacks seized control of Florence and condemned him to exile. The possibility of returning only arose when Emperor Henry VII, whom Dante supported, entered Italy in 1310, but the failure of the emperor's cause and his unexpected death (1313) put an end to Dante's hopes. The long period of exile was spent in apparently extensive wanderings, during which Dante found refuge with Cangrande DELLA SCALA in Verona and finally with Guido da Polenta in Ravenna, where he died. The *Vita Nuova* (*New Life*; 1292–1300), lyrics joined by prose commentaries, concerns Dante's love for Beatrice, a figure who later plays a major role in the DIVINE COMEDY. The historical existence of Beatrice is doubtful; she was perhaps the daughter of Folco Portinari, later the wife of Simone de' Bardi, and died in 1290. Dante says that he met her when she was nine and again when she was 18 years old. He finds solace for his grief at her death in the consolation of philosophy (as conceived by Cicero and Boethius). The *Convivio* (*Feast*; 1304–08) and the Latin treatise *De vulgari eloquentia* (*On Eloquence in the Vernacular Tongue*; after 1304) are unfinished. The former alternates poems with prose explanations but only four of the proposed 14 sections are complete. The latter discusses the origin and growth of languages and the use of the vernacular in poetry; it looks forward to issues raised in the QUESTIONE DELLA LINGUA. Among other works are *De monarchia* (*On World Government*), a treatise of doubtful date presenting Dante's argument for a temporal power centered in Rome, and *Canzoniere*, poems inspired by Beatrice but excluded from *Vita Nuova*. Dante also wrote a number of other miscellaneous poems and several Latin epistles.

**Further reading:** Patrick Boyde, *Dante Philomythes and Philosopher: Man in the Cosmos* (Cambridge, U.K.: Cambridge University Press, 1981); Cecil Grayson (ed.), *The World of Dante: Essays on Dante and His Times* (Oxford, U.K.: Clarendon Press and New York: Oxford University Press, 1980); Robert Hollander, *Dante: A Life in Works* (New Haven, Conn.: Yale University Press, 2001); George Holmes, *Dante* (Oxford, U.K.: Oxford University Press and New York: Hill & Wang, 1980); Rachel Jacoff (ed.), *The Cambridge Companion to Dante* (Cambridge, U.K.: Cambridge University Press, 1993).

**Dante chair** See FURNITURE

**Danti, Vincenzo** (1530–1576) *Italian goldsmith and sculptor*
His earliest sculpture is a monumental bronze figure, *Pope Julius III Enthroned*, outside the cathedral (1553–56) of his native Perugia. From 1557 until 1573 Danti worked as a court sculptor to Duke Cosimo I in Florence. His masterpiece there was a bronze group on the baptistery, the *Beheading of St. John the Baptist* (1571): these and all his other figures are gracefully elongated and set in balletic poses characteristic of mannerist sculpture (*see* MANNERISM). For the Medici he cast in bronze a large narrative relief of *Moses and the Brazen Serpent* for the altar frontal of a chapel and a cupboard door (1561), both now in the Bargello, as well as a statuette of *Venus Anadyomene* for the Studiolo of Francesco I in the Palazzo Vecchio (c. 1573). Danti also carved marble statuary during the 1560s (e.g.

*Honor triumphant over Falsehood* and *Duke Cosimo I*, both in the Bargello). He published in 1567 a treatise on proportion, the *Primo libro del trattato delle perfette proportioni*, and retired after 1573 to Perugia, where he was appointed public architect and was a founder member of the Accademia del Disegno. Danti's sculpture has a delicacy of detail and an elegance of line reminiscent of other goldsmiths-turned-sculptor, such as GHIBERTI and CELLINI.

**Danube School** The collective name given various 16th-century artists working in the region of the River Danube in southern Germany and Austria. Although links can be established between particular individuals, the artists never functioned as a group, and opinions differ widely on exactly which artists should be accounted members. The unifying theme of their work, however, is love of landscape for its own sake; the Danube artists can be seen to have introduced landscape painting into German art. The painters usually seen as having developed the Danube style are Lucas CRANACH in his early years, Jörg Breu (c. 1475–1537), and Rueland Frueauf the Younger, all of whom probably visited Vienna during the first five years of the 16th century. The workshop of Jörg Kölderer, court painter to Emperor Maximilian I, may have provided a focus here. Albrecht ALTDORFER is generally considered the outstanding representative of the Danube style, which was continued by Wolfgang HUBER and many other minor figures. It is usually taken to apply to painters, but sculptors, architects, and other artists were also influenced by it.

**Danzig** (Polish **Gdansk**) A city and port at the mouth of the River Vistula on the Baltic Sea, now in north Poland. First mentioned as a Polish city in the late 10th century, Danzig gained municipal self-government (1260) and became an important Hanse town (*see* HANSEATIC LEAGUE) and trading center by the end of the Middle Ages. After its long occupation by the TEUTONIC KNIGHTS (1308–1466), Danzig was regained by King Casimir IV of Poland. Under Polish rule in the 15th and 16th centuries Danzig became the most prosperous Baltic port, exporting grain and timber and developing a successful shipbuilding industry; its first warship was launched in 1572. In 1520 Danzig was involved in the Polish Teutonic war. In 1525 King Sigismund I of Poland intervened to crush the artisans who had seized church property and proclaimed the city's adherence to LUTHER.

**Datini, Francesco di Marco** ("the Merchant of Prato") (c. 1335–1410) *Italian merchant*
From his home town of Prato, near Florence, Datini built up a trading empire in northern Italy, Avignon, Aragon, and Majorca. After 1378 he settled in Florence, joined the silk guild there, and used his surplus wealth to embark on banking. His letters and account books have survived, af-

fording an unparalleled insight into the life and values of a wealthy bourgeois in 14th-century Italy.

**Further reading:** Iris Origo, *The Merchant of Prato: Francesco di Marco Datini* (London: Cape, 1957; new ed. Boston, Mass: Godine, 2002).

**Daucher, Hans** (c. 1485–1538) *German sculptor*
Active in Augsburg, Hans was the son of the sculptor Adolf Daucher (c. 1460/65–1523/24) and executed a number of works for Emperor Charles V and the dukes of Württemberg. Noted for his small decorative bronze figures, he also produced the influential group of *Christ with the Virgin and St. John* for the altar of the Fugger Chapel in Augsburg.

**Daurat, Jean** (Jean Dorat, Jean Dinemand) (1508–1588) *French humanist scholar and poet*
Daurat was born at Limoges. As principal of the Collège de Coqueret from 1547, he numbered among his pupils BAÏF, RONSARD, BELLEAU, and other members of the group that became known as the PLÉIADE, to whom he communicated his love of classical literature. His work on the texts of the Greek dramatists, whom he also translated, his lectures on Homer, and his study of Pindar and later Greek poets ensured his place in the history of scholarship. In 1555 Daurat became tutor to the children of Henry II; from 1556 until his retirement in 1567 he held the chair of Greek at the Collège de France. Daurat wrote prolifically in Greek and Latin throughout his academic career, publishing (under his Latin sobriquet "Auratus") a collection of his poetry, *Poemata*, in 1586. He did not, however, excel as a writer of French verse.

**David, Gerard** (active 1484–1523) *Netherlands painter*
He was born at Oudewater, near Gouda, and in 1484 entered the Bruges painters' guild, of which he became dean in 1501. He was admitted to the Antwerp guild in 1515, but had returned to Bruges by 1519. Few of David's works are documented, but a large group of paintings is attributed to him. His early work, such as the London *Christ Nailed to the Cross*, has a brutal realism related to Hugo van der GOES's work and the Dutch tradition. In the Bruges *Justice of Cambyses* diptych (1498) the flaying alive of the unjust judge is depicted with an excruciating objectivity. The slightly later altar shutter of *Canon Bernardinus de Salviatis and Three Saints* (London) reveals a perceptive study of the work of Jan van EYCK. A high point in David's art is reached with the strikingly monumental Bruges triptych of *The Baptism of Christ* (c. 1509). Later artists, including METSYS and GOSSAERT, began by following David's precepts before discovering a new formal vocabulary in Italian art.

**Davis, John** (John Davys) (c. 1550–1605) *English navigator*
A Devon man, like many of the other great Elizabethan sailors, Davis made three voyages in search of the NORTHWEST PASSAGE in 1585, 1586, and 1587, sailing north up the west coast of Greenland; the strait between that coast and Baffin Island was named for him. Although he was unable to advance the search for a passage westward, his experiences led him to believe that such a route was possible, as he declared in his *Worldes Hydrographical Description* (1595). Following a trip to the Azores (1590), in 1591 he took command of a ship in the fleet of the circumnavigator Thomas CAVENDISH, but became separated from him in the Straits of Magellan, and sighted the Falkland Islands in August 1592. Davis's short practical guide for sailors, *The Seamans Secrets* (1594), introduces his invention of the BACKSTAFF as an aid to navigation. Later voyages (1598, 1600–03, 1604) took him to the East Indies. He was killed in an attack on his ship by Japanese pirates off Bintan Island, near Singapore.

**Davis's quadrant** See BACKSTAFFS

**de Bry family** A family of engravers including Theodor (1528–98), a refugee from Liège, and his sons Johann Theodor (1561–1623) and Johann Israel (fl. 1570–1611). Frankfurt, a center for the production and sale of illustrated books, was their home from 1590, though Theodor worked in England in the late 1580s. All three worked on the *Collectiones peregrinationum...* (*Grands et petits voyages*), which was begun in 1590. After the death of Johann Theodor his son-in-law Matthäus Merian (1593–1650) of Basle, a member of another family of engravers, took over and finished the book in 1634. The 1590 part includes a section on America, with several pictures based on drawings by John White, an official artist with Raleigh's expedition to Virginia in 1585. Johann Theodor de Bry also produced a *Florilegium novum* in 1611, one of the most famous flower-books of the period. The de Brys' engravings set new standards in the quality of book illustration.

*Decameron* The collection of stories written by BOCCACCIO between about 1348 and 1353 and related in the fictional framework of a court set up for 10 days (hence the title) in the Tuscan countryside by 10 young people fleeing from the plague in Florence. The 100 stories (one per day from each of the seven ladies and three youths) range in tone from the most exalted and refined to the pornographic and comprise the first great masterpiece of Italian prose. Pietro BEMBO later proposed it as the ultimate model for prose writing in the vernacular. The *Decameron* also contains some of Boccaccio's greatest lyric poetry in the *canzone* with which each day ends. The work's influence throughout Europe is incalculable, with stories like that of patient Griselda, the archetypal submissive wife, being retold in many different forms in several languages.

However, despite the popularity of stories from the *Decameron*, many of which were familiar in various forms to English readers from the 14th century, the first full-scale translation of the work into English was not published until 1620. This anonymous version has sometimes been ascribed to John FLORIO. John Payne's 1886 translation is available in an edition revised and annotated by C. S. Singleton (Berkeley, Calif., 3 vols, 1982). In the 20th century the translation by Richard Aldington (New York, 1930) enjoyed a number of reprints. The Penguin Classics version (Harmondsworth, U.K., 1972) is by G. H. McWilliam, and the World's Classics version (Oxford, U.K., 1990) by Guido Waldman.

**Further reading:** Peter E. Bondella and Mark Musa (eds), *The Decameron: A New Translation: 21 Novelle, Contemporary Reactions, Modern Criticism* (New York: W. W. Norton, 1980).

**Dedekind, Friedrich** (c. 1525–1598) *German satirist*
Born in Hannover, Dedekind became a Protestant pastor. While a student at Wittenberg he wrote *Grobianus sive de morum simplicitate libri duo* (1549), one of the famous satires of the age. A book of anecdotes in Latin verse, which owes much to BRANT's *Narrenschyff*, it lampoons boorish, selfish behavior (particularly table manners) by ironically praising it. The book went into 20 editions in the 16th century, with others in the 17th. Freely translated into German in 1551, it was even more popular in this form. Dedekind's later works—two German plays and some Latin verse—are less noteworthy.

**de Dominis, Marc Antonio** (1566–1624) *Dalmatian churchman*
A brilliant student and teacher and member of the Jesuits, de Dominis left the order in 1596 and six years later became archbishop of Spalato. Siding with the Venetians in their protests against papal claims and eventually repudiating the pope's authority, he was obliged to relinquish his archbishopric (1616) and flee to England. He was warmly received by James I and made dean of Windsor and master of Savoy (1617) and the same year began publication of his classic indictment of Rome, *De republica ecclesiastica*. Personal conflicts and political considerations led to his departure from England and attempted reconciliation with Rome in 1622 by means of a vehement attack on the Anglican Church (1623). He died in Rome, a captive of the Inquisition.

**Dee, John** (1527–1608) *English mathematician, antiquary, and magus*
The son of a London gentleman, Dee was educated at Cambridge and Louvain. He led an extremely varied life, traveling widely throughout Europe, and moving easily from mathematics to antiquarianism, and from commercial activity to occultism. In this last field Dee was to be found in 1586 in Prague with the medium Edward Kelley conjuring up spirits and supposedly conversing with them. More practically, Dee advised the Muscovy Company on the possibility of a NORTHEAST PASSAGE to China and on the development of improved navigational instruments. As well as being the author of such hermetic texts as his *Monas hieroglyphica* (1564), he also contributed a famous *Preface* (1570) to the first English translation of Euclid, in which he argued eloquently for the need for technically trained workers to develop England's trade and industry. At his Mortlake home Dee had assembled one of the finest libraries in England. It was sufficiently impressive to attract visits from ELIZABETH I in 1575 and 1580, but in 1583 it was partially destroyed by a mob on account of Dee's reputation as a wizard.

**Further reading:** Peter J. French, *John Dee: The World of an Elizabethan Magus* (London: Routledge & Kegan Paul, 1972); Benjamin Woolley, *The Queen's Conjurer: The Science and Magic of Dr Dee* (New York and London: HarperCollins, 2001).

**Defenestration of Prague** (1419) The incident that marked the beginning of the HUSSITE revolution in Bohemia. Popular support for Jan HUSS expressed after his execution (1415) prompted King Wenceslas to impose upon Prague a town council of reactionary German merchants. Their persecution of leading Bohemian reformers led to a rising by the Prague mob, which culminated in the magistrates being hurled out of the windows of the town hall and impaled on pikes held by the mob below. Less than three weeks later (August 16, 1419) Wenceslas died of a stroke, and the Hussite wars began in earnest.

**Defenestration of Prague** (1618) The incident that sparked off the Thirty Years' War between rival dynastic and religious interests in central Europe. When Ferdinand (1578–1637), Archduke of Styria, was elected king of Bohemia (1617) and chosen to succeed Matthias as emperor, the Bohemian Protestants feared for their religious and civil freedom. In May 1618, invading the Hradschin Palace, Prague, they broke up a meeting of the imperial commissioners by throwing two Catholic councilors and their secretary out of the window.

**della Casa, Giovanni** (1503–1556) *Italian churchman, diplomat, and writer*
Belonging to a prominent Florentine family, Della Casa was probably born at Mugello and he studied literature and law at Bologna and Greek at Padua before going to Rome in 1532. He followed an administrative and diplomatic career in the Church, becoming archbishop of Benevento and papal nuncio to Venice in 1544. During the pontificate of Julius III he withdrew to Venice and devoted

himself to writing (1551–55). He was recalled by Pope Paul IV and made Vatican secretary of state a year before his death. The Petrarchan poems collected in *Rime* (1558) were much admired by contemporaries, but he is chiefly remembered for the influential prose work *Il Galateo* (1558), in which an older gentleman advises a younger on manners and conduct and tells stories to make moral points. It is indebted both to Boccaccio's DECAMERON for an informal un-Ciceronian style and to Castiglione's COURTIER for its ideals of behavior. *Il Galateo* was one of the most frequently translated texts in Europe during the second half of the 16th century. Robert Peterson translated it into English in 1576 under the title *A Treatise of the Maners and Behaviours*; a facsimile of this edition was produced at Amsterdam in 1969. For a modern translation see *Galateo, or the Book of Manners* by R. S. Pine-Coffin (Harmondsworth, U.K., 1958).

**della Porta, Giacomo** (c. 1537–1602) *Italian architect*
Born in Rome, della Porta trained under MICHELANGELO and was later influenced by Giacomo da VIGNOLA, developing a style based upon academic MANNERISM. He is best known for completing works by Michelangelo, including the Palazzo dei Conservatori on the Capitol and, most notably, the dome of St. Peter's basilica (1586–90), to the designs for which he and Domenico FONTANA made a number of alterations. Sometime after 1572 della Porta completed the facade for Vignola's Gesù, the mother church of the Jesuit order, and then incorporated features of Vignola's design into several of his own churches in Rome, including Sta. Maria dei Monti (1580–81), Sant' Atanasio (1580–83), and Sant' Andrea della Valle (1591).

**della Porta, Giambattista** (c. 1535–1615) *Italian natural philosopher, cryptographer, and dramatist*
After a period of study and travel throughout Europe, della Porta returned to his native Naples where he published his *Magia naturalis* (1558; translated as *Natural Magick*, 1658). An immensely successful work (some 27 editions are known), it distinguished between the magic of sorcery, which della Porta rejected, and natural magic. Under this latter term he included familiar yet mysterious phenomena taken from such fields as magnetism, hydraulics, optics, and chemistry, and sought to explain them in terms of attractions, sympathies, fascinations, and antipathies. The book also contains one of the earliest descriptions of the camera obscura. More original, although less well known, is his *De furtivis literarum* (On secret writing; 1563), a work of CRYPTOGRAPHY in which he provided solutions to a number of simple polyalphabetic ciphers. His *Phytognomonica* (1589) expounds the doctrine of SIGNATURES. Della Porta was also a leading figure in two early scientific societies. He helped to establish in Naples in 1560 the ACADEMIA SECRETORUM NATURAE, the first such modern society, and in 1610 he became a member of Federico Cesi's ACCADEMIA DEI LINCEI in Rome. In addition, from 1589 onwards, della Porta also published some 20 plays in prose and verse, some of which were translated in England and France.

**della Porta, Guglielmo** (c. 1500–1577) *Italian sculptor*
Born in Milan, Guglielmo is first recorded working with other, older members of his sculptor family at Genoa in 1534. In 1537 he went to Rome, where he became the principal sculptor to Pope PAUL III. He was appointed to the office of the papal seal (*piombatore*) upon the death of its holder, the painter SEBASTIANO DEL PIOMBO (1547), and executed busts of the pope in bronze and marble. He was an admirer of MICHELANGELO, until their dispute over the nature and location of a monument to Paul III in St. Peter's, of which Michelangelo was architect: this was Guglielmo's major work and now stands to the left of the high altar, though he had initially hoped that it would stand free under the dome. The bronze seated portrait statue of the deceased pope was a major contribution to a series in St. Peter's ranging from St. Peter himself, through POLLAIUOLO's *Pope Innocent VIII*, to the baroque figures by Gian Lorenzo Bernini and Alessandri Algardi. The reclining *Virtues* below recall Michelangelo's *Times of Day* in the Medici chapel. Della Porta was a prolific draftsman and also produced many smaller statuettes and reliefs of religious subjects in gold, silver, or bronze.

**della Robbia, Luca** (1399/1400–1482) *Italian sculptor*
Luca della Robbia's significance as a sculptor in marble and bronze has been overshadowed by the popularity of his and his family's works in terracotta. The complex steps and secret formulas which Luca invented employed the lead-based glazes already in use by ceramicists to create enameled terracotta sculpture; they became the basis for a family industry in his native Florence, which was continued by his nephew Andrea (1434–1525) and other relatives into the 16th century. Luca was trained as a marble carver, however, and his first important commission was for 10 marble reliefs for an organ loft (known as the Cantoria) for the cathedral of Florence (1431–38; Museo dell' Opera del Duomo), the classical design of which was probably suggested by BRUNELLESCHI. Luca's figures of singing, dancing, and music-making angels combine naturalism, as seen in the ease of movement and well-observed detail, with idealism, evident in the beauty of the figures and the classically balanced compositions. Luca's reliefs offer a refined degree of surface finish which is impressive but not, as VASARI was the first to point out, completely appropriate for works to be seen from a distance in the relatively dark interior of the cathedral.

More satisfying are Luca's first large colored terracotta reliefs, the *Resurrection* and the *Assumption of Christ* (1442–45, 1446–51), in lunettes above the sacristy doors and near the location of Luca's and DONATELLO's pendant

*Cantorie*: the luminous colors and lucid, Renaissance compositions of Luca's terracottas enhance their readability in the dark interior. Enameled terracotta proved an ideal and relatively economical medium for both interior and exterior architectural decoration, and Luca contributed to a number of important Florentine monuments, including MICHELOZZO's tabernacle at San Miniato (1448), Brunelleschi's Capella dei Pazzi (c. 1442–52; *Twelve Apostles*, St. Andrew, cupola), the Medici palace (c. 1460; *Labors of the Months*, for the *studietto* of Piero de' Medici, now in the Victoria and Albert Museum, London), and a ceiling with *Virtues* for the chapel of the cardinal prince of Portugal at San Miniato (1461–66). Luca also combined marble reliefs with enameled terracotta, as in the tabernacle (1441–42) now at Peretola and the monument of Bishop Benozzo Federighi (1454–57; now Sta. Trinita). Luca's blue and white *Madonna and Child* compositions are among the sweetest and most serene of Quattrocento relief Madonnas; they offer a convincing sense of physical presence in concert with a gentle humanity. He also used enameled terracotta for such free-standing sculptures as *Two Kneeling Angels Carrying Candlesticks* (1448–51; cathedral, Florence) and a *Visitation* (before 1445; San Giovanni Fuorcivitas, Pistoia).

Between 1464 and 1469 Luca collaborated with Michelozzo and Maso di Bartolommeo in the design and execution of a set of bronze doors with saints for the cathedral sacristy. The Florentine biographer Antonio Manetti (1423–97) included Luca in his *Uomini singolari in Firenze* (Illustrious men of Florence), crediting him with the innovation of enameled terracotta and praising him for his moral and intellectual qualities.

**Further reading:** Maud Crutwell, *Luca and Andrea della Robbia* (New York: AMS Press, repr. 2002); John Pope-Hennessy, *Luca della Robbia* (Oxford, U.K.: Phaidon, 1980).

**della Rovere family** A Ligurian family of obscure origins which acquired wealth, power, and status during the papacy of Francesco della Rovere (Pope SIXTUS IV; 1471–84). An enthusiastic nepotist, Sixtus generously bestowed cardinal's hats and lordships on his nephews. Giovanni della Rovere (1457–1501), whom Sixtus made lord of Senigallia, married the daughter of the last Montefeltro duke of Urbino; their son succeeded to the duchy in 1508 and the della Rovere family ruled Urbino until the extinction of the line in 1631. Sixtus made his nephew Giuliano a cardinal (1471); as JULIUS II (pope 1503–13), Giuliano proved to be one of the ablest and most efficient Renaissance popes and further enhanced his family's prestige. He was known for his opposition to simony and nepotism.

**della Scala family** The rulers of Verona from 1259 to 1387. Mastino I (died 1277) was the first to control Verona. Della Scala power in northeast Italy reached its highest point under Cangrande I (1311–29), who conquered Vicenza (1312–14), Padua (1317–18), Bellino, and Feltre and was imperial vicar of Mantua (1327). The family's fortunes declined when Mastino II (died 1351) provoked a hostile Florentine-Venetian coalition and lost all his territories except Verona and Vicenza. The VISCONTI FAMILY defeated the della Scala and annexed their territories in 1387. The della Scala were admired for their public works and patronage of scholarship and letters; DANTE was sheltered by them in Verona in the early 14th century.

**della Valle, Pietro** (1586–1652) *Italian traveler*
Delle Valle was born in Rome to aristocratic parents. From 1606 to 1614 he lived at Naples, before starting his travels in Istanbul (1614–15). From there he went to Egypt and Jerusalem, then Damascus and Baghdad (1616). In Baghdad he married a Syrian Christian girl. They traveled on to Isfahan, where he spent five years (1617–21) near the court of Shah Abbas, of whom he would write favorably in his *Delle conditioni di Abbàs rè di Persia* (1628). Leaving Persia, he headed for India; when his wife died en route he added her embalmed body to his luggage. From Goa he traveled around southern India before heading home (1624) via the Middle East and Sicily. Wherever he went delle Valle studied and became proficient in the local languages, copied inscriptions, collected manuscripts, researched the indigenous culture, and sent back meticulous reports to his Neapolitan friend Mario Schipano. However, only the first part of his *Viaggi* was published during his lifetime (1650) and then only partially.

**Delorme, Philibert** (**Philibert de l'Orme**) (c. 1510–1570) *French architect*
The son of a master stonemason in Lyons, Delorme became acquainted with contemporary Italian works, as well as with the antiquities, while living in Rome (c. 1533–36), where he executed work for Pope Paul III. Delorme returned to Lyons in 1536 and the same year designed the Hôtel Bullioud there for the finance minister of Brittany. In 1540 he was appointed controller of fortifications at Lyons and subsequently embarked (1541–47) upon his first major building, the château of St-Maur-des-Fosses near Paris for Cardinal Jean Du Bellay, whom Delorme had met in Rome. Appointed superintendent of buildings under Henry II in 1548, Delorme built for him the Château-Neuf at St. Germain-en-Laye (1557), and for Henry's mistress DIANE DE POITIERS, the Château d'Anet (1547–52) and the bridge at CHENONCEAUX (1556–59). Although Delorme fell from favor after Henry's death in 1559, he was later commissioned by Catherine de' Medici to build the palace of the TUILERIES in Paris (1564), his last major work.

Noted for his success in combining Italian humanist ideas with traditional French achitecture, Delorme also wrote two books on architectural theory, *Nouvelles Inventions pour bien bastir* (1561) and *L'Architecture* (1567); of the latter only the first part of a projected nine appeared. He designed the tomb of Francis I at St-Denis (1547), and also undertook additions to the palace of Fontainebleau (1548–58) and work on Notre Dame. Most of his buildings are now destroyed.

## Deschamps, Eustache (c. 1346–c. 1406) *French poet*

Born at Vertus and educated by Guillaume de MACHAUT, Deschamps went on to study law at Orléans and served Charles V and Charles VI in a variety of diplomatic and administrative offices, including that of *maître des eaux et forêts* in Champagne and Brie. He wrote poetry in his spare time and after his retirement, producing over 1000 ballades and nearly 200 rondeaux on patriotic and moral as well as traditional themes; one of his ballades is addressed to the English poet Geoffrey Chaucer, "grant translateur" (great translator). Deschamps's other writings include an important treatise on versification, *Art de ditier* (1392); a satire on women, *Miroir de mariage*; and a number of dramatic works, notably the *Farce de Maître Trubert et d'Antroignart*.

## Desiderio da Settignano (c. 1430–1464) *Italian sculptor*

Few facts are known about this precocious and brilliant, but shortlived, sculptor. Born in the stone-quarrying village of Settignano, near Florence, he probably learned to carve from his family and later collaborated closely with Antonio ROSSELLINO. He was influenced by DONATELLO, but cannot have been trained by him, for the master was in Padua during the relevant decade. Desiderio was a successful imitator of Donatello's shallow-relief carvings (SCHIACCIATO), which he used specially for Madonna reliefs. He was not interested in the darker, dramatic side of Donatello, but excelled in sweeter subjects, such as portraits of women and children. His two main commissions, both in Florence, were: the Marsuppini monument in Sta. Croce (c. 1453), which was an elaboration on the theme of Bernardo ROSSELLINO's Bruni monument, and the altar of the sacrament in San Lorenzo (finished 1461).

## Des Périers, Bonaventure (c. 1510–c. 1544) *French writer and humanist*

He was born at Arnay-le-Duc and after collaborating with OLIVETAN on his translation of the Bible and with Étienne DOLET on the *Commentarii linguae latinae*, Des Périers became *valet de chambre* and secretary to MARGUERITE DE NAVARRE, whom he assisted with the transcription of her *Heptaméron*. In 1537 he produced the controversial *Cymbalum mundi*, a satirical attack on Christianity in the form of four allegorical dialogues, which was banned soon after publication. Des Périers is believed to have committed suicide in 1544. His *Nouvelles Récréations et joyeux devis*, a collection of short stories providing a lively and realistic picture of 16th-century society, was published posthumously in 1558.

## Desportes, Philippe (1546–1606) *French poet*

Born at Chartres, Desportes entered the French court during the reign of Charles IX and enjoyed the patronage of the duke of Anjou, with whom he traveled to Poland. After the latter's accession to the French throne as Henry III, Desportes superseded RONSARD as court poet and received a number of lucrative benefices, including the abbacy of Tiron. Desportes' love poetry, stylistically influenced by PETRARCH, ARIOSTO, and other Italian poets, consists largely of sonnets and elegies commissioned by his patrons for their mistresses: his *Premières Oeuvres* appeared in 1573 and his *Dernières Amours* in 1583. In the latter part of his life Desportes produced a series of translations of the Psalms, which brought adverse and perhaps unmerited criticism from his enemy MALHERBE.

## Des Prés, Josquin (c. 1440–1521) *French composer*

First mentioned as a singer at Milan cathedral in 1459, he was in the employ of Duke Galeazzo Maria Sforza by 1474. After the duke's assassination (1476) Josquin joined the service of his brother, Cardinal Ascanio Sforza, with whom he traveled to Rome in 1484. From 1486 Josquin sang in the papal choir. Around 1501 he appears to have been in France, possibly as unofficial court composer to King LOUIS XII. His five-part *De profundis clamavi* may have been written for Louis's funeral in 1515. From 1503 to 1504 he was *maestro* to Duke Ercole d'Este. In 1505 Josquin was back in France, at Condé-sur-l'Escaut, where he was provost at the cathedral, and where he died.

Josquin is generally regarded as the greatest composer of the High Renaissance. In the last two decades of his life his music was disseminated through printing, and his fame is partly due to the work of the Venetian printer PETRUCCI. Josquin was a prolific composer; about 20 Masses, 100 motets, and 75 secular works survive. He developed the techniques of Mass composition, notably the canon, paraphrase, and parody styles. In the late *Missa Pange lingua* the hymn melody underlies all the movements of the work, but it is subtly paraphrased rather than being employed as a *cantus firmus*. Josquin's motets are less conservative in style. For his many chansons he elaborated on melodies from popular music of the time. The compositional techniques he employed are similar to those found in his sacred works; through abandoning the *formes fixes* in his secular music he opened the way for greater stylistic variety.

**Further reading:** Gustave Reese, *The New Grove High Renaissance Masters: Josquin, Palestrina, Lassus, Byrd, Victoria* (London: Macmillan, 1984).

## Deutsch, Niklaus Manuel (c. 1484–1530) *Swiss artist, poet, soldier, and statesman*

Born in Berne, Deutsch popularized many of the concepts of the Italian Renaissance in northern Europe and adopted them himself in portraits, drawings, and paintings, mostly executed between 1515 and 1520. Many of his works dwell on the morbid subjects of ghosts and death, as in the case of his best work *The Dance of Death*, painted for the Dominican monastery at Berne and, having been destroyed in 1660, now only known by copies. Other works include a *Judgment of Paris*, a *Pyramus and Thisbe*, and a *Beheading of John the Baptist*. Deutsch was also an active member of the Berne city councils, a proponent of the Reformation, and author of such satires on ecclesiastical affairs as *Der Ablasskrämer* (1525) and *Testament der Messe* (1528).

**Devereux, Robert, Earl of Essex** See ESSEX, ROBERT DE-VEREUX, EARL OF

**Devotio Moderna** (Latin, "Modern Devotion") A religious movement that emerged in the Netherlands in the late 14th century under the influence of the Flemish mystic Jan van Ruysbroeck (1293–1381). His ideas were put into practice by his disciple Gerard (Geert) Groote (1340–84), whose lay followers were known as the Brothers and Sisters of the COMMON LIFE. Their aim was to keep religion simple, devout, and charitable, and they played an important part in restoring monastic virtues among the laity and in the monasteries themselves. Devotio Moderna laid strong emphasis on individual spirituality, structured meditation, and moral regeneration; its leaders tended to take a skeptical view of the intricacies of scholastic philosophy and of ecclesiastical practices such as PILGRIMAGE. Lay adherents lived together under one roof and worked for a living, without taking monastic vows, but the same ideals of simple, practical Christianity also permeated certain religious houses, among which the lead was taken by the Augustinian house of Windesheim, founded in 1387 at the instigation of Groote's disciple Florentius Radewyns (1350–1400) near Zwolle in Holland. Other Dutch monasteries that associated themselves with Devotio Moderna joined "the Congregation of Windesheim," and the movement spread in the 15th century to Germany and Switzerland. It was immensely influential in the development of a powerful spiritual literature in the 15th-century Netherlands, usually written in Latin but immediately translated into Middle Dutch. The 16th-century reformers in their zeal against monasticism did not spare the Devotio Moderna houses, destroying Windesheim itself in 1581. Devotio Moderna has been criticized as anti-intellectual and antitheological, but has also been praised as the source of all religious reforms during the 16th century.

**Diana** In Roman antiquity, the virgin goddess of the hunt, frequently identified with the Greek goddess Artemis, sister of Apollo. Diana was endowed by medieval and Renaissance iconographers with many of the attributes of Artemis, in particular the latter's association with the moon. As patroness of chastity, Diana was often evoked by artists and writers who wished to compliment a lady, and in the case of ELIZABETH I of England the eulogizing of the queen as Diana, under a variety of names, became a cult, strongly promoted by the cult object herself. She appears for instance as Cynthia (one of Artemis's names) in RALEIGH's poem *The Ocean to Cynthia* and as Belphoebe in Spenser's FAERIE QUEENE (Phoebe was another of Artemis's names).

The myth of Actaeon, who surprised Artemis/Diana bathing with her nymphs and was turned into a stag and torn to pieces by his own hounds, is the subject of a fine painting by Titian (c. 1560; Harewood House). A marble statue of Diana in the character of a huntress, with stag and bow (c. 1549), which formerly stood in the grounds of DIANE DE POITIERS's Château d'Anet, is attributed to Jean GOUJON, the subject a compliment to his patroness.

***Diana, La*** (1559) A Spanish pastoral romance by Jorge de MONTEMAYOR. It was an immense success, especially among the courtly audiences previously devoted to the romances of chivalry. The prose narrative, in seven chapters with interspersed lyrics, essentially concerns the love of Sereno for Diana, who is married to Delio. The meandering story, with passages of rich descriptive detail, involves an enchantress and magicians, a magic potion, nymphs, and a number of other complications, marvels, and relationships. Love is portrayed as irrational and painful but ennobling. Though a lesser work than SANNAZARO's *Arcadia*, which it imitates, it was frequently reprinted and widely translated; it influenced a number of later pastoralists, in Spain notably Gaspar Gil Polo (*Diana enamorada*, 1564) and CERVANTES (*La Galatea*, 1585). In England it influenced Sir Philip Sidney's ARCADIA.

**Diane de Poitiers** (1499–1566) *French noblewoman*
Beautiful and talented, Diane married Louis de Brézé, grand seneschal of Normandy, in 1515. As mistress of HENRY II from the mid-1530s, she exerted considerable influence at the French court, forcing Queen CATHERINE DE' MEDICI to accept second place. Taking advantage of court rivalries between MONTMORENCY and the GUISE FAMILY she played a decisive role in the allocation of positions of power and profit. She also patronized the architect DE-LORME, who built her Château d'Anet (1547–52), and the sculptor Jean GOUJON. After Henry II's death (1559) the widowed queen took her revenge and drove Diane from court.

**Díaz del Castillo, Bernal** (c. 1492–c. 1581) *Spanish historian and soldier*
Born at Medina del Campo, he sailed to Central America with Pedro Arias de Avila in 1514. Subsequently he joined several expeditions, serving CORTÉS during the invasion of Mexico (1519) and the expedition to Honduras (1524–26). In 1568 he wrote, from the point of view of the

ordinary soldier, his *Historia verdadera de la conquista de la Nueva Espana* (The true history of the conquest of New Spain; 1632). It contains vivid eyewitness accounts of personalities, events, and places involved in the conquest of Mexico and was intended to counterbalance Cortés' self-promotion in his own letters and the eulogistic account of the conquest by Cortés' secretary, who had not even been in the New World.

**Diaz de Novaes, Bartholomeu** (died 1500) *Portuguese navigator and the first European to sail around the Cape of Good Hope (1488)*
Diaz was of noble parentage, although the date and place of his birth are unknown. His first major voyage was to the Gold Coast as navigator in 1481. King John II was impressed by Diaz and in 1487 sent him with three ships to chart the African coast and explore possible routes to India. A prolonged storm forced him southwards and by the time he sailed north again, he had unknowingly rounded the Cape of Good Hope. He followed the coast eastwards as far as the Great Fish River before discontent among his crew forced him to turn back, but he did not return before ascertaining the north-eastwards trend of the coast. This confirmed the feasibility of a route round Africa to India. Diaz was received enthusiastically when he arrived back in Lisbon, but with Vasco da GAMA established as court favorite he was never given independent command again. He was lost at sea off the Cape of Good Hope on CABRAL's expedition.

**Digges, Leonard** (c. 1520–1571) *English mathematician*
Little is known of Digges's early life other than that he was born in Kent, trained as a lawyer, and was caught up in the rebellion of Sir Thomas Wyatt. Sentenced to death in 1554, he was later reprieved. Digges belonged to the first generation of English mathematicians who sought to apply their newly acquired skills to the practical arts. To this end he produced some of the earliest surviving English texts on surveying (*Tectonicon*, 1556), geometry (*Pantometria*, 1571), and, as augmented by his son Thomas Digges (died 1595), the application of the "Science of Numbers" to military matters (*Stratioticos*, 1579).

**Dijon** A city in eastern France, formerly the capital of Burgundy. Dijon's heyday was under the 14th- and 15th-century dukes of Burgundy until the union of the duchy with the French Crown in 1477. Parts of the ducal palace survive, also a number of important churches from the 15th and 16th centuries, including St. Michel with a remarkable Renaissance facade and sculptures by Hugues Sambin (1515/20–c. 1601), a pupil of Leonardo da Vinci who ran a workshop in Dijon. The nearby Chartreuse de Champmol was founded (1383) by PHILIP THE BOLD as the burial place of his dynasty. It was wrecked in 1793 and only fragments of the Puits de Moïse, the masterpiece of

his sculptor, Claus SLUTER, survive, with further fragments in Dijon's museum.

**Leonard Digges** Woodcut illustrations appearing in his *Pantometria* (1571), an early treatise on surveying according to the principles of geometry. The surveyor in the top picture is using a theodolite, an instrument first described in Digges's work.

**diplomacy** The practice of diplomacy in the modern sense—the maintaining by a state of permanent representatives abroad—was a Renaissance development that went hand-in-hand with the older practice of exchanging ambassadors on an ad hoc basis. Such exchanges routinely took place when matters such as trade agreements, political pacts, royal marriages, or religious issues were under discussion. Aenea Silvio Piccolomini, later Pope PIUS II, who traveled extensively on Church business in the 1430s, included an account of his embassy to King James I of Scotland in his autobiographical *Commentarii*; his reception in Scotland is also recorded in the series of frescoes on his career painted by PINTURICCHIO for the Piccolomini Library in Siena. In the years before the fall of Constantinople in 1453 the Byzantine emperors sent numerous ambassadors to Catholic Europe to attempt to achieve a religious accommodation that would enable Western and Eastern Christendom to present a united front against the advancing Ottoman Turks, with Emperor John VIII Paleologus himself leading the Orthodox delegation at the Council of Florence in 1438. Prestige was also an important motivator, particularly where principals were involved, as at the FIELD OF THE CLOTH OF GOLD. The youthful French ambassadors to the court of Henry VIII in 1533 dignified their mission on behalf of FRANCIS I with a commemorative double portrait by Hans HOLBEIN the Younger.

Ambassadors often left valuable accounts of the countries they visited: the German Sigmund von Herberstein, an envoy to Russia in 1517 and 1526, wrote *Rerum Muscoviticarum commentarii*. Others who left descriptions of this then little-known country were the Englishmen Sir Jerome Horsey, Elizabeth I's envoy to tsars Ivan the Terrible and Feodor I in the 1580s, and Giles Fletcher, English ambassador to Moscow in 1588. Roger ASCHAM, who accompanied Edward VI's ambassador to CHARLES V through Germany in 1551, kept a journal in English during his travels, the bulk of which, sent home as a letter to a friend, was published as *A Report ... of the Affaires and State of Germany* (1553).

Envoys also traveled beyond the bounds of Christendom. The accession of Sultan Mehmet II in 1451 brought a flurry of embassies to his then court at Adrianople, among them envoys from Venice, Ragusa (Dubrovnik), the Knights Hospitaler on Rhodes, Serbia, and Constantinople. The importance of contact with the SUBLIME PORTE (as the Ottoman seat of government was called) grew in the 16th century as the sultan's power spread across the Mediterranean and menaced the eastern European heartlands. The suburb of Pera, north of the Golden Horn, became an established diplomatic quarter. One particularly well-documented embassy was that of Ogier Ghislain de BUSBECQ, the envoy of the Holy Roman Emperor, in 1555–62. At the end of the 15th century John II of Portugal sent Pero da COVILHÃ as his ambassador to Africa with letters for the legendary Christian ruler Prester John. In 1615 Sir Thomas Roe (c. 1581–1644), who might be accounted one of the earliest career diplomats, was sent as envoy to the Moghul emperor Jahangir to consolidate a commercial treaty on behalf of the EAST INDIA COMPANY, following up that successful mission with an equally successful embassy to the Ottoman Porte in 1621–28. Another early career diplomat was Sir Henry Wotton (1568–1639), famous for his punning witticism "An ambassador is an honest man sent to lie abroad for the good of his country."

The usefulness of having a permanent representative abroad was first demonstrated by the consuls who were maintained by the Italian city-states with trading interests in the Levant to act as the eyes and ears of their paymasters there. Venice in particular took the lead in setting up an organized diplomatic service; the reports (*relazioni*) made by its representatives at the end of their term of office were formally read out in the Senate and provide an invaluable record of the evolution of European diplomacy. In the second half of the 15th century similar arrangements began to be made by other Italian states, and the practice later spread to Spain and northern Europe, a process accelerated by the outbreak of the Wars of Italy in 1494. One condition of the 1521 treaty between Holy Roman Emperor Charles V and Henry VIII was that they should mutually appoint ambassadors. The professional diplomat Eustache Chapuys spent 16 eventful years from 1529 as imperial representative in London, while on the English side credit for the development of a formal diplomatic service is mainly due to Cardinal WOLSEY. Although the legal position of diplomats resident in foreign courts was at first sometimes ambiguous, and they could be vulnerable to accusations of spying, there were such clear advantages to all parties in having someone to keep an eye on other princes while working to maintain a peaceful and mutually satisfactory status quo that the system was steadily formalized from the early 16th century onward.

**See also:** CONSTANTINOPLE

**Further reading:** Garrett Mattingley, *Renaissance Diplomacy* (London: Cape and Boston: Houghton-Mifflin, 1955; several later editions); Joycelyne G. Russell, *Peacemaking in the Renaissance* (London: Duckworth, 1986); ~, *Diplomats at Work: Three Renaissance Studies* (Stroud, U.K.: Sutton, 1992).

**Discalced Carmelites** See CARMELITES, REFORM OF THE

**dissection** Little dissection of human cadavers took place before the Renaissance. Consequently, much of the anatomical knowledge of antiquity was derived misleadingly from the study of Barbary apes, domestic animals, and the occasional human corpse. The main source of bodies for Renaissance students were those presented for autopsy. Outside this, anatomists were forced back on their own resources. As a result medical students, as in Bologna in 1319, found themselves prosecuted for grave robbing. Although arrangements were made in 1442 to allow the medical school to receive two executed corpses annually, the supply remained quite inadequate. Consequently, VESALIUS could still be found a century later haunting cemeteries and competing with marauding dogs for skeletal remains. In his entire career he seems to have seen no more than six female corpses, although it is a female corpse on the dissecting table in the crowded theater depicted on the woodcut title page of the first edition of his *De humanis corporis fabrica* (1543; see illustration p. 491).

Even when corpses were available, the anatomical custom of the day did little to advance knowledge. The actual dissection itself was often conducted by an illiterate demonstrator while the anatomist himself merely read from a supposedly authoritative text. Given the conditions under which they had to work, it is hardly surprising that few Renaissance anatomists could feel sufficiently confident in their work to challenge the authority of their dissecting manuals.

See also: ANATOMY; GALENISM, RENAISSANCE

Further reading: Jonathan Sawday, *The Body Emblazoned: Dissection and the Human Body in Renaissance Culture* (London and New York: Routledge, 1997).

**dissolution of the monasteries** The closure of the religious houses in England under HENRY VIII. Monasteries, nunneries, and friar houses were common in Catholic England and large numbers of ascetics lived in them. These religious communities had long attracted controversy: critics lamented that members were morally lax, that their Christianity was excessively contemplative, that they venerated relics pointlessly, and that, as powerful landowners, they were institutionally corrupt. These complaints grew during the early years of Protestantism. Henry VIII, who needed revenue, exploited discontent with perceived monastic privilege to seize the assets of abbeys. Under Thomas CROMWELL's direction, the suppression of the monastic orders became a crucial moment in Protestant advancement.

The Suppression of Religious Houses Act was passed by Parliament in 1536. This initial strike was intended to remove smaller abbeys, without quashing major houses. Within months, around a third of monastic holdings had been confiscated. Anger at the state's attack on the orders partly inspired the 1536/7 PILGRIMAGE OF GRACE. The involvement of monks from large abbeys in the rebellion added impetus to Henry's drive against their orders. More comprehensive suppression of monasteries ensued. The Second Dissolution Act (1539) rubber-stamped additional seizures of land by forces sent around the country by Cromwell. Most orders had already been erased by the time of this second Act. The state compensated members of the orders, most of whom had surrendered meekly, with varying degrees of generosity or meanness. Henry's obliteration of the monastic communities impacted hugely upon his Catholic subjects. The dissolution left permanent material scars, as it caused the loss of ecclesiastical artefacts, buildings, manuscripts, and paintings through both willful destruction and subsequent neglect (*see* ANTIQUARIANISM).

Further reading: Nicholas Doggett, *Patterns of Re-use: the Transformation of Former Monastic Buildings in Post-Dissolution Hertfordshire* (Oxford, U.K.: Archaeopress, 2002); David Knowles, *Bare Ruined Choirs: The Dissolution of the Monasteries* (Cambridge, U.K.: Cambridge University Press, 1976); G. W. O. Woodward *The Dissolution of the Monasteries* (Norwich, U.K.: Jarrold, 1990); Joyce A.

Youings, *The Dissolution of the Monasteries* (London: Allen & Unwin and New York: Barnes & Noble, 1971).

***Divine Comedy*** (Italian ***La Divina Commedia***) The poem by DANTE, begun in exile in 1306 and allegorically describing the poet's (by implication mankind's) journey through life to salvation. The *Commedia* (as originally entitled, "divine" being a later addition) is the central and culminating literary work of medieval Europe. It is systematically structured in TERZA RIMA, with three *cantiche* (*Inferno*, *Purgatorio*, *Paradiso*), each having 33 *canti* (plus an introductory canto to the *Inferno*), and with each of the realms having nine subdivisions.

The action takes place in the year 1300. The poet is lost in a wood and unable to escape. VIRGIL, representing Reason, is sent by Beatrice, representing divine Revelation, to guide the poet's descent into Hell so that through a knowledge of sin he may acquire humility and finally ascend to Paradise. Dante's judgments on a number of people and issues are reflected in the historical persons who populate Hell and in the imaginative punishments meted out to them. The penitential mood continues, but with renewed hope, in *Purgatorio*, at the end of which Virgil vanishes and Dante is reunited with Beatrice. *Paradiso* is devoted to an exposition of religious life and the poetry is gradually simplified to an imagery of light as the work ends with a vision of divine love.

Manuscripts extant from the period up to Dante's death (1321) number 600. BOCCACCIO instituted the first public lectures on Dante in Florence (1373), and a vast amount of critical commentary has accumulated since. The first printed edition of the *Divine Comedy* (Foligno, 1472) was followed in the same year by others printed at Mantua and Iesi. In all, just under 50 editions appeared before 1600, and there was also a substantial secondary literature in both Latin and the vernacular. English-speaking admirers of Dante, of which there were always some from Chaucer onward, read the *Divine Comedy* in Italian until the first complete translation in blank verse by H. Boyd in 1802. It was soon superseded by Henry Francis Cary's version (1814), also in blank verse. The annotated translation by Dorothy L. Sayers (3 vols, Harmondsworth, U.K., 1955–62) is in *terza rima*. More recent verse translations include highly praised versions by John Ciardi (New York, 1977), Allen Mandelbaum (Berkeley, Calif., 1987), and Robert Pinsky (New York, 1996). For an Italian text with facing English translation and commentary see the three-volume edition by J. D. Sinclair originally published in 1939 (New York, 1961, 1981).

**Divino, El** See MORALES, LUÍS DE

**Dodoens, Rembert** (1517–1585) *Flemish physician and botanist*
His *Crūÿdeboeck* (1554) owes much to Leonhart FUCHS's herbal, including its illustrations. CLUSIUS translated it into French (1557), a version used by Henry Lyte for his *Niewe Herball* (1578). Lyte's translation and Dodoens's last book, *Stirpium historiae pemptades sex* (1583), were among John GERARD's sources for his *Herball*.

See also: HERBALS

**doge** The head of state or chief magistrate in the republic of Genoa (1339–1797) and Venice (697–1805). Influential in medieval times, the Venetian office of doge became increasingly ceremonial with real power residing in the MAGGIOR CONSIGLIO. While the dogate in Venice played an important role in the city's admired constitutional stability, the Genoese doges tended to have short and tumultuous terms of office until the 16th century when Andrea DORIA reformed the system with biennial elections to the position. The dogate in both cities was abolished by Napoleon.

**dolce stil nuovo** The "sweet new style" of lyric verse between about 1250 and 1300. The term was coined by DANTE (*Purgatorio* XXIV 57), who lists Guido Guinizelli (c. 1240–76), CAVALCANTI, and himself among the practitioners (*De vulgari eloquentia*). Later critics have added other names. It greatly influenced PETRARCH and through him many later poets. Characterized by musicality, the spiritualization of courtly love conventions, and a mystical and philosophical strain in the close analysis of love, the style was adopted in sonnets, *canzoni*, and ballads, the culminating examples being the poems inspired by Beatrice and gathered by Dante in his *Vita nuova*.

**Dolet, Étienne** (1509–1546) *French humanist and printer*
Born at Orléans, Dolet was forced to abandon his law studies at Toulouse on account of his outspoken involvement in several controversial issues. He moved to Lyons, where he produced his two major works: *Dialogus de imitatione ciceroniana* (1535), in which he defended his fellow Ciceronians (*see* CICERO) against the attacks of ERASMUS, and *Commentarii linguae latinae* (1536–38), a significant contribution to Latin scholarship. In 1538 he set up as a printer, publishing the works of his friends MAROT and RABELAIS and his own translations of classical literature and the Scriptures. He was the first to translate Platonic dialogues into French. Dolet was imprisoned at least four times: on the first occasion he had been accused of killing a painter, apparently in self-defense, for which he received a royal pardon; he subsequently faced three charges of atheism, based on his publication of allegedly heretical writings, notably a dialogue (attributed to Plato) denying the immortality of the soul. He was burned at the stake in the Place Maubert, Paris.

**Domenico da Cortona** (Le Boccador) (1470–1549) *Italian architect and woodcarver*
Domenico executed most of his best-known works in France, where he arrived in 1495 at the summons of Charles VIII. Responsible for the furthering of many Italian ideas in France, Domenico probably designed the wooden model for the Château de CHAMBORD, which was begun in 1519. A development of the designs of Giuliano da Sangallo, the model included such novel features as a double central staircase and had a profound influence upon subsequent architects in France. Other works included the design of the Hôtel de Ville in Paris (1532).

**Domenico Veneziano** (died 1461) *Italian painter*
Probably a native of Venice, Domenico was first recorded in Perugia in 1438, when he wrote to the Medici family asking for commissions; he settled in Florence in 1439. Noted for his interest in the effects of light upon color, Domenico was employed upon a fresco cycle in Sant' Egidio in Florence (1439–45), now lost, on which he was assisted by PIERO DELLA FRANCESCA. Only two signed works by Domenico survive, the earlier being the Carnesecchi tabernacle (c. 1440; National Gallery, London), which reveals the influence of Masaccio. His greatest work was the altarpiece (c. 1445; Uffizi, Florence and elsewhere) painted for the church of Sta. Lucia de' Magnoli in Florence, an early example of the SACRA CONVERSAZIONE, showing the Madonna and Child with four saints. One of the predellas from this altarpiece, an exceptionally beautiful and hieratic *Annunciation*, is in the Fitzwilliam Museum, Cambridge, U.K. Other works sometimes attributed to Domenico include several profile portraits, an *Adoration of the Magi* (date unknown; Staatliche Museen Preussischer Kulturbesitz, Berlin), and *SS. John and Francis* (Sta. Croce, Florence), which echoes the style of ANDREA DEL CASTAGNO.

**Dominis, Marc Antonio de** *See* MARC ANTONIO DE DOMINIS

**Donatello** (Donato di Betto Bardi) (1386–1466) *Italian sculptor*
A Florentine by birth, Donatello was the greatest sculptor of the early Renaissance and one of its key figures, alongside GHIBERTI, MASACCIO, BRUNELLESCHI, and ALBERTI. He was one of the pioneers of linear PERSPECTIVE. Deeply concerned with the revival of Greco-Roman culture and realism in art, he nonetheless remained sincerely Christian.

First documented as an assistant to Ghiberti on the models for the reliefs on the north doors of the baptistery (1404–07) in Florence, Donatello became a rival, allying himself with Brunelleschi. For public corporations such as the board of works of the cathedral and the guilds of Florence, he carved a succession of over-life-size statues in marble that indicate his rapid progress away from his

Gothic beginnings (e.g. the marble *David*; now Bargello, Florence), via a transitional statue, *St. John the Evangelist*, for the cathedral facade (1408; now Museo dell' Opera del Duomo, Florence), to full-blown Renaissance figures like *St. Mark* (1411–13; Orsanmichele, Florence) and *St. George* (1415; Bargello). These were followed by a series of increasingly expressive statues of Old Testament prophets for the campanile (1415–36; now Museo dell' Opera del Duomo). By imaginatively combining his study of Roman portrait statuary with his observation of contemporary Florentines, Donatello single-handedly created a new sculptural style with a maximum dramatic effect. He later pursued this vein in woodcarvings of *St. John the Baptist* (1438; Frari church, Venice) and *St. Mary Magdalene* (c. 1455–60; Museo dell' Opera del Duomo).

Donatello also invented SCHIACCIATO, a technique of very shallow carving for narrative reliefs which approximated the effect of drawing and shading on paper; this allowed the sculptor much greater freedom to suggest depths, movement, and emotion. The progressive milestones in this mode are *St. George and the Dragon* (c. 1415; Bargello); the *Ascension of Christ* (Victoria and Albert Museum, London); the *Assumption of the Virgin* (Sant' Angelo a Nido, Naples); the *Feast of Herod* (c. 1435; Musées des Beaux-Arts, Lille). These reliefs are quite unparalleled and were imitated only by DESIDERIO DA SETTIGNANO and by MICHELANGELO in his youth. His friezes of *putti* on the Cantoria of the Duomo in Florence and on the external pulpit of Prato cathedral, both carved in the 1430s, show his highly individual interpretation of antique motifs.

Donatello's favorite patron was Cosimo de' MEDICI, for whom he created many and various sculptures, including the reliefs in Brunelleschi's old sacristy and, later, the bronze pulpit in San Lorenzo, and for the newly built Medici palace the bronze statues of *David* (Bargello) and *Judith and Holofernes* (Palazzo Vecchio, Florence). Outside Florence, his greatest sculpture is in Padua, where he spent a whole decade (1443–53): this comprises the first surviving EQUESTRIAN MONUMENT since ancient times, the statue to GATTAMELATA, and statues and panels for the high altar of the basilica (il Santo).

Donatello also worked in Rome and Siena. In each of these artistic centers, his fully developed Renaissance style made a great impact on the local schools, which were fundamentally still late Gothic in character and mood. In Padua and Siena, where he worked exclusively in bronze, he founded a strong tradition—BELLANO and RICCIO in Padua, VECCHIETTA and FRANCESCO di Giorgio in Siena. In his native Florence his principal followers were, in marble carving, Desiderio da Settignano and MICHELOZZO, and, in bronze casting, VERROCCHIO, POLLAIUOLO, and BERTOLDO. The latter formed a living link between the elderly Donatello and Michelangelo.

**Further reading:** Michael Greenhalgh, *Donatello and His Sources* (London: Duckworth and New York: Holmes & Meier, 1982); Horst W. Janson, *The Sculpture of Donatello* (Princeton, N.J.: Princeton University Press, 1957); Joachim Poeschke, *Donatello and His World: Sculpture of the Italian Renaissance*, transl. Russell Stockman (New York: Harry N. Abrams, 1993).

**Dondi, Giovanni de** (1318–1389) *Italian astronomer and horologist*
Born at Chioggia, near Venice, the son of a physician and CLOCK maker, Dondi followed his father Jacopo (1293–1359) and taught medicine and astronomy at the universities of Padua and Pavia. Jacopo was reported to have built an astronomical clock in 1344 in Padua. Shortly afterwards, probably with his father's help, Giovanni began work on his own clock. Completed in 1364, it was sited in the Visconti castle in Pavia. Though long since destroyed, details of the clock are preserved in Giovanni's lavishly illustrated 130,000-word manuscript. More concerned with celestial movements than the hourly recording of time, the brass weight-driven clock had seven sides, displaying much astronomical and calendrical information. It contained the most advanced gearing then constructed and remained unsurpassed in design until the mid-16th century.

**Doni, Anton Francesco** (1513–1574) *Italian writer*
The son of a Florentine tradesman, Doni joined the Servite order at an early age but left it in 1540, thereafter supporting himself by his writings. After Pietro ARETINO, he was the most distinguished of the authors known as the *poligrafi*, whose lively vernacular works were aimed at a popular audience and printed mainly in Venice. Often critical of or disillusioned with many humanist ideals, Doni's works include *La zucca* (1551; *The Gourd*), a collection of stories and proverbs; *I marmi* (1553; *The Marble Steps*), imaginary conversation overheard on the steps of Florence's Duomo; and *I mondi* and *Gl' inferni* (1553), dialogues on seven imaginary worlds and hells.

**Don Quixote** (Spanish *El ingenioso hidalgo Don Quixote de la Mancha*) The comic prose masterpiece by Miguel de CERVANTES SAAVEDRA, published in two parts (1605, 1615). In the prologue to Part I (52 chapters), Cervantes declares his intention of ridiculing the romances of chivalry. The elderly *hidalgo* Don Quixote has gone mad from reading too many of them and so, emulating Amadís de Gaula and other knights errant, he set out from his village on his nag Rocinante in search of adventure. Sancho Panza, whose peasant realism and unheroic character contrast with Quixote's idealistic credulity, becomes his "squire." The episodes, in which Quixote's delusion transforms windmills into giants and peasant girls into princesses, range from farce to social satire and high comedy. A vast number of brilliantly sketched characters are introduced, but the action is interrupted by digressions and long interpolated tales. Part II (74 chapters), which Cervantes hastily completed because an unknown author ("Alonso Fernández de Avellaneda") had published a spurious sequel in 1614, continues the adventures but with fewer digressions and a much greater unity of action. In the course of events, the characters of Quixote and Sancho acquire a new depth until finally Quixote returns home, recovers his sanity, and dies. The book's success was immediate and its influence enduring. It was translated into English (by Thomas Shelton, 1612–20) and French (1614–18) in Cervantes' lifetime, and into Italian shortly afterwards (1622–25). Shelton's version was republished in the Tudor Translations series (1896; repr. 1967), and another edition of this version, published in 1901, has illustrations by Frank Brangwyn. J. M. Cohen's translation, *The Adventures of Don Quixote* (Harmondsworth, U.K., 1950) has frequently been reprinted in the Penguin Classics series. A more recent version is that for Norton Critical Editions by Burton Raffel (New York, 1999).

**Dorat, Jean** See DAURAT, JEAN

**Dordrecht, Synod of** See DORT, SYNOD OF

**Doria, Andrea** (1466–1560) *Genoese statesman, admiral, and patron of the arts*
After fighting for the papacy and Naples he fitted out eight galleys to defeat the Barbary pirates and the Turks in the Mediterranean and won great acclaim by defeating the Turkish fleet at Pianosa (1519). He helped FRANCIS I of France take Genoa (1527), but changed sides (1528), obtained the protection of Emperor CHARLES V, and drove the French out. He then established his authority over Genoa, suppressing conspiracies and developing oligarchic rule. As grand admiral of the imperial fleet he helped Charles V take Tunis (1535). He came out of retirement to lead the Genoese reconquest of Corsica (1559).

**Doria, Gian Andrea** (1539–1606) *Genoese nobleman, grand-nephew and heir of Andrea Doria*
When Andrea retired (1555) he handed over the command of his squadron to Gian Andrea, whose record as a naval commander proved disappointing; he failed to take Djerba (1560) and his squadron performed poorly for the imperial fleet at LEPANTO (1571). After his grand-uncle's death Gian Andrea joined the older Genoese nobility in their struggle for power against the newer nobility.

**Dort, Synod of** (1618–19) An assembly of the Dutch Reformed Church at Dordrecht (Dort), to settle disputes arising from the Arminian Remonstrance (*see* ARMINIANISM) to the states general of the United Provinces. The official delegates were all Gomarists, that is, strict Calvinists. Representatives of the REMONSTRANTS were heard, but took no part in the procedure, and they were eventually expelled. Emissaries from German, Swiss, and British churches were present, the English delegation including three future bishops and John Hales, chaplain to the ambassador. A new Dutch version of the Bible was commissioned, and arrangements were made for a new catechism and for the censorship of books. Five sets of articles were approved, asserting the doctrines of election not dependent on belief, limited atonement (for the elect only), the total depravity of man, irresistible grace, and the impossibility of the elect's falling into sin. The authority of the BELGIC CONFESSION and the HEIDELBERG CATECHISM was also endorsed. As a result of this sweeping victory for Calvinism, many Arminian ministers were deprived, GROTIUS was imprisoned, and OLDENBARNEVELDT beheaded.

See also: PREDESTINATION

**Dossi, Dosso** (Giovanni di Luteri) (c. 1480–1542) *Italian painter*
He was born in Mantua or Ferrara but little is known about his early life. The romantic approach to landscape that is particularly apparent in his early work indicates the influence of GIORGIONE. He may also have had contact with TITIAN. By 1512 he had left Venice for Mantua, where with his elder brother Battista (died 1548) he carried out for the duke of Mantua decorations which revealed the possible influence of CORREGGIO. In 1517 the brothers were working for Alfonso I, Duke of Ferrara, producing tapestries and entertainments, the latter with the poet ARIOSTO. Although Dosso Dossi has been accused of poor draftsmanship he was the leading figure in the school of Ferrara in the 16th century. One of his most famous paintings, *Circe* (1530; Galleria Borghese, Rome) is an example of the mysterious atmosphere he was able to create with effects of light. The equally well-known *Circe and her Lovers in a Landscape* (National Gallery, Washington), the second version of an earlier painting, is an example of his later work with rich exotic landscapes. Dossi died in Ferrara.

**Douai** A Flemish town (formerly in the Spanish Netherlands, now in France) particularly associated in the Counter-Reformation period with the college established there in 1568 by William ALLEN for the training of English Roman Catholic priests. The college's printing press was active in producing Roman Catholic tracts, and its scholars were responsible for the Reims-Douai translation of the Vulgate into English (New Testament 1582, Old Testament 1609). A number of the priests associated with Douai were captured and executed on their clandestine missions to England to support the Catholics there and recall the Protestants to the Catholic faith. Among them were Cuthbert Mayne, the first priest to be executed (1577), and Edmund CAMPION, who were both at Douai in the 1570s.

**Douglas, Gavin** (c. 1474–1522) *Scottish churchman and poet*
The son of the fifth earl of Angus, Douglas studied at St. Andrews University (1489–94), received his first ecclesiastical appointment in 1496, and became provost of St. Giles, Edinburgh, about five years later. The allegorical poems *The Palace of Honour* and *King Hart* (the latter possibly not by Douglas) were not published until long after his death, but were probably written between 1501 and 1513. His translation of VIRGIL's *Aeneid* into Scots, the first version of the poem made in Britain, was completed in July 1513, but not published until 1553. Douglas's prologues to each book of the *Aeneid* are some of his finest original verse, and the translation itself, in vigorous heroic couplets, makes up in energy what it lacks in accuracy (*see* TRANSLATIONS OF CLASSICAL AUTHORS). After James IV's death at the battle of Flodden (1513), Douglas's career was embroiled in politics, and he was only installed as bishop of Dunkeld (1516) with much help from the widowed queen. Further upheavals sent him into exile in London (1521), where he died.

**Dovizi, Bernardo** See BIBBIENA, BERNARDO DOVIZI, IL

**Dowland, John** (1563–1626) *English composer and lutenist*
Dowland is first mentioned as being in the service of Sir Henry Cobham, ambassador (1579–83) to France. While there he converted to Catholicism. After his return to England, probably in 1584, Dowland's music was performed at court, but on the rejection of his application for the post of queen's lutenist (1594) he went abroad again, traveling through Germany and Italy. In 1596 or 1597 he was back in England and published his *First Booke of Songes or Ayres of Foure Partes with Tableture for the Lute* (1597), an anthology of songs for solo voice and lute or four-part ayres; it was very popular and reprinted at least four times. By November 18, 1598 Dowland was lutenist at the court of Christian IV of Denmark, where he remained until his dismissal in 1606.

After his return to England, Dowland entered the service of Lord Walden. Though at this time he complained of neglect and criticism from younger lutenists, Dowland was enjoying considerable respect and popularity both in England and on the Continent. His famous *Lachrymae* (1605) was widely used in arrangements by other composers, and references to it in contemporary theatrical and literary works reflect its enormous popularity. He was finally appointed one of the king's lutes in 1612. Dowland wrote many attractive dance tunes and fantasias, but is chiefly remembered for his melancholy songs, in which chromaticism and discord are used to great effect.

**Drake, Sir Francis** (c. 1540–1596) *English sea captain and popular hero of the Elizabethan age*
Drake first became rich and famous through his exploits against Spain in the Caribbean (1567–68) and in 1572 he received a royal commission as a privateer. With ELIZABETH I's support he led the first English expedition to circumnavigate the world (1577–80), bringing back with him on the *Golden Hind* a rich cargo of treasure and spices seized from the Spaniards. The queen recognized the feat by coming on board his ship to knight him. In 1585 Drake led another successful expedition against Spain in the New World, and in 1587 his raid on CÁDIZ ("singeing the king of Spain's beard") cost the Spaniards thousands of tons of shipping and supplies. Drake played a prominent part in the defeat of the SPANISH ARMADA (1588). He died of fever off Panama, while leading yet another attack on Spain's overseas empire.

**Further reading:** R. Samuel Bawlf, *The Secret Voyage of Sir Francis Drake, 1577–1580* (New York: Walker, 2003).

**drama** See COMEDY; COMMEDIA DELL'ARTE; COMMEDIA ERUDITA; INTERLUDE; MASQUE; PASTORAL; SACRA RAPPRESENTAZIONE; THEATERS; TRAGEDY

**drawing** In Europe, drawing as an independent art form arrived with the availability of paper during the early Renaissance and was coincident with a change in artistic style. Prior to the 15th century, composition was strongly conventional, both in subject and form. Every workshop used a model-book—a collection of figures, motifs, and outline compositions that were to be copied. Very much a working tool, the model-book would be passed from master to pupil, from workshop to workshop, and, when worn out, thrown away. Consequently, few model-books survive today. Likewise, drawings of this early period tended to disappear under finished work. When materials were expensive and paper a rarity, trial sketches were made on wax tablets or on slates, to be later erased. Even as paper gradually became more available, and artists were enabled to make more trial studies before beginning a painting, these studies were still commonly considered to be of no value and were usually thrown out.

The International Gothic style of the 14th century broke with traditional forms and moved toward freer artistic expression; artists in the new style tended to guard their model-books more jealously and keep them as records of their own innovations and experimentation. A fundamental change in this period, one that underlies the whole concept of "renaissance," was that artists began to take forms and figures from life, rather than copying previous works and models.

The sketchbook of Giovannino de' Grassi (1390; Biblioteca Ciivica, Bergamo) shows what were perhaps the first representations of real animals since antiquity. In this period of transition, however, Grassi's revolutionary studies from life merely became models themselves for his contemporaries to copy. It is with PISANELLO in the first half of the 15th century that studies in motion begin. His drawings of horses, precursors to those of LEONARDO DA VINCI, show animals that are not only anatomically correct but imbued with vital spirit. Pisanello was the first artist to capture human likeness full face rather than in the customary profile, and it is in one of Pisanello's surviving sketchbooks that we find the first surviving drawn study for a major painting.

Styles in drawing varied from artist to artist. Leonardo's drawings are those of a painter; MICHELANGELO's those of a sculptor, and DÜRER's those of an engraver. In each is reflected the techniques of the primary discipline: the brush, the chisel, or the burin. At first drawing on parchment or paper was done with silverpoint—a metal style tipped with silver. This was the pencil before the discovery of graphite, and it required a surface prepared with bone and gesso. It was a difficult and merciless medium.

Cennino Cennini's handbook *Libro dell'arte* (c. 1390s; earliest known manuscript dated 1437) presents drawing as a system of training for apprentices, the "entrance and gateway" to painting. As Cennino advised, "start to copy the easiest possible subjects, to get your hand in; and run the style over the little panel so lightly that you can hardly make out what you first start to do; strengthening your strokes little by little, going back many times to produce the shadows." He describes how to draw on parchment and paper, prepared in a similar way to the panel, beginning with the silverpoint and then fixing it with ink at the points of accent and stress. "Then shade the folds with washes of ink; that is, as much water as a nutshell would hold, with two drops of ink in it; and shade with a brush made of minever tails, rather blunt, and almost always dry." Lead was also used, which had the advantage of being erasable.

From working with styles and pens, the student moved on to drawing on paper or parchment that had been tinted, using the techniques of tempera, the most popular color being green. This progression from study to finished painting mirrored the progression from apprentice to master painter. The artist began by making rough outlines in chalk or charcoal, to be fixed with silverpoint; subsequently the shadows were filled in with tonal washes and highlights made with chalk.

In FRESCO painting, the preparatory drawings would be taken from full-size cartoons, the outlines of which were pricked with pins; charcoal was pounced through the holes to form an outline on the wall. The first outlines in paint were made in a red ochre called sinopia.

When drawings were purely utilitarian preparations for paintings, they tended to be made in charcoal or chalk that could be dusted away as the study developed, with outlines being made in ink and tonal areas with ink washes and white highlights. This was the main technique of the 15th century, but artists of the High Renaissance began to explore the tonal possibilities of colored chalk on tinted paper, a supreme example being Dürer's *Praying Hands*. Red chalk, first used by Leonardo, became a favorite medium of artists such as Michelangelo and RAPHAEL.

The view that drawing was a preliminary to painting prevailed until Leonardo. In his notebooks, filled with sketches in pen and ink, he wrote of the need for a fresh approach to drawing: what matters, he said, is not a tidy finish but to capture the spirit of the subject. Drawing was a medium particularly preferred by Tuscan artists but eventually it was adopted in northern Italian schools. In the academy of the CARRACCI drawing was systematically cultivated. Although it had always been used in northern Europe as preparatory to painting, and, later, engraving, it is with Dürer and the younger HOLBEIN that drawing reached its full flowering in the north.

Drawing as an independent art form was not properly established until the 16th century, when collectors provided a market. Such was Michelangelo's fame that his admirers asked him for drawings, seeing them as works of art in themselves. At the same time VASARI was recommending the idea of collecting drawings as a record of the various styles of artists. Many of the collections begun in the 16th century now reside in museums such as the Louvre in Paris, the British Museum in London, and the Ashmolean Museum in Oxford. The largest collections of Leonardo and Holbein drawings form part of the Royal Collection at Windsor Castle.

**Further reading:** David Bomford (ed.), *Art in the Making: Underdrawings in Renaissance Paintings* (New Haven, Conn.: Yale University Press, 2002).

## Drayton, Michael (1563–1631) *English poet*
Born at Hartshill, Warwickshire, Drayton spent his youth in the household of the local Goodere family, before moving to London in about 1591. There he published the pastoral poems *Idea, The Shepheard's Garland* (1593) and the fine sonnet sequence *Ideas Mirrour* (1594). The lady celebrated in these poems, Anne Goodere, remained the object of his poetic devotion for many years, though Drayton apparently died a bachelor. Drayton was both prolific and versatile as a poet. In 1596 he published the historical poem *Mortimeriados*, which he later recast in OTTAVA RIMA as *The Barrons Warres* (1603). *England's Heroical Epistles* (1597), letters in rhyming couplets between famous English lovers such as King Henry II and Rosamond, were modeled on Ovid's *Heroides*; they were very popular and are among Drayton's best work. Around this time he was also writing for the stage, and in 1607 was associated with the Children of the King's Revels at the Whitefriars theater. Drayton's patriotism is stirringly expressed in his fine

"Ballad of Agincourt" (c. 1605) and he devoted many years to his principal work, the topographical epic *Poly-Olbion* (1622), written in hexameter couplets and divided into 30 "Songs" celebrating British landscape and history. Numerous editions of his poems appeared throughout the early 1600s and the *Muses Elizium* (1630) is the latest expression of the Elizabethan pastoral tradition.

**Drebbel, Cornelis** (1572–1633) *Dutch inventor and alchemist*
A native of Alkmaar, Drebbel trained as an engraver under his brother-in-law Hendrick GOLTZIUS, but subsequently turned his hand to hydraulic engineering. In the early 1600s he migrated to England, where he tried to attract James I's patronage by presenting him with a supposed *perpetuum mobile*. Drebbel was later involved in plans to drain fenland in East Anglia and was famous as the inventor of a scarlet dye which he and his sons-in-law exploited at their dyeworks in Bow, London. Among his many inventions was a submarine, which he demonstrated in the River Thames, apparently having found means of supplying the rowers with fresh air while the craft was under water.

**dress** See COSTUME

**Dryander, Francis** See ENZINAS, FRANCISCO DE

**Du Bartas, Guillaume de Salluste, Seigneur** (1544–1590) *French poet*
A Huguenot gentleman born at Montfort, near Auch, Du Bartas entered the service of Henry of Navarre, for whom he accomplished a number of diplomatic missions, including a visit to the court of King James VI of Scotland. His poetry was influenced in style by the techniques developed by the PLÉIADE and in content by his Protestant faith; early works include the epics *Judith* and *Le Triomphe de la foi* (1574). Du Bartas's most significant achievement was *La Semaine ou la Création du monde* (1578), a didactic account of the creation of the world in seven cantos, which was highly acclaimed in France on publication but was subsequently criticized on stylistic grounds; it was well received in England, however, in translation (*see* SYLVESTER, JOSHUA). The *Seconde Semaine*, a continuation of the Old Testament story leading to a complete history of mankind, remained unfinished at Du Bartas's death.

**Du Bellay, Joachim** (1522–1560) *French poet*
Born at Liré of noble parentage, Du Bellay was the cousin of the cardinal and diplomat Jean Du Bellay (c. 1493–1560) and the general and writer Guillaume Du Bellay (1491–1543). After studying law at Poitiers he went to Paris, where he made the acquaintance of RONSARD and joined him at the Còllege de Coqueret. He became a member of the PLÉIADE, and his early sonnets, notably *L'Olive*

(1549), the first French sonnet sequence, were heavily influenced by PETRARCH; the Pléiade's manifesto, *La Défense et illustration de la langue française* (1549; translated as *Defence and Illustration of the French Language*, 1939), was his other major work of this period. In 1553 Du Bellay accompanied his cousin Jean on a mission to Rome, a four-year exile that was to inspire some of his finest poetry: *Les Antiquités de Rome* (1558) is a melancholy contemplation of the grandeur and decadence of the ancient city; *Les Regrets* (1558) reflects his disillusionment with life at the Vatican and his homesickness for France. Du Bellay's other works include a collection of Latin poems and *Divers jeux rustiques*, both also published in 1558, after the poet's return to his native country.

**Dubroeucq, Jacques** (1500/10–1584) *Flemish sculptor and architect*
Dubroeucq, who was born near Mons, became acquainted with the ideals of the Italian Renaissance while traveling in Italy sometime before 1535; there he studied the works of Ghiberti, Michelangelo, Sansovino, and others. He executed his best works, a series of carvings for the cathedral of Ste. Waldetrude at Mons (1535–48), after his return to the Netherlands—although much of this decoration was destroyed during the French Revolution. In 1545 he was honored by the appellation of "master artist of the emperor" (Charles V) and for Charles's sister MARY OF HUNGARY, regent of the Netherlands, he built and decorated the castles of Binche and Mariemont. Dubroeucq was also notable as the teacher of the sculptor GIAMBOLOGNA.

**Dubrovnik** See RAGUSA

**Duccio di Buoninsegna** (c. 1260–c. 1318) *Italian painter*
As the first great Sienese artist Duccio's influence in Siena is comparable with GIOTTO's in Florence. Whereas Giotto's art was revolutionary in its pursuit of naturalism, Duccio kept his ritualistic art within the Byzantine framework, yet brought to it a new narrative power in his use of facial expression, his rich and subtle colors, and dramatic arrangement of scenery. Little is known of his life except that, despite several probably political clashes with the Sienese government, Duccio achieved a position of wealth and influence. His first known commission (1285) was a *Madonna* for the Florentine church of Sta. Maria Novella. It is generally agreed that this is the imposing Rucellai *Madonna* (Uffizi, Florence).

The only work that can certainly be attributed to Duccio, however, is the double-sided *Maestà*, which he was commissioned to paint in 1308 for the high altar of Siena cathedral. It was completed and carried there in procession in 1311, but was dismembered in 1771 and while much remains in the Museo dell' Opera in Siena, other panels are scattered abroad or lost. The Madonna and

Child are noted for their depth of character and solidity of form, while 60 other panels depicting the life of Christ and the saints illustrate Duccio's narrative power and the new infusion of emotion into old Byzantine models. Like the small *Madonna of the Franciscans* (1290; Pinacoteca, Siena), usually ascribed to him, the *Maestà* was remarkable also for its exquisite use of color and of gold as both decoration and an essential feature of the composition. Duccio stood for the transition from Byzantine to Gothic, influencing Sienese painters including Simone MARTINI and the LORENZETTI brothers well into the 15th century, and his sense of composition and drama heralds even later Renaissance developments.

**Further reading:** Luciano Bellusi, *Duccio: The* Maestà (London: Thames & Hudson, 1999); James H. Stubblebine, *Duccio di Buoninsegna and His School* (Princeton, N.J.: Princeton University Press, 1979).

**Ducerceau family** (**Du Cerceau family**) A French family of architects and designers, who were active from the mid-16th century to the mid-17th century. Jacques Androuet (c. 1520–c. 1585) established the family's reputation with his collections of architectural and decorative engravings, including *Les plus excellents bastiments de France* (1576, 1579), which bear witness to the influence of Italian works, with which he became acquainted during visits to that country early in his career. His patrons included the French royal family and he worked on several châteaux, although nothing now remains of these buildings. His engravings are valuable evidence for works now lost or severely damaged, such as ROSSO FIORENTINO's, PRIMATICCIO's, and Leonard Thiry's at FONTAINEBLEAU. His son Baptiste Androuet (1545–90) succeeded him as a leading architect; his only surviving work is the Pont-Neuf in Paris, begun in 1578. In 1584 Henry III made him supervisor of the royal office of works and he may have been employed on the Hôtel d'Angoulême and the Hôtel de Lamoignon (1584) in Paris. Two other sons, Jacques (c. 1550–1614) and Charles (died 1606), were also active as architects. Baptiste's son Jean (1585–1649) was a notable designer of private houses under Louis XIII, producing the Hôtel de Sully (1624–29) and the Hôtel de Bretonvillieurs (1637–43) as well as the horseshoe stairs at Fontainebleau (c. 1630).

**Dudley, Robert, Earl of Leicester** See LEICESTER, ROBERT DUDLEY, EARL OF

**Dufay, Guillaume** (c. 1400–1474) *French composer*
Dufay was probably born in Cambrai, where he sang in the cathedral choir as a boy. Some of his compositions from the early 1420s were written for the Malatesta family in Pesaro. By 1426 he seems to have been back in France and by 1430 he held benefices at Laôn cathedral, Nouvion-les-Vineux, and St. Géry in Cambrai. In 1428 Dufay

joined the papal choir. By the time he left the choir in 1433 he was one of the most famous musicians in Europe. Dufay had close associations with two famous families, the ESTE and the house of SAVOY. A notable occasion to which he contributed music was the marriage in 1434 of Louis, son of Duke Amadeus VIII of Savoy. In 1436, back in the papal choir, Dufay wrote one of his most famous works, *Nuper rosarum flores*, for the dedication of BRUNELLESCHI's dome of Florence cathedral. From 1440 Dufay was again in Cambrai as a canon at the cathedral, and apart from seven years in Savoy from around 1451, he spent the rest of his life there.

Dufay was no great innovator, but a master of the established techniques of composition. His secular works consist mainly of rondeaux; he also composed in the standard *ballade* and *virelai* form of his day. His sacred works show more development of style; the early Masses are in single and paired movements, where the later ones, such as the *Missa sine nomine*, are in cyclical, musically unified forms, as found in English Masses of the period. The motets were written for special occasions and are extraordinary in their complexity. The leading composer of his day, he greatly influenced his contemporaries, and his works were copied and performed throughout Europe.

**Further reading:** David Fallows, *Dufay* (London: Dent, 1982; rev. ed. 1987).

**Du Guillet, Pernette** (c. 1520–1545) *French poet*
Few facts are known about her life: she was born and lived in Lyons and married in 1538 but remained childless. A skilled musician and linguist, Du Guillet belonged to the Lyons school of writers, which formed a link between France and the poetry of the Italian Renaissance, and she enjoyed considerable popularity in this regional center of intellectual and academic excellence. She was an admirer of Maurice SCÈVE, whom she had met in 1536 and with whom she exchanged verses. Her creative work, which dates from 1537, took the form of *élégies* and *chansons*, as well as more satirical letter-poems and dialogues. Seventy of her poems about love and friendship were published in 1545 as *Rimes de gentille et vertueuse Dame Pernette du Guillet*. She is thought to have died of the plague. Although widely read in her lifetime, her work fell rapidly into neglect, and it was not rediscovered and republished until the 19th century.

**Dunstable, John** (c. 1390–1453) *English composer*
There are no certain details of Dunstable's career, but it is probable that he served John, Duke of Bedford; the church where he is buried, St. Stephen's, Walbrook, in London, belonged to the duke until 1432. Dunstable's importance as a composer was recognized by contemporaries both in England and on the Continent. Much of his work survives in Italian and German manuscripts. The overwhelming majority of Dunstable's surviving works are sacred and for

three voices. Many use plainsong as a basis, and complex isorhythmic techniques are frequent. Some pieces are more declamatory, and here the clear presentation of the text becomes paramount. Dunstable's style was dubbed the *contenance angloise* (English sweetness) among Continental musicians, but he cannot be regarded as an innovator. He wrote two complete Mass settings, often regarded as the earliest musically unified approaches to the genre. Though the song "O rosa bella" is well known, secular music hardly figures in his output, in which votive antiphons and motets predominate.

## Duperron, Jacques Davy (1556–1618) *Swiss-born churchman and statesman*

Duperron was born at Berne, the son of French Huguenot refugees. In 1573 he went to Paris, and studied the Fathers of the Church, the schoolmen, and Roman Catholic theologians. He was received into the Roman Church by the Jesuits (c. 1578). He became a friend of King Henry III and after the king's death (1589), he supported first Cardinal de Bourbon, then the Protestant Henry IV, whose conversion he effected in 1593. In 1595 he obtained papal absolution for the king. Duperron took part in the conference at Nantes, and in 1600 he had the advantage in a theological disputation with the Protestant DU PLESSIS-MORNAY. Since 1591 he had been bishop of Evreux, and he was made cardinal in 1604 (when he went to Rome as the king's *chargé d'affaires*) and archbishop of Sens in 1606. In 1607 he reconciled Pope Paul V and the Venetians, whom the pope had placed under an interdict on account of their defiant assertion of secular control in matters affecting the property and buildings of the Church. Duperron was a defender of ultramontanism (the doctrine of centralized papal authority) and corresponded with James I on the question of the true church.

## Du Plessis-Mornay, Philippe (1549–1623) *French politician and religious leader*

Born at Buhi in the Vexin into one of France's most distinguished families, he was converted by his mother to Calvinism and after study in Germany he became attached to the Huguenot leader COLIGNY. The MASSACRE OF ST. BARTHOLOMEW forced him to take refuge in England. On returning to France, he became an adviser to Henry of Navarre and wrote extensively in favor of the Huguenots and religious toleration; these works included his *Traité de la vérité de la religion chretienne* (1581). He was employed in many official roles—ambassador to Spain and Flanders, governor of Saumur—and after Henry's coronation as HENRY IV he acted as mediator between the Huguenots and the king, being instrumental in the promulgation of the Edict of NANTES. He lost favor after the publication of *De l'institution, usage, et doctrine du saint sacrement de l'eucharistie en l'Eglise ancienne* (1598). In 1611 he published an overt attack on the Catholic Church. After

Henry's death Marie de' Medici restored him to favor because of his efforts to avert religious war, but following the Huguenot uprising of 1620 he fell once more from grace. His standing can be gauged from his nickname, "the Pope of the Huguenots."

## Dürer, Albrecht (1471–1528) *German painter, draftsman, print maker, and art theorist*

Dürer was born at Nuremberg and initially trained as a goldsmith under his father. However, he probably never executed metalwork independently, and he began (1486) a second apprenticeship with the Nuremberg painter and woodcut designer Michael WOLGEMUT. Dürer had early experience of printing through his godfather, Anton Koberger, who printed illustrated books in collaboration with Wolgemut. In 1490 Dürer traveled on the Upper Rhine, becoming familiar with the work of the Housebook Master, and in subsequent years worked, primarily as a woodcut designer, in Strasbourg and Basle. In 1494 he returned home, married, and set up on his own account. Copying engravings by MANTEGNA seems to have motivated him to visit Venice, via the Tyrol, before the year's end.

In Italy Dürer strengthened his acquaintance with Mantegna's work, studied the paintings of BELLINI, and encountered works by artists from other regions of Italy, including POLLAIUOLO. His alpine views, executed in 1494–95, are the earliest topographical watercolors in existence. Other early drawings, such as the Berlin *Lobster* (1495), reveal his interest in natural history. After his return to Nuremberg he executed the remarkable and expressive *Apocalypse* woodcuts (1498), the first book to be conceived, executed, printed, and published by an artist. This and later series of woodcuts, such as the *Large Passion* (1510), the *Small Passion* (1511), and *The Life of the Virgin* (1511), abandoned the primitive formality of earlier northern prints for new realms of naturalism. Between 1498 and about 1520, their example transformed the woodcut as an illustrative medium.

From the beginning of his career, Dürer painted portraits. His most famous self-portraits are those of 1498 (Madrid) and 1500 (Munich). After his return from Venice, Dürer refined his Italian experiences in numerous drawings, prints, and paintings, but a work such as the Paumgärtner altarpiece (c. 1500; Munich) remains essentially a northern triptych, despite incorporating deep perspective and Italianate figure types. In 1500 Dürer became acquainted with the itinerant Venetian painter and print maker Jacopo de' Barbari, then based in Nuremberg, and his researches took a major step forward. He devoted a series of studies to the nude, which culminated in the engraved *Fall of Man* (1504), the first northern work to embody the proportional theories of VITRUVIUS. Between 1503 and 1505 Dürer also became increasingly familiar with the work of LEONARDO DA VINCI, presumably via

**Albrecht Dürer** Self-portrait in oils on a wood panel (1500; Alte Pinakothek, Munich). The image bears a striking resemblance to contemporary depictions of Christ, a fact that has provoked much discussion.
*Mansell/Time Life Pictures/Getty Images*

drawings made available to him through his friend Willibald PIRCKHEIMER. Dürer's engraved *Small Horse* (1505) utilizes Leonardo's canon of equine proportions.

Between 1505 and 1507 Dürer was based in Venice where he worked upon the altarpiece of *The Madonna of the Rosegarlands* (Budapest) for German merchants resident in the city. He wrote an account of his stay in the form of letters to Pirckheimer. Dürer was on good terms with the ageing Bellini, although he was ostracized by other Venetian artists, who presumably feared him as a competitor. Although painted after his return to Germany, his lost Heller altarpiece (1509) indicated that Dürer encountered the works of RAPHAEL and Filippino LIPPI during this visit to Italy. Magnificent preparatory drawings for the Heller altarpiece survive, one of which, *Praying Hands* (Vienna), has become a popular symbol of faith throughout Christendom. Dürer's last major altarpiece was the Vienna *Adoration of the Trinity* (1511), the Italianate frame of which survives in Nuremberg. Thereafter, both artist and city turned increasingly towards Lutheranism and the

market for large-scale religious works was considerably reduced.

Although Dürer had practiced the engraver's art with consummate skill since his youth, his finest engravings are the "Three Master Prints" of 1513–14: *The Knight, Death, and the Devil*, *St. Jerome in his Study*, and *Melancholia I* (see MELANCHOLIA). Each displays Dürer's remarkable ability to render light and texture, which caused Erasmus to dub him "the Apelles of the Black Lines." From 1512 onwards Dürer became increasingly involved with the decorative printing projects of Emperor Maximilian I, such as the *Triumphal Arch* and *Triumphal Procession* woodcut series. His 1520–21 visit to the Netherlands was ostensibly to ensure renewal of his imperial pension by the newly crowned CHARLES V. Dürer's diary of the visit and numerous drawings which he made in the Netherlands provide a detailed account of the trip. While there he made the acquaintance of several important painters, was enthralled by Aztec treasures recently brought from Mexico, and acquired a set of prints after Raphael, with whom he had previously exchanged drawings.

During his last years Dürer painted some of his finest small portraits, including those of Jacob Muffel and Hieronymus Holzschuher (both 1526; Berlin). From the same year dates his last large painting, the Munich *Four Apostles* diptych, which has a distinctly Lutheran iconography. Since 1512 he had been increasingly drawn towards theoretical studies, which culminated in the publication of his three illustrated books on geometry (1525), fortification (1527), and human proportions (1528). Dürer's publications, prints, and students, the last including ALDEGREVER, BALDUNG, and KULMBACH, broadcast his influence throughout Europe. The most significant northern artist of the Renaissance, he was also probably the greatest print maker and the most important German artist of all time.

**Further reading:** Fedja Anzelewsky, *Dürer: His Life and Art*, transl. Heide Grieve (London: G. Fraser, 1982); Giulia Bartrum (ed.), *Albrecht Dürer and his Legacy* (London: British Museum, 2002); Karl A. Knappe (ed.), *Dürer: The Complete Engravings, Etchings and Woodcuts* (London: Thames & Hudson, 1965); Erwin Panofsky, *The Life and Art of Albrecht Dürer* (Princeton, N.J.: Princeton University Press, 4th ed. 1955; repr. 1971); Victoria Salley (ed.), *Nature's Artist: Plants and Animals by Albrecht Dürer* (Munich, Germany and New York: Prestel, 2003).

**Dutch East India Company** (Dutch **Vereenigde Oostindische Compagnie**, **VOC**) An amalgamation of over 60 rival trading companies which was granted a charter by the Netherlands states general in 1602. Formed to regulate and protect Dutch trade in the Far East, the company enjoyed considerable privileges, which included the power to make treaties and establish colonies, the right to maintain armed forces, a trade monopoly, and tax exemptions. The first Dutch fleet to follow the Portuguese sea route to the East had sailed in 1595 under Cornelis HOUTMAN, and although it was a failure in terms of trade it demonstrated the possibilities that existed for encroaching on the Portuguese trading empire, and the books of Jan Huyghen van LINSCHOTEN and Willem LODEWYCKSZ. helped fuel Dutch interest in South Asia. The following 50 years saw the company setting up bases in the Indonesian archipelago (in particular Java and the Moluccas), Ceylon (Sri Lanka), numerous South Indian ports, Taiwan, and the Cape of Good Hope. From its Jakarta base the company expelled its Portuguese rivals from Ceylon (1638–58) and Malacca (1641); in 1652 it established the Cape of Good Hope colony. The company had 150 trading vessels, 40 warships, and 10,000 soldiers by 1669, but soon declined due to English competition, waning Dutch power, and rising debts. It was disbanded in 1798.

**Further reading:** Charles R. Boxer, *The Dutch Seaborne Empire 1600–1800* (London: Hutchinson, 1965; New York: Knopf, 1970); Els M. Jacobs, *In Pursuit of Pepper and Tea: The Story of the Dutch East India Company* (Zutphen, Netherlands: Walburg Pers, 1991).

**Dutch language** The language spoken in the modern kingdom of the Netherlands (where it is called Nederlands) and in northern Belgium, or Flanders (where it varies slightly from Nederlands and is called Vlaams). There are also small pockets of Dutch speakers in the French *département* of Nord, in former Dutch dependencies overseas, and in North America. The High Dutch spoken by 17th-century settlers in South Africa evolved and was simplified over 250 years until it was recognized as a distinct language, Afrikaans.

Dutch is based mainly on Old Franconian, the Germanic dialect of the northern Franks, who, with the Saxons and the Frisians, settled the area in the Dark Ages. In the early Middle Ages the dialect of Bruges, by reason of the town's dominance as a trading counter of the HANSEATIC LEAGUE, came to the fore, but in the 14th century the duchy of Brabant began to gain the ascendancy. Flanders passed to PHILIP THE BOLD, duke of Burgundy, in 1384, and in the 15th century the Burgundians were the dominant power in the Low Countries. Throughout the Middle Ages the literary influence of France was strong in the area.

Resistance to Hapsburg rule in the 16th century eventually centered on the northern province of Holland, and the form of the language there became the language of nascent nationalism. After the Spanish recapture of Antwerp in 1585, the dialects of refugees from the south affected northern Dutch in several ways; the southerners' diphthongal pronunciation of words such as *huis* (house) and *vijf* (five), formerly pronounced in the north as monothongs, became a permanent feature of the language.

The concepts of purity and correctness in language were promoted in prose by Renaissance writers such as COORNHEERT. Anna BIJNS wrote poetry that is considered a significant stage in the development of modern Dutch. The *Statenbijbel*, the Dutch translation of the Bible authorized by the Synod of DORT, contains many instances of the more formal usages of the south dignifying the colloquial language of the north.

**Du Vair, Guillaume** (1556–1621) *French statesman and philosopher*
A Parisian by birth, Du Vair became a supporter of Henry of Navarre and made his name as an orator with such speeches as *Exhortation à la paix* (1592). After Henry's accession to the French throne (as HENRY IV), Du Vair served in a number of important offices, culminating in his appointment as lord chancellor (1615) and bishop of Lisieux (1616). His writings include the treatises *De la sainte philosophie* and *De la philosophie morale des Stoïques*, translations of Epictetus and Demosthenes, and the *Traité de la constance et consolation ès calamités publiques* (1593; translated as *A Buckler against Adversitie*, 1622), which applies the philosophy of Stoicism to the Christian faith. Du Vair's influence can be traced in the poems of his contemporary François de MALHERBE and in the works of the French philosophers of the 17th century.

**Duytsche Academie (Coster's Academie)** A learned society founded in Amsterdam in 1617 by Samuel COSTER. Coster had been a member of De Egelantier (*see* CHAMBERS OF RHETORIC), but he considered its activities were too frivolous and therefore launched his own academy along the lines of the Italian Renaissance ACADEMIES, with an ambitious program of mathematical, philosophical, and linguistic instruction to be given in Dutch. The academy was also to produce plays; this was the only part of the program carried through, but the virulently anti-Calvinist stance of its dramas brought it into collision with the authorities. In 1635 it merged with De Egelantier.

# E

**East India Company** An English trading company granted a charter by Elizabeth I in 1600. Launched with £30,000 capital and a monopoly of trade to the Far East, the company dispatched its first fleet to the East in 1601, commanded by Sir James Lancaster (died 1618) who in 1591–94 had pioneered the route and established the feasibility of challenging the Portuguese trade monopoly. Over the next two decades other fleets steadily followed, both to India and to the Spice Islands; many of those who sailed with those fleets left accounts of their voyages that were published in Samuel Purchas's sequel to HAKLUYT's collections of travel narratives (*Purchas His Pilgrimes*, 4 vols, 1625).

The company's embassy in 1607 to the Great Mogul led in 1612 to the establishment of its first "factory" (trading post) at Surat on India's northwest coast, in the teeth of Portuguese opposition. In 1615–19 the company covered the costs of Sir Thomas Roe (1581–1644) as first official British ambassador to the Great Mogul. An attempt to set up a factory in Japan was short-lived, though the company established factories in Java and the Spice Islands. After conflict with the Dutch (*see* DUTCH EAST INDIA COMPANY) in the 1620s the company concentrated its trading activities on India. The decline of the Mughal empire and wars with France in the 17th and 18th centuries enabled it to accumulate extensive and wealthy territories in India, where it survived until 1873.

Many of the journals originally published in *Purchas His Pilgrimes* have been republished by the Hakluyt Society of London. Among its editions covering the early years of the Company are: *The Voyage of Thomas Best to the East Indies, 1612–14*, ed. William Foster (1934); *Diary of Richard Cocks, Cape-Merchant in the English Factory in Japan 1615–22, with Correspondence*, ed. Edward Maunde Thompson (2 vols, 1883); *The Voyages of Sir James Lancaster to Brazil and the East Indies, 1591–1603*, ed. William Foster (1877; 2nd ed. 1940); and *The Voyage of Sir Henry Middleton to the Moluccas 1604–1606*, ed. William Foster (1854; 2nd ed. 1943). Michael Strachan's and Boies Penrose's edition of *The East India Company Journals of Captain William Keeling and Master Thomas Bonner, 1615–1617* was published by the University of Minnesota Press in 1971.

**Further reading:** H.V. Bowen, Margarette Lincoln, and Nigel Rigby (eds), *The Worlds of the East India Company* (Woodbridge, U.K.: Boydell & Brewer, 2002); Antony Wild, *The East India Company: Trade and Conquest from 1600* (London: HarperCollins, 1999; New York: Lyons Press, 2000).

**Eastland Company** English trading company formed to promote trade with the Baltic area, which had formerly been a monopoly held by the HANSEATIC LEAGUE. Its heyday began with the grant of a charter from Elizabeth I in 1579. The Eastland merchants' base on the Baltic was their concession at Elbing (now in Poland), near the mouth of the River Vistula, where they exchanged English cloth for timber, hemp, and tar—raw materials vital for shipbuilding. The venture encountered increasing competition from the Dutch and the monopoly was revoked in 1673.

**See also:** MUSCOVY COMPANY

**Ebreo, Leone** See LEONE EBREO

**Eccard, Johannes** (1553–1611) *German composer*
Eccard received his earliest musical training in his native

Mühlhausen. From being a chorister at the Weimar court, he moved in 1571 to the Hofkapelle in Munich, where he was a pupil of LASSUS. In the late 1570s he was in the household of the Augsburg FUGGER FAMILY, before joining (1579) the chapel of the margrave of Brandenburg-Ansbach in Königsberg. He was assistant *Kapellmeister* until 1604 when he succeeded to the senior post. In 1608 the new elector gave Eccard responsibility for music at his Berlin court. A Lutheran composer, Eccard made much use of the chorale melodies in his works; his 1597 publication of sacred music contains simple harmonizations, but other volumes of his work develop the complex genre of the chorale motet, of which he was one of the major exponents.

## Eck, Johann (Johann Maier of Eck) (1486–1543)
*German theologian and polemicist*
Professor of theology (1510–43) and chancellor at the university of Ingolstadt in Bavaria, Eck was the first and most persistent of LUTHER's adversaries. His attack was initially launched against Luther's supporter, Andreas CARLSTADT, and led to a formal disputation with both men at Leipzig in June and July 1519. Eck's various assaults on Luther were published and widely circulated, and his accusations, including an association of Luther with Jan HUSS, forced Luther to define his position concerning the authority of the Bible, the character of Christ's Church, and the papacy and Church hierarchy. Eck helped draw up the *Confutatio* declaring Emperor CHARLES V's total rejection of Protestant principles that was read at the Diet of Augsburg (1530). He was one of the three Catholic spokesmen in the debates at the Colloquy of REGENSBURG in 1541.

## eclogue See PASTORAL

## education
In the Middle Ages education had been mainly under ecclesiastical control and was designed for those who were intended for a clerical career. This was true of the schools maintained by trade guilds no less than of the (Latin) grammar schools and choir schools supported by cathedral and collegiate churches.

From the 14th century onwards secular influences began to gain ground, and more importance was attached to training in the LIBERAL ARTS, especially RHETORIC. The Latin literature of pagan antiquity was studied for its own sake, and the revival of Greek learning in the West was begun by Manuel CHRYSOLORAS, who was invited to Florence from Constantinople in 1395. The *De ingenuis moribus et liberalibus studiis* (On gentle manners and liberal studies), written about 1402 by Pietro Paolo Vergerio (1370–1444) of Padua, argued in favor of a system of education that maintained a harmony of body and spirit. A number of boarding schools were founded in northern Italy in the early 15th century; VITTORINO DA FELTRE

founded schools at Padua, Venice, and Mantua. This last, which enjoyed the patronage of the duke of Mantua, aimed at making learning pleasant and was known as *La Giocosa*. The instruction was entirely in Latin, and the subjects were mainly those of medieval schools, but the methods were revolutionary, including the teaching of mathematics by means of arithmetical and geometrical games.

At these establishments the daughters of the aristocracy too could enjoy the benefits of a wide humanist education, but in their case, since they were unable to proceed to a university or otherwise exercise their talents in the public arena, a love of learning often had sad and frustrating outcomes for girls who developed their intellectual abilities only to come to a stultifying dead end in marriage or a nunnery. Cecilia Gonzaga (1424–51) was one of a number who opted for the latter alternative. In a later generation Battista GUARINO's two pupils Isabella (*see* ESTE, ISABELLA D') and Beatrice d'Este (1475–97) made good use of their education when they became the wives, respectively, of the dukes of Mantua and Milan, promoting the arts and humanistic culture in their husbands' courts. Less aristocratic women, such as Laura CERETA and Cassandra FEDELE, were denied such outlets, and either marriage brought an end (usually permanent) to intellectual aspirations, or family responsibilities diverted their energies, or male hostility and derision ensured that they published little or nothing.

Leon Battista ALBERTI's treatise *Della famiglia* (1435–41) emphasized the importance of the home background in education. He wrote in Italian, rather than Latin, as he wished to influence a wide public. The classical source for much of the educational theory behind these Italian projects was QUINTILIAN, whose first two books were known at the beginning of the 15th century.

In France, Spain, and England the new learning was first promoted in circles connected with the royal court. LITERACY and even scholarship began to be perceived by the upper classes as fitting attainments for gentlemen, rather than as the prerogative of despised "clerks." In England the first of the public schools (schools maintained by a corporation or body of trustees), had been founded at Winchester in 1382 by Bishop William of Wykeham, sometime lord chancellor. Many more such schools were established in the 15th and 16th centuries; in the latter part of the period some of the founders were merchants. Numerous grammar schools also originated at this time. The most important English treatises on education were *The Boke named the Governour* (1531) by Sir Thomas ELYOT and *The Scholemaster* (1570) by Roger ASCHAM, tutor to Princess (later Queen) Elizabeth. Both emphasized the importance of teaching English as well as Latin and included physical exercise as a curriculum subject. Furthermore, Ascham deplored the harsh methods used by many of his contemporaries. The elementary education

Iſ buch heyſſet Lucidarius.
das ſpricht zů teütſch alſo vil
als ein erleüchter. An diſem
buch findet mā mange groſ-
ſe lere die anderē büchern ver
borgen ſeind das vnterweiſet
vnß diß buch. In ð geſchrifft
ſo finde wir auch den ſyn diß
buchs das es genannt wirdt
Aureo gemma das bezeichnet vnß wie gůt dz buch ſey
darumb was die geſchrifft het bedecket daz hat Lucidarius alles erwecket. wer das geren leſen wil der ge-
winnet weißhept vil. die anderen büchern verborgen
ſeind vnd zů lang wären zeſůchen. Got der ye wz vñ
ymer iſt on ennd. der ſol diß büchs ein anefang weſe-
wer es geren höret leſen der ſol ſich recht verſton wie
es vmb die ſchrifft ſey gethan. der meyſter vñ ð jüger
redent miteinand. der diß büch ſchreybet ð iſt ð frager

**Education** A woodcut from the first encyclopedia printed in German; the *Lucidarius* (1479) takes the form of a dialogue between master and pupil in which the pupil receives instruction in theology, geography, astronomy, meteorology, and other sciences.

of the poorer classes mostly depended on small endow- ments given or left by the pious to parish churches. At this level provision was made for the education of girls as well as boys. The higher education of girls was practically con- fined to the home. An outstanding example was the edu- cation which Sir Anthony Cooke (1504–76), sometime tutor to King Edward VI, provided for his daughters. They were instructed in Latin and Greek, as well as the more traditional feminine accomplishments, such as music and embroidery.

In the Netherlands princely and aristocratic patron- age was less important, but the increasing wealth and power of the burghers produced a demand for a broader system of education. The ground had been prepared in the 14th century by the Brothers and Sisters of the COMMON LIFE (a mixed lay and religious association), who founded hostels for students and later, schools. ERASMUS, who was educated at their school at Deventer, became the author of several treatises embodying liberal educational ideals. He emphasized the importance of Greek and Latin and ne- glected the vernacular, but nonetheless related education to experience of life both before and after the years of for- mal schooling and regarded it as a continuous process.

In France the most influential writers were RAMUS and MONTAIGNE, and in Germany Johannes STURM, head of the academy of Strasbourg. The Spaniard Juan Luis VIVÈS, who worked in France, the Netherlands, and England in the early 16th century, wrote treatises on education, including the education of women and the poorer classes. In Germany the Reformation led to the foundation of many new primary and secondary schools. MELANCHTHON and BUGENHAGEN were responsible for a complete reorganization of the system. Religious instruction and the teaching of reading and writing were done for the first time in the German language. The work was divided into stages, and the pupils had to master the work of each before passing to the next.

The Counter-Reformation movement in the Roman Church also produced many new schools and teaching orders such as the PIARISTS. The JESUITS, following the pedagogic precepts of their founder, IGNATIUS LOYOLA, maintained a very rigid educational system, primarily intended for the training of the clergy, but very influential too in the education of laymen. Whatever utilitarian purposes may have been served incidentally by their systems of education, the preceptors of the Renaissance period never lost sight of their highest ideals, the pursuit of knowledge and the attainment of virtue.

See also: UNIVERSITIES

Further reading: Craig W. Kallendorf (ed.), *Humanist Educational Treatises* (Cambridge, Mass.: Harvard University Press, 2002); Nicholas Orme, *Education and Society in Medieval and Renaissance England* (London: Hambledon, 1989); Joan Simon, *Education and Society in Tudor England* (Cambridge, U.K.: Cambridge University Press, 1966).

## Edward VI (1537–1553) *King of England and Ireland (1547–53)*

The son of HENRY VIII and his third wife, Jane Seymour, Edward was intelligent and well educated. He succeeded to the throne under the regency of his uncle, Edward Seymour, Duke of Somerset, but by the end of 1549 John Dudley, Duke of Northumberland, had supplanted Somerset. Edward was brought up to support the Protestant cause, and during his reign Cranmer's BOOK OF COMMON PRAYER (1549) and the Forty-two Articles of Religion (1553) were published. Shortly before his death Edward was persuaded by Northumberland to exclude his half-sisters Mary and Elizabeth from the succession in favor of his cousin, Lady Jane GREY, Northumberland's daughter-in-law.

Further reading: Diarmaid MacCulloch, *The Boy King: Edward VI and the Protestant Reformation* (New York: St. Martin's Press, 2001).

## Egas, Enrique de (c. 1445–c. 1534) *Spanish architect*

He was probably born at Toledo, where his father Egas (died 1495) and uncle Hanequin (died c. 1475) were associated with work on the cathedral. Although Enrique and his brother Anton adopted the name of their father as their family name, it seems likely that the family was an offshoot of a well-known Brussels family of masons called Coeman. Enrique became cathedral architect at Toledo (c. 1498) before moving to Granada, where he designed the chapel royal (1506) and the cathedral (1521), although the latter was remodeled and completed by Diego de SILOE. Although he worked mainly in the PLATERESQUE style, Enrique was not unaware of Italian Renaissance developments. He also designed buildings in Valladolid and Santiago de Compostela, his cruciform hospital plan for the latter town (1501) being subsequently copied for the Sta. Cruz hospital in Toledo (1504) and at Granada (1511).

## Egmont, Lamoraal (1522–1568) *Dutch nobleman*

Born in Hainaut (now in Belgium), Egmont served CHARLES V in Algiers, Germany, and France. He led the Spanish cavalry to victory against France at St.-Quentin (1557) and Gravelines (1558), and served PHILIP II of Spain as councillor and governor of Flanders and Artois, where he was idolized by his countrymen. Although a loyal subject, a Catholic, and a courtier, Egmont courageously opposed Philip's harsh policies in the Netherlands. He was treacherously seized by the duke of ALBA and executed with the Count of Horn after a summary trial. His execution marked the start of the Revolt of the NETHERLANDS.

## Egyptian studies 

The Renaissance made contact with ancient Egypt almost exclusively through the medium of classical Greek and Latin literature. The second book of Herodotus's *Histories* and references scattered through Pliny's *Natural History* provided the basis for Renaissance ideas about the material life of ancient Egypt. PLUTARCH's *On Isis and Osiris* provided information about the mystical aspects of Egyptian religion. The major interest of Renaissance students was in the contribution of Egypt to hermetic, gnostic, and other pagan systems which were supposed to have affected Christianity in various ways (*see* HERMETICISM). Hieroglyphs, the ancient Egyptian system of writing, were the main focus for this interest. Early Christian writers, such as Cassiodorus and Rufinus, had taught that hieroglyphs were purely ideographic writing used by Egyptian priests to foreshadow divine ideas. Renaissance interest was stimulated by Cristoforo de' Buondelmonti's purchase, on the island of Andros in 1419, of a manuscript of the *Hieroglyphica*, attributed to Horapollo. Another early traveler to take notice of hieroglyphs was CYRIAC OF ANCONA, who visited Egypt in 1435 and copied a hieroglyphic inscription for Niccolò NICCOLI. Marsilio FICINO hailed Horapollo as a major source of information about Egyptian mysticism and its relation to Neoplatonism, and his work was mined as a source of esoteric wisdom and IMPRESE. It also influenced both the text and illustrations of the HYPNEROTOMACHIA POLIFILI (1499). The *editio princeps* of Horapollo was printed by Aldus

MANUTIUS (1505) and a Latin translation was published in 1517. Other early writers whose works on the ancient Egyptian mysteries were known to the Renaissance included PLOTINUS and Iamblichus, of whom Latin translations by Ficino appeared in 1492 and 1497 respectively.

Valeriano Bolzanio (c. 1443–1524) and his nephew Piero (see VALERIANUS, PIERIUS) summed up in their researches the state of Renaissance Egyptology in the mid-16th century. Piero's *Hieroglyphica* (Basle, 1556) is an exhaustive account of contemporary speculation which established connections between hieroglyphs and the symbolism of medieval lapidaries and bestiaries. Increased contact with Egypt in the later 16th century extended the range of primary sources available and the re-erection in Rome of the obelisks brought to the city in the time of the empire—the obelisk of Caligula in St. Peter's Square (1586) and of Augustus in front of the Lateran Palace (1588) are examples—provided a further stimulus to the study of hieroglyphs (see also BEMBINE TABLE). Pietro della Valle traveled extensively in the Levant (1614–26), bringing back with him to Italy Egyptian mummies and Coptic manuscripts. The learning of the whole period is summed up in the three massive volumes of Athanasius Kircher's *Oedipus Aegyptiacus...* (Rome, 1652–54).

**Eight of War** See EIGHT SAINTS, WAR OF THE

**Eight Saints, War of the** (1375–78) A conflict between Florence and its supporters on the one hand and the papacy on the other, over the secular power of the papacy in central Italy. The war was ended by the compromise Peace of Tivoli (1378). The threat the war posed to the security of Rome prompted Gregory XI to end the papacy's 70-year exile in AVIGNON. The "saints" referred to were the eight officials who exacted war taxes from the clergy, here confused with the Eight of War (*otto della guerra*), who conducted Florence's military operations.

**Eldorado** (Spanish, "the gilded one") The name given in the early 16th century to a South American Indian ruler believed to be located near Bogotá. According to legend, he covered his body with gold dust for religious ceremonies, then plunged into a sacred lake to wash while his subjects threw gold and jewels into the water. From 1538 Spanish adventurers searched for him; they failed to find his great treasure but the area they explored came under Spanish rule. Later the quest shifted to the Orinoco and Amazon valleys, and Eldorado came to mean a fabulously rich country. Among the many who sought its gold were Gonzalo Pizarro (in 1539), Francisco de Orellana (in 1541–42), and Sir Walter RALEIGH (in 1595 and 1617–18). The legendary gold encouraged rapid exploration and conquest of much of the Americas by Spain and other European powers.

**Further reading**: Marc Aronson, *Sir Walter Raleigh and the Quest for El Dorado* (Boston, Mass.: Houghton Mifflin, 2000).

**Elizabeth I** (1533–1603) *Queen of England and Ireland (1558–1603)*
The daughter of HENRY VIII by his second wife, Anne Boleyn, Elizabeth led an insecure life until her accession to the throne. Her father had her mother beheaded, Elizabeth was declared illegitimate (1536), and her sister, MARY I, imprisoned her in the Tower of London (1554) on suspicion of treason. Yet Elizabeth's reign would prove one of the most successful in English history. It saw the defeat of Catholic Spain, a generally acceptable religious settlement, rising prosperity, expansion overseas, a great literary age, and the emergence of England as a world power.

Elizabeth soon ended years of religious turmoil with the establishment of a moderately Protestant Anglican Church (see ELIZABETHAN SETTLEMENT). Attempts to restore Roman Catholicism continued, but Elizabeth had little difficulty in thwarting various plots, such as the NORTHERN REBELLION, to place her Catholic cousin, MARY, Queen of Scots, on the throne of England. The pope had excommunicated Elizabeth in 1570, but it was not until after the execution of Mary on Elizabeth's orders (1587) that the SPANISH ARMADA was sent to invade England (1588). The defeat of the Armada was a great triumph for Elizabeth and her navy, confirming England's status as a great power.

Elizabeth never married, but used her eligibility as a powerful weapon in diplomatic negotiations until she was well into her fifties (see FRANCIS, DUKE OF ALENÇON). She seems to have sincerely loved Robert Dudley, earl of LEICESTER. Elizabeth always retained the affection of most of her subjects, she managed the House of Commons shrewdly, and she had the ability to choose her ministers wisely; two of them in particular, William Cecil, Lord Burghley (1520–98) and Francis Walsingham (1532–90), were responsible for sound economic and administrative reforms. Elizabeth was succeeded by her Stuart cousin, JAMES I of England and VI of Scotland.

Elizabeth's record as a model Renaissance princess must be seen in the light of the political and religious stresses of her life and her ambivalent position as a woman monarch. Educated alongside her younger brother, she was taught Latin, French, and Italian, and later her stepmother Catherine PARR oversaw her education. In her late teens she had the advantage of having Roger ASCHAM as her tutor. She made translations of classical authors, notably Boethius, and also of French devotional poetry by MARGUERITE DE NAVARRE. Elizabeth was herself a proficient musician—the FITZWILLIAM VIRGINAL BOOK was for many years believed to have been her personal music book—and in her reign the Chapel Royal employed some musicians and composers of exceptional stature, among them

John BULL, William BYRD, and Thomas MORLEY. The carefully nurtured cult of Elizabeth as Gloriana, the Virgin Queen, was the source of much of the richest visual heritage of her reign, seen most notably in the portraits of the queen herself.

**Further reading:** Susan Doran (ed.), *Elizabeth: The Exhibition at the National Maritime Museum* (London: Chatto & Windus and National Maritime Museum, Greenwich, 2003); Michael Dobson and Nicola Watson, *England's Elizabeth: An Afterlife in Fame and Fantasy* (Oxford, U.K.: Oxford University Press, 2002); Leah S. Marcus, Janel Mueller, and Mary Beth Rose (eds), *Elizabeth I: Collected Works* (Chicago, Ill. and London: University of Chicago Press, 2000); David Starkey, *Elizabeth: Apprenticeship* (London: Vintage, 2001).

**Elizabethan Settlement** The measures undertaken to define England's religious identity under the regime of ELIZABETH I. Begun at her accession in 1558, they reversed Mary I's Catholic policies and reflected Elizabeth's own brand of moderate Protestantism. Papal power was again abolished in England, permanently separating England from Rome—Pius V was to excommunicate Elizabeth in 1570 (*see also* RECUSANCY). Monarchs would lead England, not popes. An Act of Supremacy declared that the Queen was "supreme of all persons and causes, ecclesiastical as well as civil." The Protestant Matthew PARKER, became archbishop of Canterbury (1559). Monasteries opened by Mary were dissolved.

A third Act of Uniformity (1559) mainly accepted Edward VI's 1552 Prayer Book (*see* BOOK OF COMMON PRAYER), though the removal of harsh antipapal rhetoric from it typifies Elizabeth's efforts to advance Protestantism without provoking violent reaction from religious conservatives. But religious strife did not end in 1558. The 1569 NORTHERN REBELLION showed that Catholic loyalists were not placated by Elizabeth, whose compromising policies were also attacked by extreme reformers. The latter resented the reintroduction of a crucifix into Elizabeth's own chapel and the insistence that clergy should again wear traditional VESTMENTS. By the mid-1580s, anti-Catholic policies (with popular actions being taken against Mary, Queen of Scots, Spain, and papists in general) were in full cry. The Settlement's tolerant spirit was replaced by a jingoistic, virulent Protestantism.

**Elizabethan style** The English architectural and decorative style associated with the reign (1558–1603) of Elizabeth I. During this period the assimilation of Renaissance models, begun in the preceding TUDOR period, gathered momentum, although much Elizabethan work was still medieval in character with an often idiosyncratic application of half-understood Renaissance motifs. One characteristic form of decoration was the low-relief carving in intricate geometrical patterns known as strapwork, which

entered England from the Low Countries and was much used on FURNITURE and on plaster ceilings. The predominantly oak furniture was usually heavily carved, with bulbous pillar supports that reached massive proportions in the 1580s and 1590s; an assortment of classical motifs (lion masks, acanthus scrolls, caryatids, Ionic columns, etc.) would also appear on the same pieces.

Architectural innovations were predominantly secular and domestic. The houses of Elizabethan magnates, such as Bess of Hardwick (*see* HARDWICK, ELIZABETH), influenced by the increasing circulation of illustrated books on architecture, began to show a bias towards symmetry; this was exemplified in the E-shaped ground plan of country houses, with a formal entrance porch in the center forming the short stroke of the E and two long wings protruding at right angles from the main block. A grand staircase and a long gallery were fashionable interior features. Fireplaces became elaborate stone edifices, often inlaid with colored marbles.

**See also:** JACOBEAN STYLE

**Further reading:** Mark Girouard, *Robert Smythson and the Architecture of the Elizabethan Era* (London: Country Life, 1966); Timothy Mowl, *Elizabethan and Jacobean Style* (London: Phaidon, 1993); Anthony Wells-Cole, *Art and Decoration in Elizabethan and Jacobean England: The Influence of Continental Prints, 1558–1625* (New Haven, Conn. and London: Yale University Press, 1997).

**Elsevir press** See ELZEVIR PRESS

**Elsheimer, Adam** (1578–1610) *German painter*
Elsheimer studied painting in his native Frankfurt, where he came under the influence of exiled Dutch landscape painters living in the area. In Italy from 1598, he visited Venice and lived in Rome, absorbing the influence of Italians such as CARAVAGGIO, VERONESE, and the Bassano family. He met RUBENS and other Dutch painters there, through whom he influenced the development of northern European art. Elsheimer's usually small, very delicate paintings, often executed in oil on copper, were widely popular. His subject matter is usually biblical or mythological, with figures and an idyllic landscape setting assuming equal importance, as in *Tobias and the Angel* (National Gallery, London). He is noted especially for his rich colors and effects of light, frequently achieved in night scenes. Elsheimer died in Rome, following his release from imprisonment for debt.

**Elyot, Sir Thomas** (c. 1490–1546) *English writer and diplomat*
His place of birth and education are uncertain, but in 1511 he became clerk of assize on the western circuit, on which his father was a judge. He attracted the patronage of WOLSEY and then of Thomas CROMWELL, becoming a close friend of the latter by 1528. After having been knighted in

1530, Elyot led embassies to Emperor Charles V in 1531 and 1535. In 1531 his first and most famous publication appeared, *The Boke named the Governour*; dedicated to HENRY VIII, it was an appeal for humanistic values in the education of the aristocracy. *Pasquil the Plain* (1532) extols the virtues of free speech against flattery. The medical treatise *The Castel of Health* (1534) was novel in that it was written in the vernacular and by a layman. Among Elyot's other works, the most significant is his Latin–English *Dictionary* (1538).

**Elzevir press** (Elsevir press) The press founded by the Elzevirs (or Elsevirs or Elseviers), a Dutch family of printers, publishers, and booksellers, who spread from a base in Leyden to The Hague, Amsterdam, and Utrecht, and were active from about 1580 to 1712. The founder of the dynasty, Louis (1546–1617) left Louvain to work for PLANTIN in Antwerp, before settling in Leyden in 1580 as a binder and bookseller, eventually associated with the local university. His publishing started in 1593 with an edition of Eutropius, and classical authors continued to be the main stock of the firm. Louis's son Bonaventura (1583–1652) and grandsons Abraham (1592–1652) and Izaak (1596–1651)—the offspring of Louis's oldest son, Matthias—began the series of pocket classics in 1629, providing accurate texts for a large market. These little thirty-twomos, with their narrow margins and solid slabs of type, often with engraved title-pages, became the family's most famous product. Izaak, who had established a press of his own in 1616, became printer to the university of Leyden in 1620, and his successors retained the office.

GROTIUS was the first contemporary author to be published by the Elzevirs, in 1609; the Amsterdam branch, established by Louis III (1604–70) in 1639, subsequently concentrated on modern books in Dutch, German, English, and French until the death of Daniel Elzevir (1626–80), Bonaventura's son, when it was wound up. The Leyden branch lasted a little longer, under the control of Abraham's grandson, Abraham II (1653–1712). The Elzevirs, from Louis I on, sold new or second-hand books throughout Europe, an activity just as important as their printing and publishing.

**emblems** Symbolic pictures to which were added a few words, often in the form of a motto or a short verse, to explain the full meaning. An emblem can be defined as the graphic expression of a thought. Emblematic devices are probably most familiar now as printers' marks, such as the ALDINE PRESS dolphin and anchor, glossed as "Hasten slowly" (see illustration on p. 200). Francis Quarles, author of the best-known English emblem book, which appeared in 1635, said "An Emblem is a silent parable."

The Renaissance taste for emblems may have grown in part from study of Roman medals and Egyptian hieroglyphs. It was reinforced by the publication of collections of them in books; the first, Andrea ALCIATI's *Emblemata*, printed in Augsburg in 1531, with woodcuts by Jörg Breu, initiated a fashion that lasted over a century. A Paris edition with better illustrations by Mercure Jollot followed in 1534, with a first French translation two years later and a German one in 1542, all issued by WECHEL. In 1546 the Aldine press printed more of Alciati's emblems, followed by Lyons printers who put them into French, Spanish, and finally Italian, in 1549. The first English emblem book, Geoffrey Whitney's *A Choice of Emblemes* (Leyden, 1586), was printed on the Continent because the stock of illustrations required was available there. Henry Peacham, on the other hand, drew his own illustrations for the manuscript book of emblems that he presented in 1609 to Henry, Prince of Wales; most of these were incorporated into his published work *Minerva Britanna, or a Garden of Heroicall Devises* 1612), in which many of the individual emblems were dedicated to members of the prince's household. The later English collections (both 1635) of Francis Quarles and George Wither were predominantly devotional in character. Dutch printers were the most prolific producers of emblem books, and the PLANTIN PRESS kept the fashion alive by diverting them to educational or spiritual themes expressed in allegories. A book of this kind marking the Jesuits' centenary, *Imago primi saeculi Societatis Jesu*, was issued by Jan Moretus in 1640.

See also: IMPRESE

**Further reading:** Peter M. Daly (ed.), *Andrea Alciati and the Emblem Tradition* (New York; AMS, 1989).

**Emser, Hieronymus** (1478–1527) *German humanist and Roman Catholic controversialist*
Emser was born at Ulm and studied at Tübingen, where he learnt Greek from Dionysius (the brother of Johann) Reuchlin, and at Basle. In 1501 he became chaplain to Cardinal Raimund von Gurk, and in 1504 secretary to Duke George of Saxony. Initially he was in sympathy with LUTHER and the reformers, but he wished rather to see the Church reformed from within, without making any doctrinal break. From 1519 he was engaged in violent controversy with Luther and in 1527 he produced a German Bible, with introduction and notes, to counteract the effect of Luther's.

**Encina, Juan del** (1469–c. 1529) *Spanish poet, dramatist, and musician*
Known as the father of the Spanish theater, he was born near Salamanca and studied there under Elio NEBRIJA. He took minor orders and from 1492 to 1495 was in the service of the duke of Alba, at whose palace he produced his first pastoral entertainments which included his own music. These were dialogues of shepherds and rustics which combined classical material—Encina had translated Virgil's *Eclogues* at age 21—with verse forms and songs of popular origin. About 1500 Encina went to

Rome, serving as choirmaster under Alexander VI and Leo X. He was ordained in 1519 and went on a pilgrimage to Jerusalem where he said his first Mass. He spent his final years as prior of León cathedral.

The first edition of his *Cancionero* (1496) contained eight plays, his lyric poetry, and an introduction on Spanish poetry. Subsequent editions (1507, 1509) printed two other plays each, and 68 of his musical compositions have survived as well. Three of his early dramatic pieces are religious *representaciones* (compare the SACRA RAPPRESENTAZIONE of Italy), written for particular days (Christmas, Good Friday, and Easter); the rest are dramatic secular pastoral plays, carefully plotted and frequently comic. They are written in octosyllabic verse in various stanzaic forms and are accompanied by music and dancing, with which almost all of them end. The best show the influence of Italian pastoral drama, for example, *Egloga de Plácida y Vitoriano*, first produced in Rome in 1512 and containing a character, the hag Eritea, based on Celestina (*see* CELESTINA, LA). Encina popularized a type of peasant speech for his comic characters that was often imitated by his successors; called *sayagués* and supposedly originating in the village of Sayago, near Salamanca, it was in fact an artificial comic invention employed by Encina simply to characterize his comic shepherds and give the impresssion of local color.

***Encomium Moriae*** See PRAISE OF FOLLY, THE

**Enderlein, Gaspar** (1560–1633) *German metalworker*
Enderlein was born in Basle but became a master in Nuremberg in 1586. He was profoundly influenced by the work of François BRIOT, whose Temperantia Dish provided the model for Enderlein's own Temperantia Dish. An accompanying ewer was modeled upon the Mars Dish by Briot and the Suzannah Dish, also probably by Briot.

**English College** Theological college established (1575) in Rome by William ALLEN, under the auspices of Pope GREGORY XIII, for the training of Roman Catholic clergy. From 1578 it was closely identified with the mission to reconvert England to Catholicism. Shortly afterward the seminary was placed under the direction of the JESUITS, who ran it for nearly 200 years.

**English language** The Renaissance period saw English evolve from the stage known as Middle English to that known as Early Modern English. Middle English was characterized by a number of dialects; the language of CHAUCER, a late 14th-century Londoner, was very different from that of his anonymous northwestern contemporary who wrote *Sir Gawain and the Green Knight*. In the 15th century pressure towards a standard form of English began to emerge. This pressure was partly administrative, as English supplanted French and Latin in official records,

and partly social or educational. As an instance of the latter, members of the Norfolk Paston family who had spent time in London or at the universities began to use word forms characteristic of London dialect rather than of their native county.

Printing was a major factor in the standardization of the language. CAXTON complained of the troublesome variety of English dialects and told the story of a north-countryman who ordered "eggys" in a Kentish hostelry, only to be chided by the hostess for speaking French; another customer intervened to explain that he wanted "eyren," then still the usual word for "eggs" in the southeast. A century later Thomas Puttenham in his *Arte of English poesie* (1589) stipulated a famous model for correct English: "the usuall speech of the Court, and that of London and the shires lying about London within 1x. myles, and not much above." It was this standard that generally prevailed among educated persons.

The superior status of Latin as an ancient, learned, and international language meant that English was at first discounted as a medium of educated discourse. Sixteenth-century writers, while acknowledging Chaucer's greatness, saw that his language had become obsolete within 150 years and feared to entrust their profoundest thoughts to such an impermanent and insular vehicle. Even in the early 17th century Sir Francis Kynaston tried to guarantee Chaucer's standing by publishing a Latin version of the latter's *Troilus and Criseyde* (1635). Among the first educationists to defend the vernacular was Richard Mulcaster, whose *Elementarie* (1582) contains a spirited defense of English as "a tung of it self both depe in conceit, and frank in deliverie"; in his opinion, no language "is better able to utter all arguments, either with more pith, or greater planesse than our English tung is." The latter point was amply proved by the many translations made in the period, in particular those of the Bible, which invested the vernacular with both dignity and authority.

To establish a standard English, attention needed to be paid to three main areas: ORTHOGRAPHY, syntax, and vocabulary. Spelling reformers considered that the system should be overhauled to enable the written language to reflect more accurately the sounds of contemporary speech; to this end John Hart even suggested in his *Orthographie* (1569) that new symbols should be introduced into the alphabet. In the field of syntax several innovations that had arisen in the Middle English period generally supplanted older usages. One important one was the use of the auxiliary verb "do" to form negative or interrogative sentences; SHAKESPEARE exhibits both kinds of question within a few lines: "Do you busy yourself with that?" (new) and "Spake you with him?" (obsolescent) (*King Lear* I ii). Another change, which manifested itself around 1600, was the use of "its" instead of "his" for the neuter form of the genitive or possessive pronoun.

Vocabulary reflected the new linguistic consciousness and the new demands made upon the vernacular. An estimated 10,000 new words were adopted from Latin, Greek (often via Latin), Italian, French, and other languages during the Renaissance period. Linguistic critics fell into two camps: those who held that English could provide from its own native resources all the words necessary and those who believed that foreign importations were the best route to an enriched vocabulary. SPENSER was praised for having taken the former option in *The Shepheardes Calender*; "he hath laboured to restore, as to their rightfull heritage such good and naturall English words, as have ben long time out of use and almost cleane disinherited" wrote "E.K." in his commendatory letter, contrasting Spenser with those who "have made our English tongue, a gallimaufray or hodgepodge of al other speches." The contemporary term for those who imported and coined words to an excessive degree was "inkhornist." Most of their bizarre affectations quickly died, but other words that had a genuine role to play in English took root and flourished.

**engraving** An intaglio printing process, in which a metal plate, usually of copper, is incised with an image. The plate is then inked and the residue of ink is wiped off so that the ink remains only in the engraved furrows of the plate. A piece of damp paper is then laid against the plate and both are rolled through a heavy press, somewhat like a clothes mangle. Under this intense pressure, the damp paper is forced into the ink-filled furrows so that an impression of the image is embossed upon the paper. The final image is a reverse impression of that incised upon the plate.

The earliest form of engraving, and that most used during the Renaissance, is line (or copper) engraving, in which a sharp metal tool with a V-shaped section is pushed by hand pressure across the plate, rather like a plough. The tool, known as a burin, throws up metal shavings and leaves a V-shaped groove, which constitutes the line subsequently inked. This technique derived from that used by sculptors to chase the surface of bronze statues. The earliest dated print executed in this technique is of 1446.

Dry-point engraving is a simpler, but less commercially viable, technique, in which the image is transferred to a metal plate by a sharp stylus of hard steel. The stylus throws up a raised metal edge to the furrow, known as "burr." The latter is retained when the plate is inked, so that it adds a rich, broken edge to the printed image. However, the pressure of printing rapidly crushes the burr, so that no more than a few dozen impressions may be made with this technique. The most outstanding early master of dry-point engraving was the Dutch Master of the Housebook, active about 1480, who was influential upon Albrecht DÜRER.

Etching is a further method of engraving, in which the plate is covered with a ground impervious to acid, upon which the engraver draws with a needle, exposing the copper where he wishes to print. The plate is then immersed in acid, which eats a line in the plate where the needle has exposed the copper, while leaving the covered area unaffected. The line produced by this technique has an irregular, broken form of greater variety than that produced by line engraving. Although Dürer experimented with etching as early as 1515, the technique was little used until the 17th century, since when it has become increasingly popular.

The earliest known engraver, the German Master of 1446, was followed by a number of outstanding northern masters, including the Master of the Banderoles, the Master of the Playing Cards, the MASTER E. S., and Martin SCHONGAUER, who refined the technique of line engraving to a high level. In Italy a number of anonymous masters started producing engravings almost contemporaneously with their northern counterparts. The earliest major Italian engravers whose names are known were Antonio POLLAIUOLO and Andrea MANTEGNA. However, both were primarily active in other fields and they produced relatively small editions of prints, which were nevertheless extremely influential. Albrecht Dürer was the greatest print maker of the Renaissance. He made numerous technical refinements, which permitted engraving to reproduce effects of light and texture with a much higher fidelity than had previously been possible. Dürer's example stimulated a remarkably accomplished series of followers, including the Germans Albrecht ALTDORFER, Urs GRAF, Hans BALDUNG, Lucas CRANACH, and Hans Sebald Beham (*see* LITTLE MASTERS (OF NUREMBERG)), as well as the Netherlander LUCAS VAN LEYDEN. In Italy the most outstanding school of engraving of the early 16th century was that of Venice, the leading masters of which were Jacopo de' BARBARI, Giulio CAMPAGNOLA, and Marcantonio RAIMONDI. Raimondi, who was profoundly influenced by Dürer, moved to Rome about 1510, where he specialized in prints after the paintings of Raphael. Subsequently, a decline in original engraving set in, which lasted until well into the following century. The growing market for prints, which expanded throughout the Renaissance, was satisfied by a highly organized print trade, in which painters prepared design drawings which were subsequently engraved by specialist engravers.

**Further reading:** David Landau and Peter Parshall, *The Renaissance Print, 1470–1550* (New Haven, Conn. and London: Yale University Press, 1994).

**Enzinas, Francisco de** (Francis Dryander) (c. 1520–1570) *Spanish scholar, translator, and reformer*
Enzinas was born at Burgos and studied at Wittenberg, where he was influenced by LUTHER's teaching. He produced the first translation of the New Testament into

Spanish, which was published at Antwerp in 1543. This translation incurred the displeasure of Charles V because it was based on the Greek text of Erasmus and because of Enzinas's marginalia, which expressed unorthodox opinions. He also printed in capitals the verses of Romans 3 which provided one of the main supports for those who endorsed JUSTIFICATION BY FAITH. Enzinas was therefore imprisoned (1543) at Brussels but he managed to escape to Antwerp two years later. He journeyed widely and in 1546 came to England, where he was professor of Greek at Cambridge until the accession of the Catholic Mary I forced him to leave. He even traveled as far as Constantinople, founding a Protestant colony there. His works included a history of religion in Spain and Spanish translations of Lucian (1550) and Plutarch (1551). He also wrote memoirs in Latin which remained in manuscript until the 19th century.

**epic** A long narrative poem written in a heightened style concerning a heroic character whose legendary or historical actions are central to his culture, race, or nation. "Primary" or traditional epics, such as the Homeric poems, derive from an heroic age and celebrate a war or similar event and the hero's role in it. "Secondary" or literary epics are by known individual poets writing in deliberate imitation of "primary" models. VIRGIL'S *Aeneid* is both the outstanding example of the literary epic and the model, in turn, for most succeeding European epic poets.

In addition to the great national or cultural significance embodied by the epic hero and his actions, there are a number of other conventional features of both types of epic. The setting is suitably extensive, often representing the whole of the known world (as in the *Odyssey*) and more, for example, the underworld in classical epics and the entire Christian cosmos in John Milton's *Paradise Lost* (1667). Divine beings or other supernatural agents take part, often actively, in the events. The exalted and ceremonial language appropriate to the action is also characterized by a number of conventions, for example, detailed catalogues of people, things, and places; set speeches reflecting the character of the speaker, who may also bear a stock epithet (*pius Aeneas, fidus Achates* in the *Aeneid*); and epic similes involving elaborate comparisons. The poem usually starts *in medias res* after an invocation of the Muse and a question put to her, the answer to which is the narrative itself. The most important early theoretical comments on the epic are contained in ARISTOTLE'S *Poetics*, though they have survived only in mutilated form.

In the Renaissance, the nature of the epic was the subject of intense discussion in 16th-century Italy following the recovery of Aristotle's *Poetics* and the dissemination of classical literary theory. Previously known mainly through a commentary by Averroes, the *Poetics* became available in much improved translations: into Latin by Giorgio Valla (1498) and Alessandro Pazzi (1536), and into Italian by

Bernardo Segni (1549). Although Aristotle had ranked epic second to tragedy in the hierarchy of genres, this judgment was ignored by Renaissance critics, and epic was promoted to top place—"the best and most accomplished" as Sir Philip SIDNEY called it (*Defence of Poesie*, 1595). The Homeric epics with which Aristotle was concerned were eventually given serious consideration, but Virgil remained the most significant epic model for Renaissance poets and critics. Thus Marco Giralamo VIDA in *De arte poetica* (1527) proclaims the epic as the noblest of all genres and Virgil as the best model. Many other critics and poets reflect or adapt Aristotelian principles in commenting on the epic. Giangiorgio TRISSINO in *La poetica* (1529) cites Aristotelian criteria; he modeled his own blank-verse epic, *La Italia liberata da' Gotthi* (1547–48), on Homer. CINTHIO in *Discorsi intorno al comporre dei romanzi* (1548) attempted to defend Ariosto and the romance by categorizing them in a separate slot from the epic as classically conceived. Minturno (Antonio Sebastiani) argued for an epic having classical unity of action while taking Christian and romance material as proper subject matter (*L'arte poetica*, 1564). CASTELVETRO (*Poetica d'Aristotele vulgarizatta et sposta*, 1570) opposed a rigid application of Aristotelian criteria to later works.

Among Renaissance poems of epic scope, the DIVINE COMEDY occupies a special place at the very beginning of the period, but it lacks an epic hero in any traditional sense. PETRARCH's *Africa*, SANNAZARO's *De partu virginis*, Vida's *Christus*, and Trissino's epic are the best representatives of humanist classicism. Owing more to the medieval romance and the poetry of chivalry, which included such "primary" material as the legends of ARTHUR and of CHARLEMAGNE and the Twelve Peers—though the *Chanson de Roland* itself was not known in the Renaissance—are BOCCACCIO's *Teseida*, with its erotic interest, PULCI's *Il morgante*, BOIARDO's *Orlando innamorato*, ARIOSTO's *Orlando furioso*, and TASSO's *Rinaldo*. Tasso's GERUSALEMME LIBERATA and, for theory, his *Discorsi del poema eroico* (1594) form a final, if inconclusive, attempt in Italy to reconcile neoclassical ideals of unity and moral purpose with the marvels, love interest, and multiplicity of event of the romance tradition.

The divergence between the "unified" classical epic and the "diversified" romantic epic manifested itself in the literatures of other European countries. In France RONSARD attempted a national epic on the theme of the French monarchy; its feeble plan, ill-advised choice of meter (decasyllables, as opposed to the more eloquent alexandrine), and wooden diction condemned *La Franciade* (1572) to abandonment after only four of the projected 24 books had been completed. In England Spenser's FAERIE QUEENE, also unfinished, combined grandeur of conception with poetic power in the execution, but its allegorical character and multiplicity of action disqualified it as an epic contender in the classical style. The most successful

Renaissance epic under the classical rules is Camões' LU-SIAD, in which the excitement of Portugal's imperial adventure in the East breathes new spirit into the ancient conventions.

Growing unease with national or family pride as warranting the high seriousness of epic treatment led some poets to turn to religious themes for their subject matter. *La Semaine* (1578) of DU BARTAS achieves epic dignity in its theme (the creation of the world) and occasionally in its treatment. The Christian theme was also exploited in 17th-century England, by Abraham Cowley in his unfinished *Davideis* (1656) and, of course, by Milton in *Paradise Lost* and *Paradise Regained* (1671).

Further reading: A. Bartlett Giamatti, *Earthly Paradise and the Renaissance Epic* (New York: W. W. Norton, 1999).

**Epicurus** (341–270 BCE) Greek philosopher. He was better known in the Middle Ages by repute than by any surviving writings, but he was generally mentioned with disapproval by Christian authors, who travestied his philosophy as teaching that the highest good is pleasure, while omitting to note that Epicurus defined pleasure as the practice of virtue. His atomism also was objectionable in that it suggested a random material origin for the world, as opposed to a divine plan. Finally, his doctrine that the gods did not involve themselves with human affairs contradicted Christian belief in divine intervention through the Incarnation. Epicureanism and atheism were therefore frequently bracketed. Debate about his philosophy was fueled in the Renaissance after the discovery of the work of his major Roman follower, LUCRETIUS.

*Epistolae obscurorum virorum* (**Letters of Obscure Men**) A brilliant satire originating in the controversy between the humanist Johann REUCHLIN and the converted Jew Johann Pfefferkorn (1469–1522). Pfefferkorn, supported by a number of theologians, wanted Hebrew literature confiscated and destroyed, while Reuchlin, who had initiated HEBREW STUDIES in Germany, pleaded for toleration; a bitter feud developed. In 1514, in self-defense, Reuchlin published some letters from eminent European scholars to him, the *Clarorum virorum epistolae* (Letters of famous men). The *Epistolae obscurorum virorum* appeared anonymously the following year, written mainly by the humanist Crotus Rubeanus; ostensibly they were letters from sycophantic academic theologians to one of Pfefferkorn's supporters, Ortivin Gratius, but they were soon recognized as a humanist joke. In them the fictitious theologians reveal themselves as petty and complacent, occupied with the most trivial scholastic problems, food, drink, and sex. Their absurd names and appalling Latin intensify the humor. In 1517 another book of letters appeared, more directly concerned with the Reuchlin affair (mainly by Ulrich von HUTTEN). The *Epistolae* resulted in much advantageous publicity for Reuchlin's stance and for the humanist cause.

**equestrian monuments** Statues of rulers or military leaders on horseback were a tradition revived in the Italian Renaissance on the basis of antique depictions of Roman emperors or soldiers. Only one freestanding imperial statue of this type survived intact: the statue of Emperor Marcus Aurelius (ruled 160–80 CE) in Rome, which was wrongly believed to be of the first Christian emperor,

**Equestrian monuments** Donatello's equestrian statue of Il Gattamelata, the Padua-born captain-general of Venice. Cast in the 1440s, it was erected in 1453 in the Piazza de Santo, Padua, where it still stands by the basilica.
*The Bridgeman Art Library*

**165**

Constantine. Ambitious Renaissance leaders recognized the symbolic force of such a monument, seeing in the rider's control over the horse a symbol of their own power over their subjects or enemies (*see* EQUITATION). By the 15th century, painted equestrian portraits were appearing on funeral monuments (for example, UCCELLO's repainted fresco of the English condottiere Sir John Hawkwood in Florence cathedral, 1436) and elsewhere (for example, the fresco of Guidoriccio da Fogliano in Siena's Palazzo Pubblico).

The bronze equestrian statue of GATTAMELATA (Piazza del Santo, Padua) by DONATELLO, made in the mid-1440s and erected in 1453, proved to be the first durable statue of its kind since classical antiquity. The stability of the horse is ensured by its having three feet on the base and the tip of the fourth hoof resting on a small sphere. VERROCCHIO in the later Colleoni statue in Venice (1485–88) shows the pacing horse with one forefoot raised. More taxing was the practical problem of sculpting a life-size rearing horse; sketches for a proposed monument to Francesco (I) SFORZA by Antonio POLLAIUOLO and LEONARDO DA VINCI show attempts at solving the difficulty. Leonardo's work got as far as a clay model of the over-life-size horse (1493) but it was never cast and was wrecked in the French invasion of Milan.

It was nearly a century before the next executed commission for a large-scale equestrian monument: the 1587 commission to GIAMBOLOGNA for a statue of Duke Cosimo I de' Medici. In 1594 the English traveler Fynes MORYSON saw the statue in the sculptor's workshop before it was erected (1595) in the Piazza della Signoria, Florence; he was particularly impressed by its size (over 14ft high) and the fact that the horse was shown walking naturally, its weight balanced on just one forefoot and one hindfoot. Giambologna also made an equestrian statue of Henry IV of France, erected in 1611 on the Pont Neuf, Paris, and began a statue of Grand Duke Ferdinand I (1608; Piazza dell' Annunziata, Florence) that was completed by his pupil Pietro Tacca in 1608. Tacca was responsible too for a statue of Philip III of Spain (1616; Plaza Mayor, Madrid), and for the statue of Philip IV of Spain (1642), in which he solved the problem of representing a rearing horse. England lagged behind Continental Europe in displaying sculpted portraits of its rulers in public places; a scheme to depict James I and Prince Charles on horseback was proposed in 1621, but the first equestrian statue to be realized in that country was the one by the Frenchman Hubert Le Sueur (c. 1595–c. 1650) of Charles I (1633; now in Trafalgar Square, London).

**Further reading:** Maureen Barraclough *et al*, *Sovereigns and Soldiers on Horseback: Bronze Equestrian Monuments from Ancient Rome to Our Times* (Ipswich, Mass.: Ipswich Press, 1999).

**Equicola, Mario** (c. 1470–1525) *Italian humanist courtier and diplomat*
Born at Alvito, Calabria, Equicola was mainly associated with the house of ESTE. As early as 1505 he composed a treatise on the phrase "Nec spe nec metu" (neither in hope nor in fear), which was Isabella d'Este's favorite motto, and in 1519 she appointed him her secretary. In this capacity he traveled with her on a pilgrimage to the shrine of St. Mary Magdalene at Ste.-Baume in Provence; his account of the trip still survives. His letters give valuable insights into the private lives of Isabella and her extensive family connections. He became involved in the quarrel between Isabella and her son Federico d'Este, and died in Mantua. His *De natura de amore* (1525) shows the influence of FICINO's theories of Platonic love.

**equitation** Medieval pageants favored horsemanship as a display of physical and military prowess. By contrast, Renaissance horsemanship developed into an art form, emphasizing the gracefulness, resourcefulness, and mutual discipline of horse and rider. A microcosm of Renaissance order, horsemanship was an emblem of the harmony of art and nature.

The idea of equitation as an art had a classical source in Xenophon, who in the early 4th century BCE recommended the harmonized interaction of animal and rider in terms of "gentling" or training the horse through instruction and exercises. The revival of equitation began in Naples, when Federico Grisone established the first purpose-built riding school. His influential and widely translated book *Gli ordini di cavalcare* (The principles of horsemanship, 1550) initiated the education of European nobility in equitation. In England, Thomas BLUNDEVILLE translated this work (1560) and dedicated it to the earl of Leicester, whom Queen Elizabeth had appointed her Master of the Horse. Early the next century the Continental fascination with equitation touched Henry, Prince of Wales, who enlisted French masters to teach him the art and ordered the building of a dedicated "riding house" in London, the first in England (1607–09).

Grisone's pupils dispersed across Europe as riding masters to kings and nobles, and continued his work of infusing the art of riding with characteristic Renaissance and humanist concerns. The noble horseman drew on the art of eloquence to instruct the horse, thereby shaping and refining its character; to please audiences, the riding masters also included music, especially during the exercise of the "courbette." (The horses of the Medici stables in Florence were particularly renowned for performances of this kind.) Each element of the horseman's art was developed in such a way that it honored the mutuality of the performance, ennobling with willed harmony and artistic skill the natural state of animal–human interaction.

The Renaissance art of equitation perhaps culminated in Antoine de Pluvinel's work in France. Pluvinel, a graduate of the Neapolitan Pignatelli school, consolidated and articulated the ethic of nobility and artistry in his own academy (established 1594). He elevated the art of discernment or judiciousness in the rider: if a horse is not obeying commands, the rider should not "break" it through spurs or switch, but determine the causes of its resistance. Equitation had become a medium of imparting education and developing leadership skills: "For horses can obey and understand us only through the diligence of caresses and flattery," he wrote (*The Maneige Royal de M. de Pluvinel*, 1623). It is through this "maneige" or exercises that the horse is molded to accept the guidance of the rider. The medieval French word "dresser" refers to preparing, or readying something—hence the word "dressage" for this kind of equine training. Writing to King Henry III of France, Pluvinel tells the king, "Your majesty will be able to control them with the aids of the thighs alone, and somewhat of the tongue, which is the spur of the mind and which we use to make the horse rise on his hind quarters." The whole apparatus of physical control—spurs, switches, ropes—gives way to an art of cooperation and coordination, which at times is presented almost as symbolic of a ruler's ascendancy over his subjects (*see also* EQUESTRIAN MONUMENTS).

Equitation as a supreme spectacle of art and nature in perfect unison continued to provide the theme in early 17th-century English texts: Gervase Markham's *Cavalrie; or, The English Horseman* (1607), Nicholas Morgan's *The Perfection of Horsemanship* (1609), and, as homage to Pluvinel's legacy, William Cavendish's *La Method Nouvelle et invention de dressage les chevaux* (1658).

**Further reading:** Roy Strong, *Splendor at Court: Renaissance Spectacle and the Theater of Power* (Boston, Mass.: Houghton Mifflin, 1973).

**Erasmus, Desiderius** (c. 1469–1536) *Dutch humanist scholar*

Erasmus, who was illegitimate, was probably born in Rotterdam. He entered Alexander HEGIUS's school at Deventer (1478), where, although the curriculum was still largely medieval, he made some contact with the new learning from Italy. In 1487 he joined the monastery of Steyn, near Gouda, but the monastic life was uncongenial and in 1495, as secretary to the bishop of Cambrai, he went to Paris to study theology. He found the course uninspiring and extended his reading in classical literature. In 1499 one of his private pupils, Lord Mountjoy, brought him to England, where he met John COLET at Oxford. Colet's historical approach to the Bible so stimulated Erasmus that when he returned to Paris (1500) he was determined to equip himself fully as a scholar. He learnt Greek and read widely. In 1504 he published *Enchiridion militis christiani* (Handbook of the Christian soldier), a plea to return to the simplicity of the early Church and the pristine doctrine of the Fathers. This he followed with an edition of VALLA's annotations on the New Testament (1505), thereby indicating his chosen path in scriptural criticism.

In 1506 Erasmus visited Italy as director of studies to the sons of Henry VII's physician. In 1508 he published at the ALDINE PRESS an expanded edition of his ADAGIA; the work made his European reputation. From Venice he went to Rome, where he was invited to stay, but Lord Mountjoy recalled him to England. He used his experiences to produce the satirical *Encomium Moriae* (1511; THE PRAISE OF FOLLY) with a dedication to his friend Sir Thomas MORE. Between 1509 and 1514 Erasmus was at work in London and Cambridge on his Greek New Testament and an edition of the letters of St. Jerome. He found a publisher in Johann FROBEN of Basle; both works appeared in 1516. Erasmus used only a few manuscripts of the New Testament and his edition lacked serious critical scholarship but, the COMPLUTENSIAN POLYGLOT apart, his text was the first Greek New Testament printed.

Erasmus had reached the peak of his fame. But the spread of the Reformation in northern Europe involved him in bitter controversy which clouded his later years. LUTHER felt that he detected seeds of radical criticism of the Catholic Church in Erasmus's writings, and he failed to understand how Erasmus could refuse to follow these lines of reasoning to their logical conclusion. The temperaments of the two men were fundamentally different; Erasmus was appalled at the vitriolic emotional tone of the reformers which seemed to him a negation of the reason that was God's special gift to man.

In 1517 Erasmus settled at Louvain where he worked on a second edition of his New Testament (1519). In 1521 religious persecution forced him to move to Basle where he helped Froben by editing an extensive series of patristic writers and produced the final version of his *Colloquia* (1526), a set of dialogues, started around 1500, in which he exemplified his ideal of civilized humane discussion of topical matters. He also wrote (1528) against Johann REUCHLIN on the pronunciation of ancient Greek (*see* GREEK STUDIES). In 1529 he was forced to leave Basle for Fribourg, but he returned in 1535 to die there.

Erasmus exercised a profound influence over the northern Renaissance, despite the apparent failure of his ideals. He exploited the printing press to the full and his published work runs into dozens of volumes, including editions of classical authors and the Church Fathers, manuals of prose style which show his characteristic common sense, works of moral instruction such as the *Institutio principis Christiani* (1516), and satirical squibs like the *Encomium Moriae*. The fundamental principle of Erasmian humanism is awareness and recognition of free will, from which follows the individual's responsibility for his own actions. Erasmus remained concerned to the last to spread true religion and unity in the fellowship of Christ through humane learning.

An edition of Erasmus's *Opera omnia*, edited by J. Le Clerc, in ten volumes (London, 1962), has an 11th volume containing a facsimile of the 1703–06 Leyden edition. Since 1974 the University of Toronto Press has been issuing a new English translation of all Erasmus's writings under the title *The Collected Works of Erasmus*; the earliest volumes to appear contain his highly readable letters, and the *Adages* and *Colloquia* occupy respectively vols 37–38 and 41–60. The *Encomium Moriae* was translated into English by Sir Thomas Chaloner in 1549, and this translation was reissued as vol. 257 in the Early English Text Society publications (Oxford, U.K., 1965). Betty Radice's modern English version, with introduction and notes by A. H. T. Levi, is in the Penguin Classics series (Harmondsworth, U.K., 1971). A convenient introduction to the *Adagia* is M. M. Phillips's *Erasmus on his Times* (Cambridge, U.K., 1968); there is a selection by William Barker in *The Adages of Erasmus* (Toronto, 2001).

**Further reading:** Arthur G. Dickens and Whitney R. D. Jones, *Erasmus the Reformer* (London: Methuen, 1994); James McConica, *Erasmus* (Oxford, U.K.: Oxford University Press, 1991); John Joseph Mangan, *The Life, Character, and Influence of Erasmus Derived from a Study of His Works* (Whitefish, Mont.: Kessinger, 2003).

**Erastianism** Secular control of the Church, even in ecclesiastical affairs. Erastianism is named after a Swiss theologian, Thomas Lüber (c. 1524–83), better known by his humanist pseudonym of Erastus. Erastus's *Explicatio gravissimae quaestionis* was published in London in 1589. This was a collection of theses circulated by Erastus after coming to Heidelberg in 1558 to serve as physician to the elector palatine. Initially written in defiance of attempts to impose Calvinist consistories and discipline upon the Palatinate, the *Explicatio* was employed to justify demands for greater state control of the Church during the late 16th and 17th centuries. The term is frequently but erroneously used to describe the Tudor view of ecclesiastical government, particularly under Henry VIII.

**Ercilla y Zúñiga, Alonso de** (1533–1594) *Spanish poet* Belonging to a noble family, Ercilla was born in Madrid and served Philip II as a page. He later spent seven years (1556–63) in America, serving as a captain with forces in Chile. On his return to Spain he married well and lived at court as a favorite of Philip II. His poem, *La Araucana* (Part I, 1569; Part II, 1578; complete edition, 1589), is the first important literary work to emerge from America and the greatest Spanish epic of the Golden Age. Its 37 cantos, written in *octava real* (hendecasyllabic eight-line stanzas, rhyming abababcc, a form introduced by BOSCÁN in imitation of ARIOSTO's *ottava rima*), are concerned with the Spanish capture of the Arauco valley in Chile. In itself a minor battle, in which Ercilla himself took part, the conflict is raised to epic grandeur, however, by striking descriptive passages. The Araucanian Indians and their leaders are sympathetically portrayed, courageous even in defeat. A section of the poem contains a "prophetic" passage on the battle of Lepanto.

**Ercole de' Roberti** (Ercole de Ferrara) (c. 1450–1496) *Italian painter* A native of Ferrara often confused with the Bolognese painter Ercole di Giulio Cesare de' Grandi, Ercole de' Roberti was influenced by Giovanni BELLINI and was probably a pupil of Francesco del COSSA. After assisting Cossa on the frescoes of the Palazzo Schifanoia and on the altarpiece of San Lazzaro (now destroyed) in Ferrara and the Griffoni altarpiece at Bologna (c. 1476), Ercole de' Roberti established his reputation with a large altarpiece, *Madonna Enthroned with Saints* (1480/81; Brera, Milan), painted for Sta. Maria in Porto at Ravenna. He then became court painter to the BENTIVOGLIO rulers of Bologna, in which post he executed portraits of Giovanni II and his wife Ginevra (National Gallery, Washington) before returning to Ferrara in 1486, where he succeeded Cosimo TURA as court painter to the Este family. Paintings from this last period included the *Harvest of the Manna* (National Gallery, London), a *Pietà* (Liverpool), and *The Way of the Cross* (Dresden).

**Eros** See CUPID

**Escorial** A royal palace, mausoleum, and Jeronymite monastery in central Spain. Sited northwest of Madrid, in the Guadarrama mountains, this massive complex, which constitutes the most important work of architecture of the Spanish Renaissance, was commissioned as a mausoleum for Emperor Charles V by Charles's son PHILIP II. Built between 1562 and 1584, the Escorial was originally designed by Juan Bautista de Toledo (died 1567) and completed by Juan de HERRERA. Philip himself, according to Fray José de SIGÜENZA, took a close interest in his "royal foundation of San Lorenzo del Escorial" and was responsible for many details. Juan de Herrera revised the plan under the influence of works by Serlio, Vignola, and Michelangelo—notably St. Peter's in Rome—and also redesigned the great church (1572) that stands at the center of the grid pattern of buildings. A library was added in 1592 and contains nearly 5000 manuscripts and 40,000 printed books. Paintings for the interior of the Escorial were commissioned from many notable artists, including TITIAN, TIBALDI, Federico ZUCCARO, FERNÁNDEZ DE NAVARRETE, and El GRECO. The principal sculptors employed were Leone and Pompeo LEONI. All Spanish monarchs since Charles V have been buried in the mausoleum here, with the exception of Alfonso XII.

**Further reading:** Mary Cable, *El Escorial* (New York: Newsweek Books, 1985); George Kubler, *Building the Escorial* (Princeton, N.J.: Princeton University Press, 1982;

repr. 1999); Rosemarie Mulcahy, *The Decoration of the Royal Basilica of El Escorial* (Cambridge, U.K.: Cambridge University Press, 1994).

**essay** The name adopted by MONTAIGNE for a short prose composition dealing with a single topic in a fairly subjective manner and relaxed style. Montaigne saw his own *Essais* as "attempts" to express in writing his personal reflections and experiences; they provided for their author a means of self-discovery and have preserved for posterity an intimate and comprehensive picture of the man himself—his physical appearance, moral attitudes, erudition, and philosophy. In Britain the essay form was adopted by Montaigne's contemporary Francis BACON. Bacon's pithy and compelling expositions on such universal topics as "Riches," "Deformity," "Gardens," "Friendship," and "Revenge" were immediately popular, though less intimately self-revelatory than Montaigne's essays.

## Essex, Robert Devereux, Earl of (1567–1601) *English nobleman, courtier, and soldier*

He was the elder son of Walter Devereux, 1st Earl of Essex, and achieved distinction at an early age as a soldier in the Netherlands on the expedition (1585) led by his step-father, Robert Dudley, earl of LEICESTER. After Leicester's death (1588), Essex became one of ELIZABETH I's favorites, despite the fact that in 1590 he married Frances, the widow of Sir Philip SIDNEY. Essex's sack of CÁDIZ (1596) marked the zenith of his career. The following year his expedition to the Azores was a failure, enabling his numerous enemies at court to seize the initiative. He was sent to crush a revolt in Ireland (1599) but disobeyed instructions, causing Elizabeth to imprison him briefly in the Tower of London. He then attempted to raise London against the aged queen, but the revolt failed; he was tried and executed for high treason. Essex was a considerable patron of writers, and his own poems were highly valued by his contemporaries.

## Est, Willem Hessels van See ESTIUS

## Este, Isabella d' (1474–1539) *Italian noblewoman*

She was the daughter of Ercole I d'Este (1431–1505), duke of Ferrara, who ensured that she received a thorough humanistic education. Battista GUARINO was among her tutors. In 1490 she married Gianfrancesco II Gonzaga, Marquess of Mantua, whose military prowess she complemented with her own skill in diplomacy. During her husband's frequent prolonged absences she ably protected the interests of Mantua and Ferrara against papal encroachments and after his death (1519) continued as a trusted counsellor to her eldest son, Federico II (1500–40).

Isabella is, however, chiefly remembered for the extraordinary cultural flowering she brought about in Mantua. Both she and her husband were keenly interested in choral and organ music, and their court was a major center for the development of the FROTTOLA. Isabella's music room survives in the Reggia de' Gonzaga, Mantua, decorated with wooden inlays of musical motifs by Tullio LOMBARDO. LEONARDO DA VINCI, TITIAN, MANTEGNA, RAPHAEL, GIULIO ROMANO, FRANCIA, and PERUGINO were among the artists she patronized. CASTIGLIONE, ARIOSTO, TRISSINO, Mantovano (Battista SPAGNOLI), and BANDELLO were beneficiaries of her literary patronage.

## Este family

A dynasty powerful in northern Italy from the 13th century, when Obizzo II became perpetual lord of Ferrara (1264), despite papal claims to the title. Este power was considerably extended by Niccolò III (lord 1393–1441), by Borso (lord 1450–71), who became duke of Modena and Reggio (1452) and duke of Ferrara (1471), and by Ercole I (duke 1471–1505), who allied his family by marriage with the royal line of Naples and with the BENTIVOGLIO, GONZAGA, and SFORZA families. Ercole I encouraged the arts; he beautified Ferrara, patronized ARIOSTO, and invited the Flemish composer OBRECHT to his court. His daughters by Eleonora of Aragon, Isabella (*see* ESTE, ISABELLA D') and Beatrice (1475–97), carried the Ferrarese enthusiasm for music, art, and literature to their husbands' courts, Isabella to Mantua and Beatrice to Milan. Other Este patrons of the arts included Niccolò II (lord 1361–88), who built the Castello Estense, Alberto V (lord 1388–93), who founded the university of Ferrara, and Leonello (lord 1441–50) who was educated by GUARINO DA VERONA and encouraged scholars and artists, among them ALBERTI, VERONESE, PISANELLO, Jacopo BELLINI, van der WEYDEN, and MANTEGNA. In 1502 Alfonso I (duke 1503–34) married as his second wife Lucrezia BORGIA; in their time the Ferrarese court was renowned for its brilliance. The tradition of patronage of the arts continued in later generations of the family: for instance, Cardinal Luigi d'Este employed the famous madrigal composer Luca MARENZIO in the 1580s. When Alfonso II (duke 1559–97) died without an heir the papacy recovered Ferrara, but a junior Este branch continued to rule Modena and Reggio.

## Estienne press (Latin *Stephanus*)

The press established by a dynasty of scholar-printers who worked in Paris and Geneva from 1502 to 1674. The first was Henry I Estienne (died 1520), whose widow married his partner, Simon de Colines. He in turn trained his stepson Robert (1503–59) who took over the press in 1526, later receiving the royal appointment to Francis I of France. Robert's Latin thesaurus (1531; enlarged edition 1543) was followed by several bilingual dictionaries, while his editions of the Bible, including a Greek/Latin New Testament (1551), the first to divide the chapters into numbered verses, combined his scholarship and his Christianity. In the 1540s five priced catalogues of his books were issued.

Robert's Calvinist sympathies took him to Geneva in 1550, while his brother Charles (1504–64) continued printing in Paris. Charles was a man of extensive learning, compiler of the popular *Praedium rusticum* (1554) collection of agricultural tracts and author of the first French encyclopedia (1553) and of the anatomical textbook *De dissectione* (1548). There he was followed by his nephew Robert II (1530–71), who also became a royal printer in 1564. In Geneva Robert I was succeeded by his sons Henry II (1528–98), who brought out a Greek thesaurus (1572) to match his father's Latin one, and Francis (1537–82). His grandson Paul (1567–1627), son of Henry II, eventually returned to Paris, where his son Antoine (died 1674) was the last of the dynasty and another royal printer.

The Estienne books combined scholarship and good design in a long series of 16th-century classical editions, from the Paris complete Cicero to the Geneva first editions of Anacreon and Plutarch.

**Estius (Willem Hessels van Est) (1542–1613)** *Dutch Roman Catholic martyrologist and commentator*
He was born at Gorinchem (Gorcum), educated at Utrecht, and from 1561 studied at Louvain under Michel Baius (*see* BAIANISM). From 1582 he was professor of theology at Douai, becoming chancellor of the university in 1595. His history of the martyrs of Gorcum (killed by the Protestants) appeared in 1603. He was the author of commentaries on the works of Peter Lombard, the epistles of St. Paul, and the catholic epistles (i.e. the letters of James, Peter, John, and Jude not addressed to specific churches), and also made notes for an edition of St. Augustine. His zeal against the Protestants was such that it led him to defend the murder of WILLIAM THE SILENT, Prince of Orange (1584).

**etching** *See* ENGRAVING

**Eugenius IV (1383–1447)** *Pope (1431–47)*
Born in Venice as Gabriele Condulmaro, Eugenius followed Pope Martin V's example in battling for restoration of papal supremacy over the Church. In December 1431 he attempted to exert this authority by adjourning the Council of BASLE and ordering its members to reassemble at some later date in Bologna. The council refused to adjourn and reasserted the counter-claim of conciliar supremacy. Eugenius gave way and in 1433 withdrew the decree of dissolution. In 1434 riots in Rome compelled him to flee to Florence, which remained his headquarters for nine years; in this time he met many leading writers and artists. Eugenius decreed the dissolution of the council again in September 1437 and ordered its removal to Ferrara to discuss the possibility of reconciliation with the Greek Church. In consequence, those who remained in council at Basle deposed Eugenius (1439) and elected in his place Duke Amadeus VIII of Savoy as Pope Felix V (1439–49). In the same year Eugenius succeeded in passing a short-lived act of union between Greek and Roman churches, thus increasing his own prestige and undermining that of the council. Although he did not succeed in getting rid of the antipope, he did manage to return to Rome (1443), where he died.

Despite the upheavals of his papacy, Eugenius found time to be a patron of humanist learning. He reestablished the university of Rome in 1431, and Leon Battista ALBERTI, Poggio BRACCIOLINI, and Flavio BIONDO were among those whom he employed in the Curia.

**Euphuism** The English prose style that took its name from the romance *Euphues* (1578, 1580) by John LYLY. Its principal characteristic is the elaborate patterning of sentences by means of antithesis, alliteration, and similar rhetorical devices. It also makes heavy use of mythological and other allusions. A typical example is the metaphor used by Philautus: "as the fish Scolopidus in the flood Araris at the waxing of the Moon is as white as the driven snow, and at the waning as black as the burnt coal, so Euphues, which at the first increasing of our familiarity was very zealous, is now at the last cast become most faithless." This highly artificial shaping of prose was a radical departure from the rambling constructions of Lyly's contemporaries and set a considerable fashion.

**Eustachio, Bartolommeo (1520–1574)** *Italian anatomist*
Born the son of a physician at San Severino, Eustachio followed his father in his choice of career. He was initially physician to the duke of Urbino and to his brother Cardinal Giulio DELLA ROVERE, and then (1549) moved to Rome where he taught at the papal college, being appointed professor of anatomy in 1562. In his best-known work, *Opuscula anatomica* (1564), Eustachio described the anatomy of the ear, identifying the eponymous Eustachian tube which joins the middle ear to the nasopharynx. The work also contained a description of the kidney in which Eustachio provided the first published account of the adrenal glands. Much of the impact of Eustachio's work, however, was lost by the absence of the illustrative plates. Discovered many years after his death, they were finally published in 1714.

**Eworth, Hans (Hans Ewoutsz.) (c. 1515–c. 1574)** *Flemish portrait painter*
Eworth was born in Antwerp and may possibly be identified with the "Jan Euworts" mentioned as a freeman of the St. Luke guild in that city in 1540; however, his fame dates from his arrival in the late 1540s in England, where he spent the rest of his life. The earliest of his dated paintings, signed with his monogram HE, is from the year 1549. Thirty-five portraits can either definitely or proba-

bly be attributed to him, many of them of Roman Catholic notables in the circle of Mary I. He was also a painter and designer for court fêtes. His early allegorical picture of Sir John Luttrell (1550; Coutauld Institute, London) shows the influence of the FONTAINEBLEAU painters; later paintings are more reminiscent of Holbein and Clouet. His masterpiece is the double portrait traditionally identified as Frances Brandon, Duchess of Suffolk, and her second husband and erstwhile secretary, Adrian Stokes (1559; private collection); a more plausible theory is that they are Mary, Baroness Dacre, and her son Gregory, 10th Baron Dacre.

**exploration** The Renaissance era was the heyday of exploration by European adventurers. During the 15th and 16th centuries, explorers from the leading European merchant nations traversed all the major seas and plotted their coastlines. Much of early Renaissance exploration was inspired by medieval tales of Prester John, the legendary African Christian king with hoards of treasure, and by the travels (1271–92) of Marco Polo, who reported on the riches of the Orient.

Although individuals like Fernão PINTO and Matteo RICCI made epic journeys by land, Renaissance explorers were predominantly mariners, sponsored by monarchs and merchants to establish trading links with Asia. The Portuguese were the first great nation of explorers. Using developments in navigational instruments and CARTOGRAPHY, they drew inspiration from the enthusiasm of Prince HENRY THE NAVIGATOR. Although serious exploration down the West African coast began in the early 15th century, it was not until 1488 that DIAZ rounded the Cape of Good Hope and turned northeast along the African coastline. In the same year COVILHÃ reached India via the "overland" route, although Vasco da GAMA did not open up the southern sea route to India until 1498.

By the mid-15th century the Spaniards had developed an interest in exploration. In 1474 an Italian named Paolo del Pozzo Toscanelli advocated sailing west to Asia—a theory based on Ptolemy's notions about the extent of the Asian land mass. The Spaniards adopted this theory and sponsored Christopher COLUMBUS, who made landfall on the Caribbean islands in 1492, believing them to be outposts of Asia. It was 20 years before the existence of America as a separate continent was established and, consequently, the intervening years saw an extensive search for a strait through America to the Orient. This meant that the east coast of America was extensively mapped within 10 years, as various explorers searched for the supposed passage north or south from the Caribbean. The first atlas of the Americas was produced by Cornelis Wytfliet in 1597.

Although the treaty of TORDESILLAS (1494) gave both Spain and Portugal spheres of influence in the Caribbean, the Spanish made best use of their opportunities, while the Portuguese continued to favor eastern routes to Asia.

By 1519 Spain had established Panama as a base for incursions into the South American mainland. Rapid colonization followed, and with it came riches beyond the wildest dreams of the explorers (see PIZARRO, FRANCISCO). Based on Hispaniola in the Caribbean, the Spaniards were well placed to explore the new continent. Juan Díaz de Solis discovered the Rio de la Plata in 1516, and CABRAL discovered the delta of the Amazon, which was navigated by Francisco de Orellana in 1542. By 1600 coastal mapping of South America was complete.

In 1521 Magellan's lieutenant del CANO achieved the first circumnavigation of the globe after Magellan had persisted with a southerly course down the coast of South America until he passed through the strait that bears his name. As exploration became global, England, Holland, and France slowly adopted increasingly active exploration policies. Although Sebastian CABOT and Jacques CARTIER made pioneering attempts to find a direct route to the Orient by searching for a NORTHWEST PASSAGE, it was not until the late 16th century that men such as LINSCHOTEN and HAKLUYT inspired widespread northern European interest in exploration. France and Holland undertook trading ventures in the Far East, while Hakluyt's *Principall Navigations* ignited exploration fever in England. The 1550s had seen England's initial search for a NORTHEAST PASSAGE and the establishment of valuable trade links with Russia (see MUSCOVY COMPANY). Between 1576 and 1578 Francis DRAKE retraced Magellan's famous voyage. He confirmed that the Atlantic and Pacific oceans met and explored the southern Pacific and the west coast of America. By the end of the Renaissance period, the explorers of the age had sailed and charted most of the world except for its farthest extremities and "the Great Southern Continent" (Australia).

**Further reading:** Peter T. Bradley, *The Lure of Peru: Maritime Intrusion into the South Sea, 1598–1701* (London: Macmillan and New York: St. Martin's Press, 1989); John H. Elliott, *The Old World and the New, 1492–1650* (Cambridge, U.K.: Cambridge University Press, 1970; new ed. 1992); John R. Hale, *Renaissance Exploration* (London: BBC, 1968; New York, 1972); Angus Konstam, *A Historical Atlas of Exploration* (New York: Checkmark, 2000); Kenneth Nebenzahl, *Atlas of Columbus and the Great Discoveries* (Chicago, Ill.: Rand McNally, 1990), as *Maps from the Age of Discovery: Columbus to Mercator* (London: Times Books, 1990); John H. Parry, *The Age of Reconnaissance: Discovery, Exploration and Settlement, 1450–1650* (Cleveland, Ohio: World and London: Weidenfeld & Nicolson, 1963; new ed. London: Phoenix, 2000); Boies Penrose, *Travel and Discovery in the Renaissance* (Cambridge, Mass.: Harvard University Press, 2nd ed. 1955); Günter Schilder, *Australia Unveiled: The Share of the Dutch Navigators in the Discovery of Australia* (Amsterdam: Theatrum Orbis Terrarum, 1976).

explosives  See GUNPOWDER

**Eyck, Hubert van** (died 1426) and **Jan van** (active c. 1422–1441) *Dutch painters*

Almost nothing is known of Hubert van Eyck, except that he was apparently Jan's elder brother and that both artists were born at Maaseyck and contributed to the GHENT ALTARPIECE. Jan is first documented at the court of the count of Holland at the Hague in 1422. In 1425 he was appointed court painter to PHILIP THE GOOD, Duke of Burgundy, at Bruges. He was highly esteemed by his master, who sent him on secret missions and embassies to Spain and Portugal, intervened when the ducal exchequer sought to reduce his salary, presented his children with baptismal gifts, and, finally, assisted his widow. Within a few years of his death, Jan's fame had reached almost legendary proportions as far afield as Italy; in the following century Vasari praised him as the "inventor" of oil painting. While this is not strictly true, Jan certainly grasped the new medium's potential for rendering effects of light and texture with a fidelity previously unimaginable.

The remarkable verisimilitude of Jan's technique was partially anticipated by earlier Franco-Flemish manuscript illuminators, but it is unlikely that he began his career as a miniaturist. The famous miniatures from the Turin-Milan Hours, which are sometimes believed to be his earliest works, are, more probably, late productions from his workshop. Jan's stunning technical virtuosity appears, already fully developed, in his earliest surviving panel paintings, such as the Berlin *Madonna in a Church* and the Washington *Annunciation*, both of which probably date from the 1420s. The latter includes numerous sculptural and architectural details which portray religious scenes related to the Annunciation. This "disguised symbolism" became a recurrent device in early Netherlandish painting, but Jan was its greatest and most sensitive exponent. The accurate forms of Romanesque and Gothic architecture with which Jan evoked the contrast between the Old and New Testaments imply a level of antiquarian research in advance even of contemporary Florentine artists.

Although the two brothers' respective contributions to the Ghent altarpiece (1432) have yet to be disentangled, the great polyptych has certain stylistic anomalies suggestive of two different hands. It seems probable that Hubert established the ambitious iconographic program of the altarpiece and painted much of its interior before his death. Between 1426 and 1432 Jan probably reworked some of his brother's panels and painted most, if not all, of the exterior. The seeds of much of Jan's subsequent artistic development are to be found in this compendium, which is the most significant northern altarpiece of the 15th century.

Jan's slightly later *Madonna of Chancellor Rolin* (Paris) includes a breathtaking panorama of a city. His *Arnolfini Wedding* (1434; London; see Plate V) records the making of a marriage vow and may have a quasi legal significance as a form of pictorial "wedding certificate." The tiniest details are painted with an almost microscopic accuracy both in this painting and the 1436 *Madonna of Canon van der Paerle* (Bruges), although the latter also reveals a new monumentality and simplification of form. Jan also painted a series of independent portraits, such as that of his wife (1439; Bruges), which are remarkable for their dispassionate naturalism. The monumentality of his conceptions belies the fact that most of his pictures are quite small; for example, the Antwerp *Virgin by the Fountain* (1439) measures less than eight by five inches. Jan's closest follower was Petrus CHRISTUS, who may have completed some pictures apparently unfinished at his master's death. Generally, however, the style of Rogier van der WEYDEN was more easily assimilated and was consequently more influential upon subsequent Netherlands painters. Although too demanding to be readily emulated, Jan's method established a permanent standard of excellence. His paintings, more than those of any other artist, defined the outlook and priorities of northern painters before DÜRER.

**Further reading:** Craig Harbison, *Jan van Eyck: The Play of Realism* (London: Reaktion Books, 1991).

# F

**Faber, Johann** (1478–1541) *German theologian*
Faber was born at Leutkirch near Memmingen and studied at Tübingen and Fribourg. In 1518 he joined the diocesan bureaucracy of the bishop of Constance. At first he sympathized with the reformers, especially with his friend ERASMUS, but later he became a strong supporter of the old order; his knowledge of philosophy and science was valuable to his side in the debate. His treatise *Malleus in haeresim Lutheranam* (1524) earned him the nickname of "hammer of the heretics." Among his diplomatic missions was the occasion when the future Emperor Ferdinand I sent him to England to enlist the support of HENRY VIII against the Turks. From 1530 Faber was bishop of Vienna.

**Faber Stapulensis** See LEFÈVRE D'ÉTAPLES, JACQUES

**Fabricius, Girolamo** (Fabricius ab Aquapendente) (1537–1619) *Italian anatomist*
A student of FALLOPPIO at Padua, Fabricius followed him as professor of anatomy in 1565. He is best known for his *De venarum ostiolis* (On the valves of veins; 1603) in which he published the first description of these valves. The work had a profound influence on his most famous pupil, William HARVEY, the discoverer of the circulation of the blood. Fabricius also worked extensively in the field of embryology, paying particular attention in his *De formato foetu* (1600) to evidence derived from a wide variety of species. He remained nonetheless an Aristotelian, concerned predominantly with the analysis of embryological development in terms of material, efficient, formal, and final causes. It was consequently within this framework that Fabricius, in his *De formatione ovi et pulli* (On the formation of the egg and chick; 1612), sought to understand the embryology of the chick.

*facetiae* (Latin, "jests") Humorous, often indecent, anecdotes and stories, akin to the medieval *fabliaux*, which circulated in Latin among the humanist scholars of the Renaissance. Poggio BRACCIOLINI's *Facetiae* or *Liber facetiarum*, the chief butts of which were the monastic orders and the secular clergy, was the first and one of the most popular books in the genre. Although *facetiae* were predominantly a neo-Latin genre, they also occur in German as *Fazetien*, and a bilingual Latin-German collection was published in 1486.

**faenza** (French **faïence**) The type of MAJOLICA that takes its name from the Italian town of Faenza, midway between Bologna and Rimini, which between 1450 and 1520 had about 40 active potteries. The most famous of these was the Ca' Pirota. Faenza products were reputed for excellent painting and the use of a fine red color. Arabesques, grotesques, and trophies *en camaieu* on blue or yellow grounds are usual. Plate backs carry concentric circles or spirals in lapis blue on pale blue.

*Faerie Queene, The* An epic poem by Edmund SPENSER. Probably begun shortly before 1580, it was left incomplete at the poet's death, with only six books and a fragment of a seventh, out of a projected 12, having been written. The first three books appeared in 1590, the second three in 1596. The poem is composed in a nine-line stanza with a demanding rhyme scheme, the so-called Spenserian stanza. Spenser's language is notable for its archaisms. The poem is dedicated to Queen Elizabeth and in one sense is an elaborate tribute to her; it is also a complicated allegory, functioning on both moral and political levels, with each book narrating the adventures of a particular knight, representing one of the 12 moral virtues. Thus the first book concerns the Red Cross Knight, or holiness, who has to liberate himself from the wiles of Duessa (the Roman Catholic Church and, on one level, Mary, Queen of Scots) in order to win Una, or truth.

**Further reading:** Elizabeth Heale, *The Faerie Queene: A Reader's Guide* (Cambridge, U.K.: Cambridge University Press, rev. ed. 2002).

## Falconetto, Giovanni Maria (1468–1535) *Italian architect*
Working chiefly around Padua, Falconetto designed a number of edifices based on classical forms, notably the loggia and odeon in Padua (1524), which later became part of the Palazzo Giustiniani. He was also responsible for the much admired town gates in Padua, the Porta San Giovanni (1528) and the Porta Savonarola (1530). Falconetto was also a painter; a fresco of the *Annunciation* (1514; San Pietro Martire) and architectural frescoes (1503; Duomo) survive in his native Verona.

## Falier, Marino (1274–1355) *Venetian nobleman*
He was elected doge (1354) after many years as ambassador and naval commander. Turning against his fellow patricians, he plotted with commoners to overthrow the oligarchy, but the plot was discovered and Falier was executed. His story inspired Byron's *Marino Faliero* (1821).

## Falloppio, Gabriele (1523–1562) *Italian anatomist*
A pupil of VESALIUS at Padua, Falloppio first served as professor of anatomy at Pisa before returning in 1551 to Padua to occupy the chair once held by his teacher. In his only published work *Observationes anatomicae* (1561), he threw considerable light on the female reproductive organs. The terms "vagina" and "clitoris" were coined and the eponymous Fallopian tubes were fully described. Despite this, he failed to identify the role of the ovaries in reproduction. Falloppio also worked on the anatomy of the head and succeeded in revealing several new structures in the ear. Before he could pursue his investigations further he died of pleurisy at the age of 40.

## families
Details on family life during the Renaissance are generally sparse, with the striking exception of Tuscany, where surviving tax records have enabled researchers to build an informative picture. Whereas in northern Europe marriage meant the formation of a new household, in Italy it did not. There the typical structure was that of the peasant family centered on the father (*capo*), in which sons remained in the house even after marriage and daughters left, either to go into service or to join their husband's households. The governing factor was economic—more

sons, more hands to work. Once the father died, the eldest son took over his role, but inheritance was shared between all sons. That a household might contain several brothers, each with his own family, led to a close kinship between cousins—*fratelli cugini*, "brother-cousins."

This structure was also found among the wealthier city families, but among the artisans and the poor the nuclear family was the norm; such households were smaller and shorter-lived than those of the peasants and the wealthy. Though the family unit was generally small, the sense of kinship was extensive. In times of plague and famine, it was the duty of the *capo* to take in distressed relatives; and, of course, any offense to the honor of the extended family was felt by all its members and could lead to factions and vendetta. When two members of the Pazzi family murdered the brother of Lorenzo de' Medici, six members of the family were executed, the rest of the males imprisoned or exiled, the females sent to convents, and all the family property put up for auction by the state (*see* PAZZI CONSPIRACY). A man's actions had consequences for all his relations.

Sons customarily inherited an equal share of the paternal estate, but daughters were excluded from inheritance. Instead they were dowered—invested with property and/or money to a value that reflected the family's wealth and status. Among the merchant and wealthier classes, it was almost impossible for a girl without a dowry to marry, and the "dowerless" girl became an object of charity. The dowry always remained the woman's property and when she was widowed she was expected either to marry again immediately or to return to her own family with her dowry. Even among the peasants and poor, a girl would be expected to take something to the husband's household, even if it was only bed linen and the products of her own needlework—a custom that has survived into modern times. The fabrics, linens, and embroideries that a girl took to her husband's house were carried and stored in marriage chests called CASSONE, often painted with lively scenes from the Bible or mythology by the painters of the day.

In Italy marriage was a civic affair and was always contracted for political or economic reasons. It was expected (and as personal accounts and letters show, often the case) that love between the partners would follow marriage, but the function of marriage was the formation of an economic unit and the production of children for the continuance of the family. The Church had some say in the proceedings, and marriage was considered a sacrament, but the ceremonies took place in the households of the bride and the groom.

After the respective parties had come to an agreement through a marriage broker, a betrothal would take place and the groom would visit the betrothed in her house, often taking sight of her for the first time. A contract would be drawn up by a notary. The age of the girl could be as young as seven, but it was more usually between 10 and 16. The *matrimonium* took place in the house of the girl in the presence of a notary, with the presentation of the nuptial ring by the groom. The couple were formally asked if they consented to the marriage, after which the bride was referred to as "pledged." The bride was then transported to the house of her husband where, for the wealthy, there would be banquets lasting several days. The usual age for marriage for a girl was 17 to 18, but for men it was commonly after the age of 25; thus the age gap between spouses was about 10 years. Widowers who remarried often chose young girls, which made the gap even greater.

A married woman had two functions: to oversee the running of the house, and to be a mother. A husband would generally instruct his wife in how to manage their domestic affairs and then leave her to do so; however, he would often reserve some rooms, such as his study, for himself alone (Cosimo de' Medici famously banished his wife from his library). As to being a mother, it was a wife's duty to produce children throughout her period of fertility, though the rigors of childbirth meant that few women attained menopause. Pregnancy, confinement, birth, and churching (when, after a month or more's seclusion a woman underwent a ceremony of purification) took almost a year. The extraordinarily high birthrate was matched only by the infant mortality rate. John COLET, dean of St. Paul's, for instance, was the only surviving child of 22. Because of the periods of confinement and churching, there were fewer opportunities for conjugal relations than the birthrate figures would suggest.

Modesty prevented women from having a physician at the birth; instead they relied on midwives. The newborn was given out to a wetnurse, usually in the countryside, where it would stay for up to two years, most of that time being spent in swaddling clothes. There was much concern about the quality of milk and of the wetnurse herself. MICHELANGELO's choice of sculpture as a profession was, his distressed father claimed, the result of the boy having been raised by a stonemason's wife. Mothers, therefore, had little to do with their children until it came to the time to begin instruction in the "petties"—teaching them their letters and numbers. The role of women in the education of children before school or private tutoring has often been overlooked.

Renaissance humanism marked a changing attitude toward the child. Leon Battista ALBERTI, himself illegitimate and a celibate bachelor, wrote a treatise on the family, *Della famiglia* (1435–41; translated into English by Renée N. Watkins as *The Family in Renaissance Florence*, 1969), mapping out the laws of prudent conduct. For him the child was less an economic factor than an individual to be nurtured. Paintings reflect this, with portrayals of a more lifelike baby Jesus, and the fondness for *putti* or cherubs may represent the souls of dead infants.

The Reformation made sweeping changes to family life. Among its other effects, the model Christian life lived in CALVIN's Geneva brought a fall in the rate of illegitimacy. The elders of Geneva had a great influence on domestic life, and would call to account quarreling neighbors, spouses, or kin so as to establish a harmonious society. Engagements had to be made before witnesses and banns read in church, where the marriage ceremony had also to take place. Marriage was no longer considered a sacrament but it was under stricter control by the Church. The loss of sacramental status technically made divorce possible, though it was rare. With the great reduction in holy days, the responsibility for Christian worship fell on the father of the family rather than on the local priest. "Every individual family must be a small separate church," wrote Calvin. For women under the reformed dispensation there could be no religious life in a convent or, indeed, outside the home.

**Further reading:** Richard W. Barber, *The Pastons: A Family in the Wars of the Roses* (London: Folio Society, 1981); Gene Adam Brucker, *Giovanni and Lusanna: Love and Marriage in Renaissance Florence* (Berkeley, Calif.: University of California Press, repr. 1988); Muriel St. Clare Byrne (ed.), *The Lisle Letters*, 6 vols (Chicago, Ill.: University of Chicago Press, 1981); Norman Davis (ed.), *The Paston Letters: A Selection in Modern Spelling* (Oxford, U.K.: Oxford University Press, 1983); Joanne Marie Ferraro, *Marriage Wars in Late Renaissance Venice* (Oxford, U.K.: Oxford University Press, 2001); Frances and Joseph Gies, *Marriage and Family in the Middle Ages* (New York, Harper & Row, 1987); David Herlihy and Christine Klapisch-Zuber, *The Tuscans and their Families: A Study of the Florentine Catasto of 1427* (New Haven, Conn. and London: Yale University Press, 1985); David I. Kertzer and Marzio Barbagli (eds), *Family Life in Early Modern Times, 1500–1789* (New Haven, Conn.: Yale University Press, 2001); Christine Klapisch-Zuber, *Women, Family and Ritual in Renaissance Italy* (Chicago, Ill. and London: University of Chicago Press, 1985); Iris Origo, *The Merchant of Prato: Francesco di Marco Datini* (London: Cape, 1957; new ed. Boston, Mass.: Godine, 2002).

**Family of Love** (Latin **Familia Caritatis**, Dutch **Huis der Liefde**) An obscure group of ANABAPTISTS founded (c. 1540) by Hendrik Niclaes (Henry Nicholas; c. 1502–c. 1580) in the Netherlands. Niclaes, who had apparently begun life as a Roman Catholic in Münster, went to Amsterdam (c. 1531) after suffering imprisonment for heresy, and while there received what he interpreted as a divine command to establish a new sect. He lived in Emden in the period 1540–60, during which time he wrote numerous books, all of which were placed on the INDEX LIBRORUM PROHIBITORUM. Despite this, he attracted a sizeable following in Holland. The Family of Love, however, became best established in England during the second half of the 16th century through to the end of the 17th. A pantheistic and antinomian sect, the Familists were persecuted by Elizabeth I during the 1580s but survived and spread, enjoying a revival of popularity during the 1650s before being amalgamated into other dissenting bodies toward the end of the century.

**Further reading:** Christopher W. Marsh, *The Family of Love in English Society, 1550–1630* (Cambridge, U.K.: Cambridge University Press, 1993).

## Fancelli, Domenico di Alessandro (1469–1519) *Italian sculptor*

A native of Settignano, near Florence, Fancelli was one of the first sculptors to introduce the ideals of the Italian Renaissance into Spain. He executed most of his work at Carrara but frequently visited Ávila and Granada to install his pieces. His major works include the tombs of Cardinal Hurtado de Mendoza (1509; Seville cathedral), of Prince John (1511; San Tomás, Ávila), and of Ferdinand II and Isabella I (1517; Chapel Royal, Granada). He died at Zaragoza.

## Farel, Guillaume (1489–1565) *French Swiss reformer*

Born at Gap, he studied in Paris and taught Greek and philosophy there. In 1521 he was converted to the reformed faith and soon fled to Basle (1524). He preached in several towns in and near Switzerland, attended a synod of the Waldensians (Vaudois), and settled in Geneva, where he invited CALVIN to join him in 1536. Both were expelled (1538) for refusing to impose the Zwinglian doctrines embodied in the usages of Berne on the Genevan church; Farel spent the rest of his life at Metz and Neuchâtel (where he died), with occasional visits to Geneva, to which Calvin had returned in 1541. His writings were extensive, but marred by hasty composition. His *Maniere et fasson* (1533) was the first reformed liturgy in French.

## Farnaby, Giles (c. 1560–1640) *English composer*

He was born into a musical family in Truro, Cornwall, but little is known of his life beyond that he was a joiner and worked mainly in London. Farnaby was one of the greatest keyboard composers of his time. He studied music at Oxford and graduated in 1592. He was a contributor to Thomas Ravenscroft's *Psalms* (1621) and is included in Thomas East's *Whole Booke of Psalmes* (1592). Farnaby also wrote a number of four-voice canzonets. His best work, however, was for the virginal, and 52 of his pieces, including one for two virginals (the earliest known for two keyboard instruments), are in the FITZWILLIAM VIRGINAL BOOK. Farnaby's most individual works are his "genre pieces," such as *Farnaby's Dreame* and *His Humour*, which show his mild disdain for contrapuntal elaboration.

## Farnese, Alessandro (1545–1592) *Duke of Parma (1586–92)*

He was the son of Duke Ottavio Farnese of Parma and Margaret, the illegitimate daughter of Emperor Charles V (*see* MARGARET OF PARMA). Brought up in Spain, Farnese accompanied his uncle, Don JOHN OF AUSTRIA, to LEPANTO and then (1577) was sent to reinforce him in the Netherlands. On Don John's death (1578) Farnese succeeded him as governor-general and proved to be an astute diplomat, winning the discontented Catholic nobles of the southern provinces over to the Spanish cause under the treaty of Arras (1579). Combining diplomacy with military skill, Farnese won back the lost Hapsburg territories, with the exception of Holland and Zeeland. He captured Antwerp in 1585 after a famous siege, but Spanish energies were then dissipated in preparations for the attack on England (*see* SPANISH ARMADA) and the Dutch, under MAURICE OF NASSAU, regained confidence. A sortie into France (1590) to assist Paris against the forces of Henry of Navarre (HENRY IV) further weakened Farnese's position and he was now fighting the Dutch in the north and the French Protestants in the south. Worn out, he died near Arras.

## Farnese, Palazzo

A Roman palace commissioned by Cardinal Alessandro Farnese (later Pope PAUL III) and designed in the Florentine style by Antonio da SANGALLO the Younger. Building began in 1517; after Sangallo died (1546) MICHELANGELO became the chief architect, introducing a number of alterations in the mannerist style. In the 1560s Giacomo da VIGNOLA took charge of the works, continuing until his death in 1573, when Giacomo DELLA PORTA took over, completing the building in 1589. The interior of the palace was decorated with frescoes by Annibale CARRACCI, notably the Galleria, which was decorated with mythological scenes. The palace is now occupied by the French embassy.

## Farnese family

A family from central Italy who ruled Parma and Piacenza from 1545 to 1731. From the 12th century the family had served the papacy in war and they owed their political power to Alessandro Farnese who became PAUL III (pope 1534–49) and made his son, Pierluigi (1503–47), duke of Parma and Piacenza. Pierluigi's eldest son, Cardinal Alessandro Farnese (1520–89), supported the arts and scholarship and completed the Palazzo FARNESE. Pierluigi's second son, Ottavio (1521–86), married Charles V's illegitimate daughter, Margaret (*see* MARGARET OF PARMA); their son, Alessandro FARNESE, was an outstanding general. When the last Farnese duke died without an heir (1731) the duchy passed to Don Carlos of Spain.

**Further reading:** Clare Robertson, *"Il Gran Cardinale": Alessandro Farnese Patron of the Arts* (New Haven, Conn. and London: Yale University Press, 1992).

**Farnesina, Villa** A villa outside Rome, built for the Sienese banker Agostino CHIGI. A fine example of Renaissance architecture, the villa was constructed between 1509 and 1521 by Baldassare PERUZZI, decorated by RAPHAEL and SODOMA, and set in gardens that reached to the bank of the Tiber. The building's two stories were divided into equal bays by Tuscan pilasters, while the exterior walls were also covered with fresco decorations. The villa acquired its modern name after its purchase (1580) by the great patron of the arts Cardinal Alessandro Farnese.

**Farrant, Richard** (c. 1528–1580) *English composer*
He appears to have joined the Chapel Royal under Edward VI and retained his post under Mary I, but resigned in 1564 to direct the music at St. George's Chapel, Windsor. He was appointed master of the Chapel Royal choristers in 1569, and kept his position as well as that in Windsor until his death. A service and three anthems are all that remain of his church music. Although not numerous, his works were popular and survive in a large number of sources. Farrant formed a dramatic company from the Windsor choristers; he wrote several plays, none of which survives.

**Fauchet, Claude** (c. 1530–c. 1602) *French magistrate and historian*
After studying law in his native Paris and in Orleans, Fauchet embarked on a successful legal career, rising to the office of president of the *cour des monnaies* (1581). He also made his name as a historian with such works as *Antiquités gauloises et françaises* (1579–1602) and *Recueil de l'origine de la langue et poésie française* (1581), a major contribution to French literary history. Forced to leave Paris after the JOURNÉE DES BARRICADES (1588), Fauchet returned in 1594 to find his library pillaged and his fortune ruined. He died in poverty.

**Faust, legend of** The story of a theologian whose thirst for knowledge leads him to sorcery and a pact with the Devil. In 1587 the Frankfurt printer Johann Spies published the anonymous and immediately popular *Historia von D. Johann Fausten*. Little is known about the historical George Faust (or Sabellicus; c. 1480–1540), a scholar and quack whose presence is recorded at various German universities in the early 16th century. Tales of his exploits combined with material from elsewhere (such as the motif of the pact with the Devil and the contemporary interest in witchcraft) to produce a legend that has resounded in literature ever since. Faust's demonic companion, Mephistopheles, for 24 years shows him the world and its pleasures, helps him with magic pranks (an important element in comic treatments of the theme), brings him Helen of Troy as his mistress—and ultimately claims his soul. The power of the legend lay in its combination of Re-

naissance and Reformation ideas. It is the ungodly arrogance of Faust's intellectual curiosity (and especially his interest in the pagan classical world) which in the eyes of the moralizing Lutheran author merits his damnation. The *Historia* was translated into English before 1592 and inspired MARLOWE's tragedy *Dr Faustus*.

**Further reading:** Eliza M. Butler, *The Fortunes of Faust* (Cambridge, U.K., Cambridge University Press, 1952; new ed. Stroud, U.K.: Sutton, 1998).

**Fedele, Cassandra** (1465–1558) *Venetian writer, orator, and humanist*
Her scholarly father encouraged her studies in Latin, Greek, classics, philosophy, and rhetoric. Her ability to conduct intellectual dialogues led to her presentation of a Latin oration at Padua university in 1487, and the beginning of an exchange of letters with leading European religious and secular scholars, as well as FERDINAND II AND ISABELLA I of Spain. Her humanist studies were cut short by her marriage (c. 1497) and five years (1515–20) spent living on Corfu. Her husband died after the couple's return to Venice, and, although she gave an oration before the Venetian Senate in 1521, Fedele's life thereafter was taken up with supporting her widowed mother and other relatives. Her appeal for financial assistance from the pope brought an appointment as lay matron of a Venetian orphanage. She delivered her last public oration at age 91, again before the Venetian Senate, to the queen of Poland. Ninety-nine of her many letters written before her marriage were published posthumously as *Epistolae et orationes* (1636).

**Feliciano, Felice** (1433–c. 1479) *Italian epigraphist, antiquary, and calligrapher*
Feliciano was born in Verona. At some time in the 1460s he devised a way to form monumental Roman capitals on mathematical rules derived from the study of ancient inscriptions at Rome, Ravenna, and elsewhere; a collection of these, dedicated to MANTEGNA, has survived in manuscript. The effect of these studies can be seen in inscriptions on many Renaissance commemorative statues. He also wrote a number of calligraphic manuscripts in a hand that exercised a considerable influence over later manuals of penmanship. His interest in antiquities earned him the name "L'Antiquario." He also wrote poetry in the vernacular, and his interests included printing and alchemy, the latter causing him to spend much time and money on the search for the philosopher's stone.

**Feltre, Vittorino da** See VITTORINO DA FELTRE

**Ferdinand I** (1503–1564) *Holy Roman Emperor (1558–64)*
Ferdinand was born at Alcalá de Henares, the younger brother of Emperor CHARLES V, whose career and person-

ality overshadowed his own. In 1521 Ferdinand married Anna of Hungary, and Charles granted him extensive territories in central Europe, in which Ferdinand acted as his brother's representative. At Vienna, which he made his capital from 1530, he gathered around him a circle of scholars and artists and founded a notable collection of books and coins. In 1531 Charles rewarded Ferdinand for his loyalty with the title of king of the Romans, thus designating him heir to the empire.

After the death of Ferdinand's childless brother-in-law, Louis II of Hungary and Bohemia, at the battle of MOHÁCS, Ferdinand was elected king of both realms (1526), but a strong Hungarian nationalist party under John Zapolya resisted. War dragged on until Hungary was split between the claimants (1538), and even after Zapolya's death (1540) Ferdinand's claim was contested by Zapolya's son, supported by the Turks and other enemies of the Hapsburgs. The rise of Protestantism in the Hapsburg lands was the second main issue of Ferdinand's reign, which he attempted to handle by negotiation and compromise.

Charles's attempts to secure the imperial succession for his son (later PHILIP II of Spain) occasioned a temporary rift between the brothers around 1550, but thereafter Ferdinand increasingly took charge of imperial business. In 1555 he achieved the important religious settlement of the peace of AUGSBURG. His own short reign as emperor, following Charles's abdication (1556) was taken up with the perennial problems of Turkish encroachments and religious strife. He was succeeded by his son MAXIMILIAN II.

### Ferdinand I (Ferrante) (1423–1494) *King of Naples (1458–94)*

He was the illegitimate son of ALFONSO I of Naples (Alfonso V of Aragon), who on his death left his Aragonese possessions to his brother John and Sicily and Naples to Ferdinand. Educated by Lorenzo VALLA, Ferdinand inherited his father's enlightened attitude to patronage of the arts and scholarship, but his reign was much troubled by papal opposition (on account of Ferdinand's illegitimacy Calixtus III refused to recognize him on his accession), wars with the Turks and with the Angevin claimant to the Neapolitan throne, and baronial insurrections. He is notorious for his massacre of his nobles in 1485 after they had surrendered on Ferdinand's unequivocal promise of an amnesty. He was succeeded by ALFONSO II, his son by Isabella of Clermont.

### Ferdinand II (1452–1516) and Isabella I (1451–1504) *King of Aragon (1479–1516) and of Castile (as Ferdinand V; 1474–1516); queen of Castile (1474–1504)*

In 1469 the marriage of these two heirs to Spain's principal kingdoms prepared the way for a united Spain. While respecting the different laws and customs of their domains Ferdinand and Isabella diminished feudal and local rights and extended the authority of the crown. They quelled overmighty lords and retrieved lands lost by earlier rulers. Relying on officials personally loyal to them, they strengthened their authority through HERMANDADES, viceroys, and a reformed conciliar system. By the time Ferdinand died their territories had been extended to cover the whole Iberian peninsula except Portugal. In 1492 they completed the Christian reconquest (*Reconquista*) with the capture of Granada, the last Moorish stronghold in Spain, and went on to take Algiers in 1510. Cerdagne and Roussillon were acquired by treaty in 1493 and Navarre was conquered by Ferdinand in 1512. He had further increased his Mediterranean empire by conquering Naples in 1504, and his and Isabella's support for Christopher COLUMBUS brought Spain great wealth and vast territories in the New World.

In 1494 Pope ALEXANDER VI recognized their loyalty to the Church by proclaiming them "the Catholic Kings" ("Los Reyes Católicos"); this loyalty was principally shown by their support for the SPANISH INQUISITION which was established in 1478 under TORQUEMADA. The Inquisition was concerned with the conversion of Jews and Moors, and was ultimately responsible for the expulsion from Spain of the Jews (1492) and the Muslim Moors (1500). The Catholic Kings presided over reforms that strengthened and purified the Church in Spain.

Renaissance learning and arts were strongly encouraged in the Catholic Kings' Spain, particularly by Isabella. She herself studied Latin, and she set up within her court a grammar school for the education of the sons of the Castilian aristocracy. Her humanist endeavors were strongly supported by two of her closest advisers, the sons of the Marqués de SANTILLANA, one of whom, Pedro González de MENDOZA, founded the college of Sta. Cruz in Vallodolid, and the other, the Count of Tendilla, was responsible for bringing PETER MARTYR d'Anghiera to Spain. Her confessor, Cardinal XIMÉNES DE CISNEROS founded the university of ALCALÁ as a major bastion of Renaissance scholarship. The royal policy of encouraging the immigration of German printers led to the rapid spread of presses in a number of towns, with Valencia becoming the site of Spain's first press in 1474. The Catholic Kings' control over the output of these presses was ensured by the licensing of printed books from 1502. In the visual arts their reign saw a number of innovations, as such artists as Pedro BERRUGUETE imported new trends from Italy to challenge the earlier ascendancy of Flemish and Burgundian influence in Spanish art. Isabella's encouragement of architecture is acknowledged in the name "Isabelline" sometimes given to the early phase of the PLATERESQUE style.

When Isabella died without a son, Castile passed to her mad daughter, Joanna, who had been married (1496) to the Hapsburg heir, Philip the Handsome of Burgundy. As Ferdinand's second marriage proved childless, at his death all the domains of Ferdinand and Isabella passed to their Hapsburg grandson, Charles I of Spain (also Emperor CHARLES V).

**Further reading:** Felipe Fernández-Arnesto, *Ferdinand and Isabella* (London: Weidenfeld & Nicolson and New York: Taplinger, 1975); H. A. F. Kamen, *Spain 1469–1714: Society of Conflict* (Reading, Mass.: Addison–Wesley, rev. ed., 1995).

**Fernández, Gregório** (Gregório Hernández) (c. 1576–1636) *Spanish sculptor*
Active chiefly in Valladolid, Fernández produced numerous painted sculptures with a religious theme, many of which were intended for use in religious processions. His best pieces included dramatic figures of the dead Christ, such as that in the San Cristo monastery at El Pardo near Madrid (1605), which bore the influence of classical works as well as the Gothic tradition. Other works, which marked Fernández out as a master of baroque naturalism, include *St. Veronica* (1614), a *Pietà* (1617; Valladolid museum), and the high altar for Plasencia cathedral (1624–34).

**Fernández, Lucas** (c. 1474–1542) *Spanish dramatist and composer*
Fernández was born and educated in Salamanca, where he was professor of music from 1522. His six plays (three religious and three secular) survive in a unique copy of a single volume entitled the *Farsas y églogas* (1514). Also in this volume, the *Diálogo para cantar* (a dialogue sung between two shepherds) is the earliest example of the *zarzuela*, a type of musical play that became popular at the Spanish court in the 17th century. His best-known work is an Easter Week play *Auto de la Pasión*, written in the style of his more famous rival Juan del ENCINA.

**Fernández de Lucena, Vasco** (Valesco di Portogallo) (c. 1410–1495) *Portuguese statesman and humanist*
Lucena was born of a noble Portuguese family and went to Bologna, Italy, to study civil and canon law. He worked for Pope Eugenius IV who appointed him advocate to the consistory and he took part in the church councils of Basle and Florence. He also served three Portuguese monarchs. He corresponded in the 1430s with Poggio BRACCIOLINI, and in the anecdotal *Vite* of Vespasiano da BISTICCI he is portrayed as a quarrelsome but learned man.

**Fernández de Navarrete, Juan** (El Mudo) (c. 1526–1579) *Spanish painter*
His nickname, "El Mudo," arose from the fact that he was a deaf-mute. Fernández was born in Logroño, studied in Italy under TITIAN, and became painter to King Philip II in 1568. Philip prized him highly for the gravity and decorum of his religious paintings, exemplified in such works as his 1574 *Baptism of Christ* (Prado, Madrid). From 1576

he also helped in the decoration of the Escorial near Madrid, producing a series of altarpieces for the church there, among them a striking *Burial of St. Lawrence* (1579). He died in Toledo.

**Fernel, Jean François** (1497–1558) *French physician*
An innkeeper's son, Fernel studied medicine at the university of Paris where, in 1534, he was appointed professor of medicine. Soon afterwards he became physician to HENRY II after successfully treating his mistress, DIANE DE POITIERS. He was also responsible with his *Medicina* (1554), a work known in some 30 editions, for one of the leading medical textbooks of his day. In a more controversial work, *De abditis rerum causis* (On the hidden causes of things; 1548), he sought to develop a more rational system of medicine by denying the relevance of astrology and other occult sciences to his profession. Much earlier Fernel had published a work of geodesy, *Cosmotheoria* (1528), in which he measured the length of a degree of meridian with notable accuracy.

**Ferrabosco, Alfonso** (1543–1588) *Italian composer*
Born at Bologna into a family of musicians (his father, Domenico Ferrabosco (1513–74), was a well-known composer in Italy), Ferrabosco was first active as a musician in Rome, but by 1562 was in England in the employ of Queen Elizabeth. He traveled abroad many times, and by 1582 had entered the service of the duke of Savoy in Turin, thus breaking his promise of lifelong service to Elizabeth. Ferrabosco did much to interest English composers in Italian music; his madrigals were particularly influential, 16 of them being included in the anthology *Musica transalpina* (1588). His son, Alfonso II (c. 1575–1628), was born in Greenwich and became a violinist, teacher, and composer at the courts of James I and Charles I. He collaborated with Inigo JONES and Ben JONSON in the production of court masques and composed fantasias for viol consort.

**Ferrante** See FERDINAND I, King of Naples

**Ferrara** A northern Italian city state on a branch of the River Po. A Lombard town in the eighth century, Ferrara became an independent commune under the papacy in the 10th century. Ferrara, with its population of about 30,000 in 1500, was too small to compete politically with the larger Italian city states, but it was an important regional power and a prosperous focus of agriculture and trade.

Under ESTE rule (1264–1597), Ferrara was an important center of letters and the arts. Its university was founded in 1391. In the 15th and 16th centuries it was the home of distinguished literary figures (BOIARDO, ARIOSTO, TASSO) and artists (TURA, the DOSSI, COSSA). The 16th-century Este court was also renowned for its music, particularly its women singers, and attracted composers, such as LUZZASCHI and GESUALDO. Notable Renaissance buildings include the Castello Estense, the Palazzo di Schifanoia, and the Palazzo dei Diamanti, which takes its name from the diamond emblem of the Este on the facade. Ferrara went into decline when the papacy regained control of the city in 1598 after the death of Alfonso II d'Este without an heir.

**Further reading:** Stephen Campbell, *Cosme Tura of Ferrara: Style, Politics and the Renaissance City, 1450–1495* (New Haven, Conn.: Yale University Press, 1998); Werner L. Gundersheimer, *Ferrara: The Style of a Renaissance Despotism* (Princeton, N.J.: Princeton University Press, 1973).

**Ferrara, Council of** See FLORENCE, COUNCIL OF

**Ferrari, Gaudenzio** (c. 1475–1546) *Italian artist*
Born at Valduggia in Piedmont, Gaudenzio worked in Lombardy, Piedmont, and Milan. Early influences upon his style included those of LEONARDO DA VINCI and PERUGINO, although he also borrowed from the works of notable German artists, PORDENONE, and Lorenzo LOTTO in developing his own highly emotional approach. His earliest works were chapel decorations executed at Varallo in northern Italy, where he also painted a major fresco cycle on the life of Christ at the Sacro Monte (begun in 1517). This cycle was unusual in that it incorporated a number of terracotta figures, also by Gaudenzio, to enhance the three-dimensional effect. Other frescoes painted in Lombardy included series in San Cristoforo in Vercelli (1529–32) and for the dome of Sta. Maria dei Miracoli in Saronno (1534), which indicates the influence of CORREGGIO.

**Ferreira, António** (1528–1569) *Portuguese poet and dramatist*
He was born in Lisbon and studied at Coimbra, where he came under the influence of the humanist Diogo de Teive. His life was spent as a judge in Lisbon, where he died a victim of the plague. His poems, *Poemas lusitanos* (1598), were published by his son. A friend and the outstanding disciple of Sá de MIRANDA, Ferreira was an admirer of Virgil and Horace and wrote epigrams, epistles, eclogues, and odes as well as Petrarchan sonnets. He strongly defended the use of Portuguese (as opposed to Latin or Spanish), urging the reform of literature through the new meters (as introduced by BOSCÁN and GARCILASO DE LA VEGA) and the revival of classical models. He wrote two mediocre prose comedies, *Bristo* and *O Cioso* 1622). His *Tragedia de Dona Inês de Castro* (written after 1553; published 1586), a five-act blank-verse play based on classical Greek models and concerned with a famous historical incident, is the most important and successful tragedy of Renaissance Portugal.

**Festa, Costanzo** (c. 1490–1545) *Italian composer*
Festa's works mark the emergence of native Italian composers from the lengthy period of dominance by Flemish musicians. Festa probably came from Tuscany, and his earliest works are found in the Medici Codex of 1518, which was compiled on the marriage of Lorenzo II de' Medici, nephew of Pope Leo X. In the early 1510s Festa seems to have been employed at the French court. In 1517 he joined the papal choir in Rome, remaining a member until his death. Despite his ecclesiastical duties, Festa's historical importance is as one of the earliest madrigalists; the first publication to use the word MADRIGAL, the anthology *Madrigali de diversi musici libro primo* (1530), contains compositions by him. His madrigals are less substantial than his motets, though they show a good deal of textural variety. Some are complex in their use of counterpoint while others are consistently homophonic.

**Feuillants** Reformed Cistercians named after Les-Feuillans, near Toulouse, where their order was founded in 1577 by Abbot Jean de la Barrière (1544–1600). Encouraged by Henry III, the Feuillants were established in Paris and played a major part in the reform of the capital. By the time they were given status as an independent order (1589), the Feuillants had spread to Italy, where they were known as Bernardines. The order became less austere during the 17th century but remained influential until its demise at the end of the Napoleonic wars.

**Fiammingo, Dionisio** See CALVAERT, DENYS

**Ficino, Marsilio** (1433–1499) *Italian humanist scholar and philosopher*
Ficino was born at Figline, near Florence, and taken at an early age into the household of Cosimo de' MEDICI. In stressing the divine origins of both Christian and pagan revelations, he played a seminal role in the Renaissance process by which the inspiration of Greek and Roman antiquity, as preserved in the Platonic and Neoplatonic traditions, was absorbed and revived in the Christian world of 15th-century Europe. In 1462 he became head of the PLATONIC ACADEMY, which was based at Cosimo de' Medici's villa at Careggi. From there Ficino corresponded with admirers all over Europe, including John COLET and Johann REUCHLIN. A proficient Greek scholar, Ficino undertook a new translation of PLATO's works into Latin. This translation, completed in 1477, aroused interest in Platonism throughout Europe and remained the standard Latin text of Plato's work for over a century. Ordained priest in 1472 and appointed a canon of Florence cathedral in 1484, Ficino made explicit his defense of Platonic philosophy in a Christian context with his influential *De Christiana religione* (1476) and *Theologia Platonica* (1482), arguing in the latter his belief in the immortality of the soul. He wrote a number of biblical com-

mentaries, but his interest in mysticism, first manifested in his work on the Hermetic *Pimander* (1471), continued to play a major role in his thought; in his later years he translated PLOTINUS (1492), (pseudo-)Dionysius the Areopagite (1496/97), and Iamblichus (1497). The mystical strain in his philosophy led in 1489 to his being accused of the practice of magic, but his influential friends saved him from the usual consequences of such a charge. The bulk of his *Epistolae*, published in 1495 and covering the period 1473–94, formulate his official pronouncements on Platonic questions.

See also: NEOPLATONISM, RENAISSANCE

**Further reading:** Konrad Eisenbichler and Olga Zorzi Pugliese (eds), *Ficino and Renaissance Platonism* (Toronto, Canada: University of Toronto Press, 1998); Paul Oskar Kristeller, *Marsilio Ficino and his Work after Five Hundred Years* (Florence, Italy: Olschki, 1987); Christine Raffini, *Marsilio Ficino, Pietro Bembo, Baldassare Castiglione: Philosophical, Aesthetic, and Political Approaches in Renaissance Platonism* (New York, Peter Lang, 1998).

**Field of the Cloth of Gold** The field near Calais where FRANCIS I of France met HENRY VIII of England in June 1520. Public and private negotiations were accompanied by a lavish court spectacle and show of friendship between the two monarchs. Henry VIII was able to display himself as a great and powerful European monarch, but the meeting had little real significance. WOLSEY was already negotiating with CHARLES V and England soon joined the emperor's anti-French alliance in 1521.

***figura serpentinata*** See CONTRAPPOSTO

**Filarete** (Antonio Averlino) (c. 1400–1469) *Italian sculptor and architect*
Filarete was born in Florence. His nickname is derived from the Greek, meaning "lover of virtue," and is typical of his rather clumsy and pedantic attempts to emulate the sculpture and architecture of antiquity. His masterpiece is the huge west door of St. Peter's, Rome, cast in bronze, with enameled and gilded decoration, about 1445. A reduced version of the Roman statue of Marcus Aurelius is the earliest datable bronze statuette of the Renaissance and was presented in 1465 to Piero de' Medici, to whom in the same year Filarete dedicated one copy of his imaginative *Treatise on Architecture*. This was devoted to an ideal city named Sforzinda, after a prominent Milanese patron. His principal surviving building is the hospital in Milan (1456–65), where Lombard ornamental brickwork is combined with Brunelleschian Renaissance forms.

**Filelfo, Francesco** (1398–1481) *Italian scholar, teacher, and rhetorician*
Born at Tolentino, he studied at Padua, where he was appointed professor at age 18. In 1419 he traveled to Con-

stantinople to learn the language and acquire Greek manuscripts. There he married Theodora, daughter of his teacher John Chrysoloras. He returned to Venice (1427) with over 40 manuscripts, but was dissatisfied with his reception there and moved on, first to Bologna, then to Florence. He quarreled with the Florentine humanists and Cosimo de' Medici and had to leave the city (1434) for Siena; eventually he reached Milan (1440) where he remained, apart from a visit to Rome (1475). In 1481 he was invited back to Florence, but died there soon afterwards. Filelfo's quarrelsome temperament made him highly unpopular. Nevertheless, at the time of his death his reputation as a scholar was deservedly known throughout Italy.

**Finiguerra, Maso** (1426–1464) *Italian goldsmith, designer, and engraver*
Born in Florence, Maso was praised by VASARI and Benvenuto CELLINI as a print maker and a master of niello, a type of decorative silverwork in which silver is incised with a black metallic compound. As a young man he may have assisted GHIBERTI on the east door of the Baptistery in Florence and he was later associated with Antonio POLLAIUOLO, several of whose paintings Maso may have reproduced in a series of copperplate engravings (1459–64). Although Maso did not actually invent the process of copper engraving as Vasari claimed, he was instrumental in developing its use as an extension of niello work. Few works by Maso survive; among those that are often attributed to him are the Thewalt cross (c. 1464; Metropolitan Museum of Art, New York) and a series of engravings, the *Seven Planets*.

**Fioravanti, Aristotele** (c. 1415–c. 1485) *Italian architect and engineer*
Born in Bologna into a family of architects, Fioravanti is remembered chiefly for his spreading of Renaissance ideas throughout Europe in the course of his many travels. After work in Rome, Bologna, and Milan, and other major Italian artistic centers, Fioravanti was invited to Hungary in 1467 where he worked for a short time for King MATTHIAS CORVINUS. In 1475 he was summoned to Russia to build the cathedral of the Assumption (*Uspenskii Sobor*) on the Kremlin, combining elements of conventional Russian church architecture with features of Renaissance design. He died in Moscow.

**Fiori da Urbino** See BAROCCI, FEDERICO

**fire** For Aristotle fire was one of the four elements. Combined from the hot and the dry, it was as much a substantial part of the universe as the other elements; earth, water, and air. The assumption, however, began to be questioned by the chemists and alchemists of the Renaissance. PARACELSUS, for example, held that matter was composed of the three elements, salt, sulfur, and mercury, with sulfur serving as the element of combustibility in matter. While man cannot live, he argued, without earth, water, or air, "it is well possible for a man to be bred, and to live without fire." CARDANO was equally dismissive of Aristotelian theory. He accepted the elemental nature of earth, air, and water but insisted, perceptively, that fire was simply a mode of motion, a view repeated later by Francis BACON in his *Novum organum* (1620). It did not, however, persist; Robert Boyle (1627–91) and later generations of chemists rejected Bacon's view and argued instead for the separate existence of particles of fire.

**firearms** Portable weapons from which projectiles are fired by an explosion (*compare* CANNON). The earliest firearms, the arquebuses, emerged in the late 14th century. They were merely long, smooth-bored barrels, with a touch-hole through which a hot iron ignited the priming powder. So cumbersome were they, and so prolonged was the loading process, that they initially required the protection of an equal number of pikemen. These weapons were soon replaced by matchlocks operating on the more convenient principle of firing the gun with the aid of specially prepared, smouldering rope. The matchlock, despite such disadvantages as being difficult to fire in the rain, was unchallenged throughout the 15th century. Shortly after 1500, however, there arose competition from the wheel-lock, designed, according to one tradition, by LEONARDO DA VINCI. In this case a piece of iron was held against a spring-loaded wheel; when the trigger was pulled the wheel revolved and the resulting sparks from the iron were directed into the priming pan. The principle was simplified in the flintlock, which began to appear from about 1620 and, in one form or another, survived until the development of the percussion cap in 1807. One further improvement was the introduction of rifling in about 1500. Although used initially in hunting weapons, rifling was put to military use by Christian IV of Denmark early in the 17th century.

**Firenzuola, Agnolo (Michelangelo Girolamo)** (1493–1543) *Italian writer*
Firenzuola was born in Florence and after studying law, he became a monk in 1517. He was released from vows in 1526 after visiting the papal court in Rome, where his literary friends included ARETINO, BEMBO, DELLA CASA, and others. He returned to Florence in 1534 and spent the rest of his life as abbot of a church near Prato. His posthumously published works were widely known in manuscript during his life. He wrote two comedies, translated Apuleius (*Asino d'oro*, 1550), and wrote treatises on feminine beauty and orthography. His major works are *Ragionamenti d'amore* (Discourses on love; 1548), comprising an uncompleted group of *novelle* imitating the DECAMERON, and *Prima veste dei discorsi degli animali* (First version of the animals' discourses; 1548), a faithful

rendering of the Spanish version of tales from India, the *Panchatantra*.

**Fischart, Johann ("Der Mentzer")** (1546–1590) *German writer*
His byname might indicate that he was born in Mainz. Following several years traveling and studying in France, Holland, England, and Italy, Fischart gained his doctorate in law at Basle in 1574. For a time he worked as a proofreader for his brother-in-law, a Strasbourg printer, before taking a post as magistrate near Saarbrücken in 1580. Fischart's writings include translations and paraphrases of Greek, Latin, French, Dutch, and earlier German works, and also many didactic satires, such as *Till Eulenspiegel* (1572), a verse account of the folk hero's adventures. As a Protestant, he frequently used satire to attack the Roman Church. Although Fischart belongs in the German satirical tradition of BRANT and MURNER, his style also owes much to RABELAIS, the first book of whose *Gargantua et Pantagruel* he paraphrased in German. His most acclaimed original work is the poem *Das glückhafft Schiff von Zürich* (1576), describing a day's boat journey; it is modeled on classical epic.

**Fisher, St. John** See JOHN FISHER, ST

**Fitzwilliam Virginal Book** A manuscript collection of English Renaissance keyboard music, named for Richard, Viscount Fitzwilliam, who bequeathed it to Cambridge University in 1816. It was collated and transcribed by Francis Tregian the younger (c. 1574–1619) who copied out this and other collections while in the Fleet Prison, London, for recusancy (1609–19). Most of the composers in the volume are Catholics: William BYRD features prominently, as do Peter PHILIPS and John BULL, both then living in exile. For many years the book was known as "Queen Elizabeth's Virginal Book" owing to an error by music historian Charles Burney in his *General History of Music* (1776–89).

**Flecha, Mateo, the Younger** (c. 1530–1604) *Spanish composer and churchman*
His uncle of the same name was also a composer. He entered the service of Maria of Hungary, wife of Emperor Maximilian II, and later became her chaplain. He traveled to Italy and was also attached to the courts of Prague and Vienna. In 1568 he became abbot of Tihany in Hungary. He eventually returned to Spain in 1599, dying as abbot of a monastery there. Like his uncle, he composed *ensaladas* (literally, "salads"), compositions consisting of four-line stanzas, often utilizing material from popular songs in various poetic meters; he included some of his own work in the publication of his uncle's *ensaladas* (1581) while in Prague. Flecha also published collections of motets and madrigals (*Il primo libro de madrigali*, Venice, 1568).

**Flémalle, Master of** See CAMPIN, ROBERT

**Fletcher, Giles, the Elder** (1546–1611) *English lawyer, diplomat, and writer*
Born in Watford and educated at Eton and Cambridge, Fletcher gained his doctorate in law in 1581. From 1587 to 1605 he was remembrancer of the City of London. A diplomatic mission to Scotland (1586) was followed by one to Germany and then to Russia (1588), where he secured important concessions for English merchants, despite a hostile reception from the tsar. His frank account of *The Russe Commonwealth* (1591) was suppressed on publication on account of the English traders' fears that it would antagonize the Russians. He also wrote a cycle of sonnets entitled *Licia* (1593) and a quantity of Latin verse. His sons Giles the Younger and Phineas were also poets.

**Fletcher, Giles, the Younger** (c. 1585–1623) *English poet*
The younger son of Giles FLETCHER THE ELDER, he was born in London, went to Cambridge in 1603, and became reader in Greek grammar there in 1615. About 1618 he left Cambridge and in 1619 became rector of Alderton, Suffolk, where he spent the rest of his life. His chief work, the long devotional poem *Christ's Victorie and Triumph* (1610), acknowledges a debt to both DU BARTAS and SPENSER.

**Fletcher, John** (1579–1625) *English dramatist*
Born at Rye in Sussex, the son of a clergyman, Fletcher is remembered for his collaboration with Francis BEAUMONT; however, it is now thought that many of the plays attributed to this team were in fact the work of Fletcher alone or in conjunction with other collaborators. His earliest known independent play is the pastoral *The Faithful Shepherdess* (1608/09); before then little is known of his life. Fletcher also probably collaborated with SHAKESPEARE on *The Two Noble Kinsmen* and with Philip Massinger, William Rowley, and Thomas Middleton. One of his solo plays, *The Island Princess* (1621), written at the time that he was the main playwright for the King's Men, is the first English play set in the East Indies and addresses contemporary issues such as interracial relationships and the clash of religions that were being raised by the EAST INDIA COMPANY's oriental ventures. He is reported to have died of the plague.

**Fletcher, Phineas** (1582–1650) *English clergyman and poet*
He was born at Cranbrook, Kent, the elder son of Giles FLETCHER THE ELDER, and was educated at Eton and Cambridge. While a fellow at King's College, Cambridge (1611–16), he wrote (1614) the pastoral play *Sicelides* (1631). He became chaplain to Sir Henry Willoughby, who in 1621 presented him to the living of Hilgay in Norfolk, where he remained for the rest of his life. The contents of his volume of verse *The Purple Island...with Piscatorie Eclogs* (1633) were written in his youth. The title poem, an allegory of the human body, is strongly influenced by SPENSER, and the "Piscatorie Eclogs" trace their origin to SANNAZARO (*see also* PASTORAL).

**Florence** A city state situated on the River Arno in Tuscany, central Italy. Florence was founded as the Roman military colony of Florentia. During the late Middle Ages it developed from a small city of moneylenders and cloth manufacturers to become a major Italian power and a dominating European influence during the period of the Renaissance. Its vernacular was the basis of the modern Italian language; in political and social development it gave Europe the model of an ideal prince and the first example of a genuine bourgeoisie. The BARDI, MEDICI, and other banking and commercial houses extended their power and influence throughout Europe. In learning and the arts Florence led the Renaissance.

During the earlier years of the Renaissance Florence's achievements were made in the face of political turmoil. Throughout the 14th century it was a battleground for the conflict of GUELFS AND GHIBELLINES, and it was constantly threatened by Milanese expansionism. Its merchant oligarchy was riven by feuds and threatened by the poorer citizens, notably in the revolt of the CIOMPI (1378). By 1434 the Medici family had established their power in the city; the rich merchant families were generally prepared to accept Medici rule, which preserved the republican forms of government, gave them stability, and extended Florence's power over Tuscany, but the city did free itself briefly from the Medici for two periods during the Wars of ITALY (1494–1512; 1527–30).

Renaissance Florence was the center for such architects, painters, and sculptors as ALBERTI, BRUNELLESCHI (who designed the cathedral dome), CELLINI, DONATELLO, GHIBERTI, LEONARDO DA VINCI, MASACCIO, MICHELANGELO, UCCELLO, and VASARI. The city was also in the forefront of musical innovation in the late 16th century. The Florentine Camerata, a small academy of musicians (both amateur and professional) and intellectuals, met at the house of Count Giovanni BARDI in the 1570s and 1580s, and the patronage of Bardi and the Medici dukes played an important role in the flowering of the city's musical tradition. Alessandro STRIGGIO was one of the musical stars of the Medici court in the 1560s. At the very end of the century their protégés the composers Jacopo PERI and Giulio CACCINI wrote the earliest operas. In letters and scholarship Florence was the center of Platonic studies under FICINO, and the home of BOCCACCIO, DANTE, GALILEO, MACHIAVELLI, and PETRARCH. It was also the birthplace of the navigator Amerigo VESPUCCI.

A large and a prosperous city with close on 100,000 inhabitants in the late 15th century, Florence is famous for

**Florence** The Duomo. Work on the cathedral was begun in 1294 by Arnolfi di Cambio (died c. 1305); Brunelleschi's dome (1420) was an outstanding 15th-century technical achievement. Giotto's fine campanile (left) has a decorative scheme illustrating the attainment of divine grace, through the arts, learning, and virtue.
*Mansell/Time Life Pictures/Getty Images*

the magnificent Renaissance buildings which have survived there. These include several fine churches (Sta. Croce, the Duomo), palaces (della Signoria, Pitti, Rucellai, Strozzi, UFFIZI), and other public works (Boboli gardens, Ponte Vecchio).

**Further reading:** Gene A. Brucker, *Renaissance Florence* (New York: Wiley, 1969; new ed. Berkeley, Calif.: University of California Press, 1983); Richard A. Goldthwaite, *The Building of Renaissance Florence: An Economic and Social History* (Baltimore, Md. and London: Johns Hopkins University Press, 1980; new ed. 1990); Christopher Hibbert, *Florence: The Biography of a City* (London and New York: Penguin, 1993); George Holmes, *The Florentine Enlightenment, 1400–1450* (London: Weidenfeld & Nicolson, 1969; rev. ed. 1992); Michael Levey, *Florence: A Portrait* (London: Cape, 1996).

**Florence, Council of** The Church council that secured a short-lived reconciliation between the Western (Roman Catholic) and Eastern (Greek Orthodox) Churches and reasserted papal supremacy over the councils. It was in fact held in three cities—Ferrara (1438–39), Florence (1439–43), and Rome (1443–45). In 1437 Pope EUGENIUS IV dissolved the Council of BASLE and ordered the next assembly to meet at Ferrara. The new council was to seek a religious reconciliation with the Greeks who were soliciting support against the OTTOMAN TURKS; Ferrara was considered to be a mutually convenient location for talks. The Council of Basle, offended by the pope's command to dissolve, continued to sit, refused to recognize the Ferrara

Council when it met in 1439, deposed Eugenius, and elected in his place Felix V (antipope 1439–49).

Despite this, negotiations began with the Greek emperor, John VIII Palaeologus, and Joseph, patriarch of Constantinople, resulting in the Decree of Union, promulgated on July 6, 1439 at Florence. By this decree the Greeks accepted the Latin statement of doctrine, including the contentious *Filioque* ("and from the Son") clause in the Creed. Although some points, including the concept of papal primacy, caused much difficulty, eventually all the Greek bishops, except Mark of Ephesus, accepted its dictates, though many were to recant shortly after. Hugely advantageous to papal prestige, the decree assured popular recognition of Eugenius's primacy in the West as well as the legality of his council at Florence. The members of the schismatic Basle assembly were excommunicated for heresy, and in 1441 the Bull *Etsi non dubitemus* declared the subservience of councils to popes. The remaining work of the council was directed at attaining further unions with other Eastern churches before its dissolution in 1445.

The Council of Florence was also significant in the incidental role it played in bringing from the East scholars of the calibre of BESSARION and PLETHON, who helped inaugurate GREEK STUDIES in Italy.

**Further reading:** Joseph Gill, *Personalities of the Council of Florence* (Oxford, U.K.: Blackwell, 1964).

**Florentine Academy** See ORTI ORICELLARI; PLATONIC ACADEMY

**Florio, John** (c. 1553–1625) *English courtier and translator of Italian descent*
His father was an Italian Protestant refugee and Florio may have spent part of his youth abroad during the reign of the Catholic Mary I. He obtained the patronage of the earl of LEICESTER in the 1570s and in 1603 became reader in Italian to the queen, Anne of Denmark. His *Worlde of Wordes*, an Italian-English dictionary which appeared first in 1598, was brought out in an enlarged edition in 1611 with a dedication to the queen. He also published a well-received translation of MONTAIGNE's *Essays* (1603). In 1620 he retired to Fulham, where he died of the plague.

**Floris, Cornelis** (Cornelis de Vriendt) (c. 1514–1575) *Netherlands sculptor and architect*
A native of Antwerp and brother of Frans FLORIS, Cornelis seems to have received his initial training from one of the early Netherlands Italianist artists, possibly Pieter COECKE VAN AELST. In 1538 he was in Rome, whence he had returned to Antwerp by the following year. Floris published two volumes of engravings: one, with various adaptions of grotesque ornament, was published in 1556 and the other, with numerous designs for funeral monuments, in 1557. He executed numerous tombs, church screens, and other ecclesiastical furnishings in the Netherlands, and as far afield as north Germany and Scandinavia. However, his most famous work was the new town hall at Antwerp (1561–66), one of the key monuments of Flemish mannerist architecture. Floris's principal student was Hans VREDEMAN DE VRIES.

**Floris, Frans** (Frans de Vriendt) (1516–1570) *Netherlands painter*
The brother of Cornelis FLORIS and the most famous pupil of Lambert LOMBARD, Floris was registered as a member of the guild in his native Antwerp in 1540. Shortly afterwards he visited Rome, where he was deeply impressed by the Italian mannerists such as VASARI, SALVIATI, BRONZINO, and ZUCCARO. By 1547 he had returned home, where he worked for William the Silent and other illustrious patrons as a painter and designer of festival decorations and the like. His most famous painting, the *Fall of the Rebel Angels* (1554; Antwerp), includes numerous direct quotations from MICHELANGELO's *Last Judgment*. His own later *Last Judgment* (1565; Vienna) utilizes an expressively dynamic asymmetrical composition which suggests the influence of TINTORETTO. Floris's style represents an extremely Italianate formulation of northern MANNERISM, although his drawing has a linearity and his subject matter a sense of fantasy, both of which recall the northern late Gothic tradition. He was also capable of remarkably naturalistic portraits, of which a fine example is the *Falconer's Wife* (1558; Caen). From the mid-16th century Floris's workshop was probably the most dynamic art cen-

ter in the Netherlands with, reputedly, more than 100 pupils.

**Flötner, Peter** (active 1522–1546) *Swiss sculptor and engraver*
Born in Thurgau, Flötner moved to Nuremberg in 1522, shortly after his first journey to Italy, which he revisited soon after 1530. His Stuttgart bronze horse (c. 1520–30) seems to reflect the naturalistic trend in late Gothic, but his masterpiece, the Nuremberg Apollo fountain (1532), is an entirely classical conception. Ultimately based upon the composition of an engraving by Jacopo de' Barbari, its formal clarity is remarkable. "Local color" is confined to its base, which incorporates an agitated crowd of *putti* and sea creatures. This contrast corresponds to certain developments in contemporary Italian MANNERISM. Flötner was deeply conscious of the distinction between the German and Italian traditions: a caption on a print which he executed during the 1530s actually describes the sculptor's ability to work in "Italian" and "German" manners. His influence was broadcast by small sculptures and engravings.

**Fludd, Robert** (1574–1637) *English physician and Rosicrucian*
Fludd was born at Bearsted, Kent, attended Oxford university (1591–97), and then traveled abroad, studying chemistry and medicine and becoming acquainted with the tenets of the shadowy Rosicrucians (*see* ROSICRUCIANISM). After several false attempts, he became a fellow of the College of Physicians (1608) and practiced successfully in London. He published an *Apologia* (1616) for the Rosicrucians, and their program underlay most of his medical and philosophical writings, all of them in Latin, all published in Continental Europe, and unkindly characterized by an early biographer as "great, many, and mystical." He was, however, shrewd enough to be one of the first of his profession to accept, in *Medicina catholica* (1631), William HARVEY's account of the circulation of the blood.

**Fontainebleau** A town and former royal château south of Paris. Set in parkland and forest, the medieval palace was used as a hunting residence but it was pulled down by FRANCIS I, who wanted to enhance his prestige by building a magnificent palace in the new Renaissance style. Two schools of painting and architectural decoration were associated with Fontainebleau during the 16th century. The first was the more important and was based on the court of Francis I, who brought a number of leading artists from Italy and other countries to work on the interior of the newly rebuilt château. Chief of these artists was ROSSO FIORENTINO, who arrived in 1530 and was responsible for the Galerie François I (c. 1533–44). PRIMATICCIO, who joined Rosso in 1532, is best remembered for the decoration of the Galerie d'Ulysse. Other visiting artists were Benvenuto CELLINI and Niccolò dell' ABBATE as well as

French and Flemish artists, such as Leonard Thiry (died c. 1550), who was strongly influenced by Rosso and Primaticcio. In the late 1530s Francis set up looms at Fontainebleau to weave the tapestries designed for the Galerie François I. Sebastiano SERLIO was invited in 1540 from Venice to contribute architectural embellishments. Although many of their decorations were later lost or damaged, Francis's artists introduced numerous ideas of the Italian Renaissance and provided the basis of the international mannerist style.

The second school of Fontainebleau was established under HENRY IV, but never equalled the impact of its predecessor. Henry greatly enlarged the château, adding the Cours des Offices and the Cours des Princes and landscaping the grounds. Artists of the second Fontainebleau school included the Flemish painter Ambroise Dubois (1543–1614), Toussaint Dubreuil (1561–1602), and Martin Fréminet (1567–1602).

**Fontana, Annibale** (c. 1540–1587) *Italian sculptor and medalist*
He was active in and around Milan, making two statues for the dome piers of Sta. Maria presso San Celso and some very fine candelabra for the Certosa di Pavia (1580). Among his portrait medals is one of LOMAZZO.

**Fontana, Domenico** (1543–1607) *Italian architect and engineer*
Born at Melide, near Lugano, he was probably in Rome by 1563 and by 1574 he was working for Cardinal Montalto (Felice Peretti), who in 1585 was elected Pope Sixtus V. Fontana thus became architect to the papacy and the following year he achieved fame by transporting the Egyptian obelisk formerly in the Circus Nero to its present site outside St. Peter's. This feat of engineering, which he described in an illustrated folio volume entitled *Della trasportatione dell'obelisco Vaticano…* (1590), marked the start of the extensive replanning, demolition, and building that he carried out in Rome. One major work was the completion, with Giacomo DELLA PORTA, of the dome of St. Peter's from Michelangelo's model (1586–90). Fontana is not considered to have been a great architect and he has been accused of destroying or spoiling a number of buildings better than his own; his Sistine library (1587–90) in the Vatican, for example, mars BRAMANTE's Belvedere court. Fontana even considered converting the Colosseum into a wool factory. Pope Clement VIII dismissed him from his post for misappropriating public money (1592), after which Fontana worked in Naples, mainly on the Palazzo Reale, remaining there until his death.

**Fontana, Lavinia** (1552–1614) *Italian painter*
The daughter and pupil of Prospero FONTANA, she married (1577) the painter Gian Paolo Zappi, by whom she had 11 children in 18 years. The couple lived and worked at her father's studio but Fontana rapidly outstripped her less talented husband, so much so that he gave up his career to support her work as a society painter. Her prolific output, of which 135 paintings survive, ranges from secular works, such as *Self-Portrait Seated at Her Desk* (1579) and *Portrait of a Noblewoman* (1580), to numerous church commissions, historical canvases, and altarpieces. The latter includes *The Stoning of St. Stephen*, for the church of San Paolo fuori le Mura, Rome, and *Holy Family with the Sleeping Christ*, commissioned in 1591 by PHILIP II of Spain for the Escorial. After her father's death Fontana transferred her studio to Rome, where she became official painter to the papal court and was patronized by popes Gregory XIII and Clement VIII. She maintained successful workshops in Bologna and Rome, was elected to the Rome Academy, and was one of the few independent women professionals of the period to achieve significant fame and riches.

**Fontana, Prospero** (1512–1597) *Italian painter*
A native of Bologna, Fontana traveled widely and assisted a number of notable artists on decorative projects, including Pierino del Vaga, Giorgio VASARI, and Federico ZUCCARO. Painting in a strongly mannerist style, he worked in such artistic centers as Genoa, Rome, Florence, and Fontainebleau, where he assisted PRIMATICCIO (c. 1560), but he is chiefly associated with the Bolognese school. Fontana was the earliest teacher of Lodovico CARRACCI, while his other pupils included his own daughter Lavinia (*see* FONTANA, LAVINIA), whose fame as a portraitist ultimately eclipsed that of her father.

**Fonte, Moderata** (Modesta Pozzo) (1555–1592) *Italian writer*
Fonte was born in Venice and lost both her parents, probably to plague, while still a baby. She received an unusually good education and continued her studies after her marriage to Giovanni Nicolò Doglioni, who encouraged her to write. In 1581 she published a volume of 13 poems using the pen name Floridoro and *Le feste*, a dramatic work that had been presented before the doge. Her other works include religious writings.

Fonte is now best known for *Il merito delle donne* (1600), a witty prose treatise arguing that women are the superior sex. This belongs to a late 16th-century genre of works in which a group debates the merits of the sexes, but it inverts the usual format by making the speakers women and the main theme the deficiencies of men. Fonte herself is usually identified with Corinna, the most forthright of the speakers. Modern feminist criticism has shown particular interest in Fonte's argument that men have appropriated language itself, making it very difficult for women to articulate their experience in its own terms. Fonte completed this provocative work shortly before her death in childbirth, and it was published posthumously.

An English translation by Virginia Cox, entitled *The Worth of Women: Wherein is Clearly Revealed Their Nobility and their Superiority to Men*, was published by the University of Chicago Press in 1997.

**food and cooking** Although agricultural yields rose slowly throughout the Renaissance period, food remained scarce and expensive and for most people hunger was an ever-present threat. The staples of the peasant's diet were root crops, especially turnips, and a coarse bread made from rye. The availability of meat seems to have varied greatly. In England, accounts dating from the very end of the period suggest that about half the population ate meat on a daily basis during times of plenty and that all but the poorest did so once a week. This, however, was the exception; in much of Continental Europe an agricultural laborer could be sure of eating meat only on high feast days—perhaps three or four times a year. It was the French King HENRY IV who declared that his wish was to put a chicken in the pot of every peasant on Sunday. The most widely eaten meats were pork and bacon, followed by mutton, goat, rabbit, and poultry; England was again exceptional in the wide availability of beef. Other animal products included many types of sausage and black pudding, in which minced pork fat would be mixed with pig's blood, crushed grains, and seasoning. The fat of pigs was also eaten with bread and was the main fat used in cooking. Although olive oil was produced in large quantities in southern Europe, it was not generally used for cooking—possibly because cooking in vegetable oil was associated with the Jews (who did not use pork fat for religious reasons). Other basic foods included eggs, cheese, and fish, which served as a substitute for meat during Lent and other periods of religious abstinence.

Within this framework, there were wide regional variations, reflecting differences in climate, soil, and custom. Consumption of fresh fruit and vegetables, for example, was notably higher in southern Europe, while more milk products were eaten in the north. The north–south divide was particularly marked in the choice of drink, with heavy wines being preferred in the Mediterranean lands and light wines or beer in northern countries. In England, beer (flavored with hops) began to replace ale (a stronger brew made without hops) from the 1520s—a change that gave rise to the common saying "Heresy and beer came into England both in a year." Both wine and beer were drunk in staggering quantities, largely for the lack of any alternative. Water had to be fetched from a well or spring and was often of poor quality; milk yields were low and mainly used to make cheese and butter; tea, coffee, and chocolate remained unknown in Europe until the late 17th century. In Britain and northern Europe, a large percentage of the cultivable land was devoted to growing barley for beer, and brewing played a major part in the economy. Cider and perry were also drunk widely in fruit-growing areas. Like beer and wine, these were often spiced, sweetened, or warmed for drinking.

In the absence of refrigeration, the preservation of meat and other food products was an urgent concern. For most of the population, fresh meat was all but unobtainable during the winter, as lack of fodder meant that most animals had to be slaughtered in the autumn (traditionally on or about St. Martin's day, November 11). Meat and fish were generally preserved by smoking in northern Europe and by salting in the Mediterranean south. The trade in salted herrings was a major operation, controlled largely by the HANSEATIC LEAGUE, which imported vast quantities of salt from Portugal. Milk products, eggs, and vegetables were preserved by various means, including the use of vinegar and lime. In the kitchens of the wealthy, expensive spices, such as cloves, cinnamon, ginger, or nutmeg were also added during the preservation process. However, the idea that such spices were used chiefly as preservatives, or to disguise the fact that meat had become tainted, is now regarded as a culinary myth. Rather, spices were valued for their rich taste and smell, and were thought to have therapeutic and medicinal properties. Their rarity and exoticism made them highly prized commodities and large fortunes could be earned in the spice trade—a factor that inspired many of the era's voyages of discovery. For the less wealthy, however, all such means of preserving or seasoning food remained prohibitively expensive. As a result, most ordinary people endured a miserably inadequate diet during the dark months of the year, relieved only by several days of feasting at Christmas.

At the close of the Middle Ages, the diet of the wealthy classes would have differed from that of the agricultural laborer more in quality and quantity than in kind. The banquets of the rich were characterized by robust, earthy fare and a fairly crude style of presentation. A valuable insight into the dining habits of the rich is provided by *Le Viander* (1375), a manuscript recipe book by Taillevent (Guillaume Tirel), chef to Charles VI of France. The menus are dominated by soups, pies, and meat dishes; sauces are heavy and highly seasoned, as if to hide, rather than enhance, the natural taste of the ingredients. The beginnings of a more subtle and refined style of eating can be traced, like so much else, to early 15th-century Italy, where the rising merchant class was responsible for a major change in taste. Typically, choice cuts of lamb, kid, or veal would be set off with delicacies such as mushrooms or truffles (often in the form of stuffing); favorite vegetable dishes included spinach, asparagus, and artichoke hearts. Minced and spiced meat was combined with pasta, as in lasagna and ravioli, or cooked in crepes or quenelles (croquettes). In Florence, such dishes were consumed for preference without sauce. Italian cooks also excelled in the production of elegant desserts—jellies and blancmanges, ice cream, biscuits, and zabagliones. At court banquets, the aim was to impress with the sheer diversity of dishes and with an elegant and fanciful presentation; castles would be built from fruit, swans fashioned from sugar, or statues sculpted from marzipan.

As the new tastes spread, the 15th and 16th centuries saw an outpouring of books on healthy, nutritious, and aspirational eating comparable to that of our own day. The first and most important of these was Il PLATINA's *De honesta voluptate et valetudine* (c. 1474; Of true pleasures and health), a humanistic work that has been called the first great classic of gastronomy. Platina extols the art of cooking by comparing it to that of medicine—both are concerned with the health of the body, both use spices, and so on. Other books of dietary advice shed a fascinating light on the fads, taboos, and prejudices of the day. Melons, cucumbers, and other watery fruits were disparaged on health grounds, and broad beans were disliked because the peeled bean was thought to resemble a human embryo. Other foods, such as brown (rye) bread, were stigmatized because of their class associations. Indeed, awareness of food as a social indicator seems to have sharpened during the Renaissance; several Italian cities tried to codify the various foods appropriate to the different social classes, while English sumptuary laws laid down the precise number of courses that should be served to various dignitaries (six for a peer of the realm but nine for a cardinal). Particular disapproval was reserved for novelties from the New World; the potato was despised for its plain appearance and like corn (maize) considered fit for only the lowest classes of peasant, while the tomato was inveighed against by moralists, who held that it incited lust (and may even have been the forbidden fruit in the Garden of Eden). One import to fare better was the turkey, which quickly found acceptance as an alternative to goose or peacock.

Another turning point in the history of gastronomy occurred with the spread of the new Italian tastes to France during the 16th century. Traditionally, this has been dated from the marriage (1533) of the future Henry II to CATHERINE DE' MEDICI, who is said to have been accompanied by a team of the most skilled Florentine cooks. Although recent food historians tend to downplay Catherine's role, arguing for a more gradual influence, it is accepted that the encounter between Italian expertise and the wealth of raw materials found in France proved seminal. By the end of the 16th century, the distinctive aesthetic of French *grande cuisine* had been established. This involved the selection of only the finest ingredients, their combination in ways designed to bring out the subtlest nuances of flavor, and an emphasis on presentation. The Italian influence was reinforced by the marriage of MARIE DE' MEDICI to Henry IV in 1600. It was probably in Marie's kitchen that the great chef François-Pierre de La Varenne began his career. La Varenne would subsequently publish *Le Cuisinier Françoise*, the book usually considered the

founding text of French gastronomy. With its detailed instructions for making stocks and sauces and its insistence on preparing foods in ways that enhance their natural flavors, La Varenne's work laid the basis for the systematization of French *grande cuisine* that occurred in the late 17th century.

**Further reading:** Ken Albala, *Eating Right in the Renaissance* (Berkeley, Calif.: University of California Press, 2002); Stewart Lee Allen, *In the Devil's Garden: A Sinful History of Forbidden Foods* (New York: Ballantine, 2002); Piero Camporesi, *Bread of Dreams: Food and Fantasy in Early Modern Europe*, transl. David Gentilcore (Chicago, Ill.: University of Chicago Press, repr. 1996); Andrew Dalby, *Dangerous Tastes: The Story of Spices* (Berkeley, Calif.: University of California Press, 2000); Stephen Mennell, *All Manners of Food: Eating and Taste in England and France from the Middle Ages to the Present* (Champaign, Ill.: University of Illinois, 2nd ed. 1995); Reay Tannahill, *Food in History* (New York: Stein & Day, 1973; rev. ed. Crown Publishing Group, 1995).

**Foppa, Vincenzo** (c. 1427–1515) *Italian painter*
Born near Brescia, Foppa probably trained in Padua, possibly as a pupil of Francesco Squarcione. He subsequently became the foremost painter in Lombardy and Milan until the advent of Leonardo da Vinci. His earliest dated work is a *Crucifixion* (1456; Bergamo), strongly influenced by Jacopo BELLINI, from whom Foppa derived his interest in color and light. Later works also bear the influence of Provençal and Flemish art, as well as the paintings of BRAMANTE, as seen in Foppa's frescoes in Milan of the life of St. Peter Martyr (1466–68) and the martyrdom of St. Sebastian (1485). Other works include *Boy reading Cicero* (Wallace Collection, London) and *Epiphany* (National Gallery, London).

**Forment, Damián** (c. 1480–1540) *Spanish sculptor*
Born in Valencia, Forment was probably trained in Florence, returning to Valencia in 1500 for nine years before establishing a studio in Zaragoza, where he remained until his death. In 1509 he began work on an altar for the cathedral of El Pilar in Zaragoza, in which he combined Gothic elements with Renaissance figures and demonstrated his artistic debt to DONATELLO. The author of numerous notable altarpieces in alabaster, Forment executed further works for Huesca cathedral (1520–24), the monastery church at Poblet (1527), and San Domingo de la Calzada (1537–40), the last of which also betrayed the influence of Alonso BERRUGUETE. During the course of these works, Forment gradually exchanged features of Gothic style for those of the Italian Renaissance, and his later pieces were some of the first mannerist works undertaken in Spain.

**Formula of Concord** See CONCORD, FORMULA OF

**Forster, Georg** (c. 1510–1568) *German doctor and musician*
Born in Amberg, Forster received his earliest musical training at the court in Heidelberg. A friend of LUTHER and MELANCHTHON, he devoted most of his life to the study and practice of medicine. His greatest contribution to music was the compilation of the *Frische teutsche Liedlein* (1539–40). In this sizeable publication he collected *Tenorlieder* by about 50 composers active during the previous half-century to form a representative and useful anthology. His achievement as a musical compiler outweighs his importance as a composer. He died in Nuremberg, where all his publications had been issued.

**fortification** The theory and practice of permanent fortification was compelled to undergo rapid development in the Renaissance owing to the threat posed from the early 15th century by the use of gunpowder in warfare. The new CANNON, superseding siege machinery such the ballista (catapult) inherited from antiquity, could easily demolish the walls of a medieval castle or town, and by the end of the 15th century mining with gunpowder was a threat to even substantial defensive structures.

Italian engineers in the mid-15th century were the first to produce an effective response to the problem. Their solutions were worked out and refined all over Europe during the succeeding centuries, and during the Renaissance period they were the acknowledged experts in the art of fortification. Outside Italy, DÜRER, motivated by the current European fear of invasion by the Turks, published an early summary of the art in his *Etliche Underricht, zu Befestigung der Stett, Schloss, und Flecken* (Nuremberg, 1527). The Dutch in particular interested themselves in the capabilities of the new-style fortifications in the course of their protracted struggle against the forces of Spain in the second half of the 16th century.

Fortress walls were vastly thickened, with their bases strengthened by a massive backing of earth and built with a slight inward slope from the bottom in order to minimize their vulnerability to the impact of cannon balls. Wide parapets and walkways were incorporated at the top to enable the defenders to maneuver and station their own guns. With the increased solidity, height became less important: the towers that were the main defensive points of a medieval castle were reduced to the same height as the walls and converted into massive projecting bastions that could function as gun platforms. Projecting out from the line of the adjacent walls, such bastions enable the defenders to cover the ground in front of the walls, thus preventing massed assaults or the approach of miners. From the early 1500s it was recognized that angular or pointed bastions performed this function better than the previous round ones.

Before the advent of the specialist military architect in the mid-16th century, architects and artists in other fields were often invited by rulers to turn their skills to the design of fortifications. LEONARDO DA VINCI, BRAMANTE, and MICHELANGELO, for instance, were all employed or invited to advise in this capacity at some stage of their careers. In Florence, Giuliano Sangallo (*see* SANGALLO FAMILY) designed fortresses for Lorenzo de' Medici in the 1470s, and in the 1530s his nephew Antonio Sangallo the Younger built the Fortezza da Basso; later still, in the 1590s, BUONTALENTI designed the Medicis' Belvedere fortress and fortified their port at Livorno. Baccio PONTELLI was responsible for both church and military edifices at Ostia. Michele SANMICHELI worked in Verona, Venice, and throughout the Venetian territories.

See also: ARTILLERY

Further reading: John R. Hale, *Renaissance Fortification: Art or Engineering?* (London: Thames & Hudson, 1977).

**Fortune** Allegorical figure. It was probably the Roman philosopher Boethius (c. 480–c. 524 CE), in his *Consolatio philosophiae*, who transformed Fortuna, the goddess of ancient Rome, into an allegorical figure that became popular throughout Renaissance Europe. The survival of this pagan deity in a Christian world reflects attempts to explain the unexpected adversities to which mankind is subject. In this sense, Fortune can be seen as a secular equivalent to Providence, both of which were beyond the influence of human beings.

Popularized by ERASMUS in his ADAGIA and in numerous emblem books, such as ALCIATI's *Emblemata*, Fortune was personified both as a literary trope and a pictorial symbol. She was typically depicted standing on a turning wheel or ball, suggesting change and instability. She was often blindfolded, indicating impartiality, and accompanied by a turbulent sea or an inconstant wind. Fortune had a long forelock which could be seized but the back of her head was bald so that once she had passed by, an opportunity to take control of one's fate had been missed. Fluellen's speech on Fortune in SHAKESPEARE's *Henry V* provides a summary of her characteristics. One of the great Renaissance descriptions of Fortune is the *De fortuna* (1501) of Giovanni PONTANO.

**Forty Martyrs of England and Wales** Roman Catholics martyred for their faith between 1535 and 1679 and canonized by Pope Paul VI in 1970. The 40 were selected from the 200 English and Welsh martyrs whom earlier popes had already beatified. Twenty of them belonged to religious orders, including Edmund CAMPION and nine other Jesuits; 13 were seminary priests; and there were seven laity (four men and three women, of whom Margaret CLITHEROW was one).

The Castle of Knowledge.

The Sphere of Destinye.

Sphæra Fati

whose go uernour is Know ledge.

The wheele of Fortune.

Sphæra Fortunæ

whose ruler is Igno raunce.

To KNOWLEDG is this Trophy set,
All learninges friendes will it support.
So shall their name great honour get,
And gaine great fame with good report

Though spitefull Fortune turned her wheele
To staye the Sphere of Vranye,
Yet dooth this Sphere resist that wheele,
And fleeyth all fortunes villanye.
Though earthe do honour Fortunes balle,
And bytells blynde hyr wheele aduaunce,
The heauens to fortune are not thralle,
These Spheres surmount al fortunes chance.

**Fortune** In this 16th-century woodcut the blindfolded goddess (right) is shown turning her wheel and standing on a revolving ball to symbolize instability. The figure on the left is Urania, the muse of astronomy.

**Foscari, Francesco** (1373–1457) *Doge of Venice (1423–57)*

Foscari was born into a noble Venetian family and held several of the highest offices in the republic before being elected doge at the early age of 49. His expansionist policies resulted in Venice's obtaining Bergamo and Brescia (1428), but war with the VISCONTI FAMILY of Milan in the 1430s weakened the republic and checked its further territorial advance. Of all Foscari's children by his two wives, only Jacopo survived into adulthood, and the doge's life after 1444, when the first accusations of corruption were brought against his son, was darkened by Jacopo's crimes and exile. Jacopo died in Candia (Crete) in January 1457,

and the elderly doge was so shattered by grief that he was unable to carry on the business of government and was forced to resign. He died two days later. This tragedy was the basis of Byron's play *The Two Foscari* (written 1821) and Verdi's opera *I due Foscari* (1844).

**Fouquet, Jean** (active c. 1443/47–81) *French manuscript illuminator and painter*

The earliest fixed point in Fouquet's career is his visit to Italy (1443/47). Previous to this, it seems likely that he studied under the Bedford Master in Paris and, possibly, in the Netherlands. After his return home (c. 1449) he was based in his native Tours, working primarily for members of the French court. In 1475 he was appointed painter to Louis XI.

Fouquet's key work of manuscript illumination is the dismembered Book of Hours of Étienne Chevalier, which probably dates from between 1452 and 1461, and of which the largest surviving part is preserved in Chantilly. The Munich Boccaccio, illuminated by Fouquet and his *atelier*, was begun about 1459; at about the same time he began decorating the Paris *Grandes Chroniques de France* for King Charles VII. In 1465 he executed a single miniature for the Book of Hours of Charles de France, brother of Louis XI. This and other undated illuminations, probably of the same decade, indicate how the Hours of Étienne Chevalier remained the model for his devotional miniatures. His frontispiece to the *Statutes of the Order of St. Michel* in Paris dates from about 1470 and his illuminations in the duke of Nemours's copy of the *Antiquités Judaïques* were completed by 1476. His latest manuscript illuminations are a series of detached pages in Paris and Amsterdam from a manuscript of the *Histoire ancienne*. Fouquet's few surviving panel paintings comprise the portraits of Gonella (Vienna), Charles VII (Paris), Guillaume Jouvénal des Ursins (Paris), the divided diptych of Étienne Chevalier and the Virgin (Berlin and Antwerp), and the large *Deposition* altarpiece (Nouans).

Fouquet's style, originally of Franco-Flemish derivation, was transformed by his experiences in Italy and his work reveals ideas appropriated from Fra ANGELICO, ANDREA DEL CASTAGNO, DONATELLO, and even GIOTTO and DUCCIO. A highly intellectual artist, he employed classical architectural details to "label" specific non-French locations, including Italy, the classical world, and even paradise. He understood ALBERTI's system of one-point PERSPECTIVE, but did not adopt it wholeheartedly as its use threatened to disrupt the unity of text and pictures in his manuscripts. The most significant French artist of the 15th century, he profoundly influenced later illuminators such as Jean Bourdichon (died 1521) and Jean Perréal (died 1530).

**Foxe, John** (1516–1587) *English Calvinist martyrologist*
He studied at Oxford and became a Fellow of Magdalen College (1539–45), but fled to the Continent on the accession of the Catholic Mary I. Moving between the main centers of the Protestant Reformation, he met other English refugees and wrote a Latin history of religious persecution (Strasbourg, 1554). He expanded this in English translation into the work with which he is forever associated: the *Acts and Monuments of these latter and perillous dayes, touching matters of the Church* (1563), universally known as "Foxe's Book of Martyrs." Foxe himself returned to England in 1559, and his book's testimony to the heroism of the Protestant martyrs under Mary, together with its vivid woodcuts, made it immensely popular. It was officially promoted by the bishops, and Foxe

brought out three further editions in his lifetime (1570, 1576, 1583).

**Fracastoro, Girolamo** (c. 1478–1553) *Italian physician, poet, and astronomer*
Coming from a wealthy Veronese family, Fracastoro was educated at the university of Padua, where he also taught briefly. In 1508 he returned to Verona to run the family estates. He managed nonetheless to produce two important medical works. The first, a poem in Latin hexameters called *Syphilis sive morbus gallicus* (Syphilis or the French disease; 1530), not only introduced the term "syphilis" to medical parlance but also contained a detailed description of the disease. In the second work, *De contagione* (1546), Fracastoro argued that some diseases spread by *seminaria contagium* (contagious seeds), in other words germs, but no attention was paid to his suggestive ideas. He was also ahead of his time in postulating that fossil mussels discovered (1517) in rocks at Verona were remains of creatures that had once lived in the vicinity. In astronomy Fracastoro proved less innovative. His *Homocentrica* (1538) insisted against Ptolemy (*see* PTOLEMAIC SYSTEM) that all heavenly bodies move, without epicycle or eccentric, around the sun in circular orbit. His dialogue *Nau-*

**Girolamo Fracastoro** A woodcut of the author appearing in his *Homocentrica* (1538), in which he insisted that all heavenly bodies rotate in circular orbits about the sun. He is holding an armillary sphere.

*gerius, sive de poetica* appeared in a collected edition of his works in 1555; it emphasizes the universality of poetry.

## Francavilla, Pietro (Pierre Francheville, Pierre Francqueville) (1548–1615) *Belgian-born French sculptor*

Francavilla was born at Cambrai. Initially discouraged from his vocation, he went to Paris as a teenager to learn drawing, before going (1566) to Innsbruck to work with a compatriot, Alexander Colyn, on the tomb of Emperor Maximilian. He was patronized by Archduke Ferdinand of Tyrol and in 1571/72 he went to Rome and Florence with a letter of introduction from Ferdinand to GIAMBOLOGNA, then established as court sculptor to the Medici. Francavilla went into partnership with Giambologna, taking on (1574) a big commission from Abbot Bracci for garden statuary (now distributed between the Victoria and Albert Museum, the Orangery, Kensington Palace, in London, and the Wadsworth Atheneum, Hartford, Conn.). Soon afterwards Francavilla assisted Giambologna on the Grimaldi chapel in Genoa and then carved two colossal statues, *Janus* and *Jupiter* (signed and dated 1585), for the Grimaldi palace there; he also carved six statues for the Senarega chapel in Genoa cathedral.

Back in Florence, Francavilla helped execute Giambologna's two great marble groups of the *Rape of the Sabines* and *Hercules Slaying a Centaur* for the Loggia dei Lanzi. He helped Giambologna with the marble statuary in the Salviati chapel (San Marco) and carved five statues of his own for the Niccolini chapel (Sta. Croce). His collaboration with Giambologna is specified in inscriptions on portrait statues of Ferdinando I de' Medici in Arezzo and Pisa.

Francavilla left Florence for France (1604) at the behest of Queen Marie de' Medici, to erect on the Pont-Neuf a bronze equestrian statue of her husband King Henry IV, which was being produced in Giambologna's Florence workshop. In his studio in the Louvre Francavilla modeled four slaves to adorn the corners of its pedestal, and after his death they were cast in bronze by a pupil; these survive (Louvre, Paris), but the statue was destroyed in the French Revolution.

Francavilla's style closely echoes Giambologna's and he frequently used his models. In his major works it is hard to determine whether he contributed anything more than competent carving in marble on a grand scale of a design by the greater sculptor. In his defense it should be noted that virtually all Giambologna's sculpture in marble or bronze was produced by close collaboration with just such skilled assistants.

## Francesco di Giorgio Martini (1439–1502) *Italian architect and architectural theorist*

Trained as a painter and sculptor in VECCHIETTA's workshop in his native Siena, Francesco subsequently turned to architecture. He wrote his influential *Trattato dell'ar-chitettura civile e militare* about 1482. Using VITRUVIUS and ALBERTI as springboards, Francesco attempted to rationalize and codify architectural practice, using illustrations to clarify his theories. His drawings display eccentric adaptations of Vitruvius's anthropomorphism and an idiosyncratic approach to classical design.

In his capacity as military engineer, Francesco traveled to Milan, Naples, and Urbino, pioneering a design for the angled bastion, and in 1477 he succeeded Luciano LAURANA as architect to Federico da Montefeltro. Moving to Urbino, he probably continued construction of the Palazzo Ducale there and provided plans for the ducal palace in Gubbio, as well as building many fortresses in the Marches. His architectural work is poorly documented, but his singular style makes attribution fairly secure. His hallmarks include the use of arches supported on piers and capitals with flat fluting, evidenced in the Palazzo Ducale, Urbino, and the Palazzo Communale, Iesi (1486–98); superimposed pilasters whose capitals are formed by the string course, executed in San Bernadino, Urbino (1482–90) and Sta. Maria del Calcinaio, just outside Cortona (completed 1516); and the deployment of classical lettering in the courtyards of the ducal palaces of Urbino and Gubbio. Having maintained professional links with Siena throughout his career, Francesco returned there in 1497 after a six-year stay in Naples to advise on military fortifications. A *Nativity* in the Pinacoteca, Siena, is a good example of his work as a painter, among several paintings in the same gallery.

## Francheville, Pierre See FRANCAVILLA, PIETRO

## Francia, Francesco Raibolini (1450–1517/18) *Italian painter and goldsmith*

A native of Bologna, Francia began practicing as a goldsmith before turning to painting in 1486. Influenced initially by the Ferrarese artists, Francia entered into partnership with Lorenzo COSTA, with whom he worked until 1506 when Costa left for Mantua. Early works, such as his *Madonna Enthroned with Saints* (Pinacoteca, Bologna), exemplify the austerity of the Ferrarese school but later works, under the influence of the paintings of Raphael and Perugino, are executed in an increasingly soft style. Other works include several pictures of the Madonna and the more personal portrait *Federico Gonzaga as a Boy* (1510; Metropolitan Museum of Art, New York).

## Franciabigio, Francesco di Cristofano (1482–1525) *Italian painter*

A notable member of the Florentine school, Franciabigio was a pupil of ALBERTINELLI and PIERO DI COSIMO and was also influenced by RAPHAEL and ANDREA DEL SARTO. He collaborated with Andrea del Sarto on a series of paintings in SS. Annunziata in Florence (1513) and in the Chiostro dello Scalzo in Florence, where Franciabigio painted a *Last Supper*. The two artists established a workshop together and Franciabigio went on to decorate the Medici villa at Poggio a Caiano with del Sarto's pupil PONTORMO, executing the celebrated *Triumph of Cicero* there. Franciabigio was also noted for his introspective portraits of young men. Other works which bear the stamp of Raphael include the *Madonna del Pozzo* (c. 1508; Accademia, Florence).

## Francis I (1494–1547) *King of France (1515–47)*

Francis was born at Cognac, the son of Charles of Valois and Louise of Savoy, and was brought up as heir-presumptive to LOUIS XII, whose daughter Claude (died 1524) he married in 1514. He and his sister Margaret (*see* MARGUERITE DE NAVARRE) both received a sound education, and Francis early manifested his lifelong love of hunting, chivalric tournaments, and other vigorous sports.

Inheriting Louis's policy of intervention in Italy, Francis soon after his accession led a campaign that resulted in his victory (1515) at Marignano, southeast of Milan; this left him in possession of Milan and Genoa and he also acquired Parma and Piacenza. By 1523, however, these gains had been negated by the intervention of the newly elected emperor, CHARLES V, and Francis's efforts to recover the territories ended in his defeat and capture at the battle of PAVIA (1525). Taken to Madrid as a prisoner, he signed a treaty renouncing his Italian ambitions (1526). After this his only territorial advance in the area was the conquest of Savoy and part of Piedmont in 1536. Although he married the emperor's sister as his second wife (1530), Francis wavered for the rest of his reign between allying himself with the Hapsburg interests and conspiring against them.

At home Francis's reign was marked by a considerable increase in the monarch's power. Initially sympathetic towards the Protestants, he became from the mid-1530s increasingly repressive in his attitude to religious dissent, culminating in a shameful massacre of the Waldenses (1545). Dominated by his mistresses and favorites, Francis was vain and extravagant, but it was through his patronage that the Italian Renaissance first made an impact upon French art and architecture (*see* FONTAINEBLEAU). He invited LEONARDO DA VINCI to France in 1515, and CELLINI, PRIMATICCIO, ROSSO FIORENTINO, and SERLIO were later and more influential Italian visitors. Prompted by Guillaume BUDÉ, Francis founded (1530) the lectureships that were the basis for the Collège de France. Among the humanist scholars and writers whom he encouraged was Clément MAROT.

**Further reading:** Robert J. Knecht, *Francis I* (Cambridge, U.K.: Cambridge University Press, 1982); Desmond Seward, *Prince of the Renaissance: The Golden Life of François I* (New York: Macmillan, 1973).

## Francis, Duke of Alençon (1554–1584) *Duke of Anjou (1576–84)*

The youngest son of HENRY II of France and CATHERINE DE' MEDICI, Francis received the duchy of Alençon in 1566. After his elder brother Henry had succeeded to the throne (1574) as HENRY III, Francis succeeded him as duke of Anjou. Although stunted in stature and scarred by smallpox, from 1572 he was an apparently favored suitor of ELIZABETH I, who nicknamed him her "petite grenouille" (little frog). He visited her in England three times and in 1581 she even announced her firm intention of marrying him. In 1580 the duke was offered limited sovereignty over part of the Netherlands in return for aid against Spain, but impatience at these limitations and military setbacks induced him to turn his troops against Antwerp (1583) in the so-called "French fury." He was repulsed and withdrew to France, where he died.

## Francis de Sales, St. (1567–1622) *French churchman and leader of the French Counter-Reformation*

Born at Sales in Savoy, he was educated in Annecy, Paris, and Padua. On being ordained (1593) he embarked on the reconversion of much of the Calvinist population of Chablais. In 1602 he was made titular bishop of Geneva, making his headquarters at Annecy. An exceptionally active preacher and prolific writer of letters, he inspired many other French Catholic reformers, including St. JEANNE FRANÇOISE DE CHANTAL, who founded the Congregation of the Visitation in 1610. He wrote two classic books of devotion, *Introduction to the Devout Life* (1608) and *Treatise on the Love of God* (1616), in which he drew up a scheme of devout life attainable by all, laity as well as clergy. He was canonized in 1665.

## Francisco da Hollanda (c. 1517–1584) *Portuguese artist and art theorist*

He was born in Lisbon, where his father, a Netherlands miniaturist, had settled. King John III sent him to Rome in 1537 to study architecture; while there he met many major artists, including Michelangelo, and made an interesting album of archeological drawings, including some of frescoes in the Domus Aurea of Nero that are now destroyed. Francisco's famous *Quatro dialogos da pintura antiga*, recording conversations in Rome in 1538, appeared in his *Tractato de pintura antiga* (1548).

## Francis Xavier, St. (1506–1552) *Jesuit missionary*

A Basque of noble extraction, Xavier was born in Navarre. He was one of the small group of original followers that IGNATIUS LOYOLA gathered together in Paris, and with him he took a vow of poverty and chastity in 1534. With Simon Rodríguez, Xavier succeeded in turning Portugal into a Jesuit stronghold by gaining both popular and royal support. In accordance with the wishes of Pope Paul III he set out for the Indies in 1541 with the intention of reasserting Christianity and making new conversions in the Portuguese colonies. Traveling via Mozambique he arrived at Goa in 1542 where he remained for five months. Having had some success among the colonists he traveled to Cochin, Ceylon, Malacca, the Moluccas, and Japan (1549), before returning to Goa in 1551. He then set right certain abuses that had developed in his absence and set sail again, this time with a view to realizing the conversion of the Chinese empire to Christianity. He is reputed to have converted many thousands on the way but never actually reached China, for he died of fever in December 1552 on an island just 30 miles short of his destination. His body was taken back to Goa, where the imposing Renaissance church of Bom Jesus was built (1594–1603) over his shrine. Although Xavier is popularly considered to have been the greatest missionary since St. Paul, his critics believe that his work would have been of more lasting effect had he concentrated his mission on a single colony or country. Together with Ignatius Loyola, he was canonized in 1622.

**Further reading:** Georg Schurhamer, *St. Francis Xavier: His Life, His Times*, 4 vols (Rome: Jesuit Historical Institute, 1973–82).

**Franck, Sebastian** (1499–1542) *German theologian and humanist*
Franck was born at Donauwörth and after studying at Ingolstadt and Heidelberg he was ordained priest. In about 1525 he became a Lutheran, but later developed an undogmatic form of religion and argued in favor of freedom of thought. This antagonized both reformers and traditionalists in Germany, and he retired to Basle. His major historical work, *Chronica*, appeared in 1531 and an index to the Bible in 1539. He also produced German versions of an anti-Anabaptist tract (1528) and of Erasmus's PRAISE OF FOLLY (1534). *Die deutschen Sprichwörter* (1541) was a major compendium of German proverbs.

**François I style** A trend in the visual arts in France initiated during the reign (1515–47) of Francis I. An enthusiastic patron of the arts, Francis modeled himself upon the Italian princes and actively encouraged the adoption of the ideals of the Italian Renaissance, chiefly through the building and decoration of a number of major French châteaux. Italian artists such as ROSSO FIORENTINO, LEONARDO DA VINCI, and PRIMATICCIO were brought to France to work at BLOIS, CHAMBORD, FONTAINEBLEAU, and elsewhere, providing the impetus for a national style incorporating both Gothic and humanist elements. As well as the châteaux, other works from this period in which this fusion of styles can be detected include tapestries, paintings, and furniture.

**Franco, Veronica** (1546–90/1) *Venetian courtesan, poet, and letterwriter*
She was briefly married to a doctor, but he died young leaving her with a son, by which time she had already embarked on her professional life. This came to epitomize the cultured and refined lifestyle of courtesans of 16th-century Venice, many of whom became well-known public figures. Franco counted numerous aristocrats among her clients and personal correspondents and was painted by TINTORETTO. Her sonnets and erotic love poems, many in epistolary form, were published as *Terze rime* (1575). These celebrated her independent life in unrepentant fashion, urging other women not to be submissive. However, her *Lettere* (1580) reveal a more somber view of the vulnerabilities of the courtesan dependent on the patronage of rich men and constantly preoccupied with fear of losing her looks. Prompted by such thoughts, Franco advocated the establishment of charitable refuges for aging courtesans; the first one opened in 1591.

**Frankfurt(-am-Main)** A city in western Germany on the River Main. Celtic in origin, the site became a Roman settlement; its name, which dates from the early sixth century, means "crossing of the Franks." In the late Middle Ages Frankfurt prospered on account of its trade fairs (from 1240) and it became an international commercial center during the Renaissance, in particular of the BOOK TRADE. Its stock exchange was founded in 1585. Despite its prosperity the city retained its rural character until the 16th century. Frankfurt became an imperial free city in 1372 and was an important base of Hapsburg power by the late 15th century. In 1485 the imperial Diet met there, and in 1519 it was the scene of the election of Emperor CHARLES V. Later the city joined the Lutheran cause until it was forced into submission by Charles (1546).

**Franqueville, Pierre** See FRANCAVILLA, PIETRO

**Frederick III** (1415–1493) *Holy Roman Emperor (1452–93)*
The son of Duke Ernest of Styria and Carinthia, Frederick was born in Innsbruck; on his father's death (1424) he was brought up by his uncle, Count Frederick of Tyrol. From 1435 he was coruler with his brother Albert (died 1463) of Styria and Carinthia. In 1440 he was chosen German king but his alliance with the papacy through the Concordat of Vienna (1448), which was engineered by the future Pope PIUS II, occasioned great discontent among his subjects, who resented his pledge of their obedience to Rome. Nonetheless Frederick was crowned emperor in Rome by Pope Nicholas V in 1452.

Friction with his brother Albert and incursions by his neighbors, the most dangerous of them MATTHIAS CORVINUS of Hungary, caused Frederick to seek to establish his position by an alliance with Duke CHARLES THE BOLD of

Burgundy. Negotiations broke down in 1473, when Charles demanded the title of king, but after Charles's death (1477), Frederick was able to bring about the marriage of the duke's heir, MARY of Burgundy, with his son, the future Emperor MAXIMILIAN I, and thus secured the great Burgundian inheritance for the house of Hapsburg. Frederick spent his last years in retirement at Linz where he indulged his passion for alchemy, astronomy, and botany.

**Frederick (III) the Wise** (1463–1525) *Elector of Saxony (1486–1525)*
An efficient ruler who urged constitutional reform in the empire, Frederick welcomed to his court at Wittenberg scholars and such great artists as DÜRER, MEIT, and CRANACH. He befriended the humanist scholar George SPALATIN and established the university of Wittenberg (1502), where he chose Martin LUTHER as professor of philosophy (1508). Frederick protected Luther, refusing to implement the papal bull against him (1520) and sheltering him at Wartburg castle after the imperial ban on him (1521). In 1524 Frederick accepted Luther's reformed doctrines.

**French language** The romance language of France, also spoken in parts of Belgium, Switzerland, eastern Canada, and in other areas of the former French colonial empire, for example in Africa and the Caribbean.

French developed from Vulgar Latin as spoken by Roman settlers in Gaul (conquered by Julius Caesar, 58–51 BCE). Pre-Roman Gaul was inhabited mainly by Celtic tribes, though there were Basques in Gascony and Marseilles had been settled by Greek and Phoenician merchants since about 600 BCE. (Provence had become a Roman colony in the second century BCE.) Vulgar Latin replaced Gaulish (Celtic) after Caesar's conquest; a few hundred French words—*chemin*, for example—are of Gaulish origin, but in vocabulary and structure the language is primarily derived from Latin. Christianity, introduced in the first century CE, spread rapidly, and a distinctive Gallo-Roman society gradually emerged with its capital at Lugdunum (Lyons). There were incursions by Germanic tribes from the third century CE. One of these, the Franks, was led by Clovis (from 481), who defeated both the other barbarian tribes and the Roman governor and established the Merovingian dynasty at Paris, where it ruled until the last Merovingian was overthrown in 751 by Pepin the Short, father of Charlemagne. A few hundred words of Frankish origin—*guerre*, *honte* ("shame"), *riche*, *danser*, for example—survive in modern French; Old French contained many more that are now no longer in use. By the ninth century French (of which there were a number of dialects) was significantly different from Latin. The earliest extant document in French, the *Serments de Strasbourg* (842), transcribed by the chronicler Nithard (a grandson

of Charlemagne), contains the oaths sworn in French and German by the sons of Louis I (Louis the German and Charles the Bald) against their brother Lothaire. The earliest literary text, the *Séquence de Ste. Eulalie* (c. 880), was written down soon afterwards.

French evolved in quite different northern and southern forms during the Middle Ages, the line of division extending roughly from the mouth of the Gironde to the Alps. South of this divide, the language came to be known as the *langue d'oc* (*oc*, "yes," from Latin *hoc*); north of it, a number of related dialects were called the *langue d'oïl* (*oïl*, "yes," from Latin *hoc ille*). From the 12th century the dialect of the Île-de-France—and of Paris, the ancient Frankish capital—gradually came to be preferred over the numerous other dialects (of Normandy, Anjou, Picardy, Champagne, etc.) of the *langue d'oïl*. And in the 13th century, the Albigensian crusade helped establish the *langue d'oïl* in the south as well. Literature in the *langue d'oc*, such as that of the Provençal troubadours, which was of major importance in the Middle Ages, began to decline after this time, though Provençal continued as a spoken language, and a number of words borrowed from it persist in modern French vocabulary (*asperge*, *bastide*, *béret*, *cadeau*).

Old French (ninth to 13th centuries) and Provençal retained two (nominative and oblique) of the six cases of the Latin noun, but otherwise changes, typical of most other romance languages, gradually occurred: indefinite and definite articles developed from *unus* and *ille*; new analytic constructions (as in the perfect tense of verbs and the comparison of adjectives) replaced Latin synthetic constructions; and complex changes took place in pronunciation and semantics. In the Middle French period (14th and 15th centuries), inflections were reduced to their modern minimal levels, resulting in a more settled word order, and the dialect of the Île-de-France became dominant. In the early 16th century French, by royal decrees (1520, 1539), supplanted Latin as the dominant language in the legal and official spheres. The authority of CALVIN's theological writings in French and translations of the Bible made French acceptable as a medium of religious discourse, while humanists and members of the PLÉIADE explored its possibilities as a literary medium on a par with the classical languages. These developments resulted in a great expansion of the vocabulary, with learned borrowings especially from Latin.

The following century was characterized by attempts to control and refine the language, mainly promoted by the Académie Française, which was founded by Cardinal Richelieu in 1635. The task of compiling an authoritative dictionary was undertaken by Claude Favre de Vaugelas (1585–1650), as editor, and the poet Jean Chapelain (1595–1674). Progress was slow, however, and the *Dictionnaire universel des arts et sciences* (1690) by the Académicien Antoine Furetière (1619–88) appeared first, the first modern encyclopedic dictionary. The Académie's *Diction-*

*naire* (1694) in four volumes originally arranged words by families (roots) rather than alphabetically and was (and remains) concerned with establishing acceptable literary and polite usage rather than describing the language in detail. Subsequent editions, of which there have been eight, have been arranged alphabetically. Other noteworthy early lexicographical works are Robert Estienne's *Dictionnaire françois-latin* (1539), Jean Nicot's *Trésor de la langue françoise* (1606), Gilles Ménage's *Dictionnaire étymologique* (1650), and César-Pierre Richelet's *Dictionnaire françois* (1680).

## Frescobaldi, Girolamo (1583–1643) *Italian composer*

Frescobaldi was born into an influential Ferrarese family and his father was also a musician. He studied music with the court organist LUZZASCHI, and his first post was as organist at the church of Sta. Maria in Trastevere, Rome (1607). In that year he visited the Low Countries with Guido Bentivoglio, his patron, and published his first work, a collection of five-part madrigals, in Antwerp. In 1608 he was appointed organist of the Cappella Giulia at St. Peter's in Rome and in the same year he published a set of 12 open-score fantasias. Apart from a period as court organist for the Medici in Florence (1628–34), during which he published two books of songs, the *Arie musicale* (1630), he remained in Rome until his death.

Frescobaldi was famous in his lifetime as a virtuoso performer on the organ, whose style of playing was innovative. The prefaces to his collections contain information on the interpretation of baroque music and indicate that his playing technique involved frequent changes of pace. He is now most famous for his compositions of instrumental works for keyboard and his contribution to the development of the trio sonata, the major form of chamber music until it was superseded by the string quartet. In 1615 he published his most famous work, his first book of toccatas, which was reprinted five times with numerous revisions and additions. The final and most substantial revision was published as *Toccate d'intavolature cimbalo e organo* (1637).

Frescobaldi's international reputation made him a much sought-after teacher, and among his pupils were Johann Jakob Froberger (1616–67). His *Fiori musicali* (Musical flowers;1635), which consists largely of three organ masses, was later famously copied out by the young J. S. Bach. He was an innovative and influential figure in early Italian baroque music who adapted and synthesized older musical forms and invested them with new and complex harmonies and rhythms. A contemporary of the Dutch composer SWEELINCK, Frescobaldi is one of the most important composers in the history of keyboard music and, through the work of his pupils, he had a strong influence on the German baroque school of the following century.

## frescoes

Wall paintings executed upon plaster, most notably by Italian artists during the 16th century. The medium of fresco (Italian "fresh") was originally developed in the ancient world before being adopted by artists of the Renaissance in the decoration of public buildings, churches, and private houses. In the most permanent form, *buon fresco*, the wall is first plastered and then the basic cartoon is transferred to this surface. Next, an area sufficient for one day's work is coated with plaster in a stage known as the *intonaco*. Dry powder pigment is mixed with water or lime-water and then painted onto the still damp plaster with which it reacts so that the paint becomes part of the actual wall as opposed to a superficial layer. In a more primitive form of fresco, *fresco secco*, the pigment is applied to dry plaster and is consequently more likely to flake off, as happened notoriously in the case of Leonardo da Vinci's LAST SUPPER in Milan.

Exponents of fresco painting in the early Renaissance included GIOTTO in Padua and Florence, MASACCIO in Florence, and PIERO DELLA FRANCESCA in Arezzo and Rimini. It reached its height, however, in the 16th century under the direction of RAPHAEL, best known for his decorations in the Stanze of the Vatican, and MICHELANGELO, whose ceiling and *Last Judgment* for the SISTINE CHAPEL in Rome provided an inspiration for many subsequent fresco artists. Other leading Renaissance artists in this medium, all of whom worked with numerous assistants and combined with other painters on certain cycles, included ROSSO FIORENTINO, ANDREA DEL SARTO, PONTORMO, VASARI, BRONZINO, BECCAFUMI, GIULIO ROMANO, CORREGGIO, and Paolo VERONESE.

**Further reading:** Eve Borsook, *The Mural Painters of Tuscany: from Cimabue to Andrea del Sarto* (1960; 2nd ed. Oxford, U.K.: Clarendon Press and New York: Oxford University Press, 1980).

## Frisius, Gemma See GEMMA FRISIUS

## Froben, Johann (1460–1527) *Swiss scholar and printer*

Froben was born at Hammelburg, Bavaria, and after studying in Basle started printing there in 1491, in partnership with Johannes AMERBACH and mostly in Greek, Latin, or Hebrew. The scholars he employed as editors included his friend ERASMUS, whose Greek New Testament (1516) he printed, as well as many of his other works. Among Froben's authors was Martin LUTHER, at least until his disagreement with Erasmus. Well-printed scholarly texts from Froben, among them St. Jerome in nine volumes (1516) were distributed all over Europe. He sold type as well as books, once he had adopted roman faces, and introduced the use of italics for quotations. His situation in Basle allowed him to employ the HOLBEINS, who contributed initials, borders, and other decorations to his books after 1516. His son Hieronymus (1501–65) and grandson Ambrosius (1537–95) continued his work.

**Frobisher, Martin** (c. 1535–1594) *English navigator*
Brought up in London after the death of his father, Frobisher was sent on his first voyage in 1554, to Guinea. His later activities in the Irish seas brought him to the attention of Queen Elizabeth and Sir Humfrey GILBERT, and he was commissioned to pursue Gilbert's vision of a NORTHWEST PASSAGE to China. He reached Frobisher Bay (on Baffin Island) on his first voyage (1576), returning with ore that he believed to contain gold. Two subsequent voyages (1577, 1578) having failed to discover either the passage westward or any gold (his mineral samples all proved worthless), Frobisher then devoted his attention to naval action against the Irish and Spaniards, distinguishing himself on DRAKE's 1585–86 expedition to the West Indies. He was knighted at sea in 1588 for his role in defeating the SPANISH ARMADA.

**Further reading:** Thomas H.B. Symons (ed.), *Meta Incognita: A Discourse of Discovery: Martin Frobisher's Arctic Voyages, 1576 to 1578*, 2 vols (Hull, Canada: Canadian Museum of Civilisation, 1999).

**Froment, Nicolas** (c. 1430–c. 1484) *French artist*
Originally from Uzès in Languedoc, Froment was active chiefly in Avignon where he established an important school with Enguerrand QUARTON in about 1450. Two documented works by Froment survive, both altarpieces: *The Resurrection of Lazarus* (1461; Uffizi, Florence) and *Mary in the Burning Bush* (1475–76; cathedral of St.-Sauveur, Aix-en-Provence). The former work was painted for RENÉ OF ANJOU and includes portraits of the king and his wife, while the latter painting demonstrates the artist's control of sculptural form. Despite the lack of polish in these works, they contributed greatly to the introduction of both the ideals of the Italian Renaissance and the realism of Flemish art in subsequent French painting.

**frottola** (plural: frottole) A form of secular Italian song that flourished at the end of the 15th century and the beginning of the 16th. Although the frottola was a specific poetic form, alternatively known as the barzelletta, it was also used as a generic term for Italian secular songs of other poetic forms, such as the strambotto, oda, or canzona. The main center for the frottola was Mantua, where Isabella d'ESTE employed two important composers in the form, Marchetto Cara and Bartolommeo Tromboncino. The major collection of frottole is in 11 books published by PETRUCCI in Venice (1504–14). Frottole are simple in style and were written for varying numbers of voices. They were given in the theater, sometimes as part of INTERMEDII. The frottola has been viewed as a precursor of the MADRIGAL, but some would argue that it represents a distinct strand in musical history.

**Frueauf, Rueland, the Elder** (c. 1445–1507) *Austrian painter*
Active in his native Salzburg from about 1478, Frueauf worked at first largely for the Benedictine monks there. His style was influenced by the work of Konrad LAIB, who had painted in Salzburg a few decades earlier; like Laib, Frueauf paid much attention to the expressive power of his figures (as in the Munich *Man of Sorrows*), which he set in carefully observed landscapes. He died in Passau, to which he had moved in 1497. His son, Rueland Frueauf the Younger (died after 1534), worked in Passau, following his father's style.

**Fuchs, Leonhart** (1501–1566) *German physician and botanist*
His *De historia stirpium* (1542), followed by a German edition (1543) and many later ones, described about 400 native plants and 100 foreigners (including North American maize) with illustrations that were copied in many other herbals. The descriptions are arranged alphabetically, with no attempt at classification.

**Fugger family** The foremost of the trading and BANKING dynasties that arose in southern Germany, and most notably in Augsburg, during the 14th and 15th centuries. The preeminent position of the Fuggers was largely the result of their acquisition of mining concessions in copper, gold, silver, and quicksilver from the Hapsburg emperors, at a time when European demand for precious metals was rising rapidly. Under the direction of Jakob Fugger ("the Rich"; 1459–1525) between 1478 and 1525, the family fortunes reached their peak, with trading interests extending from the Far East to the New World, and the family acting as bankers to the Hapsburgs and the Roman Curia. His entreprenurial drive was continued by his nephews Raimund (1489–1535) and Anton (1493–1560). During the 16th century the Fuggers were great patrons of the arts, commissioning artists and sculptors for portraits and buildings, including a family chapel in Augsburg. The mannerist sculptor Hubert GERHARD and the painters Hans von AACHEN, Georg HOEFNAGEL, and Jacopo STRADA, were among the major artists who enjoyed their patronage, as did the composer Hans HASSLER. The Fuggerei in Augsburg, a purpose-built settlement for the poor, was funded by the Fugger fortune in the second decade of the 16th century and is still in use. The house of Fugger established a network of agents and correspondents all over Europe whose letters often contained information ranging beyond immediate business matters, and the *Fugger-Zeitungen* (Fugger Newsletters) functioned as a kind of proto-newspaper. Of Raimund's sons, the eldest, Sigismund (1542–1600), became bishop of Regensburg; Johann Jakob (1516–75) was a writer and patron of art; and Ulrich (1526–84), who turned against the strongly Catholic loyalties of his family and became a Protestant, built up a collection of Greek manuscripts. Engraved portraits of family members were published in *Pinacotheca Fuggerorum* (1592). Decline set in during the later 16th century, however, when the Hapsburgs demanded increasingly large and risky loans to finance their wars and the Spanish bankruptcies of 1557, 1575, and 1607 significantly impaired the family's wealth.

**Further reading:** Victor von Klarwill (ed.), *The Fugger News-Letters: Being a Selection of Unpublished Letters from the Correspondents of the House of Fugger during the Years 1568–1605*, transl. Pauline de Clary (London: John Lane The Bodley Head, 1924).

**furniture** The Gothic tradition in domestic furnishings, extant throughout Europe before the Renaissance, was less firmly entrenched in Italy than elsewhere, so that the changes consequent on the Renaissance were more of a return to the ancient familiar classicism than the embracing of a new style.

Increasing sophistication in the style of life in Italy from the mid-15th century demanded more and better furniture. Italian Renaissance furniture, principally of walnut, is strongly influenced by classical architecture, and the function is often subordinated to the form. Much is of elegant simplicity ornamented with uncomplicated carving, but other display furniture is more elaborately shaped, covered in gesso, painted, and gilded. Several new forms appear, notably CASSONI replacing Gothic coffers and chests. A characteristic chair, with an X shape and folding construction, derives from the Roman curule chair and is known as a Dante chair. The fashion for tables with tops of marble inlaid with colored marble or semiprecious stones probably originated in Milan in the mid-16th century and was reinforced by the foundation of the *opificio delle petre dure* in Florence in 1599. Monumental sideboards of classical architectural inspiration also appeared. Beds became increasingly luxurious, with covers of rich velvets and gold embroidery, while throughout the interior fabrics and Turkey carpets were used for sumptuous effect.

In France Italian styles were first adopted after Charles VIII's capture of Naples (1495). Subsequently Italian craftsmen were employed at Amboise and Fontainebleau; other furniture-making centers were in the Île de France and Burgundy. Walnut displaced medieval oak and the refined and delicately carved furniture was often inlaid with ivory, marble, and marquetry. New forms were a light and elegant "caquetoire" (gossip) lady's chair, fixed-top (as opposed to trestle) tables, and armoires in two stages, the upper one with several small enclosed drawers. The exuberance of early Renaissance carving with its medallions and grotesques was gradually mellowed by more restrained classical features, except in the Dijon area, where a school of rich regional carving, inspired by Hugues Sambin, flourished.

In England the Italian Renaissance style was less readily absorbed and developed into an idiosyncratic formula in which basically Gothic forms were merely decorated with Renaissance motifs (*see* ELIZABETHAN STYLE). Gradually new construction techniques introduced by continental craftsmen were adopted and new ideas emerged, such as the draw-leaf tables (mid-16th century) and farthingale chairs (c. 1600). Typical Elizabethan features were heavy bulbous carved sections on legs and bed pillars, with carved strapwork often incorporating cabochons. Romayne work (a carved roundel featuring a head in profile) was especially popular in the first half of the 16th century, and is found in Italy, France, Portugal, and Spain, as well as England. In the Iberian peninsula classical motifs were often incongruously combined with the Moorish (mudéjar) style of intricate, abstract, curvilinear decoration. In Germany some cities, such as Augsburg and Nuremberg, developed a specialist decorative line in perspective work using intarsia (mosaics of inlaid wood or ivory).

# G

**Gabrieli, Andrea** (c. 1510–1585) *Italian composer*
He was a singer at St. Mark's, Venice, in 1536 and organist at San Geremia there in 1557. In 1562 he was in the service of Duke Albrecht V of Bavaria; accompanying him on a state visit to Frankfurt, he met LASSUS in Munich. From 1566 until his death Gabrieli was organist at St. Mark's. Gabrieli was a prolific composer; his works include keyboard music, notably canzonas and ricercars, which forms he developed, madrigals, and sacred music. He also wrote music for ceremonial occasions, such as the celebrations following the victory against the Turks at LEPANTO (1571). Gabrieli's compositions show the influence of Lassus and WILLAERT, and he is acknowledged as one of the foremost native Venetian composers who emerged after a long period of Flemish dominance. He was the uncle and most probably teacher of Giovanni GABRIELI.

**Gabrieli, Giovanni** (c. 1555–1612) *Italian composer*
The nephew of Andrea GABRIELI, he almost certainly studied with his uncle and like him worked for Duke Albrecht V in Munich; in 1575 he collaborated in a madrigal collection by composers who served the duke. Around 1579 he left Munich and in 1584 was back in Venice as temporary organist at St. Mark's. He obtained the permanent post, and that of organist at the Scuola Grande di San Rocco, in 1585 and kept both until his death. For both institutions Gabrieli wrote ceremonial music, much of which he published in his *Sacrae symphoniae* (1597). This contains music for two or more choirs, some with instruments, and shows a development from his earlier works which were influenced by his uncle. Around 1605 his style became more progressive; solo voices, obbligato parts for specific instruments, and basso continuo are used in varied combinations. Gabrieli also composed instrumental music; his *Canzoni e sonate* (1615) contains elaborate music for large ensembles.

**Further reading:** Denis Arnold, *Giovanni Gabrieli and the Music of the Venetian High Renaissance* (1979; repr. Oxford, U.K.: Oxford University Press, 1985).

**Gaddi, Agnolo** (c. 1350–1396) *Italian painter*
The son of Taddeo GADDI, Agnolo Gaddi worked in the Vatican as assistant to his painter brother Giovanni before embarking upon his own prosperous career. He was the last Florentine painter stylistically descended from GIOTTO and, like both Giotto and his own father, painted a series of frescoes in Sta. Croce, Florence (sometime after 1374). His most important work there was in the choir, illustrating the *Legend of the True Cross* (1388–93), in which his sacrifice of expression to design and highly decorated style anticipate the more refined paintings of his pupil Lorenzo Monaco and subsequent artists. He also designed a number of medallions, worked on statues, and painted other notable frescoes in Prato cathedral (1392–95) and San Minato al Monte, Florence (1393–96).

**Gaddi, Taddeo** (c. 1300–c. 1366) *Italian painter*
Son of the artist Gaddo Gaddi (c. 1250–1330) and godson of GIOTTO, Gaddi was a prominent member of the Florentine school of painters and worked directly under Giotto, as his chief assistant, for 24 years. His best-known fresco cycle, the *Life of the Virgin* in the Baroncelli chapel in Sta. Croce, Florence, was undertaken as an independent commission in 1332 and completed in 1338. The cycle demonstrates Gaddi's devotion to the manner of Giotto, which he later passed on to his son Agnolo GADDI, as well

as his excellence as a narrative painter in a style parallel to that of such contemporaries as Bernardo DADDI. By 1347 he was sufficiently admired to head a list of candidates to paint the altarpiece for San Giovanni Fuorcivitas in Pistoia (completed 1353). He also painted a series of scenes from the lives of Christ and St. Francis on the panels of a sacristy cupboard door, based on similar works by Giotto.

**Gaetano** See CAJETAN, THOMAS DE VIO

**Gaffurio, Franchino** (1451–1522) *Italian composer and music theorist*
A native of Lodi, he became a priest and singer at the cathedral there in the early 1470s. From 1474 he lived in various Italian cities, and in Naples he met the theorist TINCTORIS, who apparently became his closest friend. It was in Naples that he wrote his *Theoricum opus* (1479–80), his first original theoretical writing. After short periods in Lodi and Bergamo he became *maestro* at Milan cathedral in 1484, remaining there until his death. Though he left a large number of Masses and motets, Gaffurio is best known for his theoretical writings, which mainly date from his time in Milan. The *Practica musicae* (1496) is of major importance; it deals with the interpretation of chant, poetic meters and mensuration, counterpoint, and musical proportions. Most of Gaffurio's music was composed for the Ambrosian liturgy celebrated in Milan cathedral. Like his contemporary WEERBEKE, he composed for the Ordinary of the Mass.

**Gagliano, Marco da** (c. 1575–1642) *Italian composer*
Gagliano was a priest at San Lorenzo, Florence, where he was also made musical director in 1608 in succession to his teacher, Luca Bati. In the same year he was appointed court organist to Duke Cosimo II. He is primarily known as an early composer of operas and his first, *Dafne*, was staged at the Gonzaga court at Mantua in 1608. In *Dafne* he supplements the monodic recitative of the Florentine Camerata, whose members produced the earliest opera of the same name (now lost), with arias and polyphonic choruses. He wrote a number of other operas which do not survive complete, including collaborations with Jacopo PERI, *Lo sposalizio di Medoro e Angelica* (1619) and *La Flora* (1628). Gagliano was also a composer of five-part madrigals, secular duets and trios, and sacred music, including 38 motets. His song *Valli profonde* is one of the finest monodic compositions of the early baroque period.

**Galateo, Il** See DELLA CASA, GIOVANNI

**Galenism, Renaissance** The works of the Roman physician Galen (129–c. 199 CE) were considered authoritative throughout the Middle Ages and became widely available in print during the early 16th century. A Latin *Opera* was published in 1490, while the Greek *editio princeps* appeared in 1525. In addition, such important works as *On the Use of Parts*, *On Natural Faculties*, and *On Anatomical Procedures* were all available in separate Latin editions. Their main appeal to Renaissance scholars lay in the comprehensive systems of anatomy, physiology, and medicine developed in Galen's numerous works. By the mid-16th century, however, VESALIUS and FALLOPPIO began to challenge details of his anatomy, arguing there were aspects of human anatomy ignored by Galen and other features misdescribed. They therefore sought to create a more accurate and detailed system of human anatomy that depended on observation and DISSECTION.

Galenic physiology, however, proved to be more durable. The body operated, Galen argued, through three interacting systems. Natural spirits were transmitted through the venous system; vital spirits through the arterial system; and animal spirits through the nervous system, with areas of interaction in the liver, heart, and brain. Galen rejected the idea of the circulation of the blood and proposed instead that it ebbed and flowed, somewhat like the tides. Carried with it were the vital and natural spirits which, together with the animal spirits, were responsible for such distinctive vital phenomena as growth, motion, heat, and sensation. The system remained unchallenged during the Renaissance and only gradually collapsed after the publication in 1628 of HARVEY's *De motu cordis*.

Even more successful was the system of medicine constructed by Galen. Derived from Hippocratic principles, it saw man as ultimately composed of the four elements: earth, air, fire, and water. These in turn, depending on how they combined, produced the four humors: blood, phlegm, yellow bile (choler), and black bile (melancholy). If the humors were mixed harmoniously, health followed; any imbalance produced disease. The most obvious causes of such an imbalance were diet and climate. Consequently, treatment consisted largely of redressing the defects; for example, the effects of an excessively "hot and dry" diet were neutralized by switching to "wet and cold" foods and herbs. Though, in essence, the system long outlasted the Renaissance, it nevertheless faced sustained opposition from PARACELSUS and the proponents of IATROCHEMISTRY. (See illustration overleaf.)

**Galilei, Vincenzo** (c. 1525–1591) *Italian music theorist and composer*
He studied the lute in his youth, and later MUSIC THEORY with Gioseffo ZARLINO in Venice. He had settled in Pisa by the early 1560s and married (1562) a member of the local nobility by whom he became the father of GALILEO GALILEI. In 1572 he returned to Florence where his principal patron was the Florentine noble Giovanni BARDI. Galilei was at the forefront of attempts to revive the ancient Greek notion of the union of music and poetry through monody. His surviving compositions include madrigals, songs, and lute music, but he is best known for

ΓΑΛΗΝΟΥ. Α

GALENI LIBRORVM
PARS PRIMA, QVORVM IN-
DICEM VI. PAGINA
CONTINET.

ALDVS    M· R·

Ne quis alius impune, aut Venetiis aut usquam locorum hos Galeni libros imprimat, & Cle-
mentis VII. Pont· Max· & Sena-
tus Veneti decreto cau-
tum est·

**Galenism** The title page of the first printed edition (1525) of Galen's works in the original Greek. It was edited by Andrea Torresani di Asolo and Giovanni Battista Opiza and printed at the press founded by Aldus Manutius of Venice, whose anchor and dolphin device appears on the title page.

his theoretical writings. His *Dialogo della musica antica e della moderna* (1581) attacked Zarlino's theories, declaring that the Greek "modes" were quite different from the church modes, and that Greek tuning was not as Zarlino claimed. He condemned counterpoint and maintained that vocal writing should follow the form of ancient Greek music, which always had a single melodic line.

**Galileo Galilei** (1564–1642) *Italian physicist and astronomer*

The son of Vincenzo GALILEI, Galileo began to study medicine in 1581 at the university of his native Pisa, but realized that his real interest lay with mathematics, and in 1585 he left the university for Florence. There he rapidly established his scientific reputation. In 1589 he began his academic career as a mathematics lecturer at Pisa. Quarrels with colleagues forced him in 1592 to seek a comparable post in Padua. There he formed a relationship with Marina Gamba, a Venetian woman who bore him two daughters (1600, 1602) and a son (1606). While in Padua he made one of the most dramatic scientific discoveries of all time. Early in 1610 he turned the newly invented telescope to the heavens and, observing such totally unexpected phenomena as the satellites of Jupiter and the mountains of the moon, he realized immediately that he had thereby destroyed the plausibility of the still widely accepted Aristotelian COSMOLOGY. Galileo quickly published his observations in his *Sidereus nuncius* (1610;

translated as *The Starry Messenger*, 1880), a work which, though it led him into controversy, won him an international reputation.

*Sidereus nuncius* also won him the patronage of Grand Duke Cosimo II (1590–1620), who persuaded him to return to Florence. Further controversies followed. In 1613 he clashed with Christoph SCHEINER on the nature of sunspots (see illustration overleaf); during the same period he disputed with Ludovico Colombe on the issue of why thin bodies float on water. A further controversy, on the nature of comets, began in 1618 and continued for several years.

Galileo's debating skills and savage wit may well have gained him the upper hand in various disputes, but only at the expense of creating a number of powerful enemies. Consequently when they heard that Galileo was openly defending the COPERNICAN SYSTEM they protested that this belief was contrary to Scripture. Though warned by Cardinal ROBERT BELLARMINE in 1616 to be less forthright, Galileo chose to publish his thinly camouflaged views in dialogue form. When it appeared as *Dialogo dei due massimi sistemi del mondo* (1632; translated as *Dialogue on the Great World Systems*, 1953), Galileo found himself summoned to Rome. Abandoned by his patrons and friendless in Rome, Galileo had little choice, under threat of torture, other than to declare as erroneous the Copernican claim that the earth moved around the sun. He was, however, said (perhaps apocryphally) to have murmured "Eppur si muove" ("Still it moves"), referring to the earth, which the Church insisted was stationary at the center of the Universe. The Vatican cleared Galileo of heresy in 1992.

Having recanted, Galileo expected a token sentence; instead he was condemned to indefinite detention. However, his friend, the humane Archbishop Piccolomini of Siena managed to have this commuted to house arrest under his own custody, and eventually (1633) Galileo was able, though still under the supervision of the Inquisition, to move to his villa at Arcetri, close to the Franciscan convent in which his elder daughter Virginia (Sister Maria Celeste; 1600–34) was a nun. Her surviving letters show that she always had an informed interest in her father's work and a loving concern for his welfare. Her death the following year was a severe blow to him.

The enforced inaction did, however, allow him to complete a long-contemplated treatise on the nature of motion, *Due nuove scienze* (1638; translated as *Two New Sciences*, 1914). The work shows Galileo struggling to develop a new science of motion and formulating in the process an early version of the law of inertia. Further work was cut short by the blindness that had become total by the time *Due nuove scienze* was published. In his last years Galileo was attended by a pupil, Vincenzo Viviani, who acted as his ammanuensis, enabling him to keep in touch with his friends and correspondents. Viviani later wrote a biography of his master.

One further feature of Galileo's work lies in the fact that he was one of the first to appreciate the true nature of the newly emerging science. The book of nature, he declared, is written in the language of mathematics. Further, he went on, physics must concern itself with such "primary qualities" of matter as shape, size, weight, and position, which can be treated quantitatively. In this matter, while his account of motion and other such topics may have long been superseded, his vision of science and its method has been preserved largely intact.

The *Dialogo dei due massimi sistemi del mondo*, Galileo's defense of the Copernican system against a supporter of Ptolemaic cosmology, was translated into Latin in 1635, although the work was placed on the INDEX LIBRORUM PROHIBITORUM, where it remained until 1823, thus curtailing its circulation in Catholic Europe. It was translated into English in 1661 by T. Salusbury for a compilation of mathematical texts; this version, *Dialogue on the Great World Systems*, has been reprinted separately (London and Chicago, 1953). The translation by Stillman Drake, *Dialogue Concerning the Two Chief World Systems, Ptolemaic and Copernican* (Berkeley, Calif., 1953) has a foreword by Albert Einstein. There is also an abridged translation, with notes, by Maurice A. Finocchiaro (Berkeley, Calif., 1997).

**Further reading:** Stillman Drake, *Galileo* (Oxford, U.K.: Oxford University Press, 1980); Maurice A. Finocchiaro, *The Galileo Affair—A Documentary History* (Berkeley, Calif.: University of California Press, 1989); James Reston, *Galileo, a Life* (New York: HarperCollins, 1994); Dava Sobel, *Galileo's Daughter: A Historical Memoir of Science, Faith, and Love* (London and New York: Penguin, 2000).

**Gallego, Fernando** (c. 1440–c. 1509) *Spanish painter*
Mainly active in Salamanca, Gallego is noteworthy for his introduction of Flemish characteristics into Castilian painting. Dirk BOUTS is an obvious influence in Gallego's work. He painted an altarpiece of *St. Idelfonso* (c. 1467) for Zamora cathedral, a triptych of the *Virgin and Saints* for Salamanca cathedral, the now almost destroyed ceiling of the old library of Salamanca university (before 1493), and paintings of scenes from the Passion and a *Christ in Majesty* in the Prado.

**Gallican Confession** (Latin *Confessio Gallicana*) The confession of faith drawn up at France's first national synod of Protestants in 1559. It was based on a first draft prepared by CALVIN in Geneva and was revised at the synod by his pupil Antoine de la Roche Chandieu (1534–91). The confession, written in French and comprising 35 articles, restates basic Calvinist positions, including absolute PREDESTINATION. An expanded version, with 40 articles, was confirmed by the synod of La Rochelle (1571). This became the definitive statement of

**Galilei Galileo** An engraving of the author from the first edition (1613) of his *Istoria e dimostrazioni intorno alle macchie solari* (History and demonstration concerning the spots on the sun). In this work Galileo argued against Christoph Scheiner's view that sunspots were small planets circling the sun.

HUGUENOT belief and remained standard within the French Reformed Church for some 300 years; as such it was often printed in French Bibles. Its content was closely followed by the BELGIC CONFESSION of 1561, which became authoritative for the Reformed Church of the Netherlands.

**Galvão, Antonio** (c. 1490–1557) *Portuguese historian*
Galvão was the first major historian to marshal a comprehensive knowledge of the voyages of all the leading contemporary explorers, regardless of nationality. Galvão went to India in 1527 and rose to become governor of the Moluccas (1536–40), before his abilities led him to be offered the throne of Ternate Island. He declined, but on his return to Portugal (1540) he found he was out of favor and lived the rest of his life in anonymity and poverty, dying in Lisbon. His works remain among the most accurate and thorough of the period, especially *Livro dos descobrimentos das Antilhas de India*, which was published in Lisbon in 1563 and translated into English by Richard HAKLUYT in 1601.

**Gama, Vasco da** (c. 1460–1524) *Portuguese navigator*
Manuel I of Portugal employed da Gama to continue the search for the sea route to India. Sailing from Lisbon with four ships in July 1497, he successfully rounded the Cape of Good Hope in November that year. On Christmas Day 1497 he landed in Natal, naming it in honor of Christ's birthday. The expedition visited Mozambique, Mombasa, and Malindi before crossing the Indian Ocean, with the help of a local pilot, to Calicut in May 1498. Warmly received by Calicut's Hindu ruler, da Gama left some Portuguese behind and took some Hindus with him. Despite unfavorable winds and many deaths from scurvy, da Gama returned triumphantly to Lisbon in September 1499 with two ships heavily laden with spices. Rewarded with honors and a pension, da Gama returned to Calicut (1502–03) to avenge the murder of the men he had left there in 1498.

Shortly before his death in Cochin he was appointed viceroy of India.

See also: LUSIAD, THE

**Gambara, Veronica** (1485–1550) *Italian poet and patron of the arts*
Born near Brescia into a distinguished noble family, Gambara received a humanistic education, studying theology, Greek, Latin, and philosophy. In her teens, as a devoted admirer of Pietro BEMBO, she sent him her own verse, and their friendship lasted until his death (1547). In 1509 she married Count Giberto, lord of Correggio, for whom she wrote love poetry in the style of PETRARCH. She established her own salon on the Correggio estate, where she courted the political and literary elite of the day and developed friendships with Isabella d'ESTE, Bernardo TASSO, and Pietro ARETINO. Monarchs and popes were among her friends, and she promoted the career of the painter CORREGGIO (Antonio Allegri). After she was left a widow with two sons in 1518, she managed her estate with considerable skill, and in 1538 successfully resisted attack by troops of Galeotto Pico della Mirandola. Formerly a lover of high living, she graduated to a more reclusive way of life in widowhood, writing sober religious verse. The first comprehensive edition of her work, *Rime e lettere*, was published in 1759.

**Garamond, Claude** (c. 1500–1561) *French type designer, cutter, and founder*
The design and manufacture of type formed a part of printers' work until Garamond concentrated on these processes alone. He worked in Paris, where he may have been influenced by the work of the printer Geoffrey Tory, who wrote the first treatise on type design, *Champfleury*, in 1529. Garamond's family of roman types, first used by Robert ESTIENNE in 1531 in a book by Jacques Dubois (Sylvius), *In linguam Gallicam isagoge*, included capitals, small capitals, and lower-case letters. They became European standards for about 200 years, with many later versions. Garamond designed roman and italic types to complement each other, as part of the same series, so they would look harmonious on the page. His customers for type included Christophe PLANTIN, so that the best surviving collection of his punches and matrices is now in the Plantin–Moretus Museum in Antwerp.

**Garcilaso de la Vega** (1501–1536) *Spanish poet*
Born in Toledo into one of the most distinguished aristocratic families of Castile, as a youth Garcilaso served Charles V in the imperial bodyguard and, apart from a brief period of disfavor (1532), remained a member of the highest court circle. A model courtier, he successfully combined the aristocrat's profession of arms and his literary vocation. In 1525 he married the noblewoman Elena de Zúñiga, but the following year fell in love with Isabel Freire, a lady-in-waiting at the court, the "Elisa" of his poems. The unhappiness of this affair was increased by Isabel's own marriage in 1529 and by her early death in childbirth a few years later.

In 1532 Garcilaso left Spain, exiled briefly to the Danube for a minor offense that displeased the emperor. He then went to Naples where he met TASSO, Juan de VALDÉS, and others. He took part in the Tunis campaign in 1535 and the following year was fatally wounded in an unimportant skirmish near Fréjus during Charles V's invasion of France.

The greatest Spanish poet of his age, Garcilaso established Petrarchan hendecasyllabic metre and the sonnet and *canzone* in Spanish poetry. He also introduced the *lira*, a five-line stanza of 11- and 7-syllable lines rhyming *ababb*. His works, with those of his friend BOSCÁN, were published by Boscán's widow in 1543, the year which marks the beginning of Spain's *Siglo de Oro*. The poems include about 40 sonnets, five *canciones*, three eclogues, two elegies, a verse epistle to Boscán, and eight *coplas* in traditional Spanish metre. *Églogas* I and III are concerned with "Elisa"; I shows the influence of Petrarch and Sannazaro's ARCADIA and III the purely classical inspiration of Virgil and Ovid. Garcilaso also wrote the prologue to Boscán's translation of THE COURTIER (done at Garcilaso's suggestion). His oeuvre rapidly assumed the status of a classic, with editions in 1574 and in 1580, the latter by Fernando de HERRERA.

**Garcilaso de la Vega** ("El Inca") (c. 1540–1616) *Spanish writer on Inca history, rituals, and mythology*
Garcilaso was born at Cuzco, the son of a Spanish sea captain and an Inca noblewoman. He went to Spain in 1560. In 1590 his Spanish translation of the *Dialoghi di amore* by LEONE EBREO was published. His own writing displays great affection for his theme and he contradicts many Spanish chroniclers by siding with the Incas over many key issues. His most famous works are *Comentarios reales* (1609) and *Historia general del Peru* (1617).

**gardens** The designers of Italian gardens of the Renaissance revived and developed the plans of the ideal villa gardens described by the Roman author Pliny the Younger. ALBERTI directed the choice of sloping sites, with terraces giving views of the scenery beyond the garden, while within its boundaries avenues, loggias, or pergolas covered with vines provided shade, and fountains, pools, and statues added symbolic decoration to regular patterns of clipped evergreens or groves of trees. Cypress, juniper, bay, and ilex were among the plants used, with flowers or fragrant herbs often confined to a small, private, walled *giardino segreto* (secret garden) near the house, as the designs made plants subservient to symmetry. Many of these features may be seen in the illustrations to Colonna's HYPNEROTOMACHIA POLIFILI (1499). Grottoes were favorite embellishments, and hydraulic automata were almost invariably added to fountains in the most fashionable gardens, first in Italy, as at the Villa d'Este (admired by Montaigne in the 1580s), and later in France, Germany, and England. Hero of Alexandria's *Pneumatica* (first printed in Latin in 1575 and in Italian in 1589) was a source book for these toys, often of the kind known in Italy as *giochi d'acqua* (water games). They could be activated remotely, and a favorite trick was to soak the unwary visitor who came within range. The ingenuity of these and similar devices was greatly admired and commented upon by contemporary garden visitors. One of the best-documented of the later Renaissance gardens, the Hortus Palatinus at Heidelberg Castle, Germany, contrived (1615–19) by Salomon de CAUS for Princess Elizabeth, the English bride of Elector Palatine Frederick V (*see* WINTER KING), made extensive use of both grottoes and automata; there is a bird's-eye view of this complex garden in de Caus's *Hortus Palatinus* (1620).

Gardens of this kind may be said to demonstrate man's control of nature rather than the luxuriance of the plant world. In France, Charles Estienne's *Praedium rusticum* (1554) and its French version, *La Maison rustique* (1564), gave more encouragement to the enjoyment of plants arranged in parterres. However, the Italian influence, filtered through the work of such architects as Philibert DELORME and Jacques Androuet DUCERCEAU, persisted in the grandest gardens, like those of the Château d'Anet.

Around 1600 florilegia, or flower books, often records of the contents of particular gardens, show greater interest in the cultivation of an increasing variety of plants. Some were new introductions, such as the tulips brought from Turkey to western Europe in the mid-16th century. Pierre Vallet's *Le Jardin du Roy très Chrestien Henry IV* (1608) illustrates fritillaries, tulips, hyacinths, crocuses, narcissi, and lilies, among many other plants, including a selection of roses, and Basil Besler's *Hortus Eystettensis* (1613) presents a catalogue of a princely German garden in an appropriately lavish format, for systematic collections of plants were not confined to academic BOTANIC GARDENS.

**Further reading:** Terry Comito, *The Idea of the Garden in the Renaissance* (New Brunswick, N.J.: Rutgers University Press, 1978; Hassocks, U.K.,: Harvester Press, 1979); Claudia Lazzaro, *The Italian Renaissance Garden* (New Haven, Conn. and London: Yale University Press, 1990); Roy Strong, *The Renaissance Garden in England* (London: Thames & Hudson, 1979).

**Gardiner, Stephen** (c. 1490–1555) *English churchman*
Through his mother Gardiner was a second cousin of HENRY VIII. At Cambridge he was made doctor of both canon and civil law and master of Trinity Hall from 1525. He was tutor to a son of the duke of Norfolk, and in 1526 became secretary to Cardinal Wolsey, whom he accompa-

nied to France. In 1528 he went as ambassador to the pope and was active in the attempt to obtain from the universities of Europe opinions favorable to the king's divorce from Catherine of Aragon. In 1531 he was appointed bishop of Winchester. Gardiner supported the breach with Rome, but opposed the further reforms planned by CROMWELL and CRANMER. After the accession of Edward VI, he was imprisoned (1548) and deprived (1551). He was restored to his bishopric by Mary I and was also created lord chancellor, in which roles he played an important part in the Catholic reaction.

*Gargantua and Pantagruel* A cycle of four (or five) satirical novels by François RABELAIS, inspired by the successful chapbook *Les Grandes et Inestimables Chroniques du grand et énorme géant Gargantua* (1532). *La Vie estimable du grand Gargantua, père de Pantagruel*, chronologically the first novel of the series, was published in 1534, two years after *Les Horribles et Épouvantables Faits et prouesses du très renommé Pantagruel* (1532); *Le Tiers Livre des faits et dits héroïques du noble Pantagruel* and *Le Quart Livre de Pantagruel* appeared in 1546 and 1552. (The *Cinquième Livre* (1564), which continues the story of Pantagruel in the style of Rabelais, is of doubtful authenticity.) *Gargantua* deals with the birth and childhood of the giant Gargantua, son of Grandgousier; his education in Paris (an opportunity for a satirical attack on the Sorbonne); the war between Gargantua and King Picrochole; and the foundation of the abbey of Thélème, the motto of which is "Fay ce que vouldras" ("Do what you will"). *Pantagruel* tells the story of Gargantua's son, a giant of enormous strength and appetite, his friendship with the cunning rogue Panurge, and his conquest of the kingdom of the Dipsodes. Both novels are written in mock-heroic style and reveal the extent of Rabelais's learning in the fields of medicine, theology, and law. They satirize a variety of institutions, notably the Church: the intensification of these attacks in the *Tiers Livre* and *Quart Livre* led to their condemnation by the Sorbonne.

The first part of Thomas Urquhart's vigorous but free English translation, apparently the first to be published in Britain, appeared in 1653. This version was completed by Peter Motteux (1708) after Urquhart's death, and although Motteux fails to capture the spirit of either Rabelais or Urquhart this Urquhart–Motteux version was several times reprinted in the 18th and 19th centuries; C. Whibley edited it for the Tudor Translations series (3 vols, 1900). J. M. Cohen's version for the Penguin Classics series (Harmondsworth, U.K.,1955) has often been reprinted; another popular modern translation is that by Burton Raffel for Norton Critical Editions (New York, 1991).

**Garnier, Robert** (c. 1544–1590) *French tragic dramatist*
Garnier was born at La Ferté-Bernard and studied law at Toulouse, where he won prizes for his poetry at the annual

competition of the Jeux Floraux. After a period of service at the bar in Paris he was appointed to a number of important legal posts in the provinces. As a member of Henry II's Grand Conseil, he expressed his patriotism in the *Hymne de la monarchie* (1567). Garnier's dramatic works reveal his preoccupation with moral and religious issues; his early plays, which were heavily influenced by SENECA, include *Porcie* (1568), *Hippolyte* (1573), *Marc-Antoine* (1578), and *Antigone* (1580). With *Bradamante* (1582), inspired by Ariosto's ORLANDO FURIOSO, Garnier pioneered the genre of tragicomedy in French literature. The tragedy *Les Juives* (1583), generally considered to be his finest work, deals with the Old Testament story of the sufferings of Zedekiah and his family at the hands of Nebuchadnezzar.

**Further reading:** Gillian Jondorf, *Robert Garnier and the Themes of Political Tragedy in the Sixteenth Century* (Cambridge, U.K.: Cambridge University Press, 1969).

**Garofalo, Il** (**Benvenuto Tisi**) (1481–1559) *Italian painter*
The most prolific of the 16th-century Ferrarese school, Garofalo studied in Cremona and visited Venice and Rome, where he came under the influence of RAPHAEL. He served his first apprenticeship with Domenico Panetti and, after settling in Ferrara, associated with Dosso DOSSI, whose influence is evident in the treatment of landscape backgrounds in several of Garofalo's works, including his pictures of the Nativity (pre-1520) and his fine *Sacrifice to Ceres* (1526). Other works, the majority of which are competent but unoriginal, can be seen in certain Ferrarese churches, most notably the *Madonna del Pilastro* in San Francesco. He went blind in 1550.

**gastronomy** See FOOD AND COOKING

**Gattamelata, Il** (**Erasmo da Narni**) (1370–1443) *Italian soldier*
Born in Padua the son of a baker, Gattamelata served his military apprenticeship under Braccio da Montone and Niccolò PICCININO before serving in the Florentine and papal armies. It is unclear how he acquired his nickname, which means "honeyed cat." In 1434 he entered the service of Venice. During the republic's wars with the VISCONTI FAMILY of Milan, he developed a reputation for resourcefulness, determination, and leadership. His most famous exploit was to have his army drag five galleys and 25 other vessels overland from Mori on the Adige to Lake Garda to launch a surprise attack on a Milanese transport station. The tale is marred only by the failure of the raid. By the time he died, Gattamelata was captain-general of Venice, a position that earned him a state funeral and an EQUESTRIAN MONUMENT by DONATELLO, which stands outside the church of the Santo in Padua.

**Gazes, Theodore** (**Theodore Gaza**) (c. 1400–1475) *Greek scholar and teacher of Greek*
Born at Thessalonica, he came to Italy in 1430 and lived at Mantua, supporting himself by giving Greek lessons and copying manuscripts while learning Latin from VITTORINO DA FELTRE. He was made professor of Greek at Ferrara (1447) but in 1450 went to Rome at the invitation of Pope Nicholas V. In 1456 he moved to Naples and in 1459 to Calabria, where he died. He wrote a Greek grammar in Greek, which was printed in Venice (1495) and long remained a standard textbook, and he translated many Greek authors into Latin, including Aristotle, Theophrastus, and John Chrysostom.

**Gelli, Giambattista** (1498–1563) *Italian translator, dramatist, and philosopher*
Gelli had little formal education and was born of a relatively poor Florentine family. He trained as a shoemaker and tailor and in his spare time he studied Latin and Greek. He was a committed supporter of the Tuscan vernacular tongue for which he became a member of the Accademia degli Umidi (the Accademia Fiorentina from 1541). Gelli translated philosophical works from Latin, wrote comedies, and lectured on Petrarch and Dante. He is especially remembered for *I capricci del bottaio* (*The Caprices of the Cooper*; 1546), consisting of 10 dialogues between Giusto, the cooper, and his own soul; it covers satirically a range of subjects although its dominant idea is that wisdom does not ensure virtue. The book attracted the opprobrium of the Church and by 1562 it had been placed on the Index of forbidden reading (*see* INDEX LIBRORUM PROHIBITORUM). In *La Circe* (1549) the human condition is discussed in a dialogue between Ulysses and some men who had been turned into animals by Circe; they reject the chance to resume human shape because of the woes of humankind.

**Gemistus Plethon** See PLETHON, GEORGE GEMISTUS

**Gemma Frisius** (**Gemma Regnier**) (1508–1555) *Dutch mathematician, astronomer, and geographer*
Born at Dockum, East Friesland, he became a pupil of Peter APIAN and was educated at the university of Louvain, where he was appointed professor of medicine (1541). In his *Libellus de locorum describendorum ratione* (Little book on a method for delineating places), incorporated in his 1533 edition of Peter Apian's *Cosmographia*, Frisius published the first clear description of how maps could be constructed more accurately by using triangulation. Less immediate in its application (on account of the lack of sufficiently reliable timepieces at that time) was Frisius's proposal in *De principiis astronomiae et cosmographiae* (1553 ed.) that longitude at sea and elsewhere could be determined with the aid of portable clocks. His *Arithmeticae practicae methodus facilis* (1540), judging by the 59 edi-

tions known from the 16th century, proved to be one of the most successful mathematical textbooks of the period. Frisius was also known as a maker of globes, ASTROLABES, and other mathematical and astronomical instruments. His *De radio astronomico et geometrico liber* (1557) gave details of an improved cross-staff for astronomical and navigational measurements.

**Geneva** (French **Genève**, German **Genf**, Italian **Ginevra**) A Swiss city in the Rhône valley on the southwest corner of Lake Geneva. Occupied from the Stone Age, the site was first a Celtic city, then Roman, becoming the seat of a bishoric (379) and the domain of the hereditary counts of Geneva (1034–1401). After the family of the counts died out, Geneva owed a triple allegiance to its bishop-prince, its municipal government, and Savoy. During the 15th century the great trade fairs brought expansion and prosperity to the city, while its citizens resisted not only the increasing power of the bishop but also the claims of the dukes of Savoy to control its destiny.

In 1535 Guillaume FAREL persuaded the city to expel the bishop and his clergy and to adopt the reformed faith. It was Farel who invited John CALVIN to settle in Geneva, and except for a brief period when the opposition regained power Calvin spent the rest of his life in the city (1536–38; 1541–64). Under Calvin's guidance Geneva became a virtual theocracy—the "Protestant Rome"; it welcomed Protestant refugees from all over Europe, it published Calvinist tracts, and it trained theologians at its academy (*see* GENEVAN ACADEMY) and university to carry the Calvinist faith from Geneva to England, Germany, the Netherlands, Scandinavia, Scotland, and eventually to America. The refugees also played an important part in the development of Geneva's prosperous banking and watchmaking activities in the 16th century.

Late in the 16th century Geneva had to fend off aggression from Savoy; after the failure of the duke of Savoy's surprise attack (1602) Geneva's independence was guaranteed by the treaty of St.-Julien (1603). Notable buildings that have survived from the Renaissance period include St. Peter's cathedral and the town hall.

**Genevan Academy** The famous school in Geneva founded by John CALVIN in June 1559 and completed in 1564; it proved of considerable importance to the spread of Calvinism. Calvin's main intention was that his academy would prepare ministers to preach the gospel. Its outstanding academic reputation and brilliant teachers, who included BEZA, the first rector, and Jacob Arminius (1560–1609; *see* ARMINIANISM), attracted students from all over Europe. Divided into two parts, primary and secondary, the academy awarded no degrees, merely certificates of attendance. At Calvin's death it numbered 1500 students.

**Genga, Girolamo** (1472–1551) *Italian painter*
Genga was born and worked for much of his life in Urbino. He collaborated with his master Luca SIGNORELLI before going with PERUGINO to Florence (1502), where he studied perspective. Back in Urbino he was both painter and architect, completing the top story of the ducal palace there in about 1536. He also restored and decorated the Villa Imperiale near Pesaro for the duke of Urbino, endowing it with handsome wall paintings, fine stuccoed ceilings, and majolica-tiled floors.

**Gennadius (George Scholarius)** (c. 1400–c. 1468) *Greek scholar and theologian*
Perhaps born in Constantinople (the details of his early life are obscure), he came to Italy in 1438 as counselor to Emperor John Palaeologus at the Council of FLORENCE. Here he wrote works attacking PLETHON on both theological and philosophical grounds. On the schism between Eastern and Western Churches, Scholarius advocated compromise and drew up a form of agreement ambiguous enough to be accepted by both, but on his return to Greece, he completely changed his position and opposed the union. In 1448 he became a monk and took the name Gennadius. Mehmet II made him patriarch of Constantinople (1453) and he composed an exposition of Christian belief for the sultan's use, but he found the strain of being patriarch of a Muslim city too much and retired to Serres in Macedonia where he died. In addition to his theological works on such subjects as PREDESTINATION, Gennadius, who was a competent Latinist, made translations of Thomas Aquinas's works and wrote commentaries on them.

**Genoa** A northwest Italian city state and port on the Ligurian Sea. A Roman settlement (third century BCE), Genoa was frequently invaded by Arabs and Germans after the fall of Rome. By the 12th century the city had established a republic that reached the peak of its power under the Doria and Spinola families late in the 13th century. Political rivalries and foreign intervention brought years of turmoil to Genoa. The Doria and other leading noble families were expelled by Simone BOCCANEGRA (1339), but he and his successors were unable to consolidate their authority. At various times Genoa was ruled by Savoy, France, and Milan. It was conquered by France (1499) and sacked by Spain (1522) during the Wars of ITALY. In 1528 Andrea DORIA achieved a measure of political stability by expelling the French and setting up an oligarchic republic with the support of Emperor CHARLES V. The civil war (1573–76) between the old and the new aristocracy was ended by the intervention of Spain and the papacy and by the new constitutional settlement which abolished the distinctions between the old and the new nobility.

At the beginning of the Renaissance period Genoa was a major Mediterranean trading power with outposts in the Near East: during the 14th and 15th centuries its power and its trade were checked by the advances of Aragon, the loss of trading stations to the Ottoman Turks, the rivalry of Venice, and the discovery of the sea route to India. Despite these setbacks Genoa was still an important commercial power in the 16th century. Its bankers pioneered the use of credit and lent money throughout Europe.

Christopher COLUMBUS was one of its most notable citizens. Its outstanding buildings from the Renaissance period include the palaces of the Strada Nova (now the Via Garibaldi) from the second half of the 16th century and parts of the Palazzo di San Giorgio.

**Gentile de Fabriano** (Niccolò di Giovanni di Massio) (c. 1370–1427) *Italian painter*
The most accomplished exponent of the International Gothic style, Gentile first became famous for his work in northern Italy. His productions are stylistically linked with paintings of the Lombard school, in which he may have trained. In 1409 he was commissioned to execute frescoes (now destroyed) in the doge's palace in Venice, later completed by his artistic heir PISANELLO. Further commissions followed in Brescia, Siena, Florence, Orvieto, and Rome, where he painted frescoes in the basilica of St. John Lateran, which—like the greater part of Gentile's work—are now lost. The *Adoration of the Magi* (1423; Uffizi, Florence), considered to be his surviving masterpiece, is the quintessential International Gothic painting. Commissioned for a family chapel in the sacristy of Sta. Trinità, Florence, it depicts an exotic procession approaching the Virgin and Child through a fantastic landscape and is crammed with richly decorative natural detail. Among Gentile's other major extant works is the altarpiece known as the Quaratesi polyptych (1425), made for the Quaratesi family of Florence, which features a notable painting of the Madonna (London; other panels elsewhere). Such works greatly influenced the course of Florentine art.

**Gentileschi, Artemisia** (1593–c. 1653) *Italian painter*
Trained by her father, Orazio GENTILESCHI, in 1612 she was embroiled in a sensational court case when he accused her teacher, Agostino Tassi, of raping her. Tassi was eventually acquitted, but thereafter Artemisia had to live with the notoriety. In 1612 she married a wealthy Florentine painter, Pietro Antonio di Vincenzo Stiattesi. Between 1620 and 1626 she worked in Rome, where she produced some of her finest paintings, commanding high fees for her portraits, nudes, and religious scenes in the style of CARAVAGGIO. Her controversial *Judith and Holofernes* (1625; Uffizi, Florence), as well as *Penitent Magdalene*, *Rape of Proserpine*, *Portrait of a Condottiere*, and *Esther and Ahasuerus* all date from this period. In the mid-1620s she settled in Naples, where she numbered the dukes of Tuscany, Modena, and Alcalda among her patrons. After

a year painting at the court of Charles I of England (c. 1628), she undertook the important commission of *St. Januarius with Lions* for the new basilica at Pozzuoli. Despite Gentileschi's fame and wealthy clientele, much of her considerable output has not survived.

**Further reading:** Keith Christiansen, *Orazio and Artemisia Gentileschi* (New Haven, Conn: Yale University Press, 2001); Mary D. Garrard, *Artemesia Gentileschi* (Princeton, N.J.: Princeton University Press, repr. 1991).

**Gentileschi, Orazio** (Orazio Lomi) (1565–c. 1638) *Italian painter*
Born in Pisa, the son of a Florentine goldsmith, he was in Rome by 1585, painting in a late mannerist style. His friendship with CARAVAGGIO changed his fortunes and his working method and he adopted his mentor's use of CHIAROSCURO. He collaborated with the landscape painter Agostino Tassi, whom he accused in 1612 of raping his daughter (see GENTILESCHI, ARTEMISIA). After a decade working in Rome he painted altarpieces and frescoes for Fabriano cathedral and moved to Genoa in 1621. Here he painted an *Annunciation* (1623) that is often considered his masterpiece. A considerable number of his works on religious subjects have survived in Italy and elsewhere. From 1624 to 1626 Gentileschi worked in Paris for Marie de' Medici. Late in life he was invited by Charles I to execute decorative work in the royal palace at Greenwich and he died in England.

**geometry** After the great triumphs of antiquity in the *Elements* of Euclid and the *Conics* of Apollonius, advances in geometry were sparse during the medieval period. The first task facing the Renaissance scholars was to recover the texts of the ancient geometers. Erhard RATDOLT first issued the *Elements* in a Latin translation in 1482; the Greek *princeps*, edited by Simon Grynaeus, appeared in 1533. Numerous other editions, including translations, introductions, summaries, and commentaries appeared throughout the 16th century. Apollonius' *Conics* was first printed in a 1537 Latin edition, while much of Archimedes was made available in TARTAGLIA's edition of 1543.

Given the completeness of Euclid, there was in fact little for the Renaissance mathematician to add, and, when a major advance in geometry did come, it took place in analytical and not classical geometry. The roots of this discipline lay more in the works of Archimedes and Apollonius than in those of Euclid. Archimedes had worked out a number of techniques for determining the areas of curved figures. The area of a parabolic segment, for example, was shown by him to be 4/3 the area of a triangle inscribed in it. Such problems, however, only began to appeal to modern mathematicians towards the end of the Renaissance. The generally conservative nature of geometrical preoccupations is exemplified by the French mathematician Jean

Buteo whose *Opera geometrica* (1554) begins with a treatment of the shape and size of Noah's Ark as an exercise in geometry. Luca Valerio, in his *De quadratura parabolae* (1606) did little more than survey the earlier work of Archimedes. Other early attempts to develop analytical geometry were made by Simon STEVIN in his *Statics* (1586) and by KEPLER in his *Nova stereometria* (1615); it remained, however, for such later 17th-century scholars as René Descartes and Isaac Newton to develop the subject.

While not, therefore, at the center of Renaissance mathematics, classical geometry could still excite and benefit scholars in other fields. Such artists as DÜRER, for example, made a serious study of Euclid to gain a better understanding of the principles of perspective and proportion. Dürer, in fact, wrote two geometrical works: *Underweysung der Messung* (1525), on constructions with compass and ruler, and *Vier Bücher von menschlicher Proportion* (1528), on human proportion. Similar interest was shown in the subject by surveyors, astronomers, physicists, and architects. Much of the astronomy of the heavens and of the physics of motion was worked out by Renaissance savants not in the observatory or laboratory but at the drawing board, using purely geometrical techniques. Thus, COPERNICUS in his *De revolutionibus* (1545) could offer his work to the judgment of "learned mathematicians," a view echoed by LEONARDO DA VINCI who opened his lost *Trattato della pittura* with the warning: "Let no one who is not a mathematician read my works."

### George of Trebizond (c. 1395–1484) *Cretan-born teacher of Greek*

His family came from Trebizond (Turkish: Trabzon) on the Black Sea. Brought to Venice (1417) by the elder Ermolao Barbaro, who employed him as a copyist and had him taught Latin, he mastered the language so well that he became a public teacher of Latin literature at Venice, Padua, and Vicenza. Pope Eugenius IV used George's knowledge of Greek at the Council of Florence (1438) and subsequently appointed him apostolic secretary and professor at Rome, which aroused the jealousy of Italian humanists. George was a pioneer of Greek studies in Italy but his own bad temper, expressed in his feud with BESSARION, who accused him of faulty translations of Aristotle (1464), and the greater abilities of the scholars who came to Rome in the papacy of Nicholas V eclipsed his fame. He died senile and impoverished.

### Gerard, John (1545–1612) *English barber-surgeon and gardener*

Born in Nantwich, Gerard traveled abroad before settling in London to pursue his medical career. In 1596 he published a catalogue of the plants in his Holborn garden. His *Herball* (1597; with woodcuts borrowed from Frankfurt) and its revised version by Thomas Johnson (1633; with new blocks taken from PLANTIN's stock) had great influ-

ence during the next 150 years. It contains new observations on both wild and cultivated plants, combined with descriptions drawing on the work of William TURNER, Rembert DODOENS, and Matthias L'OBEL.

**See also:** HERBALS

### Gerhaert van Leyden, Nicolaus (c. 1430–1473) *Netherlands sculptor*

Born at Leyden, Gerhaert is first documented in 1462 as executing the vigorously carved tomb of Archbishop von Sierck in Trier. Between 1463 and 1467 he was in Strasbourg, after which he moved to Wiener Neustadt, where he died. Assessment of Gerhaert's development is rendered difficult by the destruction of his early sculptures in Holland and of his chief work, the high altarpiece of Constance cathedral (1465–67). The latter, in particular, was deeply influential upon south German sculptors. Only three fragments survive from his sandstone portal (c. 1464) for the new chancellery in Strasbourg. One of these astonishingly realistic heads is probably a self-portrait. Gerhaert's best-known work is the sandstone crucifix (1467) in Baden-Baden parish church. His last years were spent working on the flamboyant and expressive red marble tomb effigy of Frederick III in Vienna cathedral. Gerhaert's productions possess an entirely novel dynamism and expansiveness combined with profound characterization. The widespread diffusion of his style was stimulated both by his extensive travels, from Holland to Austria, and by numerous prints influenced by his work.

### Gerhard, Hubert (c. 1545–1620) *Netherlands sculptor*

One of the leading mannerist sculptors in Northern Europe, Gerhard was clearly influenced by his training in Italy. For the earlier part of his career he worked mainly for the FUGGER FAMILY in Augsburg (from 1581) and Duke Wilhelm V of Bavaria in Munich (from 1584). His Augsburg commissions included the Augustus fountain (erected in 1594 to celebrate the city's centenary), which first incorporated the newest Italian ideas into monumental German sculpture, and many figures and fittings for Hans Fugger's new castle at Kirchheim (1583–95), including the courtyard fountain showing Mars and Venus embracing. The first sculptor of note to work in Munich for many years, he made sculptures for Wilhelm's palace there (the Residenz) and for the church of St. Michael which Wilhelm was building for the Jesuits. After Wilhelm abdicated (1597), Gerhard moved to the court of his successor, Archduke Maximilian I, at Innsbruck.

### German language

During the period 1350–1650 (the Early New High German period) the foundations of modern German were laid. The language previously consisted of regional spoken dialects with a standardized literary language used for courtly poetry. Otherwise Latin was the usual written language. The Early New High German period saw the simplification of case endings and changes in certain vowel sounds; but the most significant development was the emergence of a standardized written language, as writing became more widespread, encompassing new spheres, from trade to expression of the emotions. The chief promoting factors were the increase in trade and business, the advent of PRINTING, and the Reformation; the impact of HUMANISM was more complex.

Humanism in Germany did not give rise directly to a vernacular literary florescence, as in Italy, France, and England. By their use of Latin for education and poetry as well as for communication, the humanists even retarded German linguistic growth. Also, the Reformation channeled the energies of many scholars away from the refinement of literary skills and into religious disputes. The humanists mainly exerted a literary influence through their translations of works in Latin and romance languages (one by-product of this was an influx of new vocabulary into German in the form of loan words from these languages). Humanist literature, however, on the whole remained separate from the popular vernacular literature (such as the SCHWÄNKE), which was flourishing by the 16th century as the new middle classes began to provide their own literary entertainment. The nationalistic concern of some humanist scholars was also significant, as they directed their attention to German literary achievements. This motivated the rediscovery of forgotten manuscripts in the vernacular, the publication of the first German dictionaries in the late 15th century, and the production of German grammars in the 16th. Scholarly interest in the German language flourished in the 17th century with the formation of societies to unify and purify the language, such as Die Fruchtbringende Gessellschaft ("the fruitful society") founded in Weimar in 1617, and with Martin Opitz's championship of German as a language fit for poetry in his *Buch von der Deutschen Poetery* (1624). Latin remained the language of scholarship until very late, however; only in 1681 did the number of German-language books printed in Germany exceed those in Latin, and German only began to be used for university lectures in 1687.

The increasing standardization of German during the period is attributable largely to the growth of trade and business. Merchants generally did not know Latin, and the prosperous activities of the HANSEATIC LEAGUE in the 14th and 15th centuries resulted in the incipient development of a standardized written language based on Low German (i.e. North German) dialects. German also came to be used as the language of documentation in the chancelleries of local princes; this was instrumental in introducing standardization in other regions in the 15th century. Most notable were a southern standard based on the *Kanzleisprache* (chancellery language) of the imperial court, and an east-central standard (in, for example, Saxony). As the economic power of the north declined, the southern and central forms gained in importance.

The process of regional standardization was furthered by printing, as it both satisfied and stimulated the growing demand for the new scholarship and literature. As printers strove to achieve the widest possible sales, they reduced regional variation in their texts and took care over orthographic consistency. The 16th century saw five regional standards of German in use among printers. Again, as the major centers of printing were in central and southern Germany, this strengthened the linguistic importance of these areas over the north.

The final step in the evolution of a written standard was LUTHER's translation of the Bible, published between 1522 and 1534. His was not the first, but it was outstanding in its scholarship and in the power of its appeal. In order to spread his message as widely and clearly as possible, Luther deliberately used everyday (even vulgar) language, introducing a new vitality and vividness to the stilted written forms then in use. A measure of his success were the 100,000 copies printed by Hans Lufft's press in Wittenberg alone between 1534 and 1584. As well as achieving a literary masterpiece, Luther exerted a decisive linguistic influence throughout Germany; even subsequent Catholic translations drew on his usage. The form of German that Luther used was east-central German, modified with usages from other areas and extended by his own innovations to cover a variety of registers. This form became the basis of modern standard German.

*Gerusalemme liberata* (1581) An epic poem in 20 cantos by Torquato TASSO. Although he had completed his masterpiece by 1575, Tasso remained dissatisfied, troubled by both aesthetic and religious qualms, and the poem underwent several revisions after its first publication. Retitled *Gerusalemme conquistata*, the latest of these appeared in 1593, a sorry testimony to Tasso's urge to appease Counter-Reformation morality and academic rules. Like BOIARDO and ARIOSTO, his predecessors at the Este court in Ferrara, Tasso wrote in OTTAVA RIMA, aiming to produce a Christian epic founded on historical truth without, however, foregoing the appeal of the chivalric and marvelous elements (*materia cavalleresca*) of earlier romances based on the legends of ARTHUR and CHARLEMAGNE and Roland. His subject was the climax of the First Crusade, the siege and conquest of Jerusalem in 1099 by the army of Godfrey of Boulogne. To the historical participants—Godfrey, Baldwin, Tancred, Raymond of Toulouse, Bohemond, Peter the Hermit, and Solyman, Sultan of Nicaea—Tasso added essential fictional characters: Rinaldo (introduced as the ancestor of the Este), the enchantress Armida, Argante, and Clorinda and Erminia, who are romantically involved with Tancredi. The Christians defeat the many stratagems of the forces of evil and the poem concludes as Godfrey leads the triumphant crusaders to the Holy Sepulcher. It was translated into English (1594, 1600) by Edward Fairfax and influenced parts of Spenser's FAERIE QUEENE. There is a modern verse translation by Anthony Esolen (Detroit, Mich., 1987).

**Gesner, Konrad** (1516–1565) *Swiss naturalist and bibliographer*
The son of a Zürich artisan, Gesner was educated at the university of Basle. After continuing his education in Paris and Montpellier, he returned to Switzerland in 1641 to become professor of Greek at Lausanne university. He later turned to medicine, becoming in 1541 chief physician of Zürich. A prolific author, Gesner wrote more than 80 works, the best known of which is his comprehensive five-volume *Historiae animalium* (1551–87). A related *Historiae plantarum*, with 1500 illustrations, appeared posthumously (1751–59). Much shorter, but more perceptive, is Gesner's *De omni rerum fossilium genere* (1565), in which he proposes a possible organic origin for fossils (*see* MINERALOGY). In the field of bibliography Gesner's major work is *Bibliotheca universalis* (1545–49) in which he tried to list and summarize all known Greek, Latin, and Hebrew works. He died in Zürich of the plague.

**Gesualdo, Carlo** (c. 1561–1613) *Italian nobleman and composer*
Born in Naples, Gesualdo held the title of prince of Venosa. Following the widely publicized murder of his wife and her lover (1590), Gesualdo retired to his estate at Gesualdo near Avellino. In 1594 he went to Ferrara to marry Leonora d'Este, niece to the reigning duke. In the same year his first two books of MADRIGALS were published in Ferrara. Gesualdo suffered from melancholy, and spent most of the rest of his life on his estate at Gesualdo; his letters from this period reveal an extraordinary sensitivity. He published in all six books of madrigals, two of motets, one of responsories, and some keyboard works. It is for his madrigals that he is chiefly remembered; chromatic harmonies and the juxtaposition of fast and slow movements result in a mannered, idiosyncratic style which was much admired, though little imitated.

**Further reading:** Glenn Watkins, *Gesualdo: The Man and His Music* (1973; 2nd ed. Oxford, U.K.: Clarendon Press, 1991).

**Ghent** The capital of the modern province of East Flanders, Belgium, situated at the junction of the Scheldt and Lys rivers. Ghent supplanted neighboring Bruges as seat of the counts of Flanders in the late 12th century but its wealthy merchant class soon gained a measure of independence from its feudal overlord and a degree of democratic self-government which was mainly in the hands of those connected with the cloth industry. Ghent passed with the rest of Flanders to Burgundian and then Hapsburg rule, and in the 16th century played a prominent role in the attempt to throw off the Spanish yoke. It rebelled and was severely crushed by CHARLES V in 1540, and in 1576 the leaders of the Netherlands patriots met there to sign the Pacification of Ghent as a compact for preserving their lands from Hapsburg despotism. It was regained for Spain by Alessandro FARNESE, Duke of Parma, but depopulation and religious persecution had wrecked its prosperity, and the closing of the Scheldt to trade (1648) ended its chances of recovery.

The cathedral of St. Bavon contains the van EYCK brothers' great masterpiece, *The Adoration of the Lamb* (*see* GHENT ALTARPIECE). The town hall has one Flamboyant Gothic facade (1518–33) and one in the Renaissance style (1595–1628).

**Ghent altarpiece** (*The Adoration of the Lamb, The Mystic Lamb*; 1432) A polyptych painted for the cathedral of St. Bavon, Ghent, by Hubert and Jan van EYCK. The subject matter of the two-tier, shuttered altarpiece is complex. The lower register of the interior features *The Adoration of the Lamb of God by the Elect* (hence the altarpiece's alternative name), and the upper shows God the Father enthroned between the Virgin and St. John the Baptist, musical angels, and Adam and Eve. On the lowest level of the exterior, Jodocus Vyd and his wife, patrons of the altarpiece, kneel in prayer before two simulated statues of St. John the Baptist and St. John the Evangelist. These figures are surmounted by an Annunciation, and, at the top, pictures of the prophets and sibyls who foresaw the Virgin Birth. Each of the polyptych's 20 separate panels has the same high finish and extraordinary attention to detail, and the relative contributions of the two brothers van Eyck remain controversial among art historians.

**Ghibellines** See GUELFS AND GHIBELLINES

**Ghiberti, Lorenzo** (1378–1455) *Italian sculptor*
Unlike many other Florentine sculptors, Ghiberti, who trained as a goldsmith, specialized exclusively in bronze casting. The Renaissance is often taken as beginning with the competition (1401) to find the executant of the doors for the Baptistery, which Ghiberti won—narrowly—from BRUNELLESCHI, both submitting specimen panels in relief of the *Sacrifice of Isaac* (Bargello, Florence). Ghiberti is famed for the two sets of great bronze doors he produced: those now on the north of the Baptistery took him the first half of his career (1403–24); those on the east, facing the facade of the cathedral (called by Michelangelo the "Gates of Paradise"), preoccupied him from 1425 until 1452. His style developed considerably from the 28 small decorative panels of the earlier doors to the 10 great panoramic narrative scenes of the later ones.

It is an oversimplification to regard Ghiberti as a Gothic artist, in diametric contrast with Brunelleschi and DONATELLO as representatives of the Renaissance, for there are many debts in his work to Greco-Roman sculpture, which he personally collected and on which he advised others. Ghiberti's genuinely transitional style was greatly appreciated in his day and was probably more popular than Donatello's demanding and dramatic mode. Ghiberti's three bronze statues for the guildhall, Orsanmichele, are also far less intensely characterized than Donatello's: *St. John the Baptist* (1412), still very Gothic in treatment; *St. Matthew* (1419), a truly Renaissance statue, derived from those of ancient Roman senators; and *St. Stephen* (1426–28), a rather bland young priest.

**Further reading:** Ross King, *Brunelleschi's Dome: The Story of the Great Cathedral in Florence* (New York: Walker, 2000); Richard Krautheimer, *Lorenzo Ghiberti* (Princeton, N.J.: Princeton University Press, 1956; repr. 1982).

## Ghirlandaio, Domenico (Domenico di Tommaso Bigordi) (1449–1494) *Italian painter*

The best FRESCO painter of his generation and extremely prolific, Ghirlandaio was the son of a Florentine goldsmith and established a flourishing workshop there with the assistance of his relatives. Later, MICHELANGELO served him as an apprentice. One reason for Ghirlandaio's popularity was his inclusion in his paintings of portraits of his friends and contemporary Florentine dignitaries, as seen in the fresco cycle *Christ Calling the First Apostles* in the Sistine Chapel in Rome (1481–82), painted in the already old-fashioned style of MASACCIO. Most of Ghirlandaio's frescoes were painted in Florence and are notable for their complex composition and technical excellence; chief

**Lorenzo Ghiberti** A panel (one of ten) from the east door of the Baptistery adjoining the Duomo of Florence, produced by Ghiberti during the period 1425–52. The panel depicts the biblical story in which Jacob tricked his father, Isaac, into believing that he was his brother Esau.
*Mansell/Time Life Pictures/Getty Images*

among them are those in the Sassetti chapel, Sta. Trinità (scenes from the life of St. Francis; c. 1485) and in the choir of Sta. Maria Novella (scenes from the lives of the Virgin and St. John the Baptist; c. 1490), which were again remarkable for their control of prosaic naturalism. Best known of his other paintings is *Old Man and his Grandson* (1480), which combines genuine tenderness with uncompromising reality. Ghirlandaio's son, Ridolfo Bigordi (1483–1561), distinguished himself as a portrait painter.

## Giambologna (Jean Boulogne, Giovanni (da) Bologna) (1529–1608) *Flemish-born sculptor*

Giambologna was born at Douai and trained under the Flemish sculptor Jacques DUBROEUCQ on the roodloft for Ste. Waldetrude, Mons (now Belgium). In about 1550 he traveled to Rome to study classical and Renaissance sculpture and met MICHELANGELO. He was encouraged to settle in Florence and by 1558 was in the pay of the Medici. He grafted an understanding of Michelangelo's style onto his fresh knowledge of classical Hellenistic sculpture, which had recently been excavated in Rome.

Giambologna developed Michelangelo's earlier ideas for sculptures with two or three figures in a series of marble masterpieces that span his career: *Samson slaying a Philistine* (1560–62; Victoria and Albert Museum, London); *Florence triumphant over Pisa* (1565–80; Bargello, Florence); *The Rape of a Sabine* (1579–83; Loggia dei Lanzi, Florence); *Hercules slaying a Centaur* (1594–99; also Loggia dei Lanzi). For the garden of Duke Francesco I de' Medici's favorite villa at Pratolino on the outskirts of Florence he created (c. 1580) a gigantic statue of the personification of the Apennines, an old man with a stalactite-like beard crouching on a rocky outcrop above a pool in the present-day Parco Demidoff (see Plate IV). Such displays of virtuosity made him the most influential and sought-after sculptor in the whole of Europe for half a century (1560–1610).

Giambologna also excelled in modeling sculpture to be cast in bronze, a medium Michelangelo had abhorred; he must have been encouraged by the success of Cellini's *Perseus*, unveiled just as he arrived in Florence (1554). His own first success was a fountain of Neptune in Bologna (1563–67), where he also invented his most enduringly successful, and widely reproduced, composition in bronze, a flying Mercury (examples at different scales in Bologna, Florence, Naples, Paris, and Vienna). Exploiting the potential of metal for statues with widely flung limbs and accessories, he produced a series of *Labours of Hercules* and other aggressively masculine subjects; his statuettes of females are composed differently, with their bent limbs wound round their bodies in a fascinating sequence of angles and sensuous curves.

Giambologna revitalized, mainly for religious themes, the Florentine tradition of narrative reliefs in bronze. But his greatest contribution to the development of sculpture was the EQUESTRIAN MONUMENT of Duke Cosimo I (1587–93; Piazza della Signoria, Florence); this gave a fresh impetus to a tradition, which was then followed throughout the capitals of Europe. His own studio produced other similar equestrian portraits of the reigning Duke Ferdinando I de' Medici (Piazza SS. Annunziata, Florence), of King Henry IV of France (Paris, destroyed in the French Revolution), and of King Philip III of Spain. These were imitated in London by Hubert Le Sueur's statue of King Charles I (1630; Trafalgar Square).

The spread of Giambologna's elegant, courtly style was ensured by the wide distribution of his bronze statuettes and the number of his pupils who went to work all over Europe. Giambologna's career links that of Michelangelo, whom he imitated, to that of Bernini, founder of the Baroque in Rome.

**Further reading:** Charles Avery, *Giambologna: The Complete Sculpture* (Oxford, U.K.: Phaidon Christie's, 1987; repr. Phaidon, 1994); Mary W. Gibbons, *Giambologna: Narrator of the Catholic Reformation* (Berkeley, Calif. and London: University of California Press, 1995).

**giant order** See COLOSSAL ORDER

## Gibbons, Orlando (1583–1625) *English composer*

He sang in the choir of King's College, Cambridge, from 1596/98 before becoming a student at the university. In about 1603 he became a member and probably organist of the Chapel Royal. In 1623 he was appointed organist of Westminster Abbey, and in 1625 is recorded as also being senior organist at the Chapel Royal and a musician in the king's private music. He died in Canterbury while awaiting with Charles I's retinue the arrival of Charles's bride, Henrietta Maria. Gibbons wrote many keyboard pieces and a number of consort works, but is most famous for his church music, all for the Anglican rite. In his verse anthems soloists and chorus alternate in an expressive treatment of the text; many of these works may be accompanied by either viols or organ.

## Giberti, Gian Matteo (1495–1543) *Italian churchman*

Giberti, who was illegitimate, was born in Genoa and as a young man he attracted the patronage of Cardinal Giulio de' Medici. When his patron became Pope Clement VII (1523) Giberti virtually ran the papal Curia and strongly encouraged the pope in his anti-imperial diplomacy. In 1524 he was appointed bishop of Verona, and after the sack of Rome (1527) he settled in his diocese and undertook far-reaching reforms, aimed at raising the quality of the Church's pastoral life and the efficacy of its ministry. His methods were studied with attention by Cardinal (later St) CHARLES BORROMEO. Under Pope Paul III Giberti continued to be a trusted papal adviser, and his work is seen as preparing the way for the Council of TRENT. He was also an able patristics scholar, publishing several editions of the Church Fathers.

## Gilbert, Sir Humfrey (c. 1539–1583) *English explorer and soldier*

He served in Le Havre (1563) and Ireland (1567–70 and 1579) and in 1572 commanded 1500 English volunteers assisting the Dutch struggle against Spanish rule. In 1566 he failed to persuade Queen Elizabeth to support his proposed search for a NORTHWEST PASSAGE from England to the East; later she rejected his plans to prey on Spanish treasure ships. Armed with a royal charter to settle heathen land, he embarked on his first and unsuccessful expedition (1578–79) to North America. On his second expedition (1583) he annexed Newfoundland for England, but went down with his ship on the homeward voyage.

## Gilbert, William (1544–1603) *English physician and physicist*

After reading medicine at Cambridge, and a period of European travel, Gilbert moved to London in 1573. His practice flourished, culminating in his becoming physician to Elizabeth I and, in 1600, president of the College of Physicians. It is, however, on *De magnete* (1600), long recognized as the first major work of British science, that Gilbert's reputation rests. Dedicated to those who seek knowledge from things, not books, the work made one of the first serious attempts to show the value of the newly established experimental method. In his most unexpected conclusion he demonstrated that the earth itself was a magnet, with lines of force running between the poles. No traditionalist, Gilbert was intensely critical of Aristotle, while at the same time supporting the claim of Copernicus that the earth rotates.

*Gioconda, La* See MONA LISA

## Giocondo, Fra (Giovanni da Verona) (1433–1515) *Italian architect*

Best known for his edition of the Roman architectural writer VITRUVIUS (1511), Giocondo was frequently consulted by other leading architects, and his collection of drawings of details of classical ruins in Rome was a valuable resource both to them and to his patrons. He worked in both Italy and France, often as architectural adviser, but also as a designer of gardens (at Naples and Blois). In his native Verona he worked on the Palazzo del Consiglio (1476–88), in Naples (1489–93) he was responsible for fortifications, and in Paris he built the Pont-de-Notre-Dame (1500–08). He also designed the defenses of Venice (c. 1506), built city walls at Treviso (1509), and, following BRAMANTE's death in 1514, became supervisor at St. Peter's in Rome, sharing the post with RAPHAEL and Giuliano da SANGALLO.

## Giolito, Gabriele (fl. 1538–1578) *Italian printer*

The most important member of a Piedmontese family of printers and publishers, Giolito settled in Venice in 1538. In the next 40 years he published about 850 books, including many editions of Ariosto and reprints of Petrarch, Boccaccio, and Dante, as well as translations. As the intellectual climate changed and the power of the Inquisition grew, Giolito concentrated on books of spiritual advice. The decorated initials and title-pages of his books, with borders and panels of printers' flowers and fine woodcut illustrations, set new fashions, like those for enclosing whole scenes in initials (an echo of manuscript illumination) or packing a series of small illustrations into one picture. His sons took over his firm, but they were less successful and it did not survive beyond 1606.

## Giorgio, Maestro See ANDREOLI, GIORGIO

## Giorgione (Giorgio Barbarelli, Giorgio del Castelfranco) (c. 1476–1510) *Italian painter*

Born at Castelfranco in the Veneto, Giorgione was a pupil of Giovanni BELLINI at Venice during the 1490s and probably met TITIAN there. Little is known of his life, and only a few paintings are firmly attributed to him; however, there is general agreement that he initiated the High Renaissance style in Venetian art. His early works, such as the Castelfranco *Madonna Enthroned* (c. 1500) with its dreamy figures and passive mood, and *Judith* (c. 1504; St. Petersburg), were profoundly influenced by the styles of Bellini, GENTILE, and (increasingly) LEONARDO DA VINCI. *The Tempest* (c. 1503; Venice) is an evocative pastoral scene in which landscape for the first time is treated for its own sake, rather than as a mere background, and established a genre in Venetian art. In this and other works, such as *Sleeping Venus* (Dresden), finished by Titian, *The Three Philosophers* (Vienna) finished by SEBASTIANO DEL PIOMBO, and *Laura* (1506; Vienna), a portrait of a young woman, Giorgione experimented with qualities of mood and mystery, experiments that Titian went on to develop after Giorgione's death in an outbreak of the plague. Among his mature portraits is a fine one of a Knight of Malta (Uffizi, Florence), with an intense, brooding gaze. Other works probably by Giorgione include *The Pastoral Concert* (Louvre, Paris), *Christ Carrying the Cross* (Boston), and *Adoration of the Shepherds* (Washington), although several works are lost. Also active as a musician and poet, Giorgione, although controversial in his time, played a crucial role in the development of High Renaissance art, as expanded in the works of Titian.

**Further reading:** Jaynie Anderson, *Giorgione: The Painter of 'Poetic Brevity'* (Paris: Flammarion, 1997); Terisio Pignatti and Filippo Pedrocco, *Giorgione* (Milan, Italy: Rizzoli, 1999).

**Giotto (di Bondone)** (c. 1267–1337) *Italian painter*
Born near Florence, Giotto, above all his contemporaries, is credited with effecting the transformation of European art from the earlier flat Byzantine model to the humanistic naturalism of the Italian Renaissance. Tradition has it that he was a pupil of the Florentine artist CIMABUE, who was lauded with Giotto in Dante's *Purgatorio* as the greatest of all artists. Giotto's early works also show the influence of PISANO and other contemporary sculptors in his adoption of a new three-dimensional realism. The work of Giotto most celebrated among his contemporaries was the mosaic *Navicella* (c. 1300) for St. Peter's, Rome, now largely destroyed.

More influential in the long term were his frescoes for the ARENA CHAPEL, Padua (begun c. 1305). This cycle, the *Lives of the Virgin and Christ*, covers most of the interior of the chapel and epitomizes Giotto's achievement as the first great creative personality of European painting. The three tiers of scenes are remarkable for their rejection of color and conventional elegance and for their concentration upon moral content, expressed with a simplicity and dignity hitherto unknown. Giotto's altarpiece of the *Madonna Enthroned* for Ognissanti, Florence (c. 1310; Uffizi, Florence) and his frescoes for the chapels of the Bardi and Peruzzi families in the church of Sta. Croce, Florence, painted during the 1320s, consolidated his reputation as the most important painter of the Trecento. Also often attributed to him is the fresco cycle in the upper church of San Francesco at Assisi (c. 1297–c. 1305). In Florence, where he was director of public works, he was entrusted with the major architectural commission for the building of the campanile of the cathedral (1334). An ugly but witty man, Giotto exercised enormous influence upon almost all the Florentine painters who succeeded him, including MASACCIO and MICHELANGELO.

**Further reading:** Bruce Cole, *Giotto and Florentine Painting, 1280–1375* (New York: Harper & Row, 1976); Andrew Lodis (ed.), *Giotto, Master Painter and Architect: Florence* (New York: Garland, 1998).

**Giovanni (da) Bologna** See GIAMBOLOGNA

**Giovanni Capistrano, St.** (John of Capistrano) (1386–1456) *Italian Franciscan*
Born in Capistrano in the Abruzzi, Giovanni studied law and was appointed magistrate at Perugia in 1412. While a prisoner of war of the MALATESTA FAMILY, he experienced a religious conversion; on his release in 1416 he joined the Franciscan Order. With BERNARDINO OF SIENA he became a leading figure in the Observants, the Franciscan faction that aimed to restore the original rule of St. Francis in all its austerity. These activities led to his trial (but acquittal) for heresy in 1429. During this period he became a famous preacher and in 1451 he was chosen by Pope Nicholas V to lead a mission to Austria, where the spread of HUSSITE teachings was causing alarm. Preaching missions to many parts of eastern Europe followed. In his last years he became preoccupied with the threat to the whole region from the OTTOMAN TURKS. Having failed to persuade other European leaders to act, he joined the Hungarian general János Hunyadi (c. 1407–56) in raising and leading a largely untrained peasant army to relieve the Turkish siege of Belgrade. The result was a remarkable victory over the Turks (July 22, 1456) but Giovanni died of illness on the return journey.

**Giovanni da Udine** (Giovanni Recamador) (1487–1561/4) *Italian painter and architect*
Born at Udine, he was a pupil of RAPHAEL in Rome and played a leading part in the decoration of the Vatican Loggie (1517–19) and the Villa Madama (1520), together with such colleagues as GIULIO ROMANO. He made extensive use of GROTESQUES in his decorative style, which lent itself particularly well to stucco and fresco, and after his return to Udine he was made responsible for all public architectural projects there (1552), as well as continuing his decorative work. His graceful style was imitated throughout Europe during the 18th century by neoclassical designers. His other works include stained-glass windows, incorporating arabesque features, in Florence.

**Giovanni da Verona** See GIOCONDO, FRA

**Giovanni di Paolo** (c. 1403–1482) *Italian painter*
A native of Siena, Giovanni may have been a pupil of Taddeo di Bartol. He probably never visited the other artistic centers in Italy, thus remaining virtually unaffected by the growing trend towards naturalism and classical humanism in such cities as Florence. Instead Giovanni was, with SASSETTA, the leading exponent of the mystical and conservative style of the 15th-century Sienese school and was dubbed the "El Greco of the Quattrocento" by the U.S. art critic Bernard Berenson. Although archaic in form, such works as *St. John in the Wilderness* (date unknown), *Purification of the Virgin* (1447–49), and the *Madonna* altarpiece in Pienza cathedral (1463) illustrate Giovanni's ability as a narrative painter. At his best Giovanni expresses a dramatic and tormented intensity, which has been seen by some to anticipate mannerist and expressionist art; at his worst he repeats the conventional formulae of medieval decoration. For many years his work was neglected, but the 20th century saw a revival in critical interest, despite the fact that he was already outmoded in his own time and had no very profound influence upon his immediate successors.

**Giovio, Paolo** (Paulus Jovinus) (1483–1552) *Italian historian and biographer*
Educated as a doctor, Giovio left his native Como to become a servant of the papacy under Leo X (1513) and

spent most of his life at the papal court, where he acquired an intimate knowledge of its affairs. Clement VII made him bishop of Nocera (1528); he withdrew from Rome in 1549, having failed to become a cardinal under Paul III, and ended his life on a visit to Florence. His major work, *Historiae sui temporis* (1550–52), covers the years 1494–1547. In Italian he wrote a commentary on Turkish affairs (1531) and a work on heraldic IMPRESE (1541). His Latin biographies of Leo X, the military leader Ferdinando d'Avalos, and others were soon translated into Italian and he encouraged VASARI to write his lives of artists. The posthumously published collection of lives of scholars, *Elogia doctorum virorum* (Antwerp, 1557), contained portraits of the subjects and poems by Ioannes Latomus Bergamus and others.

**Further reading:** T. C. Price Zimmermann, *Paolo Giovio: The Historian and the Crisis of Sixteenth-Century Italy* (Princeton, N.J.: Princeton University Press, 1995).

**Giraldi Cinthio, Giambattista** See CINTHIO

**Giuliano da Maiano** (1432–1490) *Italian architect*
A member of a leading artistic family of Florence in the 15th century, Giuliano trained with his brother, the sculptor BENEDETTO DA MAIANO, as a stone-carver and later collaborated with him on a number of projects, including the shrine of San Savino (1472; Faenza cathedral) and a chapel for Sta. Fina in the Collegiata at San Gimignano (1468). Following in the artistic footsteps of BRUNELLESCHI and MICHELOZZO, Giuliano worked on the Palazzo Pazzi in Florence (c. 1460–72) and designed Faenza cathedral (1474–86), the vaulting of the nave in the cathedral of Loreto (post-1481), and a royal villa in Naples, the Poggio Reale (1484–90), now destroyed. He also executed several notable carvings in wood.

**Giulio Romano** (Giulio Pippi) (c. 1492–1546) *Italian painter and architect*
Born in Rome, Giulio worked in RAPHAEL's workshop as a child and by the time of the painter's death (1520) had become the chief assistant there, engaged on frescoes in the Stanza dell'Incendio in the Vatican (completed in 1517) and in the Loggie (completed in 1519). After Raphael's death, Giulio completed several other works, including the Sala di Constantino frescoes at the Vatican (1524) and the *Transfiguration* (1517–22), as well as original paintings of his own, such as the altarpiece for Sta. Maria dell'Anima in Rome (c. 1523) and the *Stoning of St. Stephen* (1523) for San Stefano in Genoa.

After further work at the Villa Madama and the Villa FARNESINA with GIOVANNI DA UDINE, he moved to Mantua, where he was obliged to remain after a scandal erupted over his implication in some obscene engravings. There he dominated artistic affairs and, at the invitation of Federico II Gonzaga, embarked upon his masterpiece, the Palazzo del TÈ (c. 1525). Constructed and decorated under Giulio's direction, the palace is a monument to the mannerist style that he helped to create (*see* MANNERISM). He also worked in the Reggia dei Gonzaga in Mantua, in a style anticipating the Baroque, built a mannerist-style house for himself and his family (1544–46), and in 1545 began the rebuilding of Mantua cathedral after his own plans. He enjoyed considerable fame even beyond the borders of Italy; Shakespeare, for instance, refers to him as "that rare Italian master" (*Winter's Tale* V ii).

**Further reading:** Manfredo Tafuri, *Giulio Romano* (Cambridge, U.K.: Cambridge University Press, 1998).

**Giunti press** (**Junta press**) A printing house first established by Luca-Antonio Giunti (1457–1538) in Venice in the 1480s, specializing in liturgical works. The more important branch of the firm was at Florence, where Filippo Giunti (1450–1517) printed from 1497 until his death. The business was carried on by his descendants until the early 17th century. The Venetian branch of the family lasted until 1642, and there was a third branch printing at Lyons from 1520 to 1592. Filippo Giunti printed the first Greek edition of PLUTARCH's *Lives* (1517), but the quality of scholarship in Giunti editions was generally well below that of works from the ALDINE PRESS.

**Glareanus, Henricus** (**Henry of Glarus, Heinrich Loris**) (1488–1563) *Swiss musical theorist and humanist*
As a child and young man Glareanus studied in Berne and Rottweil with Michael Rubellus, and in 1506 he began his studies of philosophy, theology, mathematics, and music at Cologne university. He made a reputation for himself by writing Latin poems and was awarded the poet's laurel by Emperor Maximilian in 1512. In 1514 he returned to Basle, where he met ERASMUS, who became a great influence on his thinking. In 1529 Glareanus became professor of poetry at the university of Fribourg, and later professor of theology. He wrote a treatise on geography (1527) and several musical treatises, the most important being his *Dodecachordon* (1547), in which he propounds his theory of 12 church modes. This had considerable influence on late Renaissance composers.

**See also:** MUSIC THEORY

**glass** During the Renaissance the fine glass of Venice was preeminent, widely exported into northern Europe and coveted by the nobility. Venetian glass manufacture had been moved to the island of Murano in 1292 as a precaution against fire and by 1330 the famous Barovier family of glass makers was already active there. In the mid-15th century an influx of expert Islamic glass-workers into Murano stimulated the already established industry. Strictly enforced guild rules of secrecy protected the Venetian product from effective competition.

From about 1450 output included goblets, cups, and bowls of dark red, green, and blue glass, modeled on shapes used by contemporary metalworkers. These were painted in enamels in contrasting colors with historical and mythological scenes and on betrothal goblets medallion portraits of bride and groom. This style was later superseded by painted geometric and fish-scale decoration, with imitations of inset jewels.

Toward the end of the 15th century a clear colorless glass called *cristallo* was developed. Its great ductility and rapid cooling allowed glass blowers to make thin-walled vessels, tazzas, and other items of austere, unadorned beauty. Gradually this *cristallo* ware became more ornamented, with fantastic applied winged shapes and handles. Admiration for antique Roman glass led to the revival of millefiori and mosaic glass, and to the imitation of such natural stones as aventurine and chalcedony. Similarly the Roman use of rope-like decoration inspired the well-known *latticino* ware with interlaced white threads in the glass. Another widely practiced technique produced cracked-ice glass, particularly effective when used for water jugs and bowls.

Eventually migrant workers from Genoa, not bound to secrecy, enabled many northern European centers to produce imitative glassware in what was called "façon de Venise." The technique of making Venetian crystal was brought to England early in Elizabeth I's reign by glassmakers from Lorraine and Venice; in 1575 she awarded the Venetian glassmaker Giacomo Verzelini (1522–1606) a monopoly for this product. In Germany there was a different indigenous glass-making tradition, with beakers and stemmed glasses, almost always in green glass, often with prunt decoration. The classic German wine glass, the *roemer*, was an early 16th-century development. Kaspar Lehmann (1563–1622), jewel-cutter to Emperor Rudolf II, pioneered the technique of decorative glass cutting, for which he obtained a monopoly in 1609 and which he passed on to his pupil Georg Schwanhardt. This heralded the predominance of Bohemian glass in the post-Renaissance period.

Fine glass vessels such as the Venetian and Bohemian wares were always goods for the luxury end of the market. A major difference between the glass factories of the Mediterranean area and northern Europe was that the former used soda-ash obtained from various maritime plants, which was capable of yielding good-quality crystal, while the latter had to rely on potash from sundry kinds of vegetation, with more variable results. Less glamorous glass manufactories, capable of turning out utilitarian items for local use, existed in Europe throughout the Middle Ages wherever a supply of all the necessary raw materials was readily to hand: ashes (preferably of beechwood, but also of ferns or bracken, which gave rise to the French name *verre de fougère*); sand of a suitable composition; clay capable of being made into crucibles that could withstand temperatures in excess of 1200° Celsius; and an abundance of wood to fuel the furnaces. A manuscript of *Mandeville's Travels* in the British Library dated c. 1420 and probably from Bohemia contains a miniature showing various stages of glass manufacture from digging the sand to removing the finished vessels from the furnace. In England the Weald of Surrey and Sussex in the southeast of the country was probably the major center for the craft, but Cheshire and Staffordshire too had the necessary combination of materials to support a glass-making industry. The characteristics of the sand used, which usually contained small percentages of iron oxide, meant that most English medieval glass is either green or tinged with green. Flanders, Normandy, and the Rhineland were all significant northern European glass-making areas. Other items made in the humbler workshops were hanging lamps, flasks, vessels and tubes for distilling, urinals, and solid balls of glass used for smoothing materials in various industrial activities.

Until the 16th century, when specialization became common, the manufacture of glass vessels and other pieces was normally only one aspect of a workshop's output, and in many cases the making of glass for windows was the more important activity. Colored glass for stained-glass windows was considerably more expensive than white (clear) as the minerals necessary for making it often had to be imported from afar: cobalt for blue may have come from the Near East in the form of a diluted colorant called "zaffre." Copper was needed for red. The techniques for obtaining the rich colors associated with medieval church windows were already understood at the beginning of the period, and the main technological development of the later Middle Ages and Renaissance was the ability to produced larger panels of glass. The main medieval process (the "crown" method), associated particularly with the glass makers of Normandy, produced a circular disk from which the glaziers cut window panes. The more complicated "muff" technique was refined by French Huguenot makers in Lorraine who took their skill with them to other parts of Europe when they became refugees in the late 1560s.

**Further reading:** Patrick McCray, *Glassmaking in Renaissance Venice: The Fragile Craft* (Aldershot, U.K.: Ashgate, 1999).

## Goes, Hugo van der (c. 1440–1482) *Flemish artist*

Probably born at Ghent, Hugo van der Goes was accepted as a master in the painters' guild there in 1467, although few other details of his early life are known. He executed decorations for such public events as the marriage of CHARLES THE BOLD and Margaret of York (1468) and a number of paintings reflecting the influence of Jan van EYCK and Rogier van der WEYDEN, notably a diptych begun in 1467. Having been made a dean of the painters' guild in 1474, Hugo entered the Augustinian monastery of the Red

Cloister, near Brussels, as a lay brother in 1475 and, in the same year, produced his master work, the PORTINARI AL-TARPIECE (see Plate VI). Subsequent works from this period, such as two panels probably designed as organ shutters (1478–79; National Gallery of Scotland, Edinburgh) and the *Death of the Virgin* (c. 1480; Musée Communal, Bruges) demonstrate Hugo's skill as a draftsman and are characterized by a sense of religious intensity. In his last years Hugo became increasingly depressive, attempting suicide in 1481 and dying insane the following year.

**Góis, Damião de** (1502–1574) *Portuguese humanist and chronicler*
A member of a noble family, Góis was born at Alenquer and grew up at the court of King Manuel (I) the Fortunate. Manuel's son and successor, John III, appointed him secretary to a Portuguese factory in Antwerp (1523), and he later traveled widely on a number of missions as a government servant. In 1533 he resigned his post to devote his time to study, in which he was advised by his friend ERASMUS. In Padua (1534–38) he met Pietro BEMBO. After marrying Johanna van Hargen, a Dutch noblewoman, he lived for six years in Louvain. He became keeper of the Portuguese national archive in Lisbon in 1548 and in 1558 was appointed official court chronicler. Towards the end of his life, Góis was imprisoned by the Inquisition and deserted by his family. He probably died at his family estate at Alenquer, a few miles north of Lisbon. His most important works, written in both Portuguese and Latin, are the chronicles of Manuel I and John III: *Crónica do felicíssimo rei Dom Emanuel* (four parts; 1566–67) and *Crónica do príncipe Dom João* (1567). He also wrote a Latin treatise on the religion and customs of Ethiopia (1540).

**Golden Fleece, Order of the** (French *La Toison d'Or*)
The chivalric order founded at Bruges (1430) by PHILIP THE GOOD of Burgundy and pledged to uphold chivalry and the Catholic religion. The dukes of Burgundy served as grand masters and presided over the chapters, settling disputes between member knights, who had the right to trial by their peers on charges of heresy, treason, and rebellion. By the marriage (1477) of Mary of Burgundy, daughter of Duke CHARLES THE BOLD, to Maximilian (later Emperor MAXIMILIAN I) the grand mastership passed to the house of HAPSBURG.

**Goltzius, Hendrick** (1558–1618) *Dutch print maker and painter*
Goltzius was born at Mulbrecht and studied under his father, Jan Goltz II, and with Dirck Volckertsz. COORNHEERT. At Haarlem he was influenced by Bartholomäus SPRANGER. His *chiaroscuro* woodcut of *Proserpine*, an agitated mannerist conception, is typical of his early style. He was a virtuoso engraver, and his skill with the burin is exemplified by his famous print of the *Standard Bearer*. After a visit to Rome (1590) Goltzius adopted a more classical style. It was Goltzius's technical skill that most impressed his contemporaries. Van MANDER praised his ability to reproduce the styles of other artists, including Dürer, Lucas van Leyden, Raphael, and Parmigianino. Each of his six engravings of the *Life of the Virgin* is an expert imitation of a different artist's style. Goltzius also produced numerous drawings, including life-size works, such as the *Venus, Ceres, and Bacchus with a Self-Portrait* (St. Petersburg). His paintings, however, lack the immediacy of his graphic work. Goltzius's wit and audacity reflects contemporary MANNERISM and his technical mastery the northern tradition. His naturalistic studies hint at the future of 17th-century Dutch art.

**Further reading:** Stephen H. Goddard *et al*, *Goltzius and the Third Dimension* (Williamstown, Mass.: Clark Art Institute, 2001); Huigen Leeflang *et al*, *Hendrick Grotius 1558–1617: Drawings, Prints and Paintings* (Amsterdam, Netherlands: Rijksmuseum, 2003).

**Gomarists** The extreme Calvinists in early 17th-century Holland, who took their name from their leader Francis Gomar (1563–1641), the principal opponent of ARMINIANISM.
**See also:** DORT, SYNOD OF

**Gonçalves, Nuño** (mid-15th century) *Portuguese painter*
Little is known of his life and work apart from the account of FRANCISCO DA HOLLANDA, who ranked him with the great Italian masters. He was court painter (c. 1450–71) to Afonso V. Almost all his work perished in the 1755 Lisbon earthquake, but panels of an altarpiece discovered in 1882 in the convent of San Vicente, Lisbon, have been confidently ascribed to him. Depicting St. Vincent (patron saint of Portugal) surrounded by the Portuguese royal family, courtiers, and clergy, the panels show strong Flemish and Burgundian influence.

**gonfaloniere** The official responsible for a district of an Italian city. In Florence the title was attached to the chief member of the council of magistrates. The word derives from *gonfalone* (military banner), which, by extension, also came to mean a subdivision of a city with its own section of militia.

**Góngora y Argote, Luis de** (1561–1627) *Spanish poet*
Born into a prominent and cultured family at Cordova, Góngora appears to have been a precocious child. He attended Salamanca university but took no degree. As a young man, he was given to gambling, love affairs and, from about age 20, verse writing. In 1585 he became a deacon and prebendary at the cathedral of Cordova, a post that he held until 1611, traveling widely on missions for the chapter. In 1589 12 of his *romances* (ballads) appeared

anonymously in an anthology; a number of shorter poems were also anthologized later in Pedro Espinosa's *Flores de poetas ilustres* (1605). In the meantime he had met his contemporary Lope de VEGA CARPIO, whom he disliked, and while staying at the court in Valladolid had been lampooned by QUEVEDO, the first of many attacks. In 1613 two works, which had earlier circulated in manuscript, set off the great controversy over *culterano* style: *Fábula de Polifemo y Galatea*, based on Ovid (*Metamorphoses* XIII), in 504 *octavas reales* (*ottava rima*), and *Soledad primera* (1091 verses), the first of an uncompleted four-part work, *Soledades*, of which only 979 further lines of *Soledad segunda* were finished. Góngora insisted on an allegorical reading of this poem, which deals with the journey and experiences of a youth shipwrecked on a strange shore, all rendered in a style of the utmost artificiality.

In 1617 Góngora, hoping to make his way at court, moved to Madrid, was ordained, and became a chaplain to King Philip III. The decision was unfortunate; he failed to advance as expected, his debts increased, and his health worsened. While collecting his works for publication, he suffered a stroke and lost his memory, dying a few months after returning to Cordova. His works, however, were published later the same year. *Gongorismo* or *culteranismo* (*culto*: polished, learned, "witty"), which Góngora's style exemplifies—but which he himself was quite capable of parodying, as in *Fábula de Píramo y Tisbe* (1618)—is conventionally said to involve surface elaborations, excessive metaphor, Latinate word order, inversions, and other devices, and is contrasted to *conceptismo*, in which the "wit" (*agudeza*) derives from catachresis (extension of meaning), ambiguity, etc. But a simplified opposition between the two is misleading, and the *culterano* style was not a novelty, as Lope de Vega claimed. The quarrel ignited by Góngora's verse reflects older stylistic arguments over Ciceronian elegance versus Senecan brevity, and such distinctions as those made by the Roman rhetorician Quintilian between figures of speech and figures of thought. Of Góngora's shorter poems, his 94 ballads (*romances*) excel the rest. He also wrote 166 sonnets, 121 *letrillas*, and a number of other lyrics; many more are doubtfully ascribed to him.

**Further reading:** Marsha S. Collins, *The Soledades: Góngora's Masque of the Imagination* (Columbia, Miss.: University of Missouri Press, 2002).

## Gonzaga, Federico II (1500–1540) *Marquis (1519–40) and duke of Mantua (1530–40)*

Federico was a prominent military commander; appointed Captain of the Church (1521), he led the imperial forces during the siege of Pavia and in defense of Parma (1521-22). After the Peace of Cambrai (1529) his protector, Emperor Charles V, enhanced his title to duke of Mantua. In 1531 he married Maria Palaeologo, thus becoming the successor to the duchy of Monferrato. Under Federico's rule the court of Mantua enjoyed its finest period of cultural activity, as, like his mother Isabella d'ESTE, he was an enthusiastic patron of the arts. Among the villas and palaces he commissioned was Giulio Romano's famous Palazzo del TÈ. He was a patron and host to many artists and writers, including LEONARDO DA VINCI, RAPHAEL, TITIAN, CASTIGLIONE, and Pietro BEMBO.

## Gonzaga, Gianfrancesco II (1466–1519) *Marquis of Mantua (1484–1519)*

Gianfrancesco was a military captain who sided with the Holy Roman emperor Charles V following the French invasion of Italy in 1494 (*see* ITALY, WARS OF). He led the allied Italian troops of the Holy League against Charles VIII of France at Fornovo (1495), winning a victory which he celebrated by commissioning MANTEGNA's *Madonna della Vittoria* as an *ex voto*. He went on to fight in Tuscany (1505) and Bologna (1506), but was captured by the Venetians (1509) and imprisoned for a year. On his release he adopted a more peaceful strategy.

Gianfrancesco was husband to the celebrated Isabella d'ESTE, who ruled Mantua during his numerous absences; his foreign policy was consequently sometimes determined by her Ferrarese interests. His reputation and cultural achievements have been overshadowed by those of his wife, although he too promoted the arts. He was particularly active in promoting organ and choral music in Mantua cathedral. His letters reveal a man who had a fondness for representations of animals, particularly horses and dogs. He contracted syphilis and died in 1519.

## Gonzaga, Ludovico III (1412–1478) *Marquis of Mantua (1444–78)*

Ludovico distinguished himself as a military captain on the Milanese side in the wars against Venice. He was also a patron of many artists and scholars, and in 1460 he hired MANTEGNA as his court painter. Mantegna's evocative depiction of Ludovico, his family, court, and friends (1472) survives in the *camera picta* of Mantua's Castello di San Giorgio. Putting into practice the humanistic ideals of his tutor VITTORINO DA FELTRE, Ludovico was a collector of classics, particularly the works of Virgil, and sponsored a printing press in Mantua. He was in close contact with Medicean Florence, and his interest in architecture is evident in his employment of Luca Fancelli and ALBERTI on various Mantuan projects, including the innovative Vitruvian-influenced churches of San Sebastiano and Sant' Andrea.

## Gonzaga family

The dynasty that ruled Mantua (1328–1707) as marquesses (1433–1530) and dukes (1530–1707) and Montferrat as marquesses (1536–74) and dukes (1575–1707). The Gonzaga were feudal nobility near Mantua in the 12th century. During the Renaissance the family included cardinals, a saint, CONDOTTIERI, and many patrons of the arts and scholarship. Luigi was the first Gonzaga to become captain-general of Mantua (1328). His great-grandson Francesco I (1388–1407) was not only a noted military leader, who successfully withstood the expansionism of the VISCONTI FAMILY—Mantua's Castello San Giorgio dates from his time—but also a keen bibliophile whose collection contained numerous French manuscripts. Gianfrancesco (I), a brave soldier and a patron of the arts and humanist scholarship, was made marquess by Emperor Sigismund (1433). Gianfrancesco II GONZAGA and his wife, Isabella d'ESTE, made the Mantuan court a glittering center for the arts and scholarship. The first Gonzaga duke of Mantua was their son Federico II GONZAGA, who also acquired Montferrat (Monferrato) by his marriage (1531) to Montferrat's heiress, Maria Palaeologo. St. Aloysius Gonzaga (1568–91), who died shortly before his ordination, is the patron of Catholic youth. The direct male line ended in 1627, and after a war of succession Mantua passed to a French branch, the Gonzaga-Nevers.

See also: GONZAGA, LUDOVICO III; VITTORINO DA FELTRE

Further reading: Kate Simon, *A Renaissance Tapestry: The Gonzaga of Mantua* (London: Harrap, 1988).

## Gossaert, Jan (Mabuse) (c. 1478–1533/36) *Flemish painter*

Gossaert derived his assumed name of Mabuse from his family home in Maubeuge in Hainaut (now in Belgium). He was the first artist to introduce the style of the Italian Renaissance into the Low Countries. First documented as belonging to the Antwerp painters' guild in 1503, Gossaert began by producing works full of richly ornate detail and flamboyance. The influence of Hugo van der GOES, Gerard DAVID, Albrecht DÜRER, and Jan van EYCK is also evident in such early paintings as the *Adoration of the Magi* (c. 1512; London), the Malvagna triptych (c. 1511; Palermo), and the *Agony in the Garden* (Berlin).

In 1508 Gossaert visited Italy in the service of Philip of Burgundy, bastard son of Philip the Good, and was exposed for the first time to the art of the Italian Renaissance. Although he failed to understand the essence of the movement, he employed many features of the Italian style in his work on his return and continued to study it through the engravings of Marcantonio RAIMONDI and Jacopo de' BARBARI. *Neptune and Amphitrite* (1516; Berlin), his first dated work, differs greatly from earlier efforts, with its Dürer-type figures placed incongruously in a Doric temple and its much more simple and direct execution. Later paintings, such as *Venus and Cupid*, *Danäe* (Munich), and *Hercules and Deianira* (1517; Birmingham) often present nude figures in elaborate architectural settings, painted with the acuteness of observation characteristic of Flemish art. Gossaert also excelled as a portrait painter and his patrons included the Danish royal family

and Cardinal Carondelet. After Philip of Burgundy's death (1524) Gossaert retired to Middelburg, where he died.

## Goudimel, Claude (c. 1516–1572) *French composer*

Goudimel studied at Paris university and then worked with the publisher Nicolas du Chemin as proofreader and later partner. From 1557 he lived at Metz, where he composed his first complete Psalter (1564). He was killed in Lyons in the MASSACRE OF ST. BARTHOLOMEW. Although Goudimel wrote Masses, motets, and chansons, it is for his psalm settings that he is noted. These all treat French translations of the texts and range in style from motet-like works to simple harmonizations.

## Goujon, Jean (c. 1510–c. 1568) *French sculptor*

The early years of Goujon's life are obscure but he was probably born near Rouen, where he executed his first documented work, the fine Corinthian columns supporting the organ loft in the church of St. Maclou (1540). The tomb of Louis de Brézé (husband of DIANE DE POITIERS) in Rouen has also been ascribed to him and shares the same classical influence evident in subsequent works. His mature style first showed itself in a notable rood screen for St. Germain-l'Auxerrois in Paris (c. 1544; Louvre, Paris), upon which he collaborated with the architect Pierre LESCOT. Goujon also collaborated with Lescot upon his finest work, the Fontaine des Innocents (1547–49; Louvre), which is clearly influenced by the style of Benvenuto CELLINI.

Later works, similarly distinguished by strong classical elements, include decorations for the interior and exterior of the LOUVRE, notably the caryatids of the Salle des Caryatides (extensively restored in the 19th century), and—again with Lescot—work at the Hôtel Carnavalet. No works after 1562 are known and Goujon eventually died in Bologna, an exile from religious persecution. He also contributed comments on sculptural ornamentation in an appendix to the first French edition (1547) of the *De architectura* of VITRUVIUS, as well as a number of woodcut illustrations for the book.

## Gournay, Marie de (1565–1645) *French writer*

Marie de Gourney was born in Paris but spent her early years at the family estate in Picardy. In 1588 she met MONTAIGNE in Paris and after his death (1592) she became the editor of what has been accepted as the definitive text of his *Essais*, incorporating Montaigne's own annotations on his copy of the 1588 and writing the preface to the 1595 edition. As well as writing poems, autobiographical works, translations from the *Aeneid*, and a novel, de Gournay was an early advocate of equality for women in education. To this end she wrote a number of protofeminist tracts, including *Egalité des hommes et des femmes* (1622) and *Grief des dames* (1626).

**Gozzoli, Benozzo di Lese** (1420–1497) *Italian painter*
Celebrated as a painter of frescoes in the early Renaissance, Gozzoli was apprenticed as a goldsmith and worked (1444–47) with GHIBERTI on the Baptistery doors in his native Florence. He also assisted Fra ANGELICO, working with him at the Vatican and in the cathedral at Orvieto (1447), but maintained a more secular approach in his own frescoes at Viterbo and Perugia (1453–56). In 1459 Piero de' Medici, who shared Gozzoli's taste for pageantry, chose him to decorate the chapel in the Palazzo Medici-Riccardi, Florence. The *Procession of the Magi* is Gozzoli's masterpiece, covering three of the chapel's walls and revealing him as an artist of considerable decorative talent and ability as a portraitist. A large entourage coils through a typical Tuscan *crete* landscape, enabling Gozzoli to show off his mastery of perspective in the disposition of the horses and figures; in pride of place, the youthful Lorenzo de' Medici as the youngest of the Magi, a golden Renaissance prince on a richly caparisoned gray horse, gazes out at the viewer. A number of other recognizable contemporaries are depicted among the figures, including himself, wearing a cap on which his name is inscribed. A major fresco cycle of Old Testament scenes (1468–84) in the Campo Santo at Pisa, where Gozzoli died, is much damaged.

**Further reading:** C. Acidini Luchinet (ed.) *The Chapel of the Magi: Benozzo Gozzoli's Frescoes in the Palazzo Medici Riccardi, Florence* (London and New York: Thames & Hudson, 1994).

**Graces** In classical mythology, the three daughters of Zeus, the personifications of grace and beauty, known to the Greeks as Charites and to the Romans as Gratiae. Their names were Aglaia, Euphrosyne, and Thalia. They were often depicted or described in the company of the MUSES or APOLLO or as attendants on VENUS, and the Renaissance artists and poets accepted these associations as part of the iconography. Annibale CARRACCI, for instance, in a picture in the Kress Collection, National Gallery, Washington, shows the Graces adorning the goddess of love at her toilette.

Characteristically the Graces are shown linked together in a dancing group in such a way that two face the viewer and the third has her back turned, as in RAPHAEL's stucco roundel in the Loggie of the Vatican. This image was interpreted by the Stoic writers of antiquity as an allegory of liberality—giving, receiving, and returning benefits—and the interpretation was inherited by the Renaissance along with the icon. To the Neoplatonists, the dancing Graces, being closely associated with Venus, were emblematic of the operations of love in the universe, moving in a ceaseless circle (*see also* PRIMAVERA, LA).

They appear on the reverse of the personal medal of Giovanni PICO DELLA MIRANDOLA with the inscription CASTITAS–PULCHRITUDO–AMOR (chastity–beauty–love).

**Graf, Urs** (c. 1485–c. 1528) *Swiss artist, goldsmith, and designer*
Graf was born in Solothurn and was probably taught by his goldsmith father before being apprenticed at Strasbourg. He led a somewhat irregular life, but in 1509 he settled at Basle, where he executed his chief work as a goldsmith: a reliquary for the monastery of St. Urban (1514; now lost). He was exceptionally talented as a draftsman; over 200 drawings by him survive, many depicting mercenaries and courtesans and others with evocatively drawn mountain landscapes. Graf also made engravings and designs for woodcuts, stained glass, and goldsmith's work, and the Basle publisher Johan FROBEN employed him to ornament his books.

**Granada** A city in southern Spain on the slopes of the Sierra Nevada. A fifth-century BCE Iberian settlement, Granada was refounded in the seventh century CE and taken by the Moors in the eighth century. It became the capital of the Moorish state of Granada and an important center of Islamic learning and culture. The Alhambra (completed in the 14th century) is a supreme example of Moorish architecture. In 1492 FERDINAND II AND ISABELLA I completed the Christian *Reconquista* by driving the Moors out of Granada. Under Castilian and Spanish rule Granada's importance declined, and the expulsion of the Jews (1492) and the unconverted Moors (1502) deprived Granada of many enterprising citizens. The *Moriscos* (Moors who had converted to Christianity in order to avoid exile) were harried by the SPANISH INQUISITION until their final expulsion (1610).

In addition to the Alhambra the monastery of San Jerònimo (1492), the Carthusian monastery (1516), and the cathedral (1523–1703) have survived from the Renaissance period. The Catholic university of Granada was founded in 1531.

**Granjon, Robert** (1513–1589) *French type designer, type cutter, and printer*
The son of a printer, Granjon worked in his native Paris, Lyons (1556–62), and Rome (c. 1578–89), where he cut types for the Typographia Vaticana and oriental founts, including Arabic, for the religious propaganda of the Stamperia Orientale Medicea. His cursive *civilité* type was designed in 1557, but never achieved the widespread popularity of italics, though Granjon's roman and italic faces were transmitted across Europe by Dutch founders. His Greek, Syriac, and *civilité* founts were used in PLANTIN's polyglot Bible (1568–73) and he worked for the Plantin press for many years. He is credited with being the first to make printers' flowers as units of decoration to be used in borders or headpieces.

**Granvelle, Cardinal Antoine Perrenot de** (1517–1586) *Burgundian aristocrat and churchman*
He became bishop of Arras (1540), archbishop of Malines (1560), and cardinal (1561). PHILIP II appointed this loyal servant of the Spanish Hapsburg monarchy president of the council of state of the Netherlands, where he advised the regent, MARGARET OF PARMA, and was known for his strict religious orthodoxy and defense of political absolutism. His opposition to Dutch pleas for political reforms and religious toleration made him so unpopular that he was removed from the Netherlands (1564) and sent to serve Philip in various capacities in Italy (1565–79). One of his successes there was the Italy League that took on the Ottoman fleet at LEPANTO (1571). Finally, as secretary of state in Spain (1579–86) he directed the campaign against the Dutch and negotiated the union of the Portuguese and Spanish crowns (1580). Granvelle was also a great patron of artists, both on his own behalf and for Charles V and Philip II. He was a personal friend of the sculptor Leone LEONI and of TITIAN, and was a noted collector, many of whose treasures passed (1597) after his death into the collection of RUDOLF II.

**Grazzini, Anton Francesco** (1503–1584) *Italian writer, poet, and dramatist*
Grazzini was born in Florence; otherwise little is known of his early life and education. One of the founders of the Accademia degli Umidi (1540), which worked to promote the vernacular in literature, he adopted the name "Il Lasca" (Roach). In 1582 he helped found the ACCADEMIA DELLA CRUSCA. He is remembered for the realistic *novelle* about Florence collected in *Le cene* (*The Suppers*), which was not published until 1756. To contemporaries he was best known as a poet of burlesque verses and Petrarchan lyrics. He also wrote seven comedies and edited the poetry of Francesco BERNI (1548) and others.

**Great Schism** The division in Western Christendom in the period 1378–c. 1430, when rival popes existed at Rome and at Avignon in southern France.
   See also: AVIGNON, PAPACY AT

**Greco, El** (**Domenikos Theotokopoulos**) (1541–1614) *Spanish painter*
Born in Crete, El Greco (the Greek) was the most outstanding Spanish artist of the 16th century and one of the last great painters of the Renaissance. First apprenticed as a painter of religious works in the Greco-Byzantine tradition, El Greco combines in his early works standard elements of Orthodox icons with awareness of Italian trends: an undated *Dormition of the Virgin* in the church of the Koimesis tis Theotokou on the Aegean island of Syros uses the conventional 15th-century Orthodox iconography of the subject but the figures are treated in a way that shows consciousness of the mannerist trends in contemporary Venetian painting, while an *Adoration of the Magi* (?late 1560s; Benaki Museum, Athens), painted in the egg tempera favored by Byzantine iconographers shows a Western approach to perspective. He studied under TITIAN in Venice during the 1560s, inheriting from him his taste for sensuous color and also absorbing the influences of BASSANO, MICHELANGELO, and, above all, TINTORETTO. Portraits and paintings on biblical subjects survive from this time. It is said that he had to leave Italy after offending the Roman art establishment by offering to repaint Michelangelo's *Last Judgment*.

By the time he moved (1577) to Toledo in Spain El Greco had rejected the three-dimensional space and solidly depicted figures of the High Renaissance and was building his own very individual style from a fusion of Venetian Renaissance and Florentine-Roman mannerist styles (*see* MANNERISM). At Toledo, where many of his paintings still remain, he embarked upon an important series of religious paintings, beginning with two altarpieces, a *Trinity* and an *Assumption*, and the painting *The Disrobing of Christ* (1579; Toledo cathedral). *The Dream of Philip II*, also known as *The Adoration of the Name of Jesus* (c. 1580; Escorial; see Plate VII), and *St. Maurice* (1582; Escorial) represented attempts to attract Philip II's patronage but they were rejected, as their stormy harsh colors and emotional intensity were regarded as eccentric and not conducive to devotion. Relying on commissions in Toledo, where he spent the rest of his life, El Greco continued to move away from naturalism in order to express the hallucinatory quality of his supernatural vision as an artist. This is seen most clearly in such mature works as *The Burial of Count Orgaz* (1586; Santo Tomé, Toledo), *The Agony in the Garden* (c. 1597–1603), and *The Assumption* (1613). He also demonstrated his penetrating psychological insight in several portraits, including those of Cardinal Guevara (c. 1600) and Félix Paravicino (1609), visionary landscapes such as *Toledo* (c. 1595–1614), and one mythological subject, *Laocoön* (c. 1610).

Although he was too individual an artist to have many direct artistic heirs, apart from his own son Jorge Manuel Theotokopouli (1578–1631), El Greco has nonetheless had an impact upon the art of the last hundred years, with modern artists finding an affinity with his figural distortion and concentration upon the imaginary and spiritual aspects of art.

   **Further reading:** Léo Bronstein, *El Greco* (London: Idlehurst, 1951; concise ed. Thames & Hudson, 1991); David Davies *et al*, *El Greco* (New Haven, Conn.: Yale University Press, 2003).

**Greek studies** Knowledge of Greek had practically disappeared in western Europe by the eighth century CE. For the next 500 years Europe depended on translations of Greek works into Latin, either made directly by such late antique writers as Boethius or from Arabic versions of the originals. It was not until PETRARCH's time that Greek began to be taught extensively in the West, though some 12th-century scholars had a knowledge of the language. The first teachers in 15th-century Italy were either Sicilians or southern Italians who lacked idiomatic knowledge or envoys from Constantinople whose main preoccupation was with the threat from the Turks; the teaching was inevitably haphazard. It became more systematic with the appointment, at the instigation of Coluccio SALUTATI and others, of Manuel CHRYSOLORAS as professor of Greek at Florence, where he taught from 1396 to 1400. From this time Greek studies evolved steadily in Italy using the talents not only of other Greek immigrants, such as GEORGE OF TREBIZOND and Gemistus PLETHON, but eventually native Italians, such as POLITIAN. The first Greek book to be printed in the West was Constantine Lascaris's grammar, *Erotemata* (Milan, 1476).

France was the first country outside Italy in which Greek studies developed, though teaching was at first largely in the hands of Greeks, such as John Lascaris, who visited France three times between 1495 and 1534, or Italian scholars, such as Giralomo ALEANDRO; their main emphasis was on the acquisition of the language. Second-generation French Hellenists included Guillaume BUDÉ, RABELAIS, Robert Estienne (*see* ESTIENNE PRESS), and Étienne DOLET. The emphasis of this second generation was on literature, but increasingly Greek scholars in France were forced to adopt one side or the other in the Reformation struggle. ERASMUS played a key role in this controversy with his edition of the Greek New Testament (1516).

Religious controversy also accompanied the gradual extension of Greek studies into northern Europe. The activities of Johan REUCHLIN in Germany (*see also* HEBREW STUDIES) provoked a reaction by traditionalists, which led to the satirical scholarly feud of the EPISTOLAE OBSCURORUM VIRORUM. LUTHER was led to formulate some of his central doctrines as a result of his contact with the original New Testament text, though Erasmus deplored the conclusions he drew, and thereafter it was impossible to free the study of Greek in Germany from theological implications.

The study of Greek in England began at Oxford and Canterbury in the 1460s. George Neville, a younger brother of Warwick the Kingmaker, had Greek scholars attached to his household during his time as chancellor of Oxford (1453–56, 1461–72). A number of extant manuscripts were written by the scribe George Serbopoulos between 1489 and 1500 at Reading Abbey. Greek was first formally taught at Oxford (1491) by William GROCYN whose fellow-pupil in Italy was Thomas LINACRE. A chair of Greek was established at Oxford in 1516 and some years later at Cambridge where Erasmus had lectured in 1511 at Bishop (later St) JOHN FISHER's request. As in the rest of northern Europe, the study of Greek was associated in England with developments in theology and there was a strong reaction against Greek, particularly at Oxford.

One topic that occasioned much controversy was the correct pronunciation of Greek. The 15th-century Greek immigrants recognized that their pronunciation differed from that of the ancient Greeks. Reuchlin derived his pronunciation from his Greek contemporaries, rendering the vowels η ι υ and diphthongs ει οι and υι like the Italian i. His so-called itacistic pronunciation was propounded in MELANCHTHON's *Institutiones linguae Graecae* (1518) and Erasmus published his counterproposals in *De recta Latini Graecique sermonis pronuntiatione* (1528). German and Italian scholars generally retained the Reuchlinian pronunciation while the Erasmian standard prevailed elsewhere.

The importance attached to the study of Greek by the early humanists had far-reaching implications. Greek philosophy encouraged the more radical aspects of humanism and the study of the language inculcated a critical approach that insisted on close attention to the actual words of the text rather than the revamping of scholastic commentaries and interpretations. The study of Greek carried with it the seeds of many preoccupations of the 16th-century religious reformers.

**Further reading:** Nigel G. Wilson, *From Byzantium to Italy: Greek Studies in the Italian Renaissance* (London: Duckworth, 1992; Baltimore, Md.: Johns Hopkins University Press, 1993).

## Greene, Robert (1558–1592) *English writer*

Greene, who was probably born at Norwich, went to Cambridge University in 1575. There he made friends with Thomas NASHE, who later supported him against the attacks of Gabriel HARVEY. Greene then traveled abroad before settling to a life of dissipation, supported by writing, in London. He perhaps contributed to the *Henry VI* plays that were later recast by SHAKESPEARE (whom Greene attacked in his autobiographical *Groatsworth of Wit*, 1592). Of his five independent plays, the lighthearted *Friar Bacon and Friar Bungay*, acted in 1594, is the best. His prose works include the romances *Pandosto* (1588) and *Menaphon* (1589; republished as *Greene's Arcadia*, 1599). His numerous pamphlets embrace a variety of topics and moods: for example, *Euphues, his Censure of Philautus* (1587) takes up LYLY's theme and style (*see* EUPHUISM), but his most popular works were the so-called "coney-catching" pamphlets, describing in racy prose the lives and trickery of London's rogues.

## Gregoriana

The Jesuit college founded in Rome as the Collegium Romanum by St. IGNATIUS LOYOLA in 1551. Between 1582 and 1584 it was endowed and made into a university by Pope GREGORY XIII. The Gregoriana was the earliest modern seminary and the model for later foundations. The college's influence on the course of the

Counter-Reformation was very great, many of its pupils becoming missionaries and teachers in northern Europe and the Far East.

## Gregory XIII (1502–1585) *Pope (1572–85)*

Gregory was born Ugo Buoncompagni in Bologna, Italy. He studied law at Bologna University before being appointed judge of the Capitol in Rome (1539). In 1558 he was appointed bishop of Viesti and cardinal priest of San Sisto in 1564. He was elected pope in 1572. Although Gregory has become notorious for celebrating the massacre of the Huguenots on St. Bartholomew's Day (1572; *see* MASSACRE OF ST. BARTHOLOMEW) he was one of the great popes of the COUNTER-REFORMATION. Despite his many achievements in bringing about reforms within the Catholic Church he is chiefly remembered for the CALENDAR reform (1578) that resulted in the institution of the Gregorian calendar (1582).

## Gresham, Sir Thomas (1519–1579) *English merchant and financier*

Gresham was born in London, of which his father, Sir Richard Gresham (c. 1485–1549), was lord mayor in 1537. After attending Caius College, Cambridge, Gresham was apprenticed to his uncle and in 1543 became a member of the Mercers' Company. He then became the Antwerp agent for Henry VIII, Edward VI, Mary, and Elizabeth until war compelled his return to England in 1567. He was an acute financier and his name is (wrongly) associated with the formulation of the economic law that "bad money drives out good." In 1565 he proposed the building of the Royal Exchange and under his will he made provision for the rents from the Exchange to be used to found a college in London at which seven chairs were to be endowed (in astronomy, divinity, geometry, law, music, physic, and rhetoric). The early Gresham professors of astronomy and geometry, such as Henry BRIGGS, were particularly significant in establishing a practical scientific tradition in London, although the fact that the lectures were in Latin meant that Gresham's intended audience of ordinary practitioners of skills, such as navigation, were excluded.

## Greville, Fulke (1554–1628) *English statesman, courtier, and writer*

The son of a Warwickshire landowner, Greville entered Shrewsbury School (1564) where he became friends with Philip SIDNEY, whose biography he later wrote. Greville went on to Cambridge (1568) and then accompanied Sidney to court (1577) and on journeys abroad, although Queen Elizabeth, with whom Greville was a great favorite, thwarted his more ambitious travel plans. In 1583 Greville entertained Giordano BRUNO at his London home; among his friends and protégés were Edmund SPENSER, Francis BACON, William CAMDEN, and Samuel DANIEL. He first became MP for Warwickshire in the 1590s and was granted several official posts, such as secretary for Wales (1583) and treasurer of the navy (1598). James I continued Elizabeth's generous patronage of Greville, creating him Baron Brooke in 1621. Greville was stabbed to death by a disgruntled servant.

Most of Greville's literary works appeared posthumously (1633) in a volume that included his long verse tracts on humane learning, fame and honor, and war, his Senecan tragedy *Mustapha* (unauthorized first edition, 1609), and his collection of songs and sonnets entitled *Caelica*. His biography of Sidney appeared in 1652.

## Grévin, Jacques (1538–1570) *French playwright, poet, and physician*

Grévin was born at Clermont-en-Beauvaisis and studied medicine at the university of Paris. He was a friend of RONSARD and sympathetic to the latter's promotion of classical standards in French literature. *La Trésorière*, based on an earlier lost comedy called *La Maubertine*, was first performed at the college of Beauvais in 1558. His tragedy *Jules César* (1560) was based on a Latin play by Marc-Antoine MURET. Grévin's poetry, published in *Olimpe* (1560), is reminiscent of Ronsard, but about this time Grévin was converted to Protestantism and their friendship was broken off. Grévin became physician to Margaret of Savoy in 1561 and moved to her court at Turin, where he died. His *Théâtre* (1562) contains *Les Ébahis* (The dumbfounded), his most important, but also his most indecent, play.

## Grey, Lady Jane (Lady Jane Dudley) (1538–1554) *Queen of England for nine days*

Daughter of the duke of Suffolk, she had a strict Protestant upbringing, living in Catherine PARR's household until 1548. Her remaining education was conducted by humanist tutors at home. She knew French, Latin, Italian, Hebrew, and Greek and corresponded with leading European theologians. In 1553, to advance the political machinations of her father and the duke of Northumberland, she was compelled to marry Northumberland's son, Lord Guildford Dudley, as Northumberland, during his regency, had induced the boy king EDWARD VI to make Lady Jane his heir (she was a great niece of Henry VII). After Edward's death, she was proclaimed queen (July 10, 1553). But the legitimate successor, Henry VIII's Catholic daughter MARY I, entered London nine days later, and Northumberland's forces were routed. Seeing Lady Jane as a dangerous focus for Protestant opposition, Mary had her imprisoned and arraigned for treason. During the six months she was kept in the Tower of London before her execution, Lady Jane wrote poetry, letters, and prayers that are testimonies to her courage and piety.

## Grien, Hans Baldung See BALDUNG GRIEN, HANS

**Grimani, Cardinal Domenico** (1461–1523) *Italian humanist and patron of the arts*
He was the son of Doge Antonio Grimani of Venice and served the papal Curia, becoming apostolic secretary and protonotary in 1491. From 1497 to 1517 he was patriarch of Aquileia (and was succeeded by three of his nephews). He was employed by Venice as envoy to the pope. He was a collector of coins, cameos, paintings, and antique sculptures, many of which passed to the Venetian state at his death, and he owned the Grimani Breviary (now in the MARCIANA library) with illuminations by the Fleming Simon Benig.

**Grindal, Edmund** (c. 1519–1583) *English churchman, archbishop of Canterbury (1575–83)*
Grindal was educated at Cambridge and, as a devoted Protestant and Calvinist, fled to Germany during the Catholic reign of Mary I. He returned at the accession of Elizabeth I and became bishop of London (1559) before moving to the archdiocese of York (1570) and finally Canterbury. Despite his rapid promotion to high ecclesiastical office, his influence on Elizabethan Protestantism was limited. This was mainly because he provoked the wrath of Elizabeth with his support for "prophesying," or the open discussion of the Scriptures, a practice of which the queen disapproved. He was placed under house arrest and stripped of his functions in 1577; plans were afoot for his resignation on the grounds of increasing blindness when he died.

**Grocyn, William** (c. 1446–1519) *English humanist and scholar*
Very little is known about his life before his matriculation at New College, Oxford (1465). In 1481 he was appointed reader in divinity at Magdalen College. In 1488 he went to Italy to study Greek at Florence and Rome with Demetrius Chalcondyles and POLITIAN. He returned in 1491, was ordained priest, and began to teach Greek at Exeter College, Oxford, the first time in England the subject had been taught publicly; ERASMUS and Sir Thomas MORE were among his pupils. Some impression of Grocyn's character can be gained from Erasmus's letters; he comes across as a man who combined traditional scholastic theology with a respect for the new learning. Grocyn died at Maidstone, leaving a library of 105 printed books and 17 manuscripts. None of Grocyn's own writings survives; his importance today rests on his consistent encouragement of humanism in England and his embodiment of the highest standards of scholarship.

**Grolier, Jean, Viscount d'Aguisy** (1479–1565) *French nobleman and humanist bibliophile*
Grolier was born in Lyons (hence his *ex libris* "Grolerii Lugdunensis et Amicorum"—"of Grolier of Lyons and Friends") and was the friend of many distinguished humanists, including Aldus MANUTIUS, whom he met while ambassador in Italy (1510–35), and BUDÉ. Many books in Grolier's extensive library were handsomely bound with stamped patterns of interlaced geometrical designs and gold tooling; these bindings in the Grolier style are much sought after by collectors. Among the craftsmen who worked for him were Étienne Roffet (died 1548) and Geoffrey Tory (c. 1480–1533), both bookbinders to the French kings. In 1545 Grolier became treasurer of France.

**Further reading:** *Bookbindings from the Library of Jean Grolier* (London: British Museum, 1965); Anthony Hobson, *Renaissance Book Collecting: Jean Grolier and Diego Hurtado de Mendoza, Their Books and Bindings* (Cambridge, U.K.: Cambridge University Press, 1999).

**Groot, Hugo de** See GROTIUS

**Groote, Gerard** See COMMON LIFE, BROTHERS AND SISTERS OF THE; DEVOTIO MODERNA

**grotesques** Fanciful mural or sculptural decorations incorporating human, animal, and plant forms, originally used in ancient Roman buildings and revived by Renaissance artists in various media. Such decorations were found during excavations of Roman houses at the beginning of the 16th century, notably at the Golden House (Domus Aurea) of Nero: the word "grotesque" is derived from the Italian *grotteschi* (paintings found in grottoes, i.e. excavated chambers). RAPHAEL and his followers quickly established grotesque motifs as a facet of their style, particularly in their frescoes. Early examples of grotesque ornament in architecture occur in PINTURICCHIO's cathedral library ceilings at Siena (1502–07), PERUGINO's ceiling of the Cambio in Perugia (c. 1500), and SIGNORELLI's embellishments in Orvieto cathedral (1499–1504).

**Grotius** (**Hugo de Groot**) (1583–1645) *Dutch jurist, statesman, theologian, playwright, and poet*
Grotius was born at Delft and went in 1594 to study law at Leyden before visiting Orleans (1598) where he took a doctorate. He settled at The Hague (1599) to practice law. Grotius had been an accomplished Latinist at an early age, editing Martianus Capella when he was just 15 years old; he wrote some fine Latin verse and of his three Latin dramas on biblical subjects—*Christus patiens, Sophomphaneas,* and *Adamus exul*—the last is best remembered as having suggested to John Milton the subject of *Paradise Lost*. In 1603 the states general appointed Grotius official historiographer. For the Dutch East India Company, by whom he was employed as an advocate, he wrote (1604) *De jure praedae,* arising out of the company's claim to the prize of a Portuguese galleon captured in the East. This case led him to formulate his theory of the oceans being free to all nations (*mare liberum*), a concept rejected by the English lawyer John Selden in *Mare clausum* (1635). His

commission from the states general resulted in *De antiquitate reipublicae Bataviae* (1610), justifying the revolt of the United Provinces from Spain.

Grotius was made advocate-fiscal of Holland, Zeeland, and West Friesland (1607) and then in 1613 pensionary of Rotterdam, which gave him a seat in the states general. The same year he visited England and this may have encouraged him in his ARMINIANISM. The conflict between the Arminian REMONSTRANTS, under OLDENBARNEVELDT, and the GOMARISTS, or strict Calvinists, who had the support of MAURICE OF NASSAU, came to a head in 1618; as a leader on the Remonstrant side, Grotius was sentenced in 1619 to life imprisonment. In the castle of Loevestein he continued his scholarly activities, and in 1621 his wife contrived his escape, concealed in a chest that his warders thought contained books. He went via Antwerp to Paris, where Louis XIII gave him a pension, and thence to a château lent to him near Senlis. There he completed *De jure belli et pacis* (1625), which he had first drafted in 1604. This book, now recognized as a cornerstone of international law, quickly became immensely famous, but Grotius's enemies in Holland remained implacable; apart from a six-month period in 1631–32 he spent the rest of his life in exile in France or Germany and finally as France's ambassador in Stockholm. Unhappy in this post, he obtained his recall, but died at Rostock on the way south after a stormy journey. In addition to his legal and historical writings, Grotius wrote on theological matters; his *De veritate religionis Christianae* (1627) and *Via et votum ad pacem ecclesiasticam* (1642) both suggest means of reconciliation between opposing Christian sects by playing down doctrinal differences and playing up grounds for accommodation.

**Further reading:** John Dunn and Ian Harris (eds), *Grotius* (Cheltenham, U.K.: Edward Elgar, 1997).

**Groto, Luigi** (1541–1585) *Italian poet and playwright*
Known from his birthplace and disability as "Il Cieco d'Adria" (the Blind Man of Adria), Groto wrote mainly in Italian but also in Latin, Spanish, and Venetian dialect. His works, both the extravagant and metrically complex verses of *Rime* (1577) as well as the plays, show mannerist tendencies. The plays include the tragedies *Dalida* (1572), a Senecan horror drama, and *Hadriana* (1578), a dramatization of the Romeo and Juliet story. His comedies are *Emilia* (1579), *Tesoro* (1580), and *Alteria* (1584).

**Grün, Hans Baldung** See BALDUNG GRIEN, HANS

**Guarini, Battista** (1538–1612) *Italian poet*
Belonging to the Ferrarese family of the distinguished humanist GUARINO DA VERONA, he probably studied at Padua. He was appointed professor of rhetoric in Ferrara (1557–67), subsequently serving the Este court in secretarial and diplomatic roles. Guarini also succeeded TASSO as court poet after the latter's disgrace in 1577. His final years were marred by quarrels with patrons and his children. He wrote lyrical verse and madrigals, a comedy called *La idropsica* (1583; *The Dropsical Woman*), a treatise on government, and a dialogue on letter-writing.

He is remembered for the immensely popular and influential pastoral play, *Il pastor fido* (1589; *The Faithful Shepherd*), which stirred up a far-reaching critical debate. Guarini's controversial innovation was in mixing the noble and sentimental styles to create a new genre, his "pastoral tragicomedy," which went far beyond its model, Tasso's *Aminta*, in combining heroic and pastoral elements. He added his own voice to the critical discussion with his defense of tragicomedy, *Compendio della poesia tragicomedia* (1603). Admirers of the pastoral genre throughout Europe ensured the continuing popularity and influence of *Il pastor fide* for at least 150 years after its publication. Its first English translator was Sir Edward Dymoke, who had visited Guarini while traveling in Italy (c. 1590–91) and whose *Faithfull Shepheard* was published in 1602 (repr. 1633). The most enduringly popular English translation, however, was that by Sir Richard Fanshawe (1647). It has been republished in a critical edition by Peter Davidson of *The Poems and Translations of Sir Richard Fanshawe* (2 vols, Oxford, 1997–99).

**Guarino, Battista** (1434–1503) *Italian humanist scholar and educator*
He was the son of GUARINO DA VERONA and he followed his father's footsteps in his native Ferrara, teaching Greek to scholars who came to him from as far afield as Germany and England. Of his pupils, the one who probably had the greatest impact on Greek studies was Aldus MANUTIUS. In 1459 he composed the treatise *De ordine docendi et studendi*, which embodies his father's ideas on the teaching and studying of classical languages. His *Poemata* appeared in 1496, and he was also responsible for several editions and translations.

**Guarino da Verona** (Guarino Guarini) (1374–1460) *Italian humanist scholar and educator*
Guarino left his native Verona to study Greek with CHRYSOLORAS in Constantinople (1403–08), bringing back with him over 50 Greek manuscripts. Guarino taught Greek in several Italian centers—Florence (1410–14), Venice (1414–18), and Verona—before settling finally in Ferrara (1429), which he made into a showplace of humanism. As tutor to the young Leonello d'Este, Guarino was able to put into practice his theories about the education of the model prince, but he is best remembered for his services to the study of Greek, which he insisted was of equal importance with Latin. Many 15th-century scholars learnt their Greek from Guarino, including VITTORINO DA FELTRE. He used his classical studies as the basis for his influential book on the rules of grammar, *Regulae grammat-*

*icae* (1418), and translated into Latin PLUTARCH's treatise on education.

## Guas, Juan (died 1496) *Spanish architect and sculptor*

A Frenchman in origin, Guas may have trained in Brussels before emigrating to Spain in the 1450s. He was master of works at the cathedrals of Segovia (1473–91) and Toledo (1483–95) and in his capacity as architect to Queen Isabella designed one of the foremost monuments in the Gothic-plateresque idiom, the monastery of San Juan de los Reyes (1479) at Toledo.

## Guelfs and Ghibellines

Rival Italian political factions in the 13th and 14th centuries. The labels derived respectively from the German *Welf* (a Bavarian family that competed for the German throne against the Hohenstaufen in the 12th and early 13th centuries) and *Waiblingen* (a Hohenstaufen castle). Originating as factional names in Florence, they were first widely used during Emperor Frederick II's conflict with the papacy (1227–50), when a Guelf opposed the claims of the Hohenstaufen emperor to authority in Italy and was sympathetic to the pope, while a Ghibelline supported Frederick. Already, however, they were also convenient tags for inter- or intra-city political rivalries, and their original function was lost with the extinction of the direct Hohenstaufen line in 1268. The Guelf label then became associated with French ambitions and with political conservatism, while, in the early 14th century, the VISCONTI FAMILY of Milan and DELLA SCALA FAMILY of Verona emerged as the leading Ghibellines. The last conflict in Italy between the empire and papacy, in the reign of Louis of Bavaria (1324–47), temporarily revived the original significance of the terms. Thereafter their importance rapidly declined.

## Guerrero, Francisco (1528–1599) *Spanish composer*

Born in Seville, Guerrero studied music with Luis de MORALES. He sang at Seville cathedral (1542–46) until his appointment as *maestro de capilla* at Jaén cathedral. In 1549 he returned to Seville as singer, then assistant *maestro*, at the cathedral, becoming *maestro de capilla* there in 1574. In 1581 he was granted leave of absence to visit Rome, and in 1588 went to the Holy Land. Many of his works were published in France and Italy, and were performed long after his death, especially in Latin America. He wrote many secular songs with alternative sacred texts, but is chiefly remembered for his sacred compositions. He published Masses, requiems, motets, psalms, and Passions in a flowing polyphonic style; they were much admired on account of their complex canonic devices.

## Guevara, Fray Antonio de (1480–1545) *Spanish bishop, courtier, and writer*

From a prominent family, Guevara, who was born at Treceño, grew up at the court of Ferdinand and Isabella and for a time was page to their son Don Juan (died 1497). He became a Franciscan friar and left the court when Queen Isabella died (1504), returning to serve as preacher and chronicler under Charles V. He became bishop of Guadix and finally of Mondoñedo in 1537.

Guevara was steeped in classical learning and particularly influenced by CICERO; his own style, however, was extravagantly ornate, and his view of his material was medieval: he missed no opportunity to include anecdotes, digressions, and curious lore, often passing off fanciful lies as truths. The *Libro áureo de Marco Aurelio* (*Golden Book of Marcus Aurelius*; 1528) first published anonymously and extremely popular in Spain and elsewhere (it was translated into English in 1532 by Lord Berners), is presented as a series of letters addressed to the Roman emperor Marcus Aurelius on the virtues of an ideal ruler. It was later included in an enlarged, moralizing "mirror for princes" work entitled *Reloj de príncipes* (1539; translated as *The Diall of Princes* by Thomas NORTH, 1557). His *Epístolas familiares* (I, 1539; II, 1541) are 112 highly rhetorical essays, mainly cast as letters to various eminent people. Guevara's rhetorical excesses and ability to invent when it suited him were criticized even in his own day. His other works include lives of some of the Roman emperors, a handbook for courtiers, and a panegyric on rural life.

## Guicciardini, Francesco (1483–1540) *Italian historian and statesman*

A member of one of the most distinguished Florentine families, Guicciardini became related to another (the Salviati) by his marriage in 1508. He received a classical education, studied law, and as ambassador to Spain (1511) embarked on a long and active career that gave him an intimate knowledge of the political affairs of the period. After the return of the Medici to power in Florence in 1512, Guicciardini was made a member of the *signoria* (1515) and under Leo X was successively governor of Modena, Reggio, and Parma (1516–19), during which time he met and became a friend of MACHIAVELLI. Under Clement VII, he served as president of Romagna (1524), represented the pope in Florence (1530), and was governor of Bologna. After Clement's death (1534), he acted as adviser to Alessandro de' Medici until his assassination (1537) and then helped to secure the succession of Cosimo (I) de' Medici, who subsequently forced his retirement from politics.

None of Guicciardini's works was published in his lifetime, a number were left unfinished, and only his major *Storia d'Italia* (1561)—covering events from the first French invasion to the death of Clement VII (i.e. 1494–1534)—appeared during the 16th century. It was translated into English in 1579. His work represents an important advance in historical scholarship, especially in the scrupulously critical use of sources and in its psychological emphasis. Guicciardini's other works include *Storie fiorentine* (written 1508–09; published 1859), a history of Florence 1378–1509, *Ricordi* (*Maxims and Reflections*), and *Considerazioni sui discorsi del Machiavelli*.

**Further reading:** Peter E. Bondanella, *Francesco Guicciardini* (New York: Twayne, 1997); Felix Gilbert, *Machiavelli and Guicciardini: Politics and History in Sixteenth-Century Florence* (1965; repr. New York and London: W. W. Norton, 1984).

**Guise family** A prominent Roman Catholic family in 16th-century France. Claude de Lorraine was awarded the duchy of Guise (1527) for military service to FRANCIS I. His daughter, Mary of Guise, married James V of Scotland and was mother of MARY, Queen of Scots. The attack by the second duke, Francis, on Huguenots at Vassy (1562) precipitated the (French) Wars of RELIGION; Francis himself was assassinated by Huguenots in 1563. In order to avenge his father's murder, Henry, the third duke, fought bravely for the Catholics and also directed the murder of the Huguenot leader COLIGNY (1572). Determined to resist the accession of the Huguenot prince Henry of Navarre (later HENRY IV), Guise forced HENRY III to make him lieutenant-general of the kingdom with wide powers in 1588. In December that year Henry III had Guise assassinated.

**gunpowder** An inflammable mixture of charcoal, sulfur, and saltpeter (potassium nitrate), used in warfare. Greek fire, deployed in the defense of Constantinople from the seventh century, seems to have been made from naphtha, and there were other similar substances known from very early times, but all required an external power to launch them. The first reference to a different kind of weapon comes from ninth-century China with a description of a mixture of gunpowder's ingredients. By 1240 the secret had reached Islam, where it was referred to as *thalj al-Sin*, or Chinese snow. The same ingredients were noted anagrammatically in the West by Roger Bacon a few years later, and by the early 14th century the formula had become widely known. The CANNON followed soon after.

There remained two further questions to worry the Renaissance chemist. Until the 20th century only natural supplies of saltpeter, derived from manure collected in stables, were available. Supply was therefore limited and expensive. Further, the original fine powder tended to be unpredictable and to separate under field conditions.

**See also:** ARTILLERY; FIREARMS

**Further reading:** Bert S. Hall, *Weapons and Warfare in Renaissance Europe: Gunpowder, Technology, and Tactics* (Baltimore, Md.: Johns Hopkins University Press, 2002).

**Gunter's quadrants** See QUADRANTS

**Gustavus I Vasa** (1496–1560) *King of Sweden (1523–60)*
After Christian II of Denmark murdered his father and uncles (1520) Gustav Eriksson led the struggle for independence from Denmark, drove the Danes out of Sweden, and was elected king. Despite the continuing Danish threat and the resentment of the great nobles whose power he systematically reduced, Gustavus Vasa created a strong monarchy and gave Sweden years of stable government. His need for money prompted him to take control of the Catholic Church's property (1527); eventually he made Sweden Lutheran (1544). He persuaded the Diet (Riksdag) to pronounce the monarchy hereditary (1544), created a strong standing national army, and founded the Swedish navy. Although he cared little for learning and the arts, he was an expert orator and a lover of music.

**Gutenberg, Johann** (c. 1399–1468) *German printer*
Although no surviving printed work bears his name, Gutenberg is usually considered the inventor of printing from movable type. His training as a goldsmith may well have helped him to solve the problems of casting the individual letters. In the 1430s he seems to have been experimenting with printing presses in Strasbourg, but by 1448 he was back in his native Mainz, where he borrowed money from a lawyer, Johann Fust, to continue his work. Another loan helped to pay for the six presses and assistants used in the production of the 42-line (or Mazarine) Bible between about 1450 and 1456. Part of the Mainz Psalter, dated 1457, may also have been Gutenberg's work, though it was published by Fust and Peter Schöffer, Gutenberg's foreman and successor, after Fust called in his loan in 1455 and took over books, presses, and type when his debtor was unable to repay what he had borrowed. Only 48 copies of the 42-line Bible, most of them imperfect, have survived from the 200 printed, but several smaller fragments printed before 1456, including calendars, indulgences, and copies of Donatus's grammar, are also attributed to Gutenberg.

After his break with Fust, Gutenberg's life is less well documented, though he was given an appointment by the archbishop of Mainz in 1465. He still owned some printing equipment when he died, but no more books were produced during the last decade of his life.

**Further reading:** Martin Davies, *The Gutenberg Bible* (London: British Library, 1996); Janet Ing, *Johann Gutenberg and his Bible* (New York: Typophiles, 1988).

***Guzmán de Alfarache*** (Part I, 1599; Part II, 1604) A novel by Mateo ALEMÁN. One of the first PICARESQUE NOVELS, it became extremely popular, was widely translated, and established the fashion for the genre for the next 50 years. The hero recounts his life of crime, his thefts, deceits, the desertion of his rich wife (Alemán's own marriage was unhappy), and other escapades, until he is finally apprehended, condemned to the galleys, and re-pents. The novel is much longer than its predecessor, LAZARILLO DE TORMES, and has none of its mirth and satir-ical quality. Moral commentaries on each episode out-weigh the narrative element and reflect a pessimistic loathing of the nastiness of life and of man's evil nature when unredeemed by grace.

*Guzmán de Alfarache* was almost immediately trans-lated into French (1600) and in the same year (1623) that a Latin version appeared James Mabbe published his lively translation into English, under the title of *The Rogue*. This version, which admirably captures the tone of the original, was reprinted in the Tudor Translations series (4 vols, 1924; repr. 1967).

# H

**Hadrian VI** See ADRIAN VI

**Hakluyt, Richard** (c. 1552–1616) *English geographer*
Born near London of a wealthy family, Hakluyt excelled as a scholar and was educated at Westminster and Oxford. After his ordination (1578) he remained at Oxford, lecturing on both geography and navigational technology. He also took pains to befriend the great merchants and navigators of the day. In 1583 he went to Paris, where for five years he was chaplain to the English embassy and simultaneously accumulated a mass of information about foreign settlements and trade. He returned to devote his life to promoting colonial expansion through his publications, putting much emphasis on the value of America. Hakluyt's *Principall Navigations, Voyages, and Discoveries of the English Nation* first appeared in 1589, and the three-volume second edition (1598–1600) is indispensable to any study of the theme in this period. The London Hakluyt Society, founded in 1846 to promote the study and publication of early travel narratives, is named in his honor.

Hakluyt's 1589 volume was republished in a two-volume facsimile by the Hakluyt Society in 1965, edited with an introduction by D. B. Quinn and R. A. Skelton. The expanded second edition, *The Principal Navigations, Voyages, Traffiques, and Discoveries of the English Nation, Made by Sea or Over-land, to the Remote and Farthest Distant Quarters of the Earth at Any Time within the Compass of These 1500 Yeeres: Divided into Three Severall Volumes, According to the Positions of the Regions, whereunto They Were Directed,* was republished in 12 volumes by MacLehose of Glasgow, U.K., in 1903–05. There is a one-volume selection of Hakluyt's writings in the Penguin Classics series (*Voyages and Discoveries*, 1982).

**Further reading:** David B. Quin (ed.) *The Hakluyt Handbook* (2 vols, London: Hakluyt Society, 1974; repr. Cambridge University Press).

**Hamilton, Patrick** (c. 1504–1528) *Scottish Protestant martyr*
A precocious scholar, Hamilton became abbot of Fern, in Angus, while still a boy (1517). He gained an MA from the University of Paris in 1520 and later studied at both St. Andrews and Aberdeen. During this period he showed a growing attraction to Lutheran ideas and in 1527 he traveled to Germany, where he met both LUTHER and MELANCHTHON and visited the new Protestant university at Marburg. On his return to Scotland, Hamilton preached the new doctrines openly and was called to a conference at Aberdeen, where Alexander ALESIUS attempted to refute his arguments. The following year he was formally charged with heresy by James Beaton, archbishop of St. Andrews, and put to death. His courage at the stake is said to have clinched Alesius's own conversion to Lutheranism. As Scotland's first Protestant martyr, Hamilton became a revered figure in his homeland after the Reformation there. His only written work, an exposition of JUSTIFICATION BY FAITH known as the *Loci communes,* or "Patrick's Places,'" gained a wide circulation through its inclusion in FOXE's *Book of Martyrs.*

**Hamlet** The tragedy by SHAKESPEARE written about 1600 and first published in a corrupt form (Bad Quarto) in 1603 and a better version (Good Quarto) in 1604/05. The plot is based on an episode in the 12th-century Danish history of Saxo Grammaticus, which was amplified by François de Belleforest in *Histoires tragiques* (1576) and was the subject of an earlier tragedy (the socalled Ur-Hamlet), now lost, possibly by Thomas KYD. The play contains melodramatic elements common to other Elizabethan and Jacobean revenge tragedies, such as the ghost of the murder victim and the real or feigned madness of the hero, but the complexity of the character of Hamlet himself sets it apart from its fellows; the play has evoked generations of critical speculation and the title role remains perhaps the supreme challenge for an English-speaking tragic actor.

**Hampton Court Conference** (1604) A Church conference convened at Hampton Court Palace under the presidency of James I for the purpose of considering the demands of the Puritans embodied in the Millenary Petition of 1603. This petition, so called on account of its purportedly having 1000 supporters in the ministry, objected to a number of rites and ceremonies practiced by the Church of England. John RAINOLDS was the leading spokesman for the Puritans, and the archbishop of Canterbury, Richard Bancroft (1544–1610), led the bishops' side. Few concessions were made to the Puritans, and James, who maintained that the logic of their position meant "no bishop, no king," lent his support to the bishops. He did however back Rainolds's suggestion that a new English translation of the Bible should be made; a strong panel of theologians and scholars was set up to undertake the work, which was published in 1611 as the Authorized Version or King James Bible (*see also* BIBLE, TRANSLATIONS OF).

**Hampton Court Palace** A palace built on the north bank of the River Thames, 14 miles (23 km) upstream from central London. Construction began at the behest of Cardinal WOLSEY in 1515. The palace later passed into the hands of HENRY VIII, who made numerous alterations to it and adopted it as his favorite residence. Although the palace was built very much in the English TUDOR STYLE, with red-brick turreted battlements and Gothic motifs, it also includes many features reminiscent of the Italian Renaissance, with terracotta medallions (c. 1521) by the Tuscan sculptor Giovanni da Maiano adorning the gateways and much classically derived decoration. The Great Hall, for instance, combines Renaissance-style carvings and gilding with a traditional open timber roof, while the rest of the palace is laid out in the symmetrical fashion favored by the Italians.

**Further reading:** Simon Thurley, *Hampton Court: A Social and Architectural History* (New Haven, Conn.: Yale University Press for the Paul Mellon Center, 2003).

**Handl, Jacob** (Jacobus Gallus, Jacob le Coq) (1550–1591) *Slovenian composer and monk*
Born in Ribnica near Ljubljana, Handl went to Austria in the mid-1560s. In 1574 he was a singer in the chapel of Emperor Maximilian II in Vienna. After leaving there (1575) he traveled through Austria, Bohemia, Silesia, and Moravia, becoming choirmaster to the bishop of Olomouc (1579). By mid-1586 he was cantor at the church of St. Jan na Brzehu in Prague, where he remained until his death. Handl was prolific in his composition of Masses, motets, German songs, and secular works, many of which show the influence of Flemish, French, or Italian composers. Criticized during his lifetime for the complexity of his music, he included in his four-volume *Opus musicum* (1586–91) two pieces scored for 24 voices. He was sometimes referred to as "the Bohemian Palestrina."

**Hanseatic League** A league of northern European and Baltic trading towns formed in the 13th century under the leadership of Lübeck. The word *Hanse* is Middle High German for "fellowship," and the league was an association to enforce a common commercial code in an area over which no single prince could impose an effective set of laws to govern trade. Despite the opposition of the Danish kings in the 14th century, the merchants of the Hanse combined successfully in political and commercial initiatives until the rise of Dutch maritime power, which, with Burgundian encouragement, broke their monopoly of the Baltic trade. Their trading counters extended across Europe from London to Novgorod, and their wealth, privileges, and prestige, if not their political power, survived in a number of places well into the 16th century.

**Further reading:** Philippe Dollinger, *The German Hansa*, transl. and ed. D. S. Ault and S. H. Steinberg (London: Macmillan, 1970; repr. Routledge, 1999).

**Hapsburg, house of** The German princely family that took its name from Hapsburg Castle in Switzerland and supplied sovereigns of the Holy Roman Empire, Austria, Spain, Hungary, and Bohemia. Werner I, the first Count Hapsburg, died in 1096. The first Hapsburg to be elected Holy Roman Emperor (1273) was Rudolf I (1218–91); subsequent Hapsburgs ruled the empire from 1298 to 1308 and from 1438 to 1740, with successive generations enlarging their domains by diplomacy, conquest, and marriage. In 1477 the marriage of FREDERICK III's heir, Maximilian (I) to Mary, heiress of CHARLES THE BOLD of Burgundy, added the Netherlands to the Hapsburg territories. Maximilian's grandson, CHARLES V, also inherited Spain from his mother Joanna, daughter of FERDINAND II AND ISABELLA I. After Charles V's reign one branch of the family ruled Spain, the Netherlands, and the New World territories; the other branch held the imperial title and ruled the family's German lands. The death of Charles II of Spain in 1700 ended the Spanish Hapsburg line. The direct male line in Germany ended with the death of Emperor Charles VI in 1740. His daughter, Maria Theresa, married Francis of Lorraine and the Hapsburg-Lorraine family continued as emperors until the Holy Roman Empire was abolished in

1806; subsequently they ruled as emperors of Austria until 1918.

**Further reading:** I. A. A. Thompson, *War and Government in Habsburg Spain, 1560–1620* (London: Athlone Press, 1976).

## Hardwick, Elizabeth (Bess of Hardwick) (1527–1608) *English noblewoman famous for her architectural patronage*

Following her first husband's death (1544), she entered court society, meeting Sir William Cavendish, whom she married in 1547. They purchased land at Chatsworth, Derbyshire, and from 1551 onward Bess, later with her two subsequent husbands, built the first great house there. A friend of Queen Elizabeth I, Bess also had close contact with Mary, Queen of Scots, when the latter was in the custody of Bess's fourth husband, the Earl of Shrewsbury, during the 1570s; the two worked a number of surviving embroidery hangings together. Returning to Hardwick after her marriage to Shrewsbury broke down (1584), Bess remodeled the now ruined Old Hall there (1587–91) before employing Robert SMYTHSON to build a magnificent and innovative house alongside it, Hardwick New Hall, where she lived from 1597 and on which she was still working at her death.

**Further reading:** David N. Durant, *Bess of Hardwick: Portrait of an Elizabethan Dynast* (New York: Hyperion, 1988; new ed. London: Peter Owen, 1999); Kate Hubbard, *Bess of Hardwick 1527–1608: A Material Girl* (London: Short Books, 2002).

## Harington, Sir John (1561–1612) *English courtier and writer*

Born to parents who had loyally served ELIZABETH I during her perilous youth, Harington became the queen's godson. From 1582, after an education at Eton, Cambridge, and the Inns of Court, he divided his energy between place-seeking in London and beautifying his country estate of Kelston, near Bath. His wit attracted attention, but also landed him in trouble. After he had circulated around the court his translation of an indecent episode from Ariosto's ORLANDO FURIOSO, the queen banished him from her presence until he had translated the whole poem. One of the greatest Elizabethan translations, this was published in 1591.

In 1596 Harington was again in disgrace, this time with his *Metamorphosis of Ajax*, an indelicate discourse on water closets. More dangerous was his association with the earl of Essex, who knighted him (1599) in the course of his Irish expedition; on the failure of Essex's rebellion Harington managed to exonerate himself, but was unable to win Elizabeth's pardon for the earl. After James I's accession, Harington obtained little further royal patronage. His letters and other writings, giving an interesting insight into Harington's character and that of the late Elizabethan

court, were eventually published as *Nugae antiquae* (1769).

**Further reading:** Jason Scott-Warren, *Sir John Harington and the Book as Gift* (Oxford, U.K.: Oxford University Press, 2001).

## Harriot, Thomas (1560–1621) *English mathematician, astronomer, and physicist*

Born and educated at Oxford, Harriot accompanied Sir Richard Grenville as a surveyor on his 1585 trip to Virginia and published his account of the expedition in *A Briefe and True Report of the New Found Land of Virginia* (1588). Shortly afterwards he entered the service of the remarkable ninth Earl of Northumberland, the socalled "wizard Earl," Henry Percy. From 1590 until his health broke down in 1615, Harriot produced a number of important works, none of which was published until long after his death. The first to appear, *Artis analyticae praxis ad æquationes algebraicas resolvendas* (1631), revealed his power as a mathematician. He also appears to have worked out, at about the same time as KEPLER, that planets move in elliptical orbits and to have anticipated GALILEO's telescopic observations of the heavens and Willebrord SNELL's derivation of the law of refraction.

## Harvey, Gabriel (c. 1545–1630) *English scholar and literary critic*

Harvey's father was a prosperous ropemaker of Saffron Walden, Essex, who sent his son to Cambridge, where he became a fellow of Pembroke Hall (1570). There he became friendly with SPENSER, who celebrated him as "Hobbinol" in *The Shepheardes Calender* (1579) and corresponded with him on poetic topics. Part of their correspondence was published in 1580 as *Three proper and wittie, familiar Letters, with a two-letter sequel*; in one of the former Harvey writes scathingly of THE FAERIE QUEENE, a judgment for which posterity has mercilessly ridiculed him. Harvey claimed for himself the title "father of the English hexameter" and tried to introduce classical meters into English verse. His vanity, pedantry, and quick temper won him many enemies both inside the university and beyond, although his outstanding abilities were also widely recognized. In the early 1590s he was drawn into a vituperative pamphlet controversy with Robert GREENE and Thomas NASHE, which was eventually (1599) stopped by official decree and confiscation of Nashe's and Harvey's offending works. Thwarted in his attempts (1585, 1598) to become master of Trinity Hall, Cambridge, Harvey retired to his home town, where he died.

## Harvey, William (1578–1657) *English physician and anatomist, who discovered the circulation of the blood*

After studying medicine at Cambridge University he continued his studies at the University of Padua under the noted anatomist Girolamo FABRICIUS. Here he first recog-

*Figura 1.*

*Figura 2.*

**William Harvey** An engraving showing Harvey's experiments on the circulation of the blood. The arms, with tourniquets applied, show the blood vessels and the pressure points.
© *Bettmann/CORBIS*

nized a connection between the beating heart and the blood flowing through it, his interest having been quickened by Fabricius's work on the valves in the veins and VESALIUS's *De humani corporis fabrica* (On the structure of the human body). He returned to London (1604) to practice medicine and was appointed (1609) to St. Bartholomew's Hospital, where he remained for 34 years. During this period he served as physician to both James I and Charles I while continuing his own scientific research, which culminated in his discovery of the true function of the heart as the pump that circulates the blood. The publication of his *De motu cordis et sanguinis in animalitus* (On the motion of the heart and blood in animals; 1628) made him famous throughout Europe.

After attending King Charles and his sons at the battle of Edgehill (1642) in the Civil War, Harvey was appointed warden of Merton College, Oxford. Here he resumed his research on the development of chicks in hens' eggs, which led to the publication of *De generatione animalium* (On the generation of living creatures; 1651). However, he did not avail himself of a microscope for this work and so was unable to see spermatozoa; although he was led to reject the Aristotelian theory of spontaneous generation, his own interpretation is unclear. He died of a stroke at age 80.

**Further reading:** Roger French, *William Harvey's Natural Philosophy* (Cambridge, U.K.: Cambridge University Press, 1994).

**Hassler, Hans Leo** (1564–1612) *German composer*
Born in Nuremberg, he received his earliest musical training from his father. In 1584 he became one of the first German musicians to study in Venice, as a pupil of Andrea GABRIELI. In 1586 he was appointed chamber organist to Octavian II Fugger in Augsburg, where he published many works and established a wide reputation. In 1600 he returned to Nuremberg as director of the town's music. In 1604 he moved to Ulm, and in 1608 was appointed chamber organist to Christian II, Elector of Saxony, in Dresden. He died in Frankfurt as court *Kapellmeister*.

Though a Protestant, Hassler's early works are all for the Roman rite. His Masses and motets show the influence of the Venetians in their polychoral techniques and rich sonorities. He was also famous for his Italian madrigals and canzonettes. His rather conservative German church music, though often using Lutheran melodies, shows the influence of LASSUS. His lieder were widely known; the tune of his love-song, "Mein G'müt ist mir verwirret" (1601), was used for the Lutheran hymn, "O Haupt voll Blut und Wunden" which features in J. S. Bach's *St. Matthew Passion*.

**Hebrew studies** Curiosity about the Hebrew language dates in Western Christendom from the time of the Church Fathers, notably St. Jerome (337–420). During the Middle Ages, Hebrew's unfamiliar alphabet was thought by many Christians to possess talismanic powers, but isolated scholars, with the aid of learned Jews, did pursue the subject more seriously. In 13th-century France and Spain public disputations between Jews and Christians on matters of faith disseminated some knowledge of Jewish thought, but too often resulted in increased ANTISEMITISM and the burning of Hebrew books. The object of the Hebrew studies of such men as Robert Grosseteste (1175–1253) and Roger Bacon (c. 1213–c. 1294) was primarily the conversion of the Jews. Orthodox Jews continued to suspect such a motive behind Christian interest in Hebrew texts during the Renaissance, with the result that Jewish teachers or Christian pupils sometimes encountered hostility from their coreligionists.

In the Renaissance the principal spur to Hebrew studies was the desire for better understanding of the Bible. John COLET in 1497 stressed the importance of access to the original Hebrew version of the Old Testament and to Jewish commentaries on it. The idea was given wider currency by ERASMUS in his introduction to his 1516 New Testament. The Reformation, with its emphasis on the Word of God, stimulated all aspects of biblical scholarship. LUTHER and TYNDALE, as Bible translators, were both competent Hebraists, as were ZWINGLI, MELANCHTHON, BULLINGER, and CALVIN.

In the pre-printing era access to Hebrew texts had been a problem. Gianozzo Manetti (1396–1459), secretary to Pope NICHOLAS V, was instrumental in starting the collection of Hebrew manuscripts at the Vatican, where Pope SIXTUS IV later endowed Hebrew *scriptores*. The first printed Hebrew book appeared in 1475, with the first complete Hebrew Bible following in 1488 from the press of the Jewish printer Joshua Solomon of Soncino (died 1493). Before 1500 printing in Hebrew was confined to Italy, Spain, and Portugal but later members of the Soncino printing dynasty were responsible for setting up Hebrew presses further afield: in Prague (1512), Thessaloniki (1527), and Constaninople/Istanbul (1530). Gershom Soncino (died 1534) was a leader in the development of Hebrew typography; he was the first to use woodcut illustrations for Hebrew texts and also produced the first Hebrew printed book on mathematics, the *Sefer ha-Mispar* (Constantinople, 1532–33) of Rabbi Elijah Misrachi (c. 1455–1526). Two outstanding 16th-century printers of Hebrew were the Fleming Daniel Bomberg (died 1549) at Venice and the Basle printer Johann FROBEN. Both Christians themselves, they were assisted by the best Jewish and Christian Hebraists of their day. The renowned Hebrew teacher Elias LEVITA published his famous treatise on the Masoretic text of the Bible (1538) while working for Bomberg, and the following year Sebastian MÜNSTER published the second edition of Levita's work in Basle. An example of the emphasis placed by Reformation scholars on access to Hebrew texts is the Hebrew printing press set up at Isny im Allgäu, Württemberg, by the Protestant pastor Paul Fagius, which in 1541–42 was under the supervision of Levita. Later ARIAS MONTANO was a regular reader for the PLANTIN PRESS, which issued his Polyglot Bible (1568–73), in which the Hebrew text was printed with type obtained from Bomberg's descendants.

At first Hebrew studies spread mainly through personal contacts between individual scholars. Notable teachers were Levita and Obediah Sforno (1475–1550); the latter succeeded Jacob Loans (died 1506) as tutor to Johann REUCHLIN. Both Reuchlin in Germany and PICO DELLA MIRANDOLA in Italy were eminent early advocates of Hebrew studies, and through them the CABBALA became known to Renaissance scholars. Despite antisemitic prejudice, which hardened in Catholic countries during the Counter-Reformation, Hebrew teaching gradually became institutionalized as part of the enthusiasm for the new learning. Chairs of Hebrew were established at Bologna (1488) and Rome (1514) universities. In England Henry VIII founded a Hebrew professorship at Cambridge in 1540 and Hebrew was taught at the London Merchant Taylors' School from its foundation (1561).

**Heemskerck, Jakob van** See BARENTS, WILLEM

**Heemskerck, Maarten van** (1498–1574) *Netherlands painter*
He was born at Heemskerck, near Alkmaar, and after working under the obscure artists Cornelis Willemsz. in Haarlem and Jan Lucasz. in Delft, entered the studio of Jan van SCOREL at Haarlem (1527). Initially Scorel's student, he seems subsequently to have become his collaborator, and their works are sometimes confused. Between 1532 and 1536 Heemskerck was living in Italy, principally at Rome, where he recorded his impressions of classical architecture and sculpture in two sketchbooks (now in Berlin). After his return from Italy he specialized in religious paintings and classical allegories, redolent with architectural and decorative motifs copied from ancient monuments and the works of contemporary Italian mannerist painters. The flamboyancy of these narrative paintings contrasts markedly with the sober naturalism of his portraits. Both these aspects of his style find expression in the *Self-Portrait* (1553; Fitzwilliam Museum, Cambridge) in which his massive bearded head is set against the backdrop of a view of the Colosseum, like an allegory of the aspirations of northern visitors to Rome.

**Heere, Lucas de** (1534–1584) *Flemish painter*
Born in Ghent, de Heere was taught by Frans FLORIS and himself taught Carel van MANDER in the late 1560s. He worked in France and England as well as Ghent, where his *Solomon and the Queen of Sheba* (1559) is in St. Bavon's cathedral. Also attributed to him is the design of the famous Valois tapestries (1582; Uffizi, Florence), woven in Flanders to celebrate the arrival there of the soon to be discredited FRANCIS, Duke of (Alençon-)Anjou, in his role of "defender of the liberties of the Netherlands."

**Hegius, Alexander** (Alexander von Heek) (c. 1433–1498) *German humanist and educator*
He was born at Heek, Westphalia, and was at one time a pupil of Thomas à Kempis. He opened a school at Deventer, Holland, in 1474. Through this school passed many of the leading figures of the northern Renaissance, including

ERASMUS and ADRIAN VI. Hegius produced a number of works which were published posthumously but his importance rests more on his teaching methods. He rejected the formalism of medieval scholastic education and insisted on the need to go directly to the classical texts. Although Hegius stressed the importance of Greek, his knowledge of the language was considerably inferior to his grasp of Latin.

**Heidelberg** A city in southwest Germany on the River Neckar. Probably of 12th-century origins, the city was the capital of the Rhenish Palatinate until 1720. Heidelberg has the oldest university in Germany, founded by Elector Palatine Rupert I and chartered by Pope Urban VI in 1386. In the second half of the 15th century the university was a center of humanist studies, where Rudolf AGRICOLA ("the father of German humanism") taught Greek. By 1540 Heidelberg was described as the most Lutheran city in Germany. The Elector Palatine Frederick III the Pious made the Palatinate a haven for persecuted Calvinists and the university taught Calvinist youth from all over Europe. In 1562 Frederick III supported the promulgation of the HEIDELBERG CATECHISM, hoping it would provide the basis for a reconciliation between the different Protestant groups. Although no reconciliation was achieved the catechism is still widely used. Notable buildings from the Renaissance period that have survived the Thirty Years' War and the French sack (1693) include 16th-century additions to the medieval castle, the church of the Holy Ghost (1400–36), the Marstall (1590), and the Haus zum Ritter (1592). Almost nothing remains of the famous gardens laid out at the castle by Salomon de CAUS between 1615 and 1619.

See also: PALATINA, BIBLIOTHECA

**Heidelberg Catechism** (1562) A reformed confession of faith, written by Kaspar Olevianus and Zacharias Ursinus, both of Heidelberg. It maintained the doctrines of CALVIN and J. H. BULLINGER, but moderately expressed to conciliate the Lutherans. It was accepted by the annual synod of the Palatinate in 1563 and at DORT in 1619, and was translated into English in 1572.

**Helmschmied family** (Kolman family) A family of Augsburg armorers, successive generations of which worked for emperors and princes from the last quarter of the 15th century. Their work is signed with the mark of a helmet. Lorenz Helmschmied (1445–1516) made a complete set of ARMOR for horse and rider for Emperor Frederick III (1477; Vienna) and in 1491 was appointed chief armorer to Frederick's son Maximilian (I), for whom he made many fine pieces. Lorenz's son Kolman (1471–1532), who worked independently from 1500, produced complete garnitures for Charles V, such as the "K.D." garniture (c. 1526), parts of which survive in the Armería

Real, Madrid. The family workshop's tradition of creating richly decorated parade armor was further developed by Kolman's son Desiderius (1513–c. 1578) under the patronage of Philip II.

**Helvetic Confessions** (1536, 1562) Two confessions of faith of the Reformed Church in Switzerland. The earlier was compiled by J. H. BULLINGER, Oswald MYCONIUS, and others. It is sometimes referred to as the second Confession of BASLE. The second was written by Bullinger, and a revised version was published in 1566 as the official creed of the Swiss cantons. By 1578 it had been adopted by several reformed churches.

**Henri II style** A movement in the visual arts in France during the reign (1547–59) of HENRY II. Succeeding FRANCIS I as patron at FONTAINEBLEAU, Henry II continued to foster the ideals of the Italian Renaissance by favoring French artists who had assimilated Italian concepts and adapted them to traditional French modes. Talented French architects such as Pierre LESCOT and Philibert DELORME were employed upon the building of major châteaux, such as those at St.-Maur (1541) and Anet (1547–52), while the beginning of the construction of the TUILERIES was instrumental in the creation of an entirely new school of French decoration. As well as architecture, other fields in which French artists developed a national style based upon Italian ideals included tapestries and medals.

**Henri IV style** A movement in French architecture associated with the reign (1589–1610) of HENRY IV. A noted patron of the arts, Henry revolutionized contemporary attitudes towards town planning through his pragmatic redevelopment of Paris, overseeing such projects as the building of the Pont-Neuf (begun 1599), and the laying out of extensive public squares, notably the Place Dauphine (begun 1607). Henry also developed his ideas about architecture through a number of major building projects, such as the Cours des Offices at FONTAINEBLEAU (1606–09) and the Place Royale (planned in 1603).

**Henry II** (1519–1559) *King of France (1547–59)*
The second son of FRANCIS I, Henry became dauphin on the death of his elder brother in 1536. His marriage (1533) to CATHERINE DE' MEDICI gave him four sons (Francis II, Charles IX, HENRY III, FRANCIS of Alençon), but he neglected Catherine in favor of his mistress, DIANE DE POITIERS. Henry reformed his administration and established the *chambre ardente* to stamp out heresy. His Edict of Écouen (1559) paved the way for harsh measures against HUGUENOTS. Henry's foreign policy was dominated by the continuing war against the HAPSBURGS, mainly in Spain and northeast France. By the Treaty of Chambord (1552) he helped German Protestant princes against

CHARLES V in exchange for the freedom to take Verdun, Metz, and Toul. Despite successes by Francis of Guise, including the capture of Calais (1558), Henry decided on peace. Financial difficulties, some setbacks in battle, and his eagerness to concentrate his efforts on the elimination of heresy led to the Peace of CATEAU-CAMBRÉSIS (1559). Henry was mortally injured while jousting in a tournament.

## Henry III (1551–1589) King of France (1574–89)

The third son of HENRY II and CATHERINE DE' MEDICI, Henry abandoned the Polish throne, to which his mother had arranged his election (1573), in order to succeed his brother Charles IX as the last VALOIS king of France. His reign was overshadowed by religious conflict. When the Protestant Henry of Navarre (later HENRY IV) became heir to France (1584), Henry was faced with the wrath of the diehard Catholics led by the GUISE FAMILY. Losing control of Paris, Henry had to grant wide powers to the duke of Guise (1588), but then arranged Guise's assassination (December 1588) at Blois. Henry III was in turn assassinated by a fanatical friar. Henry had cultivated tastes, but his attachment to his *mignons* (effeminate young men) discredited the French court.

## Henry IV (1553–1610) King of France (1589–1610) and king of Navarre (1572–1610)

Henry was born at Pau, the son of Antoine de Bourbon and JEANNE D'ALBRET, queen of Navarre. Although brought up a Protestant, he was forced to renounce his faith following the MASSACRE OF ST. BARTHOLOMEW (1572), which took place shortly after his marriage to the king's sister, Margaret of Valois. He escaped from the French court in 1576 and rejoined the HUGUENOT forces. The political and religious conflicts intensified after Henry was designated heir to the throne (1584), but he was reconciled to HENRY III shortly before the king's assassination (1588). The dying king acknowledged Henry of Navarre as his heir.

On his accession as the first Bourbon king of France, Henry IV had first to establish his power; his conversion to Catholicism helped persuade Paris to accept him (hence his reputed comment, "Paris is well worth a Mass"), but he was still opposed by the hardline Catholics. Gradually he gained control of all France and in 1598 granted the Huguenots religious toleration by the Edict of NANTES.

Relying on trusted advisers, such as the duke of SULLY, the king started to restore order and prosperity. It was his declared aim that even the poorest peasant should be able to afford a chicken in his pot on Sundays. He reformed the administration and put the royal finances to rights. He encouraged the economy, especially agriculture and the cloth industry: the improvements in communications included an impressive network of canals. A program of public works beautified Paris. In foreign affairs Henry IV opposed Spanish power, but he helped negotiate the 1609 truce between the Netherlands and Spain. Henry IV had no children by Margaret, whom he divorced in 1599; by his second wife, MARIE DE' MEDICI, niece of the grand duke of Tuscany, he had six. He also had numerous lovers. Despite his general popularity, he was assassinated by a Roman Catholic fanatic, François Ravaillac, leaving his kingdom to his young son Louis XIII, under the regency of Marie de Medici.

**Further reading:** Mark Greengrass, *France in the Age of Henri IV: The Struggle for Stability* (London and New York: Longman, 1984; 2nd ed. 1995).

## Henry VIII (1491–1547) King of England (1509–47) and Ireland (1540–47)

The second son of Henry VII and Elizabeth of York, he was descended from the houses of both Lancaster and York. Henry was a popular and accomplished young king, with an interest in HUMANISM. Later in his reign many regarded him as a ruthless tyrant whose hands were stained with much innocent blood.

Henry first married (1509) CATHERINE OF ARAGON, widow of his elder brother Arthur. He soon embarked on an ambitious foreign policy, which proved both expensive and fruitless. He defeated France at the battle of the Spurs (1513), then confirmed an alliance with FRANCIS I at the FIELD OF THE CLOTH OF GOLD (1520), but soon afterwards was again at war with France.

Henry was well served by his chief minister, Thomas WOLSEY, until slow progress in the king's attempt to have his marriage to Catherine annulled caused Wolsey's disgrace. Catherine had borne one healthy daughter, later MARY I, but Henry wanted a son to secure the succession. With the support of Thomas CROMWELL and Archbishop CRANMER, Henry defied the pope by dismissing Catherine and marrying Anne BOLEYN (1533). This precipitated the English Reformation which made Henry the supreme head of the Church of England and the master of its wealth—a strange irony in that he had earlier been honored by Pope LEO X for his opposition to LUTHER. Anne Boleyn had a daughter, later ELIZABETH I, but was beheaded to make way for Henry's third wife, Jane Seymour (1509–37), who died shortly after giving birth to a son, later EDWARD VI. Cromwell then persuaded the king to marry the Lutheran princess, Anne of Cleves (1515–57), in order to bolster England's links with Protestant Europe, but Henry found both her and the political strategy she represented unattractive. A speedy divorce and Cromwell's execution followed. A fifth marriage to young Catherine Howard (1542) ended in her execution. Finally he married the widowed Catherine PARR, who survived him.

Henry, particularly in his early days, enjoyed a reputation as a patron of learning and the visual arts. Among his more lasting contributions to the former was the establishment of a professorship of Hebrew at Cambridge university (1540) and the refoundation of Wolsey's unfinished Cardinal College at Oxford as Christ Church (1546). In the early years of his reign he encouraged lavish court spectacles, presenting himself as the ideal Renaissance prince. He personally engaged in the religious controversies of the day with his *Assertio septem sacramentorum contra M. Luther* (1521) and is credited with writing a number of songs and ballads. HOLBEIN THE YOUNGER worked for him in the 1530s. Using assets acquired by the seizure of Church property, particularly after Wolsey's fall, Henry also embarked on major building projects, most notably at HAMPTON COURT PALACE, York Place (Whitehall), and Nonsuch, the last directly influence by FONTAINEBLEAU.

**Further reading:** James McConica, *English Humanists and Reformation Politics under Henry VIII and Edward VI* (Oxford, U.K.: Clarendon Press, 1965; repr. 1968); David Starkey (ed.), *Henry VIII: A European Court in England* (London: Collins & Brown and National Maritime Museum, Greenwich, 1991); Alison Weir, *Henry VIII: The King and His Court* (New York: Ballantine, 2001).

**Henry of Glarus** See GLAREANUS, HENRICUS

**Henry the Navigator** (1394–1460) *Prince of Portugal*
The younger son of John I of Portugal, he was renowned for fostering science and exploration. His home at Sagres was a center of information about navigation, maps, new lands, and improved shipbuilding techniques. Henry himself did not travel, but he masterminded the exploration of the Atlantic coast of Africa, and his expeditions reached the Senegal coast, Madeira, and the Azores. He alerted Portugal to the opportunities to be won by exploration and after his death the Portuguese continued his work by opening the route to India via the Cape of Good Hope and by discoveries in the Americas.

**herbals** Collections of descriptions of plants and their medicinal uses. Many derive from Dioscorides' *De materia medica*, compiled in the first century CE, of which the oldest surviving manuscript, the Codex Vindobonensis, was made in 512 in Byzantium; the family of herbals based on it, comprising manuscript or printed translations and adaptations, flourished until the 17th century. Latin versions often combine Dioscorides' text with another by pseudo-Apuleius (Apuleius Platonicus), collected from Greek sources about 400 CE and among the first to be printed, in Rome in the 1480s. The Mainz printer, Peter Schöffer, produced the Latin *Herbarius* (1484) and its larger German companion (1485), one of the first scientific books in the vernacular. The Latin one described about 150 plants, the German nearly 400. Both were illustrated, the German pictures drawn in part from nature, though the third Mainz herbal, *Hortus sanitatis* (1491) reverted to more primitive illustrations. The great herbals of BRUNFELS, FUCHS, and MATTIOLI, in Latin and the vernacular, first appeared from 1530 to 1544, still leaning on Dioscorides but also describing and illustrating new plants without medicinal uses. William TURNER, Rembert DODOENS, and Carolus CLUSIUS continued to enlarge botanical knowledge, though the influence of GERARD's *Herball* probably lasted longer than most. The doctrine of SIGNATURES, based on the supposed resemblance of particular plants to the parts of the body they affected, was explained most fully in Giambattista DELLA PORTA's *Phytognomonica* (1588). As BOTANY became an independent study, herbals were once more restricted to medicinal plants.

**Further reading:** Wilfrid Blunt and Sandra Raphael, *The Illustrated Herbal* (London: Frances Lincoln, rev. ed. 1994).

**Herbert, Mary, Countess of Pembroke** (1561–1621)
*Poet and literary patron*
The daughter of Sir Henry and Mary Sidney, she was born at Ticknell, Worcestershire; her much-loved elder brother was Sir Philip SIDNEY. Recommended to court by her uncle Robert Dudley, Earl of LEICESTER, she became the third wife of Henry Herbert, Earl of Pembroke in 1577. When Philip fell out of favor at court in 1580 he retired to the Pembrokes' house, Wilton in Wiltshire, where he collaborated with Mary on a metrical translation of the Psalms and worked on his *Arcadia*, which he wrote for her and of which Mary brought out two revised editions (1593, 1598) after his death. Her sorrow at his death in 1586 is recorded in "The Dolefull Lay of Clorinda," published by Edmund SPENSER with his own elegy "Astrophel" (1595). She also edited Sidney's poems, bringing out an authorized edition in 1598 to supersede earlier unauthorized ones. In 1590 she made two translations from French: a blank verse version of Robert GARNIER's *Anthonie* (published 1592), and *A Discourse of Life and Death* from Plessis du Mornay (1593, 1600).

She was a major patron of writers, first of all of Philip's literary protégés Spenser and Abraham Fraunce. She appointed Samuel DANIEL tutor to her son William at Wilton in the 1590s, where he wrote some of his earliest work; he dedicated a number of his publications to her. Many other writers (Nicholas Breton, Gabriel Harvey, Ben Jonson among them) recorded their admiration of her in dedications or poems; Thomas NASHE referred to her as "a second Minerva." She died in London and was buried in Salisbury cathedral. Her famous epitaph is attributed to William Browne: "Underneath this sable Herse / Lyes the subject of all verse: / Sydney's sister, Pembroke's Mother..."

**Further reading:** Margaret P. Hannay, *Philip's Phoenix: Mary Sidney, Countess of Pembroke* (Oxford, U.K.: Oxford University Press, 1990); Kim Walker, *Women Writers of the English Renaissance* (New York: Twayne, 1996).

**Hercules** (Greek **Heracles, Herakles**) The greatest of the heroes of ancient mythology, who played a leading role in a number of myths. He was the son of Zeus (Jupiter) by the mortal Alcmene and gave early promise of his great strength when he strangled two deadly serpents sent to kill him in his cradle by Zeus's jealous wife Hera (Juno). An episode from his youth became a moral fable generally referred to as the Choice of Hercules: Virtue and Pleasure appear to the hero in a dream, acquaint him with what each has to offer, and ask him to choose between them, which he does in favor of the former. This choice underlies the action of Ben JONSON's masque *Pleasure Reconciled to Virtue*. A similar decision confronts the young Scipio in the painting by RAPHAEL entitled *The Dream of Scipio* (National Gallery, London). The Florentine humanist Cristoforo LANDINO examined the moral interpretation of the Hercules myths in his *De vera nobilitate* (On true nobility), and SALUTATI too subjected them to extended allegorical scrutiny.

The most famous of Hercules' exploits are those grouped under the title of the Twelve Labors of Hercules. The first of these was the slaying of the Nemean lion; thus he is often depicted as wearing a lionskin. Another of his labors was to fetch the apples of the Hesperides, and he is also sometimes shown holding these fruits, as in the colossal Farnese Hercules, a Roman copy of a Greek original, excavated from the baths of Caracalla in Rome and known and admired in the Renaissance. The Twelve Labors and Hercules' other adventures afforded material for studies of the mature male nude in vigorous action; POLLAIUOLO, for instance, treated the subject of Hercules' wrestling with Antaeus both in a bronze statuette (Bargello, Florence) and in a painting (Uffizi, Florence), and the contest is also the subject of a painting by BALDUNG (1530; Breslau).

*hermandad* (Spanish, "brotherhood") A form of organization originally established by medieval Castilian towns to protect their interests and maintain law and order. FERDINAND II AND ISABELLA I reorganized the *hermandades* and combined them with a central council (1476). *Hermandad* tribunals of unpaid local officials (*alcaldes*) reduced crime by their savage punishment of criminals. Their police, who could call on the central council's soldiers for help, had many successes in suppressing brigandage and maintaining law and order. Partly because the system was expensive and partly because its success made it seem less necessary, Ferdinand and Isabella agreed to the abolition of the central council in 1498. After this, local *hermandades* tended to deteriorate into inefficient rural police forces.

**Hermes** In classical Greek mythology, the messenger of the gods. The Romans identified him with their indigenous god Mercurius (Mercury), patron of trade and traders, and, by a logical extension, of travelers. One of Hermes' roles was to lead the souls of the dead to Hades; ancient Greek funerary vases often depict him in this capacity of conductor of souls (*Psychopompos*). In art he is generally shown as a youth wearing a broad-brimmed, often winged hat (*petasos*) and winged sandals and carrying a serpent-entwined staff (*caduceus*). One myth tells how he invented the lyre and gave it to APOLLO to appease the senior god for the theft of some cattle; he is therefore sometimes associated in art and literature with Apollo and the MUSES and GRACES. He was also the god of eloquence and a bringer of dreams.

In the esoteric philosophy of the late antique world, Hermes was conflated with the Egyptian god Thoth, and a whole body of mystical writings was attached to his name (*see* HERMETICISM). This made him an object of special interest to the esoteric philosophers of the Renaissance, the Florentine Neoplatonists who rediscovered the ancient texts and believed that they contained profound truths that would only be revealed to the initiated. As the go-between between natural and supernatural worlds, Hermes was invested with the symbolic role of mystagogue, instructing the candidates for initiation in the divine wisdom. BOCCACCIO calls him an "interpres secretorum" (interpreter of secrets) in *De genealogiis deorum*.

**hermeticism** A body of esoteric doctrine deriving its name from its supposed author, Hermes Trismegistus (Hermes Thrice Greatest), the Greek equivalent of Thoth, Egyptian god of wisdom. From the second century CE onward a collection of treatises was formed which became known as the Corpus Hermeticum and came to include Gnostic and cabbalistic material as well as more conventionally Neoplatonic works. Some of this was known to medieval thinkers, but the main body of hermetic writings was not available until 1460 when a Greek manuscript of the Corpus Hermeticum was brought to Florence. Lorenzo de' Medici commissioned a Latin translation of it from FICINO as a preliminary to his translation of PLATO. This was published in 1471 and made available to scholars such mystical texts as the *Poimandres*, *Asclepios*, and the *Emerald Table*, which the Renaissance saw as the source of Plato's doctrines, believing that the Corpus was an authentic record of Egyptian wisdom. Hermetic doctrines formed part of the philosophical basis of PICO DELLA MIRANDOLA's 900 theses and he began his *Oratio de dignitate hominis* (1486) with a quotation from the *Asclepios*.

The association of Platonism with hermetic ideas fundamentally colored Renaissance concepts of Plato. Christian theologians selected the less magical passages of the Corpus to provide support for Christian philosophy, some enthusiasts claiming that this was the fount of the wisdom of Moses who, the Bible says, was "learned in all the wisdom of the Egyptians" (Acts 7:22). Magicians and astrologers, such as John DEE, saw in the Corpus a systematic body of ancient wisdom that supported their animism. Giordano BRUNO is a striking example of the influence of hermeticism on a Renaissance thinker; he rejected the Christian interpretation of the Corpus and saw it as a body of pure Egyptian doctrine from which he derived a complex structure of natural philosophy. The progress of a more scientific approach to ancient texts led to the discounting of an ancient Egyptian origin for the Corpus Hermeticum. Isaac CASAUBON demonstrated its post-Christian date and the doctrines gradually declined in importance, though they exercised an influence on later ROSICRUCIANISM.

**Further reading:** Ingrid Merkel and Alan G. Debus, *Hermeticism and the Renaissance: Intellectual History and the Occult in Early Modern Europe* (New York: Folger, 1988).

**Hernández, Gregório** See FERNÁNDEZ, GREGÓRIO

**Héroet, Antoine** (died 1568) *French poet and churchman*
Born in Paris, Héroet published his major work *La Parfaicte Amye* (1542) at Lyons; its idealized portrait of the beloved was heavily influenced by the Italian Neoplatonism characteristic of the writings of Maurice SCÈVE and his Lyonnaise disciples. Héroet also made some translations from the classics, but after he was ordained he gave up writing secular verse. He rose to become bishop of Digne. Clément MAROT and Pierre de RONSARD were among his contemporary admirers.

**Herrera, Fernando de** ("El Divino") (1534–1597) *Spanish poet*
Coming from a poor family of Seville, Herrera took minor orders and obtained a small benefice which allowed him to pursue his literary interests. He was a prominent member of a *Tertulia* (literary circle) associated with the Conde de Gelves, which included Juan de la CUEVA and other poets, clergymen, and scholars. Most of Herrera's Petrarchan love poetry—more elaborate but less delicate and subtle than GARCILASO DE LA VEGA's, which it imitates—was inspired by a long platonic affair with Doña Leonor de Millán, the wife of the Conde de Gelves, though she was never named in his verse or otherwise openly identified. He also wrote three patriotic *canciones*, odes stylistically indebted to the Old Testament. *Canción al señor don Juan de Austria vencedor de los moriscos en las Alpujarras* celebrates Don John of Austria's part in defeating the Moorish uprising in Granada (1568–71); *Canción por la pérdida del Rei Don Sebastián* concerns the death of the king of Portugal in a battle against the Moors in 1578; and *Canción por la victoria del Señor Don Juan* celebrates the naval victory of LEPANTO in 1571.

After Doña Leonor's death in 1591, Herrera wrote mainly in prose but most of these works are lost. He also edited the works of Garcilaso (*Obras*, 1580). In the form of *anotaciones* he included a formulation of his own poetics: he holds clarity of expression as a principle and emphasizes the craftsmanlike and learned skills of writing verse.

**Herrera, Francisco, the Elder** (1576–1656) *Spanish painter and engraver*
A native of Seville, Herrera was influenced by the mannerist Juan de las ROELAS in his early works, which also bore the influence of 16th-century Flemish prints and of CARAVAGGIO. His early pieces include an engraving of St. Ignatius Loyola (1610), a Pentecost painting (1617; Casa y Museo del Greco, Toledo), and scenes from the life of St. Bonaventura (c. 1627; Prado, Madrid, and Villandry), upon which Francisco de Zurbarán also worked. In about 1638 he moved to Madrid, shortly afterwards painting his masterpiece, *St. Basil Dictating his Doctrine* (1639; Louvre, Paris). Other notable works include the *Triumph of St. Hermengild* (c. 1624; Museo de Bellas Artes, Seville) and *St. Joseph* (1648; Museo Lázano Galdeano, Madrid). Among his pupils were his son Herrera the Younger (1622–85) and, possibly for a brief period (1611–12), Velázquez.

**Herrera, Juan de** (c. 1530–1597) *Spanish architect*
The most influential architect in Spain during the Renaissance, Herrera was born in Mobellán and educated at Valladolid, after which he traveled with Philip II to Flanders and Italy (1547–51). During this time Herrera indulged his primary interest in the sciences, but also became familiar with the ideals of contemporary Italian artists. In 1563 he was appointed assistant to Juan Bautista de Toledo (died 1567), the court architect in charge of the building of the ESCORIAL; in 1572 he was given command of the project and was able to develop the austere style, known as *desnudo* or *desornamentado*, for which he is chiefly remembered.

Herrera also designed a palace at Aranjuez (1569) and the exchange at Seville (1582), both of which were executed in his characteristic simplified manner. Later, in his role as royal inspector of monuments, he worked on but did not complete the cathedral at Valladolid (1585). His style was copied by his successors in the post of royal architect and others, and his designs inspired a large number of imitators throughout Spain and its colonies, although several of them revolted against the severity of his architectural vision. Of all his buildings, the most influential were the west facade and church of the Escorial. He also amassed a notable library of mathematical and scientific books, invented navigational instruments, and founded the academy of mathematics at Madrid (1582).

**Hervetus, Gentian (Gentien Hervet) (1499–1584)**
*French scholar and humanist*
He came from a poor family near Orleans and had to earn a living as a tutor. In Paris he met Thomas Lupset (c. 1498–1530) and published with him an edition of the Greek physician Galen. Lupset invited him to England where he became tutor to the younger brother of Cardinal Reginald POLE; he accompanied his pupil to Rome where he translated many of the Greek Fathers into Latin. He became professor at Bordeaux but then returned to Rome, to the service of Cardinal Cervini (who became briefly Pope Marcellus II, 1555) and was a participant in the Council of TRENT (1545). He died at Reims where he had been a canon since 1562. Apart from his translations Hervetus produced polemical works against the Calvinists. He also worked on the edition of the Bible projected by the Council of Trent, published a French translation of its decrees (1564), and collated the Codex Bezae (*see* BEZA). His French version of St. Augustine's *Civitas dei* (City of God) was published in 1572.

**Hilliard, Nicholas** (c. 1547–1619) *English miniaturist*
The son of an Exeter goldsmith, Hilliard was trained as a jeweler and by 1560 was already painting miniatures. He was appointed court miniaturist and goldsmith (c. 1570), and in his official role he designed a Great Seal for Elizabeth I and was sent to France (1576–78) attached to the queen's suitor FRANCIS, Duke of Alençon. Until the 1600s he remained the leading miniaturist in England, rivaled only by his pupil Isaac OLIVER. His eminent sitters included Sir Philip SIDNEY, the earl of Southampton, Sir Walter RALEIGH, Sir Francis DRAKE, Sir Christopher Hatton, the earl of Cumberland, and the queen herself. In 1600 he wrote a treatise, *The Arte of Limning*, in which he detailed his approach to miniature painting and recorded among other things the queen's agreement with him that such works were better done in a linear style without shadows. He also makes it clear that, while he regarded himself as following in HOLBEIN's footsteps, he treated miniatures as something more than small-scale oils and considered them to have a subtlety of their own, exemplified in such works as the *Young Man Among Roses* (c. 1590), which combines the artist's skills as a jeweler and a portraitist to achieve an exquisite work of art. Other notable paintings, most of which were painted on vellum mounted on card, include *Mrs Mole*. He also occasionally worked on a larger scale, for instance in his portrait of Elizabeth painted around 1575. His son Laurence (1582–post-1640) was also a limner.

**Further reading:** Mary Edmond, *Hilliard and Oliver: The Lives and Works of Two Great Miniaturists* (London: Hale, 1983).

**historiography** The study and writing of history during the Renaisance differed considerably from that of the Middle Ages. Medieval monks had written chronicles of events or "universal histories" from the Creation to the Last Judgment in an attempt to justify God's ways in human affairs. Starting in Italy, humanist historians broke with tradition and initiated the "modern" and "scientific" (because critical) study of history.

Renaissance historiography is limited by its excessive concentration on military and political history and on kings and queens. Sometimes, like BIOGRAPHY, it was mainly a vehicle for royal propaganda with little claim to be regarded as history. A notorious example in England is Sir Thomas MORE's *The History of Richard III* (first printed in a corrupt text 1543), in which the events of Richard's reign are selected and interpreted to shed the best possible light upon his Tudor successor. Yet these faults were far outweighed by the positive contributions made by Renaissance historians. First, they pioneered the division of history into three parts; ancient history until the last days of the Roman empire, the Dark or Middle Ages from the fall of Rome to the beginning of their age, and their own modern era, which they considered one of optimism and light after darkness. Second, they secularized history, looking for natural explanations rather than explaining causality in terms of the supernatural or God's will. Third, they were more selective and often focused their work on the history of one state, as, for instance, Paolo PARUTA did on Venice. Fourth, believing men and women could learn from history, they undertook comparative studies or selected events which could help people to understand the world they lived in. Finally, they generally approached previous histories with a healthy skepticism and understood the importance of using original sources where possible.

In the 15th century Florence was the nursery of a thriving school of historians, among them Leonardo BRUNI and Flavio BIONDO; MACHIAVELLI and Francesco GUICCIARDINI were later representatives of this tradition. Depending on subject matter, historians looked to Julius Caesar, LIVY, TACITUS, or Sallust as classical models for their style. BARONIUS was a pioneer in applying the new historiographical techniques to ecclesiastical history. His *Annales ecclesiastici* (1588–1607) was a sophisticated riposte on behalf of the Roman Catholic Church to the clumsy and antiquated historiographical methods used by the Lutheran CENTURIATORS OF MAGDEBURG.

Outside of Italy too the uses of history began to be appreciated in the context of nascent national pride. In Portugal João de BARROS used Livy as the model for his *Asia*, which, with its continuation by Diogo de COUTO, provides a near-contemporary view of the triumphs and disasters of the Portuguese ventures in the East. Livy provided the stylistic model too for Juan de MARIANA in his massive Latin history of Spain down to 1516, although in the matter of his sources Mariana took an uncritical approach that mars his work; he himself published a Spanish translation of his *magnum opus* in 1601. In Holland GROTIUS, who had served his scholarly apprenticeship on the study of classical history texts, was appointed official historiographer of the United Provinces in 1603 and declared he would devote himself henceforth to the annals of his own country. By reference to the Batavi, an ancient Germanic people who lived near the mouth of the Rhine and who revolted against imperial Rome, Grotius justified the Netherlands' revolt against Spain in his *De antiquitate reipublicae Bataviae* (1610). HOOFT's later *Nederlandsche Historiën*, modeled on Tacitus, also covers this struggle, and is considered a classic of Dutch prose.

The use of history, particularly near-contemporary history, as a justification or model for political action had its dangers for historians when the authorities suspected a subversive motive; as Sir Walter RALEIGH observed, "Whosoever, in writing a modern history, shall follow truth too near the heels, it may happily [by chance] strike out his teeth" (*History of the World*, 1614).

**See also:** ANTIQUARIANISM

**Further reading:** Eric W. Cochrane, *Historians and Historiography in the Italian Renaissance* (Chicago, Ill. and London: University of Chicago Press, 1981); Arthur B. Ferguson, *Clio Unbound: Perception of the Social and Cultural Past in Renaissance England* (Durham, N.C.: Duke University Press, 1979); E. B. Fryde, *Humanism and Renaissance Historiography* (London: Hambledon, 1983); Joseph M. Levine, *The Autonomy of History: Truth and Method from Erasmus to Gibbon* (Chicago, Ill.: University of Chicago Press, 1999); Donald J. Wilcox, *The Development of Florentine Humanist Historiography in the Fifteenth Century* (Cambridge, Mass.: Harvard University Press, 1969).

**Hoby, Sir Thomas** (1530–1566) *English diplomat and translator*
Born in Leominster, Hoby went to Cambridge before undertaking extensive travels on the Continent. An expert linguist, he was knighted and sent as ambassador to France in 1566, but died in Paris a few months later. His fame rests on his elegant translation of CASTIGLIONE's *Il cortegiano* (THE COURTIER), which appeared in 1561 and in four later editions before 1603. Hoby's wife Elizabeth (1528–1609) was also a skilled linguist.

**Hoefnagel, Georg (Joris Hoefnagel)** (1542–1600) *Flemish painter*
The son of an Antwerp diamond dealer, Hoefnagel traveled extensively, visiting Spain and France (1561–67), England (1569), and Italy (1577), before entering the service of first the FUGGER FAMILY and eventually RUDOLF II (from 1591). His travels, often accompanied by his friend the geographer ORTELIUS, resulted in his numerous depictions of towns in Frans Hogenberg's great topographical work *Civitates orbis terrarum* (1572–1618). In Prague he made exquisite drawings of natural history subjects and also created his masterpiece, the emblematic illustrations to a primer on calligraphy by a Hungarian, George Bocskay, written 20 years previously for Emperor Maximilian II. This primer, now in the possession of the J. Paul Getty Museum, has been published in facsimile form as *Mira Calligraphiae Monumenta: A Sixteenth-Century Calligraphic Manuscript* (J. Paul Getty Museum, 1992). Hoefnagel's son Jakob (1575–c. 1630) followed him as a miniature painter in the imperial service.

**Holbein, Hans, the Elder** (c. 1465–1524) *German painter and draftsman*
A native of Augsburg, Holbein worked there between 1494 and 1517, mainly producing altarpieces and other religious subjects in the late Gothic style for ecclesiastical patrons. His early work reveals the influence of contemporary Netherlands painters, but works of his last period, such as the *Well of Life* (1519; Lisbon), show incipient awareness of Italian Renaissance motifs. Like his more famous son of the same name, the elder Holbein was an accomplished portraitist. He died at Isenheim.

**Holbein, Hans, the Younger** (1497/8–1543) *German painter*
Born in Augsburg, the son of Hans HOLBEIN THE ELDER (c. 1465–1524), he began by training in his father's Augsburg studio. By 1515 he was working for a painter in Basle with his brother. He also executed designs for the humanist publisher Johann FROBEN, through whom he met ERASMUS in about 1516. The drawings he did for the paintings of Burgomaster Meyer and his wife (1516; Basle) were probably more mature than the paintings themselves. After visiting Lucerne and probably Italy (1517–19), Holbein returned to Basle, where he was commissioned to paint the council chamber. Disturbances connected with the Reformation, however, interrupted this work, which was not finally completed until 1530; other paintings from this period include *Bonifacius Amerbach* (1519; Basle) *Christ in the Tomb* (1521; Basle), and *Madonna and Child with Saints* (1522; Solothurn). Holbein also designed the *Dance of Death* (1523/24) and the *Alphabet of Death* (1524) series of woodcuts, illustrated the Luther Bible (1522), and painted three portraits of Erasmus (1523), which established his international reputation.

In 1526, possibly because of continuing religious unrest, Holbein moved to London and met Sir Thomas MORE, whose family he painted in the first group portrait of full-length figures in their domestic setting in European art (the painting now exists only in sketches and copies). After 18 months he returned to Basle, there executing designs for stained glass and a portrait of his own family whom he painted with an honesty he curbed with influential sitters. Then religious strife again prompted him to seek his fortunes (c. 1532) in England. As More was now

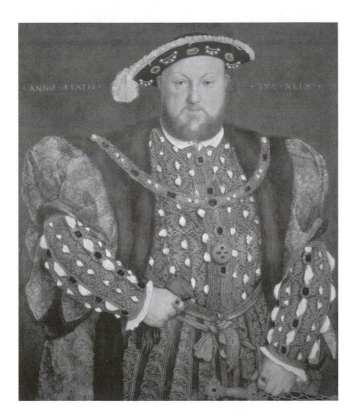

**Hans Holbein the Younger** Detail from the famous portrait of Henry VIII of England painted in 1540 when Holbein was court painter (Galleria Nazionale, Palazzo Barberini, Rome). *Photo AKG London*

out of favor at court, Holbein won the patronage of the German merchants of the Steelyard, producing for them many portraits of considerable virtuosity. Possibly through the good offices of Thomas CROMWELL he obtained the commission in 1533 for his great double portrait *The Ambassadors* (National Gallery; London) and then the patronage of HENRY VIII, for whom he undertook his most celebrated work in England, the wall painting in Whitechapel Palace of the king with his mother and Jane Seymour (destroyed in 1698 but preserved as a cartoon and in copies). Subsequent portraits for Henry VIII included *Jane Seymour* (1537; Vienna), *Anne of Cleves* (1539/40; Louvre), *Catherine Howard* (1540/41; Toledo, Ohio), and *Christina, Duchess of Milan* (1538; London). Although it seems likely that Holbein never realized the full depth of his talent at the English court, he did also produce other portraits, miniatures, and designs for goldsmiths' work which has now perished. He died in London of the plague.

**Further reading:** Susan Foister *et al*, *Holbein's Ambassadors* (New Haven, Conn.: Yale University Press, 1998); John North, *The Ambassador's Secret: Holbein and the World of the Renaissance* (London: Hambledon, 2003); Roy Strong, *Holbein and Henry VIII* (London: Routledge & Kegan Paul, 1967).

**Holl, Elias** (1573–1646) *German architect*
Holl was born into a prominent Augsburg family of masons. He visited Venice briefly (1600–01) and some Palladian influence is to be seen in his work. He was the city architect, or master builder, of Augsburg from 1602 to 1635, at a time when Augsburg was the largest city in Germany and one of the most important. It is for his Augsburg building program (which included schools, guildhalls, warehouses, houses, and city gates) that he is known, although he also executed commissions outside the city. His first building in office was the arsenal (constructed 1602–07), carrying out a design by Joseph Heintz. The style here was mannerist verging on baroque, especially in the sculpture erected over the portal. Holl's own designs are based on a primarily functional approach, symmetry, and fine proportions—in fact a far more restrained classicism, almost severe in its lack of elaborate detailing. This style can be seen particularly in St. Anne's grammar school (1613–15) and in Holl's most acclaimed building, the town hall (constructed 1615–20). This combines classical with Germanic and other features (such as onion domes) in a very plain, functional, but pleasantly proportioned building. Holl's career reflects the fate of Renaissance architecture in Germany, being brought to an abrupt close by the Counter-Reformation and the Thirty Years' War. Along with 8000 Augsburg citizens, Holl went into temporary exile when Protestant worship was forbidden in the city in 1629; in 1635 his Protestantism finally lost him his post. Widely celebrated in his own day, Holl is considered the most important German Renaissance architect.

**Holland, Philemon** (1552–1637) *English translator*
Holland was born at Chelmsford, Essex, the son of a Protestant clergyman who fled to the Continent during the reign of the Catholic Mary I. He took his MA at Cambridge in 1574 and subsequently studied medicine. He then settled in Coventry where he spent the rest of his life teaching, practicing medicine, and making his renowned translations from the classics: of the Roman historian Livy (1600), Pliny's *Natural History* (1601), Plutarch's *Moralia* (1603), Suetonius (1606), Ammianus Marcellinus (1609), and Xenophon's *Cyropaedia* (1632). In addition he translated William CAMDEN's *Britannia* into English (1610), and some medical translations were issued posthumously. His translations are characterized by immense learning combined with a fine feeling for the emotional tone of the original.

**Hollanda, Francisco da** See FRANCISCO DA HOLLANDA

**holy brotherhood** See HERMANDAD

**Holy League** Any military alliance that included the papacy. In the Renaissance period the term was applied to several such alliances. Pope JULIUS II inspired the Holy League (1511–13) of the papacy, Venice, Spain, England, and Emperor MAXIMILIAN I to fight the French threat to Italy. The French won at Ravenna (1512), but were defeated by the league's Swiss mercenaries at Novara (1513). This league collapsed after quarrels among its members and Julius II's death. In 1571 Spain, the papacy, Venice, and other Italian states formed the Holy League to fight the Turkish threat. Their navy practically annihilated the Ottoman fleet at LEPANTO (1571).

**Holy Roman Empire** During the Renaissance, a loosely organized collection of between 300 and 400 states, varying greatly in size. The term itself dates back to 1254. These mainly Germanic territories covered central Europe from the Alps in the south to the Baltic in the north, and from France in the west to Hungary and Poland in the east. The empire's population, about 20 million in 1450, was the largest in Europe.

Although the Golden Bull (1356) had established an electoral empire, heads of the HAPSBURG family ruled the empire continuously from 1438 to 1740. In many ways the emperor was a nominal ruler, and real power lay with the princes, especially the seven electoral princes; these were the archbishops of three Rhineland cities (Cologne, Mainz, and Trier), the king of Bohemia, the margrave of Brandenburg, the duke of Saxony, and the count Palatine of the Rhine.

The Holy Roman Empire faced serious problems in the Renaissance period. In the 14th and 15th centuries local and factional warfare brought it close to disintegration. Emperors often only survived because they were too weak to be a threat to their powerful subjects. In the 16th century OTTOMAN TURKS reached the gates of Vienna, the Hapsburg–Valois conflict strained the empire's resources, and the empire was torn apart by religious wars. In the 17th century it was devastated by the Thirty Years' War.

Some emperors tried to centralize the empire and to make it into a modern sovereign state like France and England, but they were defeated by its size, its diversity, and its powerful vested interests. Only CHARLES V in the 16th century might have managed to weld it into a modern European power.

**Further reading:** Peter H. Wilson, *The Holy Roman Empire 1495–1806* (New York and London: Palgrave Macmillan, 1999).

**Homer** (?ninth century BCE) *Greek epic poet*
Although the stories of the *Iliad* and *Odyssey* were known in the West in the Middle Ages, the almost universal ignorance of Greek prevented any widespread appreciation of the poems themselves. Various Latin paraphrases, commentaries, and secondary material were available (*see* TROY, LEGEND OF) and these accounted for the medieval picture of Homer as a great and venerable poet. DANTE, for

instance, refers to him in the *Divine Comedy* as "Omero poeta sovrano." The earliest humanist Latin translations of the *Iliad* and *Odyssey* were made in the 14th century at the instigation of PETRARCH and BOCCACCIO; BRUNI and VALLA in the following century were responsible for Latin prose versions and POLITIAN for one in Latin hexameters.

The growth of GREEK STUDIES in western Europe from the mid-15th century eventually ensured a readership for the Homeric poems in their original tongue. The *editio princeps* was printed in Florence in 1488. Inevitably Homer was compared with his Roman epic counterpart VIRGIL. Pierre de RONSARD was one of the earliest critics to contrast "la naïve facilité d'Homère" with "la curieuse diligence de Virgile."

**See also:** EPIC

**homilies** See PREACHING

**Hondius, Jodocus (Josse de Hondt)** (1563–1612) *Flemish cartographer*
Raised in Ghent, Hondius moved to London around 1583, where he established himself as an engraver and type founder and met many geographers and scientists, including Richard HAKLUYT. Hondius engraved the terrestrial globes developed by Emery Molyneux (1592) before moving to Amsterdam in 1593. His most celebrated works were his two world maps on the MERCATOR projection. One was the illustrated "Christian Knight" map, so called because it contained the image of a knight; the other depicted the voyages of Sir Francis Drake and Thomas Cavendish. Hondius made other maps and globes and engraved the maps for John Speed's *Theatre of the Empire of Great Britain* (1611–12), but the latter part of his career was successfully involved with the work of Mercator, whose plates he bought in 1604. He published a Mercator atlas with 37 new plates two years later. Hondius's work is less scientific but more attractive than Mercator's, and is notable for its decorative calligraphy. His sons, Jodocus (1593–1629) and Henricus (1597–1644), and also later descendants, continued his business, capitalizing on the phenomenal and enduring success of the Mercator–Hondius atlas.

**Hooft, Pieter Cornelisz.** (1581–1647) *Dutch poet, playwright, and historiographer*
Hooft's father was a prosperous merchant of Amsterdam, who obtained a good classical education for his son. Hooft then traveled in France and Italy (1598–1601); his literary encounters in these countries made a deep impression, turning him away from the indigenous tradition nurtured in the CHAMBERS OF RHETORIC (he was a member of De Egelantier in Amsterdam) and toward the Renaissance poets such as PETRARCH, ARIOSTO, TASSO, and RONSARD. His brilliance as a lyricist manifested itself not only in the love lyrics he wrote in the decade after his return but also in

the lyrical passages of his plays such as the pastoral *Granida* (1605), which is influenced by Jacopo SAN-NAZARO. After studying law at Leyden (1606–09), Hooft was appointed sheriff of Muiden, where he restored the castle and lived the rest of his life. There he played host to a distinguished literary and musical circle, known as the Muiderkring. His play *Geeraerdt van Velzen* (1613) was inspired by the story of a late 13th-century occupant of the castle at Muiden; it was followed by *Baeto* (1617), another historical drama on a Netherlands theme, and in both plays Hooft displays his interest in statecraft and the nature of power. The comedy *Ware-nar*, written in 1614, adapts Plautus' *Aulularia* to an Amsterdam setting.

Even more important than his poems and plays was Hooft's output in prose, of which he was an outstanding master. He wrote histories of Henry IV of France (1624), and the Medici (1638), but his greatest achievement was his 27-book *Nederlandsche Historiën* (1624, 1654) on the history of the Dutch struggle against Spain in the years 1555–87. Its style and presentation are deeply indebted to TACITUS. Hooft died while visiting The Hague and was buried in the Nieuwe Kerk in Amsterdam.

## Hooker, Richard (c. 1554–1600) *English theologian and scholar*

Hooker was born near Exeter into a poor family and was sent to Oxford through the generosity of Bishop John JEWEL, to whose defense of the Church of England, *Apologia pro ecclesia Anglicana* (1562), Hooker's own great work was to be deeply indebted. Hooker became a fellow of Corpus Christi College (1577) and deputy professor of Hebrew (1579) but had to leave Oxford on his marriage. About the same time (1581) he took holy orders and in 1584 was appointed rector of Drayton Beauchamp in Buckinghamshire. In 1585 he was made master of the Temple before returning to parochial duties, first (1591) in Boscombe, Wiltshire, and finally (1595) in Bishops-bourne, Kent, where he died.

The first four books *Of the Lawes of Ecclesiasticall Politie* appeared in 1594, followed by the fifth book in 1597. The remaining three books did not appear in Hooker's lifetime. The treatise is a masterly defense of the ELIZABETHAN SETTLEMENT of 1559, defending the Church of England against the implications of the Puritans' literal interpretation of the Scriptures. Hooker's interpretation of natural law as the manifestation of God's reason had important repercussions on the political theories of 17th-century writers such as John Locke. He is also important as a prose stylist, writing a clear and vigorous English that was unusual in theological debate in his time. A biography of Hooker was published by Isaak Walton in 1665.

**Further reading:** Arthur S. McGrade (ed.), *Of the Laws of Ecclesiastical Polity: Preface, Book I, Book VIII* (Cambridge, U.K.: Cambridge University Press, 1989); Nigel Voak, *Richard Hooker and Reformed Theology: A Study of Reason, Will, and Grace* (Oxford, U.K.: Oxford University Press, 2003).

## Hopfer, Daniel (Daniel Hoppfer) (c. 1470–1536) *German engraver and designer*

Hopfer was born at Kaufbeuren, but was a citizen of Augsburg from 1493. He is claimed as the first to have made prints on paper by etching iron plates (as opposed to ENGRAVING). He certainly produced some of the earliest original etched portraits, a number of religious illustrations (on Reformation lines), scenes of everyday life, such as village festivals, and a large number of reproductions of Italian art, which made him a significant popularizer of the Italian style in Germany. He was also a designer of decoration, publishing 50 plates of ornamental motifs, which included Gothic foliage and Renaissance grotesques. Like other engravers of the time, he etched decoration on ceremonial parade armor, which formed a major part of his work.

## Horace (Quintus Horatius Flaccus) (65–8 BCE) *Roman poet*

Born in the Latin colony of Venusia, Horace was educated in Rome and Athens. He lost his estate in the civil war that followed the murder of Julius Caesar, but in about 33 BCE MAECENAS gave him a farm which inspired some of his most beautiful poetry on country life. The *Odes* and *Epodes*, in a range of lyric meters, cover personal, political, and patriotic themes, and were much admired and imitated from the time of Petrarch onwards. Konrad CELTIS even had some of the odes set to music to be sung after his lectures. The two books of *Satires* were also admired for their urbanity, as were the *Epistles*. Another epistle, to Piso, is better known as the *Ars poetica*. Before the full text of ARISTOTLE's *Poetics* was in general circulation, Horace's treatise was the main source for Renaissance knowledge of literary theory in the ancient world.

## horology

The science of measurement of time. Time in antiquity was measured by several devices, chief among them the water clock or clepsydra and the sundial. The use of both, however, was limited, the former by frost and the latter by cloud or darkness. The mechanical clock emerged in the late 13th century. In its earliest forms it was powered by a descending weight and controlled by the verge and foliot form of escapement. Although free from the disabilities of clepsydrae and sundials, early CLOCKS operated more as planetaria and alarm bells than as a means of measuring time accurately. So inaccurate were they that it was only in the late 15th century that it was deemed worthwhile to fit them with a minute hand. Tycho BRAHE, for example, still used a clepsydra in the late 16th century to make his more precise measurements, and clocks only became reliable and accurate enough for sci-

**Horology** A woodcut of a 16th-century water clock, appearing in *De solaribus horologiis et quadrantibus* (editor Jean Fine; 1560).

entific use with the development of the pendulum clock in the late 17th century.

See also: WATCHES

**Further reading:** Gerhard Horn von Rossum, *A History of the Hour: Clocks and Modern Temporal Orders*, transl. Thomas Dunlap (Chicago, Ill.: University of Chicago Press, 1996); David S. Landes, *Revolution in Time: Clocks and the Making of the Modern World* (Cambridge, Mass.: Belknap Press of Harvard University Press, 1983).

**horsemanship** See EQUITATION

**Hosius, Stanislaus** (Stanislaus Hosen) (1504–1579)
*Polish churchman*
Hosius studied law in his native Cracow and subsequently

at Bologna and Padua. Having been ordained priest in 1543, he was appointed bishop of Kulm (1549) and then of Ermland (1551). In his struggle with the Protestants in his diocese he approved the use of force against them. This course of action was based on his conviction that Catholicism was the only true Christianity; Hosius attempted to prove this in his *Confessio catholicae fidei christiana* (1552–53), a work that was frequently reprinted and translated in the next 25 years. In 1558 he was summoned to Rome to advise the pope about Poland and Prussia. Two years later he became papal nuncio to Emperor Ferdinand I and reclaimed his son (later Emperor Maximilian II) for the Roman Church. He was made a cardinal in 1561 and attended the Council of Trent as papal legate. He died at Capranica, near Rome.

**Hospitalers** See KNIGHTS HOSPITALER

**Hothby, John** (c. 1410–1487) *English music theorist and composer*
Hothby was a Carmelite monk who traveled through Germany, France, Spain, and northern Italy. He had settled at Lucca by 1467, becoming choirmaster, teacher, and chaplain at the cathedral there. He died on his way back to England. Nine of his compositions survive, but he is remembered as a theorist. His treatises include texts on the rudiments of music, *musica speculativa*, notably his *Calliopea legale*, and polemical works, such as *Dialogus Johannis Ottobi Anglici in arte musica*, in which he attacks the ideas of RAMOS and defends traditional foundations of music.

**Houtman, Cornelis** (died 1598) *Dutch explorer*
Houtman was a key figure in the Dutch exploration movement inspired by LINSCHOTEN that resulted in the formation of the DUTCH EAST INDIA COMPANY. In 1595 Houtman headed a four-ship expedition which sailed from Texel in search of trade routes to Asia. Although his voyage was disrupted by illness, he eventually arrived at Java. After exploring the surrounding area and visiting Bantam, Houtman was imprisoned because the native inhabitants and the Portuguese merchants there resented the presence of the Dutch, and on his release his crew insisted on sailing home rather than trying their luck elsewhere. The voyage cost Houtman one ship and two-thirds of his men. He attempted a second voyage in 1598, during which he was killed by the inhabitants of Sumatra.

The first account of the 1595 voyage, by an anonymous crew member on Houtman's ship *Hollandia* was published in autumn 1597 as *Verhael vande Reyse by de Hollandtsche Schepen gedaen naer Oost Indien* (as *Description of a Voyage Made by Certaine Ships of Holland into the East Indies*, 1598). A revised and expanded edition, *Journael Vande Reyse der Hollandtsche Schepen ghedaen in Oost Indien* (Journal of the Voyage of the Dutch Ships to the East Indies), came out early in 1598, with French, Latin, and German translations the same year. However, the most successful narrative of this important voyage was that by Willem LODEWYCKSZ.

**Howard, Henry, Earl of Surrey** See SURREY, HENRY HOWARD, EARL OF

**Howard, Thomas, 2nd Earl of Arundel** (1585–1646) *English art collector and patron*
Son of the stubbornly Roman Catholic Philip Howard, who died (1595) in the Tower of London for his faith, Thomas spent his youth deprived of his lands and titles until the accession of James I, who restored his titles. Marriage to an heiress enabled him to make his way at court and undertake travel on the Continent (1609), where he discovered his interest in art. He was a patron of Inigo JONES, who traveled in his entourage to Italy in 1613–14. During this visit the earl carried out an archeological dig in Rome to search for antiquities, and the statuary he obtained in Italy formed the nucleus of the influential collection known as the Arundel Marbles (donated 1667 to the University of Oxford; Ashmolean Museum, Oxford).

Although James made him earl marshal (1621), the enmity of the royal favorite George Villiers, Duke of Buckingham (1592–1628) caused him to fall into temporary disfavor on Charles I's accession. In 1636 Charles sent Arundel on an abortive embassy to Emperor Fredinand II to request the return of the Palatinate to Charles's nephew, the son of the WINTER KING; the journey was recorded by another of Arundel's protégés, the Bohemian artist Wenceslaus Hollar (1607–77). Arundel amassed a renowned gallery of paintings at Arundel House, London, in addition to antique statuary, marble fragments, gems, coins, medals, and books. His zeal for collecting is documented in his correspondence with his agents in Europe and the Levant, including Sir Thomas Roe (c. 1581–1644), ambassador to Constantinople in the 1620s, and while typical of a Renaissance grandee Arundel in his role as collector is also a precursor of the 18th-century Grand Tourist.

**Further reading:** Mary F. S. Hervey, *The Life, Correspondence and Collections of Thomas Howard, Earl of Arundel* (Cambridge, U.K.: Cambridge University Press, 1921).

**Huber, Wolfgang** (c. 1490–1553) *German artist*
One of the masters of the DANUBE SCHOOL, he was born in Feldkirch (Vorarlberg) and was probably Albrecht ALTDORFER's assistant around 1510. Like him, Huber frequently depicted poetic landscapes in both drawings and paintings. He also made some experiments in figure composition and perspective, but is chiefly remembered for his studies of wind-blown trees and views of the Danube valley. From 1515 he worked in Passau, incurring the dislike of the local painters. He was also a notable draftsman and engraver.

**Hudson, Henry** (died 1611) *English navigator*
Engaged by the MUSCOVY COMPANY to search for a direct route to the spice islands via the north pole, he made his first, inevitably abortive, voyage in 1607. After an attempt the following year on the NORTHEAST PASSAGE, he switched allegiance to the DUTCH EAST INDIA COMPANY, which again dispatched him northeastward. When his crew refused to continue in that direction he sailed west across the Atlantic, reaching Nova Scotia, then turning south and exploring the lower reaches of the river that bears his name. In 1610 he led an English attempt on the NORTHWEST PASSAGE; the ship was frozen in over winter in James Bay and in June 1611 mutinous sailors set Hudson adrift in a small boat, never to be seen again. Hudson's luckless voyages

had the merit of proving to the European trading companies that neither the northeast nor the northwest passage could afford easy access to the riches of the Orient.

**Huguenots** The name given to French Protestants from the mid-16th century, apparently derived from a King Hugo in a medieval romance. By the early 1520s LUTHER's ideas were circulating in France and a reform movement was established. The first French Protestant martyr was burnt in 1523. After the appearance of posters attacking the Mass (1534) many Protestants, including CALVIN, had to leave France, but Protestantism still spread, attracting members of the nobility like Antoine de Bourbon (father of Henry of Navarre who became HENRY IV). At a synod in Paris (1559) the Huguenots drew up a confession of faith (*see* GALLICAN CONFESSION) which was strongly influenced by Calvin; hence they became a Calvinist rather than a Lutheran movement.

The Huguenots were fiercely opposed by the GUISE FAMILY and their Catholic supporters (*see* RELIGION, (FRENCH) WARS OF). After the Edict of NANTES (1598) granted them religious and political freedom the Huguenots prospered, but the revocation of the edict in 1688 drove most of them into exile.

**humanism** In general, any system of belief that places human affairs at its center. In the Renaissance context humanism is associated with the rediscovery of the culture of the Greco-Roman world, particularly Greek literature and philosophy (*see* GREEK STUDIES). The medieval world had some knowledge of classical Latin literature; indeed, individual scholars such as Alcuin (735–804) and John of Salisbury (died 1180) show an impressive range of reference, but this cannot properly be described as humanism. The term *humanismus* itself seems first to have been used by PETRARCH and his contemporaries to express the spirit of intellectual freedom by which man asserted his independence from the authority of the Church. Characteristically, Petrarch was influenced by the use of the term *humanitas* by both CICERO and the Roman scholar Varro to define their educational ideal. By the 16th century humanistic concepts had become inextricably involved with theological controversy but even the earliest humanists, by their exaltation of personal freedom, challenged the hierarchical structure of the medieval theocracy. Humanism grew up in the cities and communes of Italy which were fighting for their political autonomy against the control of pope or emperor, both personifications of fundamentally medieval institutions.

According to orthodox theology, man was born sinful and was incapable of virtue without the aid of divine grace. Humanism offered an alternative, which said that man could freely choose his destiny and by the exercise of his own will could act rightly. PICO DELLA MIRANDOLA expressed this idea most comprehensively in his *Oratio de dignitate hominis* but other humanists took up and developed the idea. For such men Prometheus, the foresighted Titan, is the prototype of the humanist "wise man." This did not necessarily mean a rejection of religion; on the contrary many humanists strove to synthesize the new approaches with Christianity, a Christianity which came more and more to depend not on the interpretations of ecclesiastical authority but on the scientific study of original texts. The methods of classical scholarship which were evolved to deal with secular literature were applied to the Scriptures and the Church Fathers (*see* PATRISTIC STUDIES) and the same standards of coherence and connection were demanded (*see* CRITICISM, TEXTUAL). The interaction of humanism with religion produced another consequence—a search for some underlying principle that would unite the warring elements of different doctrines. This search made many humanists more tolerant of religious differences; Pico for example aimed at nothing less than a demonstration of the accord between PLATO, ARISTOTLE, classical and Jewish esoteric wisdom, and the spectrum of patristic interpretation and exegesis. He felt that the diversity of belief reflected partial but not contradictory glimpses of the original One to which humanism sought to return (*see also* NEOPLATONISM, RENAISSANCE).

Renaissance humanism also helped to create the conditions that led to the scientific revolution. The revival of interest in classical doctrines of the nature of the physical universe, the insistence on autopsy of original texts, the shift away from the authoritarian *ipse dixit* ("he said") of scholasticism, all helped to stimulate a spirit of critical objective inquiry. By stressing that man is a natural being, the humanists implied that he could understand his physical environment by using the tools that nature gave him, namely his senses.

Another of the major contributions of Renaissance humanism to the stock of western European concepts is the idea of historicity. Medieval thinkers had little sense of the difference between the ancient world and their own time. The humanists, by virtue of their own self-consciousness about their relationship with the ancient world, focused sharply on precisely those differences and coined the term "Middle Ages" to express that historical awareness (*see also* HISTORIOGRAPHY).

As humanism diffused beyond the bounds of Italy it became increasingly involved in theological controversy. The potential for such controversy was always there, and frequently it was only the direct intervention of humanist popes such as Nicholas V, Pius II, or Eugenius IV that protected humanists from ecclesiastical wrath. In France and Germany humanism was associated first with the movement for reform within the Church, then with the more radical reformers; it was said that LUTHER hatched the egg that ERASMUS laid.

It is difficult to assess briefly the lasting contribution of Renaissance humanism to Western civilization. Many of its features have mainly historical interest today. But the central belief of the early humanists that the human personality is worth cultivating and developing to its fullest extent for its own sake is a continuing inspiration.

**Further reading:** Arthur G. Dickens, *The Age of Humanism and Reformation: Europe in the Fourteenth, Fifteenth and Sixteenth Centuries* (Eaglewood Cliffs, N.J.: Prentice Hall, 1972); Samuel Dresden, *Humanism in the Renaissance* (London: Weidenfeld & Nicolson, 1968); Anthony Grafton, *Bring Out Your Dead: The Past as Revelation* (Cambridge, Mass.: Harvard University Press, 2002); Jill Kraye (ed.), *The Cambridge Companion to Renaissance Humanism* (Cambridge, U.K.: Cambridge University Press, 1996); Robert L. R. Mandrou, *From Humanism to Science, 1480 to 1700*, transl. Brian Pearce (Harmondsworth, U.K.: Penguin, 1978); Charles G. Nauert Jr, *Humanism and the Culture of Renaissance Europe* (Cambridge, U.K.: Cambridge University Press, 1995); Charles E. Trinkaus, *The Scope of Renaissance Humanism* (Ann Arbor, Mich.: University of Michigan Press, 1983) ENGLAND: Roberto Weiss, *Humanism in England during the Fifteenth Century* (Oxford, U.K.: Blackwell, 3rd ed. 1967) FRANCE: Werner L. Gundersheimer (ed.), *French Humanism, 1470–1600* (London: Macmillan, 1969) ITALY: Peter Godman, *From Poliziano to Machiavelli* (Princeton, N.J.: Princeton University Press, 1998); Lauro Martines, *The Social World of the Florentine Humanists, 1390–1460* (London: Routledge & Kegan Paul, 1963); Charles E. Trinkaus, *In Our Image and Likeness: Humanity and Divinity in Italian Humanist Thought*, 2 vols (Chicago, Ill.: Chicago University Press and London: Constable, 1970; new ed. Notre Dame, Ind.: University of Notre Dame Press, 1995).

**Hurtado de Mendoza, Diego de** (1503–1575) *Spanish diplomat, humanist, poet, and historian*
Born to a noble family at Granada and a descendant of SANTILLANA, he received an excellent humanist education, learning Hebrew and Arabic as well as the classical languages. After serving with the Spanish forces at the battles of PAVIA (1525) and Tunis (1535), he entered on a distinguished diplomatic career. An early mission on behalf of Emperor CHARLES V was his vain attempt to negotiate a marriage between Henry VIII of England and Christina, duchess of Milan. As ambassador in Venice (1539) he was able to indulge his bibliophil interests: he sponsored the recovery of 300 Greek manuscripts from Greece and Mount Athos and was a patron of the ALDINE PRESS. Although he represented Spain at the Council of TRENT and at Rome (1547–54), he was recalled to Spain in 1555 on the accession of Philip II, who eventually dismissed him from court (1568). He returned to Granada and participated in suppressing a Moorish rebellion there, in the Alpujarras (1568–71). This forms the subject of *La guerra de Granada* (published 1610, 1627, 1630, in various versions), the first objective military history written in Span-

ish. Modeled on Sallust, the work is remarkable for its brilliant style and its impartiality. As a poet, Hurtado de Mendoza practiced the Italian meters introduced by BOSCÁN and his own contemporary, GARCILASO DE LA VEGA. His poems were published in *Obras* (1610). At one time he was believed to be the author of LAZARILLO DE TORMES. At his death his manuscript collection was added to that of the Escorial.

**Huss, Jan (John Hus)** (1369–1415) *Czech theologian and religious reformer*
Together with Jerome of Prague (c. 1370–1416), Huss initiated the reform movement that led to the creation of a strong national Church in Bohemia by the mid-15th century. Huss, who was rector of Prague University from 1403, first came to prominence as a keen defender of the radical English theologian John WYCLIF. As part of a growing movement that sought greater religious egalitarianism, Huss included in his demands vernacular translations of the Bible, lay communion, and a reduction of clerical power. Opposition to Huss was aroused not only because of the possible heresy in his teachings but also because he became the hero of the Czech nationalist movement. In 1408 Archbishop Zbyneck of Prague suspended him from his teaching office and in 1411 he was excommunicated by Pope John XXIII. Taking refuge in southern Bohemia, he wrote a major treatise *De ecclesia* (1413), which was to be used as the chief pretext for his condemnation by the Council of CONSTANCE. He attended the council under a false promise of safe conduct from Emperor Sigismund and was burned as a heretic upon its decision in July 1415.

Whether the charge of heresy could be substantiated is debatable, especially since he rejected many of the more obviously heretical Wycliffite claims. His execution, together with that of Jerome the following year, proved disastrous for the orthodox party, since it ensured a successful radical HUSSITE revolution in Bohemia and the spread of Hussite doctrine throughout Europe.

**Further reading:** Matthew Spinka, *John Huss: A Biography* (Princeton, N. J.: Princeton University Press, 1968).

**Hussites** Followers of the Czech reformer Jan HUSS. The main demands of the early Hussites, which owed much to the teaching of John WYCLIF, were: communion in both kinds for the laity (i.e. reception of both bread and wine at the Eucharist, a doctrine known as Utraquism); the expropriation of Church property—many Czechs believed that the region had been impoverished by the Church; freedom to preach from the Scriptures; and civil punishment of serious sinners. These aims were enshrined in the Four Articles of Prague (1420), drawn up by Jakoubek of Stríbro, successor to Huss at the Bethlehem Chapel in Prague.

The demands for religious reform were closely linked to political aspirations, with anger at the executions of

Huss (1415) and Jerome of Prague (1416) igniting an intense nationalism in all sections of Czech society. The Bohemian *Länder* had long been part of the Holy Roman Empire, and nationalist feeling was fueled by a deep resentment of German influence; Huss himself had been leader of the nationalist movement at Prague University.

In 1417 Prague University sanctioned Hussite practice, and many Czech nobles offered to protect those persecuted for their faith. In 1419, when Sigismund (emperor 1411–37) acceded to the Bohemian throne, leading Czechs asked him to guarantee that Hussite demands would be met. He refused, and in 1420 Martin V (pope 1417–31) declared a crusade against the Hussites. Several imperial and papal invasions were firmly repelled during the 1420s and the early 1430s, the Hussites being led by a brilliant general, Jan Zizka (c. 1376–1424), who also expelled thousands of Germans. Under his successor, Prokop Holý (Procopius the Great; died 1434), the defensive strategy became expansionist, with Hussite forces entering Silesia, Saxony, and Franconia.

However, the wide support enjoyed by Hussite views was also a weakness, as it became increasingly difficult to hold together factions with very different political and religious aspirations. The moderate Hussites, the Utraquists, who were mainly nobles and burghers, sought a reconciliation with Sigismund and the Church. By contrast, the Taborites, who were largely (but not exclusively) drawn from the peasantry, supported radical religious and social reforms, including the abolition of feudalism. In 1423 and 1424 Zizka (a Taborite) had suppressed several moderate factions.

Eventually, negotiations begun in 1433 at the Council of BASLE led to the Compacts of Prague, in which (bowing to pressure from Sigismund and against the wishes of the pope) the Church conceded several Czech demands. Having accepted Sigismund's main demand—an oath of loyalty—the Utraquists now joined with imperial forces to inflict a final defeat on the Taborites at the battle of Lipany (1434). In 1436 Sigismund was recognized as king of Bohemia and an independent Hussite Church came into existence.

A desire to return to the religious and social reforms of the radical Hussites persisted, however. The CZECH BRETHREN, notably, who became formally independent in 1467, spread rapidly and in time sought union with Calvinists and Lutherans, leading to the Bohemian Confession of 1575.

The Bohemian Church finally came to an end during the Thirty Years' War: in 1620 Catholic forces reasserted their control over the region through their victory at the battle of the WHITE MOUNTAIN, scattering radical Hussites and Protestant groupings and bringing the moderates back into the Catholic Church.

**Further reading:** Frantisek Michálek Bartos, *The Hussite Revolution, 1424–37* (Boulder, Colo.: East European Monographs and New York: Columbia University Press, 1986); Howard Kaminsky, *A History of the Hussite Revolution* (Berkeley, Calif.: University of California Press, 1967); Josef Macek, *The Hussite Movement in Bohemia,* transl. Vilém Fried and Ian Milner (London: Lawrence & Wishart, 1965).

**Hutten, Ulrich von** (1488–1523) *German humanist*
After an early life of apparently aimless wandering from his native Steckelberg around the universities of Germany and Italy, Hutten found fame as a controversialist and pamphleteer. His first work, an attack on Duke Ulrich of Württemberg, was inspired by a family quarrel, but about the same time (1515) Hutten also became a major contributor to the famous humanist satire EPISTOLAE OBSCURORUM VIRORUM. In 1517 Hutten entered the service of the archbishop of Mainz and the following year published an edition of Lorenzo VALLA's *Donation of Constantine* with a sarcastic dedication to the pope. In 1520 his enthusiastic support of Martin LUTHER (expressed in several Latin and German tracts) resulted in his dismissal from the archbishop's service, and Hutten resumed his wanderings. He died soon afterwards, under the protection of Ulrich ZWINGLI at Zürich.

**hydraulics** Before the development of the steam engine, and excluding animal power, much of the energy available to Western man derived from hydraulic power. Vitruvian mills, with vertical wheels and horizontal axles, were introduced into Rome in the first century BCE. They were mainly used to grind corn. From the 10th century CE new uses began to be found for them. With suitable gearing and connections a water mill could be used to power a trip hammer or a mechanical saw, to beat cloth, to pound ore, to pump water, to ventilate galleries, and to operate numerous other devices. Many of these machines can be seen illustrated in the pages of Georgius AGRICOLA and Agostino RAMELLI. Advances were also made in canal design. Pound locks replaced primitive flash locks in the 15th century and soon spread across Europe. At approximately the same time the miter-gate, reputedly designed by LEONARDO DA VINCI and still in use today, began to replace the more cumbersome portcullis.

At a more theoretical level, Renaissance mathematicians sought to advance beyond the foundations established by Archimedes in antiquity. STEVIN in his *Hydrostatics* (1586) formulated the socalled hydrostatical paradox, the principle that the force exerted by a fluid on the bottom of a vessel is proportional to the bottom's area, the height of the fluid, and its specific gravity, but is not necessarily equal to the weight of the fluid. Further insight came from Leonardo da Vinci, who presented the continuity equation, relating the flow of a volume of water to its cross-sectional area. He was less successful, however, in determining the water's velocity. This required a more sophisticated mathematics than was available to the Renaissance.

**Further reading:** Denis Cosgrove *et al*, *Water, Engineering and Landscape* (Chichester, U.K.: John Wiley & Sons, 1994).

**hymnody** In the usage of the Western Church, the hymn is a strophic poem of praise, sung in worship since late antiquity. In the medieval Church singing of hymns took place mainly in the Divine Office, the set of daily services apart from the Mass. As is the case with many forms of liturgical music, congregational performance of hymns as practiced in modern times was largely unknown until its introduction in the worship of the Reformed denominations. Nevertheless, monophonic music such as the famous hymns used in processions during Holy Week and Easter (for example, "Vexilla regis" and "Salve festa dies") was certainly known and loved by the laity well before the 16th century.

In many instances, the characteristics of the earliest multivoice hymn settings find parallels in the first stages of polyphonic PSALMODY. The liturgical context that elicited the majority of such settings in the 15th century—when these compositions first appeared in significant numbers—was the office of Vespers, particularly on important feast days. A simple, transparent style of writing predominates in these early works, with the separate voices moving mainly in the same rhythm, unlike the more elaborate compositional approaches found in contemporaneous Mass Ordinary settings and motets. As with Vespers psalms, the sectional and repetitive structure of the plainchant hymns encouraged composers to adopt alternation schemes in their polyphonic versions. Multi-voice settings of even-numbered strophes, for example, could alternate with plainchant or organ-playing for the odd-numbered strophes; likewise, the antiphonal alternation of polyphonic choirs was employed in certain hymn settings more than half a century before multichoir writing became an established style of motet composition.

The evidence of late sources, as well as the treatment of hymn melodies when reused in polyphonic compositions, suggests that plainchant hymns were sometimes sung in rhythmicized versions (reflecting the verse forms); this practice is particularly well documented in Spain. The original monophonic melodies were left completely intact in many polyphonic settings; indeed, examples from England and Germany use traditional plainchant notation for the voice carrying the hymn tune, while other voices weave more complex counterpoints around it. The better-known hymn melodies found their way into compositions for instrumental ensembles alongside popular tunes of all sorts, suggesting their use in private secular contexts.

As mentioned above, Protestant denominations took the step of establishing congregational hymn-singing, creating a new repertory that mixed music from sources of great variety: popular songs with sacred and secular vernacular texts, Catholic plainsong hymns, and nonliturgical Latin religious songs. Many of the Latin works adopted for Lutheran use were given vernacular texts, as in LUTHER's translation of "Veni redemptor gentium" as "Nun komm, der Heiden Heiland." In the music of the reformed Church of England (as elsewhere) there was a somewhat blurred line between metrical psalms and vernacular hymns, including both translations of existing Latin hymns and new texts. If the hymn in these contexts lost some of its traditional characteristics and usage patterns, nonetheless its transformation into a composition inviting congregational participation proved to be one of the greatest changes in the form's history.

**See also:** LITURGY

*Hypnerotomachia Polifili* A romance, describing a lover's search for his mistress, written by the Dominican monk Francesco Colonna (1433–1527) and published by Aldus MANUTIUS in Venice in 1499. The large book is outstanding for the beauty of its typography and woodcut illustrations, as well as for its fine printing. The unknown artist seems to have been influenced by both MANTEGNA and Giovanni BELLINI, and some of his work records contemporary garden designs. The text, a mixture of Latin and Italian, was translated into French by Jean Martin and Jacques Ghorry in 1546 and published, with extra pictures, in a format almost as beautiful as the original. *The Strife of Love in a Dreame*, an incomplete English version by Robert Dallington, appeared in a scruffy little book in 1592. An electronic facsimile of the original 1499 edition can be viewed at htpp://mitpress.mit.edu/e-books/HP/

# I

**iatrochemistry** The medical theory that disease results from a chemical reaction and that it can be both defined and treated chemically. The idea was originally associated with the remarkable Swiss physician PARACELSUS, and the Latin word *iatrochymista* (from Greek *iatrikos*, healing + chemist) appears to have originated in late 16th-century translations of his work, although it was not adopted into English until the mid-17th century. For iatrochemists the creation of the universe itself, as well as most natural processes, were essentially chemical operations; it followed inevitably that medicine would be absorbed into the scheme. Iatrochemistry was helped by the total failure of traditional medicine to control the spread of major diseases such as syphilis and PLAGUE. Its practitioners, with their use of such potent chemical medicines as arsenic and antimony, seemed initially to be successful, and the movement prospered. This early success is signaled in the growing tendency for the printed PHARMACOPOEIA to include chemical preparations. Although opposition was encountered in Paris, where the authorities declared antimony a poison and banned its therapeutic use, elsewhere, and particularly in Britain and Germany, iatrochemistry spread rapidly and widely in the 17th century.

**iconoclasm** The breaking or destruction of images set up for religious veneration, especially practiced by Protestants during the century of the Reformation. Protestants based their hostility to images on the Old Testament prohibition (Exodus 20:4–5) and on their belief that religious statues and pictures encouraged superstition among the ignorant multitude. The ANABAPTISTS at Münster were an example of the radical Protestant sects who took this line. Not all reformers shared their view: LUTHER approved of religious pictures as an aid to piety, and intervened forcibly at Wittenberg to restrain Andreas CARLSTADT and his supporters, who were bent on their destruction (1522). CALVIN, however, attacked superstitious practices with particular severity, and many of the most violent episodes were perpetrated by his followers, notably the so-called "Iconoclastic Fury" in the Netherlands (1566). Carel van MANDER records among the losses paintings by Pieter Aertsen, Hieronymus Bosch, and Jan van Scorel, and other famous works such as the Eyck brothers' GHENT ALTARPIECE only narrowly escaped destruction. Such outbursts were widely deplored, and even Protestant regimes hostile to images usually tried to secure their orderly removal, in order both to discourage riotous conduct and to prevent plunder. But undoubtedly iconoclasm resulted in the destruction of many priceless works of art and the defacement of numerous church buildings.

**Further reading:** Margaret Aston, *England's Iconoclasts: Laws Against Images* (Oxford, U.K.: Clarendon Press and New York: Oxford University Press, 1988; repr. 1991); Phyllis M. Crew, *Calvinist Preaching and Iconoclasm in the Netherlands* (Cambridge, U.K.: Cambridge University Press, 1978).

**iconography** The study of icons, that is, images which are often, though not necessarily, sacred and which express in a concentrated visual way some deep moral or spiritual truth. The Church in the Middle Ages had elaborated a complex set of rules for the interpretation of icons and these were based on assumptions about the nature of the relationship between the image and the object it depicts. The Renaissance, in this area as in so many others, took over medieval concepts and modified them.

Renaissance icons had to satisfy a number of requirements. First was the principle of decorum; the icon had to be appropriate to the situation or object. For example, a representation of Vulcan's smithy was a suitable decoration for a fireplace. However, an image had also to convey a moral message so an even better subject would be Croesus about to be burnt on his pyre and recalling Solon's saying that no man should be considered happy until he had finished his life happily. Symbols could be drawn in this way from the whole range of classical and biblical sources, and many handbooks were published classifying and explaining their application, thus evolving a shared vocabulary of symbols current throughout educated Europe. Perhaps the most representative of these was the *Iconologia* of Cesare Ripa (1593). Ripa takes as his starting point the theory of metaphor developed by ARISTOTLE in the *Rhetoric* and *Poetics*, and the fourfold definition by types of causes, material, efficient, formal, and final. The deviser of images has the same freedom to work within these four categories as the formulator of verbal definitions. Ben JONSON, for instance, is known to have owned a copy of Ripa's book and drew upon it when devising his masques.

The other strand of iconography in the Renaissance was the Neoplatonic. This owed much also to Christian mysticism, particularly the works of Dionysius the Areopagite. These fused Neoplatonic and Christian ideas to produce a theory of symbolism which made the image the medium by which the deepest truths were expressed in the most concise way. Platonism assumed that unity was superior to multiplicity and the icon seemed to Renaissance Platonists to have a precision that was denied to discursive language. This made the designing of icons one of the most serious tasks for the philosopher, as it was by means of the image that one approached the ineffable Reality which was the Divine Oneness.

From this it will be clear that the study of icons in the Renaissance requires not only an extensive knowledge of the possible sources for such images but also an awareness of the philosophical subtleties which determined the choice of a particular image in a particular situation. Thus, much ingenuity has been exercised by historians of art in expounding the Neoplatonic program that underlies the images of Botticelli's PRIMAVERA and by literary critics in explaining the inner significance of such verbal icons as those created by Edmund Spenser in such passages as the Masque of Cupid or the Bower of Bliss in his FAERIE QUEENE.

**See also:** EMBLEMS; IMPRESE; GRACES

**Further reading:** Edgar Wind, *Pagan Mysteries in the Renaissance* (London: Faber and Faber, 1958; rev. ed. Harmondsworth, U.K.: Penguin, 1967).

**Ignatius Loyola, St.** (1491–1556) *Spanish mystic, founder of the Jesuits*

Ignatius was born at his family's castle in the Basque province of Gúipuzcos, the youngest of 13 children. After his leg had been shattered in battle at Pampeluna in 1521, he went on pilgrimage and retreat for a year, during which time he drafted his *Ejercicios espirituales* (*Spiritual Exercises*), eventually printed at Rome in 1548. He was brought before the Inquisition because of his preaching, but was released. In 1534 he and six other students founded the Society of Jesus (*see* JESUITS) in Paris and took their first vows. In 1539 they presented their plans for the order to Pope Paul III, and the order was approved the following year. Ignatius was appointed the first superior-general. He sent his companions as missionaries to found Jesuit schools, colleges, and seminaries throughout Europe. Ignatius wrote the Jesuit *Constitutions*, which were adopted in 1554. These regulations created a monarchical organization and stressed absolute obedience to the pope. The Jesuits thus became a major factor in the success of the COUNTER-REFORMATION.

Ignatius was a mystic who believed in a rigorously ordered spiritual life. His ideal became the Jesuit motto: *ad maiorem dei gloriam* ("All things for the greater glory of God"). He died in Rome and was canonized in 1622.

The *Ejercicios espirituales* were translated from the Latin text into English by C. Seager in 1847. J. Norris and others worked from the Spanish text for their 1880 translation, which has been several times reprinted. The version by Thomas Corbishley S.J. appeared in 1963 and that by Pierre Wolf in 1997. English recusants (*see* RECUSANCY) of the 16th and 17th centuries were supplied with English texts based on the *Exercises* printed by Catholic presses overseas: Tomás de Villacastín's *Manual de consideraciones y ejercicios espirituales* was made available in English as *Manuall of Devout Meditations and Exercises*, published at St. Omer in 1618 (repr. 1976), with further editions in 1623 and 1624, and *Annotations to the exercise*, translated from Latin, appeared about 1630 at Rouen (repr. 1972).

**Further reading:** John Patrick Donnelly, *Ignatius of Loyola: Founder of the Jesuits* (New York and London: Pearson Longman, 2003).

*imprese* Devices embodying a picture and a motto in such a way that they reciprocally interpret each other. The *impresa* is thus a subtype of the EMBLEM; the difference, according to CARPACCIO (1592), was that the emblem had only to feed the eyes, whereas the device fed the mind. While the design of an emblem was largely a matter of personal choice, the rules of the *impresa* were fixed by the academies, and one of the tasks a court humanist would be expected to perform was the devising of suitable *imprese*. The concept of the *impresa* came into Italy from courtly French society in the reign of Louis XII, specifically during the occupation of Milan from 1499.

The correspondence of Isabella d'Este shows how much importance was attached to *imprese*, which were believed to present in a peculiarly concentrated form the various operations of mind and spirit to produce a distillation of the owner's personality; medals bearing a portrait of the owner on one side and a riddling *impresa* on the other were favorite tokens among humanist courtiers. Thus Lorenzo di Pierfrancesco de' Medici had depicted on the obverse of his medal a variation on the ancient Egyptian hieroglyph of a serpent biting its tail, an emblem of perfection or eternity; the hint conveyed to the initiated by this serpent is that the soul although descended to earth still partakes of its heavenly nature. Paolo GIOVIO (*Dialogo dell' imprese militari et amorose*, 1555) established five requisites for the *impresa*: it should show just proportion; it should not be too obscure or too transparent; it should make a fine show; there should be no human figure; the motto should be in a different language from that of the author of the device.

The fashion lasted throughout the 16th century and spread throughout Europe. Toward the end of the period RUDOLF II was a particular aficionado of *imprese* and both the *Empresas Morales* (1581) of the Spaniard Juan de Borja and the *Symbola Divina et Humana* (1601–03) of Aegidius Sadeler were published in Prague.

**incunabula** (Latin, "swaddling clothes") Books printed before the end of the year 1500. The term was first used in reference to printing by Bernard von Mallinckrodt, dean of Münster cathedral, in *De ortu et progressu typographicae* (Cologne, 1639), a bicentenary celebration of GUTENBERG's invention. The author describes the period up to 1500 as *prima typographicae incunabula* ("the time when printing was in swaddling clothes"), a phrase that other writers soon copied. In the 18th century the word "incunabula" alone began to be applied to the products of early printing. The singular form "incunabulum," now often anglicized or gallicized to "incunable," is used to refer to a single book from this period. The German equivalent is *Wiegendruck* ("cradle-book"). The choice of the year 1500 as the end of the first period suggests a clear break in the development of printing, an implication that is not confirmed by the work produced early in the 16th century.

**Index Librorum Prohibitorum** A list of books which Roman Catholics were forbidden to read, on pain of excommunication. Its aim was to protect faith and morals, especially to prevent the spread of heresy and to regulate the reading and editing of Scripture. From the fourth century onwards, the works of heretics were condemned, and several popes issued decrees listing recommended and forbidden books. From about 1540 lists of proscribed works were produced by universities and bishops. In 1557 Pope PAUL IV ordered the Congregation of the Holy Office to compile the first official printed list or Index, which condemned some authors entirely and certain works of others: there were rules for the guidance of readers. It was issued in 1559 and revised several times by the popes and by the Council of TRENT in 1562. In 1571 a separate Congregation for the Index was established, which was reorganized in 1588; the secretary was always a Dominican. The system remained substantially unchanged until the early 20th century and was finally abolished in 1966.

See also: CENSORSHIP

**indulgences** In Roman Catholic teaching, the commutation by the Church of the temporal penalty incurred by sins that have already been forgiven. There are two presumptions behind this doctrine: first, that divine justice requires temporal punishment of sins on earth and in Purgatory, even though the sinner has repented and received God's forgiveness; second, that the Church, through the merits of Christ and the saints, has the authority to remit such punishment in consideration of good works performed by the sinner. Having become deeply uneasy about both presumptions, LUTHER would challenge the whole system of indulgences in 1517–18, thus setting in train the complex series of events now known as the REFORMATION.

Although the doctrine of indulgences can be traced back to the early centuries of the Church, it did not acquire any great importance until the high Middle Ages. From the 12th century onward the granting of indulgences to repentant sinners who performed conspicuous good works, such as going on crusades or pilgrimages, became increasingly common. The doctrine was greatly extended in 1459, when Pope Sixtus IV ruled that indulgences could commute not only the penance required on earth but also sufferings endured in Purgatory. By this time, the system was already under attack for its manifold abuses. These included not only the flagrant selling of indulgences by rogue "pardoners," but, more insidiously, the Church's use of the system to encourage donations, often for specific building projects.

The chain of events leading to Luther's epoch-making protest began in 1506, when Pope JULIUS II declared an indulgence for Christians who contributed to the cost of rebuilding St. Peter's, Rome. In 1514 his successor, LEO X, made the fateful decision to extend the preaching of the indulgence from Italy to other territories. In Germany it was proclaimed in extravagant terms by Albert, archbishop of Mainz, and his agent, a Dominican named Johann Tetzel (c. 1465–1519), both of whom appeared to suggest that sins could be remitted for a simple cash payment. To Luther, already passionately committed to the idea of JUSTIFICATION BY FAITH alone, this was intolerable. His Ninety-five Theses, posted at Wittenberg on October 31, 1517, were a direct response to Tetzel's preaching; at the same time, they went beyond the issue of monetary abuse to raise deeper questions about the theology behind

**Indulgences** A 16th-century German woodcut showing Martin Luther posting his Ninety-five Theses against indulgences on the church door at Wittenberg. The lion in the center of the picture represents Pope Leo X.
*Private Collection/The Bridgeman Art Library*

the indulgence system. Although the theses were intended as an invitation to scholarly debate, rather than a statement of public defiance, they soon circulated throughout Germany and became an unofficial manifesto for those who sought thoroughgoing reform of the Church. The indulgence controversy raged throughout 1518; Rome published a list of countertheses under Tetzel's name (the socalled Fifty Theses) and Luther issued a long defense of his views. By the following year the dispute had moved beyond the immediate question of indulgences to wider issues of sin, grace, justification, and (most crucially) the true source of authority in matters of faith. When Luther refused to submit to papal authority in 1519–20, the break with Rome was inevitable.

Within the Roman Church it would be another 40 years before the worst abuses of the indulgence system were tackled (1562) at the Council of TRENT. The practice of granting indulgences for money payments was revoked by papal decree in 1567.

**See also:** PILGRIMAGE AND PILGRIMAGE SHRINES

**Inquisition** The Inquisition has a long history, starting in the 13th century. Following the crusade called (1208) by the pope and led by the northern French nobility against the Cathar heretics of southern France (which also reduced the southern French nobility), an inquisition was set up to investigate communities for the Albigensian heresy. Albigensianism, named for the town of Albi in southern France, was an extreme form of dualism which held that the material world was irredeemably evil and showed implacable opposition to the Church hierarchy and orthodox interpretations of the Bible; its adherents referred to themselves as Cathars, from Greek *katharos*, pure. The most famous investigation was that in the Bas-Pyrénées between 1294 and 1324, when Jacques Fournier (later Pope Benedict XII) conducted an inquisition into the diocese of Montaillou. The meticulous verbatim records made by the inquisitors of the examinations of accused Cathars from this area have been preserved and give an unparalleled insight into a segment of medieval French society. Except for the Languedocian region of southern France, inquisitorial activity declined in the 14th century.

After the mid-16th century, the Inquisition became an important arm of the COUNTER-REFORMATION. Individual communities (e.g., Rome, Modena, Venice, and Spain) had their own inquisitorial bodies; the most famous are the SPANISH INQUISITION and the Roman Inquisition. The former was founded by Tomás de TORQUEMADA and was infamous for its severity. In Spain, confiscated properties went to the royal coffers, and the Spanish Inquisition was entirely independent of Rome. The Roman Inquisition (reestablished in 1542) was given strict procedural rules by Francisco Peña. No matter whether in Madrid, Rome, or Modena, the Inquisition was a dreaded instrument for heresy hunting. Once charged with heresy by a delator (informer), the accused was imprisoned and intensely questioned about his heresy. It was said that in the Inquisition's prisons one's diet consisted of "the bread of sorrow and the water of tribulation." If the charge was not too severe, the accused might be imprisoned for several years or, occasionally, released after the trial and sentencing. In more serious cases, if the accused was found to be unrepentant or was a relapsed heretic, the sentence was death. The heretic was then "relaxed" to the secular authorities, who burned him or her at the stake.

In the late 16th and early 17th centuries, the local and Roman inquisitions were active against both famous intellectuals and village eccentrics whose theological ideas went beyond the rather straitened bounds of Counter-Reformation orthodoxy. Among the victims of the Inquisition's investigations during this period were the philosophers Francesco PATRIZI, Giordano BRUNO, and Tommaso CAMPANELLA, and the scientist GALILEO GALILEI. Of these, only Bruno was executed; Galileo ended his days under house arrest and Campanella spent many years in prison.

The examination and fate of the miller Domenico Scandella (known as Menoccio) from Montereale in Friuli, burned at the stake in 1599, is studied by Carlo Ginzburg in *The Cheese and the Worms* and may stand for those of thousands of obscure victims with unconventional reading habits, inquiring minds, or social eccentricities who fell foul of the Inquisition in one of its many manifestations.

**Further reading:** Carlo Ginzburg, *Il formaggio e i vermi* (1976), as *The Cheese and the Worms: The Cosmos of a Sixteenth-Century Miller* (Baltimore, Md.: Johns Hopkins University Press and London: Routledge & Kegan Paul, 1980); Emmanuel Le Roy Ladurie, *Montaillou* (New York: George Braziller, 1978); Benjamin Netanyahu, *The Origins of the Inquisition in Fifteenth-Century Spain* (New York: New York Review of Books, 2001); Edward M. Peters, *Inquisition* (Berkeley, Calif.: University of California Press, repr. 1989).

**Inquisition, Spanish** See SPANISH INQUISITION

*Institutes, The* The popular English name for CALVIN's *Christianae religionis institutio*, the principal text of the Calvinist or Reformed Church. The first edition, published at Basle in 1536, was a brief manual of six chapters based on the framework of the catechism and intended as a short textbook of reformed orthodoxy. Its success prompted Calvin to expand it considerably, so that by the time of the definitive edition of 1559 it was five times its original length. Its 80 chapters and four books now comprised a complete handbook of the reformed religion: a systematic theology based on the Bible, a manual of ethics, a guidebook to the Protestant creed, and a comprehensive survey of Reformation theological controversy. The clearest and ablest systematic exposition of the ideals that inspired the Reformation, the *Institutes* was translated into the languages of those countries influenced by Calvinism, including French (1541; by Calvin himself), Dutch (1560), and English (1561).

The English translation of *The Institutes of the Christian Religion* by John Allen (1813; first U.S. edition, 1816) was frequently reissued during the 19th and 20th centuries. An edition by John T. McNeill featuring a translation from the Latin by Ford Lewis Battles makes up vols 21 and 22 in the Philadelphia Library of Christian Classics (1960; repr. 1980). The French text appeared in a modern critical edition with notes by J.-D. Benoit (Paris, 1957–63).

**interlude** (Latin *interludium*, "between-play") In the theater, a short dramatic piece, usually comical or farcical and possibly including music, mime, and acrobatics, performed as a diversion between the acts of a longer play. In Italy the INTERMEDII or *intermezzi* of the late 15th and early 16th centuries were slight, often comic entertainments, frequently on a classical or mythological theme, inserted as relief between the acts of a more substantial work. The related French *entremets* was a similar comic or satirical interpolation. The Spanish *entremés* evolved in Castile from comic interludes performed in public theaters and became a separate independent genre, popularized especially by Luis Quiñones de Benavente (c. 1583–1631) and practiced by most Golden Age playwrights including CERVANTES and Lope de VEGA.

In England, the term "interlude" was applied to a very wide range of dramatic works written in the transitional period (c. 1500–76) between the medieval religious drama (mystery, morality, and miracle plays) and Elizabethan drama as performed in theaters by professional companies. John Heywood (c. 1497–1580) was the first English playwright to treat it as an independent dramatic genre (as, for example, his farcical interlude *The Pardoner and the Friar*). But the term continued to be used very loosely in England and could as easily describe a late mystery play or John BALE's *King John* as a "classical" comedy (for example, Nicholas UDALL's *Ralph Roister Doister*).

*intermedii* (intermezzi) Either instrumental interludes played out of sight of the audience, or, more popularly, stage spectacles by singers, dancers, and actors in costume, first performed in the Renaissance between the acts of plays. Sometimes the subject matter of the *intermedii* was connected with that of the play, though more often unrelated pastoral scenes with allegorical figures were presented. While *intermedii* were first performed in the 15th century at the court in Ferrara, the Medici court in Florence was the scene of many of the most lavish entertainments; the most spectacular was that performed in 1589 at the wedding of Christine of Lorraine and Ferdinando de' Medici, for which the music was provided by leading composers, including MARENZIO and CACCINI. In its combination of music and drama, the *intermedio* can be regarded as a forerunner of opera.

### Isaac, Heinrich (c. 1450–1517) *Flemish composer*
Though Isaac was born in Flanders, the first definite reference to him is in Innsbruck (1484) en route for Florence to enter the service of Lorenzo de' Medici. In Florence Isaac sang in the Cantori di San Giovanni and was regularly employed at the cathedral from 1485. After the death of Lorenzo (1492) Isaac met Maximilian I, and in 1497 became his court composer. While in the emperor's employ he maintained his Florentine connections and eventually resettled there in 1514. Isaac was one of the few Netherlanders active in Germany. He wrote a wide range of music; among his Masses, motets, German lieder, Italian songs, and instrumental pieces, his *Choralis constantinus* (1550–55), a posthumous collection of Mass propers, stands out as a monumental achievement. Isaac contributed considerably to the *Tenorlied*, as his skillful settings of "Innsbruck, ich muss dich lassen" demonstrate.

### Isabella, Archduchess (1566–1633) *Infanta of Spain and coruler of the Spanish Netherlands (1598–1621)*
The daughter of Philip II of Spain, Isabella married her cousin ALBERT OF AUSTRIA under an arrangement that made them joint sovereign rulers of the Spanish Netherlands. Both Archdukes were enthusiastic patrons of the arts, Isabella's taste mainly inclining towards religious art in a high Counter-Reformation vein. RUBENS painted a number of works under her patronage, and in 1625 she commissioned him to design a set of allegorical tapestries (completed 1628) with titles such as *The Victory of the Eucharist over Heresy*. Rubens and Jan BRUEGHEL painted a pair of portraits of the Archdukes (Prado, Madrid), and Hendrik Staben painted them on a visit to Rubens' studio (Musées Royaux des Beaux-Arts, Brussels). After Albert's death (1621) Isabella continued to act as governor of the Netherlands on behalf of her nephew, the king of Spain, and relied greatly on Rubens' advice, sending him on several important and successful diplomatic missions.

**Isabella (I) of Castile** See FERDINAND II AND ISABELLA I

**Isabelline style** See PLATERESQUE

**Istanbul** See CONSTANTINOPLE

**Italian language** In many respects the closest of the romance languages to Latin, Italian is used, at least as a written or second language, by more than 60 million people in Italy, Switzerland, and elsewhere. By the beginning of the Christian era, Latin had largely supplanted a number of early peninsular languages with which it originally coexisted. Ligurian, Etruscan, Oscan, Umbrian, Rhaetian, and Punic had disappeared or been reduced to insignificance, though some (Etruscan and Punic) may have survived for a while in ritual use. Greek is still spoken in areas of southern Italy, but whether it is continuous with that of Roman times is doubtful. Between 476 and 960 three waves of Germanic invaders entered Italy. Romanized Goths under Theodoric (489) had slight effect on vocabulary and were soon submerged by Justinian's reconquest (555). Lombards (Langobards) occupied areas north of the latitude of Spezia–Rimini and further south in Benevento and Spoleto, donating some 280 words to Italian and many more to various dialects. Franks (from 773) reached northern and central regions, but it is difficult to determine which Frankish words (e.g. *barone*, *feudo*, *ligio* (liegeman), *galoppare*, *bargagnare*) date from the era of Charlemagne and which from the later era of chivalry.

Evidence that a vernacular language is about to be born exists from the late eighth or early ninth century in the *Indovinello veronese*. This is a riddle, of uncertain interpretation but generally comparing ploughing to writing (plough: pen, oxen: fingers, white meadows: parchment, black seed: ink). By 960 legal documents record testimonies in the vernacular. Like all romance languages, Italian developed certain features: simplification of gender with loss of the neuter; loss of the deponent; definite and indefinite articles; a passive with *esse* and compound tenses with *habere*; prepositional constructions replacing genitives and datives; comparatives with *plus* replacing Latin synthetic comparatives; *quia* assuming a modern function (as *che*). Other typical changes can be exemplified in such words as *più* (from *plus*), *poi* (*post*), *buono* (*bonum*) and *fatto* (*factum*). The earliest literary document is the *Ritmo laurenziano* (c. 1150) and a number of other poems in various dialects are found by about 1200. In the early 13th century the Albigensian crusade caused Provençal poets to migrate to Italy and the *langue d'oc* (see FRENCH LANGUAGE) came to compete with Tuscan as a literary language in the northern courts. At the court of Frederick II, however, the poets of the Sicilian school, while writing in the troubadour tradition, did so in some variety of Italian, perhaps a refined version of the local dialect (a *volgare illustre*); their compositions was then passed to the north in tuscanized form and had an immense influence (*see* DOLCE STIL NUOVO). In Umbria, St. Francis and Jacopone da Todi inspired the writing of religious verse, such as the *Laudes creaturarum* (or *Cantico di Frate Sole*), by St. Francis (c. 1225). By the end of the 13th century, there is an awareness of Tuscan primacy in vernacular usage; the prestige of the socalled *Tre Corone*, DANTE, PETRARCH, and BOCCACCIO, eventually assured Tuscan, and Florentine, preeminence.

A temporary setback occurred in the first half of the 14th century, however, when humanist devotion to Latin radically depreciated the vernacular in all fields of learning. But the vernacular foundations were strong and the 15th century saw the triumph of a vernacular humanism cultivated by ALBERTI, POLITIAN, Lorenzo de' MEDICI, and others. Printing (from 1470), in which the earliest priorities were the works of Petrarch, Boccaccio, and Dante (in that order), in time assisted in standardizing the language. Pietro BEMBO's *Prose della volgar lingua* (1525) and the founding of the Accademia della Crusca (1582) mark the final stages in resolving the QUESTIONE DELLA LINGUA and establishing the standard embodied in the Cruscan *Vocabolario* (1612).

In speech, though Italian has now gained ground and dialects are becoming increasingly italianized, an extreme diversity persists that is due to the historical fragmentation of Italy and the lack of a centralizing impetus (before unification in 1861) able to counterbalance the civic pride of the urban centers. (It has even been suggested that Venice produced no substantial body of literature out of pique at the preference for Tuscan over her own dialect.) In *De vulgari eloquentia* (c. 1303) Dante listed major dialect groups, noting further differences within them (as between Siena and Arezzo in Tuscany) and even between districts of a city. The present picture is scarcely less complex, with up to four levels of usage occurring in one area (Italian for writing and a regional variety with two local dialects as well for spoken use in certain circumstances). The dialects may vary greatly, Piedmontese and Sardinian, for example, having less in common than Spanish and Portuguese. Recently over 200 concepts or things sur-

veyed in a study of 54 Italian regions produced only one item known to all informants by the same word (*espresso*); for other items, between two and 13 different words or expressions were used. In such conditions, the establishment of a standard language at the end of the Renaissance was an achievement of unique and lasting importance.

**Italy, Wars of** (1494–1559) A series of conflicts that involved most Italian states, Spain, the Holy Roman Empire, France, and Switzerland. They began with CHARLES VIII's triumphal invasion and coronation in Naples (1494–95), which was followed by the expulsion of France from Naples by Spain and its Italian allies (1496). In the second French invasion LOUIS XII took Milan and tried to regain Naples. Initially he cooperated with FERDINAND II of Aragon, but the Aragonese later expelled the French from southern Italy (1504).

The conflict continued when Emperor MAXIMILIAN I joined Pope JULIUS II, some other Italian states, France, and Spain in the League of CAMBRAI against Venice (1508); quarrels over the spoils then led to the formation of the anti-French HOLY LEAGUE in 1511. The Swiss entered the wars and forced Louis XII out of Milan, which his successor, FRANCIS I, regained after his victory at Marignano (1515).

In the relatively quiet period that followed, both Ferdinand (1516) and Maximilian (1519) died. War resumed in the 1520s in the wider context of the European struggle between the Hapsburgs under CHARLES V and the Valois under Francis I. At the battle of PAVIA (1525) Charles V defeated and captured Francis I, who had to renounce his Italian claims. In the anti-Hapsburg reaction that followed, France, the papacy, and other Italian states formed the League of Cognac against Charles. The notorious Sack of ROME (1527) by imperial troops followed. By 1529 several setbacks compelled Francis I again to surrender his Italian claims in the treaties of Barcelona and Cambrai. The last phase of the wars (1529–59) saw limited foreign involvement in Italy and ended with France's final renunciation of its Italian claims in the treaty of CATEAU-CAMBRÉSIS (1559).

# J

**Jacobean style** The English architectural and decorative style associated with the reign (1603–25) of James I. It is also known as Early Stuart and is a natural development of the preceding ELIZABETHAN STYLE. Its general tendency was to fine down and restrain the exuberant inventiveness of earlier craftsmen and builders in their attitude to classical models and motifs. While FURNITURE was still made predominantly of oak, some new forms of chairs and tables began to make their appearance. In architecture there was renewed interest in the correctness of classical proportions and a tendency to use stone again for important buildings. Forerunner of the revival of building according to classical canons in late Stuart England was the architect Inigo JONES, whose important commissions and careful study of the work of PALLADIO initiated the fashion for pure Italian Renaissance architecture.

**Further reading:** Timothy Mowl, *Elizabethan and Jacobean Style* (London: Phaidon, 1993).

**Jacobello del Fiore** (c. 1370–1439) *Italian artist*
The son of Francesco del Fiore, the president of the guild of painters in Venice (1415–36), Jacobello was a pupil of GENTILE da Fabriano and adopted a similar approach in the International Gothic style when he began painting in 1394. His earliest surviving work is the *Madonna della Misericordia* (1407); other works include the *Lion of St. Mark* (1415; Palazzo Ducale, Venice) and the *Coronation of the Virgin* (1438), a copy of the well-known painting by Gauriento.

**James I** (1566–1625) *King of England and Ireland (1603–25), King of Scots (as James VI; 1567–1625)*
The son of MARY, Queen of Scots, and Henry Stewart, Lord Darnley, James was the first monarch to rule both Scotland and England. His long minority was plagued by Scotland's religious and political turmoil, but after 1583 he succeeded in imposing his authority on the warring factions. In England he had less success, failing to understand the English and their institutions; they in turn mocked his personal habits and his liking for handsome young courtiers. They also resented his policy of seeking peace with Spain. In his attempts to assert himself James had bitter disputes with his parliaments, usually over money. His schooling under George BUCHANAN had given him a taste for learning, and he wrote treatises on several subjects (witchcraft, tobacco, the divine right of kings); however, his greatest contribution to literature was made in 1604 when he commissioned the Authorized Version of the Bible.

**Further reading:** W. B. Patterson, *King James VI and the Reunion of Christendom* (Cambridge, U.K.: Cambridge University Press, 1998); Alan Stewart, *The Cradle King: The Life of James VI and I* (London: Chatto & Windus and New York: St. Martin's Press, 2003).

**James IV** (1473–1513) *King of Scotland (1488–1513)*
The son of James III, he succeeded to the throne when his father was killed at the battle of Sauchieburn (1488) fighting against a rebellion of nobles. In 1503 he married Margaret, daughter of Henry VII of England. An energetic and popular ruler, he promoted efficient administration, improved the working of the judicial system, and attempted to assert royal authority in the Highlands and Western Isles. He encouraged learning, supporting the foundation of King's College, Aberdeen (1495), which became a center of humanist scholarship, patronizing the poet William Dunbar, and granting a patent to the first Scottish printers

(1507). In general he avoided war, but in 1513 treaty obligations with France compelled him to invade England. He was defeated and killed at the battle of Flodden.

**Jamnitzer family** The leading family of German goldsmiths and silversmiths in the 16th and 17th centuries, working in Nuremberg. Wenzel Jamnitzer (1508–85), the greatest of the family, moved with his father Hans (died c. 1549) and brother Albrecht (died 1555), both goldsmiths, to Nuremberg from Vienna sometime before 1534. His preeminence as a craftsman and contribution to the city's prosperity were recognized in his appointment as master of the city mint (1552) and in further civic positions. He was court goldsmith to four Hapsburg emperors. His work, which was extremely ornate, includes elaborate table centers, goblets, and a richly ornamented jewel casket. A design also exists for a magnificent bearing sword for Charles V. Particularly famous is the huge table fountain made for Emperor RUDOLF II, an allegory both of Hapsburg rule and of the various types of knowledge (1578). Jamnitzer worked in the mannerist style, and is known particularly for using naturalistic casts of insects, lizards, grasses, and shells as decoration, setting the fashion for this in Germany (it was already established in Italy). An example is his mother-of-pearl and silver-gilt ewer in the shape of a snail (c. 1570). His figures, such as the caryatids for Rudolf's table fountain, show him to have been a gifted sculptor. He also made mathematical and astronomical instruments, and published a book on mathematics, mechanics, and architecture, *Perspectiva corporum regularium* (1568).

Wenzel's son Hans (c. 1538–1603) and Albrecht's son Bartel (c. 1548–c. 1596) carried on the workshop and produced several fine pieces. Christoph (1563–1618), the son of Hans the Younger, was again a highly talented craftsman, approaching his grandfather's brilliance. His more complex work, in a mannerist style verging on the Baroque, includes a goblet in the form of an angel and a table fountain in the form of an elephant. He probably visited Italy, and he too produced work for Emperor Rudolf II. In 1610 he published his *Neuw Groteszken Buch*, a collection of decorative designs which included grotesque fantasies.

**Janequin, Clément** (c. 1485–1558) *French composer*
He may have been educated in his native Châtellerault. In 1505 he was a "clerc" in Bordeaux, and in 1523 he entered the service of the bishop there. He collected various ecclesiastical appointments, and in the 1530s was *maître de chapelle* in the cathedrals of Auch and Angers. He probably moved to Paris in the 1540s, but was certainly there from 1549, and he spent the rest of his life there. In 1530 he wrote a chanson to celebrate the entry of Francis I into Bordeaux, but it was not until the 1550s that he joined the court as a singer and then *compositeur ordinaire*. He is best remembered for his chansons, ranking with Claudin de SERMISY as the foremost exponent of the genre. His lengthy programmatic chansons such as *Le chant des oiseaux* and *La bataille* are well known, but the bulk of his output comprises short, pithy works with a good deal of imitation and clearly defined rhythmic patterns. There is often a popular or rustic aspect to these works. Janequin also set metrical versions of psalm texts and a small number of motets and two Masses. The Masses are both closely based on two of his own chansons.

**Jeanne d'Albret** (1528–1572) *Queen of Navarre (1555–72)*
She was the daughter of Henry II d'Albret, King of Navarre, and in 1548 she married Antoine de Bourbon, who succeeded to the throne of Navarre on her father's death. Like her mother MARGUERITE DE NAVARRE, she was assertively Protestant, and when Antoine died of wounds sustained in the opening hostilities of the French Wars of RELIGION (1562), Jeanne became regent for her young son Henry III of Navarre (later HENRY IV of France), bringing him up in her own faith. Shortly before her death she arranged his marriage to Margaret of Valois, sister of Charles IX of France.

**Jeanne Françoise de Chantal, St. (Jane Frances of Chantal)** (1572–1641) *French religious*
The daughter of a wealthy lawyer, she married Christophe de Rabutin, Baron de Chantal, in 1592 and bore him four children before his death (1601) in a riding accident. In 1604 she heard FRANCIS DE SALES preach in Dijon and placed herself under his spiritual direction. In 1610 she and Francis traveled to Annecy, where they formed the Congregation of the Visitandines, an association of women dedicated to contemplation and charitable works. Although this was founded especially for women who did not feel suited to an enclosed life, the Church authorities demanded that its members adopt such a rule in 1615. It became a full monastic order (the Visitation Order) in 1618 and grew rapidly under Jeanne's leadership, having 86 houses at the time of her death. It also established some of France's first schools for girls and played a pioneering role in women's education during the 17th and 18th centuries.

**Jena** A city in south central Germany on the River Saale. Probably of ninth-century origins, the city was chartered in 1230 and ruled by the Margraves of Meissen from the mid-13th century until it passed to the elector of Saxony (1423). The university, founded in 1548 and granted university status in 1577, was a stronghold of Lutheran scholarship. Notable buildings which have survived from the Renaissance period include the Black Bear inn (where LUTHER sheltered after his flight from Wartburg), the 14th-century town hall, and St. Michael's church (1438–1528).

**Jenkinson, Anthony** (died 1611) *English traveler and merchant*

After some years in the Middle East as a merchant (1546–53), Jenkinson went to Russia as an agent of the MUSCOVY COMPANY (1557–60); in 1558, searching for a possible land route to China, he became the first Englishman to visit Kazan and the northern Caspian Sea. On later visits to Russia (1566–68, 1571–72) he conducted valuable trade negotiations, despite the tsar's hostility. After a final mission to Embden to negotiate with the Danes (1577), he lived in London and Northamptonshire. His lively reports on his Russian and Persian journeys were published by HAKLUYT.

**Jenson, Nicolas** (1420–1480) *French type designer and printer*

Jenson was born at Sommevoie, near Troyes, and after learning to print in Germany, perhaps at Mainz, he settled in Venice about 1470. There he perfected the roman typeface first used in Strasbourg and Rome by 1467, following a roman manuscript hand. In the following decade he issued about 70 books, mostly Latin or Greek classics; of these Pliny's *Historia naturalis* (1472) is one of his finest productions. Many of his books were illuminated and decorated by hand, as though they were MANUSCRIPTS, and special copies of some were printed on vellum.

**Jessenius, Johannes** (Jan Jesenský) (1566–1621) *Slovak physician and polymath*

Born in Breslau, Jessenius studied medicine at Padua (1588–91). There he wrote *De divina humanaque philosophia* (1591), dedicated to Emperor Rudolf II, who rewarded him with a degree on his first visit to Prague shortly afterward. He lived in Wittenberg for some years, where he wrote a quasi hermetic treatise, *Zoroaster* (1593), published a compendium on the unity of knowledge, *Universae philosophiae epitome* (1596), and also made the acquaintance of Tycho Brahe. Jessenius moved to Prague in 1600 where he became an influential teacher at the university.

**Jesuits** A Roman Catholic religious order established to strengthen the papacy and the Catholic Church against Protestantism. The Jesuits came into being when IGNATIUS LOYOLA and ten followers, all committed to missionary work, met in Venice in 1537 to form the Society of Jesus. This put into effect plans made in Paris three years earlier, when Loyola and six companions dedicated themselves to a life of service to God. Their order was recognized by Pope Paul III in 1540.

Representing a new religious technique rather than new doctrine, the Jesuits' spiritual discipline is contained in the *Spiritual Exercises*, first composed by Loyola in 1522 but continually revised until the appearance of a printed version in 1548. The *Exercises*, reinforced by Loyola's *Constitutions* (first drafted 1547–50), are fundamental to the self-discipline and organization that are the hallmark of the society. Divided into four parts, each part to be studied for a week, the *Exercises* provide a meditative experience based upon the themes of sin, Christ's life, the Passion, and the Resurrection. The overall effect of the program was the fostering of a greater awareness of sin and salvation, continually refreshed through study and confession. United in a devotion to the pope and organized into congregations superintended by a general, the society proved to be a highly effective mission. By the time of Loyola's death (1556) it had over 1000 members and was set to become a major force in the COUNTER-REFORMATION.

Dedicated to personal humility and reliant on alms, the Jesuits soon became renowned for their courage, tenacity, and zeal, as demonstrated in the heroic exploits of one of the original companions of Loyola in Paris, FRANCIS XAVIER, whose mission lay in the Indies and Far East. The Jesuit practice by which individual priests regularly reported on their travels to their superiors is the source of much fascinating historical, geographical and ethnographic material during the 16th and 17th centuries. Reports from the Orient include accounts of some astonishing journeys: of Fathers António de Almeida and Michele Ruggieri into the interior of China (1585); of Father Nicolau Pimenta around India (1597–1600); of Brother Bento de Góis traversing Central Asia (1603–05).

The Portuguese Manuel da Nóbrega, the first Jesuit to visit the New World (1548), was instrumental in founding Salvador in Bahia, Brazil's first capital. Later Portuguese New World missions covered the Spanish colonies of New Spain (present-day Mexico and southern North America from Florida to California) and Central and South America. Jesuit activity in New Spain from 1570 to 1605 is chronicled in the eight-volume *Monumenta Mexicana* (1956–59); few of these documents have been translated. French Jesuits toiled in New France (Canada), along the eastern seaboard, in the Great Lakes area, and Louisiana. All these missions were covered by the reports, written in Latin, French, or Italian, known collectively as *Relations*, and published in English as a 73-volume set entitled *The Jesuit Relations and Allied Documents* (1896–1901).

The Jesuit mission to reconvert England, undertaken in 1578, also produced many acts of bravery and several martyrs, prominent among them Edmund CAMPION. The Jesuits were opposed by the Jansenists and other movements within the Catholic Church and were persecuted in several European countries during the late 17th and 18th centuries, but their suppression was incomplete. The society once again flourishes and plays a leading part in modern Roman Catholicism, particularly in its educational aspects (*see also* GREGORIANA).

**Further reading:** James Brodrick, *The Origin of the Jesuits* (London: Longmans, Green, 1940; new ed.

Wheathampstead, U.K.: Anthony Clarke, 1986); ~*The Progress of the Jesuits 1556–79* (London: Longmans, Green, 1946); Joseph A. Gagliano and Charles E. Ronan (eds), *Jesuit Encounters in the New World: Jesuit Chroniclers, Geographers, Educators and Missionaries in the Americas, 1549–1767* (Rome: Institutum Historicum, 1997); Jean Lacouture, *Jesuits: A Multibiography*, transl. Jeremy Leggatt (Cambridge, Mass.: Counterpoint, 1997); Edward Maclagan, *The Jesuits and the Great Mogul* (London: Burns Oates, 1932; new ed. New York: Octagon, 1972); John W. O'Malley *et al* (eds), *The Jesuits: Cultures, Sciences, and the Arts 1540–1773* (Toronto, Canada: University of Toronto Press, 2000).

**Jeux Floraux, les** See ACADEMIES

**Jewel, John** (1522–1571) *English bishop and theologian*
Jewel was born in Berrynarbor, Devonshire, and educated at Oxford, where he was influenced by the reformer PETER MARTYR Vermigli. In the reign of the Catholic Mary I he fled to Frankfurt (1555) and later traveled to Zürich, Strasbourg, and Padua. After the accession of Elizabeth I he returned to England and was a Protestant disputant at the Westminster Conference of 1559. Jewel was appointed bishop of Salisbury (1560) and in 1562 he published his famous *Apologia pro ecclesia Anglicana* (Apology for the Anglican Church), a statement defending the Church of England against the Church of Rome. His view that it should be protected by the Crown but retain spiritual autonomy was highly influential, and his protégé Richard HOOKER adopted a similar position in *Lawes of Ecclesiasticall Politie* (1594–97). In 1571 Jewel was appointed to supervise the revision of the THIRTY-NINE ARTICLES but he died before work commenced.

**jewelry** The jeweler's art flourished in the Renaissance, fueled by the rivalry between courts and noble families that expressed itself in ostentatious display. Many outstanding artists designed jewelry, among them BOTTICELLI, GIULIO ROMANO, and HOLBEIN THE YOUNGER; some even initially trained as goldsmiths. Because Renaissance jewelry was so elaborate, the value of the workmanship usually exceeded the intrinsic value of the material, and much therefore survives. Contemporary portraits offer excellent evidence of the opulence and variety of Renaissance jewelry. Women's hair ornaments emphasized the movement of loose hair and braids. Necklaces were particularly popular, either in the form of a heavy gold chain with a central pendant or multiple ropes of pearls; those of extreme length were worn looped up to the bodice. Numerous brooches and rings were worn together, pearls dangled from the points of lace ruffs and stiff caps, and frequently the whole female dress would be jewel encrusted. Men wore hat or cap badges and displayed on their chests wide jeweled and enameled collars or gold chains, often with pendants on them.

Pendants were an important form as a frame for a cameo or portrait miniature. Antique gemstones or cameos could be reused in new setting: Rudolf II had a pendant with a cameo of a Roman emperor on the obverse and an enameled reverse symbolizing his own role as a Christian emperor. Many were polychromatic with inset gemstones and enameling. Jeweled or enameled cases for miniatures and watches were also popular. Other pendants developed into complicated openwork creations in which the bizarre shape of a baroque pearl suggested to the artificer the body of a sea monster or centaur. Rings were often made in architectural high relief and some had concealed compartments for poisons or love charms; Elizabeth I had a ring with a hinged bezel that opened to reveal miniature portraits of herself and her mother Anne Boleyn, while a seal ring with the coat of arms of the Holy Roman emperor, made for Rudolf II or one of his immediate successors, opens to reveal a tiny watch by Johann Buz of Augsburg. Pendant crosses became highly decorative, their original religious significance submerged in their ornamental function.

Jewelry often shared with medals an emblematic or symbolic role. Some surviving pieces, such as the heart-shaped Darnley (or Lennox) Jewel, probably made in the 1570s for the wife of the late regent of Scotland, has a whole personal and political program concealed within its elaborate decoration. Elizabeth I in a portrait (c. 1575) by Nicholas HILLIARD wears at her breast a pendant of a phoenix rising from the flames as a symbol of her uniqueness and her chastity. Portraits of James I show him wearing in his hat a jewel called the Mirror of Great Britain, made for him in 1604 to symbolize the union of the kingdoms and comprising four main stones—three diamonds and a ruby.

**Further reading:** Yvonne Hackenbroch, *Renaissance Jewellery* (London and Totowa, N.J.: Sotheby Parke Bernet, 1980); Anna Somers Cocks, *Princely Magnificence: Court Jewels of the Renaissance, 1550–1630* (London: Debrett's Peerage and Victoria and Albert Museum, 1980).

**Jews** Followers of the Judean faith. Ever since the Romans destroyed the Jerusalem Temple (70 CE), Jewish believers have spread out from the Middle East, building synagogues and establishing a hugely diverse and influential diaspora. Jewry in postmedieval Europe was dominated by orthodox, Rabbinic Judaism. Jewish communities revered the teachings of the Hebrew Scriptures (the Old Testament of Christians), the Talmud (a compilation of oral teachings from the first millennium CE), biblical commentaries, and the tradition of the Halachah (direct practical teaching).

Like Christians, Rabbinic Jews believed in a unique, incorporeal God, a deity who created the world, engages with it, and who will ultimately redeem its flawed people. God's will, as expressed in the Scriptures and through priestly instructions (the code of the "Torah," or "Law") will eventually triumph. Worship consisted mainly of instruction on how to live according to the Torah, together with readings from the prophets, psalms, hymn-singing, and certain prayer recitations. Although sharing some tenets, Rabbinic Jews differed from Christians in a number of obvious ways: they sought to obey ancient Jewish laws; all males had to be circumcised; and they rejected the Christian belief that Jesus Christ was the expected messiah and the savior of mankind.

The demonization of Jews, which has its roots in the New Testament but dates essentially from the Roman Empire's adoption of Christianity, was particularly motivated by the Jewish rejection of Christ. For Christians (Catholic and Protestant) this was evidence enough of hellish depravity and was used to justify ferocious suppression of Jews throughout medieval and Renaissance Europe. ANTI-SEMITISM thrived. It is true that the history of Jews in the period is hugely varied, and that local factors always influenced the brutality or tolerance that was shown to this minority sect. But a general observation can be made: by 1500, the great nations of Europe were largely free of Jewish communities.

Jews had been expelled from England (1290), France (1394), Spain (1492), and Portugal (1497). Largely owing to these expulsions and related pogroms, Renaissance Jews were by necessity peripatetic. Take, for instance, the fate of the Shephardi—Portuguese or Spanish Jews. These communities had been removed from the Iberian peninsula during the 1490s, together with communities from the Spanish-held islands of Sardinia and Sicily. They moved eastwards, traveling to Ottoman Turkey, Constantinople, and Salonika (Thessaloniki in modern Greece). Western Europe's cultural loss was Eurasia's gain.

In the early 16th century Italian states generally accepted the presence of Jews, but in 1542 they were removed from Naples (which was still ruled by Spain) and were later ghettoized (by papal decree) in Mantua, Rome, and Venice. These antisemitic acts are notorious, whereas the fate of Judean communities in early 17th-century Eastern Europe is less well known. The Catholic state of Poland held controversial hegemony over Greek Catholic communities in the Ukraine. The latter rose against the Poles in 1648/9 and Jews, the common enemy, got caught in the middle. Both sides brutally massacred Jews, provoking great numbers to move west to eastern German states. At around the same time, Jewish settlements were established in Amsterdam and Hamburg. Jews would gradually be integrated into European economic affairs, in the way that they had, to some extent, been integrated (mainly as moneylenders) in the pre-expulsion Middle Ages.

It should also be recognized that Jews had a limited presence in states from which they were officially barred. In England, for instance, no Jews were officially resident between 1290 and 1656. But it is now believed that as many as 150 Jews flourished in Elizabeth I's London. Some of these Jews (marranos), who practiced their faith privately, contributed substantially to the court, the economy, and the arts. Jewish historiographers have long recognized the vitality of these communities; now, finally, non-Jewish cultural historians acknowledge the rich legacy that "illegal" Jews made to Renaissance England and to other early modern states.

See also: HEBREW STUDIES

Further reading: Jonathan I. Israel, *European Jewry in the Age of Mercantilism, 1550–1750* (Oxford, U.K.: Clarendon Press, 1985); Brian Pullan, *The Jews of Europe and the Inquisition of Venice, 1550–1670* (Oxford, U.K.: Blackwell, 1983); Cecil Roth, *The Jews in the Renaissance* (New York: Harper & Row, 1965); W. D. Rubenstein, *A History of the Jews in the English-Speaking World: Great Britain* (Basingstoke, U.K.: Macmillan and New York: St. Martin's Press, 1996); Moses A. Shulvas, *The Jews in the World of the Renaissance*, transl. Elvin I Kose (Leyden, Netherlands: Brill and Spertus College of Judaica Press, 1973).

**Jiménes de Cisneros, Cardinal Francisco** See XIMÉNES DE CISNEROS, CARDINAL FRANCISCO

**Jodelle, Étienne** (1532–1573) *French dramatist and poet* A member of the PLÉIADE, Jodelle applied the principles of the group to dramatic composition and succeeded in producing the first modern French tragedy and comedy, utterly different in every way from the morality and mystery plays then occupying the French stage. He is chiefly remembered for the tragedy *Cléopâtre captive* (acted before the court in 1552), which excited great interest in humanist circles for its careful construction, elegiac atmosphere, long declamatory speeches, and characters in the grand style. Together with *Didon* (c. 1560) and his comedy *Eugène* (1552), this play broke new ground and prepared the way for the great neoclassical dramatists Racine and Corneille. Despite these successes, Jodelle died in Paris in extreme poverty.

**Johannes de Muris** See MURIS, JOHANNES DE

**John I** (1357–1433) *King of Portugal (1385–1433), founder of the Avis dynasty* The illegitimate half-brother of Ferdinand I (king 1367–83), John of Avis took the crown after a short interregnum. He decisively defeated a much larger Castilian invasion force at Aljubarrota in 1385, assuming undisputed control of Portugal and assuring its independence from Spain for the following two centuries. The great Dominican monastery of Batalha (Battle), north of Lisbon, was founded in 1388 to commemorate this victory. John and his wife, Philippa of Lancaster (1360–1415), granddaughter of King Edward III of England, are both buried there.

## John Fisher, St. (1469–1535) *Roman Catholic martyr, churchman, and scholar*

As chancellor of Cambridge university (from 1504) Fisher encouraged Hebrew studies and brought his friend ERASMUS to England to teach. He was also bishop of Rochester from 1504 until 1534. A strong opponent of the new Protestant doctrines, Fisher led the defense of traditional Catholic teaching in England. He enraged HENRY VIII by denouncing the king's attempts to end his marriage to Catherine of Aragon and by refusing to accept Henry as supreme head of the Church of England. Shortly before Fisher's trial and execution for treason on Tower Hill the pope made him a cardinal. He was canonized in 1935.

**Further reading:** Cecilia A. Hatt (ed.), *English Works of John Fisher, Bishop of Rochester: Sermons and Other Writings 1520 to 1535* (Oxford, U.K.: Oxford University Press, 2003).

## John of Austria, Don (1545–1578) *Spanish prince*

He was born at Regensburg, the illegitimate son of Emperor CHARLES V and a local magnate's daughter, and brought up in Spain in ignorance of his parentage. Recognized in Charles's will, John was received into the royal family (1559) with the title Don Juan de Austria. His military ambitions soon manifested themselves in fighting Algerian corsairs (1568), crushing a revolt of *moriscos* in Granada (1569–70), and commanding the Christian fleet at LEPANTO (1571). PHILIP II, alarmed at his half-brother's schemes, refused to back his projects, including his short-lived capture of Tunis (1573), but instead appointed him governor-general of the now openly defiant Netherlands (1576). Having reluctantly complied with the terms of the Pacification of GHENT in 1577, Don John repudiated the agreement when he realized how strong Prince WILLIAM (I) THE SILENT had become. Reinforced by troops under Alessandro FARNESE, Don John defeated the rebels at Gemblours (1578) but was unable to follow up the success and died of fever the same autumn.

## John of the Cross, St. (Juan de Yepes) (1542–1591) *Spanish Carmelite reformer and mystic*

He was born the youngest son of a Toledan silk weaver at Fontiveros and after studying with the Jesuits in Salamanca he went to university there. He abandoned the idea of following his father's trade and joined the Carmelites in 1563 and was ordained in 1567. He soon met TERESA OF ÁVILA and promoted her cause of reforming the Carmelite order (*see* CARMELITES, REFORM OF THE). In 1568 Antonio de Heredia, José de Cristo, and he founded the male Discalced Carmelites. In 1572 Teresa of Ávila summoned John of the Cross (as he now termed himself) to Ávila to serve as the spiritual adviser to her reformed Convent of the Incarnation.

Because of a conflict with a Carmelite superior who disapproved of John's and Teresa's reformist activities, John was imprisoned for a short while in Toledo. During this period his spiritual experiences intensified and he wrote the mystical poems *The Dark Night of the Soul* and *The Spiritual Canticle*. In 1578 he escaped from prison and resumed his former activities. Finally in 1579 the Discalced Carmelites became a recognized order, one of the several new orders of the Counter-Reformation. Between then and his death John founded several new houses for the order. In 1591 his enemies managed to have him relieved of all his offices and even attempted to expel him from the order. Seriously ill, he nevertheless went to Ubeda where he received scant welcome. There he died. He was canonized in 1726 and was named Doctor of the Church in 1926.

**Further reading:** Gerald Brenan, *St. John of the Cross: His Life and Poetry* (Cambridge, U.K.: Cambridge University Press, 1973); Wilfrid McGreal, *John of the Cross* (Liguori, Mo.: Liguori Press, 1997).

## Jonas, Justus (Jodocus Koch) (1493–1555) *German Lutheran jurist and theologian*

Jonas was born at Nordhausen and proved to be an able scholar whose precocious talents attracted the notice of ERASMUS. He became professor of law at Erfurt in 1518, and in 1521 professor of theology at Wittenberg. A firm friend and admirer of LUTHER, Jonas took a prominent part in the Protestant cause. He attended both the Colloquy of MARBURG (1529) and the Diet of AUGSBURG (1530), and translated a number of Luther's Latin works into German, along with the *Loci communes* of Philipp MELANCHTHON. In 1541 Jonas left Wittenberg to take up a post in Halle, where as superintendent of the area's churches he supervised the organization of the local reform. Forced to leave Halle by the Schmalkaldic war (*see* SCHMALKALDIC LEAGUE) he eventually settled in Eisleben, where he remained until his death.

## Jones, Inigo (1573–1652) *English architect and stage designer*

The son of a London clockmaker, Jones probably trained as a painter, although little is known of his early life. He became acquainted with the ideals of the Italian Renaissance during visits to Italy (1598–1603, 1613), where he studied both classical architecture and the theories of Andrea PALLADIO. After a short period at the Danish court of Christian IV, Jones was brought to the court of James I, where he executed costume and set designs for numerous masques and plays, notably those by Ben JONSON. After being consulted on the building of Hatfield House and the New Exchange for Merchants (now destroyed), he was ap-

# Plate I

**Andrea del Sarto** *The Last Supper*

Less dramatic than Leonardo's version, this fresco in the refectory of the Vallombrosan abbey of San Salvi, just outside Florence, is nonetheless notable for its highly individualized portraits and rich coloring (c. 1527; San Salvi).
©Photo SCALA, Florence—courtesy of the Ministero Beni e Att. Culturali, 1997

**Plate II**

**Giovanni Bellini** *Sacred Allegory*

The subject is possibly taken from a medieval French allegory, *Le Pèlerinage de l'âme* (The pilgrimage of the soul) (c. 1500; Uffizi, Florence).
©Photo SCALA, Florence—courtesy of the Ministero Beni e Att. Culturali, 1990

# Plate III

**Botticelli** *The Birth of Venus*

Classical literary and graphic sources, well known to the contemporary Neoplatonists of Florence, inspired the iconography of Botticelli's vision of the new-born goddess of love wafted over the sea in her scallop shell by zephyrs. The personification of spring stands ready to cast a flowery cloak about her (c. 1485; Uffizi, Florence).

©*Photo SCALA, Florence—courtesy of the Ministero Beni e Att. Culturali, 1991*

# Plate IV

**Domenico da Cortona** (architect)  Château de Chambord
This French château built in the period 1519–47 on the River Cosson, east of Blois, has a fairyland roofscape that hides over 360 chimneys among its turrets, gables, and pinnacles.
*©Photo Graham Speake*

**Giambologna**
The colossal statue of the Apennines, symbol of untamed natural forces, gazes at its own reflection in a pool at the Villa Demidoff at Pratolino, on the outskirts of Florence (c. 1580).
*©Photo SCALA, Florence, 1990*

# Plate V

**Jan van Eyck**  *The Arnolfini Wedding*
The making of the marriage vow between Giovanni Arnolfini, a rich merchant, and Giovanna
Cenami; every detail in the scene is painted with meticulous accuracy (c. 1434; National Gallery,
London).
*©National Gallery, London*

# Plate VI

**Hugo van der Goes** The Portinari Altarpiece (central panel of a triptych) Originally set up in the church of Sant' Egidio in the hospital of Sta. Maria Nuova, this work was the first sizable example of Netherlandish art to be seen in Florence (c. 1475–77; Uffizi, Florence).
©Photo SCALA, Florence—courtesy of the Ministero Beni e Att. Culturali, 1990

**El Greco** Christ Driving the Traders from the Temple El Greco painted this subject several times, perhaps because it suggested the purging of the Church during the Counter-Reformation (c. 1600; National Gallery, London).
©National Gallery, London

# Plate VII

**El Greco** *The Dream of Philip II* (also called *The Adoration of the Name of Jesus*)
Somberly clad, Philip II of Spain kneels in the foreground, his back to a devouring hell-mouth, while men on earth and the heavenly host unite in worship of the holy monogram IHS (*I*esus *H*ominum *S*alvator—Jesus, Savior of Men) (c. 1580; Escorial, Madrid).
©*Photo SCALA, Florence, 1990*

# Plate VIII

**Leonardo da Vinci** *The Annunciation*
The angel Gabriel announcing the conception of Jesus to the Virgin Mary; an early work by Leonardo, painted while he was still apprenticed to Andrea del Verrocchio (c. 1474; Uffizi, Florence).
*The Bridgeman Art Library*

**Paolo Uccello** *St. George and the Dragon*
This fantasy, one of the first Italian paintings on canvas, enabled the artist to demonstrate his skill in depicting animals in movement (c. 1455; National Gallery, London).
*The Bridgeman Art Library*

**Plate IX**

**Michelangelo** *Ignudo*
Twenty of these naked youths adorn the vault of the Sistine Chapel in the Vatican, interspersing the religious and symbolic scheme with figures that extol human grace, beauty, and delight (1508–12; Sistine Chapel, Vatican).
©*Photo SCALA, Florence, 1990*

# Plate X

**Leonardo da Vinci** *Mona Lisa* (also called *La Gioconda*)
The sitter was the wife of a Florentine official, Francesco del Giocondo. The apparent simplicity of this famous portrait has led generations of commentators to puzzle over the sitter's enigmatic smile (1503–06; Louvre, Paris).
*The Bridgeman Art Library*

# Plate XI

**Il Parmigianino** *Madonna and Child with St. Zacharius*
Painted for Bonifacio Gozzadini of Bologna, where Parmigianino had sought refuge after the Sack of Rome, this treatment of the Madonna and Child theme is laden with foreboding, from the visionary head of St. Zacharius in the foreground to the brooding sky above. The Christ Child seems to shrink from the embrace of the infant St. John the Baptist, while behind them St. Mary Magdalene holds up her jar of ointment, emblem of Christ's Passion and death (1527–31; Uffizi, Florence).

**Plate XII**

**Bernado il Pinturicchio** Aenea Silvio Piccolomini crowned poet laureate by Emperor Frederick III
The third in a series of ten scenes from the life of Pope Pius II (1502–07; Piccolomini Library, Siena
cathedral).
©Photo SCALA, Florence—Photo Opera Metropolitana Siena, 1990

# Plate XIII

**Raphael** *The School of Athens*

Painted on the wall facing the same artist's *Disputà*, the *School of Athens* represents the noblest expression of human intellect, which the Renaissance believed to have been embodied in the philosophers of ancient Greece. Plato and Aristotle pass through the center of a vaulted portico (clearly based on the Roman Baths of Caracalla); Plato points heavenward, indicating the metaphysical nature of his speculations, while Aristotle gestures toward the physical world before him. Around them are their followers or representatives of other philosophical schools; several of these are portraits of Raphael's contemporaries and in the exteme right-hand corner Raphael has included himself and Sodoma (1509–11; Stanza della Segnatura, Vatican).

*©Photo SCALA, Florence, 1990*

## Plate XIV

**Sebastiano del Piombo** *Pope Clement VII*
Within the limits of a conventional pose for papal portraits, Sebastiano has created a powerful and subtle impression. At about the time the picture was painted Clement abandoned his former ally, Charles V, in favor of an alliance with France, a decision that led to the Sack of Rome by imperial troops the following year. Something of these political maneuvres is suggested in the sitter's half-averted head and watchful gaze (1526; Capodimonte, Naples).
©Photo SCALA, Florence—courtesy of the Mistero Beni e Att. Culturali, 1990

# Plate XV

**Luca Signorelli** *The Fall of the Damned*

Signorelli's *Last Judgment* frescoes, of which this is a part, acknowledge a debt to Dante as well as to classical and medieval Christian iconography (1495–1503; Capella della Madonna di San Brizio, Duomo, Orvieto).

©Photo SCALA, Florence, 1990

## Plate XVI

**Tapestry** *The Battle of Pavia* (detail)
These Flemish tapestries, woven to the designs of Bernard van Orley, commemorate the victory of the imperial forces over Francis I of France in 1525. It was this battle that finally established the supremacy of firearms over the cavalry lance and pike (Capodimonte, Naples).
©*Photo SCALA, Florence—courtesy of the Ministero Beni e Att. Culturali, 1990*

pointed surveyor of works to James I in 1615 and he subsequently held the same office under Charles I.

Jones's earliest surviving structure is the Queen's House at Greenwich, London (1616–35), which was built in the style of an Italian villa and was the first strictly classical English building. His greatest work, however, was the building of the Banqueting Hall in Whitehall (1619–22), which owed much to the ideas of Palladio, and subsequent designs for the rebuilding of the whole of Whitehall Palace. The only other surviving royal building by Jones is the Queen's chapel at St. James's Palace (1623–27), the first English church in the classical style. Jones also designed London's first piazza (at Covent Garden in 1630), including the Palladian church of St. Paul, and several country houses, and directed the restoration of St. Paul's Cathedral (1632–42); this last work was unfortunately lost in the Great Fire of London (1666). Jones's career ended with the civil war in the 1640s, but his influence upon later English architects was profound.

**Further reading:** Michael Leapman, *Inigo: The Troubled Life of Inigo Jones, Architect of the English Renaissance* (London: Hodder Headline, 2003); John Peacock, *The Stage Designs of Inigo Jones: The European Context* (Cambridge, U.K.: Cambridge University Press, 1995); Roy Strong, *Britannia Triumphans: Inigo Jones, Rubens and Whitehall Palace* (London: Thames & Hudson, 1980); John Summerson, *Inigo Jones* (Harmondsworth, U.K.: Penguin, 1966; rev. ed. New Haven, Conn. and London: Yale University Press, 2000).

**Jonghelinck, Jakob** (1530–1606) *Netherlands medallist and sculptor*
After studying in Milan with Leone LEONI, Jonghelinck, who was born in Antwerp, returned to the Netherlands in 1555. Between 1558 and 1566 he executed the tomb of Duke Charles the Bold of Burgundy, who had died nearly a century earlier, for the church of Our Lady in Bruges. As this tomb was situated beside the late 15th-century tomb of Charles's daughter, Mary of Burgundy, Jonghelinck imitated the style of the earlier artist, an example of antiquarianism rare in 16th-century art, which customarily eschewed the Gothic past in favor of neoclassicism. Although Jonghelinck's life-size bronze of the infamous duke of ALBA in the Antwerp citadel was destroyed during the revolt of 1577, its appearance is reflected in a bust of the same sitter now in New York. Jonghelinck's bronzes are technically very accomplished and his portraits have considerable characterization.

**Jonson, Ben(jamin)** (1572–1637) *English dramatist, poet, and critic*
Jonson received a classical education under William CAMDEN at Westminster School in his native London, but then followed his stepfather's trade of bricklaying. In the 1590s he fought in Flanders and later became an actor. His first

great success as a dramatist was *Every Man in his Humour* (1598), the forerunner of "the comedy of humors" at which he excelled, but the same year he was imprisoned for killing a fellow-actor and barely escaped hanging. He converted to Catholicism in gaol and remained a Roman Catholic for 12 years. In 1605 he was again in trouble, along with George CHAPMAN and John Marston, for anti-Scots satire in *Eastward Ho!* He nonetheless became a favorite producer of entertainments and masques for James I's court, usually in collaboration with Inigo JONES (*see* MASQUE). In 1616 the king awarded him a pension.

Johnson's great comedies—*Volpone* (1606), *Epicoene* (1609), *The Alchemist* (1610), and *Bartholomew Fair* (1614)—are outstanding for their energy and comic invention. His tragedies—*Sejanus* (1603) and *Catiline* (1611)—were less popular, but are models of classical construction and contain some fine blank verse. In 1612–13 he accompanied Raleigh's turbulent son, young Walter, as his tutor on a tour of Continental Europe. After publishing his collected *Works* (1616) Jonson abandoned the stage for a decade, but his reputation as a man of letters continued to grow. He was a great mentor to younger writers ("the tribe of Ben"), 33 of whom contributed elegies to the commemorative volume *Jonsonus Virbius* (1638) after his death. Among the troubles of his later years were a fire that destroyed his library and unpublished manuscripts (1623), the failure of several plays, a paralytic stroke (1628), financial distress, and a feud with Inigo Jones, whom he satirized in *The Tale of a Tub* (1634).

Jonson's chief work in prose was *Timber, or Discoveries made upon Men and Matter* (1640), but his recorded conversations with William Drummond of Hawthornden, whom he met in Scotland in 1618, give the most vivid impression of his ideas on poetry and people. His poetry includes some magnificent lyrics for his masques, such as "Queen and huntress, chaste and fair" from *Cynthia's Revels* (1600), and the famous epitaph on the child actor Salathiel Pavy (published in *Epigrams*, 1616).

**Further reading:** Anthony W. Johnson, *Ben Jonson: Poetry and Architecture* (Oxford, U.K.: Clarendon Press, 1994); David Riggs, *Ben Jonson: A Life* (Cambridge, Mass.: Harvard University Press, 1989); Charles J. Summers and Ted-Larry Pebworth, *Ben Jonson Revised* (New York: Twayne, 2000).

**Josquin Des Prés** See DES PRÉS, JOSQUIN

**Joubert, Laurent** (1529–1582) *French physician*
Born in the Dauphiné, Joubert studied at Montpellier, becoming chancellor of the faculty of medicine there. Appointments as Catherine de' Medici's personal physician and then as one of the king's physicians followed. Joubert was a prolific author in both Latin and French. His first treatise, though not published until 1579, was the *Traité du Ris*; his most notorious the *Erreurs populaires* (1578),

dedicated to Princess Marguerite de France, which caused scandal by its frank discussion of gynecology and obstetrics in the vernacular. In line with the Renaissance trend toward the professionalization of medicine, *Erreurs populaires* is typical of Joubert's tracts in its agenda of enhancing the status of the physician against other medical practitioners, such as apothecaries and midwives.

**Journée des Barricades** (May 12, 1588) A Catholic revolt in Paris, which was one of the decisive events in the final stages of the French Wars of RELIGION. The Parisians, many of whom supported the Catholic League by which Duke Henry of Guise (*see* GUISE FAMILY) hoped to secure his succession to the throne, had grown increasingly anxious during the 1580s about the threat from Huguenot force and they were also weary of the vacillations of the ineffectual King HENRY III. They invited Duke Henry to come to their aid, which he did in defiance of the king's ban against his entering Paris, and the Parisians then erected barricades against their sovereign. The king fled to Chartres and, unable to recover his position, determined upon the assassination of Guise and his brother in December that year.

**Julius II** (1443–1513) *Pope (1503–13)*
Giuliano della Rovere came from an impoverished noble family (*see* DELLA ROVERE FAMILY) in Liguria. When his uncle became Pope SIXTUS IV (1471) he gained a cardinal's hat and many benefices. He served on papal missions and helped defend Rome against Naples, but had to leave Rome when his enemy Rodrigo Borgia became Pope ALEXANDER VI (1492). When Alexander VI died (1503) Cardinal della Rovere returned to Rome and was elected pope after Pius III's short reign. Once elected, Julius broke his promises to continue the war against the Turks, to call a general council within two years, and to consult the cardinals on all important matters.

Julius took some interest in Church reform; he issued a bull against simony and encouraged the reform of the Benedictines. He also summoned the fifth Lateran Council in 1511. Julius was primarily a military leader and statesman who did much to restore the papacy's temporal power. After defeating Cesare BORGIA in battle (1504) he commanded an expedition which forced Perugia and Bologna to submit to papal authority (1506). He joined the League of CAMBRAI against Venice (1509) and after Venice's defeat joined the anti-French HOLY LEAGUE (1511). With the support of Emperor MAXIMILIAN I he foiled LOUIS XII's attempts to depose him and isolated France. He occupied Modena (1510) and took Mirandola (1511).

Julius was a clever financial administrator, but is best remembered for his generosity to such great artists as RAPHAEL, MICHELANGELO, and BRAMANTE. He expanded the Vatican Library, collected ancient sculpture, and laid the cornerstone of ST. PETER's basilica, Rome.

**Further reading:** Christine Shaw, *Julius II: The Warrior Pope* (Oxford, U.K.: Blackwell, 1993).

**Juni, Juan de** (c. 1507–1577) *French-born sculptor*
Although probably a native of Burgundy, Juni became a part of the Spanish artistic tradition, arriving at León in 1533 and settling in Valladolid in 1540. His early works include portrait medallions (1536) for the facade of San Marcos, León, but he is best known for the polychromed wood group *The Entombment of Christ* (1539–44; Valladolid museum), which testifies to Juni's great technical skill and emotionalism. Other pieces include a large reredos (1545–61; Valladolid cathedral) for Sta. Maria la Antigua and other altarpieces. He also executed works in Salamanca and Zamora. His later pieces anticipated the BAROQUE in Spain.

**Junta press** See GIUNTI PRESS

*juros* (Spanish *juro*, "I swear") In Spain, bonds promising a fixed rate of interest. These bonds were issued by the Hapsburg monarchs of Spain and were sold to finance the European wars of CHARLES V and PHILIP II, but became a factor in the financial crisis afflicting Spain at the end of the 16th century.

**justification by faith** In Christian theology, the doctrine that a sinner becomes or is counted righteous before God through a personal faith in Jesus Christ as savior. The idea is first clearly stated by St. Paul (Romans 1–3), who insists that salvation cannot be earned by observation of the Jewish Law, but must be accepted as a free gift through faith in Christ. The doctrine was further elaborated by St. Augustine in his dispute with the Pelagians, who held that humans could attain justification through their own merits; however, it was not generally emphasized by medieval theologians, who tended to see membership of the Church, participation in the sacraments, and the performance of good works as the way to salvation. An insistence on justification by faith alone reemerged at the Reformation, when it became a fundamental principle of Protestant teaching and led to the rejection of many traditional doctrines and practices.

LUTHER's writings express a profound, almost existential, anguish about justification. For him, the Church's insistence on good works was fundamentally flawed because, however pious, no human could ever reach God's standards—accordingly, no believer could feel secure about his or her salvation. God, for Luther, offers divine grace whether or not one strives to deserve it. When a believer accepts Christ as his or her savior, God "imputes" righteousness to this person, even though he or she remains a sinner. Protestants, generally, adopted Luther's conclusions. Contrarily, the Catholic Council of TRENT (1545–63) maintained that faith needed to be augmented by religious observance and good works. Justification by faith alone thus came to define Protestant radicalism against Catholic traditionalism.

**See also:** INDULGENCES; PREDESTINATION

**Justus of Ghent (Joos van Wassenhove)** (active 1460–c. 1480) *Flemish painter*

Between 1473 and 1475 "Giusto da Guanto" is documented as the painter of the *Communion of the Apostles* altarpiece in Urbino. He is identical with Joos van Wassenhove, active at Antwerp in 1460 and recorded at Ghent in 1464–69. A document of 1475 states that he was an associate of Hugo van der GOES and that he had gone to Rome. A handful of early pictures have been attributed to Justus by comparison with his only documented work, the *Communion* altarpiece. The most important of these is the *Mount Calvary* triptych in St. Bavon, Ghent. Justus is usually identified with the anonymous painter of a group of pictures in a Netherlandish style executed for the Urbino court: these include 28 portraits of *Famous Men* and *Federico da Montefeltro and his son Guidobaldo* (c. 1473–76) for the ducal study in Urbino, and four fragments from a series of *The Seven Liberal Arts* and *Federico da Montefeltro Attending a Lecture* (c. 1476–80) for a similar study in Gubbio. The former group is divided between Paris and Urbino; the latter between London, Windsor, and (prior to destruction in 1945) Berlin.

Justus is the only 15th-century Flemish painter with surviving works known to have been produced in Italy. These reveal his increasing mastery in the handling of illusionistic perspective and the representation of Italianate subject matter. He is thus an important forerunner of the assimilation of Italian ideas by northern artists during the early 16th century.

**Justus of Ghent** A portrait of St. Thomas Aquinas (1225–74) from the *Famous Men* series painted for the Urbino court in 1473–76. These are usually attributed to Justus, possibly working with Pedro Berruguete. (Louvre, Paris).
*Photo AKG London/Erich Lessing*

# K

**Kempeneer, Pieter de** See CAMPANA, PEDRO DE

**Kepler, Johannes** (1571–1630) *German astronomer*
Born near Wittenberg, the son of a mercenary, Kepler was educated at Tübingen university where, as a student of Michael MAESTLIN, he was introduced to astronomy and became an early convert to the COPERNICAN SYSTEM. Here also he began to consider the problem of why there were only six planets (according to the contemporary count) and why they were sited in their particular orbits. In his *Mysterium cosmographicum* (1596) he proposed that God had modeled the universe on the pattern of the five regular solids of 4, 6, 8, 12, and 20 sides respectively. Before he could advance further, he realized, he would need fuller and more accurate data.

Access to such data came in 1599 when he was invited by Tycho BRAHE, the leading observer of his day, to join him at his Prague observatory. The death of Brahe soon afterwards (1601) left Kepler in charge of all his observations. With them Kepler was able to reshape astronomy. After several years' struggling to make sense of the orbit of Mars, Kepler finally saw in 1605 that planetary orbits were elliptical, not circular as had previously been thought. This result, since known as Kepler's first law, was revealed in his *Astronomia nova* (1609). The debt to Brahe was repaid after many years with the publication of his observations in 1627 as the *Tabulae Rudolphinae* (the Rudolfine Tables, so called after Brahe's and Kepler's patron Emperor RUDOLF II). Ever convinced, however, that the universe was built to some divine design, Kepler continued to search for the key to the cosmic mystery. His final thoughts on the matter were contained in his *Harmonices mundi* (1619), a work in which he also first formulated his third law. His *Epitome astronomiae Copernicanae* (1618–21), which was the first manual of astronomy to be based on the Copernican system incorporating Kepler's own laws of planetary motion, was placed on the INDEX LIBRORUM PROHIBITORUM in 1619, after the publication of the first three books.

Kepler's personal life was to prove less successful. Although he succeeded Brahe in 1601 as imperial mathematician to Rudolf II he found the duties irksome and often unpaid. In 1612 he moved to Linz as provincial mathematician. The outbreak of the Thirty Years' War in 1618, religious controversies, domestic troubles, and the need to defend his mother against a charge of witchcraft, together with a perennial shortage of funds, ill health, and intense intellectual labors, made the latter part of Kepler's life both hectic and unpredictable. After abandoning Linz in 1627, he settled in Silesia in 1628 in the service of the statesman and general Wallenstein. He died at Regensburg, while traveling to Linz to collect a debt.

See also: ASTRONOMY

**Further reading:** Max Caspar, *Johannes Kepler*, transl. C. Doris Hellman (New York: Dover, repr. 1993); Kitty Ferguson, *Tycho and Kepler* (New York: Walker, 2002); James R. Voelkel, *Johannes Kepler and the New Astronomy* (Oxford, U.K.: Oxford University Press, 2001); ~*The Composition of Kepler's* Astronomia nova (Princeton, N.J.: Princeton University Press, 2001).

**Key, Lieven de** (1560–1627) *Netherlands stonemason and architect*
Key was born in Ghent and after working in England for some years moved to Haarlem (1591), where he remained for the rest of his life. His highly ornamental style was

largely a development of that of his predecessor in Haarlem, Willem den Abt. His finest works are the Haarlem meat hall (1602–03) and the tower of the Nieuwe Kerk (1613). Both buildings are basically traditional in type, but are distinguished by a taut sense of form and a brilliant handling of decorative details. While Key stands out in comparison with many of his 16th-century predecessors for his vigorous and personal sense of decorative design, he nevertheless remained a provincial figure, rooted in an essentially Dutch architectural tradition.

## Keyser, Hendrick de (1565–1621) *Netherlands architect and sculptor*
The son of a cabinet maker, Keyser studied in his native Utrecht under Cornelis Bloemaert and was appointed city sculptor and architect of Amsterdam in 1594. In London in 1607 he met the English sculptor Nicholas Stone, who became his assistant and son-in-law. Keyser's major buildings include the Zuiderkerk, the Westerkerk, and the exchange, all in Amsterdam, and Leyden town hall. Like Lieven de KEY, Keyser was a leading figure in the last phase of Dutch MANNERISM. However, unlike his compatriot, he outgrew this increasingly provincial tradition, to become one of the founders of 17th-century Dutch classicism.

Keyser was also the most significant Dutch sculptor of the early 17th century, working in a style loosely derived from that of the Italian mannerists. He produced numerous small bronzes and pieces of architectural sculpture. His chief sculptural work, the tomb of William the Silent in the Nieuwe Kerk at Delft, was commissioned in 1614 but was not complete by the time of his own death.

## Khair ed-Din See BARBAROSSA

## Kid, Thomas See KYD, THOMAS

## Kirchmaier, Thomas See NAOGEORGUS, THOMAS

## Klonowic, Sebastian Fabian (c. 1545–1602) *Polish poet*
Klonowic was born in Sulmierzyce but worked mainly in Lublin, where he was a teacher and held civic offices and described the social life of a Polish town in his satirical and descriptive verse. He wrote in both Latin and Polish; his major works in the former are *Roxolania* (1584) and the allegory *Victoria deorum* (1587), and in the latter *Flis* (1595) and *Worek Judaszów* (1600).

## Knights Hospitaler (Knights of the Order of the Hospital of St. John of Jerusalem) A religious order founded in the 11th century in the Holy Land for the medical care and armed defense of pilgrims. After the fall of Acre (1291) the order moved first to Cyprus and then settled in Rhodes (1309), which they held with superlative military skill against repeated Muslim attacks until 1522, when the

victorious Suleiman the Magnificent allowed them to withdraw to Crete. They then established themselves on Malta (1530), where they withstood a famous siege by the Ottoman fleet in 1565. The Knights' military prowess was a key factor in checking Ottoman naval expansionism in the Mediterranean for nearly three centuries.

## Knights of Malta See KNIGHTS HOSPITALER

## Knights of Rhodes See KNIGHTS HOSPITALER

## Knights Templar A military religious order founded in 1118 in Jerusalem to protect the holy places against the Muslims. Following the fall of Jerusalem (1187) to Saladin, the Templars continued to fight until the Christians were ejected from the Holy Land after the siege of Acre (1291), in which the master of the order was killed. Meanwhile the order prospered to the extent that their headquarters in London and Paris were repositories of immense wealth. This brought upon them the envy of the French monarchs, who, on a series of trumped-up charges, persuaded Pope Clement V to suppress the order at the Council of Vienne in 1312.

## Knox, John (c. 1513–1572) *Scottish religious reformer*
Although trained at Glasgow for the Catholic priesthood, Knox converted to Protestantism in the 1540s. He was a preacher at St. Andrews when the town was attacked by the French and suffered two years' imprisonment in France. On his release he took a leading role in Edward VI's religious reforms in England (1549–53) but fled to Geneva on the accession of the Catholic Mary I. While there he published *The First Blast of the Trumpet against the Monstrous Regiment of Women* (1558), a violent attack on Mary of Guise's regency in Scotland; the following year he returned to Scotland to join the fight against Catholicism, particularly as represented by Mary of Guise and her daughter MARY, Queen of Scots. In 1560, in the terms of the Scottish Confession, Knox shaped the moderate Calvinist doctrines of the Church of Scotland. After Mary, Queen of Scots had to abdicate (1567), Knox, with the support of the regent, the Earl of Moray, directed Scotland's religious affairs and the organization of the Church of Scotland on democratic lines.

**Further reading:** Jasper Ridley, *John Knox* (Oxford, U.K.: Clarendon Press, 1968); Douglas Wilson, *For Kirk and Covenant: The Stalwart Courage of John Knox* (Nashville, Tenn.: Cumberland House, 2000).

## Koch, Jodocus See JONAS, JUSTUS

## Kochanowski, Jan (Johannes Cochanovius) (1530–1584) *Polish poet*
A native of Sycyn, Kochanowski was educated at Cracow and Padua. He then visited Königsberg and Paris, meeting

Pierre de RONSARD in the latter. He returned to Poland (1559) with a thorough knowledge of classical and Italian literature and a sympathy with Renaissance literary ideals, which until then he had expressed only in his accomplished Latin verse. His *Foricoena*, not published until 1584, dates from this period, as do his Latin lyrics and elegies. Attaching himself to the court, where he attained (1567) the position of royal secretary, Kochanowski began to write in Polish as well as Latin. His *Szachy* (c. 1566) is based on the mock-heroic *Scacchia Ludus* by Marco Girolamo VIDA. In 1570 he retired from the court to settle on an estate at Czarnolas, where he farmed and wrote some of the masterpieces of Renaissance Polish verse; his work refined the language, exercising a formative influence upon the vernacular and upon later poets. *Treny* (1580) is a cycle of laments for his infant daughter Urszula (died 1579). *Fraski* (Trifles; 1584) is a collection of sparkling epigrams. *Pieśni* (Songs; 1586) is much influenced by the odes of Horace, as are his lyrical renderings of the psalms. He wrote one verse play, *Odprawa posłów greckich* (The Dismissal of the Greek envoys: 1578) based on an incident in the third book of the *Iliad* and modeled on the lines of classical Greek tragedy.

**Kolman family** See HELMSCHMIED FAMILY

**Kraft, Adam** (Adam Krafft) (c. 1460–1508/09) *German sculptor*
Kraft's work was all produced in his native Nuremberg, where he was given the most prestigious commissions. He was a close friend of Peter Vischer the Elder (*see* VISCHER FAMILY). As a stone carver he worked in the late Gothic style, but with a new realism and expressiveness and particular clarity and simplicity. All these qualities are apparent in his seven reliefs of the Stations of the Cross near the entrance to St. John's church (1505–08). His best-known work is the tabernacle in the church of St. Lawrence (1493–96), for which he made not only the sculptures but also the whole imaginative architectural edifice—a kind of tiered spire about 62 feet (19 meters) high. Among the numerous figures of humans and animals decorating it are portraits of Kraft and two apprentices, kneeling and supporting the base of the structure.

**Krumper, Hans** (Hans Krumpper) (c. 1570–1634) *German sculptor, architect, and painter*
Born at Weilheim, he joined the court of Duke Wilhelm V in Munich in 1584, and became a pupil of the sculptor Hubert GERHARD. He was sent to Italy to complete his training (1590–92). In 1599 he succeeded Frederik SUS-TRIS as court architect and artistic director (having already married his daughter). Wilhelm's successor, Duke Maximilian I, appointed him also court painter (1609), although Krumper's chief assignment at this time was to oversee the alterations to the Munich palace (the Residenz). He worked in the mannerist style, producing not only sculpture, but also many designs for goldsmiths (lamps, altars, reliquaries, etc.).

**Kulmbach, Hans Suess von** (1475/80–1522) *German painter*
About 1500 he left his native Kulmbach for Nuremberg, where he studied in Dürer's workshop and was also influenced by the visiting Venetian artist Jacopo de' BARBARI. In 1511 Kulmbach obtained citizenship of his adopted town and became an independent artist. As a young man, he collaborated with DÜRER in designing woodcuts, and after 1508 he designed numerous stained-glass windows. When Dürer gave up the execution of altarpieces in 1510, Kulmbach emerged as a major painter of triptychs. Of his dozen or so altarpieces, three were exported to Cracow in Poland. He also painted a number of portraits of considerable charm. Next to BALDUNG GRIEN, Kulmbach was Dürer's most important pupil, with a personal style quite distinct from that of his master.

**Kyd, Thomas** (Thomas Kid) (1558–1594) *English playwright*
Kyd was the son of a London scrivener, who sent him to the Merchant Taylors' school (1565); he seems, for a time at least, to have followed his father's profession, though the details of his life are obscure and what information there is often derives from the gossip of Kyd's contemporaries on the London literary scene. His claim to fame is the Senecan-based *Spanish Tragedy* (1594). It was probably written in the middle of the decade 1582–92 and ushered in the Elizabethan vogue for revenge tragedies. The melodramatic plot, violent actions, overwrought emotions, and murderous finale, along with such devices as the madness of the hero, appealed strongly to the contemporary audience, both in England and in Continental Europe; the play is also well constructed and its hero, Jeronimo, is a genuinely moving figure. Kyd also wrote a tragedy on the subject of Cornelia (1594), and *Soliman and Perseda* (c. 1592) is ascribed to him. His possible connection with the so-called Ur-Hamlet (*see* HAMLET) has aroused much speculation.

**Further reading:** Lucas Erne (ed.), *Beyond* The Spanish Tragedy: *A Study of the Plays of Thomas Kyd* (Manchester, U.K.: Manchester University Press, 2002).

# L

**Labé, Louise** (c. 1524–c. 1566) *French poet*
The beautiful wife of a wealthy rope maker (*cordier*), Louise Labé was nicknamed "La Belle Cordière." She was also an accomplished horsewoman, skilled in swordsmanship: one of the many legends attached to her alleged that in her adventurous youth she had ridden to war disguised as a soldier. She was a member of the group of poets, led by Maurice SCÈVE, that flourished in her native Lyons in the 16th century. Her poetic works, published in 1555, comprise three elegies and 24 sonnets, which express with intense passion and realism, inspired by personal experience, the joys and anguish of love. Also included in the volume was the prose *Débat de Folie et d'Amour*. The example Labé set to other women, encouraging them to take an interest in learning and to publish their writings, and her assertion that women should not be despised as companions to men in both private and public spheres caused a considerable amount of adverse comment, especially among strict Calvinists.

**La Boétie, Étienne de** (1530–1563) *French magistrate and man of letters*
La Boétie was born at Sarlat and became a colleague of MONTAIGNE in the *parlement* of Bordeaux: their acquaintance developed into a close friendship that was to have a profound influence on Montaigne's life and works. La Boétie is remembered for his *Discours sur la servitude volontaire* or *Contr'un* ("Against One"), an antimonarchical treatise written in his youth and published posthumously in 1576; his other works include translations of the historians Xenophon and Plutarch, the *Mémoire sur l'édit de janvier*, demanding nonviolent Catholic reform, and a number of sonnets stylistically influenced by RONSARD. La Boétie's premature death, the result of a bout of dysentery, was movingly described by Montaigne in a letter to his father, his first published work.

**Lafreri, Antonio** (**Antoine Lafréry**) (1512–1577) *French-born Italian engraver and publisher*
Born in Orgelet, Lafreri settled in Rome as an engraver (1544), but by 1553 had moved into publishing. A particularly sumptuous production was his *Speculum Romanae magnificentiae* (1575), but he was also known for his output of prints by Marcantonio RAIMONDI. Lafreri had the idea of binding sheet maps by various cartographers into a single volume according to the individual customer's requirements; these compilations, of which no two are exactly the same, are known generically as Lafreri atlases, although other publishers in Rome and Venice were naturally quick to take up this profitable scheme. Lafreri's own imprint occurs on a number of such atlases issued between 1556 and 1572, the later ones under the title of *Tavole moderne di geografia*.

**Laib, Konrad** (fl. c. 1431–1460) *German painter*
Laib was born in Swabia and is recorded as working in Nördlingen in 1431; he moved to Salzburg around 1440. An early German proponent of the realistic style, he established this style in Salzburg. His realism is apparent in his depiction of the folds of fabric and reflections in polished metal, and particularly in his portraiture and interest in facial expression. His ability to portray individuals is seen, for example, in his portrait of Emperor Sigismund (c. 1437) and in the crowds of figures in his altar panels (e.g. the Viennese *Crucifixion* of 1449).

*Lamb, Adoration of the* See GHENT ALTARPIECE

**Lambert, Francis** (1486–1530) *French-born religious reformer*

The son of a papal official at Avignon, Lambert joined the Franciscan Order there (1507) and became famous as a preacher. After 1517 he traveled through France, Italy, and Switzerland, and his study of the Bible and the religious reformers he encountered caused him to abandon his order and travel to Wittenberg (1523), where he was assisted by LUTHER. On moving to Strasbourg (1524) he met such hostility that he was forced to move on. In 1526 he was summoned by PHILIP OF HESSE, who entrusted Lambert with the setting up of a state Lutheran Church in his domains and appointed him as professor of exegesis at his new university of Marburg (1527). In 1529 Lambert openly adopted the Zwinglian line (*see* ZWINGLI, ULRICH) in the debate over the Eucharist, thus alienating his Lutheran supporters. The following year he died of the plague, leaving a number of works that include a polemic against ERASMUS (1525) and commentaries on the Song of Songs (1524) and the Book of Revelation (1528).

**Landini, Francesco (Francesco Landino)** (c. 1325–1397) *Italian composer*

A Florentine by birth, Landini was a leading exponent of the 14th-century musical style known as the ARS NOVA. Although he was blind (and was therefore referred to by contemporaries as "il Cieco"), he was famous as an organist and also played the lute and other instruments. He spent most of his life in Florence but also visited Venice, where he was highly acclaimed. As a composer he is remarkable for his madrigals and his *caccie* (canons for two voices), both forms that later underwent considerable development.

**Landino, Cristoforo** (1424–1492) *Italian humanist scholar*

Born in Florence, Landino was one of the group of able men who gathered around Lorenzo de' MEDICI in the PLATONIC ACADEMY. He became professor of poetry and rhetoric (1457), and later of Latin literature, a post which he held until his death. He published commentaries on VIRGIL and HORACE and translated Pliny's *Natural History*. His edition of Dante (1481) and lectures on Petrarch reveal the humanist interest in vernacular literature which seemed to measure up to classical standards. His *Camaldolese Disputations* (c. 1480), a dialogue modeled on the *Tusculan Disputations* of CICERO, gives an intimate glimpse of the kind of discussion engaged in by members of the Florentine Academy. The poetry of Virgil is one of the main topics, but the interpretations are still those of the medieval allegorists. The other subjects discussed, for example the comparative advantages of the active and the contemplative life, show the extent to which classical concepts permeated the Medicean circle.

**landsknechts** See MERCENARIES

**Languet, Hubert** (1518–1581) *French writer and diplomat*

Born at Vitteaux in Burgundy, he was educated by Jean Perrelle, a distinguished Greek scholar, and then studied at Poitiers (1536–39), Bologna, and Padua. In 1549, after meeting MELANCHTHON at Wittenberg, he became a Protestant. He traveled widely in Europe before entering the service (1559) of Augustus I, Elector of Saxony, whom he represented at the French court (1561–72). He narrowly escaped the MASSACRE OF ST. BARTHOLOMEW and later served Augustus at the imperial court (1573–77) before retiring to the Netherlands and dying at Antwerp. Languet's extensive correspondence is a valuable source for 16th-century history; among his friends and correspondents was Sir Philip SIDNEY. The anonymous *Vindicia contra tyrannos* (1579) expounding the doctrine of resistance to tyranny by constitutional means, is attributed to him, but this attribution is still disputed. He may also have helped WILLIAM THE SILENT draft his *Apologia* attacking the king of Spain (1581).

**Lannoy, Ghillebert de** (1386–1462) *Burgundian soldier and envoy*

Lannoy spent much of his life (1339–1450) traveling on military or civil business. After taking part in the French attack on the Isle of Wight (1403), he made a pilgrimage to the Near East (1405–06). In 1413 he was crusading in Prussia and the Baltic, and in 1419 he was in England as Burgundian representative at the marriage of Henry V and Catherine of France. PHILIP THE GOOD twice sent him to the Near East (1421, mid-1440s) to look into the prospects for raising a crusade, and employed him on embassies to Scotland, Ireland, and the Council of Basle (1433); he also attended the Congress of Arras (1435). He was made a founding member of Order of the GOLDEN FLEECE in 1430. In addition to his travel notes (*Voyaiges*), Lannoy wrote *Instruction d'un jeune prince* (c. 1440), and *Enseignements paternels*, advice to his son.

**La Noue, François de** (1531–1591) *French soldier and writer*

La Noue was born in Nantes and converted to Protestantism in 1558. He fought on the HUGUENOT side in the French Wars of Religion; his nickname "Bras de Fer" ("Iron Arm") derived from the replacement "arm" he wore after an injury sustained in battle. Following the MASSACRE OF ST. BARTHOLOMEW he spent four years in the Huguenot defense of La Rochelle. Fighting against the Spanish in the Netherlands, La Noue was captured and imprisoned for five years; he used this enforced leisure to reflect on his military career in *Discours politiques et militaires* (1587), a patriotic account of France's problems, advocating reconciliation between Catholics and Protestants, combined with his personal memoirs as a soldier. On his return to France La Noue entered the service of Henry IV and died in action.

**Larivey, Pierre** (c. 1540–1619) *French playwright*
Of Italian extraction, Larivey was born in Champagne. He was responsible for the introduction of Italian Renaissance comedy into France through his versions of nine plays by various Italian authors. Six (*Le Laquais, La Veuve, Les Esprits, Le Morfundu, Les Jaloux, Les Écoliers*) were published in 1579 and a further three in 1611.

**Las Casas, Bartolomé de** (1474–1566) *Spanish priest*
Las Casas was born in Seville and studied law before being ordained (c. 1510). In Cuba from 1512 onwards he quickly became incensed at the conquistadores' treatment of the Indians. From 1514 he devoted his life to the preservation of Indian rights, pleading their cause before the king (1515) and publishing books in their defense. Most of Las Casas's humanitarian schemes failed because of Spanish opposition and because he had overestimated the capabilities of the Indians, as highlighted by the failure of his model colony at Cumuná, Venezuela. Established in 1520, Cumuná was destroyed by an Indian revolt one year later. Back in Spain, Las Casas advised the Council of the Indies (1539–44), obtaining several decrees protecting the Indians. His tenure of the Mexican bishopric of Chiapas (1544–47) was rendered impossible by local Spanish hostility. In 1550 he had a famous debate with the humanist scholar Ginés de Sepúlveda (c. 1490–c. 1573) concerning exploitation of aboriginal populations.

**Further reading:** Raup Wagner and Helen Rand Parish, *The Life and Writings of Bartolomé de las Casas* (Albuquerque, N. Mex.: University of New Mexico Press, 1967).

**Lassus, Orlando** (1532–1594) *Franco-Flemish composer*
Lassus was born in Mons, and at the age of 12 he entered the service of Ferrante Gonzaga, a general of Emperor Charles V. Lassus accompanied him to Mantua, Sicily, and Milan, and then went to Naples and Rome, becoming *maestro di cappella* at the church of St. John Lateran in 1553. A year later he left to visit his parents and in 1555 was in Antwerp. In 1556 he was appointed as a singer at the court of Duke Albrecht V in Munich, and in 1563 took over the post of *Kapellmeister*, which he held until his death. Lassus's duties here included a wide range of liturgical responsibilities, as well as music for such special occasions as state visits, banquets, and hunting parties. In the years following his appointment he traveled much, often at the invitation of kings and dukes, and was received with high honor; in 1574 he received the Knighthood of the Golden Spur from Pope Gregory VIII. His works were published in Venice, Antwerp, Paris, Frankfurt, and Munich, and were widely disseminated.

Lassus was a prolific and versatile composer; his compositions embrace all 16th-century forms of vocal music from drinking songs to Masses. About 200 Italian madrigals and villanelles, 150 chansons, and 90 German lieder survive of his secular music, which covers a wide range of moods; Lassus was a master in all three styles. He was most prolific in motet composition; over 500 survive, in which both liturgical and nonliturgical texts are set. As in all Lassus's music, the words of the motets generate most of the expressive content of the composition. The largest collection of motets is the posthumous *Magnum opus musicum* (1604). Around 60 Masses, 101 Magnificats, and numerous other liturgical works survive, in which Lassus's skillful counterpoint, rhetorical treatment of the text, and succinct manner are demonstrated to great effect. He was more cosmopolitan than his great contemporary PALESTRINA, and their musical styles differ considerably.

**Further reading:** Gustave Reese, *The New Grove High Renaissance Masters: Josquin, Palestrina, Lassus, Byrd, Victoria* (London: Macmillan, 1984).

***Last Supper*** (*Cenacolo*) A major work by LEONARDO DA VINCI, executed in the refectory of Sta. Maria delle Grazie, Milan, between 1495 and 1497. One of Leonardo's most important paintings, the *Last Supper* is the work that effectively launched the High Renaissance. It differed from the numerous earlier treatments of the same subject by concentrating on the psychological content at the moment that Christ revealed that one among the present company would betray him. The figures of the apostles themselves were based upon some of Leonardo's contemporaries. Because Leonardo chose to paint with oil directly onto the plaster, the painting deteriorated rapidly, even within Leonardo's own lifetime, and suffered further from inadequate restoration in the 18th and 19th centuries—as well as from damage in the Napoleonic wars, in World War II, and from the monks themselves, who cut a door through it. A controversial restoration project began in 1977 and was completed in 2000.

**Further reading:** Pinin Brambilla Barcilon *et al*, *Leonardo: The Last Supper* (Chicago, Ill.: Chicago University Press, 2001); Leo Steinberg, *Leonardo's Incessant Last Supper* (New York: Zone Books, 2001).

**La Taille, Jean de** (c. 1535–c. 1607) *French dramatist*
La Taille, like his younger brother Jacques (1542–62), also a playwright, was born at Bondaroy. He is notable for having written vernacular religious tragedies in the style of SENECA—*Saül le furieux* (1572) and *La Famine, ou les Gibéonites* (1573)—and an influential treatise on dramatic theory, *De l'art de la tragédie* (1572), in which Aristotelian

principles are expounded. Of his prose comedies, *Le Négromant* is a translation from Ariosto.

**Latin studies** Throughout the Middle Ages Latin remained the language of the Church, used for a variety of purposes. It was also the language of polite literature, certainly until the 10th or 11th century when the vernacular languages first began to be used in a self-consciously artistic way. Medieval Latin had developed its own characteristics which made it a distinct language, and the rediscovery of the classical Latin writers gradually influenced humanists and scholars in their own use of Latin. The letters of PETRARCH show evidence that he had begun to assimilate the style of the recently discovered Ciceronian correspondence (*see* CICERO). For the first generation of Italian humanists, work on Latin authors took second place as a rule to the work of editing Greek texts and translating them (into Latin), but as the 15th century went on scholars became more anxious about their personal standards of Latinity. Latin gradually ceased to be a living language used with flexibility and variety and became increasingly restricted by an artificial canon of rules formulated from the works of Cicero. ERASMUS did much by ridicule and by example to weaken the influence of this Ciceronianism, but the classical writers remained the models for imitation and the criteria by which contemporary products were judged.

The study of classical Latin literature itself began with work on the interpretation of texts. The earliest humanists regarded classical Latin authors as in some sense contemporaries; Petrarch responded to the revelations of the weaknesses in Cicero's character which followed the discovery (1345) of the letters to Atticus as if responding to the discovery that a trusted friend had feet of clay. This sense of the contemporaneity of classical authors passed into a desire to produce the most accurate texts, to treat Latin authors as testimony to a remote past. This is an important aspect of that historical sense which so sharply distinguished the later Renaissance from the Middle Ages. The second half of the 15th and the 16th century saw the skills of textual analysis refined (*see* CRITICISM, TEXTUAL); Lorenzo VALLA's demonstration (1440) that the Donation of Constantine was a forgery depended on a very accurate knowledge of Latin usage in the fourth century CE. Work of this kind led finally to the encyclopedic editions of Latin authors produced by Isaac CASAUBON, Joseph SCALIGER, and others. Latin became the language of scholarship and ceased to evolve except within a very limited sphere. Once the styles of ancient Latin authors were more fully appreciated and understood, the next stage was the investigation of the material remains of the Roman world, and the late 16th- and 17th-century editions embodied the latest researches in archaeology, NUMISMATICS, and legal and religious history.

Latin also continued to be used as a medium for creative writing, and an immense quantity of Latin verse was produced by Renaissance writers on every conceivable subject. The writings of BEMBO, FRACASTORO, SANNAZARO, and SADOLETO, to name but four, show the extent to which the Latin language could be exploited by humanist poets. Often a scholar's international reputation depended on his skill as a versifier; George BUCHANAN in Scotland and John Milton in England are examples of writers whose Latin poems reached a European audience. The Latin eclogues (1498) of Mantuan (Giovan Battista SPAGNOLI) were a crucial influence upon the development of PASTORAL poetry in the vernacular throughout Europe.

**See also:** NEO-LATIN LITERATURE

**Laurana, Francesco** (c. 1430–c. 1502) *Dalmatian sculptor*
Laurana was born at Zara, but little is known of his early life. He produced works in Italy, France, and Sicily, sometimes in collaboration with his relative Luciano LAURANA. He is first recorded as working on the triumphal arch of Alfonso I at the Castel Nuovo in Naples (1453), after which he moved to the court of RENÉ OF ANJOU, for whom he executed some notable medals. Laurana is best known, however, for a series of portrait busts of women connected with the royal house of Naples, including those of Battista Sforza (Bargello, Florence) and Beatrice of Aragon (Kunsthistorisches Museum, Vienna). Besides these, he also produced a number of reliefs and worked on the Mastrantonio chapel at the church of San Francesco in Palermo, Sicily (1468).

**Laurana, Luciano** (c. 1422–1479) *Dalmatian architect*
A relative of the sculptor Francesco LAURANA, Luciano was born at Lo Vrana, near Zara, and is first recorded as working in Urbino in about 1465. By 1468 he had been appointed principal architect on the construction of the ducal palace of Urbino, which became the site of his best work. Laurana was responsible for the courtyard of the palace and the facade, which resembled the triumphal arch of Alfonso I at Castelnuovo in Naples, upon which he may have worked in the 1450s. The palace at Urbino was later completed by the Sienese architect FRANCESCO di Giorgio and is known to have inspired BRAMANTE.

**Laurenziana, Bibliotheca** A LIBRARY in Florence, originally that of the MEDICI FAMILY. The library was built to house the valuable collection of books and manuscripts founded by Cosimo de' Medici and enlarged by other members of the Medici family in the 15th and 16th centuries. It was opened to the public in 1571. The library building was designed by MICHELANGELO for Pope Clement VII (Giulio de' Medici) in 1523 in the cloisters of the church of San Lorenzo and includes such features as a carved ceiling, mosaic floor, and carved benches all made to Michelangelo's designs. The library's staircase was completed by Bartolommeo AMMANATI and Giorgio VASARI in 1559. Among the library's 10,000 manuscripts are some of the most important surviving classical texts, including a fifth-century copy of Virgil, and the oldest complete Latin Bible known, the eighth-century Codex Amiatinus. In 1808 the Medici library at the convent of San Marco (*see* MARCIANA, BIBLIOTHECA) was combined with the Laurenziana to form the present Bibliotheca Medicea Laurenziana.

*Lazarillo de Tormes* An episodic narrative published in 1554 (though evidence suggests there may have been an earlier edition). It is remarkable for its social satire, and its scathing anticlerical passages caused it to be put on the INDEX LIBRORUM PROHIBITORUM in 1559, but its continued popularity was such that Philip II authorized an expurgated edition in 1573 (*Lazarillo castigado*). Authorship has never been determined; among the candidates proposed are Fray Juan de Ortega, Diego de HURTADO de Mendoza, and the brothers VALDÉS. The tale relates the adventures of Lázaro, a boy from the dregs of society. He learns the art of survival as he moves from one corrupt or deluded master to another: as helper to a blind beggar who starves him, as altar-boy to a priest who is even meaner, as servant to an impoverished *hidalgo*, and so on. The hero ends, optimistic and contented, as a towncrier in Toledo married to the mistress of an archpriest—in other words, in a dismally low position and a cuckold. The book introduced the realistic autobiographical narrative and is thus the forerunner of the PICARESQUE NOVEL. It was translated into English in 1586.

**Lebrija, Elio Antonio de** See NEBRIJA, ELIO ANTONIO MARTÍNEZ DE CALA DE

**Lefèvre d'Étaples, Jacques** (Faber Stapulensis) (c. 1453–1536) *French humanist and theologian*
Born at Étaples, Lefèvre became a priest and a teacher of philosophy in Paris. He visited Italy in the late 15th century and embarked on the study of Greek classics, translating and editing some of the works of Aristotle. Around 1505 he was teaching Greek in Paris. He subsequently turned his attention to the Scriptures, publishing his *Commentaires sur les épîtres de Saint Paul* in 1512; by 1530 he had completed the first French translation of the Bible. Lefèvre's approach to religion and to the study of biblical texts made him a leader of the pre-Reformation movement in France and an enemy of the Sorbonne; in 1525 he was forced to abandon his post as vicar-general to the bishop of Meaux and take temporary refuge in Strasbourg. After a brief period of service as tutor to the children of Francis I he retired to Nérac, where he enjoyed the protection of MARGUERITE DE NAVARRE for the last five years of his life.

**Leicester, Robert Dudley, Earl of** (c. 1532–1588) *English nobleman, courtier, and soldier*
He was the fifth son of the duke of Northumberland and shared in his family's disgrace over the abortive attempt (1553) to place his sister-in-law, Lady Jane GREY, on the throne. However, Mary I pardoned him, and on the accession of ELIZABETH I he rapidly rose in royal favor, becoming a strong contender for the queen's hand. In 1560 his wife Amy Robsart died from a fall in suspicious circumstances; rumor had it that Dudley was implicated in her death to facilitate his marriage with the queen. This marriage was now out of the question, but he nonetheless remained a royal favorite and Elizabeth created him earl of Leicester in 1564.

Leicester was a generous patron of writers, particularly those with a strongly Protestant, even Puritan, bias; his nephew Sir Philip SIDNEY, Edmund SPENSER, and Edward Dyer were the most distinguished poets among his literary protégés. He was also a patron of Nicholas HILLIARD, apparently promoted Federico ZUCCARO's visit to England, and sat for his portrait over a dozen times. His anti-Catholic policies embroiled him in the catastrophic expedition (1585–87) to aid the Dutch against their Spanish Hapsburg overlords (*see* NETHERLANDS, REVOLT OF THE). By his marriage (1578) to Lettice, widow of the 1st earl of Essex, he became stepfather to Robert Devereux, Earl of ESSEX.

**Leiden** See LEYDEN

**Leipzig** A central European city in which Germans were settled by the early Middle Ages. After obtaining municipal status (1170), Leipzig prospered on account of its position on important trade routes. Its two annual markets, which became imperial fairs in 1497, and further commercial privileges from the Holy Roman Empire ensured continuing prosperity during the period of the Renaissance, especially from the fur trade. By the 16th century Leipzig was known for its publishing and for its annual book fairs. Its university (founded 1409) was known for its humanist and Greek studies by 1500. In 1519 Leipzig was the site of the famous disputation between LUTHER and ECK. Many historic landmarks were restored after World War II.

**Leipzig, Interim of** (1548) Articles of religion imposed on his subjects by Maurice, Elector of Saxony. The Interim was a Lutheran modification of the Interim of AUGSBURG, intended to preserve the unity of the Church until the disputed doctrines should be resolved by the Council of Trent. This compromise was abandoned at the Peace of AUGSBURG in 1555.

**Leland, John** (c. 1506–1552) *English antiquary and poet*
Leland was born in London and educated there at St. Paul's School and at Oxford and Paris. He was keeper of libraries under HENRY VIII and became the king's antiquary in 1533 with permission to search England's colleges, monasteries, and cathedrals for ancient documents, of which he made an invaluable collection. First results of his six-year tour of research were presented to Henry and published (1549) by his friend John BALE, though his full *Itinerary* only appeared in 1710–12 (9 vols, ed. Thomas Hearne). Leland also wrote some proficient Latin poems and a defense of the Arthurian legends, *Assertio inclytissimi Arthuri* (1544).

**Leo X** (1475–1521) *Pope (1513–21)*
Born Giovanni de' Medici at Florence, the second son of Lorenzo de' MEDICI ("the Magnificent"), he received a humanistic education from Marsilio FICINO, POLITIAN, and PICO DELLA MIRANDOLA and studied canon law at Pisa (1489–91). In 1492 he became a cardinal and went to live in Rome. Lorenzo's death recalled him to Florence the same year, but he was exiled with the rest of his family (1494). After traveling in Europe he returned to Rome (1500) and in 1503 he became the head of the Medici family. The revolution of 1512 allowed the Medici to return to Florence and in 1513, aged only 37, Giovanni was elected pope. He was thus able to gratify his humanistic tastes, patronizing scholars and artists and spending papal wealth lavishly on the construction of St. Peter's and on the accumulation of books and manuscripts. Foremost among the artists was RAPHAEL, who was his architect for St. Peter's from 1514, as well as designing the *Acts of the Apostles* series of tapestries for the Sistine Chapel (c. 1515–19), and painting Leo's portrait (c. 1518). Leo surrounded himself with prominent humanists: among his secretaries were BEMBO and SADOLETO, and Cardinal BIBBIENA was his treasurer-general. His patronage of music was no less notable, and he himself played and composed. In 1520 he had more than 15 musicians in his private service; the French composer Elzéar Genet was in charge of music for the papal chapel, and the madrigal composer Costanzo FESTA and the lutenist Gian Maria Giudeo were also on his payroll.

One of Leo's concerns was the removal of foreign influence from Italy; this was initially achieved by the victory of Novara (1513) over the French, but the death of LOUIS XII with the accession of FRANCIS I brought fresh hostilities. These were resolved through negotiation; by the Bull Primitiva (1516) relations between the French monarchy and the papacy were regulated and the concordat agreed at Bologna that year remained in force until 1789. The most significant event of Leo's papacy was the attack by LUTHER on the Roman Catholic Church, inspired by the sale of INDULGENCES to cover the ever-increasing costs of the papacy. Leo excommunicated Luther in 1521, and one of his last acts was to confer the title "Defender of the Faith" on HENRY VIII of England for his stance against Luther.

**Further reading:** Silvio A. Bedini, *The Pope's Elephant* (Austin, Texas: Harry Ransom Humanities Research Center, 1997; repr. New York: Penguin USA, 2000).

**Leo Africanus** (c. 1494–c. 1552) *Spanish-born Moroccan traveler*
Born Hasan Ibn Muhammad al-Wazzan in Granada, he accompanied his family to Fez while still very young. There they were well received at the sultan's court, and after studying law and theology the young man accompanied his uncle on an embassy to Timbuktu (c. 1510). Some years later, another journey encompassed Timbuktu again, also Gao, Bornu, and Egypt. Appointed an ambassador by the sultan, he went to Constantinople, visiting Tlemcen, Algiers, and Tunis, and then on to Turkey by sea. On the way back, after spending some time in Egypt, he was heading for Morocco in 1518 when the ship he was on was attacked by Sicilian pirates, who took him prisoner and handed him over to Pope LEO X. After a year's imprisonment in Castel Sant'Angelo, he converted to Christianity, and was baptized in 1520 by the pope himself, who gave him his own names Giovanni Leone (Joannes Leo) de' Medici. From that date he was also known as Leo Africanus. He taught Arabic in Rome, and while there wrote, in Italian, his most famous book, the *Descrittione dell' Africa*, which was published in Giovanni Battista RAMUSIO's *Navigationi e viaggi* (1550) and translated into French (1556), Latin (1556), and English (1600). In 1529 he returned to Africa, settling in Tunis, where he died.

His life intrigued his contemporaries and continued to exert a grip on the imaginations of later writers, including W. B. Yeats and Amin Maalouf; the latter's best-selling novel, *Léon l'Africain* (1986; in English as *Leo the African* (1988)) is a fictionalized autobiography of Leo. He is sometimes said to be the inspiration behind Shakespeare's Othello.

**León, Fray Luis de** See LUIS DE LEÓN, FRAY

**Leonardo da Vinci** (1452–1519) *Italian painter*
Giorgio VASARI justly began the third part of his *Lives of the Painters* (the High Renaissance section) with Leonardo, commenting that the artist "endowed his figures with motion and breath." Leonardo was born at Anchiano, the illegitimate child of a notary, Piero da Vinci, and a peasant woman, Caterina. By 1469 Leonardo, his father, and stepmother, had moved to Florence, where, because of his aptitude in drawing, Leonardo was apprenticed to the studio of VERROCCHIO. He became a member of guild of St. Luke in 1472; about the same time he painted portions of Verrocchio's *Baptism of Christ* (Uffizi, Florence). The kneeling angel in the left foreground displays the young artist's

deft handling of color and brush. Other early works traditionally attributed to Leonardo include the *Annunciation* (c. 1474; Uffizi; see Plate VIII) and the portrait of Ginevra de' Benci (c. 1474 or c. 1480; National Gallery of Art, Washington). The Benois *Madonna* (c. 1478; Hermitage, St. Petersburg) reveals a figurative animation which will characterize his later paintings.

Leonardo's first major independent commission was the *Adoration of the Magi* (Uffizi), begun in 1481, for the monastery of San Donato a Scopeto outside Florence. The unfinished panel contains only the underdrawing with areas of light and shadow indicated; among the preliminary studies is a fine linear perspective study for the architecture of the left background (also Uffizi). The composition of the *Adoration of the Magi* features a pyramidal grouping of Mary, the Christ Child, and the three Magi surrounded by a semicircular gathering of worshipers. The predilection for geometrical compositions reveals Leonardo's belief, common in the Renaissance, that mathematics and geometry "embrace everything in the universe." While he was working on the *Adoration* panel, Leonardo began to experiment with a more fully activated CONTRAPPOSTO figure, counterpositioning the shoulders and legs to create a vigorous movement. Leonardo's invention, explored in a drawing of *St. Sebastian* (Kunsthalle, Hamburg), would be known in the 16th century as *figura serpentinata* (serpentine figure), and would have great impact, especially on MICHELANGELO, who, like Leonardo, saw figurative movement as reflecting psychological life. Another unfinished work from this period is the painting of *St. Jerome* (Vatican museum, Rome).

Around 1482 Leonardo left Florence to seek employment at the court of Lodovico SFORZA "il Moro" in Milan. A draft of his letter to Duke Lodovico survives; the areas in which Leonardo cites expertise include the construction of bridges and irrigation canals, the designing of military weapons, and architecture, as well as painting and sculpture. He offers to construct the colossal bronze equestrian monument which Lodovico desired to have made in memory of his father Francesco. Leonardo entered the service of Lodovico, directing festivals, displaying his talent as a musician, working on architectural projects, and studying anatomy and painting; one portrait, known as the *Lady with an Ermine*, is of Cecilia Gallerani, Lodovico's young mistress (c. 1483; Czartoryski museum, Cracow). Two paintings from this time pose particular problems regarding their mutual relationship, an early *Madonna of the Rocks* (c. 1484; Louvre, Paris) and a later copy of the same painting (c. 1488, perhaps reworked c. 1506; National Gallery, London); the extent of Leonardo's hand in the London painting is uncertain. The Louvre painting skillfully demonstrates Leonardo's use of SFUMATO, a subtle modeling revealed through a thin veil of atmosphere, delicately blending the lines and colors. From 1495 to 1497 Leonardo worked on the LAST SUPPER

in the refectory of Sta. Maria della Grazie, Milan, a composition that exemplifies the ideals of High Renaissance art, with its convincing illusionism, heroic scale, and psychological reactions displayed by the apostles to Christ's prophecy of his imminent betrayal. It embodies Leonardo's maxim: "Painted figures ought to be done in such a way that those who see them will be able to easily recognize from their attitudes the thoughts of their minds."

Leonardo left Milan in 1499 just after French troops entered the city to put an end to the rule of Lodovico Sforza. He traveled to Mantua and Venice, but by April 1500 was back in Florence, where, in 1503, he had his name reinscribed in the roll of guild painters. The brilliant maturity of Leonardo's art was, according to Vasari, viewed by excited crowds of Florentines who were astonished at his cartoon of the *Virgin and Christ Child with St. Anne* (now lost). The cartoon was probably similar to the Burlington House cartoon of the *Virgin and Child with St. Anne* (1500–05; National Gallery, London) and the panel of the *Virgin and Child with St. Anne* (c. 1508; Louvre); both works displayed a masterful command of modeling, creating in illusory forms the palpability of sculpture. During this Florentine period Leonardo painted MONA LISA, whom Vasari identified as the wife of Francesco del Giocondo. Vasari praised the portrait for its naturalism; only in the 19th century did critics begin to read personal psychological revelations in the picture (see Plate X). From 1503 to 1505 Leonardo worked on the *Battle of Anghiari* (now lost, although studies for it survive) for the Sala del Gran Consiglio of the Palazzo Vecchio; Michelangelo, in 1504, was contracted to paint an adjoining fresco in the same council hall. Between 1506 and 1513 Leonardo worked in both Florence and Milan; he journeyed to Rome in 1513. A late work, *St. John the Baptist* (c. 1515; Louvre) is perhaps his most enigmatic; the intense *chiaroscuro* is prophetic of later baroque painting.

For Leonardo, art as he wrote, "truly is a science." Nowhere is his belief observed more completely than in the over 3500 surviving pages of his notebooks, which contain detailed observations on the widest variety of natural phenomena, including mathematics, perspective, modeling, color, optics, anatomy, painting media, sculpture, philosophy, architecture and urban planning, astronomy, engineering, and the earth sciences. Visual form was given to his observations and ideas in numerous drawings which, more than any other medium, express the freedom of his mind, the subtlety of his observing eye, and the talent of his hand. In 1516 Leonardo traveled to France at the invitation of FRANCIS I. Among the projects he proposed to the French king was a scheme for regulating the waters of the Loire. He died at Clos-Lucé, near Amboise, in the manor given to him by Francis.

**Further reading:** Serge Bramly, *Leonardo: The Artist and the Man* (London: Michael Joseph, 1992); Kenneth

Clark, *Leonardo da Vinci* (London: Penguin, rev. ed. 1993); Charles Gibbs-Smith and Gareth Rees, *The Inventions of Leonardo da Vinci* (Oxford, U.K.: Phaidon, 1978); Martin Kemp, *Leonardo da Vinci: The Marvelous Works of Man and Nature* (Cambridge, Mass: Harvard University Press, 1981; rev. ed. 1988); Pietro C. Marani, *Leonardo da Vinci: The Complete Paintings* (New York: Harry N. Abrams, 2000); Carlo Pedretti, *Leonardo: A Study in Chronology and Style* (Berkeley, Calif.: University of California Press and London: Thames & Hudson, 1973; repr. 1982); Jean Paul Richter, *The Literary Works of Leonardo da Vinci*, ed. Carlo Pedretti (Oxford, U.K.: Phaidon, new ed. 1977); Jack Wasserman, *Leonardo da Vinci* (New York and Leicester, U.K.: Doubleday, 1981; concise ed. London: Thames & Hudson, 1992).

**Leone Ebreo (Judah Abarbanel)** (c. 1465–c. 1530) *Portuguese Jewish philosopher and physician*
The son of Isaac ABARBANEL, he was born in Lisbon and lived in Toledo from 1483 until the expulsion of the Jews from Spain in 1492. He then practiced as a physician in several Italian towns and fell under the influence of PICO DELLA MIRANDOLA. Around 1502 he wrote, probably in Spanish or Hebrew, his *Dialoghi di amore*, first published in an Italian translation in 1535. It was soon translated into Latin and became a highly influential text for Christian Neoplatonists throughout Europe, with its doctrine that "in God the lover, the beloved, and their love are all one and the same," and that love, identified with God, is the principle underlying and animating the universe. Leone Ebreo died in Naples.

**Leoni, Leone** (c. 1509–1590) *Italian sculptor, engraver, and goldsmith*
Leoni was born at Arezzo and trained as a goldsmith, but none of his work in that medium has survived. He is best known for his bronze portraits and funerary monuments and for his medals of patrons, rulers, and artists such as Michelangelo. He is said to have rivaled Benvenuto CELLINI, not only in his work but also in the notoriety of his personal life. Leoni first worked in Venice and then in Rome, where he was coin engraver at the papal mint (1537–40). He held the same post at the mint in Milan from 1542. As court sculptor and medalist to Emperor CHARLES V (from 1546) Leoni traveled to Germany and Brussels, besides attending the emperor on his visits to Italy. Later he executed portraits of Philip II of Spain, Empress Isabella, and Maria of Portugal and collaborated with his son Pompeo LEONI on statuary for the ESCORIAL. His sculptural style was one of strong elegant naturalism. He spent the last years of his life at his base in Milan, where the tomb of Gian Giacomo de' Medici in the cathedral (1560–62) is an example of his work. Partly as a means of enhancing his social status, by presenting himself as not only a creator but also a connoisseur of works of art, Leoni assembled a major collection of sculptures and paintings by his contemporaries (among them Leonardo da Vinci, Bernardino Luini, and Michelangelo), which he displayed in a gallery in his house in Milan.

**Leoni, Pompeo** (c. 1531–1608) *Italian sculptor, goldsmith, and medalist*
Like his father, Leone LEONI, Pompeo is best known for his funerary monuments and his expressive sculpture portraits. He spent much of his life in Spain finishing bronze statues that had been cast and sent to him from Milan by his father. He also produced his own work for Spanish princes and cardinals and for his patron PHILIP II. The church of the ESCORIAL contains his most famous sculptures, the larger-than-life-size bronze statues flanking the main altar. Following his father's example, Pompeo collected paintings by his contemporaries, including Correggio, and displayed them in his grand house in Madrid.

**Lepanto, battle of** (October 7, 1571) A naval battle fought off Lepanto, in the Gulf of Corinth, in which the forces of the HOLY LEAGUE, commanded by Don JOHN OF AUSTRIA (half-brother of Philip II of Spain), defeated the OTTOMAN TURKS under Ali Pasha, governor of Alexandria. The dominant naval power in the Mediterranean for 30 years, the Turks had invaded Cyprus, Venice's wealthiest colony, in 1570. Spain joined Venice and the pope in the Holy League (1571), contributing respectively a half, a third, and a sixth of the forces, and, fired by crusading zeal against the infidel, the Christian fleet sought out the Turks in their home waters. The fleets, at 300 ships apiece, were roughly equal in strength; the Turks lost about 117, the Christians between 15 and 20. Lepanto is particularly remembered as the last naval battle at which the motive power was provided by oars pulled by galley slaves, and many thousands of Christian galley slaves were liberated in its aftermath. The victory was widely celebrated as proof that the Turks were not invincible, but the practical results were minimal: the Turks built another fleet and retained control of Cyprus, which the Venetians formally surrendered in 1573.

**Léry, Jean de** (1534–1613) *French Protestant pastor*
Born in Lamargelle, Burgundy, Léry converted to Protestantism and around 1552 moved to Geneva to study theology. In 1556 he volunteered to go as pastor to the "Ile de Coligny," the short-lived French colony set up in 1555 as a Protestant refuge off the Brazilian coast under Nicolas Durand de Villegagnon (c. 1510–71) and named for its sponsor Admiral COLIGNY. Religious disputes soon drove Léry and some companions from the island, and they had to wait on the adjacent mainland for a ship home. During this period (March 1557–January 1558), they were in daily contact with the indigenous Tupinamba, of whom Léry wrote a lively, detailed, and mainly sympathetic ac-

count in *Histoire d'un voyage faict en la terre du Brésil, autrement dite Amerique* (1578), which may have influenced MONTAIGNE's essay "Des Cannibales"; five further editions appeared during its author's lifetime (English translation by Janet Whatley, *History of a Voyage to the Land of Brazil, Otherwise Called America*, 1990). Back in Europe Léry ministered as pastor in various French towns. After the MASSACRE OF ST. BARTHOLOMEW he took refuge in the Huguenot stronghold of Sancerre, surviving the 1573 siege there, of which he wrote an account, *Histoire mémorable de la ville de Sancerre* (1574).

## Lescot, Pierre (c. 1510–1578) *French architect*
Born into a wealthy family of lawyers, Lescot probably never visited Italy but became acquainted with classical ideals through books and study of Roman ruins in France. He executed his most famous work at the LOUVRE, where he designed a square court known as the Cour Carrée (1546–51). His final design combined classical and traditional French features and was further embellished with low-relief sculptures by Jean GOUJON; it was completed under Claude Perrault in the 17th century. Other major works included the Fontaine des Innocents (1547–49) in Paris and the Hôtel de Ligneris (now the Musée Carnavalet; 1545). Other works, which exercised an important influence upon subsequent French design and decoration, have been largely destroyed.

## Leto, Pomponio Giulio (Julius Pomponius Laetus) (1428–1498) *Italian humanist*
Born in Calabria, an illegitimate member of the Sanseverini family, he was educated by Lorenzo VALLA. He was a dedicated Latinist, refusing even to learn Greek, and he deliberately cultivated an antique lifestyle, with his behavior modeled on the life of Cato the Elder. Leto was the moving spirit behind the ROMAN ACADEMY which developed in imitation of the more famous one in Florence. The academy was accused of being a conspiracy to overthrow the papal administration (1468) but Leto escaped serious punishment and the academy was revived under Sixtus IV. Leto's main influence was as a lecturer and as an example of how far enthusiasm for the ancient world would carry the humanists.

## Levita, Elias (Elijah Bachur) (1468–1549) *Jewish scholar, teacher, and lexicographer*
Levita was born at Neustadt, Bavaria, but migrated to Padua. In 1509, left destitute after Padua's failed revolt against Venice, he moved to Rome, where he lived for 13 years under the congenial protection of Cardinal Egidio di Viterbo, teaching him and others Hebrew and learning Greek himself. From this period date his Hebrew textbook *Bachur* ("Student"; 1518) and other grammatical works. Following the Sack of Rome (1527), Levita became a proof corrector for the Venetian printer Daniel Bomberg while

continuing his teaching: among his pupils and benefactors at this time was the French ambassador Georges de Selve (1509–41), who was later painted by HOLBEIN in the famous double portrait of *The Ambassadors. Masoreth ha-Masoreth* (1538), Levita's treatise on the "points" used in Hebrew Bibles, proving them to have been the invention of fifth-century CE Masoretic scholars, provoked hostility from orthodox Jews, who were already suspicious of his teaching Hebrew to Christians. After the closure of Bomberg's press, the German pastor and Hebraist Paul Fagius (1504–49) invited Levita to supervise his Hebrew printing press at Isny im Allgäu (1541–42). Among his later publications Levita produced dictionaries of the Targum (*Meturgeman*, 1541) and Talmudic and Midrashic words (*Tishbi*, 1542) and a German translation of the Psalms (1545). He eventually returned to Venice, where he died.

## Leyden (Leiden) 
A city in the Netherlands. Leyden grew up around a 12th-century castle. During the Renaissance period prosperity came to the city through the textile industry, which was first developed in the 14th century by weavers from Ypres and greatly expanded in the late 16th century by refugees from the Spanish-ruled parts of the Netherlands. During the revolt of the Netherlands Leyden bravely resisted a Spanish siege (May–October 1574) and was saved when the dykes were breached so that Dutch ships could bring supplies to the citizens across the flooded fields. In recognition of the city's heroism WILLIAM (I) THE SILENT founded the university of Leyden (1575) as a center for science, medicine, and reformed theology. The classical scholar Joseph SCALIGER held a chair at the university in the late 16th century and Arminius, leader of the REMONSTRANTS, became professor of theology there (1603; *see* ARMINIANISM). After 1580 the ELZEVIR PRESS made Leyden an important center of publishing. Van Goyen in 1596 and Rembrandt in 1609 were both born in Leyden. The PILGRIM FATHERS spent some years there before sailing for New England. Landmarks from the Renaissance period include the 15th-century Hooglandse Kerk, the botanic gardens (1587), and the Gemeenlandshuis van Rijn (1596).

## Leyden, John of See ANABAPTISTS

## Leyden, Lucas van See LUCAS VAN LEYDEN

## L'Hôpital, Michel de (1507–1573) *French lawyer*
He became councillor of the *parlement* of Paris (1537), HENRY II's envoy to the Council of TRENT (1547), master of requests, responsible for petitions to the king (1553), president of the *chambre des comptes* (1555), and chancellor of France (1560–68). As chancellor he worked for judicial reform and joined the moderate Catholics (*politiques*) in their search for a compromise to end religious conflict. He was the author of impressive presenta-

tions of the case for religious toleration. With the resumption of the Wars of RELIGION in 1567 CATHERINE DE' MEDICI lost confidence in L'Hôpital and his policy of religious toleration, so he retired to his estates and wrote. His *Epistolarum seu sermonum libri VI* appeared posthumously (1585).

## Libavius, Andreas (c. 1560–1616) *German chemist*
Born at Halle, the son of a weaver, Libavius studied at Jena university, then worked initially as a doctor. From 1588, however, he was a teacher of history and literature, first at Jena, and thereafter at Rothenburg (1591–1607) and Coburg (1607–16). A prolific writer and controversialist, he is best known for his *Alchemia* (1597; expanded edition, entitled *Alchymia*, 1606), a work often described as the first recognizable textbook of modern chemistry. A convinced Lutheran, Libavius sought to rescue the theory and practice of the chemical art, as understood in his day, from both the magical and mystical approach of the followers of PARACELSUS and the overtly Calvinistic program of RAMUS and to establish it as a distinct educational discipline. Though of little interest theoretically, the *Alchemia*, with over 200 illustrations, is a prime source for the organization of the 16th-century chemical laboratory.

Further reading: Owen Hannaway, *The Chemists and the Word: The Didactic Origins of Chemistry* (Baltimore, Md. and London: Johns Hopkins University Press, 1975).

## liberal arts
Those arts which, according to a classification made first in antiquity, were worthy of study by a free (Latin *liber*) man. In contrast with the *artes liberales* were the *artes vulgares* (or *artes sordidae*); this roughly corresponded with the distinction between intellectual occupations and those for which slaves or trained performers were engaged. The system was further refined in the early Middle Ages by Boethius (died 524), who divided the liberal arts into the *trivium* (grammar, RHETORIC, and logic) and *quadrivium* (astronomy, geometry, music, and arithmetic). It should be noted that music featured among the liberal arts purely in its theoretical form, musical performance being in the sphere of the vulgar arts. The *trivium* and *quadrivium*, together with philosophy, underpinned the entire medieval educational system. In practice the subjects often covered a wider range of topics than their names now suggest; for instance, geography was often included under geometry and some study of literature would be part of the grammar course.

The exclusion of the arts of painting and sculpture from the liberal arts category resulted in the artist's being held in low esteem. LEONARDO DA VINCI was one of the earliest to protest against this perception of the artist as a "mere" artisan; he and MICHELANGELO led the way in winning proper recognition of the great artist's creative powers and raising the status of the arts of *disegno*. One reason for the enthusiasm with which the study of PERSPECTIVE

and proportion was pursued was that it provided the visual arts with a theoretical basis and so made them a respectable intellectual subject, like music in the medieval schools.

The liberal arts themselves were often personified during the Middle Ages, following the lead of the fifth-century CE poet Martianus Capella. They were depicted as seven ladies, each holding an identifying attribute, and often accompanied by an eminent practitioner of the art they represent, for example, Pythagoras accompanying Geometry. The full scheme can be seen in the frescoes of the Spanish chapel of Sta. Maria Novella, Florence, executed in about 1355 by Andrea da Firenze and depicting the triumph of St. Thomas Aquinas. Later artists also used and sometimes expanded on the scheme. AGOSTINO DI DUCCIO combined the liberal arts with the Muses in his program of reliefs for the TEMPIO MALATESTIANO. PINTURICCHIO's decorations in the Appartamento Borgia in the Vatican (1492–95) depict the seven liberal arts enthroned and attended by groups of their adherents. They also appear, with the addition of Philosophy, Theology, and "Prospettiva," on the bronze reliefs on the tomb of Sixtus IV (1493; now Museo Storico Artistico, St. Peter's, Rome) by Antonio del POLLAIUOLO.

## Liberale, Antonio (Liberale da Verona) (c. 1445–c. 1526) *Italian miniaturist and painter*
Liberale was born in Verona, trained as a book illuminator, and spent about a decade from the late 1460s illustrating liturgical books at Monte Oliveto Maggiore, near Siena, and in Siena itself. Some of his exquisite work in this genre, together with that of Girolamo da Cremona, by whom he was influenced, is housed in the cathedral (Piccolomini) library, Siena, and the techniques of the miniaturist are visible even in his large-scale paintings. Liberale also worked in Florence and Venice, but by 1488 was back in Verona. His *Madonna with Saints* (1489; Berlin) initiated a series of religious paintings that confirmed his standing as a major representative of the Veronese school. His Munich *Pietà* is possibly his most impressive work. Other paintings are still to be found in Verona, including an *Adoration of the Magi* (1490; Duomo). His sensitivity to the decorative qualities of architecture is apparent in his *St. Sebastian* (Brera, Milan), set against the backdrop of a Venetian canal, and in his *Dido on the Pyre* (National Gallery, London).

## libraries
In the early Renaissance period collections of MANUSCRIPTS owned by princes, monasteries, cathedrals, universities, or private individuals were not a new phenomenon; however, until the second half of the 15th century the quantity of books in circulation was necessarily limited by the means of production, as was the number of people able to afford them. Aristocratic collections tended to focus on subjects that enhanced dynastic or family pres-

tige: PHILIP THE GOOD of Burgundy, for instance, believing he could trace his descent from the Trojans, owned no fewer than 17 manuscripts that supported this claim. Princely collections also often included handsomely illustrated manuscripts of historical and romance material in verse or prose, written in the vernacular and used for public reading aloud.

In the Middle Ages the scriptoria where manuscripts were copied were attached to monasteries, and their output was overwhelmingly ecclesiastical and theological and therefore in Latin. Since the earliest days of Western monasticism a library was considered an essential part of a monastery, and the rule of St. Benedict stated that monks were to borrow the monastery's books for their personal reading. Inventories and catalogues of library holdings were regularly compiled; for instance, around 1400, a Benedictine monk catalogued the libraries of nearly 200 religious houses in England and Scotland. John LELAND's notes made during his visitation of the religious houses in 1539–45 record the state of the English monastic libraries immediately before the DISSOLUTION OF THE MONASTERIES. Predictable mainstays of monastic libraries were glossed Bibles and the works of the Latin Church Fathers; books of saints' lives, other theological works, and occasional classical texts are also recorded; monasteries also made numerous copies of service-books for everyday use by the monks but these were often kept handy for the church, rather than in the main collection. The great Bibles and liturgical manuscripts with their magnificent illuminations were always hugely expensive prestige products, and the most that individuals of modest means could hope to own was a book of hours to enable them to follow the Church's cycle of devotions (although books of hours could themselves be richly decorated for wealthy patrons, such as Jean, Duc de Berry (1340–1416), who commissioned the famous Très Riches Heures).

While the embryo universities did not themselves immediately start to form libraries, their individual teachers and students undoubtedly did, generating a demand for textbooks in the subjects being taught: theology, astronomy, philosophy, canon and civil law, mathematics, and medicine. This in turn led to the secularization of the scriptoria and the beginnings of a BOOK TRADE in cities such as Paris, Bologna and Oxford. Library lists compiled for universities and colleges are invaluable sources of information for the late medieval and early modern period but need to be used with care as their survival has often been a matter of chance and they certainly do not represent the whole picture. Bequests of books mentioned in the wills of individuals are another source of information on libraries, both private and public, and some institutions even made it a requirement that their members leave their books to them on their deaths. Colleges therefore tended to amass book collections more readily than the universities of which they were part; for instance, in 1363

the entire stock of books owned by the University of Cambridge appears to have been just five, but 19 years later Clare College received a bequest of 30 volumes from a certain Thomas de Lexham.

One of the earliest individual bibliophiles whose library had a definite humanist character was PETRARCH. His activities as a collector are well documented, and he was active in searching out copies of classical manuscripts in monastic and other libraries with the aim of assembling a complete set of Latin texts that had survived from antiquity. One of his coups (1345) was the discovery of a copy of CICERO's letters to Atticus in the chapter library at Verona. Over 40 of the manuscripts that Petrarch owned have survived, such as his copy of Virgil's *Aeneid* with the commentary by Servius; this is now in Milan's Bibliotheca AMBROSIANA, founded in 1609 as a public library.

Petrarch's friend BOCCACCIO followed his bibliophilic example; on his death his library was bequeathed to the convent of San Spirito in Florence. SALUTATI, BRUNI, and BRACCIOLINI were likewise avid collectors and assembled superb libraries. Niccolò NICCOLI's collection was purchased on his death by Cosimo de' MEDICI and became the basis of the Bibliotheca MARCIANA in Florence. All these men helped inspire the formation of the Medicis' own library (later the Bibliotheca LAURENZIANA). Vespasiano da BISTICCI also played a pivotal role as agent and bookseller. Major humanist collections were assembled for other princes in Italy and beyond, including the VISCONTI and SFORZA dukes of Milan, the ESTE in Ferrara, the GONZAGA in Mantua, the Aragonese rulers of Naples, King MATTHIAS CORVINUS of Hungary, and of course the papacy. From the mid-15th century collections of Greek manuscripts came to Italy with men such as Cardinal BESSARION, whose book-collecting habit had been formed among the great libraries of Constantinople, and it was his massive collection of manuscripts that became the nucleus of the Bibliotheca MARCIANA in Venice. In 1490–92 Lorenzo de' MEDICI ("the Magnificent") sent John Laskaris (1445–1535) on a manuscript foray in the Levant, from which he returned with around two hundred Greek manuscripts for the Medici library.

To house these and similar later collections appropriately major architects were commissioned to design prestigious and lavishly appointed buildings. A surviving example of a purpose-designed room for a ducal library is the wood-paneled studiolo of Federico da Montefeltro (1422–82) in the palace at Urbino, with elaborate *trompe l'oeil* intarsia work depicting cupboards in which the books were stored. In larger monastic or princely libraries the medieval system for keeping the books—in two ranks of reading desks ranged underneath windows at right angles to the walls, with a central aisle between them—was not immediately superseded. An example of this arrangement is the Bibliotheca Maletestiana at Cesena, near Rimini in Italy, a vaulted and aisled hall designed by Matteo

Nuti in 1447–52, which survives with its original furniture intact. Books were stored on shelves below or above the reading surface, chained to horizontal metal bars. Vestiges of this plan, with shelving and benches set at right angles to the walls on either side of windows, creating bays, can still be seen in older libraries; two Oxford examples are the library of Merton College, originally built 1373–78, but refurnished under Sir Henry SAVILE in the early 17th century and Duke Humfrey's Library in the BODLEIAN. Only in the last decade of the 16th century did great libraries, such as that of the ESCORIAL in Spain, begin to have their books housed in lofty shelving built flat against the walls.

Under the impetus of the new learning, enthusiasm for book collecting spread to northern Europe. The French invasion of Italy in 1494 saw the looting of the library of the king of Naples and Aragon, and CHARLES VIII took many hundreds of its volumes back with him to France. His successor, LOUIS XII, captured the Visconti and Sforza collections on his campaign in Italy (1499–1500), as well as using his great wealth to purchase other libraries and commission the production of magnificent manuscripts. FRANCIS I consolidated the French royal collection, shifting it from Blois to his new palace at FONTAINEBLEAU and appointing the great scholar Guillaume BUDÉ to the post of librarian.

Library holdings could be augmented not only by purchase, bequest, or looting, but also through dynastic alliances. In Austria MAXIMILIAN I acquired important manuscripts as part of the dowries of his two wives: Mary of Burgundy, whom he married in 1477, and Bianca Maria Sforza of Milan (1497). Maximilian did not keep his books in a single purpose-built library, preferring to store them in portable leather chests, but he did appoint a major humanist figure, Konrad CELTIS, as his librarian. It was in 1562, during the reign of Ferdinand I, that the nascent Hofbibliothek acquired, via an agent in Constantinople, the Codex Vindobonensis, the most magnificent of the manuscript HERBALS to have survived from late antiquity and one of the greatest bibliographical treasures of all time, containing the illustrated text of Dioscorides made in 512 for a Byzantine princess. However, it was not until the appointment of Hugo Blotius as librarian in 1575 that an attempt was made to impose more regularity on the records and operations of the imperial library.

With the advent of PRINTING, personal and institutional collections expanded apace, and new patterns of acquisition become discernible. While the purchasing power of royal patrons brought about the creation of prestigious libraries that form the core of modern national collections, the scholars who were at the forefront of the new learning accumulated impressive personal libraries of both manuscripts and printed books. Central to the humanist enterprise was the quest for good manuscripts of classical texts. When such collectors died their books often found their

way into university and, later, public libraries. From the early 16th century humanist interests began to be represented in academic libraries in addition to the standard medieval theological and legal texts. In England, for instance, Queens' College, Cambridge, bought the humanist library of Henry Bullock (died 1526), a friend of ERASMUS, and Bishop Cuthbert TUNSTALL donated books on Greek to the university. At Oxford the original statutes of Corpus Christi College, founded in 1517 by Bishop Richard Foxe (c. 1448–1528) to train the clergy in Greek and Hebrew as well as Latin, made provision for a library—the *trilinguis bibliotheca*—that Erasmus predicted would become a major attraction for scholars. Foxe wished the volumes to be accessible to the students, stipulating that only the most rare or valuable were to be chained, and his own generous donation of books formed the basis of the collection. The first library of the University of Oxford had been founded by Duke Humfrey of Gloucester (1391–1447), youngest son of King Henry IV and a noted patron of learning; refounded in 1598, it is now known as the Bodleian Library after its shrewd and generous benefactor Sir Thomas Bodley.

Among the northern European humanists who formed notable libraries, the Rhineland scholar Beatus RHENANUS was unusual in bequeathing his books to the parish church in his home town of Sélestat (between Strasbourg and Colmar); even more unusually, the collection, augmented by donations from Rhenanus's humanist associates, remains there. Housed in the Bibliothèque Humaniste, it is a monument to a thriving intellectual network of the first half of the 16th century. In the same period another major collection was assembled by the wealthy Nuremberg humanist Willibald PIRCKHEIMER; this library fetched up in England in the following century, having been bought by Thomas HOWARD, Earl of Arundel, in 1636 and presented by his son to the Royal Society.

See also: LITERACY

**Further reading:** Francis Ames-Lewis, *The Library and Manuscripts of Piero di Cosimo de' Medici* (New York: Garland, 1984); Albinia de la Mare and Richard W. Hunt, *Duke Humfrey and English Humanism in the Fifteenth Century* (Oxford, U.K.: Bodleian Library, 1970); Phyllis W. G. Gordon (transl.), *Two Renaissance Book-hunters: The Letters of Poggius Bracciolini to Nicolaus de Niccolis* (New York: Columbia University Press, 1974); Anthony Hobson, *Renaissance Book Collecting: Jean Grolier and Diego Hurtado de Mendoza, Their Books and Bindings* (Cambridge U.K.: Cambridge University Press, 1999); Lotte Labowsky, *Bessarion's Library and the Bibliotheca Marciana* (Rome: Edizioni di storia e letteratura, 1979); Konstantinos Sp. Staikos, *The Great Libraries from Antiquity to the Renaissance* (New Castle, Del.: Oak Knoll Press and London: British Library, 2000); Alan G. Thomas, *Great Books and Book Collectors* (London: Weidenfeld & Nicolson, 1975); Berthold L. Ullman and Philip A. Stadter, *The Public Li-*

brary of *Renaissance Florence: Niccolò Niccoli, Cosimo de' Medici and the Library of San Marco* (Padua, Italy: Antenore, 1972).

**Ligorio, Pirro** (c. 1500–1583) *Italian architect*
Born in Naples, Ligorio is best known for his work (1550–69) on the Villa d'Este at Tivoli, which he designed for his patron Cardinal Ippolito d'Este. Incorporating both landscape features and a terraced garden, Ligorio's plan shows the influence of both Bramante and Raphael and has survived largely intact. Ligorio also built (1558–62) the Casino in the Vatican gardens for Pope Pius IV, but was later dismissed as MICHELANGELO's successor at St. Peter's after altering Michelangelo's designs (1565). He was also known as a painter and an antiquarian, although he was suspected of forging certain Roman antiquities. Several of Ligorio's buildings were also adorned with stucco decorations by him, including the Casino in the Vatican.

**Ligozzi, Jacopo** (c. 1547–1626) *Italian painter*
Ligozzi was born in Verona but moved to Florence, where he became a court painter to the Medici (1575). In this role he painted scenes from Florentine history for the Palazzo Vecchio, Florence. His paintings in Ognissanti, Florence, show his characteristic use of warm color. He was also a fine draftsman, noted for his detailed pen drawings, some of which are in the Ashmolean Museum, Oxford.

**Lily, William** (c. 1468–1522) *English educationist*
Born at Odiham, Hampshire, Lily was the godson of William GROCYN. He entered Magdalen College, Oxford (1486), graduated there, and then traveled to Jerusalem, pausing on his return journey to study Greek and Latin in Italy. He was the friend of Sir Thomas MORE, with whom he collaborated in the translation of Greek epigrams into Latin elegiacs (*Progymnasmata*, 1518), and of John COLET, who appointed him first high-master of St. Paul's School, London (1512). His Latin syntax with rules in English, *Grammatices rudimenta*, was published with Colet's *Aeditio* in 1527, and in revised forms this volume was the standard Latin grammar in England for over two centuries.

**Linacre, Thomas** (c. 1460–1524) *English physician and humanist*
Linacre was born at Canterbury and educated at Oxford. He then spent several years in Italy, where he met many humanist scholars and studied Greek in Florence and medicine in Padua. To promote the revival of classical learning he translated works of Aristotle, Galen, and Proclus from Greek into Latin. He also published Latin grammars, one of which was reprinted some 50 times before the end of the 16th century. Linacre's own career was advanced through his service at court, first (1500–02) as tutor to Henry VII's eldest son, Arthur, and then as physician (from 1509) to HENRY VIII, and finally tutor (1523) to Princess Mary. Many eminent statesmen and scholars were among his patients and friends. His most lasting contribution remains, however, his foundation (1518) of the College of Physicians, forerunner of the Royal College of Physicians.

**lingua cortigiana** See ITALIAN LANGUAGE; QUESTIONE DELLA LINGUA

**Linschoten, Jan Huyghen van** (1563–1611) *Dutch traveler and author*
A native of Haarlem, Linschoten is famous for his epic journey to India (1583–88) as clerk to the archbishop of Goa, during which he gathered information about the lands bordering the Indian and western Pacific oceans. This was published in his *Itinerario* (1595–96), which combines his personal observations with material obtained from others. The drawings illustrating his work are among the earliest accurate depictions of Asian lands and peoples to reach a European readership. He also made a two-year stay (1589–91) in the Azores following a shipwreck, and while at Flores he collected first-hand evidence of the battle there between England and Spain in 1591 involving Sir Richard Grenville of the *Revenge*. Later he played a major role in promoting Holland's search for a NORTHEAST PASSAGE, accompanying Willem BARENTS on his second voyage (1595), which he described in his *Journalen* (1601). He died at Enkhuizen.

The Linschoten-Vereeniging, founded in 1908 to publish Dutch travel accounts, is named in honor of him.

**Further reading:** Charles McKew Parr, *Jan van Linschoten: The Dutch Marco Polo* (New York: Crowell, 1964); Ernst Van Den Boogaart, *Civil and Corrupt Asia: Image and Text in the* Itinerario *and* Icones *of Jan Huygen van Linschoten* (Chicago, Ill.: University of Chicago Press, 2003).

**Lippi, Filippino** (1457/58–1504) *Italian painter*
The son of Fra Filippo LIPPI, by whom he was trained in Spoleto, Filippino was born at Prato and moved at the age of 12, after his father's death, to Florence. There he became the pupil of BOTTICELLI, whose influence is evident in early paintings attributed to him. He was commissioned to paint the *Annunciation* on two tondi in San Gimignano (now in the Pinacoteca there) in 1483 and then received a major commission in 1484 to complete the frescoes alongside those of MASACCIO in the Brancacci chapel of Sta. Maria del Carmine, Florence. The *Vision of St. Bernard* (1486; Badia, Florence) is generally considered his masterpiece.

Filippino's frescoes in the Strozzi chapel in Sta. Maria Novella illustrate his later style and his interest in classical art. In 1488 he went to Rome where he decorated the Caraffa chapel in Sta. Maria sopra Minerva. His popularity was then at its height and he was asked to replace the *Ado-*

*ration of the Magi* (completed 1496; Uffizi, Florence), which LEONARDO DA VINCI had begun in 1481 for the monks of San Donato a Scopeto near Florence and had left unfinished. During his last years in Rome he painted many panels and was able to study antique remains. As a result of this all his paintings included fragments of antiquity, brought in entirely for their own sake.

**Lippi, Filippo** (c. 1406–1469) *Italian painter*
Lippi was an orphan and became a Carmelite monk in his native Florence at the age of eight, taking orders in 1421. His earliest works, the damaged fresco of the *Relaxation of the Carmelite Rule* in the cloister of Sta. Maria del Carmine (c. 1432), is heavily influenced by MASACCIO's bold three-dimensional style, suggesting that he was indeed the pupil of Masaccio, who was painting the Brancacci chapel in the same Florentine church during the 1420s.

Filippo Lippi's first important work, the Tarquinia *Madonna* (1437), shows a lessening of this influence and an interest in DONATELLO and Flemish painting. In the Barbadori altarpiece (Louvre, Paris), also begun in 1437, with its complicated composition and decorative features there is almost none of Masaccio. In about 1438 he painted the *Annunciation* in San Lorenzo, Florence, remarkable at the time for its careful composition and use of perspective. In 1442 Filippo Lippi became the rector and abbot of the parish of San Quirico at Legnaia near Florence. Among other paintings during this period was the Bartolini tondo, a *Madonna and Child with Scenes from the Life of the Virgin* (1452; Palazzo Pitti, Florence), which shows his mastery of spatial organization.

The frescoes in the cathedral at Prato, begun in 1452 and completed 12 years later, are generally considered his finest achievement. They showed a revival of interest in Gothic features, using a Gothic landscape and an increasingly dramatic style which included several events in one area of space. In 1456 while chaplain at the convent of Sta. Margherita, where he painted a large altarpiece, he met the nun, Lucrezia Buti, who became the mother of his son, Filippino LIPPI; she is supposed to have been the model for Salome in the *Banquet of Herod* fresco in Prato cathedral. In his later years he painted several beautiful *Nativities*, notably the Uffizi *Madonna and Child*, set in landscapes filled with gold light, full of religious feeling, and more poetic than his early works. His last work was at Spoleto cathedral, where he went with his son in 1466 to paint frescoes. This cycle of scenes from the life of the Virgin, culminating in a dramatic *Coronation of the Virgin*, was unfinished at his death and completed by pupils and assistants. As well as influencing 15th-century artists such as BOTTICELLI, who was his pupil, the style that Lippi developed served as an inspiration for the Pre-Raphaelites in the 19th century.

**Further reading:** Megan Holmes, *Fra Filippo Lippi: The Carmelite Painter* (New Haven, Conn.: Yale University Press, 1999); Jeffrey Ruda, *Filippo Lippi Studies: Naturalism, Style, and Iconography in Early Renaissance Art* (New York: Garland, 1982): ~*Fra Filippo Lippi: Life and Work, with a Complete Catalogue* (New York and London: Harry N. Abrams, 1993).

**Lipsius, Justus** (1547–1606) *Netherlands scholar and teacher*
Born at Issche, Lipsius was educated at the Catholic university of Louvain and then went to Italy as secretary to Cardinal GRANVELLE. Returning via Vienna, he then taught at the Lutheran university of Jena, where he became a Lutheran. He married a Catholic and returned to lecture at Louvain. In 1579 he accepted an invitation to the Calvinist university of Leyden, where he was professor of Roman history for 12 years. He then reverted to Catholicism and spent the last 14 years of his life teaching at Louvain, where he died. His major editions of TACITUS (1574; second edition, 1600) and SENECA (1605), combine critical insight with wide knowledge of Roman social and political history. His much admired and translated *De Constantia* (1584) advocates a Christianized form of the ancient philosophy of Stoicism on which he was an acknowledged expert. RUBENS was an admirer of Lipsius and painted a posthumous portrait of him with three disciples, one of whom was Rubens himself, around a table overlooked by a bust of Seneca (c. 1612; Palazzo Pitti, Florence).

**literacy** The dictionary definition of literacy as the ability to read and write has been interpreted in various ways when dealing with early modern European societies. A distinction was drawn in medieval Europe between the literate who knew Latin and the illiterate who did not. This criterion became increasingly irrelevant for practical purposes as reading and writing skills spread among the lay nobility and the mercantile classes and individual vernacular languages attained respectability as a literary medium.

For social historians, the ability to sign one's name on a legal document is an often-used indicator of basic literacy since it is the only one consistently available—though of course it is not unproblematical, as the signatory could have acquired the knack by mere copying, and there is no guarantee that such a person would have been able to read. However, where there is evidence of elementary schools to which the children of merchants and artisans could be sent it is clear that both reading and writing were taught. These could be supplemented by the basic arithmetical skills necessary for commerce and the carrying on of a trade. Another useful indicator of literacy is ownership of books attested in wills of the period. This too has to be used with some caution, as possession of a book of hours does not necessarily mean the practice of more mundane literate skills. However, ownership of a vernacular book of devotion or self-improvement strongly suggests that the owner was in a position to read it, and among Protestants too poor to possess more than just one book a Bible in the vernacular was the popular choice.

The Renaissance is generally seen as a period in which literacy rapidly expanded across society as the new technology of PRINTING enabled books to move out of the exclusive enclaves of the Church, universities, and aristocracy. Although this general impression is correct, with book-ownership growing steadily over the period, historians have shown that the impact was patchy, with more townspeople literate than country dwellers, and more men than women; for instance, Natalie Zemon Davis quotes a survey of documents from Lyons dating from the 1560s and 1570s which suggests that even in a prosperous and sophisticated city only 28% of women were able to sign their names: almost all of those belonged to families of the city's mercantile elite (*Society and Culture in Early Modern France*, Stanford, 1975).

The reformers' emphasis on personal access to the Scriptures for the laity was undoubtedly a factor in the establishment of elementary schools where children of all social classes could be taught to read. In England the DISSOLUTION OF THE MONASTERIES closed one point of access to education but the disappearance of monastic schools was often balanced by the foundation of new grammar schools in the 1540s. Arrangements for teaching young children (age eight and under) were often informal and transient: four or five boys and girls under the tuition of the local vicar or of a woman teacher in her own house. Literacy for non-noble women was considered in theory a fine thing, provided it enabled them to function better in their sphere of household management and child rearing; in practice when a woman's reading of the Bible led her to address theological questions on her own account male Protestant theologians were generally as alarmed and dismissive as their predecessors of the unreformed Church.

See also: BIBLE, TRANSLATIONS OF; EDUCATION; VERNACULAR

Further reading: Paul F. Grendler, *Schooling in Renaissance Italy: Literacy and Learning 1300–1600* (Baltimore, Md.: Johns Hopkins University Press, 1991).

**Little Masters (of Nuremberg)** A group of 16th-century engravers, influenced by DÜRER, whose work was mainly on a small scale. The English phrase translates the German *Kleinmeister*, which would more informatively be rendered "masters in little." Hans Sebald Beham (1500–50) and his brother Bartel (1502–40) were foremost in the group, which also included Georg Pencz (c. 1500–50), Jakob Binck (died c. 1569) and Heinrich ALDEGREVER. Their characteristic work was small, finely worked illustrations of biblical, mythological, and historical scenes, with a strong decorative interest.

**liturgy** The term "liturgy" refers to a Church's public, communal worship (as opposed to private devotions), and more particularly to the Eucharistic service. The Roman Catholic MASS in pre-Reformation Europe was not a monolithic entity—for instance, there were local variants (called "uses" or "rites") associated with local saints and traditions—but there was nonetheless a degree of uniformity throughout Western Christendom. In Britain, the form of the rite used in the cathedral of Salisbury ("the Use of Sarum") had been gradually adopted by other dioceses, so that by the mid-15th century it was in widespread use in England, Wales, and Ireland. For much of the Middle Ages, unifying factors included: use of a single liturgical language (Latin); the weight of Church authority backing the core doctrines (such as TRANSUBSTANTIATION) embodied in the ritual; and general practices such as the laity receiving communion in one kind only (that is, the consecrated bread, with the consecrated wine being taken by the celebrant alone). All these were challenged and rejected by the reformers.

The use of Latin in church services was an early target of the reforming drive to wrest the monopoly in divine matters from the priesthood. Belief in an individual's right to study and reflect on the Bible and theological issues opened up the possibility—and desirability—of conducting Mass in the vernacular. Latin's supremacy as the lingua franca of the Church was already being challenged in the late 15th century, when, from 1480, the business of the papal Curia began to be conducted in Italian, and in the course of the following century its hold continued to be loosened. The HUGUENOTS in particular were enthusiastic supporters of the use of French in all religious contexts.

The extremist early reformer Andreas CARLSTADT made a comprehensive attack on the traditional Catholic liturgy in 1521, when he conducted a vernacular Christmas Day Mass in which the Host was not elevated, VESTMENTS were not worn, and the laity communicated in both kinds. The issue of the elevation of the Host (the lifting up of the consecrated bread to display it to the people for their veneration) is an example of a practice that became immensely contentious; in 16th-century England it was one of the touchstones by which priests who covertly sympathized with Catholic traditions were distinguished from true reforming clergy, and both parishioners and Church authorities avidly monitored such indicators of priests' allegiance. Similarly, the character of the vestments worn at services was another visible pointer to the thoroughness or otherwise of a reforming dispensation, a fact not lost on Calvinistically inclined critics of the ELIZABETHAN SETTLEMENT.

LUTHER's denunciation of the Roman Catholic doctrine of Purgatory entailed the reformers' rejection of a whole subtype of liturgy, the Mass for the Dead. Otherwise Luther was cautious in promoting liturgical change—even to the extent of not hastening to jettison Latin—and in largely retaining the sacramental and ceremonial character of the Mass. CALVIN's innovations were much more drastic, emphasizing the ministry of the word (PREACHING and Bible readings) over that of the sacraments and encouraging congregational psalm-singing by men and women together—a practice considered scandalous by Catholics.

The impact of both Lutheranism and Calvinism on the music of public worship was profound. The trained choirs and other musical resources of medieval cathedrals and monasteries were mainly lost in the regions where the Reformation took hold, but new developments compensated for the loss. Luther himself led the way in the writing of new vernacular hymns to be sung by the congregation (*see* HYMNODY). French, Swiss, English, and Scottish adherents of Calvin disliked the use of nonscriptural texts in worship and so promoted the composition of metrical psalms in their respective vernaculars (*see* PSALMODY).

**Livy (Titus Livius)** (59 BCE–17 CE) *Roman historian*
Livy was born at Patavium (Padua), but spent much of his adult life in Rome, where he was befriended by Augustus. He wrote the history of Rome *Ab urbe condita* (from the foundation of the city) in 142 books, of which only books 1–10 and 21–45 survived complete into the Middle Ages and so down to the present. The whole work was divided into "decads" of 10 books, and the contents of the incomplete or missing decads are known from summaries.

Livy's patriotism, idealization of the Roman republic, and flair for description of characters and events recommended him first to PETRARCH, who compiled from separate manuscripts a text that brought together almost all the surviving parts of Livy's work. Lorenzo VALLA emended the text (1448) and the first printed edition appeared at Rome in about 1469. Livy's appeal to students of statecraft received its greatest tribute in MACHIAVELLI's *Discorsi della prima deca di Tito Livio*. Despite charges of Patavinity (stylistic provincialisms), Livy was the acknowledged model for Renaissance historians until supplanted in the later 16th century by TACITUS.

**L'Obel, Matthias de (Matthias de Lobel, Lobelius)** (1538–1616) *French botanist*
L'Obel was born in Lille and studied at Montpellier under Guillaume RONDELET, who at his death (1566) left him all his papers. L'Obel moved to London with a fellow-student from Montpellier, Pierre Pena, where they published *Stirpium Adversaria Nova* (1570–71), and L'Obel was put in charge of Lord Zouche's physic garden. The printer Christophe PLANTIN enlarged and republished Pena's and L'Obel's book as *Nova Stirpium Adversaria* (1576), following it with *Plantarum seu Stirpium Icones* (1581); this was illustrated by over 2,000 woodcuts arranged by L'Obel according to his system of plant classification by the characteristics of a plant's leaves. L'Obel was William the Silent's

personal physician (1581–84), and after the latter's assassination moved to Antwerp before a final move back to England, where he was appointed (1607) James I's royal botanist (*Botanicus Regius*). He is commemorated in the plant genus name *Lobelia*.

**Lodewycksz., Willem** (before 1565–1604) *Dutch merchant*
His date and place of birth are unknown. He sailed as a merchant with the first Dutch fleet to attempt the Portuguese sea route to Asia (1595–97). Lodewyckz. gathered a great deal of material during their stay on Java, and on his return published anonymously his *Historie van Indien* (1598); illustrated with over 50 engravings after his own sketches and immediately translated into Latin and French, the book was an important source of information on the East Indies. Lodewycksz. later commanded a fleet to the Guinea Coast (1598–99) and then sailed again for the East (1603), but died on the voyage.

**Lodge, Thomas** (1558–1625) *English author and physician*
A Londoner by birth, Lodge attended the Merchant Taylors' School there before going to Oxford and then studying law. Samuel DANIEL, Michael DRAYTON, and Robert GREENE were among his literary friends. Lodge attempted several genres: literary controversy in his *Defence of Plays* (1580) against Stephen Gosson's *Schoole of Abuse* (1579); social criticism in *An Alarum against Usurers* (1584); verse romance in *Scillaes Metamorphosis* (1589; reissued as *Glaucus and Scilla*, 1610); pastoral romance in *Rosalynde, Euphues Golden Legacie* (1590), which was a successful exercise in EUPHUISM and was dramatized by Shakespeare in *As You Like It*; poetry in *Phillis* (1593); the play *The Wounds of Civill War* (1594); and satire in *A Fig for Momus* (1595). He twice made long voyages, to the Canaries in 1585 and to South America in 1591–93; the latter resulted in *A Margarite of America* (1596). Around this time he converted to Roman Catholicism and began to study medicine, which he practiced successfully in London from 1600. Apart from *A Treatise of the Plague* (1603), Lodge's later works are translations: of the Jewish historian Josephus (1602), SENECA (1614), and DU BARTAS (1625).

**Lodi, Peace of** A peace agreement signed at Lodi, near Milan, between Milan and Venice in 1454. Later the same year this was extended into a mutual nonaggression pact to which Florence and, early in 1455, the papacy and Naples also became parties. Despite periods of tension, such as that arising from papal involvement in the PAZZI CONSPIRACY, these five principal Italian powers in the main kept the peace among themselves and their adherents until the outbreak of generalized turmoil occasioned by the French invasion of 1494 (*see* ITALY, WARS OF).

**Lollards** A derogatory name for the English followers of John WYCLIF; first recorded in 1382, it is thought to derive from a word meaning "chanter" or "mumbler" (of prayers).

Initially, Lollardy was an elite movement among a small group of Oxford scholars who shared Wyclif's radical religious ideas. However, the Oxford Lollards were suppressed in 1381–82, when Wyclif's views were publicly condemned and his followers either fled or recanted. Although this deprived Lollardy of intellectual leadership, a simplified, populist version of Wyclif's teaching soon found a wider audience, mainly through the activities of unlicenced preachers. Henceforth, Lollardy would be chiefly associated with semiliterate traders and artisans, although it also found adherents among the gentry and the lower clergy.

At the heart of Lollard teaching was the insistence on the Bible as sole authority in matters of faith. From this it followed that everyone should have the right to read the Scriptures in his own language, and to interpret and expound them by the light of conscience. The first English translation of the Bible as a whole (the so-called Lollard Bible) was begun under Wyclif's aegis in the 1380s and completed by about 1396 (see BIBLE, TRANSLATIONS OF). On the basis of their reading of the Scriptures, Lollards attacked both the great wealth of the Church and many accepted teachings, notably those concerning papal authority, monasticism, clerical celibacy, pilgrimages, and TRANSUBSTANTIATION.

These points all appear in the most comprehensive statement of Lollard teaching, the so-called "Twelve Conclusions" delivered to Parliament in 1395. By this time, however, official attitudes to heresy were hardening. In 1401 William Sawtrey, a Norfolk priest, became the first Lollard martyr when he was burned at the stake; legislation making this the standard punishment for heresy was enacted later in the year. At this point, many Lollards either recanted or fell silent. The movement was finally driven underground when a Lollard uprising led by the accused heretic Sir John Oldcastle (c. 1378–1417) was crushed, with great severity, in 1414. After a further abortive uprising in 1431, Lollardy effectively vanished from public life, although there is evidence of its survival among the poorer classes. The question of the Lollards' wider influence on English religious history is much debated. While some historians argue that the Lollard tradition made England more receptive to the ideas of the Continental reformers after 1530, others regard any such link with skepticism.

**Further reading:** Margaret Aston, *Lollards and Reformers* (London: Hambledon, 1985; repr. 2003); Arthur G. Dickens, *Lollards and Protestants in the Diocese of York, 1509–1558* (London: University of Hull, 1959; repr. Hambledon, 1982); Fiona Somerset (ed.), *The Lollards and Their Influence in Late Medieval England* (Woodbridge, U.K.: Boydell & Brewer, 2003).

**Lomazzo, Giovanni Paolo** (1538–1600) *Italian painter and art theoretician*
Lomazzo was born in Milan and trained as a painter under Gaudenzio FERRARI, but at the age of 33 he went blind. He therefore turned to writing on the theory of art. His first major work was *Trattato dell'arte de la pittura* (1584), which was widely used as a handbook for over 200 years after his death. The work is in seven parts, dealing with proportion, movement, color, light, perspective, technique, and history. In 1587 his *Rime* was published, together with an autobiography and in 1590 the Neoplatonic *Idea del tempio della pittura*. His writings can be considered to represent the outlook and ideas of the later mannerists (*see* MANNERISM), particularly the renunciation of the belief in nature as the source of all beauty.

**Lombard, Lambert** (1506–1566) *Netherlands painter, architect, and art theorist*
A pupil of Jean Demeuse at his birthplace, Liège, Lombard subsequently studied under Arnold de Beer at Antwerp and Jan GOSSAERT at Middelburg. In 1537–38/39 he visited Italy, principally Rome, and he is also reputed to have visited Germany and France. Only a very small number of paintings can be attributed to him with certainty, and many have been lost, but he executed a considerable number of drawings, nearly 70 of which were engraved by Hieronymus Cock. The latter reveal his figural style to have been conditioned largely by a study of classical and contemporary Italian sculpture.

Lombard's chief significance was as an educator. In 1565 he sent VASARI details about northern artists and requested in return sketches of Italian Trecento paintings for comparison with northern stained glass. His students included Frans FLORIS and the Antwerp painter Willem Key (1515–68). Long after his death, Lombard was praised by Carel van MANDER as "a father of our art of drawing and painting."

**Lombardo family** A family of sculptors and architects, originally from Lombardy, who established a major workshop in Venice during the 15th and 16th centuries. Pietro (c. 1435–1515), born at Carona the son of the architect Martino, was the most important member of the family. He executed monuments in Padua, for example that of GATTAMELATA's son Giannantonio (died 1455) in Il Santo, before moving to Venice in about 1467. His Venetian sculptures included the monuments of Doge Pasquale Malipiero (died 1462), of Doge Pietro Mocenigo (died 1476), and of Doge Niccolò Marcello (died 1474) in the church of SS. Giovanni e Paolo, as well as the church of Sta. Maria dei Miracoli (1481–89), on which he worked as both architect and sculptor. Other works by Pietro included the effigy and tomb of Dante in Ravenna (1482), the Zanetti tomb in Treviso cathedral (1485), and the Palazzo Vendramin-Calerghi on the Grand Canal in Venice, which he completed (c. 1500–09) to designs by Mauro CODUSSI.

Pietro's sons Tullio (c. 1460–1532) and Antonio (c. 1458–c. 1516) assisted their father in his workshop and were much influenced by classical models, as seen in such works as their decoration of Sta. Maria dei Miracoli. Among Tullio's best works are the tombs of Doge Giovanni Mocenigo (died 1485) and Doge Antonio Vendramin (died 1478) in SS. Giovanni e Paolo, Venice, the effigy of Guidarello Guidarelli (1525; Accademia, Ravenna), and reliefs of classical subjects such as the marble panel with busts of Bacchus and Ariadne in the Kunsthistorisches Museum, Vienna. Antonio worked with his brother on reliefs depicting the miracles of St. Anthony for Il Santo, Padua, and worked independently (1506–16) on reliefs of mythological subjects (now mainly in St. Petersburg) to decorate the Camerini d'Alabastro in Alfonso I d'Este's Castello at Ferrara. Antonio's sons, Aurelio (1501–63), Girolamo (c. 1504–c. 1590), and Lodovico (c. 1507–75) were also active as sculptors.

**London** The capital city and port on the River Thames in southeast England. By the Renaissance period London included the two cities of London and Westminster, the buildings in the two-mile gap between the cities, the surrounding areas, and the areas south of the river that were linked to the cities by a single stone bridge, London Bridge. A Roman administrative center from the first century CE, the City of London declined in importance during the Saxon period although it was the site of the first St. Paul's cathedral (founded 597). The importance of the City of London was firmly established by the Norman rulers in the 11th and 12th centuries. The City of Westminster was important from the reign of Edward the Confessor (1042–66), when Westminster became the royal capital and Westminster Abbey was consecrated (1065).

In the 14th and 15th centuries Westminster was an administrative center, the home of parliament, the royal court, and the law courts. In 1476 William CAXTON set up England's first movable type printing press at Westminster. The City of London was the commercial and trading capital of England with great fairs and markets (such as the Corn Exchange, Leadenhall, and Billingsgate), busy docks, flourishing silk, pottery, and glass industries, and energetic mercantile communities of Danes, Dutch, Gascons, Germans, and Italians.

During the 16th century the capital expanded rapidly. Between 1530 and 1600 the City of London's population grew from 25,000 to 75,000; by the early 17th century the population of the two cities and surrounding areas was close on 250,000, probably the largest center of population in Europe. Notable 16th-century developments in-clude the development of London's commerce with the building of Gresham's Royal Exchange (1567) and the formation of such great trading companies as the MUSCOVY COMPANY (1552), the Turkey Company (1581), and the EAST INDIA COMPANY (1600).

Sixteenth-century London was externally transformed by the use of bricks in housing and by the conversion of York Place to the royal palace of Whitehall from 1529. The later 16th and earlier 17th centuries were the period of the great literary age of England, and London became a European center of culture. Most of the City of London's notable Renaissance buildings were destroyed by the Great Fire (1666).

**Further reading:** Stephen Inwood, *A History of London* (Berkeley, Calif.: Publishers Group West, 1999); Roy Porter, *London: A Social History* (Cambridge, Mass.: Harvard University Press, 1995).

**Lope de Vega** See VEGA CARPIO, LOPE FÉLIX DE

**López de Ayala, Pedro** ("El Canciller") (1332–1407) *Spanish chronicler and poet*
A member of a distinguished noble family, he was born at Vitoria, Castile, and played a prominent role at the court of Peter (I) the Cruel (1350–69), and under the succeeding Trastámara kings, Henry II, John I, and Henry III. His nickname derives from his appointment as chancellor of the realm (1399). During this period of unrest, foreign powers took part in the dynastic struggles of Castile, and Ayala was twice taken prisoner of war: briefly by the Black Prince (the English had invaded to support Peter I) and in 1385 for two years by the Portuguese. His work as official historian, the *Crónicas* (completed 1393; published 1526), cover the years 1350–90. They contain remarkably objective first-hand accounts recorded with a clarity Ayala learned from translating LIVY. The verse miscellany, *El rimado de palaçio* (1385–1407) begun during his captivity in Portugal, is penitential in tone, with satirical passages on a courtier's life. It contains a confession, an attack on contemporary corruption, a "mirror for princes" section, and concludes with an adaptation of Gregory the Great's *Moralia* on the Book of Job. It is the last example of the medieval stanzaic form known as *cuaderna vía*, though Ayala also used the new meter, the ARTE MAYOR. Ayala also translated Boethius, Isidore of Seville, and Boccaccio's *De casibus virorum illustrium* (as *Cayda de príncipes*).

**Lorenzetti, Ambrogio** (fl. 1319–1347) *Italian painter*
Brother of Pietro LORENZETTI, Ambrogio formed in style a link between the schools of his native Siena and Florence, extending a trend towards realistic narration and emotional intensity. Although probably a pupil of DUCCIO in Siena he also worked periodically in Florence between 1318 and 1332 and was a member of the painters' guild in Florence in 1324. In much of his work therefore the pre-

dominant influence is that of GIOTTO. His earliest dated work, the *Madonna and Child* (1319) at Vico l'Abate, near Florence, illustrates this influence and also that of the contemporary sculptor Giovanni PISANO. His most important works are the frescoes of *Good and Bad Government* in the Palazzo Pubblico of Siena (1337–39). Those representing good government in the town and in the country are noted respectively for the unusually accurate perspective for that time and for the exceptionally evocative representation of a landscape. Ambrogio's *Presentation in the Temple* (1342; Uffizi, Florence) again illustrates a realism and use of perspective considered to be 100 years ahead of their time. Other important panel paintings are scenes from the legend of St. Nicholas of Bari (1327–32; Uffizi) and *Madonnas* and an *Annunciation* (1344) in the Pinacoteca in Siena. It is thought that Ambrogio may have died in the plague of 1348.

**Lorenzetti, Pietro** (fl. 1305–1345) *Italian painter*
Like his brother Ambrogio LORENZETTI, Pietro was Sienese born and was influenced by the schools of both Siena and Florence. His work was similarly concerned with emotional expression and realism of form. His earliest dated painting, the polyptych in the parish church (Pieve) at Arezzo (1320), shows an already mature style but more influenced by DUCCIO than Ambrogio's works are. Of his frescoes those at the lower church of San Francesco, Assisi, are the most important, illustrating the influence of GIOTTO in their expressive simplicity. Among his paintings the altarpiece from the Carmine in Siena (1329) and *The Birth of the Virgin* (1342), both in the Museo dell' Opera, Siena, are the best known and demonstrate his narrative power.

**Lorenzo Monaco** (c. 1370–c. 1425) *Italian artist*
A native of Siena, Lorenzo settled in Florence where he entered the monastery of Sta. Maria degli Angeli (1391). His early works were influenced by Agnolo GADDI and include several altarpieces, notably two versions of the *Coronation of the Virgin* (1414), one in the Uffizi, Florence, and the other in the National Gallery, London. The decorative and naturalistic style of his early works was replaced in his mature paintings by the International Gothic approach of such artists as Lorenzo Ghiberti, as seen in the massive frescoes *Life of the Virgin* (1420–22; Bartolini chapel, Sta. Trinità, Florence) and the *Adoration of the Magi* (c. 1422; Uffizi), which was one of his best works. Lorenzo was also known as a painter of miniatures, but no such works can be attributed to him with certainty.

**Lorenzo Veneziano** (active 1356–1379) *Italian painter*
The leading Venetian painter in the latter part of the 14th century, Lorenzo may have been a pupil of Paolo Veneziano (died c. 1360). His own work was Gothic in style and comprises a number of polyptychs such as those

in the Duomo at Vicenza (1356), the Accademia, Venice (1357), and San Giacomo Maggiore, Bologna (1368). Other works are preserved in the Museo Civico, Padua, and the Museo Correr, Venice.

**Loris, Heinrich** See GLAREANUS, HENRICUS

**Lotto, Lorenzo** (c. 1480–1556) *Italian painter*
He trained in the studio of Giovanni BELLINI, probably alongside GIORGIONE and TITIAN, and later under Alvise VIVARINI in his native Venice. From 1508 to 1512 Lotto was in Rome, but although he is known to have been employed in the Vatican there is no surviving record of his work there. After leaving Rome he spent most of his life in Bergamo, where his principal frescoes were done, and in Venice and neighboring towns, where many churches contain altarpieces by him. He also worked in Ancona. His pictures reveal a wide variety of influences during this period but always retain a very personal character. His portraits, for example, though derived from Titian, are more direct and show a penetrating and highly individual insight into character, as in his portrait of a young man against a white background (c. 1505; Kunsthistorisches Museum, Vienna). Lack of material success is suggested by his account book, which he kept from 1538 onwards. In 1552 he settled in the monastery of the Sta. Casa in Loreto and became a lay brother in 1554.

**Louis XII** (1462–1515) *King of France (1498–1515)*
Louis, who was duke of Orleans from 1465, first married (1476) Louis XI's saintly but disabled daughter Jeanne. He was imprisoned for rebellion in 1488, but was reconciled to CHARLES VIII three years later. On his accession Louis agreed to support Pope ALEXANDER VI's son, Cesare BORGIA, in Romagna in exchange for the annulment of his marriage to Jeanne. He then married (1499) Anne of Brittany, widow of Charles VIII.

In Italy Louis pursued the claim to Naples inherited from Charles and the claim to Milan via his VISCONTI grandmother. He captured Milan and ruled there from 1500 to 1512. Then, in cooperation with FERDINAND II of Aragon and Castile, he conquered and partitioned Naples (1501–02), but the Spaniards later drove the French out (1504). France joined the anti-Venetian League of CAMBRAI (1508), but quarreled with its allies who then formed the HOLY LEAGUE against it (1511). The Swiss then drove the French out of Italy and invaded Burgundy, Spain took southern Navarre, and HENRY VIII invaded northern France. Peace with Henry and Louis's marriage to Henry's sister Mary (1514) partly retrieved the situation.

Although his Italian ventures caused France severe financial problems, Louis was popular. Internal peace, low taxation, judicial reforms, and measures protecting the poor from oppression earned him the title "the father of the people."

**Louvre, the** The national art gallery and museum of France. Built on the right bank of the Seine in Paris on the site of a former royal fortress and residence, the present building was begun on the orders of FRANCIS I, who commissioned the French architect Pierre LESCOT to design four wings around a square court in 1546. Noted as a great collector of Renaissance art, Francis I gathered about him many celebrated Italian artists, including LEONARDO DA VINCI, ANDREA DEL SARTO, PRIMATICCIO, and Benvenuto CELLINI, and established the basis of the royal collection to be housed in the Louvre. After Lescot had completed the west wing of the complex, with sculptures by Jean GOUJON, work on the Louvre and the adjoining TUILERIES was continued in the first place by Jean BULLANT and Philibert DELORME and then in the 17th century by Jacques Lemercier, Jacques II DUCERCEAU, and others, while the decoration of the Grande Galerie was entrusted to Nicolas Poussin and his assistants (1641). The court moved into the Louvre in 1652, after which many alterations were made to the original design by such noted artists as Bernini and Claude Perrault before the building was ded-icated as a museum in 1678. The overall complex was completed in the 19th century during the reign of Napoleon III.

**Further reading:** Nicholas D'Archimbaud, *The Louvre: Portrait of a Museum* (New York: Abradale, 2001).

**Loyola, St. Ignatius** See IGNATIUS LOYOLA, ST

**Lucas van Leyden** (c. 1489–1533) *Netherlands painter and print maker*
According to Carel van MANDER, Lucas was born in 1494, although this seems unlikely in view of the evident maturity of his earliest dated engraving, *Muhammad and the Murdered Monk* (1508). Between 1514 and 1529 the artist is repeatedly documented in his native Leyden, and in 1521 he met DÜRER in Antwerp. He is probably identical with the "Lucas of Holland" listed as a visiting artist in the registers of the Antwerp guild for 1522. According to van Mander, he visited Zeeland, Flanders, and Brabant at age 33, a journey that presumably occurred in 1522, rather than 1527. Although Lucas was apparently trained by his

**Lucas van Leyden** An engraving (1525) by the artist of his own self-portrait. *Mansell/Time Life Pictures/Getty Images*

father Huygh Jacobsz. and by Cornelis Engebrechtsz., his earliest surviving painting, *The Chess Players* (before 1508; Berlin) has a psychological intensity that is entirely novel. He was profoundly influenced by the graphic work of Dürer and Marcantonio RAIMONDI, as well as by Jan GOSSAERT and Jan van SCOREL. From these sources, without ever visiting Italy, he formulated a postclassical mannerist style which reached its ultimate expression in the Leyden *Last Judgment* tryptych (1526) and the Boston *Moses Striking the Rock* (1527). Despite his evident skills as a painter, Lucas's chief claim to fame rests upon the formal variety and technical virtuosity of his engravings, which rival those of Dürer himself. In his short lifespan he emerged as the most accomplished Dutch artist of the early 1500s.

**Lucca** A city state by the River Serchio in Tuscany, northern Italy. In turn Etruscan, Roman, Gothic, Byzantine, and Lombard, Lucca was granted an imperial charter of liberties (1118) and was the most powerful Tuscan city until overtaken by Florence in the late Middle Ages. It continued to prosper however until family feuds in the 14th century left it unable to resist domination by other Italian cities. From 1369 imperial protection brought a measure of security, although the Milanese briefly occupied Lucca between 1430 and 1433. Despite some years under a *signoria*, Lucca was generally a republican oligarchy during the period of the Renaissance. Its silk industry and position on roads linking Florence, Parma, Pisa, and Rome made the city rich. Surviving landmarks include the cathedral, completed in the 14th century, the impressive ramparts (begun in the 1560s), and several fine 16th-century palaces.

**Lucretius Carus, Titus** (c. 99–c. 55 BCE) *Roman poet*
Lucretius's long philosophical poem *De rerum natura* (*On the nature of things*) was known in the Middle Ages only through excerpts. Poggio BRACCIOLINI discovered a complete manuscript in 1417, but even after the text was printed (c. 1473) suspicion of the author's philosophy, which is heavily indebted to the notorious EPICURUS, prevented its attaining great influence. Giordano BRUNO was one of its few Renaissance followers, and Lucretius's atomism attracted some scientists, among them William GILBERT.

**Luini, Bernardino** (c. 1481–1532) *Italian painter*
Little is known for certain about his early life and work before 1512. He appears to have been influenced by Bramantino and other Milanese artists, of whose school he was a follower. At first he worked in a fresh and light-hearted style, as demonstrated in the fresco fragments from a villa at Monza, but his popularity in the 16th century, and later with Victorians such as John Ruskin, was chiefly due to his later works, which consisted of senti-

mentalized imitations of LEONARDO's style. These survive in large numbers, mainly in Milan.

**Luis de León, Fray** (c. 1527–1591) *Spanish poet, writer, and translator*
Born the eldest son of a judge at Belmonte, La Mancha, Luis de León entered the university of Salamanca (c. 1541), in which town he spent virtually his entire life, and then joined the Augustinian order, taking vows in 1544. He was elected to the chair of St. Thomas Aquinas in 1561. After the decrees of the Council of TRENT were promulgated in Spain (1564), there was pressure to impose orthodoxy on university teachers. For various reasons (a translation of the Song of Songs made privately for a cousin who was a nun, public criticism of the Vulgate Bible, and perhaps even the fact that a great-grandmother was a CONVERSA), Luis de León fell foul of the Inquisition (he was secretly denounced by rival professors) and was imprisoned (1572–76). Finally acquitted, he returned to Salamanca, holding the chairs of moral philosophy (1578) and biblical studies (1579). He became provincial of the Augustinian order in Castile shortly before his death.

Luis de León's 29 poems (not published until 1631) were influenced by Virgil, Horace, and Neoplatonic philosophy and are, like those of St. JOHN OF THE CROSS, highly personal expressions. They include odes that are among the best examples of the *lira* stanza introduced by GARCILASO DE LA VEGA. In his lifetime Luis de León was recognized as the greatest prose writer of his age. His masterpiece, *De los nombres de Cristo* (1583), is a Platonic discussion of the scriptural names of Christ (the Way, Shepherd, Bridegroom, etc.) in the form of a Ciceronian dialogue which was composed while he was in prison. He also wrote *La perfecta casada* (1583), a commentary on chapter 31 of the Book of Proverbs expounding the duties of a married woman. He was as fluent a writer in Latin as in Spanish, and also translated works by the poets Pindar and Tibullus, SENECA, Pietro BEMBO, and Giovanni DELLA CASA.

**Luis of Granada** (**Luis Sarriá**) (1505–1588) *Spanish preacher and religious writer*
After leaving his native Granada, he studied at Valladolid before moving to Cordova (1534–45), where he restored the Dominican convent and studied devotional works. In 1547 he became prior at Badajoz, and about 1555 was invited by Cardinal Infante (later King) Henry to Portugal, where he was provincial of the Portuguese Dominicans (1556–60). Among his works were *Libro de la oración* (1554) on prayer and meditation, *Guía de pecadores* (1555), a guide to the Christian virtues for sinners, and *Memorial de la vida cristiana* (1566) on the ascetic life. He was influenced by both SAVONAROLA and ERASMUS, emphasized the importance of the inner life, and regarded religious ceremonies as unimportant. In 1559 the *Libro de*

*la oración* and the *Guía* were put on the INDEX LIBRORUM PROHIBITORUM.

## Luna, Álvaro de (c. 1390–1453) *Spanish statesman and poet*

An illegitimate member of a family of wealthy CONVERSOS, de Luna rose to prominence by becoming tutor to the young King John II of Castile. When John came of age (1419) he totally relied upon de Luna, who, despite the hostility of the king's Trastámara cousins and their supporters among the old aristocracy, became virtual ruler of Castile. He was appointed constable of Castile in 1423. Although driven from court in 1427, he was recalled the following year and consolidated his power, but his attempt to raise a crusade against the Moors of Granada (1431) ultimately failed. After the Castilian defeat of the Aragonese at Olmedo (1445) he was elected grand master of the Order of Santiago. The hostility of the king's second wife, Isabella of Portugal, brought about his downfall, and he was executed at Valladolid after a show trial for witchcraft. His poems appeared in the *Cancionero de Baena* (1445) and he also wrote a treatise in defense of women, *Libro de las virtuosas e claras mugeres* (1446).

## Lusiad, The (Portuguese *Os Lusíadas*; 1572) The national poem of Portugal, by Luís Vaz de CAMÕES; one of the most important and successful epics of the Renaissance. The title refers to the Portuguese (the Lusitanians), whose heroic achievement in discovering the sea route to India the poem celebrates. Although in historical time the action spans the two years of Vasco da GAMA's voyage of 1497–98, it includes a visionary expanse of Portuguese history both backward and forward to Camões's own day. The poem, consisting of 10 cantos (1102 stanzas) of *ottava rima*, is thoroughly Virgilian and classical and yet firmly based on historical events and draws on Camões's 17 years' experience in India and the Orient. After an introduction, the invocation, and a dedication to King Sebastian, the action begins at the point when the Portuguese are sailing off the coast of East Africa in the Indian Ocean. The mythological action (with Venus protecting and Bacchus opposing the enterprise) is skillfully combined with the historical narrative, which incorporates outstanding descriptive passages and a variety of historical and fictitious episodes before its triumphant conclusion.

*Os Lusíadas* has been edited with an introduction and notes by F. Pierce (Oxford, U.K., 1973; repr. 1981). Sir Richard Fanshawe's version (1655), the first and most successful of the English verse translations, has most recently been republished in a scholarly edition by Peter Davidson of *The Poems and Translations of Sir Richard Fanshawe* (2 vols, Oxford, U.K., 1997–99). Of other English versions, Sir Richard Burton's abstruse rendering (2 vols, London, 1880), in which he labored to reproduce exactly the meter and obscurities of Camões' Portuguese, is more a curiosity than a valid interpretation for an English readership. There is a prose translation by W. C. Atkinson in the Penguin Classics series (Harmondsworth, U.K., 1952; repr. 1973) and a verse rendering by Llandeg White for Oxford World's Classics (1998).

## Luther, Martin (1483–1546) *German reformer*

The son of a prosperous copper miner at Eisleben, Luther received a thorough education, first at school in Magdeburg, then at the local university in Erfurt. He graduated MA in 1505 and began to study law, but soon abandoned his legal studies and entered the Augustinian priory at Erfurt. The year after his ordination (1507) Luther was appointed a lecturer in the new university at Wittenberg, where he became a doctor of theology in 1512 and then professor of Scripture. During his years in Wittenberg Luther's intensive theological studies brought him into an increasingly troubled relationship with established Catholic doctrine: his mounting impatience with scholastic theology and his preference for the Bible over the Church as a final arbiter in matters of faith and practice both grew steadily more apparent in his sermons and lectures. About this time (1512–15) Luther seems also to have come to his new understanding of justification, with the realization (based on his reading of St. Paul's Epistle to the Romans) that faith alone justifies without works. This doctrine, of JUSTIFICATION BY FAITH, was to be the cornerstone of his future creed.

Luther's impatience with traditional Catholic theology and its abuses finally found voice with his Ninety-five Theses against INDULGENCES posted at Wittenberg in October 1517. The indulgence granted by Pope Leo X for the renovation of St. Peter's in Rome and preached with little restraint by the Dominican friar Johann Tetzel, was widely resented in Germany, and Luther's Theses found a ready audience. Within a month they had spread throughout Germany, making their author a major public figure. In the fierce controversy that now arose Luther gradually elaborated his theology and broadened his attack on the Church. At the Leipzig Disputation with Johann ECK (1519) he made a devastating assault on Church authority, denying the primacy of the pope and the infallibility of a general council. The following year, 1520, he published the three great tracts that marked the final break with the Roman establishment. The appeal *An den christlichen Adel deutscher Nation* (*To the Christian Nobility of the German Nation*) urged the princes to take ecclesiastical reform into their own hands. *De captivitate Babylonica ecclesiae* (*The Babylonian Captivity of the Christian Church*), published in German as well as Latin, denounced Catholic abuse of the sacraments and condemned the doctrine of TRANSUBSTANTIATION. *Von der Freiheit eines Christenmenschen* (*The Freedom of a Christian Man*) developed the doctrine of salvation by faith. Finally, in December, Luther burnt the papal Bull condemning his teaching (*Exsurge domine*, June

1520), leaving the pope no alternative but to pronounce his excommunication (January 1521).

Luther's fate now depended to a large extent on political events within the empire. Summoned to appear before Emperor Charles V at the Diet of WORMS (March 1521), Luther refused to recant, but he was protected in his defiance by FREDERICK (III) THE WISE, Elector of Saxony, and in 1522 Luther was able to return to Wittenberg. Here he remained for the rest of his life, writing and watching over the gradual growth of the reformed movement. In 1534 he completed his new German translation of the Bible based on the original texts, destined to be the most enduring of his literary productions. The Greater Catechism and Shorter Catechism (1529) also played an important role in spreading his teaching among the people.

Luther also wrote an enormous number of small pamphlets and tracts in which his love of controversy and capacity for abuse found full expression. His *Contra Henricum regem Anglicanum* (1522), written in response to HENRY VIII's *Assertio septem sacramentorum* (1521), was expressed in such immoderate terms that potential English sympathizers with his cause were alienated. In the mid-1520s he was embroiled in controversy with ERASMUS, who had for some years resisted pressure to involve himself in religious controversy; Erasmus's *Diatribe de libero arbitrio* (1524), his vindication of the importance of human free will in the Christian scheme of Redemption drew a sharp response in Luther's *De servo arbitrio* (1525), which clearly set out his doctrine of determinism. Erasmus responded with *Hyperaspites* (The defender; 1526). Around this time, during the PEASANTS' REVOLT in Germany, Luther backed the Protestant aristocracy in its efforts to restore order by exterminating the disaffected mobs, thus antagonizing a large section of the German people. His later attack on the Jews, *Von den Juden und ihren Lügen* (1543), is notorious in the history of ANTI-SEMITISM, and his final published work was a bitter onslaught against his oldest antagonist, the papacy. These works are now the preserve of historians or theologians, but Luther is better remembered as a writer of hymns: he wrote both words and music for "Ein' feste Burg is unser Gott" ("A safe stronghold is our God"), a version of Psalm 46 that is still sung in Protestant churches worldwide. In middle age Luther became increasingly irascible, stubbornly resisting any attempt to develop or refine his theological insights. The result was a series of damaging disputes with other reformers, of which the Eucharistic controversy with the Swiss reformer Ulrich ZWINGLI (*see* MARBURG, COLLOQUY OF) was the most serious. By the time of Luther's death a Lutheran Church was well established over large areas of Germany, but it was increasingly troubled by internal dissensions.

Luther married a former nun, Katharina von Bora, in 1525, the year after he had finally abandoned his religious habit. They enjoyed a happy family life, and the *Table Talk*

(*Tischreden*) recorded by his students faithfully preserves the flavor of life in his household. His friendship with Lucas CRANACH resulted in a number of portraits; the reformer's uncompromising character is well captured in a 1529 painting now in the Uffizi, Florence.

**Further reading:** Ronald H. Bainton, *Here I Stand: A Life of Martin Luther* (Nashville, Tenn.: Abingdon Press, 1980; repr. New York Penguin USA, 1995); Peter N. Brooks (ed.), *Seven-Headed Luther: Essays in Commemoration of a Quincentenary, 1483–1983* (Oxford, U.K.: Clarendon Press, 1983); Arthur G. Dickens, *The German Nation and Martin Luther* (London: Edward Arnold, 1974); Robert Kolb, *Martin Luther as Prophet, Teacher, Hero: Images of the Reformer, 1520–1620* (Grand Rapids, Mich.: Baker Books and Carlisle, U.K.: Paternoster, 1999); Bernhard Lohse, *Martin Luther's Theology: Its Historical and Systematic Development*, transl. Roy A. Harrisville (Minneapolis, Minn.: Fortress Press, 1999); Lewis W. Spitz, *Luther and German Humanism* (Aldershot, U.K.: Variorum, 1996).

**Lutheranism** The movement for evangelical reform in Germany, led by Martin LUTHER. Although the term "Lutheran" was originally coined by Luther's Catholic opponents, it soon came into general use to describe his supporters. As the movement gathered pace the need for a clearer definition of doctrine than that provided by Luther's own writings became evident; this process of definition led to the establishment of a distinct Lutheran Church and to the exclusion of many non-Lutheran reformers. The first authoritative expression of Lutheran doctrine was the Confession of AUGSBURG, drawn up by Philipp MELANCHTHON with Luther's approval. Its 21 doctrinal articles included a clear exposition of JUSTIFICATION BY FAITH, together with an affirmation of the REAL PRESENCE (of Christ's body in the sacrament, the point that had already caused a breach between Luther and the Swiss reformer ZWINGLI). Although Melanchthon issued a substantially revised version in 1540 (the *Variata*), more acceptable to reformed theologians, it was the original text that was incorporated into the 1580 Book of CONCORD, the definitive statement of Lutheran orthodoxy. Also influential in defining Luther's teaching were his two catechisms (1529) and the SCHMALKALDIC ARTICLES (1537).

Lutheranism achieved its greatest success in Germany, where many cities and princes adopted the Reformation between 1524 and 1535. Lutheran state churches were subsequently established in much of the empire, including the important states of Saxony, Brandenburg, Brunswick, and Hesse. Outside Germany Lutheran churches were permanently established only in Scandinavia (in Denmark in 1530 and Sweden in 1531–37) and the Baltic lands. In other parts of Europe where the Reformation had made early headway Lutheranism was generally superseded by the more robust Calvinist tradition.

After Luther's death (1546) his movement was increasingly rent by internal divisions, resulting in the virtual exclusion of the Melanchthonite wing in the Formula of CONCORD (1577).

See also: HYMNODY; LITURGY

Further reading: Diarmaid MacCulloch, *Reformation: Europe's House Divided 1400–1700* (London: Allen Lane, 2003), as *The Reformation: A History* (New York: Penguin Viking, 2004); Bodo Nischan, *Lutherans and Calvinists in the Age of Confessionalism* (Aldershot, U.K.: Ashgate, 1999).

**Luzzaschi, Luzzasco** (c. 1545–1607) *Italian composer*
Luzzaschi studied with Ciprìen de RORE in Ferrara and in 1561 became a singer at the Este court there. In 1564 he became court organist, but was also active as a composer and teacher. FRESCOBALDI was among his pupils. Luzzaschi was also organist at Ferrara cathedral and the Accademia della Morte. By 1570 he was directing the duke's chamber music. It was here that the celebrated "singing ladies" of Ferrara, remarkable virtuoso singers, performed for private audiences, and Luzzaschi composed madrigals for them. His *Madrigali per cantare, et sonare a 1–3 soprani* (1601) contains some of these pieces with their fully notated keyboard accompaniments. From 1597 Luzzaschi served Cardinal Pietro Aldobrandini, who took over Ferrara from the Este when the city passed to the papacy. Luzzaschi wrote some sacred works, but his madrigals are his best-known compositions. His five-part madrigals were his most popular works, and, while not very innovatory in style, they are skillfully composed; the later ones show an increased use of homophony.

**Lyly, John** (c. 1554–1606) *English novelist and playwright*
The son of a Kentish gentleman, Lyly took his MA at Oxford (1575) before trying to earn his living as a writer in London. He was appointed vice-master of St. Paul's choir school (1585), and the Paul's boys gave the first performances of several of his plays before Queen Elizabeth; these highly polished prose comedies on mythological themes included *Alexander and Campaspe* (1584), *Sapho and Phao* (1584), *Endimion* (1591), *Gallathea* (1592), and *Midas* (1592). Lyly contributed the pro-bishop *Pappe with an Hatchet* (1589) to the MARPRELATE CONTROVERSY, but his main achievement in prose was *Euphues*, a romance published in two parts—*The Anatomy of Wit* (1578) and *Euphues and his England* (1580). He was MP successively for Hindon, Aylesbury, and Appleby (1589–1601), but never achieved his longed-for court post of master of the revels. If he wrote the exquisite lyrics in his plays, such as "The Fairy Song" in *Endimion* or "The Song of Daphne to the Lute" from *Midas*, he was also an accomplished poet.

See also: EUPHUISM

**Lyons** (French **Lyon**) A city in eastern France at the confluence of the rivers Rhône and Saone. Its position has made it an important focus of trade and communications ever since Roman times, when it was known as Lugdunum. From 1312 it was part of the French realm. Charles VII granted the city's silk industry a monopoly in 1450, Italian silk workers were brought in, and Lyons became famous as a producer of luxury textiles. Lyons' prime position on the trade route between northwestern Europe and Italy attracted numerous Italian merchants; in 1465 the Medici set up an office there and by 1502 around 40 other Florentine firms had followed suit. With these commercial connections, the city's annual fairs flourished in the 15th and 16th centuries, and its population expanded to around 60,000 by the mid-16th century. Italian potters made Lyons France's first important center of MAJOLICA production. Lyons' first printing press was established by 1473, and it quickly became a major focus of the book trade. BADIUS ASCENSIUS and later Robert GRANJON were printers there, as was SERVETUS. It enjoyed a thriving literary culture in the mid-16th century: the bibliophile Jean GROLIER was a native of Lyons, and a notable group of poets formed around Maurice SCÈVE. In the wars of religion, there was a Calvinist takeover of the city in 1562, but 10 years later the Catholics regained control.

**Mabuse** See GOSSAERT, JAN

**Machaut, Guillaume de** (c. 1300–c. 1377) *French composer and poet*
Probably born in Reims, Machaut entered the service of John of Luxembourg, king of Bohemia, in around 1323, and was his secretary until the king's death at Crécy (1346). Machaut was given canonries by Pope John XXII at Verdun, Arras, and Reims in the 1330s, and after the king of Bohemia's death, he was patronized by, among others, the king of Navarre, the duke of Berry, and the future King Charles V. Machaut's autobiographical poem "Voir dit" gives some insight into his compositional methods. He is generally regarded as the most important figure of the French ARS NOVA and was highly revered by his contemporaries. He wrote little sacred music, but notable among it is his *Messe de Notre Dame*, one of the earliest polyphonic settings of the Ordinary of the Mass. His secular output consists of around 20 motets and well over 100 pieces in song forms (lais, virelais, rondeaux, and *ballades*). The lais and virelais are for one voice in the troubadour tradition, but the rondeaux and *ballades* are polyphonic, based on isorhythmic tenor lines. Here Machaut is at his most innovatory, using syncopation and musical rhyme to great effect.

**Machiavelli, Niccolò** (1469–1527) *Italian political theorist and dramatist*
From 1498, after the fall of SAVONAROLA, Machiavelli served in the republican administration of his native Florence, in the chancery and as secretary (1498–1512) to the TEN OF WAR, the body concerned with diplomacy and warfare. He acquired a thorough knowledge of political affairs and traveled extensively in legations to various courts, meeting such leaders as LOUIS XII of France, Pope JULIUS II, Emperor MAXIMILIAN I, and Cesare BORGIA. With the return to power of the Medici in 1512, Machiavelli was forced to retire from public life because of his association with the republican government; he was also suspected of involvement in a plot against the Medici in 1513. Apart from insignificant and temporary appointments, he devoted the rest of his life to his writings, living at Sant' Andrea in Percussina, several miles from Florence.

Two of Machiavelli's works were published in his lifetime: *La mandragola* (*The Mandrake Root*; 1518), an instant success still acknowledged as one of the most brilliant of Italian comedies, and the treatise *Dell'arte della guerra* (*The Art of War*; 1519–20), set in the intellectual gatherings of the ORTI ORICELLARI. It was there that he read a version of his first major commentary on government, *Discorsi sopra la prima deca di Tito Livio* (*Discourses on the First Decade of Livy*; 1531), written about 1517. His other works include a history of Florence (written 1520–25), the comedy *Clizia* (written c. 1524), and his political masterpiece, *Il principe* (THE PRINCE). *Dell'arte della guerra* and *Istorie fiorentine* were translated into English in 1560 and 1595 respectively, but by that time Machiavelli's name had undeservedly become a byword for godlessness, cynicism, and treachery, exemplified in the prologue to MARLOWE's *The Jew of Malta* in which the ghost of "Machevill" is made to say, among other scandalous sentiments: "I count Religion but a childish Toy, And hold there is no sinne but Ignorance."

Despite the opprobrium loaded on the author, Henry Nevile's edition of Machiavelli's *Works* (1675) was twice reprinted before the end of the 17th century (1680, 1694).

A more recent English edition is Allan H. Gilbert's three-volume *Machiavelli: The Chief Works and Others* (Durham, N.C., 1965). The two-volume translation of the *Discorsi* by Leslie Walker SJ (*The Discourses of Niccolò Machiavelli* (London, 1950) was published as a Pelican Book in 1970 with an introduction by Bernard Crick, and later issued as a Penguin Classic (1983). John R. Hale edited *The Literary Works of Machiavelli* (Oxford, U.K., 1961).

Further reading: Sebastian de Grazia, *Machiavelli in Hell* (New York and London: Harvester Wheatsheaf, 1989; repr. 1994); Felix Raab, *The English Face of Machiavelli: A Changing Interpretation 1500–1700* (London: Routledge & Kegan Paul, 1964); Quentin Skinner, *Machiavelli* (Oxford, U.K.: Oxford University Press, 1981); Leo Strauss, *Thoughts on Machiavelli* (Seattle, Wash.: University of Washington Press, 1969; repr. University of Chicago Press, 1995); Maurice Viroli (ed.), *Machiavelli* (Oxford, U.K.: Oxford University Press, 1998).

**Machuca, Pedro** (died 1550) *Spanish architect and painter*
Machuca became familiar with Italian Renaissance theories while studying in Italy. He returned to Spain in 1520. He is best known for his design of the palace of Charles V in the Alhambra at Granada, begun in 1531. This was the first building of its kind in Spain, exhibiting many Italian features and decorated in the mannerist style; it was never completed. Other works included the coloring of a carved reredos in Jaén cathedral, several altarpieces at Granada (1521–49), and an early panel, the *Madonna del Suffragio* (1517; Prado, Madrid), executed in Italy.

**Madrid** The capital city of Spain, situated on the central Castilian plateau. At first a small Moorish town named Majrit, Madrid was reconquered by the Christians in 1083. Although its first *cortes* was summoned in 1329 and various monarchs spent some time in the city, Madrid only became an important center in 1560 when PHILIP II established his court there. Madrid was chosen presumably because it was not associated with the historic divisions of Spain. In 1607 Philip III made Madrid Spain's official capital. Surviving landmarks include the town hall and the Plaza Mayor from the early 17th century.

**madrigal** In the 14th century, a setting of a secular poem of eight to eleven lines for two voices. In the 16th century the genre re-emerged in Italy, and became the most popular secular form in the second half of the 16th century. The 16th-century madrigal was a freer musical form than its predecessor and was generally for four or five voices. The poetry of PETRARCH was revived, used, and also imitated in countless pieces. Two of the earliest exponents were Philippe VERDELOT and Costanzo FESTA; madrigals by both were published in 1530. Jacques ARCADELT published one of the most popular madrigal collections in Venice; his

first book was reprinted around 40 times before the mid-17th century. In it he uses imitative counterpoint and chordal declamation according to the contour of the text.

Venice became an important center for the publication and composition of madrigals during the 1540s; Adrian WILLAERT and his pupils composed madrigals in which the form of the music is dictated by the text. In the 1550s declamation of the text remained important, requiring a supple rhythm with a chordal texture; composers started to experiment with harmonies, using chromaticism to some effect. The influence of Willaert and Ciprien de RORE remained strong; in the second half of the 16th century composers all over Italy imitated them, notably Andrea GABRIELI in Venice and Giaches de WERT in Mantua. Gabrieli and other Venetian composers wrote in a new style which was freer, polyphonically complex, and of a light texture. From the 1580s Luca MARENZIO helped to make Rome and Ferrara centers of madrigal composition. As a new style of singing with great ornamentation, fostered in particular by the dukes of Ferrara, became established, composers wrote virtuoso music full of contrasts, both harmonic and textural.

In the 1590s another new style emerged, led by Marenzio, LUZZASCHI, and Carlo GESUALDO, in which the text was increasingly the master of the music; these texts were almost always of great emotional intensity and as such inspired the use of dissonance, bold harmonies and rhythms, and unusual melodic leaps. In the early 1600s these trends were taken still further by MONTEVERDI. The compositions of composers active in Italy were imitated throughout Europe. Philippe de MONTE was one popular and prolific composer of madrigals. Alfonso FERRABOSCO composed madrigals in England in the 1560s and 1570s, but it was not until the 1580s and 1590s that English composers interested themselves in the genre. Thomas MORLEY, Thomas WEELKES, and John WILBYE wrote with great expressiveness, depicting dramatic contrasts in the text.

Further reading: Martha Feldman, *City Culture and the Madrigal at Venice* (Berkeley, Calif.: University of California Press, 1995); Anthony Newcomb, *The Madrigal at Ferrara, 1579–1597*, 2 vols (Princeton, N.J.: Princeton University Press, 1980).

**Madrigal, Alfonso de** (c. 1400–1455) *Spanish philosopher and theologian*
Often referred to as "el Tostado," after his father Alfonso Tostado, Madrigal was born at Madrigal de la Sierra, Ávila, and first taught at Salamanca. He later went to Rome, where he came to the notice of Pope Eugenius IV. He entered the Carthusian Order at the Scala Dei monastery in Catalonia, but King John II of Castile persuaded him to leave the contemplative life and secured his appointment as bishop of Ávila. He is one of 24 eminent men at the court of Henry IV who are memorialized in the *Libro de los claros varones de Castilla* (Book of the famous men of

Castile; 1486). Madrigal was a proverbially voluminous writer in Spanish and Latin (*escribir más que el Tostado*—"to write more than el Tostado"). He is reputed to have produced six printed sheets for every year of his adult life, and his two books attacking the Jews and the Koran ran to 27 volumes. In addition to works on moral philosophy and religious subjects, he translated SENECA's *Medea* and wrote a commentary on the early Church historian Eusebius. The first edition of his *Opera omnia* (Venice, 1507–31) was published in 20 volumes.

## Maecenas, Gaius (74/64–8 BCE) *Roman statesman and patron*
He was the trusted adviser of Emperor Augustus and the friend and patron of VIRGIL, HORACE, and other major Roman poets, who eulogized him in their poetry. His name became synonymous with discerning PATRONAGE, and he is often invoked in Renaissance writers' dealings with their own patrons.

## Maestlin, Michael (1550–1631) *German astronomer*
Educated at Tübingen university, Maestlin became in 1576 a Lutheran pastor. He also served as mathematics professor at the universities of Heidelberg and Tübingen. Having observed the NEW STAR of 1572 and the comets of 1577 and 1580, Maestlin began to express privately his support for the COPERNICAN SYSTEM, but in public and in his *Epitome astronomiae* (1582) he continued to expound the PTOLEMAIC SYSTEM. He must have been more daring in conversation, for it was from Maestlin that KEPLER, as a student at Tübingen, received his first serious introduction to Copernican astronomy. Maestlin also edited Kepler's Copernican treatise, *Mysterium cosmographicum* (1596).

## Maestro Giorgio See ANDREOLI, GIORGIO

## Magellan, Ferdinand (c. 1480–1521) *Portuguese explorer*
Born near Villa Real of noble parentage, Magellan served in the court of Queen Leonor from an early age. In 1505 he sailed to the East Indies with Francisco de Almeida, acquiring during the voyage a comprehensive knowledge of navigational techniques. From then until 1510 Magellan was perpetually on the move, helping to establish a fort in Mozambique and fighting at the battle of Diu (1509), which confirmed Portuguese supremacy in the Indian Ocean. He also played a major role in the conquest of Malacca (1511), the gateway to the Far East. Back in Portugal (1512), Magellan took part in an expedition against Morocco (1513), but he then lost favor with King Manuel I.

Magellan responded by offering his services to Spain. In 1518 he and the exiled Portuguese astronomer Ruy Faleiro were commissioned by Charles I of Spain (later Emperor Charles V) to sail west and ascertain that the Spice Islands were within Spanish territory (see TORDESILLAS, TREATY OF). To reach his destination, Magellan navigated the southern tip of America, discovering the straits which now bear his name. He then took the unprecedented decision to return home by continuing to sail westwards. On September 6, 1522 the *Vittoria* arrived back in Seville, but Magellan himself had been killed a year earlier in battle against the natives of Mactan in the Philippines. Consequently, his deputy, Sebastian del CANO, is acclaimed as the first actual circumnavigator.

**Further reading:** Tim Joyner, *Magellan* (Cambden, Me.: International Marine/Ragged Mountain Press, 1992: repr. 1994).

## Maggior Consiglio (Italian, "Great Council")
The ruling body of Venice on which all adult males belonging to patrician families had a lifelong hereditary right to sit. The closure (*serrata*) of the membership to all except these families took place in 1297, and from 1325 their names were recorded in the *Libro d'oro* (Golden book). Throughout the Renaissance period the Maggior Consiglio functioned mainly as a pool from which members could be drawn for other councils and committees of state, such as the senate (with about 200 members) and the COUNCIL OF TEN, all under the chairmanship of the DOGE.

The Venetian council was copied in Florence on the fall of the Medici in 1494 and became the basis of the republican constitution there until 1512.

## magic
In the Renaissance, a specific and essentially literate view of how the universe operates. It was far from the body of superstitious beliefs held by illiterate peasants in many other cultures. One of the fullest accounts of Renaissance magic is to be found in Cornelius AGRIPPA's *De occulta philosophia* (1531). For Agrippa, the universe was divided into natural, celestial, and intellectual worlds, with influences flowing from the intellectual to the celestial to the natural world. There were, thus, three types of magic: natural magic applying to the natural world, celestial magic deriving from the stars and planets, and intellectual magic controlled by ceremony and ritual. As natural magic operated by observing the sympathies and antipathies between natural objects, such as the lodestone and iron, it approximated to some extent to Renaissance science. Celestial and intellectual magic, whatever their pretensions, soon degenerated into astrology and numerology. Much ingenuity was consequently devoted to extracting, by techniques like that of gematria, important and potent numbers, such as that of God (tetragrammaton), Christ (pentagrammaton), and the Shemhamphorash (the preeminent name). In gematria words were converted into numbers by assigning the letters arbitrary values. Thus, given that Y = 10, H = 5, and V = 6, then the name of God, YHVH (the tetragrammaton) takes the value

$10 + 5 + 6 + 5 = 26$. In this manner a verse of the Bible containing exactly 26 syllables would be taken by the Renaissance magician as being of special significance.

Less mechanical systems of magic emerged from the work of the Neoplatonists FICINO and PICO DELLA MIRANDOLA. Extracted in part from the Corpus hermeticum (see HERMETICISM) and the Jewish CABBALA, they sought to identify harmonies and resonances in the universe rather than cast spells or design amulets. From the early 17th century, however, all such traditions began to be challenged. KEPLER in his *Harmonices mundi* (1619), for example, and Marin Mersenne in his *Quaestiones in genesim* (1623), began the process of critical appraisal which thereafter inexorably assigned magic a more peripheral role in intellectual history.

See also: WITCHCRAFT

Further reading: Ioan P. Culiany, *Eros and Magic in the Renaissance*, transl. Margaret Cook (Chicago, Ill.: University of Chicago Press, 1987); William Monter, *Ritual, Myth and Magic in Early Modern Europe* (Athens, Ohio: Ohio University Press, 1980); Keith Thomas, *Religion and The Decline of Magic* (London: Weidenfeld & Nicolson, 1971); Brian Vickers (ed.) *Occult and Scientific Mentalities in the Renaissance* (Cambridge, U.K.: Cambridge University Press, 1984); Daniel P. Walker, *Spiritual and Demonic Magic from Ficino to Campanella* (London: Warburg Institute, 1958; Notre Dame, Ind.: University of Notre Dame Press, 1975).

**magus** As seen by Renaissance scholars, a man in possession of powerful esoteric knowledge gained from certain secret texts or from another noted magus. His initiation might involve various rites of purification and entailed a code of behavior of which fasting and sexual abstinence would be the most obvious features. The knowledge gained by the magus in this way was thought to give him power over nature. It could be exercised, as by John DEE, through the conjuring of demons, or, following Cornelius AGRIPPA, through the manipulation of occult sympathies, celestial influences, and numerological relationships.

See also: MAGIC

**Maier, Michael** (c. 1568–1622) *German alchemist and physician*
Maier was born in Holstein and studied medicine at the university of Basle. From about 1608 to 1612 he practiced in Prague, becoming court physician to RUDOLF II, who ennobled him as a Pfalzgraf (Count Palatine). His last years were spent as a physician in Magdeburg. His first book was *Arcana arcanissima* (Most secret secrets; 1614), which was followed by a spate of publications in the next six years. Two were defenses of ROSICRUCIANISM: *Silentium post clamores* (Silence after the uproar; 1617) and *Themis aurea* (Golden Themis [goddess of justice]; 1618). However, his most famous work is *Atalanta fugiens* (Fleeing

Atalanta; 1618), an emblem book which provides a synthesis of medieval alchemy and Paracelsian and Rosicrucian philosophy. After a visit to England he translated Thomas Norton's influential *Ordinal of Alchemy* (c. 1470s) into Latin (1618).

**majolica** A tin-glazed soft earthenware pottery made at several places in Italy during the 15th and 16th centuries. It derived from the Islamic Middle East via Spain through the Majorcan trade (hence the name). Sometimes called Raffaele ware (after the influence of RAPHAEL), majolica was particularly suited to brilliantly colored painted decoration in the Renaissance taste.

The manufactures include domestic utensils, drug jars, and ornamental display pieces. The painted decoration surpassed previous achievements and consisted of grotesques, arabesques, strapwork, armorial and commemorative statements, and narrative and mythological scenes. Many of the centers of manufacture were under noble patronage and developed individual styles. The principal products prized by collectors include wares from: Gubbio (patronized by the dukes of Urbino), famed for ruby metallic lusters by Maestro Giorgio ANDREOLI; Deruta (patronized by Cesare BORGIA), making yellow lusters edged with blue; Caffagiuolo (patronized by the Medici family), painting in bright orange, yellow, red, and green on cobalt blue; Florence, where Luca DELLA ROBBIA produced tin-glazed bas-reliefs and dark blue Gothic decoration; Castel Durante (now Urbania), remarkable for arabesques and grotesques, often on a blue ground; and Faenza (see FAENZA). The technique was brought from Castel Durante to Antwerp in the first decade of the 16th century by Guido di SAVINI and from there exported to England by his sons. An important source for knowledge of Italian majolica in the 16th century is *Li tre libri dell'arte del vasaio* (c. 1548) by the nobleman Cipriano Piccolpasso (1524–79) of Castel Durante, in which he describes the techniques used by the potters in making and decorating their wares.

Further reading: Timothy Wilson, *Ceramic Art of the Italian Renaissance* (London: British Museum, 1987).

**Malatesta, Sigismondo** (1417–1468) *Italian nobleman and condottiere*
Although the illegitimate son of Pandolfo Malatesta, lord of Fano, he succeeded his uncle as lord of Rimini in 1432. A successful condottiere, he served Pope Eugenius IV and Francesco Sforza well, but his later desertion of King ALFONSO (I) of Naples in 1447 and his rejection of PIUS II's peace terms incurred the bitter enmity of other Italian rulers. Pius II excommunicated him, launched a crusade against him, and seized most of his territories (1459–61). Although reviled on biased papal evidence as immoral, cruel, and reckless, Sigismondo was a man of culture and learning. He took a keen interest in military science and in

the work of VALTURIO in particular. Under his instruction ALBERTI replanned San Francesco in Rimini as a monument for the Malatesta family (*see* TEMPIO MALATESTIANO). He was for many years infatuated with Isotta degli Atti, whom he married in 1456 after two previous marriages; the death of his second wife, Polissena Sforza, in 1449 led his many enemies to suggest that she had been poisoned.

**Malatesta family** The rulers of Rimini and neighbouring towns in the 14th and 15th centuries. The Malatesta were originally feudal lords and CONDOTTIERI in the service of the papacy. Veruchio Malatesta became lord of the city after expelling the imperial faction (1295), and from 1355 his descendants ruled Rimini as papal vicars, loyal servants of the papacy until Sigismondo MALATESTA rashly challenged papal authority. Despite the efforts of Roberto (died 1482) the power of the Malatesta declined and they became increasingly dependent on Venice. Pandolfo V's brutal regime provoked a rebellion in Rimini (1498) and Pandolfo was expelled by Cesare BORGIA (1500). The family later made two unsuccessful attempts to reestablish itself in Rimini (1522–23, 1527–28).

**Maldonado, Juan** (c. 1485–1554) *Spanish humanist writer*
Maldonado's neo-Latin treatises covered a wide range of genres including poetry, drama, and history. An avid admirer of ERASMUS, he was at the forefront in promoting the cause of liberal humanism in Spain with his *Paraensis ad politiores literas adversus grammaticorum vulgum* (Recommendation in favour of more elegant literature against the rabble of grammarians; 1529). Other subjects on which he wrote included Spain's adventure in the New World and the Revolt of the COMUNEROS. He is sometimes confused with the Spanish Jesuit scholar and exegete Juan Maldonado (Maldonatus; 1533–83).

**Maldonado, Juan** (Maldonatus) (1533–1583) *Spanish theologian*
Maldonado, who is sometimes confused with his earlier namesake, studied at Salamanca and became a Jesuit in 1562. From 1564 he was a professor at the Jesuit college in Paris, where his lectures on theology were popular. In 1574 the Sorbonne accused him of heresy, but he was vindicated by the bishop of Paris in 1576. His important commentaries on the gospels were published posthumously (1596–97).

**Malherbe, François de** (1555–1628) *French poet and literary critic*
Malherbe was born at Caen and after studying at the universities of Basle and Heidelberg, he took the post of secretary to Henry of Angoulême, governor of Provence, in 1577. His first published poetic work was the baroque *Les Larmes de Saint Pierre* (1587); in 1605 he became court

poet to King Henry IV in Paris. Malherbe was not a prolific poet: he wrote slowly and deliberately, developing the clear pure style that was to form the basis of French classicism, in reaction against the neologisms and Latinisms of the PLÉIADE, which had been a major stylistic influence in his early works. His prose writings include translations, letters, and a number of critical works, notably a hostile commentary on the poems of his predecessor Philippe DESPORTES.

**Malines** (Mechlin, Flemish **Mechelen**) A city in Antwerp province in the Netherlands (now Belgium). Founded by St. Rumoldus, Malines was ruled successively by the prince-bishops of Liège (915–1333), the counts of Flanders (1333–69), and Burgundy (1369–1477) before passing to the HAPSBURGS. MARGARET OF AUSTRIA held a brilliant court at Malines (1507–30), making it not only the capital of the Netherlands but also a center of learning and the arts. Malines was long famed for its fine lace. The city suffered extensive war damage in the 16th and 17th centuries. Landmarks which have survived from the period of the Renaissance include the cathedral of St. Rumoldus (13th to 15th centuries), the 14th-century cloth hall, Margaret of Austria's palace, and the town hall (14th to 17th centuries).

**Mander, Carel van** (1548–1606) *Flemish painter and writer*
Born into a noble family near Kortrijk, van Mander was taught by Lucas de HEERE and visited Rome (1573) and Vienna (1577) before settling in Haarlem (1583). There he opened an academy with Hendrick GOLTZIUS and Cornelis CORNELISZ. in order to spread the ideas of the Italian Renaissance. He moved to Amsterdam three years before his death. Van Mander is best remembered as author of *Het Schilderboeck* (1604), an educational handbook for young artists largely based upon VASARI's *Lives of the Painters* (1550). Divided into three parts, *Het Schilderboeck* constitutes, despite inaccuracies, a unique guide to northern European painters from the time of the van Eycks to van Mander's contemporaries. The book also includes an instructional poem summarizing the fundamentals of Renaissance art as the author interpreted them, although this had little impact upon Dutch painting of that period. Often called the "the Dutch Vasari," van Mander was a distinguished artist in his own right, producing works in the mannerist style instilled by his Viennese mentor Bartholomäus SPRANGER. He wrote several allegorical dramas for which he also painted the scenery. His pupils included Frans Hals.

Van Mander's *Schilderboeck* is available in English translation in the two-volume *Lives of the Illustrious Netherlandish and German Painters from the First Edition of the 'Schilder-Boeck' (1603–1604)*, ed. Hessel Miedema (Doornspijk, Netherlands, 1994).

**Mannerism** A style in the arts originating in Italy during the 16th century. Deriving its name from the Italian word *maniera* (manner), the movement developed first in Rome and Florence in the wake of the High Renaissance around 1520. Mannerism extended to all branches of the arts and depended chiefly upon the exaggeration of such Renaissance features as the use of classical motifs and technical virtuosity. Its effect is one of extreme elegance and sophistication. In architecture the chief exponent in the mannerist style was GIULIO ROMANO, who was a pupil of RAPHAEL and introduced numerous distinctive devices. Mannerist architects in Florence included VASARI and AMMANATI; those in northern Europe included de VRIES, Cornelis BOS, and Cornelis FLORIS.

In painting MICHELANGELO and others developed the ideas of Raphael and executed many notable works distinguished by distortions of scale, strong colors, and elongated human figures. Italian artists in the mannerist style included PONTORMO, PARMIGIANINO, Vasari, TINTORETTO, and BRONZINO, whose allegory *Venus, Cupid, Folly, and Time* (1546; National Gallery, London) exemplifies the movement's salient characteristics. From Italy the style was exported to France, where it was used at FONTAINEBLEAU by CELLINI and others, and the Netherlands, where artists included Pieter COECKE VAN AELST, Hendrick GOLTZIUS, and Antonio MORO. Other masters associated with mannerist art include El GRECO, Pieter BRUEGHEL the Elder, and Albrecht ALTDORFER.

In the field of sculpture Mannerism achieved its highest expression in the bronze figures of GIAMBOLOGNA, who based his work largely on the late figures of Michelangelo. Cellini and Ammanati were the other most significant exponents. Eventually the style fell from fashion and by 1660 it had been absorbed by the BAROQUE. Although the term "mannerist" was later used as a derogatory phrase suggestive of artistic decadence, the movement has since been recognized as an important development in its own right.

**Further reading:** John F. Hayward, *Virtuoso Goldsmiths and the Triumph of Mannerism, 1540–1620* (London: Sotheby Parke Bernet, 1976); Linda Murray, *The High Renaissance and Mannerism: Italy, the North, and Spain, 1500–1600* (London: Thames & Hudson and New York: Oxford University Press, 1977).

**Mannerism** A detail from *Madonna dal collo lungo* (The Madonna of the long neck), painted in 1532 by Il Parmigianino. The elongated figures and distorted scale are characteristic of the mannerist style (Uffizi, Florence). *Photo AKG London/Erich Lessing*

**Manrique, Jorge** (1440–1479) *Spanish poet and soldier*
Born at Paredes de Nava, the son of a famous general, Rodrigo Manrique, count of Paredes and grand master of the military Order of Santiago, Manrique was also the grand-nephew of SANTILLANA. Like his father he was a professional soldier, fighting for the Castilian Infante Don Alfonso (against his half-brother Henry IV) and later for Alfonso's sister Isabella. He was killed in battle at Calatrava. The author of about 50 lyric poems, he is remembered for a longer elegy, *Las coplas de Jorge Manrique por la muerte de su padre* (*Stanzas of Jorge Manrique for the death of his father*; 1476). The 43 *coplas* (12-line stanzas in a pattern of eight and four-syllable lines known as *pie quebrado*) are an expression of grief but move from a conventional medieval and Christian emphasis on the brevity and vanity of human life to a more humanistic celebration of Count Rodrigo's character and worldly achievements.

**Mantegna, Andrea** (1431–1506) *Italian painter and engraver*
Born near Vicenza, Mantegna served his apprenticeship in Padua from 1441 as the pupil and adopted son of the archaeologist-artist Francesco SQUARCIONE. His earliest works were dominated by the influence of DONATELLO, who also worked in Padua, and by the archaeological detail that also characterizes many of his later paintings.

Chief of these early works was the fresco decoration for the Ovetari chapel (1448–55), in which Mantegna demonstrated his original mastery of perspective; these frescoes were largely destroyed in 1944. He married the daughter of Jacopo Bellini in 1454. Mantegna then executed an influential altarpiece for the church of San Zeno in Verona (1459), in which he depicted sacred figures in a group instead of the usual triptych (see SACRA CONVERSAZIONE), before being appointed court painter to the Gonzaga family in Mantua in 1460. Another painting, *St. Sebastian* (c. 1460; Vienna), again betrays his passion for antiquity and impressed Vasari, but it was not until 1474 that he painted his best work, the Camera degli Sposi in the Palazzo Ducale in Mantua. This painted room includes portraits of the Gonzaga family and their court, classical motifs, and an illusionistic painted ceiling later imitated by artists of the Baroque. Other major works of Mantegna's later period include the nine-canvas series of the *Triumph of Caesar* (1487–94; Hampton Court Palace), *Parnassus* (1497; Louvre, Paris), and the *Triumph of Virtue* (c. 1500; Louvre), all of which had a deeper allegorical significance. One of the most important artists of the early Italian Renaissance, Mantegna influenced many later artists, including Giovanni BELLINI and DÜRER.

**Further reading:** Suzanne Boorsch *et al*, *Andrea Mantegna* (New York: Museum of Modern Art, 1993); Jack M. Greenstein, *Mantegna and Painting as Historical Narrative* (Chicago, Ill. and London: University of Chicago Press, 1992).

**Mantovano, Battista** See SPAGNOLI, GIOVAN BATTISTA

**Mantua** A city in Lombardy, northern Italy. Protected by lakes on three sides, Mantua was first an Etruscan settlement and then Roman. In the late Middle Ages Mantua was governed by the Bonacolsi family (1276–1328) before the GONZAGA seized power and ruled for three centuries. With imperial support, astute government, sound administration, and the approval of the city's leading families, the Gonzaga gave Mantua security, independence, and political prestige. Local agriculture and textiles brought prosperity to the city, which attained a population of about 25,000 by 1500. Under the Gonzaga Mantua was a splendid center of the arts and scholarship. MANTEGNA was court painter, the architects Giulio ROMANO and ALBERTI designed a number of Mantua's buildings, and the humanist educator VITTORINO DA FELTRE made Mantua a center of learning. The writers CASTIGLIONE and TASSO also enjoyed Gonzaga patronage. Notable buildings which have survived from the period of the Renaissance include the cathedral (rebuilt in the 16th century), the churches of San Francesco (1304), San Sebastiano (1460–70), and Sant' Andrea (begun 1472), the ducal palace (begun 1292), the Palazzo della Ragione (13th to 15th centuries), and the Palazzo del TÈ (1525–35).

**Mantuan** See SPAGNOLI, GIOVAN BATTISTA

**Manuel I** (Emanuel) (1469–1521) *King of Portugal (1495–1521)*
Known as "the Fortunate," he succeeded his cousin John II ("the Perfect Prince"), whose heir, Afonso, had died in a riding accident (1490). Manuel's reign saw Portugal established as a global power, with Vasco da GAMA's voyage to India, CABRAL's landfall in Brazil, the appointment of Alfonso ALBUQUERQUE as viceroy over Portugal's Indian possessions, and the establishment of trading links with Persia and China. Hoping to unite the whole Iberian peninsula under the Portuguese crown, he married successively two daughters of FERDINAND II AND ISABELLA I. As a condition of his first marriage the Catholic monarchs insisted on the expulsion of the JEWS from Portugal (1497). A zealous builder of monasteries, Manuel gave his name to the MANUELINE STYLE of decoration.

**Manuel, Niklaus** See DEUTSCH, NIKLAUS MANUEL

**Manueline style** (Portuguese **Arte Manuelina**) A style in Portuguese architecture associated with the reign (1495–1521) of King MANUEL I, under whom numerous monasteries and churches were built. Three architects active in the early 16th century are preeminently associated with the introduction of the Manueline style: the brothers Diogo (c. 1470–1531) and Francisco (c. 1480–1547) de Arruda and Diogo de Boytac (or Boitac; fl. 1498–1525). It was contemporaneous with and partly influenced by the early PLATERESQUE in Spain and, like plateresque, incorporates *mudéjar* (Spanish Moorish) elements and represents a transition from Gothic to Renaissance modes. Its characteristic decorative motif is a carved stone rope, thickly knotted and twisted round windows and doorways, coiled around pinnacles, looped from vaulting, and in many other situations; coral, tree branches, artichokes, and other organic forms, often with a marine connection, are also worked into the designs, which are generally carved in much higher relief than their plateresque equivalents. The monasteries at Tomar, BATALHA, Belém, and Alcobaça exhibit examples of Manueline style, and it was also exported to Portuguese possessions overseas, such as Goa.

**manuscripts** Although the Renaissance period is generally seen as preeminently the era of the rise of PRINTING, manuscripts remained significant both as prizes to be sought out and collected and as prestige items to be commissioned. In the early Renaissance, rare manuscripts, particularly of classical texts, were reproduced by copyists who were often skilled calligraphers and who, with the aid of illuminators (illustrators), turned the copies into desirable objects in their own right; after the invention of printing manuscripts containing accurate texts were sought with a view to using them as printers' exemplars. Thus, in addition to a growing percentage of printed volumes, a wealthy bibliophile's library usually contained a number of manuscripts, often of great rarity or beauty, though Duke Federico de Montefeltre of Urbino (1422–82) is said to have refused to allow any printed books into his renowned library. A particularly valued but rare category of Renaissance manuscript to survive is the holograph of a contemporary writer; a famous early example is a manuscript of the *Decameron* written in BOCCACCIO's own hand (Berlin Staatliche Museen Hamilton MS 90).

PETRARCH and Boccaccio were the leading lights of the first generation of Western scholars to be active collectors of manuscripts of important classical Latin texts. Classical Greek texts came within the purview of Western bibliophiles as contacts between the western and eastern branches of Christendom increased in the early 15th century (a result of the last Byzantine emperors' attempts to achieve a rapprochement that would bring the military forces of the West to the aid of their beleaguered empire). The fall of CONSTANTINOPLE to the Ottoman Turks in 1453, followed by that of the Byzantine cultural center at Mistra in the Peloponnese (1460), accelerated the flow of scholars and manuscripts from East to West.

Wealthy bibliophiles, such as the Spanish diplomat Diego de HURTADO DE MENDOZA, employed networks of agents to track down manuscripts in the Levant. Ambassadors were themselves often used as agents in the acquisition of manuscripts; the French historian Jacques-Auguste De Thou (or Thuanus; 1555–1617) engaged the French envoy to Constantinople to find manuscripts for his patron Henry IV. On occasion manuscripts were obtained by more unusual routes: as part-exchange for a Turkish prisoner or as an element in a dowry.

The collecting of manuscripts and the commissioning of new copies were complementary in disseminating texts of the classics. Men like the Florentine bookseller Vespasiano da BISTICCI both obtained manuscripts for collectors and hired the scribes and illuminators necessary to have them copied. Other bibliophiles, such as Poggio BRACCIOLINI, went on manuscript forays in person, scouring monastic and ecclesiastical libraries for classical texts which they then either bought or had copied. If need arose, some passionate collectors such as Poggio and SALUTATI even did the copying themselves, and the versions of antique scripts produced by them and the scribes they trained ultimately influenced the development of printing types. Identification of individual Renaissance scribes is not always just a matter of paleographical detective work; a number of scribes working for important patrons signed their output, among them the Florentines Antonio Maro and Gherardo del Ciriago, both of whom were hired to work on commissions from Vespasiano. Often such people appear not to have been full-time professional calligraphers but to have undertaken copying work to supplement their incomes.

The personal notes added by scribes to the manuscripts are an invaluable source not only for the identification of the scribes themselves but also often of the person who commissioned the book and the date and circumstances of its production. Prestige manuscripts were normally decorated with the patron's coat of arms. Occasionally a manuscript produced with no particular buyer in mind has the space for the coat of arms left blank, to be filled in after purchase. The illumination of many Renaissance manuscripts is sumptuous and often deliberately modeled on antique or Carolingian motifs; opening pages have intricate multicolored borders and initials, often with other decoration such as putti, EMBLEMS, or the portrait of the person who commissioned it or for whom it was intended as a gift. Magnificent and expensive volumes were the currency of diplomacy, an acceptable present for a bibliophile monarch like MATTHIAS CORVINUS of Hungary, a pope, or other humanistically minded grandee. Even after the printed word took over as the successor to the handwritten, manuscript illuminators continued to embellish prestigious printed texts for wealthy and discerning patrons.

See also: ANTIQUARIANISM; CALLIGRAPHY; LATIN STUDIES; LIBRARIES; TYPOGRAPHY

Further reading: Leighton D. Reynolds and N. G. Wilson, *Scribes and Scholars: A Guide to the Transmission of Greek and Latin Literature* (Oxford, U.K.: Clarendon Press, 3rd ed. 1997).

**Manutius, Aldus** ((Teob)aldo Mannucci, (Teob)aldo Manuzio) (1449–1515) *Italian scholar and printer*
After studying Latin and Greek, Aldus became tutor to PICO DELLA MIRANDOLA's nephews at Carpi. There he conceived the idea of establishing a printing house at Venice to publish classical Greek texts, drawing on the resources of the Venetian libraries and the expertise of the city's community of Greek exiles. The ALDINE PRESS (founded 1494/95) produced the first printed editions of nearly all the major Greek authors, the years 1502–04 alone seeing editions of Demosthenes, Euripides, Herodotus, Sophocles, and Thucydides. The Cretan Marcus Musurus (1470–1517) undertook a large share of the scholarly work involved. Sometime before 1502 Aldus founded his NEAKADEMIA (Academy) to promote Greek studies; the names of about 40 members of this club are known and its famous visitors included ERASMUS and Thomas LINACRE. When Aldus died the press was carried on at first by his father-in-law, then after 1533 by his son Paolo, and finally by Paolo's son, another Aldus, after which it passed out of the family's hands.

See also: PRINTING; TYPOGRAPHY

Further reading: Martin Davies, *Aldus Manutius: Printer and Publisher of Renaissance Venice* (Oxford, U.K.: Oxford University Press, 1995); H. George Fletcher *In Praise of Albertus Manutius: A Quincentenary Exhibition*

(New York: Pierpont Morgan Library, 1995); Martin Lowry, *The World of Aldus Manutius: Business and Scholarship in Renaissance Venice* (Oxford, U.K.: Basil Blackwell, 1979).

**Manzoli, Pier Angelo** See PALINGENIUS

**maps** See CARTOGRAPHY

**Marburg, Colloquy of** (1529) A conference summoned by PHILIP OF HESSE to effect a reconciliation between the German and Swiss reformers. It was attended by LUTHER and Phillip MELANCHTHON on the German side and by ZWINGLI, John OECOLAMPADIUS, and Martin BUCER on the Swiss. There was agreement on most of the articles, but the Colloquy ended in failure when the Zwinglians refused to accept the doctrine of consubstantiation (*see* TRANSUBSTANTIATION).

**Marciana, Bibliotheca** (in Florence) The library of the Dominican convent of San Marco. The basis of the collection was the library of some 800 volumes accumulated by Niccolò NICCOLI and purchased on his death by Cosimo de' MEDICI; he entrusted them to the Dominicans, who housed them in a building designed by MICHELOZZO (1441). Many were dispersed and destroyed by SAVONAROLA and his followers. In 1508 the library was bought by Pope Leo X and returned to Florence in 1532 by Clement VII. In 1571 Grand Duke Cosimo I made the Marciana a public library. In 1808 the collection was amalgamated with that of the LAURENZIANA.

**Marciana, Bibliotheca** (in Venice) The library housed in the Libreria Sansoviniana on the Piazzetta. The building, begun in 1536, is considered the masterpiece of its designer Andrea SANSOVINO. It was finished by Vincenzo SCAMOZZI in the 1580s and inside it is adorned with stuccoes by VITTORIA and paintings by TITIAN, TINTORETTO, VERONESE, and Andrea SCHIAVONE.

The foundation of the collection was the gift of manuscripts made by Cardinal BESSARION to the Venetian senate in 1468. Among its treasures are the Grimani Breviary, bought in 1489 by Cardinal GRIMANI from a former Milanese ambassador in Flanders, and the CAMALDOLESE CHART. Associated from its beginnings with Greek studies, it contains many Greek items among its 13,000 manuscripts. See illustration p. 427.

**Marenzio, Luca** (1553/4–99) *Italian composer*
Born at Coccaglio, near Brescia, Marenzio probably spent his early years as a singer in the service of the Gonzagas in Mantua. He moved to Rome to join the household first (c. 1574–78) of Cardinal Cristoforo Madruzzo, and then (1578–86) of Cardinal Luigi d'Este, serving both as a singer but also publishing many MADRIGALS, for which he

became internationally famous. In 1588 he entered the employ of Ferdinando de' Medici in Florence, and contributed to his wedding celebrations (1589). Later in 1589 he returned to Rome, where his chief patron was Virginio Orsini, Duke of Bracciano. Another patron, Cardinal Cinzio Aldobrandini, recommended Marenzio as *maestro* to the king of Poland. Marenzio arrived in Poland in 1596 and remained for two years. He then returned to Rome, where he died.

Marenzio wrote a small amount of sacred music, but it is for his madrigals that he is celebrated. During his life 18 madrigal books (1580–99) for four to ten voices were published, as well as five books of villanelles and two books of motets. The early madrigals (written before 1587) are frequently settings of pastoral texts by, among others, PETRARCH; these were extensively imitated throughout Europe, and in England by Thomas MORLEY. The mood of the madrigals became increasingly serious throughout Marenzio's career, with melancholy texts and greater use of dissonance and chromaticism.

**Margaret of Austria** (1480–1530) *Regent and governor of the Netherlands for Charles V (1507–15, 1519–30)*
She was the daughter of MAXIMILIAN I and Mary of Burgundy. After her brief marriage (1497) to the Spanish heir, the Infante John, ended with his death, she married (1501) Duke Philibert II of Savoy, who died in 1504. Following the sudden death of her brother, Philip the Handsome of Burgundy (1506), Maximilian appointed Margaret guardian of her infant nephew, the future CHARLES V, and his younger sister, the future MARY OF HUNGARY. In the Netherlands Margaret extended Hapsburg domination. She pursued a foreign policy favorable to England and hostile to France, but did negotiate the "Ladies' Peace" between Spain and France at Cambrai (1529). She employed the sculptor Konrad MEIT of Worms and the painters Jan MOSTAERT and Bernard van ORLEY; the latter's portrait of her in austere dress is in the Musées Royaux des Beaux-Arts, Brussels. She also encouraged writers and scholars. The palace built for her at MALINES (1507–26) combined Renaissance decoration with a basically Gothic structure. As a memorial to herself and Philibert she commissioned the church at Brou, on the outskirts of Bourg-en-Bresse, Burgundy; it was built by the architect Lodewyk van Bodeghem (c. 1470–1540) between 1512 and 1532. Here Meit worked from 1525 to 1531 on her tomb, an ebullient concoction of late Gothic and Renaissance elements.

**Margaret of Austria** See MARGARET OF PARMA

**Margaret of Parma** (Margaret of Austria) (1522–1586) *Duchess of Parma (1547–86)*
Margaret was the illegitimate daughter of Emperor Charles V by a Flemish woman, Margaret of Ghent, and

she was brought up in the Netherlands by her great-aunt MARGARET OF AUSTRIA and aunt MARY OF HUNGARY, who were successively regents there. She was first married (1533) to Duke Alessandro de' Medici of Florence, who was assassinated in 1537, and she later (1542) married Ottavio Farnese of Parma, by whom she became the mother of the general Alessandro FARNESE. Appointed regent of the Netherlands (1559) by her half-brother Philip II, she was confronted by a gathering storm of opposition to Spanish tyranny and religious persecution, made worse by Philip's inflexible stance. After the rejection of the Compromise of Breda (1566) the revolt of the NETHERLANDS began in earnest. Resigning her post to the duke of ALBA, Margaret retired (1567) to Italy, where she lived the rest of her life.

## Marguerite de Navarre (Marguerite d'Angoulême, Margaret of Navarre) (1492–1549) *French patron and writer*

Sister of Francis I of France and widow of Charles, Duke of Alençon, Marguerite married Henry d'Albret, King of Navarre, in 1527: their daughter JEANNE D'ALBRET was the mother of the future King Henry IV of France. Marguerite was respected as a patron of literature and philosophy; her court became a place of refuge for persecuted writers and supporters of religious reform, such as LEFÈVRE D'ÉTAPLES, Bonaventure DES PÉRIERS, and Clément MAROT. Her backing, both explicit and implicit, for the right of women to read the Bible and exercise their talents in scholarship if they so wished and the fact that she herself published writings (instead of keeping them modestly in manuscript for the edification of ladies of her circle) attracted hostile comment from religious conservatives. The best known of Marguerite's own works is the *Heptaméron* (1558–59), a collection of 72 tales of love and passion influenced in form by Boccaccio's DECAMERON; she also wrote poetry, notably *Le Miroir de l'âme pécheresse* (1531; translated by the future Queen Elizabeth of England in 1544 as "The Glasse of the Synnefull Soule") and *Les Marguerites de la Marguerite des princesses* (1547), and a number of plays.

## Mariana, Juan de (c. 1535–1624) *Spanish historian*

The illegitimate son of the dean of the collegiate church of Talavera de la Reina, Mariana entered the Jesuit novitiate (1554), studied at Alcalá, and was ordained in 1561. He became a professor of theology at Rome and also lectured in Sicily, Paris, and Flanders before returning to Spain. He lived in Toledo from 1574 until his death.

*Historiae de rebus Hispaniae libri XX* (1592) was enlarged to 30 books (1605), and a two-volume Spanish version by Mariana was published in the meantime (1601). An uncritical work that drew on every source available and included a wealth of legendary and anecdotal material, Mariana's history of Spain covered events from the earliest times to the death of Ferdinand II and V (1516)

and was written in an impeccable style modeled on LIVY. He also wrote a number of essays on political theory and other subjects, several of them controversial; *De rege et regis institutione* (1599), on kingship, for instance, contained arguments in favor of tyrannicide. His works reflect an enlightened and liberal point of view and independence of judgment.

## Marie de' Medici (Marie de Médicis) (1573–1642) *Queen consort of France*

The daughter of Grand Duke Francesco I of Florence, she became the second wife of HENRY IV of France in 1600 and, after Henry's assassination, regent (1610–14) on behalf of her young son, Louis XIII. She arranged for Louis to marry the Infanta Anna and for her daughter Elizabeth to marry the future Philip IV of Spain, thus ensuring a Franco-Spanish alliance. After Louis came of age she suffered a period of banishment (1617–22), and Cardinal Richelieu, at first her protégé and adviser, increasingly took the side of the young king against her and her pro-Hapsburg policy during the later 1620s. Marie was responsible for building the Palais du Luxembourg in Paris, and in 1622 commissioned RUBENS to produce for it a major series of pictures on her life. In 1631 she fled to Flanders, to the protection of the Archduchess ISABELLA, and never went back to France.

## Marlowe, Christopher (1564–1593) *English dramatist*

Born and sent to school in Canterbury, Marlowe took his BA at Cambridge in 1584. Thereafter he lived, like other UNIVERSITY WITS, in London, or traveled abroad on secret government service. RALEIGH, NASHE, and other prominent writers were among his friends or admirers. He had a reputation for atheism, and at the time of his death at the hands of Ingram Frisar in a tavern stabbing at Deptford, a warrant was out for his arrest.

The two parts of *Tamburlaine*, Marlowe's earliest play, published in 1590, were probably written in 1587 and 1588; like his other tragedies, they were immediately successful and often revived. His mastery of blank verse (which Ben Jonson called Marlowe's "mighty line") and ability to create a powerful central character were already apparent. *Dr Faustus* (1604) and *The Jew of Malta* (1633) were probably written in, respectively, 1588/89 and 1589/90, with *Edward II* (1594), his best play in terms of construction, following in about 1593. *The Tragedy of Dido, Queen of Carthage* (1594) was completed by Thomas Nashe. All Marlowe's poems were published posthumously: his translations of Ovid's *Amores* (c. 1597) and the first book of Lucan's *Pharsalia* (1600), the erotic fragment *Hero and Leander* (1598) in heroic couplets (completed by CHAPMAN), and his famous song "Come live with me, and be my love" (in *The Passionate Pilgrim*, 1599).

**Further reading:** Clare Harraway, *Re-Citing Marlowe: Approaches to the Drama* (Aldershot, U.K.: Ashgate, 2000); Charles Nicholl, *The Reckoning: The Murder of Christopher Marlowe* (Chicago, Ill: University of Chicago Press, 1995).

**Marnix, Philipp van, Lord of Ste.-Aldegonde** (1538–1598) *Netherlands Calvinist theologian and statesman*
Born a member of the lesser Netherlands nobility in Brussels, Marnix studied in Geneva as a young man and became a personal disciple of CALVIN and BEZA. He took part in the insurrection against Spain in 1566 and was consequently forced to go into exile in Germany, where he helped organize the important Synod of Emden (1571). After returning to Holland in 1572 he became a close political and religious adviser to WILLIAM (I) THE SILENT and played a prominent part in drafting the Pacification of Ghent (1576). An author of some skill, Marnix wrote a number of influential polemical works, including the famous *De biënkorf der heilige roomsche kerche* (*The Beehive of the Holy Roman Church*; 1569), a satirical attack on the old Church in the style of Rabelais, which was translated into English in 1579.

**Marot, Clément** (c. 1496–1544) *French poet*
Clément Marot was born at Cahors, the son of Jean Marot, court poet to Anne of Brittany. He entered the service of the future MARGUERITE DE NAVARRE in 1518 or 1519 and, after the death of his father in 1526, became *valet de chambre* to Francis I. His first collection of poetry, *Adolescence Clémentine*, appeared in 1532. Twice arrested for eating meat during the Lenten period, Marot was suspected of Lutheran sympathies and found himself obliged to leave Paris in 1534. He took refuge first with Marguerite de Navarre, then with RENÉE DE FRANCE in Ferrara.

On his return to France in 1536 Marot was reinstated as court poet and continued his metrical translation of the Psalms, a task he had undertaken before his exile. The first part of this work, *Trente Psaumes* (1541), was condemned on publication by the Sorbonne; Marot was forced to flee once again, this time to Geneva, where he published a second edition of his Psalms (1543), and thence to Turin. Marot's contribution to French poetry was influenced by his periods of residence in Italy: he introduced several new forms, such as the epigram and the eclogue, and composed some of the earliest French sonnets. His other works include numerous rondeaux, ballades, and chansons; *L'Enfer* ("The Inferno"; 1542), an allegorical poem inspired by his first term of imprisonment; and editions of *Le Roman de la rose* (1527) and the works of François Villon (1533).

**Marprelate controversy** An English theological controversy initiated in 1588 by attacks on the episcopal system of Church government by an unidentified writer calling himself "Martin Marprelate." Seven Marprelate pamphlets, printed (1588–89) on a secret press, are known; they are important not so much for their content as for their vivid satirical prose style. John LYLY and Thomas NASHE were among the writers who joined in the controversy on the bishops' side. Of the two puritans arrested on suspicion of being "Martin Marprelate," John Penry (1559–93) was executed and John Udall (or Uvedale; ?1560–92) died in prison.

**Further reading:** Elizabeth Appleton, *An Anatomy of the Marprelate Controversy 1588–1596* (Lewiston, N.Y.: Edwin Mellen Press, 2001).

*marranos* See CONVERSOS

**Mars** In Roman mythology, the god of war, often equated with the Greek god Ares. The fable about him that most appealed to Renaissance artists was his affair with the goddess of love, VENUS.

**Martini, Francesco di Giorgio** See FRANCESCO DI GIORGIO MARTINI

**Martini, Simone** (c. 1285–1344) *Italian painter*
Born in Siena, Martini was the pupil of DUCCIO DI BUONINSEGNA, from whom he inherited a liking for sumptuous color. His earliest documented work was the *Maestà* (1315), an enormous fresco painted on the end wall of the Sala del Mappamondo of the Palazzo Pubblico in Siena. Retouched by Martini in 1321, this work imitates a similar piece by Duccio, although with an added Gothic element. In 1317 Martini painted a notable altarpiece *Louis of Toulouse Crowning his Brother, King Robert of Anjou* (1317; Museo di Capodimonte, Naples) and subsequently executed a number of elegant court paintings, such as the influential *Madonna* polyptych (1319; Museo Nazionale, Pisa), which reflected French Gothic art. Equally important was his *Guidoriccio da Fogliano* (1328; Palazzo Pubblico, Siena), a portrait of a Sienese general, in which the central equestrian figure is placed in a panoramic landscape—an innovation in that this was probably the first Sienese painting not serving a religious purpose. His best-known work was the *Annunciation* (1333: Uffizi, Florence), painted in collaboration with his brother-in-law, Lippo Memmi (active 1317–47). Martini spent his last years in Avignon, where he met Petrarch. Other notable works include scenes from the life of St. Martin of Tours (c. 1330; lower church of San Francesco, Assisi) and *Christ returning to his Parents after disputing with the Doctors* (1342; Liverpool).

**Martyr, Peter** See PETER MARTYR (Pietro Martire d'Anghiera)

**Martyr, Peter** See PETER MARTYR (Pietro Martire Vermigli)

**Mary, Queen of Scots** (1542–1587) *Queen of Scotland (1542–67), Queen consort of France (1559–60)*
The only child of James V of Scotland to survive him, Mary was sent to be educated at the French court (1548) and in 1558 married the future Francis II of France. From 1558 many people, including herself, regarded her as the legitimate queen of England, on the grounds that ELIZABETH I was a bastard. After Francis's death, she returned to Scotland (1561), a Catholic queen of an officially Protestant (but in fact divided) country.

At first Mary successfully pursued an even-handed course, but after her marriage (1565) to Henry Stuart, Lord Darnley, she more openly favored the Catholics. Darnley, however, earned her hatred by murdering (1566) her secretary and favorite, David Rizzio. Darnley was assassinated in 1567, probably by James Hepburn, Earl of Bothwell, whom Mary afterwards married. Scottish opinion, already discontented with her policies, was outraged, both by the marriage and Mary's widely suspected complicity in Darnley's death. A rebellion by Protestant nobles forced her abdication (July 24, 1567), and she fled to England (1568). Elizabeth I kept her confined in various castles, but she became the focus of several conspiracies. In 1586 the government acquired proof of her involvement in the plot organized by Anthony Babington (1561–86) to assassinate Elizabeth and rouse the English Catholics in support of a Spanish invasion force that would place her on the English throne. Mary was put on trial, found guilty, and, with Elizabeth's reluctant acquiescence, executed at Fotheringay castle.

**Further reading:** Marcus Merriman, *The Rough Wooings: Mary Queen of Scots 1542–1551* (East Linton, U.K.: Tuckwell, 2000); Susan Watkins and Mark Fiennes, *Mary, Queen of Scots* (London: Thames & Hudson, 2001).

**Mary I** (1516–1558) *Queen of England and Ireland (1553–58)*
The daughter of HENRY VIII and his first wife, Catherine of Aragon, Mary was declared illegitimate (1533) after the end of her parents' marriage. She remained loyal to her mother and to her faith, but was compelled to acknowledge her illegitimacy and to renounce Catholicism. In 1544 the crown was entailed upon her after any lawful child of Henry. Despite attempts to place Lady Jane GREY on the throne, Mary succeeded her half-brother, EDWARD VI, in 1553. News of her marriage to PHILIP II of Spain caused revolts among her subjects, but Mary was determined to return England to the Catholic Church, and in 1555 papal authority was restored in England. The ensuing martyrdom of around 300 Protestants (1555–58) earned Mary the nickname "Bloody Mary." In 1557 England's alliance with Spain in the war against France cost her Calais, the last English stronghold on the Continent. Mary died without a child to continue the Catholic succession and the throne passed to her Protestant half-sister ELIZABETH I.

**Mary of Hungary** (1505–1558) *Queen consort of Hungary (1522–26)*
The younger sister of Emperor CHARLES V, she was known as Mary of Austria before her marriage to King Louis II of Hungary and Bohemia in 1522. When the childless Louis was killed at the battle of MOHÁCS (1526) his realms passed to the Hapsburgs. It was Mary who persuaded an assembly of Hungarian nobles at Pressburg to elect her brother Ferdinand (later Emperor FERDINAND I) as their king, and she later mediated between Ferdinand and Charles in their quarrel over the succession to the empire. Mary was appointed regent of the Netherlands in 1531, a post that she held until 1556, the year of Charles's abdication. She retired with him to Spain, settling at the castle of Cigales, near Valladolid, where she died.

Despite the growth of Protestantism in the Netherlands during her regency, Mary's sway was generally moderate and the enforcement of edicts against heretics was carried out in a manner that did not provoke widespread discontent. She was a keen patron of the arts, employing Jacques DUBROEUCQ as architect at her castles of Binche and Mariemont and furnishing them with pictures by the great Flemish masters and by TITIAN which she took with her when she retired to Spain.

**Masaccio, Tommaso** (Tommaso di Giovanni di Simone Guidi) (1401–1428) *Italian painter*
Bynamed Masaccio ("slovenly Tom") because of his slipshod appearance, he was born at Castel San Giovanni di Altura and moved to Florence in 1417, where he joined the Arte dei Medici e Speziali in 1422. Only a handful of paintings are definitely attributed to him, the earliest of which was the polyptych painted for the church of Sta. Maria del Carmine in Pisa (1426), which is now largely destroyed. The central panel, *Madonna and Child Enthroned*, survives in the National Gallery, London, and indicates the debt Masaccio owed to GIOTTO, to BRUNELLESCHI's approach to linear perspective, and to DONATELLO's ideas about the construction of the human figure. Similar influences are evident in his fresco of the *Trinity* (1425–27), painted for Sta. Maria Novella in Florence, and again in his masterpiece, the frescoes for the Brancacci chapel of Sta. Maria del Carmine in Florence. Although some of these latter frescoes have been lost, those that remain—painted in association with Filippino LIPPI and MASOLINO—illustrate Masaccio's masterly control of *chiaroscuro* and revolutionary concentration upon the humanistic spirit of his subjects. Such scenes as *The Expulsion of Adam and Eve*, *Tribute Money*, and *St. Peter Giving Alms* in this chapel became models for subsequent

styles in combination with new techniques of free composition, and the basing of a Mass composition on a freely invented subject. Composers borrowed entire polyphonic pieces as the basis of a composition and this "parody mass" became the most popular form throughout the 16th century.

PALESTRINA became the first Italian to contribute substantially to the composition of Mass settings after a long period of dominance by northern composers. The Council of Trent instructed that all settings be intelligible to the listeners, and Palestrina paid great attention to the text. He was the most prolific composer of Masses (104) in the century, and his compositions were widely disseminated. Other figures who dominated Mass composition were VICTORIA, LASSUS, and BYRD.

See also: LITURGY

## Massacre of St. Bartholomew (August 23–24, 1572)
The massacre of some 3000 HUGUENOTS by the Paris mob. The queen dowager of France, CATHERINE DE' MEDICI, decided at the urging of the GUISE faction that it was necessary to assassinate the Huguenot leader, the comte de COLIGNY, Admiral of France. On August 22 a Guise agent shot but failed to kill him. As tension rose in Paris, Catherine panicked and persuaded King Charles IX to authorize the elimination of all the Huguenot leaders, who were gathered in the capital for the wedding of Henry of Navarre. Only a few were to be killed; the duke of Guise himself stabbed Coligny in his bed at 2 a.m. on August 24. However, the virulently Catholic Paris mob took matters into their own hands, and spontaneously began a general massacre of Huguenots.

Similar massacres occurred in provincial towns during the autumn, causing perhaps 10,000 deaths. The long-term effect was to destroy Catherine's image as conciliator and to throw the Huguenots on the defensive, making them safeguard their own position rather than seek to control France.

Further reading: Barbara B. Diefendorf, *Beneath the Cross: Catholics and Huguenots in Sixteenth-Century Paris* (Oxford, U.K.: Oxford University Press, 1997).

## Massys, Quintin See METSYS, QUINTIN

## Master E. S. (mid-15th century) *Anonymous German artist also known as the Master of 1466*
An engraver and goldsmith, he was an early user of copperplate engraving and was possibly the inventor of the cross-hatch technique, with which he produced subtle tonal effects. He was remarkable too for the extent of his works. Three hundred of the engravings attributed to him have survived, although only 18 are signed E. S. His skillful use of line engraving can be seen in his religious subjects such as the Annunciation, Nativity, or Man of Sorrows. He covered a wide range of subjects however and

progressed from technically accomplished early engravings with careful detail work to a more vigorous mature style.

## Master of Flémalle See CAMPIN, ROBERT

## Masters of Nuremberg, Little See LITTLE MASTERS (OF NUREMBERG)

## mathematics
The Renaissance was a somewhat transitional period in the history of mathematics. Its first task was to collect, edit, publish, and absorb the main classical mathematical texts. Thereafter mathematicians sought to work out a more conveneint formalism and to express within it some of the basic mathematical operations. Thus, in ARITHMETIC not only did the Hindu numerals win acceptance, but the basic algorithms of addition, multiplication, division, and subtraction were worked out for both integers and fractions. An important development at the end of the period was the invention of logarithms, first by Jost BÜRGI and then by the Englishman John NAPIER, who coined the word (Greek *logos* reckoning + *arithmos* number). Considerable advances were also made in ALGEBRA. Equations came increasingly to be written in a standard form, and general solutions were found in the 16th century to cubic equations. In TRIGONOMETRY the main functions were defined in modern terms, while comprehensive tables were provided by RHETICUS. Development was less apparent in the field of GEOMETRY, but understanding nonetheless improved sufficiently to prepare the way for the enormous advances made in the 17th century by such mathematicians as René Descartes, Pierre de Fermat, and Isaac Newton.

## Matteo di Giovanni (c. 1435–1495) *Italian painter*
A leading member of the Sienese school, Matteo di Giovanni was probably a pupil of VECCHIETTA although POLLAIUOLO also heavily influenced his decorative linear style, which made generous use of gold, particularly in his numerous *Madonnas*. In 1465 he completed a polyptych for his native Borgo San Sepolcro, of which the central panel, the *Baptism of Christ*, is now in the National Gallery, London. Other works include four versions of the *Massacre of the Innocents*, three (1482–91) painted in a realistic manner and one in inlaid marble in the floor of Siena cathedral, and an *Assumption* (1475; National Gallery, London).

## Matthias Corvinus (Matthias I Hunyadi) (1440–1490) *King of Hungary (1458–90)*
Matthias was the second son of János Hunyadi (c. 1387–1456), hero of the Hungarian resistance against the Turks, especially the siege of Belgrade (1456). Despite the opposition of some nobles, he was elected king of Hungary, but the malcontents then crowned Emperor FREDERICK III in Matthias's stead (1459) and it was not until 1464 that

Matthias had sufficiently established his position against his foreign and domestic enemies for his coronation to take place. In 1469 he was also elected king of Bohemia, but after years of fighting he was forced to relinquish his claim to Ladislaus of Poland.

Frederick III offered to recognize Matthias as king of Hungary on condition that he should succeed him if Matthias died without an heir. Matthias declared war (1481) and drove Frederick from Vienna (1485), which he occupied henceforth as his capital. He also extended his territories by conquest and consolidated his position by alliances, thus making himself the principal power in central Europe. He was still attempting to secure the succession for his illegitimate son János Corvinus (1473–1504), a plan fiercely resisted by his childless third wife, Beatrice of Naples, when he unexpectedly died.

Matthias was a ruler of outstanding qualities, combining statesmanship with military prowess, administrative adroitness with a passion for learning and the arts. He was also a noted patron of music, employing Netherlandish musicians and a renowned choir in his chapel royal. It was on his initiative that the university of Budapest was founded in 1475. Some of the greatest Italian scribes copied books for Matthias's royal library; one Florentine aptly wrote in 1489 that Matthias "means to outdo every other ruler in respect of his library—as he does in all other respects." Such a tribute is a measure of Matthias's success in presenting himself upon the European stage as the ideal of a Renaissance prince.

**Mattioli, Pier Andrea** (1501–1577) *Italian physician and botanist*

He was born in Siena, studied in Padua, and traveled widely in Italy to collect plants. His lengthy *Commentarii* on the herbal of Dioscorides (c. 40–c. 90 CE) were intended as practical advice for physicians. The book was first published in Venice in 1544 and went into many editions and translations, the first in Latin, following three Italian ones, in 1554. The commentaries go beyond Dioscorides' plants to include Mattioli's own discoveries and reports from his correspondents.

The two series of illustrations, one first published in the Venice edition of 1554, the larger ones appearing in a Prague version of 1562, and both copied repeatedly, are unusual in representing massed foliage, fruit, and flowers instead of single twigs or plants. The pearwood blocks of over 1000 of the large illustrations were bought in the 1750s by a French botanist, H.-L. Duhamel du Monceau, who used some of them to illustrate his own book on trees and shrubs. The rest remained in the possession of his family, and the last of them (about 120) were sold in London in 1989.

**Maurice of Nassau** (1567–1625) *Prince of Orange (1618–25) and Count of Nassau (1584–1625)*

The son of WILLIAM (I) THE SILENT and Anne of Saxony, he succeeded his father as commander-in-chief of the Dutch forces and became stadtholder of most Dutch provinces. In a brilliant military campaign he took Breda (1590) and had driven the Spanish out of the northern and eastern provinces by 1598. After years of inconclusive struggle he reluctantly agreed a 12-year truce with Spain in 1609, and was then embroiled in a bitter religious and political conflict with his former loyal supporter, the great statesman and advocate of the truce, Johan van OLDENBARNEVELDT. Maurice gained an infamous triumph by Oldenbarneveldt's execution (1619). In 1621 he resumed the fight against Spain, but with little success.

**Mauro, Fra** See CAMALDOLESE CHART

**Maximilian I** (1459–1519) *Holy Roman Emperor (1493–1519)*

The son of FREDERICK III and Eleonora of Portugal, Maximilian had great abilities; he was a daring huntsman and a brave knight, an expert on infantry, and a man of letters who probably wrote part of an allegory and a treatise on hunting. He was a popular ruler, but also a gullible man who embarked on unrealistically ambitious ventures. In the empire at large his reforms failed, but in Austria they laid the foundations of a unified administration. His dynastic arrangements greatly strengthened Hapsburg power and influence.

Maximilian's marriage (1477) to Mary, heiress of Burgundy, brought war with Louis XI of France, but in the name of his son, Philip, he secured Flanders and the Netherlands (1482) and Franche-Comté and Artois (1493). Maximilian expelled the Hungarians who were occupying much of Austria (1490) and drove the Turks out of Carinthia (1492). His second marriage, to Bianca Maria Sforza of Milan (1494), encouraged his Italian ambitions, but after years of futile and expensive effort he had to abandon Milan to France and Verona to Venice (1516). The Swiss effectively established their political independence from the empire in 1499.

In his attempts at reform, Maximilian persuaded the imperial diet to promulgate public peace (1495), which banned private warfare. He set up the AULIC COUNCIL and his own court of justice, but his constant absences from Germany and obstruction from its princes foiled his efforts. He was strong enough to block the efforts of the princes to increase their power in the empire and was largely responsible for the failure of the *Reichsregiment*, an executive committee of princes established in 1500.

Perhaps Maximilian's greatest achievements were dynastic. In addition to securing most of the Burgundian inheritance he obtained Tyrol (1490) peacefully by negotiation with his cousin. He arranged the marriage of his son, Philip the Handsome (1476–1506), to the Infanta Joanna, thus ensuring the Spanish inheritance for his grandson, CHARLES V. The marriage of his two grandchildren to Hungarian royalty brought Bohemia and Hungary to the Hapsburgs after the death of Louis II of Hungary at the battle of MOHÁCS (1526).

**Further reading:** Gerhard Benecke, *Maximilian I (1459–1519): An Analytical Biography* (London and Boston, Mass.: Routledge & Kegan Paul, 1982).

## Maximilian II (1527–1576) *Holy Roman Emperor (1564–76)*

Maximilian was the eldest son of Emperor FERDINAND I and Anna of Hungary. Born in Vienna but educated mainly in Spain, he was early involved in the business of empire. He married his cousin Maria, daughter of CHARLES V, in 1548. During the 1550s he was principally involved in protecting Austria against the Turks. Like his father, he adopted a tolerant policy in religious matters, and was even accused of being a crypto-Lutheran. In 1562 he was chosen king of the Romans and succeeded to the empire on his father's death (1564).

Maximilian inherited his father's taste for the arts and sciences; he tried unsuccessfully to lure PALESTRINA and GIAMBOLOGNA to his court in Vienna and employed the painters ARCIMBOLDO and SPRANGER and the architect and sculptor Hans Mont of Ghent. The business of his reign, like that of his father, was chiefly taken up with defending the empire's eastern border against the Turks and trying to ensure peaceful coexistence between Catholics and Protestants in Hapsburg lands. The ambiguity of Maximilian's own theological position is highlighted by his deathbed refusal to receive the Catholic sacrament. He was succeeded by his son, RUDOLF II.

## May, Jan See VERMEYEN, JAN CORNELIS

## Mazarine Bible See GUTENBERG, JOHANN

## Mazzoni, Guido (Paganino) (c. 1450–1518) *Italian sculptor*

Born at Modena, Mazzoni worked there and at Ferrara, Venice, and Naples, specializing in dramatic and realistic Nativity and Lamentation scenes. In 1495 he traveled with Charles VIII from Naples to France and helped to popularize the ideals of the Italian Renaissance there. In 1498 he worked on a monument to Charles VIII in the abbey of St. Denis (destroyed in the French Revolution) and later executed an equestrian statue of Louis XII at Blois, also later destroyed. Subsequently he was approached by Henry VIII of England to design a monument for Henry VII in Westminster Abbey, a project which was later undertaken by Pietro TORRIGIANO. Much of the realism in Mazzoni's works was achieved through his frequent use of both life and death masks. In 1516 he returned to Modena, where he died.

## Mechlin or Mechelen See MALINES

## medals See NUMISMATICS

## Medici, Cosimo de' (Cosimo Il Vecchio 1389–1464) *Italian financier and patron of artists and scholars*

The son of the very successful banker, Giovanni de' Medici, Cosimo was exiled from Florence by the ALBIZZI (1433) but promptly recalled by a newly elected council (1434). Thereafter he used his wealth to establish Medici power in the city. While overtly respecting republican forms of government he put his supporters in control of Florentine institutions, notably the *balìa* (committee of magistrates). Cosimo brought prosperity and stability to Florence, spending generously on art and public works. BRUNELLESCHI, MICHELOZZO, GHIBERTI, DELLA ROBBIA, ALBERTI, Fra ANGELICO, and UCCELLO all lived in Florence in Cosimo's time. Cosimo also protected Marsilio FICINO and encouraged the study of Greek.

In Italian affairs Cosimo brought the struggle against Milan to a successful conclusion at the Peace of Cavriana (1441), but his main concern was to preserve stability and freedom from foreign intervention. Cosimo played an important part in the formation of the Italian League (*see* LODI, PEACE OF). He allied Florence with Francesco Sforza, duke of Milan, from 1450. After his death he was honored with the title *pater patriae* (father of his country), which is signified by the letters P.P. carved on his chair in the posthumous portrait of him by PONTORMO (1519; Uffizi, Florence).

**Further reading:** Dale Kent, *Cosimo de' Medici and the Florentine Renaissance: The Patron's Oeuvre* (New Haven, Conn.: Yale University Press, 2000).

## Medici, Lorenzo de' (Lorenzo the Magnificent) (1449–1492) *Italian scholar-prince*

Although Lorenzo outwardly respected republican traditions and never adopted a formal title, he governed Florence with the splendor of a typical Italian Renaissance prince. His lavish entertainments made him popular and his manipulation of Florentine institutions gave him near-autocratic power. He arranged noble marriages for his family and procured a cardinal's hat for his son Giovanni, later Pope LEO X. Lorenzo integrated the administration of Florence with Tuscany and tightened his control through the Council of Seventy and the *balìa* (committee of magistrates). He clashed with Pope SIXTUS IV, whose nephew organized the PAZZI CONSPIRACY (1478), in which Lorenzo's brother was murdered at Mass. Lorenzo ended the war with the papacy that followed (1478–79) by persuading the pope's ally, Naples, to make peace.

Lorenzo supported artists and scholars such as POLIT-IAN, PICO DELLA MIRANDOLA, BOTTICELLI, and VERROCCHIO. Despite SAVONAROLA's denunciations of Florence's pagan pleasures and loss of republican freedoms from 1489, Lorenzo admired and tolerated the preacher. A massive project to publish all Lorenzo's correspondence (*Lettere*, ed. Riccardo Fubini *et al*, 1977–   ) throws light on his abilities as a ruler and exponent of realpolitik and on the means by which he asserted his ascendancy over Florence.

**Further reading:** Melissa Meriam Bullard, *Lorenzo il Magnifico: Image and Anxiety, Politics and Finance* (Florence, Italy: Olschki, 1994); Lauro Martines, *April Blood: Florence and the Plot Against the Medici* (London: Cape and New York: Oxford University Press, 2003).

**Medici family** A dynasty powerful in Florence and Tuscany from the 13th to the 18th century and renowned for its statesmanship and for its patronage of letters, music, and the visual arts. The family included four popes (LEO X, CLEMENT VII, PIUS IV, Leo XI) and two queens of France (CATHERINE and MARIE DE' MEDICI). The first prominent Medici, Chiarissimo, served on Florence's council (1201), and his descendants joined Florence's elite. After the exile of Salvestro, who supported the CIOMPI in 1378, another branch of the family headed by the banker Giovanni (died 1429) became dominant. Giovanni's son, Cosimo de' MEDICI (1389–1464), established the family's political power; Cosimo's grandson, Lorenzo de' MEDICI (1449–92), ruled Florence without any formal designation other than the courtesy

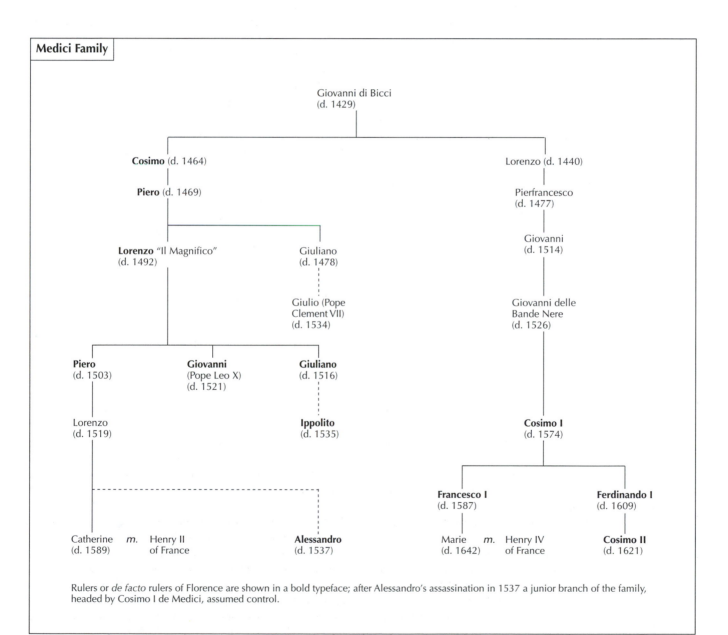

**Medici Family**

Giovanni di Bicci (d. 1429)

Cosimo (d. 1464) — Lorenzo (d. 1440)

Piero (d. 1469) — Pierfrancesco (d. 1477)

Lorenzo "Il Magnifico" (d. 1492) — Giuliano (d. 1478) — Giovanni (d. 1514)

Giulio (Pope Clement VII) (d. 1534) — Giovanni delle Bande Nere (d. 1526)

Piero (d. 1503) — Giovanni (Pope Leo X) (d. 1521) — Giuliano (d. 1516)

Lorenzo (d. 1519) — Ippolito (d. 1535) — Cosimo I (d. 1574)

Catherine (d. 1589) *m.* Henry II of France — Alessandro (d. 1537)

Francesco I (d. 1587) — Ferdinando I (d. 1609)

Marie (d. 1642) *m.* Henry IV of France — Cosimo II (d. 1621)

Rulers or *de facto* rulers of Florence are shown in a bold typeface; after Alessandro's assassination in 1537 a junior branch of the family, headed by Cosimo I de Medici, assumed control.

title of "il Magnifico." Lorenzo's son, Piero, was expelled from Florence (1494), but the family was restored in 1512. After the second expulsion of the Medici (1527–30) Pope Clement VII installed Alessandro (died 1537), the illegitimate son of his second cousin Lorenzo (died 1519), as duke of Florence. After Alessandro's assassination a junior branch of the family, headed by COSIMO I (1519–74), established a dynasty of grand dukes of Tuscany (ruled 1569–1737).

**Further reading:** Janet Cox-Rearick, *Dynasty and Destiny in Medici Art: Pontormo, Leo X and the two Cosimos* (Princeton, N.J.: Princeton University Press, 1984); Richard Fremantle, *God and Money, Florence and the Medici in the Renaissance* (Florence, Italy: Olschki, 1992); John R. Hale, *Florence and the Medici: The Pattern of Control* (London: Thames & Hudson, 1977); Christopher Hibbert, *The House of Medici: Its Rise and Fall* (Harmondsworth: Penguin, 1974; new ed. Perennial, 1999); Nicolai Rubinstein, *The Government of Florence under the Medici (1434 to 1494)* (Oxford, U.K.: Clarendon Press, 1966).

**medicine** Renaissance medicine inherited an erroneous but well-worked-out and comprehensive theory of disease. Formulated in antiquity by Hippocrates and developed by Galen (*see* GALENISM, RENAISSANCE), it assumed that man was compounded from four elements (fire, earth, water, and air) which, in turn, revealed themselves as the four humors: yellow bile (bilious or choleric), black bile (melancholic), phlegm (phlegmatic), and blood (sanguine). Any imbalance between the four humors, whether caused by diet, meteorological factors, or other conditions, led to sickness. The physicians' task was to restore the initial harmony that once existed between the humors in a person's constitution.

While the theory itself found widespread support among Renaissance physicians, there was still considerable disagreement about how best to treat an illness. Traditionalists aimed to conform to Hippocratic practice by treating disease conservatively with diet, rest, and simple herbal medicines. Such moderate therapies proved of little value against the spread of bubonic PLAGUE in the 14th century and the introduction of syphilis into Europe a century later. The failure of traditional remedies against savage epidemics of this kind invited competition from a growing number of alternative therapies. The most prominent of these was linked with the name of PARACELSUS, who saw disease as a specific rather than a general condition. It was, further, analyzable in chemical terms. Thus, whereas traditional physicians had argued that contraries cure, the Paracelsians turned from bland and harmless vegetables to powerful poisons. Syphilis was treated by the traditionalists with guaiac wood; the Paracelsians tackled it with mercury and antimony. The debate continued for much of the 16th century, with the Paracelsians being accused of using lethal poisons and the traditionalists being

pilloried as ineffective. A third tradition, linked with the name of FRACASTORO, argued that disease was caused and spread by specific contagious *seminaria*. While explaining much, there were too many obvious objections to theories of contagion to make them at all plausible. If the plague was contagious, why did some members of a household survive, despite frequent contact with their infected kin? Furthermore, talk of invisible *seminaria* accorded badly with a growing scientific reluctance to accept supposedly occult qualities as causes.

Not all patients, however, needed the services of a physician. Frequent wars, fought increasingly with artillery and firearms, had added to the calls made upon surgeons. Although they were incorporated by a royal charter in England in 1540 their status remained low; ignorant of Latin, and summoned only in the direst emergency, they could not compete in status with the learned graduates of Oxford and Padua who ran the College of Physicians. Consequently, while Henry VIII's physician received a salary of £126.13s.4d., his surgeon had to be satisfied with £26.13s.4d. a year.

Whether surgeons or physicians, Renaissance doctors had little power to help their patients. With a neo-natal mortality of over 30 per cent and with a life expectancy at birth of under 40, the quality of the average European's life was little affected by the medical profession, especially as physicians were few and expensive enough to place them beyond the reach of the bulk of the population. As a result, most people consulted herbalists, empirics, sorcerers, and anyone with a reputation for healing. Such practitioners worked well outside any tradition developed by Hippocrates and Paracelsus. The greatest failure of Renaissance medicine, however, was to ignore problems of public health. While the small populations of antiquity could escape such indifference, the growing urban concentrations of Renaissance states did so at their peril.

**See also:** ANATOMY; IATROCHEMISTRY; PHARMACOPOEIA; PLAGUE

**Further reading:** Carlo M. Cipolla, *Public Health and the Medical Profession in the Renaissance* (Cambridge, U.K.: Cambridge University Press, 1976); Margaret Pelling, *Medical Conflicts in Early Modern London: Patronage, Physicians, and Irregular Practitioners 1550–1640* (Oxford, U.K.: Oxford University Press, 2003); Nancy G. Siraisi, *Medicine and the Italian Universities, 1250–1600* (Leyden, Netherlands: Brill, 2001).

*Meistergesang* A form of sung poetry that developed in Germany during the 14th and 15th centuries and flourished in the 16th. It was performed solo by members of guilds of *Meistersinger* (mastersingers), according to strict rules of versification and music. At first religious but later also secular, it developed out of the medieval courtly song (*Minnesang*) as the practice of poetry and music became a form of relaxation for members of the urban trade guilds.

The guilds of *Meistersinger* had five hierarchies of membership, from beginner to *Meister*; the latter had to have written both words and music of at least one new song. Singing contests were held, in which the judge (*Merker*) watched for breaches of the rules. Although the best-known *Meistersinger*, Hans SACHS, the cobbler of Nuremberg, composed over 4000 songs, the rule-bound nature of the composition and the exclusiveness of the guilds condemned the form to mediocrity and prevented its development.

**Meit, Konrad** (c. 1480–1551) *German sculptor*
Meit was born at Worms and from 1506 to 1510 he worked at the court of Frederick, Elector of Saxony, in Wittenberg. The rest of his life was spent in the Netherlands, where he was court sculptor to the regent, MARGARET OF AUSTRIA. Working mainly in boxwood, alabaster, and metal, he made many small portrait busts and statuettes in a classical style. His alabaster nude *Judith* (c. 1510–15; Bayerisches Nationaalmuseum, Munich) is noted as his most successful sculpture in fusing Italian and northern elements in a sensuous and polished Renaissance style. He also produced monumental sculptures for the tombs of Margaret, her husband, and mother-in-law at Brou near Bourg-en-Bresse, Burgundy. Little work remains from Meit's period in Antwerp after Margaret's death.

**melancholia** According to Renaissance psychological theory, the humor capable of producing intellectual distinction in those in whom it predominated. This theory was grounded in the ancient physiological scheme of the four humors (*see* GALENISM, RENAISSANCE); melancholia was the cold, dry humor, which, in certain manifestations, was the hallmark of the philosopher, poet, and scholar. It was also, under the equally ancient system of astrological correspondences, linked with the planet Saturn, patron of mathematics and sciences. This concept is embodied in DÜRER's famous engraving *Melancholia I* (1514), which depicts the essence of melancholic contemplation in the figure surrounded by mathematical instruments. A verbal equivalent of Dürer's engraving is John Milton's early poem *Il Penseroso* (written c. 1632), describing the pleasures and preoccupations of the melancholic. The most extensive Renaissance treatment of the subject is Robert Burton's *Anatomy of Melancholy* (1621), which affirms that "melancholy men of all others are most witty."

Melancholia was suffered or affected by numerous eminent Renaissance figures, among them Michelangelo and Raphael. As a cult it was imported from Italy into England in the late 1580s. Melancholics, whose condition was often caused by unrequited love, advertised their plight by both dress and behavior; a black hat with a large brim (to be pulled down over the face) was *de rigueur*, as were folded arms and heavy sighs. Such affectation naturally lent itself to ridicule, and satirists were not slow to home in on a tempting target; in JONSON's *Every Man in his Humour* (1598), for instance, the two fops, Stephen and Matthew, vie with each other in their claims to melancholic distinction, as witness Matthew's boast, "I am melancholy myself divers times, sir, and then do I no more but take pen and paper presently, and overflow you half a score, or a dozen of sonnets, at a sitting."

**Further reading:** Raymond Klibansky, Erwin Panofsky, and Fritz Saxl, *Saturn and Melancholy* (London: Nelson, 1964); Bridget Gellert Lyons, *Voices of Melancholy: Studies in Literary Treatments of Melancholy in Renaissance England* (New York: W. W. Norton, repr. 1975).

**Melanchthon, Philipp** (Philipp Schwarzerd) (1497–1560) *German humanist and reformer*
He was born at Bretten, near Karlsruhe, the son of Georg Schwarzerd, a locksmith and armorer, and a great-nephew of Johann REUCHLIN, whose ideas on the pronunciation of Greek he publicized in his *Institutiones linguae Graecae* (1518). Melanchthon studied at Heidelberg and Tübingen, and in 1518 became the first professor of Greek at Wittenberg. He supported LUTHER, and in 1521 published *Loci communes rerum theologicarum* (Theological commonplaces), a systematic statement of evangelical theology. His gentle manner contrasted with Luther's vehemence. A significant figure in education, he founded secondary schools (*gymnasia*) at Eisleben, Nuremberg, and elsewhere, reformed ancient universities, and was instrumental in establishing new ones at Marburg, Jena, and Königsberg (Kaliningrad). While rejecting the debased Aristotelianism of the later scholastics, Melanchthon encouraged the study of Aristotle's own works; he was influenced by Stoicism, and his belief in natural theology and reason was partly derived from this source. In 1530 he attended the Diet of Augsburg and formulated the Confession of AUGSBURG, the "articles of religion" of the evangelical churches of Germany and Scandinavia. In 1546 he succeeded Luther as leader of the German Protestants, but was criticized for his willingness to compromise with both the Romanists and the more radical reformers. His biography was written by CAMERARIUS (1566). The *Loci communes* is available in English translation together with BUCER's *De regno Christi* in *Melanchthon and Bucer* (London: SCM Press, 1969).

**Further reading:** Sachiko Kusukawa, *The Transformation of Natural Philosophy: The Case of Philip Melanchthon* (Cambridge, U.K.: Cambridge University Press, 1995); Timothy J. Wengert, *Human Freedom, Christian Righteousness: Philip Melanchthon's Exegetical Dispute with Erasmus of Rotterdam* (Oxford, U.K. and New York: Oxford University Press, 1998).

**Melozzo da Forlì** (1438–1494) *Italian painter*
Melozzo trained in his native Forlì and in Urbino and came under the influence of PIERO DELLA FRANCESCA. Although Melozzo was acclaimed in his own time as master of illusionism in his wall-paintings and ceiling decorations, none of his frescoes have survived intact. In 1475 he moved to Rome where he painted *Sixtus IV investing Platina as Vatican Librarian* (1477; Vatican museum) and the fresco of the *Ascension* (1477–80) in the church of SS. Apostoli, now preserved in the Vatican and the Quirinale Palace, Rome. In these and other works Melozzo devised a style of extreme foreshortening known as *sotto in sù*. Other works include frescoes at Loreto and for the dome of San Biagio at Forlì (1493; destroyed in 1944).

**Melville, Andrew** (1545–1622) *Scottish churchman, reformer, and humanist*
Melville was born at Baldovie, near Forfar, and learnt Greek at Montrose grammar school from Pierre de Marsiliers. From 1564 to 1566 he read oriental languages, law, and mathematics at Paris, where he was influenced by the new methods of Petrus RAMUS, and later occupied the chair of humanity (Latin) at Geneva (1568–73). From 1574 he held academic posts in Scotland. Several times moderator of the general assembly of the church, he vehemently opposed the remnants of episcopacy and was largely responsible for the presbyterian constitution.

Although James VI of Scotland admired his learning, Melville's relationship with him was tempestuous; in one confrontation in 1596 he famously addressed the king as "God's silly vassal." Melville approved of the union of Scotland and England under James in 1603, but in 1606 he was a prime mover in the calling of a Scottish general assembly against the king's express orders. When summoned to London to explain himself he continued unabashed his attacks on royal supremacy and the episcopacy as manifested in the Church of England, and was sent to the Tower of London. After his release he went to France (1611) and spent the rest of his life as professor of biblical theology at Sedan.

**Memling, Hans** (Hans Memlinc) (active 1465–1494) *Flemish painter*
Born in Seligenstadt but based in Bruges, Memling may have been trained by Rogier van der WEYDEN, although the influence of Dirk BOUTS is also apparent in his work. He enjoyed a wide circle of patronage and several of his most important pictures were produced for foreign clients. These include the Donne triptych (London), a *Last Judgment* altarpiece (destined for Florence, but now in Gda[sk) and a *Passion* altarpiece (Lübeck). The finest collection of his work is that in the Hans Memlingmuseum (Sint Janshospitaal), Bruges. Many of his paintings are precisely datable, but Memling's style changed little and the exact chronology of his oeuvre is elusive. His numerous altarpieces and portraits are very highly accomplished but add little to the repertory established by earlier Netherlands painters.

**memory, art of** The training and exercise of the memory, partly as an adjunct to RHETORIC, widely practiced in both antiquity and the Renaissance. Its effectiveness can be judged by St. Augustine's report of a certain Simplicius, who was able to recite the whole of Virgil backwards. The classical tradition survived the medieval period and found its most extravagant Renaissance deployment in the scheme devised by Giulio Camillo (1480–1544) and published in his posthumous *L'idea del theatro* (1550). The basic idea of such a system was to aid memory by systematically linking items to be memorized to a series of striking images. Camillo thus conceived of a theater divided into a large number of blocks of seats, each one of which could be used as a memory locus. Matteo RICCI constructed a "memory palace" which he used to good effect in his missionary work at the imperial Chinese court. Alternative systems were presented by, among others, Giordano BRUNO and Robert FLUDD. For these, it has been argued, the art was more than a mnemonic device and had deep links with Renaissance occultism. Although the art continues to be cultivated today it has long since returned to its mnemonic role.

**Further reading:** Frances A. Yates, *The Art of Memory* (London: Routledge & Kegan Paul, 1966; repr. University of Chicago Press, 1974).

**Mena, Juan de** (1411–1456) *Spanish poet and writer*
Educated in his native Cordova and at Salamanca and Rome, he returned to Spain to become Latin secretary to King John II of Castile and later official court chronicler. The king and Álvaro de LUNA were his patrons, though he also maintained a friendship with Luna's great opponent, SANTILLANA. The first Spanish poet to put his vocation above all else, he showed a fine disregard for pleasing the public in his own work. He refined Spanish style, both in poetry and prose, bringing to bear the influences of Virgil, Ovid, Lucan, and Italian poets, especially DANTE and PETRARCH. In poetry one problem was the rapid, regular, strongly accented beat of traditional Spanish verse. Mena, imitating Dante and Petrarch, introduced a hendecasyllabic line and paved the way for a more varied and subtle meter. He thus popularized the ARTE MAYOR and was known as *El Ennio español* ("the Spanish Ennius," after the Roman poet who had introduced the Latin hexameter). He ignored colloquial usage, developed an elaborate syntax, introduced neologisms, and employed a range of rhetorical devices to create a new, learned humanistic poetry. His major work, *El laberinto de fortuna* (The Labyrinth of Fortune: written 1444, published 1481–88), is an allegorical vision inspired by Dante and much indebted to

Ovid. Mena was the first translator of the *Iliad* into Spanish (1519) from a medieval prose version in Latin.

## Mendes, Gracia (Gracia Hannah Nasi) (1510–1569)
*Sephardic Jewish philanthropist and patron*

Born in Lisbon at a time of enforced conversion of Portuguese JEWS, she was given the Christian name Beatrice de Luna, keeping her Jewish faith secret. She married a wealthy banker, merchant, and gem dealer, Francisco Mendes. After his death (1534) she ran his business affairs with his brother, Diogo. During the Inquisition she masterminded an underground network assisting Jews to flee Portugal and settle in areas under Ottoman rule. In 1536, she too had to flee, taking her business empire with her, first to Antwerp, then Venice, and later Ferrara, where she was at last able to live openly as a Jew. In 1553 she settled in Constantinople, where she used her wealth to endow Jewish yeshivas and synagogues as far afield as Palestine and to fund the printing of Jewish sacred texts. Her last, most visionary project was the purchase of the ancient holy city of Tiberias from the sultan. Under the supervision of her son-in-law, Joseph, duke of Naxos, she hoped to rebuild it as a city-state for Jewish refugees, but the project failed due to intervention from the papacy.

## Mendoza, Antonio de (1490–1552) *Spanish soldier and colonial administrator*

Mendoza's military experience against the Moors and diplomatic mission to Hungary fitted him for appointment as viceroy of New Spain (Mexico) in 1535. His wise and energetic policies laid the basis for Spanish rule in Mexico that lasted until the 19th century. He developed mining, industry, agriculture, and communications, backed CORONADO's expedition to New Mexico, promoted exploration in California and the Philippines, and encouraged the Catholic Church to convert and protect the native Americans. In 1551 he was appointed viceroy of Peru, but died shortly after arriving in Lima.

## Mendoza, Diego de Hurtado de See HURTADO DE MENDOZA, DIEGO DE

## Mendoza, Íñigo López de, Marqués de Santillana
See SANTILLANA, ÍÑIGO LÓPEZ DE MENDOZA, MARQUÉS DE

## Mendoza, Pedro González de (1428–1495) *Spanish churchman, soldier, and statesman*

As bishop of Calahorra from 1452 he successfully intervened in the Castilian civil wars of the mid-15th century. From being bishop of Siguenza (1468), he progressed to being cardinal, archbishop of Seville, and chancellor of Castile (1473). Supporting the claim of Princess Isabella to the Castilian crown at the battle of Toro (1476), he was instrumental in placing her on the throne (*see* FERDINAND II AND ISABELLA I). Made archbishop of Toledo (1482), "the

Great Cardinal" played a prominent role in the conquest of Granada (1492), both militarily and financially.

## Mennonites
Followers of the Dutch Protestant leader Menno Simons (1496–1561). Simons, a native of Friesland, was ordained priest in 1524 but soon fell under the influence of Luther's teachings on the Bible and Eucharist. Finding himself unable to accept the doctrine of infant baptism, he renounced the priesthood in 1536 and joined the ANABAPTISTS, at that time a small, vilified sect persecuted with equal zeal by Catholics and Protestants. For the next 25 years, often at great personal risk, Menno traveled among the scattered Anabaptist congregations of northeast Europe, striving to lift their morale and to consolidate their doctrine and organization. He also led his followers away from the revolutionary extremism of Thomas Müntzer (*see* PEASANTS' REVOLT) and other early Anabaptists.

During this time, the Mennonites (as they came to be known) developed a clear identity. In doctrine, they were distinguished by their rejection of infant baptism and the REAL PRESENCE; in organization, by a "connectionist" structure in which each congregation was permitted considerable autonomy. In both respects the Mennonites would have a direct influence on Britain's emerging Baptist movement in the early 1600s. More distinctive still, however, was their social and ethical teaching; members were forbidden to serve in the military, to take oaths, or to hold any position of secular authority.

After Menno's death, the movement developed in two quite different directions. From 1574 the Mennonites were no longer persecuted in the Netherlands and the large community there became increasingly prosperous, liberal, and influential, with a developing interest in education and social questions. However, the experience of the congregations in Switzerland and some other parts of Europe, where persecutions continued, was quite different. Here the Mennonites withdrew into closed agricultural communities and cut themselves off from secular ways (the Amish community of North America is an offshoot of the Swiss Mennonites). Persecution also encouraged wholesale emigration to the New World and elsewhere, so that the largest numbers of Mennonites are now to be found in the United States and Canada.

## "Mentzer, Der" See FISCHART, JOHANN

## Merbecke, John (c. 1508–c. 1585) *English composer and writer*

In 1531 Merbecke was employed at St. George's Chapel, Windsor, as clerk and organist. In 1543 he was condemned to death for his Calvinist views but was reprieved by HENRY VIII. His concordance of the English Bible, the first complete edition, was published in 1550. After Edward VI's accession, Merbecke compiled his *Booke of Com-*

*mon Praier Noted* (1550). The first book of its kind, it used adaptations of plainsong as well as similar melodies composed by Merbecke himself, with syllabic underlay of the text. Merbecke's other surviving compositions comprise a large-scale Mass, two motets, and an anthem.

## Mercator, Gerardus (Gerhard Kremer) (1512–1594)
*Flemish geographer and cartographer*

Mercator was born in Rupelmonde, East Flanders. He studied at Louvain before being employed by his mentor GEMMA FRISIUS as his assistant. In 1537 Mercator made a map of Palestine, followed by one of the world a year later, and a survey of Flanders (1537–40). He also published a terrestrial globe for use on board ship (1541). In 1551 Mercator presented Charles V with a celestial globe and other accessories, along with written instructions on their use.

The following year, prompted by religious persecution on account of his newly adopted Protestantism, Mercator moved to Duisburg where he established a workshop and lectured. Over the next 20 years his key works appeared. His maps of Europe in 1554 (15 sheets) and Britain in 1564 (eight sheets) set new standards in precision, presentation, and detail and broke free from the shackles of Ptolemy's geography that had hampered earlier cartographers. His masterpiece was his 1569 world chart, drawn on the "Mercator projection," which has the parallels of latitude and meridians of longitude at right angles. The sophisticated mathematics of the projection, however, militated against its immediate acceptance by mariners. Mercator spent his later years consolidating his maps into a series of publications, notably his *Atlas*, the first part of which appeared in 1585 and which was completed by his son Rumold (died 1602) in 1595.

**Further reading:** Nicholas Crane, *Mercator: The Man Who Mapped the Planet* (London: Orion, 2002).

## mercenaries
Paid professional soldiers who replaced ill-trained feudal levies in many armies of Renaissance Europe. As technological innovations made WARFARE more complex and expensive, the new princes created new armies which were heavily dependent on mercenaries. This was often seen by rulers as a better option than allowing their own subjects to bear arms, though in France Charles VII founded *compagnies d'ordonnance* (1439), French soldiers paid by the king. Monarchs however usually preferred foreign mercenaries as being less likely to become embroiled in the domestic politics of their employer's country. Highly trained and disciplined Swiss mercenaries served French kings well in the 15th and 16th centuries and the SWISS GUARD has served the papacy from the early 16th century. The German landsknechts, modeled on the Swiss, often served abroad. In Italian warfare CONDOTTIERI played a dominant part, and Venice relied on her STRADIOTTI for numerous policing and garrison duties.

The system had serious drawbacks, as noted by one contemporary critic, Machiavelli. Mercenaries were expensive and, lacking patriotic motivation, could be untrustworthy. On the eve of battle mercenary captains might demand handsome bonuses for their continued loyalty, and in peacetime mercenaries could threaten law and order by using their redundant military skills to prey on civilians.

## Mercury See HERMES

## Merulo, Claudio (1533–1604) *Italian composer and organist*

Born at Correggio, Merulo was appointed cathedral organist at Brescia (1556), and a year later as one of the organists at St. Mark's, Venice. While in Venice he composed for many official occasions, including the state visit of Henry III of France (1574). In 1586 he became organist to the duke of Parma, then organist also at Parma cathedral (1587), and in 1591 organist to the company of La Steccata, a post he held until his death. A renowned player, Merulo was also a publisher of his own and other composers' music. He wrote madrigals and church music in a style similar to that of Andrea GABRIELI, but is best remembered for his keyboard music. He developed the ricercar and canzona, but his finest works are his toccatas. Merulo moved away from the practice of basing instrumental music on vocal models; contrapuntal sections are joined by improvisatory, virtuoso passages, without the ensemble textures normally encountered in contemporary keyboard music.

## metallurgy
The craftsmen of antiquity had developed techniques for the extraction and working of gold, silver, copper, tin, and lead. They had also, since about 1500 BCE, begun to work with iron, but as they were able to attain temperatures no higher than 1200°C, well below the 1528°C melting point of iron, production was restricted to wrought iron. A major metallurgical advance, however, took place in the 15th century CE with the emergence of the blast furnace. The molten iron thus attainable could be cast into a variety of forms, using techniques learnt by working in bronze. Chief among these objects were the CANNON and cannonballs increasingly being demanded by warring Renaissance princes. Gunners at the two-month siege of Magdeburg (1631), for example, expended as many as 18,000 cannonballs daily.

Demand also increased for precious metals. While world gold production almost doubled between 1500 and 1700, silver production increased nine-fold in the 16th century alone. Much of this was made possible by improved extraction processes. Methods for separating silver from copper became established in the early 15th century, while the Mexican process for extracting silver by amalgamation was well understood by the mid-16th century.

**Metallurgy** A woodcut from a treatise (1574) on metallurgy by Lazarus Ercker.

Most of this increased production went into the mints of western Europe.

Copper also played a significant role in Renaissance industry. It was used as an ingredient of bronze in the manufacture of cannon and bells and by itself for the minting of coins. Details of all aspects of Renaissance metallurgy are available in the illustrated volumes of Georgius AGRICOLA, Agostino RAMELLI, Vannoccio BIRINGUCCIO, and Lazarus Ercker. Ercker's illustrated *Beschreibung* (Prague, 1574) is a systematic survey of metallurgical operations that has been called the earliest analytical manual of the subject.

**meteorology** Scientific understanding of the weather made little progress during the Renaissance because meteorology was still based on an outdated COSMOLOGY and time-honored texts. "Meteors" in the early modern period referred to any atmospheric phenomenon; thus "watery (or aqueous) meteors" were hail or snow; "fiery (or igneous) meteors" shooting stars. In the PTOLEMAIC SYSTEM all such meteors were features of the sublunary sphere, the region below the moon that was subject to change and decay (unlike the crystalline heavenly spheres above). Meteorology was therefore considered a branch of astronomy:

for instance, in the *Compilatio...de astrorum scientia* by the 13th-century astronomer Duke Leopold of Austria (first printed edition 1489) part six dealt with the weather.

In the absence of any natural physical explanation for their occurrence, storms or gales were likely to be ascribed to the Devil or witchcraft; following this line of thinking, the ringing of church bells could therefore be recommended as an appropriate deterrent against thunder, and holy water as a protection against lightning. There were a few honorable exceptions to the predominantly superstitious attitude to meteorological phenomena. In England William Merle (or Merlee) kept detailed records of the weather at Oxford in the period 1337–44 and used them to draw conclusions about weather patterns. Similar records were kept by his contemporary Evno (or Enno) of Würzburg from 1331 to 1355, but he used them mainly in support of astrological calculations.

Weather forecasting had important implications for farmers, sailors, and shepherds, and people depended heavily on local observations of the behavior of birds and beasts. Many of these indicators were taken over unchanged from classical authorities, such as Virgil's *Georgics*. Other texts often quoted in meteorological matters were Aristotle's *Meteorologica*, Seneca's *Quaestiones naturales*, Pliny's *Historia naturalis*, or the medieval compendium, Bartholomaeus's *De proprietatibus rerum*. For a more modern but no less traditional text containing meterological material readers could turn to DU BARTAS's *La Semaine* (1578).

**Metsys, Quintin** (Quintin Massys) (1465/66–1530)
*Netherlands painter*
Presumably trained in his native Louvain, Metsys entered the Antwerp painters' guild in 1491. His earliest work indicates points of contact with Dirk BOUTS and his followers. His Antwerp *Lamentation* triptych (1507–09) is a grand composition, drawing on the 15th-century Netherlandish tradition, and his *Banker and his Wife* (1514; Louvre, Paris) is an antiquarian exercise in the style of Petrus CHRISTUS. In the Brussels *Holy Kindred* triptych (1509) figure types derived from Robert CAMPIN coexist with classicizing architectural details of recent Italian derivation. Metsys's early interest in grotesque facial types was fortified by sketches by LEONARDO DA VINCI; works such as the Paris *Old Man* of 1513 and the presumably contemporary London *Old Woman* are probably copies after the Florentine painter's work. Metsys also excelled as a painter of more conventional portraits, of which the most famous is the divided diptych of *Erasmus* (Rome) and *Peter Giles* (Longford Castle). His two sons Jan (1509–75) and Cornelis (1511–65) became painters at Antwerp in 1531.

## Michelangelo Buonarroti (Michelangiolo di Lodovico Buonarroti-Simoni) (1475–1564) *Italian sculptor, painter, architect, and poet*

For VASARI Michelangelo, who was his friend in later years, was the "perfect exemplar" of the arts of *disegno*, representing the culmination of the previous two centuries of progress and accomplishment in Italian art.

Against his father's wishes, the young Michelangelo, who was born in Caprese, decided on a career in art and was apprenticed to the Florentine workshop of Domenico GHIRLANDAIO in 1488. Among his initial drawings are sketches after paintings by earlier masters of Italian art, including Giotto and Masaccio. Michelangelo also made, as an exercise in *fantasia*, a copy of Martin SCHONGAUER's engraving, *The Temptation of St. Anthony*. A year later Michelangelo was training under Bertoldo di Giovanni, a student of DONATELLO, who was curator of the Medici sculpture collection (whether the Medici garden was actually a school is debated by scholars). Catching the eye of Lorenzo de' Medici, Michelangelo was invited to live in the Medici palace (c. 1490–91). There he came to know the proponents of NEOPLATONISM, the philosophy that would guide many of his creative endeavors. An early relief, the *Battle of the Centaurs* (c. 1491; Casa Buonarroti, Florence), demonstrates his precocious talent and understanding of antique art; the *Battle* relief also established his penchant for the human figure, the nobility of which, for Michelangelo, must always be viewed within its symbolic significance as a microcosm, reflecting the perceived order of the universe. Continually assimilating the experience of past masters, Michelangelo carved a *schiacciato* relief, *The Madonna of the Stairs* (c. 1491; Casa Buonarroti) in the manner of Donatello.

As the French army threatened Florence, Michelangelo traveled to Bologna and Venice (1494–95). In Bologna he completed three statuettes for the tomb of St. Dominic and had the opportunity to view the expressive *furor* of Jacopo della QUERCIA's sculpted figures. Between 1496 and 1501 Michelangelo was in Rome; two surviving works from this period are the *Bacchus* (c. 1496–98; Bargello, Florence), which treats an antique theme with a new and revealing interpretation, and a *Pietà* (1498–99; St. Peter's, Rome), which displays his consummate mastery in communicating both the anatomical and psychological expression of the human form. Michelangelo returned to Florence in 1501 where, until 1504, he was engaged in carving the colossal *David* (Accademia, Florence) from a block of marble quarried in 1464 and left "misshapen" (Vasari) after earlier attempts to carve a figure from it had failed. *David's* intense scowl reflects the *terribilità* of his psychological state, while the heroically accomplished sculpture reveals the *terribilità* of Michelangelo's creative prowess. The *David*, originally conceived as part of the cathedral prophet series program, was placed at the entrance of the Palazzo Vecchio, symbolizing the virtue of Florentine republicanism, defiant against the Medici. During this time Michelangelo also worked on a cartoon (now lost) for a fresco intended as a pendant for Leonardo's *Battle of Anghiari* in the Palazzo Vecchio; this *Battle of Cascina* was never painted. With the unfinished *St. Matthew* (1504–08; Accademia, Florence) Michelangelo explored the energetic counterpositioned movement of the *figura serpentinata* (serpentine figure) which would dramatically characterize his later figurative art.

In 1505 Michelangelo was summoned to Rome by Pope JULIUS II, who then commissioned the sculptor to fashion the pope's tomb; work on the *Moses* (San Pietro in Vincoli, Rome) may have begun in 1506 or later around 1513. (The tomb project, which Ascanio Condivi, Michelangelo's biographer in 1553, called the "tragedy of the tomb," proved very burdensome for Michelangelo. It was completed, four contracts later, in 1542, in a much reduced version of the original scheme.) From 1508 to 1512 Michelangelo, again contracted by Julius II, painted the vaulted ceiling of the SISTINE CHAPEL with the story of Creation, exalting the human figure throughout the composition (see Plate IX). Following the completion of the ceiling, work resumed on the tomb project; two figures, the *Dying Slave* and the *Rebellious Slave* (c. 1514; Louvre, Paris) were begun. In 1516 Michelangelo, again in Florence, was occupied with numerous commissions. Work on the Julius II tomb continued, the triumphant *Victory* (c. 1527; Palazzo Vecchio) was carved, but the progress was slowed by Medici contracts, including the Medici Chapel (begun 1519) and the Bibliotheca LAURENZIANA (1523). The Medici Chapel combines Michelangelo's organically expressive architecture with herculean figures bearing allegorical conceits. In the vestibule of the Laurenziana Michelangelo's unique license of architectural invention is on display; here, the classical vocabulary of architecture has been refashioned to an imaginative, yet judicious aesthetic.

Late in 1533 Michelangelo settled in Rome. From 1534 to 1541 he painted a *Last Judgment* on the altar wall of the Sistine Chapel; considering the copious variety of figural positions, displayed with dramatic foreshortenings, Condivi rightly observed, "Michelangelo expressed all that the art of painting can do with the human figure, leaving out no attitude or gesture whatever." During this time Michelangelo's friendship with Vittoria COLONNA and Tommaso de' Cavalieri inspired many of his finest poems; his status as an artist rose to that of a cult figure. Two frescoes in the Pauline Chapel, *The Conversion of Paul* and *The Crucifixion of Peter*, were completed by 1550. Throughout this period Michelangelo was continually absorbed in architectural projects in Rome, including work on the Capitoline Hill, the Palazzo Farnese, and St. Peter's, of which he was chief architect from 1546. A second *Pietà* (Museo dell' Opera del Duomo, Florence) intended for his own tomb was begun before 1550; one night about 1556

Michelangelo attempted to destroy the sculpture, betraying the spiritual anxiety which found ardent expression in the late Crucifixion drawings and poems. (In the mid-1550s Michelangelo wrote, "No brush, no chisel will quiet the soul, once it is turned to the divine love of Him who, on the cross, outstretched His arms to take us to Himself.") Work on a third *Pietà* (1555–64; Castello Sforzesco, Milan) continued to a week before his death. Michelangelo died in Rome, but his body was transported to Florence for burial, with a solemn funeral in his parish church of Sta. Croce. His tomb in that church is by Vasari.

Vasari included an account of Michelangelo in his *Vite* (1550), and the highly sympathetic *Vita di Michelagnolo Buonarroti* was published three years later by Michelangelo's pupil Ascanio Condivi (1525–74). A modern translation of the latter into English is by Alice S. Wohl: *The Life of Michelangelo* (1976). James M. Saslow's *The Poetry of Michelangelo: An Annotated Translation* (1991) contains the Italian text with an English translation and commentary. Peter Porter translated the poems in George Bull's selection of Michelangelo's writings in the Oxford World's Classics series, *Michelangelo: Life, Letters, and Poetry* (1999).

**Further reading:** James S. Ackerman, *The Architecture of Michelangelo* (Chicago, Ill.: University of Chicago Press, repr. 1986); Francis Ames-Lewis and Paul Joannides (eds), *Reactions to the Master: Michelangelo's Effect on Art and Artists in the Sixteenth Century* (Aldershot, U.K.: Ashgate, 2003); Luciano Berti, *The Complete Works of Michelangelo* (New York: Reynal, 1964); Anton Gill, *Il Gigante: Michelangelo, Florence, and the David 1492–1504* (New York: Thomas Dunne, 2003); Ross King, *Michelangelo and the Pope's Ceiling* (New York: Random House, 2003).

**Michelozzo di Bartolommeo** (1396–1472) *Italian sculptor and architect*
Born in Florence and first documented (c. 1420) as assisting GHIBERTI, Michelozzo subsequently established a workshop with DONATELLO with whom he executed a number of important tombs, such as that of the antipope John XXII (died 1419) in the baptistery in Florence, as well as the pulpit (began 1428) in the Duomo at Prato. In 1420 he designed San Francesco al Bosco at Caffagiuolo, near Florence, and became increasingly involved in architectural projects. His pragmatic approach to design, involving the marrying of Gothic forms with a free use of antique motifs, endeared him to Cosimo de' MEDICI for whom he built a number of *palazzi* and villas. The Palazzo Medici-Riccardi, begun in 1444, with its heavy classical cornice and symmetrically aligned courtyard, was hailed by Flavio BIONDO as being "comparable to the work of the Roman emperors" and established the prototype for Tuscan palace architecture.

Michelozzo's work from 1437 in the cloisters and library of San Marco, Florence, displays a new formal vocabulary in the use of plain Ionic capitals and columns on pedestals. However, his centrally planned choir in SS. Annunziata (c. 1444; Florence), based on the design of the temple of Minerva Medica, Rome, sparked controversy in its disregard for the liturgical requirement to separate clergy and laity. Through his work on the Medici bank in Milan (1462) Michelozzo was responsible for the introduction of Florentine Renaissance architecture to Lombardy.

**microscopes** Early, though obscure, references to magnifying glasses can be found in the 12th-century writings of Roger Bacon. One of the first Renaissance works to deal specifically with the theory of lenses was the posthumously published *Photismi* (1611) of Francesco Maurolico (1494–1575) (*see also* OPTICS). The first work, however, to describe an optical instrument constructed with "glasses concave and convex of circular and parabolical formes" was the 1571 edition of Leonard DIGGES's *Pantometria*. The first compound microscope was constructed by Zacharias Janssen. (There were other Dutch claimants to the invention, including Cornelis DREBBEL, and GALILEO seems to have been an early user, if not maker, before 1610.) Its first published scientific use is for the series of drawings of the honeybee included in Francesco Stelluti's *Descrizzione dell'ape* (1625).

**Milan** A powerful northern Italian city state in the basin of the River Po in Lombardy. First Gallic and then Roman, Milan was devastated by Attila the Hun and the Goths, but survived to become an independent commune (1045). Under VISCONTI and SFORZA rule in the 14th and 15th centuries Milan reached the peak of its political power and cultural splendor, at times threatening to take over most of northern Italy. The Visconti ruled from 1311 until the extinction of their male line in 1447. Following the short interlude of the AMBROSIAN REPUBLIC (1447–50), the Sforza family ruled (1450–99) with great magnificence until they were displaced by the French during the Wars of ITALY. In the early 16th century the Sforza were twice restored to Milan, but in 1535 the city fell to CHARLES V, who invested his son Philip (later PHILIP II of Spain) with the duchy of Milan in 1540. Thereafter Milan continued under Spanish rule until passing to Austria in 1713.

Visconti and Sforza splendor were supported by sound administrative measures and a thriving economy. By 1500 Milan's population was probably close to 100,000. The city prospered through trade, textiles, and metalwork; it was famous for the quality of its weapons and armor (*see* MISSAGLIA FAMILY). Canals for irrigation and communication were built and agriculture was encouraged, particularly the cultivation of rice from 1475.

The first Greek book to be printed in Italy, Constantine Lascaris's *Erotemata*, was issued at Milan in 1476.

The Visconti and Sforza were generous patrons of the arts and scholarship. They encouraged humanist learning, scientific studies, and great public works. PETRARCH owed much to Visconti patronage. In the late 15th century Lodovico ("il Moro") SFORZA and his wife, the short-lived Beatrice d'Este, made their court into a showpiece of culture and learning, supporting LEONARDO DA VINCI among others; Lodovico also commissioned for Milan several buildings by BRAMANTE. Under Spanish rule in the 16th century Milan's political prestige and cultural glories were in decline, although it was then the home of one of the leading figures in the Counter-Reformation, St. CHARLES BORROMEO.

Notable buildings surviving from the Renaissance period include the enormous cathedral (begun 1386), the Dominican monastery of Sta. Maria, containing Leonardo's LAST SUPPER, the Bibliotheca AMBROSIANA (founded 1609), and the Palazzo di Brera (present facade 1615).

## Milán, Luis (c. 1500–1561) *Spanish composer*
Milán, who was born in Valencia, was one of the greatest composers of music for the vihuela, the Spanish equivalent of the lute. His most important work is *El maestro* (1536), a collection of vihuela compositions and solo vocals. It is the earliest surviving work of its kind in Spain and was intended as an instruction book for the vihuela. It contains fantasies, preludes, pavanes, Christmas carols, and sonnets by Petrarch. Milán was the first composer to write in detail about the interpretation of his music and the first to provide tempo indications for it. His book *El cortesano* (1561) is a Valencian equivalent of Castiglione's THE COURTIER.

## millenarianism
In Christianity, belief in a thousand-year reign of peace and righteousness (the millennium) to be enjoyed by the faithful at the end of human history. Opinion has differed over whether such a period will herald or follow the Second Coming of Christ. In either case, the emphasis falls on the triumph of the believing community in this world, rather than the salvation of the individual believer in the next. The only clear biblical support for millenarianism is in Revelation 20, although hints of a future reign of the elect are also to be found in St. Paul. Ultimately, the doctrine derives from popular apocalyptic traditions of the later Jewish era.

Millennial hopes, widespread among the first Christians, waned as expectations of Christ's early return receded and the Church developed from persecuted sect into powerful institution. From the fourth century onward, millenarian beliefs were ignored by most orthodox theologians and reinterpreted in a nonliteral sense by others (notably St. Augustine). Millenarianism therefore disappeared from mainstream Christian thought for a thousand years, although there were sporadic outbreaks among fringe groups, such as the Joachimites of the 13th century.

The revival of millenarian ideas that is a marked feature of the Reformation period can be explained by several factors. In the first place, reformers of all kinds shared a reverence for the word of Scripture and the beliefs of the primitive Church, both of which sanctioned such views. More generally, millennial enthusiasms tend to recur at periods of historical and intellectual crisis. Indeed, some reformers saw a precise parallel between the cosmic battle described in Revelation and the religious struggles of their own day, with the pope in the role of the great Beast or antichrist (Revelation 13), Rome as Babylon (Revelation 14), and eventual victory for the righteous guaranteed. Millenarianism had particular appeal to the more extreme Protestant groups, who sought a complete revolution in the order of things, and a special allure for the persecuted, who could look forward to a future in which the tables were turned on their oppressors.

Although there is evidence of millennial belief among LUTHER's early supporters, Luther himself did not encourage it, and it increasingly became the province of more radical groups. From the 1520s millenarianism was particularly associated with the ANABAPTISTS, whose extremism helped to bring all such notions into disrepute. For instance, in 1520 a group known as the Zwickau Prophets attempted to establish the rule of the righteous in Zwickau, Saxony; they subsequently moved to Wittenberg, where they attracted a growing following until Luther had the movement suppressed (1522). A few years later Thomas Müntzer, an early associate of the Zwickau group, saw portents of the millennium in the violence of the PEASANTS' REVOLT. Belief in the imminent apocalypse was also a distinctive belief of the Hoffmanites (or Melchiorites), followers of the former Lutheran preacher Melchior Hoffman (1498–1543), who prophesized that Strasbourg would become the site of the New Jerusalem. Taken together, such excesses led to a deep mistrust of millenarianism in the mainstream reform movements—a suspicion that remained entrenched within Lutheranism until the advent of the Pietist movement in the 17th century. In England, the mid-17th century saw an eruption of millennial ideas among the left-wing Independent groups of the Civil War and Commonwealth period.

An interesting offshoot of 16th- and 17th-century millenarianism is the fascination with utopian political ideas. In such works as More's UTOPIA (1516), CAMPANELLA's *La città del solé* (written 1602), the *Reipublicae Christianopolitanae descriptio* (1619) of the German theologian Johann Valentin Andreae, and BACON's *New Atlantis* (1627) the millennial hope is secularized and used to express an essentially Renaissance vision of human possibility.

**Further reading:** Norman Cohn, *The Pursuit of the Millennium: Revolutionary Millenarians and Mystical Anarchists of the Middle Ages* (New York: Random House, 1961; repr. 1993).

**mineralogy** In ancient, medieval, and Renaissance times no distinction was made between minerals, rocks, and fossils. All were described as "fossils," a word that meant no more than that they had been dug out of the ground. A number of medieval lapidaries survive and, like the best known of these, the *De mineralibus* (1260) of Albertus Magnus, they derive mainly from the writings of Pliny (23–79 CE) and are predominantly concerned with supposedly magical and medicinal properties of selected stones. Early texts, consequently, were full of such wonders as the bezoar, found in a toad's head and considered an antidote against all poisons. Much of this tradition survived through the Renaissance intact.

A more modern approach is first seen clearly in Georgius AGRICOLA's *De natura fossilium* (1546). While his predecessors had argued that minerals had originated either through the action of stars, or from a "petrific seed," Agricola proposed instead that they had condensed from a subterranean lapidifying juice (*succus lapidifactus*). He also replaced the traditional alphabetical listing of "fossils" with a classification based on their physical properties. In this way he distinguished between earths, rocks, metals, and stones. A more elaborate classification into 15 classes was proposed by Conrad GESNER in his *De omni rerum fossilium genere* (1565). Based on crude morphological considerations, it grouped minerals according to their resemblance to plants, geometrical shapes, animals, and other natural forms. The approach based upon a mineral's chemical composition began to emerge only in the 18th century.

**Minerva** The Roman goddess of wisdom and the arts, often identified with the Greek goddess Athene (or Pallas Athene). Like her Greek counterpart, Minerva was also associated with the arts of war, and she is generally depicted as armed with a helmet, shield, spear, and coat of mail. She was shown in Renaissance allegorical scenes as the embodiment of rational, intellectual power; in a picture now in the Louvre, Paris, but originally carried out for Isabella d'Este by MANTEGNA, the armed Minerva is shown driving a motley and grotesque crowd of personified vices from an arcaded garden pool. Perhaps the most haunting of Renaissance images of Minerva is BOTTICELLI's painting (Uffizi, Florence) of her taming a centaur, symbol of brute physical strength and passion; in this picture she does not carry the accoutrements of the classical goddess but subdues the centaur by the twist of its hair in her right hand, rather than by the huge halberd which she also carries.

**Further reading:** Marina Warner, *Maidens and Monuments: The Allegory of the Female Form* (London: Weidenfeld & Nicolson, 1985; repr. 1996).

**Miranda, Francisco de Sá de** (1481–1558) *Portuguese poet and dramatist*
The illegitimate son of a canon at Coimbra, Miranda read law, obtained a degree, and taught in Lisbon. His first works as a poet at the court of Manuel I were in the traditional forms and meters of medieval Portugal and Spain. Some of these were published in Garcia de Resende's *Cancioneiro geral* (1516). He inherited property after his father's death (1520), which allowed him to make a long visit to Italy (1521–26). Through his distant relative, Vittoria COLONNA, he met SANNAZARO, ARIOSTO, and others. He returned to Portugal through Spain, where he may have met GARCILASO DE LA VEGA and BOSCÁN. He married in 1530.

With the patronage of King John III and his inheritance, Miranda was able to devote himself to his poetry and live in rural seclusion. He introduced to Portugal the 11-syllable line and the main Italian verse forms: the Petrarchan sonnet, the *canzone*, *terza rima*, and *ottava rima*. His two plays, *Comédia dos estrangeiros* (1559) and *Comédia dos Vilhapandos* (1560), are written in prose, carefully plotted, and thoroughly classical in style. A tragedy, *Cleopatra*, is lost.

**Mirandola, Giovanni Pico della** See PICO DELLA MIRANDOLA, GIOVANNI

**Missaglia family** Italian makers of weapons and ARMOR. In the 15th century their workshop in Milan was a European leader in this field. Tommaso (died c. 1454), who retired in about 1451, handed over to his son Antonio (died c. 1495), who fulfilled commissions for a number of important clients. Some of his work is preserved in the Wallace Collection, London. After Antonio's death the family's place as leading armor manufacturers in Milan was taken by the NEGROLI FAMILY.

**Mohács, battle of** (1526) A Turkish victory over Christian forces in southern Hungary. Led by Suleiman (I) the Magnificent, the OTTOMAN TURKS destroyed the army of Louis II of Hungary before sweeping north to take Buda and Pesth and to occupy most of Hungary; from here Suleiman could threaten the very heart of Europe. Since King Louis, who drowned while fleeing from Mohács, left no male heir, the elective crowns of Bohemia and Hungary passed to his Hapsburg brother-in-law, Ferdinand (later FERDINAND I, Holy Roman Emperor). In 1687 at a second battle of Mohács the imperial Christian forces defeated the Turks.

**Molina, Luis de** (1535–1600) *Iberian Jesuit theologian*
Born in Cuenca, Spain, he entered the Society of Jesus in 1553, studied at Coimbra, Portugal, taught theology at Evora, also in Portugal, wrote many substantial works, and died as a professor at Madrid. His *Concordia liberi arbritrii* (1588) attempts to solve the problem of the relationship between God's grace and human free will. The controversial solution posited became known as "Molinism," and became widely adopted by Jesuits. God grants the ability to humans to act according to their own choices, but does not predetermine their decisions. Humans must rise to God's benevolence with proactive willingness to receive grace.

See also: PREDESTINATION

*Mona Lisa* (La Giaconda) A panel painting executed by LEONARDO DA VINCI (1503–06; Louvre, Paris). It depicts the wife of a Florentine official, Francesco del Giocondo, and ranks among Leonardo's finest works. The psychological content of the painting, epitomized by the sitter's famous enigmatic smile, together with the fantastic mountainous landscape in which she is set, profoundly influenced contemporary artists and effectively reformed the portraiture of the period. Also notable for Leonardo's SFUMATO technique of blending one color into another, the painting later provided the base for RAPHAEL's portrait of Maddalena Doni. See Plate X.

**Further reading:** Donald Sassoon, *Becoming Mona Lisa: The Making of a Global Icon* (San Diego, Calif.: Harcourt, 2001).

**Monet, Jan** (c. 1480–c. 1550) *Flemish sculptor*
Monet was born in Metz but by 1497 he was active in Barcelona. In 1512–13 he was in Aix-en-Provence, but he had returned to Barcelona by 1516. The following year he worked beside Bartolomé ORDÓÑEZ on the decoration of the choir of the cathedral there, after which he may have visited Naples. In 1521 he met DÜRER at Antwerp and the following year Emperor Charles V appointed him a court artist. From about 1524/25 until his death he was resident at Malines. Monet's chief works were alabaster altarpieces, such as those at Halle (1533) and Brussels (1538–41). In a sense, these works were the first Renaissance sculptural altarpieces in the Netherlands, in that their architectural and stylistic repertory consists entirely of classical or Italianate motifs. However, their overall compositions lack classical repose and seem to seethe with an uneasy motion, more reminiscent of Spanish late Gothic than contemporary Mannerism.

**Monluc, Blaise de** See MONTLUC, BLAISE DE LASSERAN-MASSENCÔME, SEIGNEUR DE

**Montagna, Bartolommeo** (Bartolommeo Cingano) (c. 1450–1523) *Italian painter*
Born near Brescia, Montagna probably trained as a painter in Venice and may have been a pupil of Andrea MANTEGNA, by whom he was greatly influenced. He was influenced also by Giovanni BELLINI, Antonio VIVARINI, and ANTONELLO DA MESSINA. Montagna settled in Vicenza around 1474 and was soon recognized as Vicenza's leading artist. His control of geometric composition and taste for grand architectural settings is most clearly seen in his altarpiece for San Michele, Vicenza (1499; Brera, Milan), although subsequent portraits also underline his sensitivity to character. His son Benedetto (c. 1481–c. 1558) was also a painter and engraver of note.

**Montaigne, Michel Eyquem de** (1533–1592) *French essayist*
Montaigne was born at the château de Montaigne (near Bordeaux), the son of Pierre Eyquem, a wealthy merchant whose grandfather had bought himself into the nobility; his mother, Antoinette de Louppes, was a Catholic of Spanish-Jewish origin. For the first six years of his life he spoke only Latin, his German tutor having no knowledge of the French language. He subsequently attended the Collège de Guyenne in Bordeaux and went on to study law. In 1557, after three years' service in the *cour des aides*, Montaigne became a magistrate at the *parlement* of Bordeaux, where he made the acquaintance of Étienne de LA BOÉTIE; the two men remained close friends until the latter's premature death in 1563, an event that caused Montaigne deep and lasting distress.

Never enthusiastic about his legal career, Montaigne resigned his office in 1570, two years after the death of his father, and retired to the family château to write. His translation of Raymond de Sebonde's *Theologia naturalis* had already appeared in 1569; in 1571 he published an edition of La Boétie's works and began to set down in ESSAY form the reflections inspired by his reading and his meditations on life and death. After the publication of the first two books of *Essais* (1580) Montaigne embarked on an 18-month tour of Europe, the subject of his *Journal de voyage*; although partly motivated by a writer's desire to experience the world beyond his study, the journey also had a medical purpose in that Montaigne hoped that the waters of spas in Italy and elsewhere would relieve his kidney stones. On his return to France he served for four years as mayor of Bordeaux. During a visit to Paris in 1588, possibly on behalf of Henry of Navarre (later Henry IV of France), Montaigne was arrested and briefly imprisoned in the Bastille; the main purpose of his trip had been to supervise the publication of a new edition of the *Essais*, containing the third volume. In the same year he met Marie de GOURNAY, whom he called his *fille d'alliance* (adopted daughter), who edited his final additions and amendments to the *Essais* and published the augmented work in 1595.

Of English translations of the *Essais*, that by John FLORIO (1603) was the earliest and also the most frequently reprinted, for instance in the Tudor Translations series (1892–93). Accessible modern versions include those in the Penguin Classics series by J. M. Cohen (Harmondsworth, U.K., 1958) and M. A. Screech (London and New York, 1993). The *Essais* have also been translated by Donald M. Frame in an edition of the *Complete Works* of Montaigne (Stanford, Calif., 1957); this translation was subsequently reissued separately (Stanford, 1958; New York, 1960). The travel journal was lost for many years and only rediscovered in 1770; it was published four years later as *Journal de Voyage de Michel de Montaigne en Italie, par la Suisse et l'Allemagne en 1580 et 1581* (2 vols). A modern edition is that by Fausta Garavini (1983). An English version, *The Journal of Montaigne's Travels*, appeared in 1903, translated and edited with an introduction and notes by W. G. Waters. Donald Frame's translation was published in 1983 under the title *Montaigne's Travel Journal*.

**Further reading:** Peter Burke, *Montaigne* (Oxford, U.K.: Oxford University Press, 1981); Anne Hartle, *Michel de Montaigne: Accidental Philosopher* (Cambridge, U.K.: Cambridge University Press, 2003); George Hoffmann, *Montaigne's Career* (Oxford, U.K. and New York: Clarendon Press, 1998); Dudley M. Marchi, *Montaigne Among the Moderns: Reception of the* Essais (Providence, R.I. and Oxford, U.K.: Berghahn Books, 1994).

**Montano, Benito Arias (y)** See ARIAS MONTANO, BENITO

**Montchrestien, Antoine de** (c. 1575–1621) *French dramatist, poet, and economist*
Montchrestien was a native of Falaise. As a youth he was almost killed in a fight and later had to flee abroad after taking part in a duel. He traveled in Holland and England, a keen observer of commercial activities, and established steelworks in France after his return. Although a Catholic he was killed at a tavern while fomenting a Huguenot uprising in Normandy.

Montchrestien's six tragedies (published 1601, except *Hector*, 1604)—based on classical myth and history, biblical subjects, and contemporary history—are notable for their baroque lyrical and descriptive passages. They are: *Sophonisbe*, *L'Écossaise* (on the death of Mary, Queen of Scots), *Les Lacènes* (on the Spartan king Cleomenes), *David* (on David and Bathsheba), *Aman* (on Haman, Esther, and Ahasuerus), and *Hector*. Also published in 1601 were *Susane* (a long poem on Susanna and the Elders) and *Bergerie*, a pastoral play. His *Traité de l'économie politique* (1615), one of the earliest works on the subject, influenced Cardinal Richelieu and Jean-Baptiste Colbert.

**Monte, Philippe de** (1521–1603) *Flemish composer*
Born in Malines, Monte went to Italy while still young. From 1542 to 1551 he served the Pinelli family in Naples as singer, teacher, and composer. In 1554 he traveled to England, and sang in the private chapel of the queen's husband, Philip II of Spain. In 1568 he became *Kapellmeister* to Emperor Maximilian II at Vienna. From this time he composed prolifically and published many of his works. Though he remained in the imperial service for the rest of his life, he also held various nonresidential positions at Cambrai cathedral. He died in Prague. Among Monte's friends were LASSUS and BYRD. About 48 Masses, 300 motets, 45 chansons, and an amazing 1100 madrigals survive. The Masses are largely based on motets by contemporary composers. His madrigals show close attention to the text (usually by contemporary pastoral poets such as GUARINI); later madrigals become simpler in form and tend towards increased homophony. Monte's secular music was widely sung, as the distribution of his publications and manuscripts testifies.

**Montefeltro family** A family prominent in the Romagna from the 13th to the 16th century as CONDOTTIERI and rulers of Urbino. The Montefeltro fought for the Ghibelline (imperial) forces until Guido submitted to Pope Boniface VIII in 1295. They first ruled Urbino in 1234, but lost and regained power on several occasions. Antonio, who recovered Urbino in 1377, made peace with the pope and ruled as papal vicar until his death (1403). His son, Guidantonio, papal vicar and lord of Urbino (1403–44), married a COLONNA and enjoyed papal support against the MALATESTA. Federico (1422–82), who succeeded his father in 1444, was an outstanding military leader in the service of Pope SIXTUS IV, who created him duke of Urbino (1474); he also served Lorenzo de' MEDICI. Federico consolidated his family's power and spent his earnings as a condottiere on art, his palace, and other public works. Federico's son, Guidobaldo, was the last Montefeltro to rule Urbino (1482–1508); his court, presided over by his wife Elisabetta Gonzaga, was in 1506 the setting for Castiglione's THE COURTIER.

**See also:** DELLA ROVERE FAMILY

**Montemayor, Jorge de** (c. 1519–1561) *Portuguese writer and poet*
Montemayor was born at Montemor o Velho, near Coimbra, into a Portuguese *converso* family and became a soldier and a professional musician. He served the Infanta Juana, the Spanish wife of Prince John of Portugal and mother of King Sebastian. He followed her to Spain after the death of her husband and was subsequently in the service of Philip II, whom he accompanied to England in 1554 and also probably to the Netherlands. He was killed in Italy, apparently in a duel resulting from a love affair. His works, written in Spanish, include a *Cancionero* pub-

lished at Antwerp (1554), which was reprinted with a *Segundo cancionero espiritual* (1558). The latter, which sought to render the style of the Psalms in Italianate hendecasyllabic verse, was banned by the Inquisition (1559). Montemayor's most important work, which introduced the pastoral romance from Italy to Spain, was LA DIANA.

## Monteverdi, Claudio (1567–1643) *Italian composer*

Monteverdi was born in Cremona and studied music at the cathedral there. Before moving (1591) to Mantua as a string player for Duke Vicenzo I Gonzaga, he published books of MADRIGALS and motets, a discipline he kept up throughout his career. His third book of madrigals (1592) reveals dissatisfaction with traditional harmonics. To justify his bold use of dissonance, which he saw as a resurrection of the principles of music as taught by classical antiquity, he posited two styles (or "practices"). His experiments with the "seconda prattica" in which words come before the music—as distinct from the "prima prattica" taught by Gioseffo ZARLINO—were criticized in Giovanni Artusi's *On The Imperfection of Modern Music* (1600). Monteverdi's fifth book of madrigals (1605) was the first to use *basso continuo*, a steady bass-line, which later was to become a standard feature of BAROQUE music.

His pioneering philosophy of music drew on the Platonic doctrine of correspondence. He used three styles to represent the three basic emotions: *stile concitato*, with short repeated notes on a single pitch, conveyed agitation; the softer *stile molle*, with its long notes, expressed tenderness; and *stile temperato* portrayed equanimity. *L'Orfeo* (1607) stands out for its innovative retelling of the classical tale of Orpheus who used music to draw his beloved Eurydice back from the Underworld. It is arguably the first opera in the modern sense of the term, conceived as a drama in music and depicting human psychology. Monteverdi also wrote a court opera about Ariadne abandoned on the island of Naxos by Theseus after she had rescued him from the Minotaur's labyrinth; only the famous "Lament of Arianna" survives, as a solo song and also in the form of a madrigal. The words are by Ottavio Rinuccini (1562–1621), who also wrote texts for Monteverdi's ballets, including *Il Ballo dell' ingrate* (1608) to celebrate the marriage of Francesco Gonzaga to Marguerite of Savoy, and *Il Combattimento di Tancredi e Clorinda* (published 1624) taken from Tasso's *Gerusalemme liberata*.

With aspirations beyond Mantua, in 1610 Monteverdi compiled a portfolio of sacred vocal works which he dedicated to Pope Paul V. *Vespro Della Beata Vergine* uses the traditional vesper service of the Blessed Virgin Mary to showcase the composer's versatility. These qualities later appealed to the officials at St. Mark's basilica where, in 1613, he was appointed *maestro di cappella*, a prestigious position he held for the rest of his life. From 1637 on, with the opening of public opera houses in Venice, he revived older works while also writing new ones such as *Il Ritorno d'Ulisse in patria* about Ulysses's homecoming. His last opera, *L'incoronazione di Poppaea*, celebrates the love of Nero and the courtesan whom he crowned empress. Just as his music leaves the High Renaissance behind, Monteverdi's final opera opens the way to a new kind of harmony and a vision of humanity without the gods; the result is a new kind of struggle and sweetness–and a new freedom.

**Further reading:** Denis Arnold, *Monteverdi* (London: Dent, 3rd ed. 1990); Paolo Fabbri, *Monteverdi*, transl. Tim Carter (Cambridge, U.K. and New York: Cambridge University Press, 1994); Gary Tomlinson, *Monteverdi and the End of the Renaissance* (1987; repr. Berkeley, Calif.: University of California Press, 1990).

## Montluc, Blaise de Lasseran-Massencôme, Seigneur de (c. 1500–1577) *French soldier*

Montluc was born at St.-Puy and spent his early years at court, as page and archer to the duke of Lorraine. His military career began in 1521 and culminated in his appointment as marshal of France in 1574; during the intervening years he had taken part in five pitched battles and more than 200 skirmishes. As governor of Siena (1554–55) Montluc distinguished himself in the heroic defense of that city against imperial and Florentine forces; as lieutenant-general of Guyenne and a supporter of the GUISE in the early years of the Wars of RELIGION he was remembered for his severe repression of the HUGUENOTS. Montluc's *Commentaires*, published posthumously in 1592, are an autobiographical record of his military career, its successes and its failures: his colorful description of 16th-century warfare is particularly valuable for its detailed accounts of individual operations.

## Montmorency, Anne de (1493–1567) *French soldier and nobleman*

The boyhood friend of FRANCIS I, Montmorency was made marshal of France (1522) after his bravery in the Wars of ITALY. Himself captured at PAVIA (1525), he negotiated Francis I's release from captivity (1526). He exercised great influence at court, becoming constable of France (1538) after his successes against imperial forces in Provence and Savoy, but intrigues brought about his downfall (1541).

Restored to royal favor in the reign of HENRY II (1547–59), Montmorency fought bravely against Spain until his capture at ST-QUENTIN (1557). Although the GUISE FAMILY drove him from Francis II's court (1559–60), he joined the duke of Guise in the triumvirate against Protestantism (1561) and fought on the Catholic side in the Wars of RELIGION until he was killed at the siege of Paris.

**Montorsoli, Giovanni Angelo** (1507–c. 1561) *Italian sculptor in marble*
Born at Montorsoli, near Florence, he was taught by Andrea Ferrucci and influenced by the work of MICHELANGELO, whom he assisted in the 1520s. In 1531 Montorsoli became a brother in the Servite order and during the next five years executed commissions for the Servites in the church of the SS. Annunziata in Florence. After three years in Naples, Montorsoli went to Genoa in 1539 and in 1547 to Messina in Sicily. Here, as master of the works at the cathedral, he created his two best-known works: the fountain of Orion and the fountain of Neptune. Between 1558 and 1561 he worked in Bologna before finally returning to his convent in Florence.

**Montpellier** A city in southern France renowned during the later Middle Ages and Renaissance as a center for the teaching of medicine. The school of medicine originated in the 12th century and drew a number of its earliest teachers from Montpellier's thriving Jewish community. The university was founded at the end of the 13th century. During the religious wars of the 16th and 17th centuries Montpellier suffered considerable damage, particularly in the 1620s when its Protestant defenders were eventually forced to submit after a long siege. Its botanic garden was founded in 1592. The Montpellier medical school attracted trainee physicians from all over Europe and a number of distinguished botanists were also associated with it. RABELAIS was a medical student there, as were the botanists CLUSIUS and L'OBEL, both of whom studied under the naturalist RONDELET.

**Mor, Anthonis** See MORO, ANTONIO

**Morales, Cristóbal** (c. 1500–1553) *Spanish composer*
Morales was born in Seville, where he was trained as a chorister at the cathedral. His first position was as choirmaster at Ávila cathedral (1526–29). In 1535 he joined the papal choir in Rome where he stayed for 10 years and published several collections of his compositions. During this period he traveled widely with the papal choir, which advanced his reputation as a singer and composer. He returned to Spain in 1545 and was appointed choirmaster at Toledo cathedral that same year. After a period in the service of the duke of Arcos at Marchena, near Seville, he became choirmaster at Málaga cathedral (1551), where he remained until his death.

Morales is one of the finest polyphonic composers of the Andalusian school of musicians. His output consists almost entirely of sacred works and of these his Magnificats, 16 in total, were the most popular and widely printed. He was the first composer to write Magnificats in all eight ecclesiastical modes. However, Morales regarded his Masses as his best work and he personally supervised the publication of 16 while in Rome (1544). This was quickly disseminated throughout Europe and became the earliest polyphonic collection of sacred music to be used in the New World: a copy is held at Pueblo cathedral, Mexico. His six-part motet *Jubilate Deo omnis terra* was commissioned by Pope Paul III to celebrate the peace treaty of Crépy between the Emperor Charles V and Francis I of France in 1544.

**Morales, Luís de** (El Divino) (c. 1509–1586) *Spanish painter*
Generally considered the greatest Spanish artist in the mannerist style before EL GRECO, Morales spent most of his life in his birthplace, Badajoz. He may have studied under the Dutch artist Hernando Sturmio and was influenced by the art of both the Flemish school and Leonardo's followers. Morales acquired his nickname on account of the religious intensity of his works (he never undertook profane subjects), which include a series of about 20 paintings for the church of Arroyo del Puerco (1563–68) and five panels in Badajoz cathedral. Notable works include a *Virgin and Child* (National Gallery, London) and a *Pietà* (Academia de San Fernando, Madrid). Morales also worked for a time upon the decoration of the ESCORIAL, at the behest of Philip II, and executed commissions at Elvas and Évora in Portugal. Other influences upon his highly personal style included the German artists Martin SCHONGAUER and Albrecht DÜRER.

**Morata, Olimpia** (1526–1555) *Italian humanist and scholar*
She was the daughter of Pellegrino Morata, a humanist at the Ferrarese court, and she grew up in the circle of duchess Renata (RENÉE DE FRANCE). After studying Greek and Latin, she instructed the duchess's daughters in geometry, classics, literature, and geography. She was active in a circle of humanist scholars, but came under attack during the Roman Inquisition of 1542 for her Protestant beliefs. In 1548 she was stripped of her privileges and hounded out of court. After marrying the German Lutheran physician Andres Grunthler in 1550, she went back with him to his home in Schweinfurt, from where she conducted a correspondence in Latin and Italian with her old associates in Italy. Forced to flee Schweinfurt at the onset of war, she and her husband settled in Heidelberg in 1554, but Morata died a year later after a long bout of malaria. Her husband ensured that her Latin and Greek orations, dialogues, letters, and poems were published: *Olympiae Fulviae Moratae foeminae doctissimae ac plane divinae orationes, dialogi, epistolae, carmina, tam Latina quam Graeca* (1558).

**More, St. Thomas** (1478–1535) *English statesman, scholar, and author*
The son of a London barrister, More was brought up in the household of Cardinal John Morton (c. 1420–1500), chief minister of King Henry VII, before being sent to Oxford

(c. 1492–94). There he met Thomas LINACRE (who taught him Greek) and William GROCYN. On returning to London to study law, he continued his scholarly interests and became friends with William LILY, John COLET, and ERASMUS. After four years (1499–1503) during which he seriously contemplated entering holy orders, More entered parliament instead (1504) and commenced a highly succesful legal career, which led to his becoming under-sheriff of London (1510–19). His house was a center for humanists, and he also made two journeys to France and Flanders (1508, 1515), during the second of which he sketched out his UTOPIA.

More's talents, learning, and personal charm recommended him to Cardinal WOLSEY, and from 1518 he held official posts that brought him into constant contact with HENRY VIII, with whom he was a personal favorite. Accompanying Henry to the FIELD OF THE CLOTH OF GOLD (1520), he met Guillaume BUDÉ, and later HOLBEIN came to England (1526) under More's patronage. He also used his position at court to promote the new learning in England. In 1529 he was made lord chancellor, but relations with Henry cooled on account of More's continued support for Queen Catherine during the king's attempt to have their marriage annulled. In 1532 More resigned and went into retirement, but Henry insisted on his taking the oaths recognizing the new Act of Succession in favor of Anne Boleyn's children (1534) and denying the authority of the pope. More was willing to agree to the former, but would not compromise his religious convictions by swearing to the second. He was arrested and imprisoned in the Tower of London. There he wrote *A Dialogue of Comfort against Tribulation* (not published until 1553) and other religious treatises and astounded everyone by his calm and even humorous demeanor. He was found guilty on perjured evidence of high treason and executed. He was hailed as a martyr in Catholic Europe and canonized in 1935.

More's private life is mainly known from the biography by William Roper, husband of More's favorite daughter (*see* ROPER, MARGARET); it was first published in 1626. He himself published an English version of the Latin biography of PICO DELLA MIRANDOLA (1510), but most of his works, apart from *Utopia*, were not published until long after his death. These include his biography of Richard III, Latin epigrams, Latin translations of dialogues of Lucian, and controversial pamphlets in both Latin and English.

In 1957 Loyola University, Los Angeles, issued a facsimile, edited by Frank Sullivan, of the *Complete Works* of 1557. Between 1963 and 1997 the St. Thomas More Project of Yale University published a modern edition of More's works in Latin and English, *The Complete Works of St. Thomas More* (15 vols).

**Further reading:** Peter Ackroyd, *The Life of Thomas More* (New York: Doubleday, 1998); Anthony Kenny, *Thomas More* (Oxford, U.K.: Oxford University Press, 1983); Richard C. Marius, *Thomas More: A Biography* (London: Collins, 1985).

**Moreelse, Paulus Jansz.** (1571–1638) *Dutch painter and architect*
A founder-member of the St. Lucas guild (1611), Moreelse was born and worked in Utrecht and was known chiefly as a portraitist. His portraits of children are particularly attractive. Influenced by Michiel van Mierevelt, whose pupil he was, he also produced a number of pastoral portraits of shepherds and shepherdesses. His architectural works include the Catherine gate and the facade of the Utrecht meat market.

**Moretto, Alessandro Bonvicino;** (c. 1498–1554) *Italian painter*
Moretto was a pupil of Fioravante Ferramola, with whom he decorated the choir of the cathedral in his native Brescia (1518). He worked mainly in the Brescia and Bergamo districts before visiting Milan and Verona in the 1540s. His paintings, mainly of religious subjects, are notable for their silvery colors, strength of composition, and the homely flavor which Moretto often imparted to elevated subjects. The influence of RAPHAEL can be seen in his treatment of form. He was also an outstanding portrait painter, influenced by Lorenzo LOTTO and TITIAN, and he is said to have introduced the full-length portrait into Italy (*The Nobleman*, 1526; National Gallery, London).

**moriscos** Spanish Muslims who, after the fall of Granada (1492), accepted the option of Christian baptism rather than go into exile. Despite being nominally Christian they were regarded with suspicion and, along with Jewish converts, became one of the targets of the SPANISH INQUISITION.

**Morley, Thomas** (1557–1602) *English composer*
Morley was born in Norwich, and in 1583 was appointed organist and master of the choristers at the cathedral there. He was a pupil of William BYRD, though it is not known when. In 1588 he gained the Oxford BMus. and a year later became organist at St. Paul's Cathedral, London. He was appointed a gentleman of the Chapel Royal in 1592, and in 1598 obtained the monopoly for music printing that had belonged to Byrd. His treatise, *A Plaine and Easie Introduction to Practicall Musicke* (1597), criticizes some English compositional styles and promotes Italian methods.

Morley's contribution to the madrigal in England, through the publication of Italian music and his arrangements of Italian pieces, is unrivaled. The most famous collection for which Morley was responsible is *The Triumphs of Oriana* (1601). This contains madrigals by Morley and 22 English contemporaries; one of Morley's two contributions shows the influence of CROCE, on whose *Il trionfo di*

*Dori* the collection was modeled. Morley's sacred and keyboard music is influenced by that of Byrd; his madrigals, canzonets, and balletts are more Italianate in style, but his *Consort Lessons* (1599), arrangements of English popular music for broken consort, are more typically English.

## Moro, Antonio (Anthonis Mor van Dashorst) (c. 1519–c. 1576) *Dutch painter*
Born in Utrecht, Moro was a pupil of Jan van SCOREL, whose influence can be clearly seen in Moro's *Two Jerusalem Pilgrims* (1544: Berlin). After visiting Italy Moro came under the influence of Titian, as his portrait of his patron Cardinal Granvelle (1549; Vienna) shows, although subsequent portraits by him tend towards a more austere approach. He visited Portugal and in 1554 went to London and painted his masterpiece: the portrait of Mary I commissioned by Philip II of Spain. By 1560 he had become painter to the Spanish court and was painting portraits of the Hapsburgs in Spain and the Netherlands. Other works include the portraits *Maximilian II* (1550; Prado, Madrid), *Sir Henry Lee* (1568; National Portrait Gallery, London), and the *Man with a Dog* (1569; National Gallery, Washington). Moro's pupils included Alonso Sánchez COELHO.

## Morone, Giovanni (1509–1580) *Italian churchman*
A Milanese by birth, he was appointed bishop of Modena in 1529, and in 1536 was sent by the pope on a diplomatic mission to Germany, to prepare for a general council. He was present at the diets of Hagenau (1540), Regensburg (1541), and Spires (1542). In 1542 he became a cardinal and was later also bishop of Novara (1553–60). He was imprisoned on a charge of heresy (1557–59), but later absolved, and served as the last president of the Council of TRENT from 1563. In 1570 he became bishop of Ostia, in which role he acted as protector of the ENGLISH COLLEGE in Rome.

## Moroni, Andrea (died 1560) *Italian architect*
Moroni was active in Padua, where his chief monument is the courtyard (1552) of the university, with its Tuscan and Ionic columns. He was also responsible for building the church of Sta. Giustina, modifying as he did so the original plans (1502) by Andrea RICCIO, and for the classical courtyard of the Municipio, formerly the Palazzo del Podestà.

## Moroni, Giovanni Battista (c. 1525–1578) *Italian painter*
Born near Bergamo, Moroni studied under MORETTO da Brescia and also absorbed the influence of Lorenzo LOTTO. More than any other artist of the Renaissance he specialized in portraiture, chiefly of family groups and single figures of the people of Bergamo. His most famous painting is the undated *Tailor* (National Gallery, London), although he also produced some less distinguished religious paintings for the churches of Bergamo.

## Moryson, Fynes (1566–1630) *English traveler*
Moryson was born in Lincolnshire and studied (1580–86) at Cambridge. Taking advantage of a fellowship (1590) to study law at European universities he journeyed throughout Europe (1591–95) and later in the Levant (1595–97). After a spell back in Lincolnshire he became secretary to Queen Elizabeth's deputy in Ireland (1601–06). *An Itinerary* (1617), abridged from his voluminous travel notes, is a pioneering travel book offering a fascinating view of all the lands Moryson visited, as seen by an opinionated Protestant with a remarkable eye for telling detail.

## Moser, Lukas (early 15th century) *German painter*
Although almost nothing is known about his life and only one work by him survives, Moser is generally acknowledged as one of the most important German painters at a time when a national style was beginning to develop. His altarpiece of the Magdalene (1431) at Tiefenbronn, near Pforzheim, was executed in the International Gothic style and is comparable with similar realist works by the German Swiss artist Konrad WITZ and Jan van EYCK. The painting includes a lament for the state of contemporary art: "Cry out, art, cry out and wail! No one wants you now. So alas, 1431."

## Mostaert, Jan (1472/73–1555/56) *Dutch painter*
In 1507 Mostaert was appointed dean of the painters' guild in his native Haarlem. By 1521 he was a court artist to MARGARET OF AUSTRIA, and, although she resided at Brussels and Malines, Mostaert retained his principal base in his home town. His earliest work, the Amsterdam *Tree of Jesse*, is influenced by Geertgen tot Sint Jans and even his Brussels *Passion* altarpiece (c. 1520) reveals a debt to Rogier van der WEYDEN. Mostaert's *West Indian Landscape* (c. 1542) in Haarlem has overtones of Joachim PATINIR but seems to have been partly based upon sketches brought back from the New World. He also painted numerous highly accomplished portraits, although none of his likenesses of the imperial household has survived. The landscape backgrounds of his portraits sometimes include small figure compositions, for example, the legend of St. Hubert in his Liverpool *Portrait of a Man*.

**motet** A musical work sung in Latin and, though not liturgical, often heard during church services. During the Renaissance motets were frequently composed for ceremonial events or in honor of a particular person. The medieval technique of isorhythm was continued in motet composition into the early 15th century; a late example is DUFAY's *Nuper rosarum flores*, written for the dedication of Florence cathedral (1436). In England John DUNSTABLE led the way towards the devotional votive motet, with more use of Marian texts. Continental composers used English pieces as models, experimenting with fauxbourdon and improvised counterpoint, and in France composers adopted the style of secular songs in three-part writing. In the second half of the 15th century a compositional tradition of motet writing became established in which parts were evenly balanced in polyphonic texture, and the tenor *cantus firmus* part, though retained, became less distinguishable from the others. *Cantus firmi* continued in motets throughout the 16th century, though composers also composed freely with no reference to chant; Johannes OCKEGHEM's *Ave Maria, gratia plena* is an example of free composition with equal use of counterpoint in each voice. Josquin DES PRÉS developed the motet in many ways: the canonic doubling of the tenor *cantus firmus*; the quotation of secular melodies; homophonic declamation; free counterpoint; variation in texture as duos and trios are used in alternation with the full choir; and a change of meter from binary to ternary. These compositional procedures were continued by Josquin's successors. PALESTRINA accepted chant as an important element, and in his motets imitative polyphony alternates with homophony. LASSUS's style of motet writing is more rhetorical with more depiction of the text and more homophony; this style was disseminated throughout Europe. Giovanni GABRIELI sowed the seeds of a new style in which choirs of voices or voices and instruments interchange in short homophonic phrases, paving the way for the baroque motet.

**Mudo, El** See FERNÁNDEZ DE NAVARRETE, JUAN

**Mühlberg, battle of** (1547) A victory gained at the German town of Mühlberg, on the bank of the River Elbe, by forces under the personal command of Emperor CHARLES V over a Lutheran alliance led by John Frederick, Elector of Saxony. By this triumph Charles hoped he was in a position to achieve religious harmony in his German realms and at Augsburg the following year he attempted to draw up the necessary settlement (*see* AUGSBURG, INTERIM OF).

**Müller, Johann** See REGIOMONTANUS

**Mundy, John** (c. 1555–1630) *English composer*
The son of William MUNDY, he received his bachelor of music degree at Oxford in 1586 and a doctorate in 1624. Mundy was an organist at St. George's Chapel, Windsor. His extant works include a collection of English anthems, many of which are incomplete. Five of his instrumental works are included in the FITZWILLIAM VIRGINAL BOOK.

**Mundy, William** (c. 1529–c. 1591) *English composer*
Little is known of Mundy's life. From 1543 he was a singer in the choir of Westminster Abbey and he was a Gentleman of the Chapel Royal during the reign of Elizabeth I. He is best known as a composer of sacred vocal music and

worked in a range of styles from the old Latin antiphon tradition to the new English verse anthem. Mundy also wrote Masses and Latin psalm settings. His *Vox patris caelestis* is a votive antiphon which is perhaps the greatest achievement in that tradition. His verse anthems with organ accompaniment are early examples of what was to become the principal style of English cathedral music. According to a contemporary, Robert Dow, Mundy's music was second only to that of William BYRD. He is represented in the Mulliner Book (British Museum), a manuscript collection of mid-16th-century English keyboard music.

**Munich** (German **München**) A city on River Isar in Bavaria, southern Germany. Founded by Henry the Lion, Duke of Bavaria, in 1157, the city passed to the Wittelsbach family in the late 12th century, and from 1255 it was the Wittelsbach home and capital city. In the early 14th century Emperor Louis (IV) the Bavarian greatly extended Munich. Under the leadership of the dukes of Bavaria and influenced by the Jesuits, Munich remained loyal to the Catholic faith in the 16th century and was an important center of COUNTER-REFORMATION activity. Notable buildings which have survived from the period of the Renaissance include the cathedral (1468–88), the town hall (1470–80), and the Renaissance style Michaelkirche (1583–97).

**Münster, Sebastian** (1489–1552) *German theologian and geographer*
Münster was born at Ingelheim and educated at the universities of Tübingen and Heidelberg. He became a Franciscan monk in 1505, but after converting to Protestantism in 1529 he moved to Switzerland. There he taught Hebrew at Basle university (he had been a pupil of Elias LEVITA) and was appointed to the chair of mathematics (1536). A formidable linguist, he produced Hebrew (1520) and Chaldean (1527) grammars as well as an edition of the Hebrew Bible (1534–35). He was also the first person to make a Hebrew version of any part of the New Testament: St. Matthew's Gospel (1537). He is best known for his *Cosmographia universalis* (1544), a comprehensive survey, rich in woodcuts and maps, of the known world. Although weak on the New World and Asia it contained much impressive detail on Germany and western Europe. Münster also published *Horologiographia* (1531), on the art of constructing sundials, and an edition of Ptolemy's *Geography* (1540). He died of the plague.

**Müntzer** or **Münzer, Thomas** See PEASANTS REVOLT

**Muret, Marc-Antoine** (Muretus) (1526–1585) *French humanist scholar*
Born at Muret, near Limoges, Muret attracted the attention of Julius Caesar SCALIGER and soon made a reputation for himself as a teacher of Latin. He was also friendly with

members of the PLÉIADE and sympathetic towards their poetic program. His early success, notably a course of lectures in Paris in the early 1550s attended by a numerous audience that included the French king, brought him many enemies, who succeeded in getting him thrown into prison on a charge of sexual impropriety. From 1555 he made his home in Venice, then settled in Rome under the patronage of Cardinal Ippolito d'Este. Apart from a brief return visit to France (1561–63) he remained in Rome for the rest of his life, lecturing and building up an immense reputation as a Latin stylist. MONTAIGNE, a student of his, called him "le meilleur orateur du temps." As a classical scholar he wrote commentaries on Cicero, Sallust, Plautus, and the elegiac poets, and his *Variae lectiones* was published in Venice in 1559.

**Muris, Johannes de** (c. 1300–c. 1350) *French music theorist*
Born in Normandy, he studied in Paris and spent some time at the Collège de Sorbonne there, otherwise traveling extensively through France. He knew Philippe de VITRY, and was influential in developing a theory of measured music. His *Ars nove musice* (1321) is his most important work, dealing with the notions of sound and musical proportions.

**Murner, Thomas** (1475–1537) *German satirist*
Born in Alsace, Murner grew up in Strasbourg and took orders as a Franciscan friar there (1491). He then studied theology and taught at Fribourg, Cologne, Paris, Rostock, and Cracow, and later studied law at Basle. His popular appeal was evident in both his preaching and his writing, in his use of familiar sayings and imagery combined with a love of the grotesque and scurrilous. More biting than Sebastian BRANT's gentle satire, Murner's was directed first at folly in general, as in the rhyming verses of *Die Narrenbeschweerung* (Fools' exorcism; 1512), modeled on Brant's *Narrenschyff*. Although highly critical of Church corruption, he found Luther too iconoclastic and took up the cudgels for Catholicism. In *Von dem grossen Lutherischen Narren, wie in doctor Murner beschworen hat* (Of the great Lutheran fool, as Doctor Murner has exorcised him; 1522), he vitriolically attacked the Reformation. Other works apart from satires include anti-Lutheran pamphlets, theological works in Latin, and a translation of Virgil's *Aeneid* into German verse.

**Muscovy Company** (**Russian Company**) A group of English merchants trading with Russia. The company was founded in 1552 by merchants desiring a NORTHEAST PASSAGE to China and India. In 1553 the founders sponsored a three-ship expedition under Sir Hugh Willoughby (died 1554), but only one reached Russia. Its captain, Richard CHANCELLOR, was entertained by Tsar Ivan IV, who promised free trade rights. In 1555 the company obtained a monopoly on Anglo-Russian trade. A thriving relationship with Russia developed, although attempts in the late 1550s to establish a similar link with Persia, principally through the efforts of Anthony JENKINSON, proved abortive. In the 17th century the company lost its privileges in England and Russia, and was forced to compete with other English and Dutch companies, but survived to re-emerge as a prominent force in 18th-century trading.

**Muses** The nine goddesses who, in classical mythology, were patronesses of various individual art forms. Although they were the daughters of Zeus and Mnemosyne (Memory), they are often depicted as companions of APOLLO in their role of inspirers of music and the divine creative power. Their names and the arts over which they presided were: Calliope, epic poetry; Clio, history; Erato, erotic poetry; Euterpe, lyric poetry; Melpomene, tragedy; Polyhymnia, sacred music; Terpsichore, dancing; Thalia, comedy; Urania, astronomy. Each was depicted with her conventional attributes: Urania with a staff and globe, Euterpe with a flute, etc. They feature collectively or individually in Renaissance allegorical and decorative schemes, and the appropriate Muse was conventionally invoked by writers.

**museums** See CABINETS

**music** In the Renaissance period musicians, like artists and writers, began to sense the emergence of a new age. Writing in 1477, Johannes TINCTORIS stated that music written more than 40 years previously was not worth hearing. He goes on to list the composers of his own period who had brought the art to its current state of perfection: those, like OCKEGHEM, who learned from the example set by DUNSTABLE, BINCHOIS, and DUFAY. After the barren period of the Dark Ages, composers sought models for their works. Unlike those active in other fields, musicians had no direct examples to follow in trying to resurrect the learning and styles of the classical era. This proved frustrating at a time when sculptors and architects, at least in Italy, were discovering the legacy of antiquity all around them. The musician was forced to look to trends in other arts to discover which direction his own should take.

Of the sparse references to music in classical writings the most influential was surely the Platonic dictum that the music should be subservient to the text. This continued to influence musicians throughout the Renaissance, and the principle was even cited as the reason for the advent of another "new age" which we now call the early BAROQUE. Late Renaissance enthusiasm for such humanist ideals led to some rather extreme applications, such as Jean-Antoine de BAÏF's Académie de la Poésie et de la Musique; the word setting practiced by those associated with this institution rigidly adhered to the poetic meters—

no deviation was countenanced in this *musique mesurée*. Though theorists continued to discuss music as a branch of mathematics, in practice musicians became more text-orientated, and the carefully devised numerical structures present in so much earlier music were only occasionally discernible.

Another trend in favor of verbal clarity, affecting musical idioms, manifested itself in ecclesiastical reforms, notably those of the Council of TRENT. This assembly was concerned about the lack of intelligibility of the text in composed liturgical settings. A purging of musical idioms was called for in order to right the position. Again there were a number of extreme reactions, but a more rational response to the council is evident in the works of most composers, notably PALESTRINA. Polyphonic compositions became organized in such a way that there was greater coincidence of words between the differing vocal lines; earlier this had generally been only a secondary consideration.

Italy has been regarded as the cradle of the Renaissance but, at least until the second half of the 16th century, most influential composers hailed from the Netherlands and northern France. It was not until the early 16th century that Italians themselves gained any status as composers; in fact, foreigners were crucial in the early development of the MADRIGAL, a genre that more than any other embodied a sophisticated synthesis of Italian poetry and music. Many northerners found employment in Italy at sophisticated courts and in high ecclesiastical posts. But it is questionable whether these Franco-Flemish musicians, or indeed their music, can be considered as products of the same cultural development that gave birth to contemporaneous works of literature and fine art. Their native Italian patrons were certainly men of the Renaissance, but few were equipped to exert any substantial influence on the manner in which their servants actually wrote. They could, of course, control the creative life of the musician as far as it fell to them to decide which occasions merited musical participation; the current level of prosperity determined what forces would be available for any particular event.

While musicians, like other artists, were bound by the strictures of their patrons, there was a developing sense of the composer as a creator, rather than one who merely sought to reflect the order already present in the created universe. Theoretical writings of the Renaissance demonstrate the marked decline in interest in *musica theorica* in favor of a view of music in which sound and harmony were all-important, and the ears were the ultimate judge (*see* MUSIC THEORY). Trained ears were necessary to the appreciation of the more recondite areas of musical performaance. With the emphasis on this human-centered notion of music came the practice of reflecting nature, particularly in the madrigal.

Despite the dominance of the Netherlanders in this period, music also flourished outside the courts and churches where they were active. England had a strong and individual tradition of florid church music which was brought to an abrupt end by the Reformation. In Germany a parallel, though less severe, hiatus was the result of religious changes there. In the Iberian peninsula liturgical music was produced which could worthily be heard alongside the sacred output of many musicians active in Italy.

There is no doubt that the 15th and 16th centuries were a flourishing period for musical composition. Connections can be made between some of the tendencies which emerge in the music of the period and those in fine art, the field in which the term "Renaissance" was originally applied. It is perhaps wrong to emphasize too strongly the term when dealing with the music of this period. There are certain ways—the lingering interest in numerology, for instance—in which the music is still a product of the medieval era. On the other hand, Renaissance music so closely resembles that of the Baroque in its attitude to the central issue of text that to delineate the characteristics of a single period too minutely is to misunderstand its place in the historical continuum.

**See also:** ARS NOVA; MUSIC PRINTING AND PUBLISHING

**Further reading:** Ignace Bossuyt, *Flemish Polyphony* (Louvain, Belgium: Davidsfonds, 1994); Howard M. Brown, *Music in the Renaissance* (1976; 2nd ed. Upper Saddle River, N.J.: Prentice Hall, 1999); Isabelle Cazeaux, *French Music in the Fifteenth and Sixteenth Centuries* (Oxford, U.K.: Blackwell, 1975); Peter Le Huray, *Music and the Reformation in England, 1549–1660* (Cambridge, U.K.: Cambridge University Press, 2nd ed. 1978); *New Oxford History of Music:* Vol. III *Ars Nova and the Renaissance, 1300–1540*, eds Anselm Hughes and Gerald Abraham (London: Oxford University Press, 1960; repr. 1988); ~ , Vol. IV *The Age of Humanism, 1540–1630*, ed. Gerald Abraham (London: Oxford University Press, 1968); Claude V. Palisca, *Humanism in Italian Renaissance Musical Thought* (New Haven, Conn. and London: Yale University Press, 1986); Gustave Reese, *Music in the Renaissance* (rev. ed. 1959; repr. London: Dent, 1977); John E. Stevens, *Music and Poetry in the Early Tudor Court* (London: Methuen and Lincoln, Nebr.: University of Nebraska Press, 1961; repr. Cambridge University Press, 1979).

**musical instruments** TINCTORIS's late 15th-century dictionary defines an instrument as a "body which causes sound, either by nature or by skill." In the latter category, a tremendous variety of instruments was known and cultivated during the Renaissance, affecting musical practice at every level. In recent decades, a point of particular contention has been the combination of voices and instruments in the performance of written polyphony from this period, with some scholars advocating an all-vocal (*a*

**Musical instruments** A woodcut of a group of Renaissance musicians from the title page of an early 17th-century book. The ensemble includes (left to right) an early violin, bass viol, virginal, lute, early trombone, and curtal (early bassoon); a group of singers and a recorder player can be seen at the back.

*capella*) approach to most notated music. Nevertheless, by the beginning of the 16th century at least, first-hand accounts become increasingly explicit about the performance of instrumentalists together with SINGERS in many contexts.

One benefit of the attack on instrumental participation in early polyphony has been a reduction in indiscriminately orchestrated performances. The instrumental combinations that are historically plausible in particular situations are, in fact, quite tightly circumscribed, even if the musical sources themselves only make specifications on rare occasions. The most important distinction is between *haut* and *bas* (loud and soft) instruments, which were used for separate purposes and rarely combined. Among the loud instruments, some of the most important ensemble types were wind bands, which at various points combined the shawm (a woodwind adopted centuries earlier from the East), sackbut (the early trombone, which appeared during the 15th century), and later the cornett (another woodwind, mainly used for high parts). Predominantly a Flemish and German phenomenon in its early stages, the wind band had spread to all parts of Europe by the 16th century. Highly skilled in improvisation, these ensembles were definitely playing mainstream vocal music as well by the later 15th century, and grew gradually from three players to five or six in the next century. Other loud ensembles were considerably more removed from the world of written art music. The large trumpet groups retained at major courts mainly played straight and

S-shaped instruments, which had a limited selection of notes available; their fanfares marked the entrances of sovereigns, the switching of courses at banquets, or the conclusions of spectacular royal Mass celebrations. Trumpets also retained their traditional military functions, for signals in army movements and battles. In this purpose, they were joined by drumslades who played large side drums (unrelated to the "pipe and tabor," a combination of small drum and one-handed flute which played regularly with soft instruments).

In the soft music (reserved most often for an indoor chamber context, and suited to a different style of singing from that used in churches), wind instruments included not only recorders and other flutes, but also quieter relatives of loud instruments. Bowed string instruments of an earlier period which were retained in common use through much of the 16th century include the small rebec, often with only two or three strings, and the larger fiddle of five or more strings. The viol (*viola da gamba*), distinguished by being played upright on the leg, probably developed from the Spanish *vihuela de mano* (a plucked instrument) during the later 15th century. During the 16th century the viol gained rapidly in popularity throughout Europe, and was developed into a family of different-sized instruments which could play polyphonic pieces in consort. In England and on the Continent, a set of viols became a fixture of the growing activity of domestic music-making. The violin, on the other hand, developed its modern form out of the fiddle by the mid-16th century, and remained largely in the hands of minstrels and professional musicians.

The main plucked string instruments were the harp and lute, the latter of which became very important for solo performance. Derived from the Arabic 'ūd, the European lute was widespread by the mid-14th century, although it was only in the later 15th century that solo players began to use it for playing multivoice compositions. As with the similar Spanish vihuela, 16th-century musicians translated thousands of polyphonic works into notation for the lute ("tablature"). When members of the nobility and royalty were taught music, it was frequently the lute and keyboards that they learned. Among the keyboard instruments of the period, the most venerable and widespread was certainly the organ, used in many churches and cathedrals since at least the 10th century. It is also a special case, since it was an ecclesiastical instrument, and those who received training on it and theorized about its construction were church singers. These players were always more closely associated with the sacred musical traditions than were other instrumentalists. The keyboards that came into use in secular spheres included smaller portable organ types, like the regals, as well as various string instruments (virginals and other harpsichords).

**Further reading:** Curt Sachs, *The History of Musical Instruments* (London: Dent, 1942); Howard Mayer Brown and Keith Polk, "Instrumental Music, *c.* 1300–*c.* 1520," in *Music as Concept and Practice in the Late Middle Ages*, ed. Reinhard Strohm and Bonnie J. Blackburn (*The New Oxford History of Music* Vol. III.1, Oxford, U.K.: Oxford University Press, 2002), pp. 97–161.

**music printing and publishing** During the first half-century of Western printing, the vast majority of printed music appeared in plainchant books, produced from the 1470s onward in numerous towns in Italy, Spain, and Germanic regions. Printed chant books created for the Sarum rite in England were imported from the Continent, with the first native English example being Richard Pynson's missal of 1500. As with many printed books of this period, the early plainchant prints closely imitated professionally written manuscripts, and achieved a remarkable state of elegance and sophistication. The problem of printing notes over horizontal four-line staves led to the development of a double-impression technique, in which each page went through the printing process twice: first for the empty staves, then for the notes.

Polyphonic music used a notation system somewhat different to that of plainchant, mainly on account of the specification of rhythm. The first examples of printed polyphony are found mainly in theoretical tracts such as the *Musices opusculum* (1487) of Nicolaus Burtius and the *Practica musice* (1496) of Franchino GAFFURIO. In these books, short multivoice compositions were printed from

woodcuts, requiring a significant investment of labor for each example. The few other late 15th-century ventures into the printing of polyphony likewise relied on woodcuts, serving to reproduce occasional musical items in mainly textual contexts.

The watershed year for the printing of polyphonic music was 1501, which saw the appearance of the collection *Harmonice musices odhecaton A*, published in Venice by Ottaviano PETRUCCI. In Petrucci's early prints, a triple-impression method separated the printing of staves, music, and text; the precision of alignment required for the task was considerable, but the results were visually superb. With the collaboration of an editor, Petrus Castellanus, Petrucci issued a wide variety of prints, including both vocal and instrumental music, for years before any other music publishing houses began work. Petrucci's activities in music printing appear to have wound down around 1520, with one exception (and possibly more) in 1538.

The first followers of Petrucci in the trade of printing music collections worked in Germany; in the 1510s; however, Andrea Antico created extensive music prints completely from woodcuts in Rome (and later, Venice). In the Low Countries, early examples of printed polyphony occur in a 1515 book printed by Jan de Gheet in Antwerp, where two motets by Benedictus de Opiciis are included as incidental items, reproduced from woodcuts alongside texts and illustrations. Antwerp would later become one of the great centers of music printing, home to the firms of Susato, Waelrant, and Phalèse, among others.

The French printer Pierre Attaignant is commonly credited with the introduction of single-impression music printing, in which individual pieces of type included segments of music staves; this process considerably simplified the technical aspects of printing, and eventually became the standard method of music printing throughout Europe. Attaingnant's first single-impression print of 1527/8, however, was actually preceded by some years by several songs printed in London by John Rastell, using the same technique. Rastell's examples represent the only English printing of polyphonic music until the isolated (and now fragmentary) *Book of XX Songes* in 1530. The real bulk of music printing activity in England, particularly after the middle of the 16th century, was directed toward the needs of the reformed Church, with John Day issuing edition after edition of simple vernacular psalm settings (*see* PSALMODY). These prints were inspired by models from Continental Europe, where vast collections of psalms in Dutch, German, and French played an important role in the distribution of Protestant music.

Of course, printing became an equally vital element in the traditional spheres of Latin art music for the Catholic Church and secular forms (CHANSON, MADRIGAL, instrumental music, etc.). Beginning in the late 1530s, the firms of Antonio Gardano and Girolamo Scotto in Venice made the first extended use of single-impression printing in Italy, publishing vast quantities of madrigals as well as motets, masses, and other liturgical polyphony. For the mid-century generation of composers such as Nicolaus Gombert, Jacobus CLEMENS (NON PAPA), and Adrian WILLAERT, printing took on a greater importance than ever before in establishing reputations. The process worked posthumously and conversely as well: the indiscriminate application of Josquin DES PRÉS's name to spurious compositions in 1530s editions by German printers led to the remark that "now that Josquin is dead, he is producing more compositions than when he was alive." By the end of the century, the printing of secular works and Latin-texted sacred music (even in England) was at a high point of activity. It was in later periods that economic realities caught up with the music printing field and stemmed the enormous expansion that marked its first century.

See also: PRINTING

**Further reading:** Iain Fenlon, *Music, Print and Culture in Early Sixteenth-Century Italy* (London: British Library, 1995); A. Hyatt King, *Four Hundred Years of Music Printing* (1964; 2nd ed. London: British Library, 1968); Jeremy L. Smith, *Thomas East and Music Publishing in Renaissance England* (New York: Oxford University Press, 2003).

**music theory** What is now considered "music theory" includes many different kinds of writing about music and encompasses both the major elements characterized in early treatises as *musica theorica* and *musica practica*. A division of music into practical and theoretical elements had been known in the ancient world, and was taken up again in the monumental *Speculum musice* of Jacobus of Liège (died after 1330), eventually becoming a standard structuring device. The theoretical branch of music consisted of the mathematical study of ratios, for the construction of musical intervals and scales, along with speculation concerning the causes, effects, and classifications of music in the world and the cosmos. For this type of learning, by far the most influential work throughout the Middle Ages, and continuing into the 16th century as a basic university text, was the sixth-century *De institutione musica* of Boethius. The 14th-century writings of Johannes de MURIS would achieve a similarly wide distribution for two centuries, with the *Musica speculativa secundum Boetium* and *Notitia artis musicae* reaching a university audience.

The other side of music theory, *musica practica*, dealt mainly with elements of notation and performance. In the writings of Muris and certain contemporaries, we find a major development, known as the ARS NOVA, which involved the creation of a new system of rhythmic notation. Simultaneously, the theorist Marchetto of Padua experimented with new approaches to tuning in polyphony, introducing controversial theoretical constructs to accommodate microtonal divisions of the pitch space. After later 14th-century experimentation with new notational symbols and complexities of rhythmic detail, the major steps of the 15th century involved formulations to exert closer control over the interactions of voices in polyphony. The most significant contribution to the study of music in the later part of the century was made by Johannes TINCTORIS, whose writings attempt to cover every aspect of contemporary practice in a systematic manner. In the texts of Tinctoris and major contemporaries such as Franchino GAFFURIO, the influence of classical rhetorical models affects the style and language of the treatises, particularly in the increasing attention paid to named composers and the citations from specific compositions in examples. Nevertheless, the aims and teachings of these books is still largely traditional, and issues concerning details of music notation give rise to the theorists' most heated debates. The only major British theorist to appear between the later 14th and 16th centuries was John HOTHBY, who spent the greater part of his career in Italy in the later 15th century. Hothby was an influence on a number of Italian theorists,

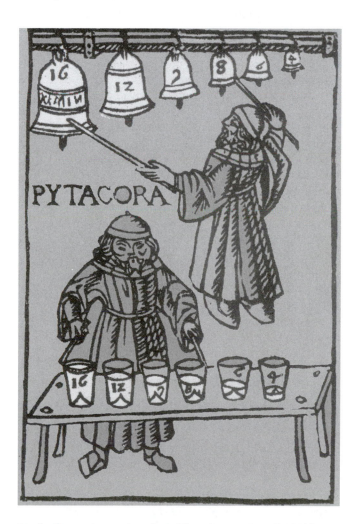

**Music theory** A woodcut from *Theorica musicae* (1492) by Franchino Gaffurio, showing experiments to establish the mathematical relationships between musical intervals.

while his English contemporaries experimented with idiosyncratic approaches to combining speculative theory with the realities of performance.

In the 16th century, major compendia of music theory, mainly printed, compose the bulk of significant new writing. Italian treatises such as Pietro Aaron's *Toscanello in musica* (first printed in 1523) and Gioseffo ZARLINO's *Istitutioni harmoniche* (1558) became classic expositions of the foundations of 16th-century musical style. Large-scale vernacular music primers were also printed in France, Britain, and the Germanic and Iberian regions. One of the major treatises of the period appeared publicly in 1547, the *Dodecachordon* by the Swiss humanist Heinrich GLAREANUS. Glareanus's book raised the idea of recovering the effects of ancient music through a reform of the system of modes; these were linked to specific emotional characteristics, and had always been associated with the legendary powers of music in the ancient world. Nicola VICENTINO's *L'antica musica ridotta alla moderna prattica* (1555), on the other hand, sought to reinstate the ancient "chromatic" and "enharmonic" melodic genera (alongside the diatonic, which was the only one in practical use). A third means by which 16th-century writers tackled the crucial problem of affect was experimentation with classical quantitative poetic meters, expressed in a direct and strict manner through musical rhythms. The most famous example is the style of *musique mesurée à l'antique* produced at Jean-Antoine de BAÏF's Parisian academy in the 1570s.

In the end, the most significant impact on musical style came from the circle of Giovanni de' BARDI, whose Florentine Camerata experimented with a new recitative compositional style, supposedly in imitation of ancient Greek music. Treatises by Girolamo Mei (1573), Vincenzo GALILEI (1581), and Bardi himself (1578) rejected fundamental principles of earlier musical practice as having no grounding in ancient tradition and confounding the expressive delivery of texts. It was this environment which, at the end of the century, gave birth to the earliest forms of opera. Ironically, the most concerted efforts to revive the classical world in music are traditionally seen as marking the end of the musical "Renaissance."

**Further reading:** Bonnie J. Blackburn, Edward E. Lowinsky, and Clement A. Miller (eds.), *A Correspondence of Renaissance Musicians* (Oxford, U.K.: Clarendon Press, 1991); James Haar, *The Science and Art of Renaissance Music* (Princeton, N.J.: Princeton University Press, 1998); Claude V. Palisca, *Humanism in Italian Renaissance Musical Thought* (New Haven, Conn. and London: Yale University Press, 1985).

**Muziano, Girolamo** (1528–1592) *Italian painter and engraver*
Based in Brescia, near his birthplace of Acquafreddo, Muziano was a pupil of ROMANINO, by whom he was greatly influenced. Muziano also shared with Titian a taste for strong color and dramatic landscape, as seen in his *St. Jerome* (Accademia Carrara, Bergamo). Around 1548 he went to Rome and was influenced by the work of Michelangelo and Raphael. He produced some attractive landscape drawings, now in the Uffizi, Florence.

**Myconius, Oswald** (Oswald Geisshäusler) (1488–1552) *Swiss reformer*
One of the pioneering figures of Swiss humanism, Myconius was born at Lucerne and studied in Rottweil and Basle before coming to Zürich to teach in the cathedral school there. He played an influential role in securing the appointment of his friend Ulrich ZWINGLI as minister and was a close collaborator in his reforming work. In 1531 Myconius was called to Basle, where he succeeded John OECOLAMPADIUS as chief minister and remained for the rest of his life. He supervised the publication of the Basle Confession of 1534 and helped draft the first Helvetic Confession of 1536. His writings included a number of biblical commentaries and the first biography of Zwingli (1536).

**mythology** The classical myths had caused serious problems for the Middle Ages. Their solution was either to characterize the pagan gods as devils, a method sanctioned by St. Augustine, or to allegorize them as symbols of Christian ethics and morality, a method exemplified in the countless manuscripts of the work known as *Ovid Moralized*. Renaissance scholars inherited both these approaches and added something of their own. A number of handbooks of mythology had been transmitted to the Renaissance; the *Bibliotheke* (*Library*) *of Apollodorus* and two works attributed to Julius Hyginus provided a basis for the study of the classical myths. The late antique period produced a number of commentaries—Servius's on Virgil (early fifth century) is the best known—which supplemented the handbooks.

The first Renaissance scholar to draw on these resources was BOCCACCIO, who compiled (1350–75) *De genealogiis deorum*, an encyclopedia of mythology, geography, and history. He also made use of Leonzio Pilato's notes to his translation of Homer and of Lactantius Placidus's commentary on the *Thebaid* of Statius. For Boccaccio a knowledge of classical mythology is an essential part of a poet's equipment; the 14th book of the *Genealogia* is in fact devoted to this proposition. He adopted the Stoic position that myths are allegories of deeper truths, and this was to have a profound influence on later students of mythology. Boccaccio's popular work circulated widely in manuscript and was printed with a commentary by Micyllus in 1532. It was the primary source of information about classical myth for poets and artists; Chaucer made use of it and its influence can be seen in the Renaissance painter's love of allegory. It was finally superseded by the *Mythologia* of Natalis Comes (1551), which provided a codification, with emblematic illustrations, of contemporary knowledge of classical mythology.

Mythology not only provided the raw material for decoration; it was also a way of conveying the truths of Neoplatonic philosophy. Plato himself had used myth as an integral part of his dialectic method. The first Neoplatonists, particularly PLOTINUS and Porphyry (232–305 CE), developed this aspect of their master's work to an extravagant degree and the theologian Origen (c. 185–c. 254 AD) made the technique respectable from the Christian point of view. The Florentine Platonists found this approach especially congenial. The choice of HERCULES, the judgment of the arms of Achilles, and the cave of the nymphs are typical of the classical myths which received allegorical or mystical interpretations. In the visual arts BOTTICELLI led the way for this kind of treatment in his introduction of pagan subject matter in major paintings.

Renaissance scholars frequently misunderstood their authorities and these misunderstandings were sometimes more fruitful than a more pedantic accuracy would have been. Boccaccio for example begins his genealogy of the gods with Demogorgon, who went on to have a long history in the works of many European writers. The reference comes from a misreading by a medieval scribe of a word in Lactantius Placidus's commentary on Statius.

**See also:** ICONOGRAPHY

**Further reading:** H. David Brumble, *Classical Myths and Legends in the Middle Ages and Renaissance* (Westport, Conn.: Greenwood, 1998); Joscelyn Godwin, *The Pagan Dream of the Renaissance* (Grand Rapids, Mich.: Phanes, 2002).

# N

**Nanni di Banco** (Giovanni di Antonio di Banco) (c. 1384–1421) *Italian sculptor*
A native of Florence, Nanni trained under his father, the sculptor Antonio di Banco, with whom he worked on pieces for Florence cathedral. His first major work was the life-sized marble figure *Isaiah* (c. 1408), a companion piece to Donatello's marble *David* that was executed in a notably Gothic manner. A more classical influence is evident in his masterpiece, the *Quattro Santi Coronati* (Four crowned saints; c. 1411–13), a group of marble figures depicting early Christian martyrs for Orsanmichele, Florence. His last major work was the *Assumption of the Virgin Mary* (begun c. 1414) over the Portale della Mandorla of Florence cathedral; it was probably finished by Luca DELLA ROBBIA, who may have been Nanni's pupil.

**Nantes, Edict of** (April 1598) The proclamation by HENRY IV of France that ended the Wars of RELIGION. By it the HUGUENOTS were granted some religious toleration, including complete freedom of conscience and the right to worship freely in parts of France. Their pastors were paid by the state. They enjoyed full civic rights and were assigned certain towns as strongholds. A special Catholic and Huguenot court was to judge disputes arising from the settlement. The Catholic Church resented the edict; Cardinal Richelieu revoked the poli-tical clauses (1629) and Louis XIV revoked the entire edict in 1685. The revocation was followed by the emi-gration of hundreds of thousands of Huguenots, depriving France of many industrious and enterprising citizens.

**Naogeorgus, Thomas** (Thomas Kirchmaier) (1511–1563) *German polemical dramatist*

Naogeorgus was born near Regensburg and became a Protestant pastor. He used the Latin drama, revived by the humanists, as a vehicle for his Reformation polemic against the pope and higher echelons of the Catholic Church. His *Pammachius* (1538), representing the pope as Antichrist, is one of the best examples of this drama and was acted in Cambridge in 1545. *Mercator* (1540) is an Everyman play in which, in line with Lutheran doctrine, faith is privileged over good works. The many plays that followed were less successful. Naogeorgus also wrote a verse epic attacking the papacy (*Regnum papisticum*, 1555; English translation by Barnabe Googe, 1570) and translated Sophocles' tragedies into Latin.

**Napier, John** (1550–1617) *Scottish mathematician*
The son of a wealthy laird, Napier was born at Merchiston Castle near Edinburgh. After attending St. Andrews University and a period of foreign travel, he returned to Scotland to manage the family estates. A fanatical Protestant, Napier sought to demonstrate the identity of the pope and antichrist in his *Plaine discovery of the Whole Revelation of St. John* (1593), a work that also predicted that the world would end between 1688 and 1700. Today Napier is remembered for his *Mirifici logarithmorum canonis descriptio* (1614; translated by Edward WRIGHT as *A Description of the Admirable Table of Logarithmes*, 1618), the work that introduced logarithms to the world. Other methods of computing, of which the best known is "Napier's bones" (a set of 10 wooden or ivory rods), are described in his *Rabdologiae* (1617).

See also: BÜRGI, JOST

**Naples** (Italian **Napoli**) A city and port in Campania, southern Italy, formerly capital of the kingdom of Naples. Originally colonized by Greeks, Naples was in turn Roman, Byzantine, and Norman before it was ruled by the Angevins (1282–1442), the king of Aragon (1442–58), and the illegitimate Aragonese line (1458–95). Much of the political turmoil that afflicted Naples in the later years of Angevin rule was due to the fact that two of the legitimate rulers were queens—Joanna (Giovanna) I of Anjou (reigned 1343–81) and Joanna II of Durazzo (reigned 1414–35)—with no clear candidate to succeed them. In pursuit of the Angevin claim, CHARLES VIII of France briefly took over Naples (1495–96); after a period of confusion the city and kingdom of Naples were restored to Aragonese and Spanish rule (1504). Naples was then ruled by Spanish governors until the early 18th century.

During the 14th and 15th centuries Naples was the capital of a kingdom still organized largely on feudal lines; it lacked a substantial middle class and its commercial and economic development lagged behind that of cities in northern Italy. The prosperity of the city depended on the presence of the royal court and on the agriculture of the region. Yet, the growth of the city's population in the Renaissance era was remarkable, rising from about 30,000 in 1300 to about 60,000 in 1400 and close to 300,000 in 1600.

Royal patronage made Naples an important center of learning and the arts. ALFONSO I "the Magnanimous", who resided permanently in Naples after 1443 set the trend with his patronage of, among others, Lorenzo VALLA and Antonio BECCADELLI. His successor FERDINAND I (Ferrante) continued to support the arts and scholarship, with the humanist PONTANO as his secretary of state. In the 1480s Ferdinand's son, the future Alfonso II (reigned 1494–95), oversaw building works that transformed Naples into a Renaissance city. The city had a fine university (founded 1224), schools of humanist studies in the second half of the 15th century (*see also* NEAPOLITAN ACADEMY), printing presses (from 1471), and one of the oldest conservatories of music (founded 1537). In the 1530s the influential religious thinker and reformer, Juan de VALDÉS, studied and wrote in Naples. The composer Philippe de MONTE worked in Naples in the 1540s, as did GESUALDO later in the century. CARAVAGGIO painted for the Neapolitan court in the late 16th and early 17th centuries. Neapolitan monarchs encouraged grand public works in their capital city; the Castel Nuovo (1279–82), the cathedral (1294–1333), and the Castel Sant Elmo (rebuilt 1537–46) are among the buildings that have survived. Alfonso I's triumphal arch erected (1453–66) by Pietro da Milano at the Castel Nuovo is adorned with reliefs by Francesco LAURANA; later sculptors to work in the city included the Spaniards Diego de SILOE and Bartolomé ORDÓÑEZ.

**Further reading:** Jerry H. Bentley, *Politics and Culture in Renaissance Naples* (Princeton, N.J.: Princeton University Press, 1999).

**Nardi, Jacopo** (1476–1563) *Italian politician and historian*
Nardi was born in Florence and belonged to the intellectual circle of the ORTI ORICELLARI. His earliest works were two comedies based on tales in Boccaccio: *L'Amicizia* (written between 1502 and 1512) and *I due felici rivali* (performed in 1513). A committed republican, he held various offices after the exiling of the Medici in 1494 and played an active role in their second expulsion in 1527. On their return in 1530 Nardi himself was exiled. Most of the rest of his life was spent in Venice. His chief work *Istorie della città di Firenze* (1582), covering the period 1498–1537, is mainly valuable for the period 1512–30, when Nardi was in the thick of political events on the anti-Medicean side.

**Nashe, Thomas** (Thomas Nash) (1567–c. 1601) *English writer*
Nashe was born in Lowestoft, went to Cambridge university (1582), and then traveled in France and Italy before settling (c. 1588) in London. There he quickly embroiled himself in literary feuds, publishing his *Anatomie of absurditie* (1589) in which he attacked recent writers, and under the pseudonym of Pasquil he contributed pro-bishop pamphlets to the MARPRELATE CONTROVERSY. The Cambridge pedant Gabriel HARVEY was a special target of Nashe's lively satire until, after the publication of Nashe's *Have with you to Saffron Walden* (1596), officialdom intervened to terminate the dispute. The picaresque novel *The Unfortunate Traveller, or the Life of Jack Wilton* (1594) shows Nashe's narrative and inventive powers at their best, while *Lenten Stuffe* (1599), a mock panegyric on Yarmouth herrings, is a bravura performance in burlesque. Nashe also wrote for the stage; in 1597 he was imprisoned for his share in the lost comedy *The Isle of Dogs*. Another comedy, *Summers Last Will and Testament*, was published in 1600, and he completed MARLOWE's *Dido, Queen of Carthage* (1594) after Marlowe's death.

**natural philosophy** Throughout the Renaissance, and indeed long after, this was the term widely used to refer to the systematic investigation of nature. Science, as we know it today, emerged in the 17th century but its roots lay in Renaissance thought. This is most clearly seen in astronomy. The work of COPERNICUS had shown that the universe is heliocentric and was followed by KEPLER's discovery of the three laws of planetary motion. What, though, of motion itself? Two problems faced the Renaissance natural philosopher: to develop techniques to describe and analyse all kinds of motion and to explain its various forms. On the first issue scholars began with the work of medieval mathematicians, such as Nicolas ORESME, who had developed simple graphical techniques to describe the motion of bodies, whether uniform or accelerating. Using their techniques, GALILEO succeeded in deriving the basic equations of motion relating acceleration, time, distance, and velocity. They were, however, expressed as geometrical ratios rather than the algebraic equations familiar today. Galileo's grasp of the nature of motion was equally limited. Although he was able to break with tradition in a number of respects, he failed to recognize the essential role of inertia in physics.

Nor was any greater progress made when scholars turned their attention to the nature of matter. While some rejected the traditional four-element theory of matter (*see* ARISTOTELIANISM, RENAISSANCE), few could agree on its replacement. PARACELSUS and his followers argued that bodies were composed of salt, sulfur, and mercury, without ever making it clear what was meant by these terms. Others, however, proposed the existence of two, four, five, or more elements. With no clear concept of the nature of an element, and without an authoritative theory, Renaissance chemistry inevitably lacked cohesion. This condition was made worse by the secretiveness and suspicion brought about by the close contact between Renaissance chemistry and ALCHEMY.

If old disciplines proved hard to reform, more impressive results were achieved in newer areas of research. Thus William GILBERT in *De magnete* (1600), with no traditional constraints to worry about, virtually founded the scientific study of magnetism. Galileo, too, in his *Due nuove scienze* (1638), could achieve similar results on the cohesion of bodies and the resistance they offer to fracture. Much of this success depended on the growing reliance on experiment and observation, exemplified especially in the works of Gilbert and Galileo. The theory justifying this approach was presented by Galileo himself and, even more so, by Francis BACON.

Less progress was made in the study of organic nature. While knowledge, of sorts, was accumulated, and some fresh attempts were made to systematize that knowledge (*see* ZOOLOGY), the subject remained too constrained by its own theological assumptions to develop into new areas. At a more fundamental level natural philosophy during the Renaissance found itself under strong attack from supporters of MAGIC. To an uncommitted 16th-century witness it cannot have been entirely clear whether a better understanding of nature could be derived from the magical techniques of someone such as Cornelius AGRIPPA, or the work of the young mathematician Galileo. In the event, the vision of Galileo and Kepler prevailed over that of FICINO and Agrippa and prepared the way, in the process, for the science of Descartes and Newton later in the 17th century.

**Further reading:** Allen G. Debas and Michael Thomson Walton (eds), *Reading the Book of Nature: The Other Side of the Scientific Revolution* (Kirksville, Miss.: Truman State University Press, 1998); James R. Jacob, *The Scientific Revolution: Aspirations and Achievements, 1500–1700* (Amherst, N.Y.: Humanity, 1998); Howard Margolis, *It Started with Copernicus: How Turning the World Inside Out Led to the Scientific Revolution* (New York: McGraw–Hill, 2002).

**Naumburg Convention** (1561) A meeting of German princes and Protestant theologians, designed to achieve doctrinal unity in accordance with the Confession of AUGSBURG. It failed because the Lutherans insisted on the original articles of 1530 (*invariata*) and the Calvinists preferred those of 1540 (*variata*). A papal invitation to send delegates to the Council of TRENT was declined.

**Navagiero, Andrea** (1483–1529) *Italian scholar, historian, poet, and diplomat*
Navagiero was born into an eminent Venetian family. He studied in Padua where he learned Greek and particularly interested himself in the odes of the poet Pindar (518–438 BCE); the Greek *editio princeps* of Pindar (1513) was dedicated to Navagiero by Aldus MANUTIUS, for whose press Navagiero edited Latin authors, most notably Cicero. In 1506 Navagiero was appointed to succeed Marcantonio SABELLICO as librarian of San Marco and this position, together with his membership of the NEAKADEMIA, placed him in the center of Venetian intellectual life. Among his friends was Giralamo FRACASTORO, who made Navagiero the mouthpiece for his views on poetry in the dialogue *Naugerius* (1555); the garden setting for this dialogue recalls Navagiero's own interest in natural science and his renowned garden at Murano. He was also friendly with Pietro BEMBO, with whom he visited Rome, with RAPHAEL, who painted his portrait, and with the geographer RAMUSIO.

Besides writing a history of Venice, Navagiero served the republic as ambassador. In 1526 he was in Spain, where he met BOSCÁN and introduced him to Italian poetic meters, which Boscán was the first to naturalize in Spanish. Navagiero brought back with him from Spain to Italy the then newly discovered potato and other exotics, including possibly a banana. He was next sent on an embassy to Francis I of France, but died while at Blois. His *Orationes duae carminaque nonnulla* were published posthumously at Venice (1530).

**Navarrete, Juan Fernández de** See FERNÁNDEZ DE NAVARRETE, JUAN

**navigation** Renaissance navigation was fundamentally a combination of the Arab astronomy that guided medieval travelers and some latter-day technological developments. The forerunner of the numerous scientific navigational instruments created by Renaissance inventors was the compass in the 13th century. In the wake of its popularization, the first known navigational book, *Lo compasso di navigare*, began to circulate in 1296. Around the same time, the Carta Pisana (Pisan chart) displayed the horizon in terms of compass points, although directions, especially in the Mediterranean area, were still mainly determined by major winds. Also, early compasses were based on dead reckoning, with no allowances for magnetic variation, the principle of which was not understood until the mid-16th century.

Along with instruments, CARTOGRAPHY flourished during the Renaissance period. In the 15th century Portuguese cartographers developed the use of latitude to permit navigators unprecedented certainty in determining their whereabouts; it was assessed by the position of either the Pole Star or the midday sun. Various methods were proposed to establish longitude; GEMMA FRISIUS suggested the use of a clock in 1530, but a sufficiently accurate timepiece was not available until the chronometer was developed in the 18th century, and mariners until then had to rely on very uncertain methods of dead reckoning.

Although navigational techniques improved throughout the Renaissance period, most of the major gaps were filled by instruments invented by German or Flemish scientists, such as APIAN and REGIOMONTANUS in the late 15th and early 16th centuries. Improvements to ASTROLABES

**Navigation** A woodcut from the Italian translation (1537) of Sacrobosco's *Tractatus de sphaera*. It shows the author with two globes, one of which includes (South) America.

made them more useful to mariners, while QUADRANTS, cross-staffs, and BACKSTAFFS were also invented or refined. The development of practical literature and of printing processes suitable for cartography was invaluable to the spread of navigational knowledge. Regiomontanus's *Ephemerides* (1474) proposed the principle of working out longitude from lunar distances, and the idea was taken up again by Apian (1524), Gemma Frisius (1530), and Pedro NUNES (1560).

The most comprehensive 16th-century treatise on navigation was by the Aragonese cosmographer Martin Cortés de Albacar, the *Breve compendio de la sphera y la arte de navegar* (Seville, 1551) it deals with practical navigation, the construction of navigational instruments (including the nocturnal for telling the time at night), the drawing of charts, and the rules for plotting ships' courses. Cortés de Albacar was apparently the first person to realize that the magnetic pole and the true pole might not be the same, enabling him to give the first clear account of the magnetic variation of the compass. Nine editions of the English translation of the *Breve compendio* are known from the period 1561–1630. An important home-produced English handbook on navigation was John DAVIS's *The Seamans Secrets* (1594).

**Further reading:** William J. H. Andrewes (ed.), *The Quest for Longitude* (Cambridge, Mass.: Harvard Collection of Historical Scientific Instruments, 1996); J. E. D. Williams, *From Sails to Satellites: The Origin and Development of Navigational Science* (Oxford, U.K.: Oxford University Press, 1993).

**Neakademia** (New Academy, Aldine Academy) The academy founded by Aldus MANUTIUS in Venice around 1500 for the propagation of Greek scholarship. Under its constitution, which was drawn up in Greek, only Greek was to be spoken at its sessions; fines for violation of this rule were accumulated to provide occasional banquets in imitation of Plato's symposia. The Neakademia had between 35 and 40 members, about a third of them Greeks. Members were divided into sections to undertake specific publishing projects for the ALDINE PRESS, with proofreaders and correctors attached to each section. Girolamo ALEANDRO and Pietro BEMBO were among its distinguished members, and the academy also welcomed visiting scholars such as ERASMUS and Thomas LINACRE.

**Neapolitan Academy** A literary society that first emerged as a coherent group in Naples in the 1440s under the patronage of ALFONSO (I) the Magnanimous and the leadership of Antonio BECCADELLI. A little later it became known as the Accademia Pontaniana after its new leading member, Giovanni PONTANO.

**Nebrija, Elio Antonio Martínez de Cala de** (Elio Nebrissa, Elio Nebrixa) (1444–1522) *Spanish humanist*
He was born at Lebrija (Latin name: Nebrissa), Seville, and studied at Salamanca and from 1461 to 1470 at Bologna, concentrating on classical languages but reading widely in law, medicine, and theology. He taught grammar and rhetoric at Salamanca from 1475. In 1502 he was one of the group of scholars gathered by Cardinal XIMÉNES DE CISNEROS at Alcalá to produce the COMPLUTENSIAN POLYGLOT Bible. He was also appointed royal chronicler (1508–09). Failing to succeed to the chair of grammar at Salamanca in 1513, he moved to the university of Alcalá. His daughter Francisca also became a professor at Alcalá, and one of the first women to teach at a European university.

The greatest Spanish humanist of the Renaissance, Nebrija published in 1481 his Latin grammar *Introductiones latine*, which he later translated into Spanish for Queen Isabella. The *Introductiones* was designed to supersede the medieval Latin grammars then in use by setting a new humanist standard for teaching the language, and, with the help of the new technology of the printing press, it quickly became a bestseller across Europe. *Interpretatio dictionum ex sermone latino in hispaniensem* (1492), a Latin–Spanish dictionary, listed 30,000 words. In the same year he published the first scientific grammar of any European vernacular language, *Gramática sobre la lengua castellana* (1492). He also published a Spanish–Latin dictionary (c. 1495, expanded 1516), a volume attempting to regularize spelling (*Reglas de orthographía en la lengua castellana*, 1517), a classics-based educational manual, and commentaries on the Latin poets Persius and Prudentius.

**Negretti, Jacomo** See PALMA VECCHIO

**Negretti, Jacopo** See PALMA GIOVANE

**Negroli family** Italian makers of weapons and ARMOR. They succeeded the MISSAGLIA FAMILY as the leading Milanese manufacturers in this field in the first half of the 16th century. Leading members were Jacopo and Filippo (active 1525–50) who made embossed parade armor as well as more practical suits. Among their clients were Emperor Charles V and Francis I of France.

**neo-Latin literature** The quantity and quality of original Latin writing in the Renaissance tend to be underestimated as few people now possess the necessary facility in Latin to appreciate it, very little of it has been translated, and interest has generally been focused upon the emergent literature in the VERNACULAR. In these circumstances it is easy to forget that the Latin writings of PETRARCH were as widely known and imitated as his innovatory Italian poems (*see* SONNET), since Latin as the universal language of the learned easily transcended national boundaries. The major controversy connected with the creation of a body of humanistic Latin literature—the Ciceronian debate (*see* CICERO)—also flourished across Europe. Virtually every humanist demonstrated his proficiency in Latin with a volume of Latin verse, though these were often juvenile or occasional productions; other writers produced Latin poetry that had a major impact upon poetic developments in the vernaculars (*see* LATIN STUDIES; PASTORAL). Women too showed off their humanist credentials in Latin verse, although publication of their work was comparatively uncommon; an exception was Elizabeth Jane WESTON, known as Westonia, who gained international acclaim with her *Parthenicon* (1602).

In prose SALUTATI was one of the first humanists to win renown as a stylist, followed by BRUNI, FICINO, PICO DELLA MIRANDOLA, and other Florentine writers. Juan Luis VIVÈS was the leading Spanish Latinist, and in northern Europe ERASMUS and Marc-Antoine MURET were among those whom contemporaries singled out as stylistic models, the former colloquial and fluent, the latter more polished and correct. Other northern European humanists held in high regard for their Latin prose or versification were CELTIS in Germany, SECUNDUS and GROTIUS in Holland, Sir Thomas MORE and his circle in England, and George BUCHANAN in Scotland.

See also: EPISTOLAE OBSCURORUM VIRORUM

**Further reading:** Grahame Castor and Terence Cave (eds), *Neo-Latin and the Vernacular in Renaissance France* (Oxford, U.K.: Clarendon Press and New York: Oxford University Press, 1984); Ian D. McFarlane (ed.), *Renaissance Latin Poetry* (Manchester, U.K.: Manchester University Press and Totowa, N. J.: Barnes & Noble, 1980); Alessandro Perosa and John Sparrow (eds), *Renaissance Latin Verse* (London: Duckworth, 1979).

**Neoplatonism, Renaissance** Neoplatonism developed in the second and third centuries CE, mainly in Alexandria where Greek, Jewish, and oriental ideas had a natural meeting place. Its greatest exponent was PLOTINUS, who in the *Enneads* developed a complex structure of mysticism and allegory which, while using aspects of PLATO's doctrines as a starting point, introduced an element of the irrational which was far removed from Plato's own ideas. Gnostic concepts were also incorporated and in its fully developed form the system constituted a serious challenge to Christianity. This philosophical school never completely died out in Constantinople and when Greek teachers migrated to Italy in the 15th century they brought with them Neoplatonism in its Byzantine form.

Gemistus PLETHON's work is typical of the writings that conveyed Neoplatonic ideas to the Renaissance. Though ostensibly a Platonist, he was heavily influenced by the Alexandrian school, and by Stoicism and oriental religions such as Zoroastrianism. In his major work *Nomoi*

(*Laws*) he attributed souls to the stars, accepted metempsychosis (transference of souls), and derived his social morality from natural law in a way that scandalized the orthodox Western Christians. These and similar ideas were congenial to many Renaissance thinkers, and Neoplatonism spread from Florence to other Italian centers. The work of Marsilio FICINO, who translated Plotinus into Latin in 1492, and of PICO DELLA MIRANDOLA helped to popularize Neoplatonic ideas, and the transcendentalism of Plethon's philosophy appealed to those who were looking for a unifying principle and already using MAGIC, hermetic theories, and heterodox Christian mysticism as elements to further that search (*see also* EGYPTIAN STUDIES). Neoplatonism exercised a powerful influence on creative writers in the Renaissance. Its characteristic mode was allegory and the exegetical potential of the allegorical approach was attractive to both poets and prose writers. Spenser's FAERIE QUEENE, for instance, has many Neoplatonic elements.

It is in fact almost impossible to draw rigid distinctions between Platonism and Neoplatonism in the Renaissance; striking evidence of this is the fact that the discussions of the PLATONIC ACADEMY at Florence were concerned far more with essentially Neoplatonic ideas than with authentic Platonism.

See also: PLATONISM, RENAISSANCE

**Further reading:** Konrad Eisenbichler and Olga Zorzi Pugliese (eds), *Ficino and Renaissance Neoplatonism* (Toronto, Canada: University of Toronto Press, 1988).

**Neri, St. Philip** See PHILIP NERI, ST

**Neri di Bicci** (1419–c. 1491) *Italian painter*
Born in Florence, Neri trained under his father Bicci di Lorenzo (1373–1452), although the influence of other eminent contemporary Florentine artists, such as Fra Angelico and Fra Filippo Lippi, can also be seen in his large output. He himself became a sought-after teacher. Examples of his work are to be found in several Florentine churches, and his journal, covering the years 1453–75, is in the Uffizi, Florence.

**Neroccio (di Bartolommeo) dei Landi** (1447–c. 1500) *Italian painter and sculptor*
Based in his native Siena, Neroccio was the partner of FRANCESCO di Giorgio for several years (1467–75) and typified the charming poetic quality of the Sienese school. His most important works include *Madonna with Saints, Antony and Cleopatra*, and *Portrait of a Girl*, all in the National Gallery, Washington. Two particularly attractive treatments of the *Madonna and Child* theme are in the Pinacoteca in Siena.

**Netherlands, Revolt of the** (1566–1609) The Dutch rebellion against Spanish rule, caused by Spanish attempts

**Revolt of the Netherlands** The sack of Antwerp during the "Spanish fury" of 1576, in which Spanish troops destroyed about a third of the city and massacred some 7000 citizens; an engraving from Michael von Eytzinger's *De leone Belgico* of 1583. *By permission of the British Library (155.a.4)*

to suppress Dutch Calvinism and political freedoms. Mounting discontent led wealthy Dutch burghers and noblemen to draft the Compromise of BREDA (1566), which they presented to the regent, MARGARET OF PARMA, as a petition. The scornful rejection of the petitioners as "ces gueux" (these beggars) was followed by attacks on Catholic clergy and churches.

In 1567 PHILIP II of Spain sent the duke of ALBA with 20,000 troops to crush the rebel Dutch, and a reign of terror was instituted by the Council of Troubles, nicknamed the TRIBUNAL OF BLOOD. Led by WILLIAM (I) THE SILENT from 1568, the Dutch suffered setbacks, but Spanish repression only stiffened their resistance.

After the SEA-BEGGARS seized Brill (1572) and took towns in Holland and Zeeland, Alba was recalled to Spain in disgrace (1573). The struggle continued inconclusively under the governor-generalship (1573–76) of Luis de Requesens and then under Don JOHN OF AUSTRIA until the conciliatory policies of Alessandro FARNESE, Duke of Parma (governor 1578–92), won the southern Catholic provinces back to Spain. It was too late to win back the

north, where the seven provinces had organized themselves into the Union of Utrecht (1579) and in 1581 proclaimed their independence as the Republic of the United Netherlands, with William the Silent as their hereditary stadtholder.

After William's assassination (1584), MAURICE OF NASSAU led the Dutch and drove the Spanish out of the seven northern provinces by 1594. The struggle continued until Spain came close to recognizing Dutch independence in the truce of 1609. By the Treaty of Westphalia (1648) the European powers formally recognized Dutch independence.

**Further reading:** Pieter Geyl, *The Revolt of the Netherlands 1555–1609* (London: Williams & Norgate, 1932; new ed. Cassell History, 1988); Edward Grierson, *The Fatal Inheritance: Philip II and the Netherlands* (London: Gollancz, 1969).

**new star** (Latin *stella nova*) The supernova (a star that temporarily becomes up to one hundred million times brighter than the sun) observed in 1572 in the constellation Cassiopeia by Tycho BRAHE. Its observation among the so-called "fixed stars" challenged the Aristotelian view, already under attack from the Copernican (heliocentric) hypothesis, that the celestial region was immutable. The mathematician and leading English Copernican Thomas Digges (died 1595) wrote his own observations on the new star (in *Alae seu Scalae Mathematicae*, 1573), which were commended for their accuracy by Brahe himself. John DEE's *Parallaticae Commentationis Praxeosque* (also 1573) was inspired by the same supernova. Another new star, often referred to as "Kepler's supernova," appeared in 1604 in the constellation of Serpentarius and was written up by KEPLER in his *De stella nova in pede Serpentarii* (1606). (The word "nova" was not used in English for this phenomenon until Sir John Herschel in the late 19th century.)

See also: ASTRONOMY; COSMOLOGY

**New World chronicles** Sixteenth-century descriptions of the newly discovered Americas and Europeans' first encounters with their inhabitants. The three instalments (1511, 1516, 1530) of PETER MARTYR d'Anghiera's *Decades de novo orbe* give an early overview of the Spanish conquests in Central and South America. CORTÉS's campaign in Mexico is narrated by his secretary-chaplain Francisco López de Gómara in *Historia de las Indias y conquista de México* (1552). This work inspired Bernal DÍAZ DEL CASTILLO in 1568 to write his own *Historia verdadera de la conquista de la Nueva España*. The *Brevissima relación de la destruyción de las Indias* (1552) by Bartolomé de LAS CASAS is bitterly critical of the Spaniards' brutal treatment of the Indians. CIEZA DE LEÓN's *Crónica del Perú* (first part 1553) attempts a just appraisal of the Spanish destruction of the Inca empire.

An English contribution to the genre is Sir Walter RALEIGH's account of his voyage in search of the legendary golden city of ELDORADO, *The Discoverie of the Large, Rich and Bewtiful Empyre of Guiana* (1596). To promote the colonization of Virginia by describing the benefits to be found there, Thomas HARRIOT wrote his *Briefe and True Report of the New Found Land of Virginia* (1588), a text that was incorporated in the *America* section (1590) of the DE BRYS' *Collectiones peregrinationum...*; the engravings illustrating this, based on the drawings of Harriot's fellow traveler John White, were the first accurate depictions of North American Indians seen by the European public.

**Further reading:** Bernadette Bucher, *Icon and Conquest: A Structural Analysis of the Illustrations of de Bry's Great Voyages* (Chicago, Ill.: University of Chicago Press, 1981); Fredi Chiappelli (ed.), *First Images of America: The Impact of the New World on the Old*, 2 vols (Berkeley, Calif.: University of California Press, 1976); Stephen J. Greenblatt, *Marvelous Possessions: The Wonder of the New World* (Chicago, Ill.: University of Chicago Press, and Oxford, U.K.: Clarendon Press, 1991); Samuel Eliot Morison, *The European Discovery of America*, 2 vols (New York: Oxford University Press, 1971, 74); Anthony Pagden, *European Encounters with the New World: From Renaissance to Romanticism* (New Haven, Conn. and London: Yale University Press, 1993).

**Niccoli, Niccolò** (1363–1437) *Italian bibliophile*
A member of the learned Medici circle in Florence, Niccoli avoided public life and concentrated on the collecting of manuscripts and on encouraging scholars to edit, copy, and translate classical texts. In this he was helped by Cosimo de' MEDICI who gave him unlimited credit at the Medici bank. Niccoli also exploited the Medici commercial network, using their agents to search for manuscripts; among those he discovered was the oldest manuscript of the minor works of Tacitus. Despite his collection of Greek manuscripts Niccoli knew no Greek himself. He was noted for the elegance of his lifestyle and the generosity with which he opened his library to scholars. On his death he left his library to a group of trustees, including Leonardo BRUNI. Cosimo took over the collection to cancel Niccoli's overdraft, and it was housed in the monastery of San Marco and catalogued by Tommaso Parentucelli, later Pope NICHOLAS V. Niccoli's life was written by Vespasiano da BISTICCI.

**Niccolò dell'Arca** (c. 1440–1494) *Italian sculptor*
Sometimes known as Niccolò di Bari or Niccolò da Puglia after his birthplace, Bari in Apulia, he worked in Venice in the 1460s, but his main work was executed in Bologna—hence his other name of Niccolò da Bologna. In 1469 he undertook the contract for the decorated canopy of the tomb (*arca*) of St. Dominic in the church of San Domenico, Bologna; he also contributed some of the small free-standing figures on the tomb. Elsewhere in Bologna are several fine terracottas by him, including a *Madonna* (1478) in the Palazzo Communale and a *Pietà* (post-1485) in Sta. Maria della Vita.

**Nicholas V** (1397–1455) *Pope (1447–55)*
He was born Tommaso Parentucelli at Sarzana, and after studying law at Bologna, he acted as tutor to two Florentine families who introduced him to humanistic ideas. He was the friend of Cosimo de' MEDICI, whom he advised (1439–40) on the collection of texts for his library. In 1444 he was made bishop of Bologna by EUGENIUS IV, whom he succeeded as pope three years later. In 1449 he resolved the schism occasioned by the Council of BASLE, and the following year he proclaimed a jubilee at Rome. In 1452 he crowned FREDERICK III emperor, the last time such a coronation took place in Rome.

Nicholas V was the first humanist pope. He employed dozens of scholars to edit and copy classical texts and founded a library which had grown by his death to 9000 volumes; this collection formed the basis for the VATICAN

LIBRARY. His own library room was decorated (1449) with portraits of pagan and Christian authors by Fra ANGELICO. Himself a scholar, Nicholas mixed on equal terms with the humanists who crowded to Rome, among them, VALLA, FILELFO, and BESSARION. The most significant event of his pontificate was the fall of Constantinople (1453) to the Ottoman Turks, which Nicholas saw as a blow to scholarship as much as to religion. He called a crusade to eject the Turks, but could arouse no response. His plan for extending and beautifying Rome, over which he consulted ALBERTI, among others, met with serious opposition, and in 1453 there was an unsuccessful conspiracy to overthrow him.

## Nicholas of Cusa See CUSANUS, NICHOLAS

## Ninety-five Theses See INDULGENCES; LUTHER, MARTIN

## Niza, Marcos de (c. 1500–1558) *Italian missionary in the New World*

Niza, a native of Nice (now France), became a Franciscan missionary and led the first group of Franciscans to Peru in 1531. After moving to Mexico (1537), he was sent by Viceroy Antonio de MENDOZA to search for the fabled golden cities of Cíbola and became the first European to reach Arizona (1539). The following year he accompanied CORONADO's expedition to New Mexico. He remained in Mexico as father provincial of Franciscan missionaries until his death.

## Nogarola, Isotta (1418–1466) *Italian humanist scholar*

Her cultured, aristocratic Veronese family enabled her and her sister Ginevra to study classics with a leading tutor, Martino Rizzoni, and while still a teenager she began corresponding with fellow humanists. Her extraordinary intellectual gifts attracted such attention that she was named La Divina Isotta, but adulation from male humanists did not bring with it acceptance into a world closed to women. In 1438, after a baseless charge of promiscuity and incest was brought against Nogarola, her brother, and sister, they moved to Venice. Three years later she returned to Verona. Resolute that she would not marry, and unwilling to enter a nunnery, she undertook long periods of contemplation and religious study in the confines of her own home. The remaining 25 years of her life were interrupted only by an intense period of intellectual correspondence (1451–53) with Ludovico Foscarini, which prompted the writing of her two books, *De pari aut impari Evae atque Adae peccato* (1451) and her treatise on St. Jerome *Oratio in laudem beati Hieronymis* (1453).

## Noot, Jan Baptista van der (Jonker Jan van der Noot) (c. 1540–c. 1595) *Dutch poet and prose writer*

Noot was born in Brecht and was sheriff of Antwerp until (1567) he was forced to take refuge in England on account of the political and religious turmoil. He later moved on to France and Germany. Noot was deeply affected by the Renaissance ideals embodied in the work of the PLÉIADE, especially RONSARD, and his *Het Bosken*, published in London in 1570 or 1571, is the first true volume of Renaissance verse in Dutch. *Het Theatre oft toon-neel* (1568), a Calvinistic prose tract, was also published in London and was translated into French the same year, into English (possibly partly by SPENSER) in 1569, and German in 1572. In 1578 Noot returned to Antwerp where he struggled to make a living by writing and eventually died. His *Olympiados* (1579) is an epic interspersed with sonnets; the full text is known only from a German translation, *Das Buch Extasis* (1576).

## North, Thomas (1535–c. 1601) *English translator*

Born into a good London family, North seems to have suffered financial difficulties throughout his life. In 1574 he accompanied his brother on a embassy to France and about 1591 he was knighted. Otherwise his fame rests entirely on his translations. The first of these to appear was of Antonio de GUEVARA's *Reloj de príncipes*, via an intervening French version, under the title *The Diall of Princes* (1557). *The Morall Philosophy of Doni* (1570) was a translation of a collection of oriental fables made by the Italian Anton Francesco DONI. *The Lives of the Noble Grecians and Romans* (1579), dedicated to Queen Elizabeth, is a translation of Amyot's 1559 French version of PLUTARCH; as such it is neither scholarly nor accurate, but it was nonetheless immensely and deservedly successful, not least because of North's clear and vigorous style. SHAKESPEARE drew heavily upon North's Plutarch for his Roman plays.

## northeast passage

A passage from western Europe to China and India through northern European and Russian waters. The merchant Robert Thorne (died 1527), writing to Henry VIII in 1527, proposed a northeast, northwest, or polar route to the Indies as being shorter than the southerly routes taken by the Spaniards and Portuguese. Sir Hugh Willoughby led the first of many unsuccessful attempts at discovery in 1553, perishing in the endeavor (*see* MUSCOVY COMPANY). Another notable but unsuccessful explorer in this direction was the Dutchman Willem BARENTS, and all attempts over the next three centuries were defeated by the harsh climate and dangerous currents. The first successful passage was achieved in 1878 when a Norwegian ship, *Vega*, sailed to Japan via the Arctic Ocean.

**See also:** NORTHWEST PASSAGE

**Further reading:** Tryggvi J. Olesen, *Early Voyages and Northern Approaches, 1000–1632* (London and New York: Oxford University Press, 1964).

**Northern Rebellion** (1569–70) An uprising in the north of England led initially by Thomas Howard, 4th Duke of Norfolk (1536–72). Howard, a cousin of ELIZABETH I, resented William Cecil's influence over her, and plotted to marry the exiled MARY, Queen of Scots as her fourth husband, to restore the Scottish crown to her, and to have her recognized as Elizabeth's successor on the English throne. After Howard was sent to the Tower of London in October 1569, disaffected northerners whose main motive was to see Roman Catholicism restored took up arms against Elizabeth, but were easily defeated by government forces. Some 800 were executed, and early in 1570 the pope issued the Bull *Regnans in Excelsis* excommunicating Elizabeth.

**northwest passage** A route from Europe to China and India along the northern coast of America. An intense search for this passage was sponsored by English, Dutch, and French merchant companies in the 16th century, as Europe yearned for rapid access to Asia's riches, but the adverse climatic conditions rendered most expeditions abortive and claimed many lives. Sebastian CABOT in 1509 sailed northwest from Newfoundland, perhaps as far as the Hudson Strait, until ice and threatened mutiny forced him to retreat. French expeditions followed (1523, 1534), leading to the exploration of Canada (see CARTIER, JACQUES), and in 1576 Sir Humfrey Gilbert refired enthusiasm for the search with his *Discourse of a Discoverie of a new passage to…Cathay*. This resulted in the voyages (1576–78) of Martin FROBISHER, John DAVIS (1585–87), Henry HUDSON (1607–10), and William BAFFIN (1615–16)—all names commemorated on the map of Canada's Arctic region—but the question of a route northwest from Hudson Bay remained unresolved for more than two centuries.

See also: NORTHEAST PASSAGE

**Further reading:** James P. Delgado, *Across the Top of the World: The Quest for the Northwest Passage* (Collingdale, Pa: DIANE, 1999); Ann Savours, *The Search for the North West Passage* (New York: St. Martin's Press, 1999).

**Nostradamus** (**Michel de Nostredame**) (1503–1566)
*French astrologer*
Born at St.-Remy, Provence, the son of a Jewish-Italian doctor, Nostradamus studied medicine at Montpellier (1522–25). He then spent four years tending sufferers from plague, acquiring a reputation as a healer. Moving to Agen, he married (c. 1534), but his family was killed by plague. In 1538 he was accused of heresy and left Agen to wander across Europe, and it was during this time that stories of his prophetic powers began to circulate. From 1550 onward he produced a yearly almanac. In 1555 the first part of his *Centuries*, a book of prophecies, was published and made a great impression, resulting in a summons to the French court (1556). However, the remainder of the work was not published until 1568, probably because of the dangers of investigation for practicing magic. For the same reason, the *Centuries* were written in a deliberately obscure style. They still exert an influence in occult circles.

**novella** The prose tale, ancestor of the short story, originated and flourished in Italy from the 13th to the 17th century. It was established as a respectable literary genre by Boccaccio's DECAMERON, though Boccaccio invented neither the term *novella* nor the form. *Novelle* drew on many sources for their plots, which were straightforward, often anecdotal. Folk tales, classical and oriental sources, the Bible, *exempla*, romances of chivalry, and *fabliaux* all provided material. The narratives were direct, sometimes conversational in style, reflecting contemporary everyday life, especially of the urban merchant class. They were published in collections, usually with a frame (*cornice*) in imitation of the *Decameron*. The outstanding collection before the mid-14th-century *Decameron* is the anonymous Tuscan *Cento novelle antiche* (or *Novellino*), anecdotal narratives presented as models for inculcating polite speech and manners. Fourteenth-century collections written after the *Decameron* include the *Trecentonovelle* (223 stories) of Franco SACCHETTI, who dropped the framing device and wrote in a lively colloquial style; *Percorone* (*Numskull*, a reference to a number of stupid characters in the tales; c. 1378) by Ser Giovanni Fiorentino, with 50 stories including one having the plot of Shakespeare's *Merchant of Venice*; and the 155 *Novelle* of Giovanni Sercambi of Lucca (1347–1424), much indebted to the oral tradition of storytelling.

Resembling secular *novelle* in some respects are the exemplary tales found in two religious works, *Vite dei santi padri* by Domenico Cavalca (1270–1342) and *Lo specchio di vera penitenza* by Jacopo Passavanti (c. 1302–57). Fifteenth-century humanist Latin examples are *Historia de duobus amantibus* (1444) by Aenea Silvio Piccolomini (later Pope PIUS II) and the bawdy *Facetiae* of Poggio BRACCIOLINI. Giovanni Gherardi da Prato (c. 1366–c. 1446) in *Paradiso degli Alberti* (c. 1426) portrays a learned gathering, which includes Coluccio SALUTATI and Luigi Marsigli, telling tales but mainly conversing during a stay at Antonio degli Alberti's villa (Paradiso) in 1389. The *Novelle* (1424) of Gentile Sermini of Siena and the Bolognese Giovanni Sabadino degli Arienti's *Le Porrettane* (The Ladies of Porretta; 1475) refer, in their frames, to life at spas, which permitted a certain license and relaxed humor. The 50 tales in the *Novellino* of Masuccio Salernitano (c. 1415–c. 1480) are notable for harsh polemical passages against friars and women; one story is a source for the *Romeo and Juliet* plot.

Contributions during the 16th century include FIRENZUOLA's uncompleted *Ragionamenti d'amore* (10 *novelle*), DONI's *La zucca* (1551), the *Novelle de' novizi* (1560) by

Pietro Fortini (1500–62), *Le cene* by Anton Francesco GRAZZINI, the 75 *novelle* of *Le piacevole notte* (1550, 1553) by Gianfrancesco Straparola (c. 1490–1557), the 214 *Novelle* (1554, 1573) by Matteo BANDELLO, source of many plots for later playwrights, DELLA CASA's *Galateo* (1558), and CINTHIO's *Hecatommithi* (1565), which contained the sources for Shakespeare's *Othello* (III, 7) and *Measure for Measure* (VIII, 5).

**Further reading:** Gloria Allaise (ed.), *Italian Novella* (London and New York: Routledge, 2002); Corradina Caporello-Szykman, *The Boccaccian Novella: Creation and Waning of a Genre* (New York: Peter Lang, 1990).

**Noye, Sebastian van** (Sebastian van Noyen, Sebastian van Oye) (c. 1493–1557) *Netherlands architect*
Noye was born in Utrecht and worked as military architect for Emperor Charles V; the star-shaped fortress at Philippeville (now in Belgium) was one of his constructions. In 1550 he also built the Brussels palace of Cardinal GRANVELLE, an important building in true Italian Renaissance style.

**numismatics** The collecting and studying of coins and medals. The science of numismatics originated with the enthusiasm of Italian noblemen for all aspects of the classical world during the early Renaissance. Such scholars as PETRARCH formed large collections of Greek and Roman coins, especially prizing specimens of particular historical interest or rarity. The popularity of coin collecting in Italy also precipitated the growth of a lucrative trade in counterfeits. Jacopo STRADA in the 1550s was one of the earliest collectors to publish his coin collection. The Medagliere Mediceo, a vast collection of Italian medals, was begun by Lorenzo de' Medici and is now housed in the Bargello, Florence.

The striking of medals, usually as commemorative items, was known in the classical world but was extensively revived during the Renaissance, when it reached its highest level of artistry. The usual formula for the design of medals reflected the practice of imperial Rome: a portrait head in profile on the obverse and on the reverse a symbol or device. Considerable ingenuity was often expended in the Renaissance upon the choice of IMPRESE for the reverses of medals. The metals commonly used were lead or bronze. PISANELLO effectively launched the art of the Renaissance medal with his bronze medal of the Byzantine emperor John VIII Palaeologus in 1438. This was the first of a series of notable portrait medals; among those who commissioned medals from him were several members of the Gonzaga family, Duke Filippo Maria Visconti of Milan (1441), Leonello d'Este (1442), Sigismondo Malatesta (1445), and Alfonso I of Naples (1449).

Pisanello's success inspired a number of contemporary imitators, among them Antonio Marescotto of Ferrara (active 1444–62), Matteo de' PASTI of Verona, and, slightly later, ADRIANO FIORENTINO. All early medals were cut entirely by hand but innovations were gradually made by leading medalists, such as the architect Donato BRAMANTE, who invented a press for leaden seals. Preeminent among medalists of the 16th century was Benvenuto CELLINI, who also made improvements in methods of engraving dies. Other important Italian medalists included Savelli SPERANDIO in Ferrara, Bologna, and Venice, Niccolò Fiorentino (Niccolò Spinelli; 1430–1514) and Cellini's pupil Pier Paolo Romano (c. 1520–84) in Florence, Caradosso (Cristoforo Caradosso Foppa; 1452–1527) in Rome, ANTICO in Mantua, and Pastorino de' Pastorini (1508–92) in Siena.

Outside Italy, there developed a notable medal-striking tradition in Germany during the first half of the 16th century, where Peter FLÖTNER, Ludwig Krug (c. 1490–1532), and others established a leading school at Nuremberg. Albrecht Dürer also produced several designs, although he probably never actually struck the medals himself. The Milanese Antonio Abondio (1538–91) made bronze medals in Vienna for the emperors Maximilian II and Rudolf II, and his son Alessandro (1575–c. 1645) followed in his footsteps. French medalists dominated the art during the 17th century, especially François BRIOT, Guillaume Dupré (c. 1576–1643), who was also in charge of France's coinage, and Jean Warin (1604–72). A younger relative of François Briot, Nicolas Briot (1580–1646) settled in England (1625), worked for the Mint, and instructed the English medalists and engravers Thomas Rawlins (c. 1620–70) and Thomas Simon (1618–65). Thomas Simon's brother Abraham (1617–92) and the Antwerp-born John Roettiers (1631–1703) maintained a belated Renaissance medallic tradition after the Restoration; among the Simon brothers' notable medals were a famous portrait of Oliver Cromwell (1656) and a gold one of General Monck (1660).

**Further reading:** John Cunnally, *Images of the Illustrious* (Princeton, N.J.: Princeton University Press, 1999); Stephen K. Scher, *Perspectives on the Renaissance Medal* (New York: Garland, 1999).

**Nunes, Pedro** (1492–1577) *Portuguese geographer and mathematician*
Born at Alcacer do Sal, Nunes was a brilliant student and quickly rose to become professor of mathematics at Lisbon. In 1529 he was appointed royal cosmographer to promote Portugal's claim to possession of the Spice Islands. He translated part of Ptolemy's works (1537) and wrote a treatise *De arte atque ratione navigandi* (1546). He recognized (1537), but did not pursue, the navigational problem solved by MERCATOR in his projection, and in *De crepusculis* (1542) explained the phenomenon of afterglow, or second twilight. His *Libro de Algebra en Arithmetica y Geometria* appeared in 1567. Between 1538 and

1544 he worked in Spain but he died at Coimbra as professor of mathematics.

**Núñez Cabeza de Vaca, Álvar** (c. 1490–c. 1557)
*Spanish explorer and soldier*
In 1527 he joined the New World expedition of Pánfilo de Narváez, but after landfall in Florida, disaster after disaster overtook the expedition. He and only three others reached Sonora, Mexico, in 1536, after an eight-year overland trek from Texas. *La Relación* (1542) tells the story of their epic journey, the first crossing of the North American continent by Europeans. In 1540 Cabeza de Vaca was sent as governor of Rio de la Plata province (now Paraguay). Landing in Brazil, he traveled overland from Santos to Asunción (1541–42) and later explored the interior of Paraguay. Usurped in his role of governor (1544), he was deported to Spain. In 1555 he published *Comentarios*, relating his South American experiences. Both his books are valuable anthropological and geographical accounts of territories previously undescribed.

**Nuremberg** (German **Nürnberg**) A city on the River Pegnitz in Bavaria, southern Germany. During the 13th century Nuremberg became an imperial free city and joined the Confederation of the Rhine. By the early 14th century its craftsmen had brought prosperity to Nuremberg, and in the 15th century further prosperity arose from its situation on the trade route linking Italy and the Netherlands. There were rich metal and mineral deposits nearby and Nuremberg produced very fine gold and silver plate. Surplus capital was used to make Nuremberg one of the first major European banking centers outside Italy.

Prosperity and close links with Italy placed the city at the forefront of the northern Renaissance. Willibald PIRCKHEIMER made it a center of humanist scholarship, and the astronomer and mathematician REGIOMONTANUS also worked there. The Nuremberg geographer Martin Behaim made the oldest surviving terrestrial globe in 1492, epitomizing the city's reputation as a producer of scientific instruments. Anton Koberger set up the city's first printing press in 1470 and produced at least 236 books there between 1473 and 1513. Other distinguished citizens included the painter and engraver Albrecht DÜRER, the woodcarver Veit STOSS, the bronze-founder Peter VISCHER, the sculptor Adam KRAFT, and the poet and dramatist Hans SACHS. Buildings that have survived, although extensively restored after World War II damage, include the Marthakirche and Frauenkirche (both 14th century), and the Lorenzkirche (13th to 15th centuries).

**Nuremberg, Little Masters of** See LITTLE MASTERS (OF NUREMBERG)

**Obrecht, Jacob** (c. 1450–1505) *Flemish composer*
In 1476 Obrecht became master of the choristers at Utrecht, then (1479–84) held the same post at the church of St. Gertrude, Bergen-op-Zoom (probably his native town), and at Cambrai cathedral (1484–85). He was appointed succentor at St. Donatien, Bruges, in 1486, and became *maître de chapelle* there in 1490, after a visit to Ferrara at the invitation of Duke Ercole I d'Este in 1487. In 1494 he was employed at the church of Notre Dame in Antwerp but in 1496 was again in Bergen-op-Zoom. After further short spells in Antwerp and Bruges he retired in 1500, made a second trip to Ferrara in 1504, and died there of the plague. As Duke Ercole d'Este's invitation to Obrecht testifies, he was greatly respected as a composer in his day, regarded as second only to Josquin DES PRÉS.

Obrecht wrote some secular music, notably chansons and arrangements of Dutch popular tunes, but is best known for his writing of sacred music, in particular for the Mass. Some 26 Masses survive, in which Obrecht uses the *cantus firmus* in varying ways. Sometimes, as in the *Missa je ne demande*, the melody on which the work is based is segmented, while in the *Missa sub tuum prae-sidium* the plainsong *cantus firmus* melody is joined progressively by three other borrowed melodies, all four combining together in the Agnus Dei.

**Ochino, Bernardino** (1487–1564) *Italian monk turned reformer*
Born in Siena, Ochino became a Franciscan and later (1534) a Capuchin. Sensationally, he avoided an Inquisition summons to Rome in 1542 by fleeing to Geneva, where he promoted evangelical Protestantism. After moving to England (1547), he preached to Italian exiles and wrote a virulent attack on papal authority. However he also rejected PREDESTINATION in *Laberinti* (*Labyrinth*; Basle, 1561). On the accession of the Catholic Mary I he became a pastor in Zürich, but in 1563 controversy over his supposed countenance of polygamy made him flee Switzerland. He died in exile in Slavkov (Moravia).

**Ockeghem, Johannes** (c. 1410–1497) *Franco-Flemish composer*
The first mention of Ockeghem is as a singer at Notre Dame, Antwerp, in 1443. It is thought that he studied with BINCHOIS and had connections with the ducal chapel of Burgundy. He entered the employ of Charles, Duke of Bourbon, around 1445, and was active in the court of King Charles VII of France in 1453, being favored with the office of treasurer of the church of St. Martin-de-Tours. On Charles VII's death (1461) Ockeghem continued in the service of Louis XI, and in 1463 became a canon at Notre Dame, Paris. In 1470 he traveled to Spain as part of a diplomatic retinue and sometime probably visited Italy. He died in Paris, still in the service of the French court.

Even in his own day, Ockeghem was renowned as a composer and as a singer. He wrote some secular works (around 22 chansons in a traditional style survive), but it is his sacred works, particularly his Masses, which are important. Although his output is comparatively low—10 complete Masses, some settings of the Ordinary, and a few motets—he is regarded as one of the greatest composers of the second half of the 15th century. The Masses are of two kinds; those based on pre-existing material, like the *Missa L'homme armé*, and those which are freely composed. In both kinds smooth counterpoint is used to great effect, with a skillful use of varied textures.

**Oecolampadius, John** (Johann Hussgen) (1482–1531)
*German theologian and reformer*
Oecolampadius was born at Weinsberg, at that time in the Palatinate. After visiting Bologna, he studied theology at Heidelberg and in 1515 was appointed preacher at Basle cathedral, where his strong reforming tendencies became plain. In 1520 he published a Greek grammar and was invited to preach in Augsburg, but a period of doubt then caused him to withdraw for a time to a monastery. In 1522, his reforming faith restored, he moved to Ebernburg, and then returned to Basle where he spent the rest of his life as a leader among the reformers. In 1528 he married, and the same year he and Ulrich ZWINGLI caused the reformed faith to be adopted at Berne and the Mass to be discontinued at Basle. In 1529 he attended the Colloquy of MARBURG.

**Okeghem, Jean de** See OCKEGHEM, JOHANNES

**Oldenbarneveldt, Johan van** (1547–1619) *Dutch statesman*
Oldenbarneveldt was born at Amersfoort. He studied law at Louvain, Bourges, and Heidelberg, where he became a Protestant, and in 1568 he supported the revolt against Spain. In 1579 he joined WILLIAM THE SILENT, Prince of Orange, in negotiating the Union of Utrecht, which united the northern provinces of the Netherlands. He was attorney-general of the union and secretary to the provincial estates of Holland. After the assassination of William the Silent in 1584, he took charge of domestic and foreign affairs, while Prince MAURICE OF NASSAU commanded the armed forces. He negotiated an alliance with France and England in 1596 and a controversial 12-year truce with Spain in 1609. He worked to maintain the dominance of the province of Holland within the union and in religious affairs supported the Arminians (*see* ARMINIANISM) against the Calvinists; this brought him into conflict with Maurice. Accused of subverting church and state, he was beheaded at The Hague.

Further reading: Jan den Tex, *Oldenbarnevelt*, transl. R. B. Powell, 2 vols (Cambridge, U.K.: Cambridge University Press, 1973).

**Oliver, Isaac** (c. 1560–1617) *English painter*
Born in Rouen, the son of French Huguenots, Oliver was brought to England in 1568 and studied painting under Nicholas HILLIARD. Although he also painted life-size portraits and religious and classical scenes, Oliver is remembered chiefly as a painter of miniature portraits. He traveled in the Netherlands (1588) and to Venice (1596) and by 1595 he had become Hilliard's chief rival. Oliver's patrons included Anne of Denmark (1604) and later Henry Frederick, Prince of Wales, of whom he painted a striking portrait miniature (c. 1610). The large-scale equestrian portrait of the prince in the Venetian manner, formerly attributed to Oliver, is now assigned to Robert Peake. In his later years Oliver adopted a more naturalistic style and painted historical and biblical scenes in the mannerist tradition. His son Peter (1594–1647) also executed paintings in his father's later style.

**Olivetan** (Pierre Robert) (c. 1506–1538) *French Protestant reformer and translator*
Born at Noyon, Picardy, a cousin of John CALVIN, Olivetan was forced to abandon his studies at Orleans and flee to Strasbourg after his conversion to Protestantism. He became actively involved in the Reformation, preaching to the Waldenses in Piedmont, and undertook the translation of the Bible into French; this was published at Serrières, near Neuchâtel, in 1535. Extensively revised by Calvin and others during the 16th century, Olivetan's Bible ranked with that of LEFÈVRE D'ÉTAPLES as a major source for subsequent French translations of the Scriptures.

**Ollanda, Francisco d'** See FRANCISCO DA HOLLANDA

**O'Malley, Grace** (Gráinne Ni Mháille) (c. 1530–c. 1603) *Irish sea queen and nationalist leader*
A scion of the hereditary chieftains of the Barony of Murrisk, she held sway with her first husband, Donal O'Flaherty, at Bunowen Castle, County Galway. After his death in clan fighting she took control of his ships and preyed on British vessels along the Scottish coast. Around 1566 she married the clan chief Richard Burke of Mayo, and became an important local powerbroker during the years of revolt against English control. Widowed once again (1586), she was captured at her Clew Bay castle by British forces intent on suppressing her piracy in the Aran Islands. She was taken to Dublin to be hanged, but freed on her son-in-law's intercession. When the English fleet attacked Clew Bay (c. 1592) she fled to Ulster. In 1593 she sailed to England and petitioned Elizabeth I for restoration of her husband's estates; these were handed over, not to her, but to her son Theobald. At age 70 she was still leading attacks on ships of other Irish clans that strayed into O'Malley waters.

**optics** Considerable advances were made in antiquity in the study of geometrical optics. Ancient scientists distinguished between "catoptrics", the study of reflection, and "dioptrics", the corresponding study of refraction. While they had managed to formulate the basic laws of reflection they were less successful in their work on refraction. Ptolemy had established no more than that the angle of incidence was always greater than the angle of refraction, whatever the media. It was not until the early 17th century that Willebrord SNELL established the true relationship. The ratio of the sines of the angles of incidence and refraction, he demonstrated, were constant for any media.

Renaissance scientists also made significant advances in the development of optical instruments. The period of the late 16th and early 17th centuries is especially significant as the time when the MICROSCOPE and the TELESCOPE were invented. Equally of concern to scientists was the nature of light and its mode of propagation. Two main theories had emerged in antiquity. Some considered that light was emitted from the eye, the object, or both, and operated by traveling between the eye and the visible object. Others, following Aristotle, denied that anything traveled between eye and object, and argued instead that light was a state of the medium acquired instantaneously from the presence in it of a luminous object. Aristotle's view found wide acceptance among Renaissance scholars. If light did travel, it was asked, why, unlike sound, was no interval noted between the occurrence of an event and its perception? Against this view, supported by KEPLER and René Descartes, scholars such as Francesco Maurolico (1494–1575), in his posthumously published *Photismi* (1611), argued that light emanated from the observed body and traveled directly and rectilinearly to the eye of the observer. It was not clear, however, where the image of the object was formed. Traditionally it had been supposed that the lens was the recipient of vision and that the lens was placed in the center of the eye. The lens was first sited correctly by the anatomist Matteo Colombo (c. 1516–59), while the retina was first proposed as the site of image formation by Felix PLATTER in 1583. LEONARDO DA VINCI had earlier recorded how the image, as it formed on the retina, became inverted, a phenomenon that was duly accounted for by Kepler in his *Ad Vitellionem* (1604).

There remains the question of color and such related phenomena as the rainbow and the prism. No one before Isaac Newton (1672) suspected that white light was a compound mixture of the primary colors. Aristotle had thought, and in this he had been followed by all medieval and Renaissance scholars, that white light was a simple quality; color was produced by a weakening or modification of light as it was reflected, refracted, or corrupted by the medium. The rainbow, consequently, had been held to be caused by reflection from the drops of water sited in a conveniently placed cloud. Against this Maurolico argued that the rainbow resulted from internal reflections within the raindrop, while Kepler considered it to be due to both internal reflections and refractions. Further progress in this and other optical problems awaited a clearer understanding of the nature of light.

**Further reading:** David Park, *The Fire Within the Eye* (Princeton, N.J.: Princeton Univesity Press, 1999); Arthur Zajonc, *Catching the Light: The Entwined History of Light and Mind* (Oxford, U.K.: Oxford University Press, 1995).

**Oratorians** See PHILIP NERI, ST

**Orcagna** (**Andrea di Cione**) (c. 1320–c. 1368) *Italian painter, sculptor, and architect*
The son of a goldsmith, Orcagna (whose name was Florentine argot for "archangel") was admitted to the guild of painters in his native Florence in about 1343 and to the guild of stonemasons nine years later. Inclined to paint in a fashion that predated GIOTTO, Orcagna painted an altarpiece in the Strozzi chapel of Sta. Maria Novella, Florence (1354–57), which is now the only painting definitely attributed to him. Probably also by him was the trilogy of frescoes for the nave of Sta. Croce, Florence (c. 1350), and the *St. Matthew* altarpiece (1367; Uffizi, Florence), which was finished by his brother Jacopo di Cione (died 1398) after Orcagna fell ill. His best-known sculptural work was the ambitious tabernacle in Orsanmichele (1359). As an architect he directed the construction of the cathedral in Orvieto (1359–62) and also advised on the building of the cathedral in Florence.

**Further reading:** Gert Kreytenberg and David Finn, *Orcagna's Tabernacle in Orsanmichele, Florence* (New York: Harry N. Abrams, 1994).

**Ordóñez, Bartolomé** (c. 1490–1520) *Spanish sculptor*
Born into a wealthy family in Burgos, Ordóñez studied in Italy, probably under Andrea SANSOVINO in Florence, and later imported many features of the High Renaissance into his native Spain. While still in Italy, he produced a marble relief, the *Epiphany* (c. 1516–18), for the Caracciolo chapel in Naples, on which he worked with Diego de SILOE, and the marble tomb of Andrea Bonifacio (c. 1518; SS. Severino e Sosia, Naples). He then moved to Barcelona, where he executed important wood and marble carvings for the cathedral. In 1519 he was commissioned by Charles V to produce the tomb for Philip the Handsome and Joanna the Mad in the royal chapel in Granada cathedral; when Ordóñez died the following year at Carrara, where he was working on the monument, the commission was almost completed. After his death his style was much imitated, especially in Naples and Flanders.

**Oresme, Nicolas** (c. 1320–1382) *French mathematician and physicist*
Oresme, who was born at Caen, flourished under the patronage of Charles V of France, and after serving as tutor to the future Charles VI he was appointed bishop of Lisieux in 1377. In his most original work, *De configurationibus qualitatum* (c. 1350), Oresme tried to show in the inadequate mathematics of his day how changing "qualities," such as speed, could be handled geometrically. He also, in his *Livre du ciel et monde* (c. 1377), a commentary on Aristotle's *De caelo*, considered the question of the earth's rotation. Despite appearing to have disposed of the traditional objections to such a possibility, he affirmed, nonetheless, his commitment to the PTOLEMAIC SYSTEM. In a further work, the *Algorismus proportionum*, he intro-

duced into mathematics for the first time the notion of fractional exponents.

**Orichovius** See ORZECHOWSKI, STANISŁAW

*Orlando furioso* The epic written by Ludovico ARIOSTO continuing the story begun in the *Orlando innamorato* of BOIARDO. The poem is structurally very elaborate, often seeming to be a tangled web of adventures sustained only by the tremendous energy of Ariosto's narrative, but three main strands of story are clearly discernible: the madness of the hero Orlando, chief of Charlemagne's paladins, on account of his love for the beautiful princess Angelica; the wars between Christians and Saracens; and the love story of Ruggiero and Bradamante, destined to marry and found the house of Este (*see* ESTE FAMILY), in whose service Ariosto passed his life and in whose celebration the poem is ostensibly written.

*Orlando furioso* appeared in three editions during Ariosto's lifetime (1516, 1521, 1532), and in its final form comprised 46 cantos written in *ottava rima*. This third edition, in particular, reveals the influence of Pietro BEMBO in matters of language and style. The poem successfully welds together medieval chivalric and folk traditions with humanistic neoclassicism to form a complex whole of which the dominant note is one of brilliant gaiety. (This gaiety is excellently captured in the English translation (1591) by Sir John HARINGTON.) It was immediately accepted as a classic, and during the late 16th-century controversy on EPIC it became the representative of one form of the genre against the more unified concept exemplifed in Tasso's GERUSALEMME LIBERATA.

*Orlando furioso* soon achieved a following beyond Italy, with a Spanish version in 1549 and a French prose version in 1555. Sir John Harington's translation "in English heroical verse" has been edited by Robert McNulty and published with plates from the 1591 edition (Oxford, U.K., 1972). Modern prose translations have been made by A. H. Gilbert (New York, 3 vols, 1954) and by Guido Waldman; the latter, which first appeared in 1974, was reissued in the World's Classics series (Oxford, U.K., 1983). A verse translation by B. Reynolds was published by Penguin (Harmondsworth, U.K., 1975).

**Further reading:** Peter V. Marinelli, *Ariosto and Boiardo: The Origins of* Orlando Furioso (Columbia, Mo.: University of Missouri Press, 1987).

*Orlando innamorato* See BOIARDO, MATTEO MARIA

**Orley, Bernard van** (c. 1492–1542) *Netherlands painter and designer of tapestries and stained glass*
Trained by his father Valentin van Orley, Bernard was principally active in his native city of Brussels. In 1515 he was commissioned to paint portraits of the children of Philip the Handsome for presentation to the king of Denmark.

Three years later he was formally appointed a court painter to the regent, MARGARET OF AUSTRIA. In 1530 he accepted a similar position from her successor, MARY OF HUNGARY. Van Orley was influenced by the Italianate repertory of Jan Gossaert and by Dürer, whom he met in 1520/21. Although he does not appear to have visited Italy, he appropriated motifs from a range of Italian prints and was personally familiar with the Raphael cartoons for the Sistine Chapel, which were woven into tapestries in Brussels between 1514 and 1519. There is a tension in van Orley's work, between the northern naturalistic tradition in which he was principally trained and the Italianate schooling which he received as a young painter. For example, in his Job altarpiece (1521; Brussels), the careful observation of individual details actually makes the overall composition more difficult to read as a single entity. By contrast, the manificent landscape vistas in van Orley's tapestry cycle of the *Hunts of Maximilian* (c. 1550; Paris) belong beside the paintings of Pieter BRUEGHEL as major monuments of the Netherlandish landscape tradition. See Plate XVI

**Orpheus** In classical legend, a Thracian poet who was given a lyre by APOLLO and taught by the MUSES to play it so exquisitely that wild animals, and even inanimate trees and rocks, were drawn to its sound. When his wife Eurydice died of a snake bite, Orpheus journeyed to Hades, hoping to win her back by his music; this he succeeded in doing, but lost her forever when he broke the conditions imposed upon him and looked back at her before they had reached the upper world. Grief then led him to fall foul of the maenads, who tore him to pieces in their frenzied worship of BACCHUS.

There are several elements in this story attractive to graphic artists, but the "Orpheus and the animals" theme gained particular favor. Allegorically interpreted, it demonstrated the power of art to subdue nature. It also afforded scope for depicting an exotic assemblage of creatures, a kind of pagan Garden of Eden in which no creature injures or preys upon another. The human figures predominate in Giovanni BELLINI's treatment of the theme (Widener Collection, National Gallery of Art, Washington), but are totally overwhelmed by the fauna and the landscape in the numerous versions by the mannerist Roelant SAVERY.

As the supposed author of the Orphic hymns and source of the mystic cult of Orphism in ancient Greece, Orpheus was a subject of intense interest to the Florentine Neoplatonists. PICO DELLA MIRANDOLA in *De hominis dignitate* states his belief that the Orphic hymns contain profound religious revelations under the guise of poetic fables and that the concealed truth is apparent only to a small band of initiates. Both Pico and Lorenzo de' MEDICI (prompted by Plato's exegesis in the *Symposium*) read the

Eurydice episode as a fable of the proximity of love and death in the experience of religious initiates.

The Orpheus legend, of course, also lent itself to musical and dramatic treatment. POLITIAN's pastoral drama *Orfeo*, performed in Mantua in 1480, contained songs which set the subject on the road towards opera. The earliest surviving works that count as true opera were produced in Florence in 1600 and 1602; these are two settings of Ottavio Rinuccini's text *L'Euridice*, the first by Jacopo Peri (1561–1633) with additions by CACCINI and the second by Caccini alone. This pastoral treatment of the story has a happy ending (*lieto fine*), as does the *L'Orfeo* of MONTEVERDI, produced in Mantua in 1607.

**Further reading:** Elisabeth Henry, *Orpheus With His Lute: Poetry and the Renewal of Life* (Carbondale, Ill.: Southern Illinois University Press, 1992).

**Orsi (da Novellara), Lelio** (1511–1587) *Italian painter*
Born at Novellara, Orsi became a prominent figure of the Parmesan school. He was influenced by CORREGGIO and MICHELANGELO as well as by German woodcuts. *The Walk to Emmaus* (National Gallery, London) reveals a taste for dramatic lighting, while other works such as *The Rest on the Flight into Egypt* (York) are more elegant and subtly colored, in the style of PARMIGIANINO. The majority of his frescoes are lost.

**Ortelius, Abraham** (Abraham Oertel) (1527–1598)
*Dutch cartographer*
Born at Antwerp, Ortelius trained as an engraver before establishing himself as a dealer in maps and more general antiquities. He traveled widely to collect and sell maps, many of which he illustrated or colored before sale. He made many contacts (*see* HOEFNAGEL, GEORG), but it was his friendship with MERCATOR that prompted his active involvement in cartography. Throughout the 1560s Ortelius built his reputation as a map maker. His most famous creation was a heart-shaped map of the world (1564), followed by maps of Egypt and Asia.

Ortelius's masterpiece was a collection of maps by 87 different cartographers including himself. Entitled *Theatrum orbis terrarum* (1570), it consisted of special engravings of the best maps in the world and covered all areas of the globe. It ran to seven editions by the end of the century, and translated and abridged versions also appeared. In 1575, despite suspicions that he might have Protestant inclinations, Ortelius was appointed geographer to PHILIP II of Spain.

**Further reading:** Paul Binding, *Imagined Corners: Exploring the World's First Atlas* (London: Hodder Headline, 2003).

**orthography** Interest in spelling reform and standardization was an aspect of interest in the VERNACULAR which manifested itself in most European countries during the Renaissance. The wide dissemination of books made possible by PRINTING increasingly rendered unacceptable the variations in spelling that reflected various dialectal pronunciations; when printers could adopt a standard and adhere to it, the prospects for reliable versions of texts were brighter than in the situation when individual scribes could "myswrite" or "mysmetre for defaute of tonge"—as CHAUCER feared would befall his *Troilus and Criseyde* (V 1795–96). However, two centuries later Gabriel HARVEY was still maintaining, in a letter to Edmund SPENSER published in 1580, that the one essential prerequisite for a proper grammar and prosody of English was "universally to agree upon *one and the same Ortographie*"; for lack of a better, he recommended the system proposed by Sir Thomas SMITH, which had originated in the latter's interest in the controversy over the pronunciation of Greek (*see* GREEK STUDIES).

Thoughtful users of the vernaculars recognized that the Roman alphabet was inadequate to render all the sounds current in speech, so proposals for rationalization of spelling abounded. An early entrant in the field was the Spanish humanist NEBRIJA. Giangiorgio TRISSINO evolved a system for Italian, which he promoted vigorously in the 1520s; among other innovations the Greek letters ε and ω were drafted in to render the different sounds expressed in written Italian by the simple vowels e and o. TOLOMEI, in his *Il Polito* (1525), was one of those who opposed Trissino's scheme. In France Louis Meygret (1545), Jean-Antoine de BAÏF, and RAMUS tried and failed to achieve a rational phonetic spelling in place of a learned, etymologically based standard. The use of grave and acute accents (è and é) to denote different qualities of e became standard French printing practice in this period. The most thorough-going phonetician in England was John Hart, whose *Orthographie* (1569) sets out an admirable phonetic alphabet which he claims would be equally applicable to Italian, Spanish, German, and French.

**Orti Oricellari** (Rucellai Gardens) The gardens in Florence that became the meeting place for the revived Florentine Academy, successor to FICINO's Accademia Platonica. The grounds were laid out by Bernardo Rucellai (1448–1514), who assembled there statuary looted from the Medici after their expulsion in 1494. MACHIAVELLI attended the discussions in the Orti Oricellari in the period after 1513 and read his *Discorsi* (1513–21) to the members, some of whom he made participants in his dialogues *Dell'arte della guerra* (1521).

**Orzechowski, Stanisław** (Orichovius) (1513–1566)
*Polish polemicist and theologian*
Born at Przemyśl, Orzechowksi was a Roman Catholic priest and a zealous participant in all manner of controversies. Among his Latin works are tracts urging a crusade against the Turks (1543) and opposing celibacy (1551).

He also wrote in Polish on the benefits of theocracy (1563, 1564). His history of Poland from the reign of Sigismund I was published posthumously (1611). Orzechoswki's vigorous prose style was important in the development of vernacular prose writing.

## Osiander, Andreas (1498–1552) *German Protestant theologian*

After studying in Ingolstadt and being ordained (1520), Osiander returned to Nuremberg, near which he had been born, and became a leading figure in the local reforming movement. He represented the city at both the Colloquy of MARBURG (1529) and the Diet of AUGSBURG (1530), and was one of the original signatories of the Schmalkaldic Articles (1537). Forced to leave Nuremberg by the imposition of the AUGSBURG INTERIM (1548), Osiander settled in Königsberg, where he became professor at the newly founded university. His controversial views on justification (*De iustificatione*, 1550) brought him into conflict with Philipp MELANCHTHON and were eventually repudiated by the Lutherans in the Formula of CONCORD (1577). His other writings include a revised edition of the Latin Vulgate and a harmony of the gospels, the first of its kind. His niece Margaret married Thomas CRANMER.

*ottava rima* An Italian stanza form usually comprising eight lines of eleven syllables each, rhyming ababab cc. Its virtues as a vehicle for narrative were most amply demonstrated by Ariosto's ORLANDO FURIOSO. It was adopted into English in the 16th century using the English five-stress (decasyllabic) line, often with a feminine rhyme. One of the earliest practitioners was Michael DRAYTON, who, on rewriting his *Mortimeriados* (1596) as *The Barrons Warres* (1603), changed the seven-line stanza of the former to *ottava rima* and observed "this sort of stanza hath in it majesty, perfection, and solidity."

## Ottoman Turks

A Turkic people who migrated from central Asia to Asia Minor, where they adopted Islam. They took their name from their first sultan, Osman (ruled c. 1288–1326), who founded a state in Anatolia, bordering on Christian territory. At this time they adopted the concept of *jihad* (holy war to extend Islam). As the Renaissance developed in Italy the Ottomans established their first settlement in Europe (1354) and took Adrianople in Thrace (1361). From Thrace they advanced to conquer the Balkans, overrunning Bulgaria (1382), Serbia (1459), most of Greece (1461), and Bosnia (1463). Taking advantage of the Byzantine empire's weakness, they occupied the eastern Mediterranean and conquered CONSTANTINO-PLE itself (1453), which became the Ottoman capital. By the early 16th century they had conquered Persia, Syria, and Egypt, and Suleiman (I) the Magnificent (sultan 1520–66) took the *jihad* into the heart of Europe. He captured Belgrade (1521) and, after crushing the Christian army at Mohács (1526), occupied most of Hungary. By 1529 the Ottoman forces had reached the gates of Vienna, but they returned to Constantinople after a short siege. Although the main expansionist drive of the Ottomans to the northwest was now over, Renaissance Europe remained aware of them as a constant threat on its eastern and southern flanks, to be contained by crusading ventures such as the battle of LEPANTO (1571). Another highly significant victory for Christendom was the heroic repulse of the Ottoman fleet by the KNIGHTS HOSPITALER on Malta after a dramatic siege in 1565, thus denying the Turks an invaluable foothold in the western Mediterranean, though they were still able to make a nuisance of themselves at sea through the activities of Barbary pirates operating out of ports on the North African coast. In 1683 Ottoman troops again reached the gates of Vienna, but were repulsed by the Christian forces.

**Further reading:** Jerry Brotton, *The Renaissance Bazaar: From the Silk Road to Michelangelo* (Oxford, U.K.: Oxford University Press, 2002); Lisa Jardine and Jerry Brotton, *Global Interests: Renaissance Art Between East and West* (Ithaca, N.Y.: Cornell University Press, 2000).

## Overbury, Sir Thomas (1581–1613) *English courtier and prose writer*

Overbury was born at Compton Scorpion, Warwickshire, and educated at Oxford before becoming a member of the Middle Temple (1597). Robert Carr, Earl of Somerset, was his friend and patron, but when Overbury opposed the earl's marriage with the divorced countess of Essex, he was imprisoned in the Tower of London on a trumped-up charge and slowly poisoned by the countess's agents. The murder came to light and at the ensuing trial, for which the prosecution was conducted by Francis BACON, the earl and countess were found guilty and condemned to house arrest; four of their accomplices were hanged. Apart from his lead role in "the Overbury Affair," Overbury is remembered as a writer of "characters"; these are a subform of the essay evolved by the third-century BCE Greek Theophrastus and comprise short and vivid descriptions of various human types and their characteristic behavior.

**Further reading:** Alastair Bellamy, *The Politics of Court Scandal in Early Modern England: News Culture and the Overbury Affair 1603–60* (Cambridge, U.K.: Cambridge University Press, 2003); Anne Somerset, *Unnatural Murder at the Court of James I* (London: Weidenfeld & Nicholson, 1997).

## Oviedo y Valdés, Gonzalo Fernández de (1478–1557) *Spanish soldier, administrator, and historian*

Born in Madrid and brought up as a page in the royal household, Oviedo was present at the siege of Granada in 1492. He went to Panama in 1514 as overseer of the gold mines there, later becoming governor of Cartagena (1526) and holding a succession of official posts before returning to Spain in 1545. As official historian of the enterprise of the Indies, he wrote his vast *Historia general y natural de las Indias Islas y Tierra-Firme del Mar Oceano*, published over many years, a massive apologia for Spain's colonial enterprise.

## Owen, John (c. 1560–1622) *Welsh schoolmaster and epigrammatist*

Born in Caernarfonshire, Owen was educated at Oxford and became headmaster of Henry VIII's School, Warwick (c. 1594). His neo-Latin epigrams, the first book of which was published under the Latinized form of his name "Audoenus," came out in 11 books from 1606 onward. His polished and witty lines, imitative of the Roman poet Martial, were widely applauded, and were translated into English by several hands during the 17th century (1619, 1628, 1653, 1659, 1677). A collected edition was published in Amsterdam in 1624, and there were also 17th-century translations into German (1653) and Spanish (1674–82).

## Oye, Sebastian van See NOYE, SEBASTIAN VAN

# P

**Pacheco, Francisco** (1564–1654) *Spanish painter and art theorist*

Pacheco was born at Sanlúcar de Barrameda, but when still young he moved to Seville, where he became a canon at the cathedral and opened an art academy which attracted numerous pupils. An enthusiast for Italian art, Pacheco collected Italian Renaissance drawings, but his own work chiefly comprised academically correct, if somewhat lifeless, religious paintings. Many of these are still to be seen in or around Seville. He was also a sought-after portraitist. A visit to Madrid and Toledo (1611) brought him into contact with EL GRECO, whose interest in *chiaroscuro* he then came to share. Pacheco's *Arte de la pintura* (c. 1640) is a significant text in the development of Spanish art. Velázquez was his son-in-law and most famous pupil.

**Pacher, Michael** (active 1462–1498) *Austrian sculptor and painter*

Pacher is first recorded in 1467, at Bruneck in the Tyrol; it seems likely that he was born in this region, though he traveled extensively. His key surviving works are the incomplete altar at Gries, near Bolzano (1471–88), the high altar at St. Wolfgang, near Salzburg (1471–88), and the painted *Fathers of the Church* altarpiece in Munich (c. 1479–82). At the time of his death, he was putting the finishing touches to his colossal high altar at Salzburg parish church, which was almost entirely destroyed during the 18th century.

Early influences upon Pacher were Hans Multscher (active in the Tyrol during the 1450s) and Nicolaus GERHAERT VAN LEYDEN (active 1462–73), whose sculptural style was disseminated by the engravings of the MASTER E. S. Pacher's Gries and St. Wolfgang altars suggest that he visited the Netherlands between 1469 and 1471, where he encountered the paintings of Hugo van der GOES and Jan van EYCK. His fragmentary and undated altarpieces of St. Thomas (Graz) and St. Lawrence (Vienna and Munich) indicate that he visited Padua, probably before 1465, where he was profoundly influenced by the frescoes of MANTEGNA and took note of the altar by DONATELLO in the Santo. Pacher ignored the classical formal vocabulary of Italian art, but became a master of one-point perspective and foreshortening. In his large composite altars, with polychromed carved central panels and pinnacles and painted shutters, his mastery of pictorial space helped to bridge the gap between sculptural and pictorial elements. Out of his various sources Pacher forged a lyrical and expressive style that breathed new life into the traditional German carved wooden altar. He had a large circle of followers.

**Pacification of Ghent** See GHENT

**Pacioli, Luca** (c. 1445–1517) *Italian mathematician*

Little is known about Pacioli's life other than that he was born at Burgo in Tuscany, became a Franciscan friar some time after 1471, taught mathematics in several towns of northern Italy, and was a friend of LEONARDO DA VINCI. He wrote numerous mathematical works, the best known of which, *Somma di aritmetica, geometria, proporzioni e proporzionalità* (Venice, 1494), is one of the earliest printed mathematical texts. Though entirely derivative, it manages to convey in the vernacular, and in an improved notation, the new mathematics first developed by Leonardo of Pisa in his *Liber abaci* (1202). Pacioli was well aware of the needs of commerce and consequently devoted considerable space to the application of the new arithmetic to book-keeping and trade; the *Somma* is claimed to be the first text to cover double-entry book-keeping. He was also responsible for a Latin translation of Euclid (1509) and a more original geometrical text, *De divina proportione* (1509), including designs after Leonardo da Vinci; the latter is also significant in the history of type design and the evolution of the roman letter.

## Paciotto, Francesco (Francisco Pachote) (1521–1591) *Italian architect*

A native of Urbino, Paciotto was a pupil of Girolamo GENGA. Around 1540 he was in Rome but in 1553 he was appointed tutor to Alessandro FARNESE, for whose mother, MARGARET OF PARMA, he designed the never-completed Cittadella at Piacenza (1558). The same year he accompanied Philip II to the Netherlands where he was commissioned to design a palace for the Hapsburg governors of the Netherlands in Brussels. This was never built. Paciotto also worked on harbor defenses at Nice for the duke of Savoy (1559) and in 1561 went to Spain where he contributed to the plans for the ESCORIAL. He was much in demand as a military architect, building a fortress at Antwerp (1564) and working for several Italian princes from his base at Urbino, where he spent his latter years.

## Padua (Italian Padova)

A city on the River Bacchiglione in Veneto, northern Italy. Padua was known to the Romans as Patavium and survived to become an important and prosperous commune in the later Middle Ages. During the Renaissance it was ruled by *signori* from the Carrara family (1318–1405) before being annexed by Venice (1405–1797). Venice allowed Padua's municipal government considerable power and dignity, even after Padua's unsuccessful rebellion in 1509.

During the Renaissance Padua was an important center of learning and the arts, and its university (founded 1222) was famous for its medical, legal, and philosophical faculties. Celebrated figures connected with the university include the teachers and anatomical researchers VESALIUS and FALLOPPIO, William HARVEY, who graduated as a doctor there (1602), and GALILEO, who held the post of professor of mathematics (1592–1610). The philosophers followed Averroes and the Aristotelian tradition and Elia del Medigo was the leading student of Hebrew philosophy. The BOTANIC GARDEN, founded in 1545, is the second oldest in Europe. Great artists who worked in Padua include GIOTTO and DONATELLO.

Surviving buildings from the Renaissance period include the ARENA CHAPEL or Capella degli Scrovegni (1303–05) with its Giotto frescoes, Il Santo or the basilica (1232–1307) of the town's patron saint, St. Anthony, which has in front of it Donatello's famous equestrian statue of GATTAMELATA (1453), the rebuilt cathedral (1552), the Palazzo della Ragione (rebuilt 1306), and the Palazzo del Capitano (1532).

## Páez, Pedro (Pero Paez) (1564–1622) *Spanish Jesuit missionary*

Páez joined the Jesuits in 1582 and went as a missionary to Goa in 1588. He joined a mission to Ethiopia (1589), but the priests were shipwrecked in southern Arabia, captured by pirates, imprisoned, and forced to serve as galley slaves until eventually ransomed in 1596. Páez resumed mission work in India, but in 1601 set out again for Ethiopia, which he finally reached, disguised as an Armenian merchant, in 1603. He was successful in his work at the Ethiopian royal court, eventually converting King Susenyos to Catholicism. From 1613 he worked on his *Historia Aethiopiae*, based on oral testimonies, Ethiopian historical manuscripts, and his own observations, which dispelled many myths about the country and laid the basis for an accurate map, including the origin of the Blue Nile in Lake Tana. He died of fever in Gorgora.

## Paganino See MAZZONI, GUIDO

**painting** If the key term "Renaissance" is used in its widest, general sense as no more than a historical label for the two centuries of European history between about 1400 and 1600, then all paintings produced in this area and period may be described as "Renaissance" artefacts. However, in the context of the visual arts, this key term has a very specific meaning which, if analysed, permits the categorization of two hundred years of European painting into a series of sub-groups, more or less closely identified with "Renaissance" values.

At the heart of the matter lies the rebirth of interest in classical antiquity which started in Italy during the early 15th century and subsequently spread to most other regions of western Europe. Originally a purely literary movement, the roots of which may be traced back to the middle of the 14th century, its influence on the visual arts was somewhat belated. Given that Roman sculptural remains constituted its principal visual source, it is not surprising that sculptors, such as DONATELLO, were motivated by the rebirth earlier than painters, such as MASACCIO. What made *the* Renaissance different from earlier, analogous movements, such as the so-called "Carolingian Renaissance," is that it entailed an appreciation of both classical form *and* content, rather than of the one or the other in isolation. Together with this imitation of antique style and subject matter came a growing interest in naturalistic values. In part the latter was fostered by the former. For example, there can be no doubt that Masaccio's study of ancient marbles assisted his portrayal of human character and emotion. However, other tools utilized by the Renaissance artist in pursuit of naturalistic visual effects, such as one-point PERSPECTIVE, were original inventions unknown to the ancients. It must be stressed that, while the revival of classical form and content was central to the Renaissance, naturalism was secondary. It is because GIOTTO's profoundly innovatory and naturalistic style neither derives from nor reflects the values of classical antiquity that it cannot meaningfully be labeled as a manifestation of Renaissance art.

Florence was the principal home of literary humanism and had also been, for more than a century, the home of the most innovatory school of painting in Italy before it became the birthplace of Renaissance painting. These first stirrings were promoted by a wealthy and erudite bourgeois ruling class which commissioned works of art both individually and corporately. Without such patrons as Felice Brancacci, for whom Masaccio executed the revolutionary fresco cycle in Sta. Maria del Carmine, there would have been no material basis for the Florentine awakening which set the tone of most subsequent developments in Renaissance painting. Although Masaccio's *Trinity* fresco (c. 1427) in Sta. Maria Novella demonstrates a familiarity with classical forms of drapery and architecture and reveals the power of one-point perspective, the manifesto of Renaissance painting, Leon Battista ALBERTI's treatise *Della pittura* (1435), was written by a humanist observer from the Florentine ruling class, rather than a professional artist. The Florentine painters Fra ANGELICO, DOMENICO VENEZIANO, Paolo UCCELLO, and ANDREA DEL CASTAGNO elaborated further on the three essential tools of the QUATTROCENTO avant-garde: the study of antique remains, use of one-point perspective, and direct observation of the human body and, especially, the nude.

Gradually these originally Florentine preoccupations spread more widely in Italy. At Borgo San Sepolcro in the Marches of central Italy, PIERO DELLA FRANCESCA had an appreciation of weight and volume and an understanding of light effects which far surpassed that of the painters of Florence, where he was trained. His contemporary, the Paduan Andrea MANTEGNA, who worked principally as a court artist of the Gonzaga princes of Mantua, developed a hard-edged style informed by a meticulous study of antique remains and was the most virtuoso exponent of one-point perspective of his generation. In Venice, Giovanni BELLINI evolved a more contemplative manner, combining classicizing forms and one-point perspective with delicate light effects, the latter derived partly from Netherlandish models. In Florence, during the second half of the 15th century, Antonio POLLAIUOLO refined the depiction of the nude in motion and devised tightly structured symmetrical compositions. The last principal element of Renaissance style to fall into place, the reunification of classical form and classical subject matter, did so only towards the end of the century, in such pictures as BOTTICELLI's *Birth of Venus* (c. 1485).

Many hundreds of miles to the north, in the Netherlands, a new school of naturalistic painting was established almost simultaneously with the new developments in Florence. The style of its founder, Jan van EYCK, may be seen, already fully formed, in his earliest dated work, the GHENT ALTARPIECE of 1432. Jan's success depended upon a seemingly infinite patience in the rendering of the minutest detail, embodied by a newly developed method of painting, in superimposed translucent glazes of oil paint, which permitted effects of light and texture to be delineated with a fidelity hitherto beyond the reach of artists working with opaque tempera. At about the same time, in Tournai, a similar but rather less accomplished style was formulated by Robert CAMPIN, sometimes known as the Master of Flémalle. Jan's pupil, Petrus CHRISTUS, had few followers, but Campin's student, Rogier van der WEYDEN, became the most influential northern painter of the 15th century.

Abroad, the style of the early Netherlandish painters was introduced to Germany, Austria, and Switzerland by Lukas MOSER, Konrad LAIB, and Konrad WITZ, to France by the Master of Aix, and to Spain by Luis DALMAU. In Sicily ANTONELLO DA MESSINA was trained by a Netherlander. Even the Florentine painters were affected by such works as Hugo van der GOES's PORTINARI ALTARPIECE, imported from Ghent in the late 1470s. Jan van Eyck was something of an antiquarian in as much as he was intrigued by 12th-century architecture, but the early Netherlandish painters had little or no interest in classical antiquity. Nevertheless, northern painters of the 15th century are best considered under the "Renaissance" head of account, because they were contemporary with the Italian avant-garde, were commonly interested in naturalism, devised the oil technique subsequently adopted throughout Europe, and fathered the Italianate northern schools of the 16th century.

The term "High Renaissance" is customarily reserved for the three decades of Italian art from the beginning of the 16th century to the Sack of Rome in 1527. Central to this epoch are the earlier works of MICHELANGELO, the mature period of RAPHAEL, and most of LEONARDO DA VINCI's paintings. To this pantheon may be added the Florentines Fra BARTOLOMMEO and ANDREA DEL SARTO and, with less assurance, the Venetians GIORGIONE and the young TITIAN. No northern painters are included, although it may be argued that Albrecht DÜRER's work of the period between about 1500 and 1509 has much in common with what we traditionally perceive as "High Renaissance" values. The view of this period as one in which painters in assured control of the techniques forged in the previous century attained a pure, classical harmony, free of superfluous detail, may be traced back to that of Giorgio VASARI, whose *Lives* was first published in 1550. While the validity of this concept, which derives from the evolutionary cycle of rise, maturity, and decay, is highly suspect, it has proved remarkably alluring. Like the brief "classical" epoch of Greek art, the High Renaissance remains one of the essential fixed points in Western art history.

Some great northern painters, principally Michael PACHER, Jean FOUQUET, and JUSTUS OF GHENT, visited Italy during the 15th century and devised Italianate styles of considerable distinction. Nevertheless, they constitute the exceptions that prove the general rule that most northerners were indifferent to the achievements of the Italians. Albrecht Dürer's visits to Venice in 1495 and 1505–07 were fundamentally different to those of his predecessors in that they stimulated the artist to seek a thorough understanding of the first principles of perspective and proportion. These Dürer publicized not only in paintings and numerous prints, but also in a series of treatises.

Dürer had little, if any, first-hand experience of ancient art. The first northern painters to retrace the steps of Masaccio and Mantegna to the antiquities of Rome were the Netherlanders Jan GOSSAERT, Jan van SCOREL, and Maarten van HEEMSKERCK. By the fourth decade of the 16th century, three principal centers of Italianate northern painting had been established: southern Germany, the Netherlands, and FONTAINEBLEAU, where Francis I entrusted the decoration of his palace to expatriate Italians. Thence a variety of more or less Italianate styles rapidly became the norm throughout northern Europe. Remarkably, the most outstanding northern painter of the mid-16th century, Pieter BRUEGHEL, eschewed the trappings of contemporary Italianism in favor of a more traditional naturalism, which drew upon 15th-century Netherlandish painting and was yet prophetic of Dutch landscape pictures of the following century.

Widespread use of the term MANNERISM in different contexts has dissipated its meaning, which was originally quite specific. Vasari regarded *maniera* as a positive quality, evocative of stylishness. Its principal exponents were ROSSO FIORENTINO, PONTORMO, and GIULIO ROMANO. While deeply attached to traditional Italian artistic precepts, especially the primacy of figure drawing, these painters rejected the serenity of High Renaissance art in favor of a powerful but subjective and emotional style, which drew somewhat upon Raphael's last paintings and was profoundly influenced by Michelangelo's late grand manner. The principal northern Italian exponent of this style was PARMIGIANINO. Venice was too profoundly conditioned by the work of Titian to be much affected by these new developments, although some aspects of TINTORETTO's style have been characterized as mannerist.

It was largely as a result of the initiative of these "first generation" mannerists that a new canon of drawing, which emphasized complexity of pose and gesture and popularized elongated figure types, became widely established. In northern Europe where the mainstream of painting had been abruptly redirected, Mannerism found fertile soil. Its principal Flemish exponent, Frans FLORIS, established a trend which endured, through the paintings of such artists as Joachim Wittewael (c. 1566–1638), Hans von AACHEN, and Hendrick GOLTZIUS. Ultimately "Mannerism" as broadly applied, constituted the final international phase of Renaissance painting. Moreover, it set the scene for the more truly European style which was to follow, the BAROQUE.

**Further reading:** John White, *The Birth and Rebirth of Pictorial Space* (London: Faber, 1957; 3rd ed. 1987); Marcia B. Hall, *Color and Meaning: Practice and Theory in Renaissance Painting* (Cambridge, U.K.: Cambridge University Press, 1992) ENGLAND: Karen Hearn (ed.), *Dynasties: Painting in Tudor and Jacobean England 1530–1630* (London: Tate Gallery, 1995); Roy Strong, *The English Icon: Elizabethan and Jacobean Portraiture* (London: Routledge & Kegan Paul and New York: Paul Mellon Foundation for British Art, 1969) FRANCE: Anthony Blunt, *Art and Architecture in France 1500–1700* (London: Penguin, 1953; 5th ed. New Haven, Conn. and London: Yale University Press, 1999); Grete Ring, *A Century of French Painting, 1400–1500* (London: Phaidon, 1949; New York: Hacket Art Books, 1979) ITALY: Michael Baxandall, *Giotto and the Orators: Humanist Observers of Painting and the Discovery of Pictorial Composition, 1350–1450* (Oxford, U.K.: Clarendon Press, 1971; corr. repr. 1986); Bruce Cole, *Italian Art 1250–1550: The Relationship of Renaissance Art to Life and Society* (New York and London: Harper & Row, 1987); David Franklin, *Painting in Renaissance Florence, 1500–1550* (New Haven, Conn.: Yale University Press, 2001); Marcia B. Hall, *After Raphael: Painting in Central Italy in the Sixteenth Century* (Cambridge, U.K.: Cambridge University Press, 1998) NETHERLANDS: Maryan Wynn Ainsworth (ed.), *Early Netherlandish Painting at the Crossroads* (New Haven, Conn.: Yale University Press, 2002); Dirk De Vos, *The Flemish Primitives* (Princeton, N.J.: Princeton University Press and Amsterdam, Netherlands: Amsterdam University Press, 2003); Rudolf H. Fuchs, *Dutch Painting* (London: Thames & Hudson, 1978).

**Palatina, Bibliotheca** Originally the LIBRARY of the university of Heidelberg, which was founded in 1386. The library was named in honor of the electors of the Palatinate, several of whom increased its holdings, especially Philip, Ludwig III, Ludwig V, Friedrich, and Otthenrich, the first Protestant elector, who lived in Heidelberg from 1556 to 1559. In 1584 it received a donation of manuscripts and books from Ulrich FUGGER of the Augsburg bankers. When Heidelberg fell to the Catholic League in 1622, Maximilian I of Bavaria presented its 3542 manuscripts and 5000 books to Pope Gregory XV; these form the Palatini collection in the VATICAN LIBRARY, except for 852 manuscripts returned to Heidelberg by the Vatican in 1816.

**Palatinate** A territory on the middle Rhine, inherited by Conrad, half-brother of Emperor Frederick I, who made Conrad count palatine in 1155. Conrad combined his administrative and judicial duties in the empire with his inherited territories. Both office and territories passed to a branch of the Bavarian Wittelbachs, who were confirmed as counts palatine by the treaty of Pavia (1329). The Golden Bull (1356) confirmed the count palatine as one of the seven imperial electors. Frederick III, Elector Palatine, established Calvinism in the Palatinate in 1563. The defeat of Frederick V (see WINTER KING) by Catholic forces in the Thirty Years' War led to a reduction of the elector palatine's powers, and the treaty of Rijswijk (1697) restored Catholicism in the Palatinate.

## Palestrina, Giovanni Pierluigi da (1525–1594) *Italian composer*

Palestrina is arguably the most important composer of the late 16th century and he was widely admired and imitated in his day. Palestrina was probably born in the town of that name outside Rome, and by 1537 was a choirboy at the Roman church of Sta. Maria Maggiore. In 1544 he became organist at the cathedral in Palestrina, where he remained until 1551. In that year he was appointed *maestro* at St. Peter's, and in 1554 his first book of Masses, the earliest by an Italian composer, was published. This was dedicated to Pope Julius III, his most powerful patron. In 1555 he became a member of the Cappella Sistina and *maestro di cappella* at St. John Lateran, but left the latter post after a dispute over funds for musicians (1560). He returned to Sta. Maria Maggiore, and in the summer of 1564 organized music at the Villa d'Este for Cardinal Ippolito II d'Este, whose service he entered in 1567. His fame was spreading, and he was offered the post of *maestro* at the court of Emperor Maximilian II in Vienna, but declined. He was also patronized by the Gonzaga family in Mantua. In 1571 Palestrina returned to Rome, to the Cappella Giulia, and remained there until his death.

Palestrina was a prolific composer; 104 Masses, around 375 motets, and many other liturgical works survive. He also composed around 140 spiritual and secular madrigals and eight *ricercari*. His sacred music, written in a conservative but uniquely harmonious style much influenced by the precepts of the Counter-Reformation, ensured Palestrina's fame and earned him the sobriquet "The Prince of Music." The Council of Trent advised that sacred texts set to music should be intelligible and that the music should contain no secular elements; it is possible that the famous *Missa Papae Marcelli* was composed for a commission of cardinals assembled to hear Masses and check that the words were intelligible. Many of Palestrina's early Masses are based on *cantus firmi*, whereas the later ones frequently employ the more modern "parody Mass" technique, and are based on pre-existing polyphonic compositions by himself and other composers. Despite the 18th-century codification of the Palestrina style by Johann Joseph Fux, his later works provide evidence of a developing musical trend which in its harmony and texture was clearly heading in the direction of the BAROQUE.

**Further reading:** Gustave Reese, *The New Grove High Renaissance Masters: Josquin, Palestrina, Lassus, Byrd, Victoria* (London: Macmillan, 1984).

## Palingenius (Pier Angelo Manzoli) (c. 1500–c. 1543) *Italian poet*

He was born at La Stellata, near Ferrara, and was attached to the court circle of RENÉE DE FRANCE, who married Ercole d'Este in 1528. She provided a refuge for persecuted French Calvinists at Ferrara, and Palingenius's only work, the *Zodiacus vitae* (1535–36), reflects the Calvinist outlook. This extensive moralistic poem in Latin hexameters was banned by the Inquisition, but was well received in Protestant Europe. The Polish moralist Mikołaj REJ based his *Wizerunek* (1558) on it, and an English translation by Barnabe Googe (c. 1540–94) of the first six books appeared in 1565.

## Palissy, Bernard (c. 1510–1590) *French naturalist and potter*

Trained as a glass painter, Palissy settled in Saintes in about 1540 and tried to develop his own distinctive style of pottery. His pond-like dishes bordered with realistically modeled animals soon won him commissions from the French court. They also gained him, as a Huguenot, some much needed protection. Although he escaped the 1572 St. Bartholomew massacre the respite proved only temporary; he was arrested in 1586 and died in the Bastille. In 1580 he published his *Discours admirables* in which "Practice" instructs "Theory" on, among other things, the origin of springs and rivers, and in which he argues for the organic origin of marine fossils; the 10th section of this work expounds his own discoveries in the arts of ceramics and enameling.

## Palladio, Andrea (1508–1580) *Italian architect*

A native of Padua, Palladio was born Andrea di Pietro della Gondola and began his career as a stonemason in Vicenza, where much of his work survives. In 1536 he came under the influence of the humanist poet Giangiorgio TRISSINO, who became Palladio's patron and was responsible for renaming the young mason after the mythological patron of the arts, Pallas Athene. Trissino encouraged Palladio's interest in the buildings of antiquity and introduced him to leading scholars of the time, probably including the mannerist architect Sebastiano SERLIO. In 1540–42 Palladio executed his first design for a villa, the Villa Godi-Valmarana at Lonedo, north of Vicenza, which incorporated many of the features of classical buildings, such as symmetrical wings and a walled courtyard, that were to become hallmarks of his style. At about this time Palladio also designed his first palace, the Palazzo Civena, which again made use of classical models.

In 1541 Palladio had visited Rome with Trissino for the first time and made an extensive study of the many an-

**Palladio** The Church of Il Redentore, Venice, built as a thanksgiving for the termination of the plague that struck the city in 1576. Constructed 1577–92, it is usually considered to be Palladio's most successful church using Roman architectural principles. *Photo AKG London/Erich Lessing*

cient buildings there; his findings were published as the treatise *Le antichità di Roma* (1554). (Two years after this publication he collaborated with Daniele BARBARO on a new edition of *De architectura* by VITRUVIUS, thus identifying himself further with the geometry and harmony of classical architecture.) In 1545 Palladio was given his first important commission, the rebuilding of the Basilica in Vicenza, which provided him with an opportunity to put into practice his understanding of the proportions and motifs of antiquity. Subsequent Vicentine buildings of note that echoed ancient ideals included the Palazzo Chiericati (1550), the Palazzo Iseppo da Porto (1552), the Palazzo Antonini (1556), and the Palazzo Thiene (c. 1545–50). In the 1560s Palladio also designed a villa for Barbaro at Maser, near Asolo, which was decorated by VERONESE and VITTORIA.

Of his later works, which included churches, palaces, and country villas, probably the most influential was the Villa ROTONDA in Vicenza, which imitated the design of the Roman Pantheon both in its symmetrical structure and in its classical ornament. He built two highly successful churches in Venice: the Redentore (begun 1577), which was built in thanksgiving for Venice's deliverance from the plague in the preceding year, and San Giorgio Maggiore (1565–80), conspicuously situated on an islet across the Canale di San Marco. Although some of Palladio's designs owed a small debt to the ideas of contemporary mannerists, they were derived chiefly from the architect's understanding of antique structures, which he explored most fully in the hugely influential *Quattro libri dell' architettura* (1570), which took 20 years to complete and profoundly influenced architects throughout Italy and the rest of Europe, including Inigo JONES in England. Palladio's last commission (c. 1579) was for the Teatro Olimpico in Vicenza, completed by his pupil Vincenzo SCAMOZZI in 1585 (*see* THEATERS).

**Further reading:** James S. Ackerman, *Palladio* (Harmondsworth, U.K.: Penguin, 1966; 2nd ed. 1991); Witold Rybczynski, *The Perfect House: A Journey With Renaissance Master Andrea Palladio* (New York: Scribner, 2000); Robert Tavernor, *Palladio and Palladianism* (London: Thames & Hudson, 1991); Manfred Wundram, *Andrea Palladio, 1508–1580: Architect between the Renaissance and the Baroque* (Cologne, Germany: Taschen, 1993).

**Pallas (Athene)** See MINERVA

**Palma Giovane (Jacopo Negretti)** (1544–1628) *Italian painter*
He was born in Venice, the great-nephew of PALMA VECCHIO and the son of Antonio Negretti. His first training was with his father and probably with TITIAN, whose *Pietà* he completed after Titian's death. He then visited Urbino and studied in Rome for about three years. Following his return to Venice (c. 1570) he produced pictures for the doge's palace and Venetian churches in a style that combined the influence of Mannerism with that of Titian and VERONESE and of TINTORETTO, whose style dominated

Venetian painting at that time. Palma increasingly rivaled Tintoretto and became the dominant figure in Venice after the latter's death.

## Palma Vecchio (Jacomo Negretti) (1480–1528) *Italian painter*
He was born at Serimalta, near Bergamo, and was almost certainly trained in the studio of Giovanni BELLINI, possibly with TITIAN and GIORGIONE, although the first mention of Palma in Venice is not until 1510. It was at about this time that he began to paint the pictures of ample female figures that made him so popular and which he continued to produce throughout his career. These ladies appeared sometimes as mythological and sometimes biblical personages in rich, sensuous pictures of simple composition, such as the *Flora* (c. 1520) in London's National Gallery. Many of the works are *sacre conversazioni* with several female saints, such as his masterpiece *Sta. Barbara and Other Saints* in Sta. Maria Formosa, Venice. Among the artists that he influenced are Alessandra MORETTO and Girolamo ROMANINO.

## Palmieri, Matteo (1406–1475) *Italian writer and poet*
Born into a Florentine mercantile family, Palmieri studied under some of the leading humanists of his day and held a number of governmental posts in the republic. He wrote several historical works in Latin, including a history of Florence (*Historia florentina*, published in the 18th century), and in the vernacular a lengthy religious poem, *La città di vita*, heavily indebted to Dante. His major work, written about 1430, is the dialogue *Della vita civile* (1529). Drawing on arguments in CICERO and QUINTILIAN, the treatise is a discussion and a defense of the active life of civic responsibility based on humanist principles, as against a life of contemplative scholarship.

## Paludanus, Guilielmus (Willem van den Broeck) (1530–1580) *Netherlands sculptor*
Posibly born at Malines, he matriculated in St. Luke's guild of artists in Antwerp (1557) and was granted citizenship two years later. He carved architectural details for the Antwerp town hall, built by Cornelis FLORIS, as well as two reliefs of Christ's Passion for Augsburg (1560–62). Paludanus is not recorded as having traveled to Italy, but his style shows a knowledge of the Italian High Renaissance, possibly gained from studying engravings and the work of Leone LEONI, who visited the imperial court in Brussels (1556–59). A male anatomical statuette of *St. Bartholomew*, excellently modeled in terracotta (dated 1569; Kunsthistorisches Museum, Vienna) attests his skill and possible contact with GIAMBOLOGNA. In 1571 he made narrative reliefs for the base of Jacques JONGHELINCK's monument in Antwerp to the duke of Alba (destroyed) and began a choir screen for export to San Leonardo, Alba

(Spain), also now lost. An altar in Antwerp cathedral was destroyed (1582) during the wars of religion.

## Pannemaker family
The most famous of the 16th-century Flemish tapestry weavers, based in Brussels. Pieter I Pannemaker (active from 1510) was a follower of Pieter van Aelst, who in 1514 was commissioned by Pope Leo X to weave the tapestries from Raphael's cartoons of New Testament subjects. In 1518 Pieter was the first of his family to gain imperial patronage, with a commission from Maximilian I, and he subsequently (1523) also worked for MARGARET OF AUSTRIA. Pieter II and Willem continued to work for the Hapsburgs. Among their prolific output was the series of 12 tapestries depicting Charles V's campaign to capture Tunis (1535), after designs by Jan Cornelis VERMEYEN. At the end of the 1570s the preeminence of the Pannemakers was overtaken by the Geubels family.

## *Pantagruel* See GARGANTUA AND PANTAGRUEL

## Panvinio, Onofrio (1529–1568) *Italian humanist scholar*
Panvinio studied in his native Verona, in Padua, and in Naples. His first published work was an edition of the *Fasti Consulares* (1556). He also published studies of the pedigrees of contemporary Roman families, ancient games, the Roman triumph, sacrifices, and the Sibylline books. Most of this antiquarian work was based on the collection of nearly 3000 inscriptions which he hoped would eventually form the basis for a complete edition of Roman inscriptions. In 1568 he visited Sicily and died at Palermo; he was buried at Rome. Panvinio's work typifies the sort of antiquarian studies characteristic of the later Renaissance. His manuscript collections are now in the Vatican. TITIAN painted a fine portrait of him.

## Paracelsus, Philippus Aureolus (Theophrastus Bombastus von Hohenheim) (1493–1541) *German physician, chemist, and alchemist*
The son of a physician, Paracelsus was born near Zürich and began his career working the Fugger silver mines at Hutenberg. He soon abandoned mining for medicine and in 1526 began to practice in Basle. He immediately gained a notable success by curing the famous printer FROBEN of a leg infection while his orthodox rivals were advising amputation. Although appointed city physician Paracelsus proved to be too quarrelsome ever to occupy an official post more than briefly: nor was his tenure helped by the sudden death of Froben in 1527. Thereafter Paracelsus led the life of an itinerant teacher and physician, traveling through, but never long welcome in, the provinces of Austria, Bohemia, Switzerland, and Bavaria. As a physician he proclaimed the total inadequacy of the classical tradition, burning the works of Avicenna in 1527, and declaring in his own adopted name that he had advanced well beyond

ALTERIVS NON SIT,QVI SVVS ESSE POTEST.

LAVS DEO, PAX VIVIS, REQVIES ÆTERNA SEPVLTIS.

OMNE DONVM PERFECTVM Á DEO,IMPERF. Á DIABO.

AVREOLVS PHILIPPVS THEOPHRASTVS

**Paracelsus** A woodcut portrait appearing in his *Astronomica et astrologica* (1567).

the Roman authority Celsus. His main innovation involved the adoption of such therapeutic drugs as mercury and antimony rather than pursuing the humoral approach of traditional medicine (*see* IATROCHEMISTRY). In chemistry his name is linked with the claim that matter was ultimately reducible to the three elements: salt, sulfur, and mercury. Both proposals were fertile enough to establish a Paracelsian tradition, which survived late into the 17th century.

**Further reading:** Allen G. Debus, *The Chemical Philosophy* (New York: Science History Publications, 1977; new ed. Dover, 2002); Gerhild Scholz Williams and Charles D. Gunnoe, Jr (eds), *Paracelsian Moments: Science, Medicine, and Astrology in Early Modern Europe* (Kirksville, Mo: Truman State University Press, 2003); Charles Webster, *From Paracelsus to Newton: Magic and the Making of Modern Science* (Cambridge, U.K.: Cambridge University Press, 1982).

**Paré, Ambroise** (c. 1510–1590) *French surgeon*
The son of an artisan at Laval, Paré qualified as a master barber-surgeon in 1536. He immediately joined the army with which he practiced his skill on a number of campaigns. He also served as court surgeon to Henry II, Charles IX, and Henry III. One of the major problems facing the military surgeon of Paré's day was how to deal with the fearsome wounds produced by cannon and other

firearms introduced into warfare in the 14th century. The orthodox technique of cauterization could prove as crippling as the wound itself. During the siege of Turin in 1536, Paré tried instead the alternative technique of applying dressings; he found it just as satisfactory. Later, in his *Dix livres de la chirurgie* (1563), he described a second and even more revolutionary technique: the use of the ligature in such wounds, an innovation that would eventually permit surgery to extend its domain considerably. Paré's attitude to his art is epitomized in his dictum: "I treated him, God cured him."

**Paris** The capital city of France on the River Seine in northern France. Paris was founded by the Parisii, a Gallic tribe, and (as Lutetia) was a capital under the Romans, and later under the Merovingians and the Capetian founders of modern France. As the Capets restored order and stability during the later Middle Ages the population and prosperity of Paris grew. The 12th century saw the establishment of the first guilds. In the 13th century the university of Paris gained royal recognition (1200), the Sorbonne was founded (1257), and a royal charter gave Parisians the right to levy duties on incoming goods (1220).

At the beginning of the 14th century Paris probably possessed the largest urban population in Europe, about 100,000; this was halved by the Black Death (1348–49) and the Hundred Years' War (1337–1453). Paris was torn apart by the struggle between the Burgundian and Armagnac factions (1407–35) and occupied by the English and the Burgundians in 1418. After Paris was recaptured by Charles VII's forces (1435) the city enjoyed a period of comparative peace and its population rose to 200,000 by the middle of the 16th century. The municipality was reorganized (1450) and the *parlement* of Paris became France's most powerful court of justice. The installation of the first printing press (1470) was followed by the development of Paris as most prolific center of publishing in Europe; during the 16th century 25,000 editions were published in Paris.

During the second half of the 15th century many churches were restored and work started on such magnificent private residences as the Hôtel de Sens and the Hôtel de Cluny. The first half of the 16th century saw the start of work on the rebuilding of the LOUVRE and the construction of the Hôtel de Ville. During the second half of the 16th century the Louvre became the royal residence, and work was begun on the TUILERIES palace.

Paris prospered and its population expanded until the sectarian turmoil (*see* RELIGION, (FRENCH) WARS OF) of the second half of the 16th century. Although Paris had been a center of humanist scholarship under the inspiration of LEFÈVRE D'ÉTAPLES in the late 15th century, it became a stronghold of Catholic reaction during the Reformation. In 1535 the appearance of placards denouncing the Mass led to the first persecution of French Protestants (HUGUENOTS). Although French Protestants held their first synod in Paris (1559), later in the century it was the scene of the MASSACRE OF ST. BARTHOLOMEW (1572) and the bastion of the Catholic League and the GUISE FAMILY. By the time Paris finally accepted HENRY IV as its king (1594) its population had dropped to about 180,000.

Notable landmarks that have survived from the period of the Renaissance include the LOUVRE and the Pont-Neuf (1599–1604).

**Further reading:** David Thomson, *Renaissance Paris: Architecture and Growth 1475–1600* (Berkeley, Calif.: University of California Press, 1985).

**Parker, Matthew** (1504–1575) *English clergyman and scholar*
Born at Norwich and educated at Cambridge, Parker was ordained in 1527 and rose in the ecclesiastical hierarchy to become chaplain to Anne Boleyn in 1535. During the reign of the Catholic Mary I (1553–58) he found it necessary to retire into private life, but under ELIZABETH I he was consecrated archbishop of Canterbury (1559). In this role he staunchly defended the moderate character of the Church of England against Puritan extremism. Parker was also a scholar of note, being particularly concerned with the collection and preservation of the many medieval documents released by the DISSOLUTION OF THE MONASTERIES. Some of these he edited and published, such as the chronicle of Matthew Paris (1571), while others formed the basis for his *De antiquitate ecclesiae* (1572), in which he contentiously tried to trace the roots of the ELIZABETHAN SETTLEMENT of the church back to St. Augustine.

**Parma** A city in the Emilia-Romagna region of northern Italy. Parma was originally Etruscan, then Roman, and emerged in the late Middle Ages as an independent commune. Threatened by Milan and Verona and weakened by rivalry between the Correggio and Rossi families, Parma enjoyed only short spells of independence before long periods of subjection to Milan (1346–1447, 1450–1500). Under both the VISCONTI and SFORZA rulers of Milan Parma was allowed a good measure of self-government. During the wars of Italy Parma was subject in turn to France (1500–12), the papacy (1515–15), France (1515–20), and the papacy again (1520–45). In 1545 Pope PAUL III made Parma and Piacenza into a duchy for his illegitimate son, Pierluigi Farnese. The FARNESE, who made the ducal court a center of arts and learning, ruled Parma until the 18th century.

Although its population was modest (about 15,000 in 1500), Parma prospered on account of local agriculture and the woolen industry. It boasted two great 16th-century artists: CORREGGIO and PARMIGIANINO. Notable churches that have survived from the period of the Renaissance include San Giovanni Evangelista (rebuilt 1498–1510), with frescoes by Correggio and Parmigianino, the baroque SS. Annunziata (1566), and the church of Sta. Maria della Steccata, reputedly built (1521–39) to BRAMANTE's original plan for St. Peter's, Rome. Secular buildings include the Palazzo Ducale (1564) and the unfinished Palazzo della Pilotta (begun 1583), which housed the wooden Teatro Farnese (built 1618–28) designed by Giovanni Battista Aleotti.

**Parmigianino, Il** (Francesco Mazzola) (1503–1540)
*Italian painter and graphic artist*
In the early 1520s he was already executing commissions for frescoes in the cathedral in Parma, his birthplace and the city after which he was named, and in the church of San Giovanni Evangelista, where CORREGGIO was also working. Although Parmigianino's personal mannerist style was already established, his work was influenced by Correggio and later by the painting of PORDENONE, RAPHAEL, and MICHELANGELO. Around 1523 he left for Rome, where he appears to have concentrated on graphic arts, particularly etching. He was one of the first artists to produce original etchings from his own designs, and these, which were widely distributed, together with reproductions of his paintings in engravings and woodcuts, helped to increase the extent of his influence in Italy and the rest of Europe.

At the Sack of Rome (1527), Parmigianino was captured, but he soon escaped to Bologna. He began to experiment with the use of landscape as a background and his work influenced Niccolò dell' ABBATE. After visiting Verona and Venice he spent the 1530s in Parma. To this period belongs the well-known *Madonna dal collo lungo* (Uffizi, Florence), one of the most extreme examples of Parmigianino's mannerist elongation of limbs, particularly, in this case, of the neck and hands (see illustration p. 298). His main commission during these years was a series of frescoes in Sta. Maria della Steccata but so little of it was completed that he was imprisoned briefly in 1539 for breach of contract. According to VASARI he had by this time undergone a change of personality from an amiable and elegant person to a long-haired, untidy, and almost savage man. The following year Parmigianino's short career came to an end in Casalmaggiore. As well as the types of work already mentioned he also left behind him a number of portraits, such as the self-portrait in a mirror (1521; Kunsthistorisches Museum, Vienna) and the portrait of a woman (Museo di Capodimonte, Naples), probably his mistress, Antea "La Bella"; many of these convey a sense of deep spiritual insight. See Plate XI.

**Further reading:** Cecil Hilton Monk Gould, *Parmigianino* (New York: Abbeville, 1995).

## Parr, Catherine (1512–1548) *English queen, sixth wife of Henry VIII*

Catherine married HENRY VIII reluctantly in 1543; already twice widowed, she had wished to marry Sir Thomas Seymour. A scholar herself, she took advantage of her position at court to become a notable patron of Protestant humanism. As nurse to Henry, and his intellectual equal, she exerted a restraining influence, encouraging him to greater religious toleration. Under Catherine's influence Henry founded Trinity College, Cambridge, and reformed Wolsey's Cardinal College at Oxford as Christ Church. Herself childless, Catherine oversaw the education of Henry's three children with care and kindness, influencing the Protestant faith of Elizabeth and encouraging her and her half-sister Mary to publish their own translations. She herself commissioned translations of key Reformation texts, among them Erasmus's *Paraphrase of the Gospels*, and published her own devotional writings *Prayers, or Meditacions* (1545) and *Lamentacion or Complaynt of a Sinner* (1547). After Henry's death (1547) she married Seymour, but died in childbirth a year later.

## Parsons, Robert (Robert Persons) (1546–1610) *English Jesuit*

Parsons held a post at Oxford (1568–74) which he abandoned in order to join the Roman Catholic Church at Louvain. In 1575 he became a Jesuit in Rome and later joined Edmund CAMPION on the first Jesuit mission to reconvert the English. He escaped back to the Continent and continued to direct Jesuit policy concerning England, but his plots with hardline English Catholics against Elizabeth I had the effect of provoking her to clamp down vigorously on RECUSANCY. In 1594 he published pseudonymously a book claiming the right of a people to reject an heir to a throne on religious grounds and supporting the claim of the impeccably Catholic Infanta of Spain to the English crown.

## Paruta, Paolo (1540–1598) *Italian historian*

A member of a patrician Venetian family, Paruta was educated at Padua and from 1561 occupied a number of official positions in the republic, among them that of city historian, an office previously held by BEMBO, to which he was appointed in 1579. In this capacity he was able to consult state records and his careful use of these sources lend a special interest to his historical works in Italian which he was officially commissioned to write. These include *Istorie veneziane* (1605), a history of the republic from 1513 to 1552, and *Storia della guerra di Cipre* (c. 1573), a history of the Cyprus war (1570–73). The conservative and reflective viewpoint of a Venetian nobleman informs the works written on his own account. The dialogue *Della perfezione della vita politica* (1579) is a discussion of civic ideals in which Paruta supports the argument for the active life of political involvement against the contemplative religious life. His *Discorsi politici* cover questions in history and politics earlier introduced by MACHIAVELLI, for example, the causes of the greatness of ancient Rome and the character of the ideal state.

## Pasquier, Étienne (1529–1615) *French lawyer and man of letters*

Pasquier studied law at Toulouse and was called to the bar in his native Paris in 1549. He made his name as a lawyer with his successful defense of the university of Paris in its suit with the Jesuits (1565), who had demanded the right for their order to be admitted to teach there. Having served as commissioner in the assize courts of Poitiers and Toulouse, in 1585 he was appointed advocate-general for Henry III at the *chambre des comptes* in Paris. In 1560 Pasquier produced the first volume of his *Recherches de la France*, an encyclopedic collection of information on the country's history, culture, and institutions; this major work was to occupy much of his leisure time in the later years of his life and was first published in its entirety in 1621. His other writings include the anti-Jesuit pamphlet *Le Catéchisme des Jésuites* (1602), *Lettres* (1586, 1619), and a number of collections of poetry.

## Passarotti, Bartolommeo (1529–1592) *Italian painter*

Born in Bologna, he studied with Giacomo Barozzi da VIGNOLA and then became the assistant of Taddeo ZUCCARO in Rome, where he lived from about 1551 to about 1565. His *Martyrdom of St. Paul* can be seen in the church of San Paolo alle Tre Fontane. On his return to Bologna he continued to paint altarpieces and also portraits, mainly of popes and cardinals, at which he excelled. He created a type of genre and still-life painting depicting peasants with flowers and fowls and he produced a number of etchings. As his style moved further towards the BAROQUE, his studio became a focal point for many of Bologna's artists, among whom his most distinguished disciple was the painter and engraver Agostino Carracci (1557–1602).

## Passerat, Jean (1534–1602) *French poet and humanist*

Passerat was born at Troyes and after studying at the university of Paris and teaching at the Collège du Plessis, he was appointed to the chair of Latin at the Collège de France (1572). His prose writings include commentaries on Catullus, Propertius, and other Latin poets; among his better-known poetic works are the ode "Du premier jour de mai" and the villanelle "J'ai perdu ma tourterelle." A supporter of Henry of Navarre (later Henry IV), Passerat was one of the authors of the SATIRE MÉNIPPÉE (1594). His *Recueil des oeuvres poétiques* was published in 1606.

## Pasti, Matteo de' (c. 1420–c. 1467) *Italian architect and artist*

Pasti was born in Verona and executed a number of works in Venice. He included Sigismondo MALATESTA, Leonello d'Este, and Piero de' Medici among his patrons. Notable examples of his work in various genres are the illuminations for Piero de' Medici's copy of Petrarch's *Trionfi* (1441), the Palazzo Rucellai in Florence (c. 1446–c. 1451) as designed by ALBERTI, and several portrait medals in the style of PISANELLO, of whom he was a follower. Other works included the unfinished reconstruction of the church interior of San Francesco in Rimini, on which he also collaborated with Alberti (*see* TEMPIO MALATESTIANO).

**pastoral** A type of literature concerned with idealized rustic life, especially the lives and loves of shepherds living in a golden age of simplicity and innocence. The style is often artificial, always unrealistic, and frequently colored by the nostalgia felt by the urbanized author and his or her audience. Pastoral (or bucolic) elegy, romance, and drama developed as important genres in the Renaissance.

The pastoral poem originated in Sicily. The *Idylls* of Theocritus, who was probably born at Syracuse around 270 BCE, include six pastorals (nos. 1, 3, 4, 5, 6, 10) which reflect ancient Sicilian life and are structured dramatically as verse dialogues or contests (known as Amoebean or "responsive" verses) between rural characters. Other of the *Idylls* contain pastoral elements, for example, no. 15: although set in Alexandria, it describes the Adoniazusae or festival of Adonis and concludes with a hymn in his honor. Idyll 1 contains a "Lament for Daphnis," the legendary Sicilian shepherd who invented the pastoral (in Theocritus's version, he dies of unrequited love visited on him by Aphrodite as a punishment for his having earlier refused love himself). Theocritus's successors were Bion, born at Smyrna (c. 100 BCE), and the Syracusan Moschus (born c. 150 BCE). Bion wrote six pastorals, imitating Theocritus most successfully in his "Lament for Adonis." The "Lament for Bion," traditionally attributed to Moschus but probably by one of Bion's disciples, completes the Greek models for what in the Renaissance was conventionalized as the pastoral elegy. John Milton's *Lycidas* (1638) is the outstanding English example of the type.

VIRGIL's 10 *Eclogues* (c. 42–37 BCE) imitate Theocritus and refine pastoral conventions: the unrequited love of Corydon for Alexis (2), song and verse contests between shepherds (3, 7), the death of Daphnis (5). The fourth eclogue, which foretells the return of a golden age under the rule of a newborn child, was read by early Christians as a Messianic prophecy of the coming of Christ, and Virgil's use of allegory in the *Eclogues* exercised a strong influence on later poets. Far removed from the classical tradition, the medieval *pastourelle* (Provençal *pastorela*) was especially popular among Old French poets in the 13th century, though it was Provençal in origin. A short narrative poem about the meeting of a knight and a shepherdess, it had no characteristic formal features and was defined merely by its often crude subject matter. CAVALCANTI's "In un boschetto trova' pasturella" is an example.

The classical pastoral, with a decided allegorical emphasis, was revived in the Latin poems of DANTE (two eclogues), PETRARCH (12 eclogues), and in BOCCACCIO's *Bucolicum carmen*. His "Ninfale fiesolano" (Nymph of Fiesole; 1344–46), which qualifies as the first vernacular idyll, dealt with Ovidian transformations to explain Tuscan river names and incorporated pastoral elements. PONTANO's Latin eclogues and idylls (three of each; Aldine edition, 1518) stand at the beginning of a Neapolitan revival of the pastoral tradition which culminated in Jacopo SANNAZARO's *Arcadia*. (Sannazaro's innovative *Piscatoria* (1526) substituted fishermen for shepherds; in this he was imitated by Phineas FLETCHER.) Among BOIARDO's earliest poems are Italian eclogues imitating Virgil. SPAGNOLI's (Mantuan's) 10 Latin eclogues (1498) developed satirical motifs by using conventional pastoral characters to attack the follies of church, court, and the female sex.

The pastoral romance is usually traced to Boccaccio's *Ameto* (1342), which mixed a long prose narrative with *terza rima* lyrics in a complicated plot involving pastoral characters. *Ameto* owes most, however, to medieval allegory. Sannazaro's *Arcadia* (1504) was the first true, and definitive, pastoral romance, the model for later authors (*see also* ARCADIA). The pastoral drama of the 16th century developed in the wake of the immense popularity of *Arcadia* and drew on the dramatic potentials of the pastoral eclogue: the dialogues and verse contests, the loves of shepherds and nymphs, the allegorical elements and allusions to contemporary people and events, and the contrast between the golden age of rustic simplicity and the sophistication of the court life of the audience. The court of Ferrara in particular gave the impetus to these developments and its poets produced the two most influential pastoral plays: TASSO's *Aminta* (1573), the best example of the type, which became the model for GUARINI's *Il pastor fido* (1589), the first pastoral tragicomedy. Other important Italian pastoral plays (or plays with significant pastoral elements) are POLITIAN's *Favola di Orfeo* (1472), Epicuro's *Mirzia* (1535), CINTHIO's *Egle* (1545), and Agostini Beccari's *Il sacrificio* (1554).

The fashion for pastoral spread throughout Europe, encouraged by the Italian example or by direct contact with the classical models. The eclogues of Alexander Barclay (c. 1475–1552), the earliest in English (1515, 1521), are based directly on Spagnoli's, as are the pastoral poems of Clément MAROT in French. Both Mantuan (Spagnoli) and Marot are acknowledged by SPENSER as sources for his *Shepheardes Calender* (1579).

In the field of pastoral romance, LA DIANA (1559) by Jorge de Montemayor was immensely popular in its original Spanish and in translation. SIDNEY's *Arcadia* (1590) is one of its offspring, and several Elizabethan prose writers tried their hand at the genre, most successfully perhaps in the case of Thomas LODGE, whose *Rosalynde* (1590) is the source for SHAKESPEARE's *As You Like It*. In France the best-known novel in this kind is Honoré D'URFÉ's *L'Astrée* (1607–27).

Besides plays, pastoral also had its uses in court entertainments and MASQUES; rustic characters could be introduced for merriment while more refined shepherds and shepherdesses could pay delicate compliments to the powerful and sophisticated audience, and courtiers could themselves take on bucolic roles and enjoy the game of pastoral make-believe.

**Further reading:** Bruno Damiani and Barbara Mujica, *Et in Arcadia Ego* (Lanham, Md: University Press of America, 1990); Reinhold Grimm and Jost Hermand (eds), *From the Greeks to the Greens: Images of the Simple Life* (Madison, Wis.: University of Wisconsin Press, 1990).

**Pastor fido, Il** See GUARINI, BATTISTA; PASTORAL

**Patinir, Joachim** (Joachim Patinier, c. 1480–1524) *Netherlands painter*
Patinir, who was born at Dinant, is first recorded in 1515 on his admission to the painters' guild at Antwerp, where he remained for the rest of his life. In 1521 he met Dürer who described him as "the good landscape painter." An early inventory states that the figures in Patinir's Madrid *Temptation of St. Anthony* are by Quentin METSYS. The landscape background in Joos van Cleve's Liverpool *Virgin and Child with Angels* is identical with one in a painting by Patinir in Lugano and may actually have been painted by him. Accordingly, Patinir emerges as the first landscape specialist, initiating a trend which flourished in Flemish painting of the early 16th century. Patinir's dramatic late landscapes, such as the Oxford *Destruction of Sodom and Gomorrah*, with heaped-up rocks of great size and irregular shape, strongly influenced subsequent Flemish mannerist landscapes.

**patristic studies** Early humanists made no distinction between the texts of classical authors and those of the Church Fathers. PETRARCH collected texts of CICERO and St. Augustine with equal enthusiasm and studied both for their moral content, preferring, as he himself said, to be made good rather than learned. As philological awareness advanced, however, scholars realized that there was a difference between the Latin prose style of Cicero and that of third- or fourth-century CE writers. Lorenzo VALLA, a leader in this field of study, observed in his *Elegantiae* (1444) that the Church Fathers were indebted to Cicero for their eloquence and exalted Ciceronian Latin as the model to be followed. He castigated St. Jerome for deficiencies in his Latin style that he considered deformed the "truth" of the Greek original text of the New Testament which Jerome translated. An important early figure to show an interest in the writings of the Greek Church Fathers was the monk Ambrogio TRAVERSARI who collected Greek patristic manuscripts and translated some into Latin; his version of a work by St. John Chrysostom (c. 350–407) defending monasticism was issued as early as 1417.

As the religious controversies of the 16th century got under way, Catholics and Protestants alike appealed to the venerable authority of the Church Fathers for guidance on biblical interpretation and for their teaching on such matters as JUSTIFICATION BY FAITH and the operation of divine grace. To do this it was necessary for authoritative texts to be available. An early leader in the field of patristic printed texts was Johannes AMERBACH at Basle, whose successor, FROBEN, was the chief publisher of ERASMUS. Erasmus showed phenomenal zeal in his patristic publications: his nine-volume St. Jerome appeared in 1516, his 10-volume St. Augustine in 1529, and his two-volume Origen, which had taken up the last months of his life, in 1536; these were in addition to texts of Sts. Ambrose, Cyprian, Hilary, Irenaeus, and John Chrysostom.

The Council of TRENT explicitly endorsed the authority of the Fathers in biblical exegesis, thus giving a further stimulus to patristic studies in Catholic countries. The first important printed collection of patristic texts, the *Bibliotheca SS. patrum*, appeared in Paris in eight volumes in 1575, and in increasingly expanded editions over the next century. Apologists of the Church of England found the Fathers an invaluable source of doctrine, uncontaminated, as they saw it, by Romanist corruptions. Isaac CASAUBON and Georg CASSANDER were just two scholars who were greatly influenced in their theological opinions by their patristic studies.

**Further reading:** Charles L. Stinger, *Humanism and the Church Fathers: Ambrogio Traversari (1386–1439) and Christian Antiquity in the Italian Renaissance* (Albany, N.Y.: State University of New York Press, 1977).

**Patrizi, Francesco** (Franjo Petril, Patritius) (1529–1597) *Dalmatian philosopher, mathematician, and scholar*
Born at Cherso, Istria, he studied at Padua and Venice where he developed an interest in Platonism through reading the *Theologia Platonica* of Marsilio FICINO. After service in France, Spain, and Cyprus he became professor of Platonic philosophy at Ferrara (1578). In 1592 he was called to Rome by Pope Clement VIII and died there as professor of philosophy at the university. Pure scholarship was not his only interest; he also published practical manuals of military strategy. He produced a number of works presenting art, history, and philosophy in a Platonic interpretation challenging the dominant Aristotelianism of his day, most notably *Della historia* (1560), *Della retorica* (1562), and *Nova de universis philosophia* (1591). Patrizi sought to combine Christianity, Platonism, and the hermetic writings in a metaphysical synthesis but failed through lack of a sufficiently rigorous method of argument.

**patronage** In considering the cultural bond linking creative artists and the grandees who supported them, the Renaissance looked back for its model to a famous relationship in classical antiquity: the patronage bestowed by Maecenas, the friend and minister of the Roman emperor Augustus, upon the epic poet Virgil. As the epigrammatist Martial said, "Sint Maecenates, non deerunt…Marones" (As long as there are Maecenases… Virgils will not be lacking). Maecenas was thus perceived as the epitome of the liberal and discerning patron, and it was a standard compliment from Renaissance literati to refer to an actual or intended patron as a "Maecenas" (*see* SIDNEY, SIR PHILIP).

At its most basic, the patron's duty was to provide the artist with financial security, either through long- or short-term employment or by commissioning specific works from him. The degree of enlightened encouragement that a patron could provide naturally varied with the patron's own tastes, discernment, and funds. Poets, musicians, and painters, along with competent falconers or riding masters, might well be considered little more than desirable personnel in the entourage of any nobleman who wished to cut a dash among his fellows, but ideally both sides conceived the patronage relationship as considerably more than a crude transaction whereby monetary advantage was traded for gross flattery. Present enjoyment and display naturally mattered to a patron, but the quality of his artists' output mattered too, because in a world in which military glory and political power were seen to be frail and transitory the discriminating prince could hope to achieve lasting renown through his association with works that would be admired by future generations.

This idealistic view of patronage applied particularly to literature, less so to the visual arts, and hardly at all in the case of music. Even so, writers were seldom primarily employed for literary ends, as was the case with ARIOSTO, who was sent on various diplomatic missions by his ESTE employers. The relationship between painters, sculptors, and architects and their patrons varied considerably. Some artists had little, if any, more status than other household employees, but great figures such as MICHELANGELO, Titian, and Cellini were highly mobile and were sought after by popes and emperors. On the other hand, such artists needed the scope provided by huge and expensive projects for such patrons as POPE JULIUS II, Emperor Charles V, and Francis I of France to realize their artistic vision. Music, while an integral part of Renaissance life, is scarcely included within the exalted concept of patronage; popes, princes, great churches, or municipal corporations generally just hired the best men available to compose and perform music for grand occasions and for everyday requirements.

While some patronage relationships in the visual arts are well documented, especially the stormy ones like that between Michelangelo and Pope Julius II, most evidence for the system in the Renaissance derives from literature. Compliments to patrons could be integral to the work itself (as in Ariosto's glorification of the Este dynasty in the storyline of ORLANDO FURIOSO) or the patron's association with it could be proclaimed via the dedication. With the spread of printing the latter practice was easily debased, with some authors claiming as "patrons" eminent persons whom they scarcely knew, in the hope of a cash hand-out.

**Further reading:** Alison Cole, *Virtue and Magnificence: Art of the Italian Renaissance Courts* (Upper Saddle River, N.J.: Prentice Hall, 1995); Mary Hollingsworth, *Patronage in Renaissance Italy: From 1400 to the Early Sixteenth Century* (Baltimore, Md: Johns Hopkins University Press, 1996); Dale Kent, *Cosimo de' Medici and the Florentine Renaissance: The Patron's Oeuvre* (New Haven, Conn.: Yale University Press, 2000); Guy F. Lytle and Stephen Orgel (eds), *Patronage in the Renaissance* (Princeton, N.J.: Princeton University Press, 1981); David C. Price, *Patrons and Musicians of the English Renaissance* (Cambridge, U.K.: Cambridge University Press, 1981); Hugh Trevor-Roper, *Princes and Artists: Patronage and Ideology at Four Habsburg Courts 1517–1633* (London: Thames & Hudson, 1976).

**Paul II** (1417–1471) *Pope (1464–71)*
A wealthy Venetian by birth, at age 23 Pietro Barbo was created a cardinal by his uncle, Pope EUGENIUS IV. As Paul II, he failed to gain Emperor Frederick III's cooperation in organizing a crusade against the Turks, but he enjoyed more success in his fight against heresy in Bohemia, where he excommunicated and deposed King George of Podebrady for his Hussite sympathies. Paul supported the candidature of the more loyal Catholic, King MATTHIAS CORVINUS of Hungary, who was elected king of Bohemia in 1469. Paul II made little progress in restoring papal authority in the Papal States, but his restoration of ancient monuments made Rome a more worthy papal capital; he also amassed a collection of ancient coins and bronzes, many of which passed into the ownership of Lorenzo de' Medici ("the Magnificent") at his death. During his pontificate the first printing presses were founded in Rome, but Paul clashed with the humanist scholars of the ROMAN ACADEMY, led by Pomponio LETO. He temporarily closed the academy in 1468 and arrested its members; one of them, PLATINA, was tortured. At the root of these incidents was Paul's view that the study of the pagan writers of classical antiquity was an unsuitable activity, particularly on the part of members of the papal staff. In his opinion, such an activity would be likely to lead to paganism or heresy; in fact it led to his humanist opponents portraying him as a bigoted opponent of all learning.

**Paul III** (1468–1549) *Pope (1534–49)*
After enjoying the benefits of a humanist education in the circle of Lorenzo de' MEDICI, Alessandro Farnese became

through papal patronage cardinal deacon (1493), bishop of Parma (1509), and papal legate to the Lateran Council (1512). Despite fathering several illegitimate children, he gave up his mistress before his ordination (1519) and subsequently led an irreproachable private life, although as pope he indulged in nepotism. Paul III wished to unite Catholic Europe against Turks and Protestants, but could not persuade Emperor CHARLES V and FRANCIS I of France to settle their differences.

By supporting agriculture, the construction of fortifications, and major projects in Rome Paul III brought prosperity and security to his domains, but his attempts to assert his authority elsewhere provoked the Perugian SALT WAR. He supported reform within the Roman Church, appointed virtuous men as cardinals, favored such new religious orders as the JESUITS, and established the Holy Office of the Italian Inquisition (1542). He summoned the Council of TRENT, the first meeting (1545) of which marked the beginning of the COUNTER-REFORMATION and led to major administrative and spiritual reforms. A patron of the arts and learning, Paul III added to the Vatican Library, restored the university of Rome, completed the plans for the new St. Peter's, and persuaded MICHELANGELO to finish *The Last Judgment* in the SISTINE CHAPEL. In 1543 he commissioned a portrait from TITIAN and in 1546 the artist began a famous but unfinished portrait of the elderly Paul III with two of his "nephews," i.e. grandsons (Museo Nazionale, Naples). Cristóbal MORALES was one of those who benefited from Paul's discerning patronage of music.

## Paul IV (1476–1559) *Pope (1555–59)*

Giampietro Caraffa was born into an aristocratic Abruzzi family. Having served as papal nuncio in England and acted as adviser to the papacy on means of counteracting heresy, he was co-founder of the THEATINE ORDER (1524). As cardinal archbishop of Naples from 1536 he was an active ecclesiastical reformer whose reorganization of the Italian Inquisition made it a feared defender of Catholic orthodoxy. An austere and authoritarian pope, he curbed clerical abuses in Rome, disciplined erring clergy, and forced JEWS to live in a Roman ghetto and to wear badges. He joined France in a war against Spain, but Spain's victory compelled him to make peace with PHILIP II (1557). Paul's unwillingness to compromise led him to charge Cardinal POLE with heresy and facilitated the Protestant victory in England. In 1559 Paul issued the first INDEX LIBRORUM PROHIBITORUM.

## Paumann, Konrad (c. 1410–1473) *German composer and organist*

Paumann, who was born blind, was organist at the church of St. Sebald in his native Nuremberg from at least 1446; the next year he was appointed town organist. In 1450 he became court organist to Duke Albrecht III of Bavaria in Munich, a post he retained for the rest of his life. Famous throughout Germany as an organist, from 1450 Paumann traveled widely through France, Italy, Germany, and Austria, playing and examining instruments at the courts of dukes and princes. Few of Paumann's compositions survive, probably because he was unable to write them down; it is thought by some, however, that he was the inventor of German lute tablature. His treatise, *Fundamentum organisandi* (1452), gives examples of the ornamentation of chant, with keyboard arrangements of chants and secular melodies.

## Pavia, battle of (February 24, 1525)

A victory by the forces of Emperor CHARLES V, numbering some 23,000, against FRANCIS I of France. Francis had invaded Italy in 1524 and beseiged Pavia, near Milan, with 28,000 men, as a preliminary to attacking Milan itself. The imperial force's attempt to relieve the town resulted in a battle in which the French army was destroyed and the king captured. The battle established the Hapsburgs as the dominant power in Italy, and Charles was able to dictate the terms of Francis's release in the treaty of Madrid (1526); but France's power was not broken, and the threat of Hapsburg domination in Europe attracted allies to the French king. Pavia was also significant in conclusively demonstrating the superiority of FIREARMS over cavalry lances.

See also: ITALY, WARS OF

## Pazzi conspiracy (1478)

A plot by Francesco and Jacopo Pazzi, of the Florentine banking family who were longtime rivals to the MEDICI, to assassinate Lorenzo de' Medici and his brother Giuliano. Their fellow-conspirators included the archbishop of Pisa, and the plot had the tacit support of Pope Sixtus IV (whose nephew, Girolamo Riaro, was among the plotters) because of Lorenzo's efforts to thwart consolidation of papal rule over the Romagna. The Medici brothers were to be killed in the cathedral in Florence after Mass on Easter Day (April 26); in the event, Giuliano was killed, but Lorenzo escaped with only slight injuries. Simultaneous attempts to raise the populace against the Medici met with no support. Subsequent executions (including that of the archbishop of Pisa) and exiles broke the influence of the Pazzi family and strengthened the Medici hold on Florence.

**Further reading:** Lauro Martines, *April Blood: Florence and the Plot against the Medici* (London: Cape and New York: Oxford University Press, 2003).

## Peasants' Revolt (1524–26)

An abortive insurrection of German peasants. Although its leaders claimed many specific grievances, the underlying cause of the revolt was the deteriorating economic situation of the peasantry in the early 16th century. A mood of unrest was also stimulated by the spread of new religious ideas, including LUTHER's emphasis on "the liberty of Christian men." In the main statement of rebel claims, the 12 Articles of March 1525, the Swabian peasants demanded not only the abolition of serfdom and the remission of certain taxes, but also the freedom to elect their own pastors.

Disorganized rebellions began in the Black Forest area in the summer of 1524 and spread through most of south and east Germany during the following year. In April–May 1525 the rebels overthrew the civil and religious authorities in Mühlhausen, Thuringia, where they found an uncompromising leader in the radical preacher Thomas Müntzer (c. 1490–1525). In Müntzer's apocalyptic view, the destructive fury of the rebels was the instrument of God's judgment on a corrupt world. Although the rebels had originally found some support in the middle class and lesser nobility, this evaporated as chaos and destruction mounted. Luther, who had earlier shown some sympathy with peasant grievances, denounced the rebellion in his broadsheet *Against the Murdering and Thieving Hordes of Peasants* (1525). His call for Protestant rulers to unite and crush the rebels without mercy was answered when an alliance of princes defeated the poorly led peasant army at Frankenhausen (May 1525). The reprisals were general and bloody. Although a small force of rebels held out in the Austrian mountains until 1526, this was effectively the end of the revolt. Its main effect was to confirm the emerging power of the Protestant rulers of north and east Germany.

**Further reading:** James M. Stayer, *The German Peasants' War and Anabaptist Community of Goods* (Montreal and London: McGill-Queen's University Press, 1991).

## Pecock, Reginald (c. 1393–1461) *English churchman*
He was born in Wales, became a fellow of Oriel College, Oxford, and in 1431 was appointed master of Whittington College, London. He was created bishop of St. Asaph, in Wales (1444), and of Chichester (1450) and he was also made a privy counsellor. He wrote extensively and preached against the LOLLARDS; many of his works have not survived. The Lancastrian dukes of Gloucester and Suffolk were his patrons, and the hostility of the Yorkists resulted in his expulsion from the privy council and citation before the archbishop of Canterbury for denying the authority of the Apostles' Creed (1457). Despite a public recantation he had to resign his bishopric, and from 1459 he was confined in Thorney Abbey, near Cambridge, where he probably died. His writings are remarkable for their clarity, rationality, and critical power in presenting a theological argument, but read oddly on account of his having frequently to coin words or borrow foreign expressions to make up for the limitations of the unsophisticated vernacular in this period.

## Peele, George (c. 1558–c. 1597) *English poet and dramatist*
Little is known for certain of Peele's life except that he was at Oxford in the early 1570s and in 1579 was ejected from his father's house in Christ's Hospital, London, for dissipation. He wrote a number of plays and pageants in the 1580s and 1590s; these are notable principally for their highly accomplished lyrics. *The Arraignment of Paris* (1584), a pastoral comedy, was his first play, performed perhaps as early as 1581. It was followed by the chronicle play *Edward I* (1593), *The Battle of Alcazar* (1594), *The Old Wives Tale* (1595), and *The Love of King David and fair Bethsabe* (1599).

## Peffenhauser, Anton (Anton Pfeffenhauser, c. 1525–1603) *German armorer*
Peffenhauser came from an Augsburg family of armorers. As plate ARMOR was by then solely for ceremonial parade purposes rather than protection in battle, it was magnificently decorated; Peffenhauser's work was both extremely elaborate and beautifully crafted. His clients included German princes and members of the court of Philip II of Spain. The suit of armor made for King Sebastian of Portugal is one of the most ornate ever made. Examples of his work still survive, for instance in the Tower of London.

## Pellegrini, Pellegrino de See TIBALDI, PELLEGRINO

## Pérez, Antonio (c. 1540–1611) *Spanish courtier and writer*
Pérez was born in Madrid, the illegitimate son of an imperial secretary. Educated in Italy and Flanders, he himself rose to become the favorite minister of PHILIP II; in 1573 he was appointed head of the bureau through which Philip governed his domains. In 1578 Pérez engineered the assassination of one of Philip's enemies, an act that eventually brought about his downfall, when the king, to prevent his complicity in the murder becoming public knowledge, arranged for Pérez's imprisonment and torture by the Inquisition (1589). Pérez escaped, leaving behind in Spain a fine picture collection, which Philip promptly confiscated.

Received first at the Navarrese court at Pau, Pérez subsequently moved to Paris and then England. His *Relaciones* (1598) and epigrammatic letters effectively blackened the character and conduct of Philip while exonerating his own. Despite later efforts to win a pardon from Philip III, Pérez died in exile in Paris.

## Peri, Jacopo (1561–1633) *Italian composer and singer*
Peri was probably born in Rome and moved to Florence when he was young. He studied music with the organist and composer Cristofano Malvezzi and was organist at the Badia, Florence (1579–1606), singer at San Giovanni Battista (from 1586), and court musician to the Medicis (from 1588). After 1600 he was also associated with the court of Vicenzo Gonzaga at Mantua. Peri wrote a number of madrigals and incidental music for plays and court entertainments. However, he is best known, in collaboration

with the librettist Ottavio Rinuccini, for producing the first opera, *Dafne* (c. 1597). Although this work is now lost, it is known to have been performed at the Palazzo Pitti during the 1597 Florence carnival. Peri also collaborated with Rinuccini and Giulio CACCINI on *Euridice* (1600), the first opera that does survive. These early operas were probably inspired by Peri's association with Count Giovanni BARDI's Florentine Camerata and the efforts of some of its members to reproduce the classical Greek tragedies. The new monodic musical style associated with the Camerata, *stile recitativo*, was a type of singing that balanced speech and song without obscuring the text. A skillful singer, Peri also performed in these early operas.

**perspective** The graphical representation of three-dimensional objects on a two-dimensional surface, as developed chiefly during the Italian Renaissance. There are generally three recognized types of perspective: visual, linear, and aerial. Visual perspective—the simple overlapping of objects—was known to the ancient Greeks and Romans, but the laws governing the use of linear perspective, in which objects are arranged along parallel lines that apparently converge on a distant point (the "vanishing point") on the horizon line, were only discovered by BRUNELLESCHI in the 15th century. These properties were also explored by such notable artists as ALBERTI (who wrote an early treatise on the subject) UCCELLO, PIERO DELLA FRANCESCA, and MASACCIO. LEONARDO DA VINCI also used linear perspective in some of his greatest paintings, including his LAST SUPPER, in which the parallel lines converge on the vanishing point of Christ's head. Other leading artists, such as MANTEGNA, MELOZZO DA FORLÌ, BOTTICELLI, and Fra Filippo LIPPI refined the Italian idea of perspective, sometimes using more than one vanishing point in order to intensify the illusion of depth. Considerable use was also made of the third type of perspective, aerial perspective, in which distant colors are made paler and outlines of distant objects are less clearly defined. The perspective construction known by its Italian name *sotto*

**Perspective**  A woodcut by Albrecht Dürer showing how to make a perspective drawing of a lute. This appears in his *Underweysung der Messung* (1525), the first mathematical book to be published in German.

*in su* (below to above) situated the viewer's eye below the ground line of the pictorial space in an extreme form of foreshortening.

The status accorded to the theory of perspective in the Renaissance is tellingly indicated by the appearance of the personification of "Prospettiva," along with the traditional seven liberal arts, in the bronze reliefs made in 1493 by Antonio del POLLAIUOLO for the tomb of Pope Sixtus IV. During the 16th century treatises on the subject proliferated, not all of them written by practicing artists as mathematicians too became interested. Daniele BARBARO's *La Practica della perspettiva* (1568/69), which drew heavily on Piero della Francesca's *De prospettiva pingendi*, was one of the most widely read of these works. The mathematician Giovanni Battista Benedetti (1530–90) made an important contribution to understanding the geometrical aspects of the subject with his *De rationibus operationum perspectivae*, published as part of his *Diversarum speculationum physicarum et mathematicarum liber* (1585). It was even considered an appropriate field of study for princes: Salomon de CAUS, dedicating his *La Perspective* (1612) to Henry, Prince of Wales, mentions that he had given the prince lessons in perspective over the past two or three years.

See also: ANAMORPHOSIS

**Further reading:** Judith Veronica Field, *The Invention of Infinity: Mathematics and Art in the Renaissance* (Oxford, U.K.: Oxford University Press, 1997); John White, *The Birth and Rebirth of Pictorial Space* (London: Faber, 1957; 3rd ed. 1987).

**Perugia** A city in Umbria, central Italy. Perugia was originally an Umbrian foundation, then Etruscan, Roman, and Lombard. It was annexed by the papacy in 1303. During the 14th and 15th centuries Perugia was the scene of bitter internal conflicts from which the BAGLIONI FAMILY had emerged with the greatest success in the 15th century. Rome allowed Perugia considerable autonomy until 1540, when Pope PAUL III abolished Perugia's municipal powers after the city's unsuccessful revolt against papal authority in the SALT WAR.

During the 14th century the university of Perugia (founded 1308) was an important center for the study of Roman law under the direction of Bartolus of Sassoferrato. In the 15th century it was the focus of the Umbrian school of painting, with which such distinguished artists as PERUGINO, PINTURICCHIO, and the young RAPHAEL were associated. Notable Renaissance landmarks include the 13th-century city walls, the cathedral (1345–1430), the oratory of San Bernardino (1457–61) with its facade by AGOSTINO DI DUCCIO, and the Collegio del Cambio (1452–57) with frescoes by Perugino.

**Perugino, Pietro Vanucci** (c. 1445–1523) *Italian artist*
Born at Città della Pieve, near Perugia, Perugino possibly began his career under the tutelage of PIERO DELLA FRANCESCA, although little is known for certain about his early training. He then moved to Florence, where he probably worked in the workshop run by VERROCCHIO—possibly alongside Leonardo da Vinci—and became familiar with oil painting techniques. In 1472 he was listed as one of the painters of the company of St. Luke in Florence, and by 1481 he was well known enough to be employed by Pope Sixtus IV on the frescoes for the Sistine Chapel. Working there alongside ROSSELLI, GHIRLANDAIO, BOTTICELLI, and others, and with PINTURICCHIO as his assistant, Perugino executed such influential paintings as *Christ Delivering the Keys to St. Peter* (1482), upon which his reputation was established. Other works from this period included an important altarpiece, the *Crucifixion with Saints* (1481; National Gallery of Art, Washington), which is remarkable for its use of an extensive landscape as a setting. Such a sense of space, with the figures close to the front of the composition, is characteristic of much of Perugino's work.

During the 1490s Perugino, who was always prolific, produced further notable works, including the *Vision of St. Bernard* (1491–94; Alte Pinakothek, Munich), a *Pietà* (1494–95; Uffizi, Florence), and a *Madonna with Saints* (1491–92; Louvre, Paris). Between 1498 and 1500 Perugino undertook the decoration of the audience chamber of the Collegio del Cambio at Perugia, working alongside his pupil RAPHAEL; among the biblical, allegorical, and classical figures there is Perugino's famous self-portrait in a red cap. This shows the naturalism that appears in several of his portraits, for example that of Francesco delle Opere in the Uffizi, in contrast to the idealized and gracefully decorative figures of his religious and allegorical pictures. After Raphael's death, Perugino completed several of his unfinished paintings, although his own works after 1500 showed a marked decline in standard, becoming increasingly sentimental in tone. Among his later works is the fresco of the *Adoration of the Magi* (1504) in the church of Sta. Maria dei Bianchi in his native town. By 1506 his style had become outmoded and Perugino retired to Perugia, where he died.

**Further reading:** Joseph Antenucci Becherer *et al*, *Pietro Perugino, Master of the Italian Renaissance* (Milan, Italy: Rizzoli, 1997).

**Peruzzi, Baldassare (Tommaso)** (1481–1536) *Italian painter, architect, and stage designer*
Born in Siena, Peruzzi moved to Rome in 1503, where he came under the influence of Bramante and Raphael and contributed designs for St. Peter's. Peruzzi's first major architectural achievement was the Villa FARNESINA (1509–21) in Rome, a building in the High Renaissance style in which he also executed notable frescoes and experi-

mented with the use of false perspectives. Peruzzi continued in his attempts at illusionist architectural painting when he became (1520) one of the architects for St. Peter's; on this he worked until the Sack of Rome in 1527, once again producing designs that employed the use of multiple perspectives. After a period in Siena he returned to Rome in about 1532 to embark on his last major architectural undertaking, the Palazzo Massimo alle Colonne, which was completed in about 1535. With its dramatic portico and curved facade, this was one of the first mannerist buildings and is unusual in its decorations and irregular plan. Other works by Peruzzi include frescoes in the Cappella San Giovanni in Siena cathedral and stage designs, most of which are now lost.

## Peter Canisius, St. (Pieter Kanijs) (1521–1597) *Jesuit theologian*

Born in Nijmegen, the Netherlands, he studied in Cologne and Louvain, becoming a Jesuit in 1543. A key figure in the COUNTER-REFORMATION, he played a major role in the restoration of Catholicism in southern Germany. He visited in Austria, Bohemia, Poland, and Italy, and attended the Council of TRENT. In 1556 he became the Jesuit provincial of Germany, and then papal legate. He published theological and polemical work, and a popular catechism, *Summa doctrinae christianae* (1554). He was canonized in 1925.

## Peter Martyr (Pietro Martire d'Anghiera) (1459–1526) *Italian humanist*

Born in Angera, near Arona on Lake Maggiore, he used his humanist education to secure secretaryships in Rome. From there he accompanied the Castilian ambassador back to Spain (1487), where he spent the rest of his life in the service of the Spanish crown. He fought in the campaigns that resulted in the reconquest of Granada (1492), ran a school to introduce young courtiers to the elements of humanist learning, went on an embassy to Cairo (1501–02), and was increasingly employed in matters relating to administration of Spain's overseas empire, becoming an official historian to the council for the Indies in 1510.

Peter Martyr had taken a keen interest in the voyages of COLUMBUS and seems quickly to have grasped the significance of the great navigator's discoveries; in a letter dated 1494 he is apparently the first person to use the phrase "western hemisphere." His *Decades de orbe novo* appeared in three instalments: 1511, 1516, and (first complete edition) 1530. The work was the first full public chronicle of the voyages of discovery and was responsible for spreading knowledge of Spain's explorations throughout Europe; its accuracy and completeness appear even to have embarrassed the Spanish authorities, who would have preferred to keep some of the information secret. Peter Martyr was renowned for his pleasant Latin style,

which was particularly apparent in his history of the years 1488–1525, written in the form of letters and published as *Opus epistolarum* (1530).

## Peter Martyr (Pietro Martire Vermigli) (1500–1562) *Italian reformed theologian*

A native of Florence, Peter Martyr became a member of the Augustinian order and held several important offices before his evident sympathy for the evangelical movement led to accusations of heresy by the Inquisition. After sheltering for a time in Rome, in 1542 he left Italy and settled in Strasbourg, where Martin BUCER secured for him an appointment as professor of theology. In 1547 he was invited to England by Thomas CRANMER and appointed regius professor of divinity at Oxford, where he defended the reformed doctrine of the Eucharist in an important disputation (1549). Forced to leave England in 1553 by the accession of the Catholic Mary I, he first returned to Strasbourg and then moved to Zürich (1556), where he remained until his death. A prolific writer, Peter Martyr upheld a Zwinglian view of the sacraments (*see* ZWINGLI, ULRICH) but was temperamentally inclined to ecumenicism. His most popular work, the *Loci communes* (Commonplaces), was published posthumously in 1563.

During his first spell in Strasbourg Peter Martyr married as his first wife a former nun, Catherine Dammartin of Metz, who was posthumously involved in a bizarre episode of religious bigotry. She died in 1553 and was buried in Christ Church Cathedral, Oxford, near the tomb of St. Frideswide, the city's patron saint. In 1557, on Cardinal POLE's orders, her corpse was disinterred and thrown onto a dungheap in the stables of the dean of Christ Church. The following year, after Mary's death, Catherine's remains were mingled with the supposed relics of St. Frideswide and reinterred in the cathedral by the Calvinistic divine James Calfhill; the oration made over them concluded with the words *hic requiescit religio cum superstitione* (here lies religion with superstition).

## Peter of Alcántara, St. (Pedro Garavito) (1499–1562) *Spanish mystic, founder of the Discalced Franciscans*

He studied at Salamanca and became a Franciscan Observant friar (1515). Ordained priest, he preached in Estremadura, where he was elected provincial of his order in 1538. His desire for a yet more rigorous observance of the rule led him to establish a friary at Pedrosa (c. 1556), from which his movement for reform spread. The Discalced Franciscans went barefooted, consumed no meat or wine, and spent much time in solitude and contemplation. As confessor to St. TERESA OF ÁVILA he encouraged her to initiate reform among the Carmelites. He was the author of a popular treatise on prayer and meditation, *Tratado de la oración y meditación* (1556).

**Peter's Pence** An ecclesiastical tax, paid by English subjects to the papacy ("Peter") from the eighth century. The financial burden was reduced during the 12th century; subsequently, although the tax was charged on all but the poorest houses, the money demanded was small—a mere symbol of adherence to Rome. In 1534 HENRY VIII abolished the tax, thus demonstrating that the papacy could no longer make demands on English monarchs or subjects. A regulated collection for payment to Rome was revived in the late 19th century by the restored English Catholic hierarchy.

**Petrarch** (Francesco Petrarca) (1304–1374) *Italian poet and humanist*
Petrarch was born in Arezzo after his father, a notary, was exiled from Florence by the Black faction of the Guelph party. In 1311 the family settled in Provence, soon after the establishment of the papacy at AVIGNON. Apart from his travels, chiefly to Italy, Petrarch lived in Provence, mainly at his villa in Vaucluse, until 1353. Thereafter he lived in Italy under the protection of powerful rulers: in Milan, of the Visconti; in Venice, of the senate; and in Padua, of Francesco da Carrara, Il Vecchio. He first studied at Carpentras under Convenevole da Prato, a Tuscan; after reading law at Montpellier and Bologna, he returned to Avignon in 1326 and in 1330 took minor orders, which required a vow of celibacy but little else. Nevertheless he had two illegitimate children: Giovanni (born 1337) and Francesca (born 1343). The Colonna became the first of many patrons and this support, together with the benefices he received, enabled Petrarch to devote himself to writing and to cultivate classical scholarship, which was to assure him an unassailable reputation in the eyes of humanists of the 15th century.

On April 6, 1327 Petrarch had his first glimpse of Laura (Sonnet 211). (Historically little is known of her; she died in the plague of 1348.) His love for her is the central theme of 366 Italian poems collected in *Canzoniere*, a work that had a momentous effect on European poetry. Petrarch did not invent the SONNET that bears his name or introduce other innovations in the *Canzoniere*; rather, he brought a refinement and subtlety to the tradition of Provençal and Sicilian verse that led his successors to rank him even above DANTE and inspired a host of "Petrarchan" imitators, especially in the 16th century. (*See also:* CONCETTO; DOLCE STIL NUOVO; QUESTIONE DELLA LINGUA; STILNOVISMO.)

Except for an unfinished allegorical poem, *I trionfi* (written after 1350), Petrarch's other works and all of his prose were written in Latin. The epic *Africa* on Scipio Africanus, which he considered his greatest poetic achievement, and a collection of Roman biographies, *De viris illustribus*, were started before his coronation but never completed. In Rome on April 8, 1341 he was crowned poet laureate, the first modern poet so honored, after being examined by ROBERT OF ANJOU, King of Naples. *Secretum* (1342–43) reflects a tension discernible in other works between Petrarch's humanistic ideals and an otherworldly Augustinian tendency. *De vita solitaria* (1346) attempts to strike a balance and in several invectives, especially *Contra medicum*, Petrarch vigorously defended humanistic pursuits, but the medieval and Christian view dominates again, for example, in the later dialogues of *De remediis utriusque fortunae*. His history, *Rerum memorandum libri* (begun 1343), was left unfinished.

Petrarch continually worked to unearth and emend classical texts. By his early twenties he was at work on putting together a complete text of the historian LIVY, obtaining exemplars from as far away as Chartres cathedral. His researches turned up texts of the poet Propertius, CICERO's *Pro Archia*, and Seneca's tragedies, and the discovery of Cicero's letters to Atticus at Verona (1345) inspired the collection of his own *Epistolae familiares* and *seniles*. Around 45 surviving manuscripts have been identified as having belonged to Petrarch's personal collection; among them is his copy of Servius's commentary on Virgil, written about 1325 in Avignon, to which a frontispiece by Simone MARTINI was later (c. 1340) added (Bibliotheca Ambrosiana, Milan).

The republican cause of Cola di RIENZO at first attracted his enthusiastic encouragement, but he took no part in political activity after its defeat (1347), a change of heart also probably related to the deaths of Laura and his patron Cardinal Colonna in 1348. The final six years of his life were spent at Arquá, near Padua, on land presented to him by Francesco da Carrara.

The huge quantity of early modern translations and imitations of Petrarch, particularly of poems in the *Canzionere*, is an indication of the esteem in which he was held in the Renaissance. A selection from the *Canzionere* in a modern English translation by Anthony Mortimer, with facing Italian text, has been published in the Penguin Classics series (2003). Of Petrarch's other works, *De remediis utriusque fortunae* was translated into both Middle High German and Late Middle English, the latter edited by F. N. M. Diekstra and published with the Latin text under the title *A Dialogue between Reason and Adversity* (Assen, 1968). Thomas Twyne's version of the same work, *Phisicke against Fortune, as well Prosperous as Adverse,* 1579) was one of spate of 16th-century translations (Italian, German, Spanish, and French). A modern translation is *Petrarch's Remedies for Fortune Fair and Foul* by Conrad H. Bawski (Bloomington, Ind., 1991). Henry Parker, Lord Morley (1476–1556) translated *I trionfi* as the *Tryumphes of Fraunces Petrarcke* (c. 1555).

**Further reading:** Leonard W. Forster, *The Icy Fire: Five Studies in European Petrarchism* (Cambridge, U.K.: Cambridge University Press, 1969); Nicholas Mann, *Petrarch* (Oxford, U.K.: Oxford University Press, 1984); Anthony Mortimer, *Petrarch's Canzoniere in the English*

*Renaissance* (Bergamo, Italy: Minerva italica, 1975); Marjorie O'Rourke Boyle, *Petrarch's Genius: Pentimento and Prophecy* (Berkeley, Calif.: University of California Press, 1991); Charles E. Trinkaus, *The Poet as Philosopher: Petrarch and the Formation of Renaissance Consciousness* (New Haven, Conn.: Yale University Press, 1979).

**Petri, Olaus** (Olof Petersson) (1493–1552) and **Laurentius** (Lars Petersson) (1499–1573) *Swedish reformers*
The brothers were born at Örebro, and Olaus studied at Wittenberg (1516–18), where he was taught by LUTHER and Philipp MELANCHTHON. He returned to Sweden as a teacher, supported the breach with Rome in 1527, and helped to produce the first Swedish New Testament (1526) and liturgies (1529, 1531). He became a favorite of King Gustavus Vasa and was made chancellor (1531–33) but he fell out with the king and in 1540 was condemned to death for treason. This sentence was commuted to a fine. He later became pastor of the principal church (the Storkyrkan) in Stockholm.

Laurentius became the first Protestant archbishop of Uppsala in 1531. He and Olaus were chiefly responsible for the Swedish Bible (the Gustavus Vasa Bible) of 1541. Laurentius's book on church order (1571) helped to make the Swedish church less subject to the state than other Lutheran churches.

**Petrucci, Ottaviano** (1466–1539) *Italian music printer*
Petrucci was probably educated at the court of Guidobaldo I, Duke of Urbino. Around 1490 he went to Venice and in 1498 the doge granted him the exclusive right to print measured music. Until then only chant had been printed in Germany and Italy, but Petrucci's new method meant that polyphony could be printed from type; in his first publication, *Harmonice musices odhecaton A* (1501), a collection mainly of French chansons, the new process is used. This entailed three impressions—one of staves, one of notes, and one of the text. In 1507 Petrucci published lute tablature. In 1511 he returned to his native Fossombrone and continued to print music, obtaining a privilege from Pope Leo X to print mensural music and organ tablature in the Papal States. Back again in Venice from 1536 he printed Latin and Italian classical texts. Petrucci's success meant that the works of composers such as Josquin DES PRÉS and Jacob OBRECHT were widely disseminated in their day.

**Peurbach, Georg** (1423–1461) *Austrian mathematician and astronomer*
Educated in Vienna and Italy, Peurbach began his career as court astrologer to Ladislaus V of Hungary. He was appointed later to the chair of mathematics and astronomy at Vienna. Much of Peurbach's short life was devoted to the study of the *Almagest* (see PTOLEMAIC SYSTEM). With

Cardinal BESSARION he planned to obtain an accurate copy of the Greek text, but died before he could even begin the project. He did succeed in drafting the first six chapters of his *Epitoma in almagestum Ptolemei*, a work completed by his pupil REGIOMONTANUS, and managed to finish his *Theoricarum novarum planetarum*; this elementary survey of planetary astronomy served as a popular textbook throughout the 16th century. His *Tabulae eclypsium*, probably completed in 1459, were also used for many years; the first printed edition appeared in 1514 in Vienna.

**Peutinger, Konrad** (1465–1547) *German humanist scholar*
Between 1482 and 1488 Peutinger traveled in Italy, where he met POLITIAN and PICO DELLA MIRANDOLA, and became deeply imbued with the spirit of the Italian Renaissance. He remained in correspondence with his Italian teachers, published extracts from their lectures, and copied Pomponio Leto's ROMAN ACADEMY in the foundation of his Sodalitas Literaria Augustana in his native Augsburg. As town clerk of Augsburg (1497) Peutinger was on terms of friendship with Emperor Maximilian I. He published Roman inscriptions, and among his collection of antiquities was the map known as the *Tabula peutingeriana*, a 13th-century copy of the late Roman original depicting military roads, which he inherited (1508) from Konrad CELTIS.

**pharmacopoeia** A standard list of drugs with information on their preparation and use. In antiquity scholars, of whom Dioscorides is the best known, produced *materia medica* devoted almost exclusively to the medicinal properties of plants. The tradition persisted throughout the medieval period with Albucasis, a 10th-century Arab physician and other scholars, adding to the classical heritage. Albucasis's work, the *Liber servatoris*, first published in the West in 1471, became well known to Renaissance physicians. Thereafter the modern pharmacopoeias began to appear. Initially they began as local collections representing the medical wisdom of a particular area. The first appeared in Florence (1498) and was followed by similar items from Nuremberg (1546), Augsburg (1564), Cologne (1565), and London (1618). One feature of the pharmacopoeias was their growing willingness to accept the chemical remedies proposed by PARACELSUS and his followers. Thus, though absent from early issues of the Augsburg pharmacopoeia, they were introduced into the 1613 edition.

**Philip II** (1527–1598) *King of Spain (1556–98)*
He was born at Valladolid, the son of Emperor CHARLES V and Isabella of Portugal. Philip's first wife, Maria of Portugal, died in 1545. During his second marriage (1554–58), to MARY I of England, he was joint sovereign of her realms. His third marriage, to Elizabeth of Valois (1559–68), pro-

duced two daughters. His heir, the ineffectual Philip III (1578–1621), was the only surviving son of his fourth marriage (1570–80), to Anne of Austria.

Even without the Hapsburg possessions in Germany, which went to Charles's brother, FERDINAND I, Philip inherited vast territories. He ruled Spain, Milan, Naples and Sicily, the Netherlands, and the New World territories of the Caribbean, Mexico, and Peru. In 1580 he annexed Portugal.

As a young man Philip traveled in Italy, Germany, and the Netherlands, but as king he preferred the semi-seclusion of El ESCORIAL, the palace he had built near Madrid (1563–84). From his study he used viceroys to govern his provinces. His officials were obliged to submit regular and exhaustive reports and to obey his detailed instructions. Philip's ability to deal with up to 400 documents a day led one historian to describe him as the "arch bureaucrat."

Philip saw himself as a devout Catholic and a staunch opponent of both Turk and Protestant. At times he seemed to be trying to establish a Spanish Catholic hegemony over Europe. He and his allies checked the OTTOMAN TURKS at LEPANTO (1571), but he enjoyed less success against the Protestants. The destruction of the SPANISH ARMADA (1588) demonstrated his inability to subdue the English, and he failed to suppress the revolt of the NETHERLANDS. Yet, he was a leading force in the COUNTER-REFORMATION and did much to secure the Catholic faith in Italy, Spain, and Belgium.

Despite his reputation as the "most Catholic King," Philip was prepared to use the SPANISH INQUISITION not just as a weapon against heresy but also as an instrument of his royal power, as in the case of Antonio PÉREZ. He also did not hesitate to oppose papal policies that seemed hostile to the Hapsburg interests. An austere and dedicated ruler, Philip lived frugally, but he spent lavishly on the books and paintings he loved, continuing his father's patronage of TITIAN and Leone LEONI. Juan FERNÁNDEZ DE NAVARRETE (El Mudo) was the king's official painter from 1568, and after his death in 1579 Philip failed to take the opportunity to install El GRECO in the vacant post, turning instead to Federico ZUCCARO. When Zuccaro's work for the Escorial failed to please him, Philip sent for Pellegrino TIBALDI, who worked for him from 1588 to 1596. See Plate VII.

**Further reading:** Fernand Braudel, *The Mediterranean and the Mediterranean World in the Age of Philip II* (1949; 2 vols, London & New York: Harper & Row, 1972–73); Henry Kamen, *Philip II of Spain* (New Haven, Conn. and London: Yale University Press, 1997); Rosemarie Mulcahy, *Philip II of Spain, Patron of the Arts* (Dublin, Ireland: Four Courts Press, 2003).

**Philip Neri, St.** (1515–1595) *Italian religious, founder of the Oratorians*
The son of a lawyer in Florence, Neri abandoned an intended commercial career for a life of lay piety. After moving to Rome (1533), he tutored and lived an ascetic life. Neri then founded the Oratory in Rome, composed of like-minded laymen and clergy living together without vows for the purpose of prayer, fasting, and a more intense spiritual life. The Roman Oratory also organized help for Roman children, the sick, and pilgrims visiting the Holy City.

Neri's was but one of several confraternities organized during the Catholic Reformation of the early-to-mid-16th century, and it lies at the heart of that movement. The Oratory used traditional medieval mystical texts, and its themes were joy and love. Neri's prayer meetings were often accompanied by the music of his friend PALESTRINA, and this gave birth to the "oratorio." Neri finally took priestly vows in 1551. He led afternoon excursions to Roman churches, music sessions, and picnics, practices censored by Pope Paul IV because the pope had been warned that Neri had formed a heterodox sect. However, Pius IV restored Neri's reputation and he was allowed to build a new church on the site of Sta. Maria in Vallicella. In 1575 Gregory XIII recognized the Oratorians as a congregation. Neri's most famous follower was Cesare BARONIUS, and his advice was sought by such leading figures as IGNATIUS LOYOLA, CHARLES BORROMEO, and FRANCIS DE SALES. He has been called the "Apostle of Rome." He died in Rome and was canonized in 1622.

**Philip of Hesse** (Philip the Magnanimous) (1504–1567) *Landgrave of Hesse (1509–67)*
Philip assumed the government of Hesse at age 14 and quickly proved an able and energetic ruler. After prolonged study, he came down on the Lutheran side of the religious question in 1524 and a year later led the alliance of Lutheran princes that crushed the PEASANTS' REVOLT. In 1526–27 he created a state Lutheran Church in Hesse, converted monastic estates into hospitals for the insane (the first in recorded history), and established the first Protestant university at Marburg. Philip's ambitious strategy was to unite the Protestant estates of north and east Germany against any threat from the Catholic south and the Holy Roman Emperor CHARLES V. Aiming to end doctrinal divisions, he made an unsuccessful attempt to mediate between Lutherans and Zwinglians at the Colloquoy of MARBURG (1529). That same year Philip was the most prominent of those who rejected the decision of the second Diet of SPIRES, which revoked the toleration of Lutheranism (see PROTESTANTS). He was also the prime mover in the creation of the SCHMALKALDIC LEAGUE, a defensive alliance of Protestant rulers, in 1531. Although the league proved an effective block to Hapsburg aims in the 1530s, it fell into disunity after 1540, when Philip con-

tracted a marriage that was generally considered biga-
mous. Charles V seized his moment to attack in 1546 and
Philip had little choice but to capitulate, remaining a prisoner until 1555. He was restored to Hesse after the Peace
of AUGSBURG but never regained his position of regional
leadership. He was succeeded by his son, WILLIAM (IV) THE
WISE.

**Philips, Peter** (c. 1560–1628) *English composer and
organist*
Philips sang in the choir of St. Paul's Cathedral as a boy. In
1582 he fled to Rome because of his Catholicism, and was
received there at the ENGLISH COLLEGE, of which he became organist. In 1585 Philips entered the service of Lord
Thomas Paget, and in the next five years traveled through
Italy, Spain, and France, settling in Brussels in 1589. On
the death of Paget (1590) Philips moved to Antwerp. In
1593, returning from a visit to hear SWEELINCK play in
Amsterdam, he was arrested on suspicion of being party to
a plot to assassinate Queen Elizabeth. He was released,
and in 1597 entered the Brussels household of Archduke
Albert, where he remained until the archduke's death in
1621. Philips was probably the most famous English composer in northern Europe. His collections of madrigals
and motets were reprinted many times in Antwerp; these
are Roman in style, with Italianate word-painting and
polyphony. Philips also wrote much keyboard music,
some of which is preserved in the Fitzwilliam Virginal
Book. This belongs to the English tradition, the most inventive pieces being those based on madrigals and chansons.

**Philip the Bold** (Philippe le Hardi) (1342–1404) *Duke
of Burgundy (1363–1404) and count of Flanders
(1384–1404)*
The title of "the Bold" was given him for his conduct at
the battle of Poitiers (1356), after which he accompanied
his father, John II of France, into captivity in England.
When the duke of Burgundy died without an heir, his domains reverted to the French crown, and John II granted
the duchy to Philip in 1363. Philip's domains were further
enlarged through his marriage (1369) to Margaret, heiress
of Flanders, Artois, and Franche-Comté. During the minority (1380–88) of his nephew, Charles VI of France,
Philip was regent. When Charles went mad in 1392 Philip
resumed the regency and, despite the rival claim of the
duke of Orleans (Charles VI's brother), virtually ruled
France until his death. He fought England and the Netherlands, and tried to heal the GREAT SCHISM within the
Church. In 1383 Philip founded the Chartreuse de
Champmol, Dijon, to be the burial place of the Burgundian ducal dynasty and hired the sculptor Claus SLUTER to
adorn it.
**Further reading:** Richard Vaughan, *Philip the Bold:
The Formation of the Burgundian State* (London: Longman,

1962; new ed. Woodbridge, U.K.: Boydell & Brewer,
2002).

**Philip the Good** (Philippe le Bon) (1396–1467) *Duke of
Burgundy (1419–67)*
Philip succeeded his assassinated father, John the Fearless.
During his reign the Burgundian court was the most
splendid in Europe and his domains enjoyed their greatest
eminence and prosperity, but he failed to create a national
state out of his inheritance. The splendor and chivalric aspirations of his court were most clearly expressed in his
institution of the Order of the GOLDEN FLEECE (1429) to
honor his marriage to Isabella of Portugal. Jan van EYCK
was the most famous of the artists associated with Philip's
court, and the composer Gilles de BINCHOIS was for many
years attached to the ducal chapel. Philip was an ally of
England from 1420 to 1435, recognizing Henry VI of England as king of France, but subsequently he supported the
French king. When the dauphin, later Louis XI, fled
(1456) from his father, Philip gave him asylum, and later
recognized his accession (1461). Philip was much troubled by rebellions in the Netherlands, most notably in
Ghent (1432, 1448, 1453).
**Further reading:** Richard Vaughan, *Philip the Good:
The Apogee of Burgundy* (Harlow, U.K.: Longman, 1970;
new ed. Woodbridge, U.K.: Boydell & Brewer, 2002).

**philosophy** See ARISTOTELIANISM, RENAISSANCE; NATURAL
PHILOSOPHY; NEOPLATONISM, RENAISSANCE; PLATONISM, RE-
NAISSANCE

**physic gardens** See BOTANIC GARDENS

**Piagnoni** (Italian, "Snivellers") The derogatory name
given to the most devout supporters of SAVONAROLA. *See*
ARRABBIATI.

**Piarists** (Latin *Regulares pauperes Matris Dei scholarum
piarum*) A teaching order founded in Rome in 1602 by the
Spanish priest (later St) Joseph Calasanctius (1556–1648).
It grew from his work among the neglected and homeless
children of the city, for whom he had set up a free elementary school in 1597. In 1621 Pope Gregory XV recognized the Piarists as an order, whose members took a
vow to dedicate themselves to the teaching of children. It
subsequently flourished in many parts of southern Europe
and spread from Spain to Latin America.

**picaresque novel** In 16th- and 17th-century Spain, a
popular realistic episodic narrative in autobiographical
form relating the life of a rogue (*pícaro*) in a corrupt
world, with moral or religious reflections giving the final
views of the repentant sinner. LAZARILLO DE TORMES
(1554) established the model of lowlife first-person narrator, but typical picaresque novels are later in date, for ex-

ample GUZMÁN DE ALFARACHE (1599, 1604) by Mateo ALEMÁN, the earliest, and *El Buscón* (*The Rogue*; written 1603–08, published 1626) by Francisco Gómez de Quevedo y Villegas (1580–1645), perhaps the most brilliant and malicious of the type. Others are *La pícara Justina* (1605), with a female protagonist, *Marcos de Obregón* (1618), *Alonso, mozo de muchos amos* (*Alonso, Servant of Many Masters*; 1624–26) by Jerónimo Alcalá Yáñez, and *Estebanillo González* (1646), an apparently genuine autobiography set in the Thirty Years' War, after which the vogue for the picaresque died out. Two of CERVANTES's *Novelas ejemplares*, *Rinconete y Cortadillo* and *La ilustre fregona* (*The Illustrious Kitchenmaid*; both 1613) are shorter examples. The picaresque represents a reaction against idealized chivalric literature. There is no reason to discount the moral content of the novels, however, as merely a means to appease the censor.

A forerunner of the picaresque novel in England was *The Unfortunate Traveller* (1594) by Thomas NASHE.

**Piccinino, Niccolò** (1386–1444) *Italian condottiere*
Born near Perugia, Piccinino took up the profession of mercenary to escape from following his father's trade as a butcher. In 1424, on the death of his commander, Piccinino assumed leadership of the band, selling their services first to Florence and then (1426) to Duke Filippo Maria Visconti of Milan. His ambitions and his military prowess however soon alarmed his employer, who sought to win Francesco Sforza, at that time commander of Venice's forces and a personal enemy of Piccinino, over to his side. The uneasy relationship between the Milanese duke and the two condottieri on whom, in their different ways, he relied continued throughout the 1430s, but in 1443 Sforza resoundingly defeated Piccinino in battle. Piccinino died of dropsy the following year.

**Piccolomini, Aenea Silvio** See PIUS II

**Piccolpasso, Cipriano** See MAJOLICA

**Pico della Mirandola, Giovanni** (1463–1494) *Italian philosopher and humanist*
The nephew of Marsilio FICINO, he was born at Mirandola near Modena. He studied law at Bologna but found these studies unsatisfying and at age 18 traveled extensively in France and Italy, accumulating a large library and acquiring a wide range of knowledge sacred and profane, which his prodigious memory made readily accessible. In 1486 he arrived in Rome and proposed 900 theses or propositions, dealing, as he said, "de omni re scibili" (with everything knowable), inviting all comers to debate them with him and offering to pay their traveling expenses if poverty prevented their taking up the challenge. However, Pope Innocent VIII intervened by a Bull in 1487 to prevent the discussion. Thirteen of the theses were singled out and condemned as heretical. Pico withdrew to Florence and defended himself in an *Apology* (1489) but the attacks continued until Alexander VI absolved him of the taint of heresy and protected him from further persecution. Under the influence of SAVONAROLA, Pico adopted a life of austere piety and died of fever at age 31.

Like so many Renaissance philosophers Pico sought to reconcile theology and philosophy. He approached the problem through a variety of avenues, notably the study of the CABBALA, in which he believed he had found the quintessential truth that would harmonize the Scriptures and secular philosophy. A graphic description of the impact of Pico's personality on contemporaries comes from POLITIAN, who described him as "the Phoenix of the wits." Pico's biography was written by his nephew Giovanni and translated into English (c. 1510) by Sir Thomas More.

**Pienza** The model Renaissance city created out of the rebuilding of the village of Corsignano, near Siena, birthplace of Pope PIUS II. The pope initiated the project in 1459, with Bernardo ROSSELLINO as architect in charge. In 1462 the town's name was changed from Corsignano to Pienza by papal Bull. The main piazza was handsomely constructed in Florentine style and a grid of streets was also laid out, the earliest Renaissance example of symmetrical town planning. The deaths of both pope and architect in 1464 brought work at Pienza to an end before more than a few houses could be built. Nonetheless the Palazzo Piccolomini, begun in 1460, is considered to be Rossellino's masterpiece; other notable buildings from this period are the cathedral, the Palazzo Communale, and the Palazzo Vescovile.

**Pierino da Vinci** (c. 1530–c. 1554) *Italian sculptor and silversmith*
Born at Vinci, the nephew of LEONARDO DA VINCI, Pierino attended the academy of BANDINELLI in Florence from age 12 and was a pupil of Niccolò TRIBOLO. He then spent a year in Rome before moving to Pisa. His work illustrated the influence of MICHELANGELO on composition in sculpture; with this influence he combined an engaging tender quality typical of Tuscan art. A number of his sculptures can be seen in the palaces of Florence and there are also examples in European museums. He died of a fever in his mid-twenties.

**Pierino del Vaga** (Pietro Buonaccorsi) (c. 1501–1547) *Italian painter*
Born near Florence, he lost his indigent parents when young and was put under the protection of an artisan named Andrea de' Ceri. After studying under Ridolfo Ghirlandaio, he adopted the name of Pierino del Vaga and went to Rome. In Rome he worked under RAPHAEL with GIULIO ROMANO and others executing designs in the Vatican, and after Raphael's death he was among those em-

ployed to finish these works. According to VASARI he was very highly regarded as a designer. He fled to Genoa after the Sack of Rome (1527) and worked there on the decoration of the Palazzo Doria. Returning to Rome (1540) he was put in charge of decorative schemes in the Vatican and Castel San Angelo.

**Piero della Francesca** (1410/20–1492) *Italian painter*
Piero was born the son of a shoemaker at Borgo San Sepolcro, with which he maintained a lifelong connection and where he eventually died. In 1439 he is recorded as assisting DOMENICO VENEZIANO on the frescoes of Sant' Egidio in Florence (now destroyed). He returned to his birthplace in 1442, was made a councilor there, and in 1445 was commissioned to paint the *Madonna della Misericordia* polyptych (Palazzo Communale, Borgo San Sepolcro), which apparently shows the influence of MASACCIO. His *Baptism of Christ* (National Gallery, London) probably dates from this time or a little later, and he also worked in Ferrara for the Este family before going to Rimini to paint a fresco in the TEMPIO MALATESTIANA, showing Sigismondo MALATESTA kneeling before his patron saint (1451). There he met and was deeply influenced by ALBERTI, whose interest in perspective and architectural practice is reflected in many of Piero's later paintings; notable among these is the *Flagellation of Christ* (c. 1457; Palazzo Ducale, Urbino), with its enigmatic foreground figures and complex mathematical construction.

The work generally acclaimed as Piero's masterpiece is the fresco cycle of the *Legend of the True Cross* in the church of San Francesco at Arezzo (c. 1452–c. 1464). These frescoes show Piero's skill in handling a range of scenes and emotions from the pathos of the dying Adam to the drama of the discovery of the True Cross, from the motionless figures of the dream of Constantine to the hectic action of Heraclius's victory over Chosroes. During this period Piero also worked in the Vatican on frescoes (later painted over by Raphael) and painted the *Madonna del Parto* for the cemetery chapel of Monterchi (his mother's birthplace). In the late 1460s he painted the portraits in profile of Federico da Montefeltro of Urbino and his wife, Battista Sforza, in a diptych on the reverse of which are allegorical "triumphs" (Uffizi, Florence). For Borgo San Sepolcro in the same period he painted the powerful and moving *Resurrection* (Palazzo Communale), one of his finest works, and the now dismembered polyptych for the high altar of the church of Sant' Agostino (panels in Lisbon, Milan, London, and New York).

From about 1470 Piero's vigor as an artist began to decline, perhaps on account of failing eyesight. His latest commission from Federico da Montefeltro, an altarpiece depicting the duke adoring the Madonna and Child with saints and angels (Brera, Milan) shows his skill at depicting imposing and solemn figures in an opulent architectural setting, but increasingly Piero's later work relied upon the help of assistants. His interest in the mathematical aspects of aesthetic theory was set down in treatises from his last years. *De prospettiva pingendi*, dedicated to Federico da Montefeltro, was written sometime before 1482 and an autograph manuscript in Italian survives in Parma; a Latin version, with autograph notes by Piero, is in Milan. His other works, one in Italian on geometry and arithmetic and the other in Latin on the five regular solids, survive in Florence and the Vatican in autograph or partially autograph form.

**Further reading:** Marilyn Aronberg Lavin, *Piero della Francesca* (London: Phaidon, 2002); Kenneth Clark, *Piero della Francesca* (complete ed., Oxford, U.K.: Phaidon, 1981); Bruce Cole, *Piero della Francesca: Tradition and Innovation in Renaissance Art* (New York: Icon Editions, 1991); Carlo Ginzburg, *The Enigma of Piero: Piero della Francesca*, transl. Martin Ryle (London and New York: Routledge, 1985; new ed. 2002); Roberto Longhi, *Piero della Francesca*, transl. David Tabbat (Riverdale-on-Hudson, N.Y.: Sheep Meadow, 2002).

**Piero di Cosimo** (1462–c. 1521) *Italian artist*
A native of Florence, Piero was born Piero di Lorenzo but later assumed the Christian name of Cosimo ROSSELLI, of whom he was a pupil. In about 1481 he was assisting Rosselli with the frescoes in the Sistine Chapel. Piero's early conventional religious scenes show the influence of Botticelli and Ghirlandaio, but subsequent works owe more to the style of Signorelli and Leonardo da Vinci. Piero was renowned for his unconventional character, and his eccentricity expressed itself most clearly in the mythological paintings for which he is best known. Such works as *The Discovery of Honey* (c. 1500; Worcester, Mass.), *The Battle of the Centaurs and the Lapiths* (1486; National Gallery, London), and *A Forest Fire* (c. 1486; Ashmolean Museum, Oxford, U.K.) bear witness to Piero's taste for the bizarre and idiosyncratic with their depictions of distorted humans and wild animals. His masterpiece, *The Death of Procris* (c. 1490–1500; National Gallery, London), combines a sense of tenderness with elements of both mythology and natural detail. Other works include such portraits as the head-and-shoulders of Simonetta Vespucci (c. 1498; Musée Condé, Chantilly). Piero was a recluse in his later years, often painting purely for his own pleasure. His pupils included ANDREA DEL SARTO.

**Further reading:** Sharon Fermor, *Piero di Cosimo: Fiction, Invention and Fantasia* (London: Reaktion Books, 1993).

**pietà** A painted or sculpted representation of the Virgin Mary with the body of her son, Jesus Christ. The image, which extols Mary's emotional sacrifice, was popular in Catholic Europe during the Renaissance. The most famous *Pietà* is MICHELANGELO's marble sculpture in St. Peter's, Rome (1499): the sense of the Virgin's anguish is

**Pietà** Michelangelo's first (1498–99) *Pietà*, which stands in St. Peter's, Rome. When challenged over the youthfulness of the Virgin Mary, in whose arms lies the dead Christ, Michelangelo is said to have replied that chaste women retain their beauty longer than others.
*The Bridgeman Art Library*

enhanced as it shows her physically supporting the body, so mourning her dead son is a physical torment as well as a mental one. The English Catholic tradition of the pietà is best exemplified by the fine work on a church window at Long Melford, Suffolk.

**Pigafetta, Antonio** (c. 1491–c. 1526) *Italian historian*
Raised in Vicenza by his well-to-do family, Pigafetta is known as the official historian of MAGELLAN's circumnavigation of the world. His journal of the voyage, first published in 1525, is a vivid and detailed account, both flawed and colored by lengthy accounts of Pigafetta's personal feelings and experiences. The work is of great historical significance and presents particularly valuable accounts of the discovery and passage of the Magellan Straits. Pigafetta also claims to have tried to dissuade Magellan from the battle on Mactan in which Magellan was killed; Pigafetta himself was wounded. Pigafetta's reports of the voyage earned him a reception at the court of FRANCIS I of France in 1523, a meeting that inspired Francis to promote France's belated entry into the realm of exploration.

**pilgrimage and pilgrimage shrines** In Renaissance Europe the survival of the great pilgrimage shrines of the Middle Ages was closely connected with the degree to which the Roman Catholic Church was able to withstand criticism and reform. Relics (items believed to have been associated with Christ or the Holy Family, such as a splinter from the Cross or the girdle of the Virgin Mary, and the bodily remains of saints) were the focal points of the medieval pilgrimage shrines that had grown up all over Christendom. People traveled both locally and over considerable distances to venerate the relics, either as a means of eliciting supernatural assistance, or as an act of penitence, or to give thanks for benefits received. The Church linked the practice with the system of INDULGENCES, and when both indulgences and relics came under attack from the earliest reformers, pilgrimage too was in the firing line.

In the Middle Ages enterprising pilgrims could cover astonishing amounts of ground; even the Saracen capture of the Holy Land failed to deter the particularly pious and intrepid. As a young man in 1405–06 the life-long Burgundian traveler Ghillebert de LANNOY made the first of his three journeys to the Holy Land, visiting St. Catherine's monastery in Sinai, and in 1450 he went to Rome for the jubilee declared that year; his autobiographical *Voyaiges* contains the record of all the indulgences he earned by visiting the various holy sites. Chaucer's Wife of Bath had been to Jerusalem, Santiago de Compostela, and Rome, before heading for Canterbury, a record matched by her redoubtable real-life counterpart, Margery Kempe, who in the early 15th century notched up Jerusalem, Canterbury, Walsingham, Compostela, and Wilsnack and Aachen in Germany. Higher up the social scale, the pilgrimage of Isabella d'ESTE to visit the relics of St. Mary Magdalene at St.-Maximin-La-Ste.-Baume, Provence, was recorded by her secretary, Mario EQUICOLA in *De Isabella Estensis iter in Narbonensem Galliam* (c. 1517).

Authors of medieval Holy Land pilgrimage narratives include: the Tuscans Lionardo Frescobaldi, Giorgio Gucci, and Simone Sigoli who visited in 1384; several of the international band of pilgrims who took ship from Venice in 1458 (accounts by six of them were collected and edited by Rosamund Mitchell in *The Spring Voyage*, 1965); Friar Felix Fabri, who wrote up his 1480–83 pilgrimage for the benefit of his fellow friars in Germany; and the 67-year-old Milanese churchman Pietro Casola, who made his pilgrimage in 1494 and left one of the most detailed descriptions of the Holy Places. William Wey, one of the pilgrims in Mitchell's collection, made the pilgrimage to Santiago in addition to his two journeys to the east. The capture of the Holy Land by the Ottoman Turks and the onset of the Reformation meant that one of the last recorded Englishmen to make the pilgrimage to Jerusalem via Venice was Sir Richard Torkington in 1517. Rome remained a major draw for pilgrims, particularly in a so-called Holy Year, or jubilee, when the pope offered a special indulgence to those who visited the chief pilgrim churches of the city. Instituted in 1300, the jubilee was proclaimed every 25 years from 1470 onwards, and its benefits were later expanded to cover churches and local shrines worldwide.

In attacking relics, the early 16th-century critics of what they saw as blatant abuses and absurdities in the Church were attacking pilgrimage at its heart. ERASMUS wrote a satire on the subject, *A Pilgrimage for Religion's Sake* (1526). Among the reformers, LUTHER sarcastically remarked how strange it was that the bodies of no fewer than 18 apostles were buried in Germany when Christ had contented himself with a mere 12; he also specifically attacked pilgrimages in his *An den christlichen Adel deutscher Nation* (1520). CALVIN weighed in with a treatise on relics that ridiculed the proliferation of dubious items; if the Virgin had been a wet-nurse throughout her life she could scarcely have produced enough milk to fill all the phials of the purported substance venerated across Europe. Even supposing a particular relic to be genuine, it was Calvin's opinion that veneration of it distracted the laity from the true Christian path by seeming to offer a shortcut to holiness which could only properly be attained by following the Gospels. The general consensus among reformers was that the Church was at fault in both encouraging superstition among the gullible and then profiting financially from their credulity.

As the Reformation spread, pilgrimage shrines, along with other Catholic institutions in newly Protestant lands, became targets for ICONOCLASM. Calvinists were particularly zealous in their destruction of the material expressions of Roman Catholic piety—or, as they saw it, "popish superstition." In Britain, the DISSOLUTION OF THE MONASTERIES, was slightly different in that it was primarily instigated by the monarch for political ends and its purpose was plunder, not godliness, but the effect was the same: all the great pilgrimage shrines (Thomas à Becket's in Canterbury cathedral, of Our Lady at Walsingham, of the Holy Blood at Hailes Abbey) were destroyed along with the religious houses associated with them. Pilgrimages were specifically targeted in HENRY VIII's royal injunctions of 1538, with the clergy instructed to preach against "wandering to pilgrimages, offering of money, candles, or tapers to images or relics, or kissing or licking the same…".

In the Catholic lands the practice of pilgrimage continued and played its part in the growth of popular piety fostered by the Council of TRENT and the COUNTER-REFORMATION. However, even here new Catholic pilgrimage locations came gradually to focus less on bodily relics and more on miraculous happenings such as a vision (very often of the Virgin Mary) or the finding of a concealed holy statue or painting. For instance, a Spanish Dominican, Narciso Camós, visited the major Marian shrines of Catalonia in 1651–53, and noted that out of 182 shrines 117 had foundation legends involving the miraculous discovery of an image.

**Further reading:** James Bentley, *Restless Bones: The Story of Relics* (London: Constable, 1985); Wes Williams, *Pilgrimage and Narrative in the French Renaissance: The Undiscovered Country* (Oxford, U.K.: Clarendon Press and New York: Oxford University Press, 1998).

**Pilgrimage of Grace** (1536–37) A rebellion provoked by Henry VIII's DISSOLUTION OF THE MONASTERIES and the attempts of Thomas CROMWELL, the king's chief minister, to increase control of the north of England. The revolt was supported by the nobility of the northern counties. The most serious rising was led by the lawyer Robert Aske who seized York with 9,000 insurgents. The rebels' demands included the return of England to papal obedience and a parliament free from royal influence. The uprising was crushed in the early months of 1537 and around 250 men, including Aske, were subsequently executed.

**Further reading:** R. W. Hoyle, *The Pilgrimage of Grace and the Politics of the 1530s* (Oxford, U.K.: Oxford University Press, 2002); Geoffrey Moorhouse, *The Pilgrimage of Grace: The Rebellion That Shook Henry VIII's Throne* (London: Weidenfeld & Nicholson, 2003).

**Pilgrim Fathers** The usual modern name for the English founders of the colony of Plymouth, Massachusetts, who sailed for the New World in the *Mayflower* in September 1620. As members of the more strictly Calvinistic wing of the English Church (see PURITANS), they were opposed to current ecclesiastical and political trends in England, which they saw as tending toward "popery."

**Pilon, Germain** (1537–1590) *French sculptor*
Born in Paris, Pilon was the son of a sculptor and specialized in monumental tombs executed in an elongated mannerist style. He was heavily influenced by PRIMATICCIO, with whom he worked on a monument for Henry II (c. 1560; Louvre, Paris), as well as by Domenico del Barbiere and Pierre BONTEMPS. His later works were executed in the more fluid naturalistic manner of PONTORMO and MICHELANGELO, as seen in his finest piece, the tomb (1563–70) for Henry II and his wife Catherine de' Medici. As sculptor royal from 1568, Pilon also served in the post of controller of the mint and produced many notable portrait medals as well as busts of the French royal family. Other works include a bronze figure of René de Birague (1583–85; Louvre), a contribution to the tomb of Francis I at St.-Denis, an *Annunciation* in the Chapelle de la Vierge at Valmont, a statue of the Virgin in Notre-Dame-de-la-Couture, Le Mans (1571), and a bronze bust of Charles IX (Wallace Collection, London).

**Pinto, Fernão Mendes** (1510–1583) *Portuguese writer and adventurer*
Born near Coimbra, Pinto enjoyed a lifetime of varied and pioneering activity. He sailed for Goa in 1537, and there-

after lived as a soldier, pirate, and merchant, working from East Africa to Japan. In 21 years he was captured 13 times, enslaved 17 times, and shipwrecked on several occasions.

Pinto's voyages to Indo-China opened new trade markets for Europeans, although his greed caused the Chinese to torture him after he robbed a sacred tomb at Calempluy. After escaping from China, he became one of the first Europeans to visit Japan. He later met St. FRANCIS XAVIER and subsequently became a Jesuit novice. However, he was unsuited to the life of the Jesuits and returned to Portugal (1558), where he married and settled in Almada to compose his famous book. Pinto's life story, the *Peregrinação*, was not published until 1614. He had done so much that the book was considered a fantasy (the possible reason for the delay in publication), but it is now acknowledged as thorough and accurate, if somewhat embellished by fanciful first-person escapades. Whatever the doubts about its strict veracity, it was hugely popular and in the course of the 17th century was translated into Spanish, French, Dutch, English, and German.

## Pinturicchio, Bernardo, il (Bernardino di Betto) (c. 1454–1513) *Italian painter*
Pinturicchio was a native of Perugia. Among his earliest work are two panels in a series depicting the miracles of St. Bernardino of Siena (c. 1473; Galleria Nazionale dell' Umbria, Perugia). In the early 1480s Pinturicchio accompanied PERUGINO to Rome and collaborated with him on two frescoes in the Sistine Chapel, but he also became a member of the painters' guild in Perugia (1481) and executed work there, including a number of decorative *Madonnas* of a type for which he became famous.

He was also much in demand as a painter of frescoes, and examples of his work in this genre survive in several towns in Umbria. His first major independent commission however was in Rome: the cycle on St. Bernardino of Siena in the Bufalini chapel in Sta. Maria in Aracoeli (c. 1485–90). Cardinal Giuliano DELLA ROVERE (later Pope JULIUS II) commissioned him soon afterwards to decorate part of the Palazzo Colonna, and della Rovere patronage continued in commissions for decorations for chapels in Sta. Maria del Popolo, Rome. Pope Innocent VIII was another patron, but Pinturicchio's work for him on the Belvedere at the Vatican is almost entirely lost. Innocent VIII's successor, ALEXANDER VI, employed Pinturicchio on the great decorative scheme for the Borgia apartments in the Vatican (1492–95). Outside Rome, Pinturicchio worked in the 1490s on frescoes in the Eroli chapel in the cathedral at Spoleto (1497). One of his best paintings also dates from this period, the *Madonna and Saints* altarpiece for a Perugian church (1495; Galleria Nazionale dell' Umbria).

In the early 1500s Pinturicchio was at work in Siena. One of his most successful decorative schemes is the cycle of frescoes (1502–07) in the Piccolomini library there; 10 scenes from the life of Pope PIUS II are placed in attractive architectural settings and peopled with varied and graceful figures (see Plate XII). At about the same time he also painted frescoes in the chapel of St. John the Baptist in the cathedral and in about 1509 he decorated the Palazzo del Magnifico (his paintings from there are now dispersed, with a number in the Metropolitan Museum, New York). In 1507 he paid a final visit to Rome to decorate the choir of Sta. Maria del Popolo for his old patron, Julius II. He continued his prolific output right up to his death in Siena.

## Piombo, Sebastiano del See SEBASTIANO DEL PIOMBO

## Pirckheimer, Caritas (1467–1532) *German nun, humanist, letter writer, and poet*
Sister of the humanist Willibald PIRCKHEIMER, she was well educated and took religious vows as a Franciscan nun at age 16, entering a convent in Nuremberg. Here she became one of the outstanding female scholars of 16th-century Germany, thanks to her correspondence (in Latin) with intellectuals of the day who supported reform within the Church. In 1503, having been elevated to abbess, she wrote a history of her convent. As a staunch Roman Catholic, she held out against the tide of Protestantism sweeping across Germany, but her beleaguered order rapidly disintegrated. Her spiritual testimony of the battle to preserve her faith and religious practice is her *Denwürdigkeiten* (1524-28), which is also a valuable account of the intellectual debates concerning the Reformation in contemporary Nuremberg.

## Pirckheimer, Willibald (1470–1530) *German humanist*
Pirckheimer was born at Eichstätt into a wealthy Nuremberg commercial family with scholarly interests. His sister Caritas PIRCKHEIMER was also renowned for her learning. He was sent to Padua and Pavia to study law, but showed more interest in Greek, philosophy, the sciences, and other subjects. From his return in 1495 until 1523 he was a Nuremberg city councilor, and he led a contingent from Nuremberg in the Swiss war of 1499. This experience resulted in his vivid historial account of the war, *Bellum Helveticum*, not published until 1610.

A renowned scholar, Pirckheimer edited Greek and Latin works and made many translations from Greek into Latin and from Greek and Latin into German. At the request of Emperor Maximilian I, he translated the *Hieroglyphica* of the Egyptian Horapollo from Greek into Latin, with illustrations by his lifelong friend Albrecht DÜRER. This work introduced German scholars to EGYPTIAN STUDIES. In recognition of this and other imperial commissions, Pirckheimer was appointed imperial councilor. His wealth enabled him to build up one of the largest private libraries in Germany, to collect ancient coins, and to hold open house for other scholars. He corresponded with many other humanists, including CELTIS, ERASMUS, von HUTTEN, MELANCHTHON, and REUCHLIN.

**Pisa** A city state on the River Arno in Tuscany, central Italy. Pisa was a Roman colony from 180 BCE and by the late Middle Ages it was a major Tuscan city state, with a population of about 40,000 in 1300. Despite the destruction of its fleet by Genoa (1284), Pisa continued as a major port during the period of the Renaissance. Even after silting blocked the passage of laden galleys up the Arno, Pisa maintained its sea trade by using the nearby port of Livorno, which was linked to Pisa by a canal. Tanning, textiles, and the manufacture of soap and hats also brought prosperity to the city.

Political feuds weakened Pisa and brought about its annexation by Florence in 1406. During the wars of Italy Pisa declared its independence (1495), but it was soon reconquered by Florence (1509) after the Pisan war. Despite public works and the reopening of the university of Pisa (1543) by COSIMO I DE' MEDICI, Pisa suffered economic and cultural decline during the 16th century. After the PISANO family of sculptors in the 13th and early 14th centuries Pisa produced no great artists, but it was the birthplace of Galilei GALILEO, who studied and taught at the university of Pisa before going to Padua.

The romanesque Duomo and Gothic baptistery contain important sculptures by Niccolò and Giovanni Pisano, and the campanile ("Leaning Tower") is a famous landmark, completed in the mid-14th century. It stands 59 meters (194 ft) high and by the 1980s was some 5 meters (17 ft) out of the perpendicular. Work to prevent the tower from falling over was completed in 2001. VASARI designed the church of San Stefano dei Cavalieri (1565–69) and modernized the Palazzo dei Cavalieri for the Knights of St. Stephen, an order founded (1561) by Cosimo I. Several Renaissance *palazzi*, the university courtyard (1550), and the Logge di Banchi (1603–05) also survive, despite the damage suffered by Pisa in World War II, in which the Camposanto (cemetery) was wrecked, with the loss of many antique, medieval, and Renaissance monuments and frescoes. Its botanic garden (c. 1543) is considered to be the oldest in Europe.

**Further reading:** Nicholas Shrady, *Tilt: A Skewed History of the Tower of Pisa* (New York: Simon & Schuster, 2003).

**Pisa, Council of** (1409) A Church council convened at Pisa to deal with the situation arising from the GREAT SCHISM—the existence of two popes, at that time Gregory XII at Rome and Benedict XIII at Avignon. The council deposed both and elected Alexander V, who resided at Bologna, but the others refused to submit. It was not until the Council of CONSTANCE that Gregory abdicated, and the other claimants were deposed. It is consistent to regard Gregory as the only lawful pope till his abdication, and his

deposition by the prelates at Pisa as unlawful. The Pisan council's further resolution to reform ecclesiastical abuses was not effective.

**Pisanello** (**Antonio Pisano**) (c. 1395–c. 1455) *Italian painter and medalist*
After training in Verona, probably under Stefano da Zevio, Pisanello collaborated with GENTILE da Fabriano on frescoes at the doge's palace in Venice (1415–20) and at the Lateran Basilica in Rome (1431–32), all now destroyed. The only surviving fresco cycles by Pisanello are the *Annunciation* (1423–24; San Fermo, Verona) and the *St. George and the Princess* (c. 1437–38; Sta. Anastasia, Verona), in both of which fantasy and fact are combined in the International Gothic style favored by Gentile da Fabriano. Richness of detail characterizes other works such as the *Vision of St. Eustace* and the *Madonna with SS. Anthony and George* (both National Gallery, London), but Pisanello's best works, for which he was most celebrated in his day, were his portrait medals. Drawing upon similar works produced in antiquity, Pisanello made the finest and most delicate medals of his period for several of the contemporary ruling families, notably for ALFONSO I of Naples, for whom he executed a whole series (*see* NUMISMATICS). He also painted a number of striking portraits, including those of Margherita Gonzaga (c. 1438; Louvre, Paris) and Leonello d'Este (c. 1440; Accademia Carrara, Bergamo). Pisanello's keen sense of observation also shows itself in the Vallardi Codex (Louvre), an important collection of animal studies and miscellaneous sketches.

**Further reading:** Luke Syson and Dillian Gordon, *Pisanello: Painter to the Renaissance Court* (London: National Gallery, 2001).

**Pisano, Andrea** (**Andrea da Pontedera**) (c. 1290–c. 1348) *Italian sculptor*
Born in Pontedera and possibly trained in Pisa, Pisano is first recorded through his commission (1329) for a pair of bronze doors for the south portal of the baptistery of Florence cathedral. Consisting of 20 scenes from the life of St. John the Baptist and depictions of eight Virtues, the doors were decorated in the Italian Gothic style practiced by GIOTTO and influenced GHIBERTI's baptistery doors of 50 years later. In 1337 Pisano succeeded Giotto as the chief architect of the campanile of Florence cathedral and executed several marble panel reliefs; statues of David and Solomon there have also been attributed to him. In all these works, and the few others sometimes credited to him, Pisano demonstrates his artistic restraint and debt to Giotto. He died while master of works at Orvieto cathedral, and his son Nino (died ?1368), noted by his contemporaries as a goldsmith, architect, and sculptor, succeeded him there. Nino produced a number of freestanding life-size marble sculptures of sacred subjects.

**Further reading:** Anita F. Moskowitz, *The Sculpture of Andrea and Nino Pisano* (Cambridge, U.K.: Cambridge University Press, 1986).

**Pisano, Giovanni** (c. 1250–c. 1314) *Italian sculptor and architect*
The son of Niccolò PISANO, Giovanni was born in Pisa and was trained by his father, whom he assisted from the mid-1260s, first with the Sienese pulpit and later with the great fountain in Perugia. Before 1284 Giovanni produced a series of monumental figures of saints and prophets for the exterior of the Pisan baptistery, and after this date he worked in Siena on the lower part of the facade of the cathedral. This great Gothic sculptural scheme was designed to glorify the Virgin Mary.

Giovanni also contributed to the cathedral of San Cerbone at Massa Marittima (1287) and carved pulpits for the church of Sant' Andrea at Pistoia (1301) and Pisa cathedral (1302–10). He executed several sculptures on the Madonna and Child theme, among them a small ivory in the sacristy of Pisa cathedral, a majestic standing Madonna in the ARENA CHAPEL, Padua (c. 1305), and the *Madonna della Cintola* (c. 1312) in Prato cathedral. His last known commission (1313) was for the tomb of Margaret of Brabant (died 1311), wife of Emperor Henry VII, in the former church of San Francesco, Genoa; a portrait head from this tomb survives in the Palazzo Bianco, Genoa. Widely acknowledged as the greatest Italian sculptor of his day and occupying a position comparable to that of GIOTTO in painting, Giovanni Pisano exercised a profound influence on later TRECENTO artists in his integration of classical and Gothic elements.

**Pisano, Niccolò** (c. 1220–c. 1278) *Italian sculptor*
He began his career in Apulia, at a time when Emperor Frederick II was encouraging artists there to take a renewed interest in classical motifs, and he then moved to Pisa, probably shortly before 1250. His first known work there was the hexagonal pulpit in the baptistery (c. 1260), on which the relief scenes from the life of Christ are composed along the lines of the scenes on the antique sarcophagi in the Camposanto. Between 1265 and 1268 Niccolò produced an even more magnificent octagonal pulpit for Siena cathedral, although in this work the influence of French Gothic predominates over the classicizing impulse in his Pisan sculptures. His last major commission, in which he was assisted, as on the Sienese pulpit, by his son Giovanni PISANO, was the fountain (c. 1275) for the former Piazza dei Priori (now Piazza IV Novembre), Perugia. Besides Giovanni, Niccolò's followers included Fra Guglielmo da Pisa (1256–c. 1312), who carved the pulpit of San Giovanni Fuorcivitas, Pistoia, and the Arca di San Domenico, Bologna, and Arnolfo di Cambio (died c. 1302), who was an architect as well as a sculptor, working in Florence and Rome.

**Pistorius, Johann, the Younger** (1546–1608) *German physician and theologian*
Pistorius was born at Nidda, the son of Johann Pistorius the Elder (1503–83), one of the first Catholics to convert to Lutheranism. He studied theology, law, and medicine at Marburg and Wittenberg and in 1575 became court physician to Charles II, margrave of Baden-Durlach. He became disillusioned with Luther's doctrines and after a brief period as a Calvinist he returned to the Catholic faith. He published polemical religious works in Latin and in German, edited collections of the works of early German and Polish historians, and produced a volume of cabbalistic texts and studies, *Artis cabalistica* (1587).

**Pius II** (1405–1464) *Pope (1458–64); Italian humanist and historian*
Aenea Silvio Piccolomini was born at Corsignano, near Siena, the eldest of 18 children of an impoverished aristocratic family. His extensive knowledge of classical literature came largely from private study, though he was for a time a pupil of Francesco FILELFO in Florence. He attended the Council of BASLE (1432) with the cardinal of Fermo, then traveled in Germany and to Scotland. He was crowned poet laureate by Emperor FREDERICK III (1442) and worked in the emperor's chancery for the following 13 years, though not exclusively as Eugenius IV made him a papal secretary in 1445, overlooking his previous service to the antipope Felix V. His rise through the ecclesiastical hierarchy was steady; he became bishop of Trieste (1447) and of Siena (1450) and was made cardinal in 1456. He was elected pope with the help of Rodrigo Borgia, later Pope ALEXANDER VI, and assumed the name Pius in reference to Virgil's hero "pius Aeneas." At the Congress of Mantua (1459) he was active in organizing a crusade against the Turks to avenge the fall of Constantinople (1453). He died at Ancona, where he had gone to assemble his fleet for this expedition.

Pius wrote a history of the Council of Basle and an autobiography (*Commentarii*), as well as more secular works. The *Commentarii* gives a frank picture of his attitudes and motivations. His letters, a precious source of information, are models of humanistic Latin. His career is the subject of frescoes by PINTURICCHIO in the Piccolomini library of Siena cathedral (see Plate XII). Pius was also important for the stimulus he gave to classical studies in northern Europe; in 1459 he signed the foundation charter for the university of Basle, which thus began its existence as a center of humanistic learning. He also encouraged humanists to join the college of papal secretaries—PLATINA was one employed in this way—but he demanded rather stricter standards of Christian conduct than his predecessor, NICHOLAS V. Pius II's works were published in folio at Basle in 1551, and his other lasting monument was his model city of PIENZA. The translation of the *Commentarii* into English by Florence A. Gragg was published in an abridged version under the title *Memoirs of a Renaissance Pope: The Commentaries of Pius II* (1960).

**Further reading:** Zweder von Martels and Arjo Vanderjagt (eds), *Pius II: Selected Studies on Aeneas Silvius Piccolomini* (Leyden, Netherlands: Brill, 2003); Rosamund J. Mitchell, *The Laurels and the Tiara: Pope Pius II, 1458–1464* (London: Harvill, 1962).

## Pius IV (1499–1565) *Pope (1559–65)*

Born Giovanni Angelo de' Medici in Milan, he was educated at Pavia and Bologna where he studied philosophy and medicine and took a doctorate in law. He became an archbishop in 1545 and cardinal in 1549. After being elected pope in 1559 he reconvened the Council of TRENT for its final and most important session (1562–63). Pius produced a new Index of Forbidden Books (1564) and prepared a new edition of the Roman Catechism. He was a patron of MICHELANGELO and oversaw the erection of many public buildings.

## Pius V, St. (1504–1572) *Pope (1566–72)*

Born Michele Ghislieri near Alessandria, Italy, he became a Dominican and in 1528 was ordained priest. He became bishop of Nepi and Sutri in 1556 and a cardinal in 1557. As pope he was a resolute reformer, implementing the recommendations of the Council of TRENT, revising the liturgy, and reorganizing the papal household. Pius instigated the Christian alliance that in 1571 won the decisive naval battle against the Turks at LEPANTO, and he also successfully halted the advance of the Reformation in Italy and Spain, but had little success in England. He excommunicated ELIZABETH I (1570), forbidding English Catholics to give her their allegiance, which caused widespread anti-Catholic feeling there (*see* RECUSANCY). He was canonized in 1712.

## Pizarro, Francisco (c. 1471–1541) *Spanish soldier, conqueror of Peru*

Born in Trujillo, Estremadura, Pizarro was illegitimate and illiterate. He went to Darien in 1509 and accompanied BALBOA on his expedition to the Pacific (1513) before settling in Panama. In 1522 Pizarro and Diego de Almagro were commissioned to claim Peru for Spain. Their first expedition (1524–25) was abortive, but the following year, sailing down the west coast of South America, they reached the Isla del Gallo. Pizarro then continued to the Peruvian coast with about 12 men. Returning to Spain (1528), Pizarro appealed to the emperor, who appointed him governor of Peru (New Castile) in 1529. In 1531 he marched with 183 men, including his two brothers, to Cajamarca, where he seized the Inca Atahuallpa, extorting a huge ransom. Reinforced by Almagro, Pizarro murdered Atahuallpa in 1533 and entered the Inca capital at Cuzco. He founded Lima in 1535, but soon afterwards territorial disputes broke out between Pizarro and Almagro. The lat-

ter was defeated and executed (1538), but his supporters then conspired and assassinated Pizarro at Lima.

## plague

An infectious disease transmitted by rat fleas, especially in overcrowded or insanitary conditions. In 1348 three galleys brought bubonic plague to Genoa from the East. The Black Death, as it became known, spread with great rapidity and fearsome mortality throughout Europe. By 1350 the first wave of the disease had worked itself out, killing about a third of Europe's population—some 25 million deaths, including one and a half million in England alone. At frequent intervals over the following three centuries the plague returned, bringing with it disruption and death. At Venice, for example, some 20 epidemics of bubonic plague are recorded between 1348 and 1630. The impact on society was considerable. The decline in the market and the labor shortage resulting from the Black Death were largely to blame for the economic depression of the late 14th century. The safest strategy, open only to the rich and powerful, was flight and isolation. Of those who stayed in the towns and were forced back on their own or other's remedies, many died. In the face of panic and desperation there was little room for any medical orthodoxy to emerge. While a few physicians, such as FRACASTORO, began to suspect that the disease spread by contagion, the majority attributed the epidemic outbreaks to astrological, theological, or meteorological conditions, against which they were helpless.

**See also:** MEDICINE

**Further reading:** Paul Slack, *The Impact of Plague in Tudor and Stuart England* (London and Boston, Mass.: Routledge & Kegan Paul, 1985; repr. Oxford, U.K.: Clarendon Press, 1990).

## Plantin press

The printing house founded in Antwerp by Christophe Plantin (c. 1520–89). Plantin was a Frenchman who had worked in Caen and Paris before settling in Antwerp as a bookbinder in 1548. The first book from his press, Giovanni Bruto's *La institutione di una fanciulla nata nobilmente* (1555) has a parallel text in Italian and French. It was followed by about 1500 others, including liturgical, scientific, and medical books, classics, dictionaries, Waghenaer's navigational guide *Spieghel der Zeevaerdt* (1584–85) (*see* WAGGONERS), and the Antwerp Polyglot Bible or *Biblio regia* (1568–73) subsidized by Philip II of Spain and edited by ARIAS MONTANO. By 1576 Plantin had 16 presses at work. He also published books produced by other printers. His illustrated books, among them many HERBALS, used the products of a team of draftsmen led by Pieter van der Borcht, reproduced at first in woodcuts and later in engravings. The Plantin stock of pictures was used by other printers too; for example, the second edition of GERARD's *Herball* (1633) drew its illustrations from this source, though even the first (1597) had a dragon tree based on a Plantin orginal. Type was also carefully chosen and arranged, with Robert GRANJON among the designers commissioned.

Plantin was driven from Antwerp by the Spanish attack of 1576. He remained in exile until 1585, leaving the press in the hands of his sons-in-law Francis Raphelengius (who in 1585 succeeded Plantin as printer to the university of Leyden) and Jan Moretus, whose descendants kept the press going until 1876. In that year the city of Antwerp bought the archives, library, presses, and other material to found the Musée Plantin–Moretus, which encapsulates the history of printing.

**Further reading:** Colin Clair, *Christopher Plantin* (London: Cassell, 1960); Léon Voet, *The Golden Compasses: A History and Evaluation of the Printing and Publishing Activities of the Officina Plantiniana*, 2 vols (Amsterdam, Netherlands: Van Gendt, and New York: Abner Schram, 1969–72).

## Plat, Hugh (Hugh Platt) (1552–c. 1611) *English horticulturist*

Plat was a renowned gardener who devoted much of his time to writing. His *Jewell House of Art and Nature* (1594) contained many "rare and profitable inventions," including how to pump water into kitchens, preserve food, manure pastures, and make garments "sufficient against all rainie weather." *Delightes for Ladies* (1600) was a popular collection of herbal recipes and helpful tips for householders. Plat was the first to suggest means of protecting and cultivating exotic plants. For his experimental efforts, all aimed at increasing agricultural productivity, he was knighted (1605) by James I.

## plateresque

A style of architecture and ornament in Spain during the early Renaissance. Meaning "silversmith-like," the word *plateresco* was apparently first used in an architectural context in reference to the facade of León cathedral by the humanist writer Cristóbal de Villalón in 1539. The salient feature of plateresque decoration is the richness of its detail, a feature that it shared with much contemporary metalwork. Heraldic shields, pilasters, roundels, and trellis patterns were carved, usually in low relief, on surfaces with little reference to an overall structural unity, except that imposed by the presence of strong horizontal lines, as on the portal of the university library at Salamanca.

The plateresque is generally regarded as being divided into two phases. The first, often known as Gothic-plateresque, was in the ascendant in the last two decades of the 15th century and the first two of the 16th; it combined traditional Spanish features with others imported from the Netherlands and Germany. Exponents included Juan GUAS and Enrique de EGAS. The Capilla del Condestable (1482–94) at Burgos, designed by Simón de COLONIA (whose family, as the name suggests, came from Cologne), is a prime example of the early plateresque style. Another name for this style is Isabelline, in acknowledgment of the impetus given to its development by the patronage of Queen Isabella (*see* FERDINAND II AND ISABELLA I).

The second phase, often called Renaissance-plateresque, entailed the rejection of the more ornate features of the first phase as the influence of the Italian High Renaissance reached Spain. The architectural theorist Diego de Sagredo encouraged the change of emphasis with his publication of *Medidas del Romano* (1526), which promoted Vitruvian canons. Examples of this phase include the facades of the universities of Salamanca (completed 1529) and Alcalá de Henares (1541–53), Diego de RIAÑO's Ayuntiamento at Seville, and the chancel screen of Toledo cathedral (1548) by Francisco Villalpando. The plateresque style was also utilized in Mexico and other Spanish possessions in the New World, for example, in the facade of San Domingo cathedral and in the ruined cathedral of Antigua, Guatemala (both 1540s).

## Platina, Il (Bartolommeo Sacchi) (1421–1481) *Italian humanist and biographer*

Called after his birthplace, Platina, near Cremona, he studied at Mantua after a military career, then moved to Florence to perfect his knowledge of Greek. During the five years he spent at Florence he formed a close friendship with the Medici. In 1467 he became secretary to Cardinal Gonzaga. As a leading member of the ROMAN ACADEMY he was closely associated with its founder Pomponius LETO. When Pope Paul II suppressed the academy in 1468, Platina, along with other leading figures, was imprisoned and tortured. After his release he became Vatican librarian (1475–81) under Sixtus IV. His works include biographical studies of the popes and ethical treatises on true and false goodness and on true nobility. The first anniversary of Platina's death was commemorated with ceremonies described by Jacopo Volterrano.

## Plato (c. 427–348 BCE) *Greek philosopher*

From about 407 he was the pupil of Socrates in Athens, and after Socrates' death he traveled abroad before returning to Athens to found his Academy. This was the model for the PLATONIC ACADEMY in Quattrocento Florence, where discussion was based upon the understanding of the methods of Plato's school obtained from his dialogues. Greek manuscripts of these began to reach the West from Constantinople around 1400, and Marsilio FICINO translated the entire corpus into Latin. Among the dialogues were many that raised matters of key interest to later philosophers: for example, the *Theaetetus* on the nature of knowledge, the *Timaeus* on the nature and origin of the universe, the *Phaedo* on Socrates' views on death and the immortality of the soul, the *Symposium* on the nature of love, the *Phaedrus* on true rhetoric, the *Meno* on the teaching of virtue, and the *Laws* on legislation for a new state.

The Platonic theory of Ideas, developed in the *Republic*, deals with the relationships between the unseen eternal world and the phenomenal world; the supreme Idea of the Good was particularly assimilable by Christian philosophers.

In the understanding of medieval and Renaissance scholars, Platonism often merged with Neoplatonism, the elaboration of Platonic thought in the later antique world by PLOTINUS and his followers (*see* NEOPLATONISM, RENAISSANCE; PLATONISM, RENAISSANCE).

**Platonic Academy** An informal body of scholars and humanists first assembled in Florence around Cosimo de' MEDICI after the Council of Florence (1439). The main influence was Gemistos PLETHON, who had come to Florence to represent the Eastern Orthodox Church at that council. Subsequent leading members of the academy were Marsilio FICINO, who translated the dialogues of Plato, POLITIAN, Cristoforo LANDINO, and PICO DELLA MIRANDOLA. ALBERTI, MICHELANGELO, and Luigi PULCI were all at one time or another members of this or successor associations (*see* ORTI ORICELLARI). The main preoccupation of the 15th-century academicians was the reconciliation of Christian and pagan philosophy; the method used was mysticism rather than exact reasoning, and the allegorical approach derived more from medieval exegesis than from the approaches that were being developed for contemporary literary criticism.

**Platonism, Renaissance** To the Middle Ages the main classical philosopher was Aristotle. His works circulated in Latin translations, many of them translated from Arabic versions. The late 13th-century *Summa Theologica* of Thomas Aquinas achieved a fusion of Christian and Aristotelian ideas that became the basis for subsequent theological training. The emphasis was on logic and on an appeal to the subtleties of the intellect. As part of the general reaction against medieval ideas, the Renaissance inevitably turned to PLATO as a challenge to the dominance of Aristotle (*see* ARISTOTELIANISM, RENAISSANCE).

There were two important problems associated with the study of Plato in the Renaissance. The earliest Platonists were Greeks from Constantinople, whose adherence to the Orthodox Church (in schism since the 11th century) made their ideas suspect to traditionalists in Western Christendom. Furthermore it was difficult to make direct contact with Platonic texts because the founder of Platonic studies in Italy, Gemistus PLETHON, was himself strongly influenced by Neoplatonic ideas. The mysticism inherent in some, though not the most characteristic, parts of Platonic philosophy appealed to Renaissance thinkers. They saw it as the major difference from the rationalism of Aristotle and it seemed to offer a greater possibility of reconciliation with Christianity. Moreover it made a powerful appeal to the emotions.

The influence of Plethon can be seen in his disciples FICINO and PICO DELLA MIRANDOLA. Their approach was uncritical and eclectic; their admiration for Plethon blinded them to the many absurdities and inconsistencies in his system. They failed to see that Platonic theology was only a background to Plato's ethical, political, and educational theories, and they were thus prevented from using these theories as a starting point for their own speculations. The allegorizing which was so characteristic of Byzantine Platonism struck a responsive chord in men who were already familiar with the method as used by Christian exegetes.

The contribution of the Renaissance to the serious study of Plato is now only of historical importance. The willingness of scholars to accept the amalgam of Near Eastern theosophy and Neoplatonic mysticism as authentic Platonism made it almost impossible to develop any serious discussion of Plato's ideas (*see* NEOPLATONISM, RENAISSANCE). The most lasting contribution the Renaissance Platonists made was in the sphere of translation. Even after the ALDINE PRESS's publication of Marcus Musurus's *editio princeps* of Plato (1513), the Latin translation (1482) made by Ficino in 1477 continued to circulate, and the availability of a complete Plato in the original and in accurate translation increased the accessibility of authentic texts.

**Further reading:** James Hankins, *Plato in the Italian Renaissance*, 2 vols (Leyden, Netherlands: Brill, 1990; 3rd ed. 1994); Robert Merrill, *Platonism in French Renaissance Poetry* (New York: New York University Press, 1957); Christine Raffini, *Marsilio Ficino, Pietro Bembo, Baldassare Castiglione: Philosophical, Aesthetic, and Political Approaches in Renaissance Platonism* (New York: Peter Lang, 1998).

**Platter family** Two generations of a Swiss family from Basle, comprising Thomas Platter the Elder (1499–1582) and his physician sons, Felix (1536–1614) and Thomas the Younger (1574–1628). They are remarkable for their autobiographical records, starting with the elder Thomas's memoir (*Lebensbeschreibung*), written for Felix's benefit. It describes his impoverished youth and early struggles before he became a printer (1536–44) and finally headmaster (1544–78) of the Latin school in Basle, and gives an interesting account of day-to-day life during the Reformation there. Felix achieved his father's thwarted ambition to study medicine, and kept journal notes covering his boyhood and his student life at Montpellier, though he did not write up his own *Lebensbeschreibung* until 1609. Settling (1557) in Basle to practice medicine, he wrote detailed records of outbreaks of plague there to 1611. Felix encouraged his half-brother, the younger Thomas, to keep a journal of his travels (1595–1600) after he had completed his medical studies, and this lively account of experiences in Spain, France, Flanders, and

England contains much interesting detail, including seeing Shakespeare's *Julius Caesar* at the Globe in London on September 21, 1599.

**Plautus, Titus Maccius** (c. 254–184 BCE) *Roman comic playwright*
Twenty of his plays, which are largely based on earlier Greek comedies, have survived. They have a background of Roman middle-class life and generally feature a number of stock characters: the young lovers (whose romance is complicated by the girl's being a slave until it is discovered that she is really of free birth), a devious slave who promotes their interests, a braggart soldier, a miserly or lecherous old man, and a grasping pimp. Eight of Plautus's plays were known in the 14th century, and Nicholas CUSANUS found a manuscript with 12 more in Cologne in 1425. The staging of Plautine comedies began in earnest in Ferrara, in 1486, under the patronage of the Este family. Meanwhile translations and imitations of Plautus began to proliferate, and, with TERENCE, he can be accounted the founder of the modern tradition of COMEDY.

**Pléiade** A group of seven French poets of the 16th century. They were Pierre RONSARD, Joachim DU BELLAY, Rémy BELLEAU, Jean-Antoine de BAÏF, Pontus de TYARD, Étienne JODELLE, and either Peletier du Mans or Jean DAURAT (according to some scholars Daurat became a member of the Pléiade after the death of Peletier; others reject his membership altogether). The name was originally applied to seven tragic poets of the third century BCE and is ultimately derived from the seven stars of the constellation known as the Pleiades. Originally known as the "Brigade," the group was formed by Ronsard with some of Daurat's other students at the Collège de Coqueret; the name "Pléiade" was adopted in 1556. Its principal aims, set out in Du Bellay's manifesto *Défense et illustration de la langue française* (1549), involved the reform of French poetry and the French language through imitation of the linguistic and stylistic techniques of classical antiquity and the Italian Renaissance, notably the odes of Pindar and Horace, the epics of Virgil and Homer, and the sonnets of PETRARCH, and through the revival of archaisms, the adoption of dialect words and technical terms, and the coining of neologisms.
**Further reading:** Grahame Castor, *Pléiade Politics: A Study in Sixteenth-Century Thought and Terminology* (Cambridge, U.K.: Cambridge University Press, 1964).

**Plethon, George Gemistus** (c. 1355–1450) *Greek philosopher*
Plethon was born in Constantinople and became the leader of the Platonic school of philosophy at Mistra. Brought to the Council of FLORENCE (1438) by Emperor John Palaeologus, he vigorously opposed the prevailing Aristotelianism of the Italians. In Florence he became an inspiration to the circle of humanists around Cosimo de' MEDICI. Plethon (the name is a synonym for Gemistus—both mean "full"—and also close to Plato in pronunciation) developed a philosophical system that owed much to the Neoplatonism of Alexandria. He emphasized the mystical side of Plato's teaching and evolved a system in which Greek mythology fused with Greek logic. This blend struck a chord in the Florentines; his followers regarded him as the reincarnation of Plato. Some time before 1441 Plethon returned to Greece where his ideas were attacked by GENNADIUS, who accused him of paganism. In 1455 Plethon's body was exhumed and reburied in the TEMPIO MALATESTIANO at Rimini by Sigismondo MALATESTA. Plethon's influence on FICINO and PICO DELLA MIRANDOLA was fundamental in determining the mystical character of Florentine Platonism.
**See also:** PLATONISM, RENAISSANCE
**Further reading:** C. M. Woodhouse, *George Gemistus Plethon: The Last of the Hellenes* (Oxford, U.K.: Clarendon Press, 1992).

**Plotinus** (c. 205–c. 262) *Egyptian-born philosopher*
He settled around 244 at Rome, where he included among his disciples the Greek philosopher Porphyry, who later edited his *Enneads*. His profoundly mystical nature strongly influenced his interpretation of Platonic philosophy, and he is hailed as the founder of Neoplatonism. A Latin translation with commentary was published (1492) by Marsilio FICINO, but the Greek text was not printed until 1580.
**See also:** NEOPLATONISM, RENAISSANCE

**Plutarch** (c. 46–c. 120) *Greek biographer and moral philosopher*
Plutarch exercised a major influence on two Renaissance literary genres: on BIOGRAPHY through his *Parallel Lives* of Greek and Roman notables and on the prose treatise through his *Moralia*. The *Lives* appealed to the Renaissance emphasis on the individual and the *Moralia* to the prevailing interest in ethics. Lost to the Middle Ages, Plutarch's works first became accessible to humanists through epitomes and through the Latin translations of Leonardo BRUNI, GUARINO DA VERONA, and others, and these texts, of variable accuracy, became the basis for subsequent vernacular versions. The translations of the *Lives* into French (*see* AMYOT, JACQUES) and English (*see* NORTH, THOMAS) were enormously influential in their respective countries, and MONTAIGNE and Francis BACON were indebted to the *Moralia* in their development of the ESSAY form. The *editiones principes* of the Greek texts were the work of the ALDINE PRESS, the *Moralia* appearing in 1509 and the *Lives* in 1519.

**podestà** An administrator responsible for law and order in an Italian city. If conditions were right, an opportunist official could turn this post into the basis for the acquisition of permanent power.

**poesy** (poesia) In art, a painting of a mythological or arcadian character, created purely for aesthetic pleasure and without ideological or symbolic content. The most famous paintings of this kind are probably the "Poesy" series painted in the 1550s by TITIAN for Philip II of Spain, depicting eight scenes from Ovid's *Metamorphoses*.

**Poggini, Domenico** (1520–1590) *Italian sculptor, medalist, and goldsmith*
Poggini was born in Florence and worked mainly there until he moved to the court of Pope Sixtus V in Rome in 1585. From the 1550s he produced an interesting series of medals. As a sculptor he was more successful in bronze than in marble. His elder brother Gianpaolo (1518–c. 1582) was also a medalist who worked for Philip II in Brussels and from 1559 in Madrid.

**Poggio Bracciolini** See BRACCIOLINI, POGGIO

**Pole, Cardinal Reginald** (1500–1558) *English Catholic churchman*
Pole was the grandnephew of King Edward IV. He was educated at Oxford and spent some time in Italy from 1521. After challenging HENRY VIII's assumption of supremacy over the English Church he was forced into exile (1532), and his rebuke to the king, *Pro ecclesiasticae unitatis defensione*, was presented to Henry in 1536, causing deep offense. Pole's home at Viterbo became a center for Catholic reformers, and his saintly character and hostility to the English Reformation earned him a cardinal's hat in 1536. The infuriated Henry attainted his family (1539) and executed his mother (1541). Pole returned to England as papal legate (1554) and was MARY I's close adviser during the Catholic reaction. He became the last Roman Catholic archbishop of Canterbury in 1556, but clashed with Pope PAUL IV, who deprived Pole of his authority on suspicion of heresy. Pole died just 12 hours after Mary I.

**Polidoro Caldara da Caravaggio** (c. 1500–1543) *Italian painter*
A pupil of RAPHAEL, he spent the early part of his career in Rome, where he became famous for the masterly monochrome imitations of classical reliefs with which he decorated house facades. He also worked as an assistant on decorative works in the Vatican. He was one of the earliest classical landscape painters, and works such as his fresco in the church of San Silvestro al Quirinale anticipate the paintings of Claude Lorraine and Nicolas Poussin. Following the Sack of Rome (1527), Polidoro worked in Naples and in Messina, where he was murdered.

**Politian** (**Angelo Ambrogini**) (1454–1494) *Italian humanist scholar and poet*
Politian (or Poliziano) took his adopted name from his birthplace of Montepulciano. Entering the university of Florence at age 10, he was taught Latin by Cristoforo LANDINO, Greek by John ARGYROPOULOS, and philosophy by Marsilio FICINO. Lorenzo de' Medici appointed him tutor (1475) to his sons Piero and Giovanni. In 1480, after a brief sojourn in Mantua, he became professor of Greek and Latin at Florence and won a Europe-wide reputation. He translated the *Iliad* into Latin hexameters, lectured on Hellenistic Greek writers, and produced material for an edition of the *Pandects* of Justinian which is still of critical value. His prologues to his lectures were elegant poems in Latin hexameters, published under the title *Silvae*, and he even composed Greek epigrams. Unusually for a classicist, he was also a very competent writer in the vernacular: his pastoral drama, *Orfeo*, was produced at Mantua in 1480, and he published a collection of Tuscan ballads and songs entitled *Rime*. His *Stanze per la giostra del Magnifico Giuliano*, begun in 1475 but never finished, commemorates the victory of Giuliano de' Medici (died 1478) in a tournament and Giuliano's love for Simonetta Vespucci (died 1476).

Politian was the first Western scholar who could compete with the Greek immigrants in knowledge of the ancient language. Evidence for Politian's scholarship comes from the books in his own library which were extensively annotated with readings from his collations of manuscripts. He also seems to have invented the method of designating manuscripts by an individual letter (*siglum*) which made for easy reference. His major scholarly publication was his *Miscellanea* (1489) in which he offered critical comments on a wide range of Greek and Latin texts. As a teacher his influence was very great; his pupils included Johann REUCHLIN, Thomas LINACRE, and William GROCYN. His private life was marred by scandal and his personal reputation at his death was dubious.

**Pollaiuolo, Antonio del** (1432–1498) *Italian painter, sculptor, engraver, and goldsmith*
With his brother, Piero (c. 1441–96), he ran one of the most successful, innovative, and influential workshops in their native Florence. It is usually assumed that their better paintings were executed mainly or wholly by Antonio because they reveal a mastery of the human form which can only be matched by the bronze works of Antonio and not in works known to have been done by Piero alone. Influences visible in Antonio's work include DONATELLO, MANTEGNA, and ANDREA DEL CASTAGNO, under whom Antonio's brother may have studied. But the most important factor that shaped Antonio's work was his analysis of the human form. He was one of the first scientific artists who practiced dissection in order to understand muscular structure, as LEONARDO DA VINCI was to do later. His

drawings and engravings such as *Battle of the Nude Men* (c. 1470) exemplify the link between art and research into nature that was to be such a feature of Leonardo's work. In this engraving and in Pollaiuolo's masterpiece, the *Martyrdom of St. Sebastian* (1475; National Gallery, London), the figures have clearly defined muscular structures and the pictures are composed to show poses from a variety of angles.

Pollaiuolo's second main innovation was the introduction of landscape interest to Florentine art through paintings such as *Hercules and Nessus* (Yale Art Gallery, New Haven), which set the figures in a lyrical landscape. His most important sculptures were carried out with Piero in St. Peter's in the 1490s. They are the bronze tombs of Sixtus IV (1493) and of Innocent VIII (c. 1495). The latter included the first sepulchral effigy to depict the living man, and features of both tombs were widely copied.

**Further reading:** Leopold D. Ettlinger, *Antonio and Piero Pollaiuolo* (Oxford, U.K.: Phaidon and New York: Dutton, 1978).

**Pollaiuolo, Simone del** See CRONACA, SIMONE, IL

**Polybius** (c. 202–120 BCE) *Greek historian*
Polybius had a distinguished career in Greek public life, was the friend of the great Roman general Scipio Aemilianus, and after 146 BCE organized the Roman administration in Greece. His wide military and diplomatic experience made him exceptionally well qualified to observe and discuss the causes of Rome's rise and the decadence of the Greek cities. Much of his narrative and viewpoint in the first five books of his *History* (all that survive intact out of the original 40) was exceptionally interesting to Renaissance students of statecraft, warfare, and the role of the individual in history. Fragments of the sixth book survive in excerpts, including a passage on the Roman constitution that appears to have influenced MACHIAVELLI. A Latin translation, made in 1452–53 for Pope Nicholas V, was printed in 1473, and the *editio princeps* appeared in 1530.

**Pomponazzi, Pietro** (1462–1525) *Italian physician and philosopher*
Pomponazzi was born at Mantua. After medical studies at Padua (1487) he was appointed professor of philosophy there and lectured on Aristotle's *Physics* until 1509, when the closure of the Paduan schools sent him to Ferrara. There he began the studies in Aristotelian psychology which were to lead him to develop heretical views concerning the nature of the soul. In 1512 he went to Bologna as professor of natural and moral philosophy, a post which he held until his death. In 1516 he published *De immortalitate animae*, a treatise on the immortality of the soul that generated much opposition, as it conflicted with both the accepted (Thomist and Averroist) views on Aristotle.

Pomponazzi tried to separate his speculations from his own personal belief and made a formal submission to the Church on matters of faith, but it required the intervention of Cardinal BEMBO with Pope Leo X to save him from suffering as a heretic.

**Ponce de León, Juan** (1474–1521) *Spanish explorer, conquistador, and administrator*
Having fought against the Moors of Granada, he volunteered for COLUMBUS's 1493 West Indian voyage. In 1502 he joined another West Indies expedition and in 1506 led the subjugation of present-day Puerto Rico. Following a spell as a colonial governor (1509–12), he sailed in search of the mythical island of Bimini with its Fountain of Youth, and in March 1513 made landfall in the land he named Florida. His ship's log of this voyage (now lost) was used by the historian Antonio de Herrera (1559–1625) in his *Historia general de los hechos de los castellanos en las islas i tierra firme del Mar Océano* (1601–15). After five years (1515–20) in Puerto Rico, he sailed again for Florida but suffered a fatal arrow wound en route and died in Havana.

**Pontano, Giovanni** (1422–1503) *Italian humanist statesman and poet*
Educated in his native Umbria, he entered the service of the Aragonese king of Naples, ALFONSO I, becoming a royal secretary. Under his successor FERDINAND I (Ferrante), Pontano was appointed secretary of state (1486) and played a leading role in the political and military affairs of the kingdom until the conquest by the French under Charles VIII (1495).

Early in his career Pontano had become a dominant influence in the NEAPOLITAN ACADEMY and acted as its official head from 1471. His devotion to classical learning, which led him to adopt the name Jovianus (or the Italianized form, Gioviano) Pontanus, inspired his many and varied Latin works in prose and verse. His prose works include a number of stories and essays or dialogues, often on conventional moral subjects (generosity, fortune, etc.) and on philology and astrology; and a history, *De bello napoletano*, on the war between the French and the house of Aragon. His poetry was held by some contemporaries, among them Erasmus, to rival or surpass its classical models, such as Theocritus and Virgil. It includes three PASTORAL eclogues (*Acon, Quinquennius, Maeon*) and three idylls (*Meliseus, Lepidina, Coryle*), published by the Aldine press in 1518, that greatly influenced the revival of interest in classical pastoral verse in the Renaissance.

**Pontelli, Baccio** (1450–c. 1492) *Italian architect*
Pontelli, who was born in Florence, first trained as a woodcarver and worked in the cathedral in Pisa and in Urbino. He probably learned the technique of castle construction from FRANCESCO DI GIORGIO MARTINI and during

the 1480s and 1490s he built fortresses in Ostia, Iesi, Osimo, and Senigallia. He also fortified the Santuario della Sta. Casa at Loreto (1490–94) and built other churches and religious buildings, many of them for the popes Sixtus IV and Innocent VIII. He died in Urbino.

## Pontormo, Jacopo da (Jacopo Carrucci) (1494–1557)
*Italian painter*
Born near Empoli, the son of the painter and draftsman Bartolommeo Carrucci, Pontormo probably became a pupil of Leonardo da Vinci in about 1511. He was then apprenticed to ALBERTINELLI and PIERO DI COSIMO before becoming the assistant of ANDREA DEL SARTO, by whom he was profoundly influenced. Early works in the style of Andrea del Sarto include the *Visitation* (1514–16; SS. Annunziata, Florence), but a more individual approach is evident in the complex painting *Joseph in Egypt* (1518–19; National Gallery, London), which owes a clear debt to DÜRER and includes a portrait of Pontormo's pupil and adopted son Angelo BRONZINO. In about 1520 Pontormo decorated the Medici family villa at Poggia a Caiano with mythological scenes, after which he executed further decorations for the Certosa near Florence in a mannerist style. Pontormo then embarked upon his masterpiece, a cycle of paintings in the Capponi chapel of Sta. Felicità, Florence (1525–28), loosely based upon MICHELANGELO's *Pietà*. These works included an entombment scene with a self-portrait of the artist and the *Deposition*. Later works include the *Visitation* (1528–30; Carmignano, Pieve) and fresco decorations for the choir of San Lorenzo, Florence (1554–57), a major work, influenced by Michelangelo, of which only the original drawings survive. A recluse in his later years, Pontormo wrote a diary (1554–57) that vividly illuminates his obsessive and neurotic character.

## Pordenone (Giovanni Antonio de Sacchis) (c. 1484–1539) *Italian painter*
Born in Pordenone in Friuli, Pordenone was a pupil of Pellegrino da San Daniele, although early influences also included Giorgione and Mantegna. In about 1515 he moved to Rome where he was further influenced by the works of Michelangelo, Correggio, and Raphael and developed his taste for highly dramatic illusionistic painting. His masterpiece was the cycle of frescoes on the Passion in Cremona cathedral (c. 1521), painted in a distinctly mannerist style that is also evident in his painted dome in Treviso cathedral (1520–22) and his frescoes at Piacenza (1531; Madonna di Campagna). He eventually settled in Venice where, for a brief time, he rivaled TITIAN. Both Titian and RUBENS adopted elements of his style.

## Porta, Giacomo della See GIACOMO DELLA PORTA

## Porta, Giambattista della See GIAMBATTISTA DELLA PORTA

## Porta, Guglielmo della See GUGLIELMO DELLA PORTA

## Portinari altarpiece (c. 1475/77) A large-scale triptych commissioned from Hugo van der GOES by Tommaso Portinari, the Italian agent of the Medici in Bruges, for the church of the hospital of Sta. Maria Nuova, Florence (now in the Uffizi, Florence) The Adoration scene on the central panel is flanked by portraits of the donor and his family with their patron saints on the wings. An Annunciation, painted in grisaille, is revealed when the wings are closed. See Plate VI.

## portolans Sailors' charts based on practical navigational experience and giving details of features of interest to ships' pilots. Inland features are seldom marked. In use from at least the late 13th to the late 15th century, the portolans' main function was to record bearings, distances, coastal landmarks, and hazards for the guidance of mariners. They were generally hand written on parchment, and were based on the assumption that the Earth is flat. Most portolans were of southern European origin and many famous ones can be found in the 13th-century *Compasso di navigare*, a comprehensive survey of the Mediterranean and the Black Sea.

**See also:** CATALAN ATLAS

## Portuguese language The Romance language of more than 85 million speakers in Portugal, Brazil, the Azores, and a few formerly colonial areas of Africa and Asia. Galician or Galego, spoken in northwestern Spain, is a dialect of Portuguese. Brazilian Portuguese differs in generally minor details of pronunciation, vocabulary, and grammar from the language of the mother country. The region of the Iberian peninsula known as Lusitania took its name from the Celts who settled there about 1000 BCE and were particularly concentrated in the Serra da Estrela. Some of these tribes for a time successfully resisted Roman attempts at colonization in the second and first centuries BCE, while others, such as the Conii in Algarve, accepted Roman rule. Roman conquest of the region was completed by Julius and Augustus Caesar.

Portuguese derives from the Vulgar Latin spoken in the province, but, like Spanish, reflects the influences of later invasions (Germanic and Arabic) and the country's subsequent cultural (French and Italian borrowings) and imperial (African and Amerindian words) history. Germanic tribes invaded the whole of the Iberian peninsula in the fifth century CE. The kingdom of the Suevi (Swabians) in the north was taken over by the dominant Visigoths towards the end of the sixth century. In 711 the Moors occupied all areas except Asturias (east of Galicia, the present province of Oviedo) and the Basque homeland. Portugal's national identity, which assured the separate development of the language, evolved during the slow process of the reconquest. The Moors were driven from

Galicia in the eighth century and from Coimbra in 1064 (by Ferdinand I of Castile), and by the 12th century the foundation of national independence had been established.

The earliest extant documents in which Portuguese has quite distinctive features date from about 1190, but the language had probably developed its characteristics by the 10th century. The earliest literary texts (Portuguese and Galician) are the three 13th-century CANCIONEIROS (*da Ajuda*, *da Vaticana*, and *Colocci-Brancuti*), which reveal a thorough absorption of Provençal poetry. Portuguese was standardized in the 16th century on the basis of the dialect of Lisbon and Coimbra, though the orthography of some words remains unsettled, despite several official efforts to reform spelling. Grammatically the language retains some complex features lost in modern Spanish, for example a number of subjunctives. Among phonetic characteristics are the nasalization of vowels and diphthongs (which can be indicated by the tilde) and the tendency to pronounce final *s* and *z* as a sound like English *sh*. As in French, acute, grave, and circumflex accents are used to indicate pronunciation, mark contractions, and distinguish homonyms. Important early lexicographical works include the bilingual *Dictionarium lusitanico-latinum* (1611) by Bishop Augustinho Barbosa (1590–1649) and the *Diccionario de lingua portugueza* (1789) by Antonio de Moraes e Silva (1755–1824), which has been continually revised and reissued.

**Postel, Guillaume** (1510–1581) *French orientalist, linguist, and visionary*
Postel was born at Barenton. A member of Francis I's embassy to Constantinople in 1537, he traveled in the Middle East before returning to Paris; at the Collège de France he taught Greek, Hebrew, and Arabic and became the first professor of oriental languages. He entered the priesthood (1544) and returned to the Orient to preach reconciliation between Christians and Muslims. In Italy, where he spent 10 years, he was imprisoned by the Inquisition. In his writings Postel expounded his ideal of the *concordia mundi*: his works include *De orbis terrae concordia* (1544), *Protévangile de Jacques* (1552), and *Les Très Merveilleuses Victoires des femmes* (1553).

**Pourbus family** A family of Flemish artists who in three generations were active as portrait painters. Pieter Pourbus (c. 1510–84) was a native of Gouda but by 1538 was in Bruges as the pupil of Lancelot BLONDEEL. A *Last Judgment* in Bruges museum shows a debt to Michelangelo. He also worked as a surveyor for Charles V and for the city of Bruges and painted a number of portraits, among them one of Jan van der Gheenste (1583; Brussels museum). His son, Frans the Elder (1545–81), was born in Bruges and became a disciple of Frans FLORIS. His altarpiece of *Christ and the Doctors* (1571; St. Bavon,

Ghent) contains portraits of some eminent contemporaries, and he also practiced as a portraitist in a more conventional sense. Frans's son, Frans the Younger (1569–1622), was born in Antwerp and became one of the most distinguished court portraitists of his time. He worked from 1592 for the Hapsburg archducal court at Brussels before moving in 1600 to Mantua, where he worked at the court of Duke Vincenzo I Gonzaga. Examples of his output in Italy are in the Pitti gallery, Florence. In 1609 he was summoned to Paris by Queen Marie de' Medici, for whom he worked until his death.

**Prague** (Czech **Praha**) The capital city of Bohemia (now part of the Czech Republic), situated on the River Vltava. Celts, Slavs, and Avars lived on the site before Prague was founded in the ninth century. Under Püremyslid rule from the ninth century to 1306, Prague was the nucleus of Bohemia, and the city prospered on account of its position on important trade routes during the late Middle Ages. Prague developed as a major European city during the reign (1346–78) of Emperor Charles IV, who founded the Charles University (1348) and encouraged civic expansion. By the late 16th century Prague's population had risen to over 50,000.

During the early 15th century Prague became a center of the HUSSITE reformers (*see* HUSS, JAN); there followed the first DEFENESTRATION OF PRAGUE and the popular rising (1419) that led to the Hussite wars. After the death of King Louis II of Hungary at MOHÁCS (1526), Prague and Bohemia passed to the Catholic Hapsburgs who were determined to suppress Bohemian Protestantism; in the 1540s a Jesuit school for young nobles was founded in Prague. RUDOLF II made his permanent residence in Prague's Hradschin palace and there assembled his great art collection. In 1618 the second DEFENESTRATION OF PRAGUE was followed by the outbreak of the Thirty Years' War (1618) and the crushing of Bohemian Protestantism at the battle of the WHITE MOUNTAIN near Prague (1620).

The Charles University was an important center of mathematical and astronomical studies, which in the reign of Rudolf II attracted Tycho BRAHE and Johannes KEPLER. St. Vitus's cathedral was begun in 1344 and parts of the new town and the Jewish ghetto survive from the 14th century.

**Further reading:** Angelo Maria Ripellino, *Magic Prague*, transl. David Newton Marinelli (London: Macmillan, 1994).

**Prague, Compacts of** See BASLE, COUNCIL OF

***Praise of Folly, The*** (Latin *Encomium Moriae*) A prose satire written in Latin by ERASMUS in 1509 and first published in 1511. It was composed in its earliest form at the Chelsea home of Sir Thomas MORE, and its original title is a pun on More's name, as Erasmus's dedication to him makes plain. In it the goddess Folly, in a formal oration, addresses the multitude of her disciples and congratulates herself on how all mankind is enrolled in her train: princes, courtiers, statesmen, scholars, poets, lawyers, philosophers, and, most pointedly, theologians. The satire on the follies of churchmen was the heart of the work and provoked much fury from its victims. The work was an extraordinary best-seller: 42 Latin editions appeared in Erasmus's lifetime and it was soon translated into French (1520), German (1520), and English (1549).

**Prato** A town in Tuscany 12 miles from Florence. It was a prosperous wool-manufacturing center as early as the 13th century. Its cathedral exhibits fine work by DONATELLO, MICHELOZZO, and Fra Filippo LIPPI, and from 1141 housed the famous relic known as the Holy Girdle of the Virgin Mary. The church of Sta. Maria delle Carceri (1485–91) is by Giuliano SANGALLO. The "Merchant of Prato," Francesco di Marco DATINI, is buried in the church of San Francesco.

**preaching** The practice of delivering sermons underwent some important changes during the Reformation, not least in terms of their role within the church service. Although formal Latin sermons were given in medieval monasteries and universities, it was recognized early on that exposition of Christian doctrine also needed to be carried out in the vernacular for the benefit of the unlearned. From its foundation in the 13th century the Dominican Order (the Friars Preachers; Latin: Ordo Praedicatorum) spread all over Europe, with preaching and the hearing of CONFESSION as key aspects of its mission. There is much anecdotal evidence of the enthusiasm with which sermons were attended in towns and cities, and celebrity preachers such as BERNARDINO OF SIENA drew large crowds. Sermons were often delivered outdoors, sometimes from pulpits attached to the exterior walls of churches; inside churches, preachers often spoke from the rood-loft, although pulpits, normally placed on the north side of the nave, came into increasing use from the later Middle Ages. Parish priests were expected to supplement the instruction given by itinerant friars, and as some of them were ill-equipped to do so manuals were written containing suitable material; in England, for example, the *Festial* of John Mirk (or Myrc; fl. c. 1400) provided sermons for all major occasions in the Church calendar. The sermon on penitence delivered as part of his contribution to the entertainment by the Parson in CHAUCER's *Canterbury Tales* may seem to modern readers a downbeat note on which to end the book, but, like the Parson himself, it is exemplary of its kind and the preamble makes it plain that it is to be taken seriously.

In their drive to educate the laity about their faith, the reformers laid great emphasis on the "ministry of the word"—that is, Bible readings and preaching. Pictures of the austere interiors of Dutch Calvinist churches show the pulpit as the building's focal point, with the chancel—the focal point of sacramental worship—almost irrelevant. A mid-1560s painting of worship in the Huguenot "temple" named "Paradis" at Lyons (1564–67; Geneva museum), shows the whole building constructed around the high wooden pulpit. Sermons expounding the Bible and applying scriptural doctrine to the hearers' lives were preached frequently and at length. However, religious and secular authorities were both fully aware that, without some sort of control, ignorant or disaffected preachers were a menace to orthodoxy and civil order—as the example of SAVONAROLA in Florence showed. For instance, in the years preceding the uprising of the Dutch against their Spanish Catholic overlords (*see* NETHERLANDS, REVOLT OF THE) radical Calvinist preachers took to the fields to press the religious case for rebellion. Some Protestant radicals, reverting to what they believed was the practice of the primitive Church, encouraged "prophesyings" in public worship, thus allowing the laity, both men and women, to speak publicly on doctrinal matters. A few doughty Protestant women, such as the ex-nun Marie Dentière in the first half of the 16th century, stood up for a woman's right to be heard in public on religious matters, but male Protestant clergy were as insistent as their Catholic counterparts on St. Paul's injunction that women should keep silent in church.

Various measures were taken to control preachers and the content of their sermons. In Roman Catholic countries the INQUISITION could investigate preachers who deviated from the orthodox line. In England, approved set texts were issued in the form of two books of homilies (1547, 1571), with the sermons written by distinguished contributors, among them Thomas CRANMER for the first book and JEWEL and GRINDAL for the second. In article 35 of the THIRTY-NINE ARTICLES the titles of the homilies in the second book are listed and they are recommended as "godly and wholesome Doctrine…to be read in Churches by the Ministers, diligently and distinctly, that they may be understanded of the people." The books of homilies, of course, did not preclude the learned from writing their own texts; Lancelot ANDREWES and Richard HOOKER were both renowed for their sermons.

See also: LITURGY

**predestination** In Christianity, the doctrine or belief that God has foreordained the salvation of certain individuals, who have been chosen not for any merits of their own, but wholly according to God's purposes and grace. Such a doctrine is implied by several passages in the Bible and stated explicitly by St. Paul (e.g. Romans 8: 28–30), who uses it to bolster his central teaching that salvation is the free unmerited gift of God. In later centuries, these hints were developed by systematic theologians (most notably CALVIN) in ways that entail huge moral and intellectual difficulties. In particular, predestination appears to destroy human free will and responsibility and—in its extreme Calvinist form—to imply a God terrifyingly remote from human ideas of morality and justice.

A rigorous doctrine of predestination was first set out in the 5th century by St. Augustine of Hippo, largely as a corrective to the Pelagian view that humans can merit salvation through their own efforts. Augustine avoided complete determinism by arguing that humans have the freedom to choose whether or not to accept God's salvation. He also avoided the doctrine of so-called double predestination, which holds that God foreordains not only the salvation of the elect but also the damnation of the nonelect—a doctrine subsequently condemned as heresy. The standard medieval position sought to balance Augustine's severe analysis with a strong emphasis on God's universal saving will and a recognition of human freedom and responsibility; salvation is entirely owing to God's grace, damnation to man's sin and guilt.

There was little controversy over this prevalent view until the early 16th century, when the reformers' insistence on JUSTIFICATION BY FAITH alone drew LUTHER and others back to the Augustinian position. Indeed, Luther's teaching here is hardly to be distinguished from Augustine's: humankind is in complete bondage to sin and wholly unable to choose the good and to do it; nevertheless, individuals have the capacity to accept God's free offer of grace; God therefore predestines the elect to salvation but cannot be said to predestine the nonelect to damnation. There is, however, no systematic teaching on predestination in Luther's works, and he gives the impression of regarding the whole question as an inscrutable mystery.

In contrast, predestination became a cornerstone of the system devised by Calvin and elaborated by his followers. Remorselessly logical, Calvin insisted on the conclusion that most of his predecessors had struggled to avoid: that God foreordains the fate of the damned in exactly the same sense as that of the saved, decreeing membership of the elect or the nonelect with no reference to an individual's faith or works. Calvin therefore rejected the idea of God's universal saving will and the belief that Christ's death was offered for the whole of humanity, both of which were firmly upheld by Luther. Any vestiges of free will are removed by Calvin's insistence that divine grace is both irresistible (it cannot be refused) and indefectible (it cannot be forfeited once conferred). However dreadful it may seem, such a system is perfectly consistent with both justice and goodness, since the damned receive the just reward for their sins and the saved are favored beyond their merits.

In the years after Calvin's death these doctrines became ever more central to the teaching of the Reformed Church. Differences of opinion were limited to the question of whether God destined a portion of the human race to damnation before the beginning of time (supralapsari-

anism) or only after the Fall (sublapsarianism). A more fundamental challenge arose at the turn of the 17th century, when Jacobus Arminius (*see* ARMINIANISM), a theologian of the Dutch Reformed Church, reacted against Calvin's determinism by affirming free will in humans and denying that Christ died for the elect alone; predestination was best understood as God's foreknowledge of those who would persevere in faith and good works. The definitive statement of Arminian views in the so-called Remonstrance of 1610 (*see* REMONSTRANTS) sparked a long and bitter controversy in Holland, which impinged upon political issues. Following the Synod of DORT's reaffirmation of strict Calvinist doctrine (1618), many leading Arminians were exiled or imprisoned (the latter including GROTIUS). The breach between Calvinist and Arminian tendencies would for centuries remain an important faultline within the Protestant Churches generally.

In the Roman Catholic Church, the issue of predestination received renewed attention in the intellectual ferment of the COUNTER-REFORMATION, which saw various attempts to reconcile human free will with the doctrine of divine election. The most notable of these was that of Luis de MOLINA, who reinterpreted predestination as divine foreknowledge of free human choices. This was widely taken up by the JESUITS but vigorously attacked by more conservative thinkers, especially those in the Dominican tradition. Controversy continued until 1607, when the pope ruled that neither Molina's view nor its denial should be considered heretical—a position that the Church has since maintained.

**Primaticcio, Francesco** (1504–1570) *Italian painter and architect*
Bolognese by birth, Primaticcio learned his decorative skills as the assistant of GIULIO ROMANO during the decoration of the Palazzo del TÈ, Mantua (1525–32). In 1532 he was summoned to France by FRANCIS I to work on the decoration of the château at FONTAINEBLEAU. Although much of the important work he did there has been destroyed, some rooms, such as the Chambre de la Duchesse d'Étampes (c. 1541–45) and the Galerie Henri II (1552–56), survive in an altered form. After the death of ROSSO FIORENTINO, with whom he worked there, Primaticcio became head of the workshop at Fontainebleau, despite the opposition of CELLINI, and continued to produce sumptuous paintings in a mannerist style that favored mythological subjects and elongated nudes after the fashion of Parmigianino. Other works include the Valois chapel at St.-Denis and the Aile de la Belle Cheminée at Fontainebleau (1568).

**Primavera, La** One of a series of paintings on pagan mythological subjects made by BOTTICELLI probably in the early 1480s. It is likely that it was commissioned by Lorenzo di Pierfrancesco de' Medici for the Villa di

**La Primavera** (c. 1480) One of a series of paintings in which Alessandro Boticelli reimagined pagan myths in terms of Neoplatonic allegory (Uffizi, Florence).
*Mansell/Time Life Pictures/Getty Images*

Castello just outside Florence. The picture shows the entourage of Venus, as conceived in Horace's *Odes* and Ovid's *Fasti* and expounded in Renaissance Florence by POLITIAN; but the significance of the figures in terms of Neoplatonic allegory has been much debated. Over the head of Venus in the center of the picture, blindfolded Cupid aims his dart at the central one of the three dancing GRACES, while the god Mercury (*see* HERMES) stands on the left. In the right of the picture Zephyr, the wind of spring, catches hold of the nymph Chloris, who is instantly transformed into the goddess Flora, spreading the earth with flowers, a metamorphosis described in the *Fasti*.

Further reading: C. Dempsey, *The Portrayal of Love: Botticelli's* Primavera *and Humanist Culture at the Time of Lorenzo the Magnificent* (Princeton, N.J. and Oxford, U.K.: Princeton University Press, 1994).

**Prince, The** (Italian *Il principe*; 1532) A political treatise in 25 chapters by MACHIAVELLI, with a conclusion urging the redemption of Italy from barbarian forces. It was originally written in 1513 and dedicated to Giuliano de' Medici but was revised in 1516 and dedicated to Giu-

liano's nephew Lorenzo before he became duke of Urbino. Machiavelli's ideas had developed during his active career (1498–1512) in the Florentine republic, when he had become familiar with all manner of political problems and conflicts and had, as a member of important missions, directly dealt with such powerful figures as Cesare Borgia.

*The Prince* concerns what is necessary for the successful seizure and exercise of political power and considers the means available to achieve this end, without reference to individual morality or ultimate religious truths. The secular point of view and the ambiguous tone arising from Machiavelli's procedure of presenting his firmly held opinions in a purely descriptive guise were largely responsible for the work's unjustified reputation in the later 16th century as an epitome of atheism and wickedness. It and its author were frequently alluded to in Elizabethan writings. *Il Principe* was the subject of an anonymous Tudor translation of about 1560, which was edited by Hardin Craig and first published at Chapel Hill in 1944. The first printed English translation (1640), by E. Dacres and entitled *Nicholas Machiavel's Prince,* was reprinted in the Tudor Translations series (1905). *The*

HAEC ACCVRATA RECOGNITIO TRI-
VM VOLVMINVM / OPERVM CLA-
RISS.P.NICOLAI CVSAE CARD.
EX OFFICINA ASCENSIA-
NA RECENTER EMISSA
EST.CVIVS VNI-
VERSALEM IN-
DICEM /
PRO-
XIME SEQVENS PAGINA MONSTRAT.

VAENVNDANTVR CVM CAETERIS
eius operibus in Aedibus Ascensianis.

**Printing** The title page of a book printed in Paris by Jodocus Badius Ascensius showing the operation of an early 16th-century printing press. The pressman pulls the bar that makes the press descend, an assistant behind him on the left rubs two inkballs together, and the compositor on the right sits at the type frame.

*Prince* is included in A. H. Gilbert's *The Chief Works of Machiavelli* (Durham, N.C., 1965). George Bull's translation was first issued in the Penguin Classics series in 1961, and there is also an Oxford World's Classics edition by Peter Bondanella, with the translation by Bondanella and Mark Musa (Oxford, 1984). Parallel Italian and English texts feature in Musa's earlier edition of the work (New York, 1964).

**Further reading:** Leo Paul S. de Alvarez, *The Machi-avellian Enterprise: A Commentary on* The Prince (DeKalb, Ill.: Northern Illinois University Press, 1999).

**printing** After GUTENBERG began printing in Mainz, other craftsmen, many of them German, soon followed his example elsewhere. Cologne, Strasbourg, and Basle had their own printers by the mid-1460s, followed closely by Nuremberg and Augsburg. Printers found it sensible to settle in thriving commercial towns, so that the BOOK

TRADE grew alongside others, making use of the fairs already in existence at Frankfurt and Lyons and supplying buyers all over Europe. University cities were also obvious centers, providing a ready market for the sale of quantities of identical copies of essential texts.

In Spain, the Catholic Monarchs FERDINAND II AND ISABELLA I encouraged the immigration of printers, mainly German, from the 1470s onward; by 1500 commercial printers were operating in around 20 towns, including the university cities of Zaragoza (1477), Salamanca (1481), and Valladolid (1482), while the press at Alcalá de Henares (1502) was shortly to issue the COMPLUTENSIAN POLYGLOT, a formidable technical achievement.

Paris had its first press in 1470, under the wing of the Sorbonne, and BADIUS and the ESTIENNE family continued the scholarly tradition. Italian printing was started at Subiaco, near Rome, by the Germans Arnold Pennartz and Conrad Schweinheim in 1464/65, but Venice, beginning in 1469, attracted more 15th-century printers than any other town, with the greatest of them, including Nicolas JENSON and Aldus MANUTIUS, having a profound influence on both the TYPOGRAPHY and the content of early printed books. Once the Italian introduction of roman and italic types made smaller and cheaper formats a possibility, books were able to be acquired easily by individuals as well as by institutional libraries for private study. Pocket editions of the classics were a great improvement on chained folios in libraries.

Printing in VERNACULAR languages soon began to outstrip Latin and other learned tongues. A good example is William CAXTON's production, nearly three-quarters of which was in English, starting even before he took his press to London in 1476. Private patrons were important in Caxton's success, as they were in that of other contemporary printers. Books in the vernacular, one more way of bringing new ideas to the growing number of those able to read, facilitated other changes too, among them those promoted by Martin LUTHER, who was the making of the Wittenberg printer, Hans Lufft. Thirty vernacular Bible translations, mostly German, appeared before 1500, and during the 16th century virtually every part of Europe acquired its own version. As printed books became more familiar objects they inevitably began to standardize the languages in which they were written (see ORTHOGRAPHY). Caxton was influential once again in the stabilization of written English (see ENGLISH LANGUAGE), while Robert Estienne gave French its acute and grave accents. The demands of the market affected the choice of material from the earliest days, for the first vernacular scientific book was a HERBAL printed by Peter Schöffer in 1485.

The first half of the 16th century has been labeled a golden age of printing, helped by the development of ENGRAVING and the consequent improvement in BOOK ILLUSTRATION, with engraved or decorated title-pages as well as vignettes or head- or tail-pieces in the text. Many printers became publishers of other people's books as well, like Christophe PLANTIN, or even left printing for publishing, like Anton Koberger of Nuremberg. The influence of Italy was later overtaken by that of Germany and the Netherlands, with Plantin in Antwerp and the ELZEVIRS further north all flourishing once Spanish control of the region was ended.

The basic equipment, the wooden printing press, changed very little until the 18th century, except for the enlargement of the printing surface and consequently the output of printed sheets. However, as the power of the press became evident, both Church and state attempted to impose some control over the material being disseminated. Such measures included the foundation of the Stationers' Company in London in 1557 as the self-regulating body of the English book trade and the establishment of the INDEX LIBRORUM PROHIBITORUM in Rome in 1559 (see also CENSORSHIP).

**See also:** MUSIC PRINTING AND PUBLISHING

**Further reading:** Guglielmo Cavallo, *A History of Reading in the West*, transl. Lydia G. Cochrane (Amherst, Mass.: University of Massachusetts Press, 1999); Elizabeth Eisenstein, *The Printing Press as an Agent of Change: Communications and Cultural Transformations in Early Modern Europe*, 2 vols (Cambridge, U.K.: Cambridge University Press, 1979; concise ed. 1993); Leonardas Gerulaitis, *Printing and Publishing in Fifteenth-Century Venice* (Chicago, Ill.: American Library Association, 1976); Martin Lowry, *Nicholas Jenson and the Rise of Venetian Publishing in Renaissance Europe* (Oxford, U.K.: Blackwell, 1991); Arthur F. Marotti and Michael D. Bristol (eds), *Print, Manuscript, and Performance: The Changing Relations of the Media in Early Modern England* (Columbus, Ohio: Ohio State University Press, 2000); Brian Richardson, *Printing, Writers, and Readers in Renaissance Italy* (Cambridge, U.K.: Cambridge University Press, 1999).

**Protestants** The term was originally applied to the Lutheran minority at the 1529 Diet of SPIRES who protested against the Catholic majority's revocation of toleration of dissenters in their territories. Later it was extended to include all the reformed churches (although rejected in some quarters of the Church of England).

**See also:** HUGUENOTS

**Provoost, Jan** (c. 1465–1529) *Flemish painter*
He was born at Bergen and trained at Brussels and Valenciennes, where he married the widow of the miniaturist Simon Marmion (died 1489). From 1494 he worked in Bruges, where he painted a *Last Judgment* (c. 1524; Bruges museum) for the town hall. His other works, none of which is signed, show him moving away from a style predominantly influenced by Gerard DAVID towards one with an Italianate flavor. Provoost entertained DÜRER on the latter's 1521 visit to the Netherlands.

**Prutenic Tables** See ASTRONOMY

**psalmody** The performance of psalms, one of the oldest musical traditions in Christian and Jewish worship, retained its importance in the Western Church throughout the Middle Ages. In the Roman Catholic rites, plainchant recitation at the monastic hours (the Divine Office) remained the most frequent form of psalm-singing well after the 16th century, and it is this which guided many early psalm settings in polyphony. The musicians of the later 15th and the 16th centuries who began to create multivoice psalm compositions for liturgical use—mainly for the important Office of Vespers—often adopted structuring elements from monophonic psalmody: strict musical division by verse, binary alternation patterns p(for example, by setting only every other verse in polyphony), and the use of the appropriate recitation formula in one voice. Such approaches could have wider effects; as an example, the alternation of two choirs for different verses provided an early impetus for "polychoral" composition, which would become an important form for writing in numerous genres by the later 16th century.

A significant development of the early 16th century was the use of psalm texts as the basis for polyphonic motet compositions with no specific liturgical functions. The psalm-motets of composers such as Josquin DES PRÉS represent an approach to text setting that differs considerably from the practices employed in liturgical psalm-settings. Whereas the latter were structured clearly—either by the traditional recitation formulae, which they elaborated polyphonically, or by the binary verse form—the new style of psalm setting relied on a freer treatment designed to present the text rhetorically. By the middle of the century, composers were creating freely composed, nonliturgical Latin motets based on psalm texts with some frequency. The form had already been introduced to England in the first decades of the 16th century in foreign manuscripts, and native composers showed a substantial interest in writing such motets during the second half of the century.

Psalm settings would prove particularly important in the reformed branches of the Church. From the earliest decades of the Reformation, poets such as Clément MAROT set about translating the psalms into vernacular metrical versions, which were particularly suitable for musical treatment and amateur performance. Edition after edition of such settings appeared throughout the century in every country with a Protestant population. Reformers showed themselves willing to adopt popular secular tunes to their own use: the well-known collections of *Souterliedekens*, settings of Dutch metrical psalm translations printed in Antwerp from 1540 onward, indicate explicitly on each page the original tune that has been recast as a psalm. Originally published monophonically, these psalms were worked into more elaborate settings for multiple voices by Jacobus CLEMENS (NON PAPA) and Gherardus Mes. As the prints themselves inform us, the settings in these books were suitable for domestic recreation (as a deterrent from other entertainments) and could be played equally well on instruments.

See also: HYMNODY; LITURGY

**Psyche** The heroine of a fable in Apuleius's *Golden Ass*, whose name is Greek for "soul." The tale of the many vicissitudes that befell her as the result of her love for CUPID and her eventual union with him in heaven was allegorized in the Renaissance as the yearning of the human soul for divine love. The story inspired the fresco cycle designed by RAPHAEL for the Villa Farnesina (c. 1518).

**Ptolemaic system** The definitive system of ancient astronomy as fully described by Ptolemy (fl.127–161 CE) in his *Almagest*. Manuscripts of this work had been known throughout the Middle Ages, and the first printed edition (Venice, 1515) was of the 12th-century Latin translation made by Gerard of Cremona from the Arabic. A Latin translation made from the Greek text by GEORGE OF TREBIZOND in 1451 was printed in 1528, with the full Greek text, edited by Simon Grynaeus, first appearing at Basle in 1538. Erasmus REINHOLD brought out a combined Greek and Latin edition at Wittenberg in 1549 under the title *Mathematicae constructionis liber primus*. At the instigation of Cardinal BESSARION, Georg PEURBACH had begun work on an *Epitome* (or *Epitoma in Almagestum Ptolemaei*) with a view to establishing a correct text, shorn of later accretions; after Peurbach's death his pupil REGIOMONTANUS completed the work (1463), though it was not published until 1496.

All observation suggested that the heavens revolved around the earth; it also seemed obvious, given the stability of buildings and the behavior of falling bodies, that the earth was stationary. It was further assumed that all celestial motion was "perfect" and as such must be both circular and uniform (*see* COSMOLOGY). These assumptions were, however, too simplistic and soon required considerable modification. They could not, for example, account for the varying brightness of Venus, or for the unequal length of the seasons. The system was consequently adapted in a number of ways. Planets, such as Venus, were assigned a secondary epicyclic motion. Or, as with the sun, they could be given an eccentric orbit. A third and more controversial construction, the equant, identified a point distinct from both the earth and the planet's orbital center, around which the planet moved uniformly. Despite these, and other complications, the Ptolemaic system survived intact until the 16th century when it was slowly replaced by the COPERNICAN SYSTEM. See illustration overleaf.

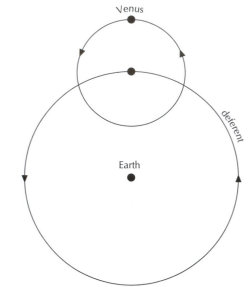

Fig. 1. Epicycle and deferent

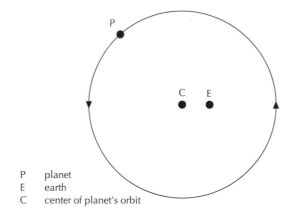

P    planet
E    earth
C    center of planet's orbit

Fig. 2. Eccentric orbit

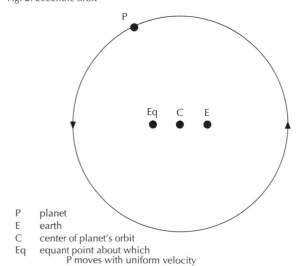

P    planet
E    earth
C    center of planet's orbit
Eq   equant point about which
     P moves with uniform velocity

Fig. 3. Equant

**Ptolemaic system**

**Further reading:** Liba Chaia Taub, *Ptolemy's Universe: The Natural, Philosophical, and Ethical Foundations of Ptolemy's Universe* (La Salle, Ill.: Open Court, 1993).

**Puglia, Niccolò da** See NICCOLÒ DELL'ARCA

**Pulci, Luigi** (1432–1484) *Italian writer and poet*
Born into a patrician but impoverished Guelph family in Florence, Pulci was helped by a friend who was close to Pierfrancesco de' Medici, in whose house he studied under the poet and humanist Bartolommeo SCALA. From age 29, Pulci was a member of Lorenzo de' MEDICI's circle, and his numerous poems reflect Lorenzo's enthusiastic interest in popular Tuscan verse. His masterpiece, the epic *Il Morgante* (1478; expanded version, 1483), draws on such anonymous popular material: a 14th-century version of the Roland story and an account of the adventures of Charlemagne's peers (*see* CHARLEMAGNE, LEGEND OF). Though loosely structured and digressive, Pulci's fantastic chivalric epic is enlivened by some mock-heroic comic inventions, especially the giant Morgante, dedicated to gluttony, and the demigiant Margutte, who manages to confess to 77 mortal sins. (RABELAIS was much indebted to the comic grotesque of *Il Morgante*.) The irreverent and occasionally bitter note in Pulci's writings contributed to his being charged, by FICINO among others, with heresy, and he was not afforded a Christian burial. His other works include *Vocabolista* (*Lexicon*; 1465), a compilation of Latinisms, and *La Beca de Dicomano* (before 1470), which parodies *La Nencia da Barberino*, a pastoral by Lorenzo de' Medici.

Pulci's brothers Luca (1431–70) and Bernardo (1438–88) were also poets. Luca, like Luigi, exploited the *materia cavalleresca* in his *Ciriffo Calvaneo*, and Bernardo's best-known work is the sacred play *Barlaam e Josafat*.

**Further reading:** Mark Davie, *Half-Serious Rhymes: The Narrative Poetry of Luigi Pulci* (Dublin: Irish Academic Press, 1997).

**Purchas, Samuel** (1575–1626) *English clergyman and editor of travel accounts*
Following his ordination Purchas held church appointments in London and Essex. His first publication, *Purchas His Pilgrimage; or, Relations of the World and the Religions Observed in all Ages and Places Discovered, from the Creation unto this Present* (1613), was a historical geography of religion, drawing on a vast array of sources as well as information from contemporaries, including Sir Walter RALEIGH. He was also assisted by Richard HAKLUYT, whose unpublished manuscripts he obtained around 1620. These formed the basis for his monumental four-volume *Hakluytus Posthumus; or, Purchas His Pilgrimes: Contayning a History of the World, in Sea Voyages, & Lande-Travells, by Englishmen & others* (1625). It was invaluable in preserv-

ing accounts of earlier English voyages that might otherwise have been lost.

**Puritans** In England, those Protestant reformers who rejected the ELIZABETHAN SETTLEMENT of 1560, which sought a compromise between Roman Catholicism and the reforming forces of CALVINISM and LUTHERANISM. The Puritans placed emphasis above all on the Bible as the Word of God, on the validity of an individual's conscience, and on preaching, and their uncompromising world-view was informed by the Calvinist doctrine of PREDESTINATION. The Puritans objected to what they saw as superstition in church services, including religious images and the wearing of VESTMENTS by priests, and propagated a form of worship stripped bare of the ceremonial and trappings of the old Catholic faith, for which they said there was no biblical warrant. Although united in their opposition to Catholicism and in their insistence on simplicity in religious practice, Puritans disagreed on matters of doctrine and ecclesiastical government. The three principal sects in England were Presbyterians (Calvinists), Congregationalists (known as Brownists in the 16th century—*see* BROWNISM) and, from the early 17th century, Baptists.

Puritanism, insofar as it was a coherent religious movement, originated in England with people who had fled to Europe to keep their faith pure during the reign (1553–58) of the Catholic MARY I. This impulse extended on their return to rejection of the BOOK OF COMMON PRAYER along with vestments; in the 1560s ELIZABETH I, determined to impose uniformity of worship, told her bishops to insist on conformity. From this grew wider conflict in the 1570s as the Puritans questioned the authority of the episcopal hierarchy—which ultimately challenged Elizabeth's position as Supreme Governor of the Church of England. Elizabeth was more concerned with order in her realm than with individual religious conscience, and it was on the authority issue, rather than religious opinion, that Puritan academics such as Thomas Cartwright (1535–1603) lost their posts, Puritan extremists ended up in the Tower of London, the Puritan John Stubbs (c. 1543–91) had his right hand cut off (1579) for his tract attacking Elizabeth's proposed French marriage, and the ringleaders in the MARPRELATE CONTROVERSY of 1588–89 were sentenced to death. Puritan sympathizers however existed even in the highest echelons of the Anglican Church, notably Archbishop GRINDAL. It was the Puritan Millenary Petition presented to James I in 1603 that led to the calling of the HAMPTON COURT CONFERENCE and ultimately to the Authorized Version of the Bible.

Puritanism is often thought to imply antagonism toward the arts. In England Puritans engaged in a sustained pamphlet war against the theater, partly based on the premise that playhouses were places of moral depravity. Yet it was also a result of the strict Puritan emphasis on truth and a corollary distrust of fiction, thought to be synonymous with lying. However, such Puritan writers as Sir Philip SIDNEY, Edmund SPENSER and John Milton (1608–74) produced poetry that is widely held to embody the spirit of the English Renaissance.

**Further reading:** Margo Todd, *Christian Humanism and the Puritan Social Order* (Cambridge, U.K.: Cambridge University Press, 1988).

**quadrants** Observational instruments consisting of a quarter circle, the curved edge of which is graduated from 0° to 90°, and which is fitted with a movable sight and plumb line. It was first proposed by Ptolemy who recognized that an arc was easier to graduate than a full circle. Quadrants reappeared in Western astronomy in the 16th century when astronomers, such as Tycho BRAHE, first began to appreciate the serious inaccuracies in the available planetary tables. Accordingly in 1568 he designed a 19-foot oak quadrant divided into 5400 minutes. When he moved to Uraniborg some years later he designed for his own use a seven-foot mural quadrant. As the fixed position of such an instrument could be unduly restrictive Brahe also built a rotatable quadrant mounted on a pillar. Such large instruments, however, tended to warp if made of wood or suffer from thermal expansion if made of metal. Small quadrants, on the other hand, proved difficult to graduate accurately. Suitably modified, the basic quadrant also found use among surveyors, navigators, engineers, and gunners. A specialized form, Gunter's quadrant, was described by Edmund Gunter (1581–1626) in his *De sectore et radio* (1623). Also known as the astrolabe quadrant, it allowed, in the manner of ASTROLABES, the time to be determined.

**Quarton, Enguerrand** (**Enguerrand Charton, Enguerrand Charonton**) (c. 1410–c. 1461) *French painter*
Virtually nothing is definitely known of Quarton's life except that he came from the area of Laôn in northern France and was active in Avignon in the period 1447–61. Like his contemporary Nicolas FROMENT, he shows the influence of both Italian and Flemish art in the two works definitely attributable to him: the deeply moving *Avignon*

*Pietà* (1452; Musée Condé, Chantilly) with SS. John and Mary Magdalene and donor, and the magnificently cosmic *Coronation of the Virgin* altarpiece (1453–54; Villeneuve-les-Avignon), the details of which were specified in the extraordinarily minute commission from the donor.

**Quattrocento** (Italian, "four hundred") The period of artistic and cultural development in Italy during the 15th century. Beginning with the competition to design the baptistery doors in Florence in 1401 and ending with the election of Pope Julius II in 1503, this period saw the revival of classical ideals in Italian culture and a flowering of scholarship and the visual arts. Leading figures of the time, who prospered in such artistic centers as Florence, Rome, Naples, Ferrara, Venice, and Padua, included BOIARDO in literature, BRUNELLESCHI, ALBERTI, the elder SANGALLO brothers, and FILARETE in architecture, DONATELLO, GHIBERTI, and DELLA ROBBIA in sculpture, and MASACCIO, UCCELLO, Fra ANGELICO, BOTTICELLI, the BELLINI family, PIERO DELLA FRANCESCA, and MANTEGNA in painting.

**Quercia, Jacopo della** (c. 1374–1438) *Italian sculptor*
Born in Siena, Quercia was an unsuccessful candidate for the first set of doors for the baptistery in Florence (1401), later executed by GHIBERTI. His earliest surviving work is the marble tomb of Ilaria del Carretto (c. 1406) in the cathedral of Lucca, in which elements of both classical and Gothic styles are combined. Subsequent works include the statue of the Virgin and Child in Ferrara (1408; Museo dell' Opera del Duomo), marble reliefs in the Trenta chapel at San Frediano in Lucca (c. 1413–22) and the Fonte Gaia for the Piazza del Campo in Siena

(1414–19; Palazzo Pubblico, Siena). From 1417 to 1434 he worked on reliefs for the baptistery in Siena, on which DONATELLO and Ghiberti also worked, before embarking upon his greatest decorations, the biblical reliefs on the main portal of San Petronio in Bologna (1425–38). This last work was much admired by Michelangelo. In 1435 della Quercia was appointed architect of Siena cathedral.

**Further reading:** James H. Beck, *Jacopo della Quercia* (New York: Columbia University Press, 1992); Anne Coffin Hanson, *Jacopo della Quercia's Fonte Gaia* (Oxford, U.K.: Clarendon Press, 1965); Charles Seymour, *Jacopo della Quercia, Sculptor* (New Haven, Conn. and London: Yale University Press, 1973).

*questione della lingua* The controversy over what should be the preferred form of national language in Italy that reached its climax in the early 16th century. The roots of the problem lay in the competing dialects of the urban centers (with their dependent regions) and the political fragmentation of the peninsula. In effect, the controversy concerned the establishment of a literary or written standard, and to this extent the question was successfully resolved by the early 17th century; however, dialectal diversity in speech and in many nonliterary works (private correspondence, diaries, and official documents) continued up to the 20th century, and only quite recently has something approaching the uniformity of written Italian begun to emerge in the spoken language.

Although BOCCACCIO could still question DANTE's choice of the VERNACULAR to treat the weighty matters of the *Divine Comedy*, the vernacular in literary composition had apparently won the day against Latin during the 13th century. There remained, however, the issue of which of the many regional dialects was the best. In *De vulgari eloquentia* Dante examined a number of them (for the purposes of poetic composition only), finding none perfect but each with useful features. Tuscan had early acquired a certain advantage since the works of the poets of the Sicilian School (written under Frederick II and his son Manfred, between about 1230 and 1266) had been transcribed in a Tuscanized form by copyists and so passed to later poets.

Several positions were taken in the controversy. Giangiorgio TRISSINO and CASTIGLIONE argued for an eclectic *lingua cortigiana*, of mixed usage but essentially Tuscan, such as already prevailed in the great courts of Milan, Rome, and Ferrara, where courtiers of diverse backgrounds communicated in the same language. MACHIAVELLI argued for current spoken Florentine. The position that eventually triumphed was that taken by Pietro BEMBO in *Prose della volgar lingua* (1525). Just as Virgil and Cicero had become the paradigms of Latin style, so Bembo proposed PETRARCH and Boccaccio as models for Italian. Their 14th-century language was not, he pointed out, that of contemporary Florence and Tuscany. His views,

strongly supported by Leonardo SALVIATI, were adopted by the ACCADEMIA DELLA CRUSCA and so reflected in the Cruscan *Vocabolario* (1612), which settled most aspects of spelling, grammar, and vocabulary.

See also: ITALIAN LANGUAGE

## Quevedo y Villegas, Francisco Gómez de (1580–1645) *Spanish satirist, poet, and novelist*

Quevedo's parents held positions at court in Madrid, where he was born, but his father died soon after his birth and his mother left him in the charge of tutors. Although born lame and with poor eyesight, he attended the university of Alcalá; there he developed an active, belligerent character and intellectual brilliance, mastering Greek, Latin, and Hebrew, and later Italian, French, and some Arabic. About 1600 he was at the court in Valladolid and moved with it to Madrid in 1606. He produced a constant flow of satirical verses and pamphlets, made a lifelong enemy of GÓNGORA, cultivated a friendship with CERVANTES, and corresponded with Justus LIPSIUS. He wrote an outstanding PICARESQUE NOVEL, *El Buscón* (1603–08), and in 1606 the first of five *Sueños* (Visions). Published in 1627, these scathing prose satires, influenced by Dante and Lucian, contain passages of grotesque brilliance.

In 1611 Quevedo was forced to leave court—according to rumor, for having murdered a man—and in 1613 became an agent of the duke of Osuna in Italy. Deeply involved in Osuna's plots against Venice, Quevedo, thanks to excellent Italian, barely escaped with his life when the Venetians struck back at the conspirators. When the duke of Olivares came to power on the accession of Philip IV (1621), all former ministers of Osuna were punished. Quevedo, however, eventually regained favor by dedicating to Olivares a "mirror of princes" work (which he thought his best), the *Política de Dios* (1617; published 1626). The period to 1639 was the happiest of his life, despite an unfortunate marriage (1634); both parties welcomed an agreed separation in 1636. In 1639 Philip IV found under his napkin at table some anonymous verses attacking Olivares. Quevedo was held to be guilty—how, exactly, he was involved is not certain—and was confined in a monastery in León until after Olivares' death in 1643. Too ill to return to court, he spent his final years on his estate.

Quevedo was unexcelled as a stylist, his works being particularly associated with the "wit" (*agudeza*—a term approximating the "wit" of English Metaphysical poetry) of *conceptismo* (often, inaccurately, taken as the antithesis of the mannered rhetorical style of Góngora and *culteranismo*). He carried on a continual polemic against Góngora and his followers and edited the works of Fray LUIS DE LEÓN as a corrective against *culteranismo*. Over 1000 of his poems were anthologized posthumously, but an accurate edition of his prolific output is more recent, the first volume of *Obras completas*, ed. J. M. Blecua, appearing in 1963.

**Further reading:** George Mariscal, *Contradictory Subjects: Quevedo, Cervantes, and Seventeenth-Century Spanish Culture* (Ithaca, N.Y.: Cornell University Press, 1991).

## Quiñones, Francisco de (1480–1540) *Spanish Franciscan reformer*

Quiñones, who was born at León, adopted the name Francisco de los Angeles when he joined the Order of Friars Minor sometime before 1507. He served as minister-general of the order (1523–28), was named cardinal (1527), and was bishop of Coira (1531–33). Quiñones was a pre-Tridentine reformer (*see* TRENT, COUNCIL OF), advocating humanist learning, the training of Franciscan youth, and the use of retreat houses to promote an intense spiritual life. He was also interested in missionary activity and in 1523 sent the mission of the "Twelve Apostles" to New Spain, to which he hoped to go as papal nuncio and Spanish viceroy. Pope Clement VII instead employed him on secret missions to Charles V's court where, following the Sack of ROME (1527), he won the pope's freedom and prepared the treaties of Barcelona (1528) and of Cambrai (1529).

At the pope's behest, Quiñones prepared a simplified breviary, often referred to as "the Breviary of the Holy Cross." Between 1535 and 1558, 100 editions were published, totalling about 100,000 copies, and it influenced the Church of England's BOOK OF COMMON PRAYER. The Council of Trent suppressed the Quiñones breviary. Quiñones died in Veroli, Italy.

## Quintilian (Marcus Fabius Quintilianus) (c. 35–c. 95) *Spanish-born Roman rhetorician*

After a distinguished teaching career in Rome, Quintilian devoted the remainder of his life to writing the *Institutio oratoria*. Despite the title, it deals not only with the training of orators but with the general principles of EDUCATION. After suffering an eclipse in the Middle Ages, the work was immensely important to the Renaissance; PETRARCH knew it only through an imperfect copy, Poggio BRACCIOLINI unearthed a complete text (1416), and it was first printed in 1470. The *Institutio*'s insistence upon linking knowledge and oratorical ability with excellent moral character was the keynote of most Renaissance educational programs—in the words of Sidney, "the ending end of all earthly learning being verteous action" (*Defence of Poesie*). Quintilian's assessment of ancient authors in his 10th book played a significant role in Renaissance literary judgments.

# R

**Rabelais, François** (c. 1483–1553) *French satirist, humanist, and physician*
The son of a wealthy lawyer, Rabelais was born near Chinon. He may have studied law before entering the Church, becoming a Franciscan novice at La Baumette, near Angers, and subsequently moving to the convent of Puy-St.-Martin at Fontenay-le-Comte, where he was ordained priest. Suspected of heretical tendencies on account of his study of Greek, he transferred to the Benedictine convent of Maillezais (1524) and became secretary to Geoffroy d'Estissac, bishop of Maillezais.

By 1530 Rabelais had abandoned religion for medicine, which he studied at Montpellier; in 1532 he was appointed physician to the hospital of the Hôtel-Dieu in Lyons. The same year saw the publication of his edition of Hippocrates' *Aphorismes*; the satirical *Pantagruel*, the first novel of his GARGANTUA AND PANTAGRUEL cycle (which appeared under the anagrammatic pseudonym Alcofribas Nasier); and the *Pantagruéline Prognostication*, a parody of the almanacs that were fashionable at the time. As physician to the brothers Jean and Guillaume du Bellay (*see* DU BELLAY, JOACHIM), Rabelais accompanied the former on diplomatic missions to Rome and the latter to Piedmont, relinquishing his post at the Hôtel-Dieu. After the publication of *Gargantua* in 1534 he appears to have written nothing until the *Tiers Livre* (1546), the third and finest novel of the cycle, which was dedicated to MARGUERITE DE NAVARRE. The Sorbonne's condemnation of this work on grounds of heresy forced Rabelais into temporary exile at Metz; his *Quart Livre*, which first appeared in its entirety in 1552, was also banned on publication. Rabelais died in Paris, probably in 1553, having resigned his benefices at Meudon and Jambet. The authenticity of the *Cinquième Livre*, published posthumously in 1564, has been disputed.

One of the most influential French writers of the Renaissance, Rabelais combined insight and imagination with a talent for verbal invention that made a profound impression on his contemporaries and has been a valuable and lasting source of inspiration for subsequent satirists and humorous writers in France and beyond.

**Further reading:** Mikhail Bakhtin, *Rabelais and His World*, transl. Helene Iswolsky (Bloomington, Ind.: Indiana University Press, 1984; repr. 1988); Jean-Claude Carron (ed.), *François Rabelais: Critical Assessments* (Baltimore, Md.: Johns Hopkins University Press, 1995); Michael A. Screech, *Rabelais* (London: Duckworth, 1979).

**racism** The attitudes of early modern Europeans toward the people of other races that they encountered during their voyages of exploration were generally of a kind that would now be considered blatantly racist. Expectations of the strangeness of peoples living in distant climes were fed by medieval yarns such as Sir John Mandeville's *Travels*, and xenophobia, particularly directed against non-Christians, was fueled by the menace of Islam on Christendom's eastern and southern flanks. The cruel and treacherous "paynim" (literally, "pagan" but often used of a Turk) was a commonplace villain in medieval romance and Renaissance epic. SHAKESPEARE gives a nuanced picture of Renaissance racism in his portrayal of Venetian attitudes toward the Moor Othello; as a soldier Othello is admired and necessary to the state but it is nonetheless a matter for incredulity and revulsion that the white girl Desdemona should love and marry him. Dark skin was considered at best undesirable, at worst an indicator of moral degeneracy. In *The Masque of Blackness*, performed before James I in 1605, blacked-up court ladies played the daughters of the black god Niger, who could only achieve their ambition of becoming white under the benign influence of James.

In real life, distrust and contempt characterized most European dealings with people of color, and relatively objective accounts of native peoples, such as Hans STADEN's of the Brazilian Tupinambá, are uncommon. People of newly encountered tribes who were brought to Europe by explorers were looked upon as freaks and exploited for their rarity value; the considerate treatment accorded to LEO AFRICANUS was a rare exception. In explorers' accounts African and Native American societies are described in sensationalist terms: nakedness, polygamy, and cannibalism are all avidly reported, but in the writers' eyes the fundamental defect in all such peoples was their ignorance of Christianity. It very often followed from this that Europeans saw indigenous peoples simply as savages to be exploited. A typical proponent of this view was the Spanish theologian Juan Ginés de Sepúlveda who, at a special session of the Council of the Indies in Valladolid in 1550, presented the argument that the indigenous people of America should be conquered by force and used as slaves. A more humane voice was that of his opponent, Batholomé de LAS CASAS, who devoted his life to the defense of Native American rights against brutal oppression. Some few people carried compassion for people of different race to an extent extraordinary even today, such as the Spanish Jesuit Peter Claver (born 1585) who ministered for decades to sick Black slaves imprisoned at Cartagena in conditions of extreme squalor and degradation.

See also: ANTISEMITISM; SLAVERY

**Further reading:** Olive Patricia Dickason, *The Myth of the Savage and the Beginnings of French Colonialism in the Americas* (Edmonton, Canada: University of Alberta Press, 1984; 2nd ed. 1992).

**Raffaele ware** See MAJOLICA

**Ragusa** (Serbo-Croatian **Dubrovnik**) A Dalmatian city and port on the Adriatic. Founded in the seventh century by Roman refugees, Ragusa enjoyed considerable autonomy under Venetian suzerainty (1205–1358). After a period under Hungarian rule (1358–1420) Ragusa was restored to Venice, but became a free city in all but name. During the period of the Renaissance shipbuilding, commerce, and the Ottoman trade brought prosperity to Ragusa. By the 16th century Ragusan ships were sailing to the Indies and the Americas (the word "argosy," meaning a ship with a rich cargo, derives from the Italian phrase for "ship of Ragusa"). A number of refugees fled to Ragusa ahead of the Ottoman advance into eastern Europe, making the city an important literary and artistic center from the 15th to the 17th centuries and earning it the title of

the "Athens of the South Slavs." Fine paved streets and handsome palaces still bear witness to the enlightened civic policies and wealth of Ragusa's rulers at this time.

**Raibolini, Francesco** See FRANCIA, FRANCESCO RAIBOLINI

**Raimondi, Marcantonio** (c. 1480–1534) *Italian engraver*
Born near Bologna, Raimondi was trained by the goldsmith and painter Francesco FRANCIA and is notable chiefly for his engravings of paintings by his contemporaries. After moving to Venice in about 1506, and later Rome (c. 1510), he was greatly influenced by the woodcuts of DÜRER and became famous for his engravings of works by Raphael, Michelangelo, and others. Although he became financially very successful, his reputation suffered after his arrest for engraving obscene designs by GIULIO ROMANO and he died in obscurity in Bologna. The technique of engraving brought by Raimondi to a high degree of perfection enabled accurate copies of works of art to be produced and disseminated in large quantities, thus contributing greatly to the spread of iconographic and stylistic information in the Renaissance.

**Rainolds, John** (1549–1607) *English divine and humanist*
Rainolds was born at Pinhoe, near Exeter, and became (1568) a fellow of Corpus Christi College, Oxford, where he was tutor to Richard HOOKER. From 1573 he was college reader in Greek and lectured on Aristotle's rhetoric. Owing to internal disputes in his college, he resigned in 1578, and became a fellow of Queen's. Although two of his brothers, William and Edmond, were Roman Catholics, John was a Calvinist; in 1592 he was rebuked by Queen Elizabeth for his reforming zeal. In the following year, he became dean of Lincoln, but returned to Oxford in 1598 as president of Corpus Christi College. In 1604 he led the Puritan faction at the HAMPTON COURT CONFERENCE and was designated one of the translators of the Authorized Version of the Bible (1611).

**Raleigh, Sir Walter** (c. 1552–1618) *English mariner and writer*
The son of an obscure Devonshire gentleman, Raleigh attended Oxford University but did not graduate. He then fought in the French Wars of Religion and in Ireland. From 1581 he was in attendance on Queen ELIZABETH I, where his wit, sincerity, and handsome appearance established him as a favorite. His long poem *The Ocean to Cynthia* expresses aspects of their relationship. Knighted in 1584, Raleigh gained grants of land and trading privileges from Elizabeth, guaranteeing his financial security. An expedition sponsored by him (1584) claimed Virginia for England, naming the territory in Elizabeth's honor. Over the next three years Raleigh spent £40,000 trying to establish a colony in Virginia; despite the failure of this pro-

ject, it drew attention to the merits of expansionism and the economic possibilities of America.

From the late 1570s Raleigh had been involved in various seafaring adventures, mainly against Spain, and in 1592 he was recalled from one and thrown into the Tower because of his clandestine marriage to one of Elizabeth's maids of honor. His expedition to Guiana (1595) and key role in the sacking of Cádiz (1596) more or less restored him to favor, although Essex was now Elizabeth's principal favorite. On the accession of JAMES I, with his policy of peace with Spain, Raleigh's numerous enemies ensured his downfall; in 1603, at a sham trial, he was convicted of treason. Given an 11th-hour reprieve from the scaffold, he then spent 12 years in prison, where he made alchemical experiments and wrote many letters and poems, as well as his influential (but inappropriately titled) *History of the World* (1614). In 1616 James released him to search for gold along the Orinoco River. The expedition was a disaster, and, contravening James's explicit instructions, Raleigh's followers attacked a Spanish settlement. On his return to England Raleigh was beheaded on the 1603 charge.

**Further reading:** Marc Aronson, *Sir Walter Raleigh and the Quest for El Dorado* (Boston, Mass.: Houghton Mifflin, 2000); Raleigh Travelyan, *Sir Walter Raleigh* (London: Allen Lane, 2003 and New York: Henry Holt, 2004).

**Rambaldoni, Vittorino de'** See VITTORINO DA FELTRE

**Ramée, Pierre de la** See RAMUS, PETRUS

**Ramelli, Agostino** (c. 1537–c. 1608) *Italian engineer*
Ramelli was born at Ponte Tresa, near Como, and is first heard of as a military engineer in the service of Gian Giacomo de' Medici. He later moved to France where he seems to have settled sometime in the 1570s. Ramelli is remembered today as the author of *Le diverse et artificiose machine* (1588), a volume published with French and Italian texts on facing pages. The 195 full- or double-page illustrations serve as a primary source for the state of Renaissance technology. About a hundred depict pumps and pumping machinery; the remainder show a variety of devices, including windmills, tilt hammers, screw jacks, water wheels, and revolving bookcases. Many of these, though feasible designs, were likely to have been beyond the capacity of the craftsmen of Ramelli's day. See illustration overleaf.

**Ramist controversy** The long-running dispute over the issues with which Petrus RAMUS chose to concern himself, namely, the nature of logic, dialectic, and rhetoric. Ramus rejected the Aristotelian tradition, opting instead to follow CICERO as he had been presented by Rudolf AGRICOLA. Whereas Aristotle had distinguished between logic, which argued to a necessary conclusion, and dialectic, which

permitted only probable conclusions, Ramus insisted there was only one *ars disserendi* (art of discourse), called indifferently by him logic or rhetoric. At a less abstract level he extolled the virtues of the practical over the theoretical, and the particular over the general. Thus, geometry was defined by him as "the art of measuring well," while ethics, he said, should be taught through biography and history. This practical approach to philosophy was echoed in the work of John DEE, William GILBERT, and Francis BACON. It was also readily accepted throughout much of Protestant Europe and found support in Puritan New England. Such support was still being expressed long after the death of Ramus in the writings of John Milton and G. W. Leibniz, among others.

Opposition arose, however, in Catholic Europe. Jacques Charpentier in France, and other so-called anti-Ramists, insisted upon the distinction between logic and dialectic and argued that "the standard and norm of logic" lay elsewhere than in the popular speech studied by the Ramists. A third group, the curiously named semi-Ramists, or Philippo-Ramists, was identified by Franco Burgersdyck in 1626; this group sought a compromise between the Ramists and the followers of Philipp MELANCHTHON. Despite the intensity of the dispute, its historical significance was limited by the emergence of the more central concerns and potent method of René Descartes in the 1630s and 1640s.

**Further reading:** James Veazie Skalnik, *Ramus and Reform: Church and University at the End of the Renaissance* (Gonic, N.H.: Odyssey Press, 2002).

**Ramos de Pareja, Bartolomé** (c. 1440–c. 1491) *Spanish music theorist*
Ramos taught music at the university of Salamanca and appears to have gone to Bologna in about 1472, where he lectured in music. After 1484 he went to Rome and was still there in 1491. Ramos wrote several theoretical works, but only his *Musica practica* (1482) survives. In it he attacked contemporary musical procedures, such as notation, classification of the modes, and, in particular, the theories of the Roman philosopher Boethius on tuning. Ramos argued that many of the theories of the past were too complicated and impractical for performers. Although he was widely criticized, his ideas were used by later theorists, including Henricus GLAREANUS and Gioseffo ZARLINO.

**Ramus, Petrus** (Pierre de la Ramée) (1515–1572) *French logician and humanist*
Ramus was born near Soissons and educated at the university of Paris. In 1536 he defended for his MA the thesis that everything written by Aristotle is false. The claim was made more publicly in his *Aristotelicæ animadversiones* (1543) and resulted in a ban forbidding him from teaching philosophy. The ban was lifted in 1547 by Henry II,

FIGVRE IX.

**Agostino Ramelli** An engraving from *Le diverse et artificiose machine* (1588) illustrating a water wheel and associated gearing. This book contains a number of remarkable illustrations depicting the state of hydraulic and military engineering toward the end of the 16th century.

and in 1551 Ramus was appointed professor of philosophy at the Collège Royal in Paris. Much of his later work was concerned with the reform of traditional logic, thought, and education (*see* RAMIST CONTROVERSY). His views were widely disseminated in his best-known work, *Dialectique* (1555), the first work on logic to be published in French, and his books on arithmetic and geometry appeared in many editions.

After converting to Calvinism in 1561 Ramus abandoned France for some time to avoid the dangers of the religious wars. He settled once more in Paris in 1570 and died as one of the victims of the MASSACRE OF ST. BARTHOLOMEW.

**Further reading:** Walter J. Ong, *Ramus: Method, and the Decay of Dialogue: From the Art of Discourse to the Art of Reason* (Cambridge, Mass.: Harvard University Press, 1958; repr. 1975).

**Ramusio, Giovanni Battista** (1485–1557) *Italian writer and geographer*
Born at Treviso, Ramusio was raised in an environment of discovery and innovation. He worked in the Venetian public service, rising steadily to become secretary of the Council of Ten by 1533. Around 1520 he became friends with Girolamo FRACASTORO, who inspired him to collect a diversity of geographical material, much of it gathered

through personal contact with leading explorers and humanists of his day. This was published as the three-volume *Delle navigationi et viaggi* (1550–59), a masterpiece widely acknowledged as the definitive geography sourcebook of the 16th century. Subsequent early editions (1563 for vol.1, 1583 for vol.2, 1606 for vol. 3) have been reprinted in facsimile as *Navigationi et viaggi: Venice 1563–1606* (Amsterdam: Theatrum orbis terrarum, 1967–70), with an introduction by R. A. Skelton and an analysis of the contents by George B. Parks.

**Raphael** (**Raffaello Sanzio**) (1483–1520) *Italian painter and architect*
Raphael was born in Urbino, the son of the painter Giovanni Santi, but little of his early career is documented. He probably joined PERUGINO's workshop before 1500, establishing contacts within the Urbino court as well as with important patrons in Perugia and Città di Castello. The St. Nicholas altarpiece (fragments in Capodimonte, Naples, and Pinacoteca Tosio-Martinengo, Brescia) shows that by 1500 Raphael had already established a reputation as a competent artist. The Mond *Crucifixion* (c. 1502; National Gallery, London) demonstrates his ready assimilation of Perugino's style.

By 1504 he had learnt all his master had to teach him and, armed with an introduction from the Urbino court, Raphael went to Florence to face the artistic challenges posed by LEONARDO DA VINCI and MICHELANGELO. Drawings played a vital role in Raphael's absorption of the Florentine concerns with mass, form, light, and movement. A drawing in the British Museum adapting the *contrapposto* of Leonardo's *Leda* onto a representation of Michelangelo's *St. Matthew* displays an eclecticism typical of Raphael. The evolution of Raphael's style from the static Umbrian mold towards a more fluid and emotive idiom is documented in the series of drawings connected with the Baglioni *Entombment* (1507; Galleria Borghese, Rome). Raphael began with a Peruginesque *Lamentation*, which subsequently developed into a dramatic, if not wholly successful, composition imbued with the Florentine emphasis on emotive narrative compositions.

One of Raphael's earliest Florentine works, the *Madonna del Granduca* (c. 1505; Palazzo Pitti, Florence) displays a new simplicity of form and unity in composition that suggests contact with Fra BARTOLOMMEO and Leonardo. Motifs from Leonardo's cartoon *Virgin and Child with St. Anne* (c. 1501; now lost) are reflected in a number of Raphael's Madonna compositions, particularly that of the Carnigiani *Holy Family* (c. 1505; Prado, Madrid), where the figures, placed in a pyramidal composition, relate to one another in a significant and harmonious fashion. Leonardo's MONA LISA introduced a new portrait type taken up in Raphael's *Maddalena Doni* (c. 1507; Palazzo Pitti, Florence), while Leonardo's *Adoration of the Magi* (1481; Uffizi, Florence) which incorporated over 40 fig-

**Raphael** An engraving based on a self-portrait (c. 1508–11) of the artist in his twenties.
*Popperfoto*

ures circling in and out of a dark penumbra, was to influence many of Raphael's works, including drawings for the *Disputà* (1509; Vatican).

In 1508, possibly at the behest of fellow Umbrian BRAMANTE, Raphael went to Rome. Pope JULIUS II had commissioned a team of artists to redecorate part of the Vatican palace, but by 1509 Raphael had been made solely responsible for the designs of the Stanze, the new papal apartments. The theme of the Stanza della Segnatura (painted 1509–11) is human versus divine intellect. In their harmonious repose and classical purity, the frescoes in this room represent the zenith of High Renaissance painting (see Plate XIII). Clarity and logic dominate the designs, particularly in the *Disputà*, where the elevated Host acts as both the vanishing point and the narrative pivot linking earthly with heavenly realms. The Stanza dell' Eliodoro (1511–14), representing divine intervention on behalf of the Church, was executed in a more theatrical vein, befitting the drama of the potent political message. The Stanza dell' Incendio (1515–17) was mainly the work of assistants, for by now Raphael was beleaguered by commissions. He executed a number of works for the wealthy banker, Agostino CHIGI, decorating his villa in Trastevere (*see* FARNESINA, VILLA), with a classically inspired fresco cycle of *Cupid and Psyche* (c. 1518) and designing his chapel in Sta. Maria del Popolo (c. 1513–16), where antique funerary motifs, expressed in architecture, sculpture, and painting, proclaimed the ascent of Chigi's soul to heaven. Raphael was also much in demand as a portrait painter; his *Julius II* (c. 1511; National Gallery, London) and *Baldassare Castiglione* (c. 1515; Louvre, Paris) are just two outstanding examples of his skill in this field.

In 1514 Pope Leo X appointed Raphael architect of St. Peter's and in 1515, superintendent of Roman antiquities. Raphael's architectural works displayed his increasing appreciation of classical vocabulary. His design for the Chigi stables (1514–18; now destroyed) incorporated column bases modeled on those of the Forum of Nerva, while the incomplete Villa Madama (c. 1518) owes much to the classical villas of Pliny the Younger. While Raphael's TAPESTRY cartoons of the *Acts of the Apostles* (c. 1515–19; Royal Collection, Victoria and Albert Museum, London) still display a classical majesty, his last work, the *Transfiguration* (1518–20; Vatican museum, Rome) suggests a new departure in its dramatic chiaroscuro and violently twisting figures. Unfinished at his death, it was displayed over his coffin in the Pantheon.

**Further reading:** Luciano Berti, *Raphael* (London: Weidenfeld & Nicolson, 1961); Leopold D. and Helen S. Ettlinger, *Raphael* (Oxford, U.K.: Phaidon, 1987); Antonio P. Graziano *et al*, *Michelangelo and Raphael in the Vatican* (Rome: Treasures Inc., 1997); Christiane L. Joast-Gaugier, *Raphael's Stanza della Segnatura: Meaning and Invention* (Cambridge, U.K.: Cambridge University Press, 2002).

**Ratdolt, Erhard** (c. 1447–1528) *German printer and type cutter*
He worked in Venice for 10 years from 1476 and, on his return to his native Augsburg (1486), issued the first known specimen sheet, showing 10 sizes of gothic type, three roman, and one Greek. In Venice his innovations included the first title-page (in REGIOMONTANUS's *Kalendarius* (1476), which also had diagrams of solar and lunar eclipses printed in color) and the 400 diagrams in his edition of Euclid's *Elementa* (1482), the first to be printed. Decorated initials and borders were used with woodcuts in the missals and breviaries that Ratdolt also produced.

**Ratisbon, Colloquy of** See REGENSBURG, COLLOQUY OF

**Raymond of Sebonde** (died c. 1436) *Spanish philosopher, doctor, and theologian*
He was born in Barcelona and in the 1430s he was professor at Toulouse, where he died. There he composed his most important work, the *Liber creaturarum seu naturae*, which was printed about 1480 under the title *Theologia naturalis*. Raymond sought to reach an understanding of God through the "two books," that of the creatures and that of sacred Scripture. This approach united the claims of reason and faith. Raymond's work attracted the criticism of the Church, and the prologue to the *Theologia* was suppressed and put on the INDEX LIBRORUM PROHIBITORUM (1595). MONTAIGNE translated the work into French (1569), and one of his best-known essays is *L'Apologie de Raimond Sebon*, defending the Spaniard's emphasis on the "book of nature."

**Real Presence** Any doctrine of the Eucharist which maintains that Christ is actually present in the sacrament, as opposed to the view of more radical Protestants that Christ's presence is merely figurative. The term can include the Catholic doctrine of TRANSUBSTANTIATION, but is more often used of moderate Protestant doctrines such as that of LUTHER, who held that Christ's body and blood are present "in, with, and under" the bread and wine, and that of CALVIN, who held that the bread and wine remain physically unaltered but that believers are blessed by Christ's "spiritual presence" in the sacrament. The term is particularly associated with the Anglican Church, which found it a usefully imprecise formula. The Real Presence is mentioned in Foxe's *Book of Martyrs* (1563) as a tenet of Bishop Hugh Latimer (burnt for heresy in 1555 under Mary I), and the Anglican position on it is set out in Jeremy Taylor's 1654 book, *The Real Presence*.

**recusancy** In Elizabethan and Jacobean England, the legally defined position of those Roman Catholics who refused to attend services of the established Church. In the early part of ELIZABETH I's reign the great majority of Catholics chose outward conformity and were not harassed for their faith. However, this changed abruptly in 1570, when the pope excommunicated and anathematized Elizabeth, effectively forcing English Catholics to choose between their religion and their allegiance. The growing strength of recusancy, encouraged from 1580 by Catholic missionaries such as Edmund CAMPION dispatched from the Continent, became a serious concern to the authorities, especially as the threat of a Spanish invasion loomed in the 1580s. Accordingly, the existing Acts of Uniformity were bolstered by further statutes (1581, 1586–87, 1593) imposing harsh penalties on recusants. Failure to attend church incurred a heavy fine, with persistent offenders liable to confiscations of their goods and estates; hearing Mass was punishable by imprisonment; making or becoming a convert to Catholicism was defined as an act of treason. However, the extent to which these laws were enforced varied greatly, and in some predominantly Catholic areas, such as northwest England, they seem to have been widely evaded. For this reason the true number of recusants is hard to compute. Figures from 1603 show that 8,630 people were indicted for recusancy that year, but it seems probable that the number of recusants who found ways of bystepping the law was much higher than this.

*rederijkers* See CHAMBERS OF RHETORIC

**Reformation** The movement for the reform of Western Christianity that led in the 16th century to its division into opposed Catholic and Protestant churches. The roots of the Reformation are now usually seen in the reform movement of the medieval period, the failure of which left many still dissatisfied with numerous aspects of Church government and teaching. This dissatisfaction found an important outlet in the writings of humanist scholars, such as ERASMUS and Johann REUCHLIN. By their sustained criticism of abuses within the Church, and still more by their encouragement of textual analysis (thereby undermining the claims of the Church to be the final arbiter on matters of faith), such scholars played an important role in creating the climate of opinion in which protest against unpopular papal practices could gain a following (see HUMANISM).

LUTHER's protest against INDULGENCES in 1517 thus belonged to a well-established tradition; its novelty lay in the speed with which it spread throughout Germany (its diffusion assisted by printing, a comparatively recent invention) and the determination with which Luther pressed home his charges of papal corruption. In his great tracts of 1520 Luther developed his criticism into a systematic denunciation of the old Church, emerging as a worthy leader of the movement; the Roman hierarchy, in contrast, responded with hesitation and indecision, influenced by political considerations that dictated caution in dealing with the German princes and with Emperor Charles V. With this encouragement, the evangelical movement spread very rapidly. By 1535 most of the imperial free cities and many of the princely states had embraced the Reformation. When they banded together in a military association to defend Protestantism (see SCHMAL-KALDIC LEAGUE) its future within the empire was largely secure.

The great interest shown in Luther's writings outside Germany strongly assisted the spread of the Reformation. In Switzerland the lead was taken by Ulrich ZWINGLI, who between 1522 and 1525 introduced in Zürich a radically reformed church polity. Zwingli's teaching, with its greater emphasis on communal values and a more emphatic rejection of Catholic practice, achieved a substantial following in Switzerland and south Germany, despite a serious disagreement with Luther over sacramental doctrine which a personal meeting failed to resolve (see MARBURG, COLLOQUY OF). After Zwingli's death the leadership of the Swiss Reformation passed eventually to John CALVIN, the reformer of Geneva. Calvin introduced into Geneva a strongly theocratic church polity, based on a tightly organized reformed theology that preserved much of the best from both the Lutheran and non-Lutheran reforming traditions (see INSTITUTES, THE).

The spread of CALVINISM after 1550 helped revive a movement that showed signs of flagging in the face of an increasingly determined Catholic counteroffensive. In France early interest in reform (characterized by groups such as Guillaume Briçonnet and the Circle of Meaux) had given way to a sustained persecution, which forced most of the leading French Protestants to seek safety in exile. But between 1555, when the first church was founded in Paris, and 1562 over 2000 Calvinist communities were planted (see HUGUENOTS), a rate of growth that destabilized the weak French monarchy and precipitated the French Wars of RELIGION. Although the Reformation never attained full success in France, the Edict of Nantes (1598) guaranteed the Huguenot churches the status of a privileged minority. In the Netherlands Calvinism also made rapid progress, building on the foundations established by a robust native evangelical tradition. Although forced to take their first constitutional steps in exile (Synod of Emden, 1571) the Calvinist communities returned in time to play a major role in the war of independence that freed the northern Netherlands from Spain. In 1622 Calvinism was established as the official state religion of the United Provinces. Calvinism also achieved a notable triumph in Scotland, where the Reformation again prevailed as part of a movement of national self-determination (1559–61). Under the leadership of John KNOX the Scottish ministers succeeded in establishing a strongly presbyterian church order. Other important Calvinist churches were planted in central Europe (Bohemia, Poland, Hungary), while Lutheranism achieved permanent success outside Germany only in the Baltic and Scandinavia.

The Reformation in England conformed fully to neither of these patterns, the breach with Rome having been initiated by the otherwise orthodox King HENRY VIII for entirely political reasons. The introduction of a genuine Protestant polity was achieved only in the reign (1547–53) of Henry's son EDWARD VI under the guidance of Thomas CRANMER, who was responsible for the BOOK OF COMMON PRAYER (1549). After a brief Catholic restoration (1553–58) under Mary I, the accession of Elizabeth signaled the final triumph of Protestantism. The Anglican Church preserved its individuality in a unique form of church government that is often described as Erastian (see ERASTIANISM), although in doctrinal terms it was essentially Calvinist.

The Reformation inevitably spawned a great variety of religious thinkers who owed allegiance to none of the major church leaders. Luther was confronted with the problem of radical dissent in Wittenberg as early as 1521 (Thomas Müntzer and the Zwickau Prophets; see ANABAPTISTS), and Zwingli faced a similar challenge from the Swiss Brethren. The most coherent force beyond the Protestant mainstream was the Anabaptist movement, which made rapid progress in Germany and northern Europe. Drawn together by a shared practice of adult baptism, the ANABAPTISTS were persecuted by Catholics and Protestants alike, particularly after the collapse of the radical Anabaptist kingdom of Münster (1535). Anabaptism, however, proved extremely resilient, particularly in the Netherlands under the leadership of Menno Simons (1496–1561), whose followers became known as MEN-NONITES.

The cultural and political effects of the Reformation were profound if unpredictable. Ultimately, it may be said to have assisted the process of nation-building by breaking the moral and economic power of the old Church—although for a time Calvinism mounted its own challenge to the developing trend towards absolutist monarchies. In cultural terms, the negative impact of the reformers' hostility towards traditional religious art was balanced by their encouragement of church music and the incentive they provided for a new artistic tradition, as in the case of Rembrandt. Certainly, the Reformation helped create the magnificent diversification of European culture that marked the succeeding centuries.

**Further reading:** Owen Chadwick, *The Early Reformation on the Continent* (Oxford, U.K.: Oxford University Press, 2001); Brian Cummings, *The Literary Culture of the Reformation: Grammar and Grace* (Oxford, U.K.: Oxford University Press, 2002); Arthur G. Dickens, *Reformation and Society in Sixteenth-Century Europe* (London: Thames & Hudson, 1966); Harold J. Grimm, *The Reformation Era, 1500–1650* (New York: Macmillan, 2nd ed. 1973); Carter Lindberg, *The European Reformations* (Oxford, U.K.: Blackwell, 1996); Diarmaid MacCulloch, *Reformation: Europe's House Divided 1490–1700* (London: Allen Lane, 2003), as *The Reformation: A History* (New York: Penguin Viking, 2004) ENGLAND: Patrick Collinson, *The Religion of Protestants: The Church in English Society 1559–1625* (Oxford, U.K.: Clarendon Press, 1982); Arthur G. Dickens, *The English Reformation* (London: Batsford, 1964; 2nd ed. 1989); Eamon Duffy, *The Stripping of the Altars: Traditional Religion in England c. 1400–c. 1580* (New Haven, Conn. and London: Yale University Press, 1992); ~, *Voices of Morebath: Reformation and Rebellion in an English Village* (New Haven, Conn. and London: Yale University Press, 2001); Felicity Heal, *Reformation in Britain and Ireland* (Oxford, U.K.: Clarendon Press, 2003); Norman Jones, *The English Reformation: Religion and Cultural Adaptation* (Oxford, U.K.: Blackwell, 2001) GERMANY: C. Scott Dixon, *The Reformation in Germany* (Oxford: Blackwell, 2002); Robert W. Scribner, *The German Reformation* (London: Macmillan, 1986; 2nd ed. Basingstoke: Palgrave Macmillan, 2003); ~, *For the Sake of Simple Folk: Popular Propaganda for the German Reformation* (Cambridge, U.K.: Cambridge University Press, 1981; 2nd ed. Oxford, U.K.: Clarendon Press, 1994) NETHERLANDS: Phyllis M. Crew, *Calvinist Preaching and Iconoclasm in the Netherlands* (Cambridge, U.K.: Cambridge University Press, 1978).

**Regensburg, Colloquy of** (1541) A conference of Roman Catholic and Protestant theologians convened by Emperor CHARLES V in the Bavarian city of Regensburg (formerly Ratisbon). The Roman Catholic representatives were Johann ECK, Julius Pflug (1499–1564), and Johann Gropper (1503–59); Cardinal Gasparo CONTARINI was papal legate. The Protestants were represented by Martin BUCER, Philipp MELANCHTHON, and Johann Pistorius the Elder (1503–83). The quest for reconciliation on doctrinal issues was largely successful, but the colloquy had no practical outcome, mainly due to Luther's implacable opposition to any compromise with Rome.

**Regiomontanus (Johann Müller)** (1436–1476) *German mathematician and astronomer*
His Latin name derives from his birthplace, Königsberg. Educated at Vienna university, Regiomontanus traveled to Italy with Cardinal BESSARION in search of important Greek scientific texts. After six years in Italy, and a brief period at the Hungarian court of MATTHIAS CORVINUS, Regiomontanus settled in Nuremberg. He planned to set up the world's first printing press devoted primarily to the publication of scientific texts, and a catalogue of 22 titles was issued. Called to Rome in 1476 to advise on calendrical reform he died suddenly, reportedly of poison, his program scarcely begun. He did, however, complete the first printed *Ephemerides* (1474), and his *De triangulis* (1533) is one of the earliest works of modern trigonometry. He also completed the *Epitoma* of his teacher Georg PEURBACH, which finally appeared in 1496, long after the deaths of both scholars; it was an important text in the astronomical debates of the following century (*see* PTOLEMAIC SYSTEM), being read by Copernicus, among others.

**Régnier, Mathurin** (1573–1613) *French satirical poet*
A nephew of Philippe DESPORTES, Régnier was born at Chartres, entered the Church at the age of nine, and accompanied the Cardinal de Joyeuse on a number of diplomatic missions to Rome. His lack of discretion and dissolute behavior, however, prevented him from fulfilling his parents' aspirations and from inheriting the lucrative benefices enjoyed by his uncle. In 1609 he became a canon of Chartres cathedral. In his *Satires* (1608–09) Régnier imitated the style of the classical satirists Horace and Juvenal and was heavily influenced by a number of other Renaissance writers, notably ARIOSTO, RABELAIS, and RONSARD. He attacked the purist literary reforms proposed by MALHERBE and, in lighter vein, painted lively and realistic portraits of a wide range of characters from all walks of life: poets and courtiers, prostitutes and procurers. His 13th satire, *Macette*, against religious hypocrisy, is generally considered his masterpiece.

**Reinhold, Erasmus** (1511–1553) *German astronomer*
Appointed professor of mathematics at Wittenberg university, Reinhold, together with his colleague RHETICUS, became one of the first astronomers to embrace publicly

**Regiomontanus** A woodcut from *Epitoma in almagestum Ptolemei* (1496), showing the seated figures of Regiomontanus (right) and Ptolemy beneath an armillary sphere. In fact, Regiomontanus only completed this book, the first six chapters of which were written by his teacher Georg Peurbach.

the newly published COPERNICAN SYSTEM. He saw his immediate task as that of compiling a new set of tables, based on Copernican assumptions, to replace the inaccurate 13th-century Alfonsine Tables. The resulting Prutenic Tables (1551) proved to be no more than a marginal improvement. Reinhold died in his native Saalfeld, having fled Wittenberg in the previous year (1552) to escape the plague.

**Rej, Mikołaj** (1505–1569) *Polish poet, playwright, and prose writer*

Rej was a country gentleman at Nagłowice, born at Żórawno and largely self-educated. His conversion to Calvinism (1546) emphasized the moralistic stance adopted in his numerous works in different genres. His first important work (1543) was a satirical dialogue in verse. His plays *Żywot Józefa* (1545) and *Kupiec* (1549) are based respectively upon the *Coemedia sacra Joseph* by Cornelius CROCUS and *Mercator* by Thomas NAOGEORGUS. The long poem *Wizerunek* (1558), based on the *Zodiacus vitae* by PALINGENIUS, describes the moral education of a young man. He also wrote miscellaneous volumes in verse and prose; one of his most famous prose pieces describes the ideal life of a Polish country gentleman. His grasp of theology is demonstrated in his works of biblical exegesis and he also made an influential prose translation of the psalms, *Psałterz Dawidów* (1546). As the first major writer to make exclusive use of Polish, Rej made an important contribution to acceptance of the vernacular in several literary genres.

**relics** See PILGRIMAGE AND PILGRIMAGE SHRINES

**Religion, (French) Wars of** (1562–98) French civil wars between Catholics and Protestants (HUGUENOTS). During the 1550s tension grew between Huguenots eager to make converts to Calvinism and Catholics who felt that their faith was threatened. CATHERINE DE' MEDICI, then regent for Charles IX, sought a compromise through the Edict of St.-Germain (January 1562), granting Huguenots freedom of conscience and the right to worship away from town centers. The discovery of Huguenots worshiping in Vassey led to the first war (1562–63), ended by the Pacification of Amboise. Uneasy peace followed; it was broken in 1567 by the Huguenot attempt to seize both regent and king at Meaux, leading to the second and third wars (1567–68, 1568–70). The Catholics, having failed to follow up their victories, agreed to a compromise peace at St.-Germain (1570), but, remembering Meaux, the regent decided to end the Huguenot threat with the MASSACRE OF ST. BARTHOLOMEW (1572). Shocked by the death of thousands of their fellows, the Huguenots defied the Crown and established governments in southern and western France. The war (1572–73) that followed ended with the granting of liberty of conscience and the right to worship freely in Huguenot towns. At the end of the fifth war (1575–76) the Huguenots made further gains, but the sixth and seventh wars (1577, 1580) were inconclusive. Finally, the War of the Three Henrys (1585–89) was provoked by the Catholic GUISE faction, which feared the accession of the Huguenot Henry of Navarre. He survived to become HENRY IV (reigned 1589–1610), but had to convert to Catholicism.

See also: NANTES, EDICT OF

Further reading: Robert J. Knecht, *The French Wars of Religion, 1559–1598* (London: Longman, 1989; 2nd ed. 1996); ~, *The French Religious Wars, 1562–1598* (London: Osprey, 2002).

**Remonstrants** The followers of Arminius (1560–1609), the Dutch theologian whose lectures at Leyden challenged the orthodox Calvinist doctrine of PREDESTINATION. After Arminius's death, his followers drew up the Remonstrance of 1610 setting out the Arminian position. They held that predestination is not absolute, but conditioned by man's response (thus reintroducing an element of free will); that grace may consequently be received or denied; and that the offer of salvation is directed to all men. Their manifesto provoked the Contra-Remonstrance of 1611, setting

out the orthodox position, and a bitter controversy ensued. This quickly achieved a political dimension, since the advocate of the States of Holland, OLDENBARNEVELDT, took the side of the Remonstrants, and MAURICE OF NASSAU the contrary position. The Arminians were finally condemned at the Synod of DORT (1618–19), and more than 200 ministers were ejected from their pulpits, although a degree of toleration returned after Maurice's death (1625).

See also: ARMINIANISM

**Renée de France** (1510–1575) *Duchess of Ferrara (1534–59)*
Born at Blois, the daughter of King LOUIS XII of France and Anne of Brittany, Renée was the subject of several abortive wedding negotiations before she was married (1528) to Ercole d'Este, heir to the dukedom of Ferrara. She encouraged men of letters at her court, particularly those who favored the reforming side in religion; among these were PALINGENIUS and Clément MAROT, and in April 1536 CALVIN himself paid a brief visit to Ferrara under an assumed name. Renée subsequently embraced Calvinism, much to the anger of her husband who adopted draconian measures to force her to renounce her new faith, at least as far as outward forms were concerned. Returning to her lands in France after Duke Ercole's death (1559), Renée made her château at Montargis in Loiret a stronghold of the Protestant faith. In 1562 it was besieged by her son-in-law, the duke of GUISE, and she suffered harassment by Catholic forces on other occasions during the Wars of Religion.

**René (I) of Anjou** (1409–1480) *Duke of Bar (1430–80), Duke of Anjou and Count of Provence (1434–80)*
As duke consort of Lorraine, titular king of Naples, and claimant to Sicily and Jerusalem, René spent his youth vainly trying to establish his wife's claim to Lorraine and his own claims to Naples, where he had been chosen as successor by Queen Joanna (Giovanna) II (*see also* ALFONSO I). In his last years, after quarreling with Louis XI of France, he spent more time in his French domains, where his interest in legal reforms and his patronage of literature and the arts earned him the title of "René the Good." It has even been suggested that the manuscript illuminator known as the Master of King René, who illustrated *Le livre des tournois du roi René* (c. 1446; Bibliothèque National, Paris) and a manuscript of Boccaccio's *Teseida* (1468; Vienna), was King René himself. At his death without a male heir his territories and the Angevin claims passed to the French crown.

**Reni, Guido** (1577–1642) *Italian painter*
He spent most of his life in his native Bologna, where he was a pupil of Denys CALVAERT. Much influenced by Lodovico CARRACCI and during a period in Rome

(1600–14) by the naturalism of CARAVAGGIO, he soon developed his own style in the Renaissance tradition of RAPHAEL. His classicism is evident in his two best-known works: *Aurora*, a fresco painted for the Casino Rospigliosi in Rome (1613), and *The Massacre of the Innocents* (1611; Pinacoteca, Bologna). His religious compositions brought him great popularity during his own lifetime among the fashionable circles of Rome and Bologna, but were later criticized by John Ruskin for their sentimentality, causing a sharp fall in his reputation in the 19th century. His style, particularly latterly, was noted for its simple sketchlike designs, pale colors, and soft outlines. He also painted portraits and mythological subjects, among the latter the Naples *Atalanta and Hippomenes* and the Munich *Apollo and Marsyas*.

**Reuchlin, Johann** (**Capnion**) (1455–1522) *German humanist scholar*
Reuchlin was born at Pforzheim and educated at Fribourg and Paris, where he began to study Greek. After periods in Basle and Orléans, he joined the entourage of Eberhardt, Count of Württemberg, with whom he traveled to Italy (1482). There he completed his Greek studies with John ARGYROPOULOS. On his second visit to Italy (1490), he met PICO DELLA MIRANDOLA, who introduced him to Jewish mystical literature. From 1492, with the help of the Jewish physician Jacob Loans, he mastered Hebrew and began to study the CABBALA, on which he published *De verbo mirifico* in 1494. His pro-Jewish sympathies brought him into conflict with the bigoted Jewish convert Johann Pfefferkorn (1468/9–1522), who advocated such antisemitic measures as the destruction of Hebrew books. The resulting controversy (*see* EPISTOLAE OBSCURORUM VIRORUM) involved nearly all the northern humanists, becoming a war between Renaissance intellectual inquiry and ecclesiastical authoritarianism. Reuchlin's Latin comedy *Sergius* (1496) is a devastating satire on the monkish obscurantists. After years of virulent controversy, the case against Reuchlin was referred to Pope LEO X, who quashed it (1516). Reuchlin spent his last years quietly teaching and studying in Ingolstadt and Tübingen. *De arte cabalistica* appeared in 1517 and the following year MELANCHTHON published Reuchlin's advocacy of the manner of pronouncing Greek used by contemporary Greeks (against the supposed "ancient" pronunciation advocated by ERASMUS). However, perhaps the most important of all his works was his Hebrew grammar and lexicon, *De rudimentis hebraicis* (1506), which laid the foundations of Hebrew scholarship for later humanists.

**Rhenanus, Beatus** (1485–1547) *German humanist scholar*
Rhenanus studied in Paris (1503–07) and from 1511 studied Greek in Basle under Johann Cuno, becoming attached to the circle of scholars around Johann FROBEN, for whose press he edited classical and patristic texts. In 1526 he returned to his native Schlettstadt (now Sélestat in Alsace). His *Rerum germanici libri tres* (1531) was a significant contribution to German historical research. A disciple and friend of ERASMUS, he published the first collected edition of the latter's works, in nine volumes (1540–41), including Rhenanus's life of the great humanist. Rhenanus's fine library was bequeathed to his native town, where it remains.

**Rheticus** (**Georg Joachim von Lauchen**) (1514–1576) *Austrian astronomer and mathematician*
Born at Feldkirch, he called himself after his native region of Rhaetia. The son of a physician beheaded for sorcery in 1528, Rheticus was appointed (1536) to teach mathematics at Wittenberg university. In 1539 he visited COPERNICUS in Frauenburg and thereafter, as an ardent disciple, strove to both publicize and publish his work. To this end he published the first account of the Copernican system in his *Narratio prima* (1540). Subsequently he persuaded Copernicus to allow him to publish his long since completed *De revolutionibus*. Academic duties, however, forced Rheticus to leave the task to others, and in 1542 he became professor of mathematics at Leipzig university. Forced to resign in 1551 as a result of a sexual scandal, Rheticus spent the rest of his life practicing medicine in Poland and Hungary. His *Opus Palatinum de triangulis*, a comprehensive set of trigonometrical tables, appeared posthumously in 1596.

**rhetoric** One of the seven liberal arts taught in the Middle Ages and defined as the art of using language to persuade or influence others. In the medieval academic scheme rhetoric was in the lower group, called the *trivium*, which also included grammar and logic. During the Renaissance period, its importance increased, and it was recognized, with grammar, history, poetry, and morals, as one of the *studia humana* (humane studies). The traditional teaching of Aristotle, CICERO, and QUINTILIAN was modified by the influence of RAMUS; there was less connection with logic and more importance was attached to elocution, pronunciation, and gesture. Figures of speech were elaborated, but mere verbal decoration was to be avoided; there was always a moral purpose, to unite an elegant style with the promotion of virtue. The application of rhetorical principles to works and speeches in the vernacular languages was studied no less than traditional Latin oratory.

In the 15th century Lorenzo VALLA, in his *Dialecticae disputationes* and *Elegantiae linguae Latinae*, attacked the received ideas and tried to reduce the number of traditional categories. A far more conservative treatise was *The Arte of Rhetorique* (1553), by Thomas Wilson (c. 1525–81), English secretary of state, who maintained the classical teaching of Aristotle and denounced the pedantry of French and Italian idiom. Abraham Fraunce's *Arcadian Rhetorike* (1588) follows the Ramist approach in English and draws its examples from the best ancient and contemporary European writers, including Tasso and Boscán. The most important French treatises were those pnof André de Tonquelin (1555) and Pierre de Courcelles (1557).

The political climate created by authoritarian rulers may have limited the scope of public oratory, but there was a greatly increased demand for sermons in the vernacular; among the most effective preachers were SAVONAROLA, LUTHER, and John KNOX (*see* PREACHING). At the same time, there was a great increase in international diplomatic activity and in written communications between heads of state; this called for a class of men skilled in the art of persuasive argument, from which the ambassadors, ministers, and secretaries could be recruited. Eloquence as well as knowledge was required of those who practiced as advocates in the law courts. The spoken word was of paramount importance in education, which was still largely oral. Public disputations on subjects of academic controversy were still frequently held at the universities. Sir Henry Wotton (1568–1639) provost of Eton, advised the boys there "not to neglect rhetoric, because Almighty God has left mankind affections to be wrought upon" (Isaak Walton's *Lives*). The influence of Renaissance rhetorical teaching lasted well into the 19th century, especially in the grammar schools.

**Further reading:** Wayne A. Rebhorn, *The Emperor of Men's Minds: Literature and the Renaissance Discourse of Rhetoric* (Ithaca, N.Y.: Cornell University Press, 1995); ~, *Renaissance Debates on Rhetoric* (Ithaca, N.Y.: Cornell University Press, 1999).

**Riaño, Diego de** (died 1534) *Spanish architect*
Riaño worked mainly in southern Spain and in 1523 was appointed cathedral architect at Seville. His masterpiece, however, was the Renaissance-plateresque Ayuntiamento (city hall) of Seville (1527–35), in which classical motifs are applied with extraordinary exuberance and inventiveness to give an effect of great richness and variety.

**Ribadeneyra, Pedro de** (Pedro Rivadeneyra, Pedro Ribadeneira) (1527–1611) *Spanish biographer and religious writer*
Born Pedro Ortiz de Cisneros at Toledo, he adopted the name of his maternal grandmother. The turning point of his life occurred in Rome, where he met IGNATIUS LOYOLA, whose friend and devoted disciple he became and to whom he was affectionately known as "Perico." He joined the recently constituted Society of Jesus (its statutes had been approved in 1540). In the year of Ignatius's death and beatification (1556), Ribadeneyra was given charge of the Jesuit mission to Belgium. Although Loyola left his own account of his life (*Autobiografía y Diario espiritual*), Rib-

adeneyra's *Vita Ignatii Loyolae* (Naples, 1572) became the classic biography of the future saint. His Spanish translation of it was published in 1583. Ribadeneyra also wrote a two-volume history of the "schism" in England (*Historia ecclesiástica del scisma del Reyno de Inglaterra*; 1588, 1593), a consolatory work addressed to Spaniards after the disaster of the SPANISH ARMADA (*Tratado de la tribulación*; 1589), and two volumes of saints' lives (*Flos sanctorum*; 1599, 1601).

**Ribalta, Francisco de** (c. 1565–1628) *Spanish artist*
Born in Valencia, Ribalta probably trained at the ESCORIAL under Juan FERNÁNDEZ DE NAVARRETE and at Madrid. His earliest known work is *Christ nailed to the Cross* (1582; Hermitage, St. Petersburg), a minor mannerist painting, but after moving to Valencia in about 1599 and establishing a large studio there he adopted a grander realist style, influenced by CARAVAGGIO. Later works, typical of the Spanish Baroque, include *The Vision of Father Simeon* (1612; National Gallery, London) and two paintings commissioned by the Capuchins in about 1620: *The Vision of St. Francis* (Prado, Madrid) and *St. Francis embracing Christ* (Valencia museum). His son Juan (c. 1597–1628) was also a painter.

**Ribeiro, Bernadim** (1482–1552) *Portuguese poet and novelist*
Ribeiro, who was born at Torrão, was a friend of Sá de MIRANDA, was perhaps a converted Jew, and belonged to the group of courtly poets whose works appeared in Resende's *Cancioneiro geral* (1516). Little else is known of his life. His *Éclogas* were the first written in Portuguese and established a fashion for this type. These and a fragmentary pastoral novel, *Minina e Moça*, which is extremely sentimental in rendering the lovers' unappeasable passion, were published posthumously (1554), together with the *Trovas de Crisfal* attributed to Cristóvão Falcão (c. 1518–c. 1554). This work, if not in fact by Ribeiro, is a very close and successful imitation of his style.

**Ricci, Matteo** (1552–1610) *Italian Jesuit missionary and writer*
Born in Macerata, Ricci obtained a wide-ranging education in Rome and joined the Society of Jesus in 1571. He went to Goa in 1578 and Macao in 1582, before following the Jesuit missionary Michael Ruggieri to China. After an unsettled beginning, Ricci developed a comprehensive knowledge of Chinese language and culture, before settling at Chao-king (Zhaoqing) in 1583. In 1589 the new viceroy finally expelled him and he moved on to Shaochow, then Nanking (1599), and Beijing (1601), where in the same year he was received by the emperor. Wherever he went, Ricci shone as a missionary of outstanding ability. He achieved numerous conversions by placing Christian doctrine within the context of Chinese culture, rather

than attempting to inflict alien values on confused or resistant proselytes. Ricci also impressed the Chinese with many European innovations, including clocks and maps. His methods upset the religious hierarchy in Europe, but delighted the Chinese. He wrote a number of works in Chinese, notably *The True Doctrine of God* (1595), and translated Christian texts for missionary work into their language. Ricci wrote his own account of his missionary travels around China in *Dell'Entrata della Compagnia di Gesù e Cristianità nella Cina* (1609). He died and was buried in Beijing. The earliest biography of him was written in Portuguese by his confessor, Sabatino de Ursis, in Beijing in 1611.

## Riccio, Andrea di Ambrogio Briosco (c. 1470–1532)
*Italian sculptor and goldsmith*
Born in Trento, Riccio was probably a pupil of Bartolommeo BELLANO and an assistant of DONATELLO, and had settled in Padua by about 1497. His most famous work is the sumptuous bronze Easter candelabrum in San Antonio at Padua (1507–16), which is notable for its classical figures and technically brilliant decoration. He also executed many small bronze statuettes in the humanist style then prevalent in Padua, including *Boy Milking a Goat* (Bargello, Florence), *Shouting Warrior on Horseback* (Victoria and Albert Museum, London), and *Arion* (Louvre, Paris). He also executed numerous small items in terracotta.

## Richier, Ligier (c. 1500–1567) *French sculptor*
Born at St. Mihiel, Richier worked mainly for the dukes of Lorraine, but in later life became a Protestant and was compelled to move to Geneva. The tomb (1545) of René de Chalons in the church of St. Etienne at Bar-le-Duc is considered to be Richier's masterpiece, featuring a gruesomely realistic cadaver. There is a wooden Christ by Richier in the church of Notre-Dame in the same town, and a *Christ carrying the Cross* in the church of St. Martin at Pont-à-Mousson is also attributed to him. His recumbent effigy of Philippe de Gueldres, Duchess of Lorraine (died 1547), is in the former church of the Cordeliers, Nancy. He also sculpted an *Entombment* (1553) for the church of St. Etienne in his native town.

## Riemenschneider, Tilman (c. 1460–1531) *German woodcarver and sculptor*
Although born in Osterode am Harz, Riemenschneider was based in Würzburg from 1483, eventually becoming mayor of the town (1520–21). He is particularly famous for his beautiful limewood carvings, both individual figures and whole altarpieces, which combine the powerful emotionalism of Veit STOSS with Adam KRAFT's vigorous realism. Of his works in stone, the most famous is in Bamberg cathedral, the magnificent marble tomb (c. 1513) of the cathedral's founder, Emperor Henry II

**Tilman Riemenschneider** *Mary Salome and Zebedee* (c. 1520). These glazed limewood figures formed part of a group of the Holy Kindred.
*V & A Picture Library*

(died 1024) and his wife Cunigunde. As well as his major commissions for Würzburg and Bamberg, Riemenschneider also produced work for churches in several neighboring towns: an altarpiece for Münnerstadt (1490–92), a triptych for Windsheim (c. 1508), and a sandstone *Lamentation* group for Maidbronn (1519–23), among others.

**Rienzo, Cola di** (Nicolà di Rienzo) (c. 1313–1354) *Italian populist leader who tried to restore the greatness of Rome*
Rienzo summoned a Roman assembly on the Capitoline Hill in May 1347 and assumed the title of tribune with dictatorial powers, his aim being to replace the power of the aristocrats and the absentee pope (then resident in Avignon) with a popular government in Rome. He executed reforms and prepared for the election of a Roman emperor of Italy, but was overthrown by the Roman nobles (December 1347). He went into exile, but triumphantly resumed power in August 1354. His dictatorial style made him unpopular and he was hacked to death by a Roman mob soon afterward. Nevertheless, he has been honored in literature and his life inspired Richard Wagner's opera *Rienzi*.

*rilievo schiacciato* or *rilievo stiacciato* See SCHIACCIATO

**Rimini** An Adriatic port and city state in Emilia-Romagna, northern Italy. At first Umbro-Etruscan, Rimini was subsequently under the sway of Romans, Byzantines, Goths, Lombards, and Franks. By the early 14th century Rimini had accepted papal suzerainty, but was actually governed by the MALATESTA FAMILY, who were recognized as lords of Rimini from 1334. In return for political and military support successive popes supported the creation of a city state based on Rimini. In the mid-15th century Sigismondo MALATESTA's quarrel with Pope PIUS II and his defeat (1463) led to Sigismondo's exile and the restriction of the Malatesta state to Rimini itself. The fortunes of Rimini declined, and after some years of conflict Rimini became directly subject to Rome (1527). Notable landmarks have survived from the period of the rule of Sigismondo Malatesta. These include the fortifications, the castle, and the so-called TEMPIO MALATESTIANO.

**Rivadeneyra, Pedro de** See RIBADENEYRA, PEDRO DE

**Rizzo, Antonio di Giovanni** (c. 1440–c. 1500) *Italian sculptor and architect*
A native of Verona, Rizzo worked chiefly in Venice, where he settled in 1466. He worked with Giovanni AMADEO on the Certosa di Pavia, but is better known for his tomb of Doge Niccolò Tròn (c. 1480; Sta. Maria dei Frari, Venice), which is notable for its scale and detail. Later works included *Adam and Eve* (c. 1485) for the Arco Foscari of the Palazzo Ducale, Venice, upon which he worked with Antonio Bregno (c. 1420–1501), clearly under the influence of Flemish or German artists. The Scala dei Giganti of the palace is likewise his work, as is the facade on the eastern side of the Cortile, rebuilt after the fire of 1483.

**Robbia, Luca della** See DELLA ROBBIA, LUCA

**Robert Bellarmine, St.** (Roberto Francesco Romolo Bellarmino) (1542–1621) *Italian cardinal and theologian*
He was born at Montepulciano, entered the Society of Jesus in 1560, and studied in Rome, Mondovi, and Padua, before being sent to Louvain in 1569. The following year, after ordination, he began lecturing, and achieved celebrity upon his return to Rome (1576) as professor at the Jesuit Collegium Romanum (*see* GREGORIANA). He lectured and wrote on a variety of controversial subjects, and was both applauded and castigated for treating Protestant views fairly. His most important writings were the three volumes of lectures published under the title *Disputationes de controversiis Christianae fidei adversus huius temporis haereticos* (1586–93). These contained a scholarly and cogent appraisal of Roman Catholic doctrine, which was divided into four sections: the Church, the sacraments, Christ, and the grave.

Pope Clement VIII made Bellarmine a cardinal in 1599, and he was archbishop of Capua (1602–05) until ill health caused his retirement; he moved first to Montepulciano and then to Rome, where he eventually died. Bellarmine continued to write prolifically, his most important work in later life being *De scriptoribus ecclesiasticis* (1613). He was also an early critic of GALILEO, and the two men shared a mutual respect. He was not canonized until 1930 because of his opposition to papal authority in temporal matters.

The stoneware wine jugs with a bearded face that were popular in the Rhineland from the mid-16th century were called "Bellarmines," apparently because they were based on Protestant caricatures of the cardinal.

**Roberti, Ercole de'** See ERCOLE DE' ROBERTI

**Robert of Anjou** (1278–1343) *King of Naples (as Robert I, 1309–43)*
Son of Charles II of Naples, Robert spent much of his youth as a hostage in Aragon. His ambitions led him to support the Guelf faction in their struggle against the papacy—with little success. He was known as a patron of literature and the arts, numbering GIOTTO and Simone MARTINI among his protégés, and was particularly interested in HUMANISM. He is also credited with the authorship of moral and theological treatises.

**Robusti, Jacopo** See TINTORETTO

**Rodiana, Onorata** (died 1452) *Italian fresco painter and soldier*
Born at Castelleone, Cremona, she was commissioned by Marchese Gabrino Fondolo to paint murals in his palace. When one of his courtiers attempted to rape her, she stabbed him and escaped disguised as a man. She was caught and tried for murder, but Gabrino pardoned her. She then joined a band of condottieri and in 1423 em-

barked on a 30-year military career, during which she continued to paint. As soldier and bandit, she was in the service of a succession of warring lords, eventually holding formal military rank. In 1452 she was killed while attempting, with Conrado, brother of the duke of Sforza, to lift the siege of her home town by the Venetians. Her surviving wall-paintings are thought to be those in the Palazzo Galeotti-Vertue at Castelleone.

**Roelas, Juan de las** (c. 1558–1625) *Spanish painter*
The son of an admiral, Roelas was born in Seville but became acquainted with Italian art while a student in Venice, being especially influenced by TITIAN and TINTORETTO. In 1603 he was appointed prebendary of the chapel at Olivárez, where after some years in Madrid and Seville, he lived from 1624. Roelas was recognized as the most important artist in Seville and did much to free the Seville school from the last influence of Romanism. His best paintings, all still in Seville, included the *Circumcision* (c. 1606; university church), the *Martyrdom of St. Andrew* (1609–13; museum), and a *Pentecost* (1615). His pupils included Pablo Legote (c. 1598–1671) and Francisco de Zurbarán (1598–1664).

**Rojas, Fernando de** (c. 1465–1541) *Spanish writer*
Born the son of converted Jews (*conversos*) at Puebla de Montalbán, Toledo, Rojas studied at Salamanca. He moved from his birthplace because of discrimination against *conversos* and settled in Talavera, where he became mayor and lived the rest of his life. The work for which he is known was first published anonymously at Burgos with the title *La comedia de Calisto y Melibea* (1499), a novel in dramatic form in 16 acts (*auctos*). In a later, expanded version of 21 acts, it was retitled *La tragicomedia de Calisto y Melibea* (1502), and Rojas's authorship is announced acrostically and in a prefatory claim that he completed the work of an anonymous original author. The most influential work of 16th-century Spain, the novel was apparently intended for dramatic reading aloud and not as a play. It is better known by its popular name, that of a central character, LA CELESTINA.

**Roman Academy** The society founded in Rome in the late 1450s by Pomponio LETO with the aim of encouraging scholarly interest in all aspects of classical Roman culture. Its members adopted Latin or Greek names and met at Leto's house on the Quirinal. Its fame spread all over Europe, but its enthusiasm for all things Roman, including pagan rituals, caused Pope PAUL II to imprison and even torture its leading members and to order its closure (1468). Later it was revived and numbered two popes (JULIUS II and LEO X) among its members, but it was finally dissolved after the Sack of Rome (1527).

**Romanino, Girolamo** (c. 1484–c. 1562) *Italian artist*
A native of Brescia, Romanino was a fellow-pupil of Alessandro MORETTO and was profoundly influenced by GIORGIONE, to whom several of his paintings have been attributed, as well as by Titian, Savoldo, and Lotto. He executed numerous sacred pictures and frescoes in provincial churches throughout northern Italy, including an *Enthroned Madonna with Saints and Angels* (Museo Civico, Padua) and *St. Matthew and the Angel* (San Giovanni Evangelista, Cremona). His best works are the frescoes with mythological figures at the Castello del Buon Consiglio at Trento; other works include portraits and the *Passion* at Cremona cathedral (1519).

**Romano, Gian Cristoforo** (Giovanni Romano) (c. 1470–1512) *Italian sculptor*
Born in Rome, he studied under Andrea BREGNO before working in a number of northern Italian cities—Cremona, Ferrara, Milan, Mantua, Pavia, and Urbino—to which he introduced elements of the Roman classical style. His most important work is the tomb of Giangaleazzo Visconti in the Certosa di Pavia (1493–97). He had considerable talent as a portraitist; Federico da Montefeltro and Francesco Sforza were among his sitters (both Bargello, Florence), and of Isabella d'Este he made a portrait medal as well as the marble bust now in the Louvre, Paris.

**Romano, Giulio** See GIULIO ROMANO

**Rome** The capital city of Italy situated on the River Tiber 15 miles (24 km) from the Mediterranean in central Italy. During the Middle Ages and early Renaissance Rome was a wretched place, described as a city filled with huts, thieves, and vermin. Bitter factional strife and conflict between imperial, papal, and republican forms of government brought such chaos to Rome that the papacy removed itself to AVIGNON (1309). During the Avignon papacy, disorder and the Black Death (1348–49) devastated Rome and reduced its population to little more than 20,000. In 1347 and 1354 Cola di RIENZO tried in vain to reestablish the glories of ancient Rome and the powers of its citizens. The return of the papacy to Rome (1378) was followed by the GREAT SCHISM, which only ended in 1417 with the election of Pope Martin V, who began to lay the foundations of a system of government that made Rome the capital of a major Renaissance power—the Papal States.

NICHOLAS V (pope 1446–55) was the first of the Renaissance popes; he and his successors embarked on the rebuilding of Rome and attracted artists and scholars to the city. By the late 15th century Rome had become an important center of humanist and Greek studies, following the initiative of Nicholas V in organizing the translation of Greek classics and the work of the ROMAN ACADEMY under the leadership of Pomponio LETO. By 1500 Rome's financial basis was secured by the local alum deposits and banking.

It was during the early 16th century that the efforts of JULIUS II (pope 1503–13) and LEO X (pope 1513–22) and the genius of such artists as BRAMANTE, MICHELANGELO, and RAPHAEL enabled Rome to displace Florence as the preeminent Renaissance city. The beginning of the rebuilding of St. Peter's basilica during Julius II's pontificate provided many opportunities which attracted men of talent and genius to Rome.

The Sack of Rome (1527) by CHARLES V's troops was a setback from which the city recovered later in the century under such COUNTER-REFORMATION popes as Sixtus V (pope 1585–90), the initiator of Domenico FONTANA's huge program of civic planning. By the late 16th century Rome was again prosperous and cosmopolitan, with a population of about 100,000.

Buildings that have survived from the 15th century include the Palazzo Venezia (1445), Sta. Maria del Popolo (1472–77), Sant' Agostino (1479–83), and the Cancelleria (1486–98). During the 16th century the new St. Peter's (from 1506) and the Quirinal palace (1574) were built, and the Lateran and Vatican palaces were remodeled. Two great works of art that have survived are Michelangelo's frescoes in the SISTINE CHAPEL (1508–12) and Raphael's frescoes in the papal apartments (begun 1509).

**Further reading:** Anthony Grafton (ed.), *Rome Reborn: The Vatican Library and Renaissance Culture* (New Haven, Conn.: Yale University Press, 1993); George Holmes, *Florence, Rome and the Origins of the Renaissance* (Oxford, U.K.: Clarendon Press, 1986); Peter Partner, *Renaissance Rome, 1500–1559: A Portrait of a Society* (Berkeley, Calif.: University of California Press, 1976); Loren Partridge, *The Art of Renaissance Rome* (Upper Saddle River, N.J.: Prentice Hall, 1996); Ingrid D. Rowland, *The Culture of the High Renaissance: Ancients and Moderns in Sixteenth-Century Rome* (Cambridge, U.K.: Cambridge University Press, 1998).

**Rome, Sack of** (1527) The pillage of Rome by imperial troops after their commander was killed in their successful assault on the city. Following the battle of PAVIA, Pope Clement VII joined (1526) the French-led League of Cognac to resist the threatened Hapsburg domination of Europe. Emperor CHARLES V appealed to the German diet for support and raised an army, which entered Italy in 1527 and joined the imperial forces from Milan, commanded by the duke of Bourbon. This army marched on Rome, hoping to detach the pope from the league. The many Lutherans in its ranks boasted that they came with hempen halters to hang the cardinals and a silk one for the pope; in addition, by the time they reached Rome, the troops were mutinous because of lack of pay. Rome fell on May 6, 1527, Bourbon being killed in the first assault. Discipline collapsed, and the city was savagely pillaged for a week

before some control was restored. The pope initially took refuge in the Castel Sant' Angelo before surrendering. The imperial army occupied Rome until February 1528. While achieving its immediate objective by bringing the pope firmly under imperial control, the sack shocked the Christian world. Charles's enemies were quick to take advantage, France and England declaring war on him in 1528.

**Further reading:** Luigi Guicciardini, *The Sack of Rome*, transl. James H. McGregor (New York: Italica, 1993).

**rondeau** A verse form used in French song from the 13th century and in French poetry in the 15th century. The typical rondeau consists of three stanzas of five, three, and five lines, based on two rhymes, usually in the pattern aabba, aab, aabba; the opening words (or, in the sung rondeau, the opening lines) of the first stanza are repeated as a refrain at the end of the second and third stanzas. The rhyming pattern, number of stanzas, and overall length of the rondeau are subject to considerable variation: the *rondeau redoublé* consists of six four-line stanzas in the pattern abab, baba, etc., in which the four lines of the first stanza are used in turn as the fourth lines of the second, third, fourth, and fifth stanzas. Notable exponents of the rondeau include Guillaume DUFAY, Clément MAROT, and Charles d'Orléans (1394–1465).

**Rondelet, Guillaume** (1507–1556) *French zoologist*
Although trained in medicine Rondelet was enabled to indulge his interest in natural history while traveling throughout Europe with his patron, Cardinal Tournon. He returned to his native Montpellier in 1545 to teach medicine. Among his distinguished pupils were the botanists Jacques d'Aléchamps (1513–88) and Matthias de L'OBEL. In the main work of his life, *Universae aquatilium historiae* (1555) he described 245 species of marine animals; it remained the standard work on the subject for over a century.

See also: ZOOLOGY

**Ronsard, Pierre de** (c. 1524–1585) *French poet*
Born near Couture into a noble family of the Vendôme, Ronsard entered the French court in 1536 as page to the royal family. He visited Scotland in the course of his duties and subsequently accompanied Lazare de Baïf, father of the poet Jean-Antoine de BAÏF, on a diplomatic mission to Alsace. Forced to abandon his court career after an illness that left him partially deaf, Ronsard turned to literature; at the Collège de Coqueret he studied Greek and Latin poetry under the humanist Jean DAURAT and, in association with Joachim DU BELLAY, Baïf, and others, formed the school of poets that became known as the PLÉIADE. Ronsard's early verse collections, *Odes* (1550, 1552), containing the famous "Mignonne, allons voir si la rose...," and *Amours* (1552), were heavily influenced by Pindar, Ho-

race, and PETRARCH; his *Bocage* (1554) and *Continuation des Amours* (1555) were inspired by the Greek poet Anacreon and the *Hymnes* (1555–56), a series of longer poems, by Callimachus. By 1560 Ronsard had become established as court poet to Charles IX. During the Wars of RELIGION his ardent and patriotic support of the royalist and Catholic cause found expression in the political poems *Discours des misères de ce temps* (1562), *Remonstrance au peuple de France* (1562), and the unfinished epic *La Franciade* (1572). Under Henry III, however, Ronsard found himself supplanted by Philippe DESPORTES; in semi-retirement at his priory of St.-Cosme at Tours he continued to write, publishing the *Sonnets pour Hélène*, one of his best-known collections of love poetry, in 1578. His nostalgic *Derniers Vers* appeared in 1586, the year after his death. Ronsard had numerous imitators and translators among 16th-century English poets, but the criticisms of François de MALHERBE, Nicolas Boileau, and other proponents of classicism led to a decline in his reputation in France in the 17th and 18th centuries. Sainte-Beuve's *Tableau historique et critique de la poésie française et du théâtre français au XVI<sup>e</sup> siècle* (1828), however, brought about a new appreciation of Ronsard's work and reestablished his position among the principal French poets of the Renaissance.

**Further reading:** Elizabeth T. Armstrong, *Ronsard and the Age of Gold* (Cambridge, U.K.: Cambridge University Press, 1968).

**Roper, Margaret** (1505–1544) *English woman of letters and favorite daughter of Sir Thomas More*
A scholastic prodigy, she grew up in her father's humanist milieu. MORE educated Margaret, her siblings, and a collection of wards, stepchildren, and other relatives in his own experimental and domestic "school of More." Thanks to his advocacy of private study for women, Margaret received an exceptional and rigorous education, being tutored in Latin, Greek, logic, theology, rhetoric, philosophy, mathematics, medicine, and astrology. Renowned for her modesty and virtue, she married William Roper in 1521, confining herself to the domestic sphere as exemplary wife, mother, and intellectual companion. She retained her interest in learning, translating (1524) from Latin Erasmus's *Precatio Dominica* (1526) and Eusebius's ecclesiastical history from Greek into Latin, as well as writing poetry. She was devoted to her father; the moving letters she wrote to him during his incarceration in the Tower of London (April 1534–July 1535) were published in 1947. It is said that she preserved her father's severed head after his execution, and requested it be buried with her.

**Rore, Ciprien de** (c. 1515–1565) *Franco-Flemish composer*
Born at Malines, Rore appears to have been in Venice in the 1540s, and by 1547 was *maestro di cappella* at the Este court at Ferrara, where he remained until the death of Duke Ercole II (1559). After a brief period of employment with MARGARET OF PARMA, governor of the Netherlands, in 1561 he entered the service of her husband, Ottavio Farnese, in Parma. In 1563 he succeeded Adrian WILLAERT as *maestro* at St. Mark's, Venice, but returned to Parma a year later, where he died. Rore composed much sacred music; his parody Masses and motets follow the style of composers of the previous generation, but it is for his madrigals that he is chiefly remembered. Of these, 125 survive; Rore set many Petrarchan texts in his earlier madrigals, and in the later ones sensitive treatment of the text became increasingly important. He is recognized as a strong influence on MONTEVERDI.

**Rosicrucianism** The movement that combined several strands of esoteric wisdom—HERMETICISM, the CABBALA, and ALCHEMY—in a mysterious secret society of the learned that apparently originated in Protestant Germany in the early 17th century. The two basic Rosicrucian texts were both printed in Kassel: the German *Fama Fraternitatis*, of which the first known printed edition appeared in 1614 (it had earlier circulated in manuscript), and the Latin *Confessio Fraternitatis R.C.* (1615). The *Fama* relates how "Christian Rosencreutz," who was purportedly born in 1378, journeyed to the East and returned with secret wisdom, which he then imparted to members of the order he founded; the "discovery" (dated to 1604) of the emblematic tomb of "Rosencreutz" and his disciples is then described, together with the refounding of the order. The *Confessio* sets out the order's program for universal Christian reformation and enlightenment. The author or authors of the *Fama* and *Confessio* are unknown, but the Lutheran pastor and mystic Johann Valentin Andreae (born 1586) was indisputably the author of a third Rosicrucian text *Chymische Hochzeit Christiani Rosencreutz* (1616), and the anonymous writers probably belonged to his circle in Württemberg and the Palatinate.

The Rosicrucian manifestos caused a stir throughout Europe. Several English scholars, among them Robert FLUDD, claimed to be or to be in touch with a member of the society. Disillusionment set in when the "brothers of the Rosy Cross" remained obstinately invisible and elusive. However, some of the Rosicrucian enthusiasm for utopian restructuring of society through knowledge resurfaced in the ideals of early members of the Royal Society.

**Further reading:** Susanna Åkerman, *Rose Cross over the Baltic: The Spread of Rosicrucianism in Northern Europe* (Leyden, Netherlands: Brill, 1998); Frances A. Yates, *The Rosicrucian Enlightenment* (London: Routledge & Kegan Paul, 1972; repr. 1999).

**Rosselli, Cosimo** (1439–1507) *Italian painter*
The pupil of Benozzo GOZZOLI, Rosselli established an important workshop in his native Florence, where his own

pupils included Fra BARTOLOMMEO and PIERO DI COSIMO. He produced a number of fairly pedestrian works himself, including frescoes in the cloister of the Annunziata and the church of Sant' Ambrosius in Florence. In 1481 he was also commissioned to help with the frescoes for the Sistine Chapel, despite the fact that few would class him with such colleagues on the project as BOTTICELLI and GHIRLANDAIO.

**Rossellino, Bernardo** (1409–1464) and **Antonio** (1427–1479) *Italian sculptors*
The brothers were born in Settignano and worked in Florence, where Bernardo executed a number of architectural works, including the Palazzo Rucellai (1446–51). His masterpiece, however, is the Palazzo Piccolomini (1460–63) in PIENZA. Bernardo's most notable sculptural achievement is the tomb of Leonardo BRUNI in Sta. Croce in Florence (1444–47), which was based upon DONATELLO's classical tomb of Pope John XXII. He was also employed for a time on work at St. Peter's in Rome (1451–53) by Pope Nicholas V.

Bernardo's younger brother Antonio was also influenced by Donatello and for a while was Bernardo's pupil. His greatest work, the tomb of the cardinal-prince of Portugal in San Miniato al Monte in Florence (1461–66), was highly innovative and more sophisticated than his brother's work. Other works by Antonio include the portrait busts of Giovanni Chellini (1456; Victoria and Albert Museum, London) and of Matteo Palmieri (1468; Bargello, Florence). Both brothers also executed decorative works.

**Rossi, Properzia de** (c. 1490–1530) *Italian sculptor and painter*
Born in Bologna, she studied drawing with Marcantonio RAIMONDI. She became known for her skillful carving in miniature—on peach, apricot or cherry stones—executing a much-admired filigree coat of arms commissioned by the Grassi family, and becoming adept at religious subjects, such as the Crucifixion. In her thirties she began working on life-sized sculptures and busts in marble and won commissions for bas-reliefs at the church of the Madonna del Barracano in Bologna and at San Petronio in Rome. Rossi was one of the earliest recorded women artists, and according to VASARI, who, in 1568, was among the first to celebrate her work, she was much envied and persecuted by male painters. Despite her gifts, she died young and in penury, at the Ospedale della Morte in Bologna.

**Rosso Fiorentino** (Giovanni Battista di Jacopo) (1495–1540) *Italian painter*
Rosso probably trained with PONTORMO under ANDREA DEL SARTO, whose influence is strong upon Rosso's early painting. Rosso's earliest surviving work is the fresco of the Assumption (1517) in the church of SS. Annunziata in

Florence, in which his taste for drama and violent color is already evident. Equally emotional in treatment was the famous *Deposition* (1521; Galleria Pittorica, Volterra), which Rosso painted shortly before leaving for Rome, where he came under the influence of MICHELANGELO. After the Sack of Rome (1527) Rosso wandered Italy for several years before being summoned to France by Francis I to work on the design and decoration of the château at FONTAINEBLEAU. Here, with PRIMATICCIO, he founded the French mannerist school, executing such influential works as the Galerie François I. Other major works include the impressive *Moses and Jethro's Daughters* (c. 1523; Uffizi, Florence) and *Dead Christ with Angels* (1525–26; Museum of Fine Arts, Boston).

**Rotonda, Villa** An Italian villa designed by Andrea PALLADIO and built on a hilltop site at Vicenza. The Villa Rotonda, which is also known as La Rotonda or the Villa Capra, was begun in about 1549 for Giulio Capra but not completed until 1606 by SCAMOZZI. It consists of a domed central hall with four symmetrical rooms leading off it, each with an identical Ionic portico. The proportions, balance, and classical ornamentation of the villa caught the imagination of architects throughout Europe. Chiswick House (1730–36) in west London is one of the numerous buildings to be built in imitation of the Villa Rotonda.

**Rovere family** See DELLA ROVERE FAMILY

**Rubens, Pieter Paul** (1577–1640) *Flemish painter*
Rubens was born in the German town of Siegen, to which his father, a devout Protestant, had fled to avoid religious persecution. The family moved back to Antwerp in 1587 following the latter's death, and Rubens was raised as a Catholic. In 1591 he began his artistic training in the studio of the landscape painter Tobias Verhaecht (or Van Haecht; 1561–16), and in the following year he moved to the studio of the portrait painter Adam van Noort (c. 1562–1641), where he remained for four years. He completed his training under Otto van VEEN who instilled in Rubens a sense of the dignity of the professional painter. In 1598 he was admitted to the painter's guild in Antwerp and in 1600, probably encouraged by van Veen, he set off for Italy.

His first port of call was Venice where he saw paintings by TINTORETTO, TITIAN, and VERONESE. These artists, especially Titian, were to be highly influential in Rubens's mature work. He also assimilated the work of many other Italian masters, whose works he was employed to copy by Vicenzo Gonzaga, duke of Mantua. In 1601 Rubens made his first visit to Rome where he came under the influence of the new BAROQUE style of CARAVAGGIO and CARRACCI. His first commission in Rome was to paint three large altarpieces for the crypt chapel of St. Helena in the Basilica of Sta. Croce (1601–02). His first diplomatic mission was

**Pieter Paul Rubens** An anatomical drawing of a man striding forward with his hands behind his back. The artist has paid great attention to the subject's musculature.
© *Christie's Images/CORBIS*

in 1603 when he presented a number of paintings to Philip III of Spain on behalf of Vincenzo Gonzaga, after which he returned to Italy. His other major commissions during this period were for a painting over the high altar of the church of Sta. Maria in Vallicella and an *Adoration of the Shepherds* for the church of San Filippo in Fermo, a painting which owes much to the influence of Caravaggio. Rubens returned to Antwerp in 1608 to attend his mother's deathbed, but she died before he could reach her.

The following decade saw Rubens establish himself as the foremost artist of the COUNTER-REFORMATION, an ascendency that was partly enabled by the Twelve Years' Truce (1609–21). This period of relative peace facilitated the refurbishment of many Flemish churches, and Rubens received numerous commissions for altarpieces. Among these are *The Raising of the Cross* (1610–11) and *The Descent from the Cross* (1611–14), both for Antwerp cathe-

dral. During this period he married Isabella, daughter of Jan Brant, a prominent Antwerp humanist, and he became court painter to the Hapsburg regents, the Archduke Albert and Archduchess Isabella. In addition to his large number of religious works in the second decade of the century, Rubens produced many secular paintings. These include portraits, allegories, hunting scenes, and complex mythological works, such as the *Rape of the Daughters of Leucippus* (c. 1617–18).

During the next decade (1620–30) he engaged in a number of diplomatic missions, which culminated in the peace treaty between England and Spain (1630). However, his artistic output did not diminish. In 1622 he was commissioned to paint a cycle of 21 large pieces (now in the Louvre, Paris) for the Palais du Luxembourg, Paris, chronicling the life of Queen Marie de' Medici. He also designed a number of tapestry cycles, including *The Triumph of the Eucharist* (1625–27), a sequence of 20 hangings. They are masterpieces of Baroque illusionism, featuring an elaborate *trompe l'oeil* architectural framework and tapestries-within-tapestries. Rubens also undertook a number of ecclesiastical commissions in this period, including the richly expressive *Adoration of the Magi* (1624) for the abbey of St. Michael and *The Assumption of the Virgin* (1624–27) for Antwerp cathedral.

In the final decade of his life (1630–40) Rubens produced some of his finest paintings. For Charles I of England he designed and painted nine canvases (1629–34) for the ceiling of Inigo JONES's newly rebuilt Banqueting House at Whitehall Palace; they show the apotheosis of Charles's father James I as the *Rex Pacificus*, the Royal Peacemaker. This period can also be characterized by a broadening of his style. For example, his *Landscape with a Rainbow* (c. 1636), painted at his country estate, is an almost impressionistic celebration of rural life. He also painted intimate portraits of his family, especially his second wife, Hélène Fourment, who also features as Venus in such allegorical paintings as *The Garden of Love* (1634). A self-portrait of c. 1631 shows him with Hélène and their son Nicholas, walking among their poultry in their Antwerp garden (Bayerische Staatsgemäldesammlungen, Munich).

Rubens was one of the most productive and influential figures of Western art, producing or supervising over 2,000 works covering religious and mythological subjects, portraits, and landscapes. Famous for his robust female figures, Rubens exemplifies the Baroque art of 17th-century Europe. His painting, a synthesis of Italian Renaissance classicism and Flemish realism, influenced many distinguished artists during his own lifetime, among them Diego de Velázquez and Anthony van Dyck. Later artists whose work was directly influenced by Rubens include the Rococo artist Antoine Watteau, the French Romantic painter Eugène Delacroix, and the English landscapist Thomas Gainsborough.

**Further reading:** Svetlana Alper, *The Making of Rubens* (New Haven, Conn.: Yale University Press, 1995); Kristin Lohse Belkin, *Rubens* (London: Phaidon, 1998); Kerry Downes, *Rubens* (New York: Hippocrene, 1981; repr. 2004).

**Rucellai family** Wealthy Tuscan merchants who, from the late 13th century onward, lived in Florence studying and cultivating the arts. ALBERTI designed the Palazzo Rucellai for Giovanni (1403–81), whose son, Bernardo (1448–1514), designed the Rucellai Gardens; Bernardo was a humanist historian who was an early user of the phrase "the balance of power" in his history of Charles VIII's invasion of 1494–95. Giovanni's grandson, also Giovanni (1475–1525), was a didactic poet, the author of *Le Api* (1539), based on Virgil's fourth *Georgic*, and *Rosamunda* (1525), a classical tragedy in verse based on an incident in Lombard history. Cosimo, Bernardo's grandson, presided over gatherings of intellectuals in the Rucellai Gardens (*see* ORTI ORICELLARI).

**Rudolf II** (1552–1612) *Holy Roman Emperor, king of Bohemia and Hungary, archduke of Austria (1576–1612)*
Rudolf was the son of Emperor Maximilian II and Mary, daughter of Emperor CHARLES V. A scholar who suffered from poor health, he spent many years in semi-seclusion in Prague. He dabbled in chemistry, medicine, astronomy, alchemy, and astrology and, with the help of his court antiquary Jacopo STRADA, acquired an impressive collection of rare works of art. He was a patron of ARCIMBOLDO, Roelant SAVERY, and Batholomäus SPRANGER, and, in the scientific realm, of Tycho BRAHE and Johannes KEPLER. His *Hofkapelle* in Prague employed around 60 singers and instrumentalists, with the prolific and eminent Netherlandish composer Philippe de MONTE as director of music; other significant composers patronized by Rudolf were the Spaniard Mattheo FLECHA, the Slav Jacob HANDL, and the Czech Krystof Harant of Polzice (1564–1621). Perhaps because he was educated in Spain, Rudolf was an uncompromising Catholic, determined to eradicate Protestantism in his domains. He reversed the tolerant religious policies of his father and supported the Jesuits and the other religious orders in their efforts to further the COUNTER-REFORMATION.

By the beginning of the 17th century Rudolf was suffering from fits of morbid depression which made him incapable of governing effectively. His attacks on Protestantism in Austria led to the collapse of government and the division of the country into warring religious leagues, and similar campaigns against political and religious liberties in Hungary occasioned a revolt (1604–05) that only terminated when the Hapsburg archdukes insisted that Rudolf entrust the government of Hungary to his brother, Matthias. Under similar circumstances he was forced in 1608 to hand over the government of Austria and Moravia

**Rudolf II** Wenzel Maler's wax relief (1606) of the emperor with his hound.
*V & A Picture Library*

to Matthias. Bohemia, where Protestantism was very well established, rebelled, and in 1611 Rudolf had to abdicate and to accept the election of Matthias by the Bohemian estates as king of Bohemia.

**Further reading:** R. J. W. Evans, *Rudolf II and His World: A Study in Intellectual History 1576–1612* (Oxford, U.K.: Clarendon Press, 1973; new ed. Thames & Hudson, 1997); Angelo Maria Ripellino, *Magic Prague*, transl. David Newton Marinelli (London: Macmillan, 1994).

**Rudolfine Tables** See ASTRONOMY; BRAHE, TYCHO; KEPLER, JOHANNES

**Rueda, Lope de** (c. 1510–1565) *Spanish actor and playwright*
The first Spanish professional actor about whom anything

is known, Rueda was born in Seville and as a youth joined a troupe of wandering actors performing at inns or other venues permitted by town councils. He became an actor-manager, performing before the future Philip II in 1551 and in plays staged in Philip's honor in 1554. Rueda's works were published posthumously in three series (1567–70). With one exception his several comedies are in prose. Crudely constructed and with no attempt to develop characterizations, they draw on Italian material. The best, *Eufemia*, is based on a tale in Boccaccio's *Decameron*. More important are his *pasos*, one-act farcical interludes with realistic dialogue and stereotypical characters borrowed from COMMEDIA DELL'ARTE: the *fanfarrón* (braggart), *rufián* (pimp), *gracioso* (the wit, or comic servant), and others. Twenty-four of some 40 *pasos* survive; about half were written for interpolation in his own comedies. By the end of Rueda's life, acting acquired the status of a full-time profession and permanent public theaters soon opened in Madrid (Teatro de la Cruz, 1579), Seville, and other cities.

**Ruiz de Alarcón y Mendoza, Juan** (1580–1639) *Spanish dramatist*
The son of a wealthy superintendent of mines, Alarcón was born in Mexico City. He went to Spain, was educated at Salamanca, and settled in Madrid (1611). Between 1615 and 1625 he wrote 25 plays, which established him as a leading playwright of the SIGLO DE ORO. In the meantime he was appointed to the Council of the Indies, an office he held for the rest of his life.

As a hunchback Alarcón was mercilessly ridiculed by literary rivals, such as Lope de Vega, Góngora, and Quevedo. These attacks did nothing, however, to obscure the outstanding quality of his plays, which were written with much greater care than those of contemporaries, who were accustomed to turning them out by the hundreds. Most of his plays were collected for print during his life:

*Parte primera de las comedias* (1628) contained eight plays and *Parte segunda* (1634), 13, including his best known, *La verdad sospechosa*, concerning a hero incapable of telling the truth. Alarcón's subjects cover a wide range but the plays dealing with contemporary manners have a moral and comic subtlety, matched by a classical construction and versification, that associates them more with 18th-century comedy than with the baroque style of Counter-Reformation Spain.

**Russian Company** See MUSCOVY COMPANY

**Rustici, Giovanni Francesco** (1474–1554) *Italian sculptor*
Nothing is known about Rustici's early years but that he was born at Florence and as a young man became a close friend of LEONARDO DA VINCI. His best-known works are the three bronze figures of John the Baptist preaching, flanked by a Levite and a Pharisee, over the north door of the baptistery in Florence, begun in 1506 and installed in 1511. A number of his marble statues, less assured than his work in bronze, are now in the Bargello and the Palazzo Vecchio, Florence; he also worked in terracotta (statue of a victorious knight in the Museo Horne, Florence). Two paintings in the Uffizi, Florence, may be his; his drawings have all been lost. In 1528 Rustici went to France at the invitation of Francis I to work on an equestrian monument, which he never finished. He died in Tours.

**rutters** Mariners' charts. The English word derives from the French *routier*. Rutters were mainly manuscript compilations until the publication of Lucas Jansz. Waghenaer's *Spieghel der Zeevaerdt* (1584–85) introduced a more sophisticated kind of guide for pilots (*see* WAGGONERS).

# S

**Sabellico, Marcantonio** (Marcantonio Coccio) (c. 1436–1506) *Italian humanist scholar and historian*
He lived and worked in Venice, where he lectured and held the post of librarian of San Marco, in charge of the bequest of books by Cardinal BESSARION, which formed the nucleus of the Bibliotheca MARCIANA. He wrote *Historiae rerum Venetarum* (1487), commissioned by the Venetian state, and followed this with a universal history, *Enneades* (1498–1504), as well as the vernacular treatise *Del sito di Venezia città* (1502). His two-volume *Opera* were published posthumously (1538).

**Sacchetti, Franco** (c. 1333–1400) *Dalmatian-born writer and poet*
Although he was born at Ragusa (Dubrovnik), Sacchetti was from an old established Florentine family and played an active role in the public life of Florence, holding many important posts. He claimed to have little learning or knowledge of Latin, but it is obvious he was widely read in vernacular literature. A prolific poet, he wrote some of the outstanding lyric poems of the 14th century and collected his verse in *Libro delle rime* (c. 1362). His major prose work, *Trecentonovelle* (*Three Hundred Tales*; 1392–97), of which 223 complete tales survive, acknowledges BOCCACCIO as model but is very different from the *Decameron*. There is no frame and no complexity in point of view; the tales are short, anecdotal, with explicit morals, like *exempla*; historical characters (e.g. Pope Boniface, Dante) appear occasionally; the comedy is low, often involving a cruel practical joke (*beffa*), but seldom indecent; the language is conversational. Sacchetti is also the author of a short burlesque epic poem and of vernacular prose commentaries on the Gospels, *Sposizioni di vangeli* (1381).

**Sachs, Hans** (1494-1576) *German dramatist, poet, and composer*
Sachs was born the son of a tailor in Nuremberg, and trained as a shoemaker. He became the most famous and prolific of the *meistersingers* (professional songwriters) of Nuremberg. He traveled throughout Germany from 1511 to 1516, visiting the schools of the *meistersingers*. He wrote over 4,000 master songs and more than 2,000 fables, farces, morality plays and tales in verse (*schwanke*). Sachs was an enthusiastic follower of LUTHER and much of his work celebrates the Reformation; the verse allegory *Die Wittembergisch Nachtigall* (The nightingale of Wittenberg; 1523) was written in honor of Luther and the advancement of Protestantism. His Shrovetide plays (*Fastnachtsspiele*) are celebrations of common life written in an energetic and graphically descriptive style, giving a vivid portrait of life in 16th-century Nuremberg. Many of his songs were later adapted as Protestant hymns. He is most famously celebrated in Richard Wagner's opera *Die Meistersinger von Nürnberg* (1868).
**See also:** MEISTERGESANG

**Sack of Rome** See ROME, SACK OF

*sacra conversazione* (Italian, "sacred conversation") A pictorial formula favored especially in the Italian Renaissance, in which the Madonna and Child are depicted enthroned and flanked by a small intimate group of saints. The saints are usually clearly identifiable by their dress or the emblems that they carry (St. Peter with his keys, St. Catherine with her spiked wheel, etc.); sometimes particular saints are featured because they have a connection with the church or locality for which the picture was painted or because the picture's donor had a special devotion toward them. They may be depicted as absorbed in meditation or study or in contemplation of the central figures, as in Giovanni BELLINI's 1505 altarpiece of the Virgin with four saints in the church of San Zaccaria in Venice. This style of composition, with central and flanking figures occupying the same pictorial space, succeeded earlier altarpieces in which the various figures were painted on separate fields or panels. Other Renaissance artists who employed this composition include MANTEGNA, Fra ANGELICO, Fra Filippo LIPPI, TITIAN, HOLBEIN, Guido RENI, and TINTORETTO.

*sacra rappresentazione* (Italian, "sacred representation") A form of sacred drama of popular origin performed in public squares or other open spaces, especially in 15th-century Tuscany. The plays, often by anonymous authors and mainly written in *ottava rima*, dealt with biblical events, saints' lives, or similar religious subjects but included elements of realistic characterization and description and allusions to contemporary life. There were no divisions into acts and scenes and no fixed length, but a variety of sets were used with scene changes as required. Presentations were sponsored by lay confraternities.

The plays apparently evolved from sung or spoken dialogues that developed in the singing of the *lauda*, a popular religious song of praise derived from the liturgy. *Laudes* flourished in Umbria among the flagellants (c. 1260), and the form, with its octosyllabic line, was adopted by the Franciscan Jacopone da Todi (1236–1306) and spread to the rest of Italy. Among writers of the *sacra rappresentazione* are Feo Belcari (1410–84), author of *La rappresentazione di Abram ed Isac* (1449), SAVONAROLA, Jacopo NARDI, and Lorenzo de' MEDICI, whose *Rappresentazione dei SS. Giovanni e Paolo* (1491) was performed towards the end of his life. During the 16th century texts of the plays were published but public performances gradually declined.

**Sadeler family** A dynasty of late 16th- and 17th-century artists, best known for their vast output of engravings, mainly reproduced after the designs of other painters. The head of the family was Johannes I (1550–c. 1600), who was born in Brussels, a member of the Antwerp guild, and was also active in Frankfurt and at the court of Wilhelm V of Bavaria, as well as in Florence, Verona, Rome, and Venice. His brother Raphael I (1560–1628/32), born in Antwerp, accompanied him to Germany. His son Justus (1583–1620) was also an editor, and his nephew Aegidius (c. 1570–1629) was both painter and engraver. After visiting Germany and Italy he moved to the court of Rudolf II at Prague (1597), where he died. Raphael I had three sons, Raphael II (1584–1632), Philip (active 1610s), and Johannes II (died 1665), all of whom were active at Munich. As a number of their prints are signed simply with an initial, it is sometimes difficult to distinguish the work of one member of the family from that of another.

**Sadoleto, Cardinal Jacopo** (1477–1547) *Italian humanist and churchman*
Sadoleto was born in Modena and studied Latin at Ferrara and Greek at Rome. He gained a reputation for his Latin style and for his hexameter poem on the newly discovered (1506) late first-century-BCE statuary group (now in the Vatican) depicting the punishment of the Trojan priest Laocoön, who with his sons was strangled by a serpent after Laocoön had attempted to warn his fellow-citizens against taking the Trojan Horse into Troy. Pope Leo X made him his secretary (1513) and bishop of Carpentras (1517). He wrote many moral and pastoral works and a commentary on the Epistle to the Romans which was placed on the Index because of suspicions that it contained crypto-Protestant ideas. Sadoleto certainly felt that the Church was in need of serious reform and was sympathetic to those pressing for change, but he did not advocate the rejection of papal authority, and in 1539 he attempted to win Calvinistic Geneva back to the Catholic Church with an eloquent appeal to Christian unity. In a letter to Clement VII after the Sack of Rome (1527), he interpreted the catastrophe as a divine punishment. In 1536 he was made a cardinal by Paul III. He was buried in San Pietro in Vincoli, Rome. His correspondence is a valuable primary source because of his contacts with many of the leading noble Italian families. He also wrote the educational treatise *De pueris recte instituendis* (1533).

**Sahagún, Bernardino de** (1500–1590) *Franciscan missionary and ethnographer*
Sent (1529) to New Spain (Mexico) to evangelize the native Americans, Sahagún learned Nahuatl and began a lifelong study of Aztec culture. This pursuit sometimes brought him into conflict with civil or Church authorities; for instance, Philip II ordered in 1577 that all research on Indian cultures should stop. However, through the backing of his superior Fray Rodrigo de Sequera, Sahagún's 12-book *Historia de las cosas de Nueva España*, was preserved and translated from Latin into Spanish. The work is a milestone in ethnography as Sahagún obtained information by the revolutionary method of conducting interviews with old people who had experienced the former Aztec regime.

**St. Bartholomew's Day, Massacre of** See MASSACRE OF ST. BARTHOLOMEW

**St. Peter's, Rome** The central basilica of the Roman Catholic Church. The first church, often referred to as Old St. Peter's, was dedicated in about 330 CE by Constantine I but was demolished in the 16th century after it had fallen into a state of disrepair. In 1506 Pope JULIUS II commissioned BRAMANTE to design a new church over the tomb of St. Peter. The new building, often called New St. Peter's, was originally modeled on a Greek cross plan, although the designs underwent many changes after Bramante's death (1514), with modifications being made by his successors, who included RAPHAEL, Fra GIOCONDO, Baldassare PERUZZI, and Antonio SANGALLO the Younger. In 1546 MICHELANGELO was appointed chief architect; he made a number of changes to Bramante's centralized plan, enlarged the size of it, and worked on the massive dome, which was completed after Michelangelo's death by Giacomo DELLA PORTA. The two small cupolas were the work of Giacomo da VIGNOLA. Further extensions were executed by Carlo Maderno in the 17th century, when St. Peter's Square was also laid out (1656–67) by Giovanni Bernini. The present basilica contains many notable works of art, including the first great PIETÀ (1498–99) by Michelangelo.

## St.-Quentin, battle of (August 10, 1557) A Spanish victory over the French at St.-Quentin in northern France. In March 1557 a French army entered Italy to challenge Hapsburg domination there and in reply a Spanish army invaded France from the Netherlands. The Spanish general beseiged the fortress of St.-Quentin; a relief force under Anne de MONTMORENCY, Constable of France, was destroyed. Montmorency and many other nobles were captured and the way to Paris lay open, but a bankrupt Spain was unable to press home its advantage.

See also: CATEAU-CAMBRÉSIS, PEACE OF

**Salamanca** A city in western Spain on the River Tormes. The town was captured by Hannibal (222 BCE) from the original inhabitants and then passed to the Romans, Visigoths, and Moors; the Moors were finally expelled around 1055. Salamanca's fame in the Middle Ages and Renaissance depended on its university, founded about 1230 by Alfonso IX of León and renowned throughout Europe first for its faculties of canon and civil law and later for its theology school. In the last decades of the 15th century, with scholars of the caliber of NEBRIJA on its staff and a rapidly growing student body, it was at the forefront of the introduction of humanist learning into Spain. The city was also one of the earliest centers for printing in Spain (1481). The new cathedral, begun in 1509 and from 1513 constructed to designs by Juan Gil de Ontañon, and several other ecclesiastical and university buildings date from the Renaissance period.

Notable among Salamanca's secular buildings is the Casa de las Conchas (House of the Shells), which is heavily adorned with scallop shells carved in high relief to reflect its late 15th-century owner's membership of the Military Order of Santiago, whose emblem was the scallop shell of St. James the Great.

**Sales, St. Francis de** See FRANCIS DE SALES, ST

**Salinas, Francisco de** (1513–1590) *Spanish organist and music theorist*
Salinas, who was born at Burgos, went blind about age 10. He studied philosophy and classics at Salamanca and then entered the service of Pedro Sarmiento de Salinas, who in 1538 became a cardinal. Salinas accompanied his employer to Rome, where he was ordained a priest. He became organist at the viceregal chapel at Naples (1553–58), and in 1559 organist at Sigüenza cathedral. He later became organist at León and, in 1567, professor of music at Salamanca. Salinas's theoretical work, *De musica libri septem* (1577) deals with the questions of consonant and dissonant intervals and proportions.

**Salt War** (1540) A rebellion by the city of Perugia against Pope PAUL III's authority. In 1538 Pope Paul III raised the price of salt by 50% throughout the Papal States. Perugia claimed his action violated an agreement not to increase its tax burdens, but the pope rejected this claim and excommunicated the city (March 1539). The Perugians chose 25 citizens as leaders and put Ridolfo Baglioni in command of their army. Paul III sent his son, Pierluigi Farnese, to Perugia with 13,000 soldiers. After minor skirmishes the Perugians submitted to papal power. Perugia had to accept rule by a papal legate and to pay for the construction of Paul III's fortress, the Rocca Paolina, in their city.

**Salutati, Lino Coluccio** (1331–1406) *Italian humanist and politician*
Salutati was born near Lucca and educated in rhetoric at Bologna. He became chancellor of Florence in 1375. Salutati rejected PETRARCH's abstract patriotism and for 30 years was an active politician; he united *studia humanitatis* with the life of action and this had a profound influence on the development of Renaissance Florence. His voluminous correspondence has still not been fully edited. In 1392 he arranged for an ancient manuscript of CICERO's *Epistolae ad familiares* to be copied; this work made a lasting impact on Renaissance concepts of the interaction between literary culture and political activity. Salutati accumulated a large library—over 800 volumes, 111 of which are still extant and identified—and he opened it to scholars. In his youth he wrote poetry and he always maintained the superiority of poetry to prose. His major work was an allegorical treatment of the labors of HERCULES, begun 1378–83 and left incomplete at his death. He was not a fruitful scholar and he knew only a few words of Greek but he was instrumental in bringing the Greek teacher CHRYSOLORAS to Florence.

**Further reading:** Berthold L. Ullman, *The Humanism of Coluccio Salutati* (Padua, Italy: Antenore, 1963); Ronald G. Witt, *Hercules at the Crossroads: The Life, Works and*

*Thought of Coluccio Salutati* (Durham, N.C.: Duke University Press, 1983).

## Salviati, Francesco (Il Cecchino) (1510–1563) *Italian painter*

He was born in Florence and having studied with ANDREA DEL SARTO, he moved to Rome, where he was patronized in the early 1530s by Cardinal Giovanni Salviati, whose surname he adopted. In 1539 he went to Venice via Parma, where the paintings of PARMIGIANINO influenced him. Other influences on his work were MICHELANGELO, PONTORMO, and the Venetians. He became a notable portrait painter and one of the leading fresco painters of the Florentine-Roman school. He decorated part of the Palazzo Vecchio in Florence in the 1540s, and in 1554 he was invited to the French court, but his restless nature brought him back to Rome the following year. His most important work in Rome was a set of frescoes in the Palazzo Farnese.

## Salviati, Leonardo (1540–1589) *Italian scholar and academician*

Born into an eminent Florentine family, Salviati studied under Piero VETTORI and rapidly established himself in literary circles, first publishing a *Dialogo dell' amicizia* (c. 1560), indebted to Cicero's *De amicitia*. His life's work, the promotion of the Tuscan vernacular, was announced in his *Orazione in lode della fiorentina favella* (1564) delivered before the Accademia Fiorentina. In the funeral oration for Benedetto VARCHI (1565), Salviati revised the definition of HUMANISM to include, in addition to classicists, those teaching and writing the language of Florence. A purist for whom BOCCACCIO was the ideal model, Salviati criticized TASSO's style on the publication of *Gerusalemme liberata* (1581). He was one of the founders of the ACCADEMIA DELLA CRUSCA, taking the academic name l'Infarinato ("the one covered with flour"), and his linguistic views were effectively embodied in the Cruscan *Vocabolario* (1612). He produced an expurgated version of the DECAMERON (1582), not from prudishness but in order to end suppression of the text (it had been placed on the INDEX LIBRORUM PROHIBITORUM in 1559) and restore its influence. Of continuing interest are his linguistic comments in *Avvertimenti della lingua sopra'l Decamerone* (*Remarks on the Language of the Decameron*; 1584–86). He also wrote two comedies, *Il granchio* (*The Crab*; 1566) and *La spina* (*The Thorn*; 1592).

**See also:** QUESTIONE DELLA LINGUA; VERNACULAR

## Sánchez Coelho, Alonso See COELHO, ALONSO SÁNCHEZ

**Sangallo family** Italian architects. The family originated in the vicinity of Florence. Giuliano (c. 1443–1516), who was also a sculptor in wood and a military engineer, was a follower of BRUNELLESCHI, whose influence is clear on several of Giuliano's buildings. Giuliano's church of Sta. Maria delle Carceri, Prato (1485–91) combines features of Brunelleschi's Pazzi chapel in Florence and of Alberti's San Sebastiano in Mantua. As Lorenzo de' MEDICI's favorite architect, Giuliano also executed work for the Medici family in Florence, notably the villa at Poggia a Caiano (1485), and designed Florence's defensive fortifications (1478). Other works include designs for St. Peter's in Rome, as BRAMANTE's successor, and for the facade of Brunelleschi's San Lorenzo in Florence (1516). Giuliano's son Francesco (1494–1576), known as Il Margotta, was also active as a sculptor and medalist.

Antonio I (1455–1535), Giuliano's younger brother and pupil, also executed work as a military engineer but is best known for his one great work, the church of the Madonna di San Biagio at Montepulciano (c. 1518–29). This dramatic classical building draws on Giuliano's church at Prato but is much more powerful in impact, despite the fact that it was never finished. Antonio II (1483–1546), the nephew of Giuliano and Antonio I, was influenced chiefly by Bramante for whom he worked in Rome (c. 1503). He undertook several projects for the Farnese family, including the initial stages of the Palazzo FARNESE. Other works include designs for St. Peter's, of which he was an architect from 1520, and the Palazzo del Banco di San Spirito (1523–34) in Rome. Another member of the Sangallo clan was Antonio I's nephew Aristotele (1481–1551), also called Bastiano, who was a painter and theater decorator at the Medici court.

**Further reading:** Christoph L. Frommel and Nicholas Adams (eds), *The Architectural Drawings of Antonio da Sangallo and His Circle*, 3 vols (Cambridge, Mass.: MIT Press, 1994– ).

## Sanmicheli, Michele (1484–1559) *Italian architect*

The son of a Veronese architect, Giovanni Sanmicheli, he trained at a very early age in Rome, where he was influenced by BRAMANTE, RAPHAEL, and the SANGALLO FAMILY. From 1509 to 1528 he worked in Orvieto as *capo-mastro* (master builder) of the cathedral. Among his works in Orvieto is the Capella Petrucci in the church of San Domenico. Returning to Verona, he began a career as a military architect, working in an elaborate mannerist style throughout the Venetian empire and in Cyprus and Crete. His two fortified gates in Verona, the Porta Nuova and the Porta Palio (1533–41), are among his best works. From the 1530s Sanmicheli also built a number of palaces, mainly in Verona, showing the influence of Bramante, GIULIO ROMANO, and Roman antiquity. Notable examples are the Bevilacqua, Canossa, and Pompei palaces.

## Sannazaro, Jacopo (1457–1530) *Italian poet*

Of aristocratic birth, Sannazaro spent almost all his life in or near his native Naples. With the backing of Giovanni PONTANO he became a member of the Neapolitan Academy, taking the academic name Actius Syncerus. King Federico also recognized his erudition, giving him the Villa Mergellina in 1499. He remained devoted to the Aragonese royal house after its downfall and followed the king into exile in France in 1501, returning to Mergellina after Federico's death in 1504. He thereafter lived in retirement and was buried in Sta. Maria del Parto in a tomb he had himself designed.

Sannazaro's earliest poetry, about a hundred Petrarchan sonnets and *canzoni*, was published posthumously (*Rime*, 1530). By the end of the 1480s he had completed most of his major work, the PASTORAL romance *L'Arcadia*, in which poetic eclogues alternate with prose narrative (*see* ARCADIA). It appeared in some 50 editions in the 16th century, from 1504 onward. Initially depicting the tranquil idyllic world of shepherds, the poem shifts to a more dramatic and tragic mood with the introduction of themes of mutability, unrequited love, and political protest. The principal figure, Sincero, suffers from MELANCHOLIA, the first of many heroes thus afflicted. Although anticipated by BOCCACCIO's *Ameto* (1342), *L'Arcadia*, which rifled virtually the entire classical heritage of bucolic poetry, established the pastoral in European verse for the next two centuries. Sannazaro's Latin poems, influenced by Pontano, are among the outstanding examples of the Renaissance. These include epigrams and three books of *Elegies* (1535), five *Eclogae piscatoriae* (1526), in which fishermen replace the conventional shepherds, and *De partu virginis* (*On the Parturition of the Virgin*; 1526), a Christian epic in Virgilian hexameters dedicated to Pope Clement VII.

**Further reading:** William J. Kennedy, *Jacopo Sannazano and the Uses of Pastoral* (Hanover, N.H.: University Press of New England, 1983).

## Sano di Pietro (Ansano di Pietro di Mencio) (1406–1481) *Italian painter*

Born in Siena, Sano di Pietro was a pupil of Stefano SASSETTA and GENTILE da Fabriano and established a reputation for his decorative and religious paintings and illustrations. His large body of work includes altarpieces, panels, predellas, and numerous scenes from the life of St. BERNARDINO, of whom he was a follower. Most notable of these is the *Sermon of St. Bernardino* (Siena cathedral); other works are the *Coronation of the Virgin* (Palazzo Pubblico, Siena) and *St. Francis receiving the Stigmata* (Nantes).

## Sansovino, Andrea (Andrea Contucci) (c. 1460–1529) *Italian sculptor and architect*

He was born at Monte San Sovino, near Siena, and having trained in Florence under Antonio POLLAIUOLO and BERTOLDO he worked there until 1491, when he was sent by Lorenzo de' Medici to Portugal. The years 1493–96 he spent in Florence working on the Baptistery and he then returned to Portugal until 1499, but very little is known of the reason for his two visits there. After his eventual return to Florence he began one of his best-known works: the *Baptism of Christ* over the central door of the baptistery. The style of this work, which was completed by Vincenzo DANTI nearly 70 years later, reflects the transition to the High Renaissance. It was, however, during his stay in Rome (1502–12) that he executed his most famous works: the tombs in Sta. Maria del Popolo of the cardinals Ascanio Sforza (1505) and Girolamo DELLA ROVERE (1507). These were influential works and the sleeping attitudes of the deceased were an innovation that was widely copied. In his later years Sansovino worked mainly in Loreto, supervising decorative and building work. He died in Monte San Sovino.

## Sansovino, Jacopo (Jacopo Tatti) (1486–1570) *Italian sculptor and architect*

A Florentine by birth, he was the pupil and most important follower of Andrea SANSOVINO, whose name he adopted. In 1505 he went to Rome to carry out a commission for Pope Julius II to restore ancient statues. With the Florentine architect Giuliano SANGALLO he also studied examples of ancient architecture. Before his move to Venice in 1527, Sansovino worked in Florence and then again in Rome, producing mainly sculptures; some of these showed the influence of MICHELANGELO, while others derived more from ancient models and from the style of Andrea Sansovino. However, like many other artists, he fled after the Sack of Rome in 1527 and two years after his arrival in Venice he was made chief architect of the city. It was in this post, which he held until his death, that he carried out the designs for which he is most famous. Chief among these was the Libreria Sansoviniana on the Piazzetta (1536; *see* MARCIANA, BIBLIOTHECA, Venice) one of the major architectural works of the 16th century and one which PALLADIO described as the richest and most ornate building since antiquity. Sansovino's other designs in Venice include the Palazzo Corner della Ca' Grande (1533) and the Zecca (mint) (1537). His most famous sculptures are the large statues of Mars and Neptune (1554–56) on the Scala dei Giganti of the doge's palace, which show his severe late style. He remained an exponent of the restrained style of the High Renaissance despite the increasing dominance of Mannerism in Italy.

**Further reading:** Bruce Boucher, *The Sculpture of Jacopo Sansovino* (New Haven, Conn.: Yale University Press, 1992); Deborah Howard, *Jacopo Sansovino: Architecture and Patronage in Renaissance Venice* (New Haven, Conn. and London: Yale University Press, 1975; repr. 1987).

## Santi di Tito (1536–1603) *Italian painter*

He was born at Borgo San Sepolcro, near Florence, and was trained by BRONZINO and then probably by BANDINELLI. He also studied in Rome, where he was influenced by the Roman masters and by antiquity, before returning to settle in Florence. VASARI says that he painted in the Belvedere of the Vatican and on the catafalque of MICHELANGELO but his best-known works are to be seen in the churches of Florence, such as his *Madonna* in San Salvatore and *Burial of Christ* in San Giuseppe. Many of his paintings are notable for their use of architectural perspectives. He was also a portrait painter and there are examples in the Uffizi, Florence.

## Santillana, Íñigo López de Mendoza, Marqués de
(1398–1458) *Spanish, poet, critic, and patron*
The son of the admiral of Castile and nephew of LÓPEZ DE AYALA, Santillana was born at Carrión de los Condes, near Burgos. The most powerful man in Castile after his defeat of the Infantes Juan of Navarre and Enrique of Aragon at the battle of Olmedo (1445), he also led the successful opposition to the constable Álvaro de LUNA, the favorite of King John II. Though he could not read Latin or Greek, he collected classical manuscripts and formed a great library at his palace at Guadalajara, open to all who wished to use it. He commissioned translations of the *Iliad*, *Aeneid*, Seneca's tragedies, and the *Divine Comedy*, and had PETRARCH's *Canzoniere* copied in the original Italian, which he read fluently.

Santillana's *Prohemio*, introducing a selection of his own poems sent to Don Pedro, the constable of Portugal, is the first work of literary criticism in Spanish (*Prohemio é carta... envió al condestable de Portugal*; 1449). In it he calls for a patron of Iberian poets and discusses the importance of studying Italian and French models, while ranking poetry in Latin and Greek highest (cultivated ver-

**Jacopo Sansovino** The library of San Marco (Bibliotheca Marciana) is housed in the Libreria Sansoviniana on the Piazzetta, Venice. Begun by Sansovino in 1536, it was eventually completed by Vincenzo Scamozzi in the 1580s.
*Anthony Kersting, London*

nacular poetry is only middling and popular ballads are lowest in rank). Despite this judgment, his own most memorable verses are short lyrics belonging to the popular troubadour tradition, especially 10 *serranillas*, poems similar to the *pastourelle*, in which a knight encounters a mountain girl (a *serrana*). His 42 less successful *Sonetos fechos al itálico modo* (1438–58) are the first Petrarchan sonnets in Spanish. He also wrote a number of longer allegorical, dream-vision, and didactic poems, mainly in octosyllabic verse.

**Saragossa** See ZARAGOZA

**Saravia, Hadrian à** (1531–1613) *Protestant theologian*
Born in Hesdin, Artois, of Hispano-Flemish parentage, Saravia came to England as a religious refugee in 1559. He interspersed periods serving as a minister in the Netherlands with 10 years as a schoolmaster in Guernsey and Southampton (1563–66, 1571–78). He settled in England permanently in 1587, and wrote a number of important tracts defending episcopacy and the ELIZABETHAN SETTLEMENT. His *De diversis ministrorum evangelii gradibus* (1590) provoked a Calvinist response from BEZA, to which Saravia in turn replied (*Defensio*, 1594). A further treatise of 1593 (*De imperandi authoritate*) was an early exposition of the divine right of kings. Saravia also contributed to the new translation of the Bible which became the Authorized Version of 1611.

**Sarpi, Fra Paolo** (1552–1623) *Italian philosopher, historian, and theologian*
Sarpi, who was born at Venice, entered the Servite order around 1565, was elected provincial in 1579, and later held the office of procurator-general (1585–88). His friendly relations with Protestants, including the British ambassador to the Venetian republic, Sir Henry Wotton (1568–1639), made him suspect in Rome. He also maintained an extensive international circle of correspondents. In 1606 he became theological counsellor to the republic during its dispute with Pope Paul V concerning secular controls over ecclesiastical buildings and the donation of property to the Church; he helped to render the papal interdict on the Venetians ineffective, though at the cost of his own excommunication (1607). His *History of the Council of Trent* was published in Latin and English in 1619 under the pseudonym Pietro Soave Polano (an anagram of Paolo Sarpi Veneto), strongly influencing northern views on papal machinations at the council. His letters indicate sympathy with some forms of Protestantism, but his secret *Pensieri filosofici* suggest an altogether more skeptical outlook on Christianity. He had a genuine interest in contemporary science, especially optics.

**Further reading:** David Wootton, *Paolo Sarpi: Between Renaissance and Enlightenment* (Cambridge, U.K.: Cambridge University Press, 1983).

**Sarto, Andrea del** See ANDREA DEL SARTO

**Sassetta, Stefano di Giovanni** (1392–c. 1450) *Italian painter*
Probably trained in his native Siena, Sassetta was influenced by the International Gothic style of MASOLINO and GENTILE da Fabriano, which he combined with Florentine realism. His first work was an altarpiece for the Arte della Lana chapel in Siena (1423–26), which was followed by another altarpiece, the *Madonna of the Snow* (1423–26; Contini Bonacossi Collection, Florence), painted for Siena cathedral. His masterpiece was the double-sided altarpiece (1437–44) executed for San Francesco, Borgo San Sepolcro, which includes panels illustrating the legend of St. Francis (National Gallery, London and Musée Condé, Chantilly) and fuses religious sincerity with naturalistic observation. Other works include a polyptych painted for San Domenico at Cortona (c. 1437) and scenes illustrating the legend of St. Anthony Abbot (Yale University Art Gallery, New Haven). Noted for his mystical imagination, Sassetta bridged the gap between the traditional Gothic style and the humanism of the High Renaissance. He died in Siena.

**Sassetti, Filippo** (1540–1588) *Italian merchant and humanist*
Sassetti was born into a noble Florentine family, studied philosophy at the university of Pisa (1568–73), and became a member of the Accademia Fiorentina. In 1577 his trade took him to Spain and Portugal, and in 1582, as superintendent of pepper supplies, to the Portuguese colony of Goa. Here he studied Indian customs, history, religions, and languages, about which he wrote letters home that he probably intended to revise for publication. However, he died in Goa before he could return to Europe, and the letters were not published collectively until 1855. His Indian letters reveal he was the first European to discover a common link between Sanskrit and the Germanic languages and Latin.

*Satire Ménippée* A satirical pamphlet in prose and verse published in 1594 by opponents of the French Catholic League. A parody of the league's *États géneraux*, convoked (1593) to elect a king other than the Protestant Henry of Navarre, the *Satire Ménippée* was compiled by Jean Leroy, a canon of Rouen, in collaboration with a number of scholars, lawyers, ecclesiastics, and others, notably Pierre Pithou, Jacques Gillot, Nicolas Rapin, Florent Chrestien, and Jean PASSERAT. The most important and influential element of the work, a solemn and eloquent harangue by a representative of the Third Estate, is preceded by a burlesque introduction, satirical attacks on prominent members of the league, and a series of comic speeches; the final part of the composition takes the form of a collection of satires and epigrams. The immense success of the *Satire*

*Ménippée* is attributable not only to its literary merit but also to its strategic publication at the moment of the league's final defeat.

**Saturn** In Roman mythology, the god of agriculture, who was later identified with the Greek Kronos. His reign, after he had overthrown his father Uranus, was a legendary Golden Age, the *Saturnia regna* celebrated by VIRGIL in the fourth eclogue. He was believed to be the father of Jupiter (Zeus) and several of the other major deities in the pagan pantheon.

In astrological terms the planet Saturn was predominantly a malign force. The metal associated with it was lead, and the qualities of slowness, coldness, and heaviness were supposed to manifest themselves in the characters of those under the planet's influence. In certain cases the gloomy temperament of the saturnine man was accompanied by intellectual and creative prowess (*see* MELANCHOLIA).

**Savery, Roelant** (c. 1576–1639) *Flemish painter*
He was born in Courtrai but studied in Amsterdam under Jacques Savery (died 1602), who was probably his brother. Around 1604 he entered the employment of Emperor RUDOLF II and spent about eight years in Prague, where he became one of the emperor's favorite artists in the symbolic mannerist mode that Rudolf particularly liked. Savery specialized in precise depiction of animals, observing from life some of the more exotic species in the emperor's menagerie; he painted at least 20 variations on the theme of ORPHEUS and the animals, and his famous *Paradise* (National Gallery, Prague) is another example of his fantastic *mélanges* of exotic and domestic birds and beasts. He also produced some fine mountain landscapes, the fruit of travels in the Alps and Tyrol (1606–08) at the emperor's behest. His exquisite flower paintings are among the earliest of their kind, although not so frequent in his prolific output. After working for Rudolf's successor, Matthias, in Vienna (1612–16), Savery returned to the Netherlands and settled at Utrecht in 1619, where his fame and ability brought him many admirers and followers.

**Savile, Sir Henry** (1549–1622) *English mathematician and humanist*
Savile was born at Bradley, near Halifax, and educated at Oxford University, where he was appointed warden of Merton College in 1585. He also served Queen ELIZABETH I as Greek tutor and Latin secretary, and from 1596 he was provost of Eton. He wrote or edited a number of books, the most substantial being his eight-volume Greek edition of St. John Chrysostom (1610–13) to which he contributed £8000 of his own money. He also helped his friend Thomas Bodley to found the BODLEIAN LIBRARY. He is best remembered, however, for his attempt to reintroduce science into Oxford by founding in 1619 the Savilian chairs of geometry and astronomy, the first recognizably scientific professorships to be established at any English university.

**Savini, Guido di** (Guido Andries) (died 1541) *Italian potter*
He first worked at Castel Durante (now Urbania), near Urbino, but by 1508 had moved to Antwerp, where he introduced the making of MAJOLICA. Three of his sons were later responsible for transferring the technique to England.

**Savoldo, Giovanni Girolamo** (c. 1480–c. 1548) *Italian painter*
Born in Brescia, Savoldo trained in Florence but worked chiefly in Venice, apart from a few years spent in Milan (c. 1529–35). He was influenced by TITIAN, GIORGIONE, BELLINI, and Lorenzo LOTTO and became known for his skillful handling of light effects, especially in night scenes. His masterpiece, the *Transfiguration* (Uffizi, Florence), anticipates the realism of CARAVAGGIO, while other paintings such as *Magdalene* (National Gallery, London) and *Gaston de Foix* (Louvre, Paris), which follows the contemporary fashion of linking painting with sculpture, illustrate Savoldo's mastery of texture and materials. Other works include the *Nativity* (1527; Hampton Court, London), the altarpiece for Sta. Maria, Verona (1523), and *St. Jerome* (National Gallery, London).

**Savonarola, Girolamo** (1452–1498) *Italian preacher and politician*
Savonarola was born in Ferrara and became a Dominican friar at Bologna in 1475. From 1482 he lectured at the convent of San Marco, Florence, of which he became prior in 1491. Despite the patronage of Lorenzo de' Medici, he preached in favor of ecclesiastical reform and against the high-handed and materialistic rule of the MEDICI; the emotional power of his sermons made him a valuable ally for the forces in Florence that brought about the exile of the Medici in 1494. His moral teaching was narrow-minded and puritanical, and during his ascendancy he presided over bonfires of "vanities," exercised strict control over religious art, and tried to eliminate gambling and licentious dress and behavior. His influence was extraordinary, especially with the young.

In 1494 he became *de facto* leader of a republic that revived Florence's ancient democratic institutions, which had fallen into disuse under the Medici. His actions, especially his support for Charles VIII's invasion of Italy, incurred the enmity of the duke of Milan, Pope Alexander VI, and the Franciscans. He also ignored papal briefs summoning him to Rome, ordering him to return to Bologna, and forbidding him to preach. In 1496 he was deprived of his post at San Marco by the amalgamation of the congregation there with that of another church. He responded by calling for a general council of the Church, maintaining that it could and should depose the pope. One of his disciples unwisely accepted a challenge to resort to ordeal by fire in order to settle his disputes with his opponents; this proved a fiasco, and the tide of popular opinion turned against Savonarola. In spite of the fact that he was an orthodox Catholic in all matters but papal authority, he was tried for heresy, tortured, and condemned by the ecclesiastical authorities to be hanged and burnt.

Among his works are Latin poems against worldly and ecclesiastical corruption, *De ruina mundi* (1472) and *De ruina ecclesiae* (1475), a tract *Della semplicita della vita Christiana* (1496), and writings against astrology.

**Further reading:** Lorenzo Polizzotto, *The Elect Nation: The Savonarola Movement in Florence 1494–1545* (Oxford, U.K.: Clarendon Press, 1995); Roberto Ridolfi, *The Life of Girolamo Savonarola*, transl. Cecil Grayson (London: Routledge & Kegan Paul, 1959; repr. Westport, Conn.: Greenwood, 1976); Pasquale Villari, *The Life and Times of Girolamo Savonarola* (1888; New York: Haskell House, 1969; repr. West Richard, 1988).

**Savoy, house of** The Franco-Italian noble family originally based on the western Alps, where France, Italy, and Switzerland now converge. The founder of the family, Humbert I, held the county of Savoy and other territories east of the Rhône River and south of Lake Geneva in the 11th century. His successors expanded their inheritance by marriage, conquest, and diplomacy until they eventually ruled Italy (1861–1945). Amadeus VII (count 1383–91) acquired Nice (1388). Amadeus VIII (1383–1451), who annexed Piedmont, was created duke of Savoy by Emperor Sigismund (1416), but abdicated (1439) to become the antipope Felix V (1439–49). The fortunes of the house of Savoy then declined and France occupied most of its territory (1536–59). After the restoration of Savoy to its ruling house (1559) Emanuel Philibert (duke 1553–80) reconstructed and enlarged his inheritance. He encouraged commercial and agricultural development and successfully welded the feudal lords and cities of Savoy into a centralized state by the time of the accession of his son CARLO EMANUELE I.

**Saxon Confession** (1551) A statement of Lutheran doctrine, drawn up by Philipp MELANCHTHON at the request of the Emperor Charles V, for submission to the Council of TRENT. It was less conciliatory than the Confession of AUGSBURG. The argument was developed from two articles of the Creed, concerning the forgiveness of sins and the Church; it held that the former excluded the doctrine of merit, or justification by works (see JUSTIFICATION BY FAITH), and that the latter referred to a spiritual community of believers. The principle that the sacraments are valid only in use was maintained.

**Saxton, Christopher** (c. 1542–1611) *English cartographer*
Saxton, who was born in Yorkshire, is renowned as the compiler of the first provincial atlas of any country. In 1572 the MP and court official Thomas Seckford commissioned Saxton to map the counties of England and Wales, an undertaking supported by the queen herself, who granted a royal license in 1577. Enhanced by expert engraving, the maps were published in 1579 as *An Atlas of the Counties of England and Wales*, a work that influenced English CARTOGRAPHY for many years. Saxton's subsequent works included an engraved map of England and Wales (1583).

**Scala, Bartolommeo** (1430–1497) *Italian humanist*
Born the son of a miller at Florence, Scala received a sound education and studied law first in Florence and then in Milan under the humanist Francesco FILELFO. He was appointed to a post in the household of his patron Pierfrancesco de' Medici before becoming secretary to the Parte Guelfa (1459). Supported by the Medici, he held the chancellorship of Florence from 1465 during the lifetime of Lorenzo de' Medici, but later wrote a defense of the republic under SAVONAROLA. He was knighted (1484) by Pope Innocent VIII. In addition to some unremarkable philosophical works, he wrote (c. 1480–97) a history of Florence from the foundation of the city to 1450.

**Scala family** See DELLA SCALA FAMILY

**Scaliger, Joseph Justus** (1540–1609) *French scholar and editor of Italian descent*
He was educated briefly at Bordeaux but mostly by his father Julius Caesar SCALIGER. Though his training was mainly in the classics he also developed an interest in science. His father disapproved of Greek, and it was not until the latter's death that the younger Scaliger, aged 19, went to Paris to learn it. He mastered the language with amazing speed and within two years had read all the available Greek literature, translating much of it into Latin. He also studied oriental languages. He was attached to an aristocratic Poitevin family for 30 years (1563–93) and with one of them traveled in Italy collecting inscriptions. He became a Calvinist (1562 or 1566) and was involved on the fringes of the religious wars. In 1593 he went to Leyden where he held a nonteaching post until his death. Scaliger is a giant among classical scholars; he had an outstanding knowledge of archaic Latin, edited many texts, and made fundamental contributions in several areas of study, notably ancient chronology, on which he wrote the revolutionary *Opus novum de emendatione temporum* (1583; see ANTIQUARIANISM). His *Thesaurus temporum* (1606) made the ancient sources available with a brilliantly intuitive commentary.

**Further reading:** Anthony and Sue Grafton, *Joseph Scaliger: A Study in the History of Classical Scholarship,* 2 vols (Oxford, U.K. and New York: Oxford University Press, 1983, 93; repr. 1997).

**Scaliger, Julius Caesar** (1484–1558) *Italian humanist*
Scaliger was born at Riva, Lake Garda, and, according to his own account, from the age of 12 he served Emperor Maximilian as a soldier for 17 years before studying at the university of Bologna. He migrated to France (1526) and settled at Agen. In the quarrel with ERASMUS over Ciceronianism he championed the Ciceronians' cause (*see* CICERO). He published several volumes of Latin verse and his *Poetices* (1561) was a key text in Renaissance literary theory, especially in its formulation of Aristotle's doctrine of the unities in tragedy. His main importance is as a philosopher; his commentaries on Aristotle and Theophrastus show acute power of reasoning and wide knowledge but retain a fundamental acceptance of the authority of Aristotle.

**Scamozzi, Vincenzo** (1552–1616) *Italian architect and theorist*
Born in Vicenza, Scamozzi was trained by his father and executed important commissions in Rome and Padua. He was greatly influenced by Andrea PALLADIO, three of whose buildings he completed after Palladio's death, including the Villa ROTONDA on which Scamozzi modeled his own Rocca Pisani at Lonigo (1576). Scamozzi's original works incorporate many Palladian features, notably in the Procuratie Nuove in Venice, begun in 1584. He was also the architect of two THEATERS, the Teatro Olimpico in Vicenza (1584) and the Teatro di Vespasiano Gonzaga in Sabbioneta (1588). Scamozzi traveled widely and was the author of an influential treatise, mainly written in the 1590s, *L'idea dell'architettura universale* (1615); this summarized his views of baroque art and had a considerable impact upon English neoclassical architecture. He also produced designs for Salzburg cathedral and the Italian fortress of Palmanova.

**Scève, Maurice** (c. 1501–c. 1564) *French poet*
The son of a magistrate, Scève made his name in the literary world with his alleged discovery of the tomb of PETRARCH's Laura at Avignon and with his first anthology, *Blasons* (c. 1536). He became leader of a group of poets in his native Lyons, whose other members included Antoine HÉROET, Pernette DU GUILLET, and Louise LABÉ: Pernette du Guillet is believed to have been the inspiration for much of Scève's poetry. *Délie, objet de plus haute vertu* (1544) is a series of 449 decasyllabic 10-line stanzas that deals in symbolic and metaphysical terms with the subject of love, and is heavily influenced by Plato and Petrarch; the title of the poem has been the subject of some speculation, "Délie" being interpreted by certain scholars as an anagram of "l'idée" ("the idea"). Scève's other works include the pastoral poem *La Saulsaye, eglogue de la vie solitaire* (1547) and *Microcosme* (1562), an epic account of the fall and redemption of mankind.

**Schardt, Jan Jorisz. van der** (c. 1530–1581) *Netherlands sculptor*
Born at Nijmegen and initially trained in the Netherlands, Schardt was active in Italy during the 1560s. After executing works for Emperor Maximilian II and King Frederick II of Denmark, he had arrived in Nuremberg by 1570. There he executed such works as the life-size terracotta bust of Willibald Imhof (Berlin) and the painted faience medallions of Paul von Praun (now divided between Nuremberg and Stuttgart). Although the latter is known to have owned dozens of terracottas and some bronzes by Schardt, very few of these can be traced. Schardt's severe realism owes more to the Italian tradition than to his experiences in Italy. Although a foreigner, he may be

**Vincenzo Scamozzi** The symmetry of the exterior of the Rocca Pisani at Lonigo, near Vicenza, is repeated in the plan of the interior, as shown in an illustration from Scamozzi's *L'idea dell'architettura universale* (1615).
*By permission of the British Library (50.f.13)*

counted as the last major luminary in the 16th-century Nuremberg school of sculptors.

## Schäufelein, Hans Leonhart (c. 1480–c. 1538) *German painter and illustrator*

A pupil of DÜRER in his native Nuremberg, Schäufelein clearly shows his master's influence, especially in his early work. He also worked for Hans HOLBEIN THE ELDER in Augsburg for a while (c. 1509). In 1515 he became a citizen of Nördlingen, his home until his death. His own style, particularly suited to characterization and portrait painting, was imaginative, sensitive, and tasteful. His paintings include a number of altarpieces and paintings for churches, such as the *Dead Christ* for Nuremberg cathedral, and a fresco of the siege of Bethulia for Nördlingen town hall. A gifted book illustrator, and one of the most prolific of his time, he drew the designs for numerous woodcuts and engravings, although he did not execute them himself. He provided many of the illustrations for the allegorical poem *Theuerdank* (1517), an account of Emperor Maximilian I's journey to marry Mary of Burgundy.

## Scheiner, Christoph (1573–1650) *German astronomer*

A prominent Jesuit, Scheiner was appointed professor of mathematics and Hebrew at Ingolstadt university in 1610. He served later at the court of Maximilian I, Elector of Bavaria, and in Rome from 1624 to 1633. In 1612, under the pseudonym Apelles, he published the first account of sunspots. The work led to a long and bitter controversy with GALILEO. The issue was revived once more by Scheiner in his privately printed *Rosa ursina* (1626–30) and ended only with Galileo's summons to Rome in 1632. Scheiner himself, it was widely believed, was not unconnected with the decision to prosecute his rival. One of the engravings in *Rosa ursina* shows Scheiner's invention of the first equatorially mounted telescope, the heliotrope; other illustrations include his important moon map and his sunspot observations. Scheiner was also one of the first scholars, in his *Oculus hoc est: Fundamentum opticum* (1619), to identify the retina as the seat of vision.

## schiacciato (stiacciato)

A technique of marble carving in a very low relief, evolved by DONATELLO and also practiced in the Quattrocento by DESIDERIO DA SETTIGNANO and AGOSTINO DI DUCCIO. Despite the shallowness of the carving, the sculptors' understanding of perspective enabled them to achieve effects of depth comparable to those produced by contemporary painters.

## Schiavone, Andrea Meldolla (c. 1515–1563) *Italian painter*

Born in Sebénico, Dalmatia, Schiavone was known as "the Slavonian" on account of his origin. He settled in Venice, where he produced a number of religious and mythological scenes and may have been a pupil of PARMIGIANINO, whose influence is apparent upon his engravings and etchings. He combined this mannerist element with the rich colors of TITIAN in a style that was much admired by TINTORETTO and imitated by him in his early works. Schiavone also painted several secular subjects and portraits, including pictures of philosophers in the great hall of the Bibliotheca MARCIANA, Venice.

## Schidone, Bartolommeo (c. 1570–1615) *Italian painter*

He was born at Modena, but little else is known about Schidone's life. He may have received his training under the CARRACCI brothers but his work bears little resemblance to theirs and indicates more the influences of CORREGGIO and CARAVAGGIO. He spent most of his life in Parma, apart from the period 1602–06, when he worked for the duke of Modena. His most important work in Modena was his series of emblematical figures in the Palazzo Pubblico depicting the history of Coriolanus. Many of his other paintings are in the museums of Parma and Naples. His later works reveal the influence of baroque trends in Rome. He is said to have been a gambler and to have died in Parma after amassing in one night a huge debt that he could not pay off.

## Schmalkaldic Articles (1537)

A statement drawn up by LUTHER at the request of John Frederick, elector of Saxony, for submission to a council of the Church to be held at Mantua. The first part, which was not controversial, dealt with the Creeds; the second, concerning the office of Christ, attacked the doctrine of the Mass and other Roman teachings; the third was about differences between Protestants in Eucharistic doctrine. An appendix by MELANCHTHON conceded the supremacy of the pope by human right. The articles were approved by a convention of theologians at Schmalkald, in Germany and, though never formally adopted by the evangelical churches, they were widely accepted.

## Schmalkaldic League

An alliance of Protestants formed in 1531 at Schmalkald, in Germany, against Emperor CHARLES V. It united Lutherans and Zwinglians, north German princes and southern cities, including Strasbourg. It was ruined by the defection of Maurice of Saxony and defeated by Charles at the battle of MÜHLBERG in 1547.

See also: PHILIP OF HESSE

## Scholarius, George See GENNADIUS

## Schongauer, Martin (c. 1440–1491) *German engraver and painter*

He was the son of Kaspar Schongauer, a goldsmith from Augsburg who had settled in Colmar, where Martin was born and spent most of his life. The only painting definitely attributed to him is the altarpiece for the church of

St. Martin, Colmar, the so-called *Madonna in the Rose Bower* (1473); this shows the attention with which Schongauer must have studied the work of 15th-century Flemish artists, especially Rogier van der WEYDEN. Schongauer's main importance resides in his innovative copper engravings of religious subjects; 113 of them are known, signed with his initials. These were widely disseminated, spreading Schongauer's influence far beyond the school for engravers he ran at Colmar; some of the works of the LITTLE MASTERS (OF NUREMBERG) show a clear debt to him, and had it not been for Schongauer's death DÜRER would have carried out his intention of studying with him when he visited Colmar in 1492.

**Schuyt, Cornelis** (1557–1616) *Dutch composer*
Schuyt was born in Leyden and trained as a chorister at St. Pieterskerk, where he succeeded his father as organist (1601). He was one of the leading Dutch madrigalists and a contemporary of the organist Jan Pietersz. SWEELINCK. He published two collections of MADRIGALS, the first in 1600 for five voices and another in 1611 for six voices. He is known to have traveled to Italy, probably in the 1570s, and this had a strong influence on his work. His madrigals, for instance, include settings of verse by the Italian poet Torquato TASSO.

**Schwabach, Articles of** See AUGSBURG, CONFESSION OF

*Schwänke* Comic anecdotes written in prose or verse, collections of which were popular reading matter in 15th- and 16th-century Germany. They often centered on the exploits of legendary rogues, such as the hero of *Till Eulenspiegel* (1515), a witty mischief-maker who reveled in tricking good citizens. Another extremely successful collection was *Das Rollwagenbüchlein* (1555) by Jörg WICKRAM. During the 16th century the *Schwank*, in the form of the humorous everyday scene, also served as the basis for drama in Shrovetide plays (*Fastnachtspiele*). The *Schwank* reflected the shift of emphasis in German literature from courtly chivalric concerns to the homelier ones of town and village. It also represented one of the earliest forms of German prose literature, which scarcely existed before the 13th century. Hans SACHS, the cobbler of Nuremberg, was a master of the *Schwank*.
**See also:** FACETIAE

**Schwarz, Hans** (c. 1492–post-1532) *German medalist and sculptor*
Schwarz was born in Augsburg but traveled extensively in northern Europe. A talented portraitist, he produced numerous portrait medallions in the Italian style, showing faces in profile or three-quarters view. As a sculptor, he worked particularly in low relief, using fine stone, and followed the style of paintings of the period by including effects of perspective and even elements of landscape. His work includes sculptures for the FUGGER FAMILY chapel (executed from sketches by DÜRER).

**science** See NATURAL PHILOSOPHY

**Scorel, Jan van** (1495–1562) *Netherlands painter*
He was born at Schoorl, near Alkmaar, and was probably first trained by Cornelis Buys the Elder in Alkmaar. Scorel was then apprenticed to Jacob Cornelisz. van Oostsanen in Amsterdam in 1512. In about 1517/18 he may have visited Jan GOSSAERT in Utrecht. In 1519 he undertook an extensive trip to Carinthia via Basle and Nuremberg, where he may have worked briefly in DÜRER's shop. In Obervellach, in Carinthia, he executed an altarpiece heavily influenced by Dürer. By 1520 Scorel was in Venice, whence he took ship for Jerusalem. His *Entry of Christ into Jerusalem* (1527; Utrecht) includes a vista of the holy city which reveals a personal study of its topography. In 1521 Scorel was back in Italy, first at Venice and subsequently in Rome. The following year the Dutch Pope Adrian VI appointed him curator of the papal collection of antiquities in the Belvedere. However, Scorel's tenure was terminated by the pope's death (1523) and he returned home. From 1524 he resided in Utrecht, save for short visits to the southern Netherlands and France and a period in Haarlem between 1527 and 1529/30.

Scorel was deeply influenced by a range of Italian artists, including MICHELANGELO, RAPHAEL, GIORGIONE, and PALMA VECCHIO. His *Death of Cleopatra* (c. 1522; Amsterdam) repeats a formula of reclining female nude popular in Venice, but with a musculature reminiscent of Michelangelo's sculptures. While the composition of his *Baptism of Christ* (c. 1528; Haarlem) harks back to Dirk BOUTS in some respects, it includes figure types derived from both Raphael and antique art. His *Rest on the Flight* (c. 1530; Washington) incorporates a background heavily indebted to ancient Roman wall paintings, with which the artist would have become familiar as curator of the Belvedere. Scorel was also a fine portrait painter of both individual figures and groups. A key figure in the assimilation of Italian style in northern Europe, Scorel has a significance in the development of the 16th-century Dutch school second only to that of LUCAS VAN LEYDEN. The style of Scorel's pupil, Maarten van HEEMSKERCK, is a creative development of his own, but seems mannered and uneasy by comparison.

**sculpture** Like its sister arts, PAINTING and ARCHITECTURE, sculpture was a medium that gave tangible form to Renaissance ideals, reflecting the progress of cultural and intellectual currents. Accordingly, the origins of Renaissance sculpture are to be found in those of the period itself. The newly matured humanist movement stimulated a historical self-consciousness which prompted comparisons of contemporary culture with that of the ancient

Greeks and Romans. Ancient texts about art became a source of inspiration and a touchstone against which to measure artistic achievements. Verisimilitude, the imitation of nature, gained signal importance in the artists' vocabulary. Contemporaneously, the lay spirituality of the Franciscan movement gave force to the renewed interest in nature and man.

Monumental stone sculpture had been revived as a component of architectural decoration in the Romanesque period. Figural sculpture was reintroduced into the artistic vocabulary of Europe in the Gothic period principally through the evolution of portal jamb colonnettes into jamb figures. This process adumbrated the revival of the ancient Vitruvian association between the human form and the column. In Italy, ingrained classical traditions ensured that figures and reliefs on pulpits, tombs, and church facades had a greater independence from their architectural setting than did those on northern Gothic structures.

Classicism and Gothic naturalism combined in the art of Niccolò PISANO, a sculptor from Apulia, working in Tuscany. His son, Giovanni PISANO, a contemporary of Giotto, enlarged the expressive capabilities of figures. Quotations from classical sculpture continued to appear side by side with stylistic elements imported from the Gothic north throughout the Trecento. By the end of the century, the Italian and northern traditions merged momentarily, producing the phenomenon of the International Gothic style, whose chief exponent in the north was Claus SLUTER.

A series of commissions for public sculpture in Florence in the first decades of the Quattrocento was the catalyst for the emergence of new directions in sculpture. The protagonists were a group of young craftsmen, mostly trained as workers of precious metal or stone in the International Gothic style. Challenged to give tangible form to a new ideal of the individual—of man's special place in the world order—they carved and cast a race of heroes, saints, and gods and won acclaim for their own genius. This concept of virtu, represented by the image as well as the maker, became a leitmotif of Renaissance sculpture.

Within this context, two strains in sculpture emerged, a refined, elegant mode and a vigorous, classical one, sparked respectively by the different temperaments of the two leading artists, Lorenzo GHIBERTI and DONATELLO. Throughout the century materials, motifs, and formats were reintroduced under the guidance of ancient art. Figures in classical CONTRAPPOSTO stance, clothed or nude, life-size and over life-size, sometimes free-standing, reappeared. Artists in the service of the cult of the individual created portrait busts, equestrian statues, and a special brand of funerary monument for a clientele who wished to perpetuate their memory or to commemorate their achievements. Donatello, a leader in these developments and undisputed creative genius of his generation, also evolved a new method of low-relief carving (SCHIAC-

CIATO). He took advantage of that method to offer provocative interpretations of traditional subjects, heightening psychic energy and incorporating the newly developed Brunelleschian one-point perspective into complex vistas. In addition to marble and bronze, terracotta was revived as a primary sculptural material; among the most important workshops, that of the DELLA ROBBIA family produced glazed, polychromed reliefs and statues, meant principally to decorate the coolly rational pietra serena and plaster spaces of the new architectural style. The third quarter of the century witnessed the emergence of a group of virtuoso marble carvers (DESIDERIO DA SETTIGNANO, Antonio ROSSELLINO, BENEDETTO DA MAIANO) working in the so-called "sweet style." Perhaps best known for their reliefs of the smiling Virgin and Child, they focused their production on church furnishings, including pulpits and tabernacles. By the last quarter of the Quattrocento, technical mastery of materials and an emerging scientific knowlede of anatomy combined in a new ability on the part of sculptors to display the body in motion. A primary vehicle for the exploration of the figure in action (and in the round) was the bronze statuette, though experiments of this kind found their way into sculpture on a large scale as well. Leading the field were VERROCCHIO and Antonio del POLLAIUOLO, masters who were distinguished by the fact that they were also painters. Greater facility gained through the combined use of drawings and models further enhanced the potential for experimentation.

The Tuscan style was disseminated to other cultural centers; Donatello spent about a decade in Padua, while artists of lesser rank sought work in the courts of northern and southern Italy or in Rome. In most cases Quattrocento sculpture outside Tuscany was characterized by a more sharply exaggerated local classicism, meant to suggest ties to Roman and early Christian traditions specific to that area.

In general, 15th-century sculptors outside Italy continued working in a late Gothic idiom which featured figures of either tall, slender proportions or Sluteresque robustness swathed in drapery. The figures, for the most part, appear embedded in fantastic and elaborate Gothic settings as part of architectural schemes or church furnishings. Sculptors worked primarily in wood and stone; polychromy was a significant feature. Among the greatest northern sculptors are counted Hans Multscher (c. 1400–67), Nicolaus GERHAERT VON LEYDEN, Tilmann RIEMENSCHNEIDER, Veit STOSS, and Adam KRAFT. Of the sculpture that was independent of an architectural framework, votive figures, such as PIETÀ groups and Madonnas, were especially popular. In France the popularity of groups of near lifesize figures in stone (representing, most typically, Entombments, as at Auch and Bourges) may have inspired a similar phenomenon in Italy, although in terracotta. Niccolò dell' ARCA exploited the latter medium, producing highly active figures charged with great expression. The appeal of tableaux vivants (which also included Annunciation and Nativity scenes) in polychromed terracotta, wood, or wax, is explained by their uncanny realistic qualities. This vogue culminated in the episodic set of tableaux of the life of the Virgin and of Christ at the Sacro Monte of Varallo in the Sesia valley northwest of Milan.

A number of conditions continued to affect the course of the development of sculpture in Italy, which was virtually dominated by the Florentines in the 15th and 16th centuries. The technological advances of the Quattrocento and the increasing significance of archaeological finds (such as the discovery of the first-century-BCE Laocoön statue in Rome in 1506) inspired a concept of perfection which characterizes the art of the 16th century. The study of collections of antiquities, like that of Lorenzo de' MEDICI, inspired young sculptors in the 1490s to formulate a new ideal of beauty, grace, and harmony. The challenge not only to match but also to outdo antique sculpture prompted a shift to colossal scale in sculpture for public places and funerary projects. The relationship of sculpture and its architectural setting was tuned to a perfect harmony. The creative power of the artist, filtered through an aesthetic vision of perfection, provided the potential to surpass nature; expression of the artifice of art replaced verisimilitude as the primary objective. The evolution of art theory in the 16th century and the corollary notion of the artist-philosopher was critical to the formulation of the concept of the artist as genius and led to the establishment of academies of design by mid-century. MICHELANGELO, the premier artist of the age and recognized master of painting, sculpture, and architecture, became the principal exponent of the concept of *disegno*, explaining it as the unifying factor among those arts. His avowed allegiance to sculpture above all secured the principal position in the hierarchy for this medium.

The political and religious climate that followed the Sack of Rome in 1527 and accompanied the gathering COUNTER-REFORMATION further affected artistic production. The strengthening of a powerful international aristocracy was mirrored by the growing importance of more localized Italian courts. Patrons favored suave, attenuated figures crafted of precious materials which represented intellectualized encores of the work of Michelangelo, Raphael, and Leonardo, either on a grand scale or translated into decorative motifs on *objets de virtu*. CELLINI, Vincenzo DANTI, and Bartolommeo AMMANATI were among the most important exponents of this style. In contrast, the new Counter-Reform piety in Rome and strong tendencies towards realism in Venice tempered the excessive refinements of the *maniera* (*see* MANNERISM) in those cultural centers.

From the late 15th century, but especially in the 16th century, Italian artists in all media were called to work in the courts of England, France, Spain, Portugal, and Poland; artists from the north and from Spain traveled to Italy to gain firsthand experience. Most artistic production throughout Europe carried an Italianate stamp. In Germany, Konrad MEIT, for example, produced small statuettes in alabaster, bronze, and wood, classical in style and subject. Florentine Mannerism enjoyed primacy at the French court, evoking a response from the talented native sculptors Jean GOUJON, Germain PILON, and Ligier RICHIER. Appropriately, in the last decades of the 16th century, northern and southern traditions fused in the work of the Flemish sculptor GIAMBOLOGNA, who lived principally in Florence. His technical and compositional virtuosity represented a culmination of Renaissance ideals and set a course for the development of the European Baroque.

**Further reading:** Phyllis P. Bober and Ruth Rubinstein, *Renaissance Artists and Antique Sculpture: A Handbook of Sources* (London: Harvey Miller, 1986) GERMANY: Michael Baxandall, *The Limewood Sculptors of Renaissance Germany* (New Haven, Conn. and London: Yale University Press, 1980) ITALY: Charles Avery, *Florentine Renaissance Sculpture* (London: John Murray, 1970); Suzanne B. Butters, *The Triumph of Vulcan: Sculptors' Tools, Porphyry, and the Prince in Ducal Florence* (Florence, Italy: Olschki, 1996); John Pope-Hennessy, *Italian Renaissance Sculpture* (1958; 3rd ed. Oxford, U.K.: Phaidon, 1986); ~ , *Italian High Renaissance and Baroque Sculpture* (1963; new ed. Oxford, U.K.: Phaidon, 1986).

**sea-beggars** Dutch Calvinist privateers who played a vital part in the successful Dutch revolt against Spanish rule. They took their name from a scornful reference by a Spanish nobleman to Dutch petitioners for religious toleration in the Compromise of BREDA (1566). In 1572 they achieved an important breakthrough in their struggle against Spain when they took the port of Brill in the name of WILLIAM (I) THE SILENT. The conquest of Flushing soon followed.

**See also:** NETHERLANDS, REVOLT OF THE

**Sebastiano del Piombo** (**Sebastiano Luciani**) (c. 1485– 1547) *Italian painter*
Born in Venice, Sebastiano trained and studied under PALMA VECCHIO, TITIAN, Giovanni BELLINI, and GIORGIONE. After Giorgione's death (1510) Sebastiano completed several of his paintings, while his own work *Salome* (1510; National Gallery, London) is clearly influenced by Giorgione's style. In 1511 Sebastiano settled in Rome, where he remained, apart from a brief period in Venice (1528–29). He became one of RAPHAEL's circle, working upon the Villa FARNESINA, before falling out with Raphael and becoming an adherent of MICHELANGELO. Sebastiano's *Raising of Lazarus* (c. 1517–19; National Gallery, London) was painted for Cardinal Giulio de' Medici in direct competition with Raphael, while Michelangelo himself contributed the cartoon for Sebastiano's *Pietà* (c. 1520–25; Musico Civico, Viterbo). Sebastiano also painted a num-

ber of notable portraits, including those of Pope Clement VII (1526; Capodimonte, Naples; see Plate XIV) and Cardinal Pole (c. 1537; St. Petersburg). In 1531 he received a papal sinecure as keeper of the curial seal (which was made of lead—hence his nickname "Piombo"); after this he executed few further works. Other major works include *St. John Chrysostom with other Saints* (1510–11; San Giovanni Crisostomo, Venice), *Portrait of a Young Man* (1514; Uffizi, Florence), and *Holy Family with a Donor* (1517–18; National Gallery, London).

Further reading: Michael Hirst, *Sebastiano del Piombo* (Oxford, U.K.; Clarendon Press and New York: Oxford University Press, 1985).

## Secundus, Janus (Jean Second, Jan Nicolaesz. Everaerts) (1511–1536) *Netherlands poet*

Secundus was born at The Hague into a distinguished Netherlands family and studied law at Bourges before becoming secretary (1533) to the archbishop of Toledo. It was while he was in Spain that he wrote his *Basia*, a series of amatory poems that show the influence of Catullus; written, like all Secundus's work, in elegant humanist Latin, the *Basia* has been translated into many languages. In 1534 Secundus accompanied Emperor CHARLES V to Tunis before returning briefly to the Netherlands to become secretary to the bishop of Utrecht. His increasing fame as a writer of Latin verse led Charles to offer him the post of private Latin secretary, but he died of fever near Tournai en route to join the emperor in Italy. Besides *Basia*, Secundus also wrote odes, epigrams, elegies, and an account of his travels. He was interested in painting and sculpture and several portrait medals have been attributed to him.

## Sellaio, Jacopo del (1442–1493) *Italian painter*

A Florentine by birth, Sellaio was known by the name that reflects his father's trade of saddlemaker. He was a pupil of Filippo LIPPI and also influenced by Botticelli and Ghirlandaio. He is represented by Madonnas in the Palazzo Pitti, Florence, and in the Ca' d'Oro, Venice, and by panels depicting the triumphs of love, chastity, and time in the Museo Bandini, Fiesole.

## Sendivogius, Michael (Michael Sendivow) (1556–after 1630) *Polish alchemist*

Sendivogius was widely known in his day as the possessor of a powder obtained from the Scot Alexander Seton (died 1604) and supposedly capable of transmuting lead into gold. Successful demonstrations were reportedly given to RUDOLF II in Prague and to King Sigismund of Poland in Warsaw. Shortly afterward, in 1607, Sendivogius lost the remainder of Seton's dwindling stock of powder. Thereafter little is known of him until 1625 when he reappeared in Warsaw peddling a variety of nostrums. There was, however, a more serious side to Sendivogius. In such

works as *Novum Lumen Chemicum* (1604; translated as *A New Light of Alchemy*, 1650) he developed a theory of metals which was to prove highly influential among a later generation of alchemists and chemists.

## Seneca, Lucius Annaeus, the Younger (c. 4 BCE–65 CE) *Roman philosopher and dramatist*

He was the son of the rhetorician Lucius Annaeus Seneca, the Elder (c. 55 BCE–c. 37 CE), and became a leading Stoic philosopher in Rome, as well as participating in public life there. His literary reputation brought his appointment as tutor to Nero, over whom at first he exercised some beneficial influence, but he was eventually ordered by the emperor to commit suicide. His calmness and courage at his death contributed substantially to his standing as a moralist. The humane and noble qualities of Seneca that so attracted his Renaissance admirers are captured in RUBENS' striking *Death of Seneca* (c. 1609–10; Bayerische Staatsgemäldesammlungen, Munich), painted from a famous Roman statue that was then believed to depict this subject.

In the Middle Ages Seneca was known as the author of a book on natural phenomena but primarily for his philosophical dialogues, treatises, and epistles. The temper of these was so congenial to the medieval mind that many people believed that Seneca had been a Christian, and the appeal of both his sentiments and style continued unabated among the Florentine philosophers of the 15th century. His tragedies too were known and their moral character highly praised. The medieval definition of TRAGEDY as a great man's fall from prosperity to adversity owes much to the argument of Seneca's plays.

It is no exaggeration to say that the revival of tragedy on the Renaissance stage was entirely founded on Seneca's nine dramas on Greek mythological subjects. Although probably based on ancient Greek originals, they deviate considerably in mood and treatment from surviving Greek tragedies. The latter were barely accessible to the 15th century, as no printed texts existed and very few people could have read them if there had been any, so Seneca's plays were the sole ancient models available. It is likely that they were written for recitation rather than acting, and their style is highly rhetorical, declamatory in tone, and recondite in allusion, combining excessive moralizing with bizarre horrors. These features were avidly incorporated in neo-Latin and vernacular imitations.

Further reading: Gordon Braden, *Renaissance Tragedy and the Senecan Tradition: Anger's Privilege* (New Haven, Conn.: Yale University Press, 1985); Lorraine Helms, *Seneca By Candlelight: And Other Stories of Renaissance Drama* (Philadelphia, Pa: University of Pennsylvania Press, 1997).

## Senfl, Ludwig (c. 1486–c. 1542) *Swiss composer*

From 1496 to 1513 Senfl sang in the *Hofkapelle* of Emperor Maximilian I in Vienna, Augsburg, and Constance.

He worked with his teacher, the *Kapellmeister* Heinrich ISAAC, in copying a large amount of music which was later published as part of Isaac's *Choralis constantinus* (1550–55), a task Senfl completed in around 1520 after Isaac's death. He took over Isaac's position at the *Hofkapelle* in 1517. After Maximilian's death (1519) Senfl traveled extensively. In 1523 he became court composer in the *Hofkapelle* of Duke Wilhelm of Bavaria in Munich, where he remained until he died. Senfl did compose some sacred music, but his numerous German lieder are his main achievement; traditional German melodies are treated in imaginative ways, ranging from chordal harmonization to canons.

## Serlio, Sebastiano (1475–1554) *Italian architect, painter, and architectural theorist*

Born in Bologna, Serlio trained as a painter under his father before moving to Rome, where he studied architecture and antiquarianism under Baldassare PERUZZI. After the Sack of Rome (1527) Serlio traveled to Venice; there he remained until 1540, when he was invited to France by Francis I to help in the building of the palace at FONTAINEBLEAU. By this time Serlio was already famous for the first installment of his great treatise *Tutte l'opere d'architettura e prospettiva* (1537–75), in which he set out the principles of classical architecture with accompanying illustrations by BRAMANTE, Peruzzi, and his own hand. This influential work helped to spread Renaissance ideas in northern Europe, appearing in Dutch in 1606 and English in 1611, and was the first such work to manifest a practical rather than a theoretical approach to architecture. Serlio also produced a short book on portals, the *Libro extraordinario* (1551), and introduced innovations in stage design based upon the classical theories of VITRUVIUS. The only two surviving architectural works by Serlio are a doorway at Fontainebleau and the château at Ancy-le-Franc (begun in 1546).

## Sermisy, Claudin de (c. 1490–1562) *French composer*

Known as Claudin in his day, Sermisy sang at the Ste.-Chapelle and in the king's private chapel. He may have accompanied Francis I to Bologna in 1515 and to the FIELD OF THE CLOTH OF GOLD (1520). In 1532 he was *sous-maître* at the royal chapel and in 1533 was nominated canon at the Ste.-Chappelle. Sermisy must have lived in Paris for much of this period and eventually died there. He wrote about 110 sacred works, including motets, Masses, and a Passion, but is chiefly remembered for his 175 or so chansons. These are in a simpler, more homophonic and syllabic style than those of his contemporaries, with attractive melodies. Many were so popular that other composers arranged them for all kinds of vocal and instrumental forces.

**sermons** See PREACHING

## Servetus, Michael (1511–1553) *Spanish theologian and physician*

The son of a notary, Servetus traveled and studied in Spain, France, Italy, and Germany before settling (1532) in Lyons, where he worked, under the pseudonym Michel de Villeneuve, as a publisher. This cover was adopted to protect him from the notoriety gained by his earlier antitrinitarian work, *De trinitatis erroribus* (1531). Servetus's interests then turned to medicine and, after graduating from the university of Paris, he worked in France as a physician to the archbishop of Vienne (1541–53). He then produced a further antitrinitarian work, *Christianismi restitutio* (1553), in which he described the circulation of the blood from the heart's left side via the lungs to the right side. Charged with heresy, he fled, but, most unwisely, went to Geneva where, under the direction of CALVIN, he was burnt at the stake as a heretic.

## Seusenhofer family

One of the most important German families of armorers in the 15th and 16th centuries. Konrad Seusenhofer (1460–1517) moved from Augsburg to Innsbruck in 1504 to set up a court armory for Emperor Maximilian I, and was later succeeded as court armorer by his brother Hans (1470–1555) and Hans's son Jörg (c. 1505–80). During the 16th century, when plate ARMOR had become ceremonial rather than practical, the family made richly elaborate armor, often decorated by inlaying, gilding, etching, or carving, for the European monarchies. Konrad was instrumental in evolving the type of fluted armor, known as "Maximilian," popular in the first three decades of the 16th century (a fusion of the German and Italian styles of armor). A fashion in armor during the 1520s was to simulate the puffing and slashing of the dress of the period, an early example being the armor made by Konrad for Archduke Charles in 1514. Other clients of Konrad's included Henry VIII of England and James IV of Scotland.

Another fashion of the mid-16th century was for garnitures—complete "wardrobes" of matching pieces of armor for different occasions. A famous example of this is the "Eagle" garniture made by Jörg Seusenhofer for Ferdinand, Archduke of Tyrol, in 1547, which comprised over 60 separate pieces.

## Seville

A city and river port on the Guadalquivir in Andalusia, southern Spain, 54 miles (86 km) from the Atlantic. Seville was in turn Roman, Visigothic, and Moorish before its Christian reconquest (1248). By the early Renaissance period Seville's silk and woolen textile industries had brought it prosperity, but it was the establishment in 1503 of the city's Casa de Contratación (house of trade), with a monopoly of trade with the Americas, that made Seville very rich. Foreign merchants flocked in, and Seville's population increased from 25,000 in 1517 to 90,000 in 1594, making it Spain's largest city.

During the 17th century competition from Cádiz led to Seville's decline.

Seville's religious history was troubled. It was a prime center of the activities of the SPANISH INQUISITION; Jews were expelled as early as 1483 and altogether some 2000 suspected heretics were burned in *autos da fé* there during the 1480s. In the early years of PHILIP II's reign further *autos da fé* (1559, 1560) brutally suppressed the city's incipient Protestant movement. Notable buildings from the Renaissance period include one of the largest cathedrals in the world (1403–1506). PACHECO established his painting academy in Seville, and Francisco HERRERA the Elder and ROELAS both worked in the city.

## Sforza, Caterina (c. 1462–1509) *Milanese noblewoman, countess of Forlì*

An illegitimate daughter of Duke Galeazzo Maria SFORZA, Caterina married (1473) Girolamo Riario, with whom she ruled Imola and, from 1480, Forlì. After her husband's assassination (in 1488 in belated revenge for his role in the PAZZI CONSPIRACY), Caterina fought off anyone who threatened her rule as regent for her young son until forced to surrender to Cesare Borgia (1500), who is said to have raped her. She was imprisoned at Rome but released (1501) on relinquishing claim to her lands and retired to Florence. By her marriage (1496) to a member of a junior branch of the Medici family, she was mother of the condottiere Giovanni della Banda Nere (1498–1526), whose son Cosimo became Grand Duke COSIMO I DE' MEDICI.

## Sforza, Francesco (I) (1401–1466) *Italian condottiere who became the first Sforza duke of Milan (1450)*

After successful service in the wars of Duke Filippo Maria Visconti of Milan, Sforza obtained the duke's daughter as bride (1441) and the promise of the duchy. He took possession of Milan after the collapse of the AMBROSIAN REPUBLIC, greatly enhancing its standing as a regional power and embarking on important military and civil construction projects in and around the city. Leading humanists were attracted to his court, among them Francesco FILELFO who wrote his *Sforziade* in Francesco's honor.

## Sforza, Galeazzo Maria (1444–1476) *Second Sforza duke of Milan (1466–76)*

Galeazzo Maria received a thoroughgoing humanist education at his father's court, and in his early adult years he was a condottiere like his father Francesco (I) SFORZA. As duke he was a patron of music, establishing a choir for his chapel (1472) and employing Josquin DES PRÉS. His rule over Milan was harsh, however, and he was assassinated in the porch of the cathedral by three Milanese noblemen, leaving his young son Giangaleazzo under the regency of his widow, Bona of Savoy.

## Sforza, Lodovico ("Il Moro") (1451–1508) *Fourth Sforza duke of Milan (1494–1500)*

In 1481, five years after the assassination of his elder brother Galeazzo Maria SFORZA, Lodovico usurped the regency of his brother's widow over his nephew, the young Duke Giangaleazzo. Following the death (or possibly murder) of Giangaleazzo, Lodovico became duke. He and his wife Beatrice d'Este (1475–97) made the Milanese court a magnet for artists, scholars, architects, and musicians: LEONARDO DA VINCI and BRAMANTE carried out commissions for him; CASTIGLIONE and the mathematician PACIOLI were among his protégés. Lodovico's entanglements with the political alliances and events leading up to the French invasions of Italy brought about his downfall when Louis XII of France captured Milan (1499). Lodovico was definitively defeated the following year and taken to France, where he died eight years later, still a prisoner.

## Sforza family

A family of prosperous farmers from Romagna, who became dukes of Milan. Their fortunes were made by two noted condottieri. The family's founder was Muzio Attendolo (1369–1424), who assumed the name Sforza (force). His son Francesco SFORZA, also a condottiere, was hired to protect the short-lived AMBROSIAN REPUBLIC (1447), but having married (1441) Bianca Maria, illegitimate daughter of the last VISCONTI duke, instead made himself duke of Milan (1450). He gave Milan great public works and lavish entertainments to make his despotism acceptable. He also initiated a tradition of patronage of learning and the arts that made Milan a cultural beacon in the second half of the 15th century. Francesco's son Galeazzo SFORZA ruled capably and encouraged agriculture, commerce, communications, learning, and the arts. After his assassination (1476) he was succeeded by his young son Giangaleazzo (1469–94), whose power was usurped by his ruthless and unpopular uncle, Lodovico "il Moro" SFORZA, husband of Beatrice d'Este (*see* ESTE FAMILY). Lodovico was expelled by Louis XII of France (1499). Lodovico's son Massimiliano was briefly restored (1513–16) by the Swiss and then expelled by the French and Venetians. Finally, CHARLES V supported the rule (1522–35) of Massimiliano's brother Francesco Maria, but when Francesco died without heirs Milan passed to Charles.

See also: SFORZA, CATERINA.

Further reading: Paul A. and Lora I. M. Merkley, *Music and Patronage in the Sforza Court* (Turnhout, Belgium: Brepols, 1999).

*sfumato* The technique of effecting a gradual transition from one color to another, practiced by many painters of the High Renaissance. To critics such as VASARI it was an indicator of the maturity of art as manifested in the paintings of LEONARDO DA VINCI and GIORGIONE, in contrast to

**Sforza Family**

The Sforza dukes of Milan. Through her third marriage (1496), to Giovanni di Pierfrancesco de' Medici, Galeazzo Maria's illegitimate daughter Caterina became the grandmother of Duke Cosimo (I) of Florence.

the hard outlines and abrupt color transitions of Quattrocento painters. Taking its name from the Italian word *sfumare*, meaning "to evaporate like smoke," *sfumato* was used in both paintings and drawings for various purposes, including the emphasis of relief effects. Leonardo and other major artists also advocated its use on more philosophical grounds, stressing its value as a means of merging human figures with the natural landscapes in which they are set.

### Shakespeare, William (1564–1616) *English dramatist and poet*

Shakespeare was born and educated at Stratford-upon-Avon, Warwickshire, the eldest son of a prosperous glover who had married into the local gentry. Little is known (though much is conjectured) about Shakespeare's early life. In 1582 he married Anne Hathaway and possibly supported her and their children, Susanna (born 1583), and the twins Hamnet and Judith (born 1585), by working as a schoolmaster. At some unknown date, maybe in the late 1580s, Shakespeare moved to London.

The erotic poems *Venus and Adonis* (1593) and *The Rape of Lucrece* (1594), with dedications to the earl of Southampton, were Shakespeare's first published works, but he had already had several plays produced (the three parts of *Henry VI*, *Richard III*, and the Plautine *Comedy of Errors*). He was also probably writing sonnets, about which speculation has continued to rage since their col-

lection and publication in 1609. From 1594 Shakespeare's theatrical company was the Lord Chamberlain's Men, for whom in the next five years he wrote the plays of his early maturity, among them *Romeo and Juliet*, *A Midsummer Night's Dream*, *Much Ado about Nothing*, *As You Like It*, *The Merchant of Venice*, and the history plays *Richard II*, *1 and 2 Henry IV*, and *Henry V*. In 1596 his father acquired a grant of arms and the following year Shakespeare purchased New Place at Stratford, both evidence of the family's standing and prosperity.

The Globe Theatre at Bankside, south of the Thames in London, was opened in 1599, and for it Shakespeare wrote his seven great tragedies (*Julius Caesar*, HAMLET, *Othello*, *King Lear*, *Macbeth*, *Antony and Cleopatra*, and *Coriolanus*). Apart from *Twelfth Night*, his comedies of the period 1599–1608 (*Measure for Measure*, *All's Well that Ends Well*, and *Troilus and Cressida*) are more somber and ambiguous than those of the 1590s. In 1608 Shakespeare's company, known since 1603 as the King's Men, took over the indoor Blackfriars Theatre, for which Shakespeare wrote the romantic comedies *Pericles*, *Cymbeline*, *The Winter's Tale*, and *The Tempest*; the last, probably written in 1611, is generally read as the playwright's farewell to the stage. Shakespeare retired to Stratford, where he died. In 1623 his old friends and colleagues in the theater, John Heminge and Henry Condell, published the first collected edition of Shakespeare's works, known as the First Folio;

it contained 36 plays, of which only 19 had been printed during the playwright's lifetime.

**Further reading:** Jonathan Bate, *The Genius of Shakespeare* (Oxford, U.K. and New York: Oxford University Press, 1998); Jonathan Bate and Russell Jackson (eds), *The Oxford Illustrated History of Shakespeare on Stage* (Oxford, U.K. and New York: Oxford University Press, 2001); Katherine Duncan-Jones, *Ungentle Shakespeare: Scenes from His Life* (London: Arden Shakespeare, 2001); Frank Kermode, *Shakespeare's Language* (New York: Farrar, Straus & Giroux, 2000).

**Sibyls** Classical prophetesses, originally associated with oracles of Apollo, but famous in post-classical times as the reputed authors of the Sibylline Oracles. This collection of prophecies had supposedly been obtained from the Sibyl of Cumae and was kept in the Capitol in ancient Rome and only consulted in national crises. The Capitoline collection was destroyed in 405 CE, but meanwhile purported texts of the prophecies had been put into circulation and overlaid with Jewish and Christian accretions, making them of great interest to the Middle Ages. The Sibyls therefore passed into medieval and Renaissance lore as true prophets, fit to associate in iconographical schemes with the biblical seers.

Most commonly, the number of Sibyls was computed at nine: Cumaean (alternatively known as the Erythraean), Tiburtine (or Albunean), Hellespontine, Samian, Eritrean, Delphic, Libyan, Persian, and Cimmerian. The list, however, can vary. The Tiburtine Sibyl was particularly famous, as among her supposed utterances was one foretelling the coming of Christ, and she is sometimes shown without her sisters, as in a fresco (1528) by PERUZZI over the altar of the Fontegiusta church, Siena, in which she announces the birth of Christ to the Roman emperor, Augustus. The Sibyls were portrayed as either young or very old women holding scrolls or books. They are depicted in inlaid marble slabs in the pavement of the aisles of Siena cathedral (mainly 15th century), and in association with prophets in the TEMPIO MALATESTIANO, in Michelangelo's ceiling in the SISTINE CHAPEL, and in scores of humbler decorative schemes, even in domestic surroundings, as at Chastleton House, Oxfordshire, England (early 17th century).

**Sidney, Sir Philip** (1554–1586) *English writer, courtier, and soldier*
Born on his father's estate at Penshurst, Kent, Sidney was brought up in court circles, went to Shrewsbury school (1564) and Christ Church, Oxford (1568–71), and then spent three years traveling on the Continent, where he made a profound impression on many eminent scholars and statesmen. On his return he was much favored by Queen ELIZABETH I. He wrote the entertainment *The Lady of May* (1578) for her, but in 1579 quarreled with the earl

of Oxford and, rejecting the queen's wish that he should apologize, he retired from court. He then incurred further displeasure by sending her, at the instigation of his uncle, the earl of LEICESTER, an outspoken memorandum (1580) against her proposed marriage with Duke FRANCIS of (Anjou-)Alençon.

While in retirement at Wilton, home of his sister Mary HERBERT, Countess of Pembroke, Sidney probably completed the first version of ARCADIA and with Mary composed metrical versions of the Psalms. In 1581 his prolonged courtship of Penelope Devereux (c. 1562–1607) was terminated by her marriage to Lord Rich; Sidney, who had been addressing sonnets to her under the name "Stella," expressed his continuing passion in some of the finest sonnets in the sequence *Astrophel and Stella* (1591). In the early 1580s he also wrote his famous *Defence of Poesie* (1595; also entitled *Apologie for Poetrie*), justifying the social utility of verse as "delightfull teaching." In 1583 he was knighted and married Frances Walsingham, daughter of the queen's adviser, both events taking place with the queen's reluctant consent, but two years later he made peace with the queen and was appointed governor of Flushing on Leicester's expedition to the Netherlands. The following autumn he was mortally wounded while fighting the Spaniards at Zutphen and died at Arnhem.

Sidney's lifelong friend Fulke GREVILLE wrote (c. 1610–14) a biography of Sidney (1652) which idealizes him as the embodiment of Elizabethan greatness and Christian chivalry. His integrity, charm, courage, and learning made him universally mourned. He was a considerable patron of writers (Greville calls him "a generall MAECENAS of learning"); among his protégés was SPENSER, who wrote the pastoral elegy "Astrophel" upon his death. The Countess of Pembroke published the revised *Arcadia* (1590), more moralistic in tone than the original "toyfull booke," and continued to encourage her brother's literary dependants.

**Further reading:** John Buxton, *Sir Philip Sidney and the English Renaissance* (London: Macmillan and New York: St. Martin's Press; 3rd ed. 1987); Katherine Duncan-Jones, *Sir Philip Sidney: Courtier Poet* (London: Hamish Hamilton and New Haven, Conn.: Yale University Press, 1991); Alan Stewart, *Philip Sidney: A Double Life* (New York: St. Martin's Press, 2001).

**Siena** A city and city state in Tuscany, central Italy. Siena was subject to, in turn, Etruscans, Romans, and Lombards before attaining its independence in the 12th century. By the early 14th century Siena was a great banking and commercial center, but its economy and population then declined on account of foreign warfare, raids by mercenaries, the Black Death (1348–49), Florentine expansionism, divisive constitutional arrangements, and Florence's commercial supremacy in Tuscany. Siena was briefly ruled by the VISCONTI of Milan (1399–1404), but then resumed its communal constitution until the *signoria* of the Petrucci family (1487–1524). From 1530 the city had to accept a Spanish garrison, but rebelled against CHARLES V's plan to build a fort there (1552). Spanish and Florentine forces subdued Siena (1555) and Spain sold Siena to Florence two years later.

Siena had a university (founded 1240) and a 16th-century literary society called the Intronati, but it is best known for its 14th-century school of artists (DUCCIO, Simone MARTINI, Ambrogio LORENZETTI). PINTURICCHIO lived in Siena in the early 16th century. The architects FRANCESCO DI GIORGIO MARTINI and Baldassare PERUZZI were Sienese-born, as was the sculptor Jacopo della QUERCIA. Renaissance Siena boasted two saints: CATHERINE OF SIENA and BERNARDINO OF SIENA. Surviving landmarks include the Palazzo Pubblico (1297–1310), the Torre del Mangia (1338–48), and numerous handsome palaces such as the Palazzo Piccolomini "delle Papesse," begun in 1460 to designs by Bernardo ROSSELLINO.

**Further reading:** Giuletta Chelazzi Dini *et al*, *Sienese Painting: From Duccio to the Birth of the Baroque* (New York: Harry N. Abrams, 1998).

**Siglo de Oro** The "golden age" of Spanish literature, roughly the 16th and 17th centuries. The term, first applied by a minor 19th-century Romantic writer, is imprecise, there being no agreement on the exact boundaries of the period. The accession of FERDINAND (II) AND ISABELLA I (1474) or 1500 have been advanced as *termini a quo*, and as *termini ad quem*, the death of the last major writer, Calderón (1681) or 1700. In either case, most Spanish "classics" fall within the period. Literary developments do not parallel but lag behind those of Renaissance Italy; nevertheless, a new European orientation emerged during this era as writers responded to humanist ideals. Particularly notable, from this point of view, are (in poetry) the publication of the works of BOSCÁN and GARCILASO DE LA VEGA (1543), and (in prose) Boscán's translation (1534) of THE COURTIER and the Erasmian influence spread by the works of the brothers VALDÉS.

**signatures, theory of** A theory that seems to have originated with PARACELSUS, who stated: "By the outward shapes and qualities of things we may know their inward Vertues, which God hath put in them for the good of man." Thus, St. John's wort was held by Paracelsus to be good for wounds because the leaves had a similar "porositie" to that of the skin, and its flowers "when putrified are like blood." Paracelsus went on to derive the secondary principle that "what Climate soever is subject to any Particular disease, in the same place there grows a Cure." Consequently, it was pointless to search for foreign drugs. But what of the objection that not all plants clearly advertised their virtues? God, it was answered, has signed some

plants to put man on the right track. Thereafter man must search more strenuously. The Paracelsian doctrine was picked up and publicized by Giambattista DELLA PORTA in his *Phytognomonica* (Plant Indicators; 1588), after which it remained current for many years although rejected by such botanists as John Ray (1627–1705).

**Signorelli, Luca** (c. 1441–1523) *Italian painter*
Signorelli was born in Cortona, the cathedral of which houses some of his major late works, including *The Institution of the Eucharist* (1512). His earliest known works, fragments in Città di Castello (1474), show some influence of PIERO DELLA FRANCESCA, whose pupil he is thought to have been; this is evident in the sculptural style of his figures. He was greatly influenced however by the contemporary Florentine school of POLLAIUOLO and VERROCCHIO, as is shown by his interest in the representation of movement and exaggerated muscular development. Between 1479 and 1481 he painted frescoes in the cupola of the sacristy of the Santuario della Sta. Casa at Loreto, and in the 1480s he worked on the Sistine Chapel frescoes with PERUGINO, BOTTICELLI, ROSSELLI, and others. In 1497 he was commissioned to paint scenes from the life of St. Benedict in the cloister of the monastery of Monte Oliveto Maggiore, south of Siena, but abandoned his work there after only nine panels, leaving the remainder to be completed by SODOMA.

His masterpiece is the fresco cycle at Orvieto cathedral (1499–1503). Begun by Fra ANGELICO in 1477, it is a series of compositions entitled *The End of the World* and *The Last Judgment*. Signorelli uses the grotesque to convey his vision of the theme with brutal intensity, as in the packed, writhing figures in *The Fall of the Damned* (see Plate XV). The frescoes are also noted for their brilliant draftsmanship and the representation of nude figures in action, which influenced MICHELANGELO. The interest in the nude was also manifest in the overtly pagan *Pan and other Gods* (c. 1490), which was destroyed in Berlin during World War II.

**Further reading:** Tom Henry and Laurence Kanter, *Luca Signorelli: The Complete Paintings* (Milan: Rizzoli, 2002).

*signoria* (Italian, "lordship") The characteristic form of government in Italian city states from the 13th to the 16th century. It replaced the older republican governments which were often torn apart by rival factions. The lord or despot of the *signoria* was ideally a strong ruler who ensured efficient government and peace for his people; he fostered civic pride through magnificent public works and lavish patronage of arts and letters. The *signoria* helped pave the way for the modern nation state. In Florence the ruling magistrates formed the *signoria*.

## Sigüenza, Fray José de (c. 1544–1606) *Spanish historian*

Named after his birthplace, Sigüenza was librarian of the ESCORIAL and later became prior of the Jeronymite monastery there. He is known for one work of dull but authoritative scholarship, *Historia de la Orden de San Jerónimo* (*History of the Order of St. Jerome;* three volumes, 1595, 1600, 1605), of which order he had been a friar since 1567. The third volume contains a full description of the Escorial that has never been superseded and the work offers fascinating glimpses of PHILIP II's role in the building of the great complex and his relationships with artists who decorated it.

## Siloe, Diego de (c. 1495–1563) *Spanish architect and sculptor*

Born in the city of Burgos, Diego was the son of the sculptor Gil de SILOE and was trained largely in Italy. His earliest documented piece is the marble Caraccioli reredos (1514–15; San Giovanni a Carbonara, Naples), on which he collaborated with his fellow-Spaniard Bartolomé ORDÓÑEZ. In 1519 he returned to Burgos, where he executed a number of designs, including one for the tower of Sta. Maria del Campo. His major work in that city, however, was the Escalera Dorada (1519–26), a magnificent gilded staircase in the cathedral. Diego is best known for his design of Granada cathedral (1528–43), where he succeeded Enrique Egas as architect. On Egas's Gothic foundations Diego erected a great domed church that combined elements of Italian, Gothic, and Spanish Muslim styles in the manner known as PLATERESQUE, also employing features of the design of the Church of the Holy Sepulcher in Jerusalem. Later works included the church of El Salvador at Ubeda (1536), the cathedrals of Málaga and Guadix (1549), and San Gabriel at Loja.

## Siloe, Gil de (active 1486–1499) *Spanish sculptor*

Possibly born in Orleans or Antwerp, Gil was one of the last great sculptors in the Gothic style in Spain. The few works by Gil that have survived include a number of elaborate tombs, including those of John II of Castile and his second wife Isabella of Portugal, Infante Alfonso, and Juan de Padilla (1489–93; all in La Catuja, Miraflores). Also for the monastery of Miraflores near Burgos, Gil executed a notable altarpiece (1496–99); other works include four reredoses for churches in Valladolid and Burgos. All his works show the influence of Spanish Muslim and Flemish styles but themselves had little artistic impact upon subsequent sculptors working in the Italian style, such as his son Diego de SILOE.

**Simone Martini** See MARTINI, SIMONE

**Simons, Menno** See MENNONITES

## singers

Before the later 16th century, the history of European singing is mainly a story of ecclesiastical musicians, who also acted as directors, composers, teachers, and theorists. The Church provided livings for clerics who were expected to sing multiple daily services, and it is in this context that the literate and educated musical world found its broadest support. Increasingly during the 14th and 15th centuries, endowments from private donors for chapels provided a vehicle for the introduction of regular polyphonic singing alongside the traditional (and much more commonly performed) plainchant. With the combination of the revenues from these endowments, from the late 14th century onward churches were able to provide permanent employment specifically for singers.

The ecclesiastical training provided to singers—men and choirboys—was of a thoroughly different character to that known today. For many, musical knowledge was limited to a proficiency in monophonic singing, allowing them to perform plainchant from memory and to read it as notated in chant books (without rhythm). In the ever-growing number of institutions that supported polyphonic music, however, instructors grounded their singers in numerous more advanced practices. Well-developed aural skills and a good working knowledge of improvisational styles were key elements in the education of such singers; other skills, such as organ-playing and reading polyphonic notation, were important but not as common. The singer's role was very much a productive one, and the line between singer and composer only began to take on real definition in the late 15th century. Throughout the 16th century, the majority of successful composers were hired as singers and chapel directors.

Specific information on the use of different voice types in polyphony from this period is notoriously difficult to come by. The issue is complicated by the fact that the names of voice parts in the musical sources refer primarily to function, rather than range. Furthermore, the notational system in use did not presuppose a fixed pitch standard, so a single piece could be performed at different pitches to suit different performing ensembles. From the 14th to the 16th centuries, the array of voice parts used in composed pieces underwent a gradual expansion and refinement, arriving eventually at a common disposition very close to the modern choral ensemble of soprano, alto, tenor, and bass. Boy trebles were used for polyphonic singing in numerous institutions by the later 15th century, both in England and on the Continent. Chapels without boys would employ adult males singing in falsetto (head voice) for the top parts in polyphony, but the use of this voice type in other contexts is disputed. Particularly difficult for modern choral performance is the existence of parts that could be performed either by high tenors (singing in chest voice) or by male altos extending into lower ranges; a common hypothesis is that male singers in the 15th and 16th centuries developed the ability to switch readily between chest and head voice for such parts. It was in the second half of the 16th century that castrati (men who had been castrated before puberty, to retain a soprano range) began to appear, mainly at Italian centers; only in the 17th and 18th centuries, however, did these singers made a significant impact on musical culture. Women and girls had opportunities to learn to sing, both in convents and in secular contexts, and could achieve occasional success as professional singers even in the 15th century.

Indeed, female singers were associated with a number of important developments in late 16th-century musical style, in connection with the rise of solo virtuoso performance. Highly elaborate ornamentation had been practiced regularly by singers as well as instrumentalists at earlier periods, and examples in embellishment manuals offer a glimpse of these practices; likewise, solo singing and amateur singing by noblewomen were known in the middle of the 16th century. However, the formation of a group of three to four professional singing ladies at the court of Ferrara in 1580–1581 (the famous *concerto delle donne*) impacted on later musical practice in significant ways. The works that the leading composers of the day wrote for the Ferrarese ladies made use of their considerable capabilities, and theorists looking for new modes of musical expression were affected by their performance style. The characteristic elements of this style—highly dramatic delivery of the text, speechlike recitation, and skillful ornamentation, for example—were cornerstones of the music in early opera and oratorio, the new forms born during these years.

**Further reading:** Rob C. Wegman, "From maker to composer: Improvisation and musical authorship in the Low Countries, 1450–1500," *Journal of the American Musicological Society* 49 (1996), pp. 409–79; Anthony Newcomb, *The Madrigal at Ferrara, 1579–1597*, 2 vols (Princeton, N.J.: Princeton University Press, 1980).

**Sistine Chapel** The papal chapel in the Vatican Palace, Rome. Commissioned by Pope Sixtus IV, the chapel was built (1473–81) under the supervision of Giovanni de Dolci and is famous as the meeting place of the Sacred College of Cardinals. The chapel is also celebrated for its series of 14 frescoes, commissioned between 1481 and 1483 and painted by leading artists of the day. The south wall is decorated with frescoes by PINTURICCHIO, BOTTICELLI, ROSSELLI, PIERO DI COSIMO, Luca SIGNORELLI, and Bartolommeo della Gatta (1448–c. 1502). The north wall has frescoes by PERUGINO, Pinturicchio, Botticelli, GHIRLANDAIO, Rosselli, and Piero di Cosimo. Most remarkable of all the paintings in the chapel, however, are those by MICHELANGELO. The west wall is covered by Michelangelo's *The Last Judgment* (1533–41), while the barrel-vaulted ceiling was also decorated by him with scenes from Genesis (see Plate IX). On ceremonial occa-

sions parts of the side walls are covered by tapestries depicting biblical scenes, designed by RAPHAEL and woven in Brussels (1515–19). The chapel also contains a marble screen and cantoria probably made in the Roman workshop of Andrea BREGNO.

**Further reading:** Leopold D. Ettlinger, *The Sistine Chapel Before Michelangelo* (Oxford, U.K.: Clarendon Press, 1965); Ross King, *Michelangelo and the Pope's Ceiling* (New York: Random House, 2003); Fabrizio Mancinelli, *The Sistine Chapel* (Rome: Vatican Museum, rev. ed. 1996).

**Six Articles, Act of** (1539) Act of Parliament by which HENRY VIII reaffirmed traditional Catholic doctrines after his break with Rome. The Articles upheld TRANSUBSTANTIATION and communion in one kind, clerical celibacy and the permanence of monastic vows, and the use of private Masses and auricular CONFESSION. Denial of any of these became punishable by imprisonment for a first offense and death for a second.

Drawn up by Henry himself, the Articles had two main purposes: to stop the religious ferment of the immediate past and to deflect threats from the European Catholic powers. English reformers, who referred bitterly to the "whip with six strings," reacted with deep anger and dismay. Two bishops resigned in protest and the bill was opposed in the Lords by Archbishop CRANMER, who was obliged to send his own wife abroad when it passed. In practice, however, it proved much less draconian than its opponents had feared.

**Sixtus IV** (1414–1484) *Pope* (1471–84)
Born Francesco della Rovere of a poor family near Savona, he became a Franciscan friar and teacher. He was made minister-general of the Franciscans (1464) and cardinal (1467). As pope, Sixtus initially campaigned unsuccessfully for a crusade against the Turks, but later concentrated more on Italian politics and the aggrandizement of the DELLA ROVERE FAMILY. Like other Italian princes he ruled his domains firmly and became involved in Italian quarrels, notably wars against Florence (1478–79) and Venice (1482–84).

In foreign affairs, relations with France were strained over the Pragmatic Sanction of BOURGES, in which the French Church claimed the right to regulate its own affairs; somewhat inconsistently, he allowed FERDINAND (II) AND ISABELLA I of Spain to establish the SPANISH INQUISITION (1478) and to make ecclesiastical appointments in Spain and the New World. Although a great nepotist who made five nephews and one grand-nephew cardinals (one of them was later Pope JULIUS II), Sixtus IV administered the church and its domains well. He was personally devoted to the Blessed Virgin Mary and instituted (1476) the Feast of the Immaculate Conception. As a patron of letters and the arts, Sixtus IV repaired Roman churches, had the

SISTINE CHAPEL built, established the Sistine choir, commissioned BOTTICELLI and POLLAIUOLO, and opened the Vatican Library to scholars.

## Sixtus V (1521–1590) *Pope (1585–90)*

Born in Ancona of a poor family, Felice Peretti joined the Franciscans at age 12. He became known as a harsh reformer, especially when inquisitor-general in Venice (1557–60). He was vicar-general of the Franciscans (1566–72) and was created cardinal in 1570.

As pope he was concerned with the lawlessness and the financial problems of the Papal States, dealing ruthlessly with the bandits and making the papacy rich by introducing heavy new taxes. He embarked on an expensive building program, including the completion of St. Peter's dome and work on the Lateran Palace and the Vatican Library. Sixtus V reorganized the Curia, limiting the number of cardinals to 70 and establishing 15 congregations (or departments) to perform the work of the papacy. He also inaugurated (1589) a revision of the Vulgate Bible, the *editio Sistina*.

## Skarga, Piotr (1536–1612) *Polish theologian and writer*

Skarga was born into a bourgeois family at Grójec and joined the Jesuits in 1569. His appointment in 1579 as head of the academy at Vilna gave him scope for the Counter-Reformation teachings for which he became famous. His book on the lives of the saints, published the same year, became a classic. In 1588 he became a preacher at the court of King Sigismund III, where his influence exacerbated the religious intolerance then beginning to afflict Poland. Nonetheless he gained a unique eminence as a Polish patriot on account of his *Kasania Sejmowe* (Parliamentary sermons; 1597); these combine moral and political exhortation, prophecies of the downfall of the Polish state, and patriotic sentiment, expressed in powerful and compelling prose that won many admirers.

## slavery

Slavery had been practiced in various forms in Europe since classical antiquity. It was sanctioned by Aristotle's opinion that "barbarians," that is those who lived beyond the bounds of the "civilized" Mediterranean world, were natural slaves. Wars, piracy, and raids into barbarian territory all yielded chattel slaves who could be bought and sold as any other livestock. High prices were paid for slaves with particular talents or skills. Such slaves should be differentiated from unfree members of their own societies, most of whom owed their slavery to some form of severe misfortune: among these were children who had been sold into slavery in time of famine and penal slaves who were enslaved as punishment for a crime. The Church accepted the practice of slavery, although with some unease, and it was considered a virtuous act for a Christian to manumit slaves (restore their freedom).

Piracy was a great source of slaves throughout the Mediterranean world from antiquity onward, and both Christian and Muslim pirates sold off the crews and passengers of captured ships. Able-bodied men often ended up as galley slaves, rowing the ships of their captors. Large numbers of galley slaves provided motive power at the battle of LEPANTO in 1571, and the victorious Christians claimed to have freed over 12,000 of their coreligionists from the Ottoman fleet. Seventeen years later over 2000 galley slaves were on the complement of the SPANISH ARMADA.

The trade in Black African slaves had long been a feature of Muslim North and East Africa, and from around 1380 Aragonese merchants were buying slaves from both the North African littoral and the Black Sea shores. During the latter half of the 14th century, after the Black Death had wiped out much of the population of western Europe, causing a severe labor shortage, Genoese and Venetian merchants trading to Constantinople imported Russian, Tartar, and Circassian slaves. In Spain the final stages of the Reconquista under FERDINAND (II) AND ISABELLA I saw the enslavement of many Jews and Moors; at the fall of Malaga in 1487, for example, a third of the population was enslaved, a further third was exchanged for Christians held captive in Muslim North Africa, and a massive ransom was demanded for 450 Malagan Jews to save them from being sold into slavery. The Portuguese began building up an organized slave trade in Africa in the mid-1400s as a result of their raids into northern Mauritania. As their ships ventured further south, into the Gulf of Guinea, in the early 1460s the acquisition of Black slaves became a major objective. By the mid-1550s slaves from the Portuguese colonies accounted for around 10% of Lisbon's population.

In the New World, the Spanish operated a system known as *encomienda*, under which royal grants of land included the native inhabitants as forced laborers. This in practice reduced the status of native Americans to that of slaves, and the humanitarian Spanish priest LAS CASAS devoted most of his life to inveighing against it. However, even he was not initially opposed to slavery as such, since his early writings recommend the importation of Africans to be used as slaves in place of the native Americans; later he regretted this, and published a treatise condemning the African slave trade (1546).

See also: RACISM

**Further reading:** David Eltis *et al* (eds), *The Transatlantic Slave Trade* (Cambridge, U.K.: Cambridge University Press, 2000); Barbara L. Solow (ed.), *Slavery and the Rise of the Atlantic System* (Cambridge, U.K.: Cambridge University Press, 1991).

**Sleidanus, Johannes** (1505–1556) *German religious historian*
He was born at Schleiden, near Aachen, and having studied both law and the classics, in 1537 he entered the service of France as secretary to Cardinal du Bellay. Between 1537 and 1544 he represented Francis I in several important negotiations with the German Protestant powers. In 1544 he was appointed on the recommendation of Martin BUCER as official historian of the Reformation and was granted access to archive material in Saxony, Hesse, and the Palatinate. His work *De statu religionis et republicanae Carolo V Caesare commentarii*, which was published in Strasbourg in 1555, was an immediate success and was translated into many languages (first English edition, 1560). It remains the most valuable contemporary record of Reformation times, largely on account of its extensive assemblage of documents.

**Sluter, Claus** (c. 1350–1406) *Netherlands sculptor*
Possibly born at Haarlem, Sluter worked for PHILIP THE BOLD of Burgundy on the Charterhouse (Chartreuse) of Champmol on the outskirts of Dijon, where he was master of the works from 1389. He worked first on the portal of the church, but his masterpiece is the calvary (1395–1404) there, of which the base, known as the Puits de Moïse, survives. Fragments of the rest are preserved in the Musée Archéologique, Dijon, including a magnificent head of Christ. The imposing figures of the prophets on the Puits de Moïse confirm Sluter's position as one of the great innovators in the history of sculpture; in their powerful realism and characterization they represent a complete break with the decorative formulae of earlier northern European art. Sluter also executed the tomb of Philip the Bold at Champmol (now in the Musée Archéologique), notable particularly for the treatment of the drapery of the mourning figures. In 1404 Sluter retired to the Augustinian monastery at Dijon. His influence continued long after his lifetime and far beyond the boundaries of Burgundy.

**Smith, John** (1580–1631) *English soldier of fortune and colonial entrepreneur*
Born in Lincolnshire, Smith was apprenticed to a merchant (1595), but in 1597 enlisted for military service in the Netherlands. He then traveled to Hungary to join the Austrian army against the Ottomans (1601). His dramatic adventures in this enterprise are narrated in his *True Travels* (1630). In 1606 he went to the New World for the Virginia Company, establishing the colony at Jamestown, Virginia (1606–08). His adventures continued: he was captured by native Americans and apparently only saved from death by the chief's daughter, Pocohontas (1607). Having returned to England (1609), he wrote a number of works to promote colonization in the area he named "New England, " including *A Map of Virginia* (1612), *A Description of New England* (1616), and *The Generall Historie of Virginia, New-England, and the Summer Isles* (1624). A three-volume modern edition of his *Complete Works*, edited by Philip L. Barbour, was published in 1986.

**Further reading:** Philip L. Barbour, *The Three Worlds of Captain John Smith* (Boston, Mass.: Houghton Mifflin and London: Macmillan, 1964); ~ *Pocahontas and Her World* (Boston, Mass.: Houghton Mifflin, 1970); J. A. Leo Lemay, *Did Pocahontas Save Captain John Smith?* (Athens, Ga: University of Georgia Press, 1992).

**Smith, Sir Thomas** (1513–1577) *English statesman, lawyer, and scholar*
The son of a wealthy landowner at Saffron Waldon, Smith was educated at Cambridge. After a period of foreign travel he returned to Cambridge in 1544 as regius professor of civil law. He also served from 1547 to 1554 as provost of Eton and was first elected to parliament in 1559. Later much of his time was spent at court, advising Queen Elizabeth on a number of issues. From 1562 to 1566 he served as ambassador to France, negotiating at the Peace of Troyes (1564) Elizabeth's abandonment of her claim to Calais. Smith's most famous work, *De republica anglorum* was published posthumously (1583); in it he describes the basis of the Tudor constitution.

**Smythson, Robert** (c. 1535–1614) *English architect*
The most original Elizabethan architect, Smythson was the first English builder to create a convincing synthesis of strong English traditions of domestic architecture, elements of north European decoration, and the classical forms spreading through Europe from Renaissance Italy. The prosperity of Elizabethan England, combined with the growth of humanist education, meant that Smythson's patrons almost certainly encouraged his confident adoption of classical forms, the main sources being editions of SERLIO and Jacques Androuet DUCERCEAU, and also (especially for decorative features such as strapwork) Flemish pattern-books. Innovative features of his country houses include a coherent use of classical orders and decoration; a striving for symmetry and harmony in both plan and facade; a shift of emphasis from the courtyard to the facade; and the use of extensive fenestration as an element of expressive design. His most important designs include Longleat, Wiltshire (from 1568; with Alan Maynard), Wollaton Hall, Nottinghamshire (1580–88), and Hardwick New Hall, Derbyshire (1590–97). Smythson's son John (died 1634) was also an architect.

**Further reading:** Mark Girouard, *Robert Smythson and the Elizabethan Country House* (New Haven, Conn: Yale University Press, 1983).

## Snell, Willebrord (1581–1626) *Netherlands physicist and mathematician*

The son of Rudolf Snell (1546–1613), a mathematician at Leyden, Snell succeeded his father as professor of mathematics at Leyden university in 1613. He published a number of mathematical books, notably *Eratosthenes Batavus* (1617), a fundamental work in the science of geodesy that dealt with the practical problem of measuring, by triangulation, the length of a degree. He is best known, however, for his discovery in 1621 of the law of refraction (for any two media, the ratio of the sine of the angle of incidence to the sine of the angle of refraction is constant), since known as Snell's law. The law itself, possibly derived from Snell's unpublished manuscripts, was first published in *Dioptrique* (1637) by René Descartes.

## Society of Jesus See JESUITS

## Soderini, Piero (1452–1522) *Italian nobleman*

A member of a prominent Florentine family, Piero Soderini came to power during the period of the Medici exile from the city after the ejection of Piero de' Medici in 1494. As the egalitarian system of government set up by SAVONAROLA faltered, Soderini was proclaimed *gonfaloniere* for life (1502). It was under his leadership that Florence recaptured Pisa, but this success could not stem the rising tide of opposition to Soderini's increasingly oligarchic rule. In 1512 the opposition of Medici supporters within the city, the withdrawal of his French allies from Italy, and the threatened attack on Florence by the Spanish papal army forced Soderini to resign, and he went into permanent exile in Ragusa (Dubrovnik).

## Sodoma (Giovanni Antonio Bazzi) (1477–1549) *Italian painter*

According to VASARI, Sodoma earned his nickname for his homosexuality and his outrageous behavior, which made him notorious. He trained in his native Vercelli under the Piedmontese artist Giovanni Martino Spanzotti (c. 1456–c. 1526), although the influence of LEONARDO DA VINCI is strong upon his early work. His earliest known works are the frescoes in Sta. Anna in Camprena, Pienza (1503–04), and the 31 frescoes of the life of St. Benedict at Monte Oliveto Maggiore, near Siena (1505–08). In 1508 Sodoma visited Rome and came under the influence of RAPHAEL and Baldassare PERUZZI. His most notable works are the frescoes painted at the Villa Farnesina, Rome, including *The Marriage of Alexander and Roxane* (c. 1514); his other major fresco cycle is *The Life of St. Catherine* (1526; San Domenico, Siena). His reputation as Siena's greatest artist of the 16th century was later eclipsed by BECCAFUMI.

## Solis, Virgil (1514–1562) *German engraver, designer, and illustrator*

Solis's birthplace is not known, but his workshop in Nuremberg was producing engravings and woodcuts from around 1540. Among editions he illustrated were the Bible and Walter Rivius's famous *Vitruvius Teutsch* (1548). His workshop also produced a large number of engraved designs for the construction and decoration of gold- and silverware and for jewelry and other items. These were primarily fashionable rather than original, but were widely popular until after the turn of the century, not only among metalworkers but also among cabinet makers and stuccoists. The styles used ranged from early Renaissance (basically late Gothic with classical motifs) to the mannerist grotesque (for example, a ewer with lizards crawling over its surface and a snake as its handle), employing motifs popularized by the JAMNITZER FAMILY.

## sonnet (from Italian *sonetto*, "little song")

A 14-line poem in iambic pentameter (in France, typically iambic hexameter), the main types of which are customarily distinguished by their different rhyme schemes. The earliest, the Italian or Petrarchan sonnet, both in rhyme and logical construction consists of an octave (abbaabba) and a sestet (cdecde or cdcdcd). The English or Shakespearean sonnet, more suited to the difficulty of rhyming in English, consists of three quatrains and a couplet (abab cdcd efef gg). Other types are the Spenserian (abab bcbc cdcd ee) and the Miltonic, which is Petrarchan in rhyme but often with an extended logical development which blurs the *volta*, or turn in thought, between the octave and sestet.

The sonnet seems to have derived from the lengthening of a very early Italian single-stanza form, the Sicilian *strambotto*, which rhymed variously; in Sicily it was usually eight hendecasyllabic lines, in Tuscany the preferred length was six lines. The poems of Jacopo da Lentino (c. 1215–33) are considered the earliest forms of sonnet (ababab cdecde), and the division into octave and sestet was fixed by his contemporaries. Guittone d'Arezzo (1230–94) introduced the octave rhyming abbaabba, which was adopted by DANTE and PETRARCH and so firmly established.

As the vogue for the sonnet spread throughout most of Europe during the 15th and 16th centuries, the form tended to become trivialized as the vehicle for standard Petrarchan love sentiments. It was given new life, however, by TASSO, MICHELANGELO, BEMBO, and CASTIGLIONE. The earliest theoretical comment on the form is found in Antonio da Tempo's *Summa artis rithimici* (1332). Besides the famous Italian sonneteers, the form was practiced in England by WYATT, SURREY, SIDNEY, SHAKESPEARE, and SPENSER, among others; in France by members of the PLÉIADE; in Spain by BOSCÁN and GARCILASO DE LA VEGA; and in Portugal by CAMÕES.

## Sorel, Agnès (c. 1422–1450) *Mistress of Charles VII of France*

Agnès was born into a family of the lesser nobility in Touraine and entered the household of René of Anjou, the king's brother-in-law. In this way she met Charles, who became infatuated with her beauty and took her as his mistress in 1444. For the remainder of her life Agnès enjoyed an unprecedented semiofficial status as the king's companion and was treated with the respect due to a queen. Charles showered her with lands, castles, and treasures, and is said to have relied on her shrewd advice in many political matters. She also bore him four children. Inevitably, Agnès's position led to jealousy and intrigue and made her powerful enemies, most notably the dauphin (the future Louis XI). When Agnès died suddenly, probably of dysentery, she was widely believed to have been poisoned by Louis. A trumped-up charge of murdering Agnès was also used to bring about the downfall of the politician and financier Jacques Coeur (c. 1395–56). After her death Agnès became the focus of romantic legends, notably the idea that she had been the chief instigator of Charles's later victories in the Hundred Years' War.

## Soto, Hernando de (c. 1496–1542) *Spanish conquistador and explorer*

Soto first landed in the New World in 1514 and earned a high reputation as a soldier in expeditions along the Central American coast (1516–20) and during the conquest of Nicaragua (1524). Joining PIZARRO's expedition to Peru (1532), he was the first to encounter the Inca emperor Atahuallpa. Enriched by Inca spoils, he returned to Spain (1536) and obtained the governorship of Cuba with a grant to colonize Florida. From Tampa Bay he explored throughout southeastern North America (1539–42) in search of gold before dying of fever beside the Mississippi.

## Spagnoli, Giovan Battista (Battista Mantovano, Mantuan) (1448–1516) *Italian poet and author of biographical and religious works*

Commonly known as Mantovano or Mantuan after his birthplace, Spagnoli was educated at Padua, became a Carmelite, and was elected Carmelite vicar-general in Mantua in 1483. From 1513 until his death he served as head of the order as a whole. He was canonized by Pope Leo XIII in 1883. His literary reputation mainly rests on 10 Latin pastoral eclogues, eight of which were composed while he was a student and two after he entered the Carmelites. Imitations of VIRGIL and of Petrarch and Boccaccio, the eclogues were published in 1498; they were widely influential in Europe and were imitated in turn, as in SPENSER's *Shepheardes Calender* (1579). *Parthenices* (*Hymns to the Virgin*; 1481), a series of seven poems, contains a depiction of hell and an assembly of fallen angels that became a source for comparable passages in Milton's *Paradise Lost*.

## Spalatin, Georg (Georg Burckhardt) (1484–1545) *German theologian and humanist reformer*

Spalatin took his name from Spalt, near Nuremberg, where he was born. He was educated at Nuremberg and Erfurt. He became a close friend of LUTHER and in 1514 was appointed chaplain and secretary to FREDERICK (III) THE WISE, Elector of Saxony. From then on his activities involved him with most of the events of the German Reformation. His close connection with Frederick took him to the Diet of Augsburg (1518) and he shared in the negotiations with Thomas de CAJETAN. He also attended the Diet of WORMS. After Frederick's death (1525) Spalatin served his successor John and in his later years he concerned himself mainly with reforming churches and schools in Saxony. His works included Latin translations of the writings of Luther and MELANCHTHON and a German translation of ERASMUS. He also wrote a history of the Lutheran reform movement, the *Chronicon et annales reformationis*, covering the years 1463–1525. He died in Altenberg, where he had lived since 1525.

## Spanish Armada

The fleet sent by PHILIP II of Spain to invade England (1588). The 130 ships and 27,000 men under the inexperienced command of the duke of Medina-Sidonia reached the English Channel in July. Hampered by unfavorable winds and harassed by English ships, the Armada made its way to Calais, France, and waited in vain to rendezvous with the duke of Parma's army from the Netherlands. Taking advantage of the English fleet's greater mobility and its able captains, its commander, Lord Howard of Effingham, ordered the attack on August 8, 1588. The Armada suffered heavy losses off Gravelines and fled north, suffering further losses in storms off Scotland and Ireland. Just 76 ships limped back to Spain. The defeat of the Armada foreshadowed Spain's decline and England's emergence as a naval and imperial power.

**Further reading:** P. Gallagher and D. W. Cruickshank (eds), *God's Obvious Design: Papers Read for the Spanish Armada Symposium, Sligo, 1988* (Woodbridge, U.K.: Boydell & Brewer, 1990); Neil Hanson, *The Confident Hope of a Miracle: The Real History of the Spanish Armada* (New York and London: Doubleday, 2003).

## Spanish Inquisition

At the request of FERDINAND (II) AND ISABELLA I, Pope Sixtus IV in 1478 united the inquisitions of the Spanish kingdoms under the control of Tomás de TORQUEMADA. The Spanish monarchs wanted to deal with the "problem" of CONVERSOS or *morranos* (Jewish converts to Christianity who secretly practiced their ancestral faith and rites). Torquemada has the reputation of a cruel monster; a more accurate characterization might be to say that he was an energetic administrator who shared the intolerance of his age and who tried to regulate the affairs of the Spanish Inquisition and prevent it from pursuing policies intended only to aggrandize or enrich the inquisitors. Devoid of personal ambition, Torquemada imprinted his own austerity on the entire institution of the Inquisition in Spain. The Spanish Inquisition was also aimed against MORISCOS (converted Muslims who were thought still to be secret practitioners of the Islamic faith). They were brutally treated by Diego Lucero, the inquisitor of Cordova, after the expulsion of the Moors from Spain in 1492, but his brutality was so blatant that he was eventually removed from office and imprisoned (1507). The Spanish Inquisition was also active in the 16th century against *alumbrados*, spiritualists whose mystic tendencies went beyond orthodox bounds. This illuminism was practiced especially in Franciscan circles, although it may have had its origins in Jewish and Muslim mystical traditions in Spain which had influenced radical Franciscans. As Spain closed its borders to outside ideas in the course of the 16th century—against Erasmian currents and Lutheran heterodoxy especially—the Spanish Inquisition acted as the safeguard of Spanish Catholic orthodoxy.

The most notorious feature of the Spanish Inquisition was its *autos de fe* (Portuguese: *autos-da-fé*). These were ceremonies in which the inquisitors publicly charged their prisoners with and convicted them of various heresies; afterward, those convicted of unrepentant heresy or of having relapsed into heresy were burned at the stake. Others, convicted of lesser charges, were imprisoned, had their property confiscated (which then went into royal coffers), were turned over to the Spanish galleys, or suffered other humiliations.

The Inquisition also reached New Spain. There were many *autos-da-fé* in Mexico, but there charges were not directed against *conversos*, *moriscos*, or *alumbrados*, but against "sorcerers". Thus, the Spanish Inquisition rarely acted against theological heresy in the New World, but more often against what was called demonic magic. The Spanish Inquisition survived until the 19th century when it was suppressed by Napoleon (1808) and, after his fall, by royal decree in 1834.

**Further reading:** Henry Kamen, *The Spanish Inquisition: An Historical Revision* (London: Weidenfeld & Nicolson, 1965; repr. Phoenix, 2000); ~ , *Inquisition and Society in Spain: The Sixteenth and Seventeenth Centuries* (London: Weidenfeld & Nicolson, 1985); Benjamin Netanyahu, *The Origins of the Inquisition in Fifteenth-Century Spain* (New York: Random House, 1995).

**Spanish language** The romance language deriving from the dialect of Castile, which is spoken in the Iberian peninsula (together with Catalan, Basque, and Galician-Portuguese), in part of Morocco, and in the countries of the former Spanish empire (chiefly those of Central and South America, with the major exception of Brazil). Like other romance languages, Spanish descends from spoken or Vulgar Latin, the day-to-day speech of Roman colonists, and has evolved by acquiring distinctive features different from Latin: a heavy stress accent (with certain effects on the stressed vowel and the unstressed syllable, as *tierra* from *terra* (land), *mesa* from *mensa* (table), and *ojo* from *oculus* ("eye"), for example); a simplification of genders and inflectional endings (replaced by analytic structures, like prepositional phrases); definite and indefinite articles; differences in the method of forming verbal tenses; and many semantic developments.

Spanish also reflects, in varying degrees, a number of other influences, both pre- and post-Roman. Among pre-Roman influences are the Phoenicians (and Carthaginians), Greeks, Iberians, Basques, and Celts. Later, Germanic, Arabic, and Amerindian languages also affected the character of Spanish. Pre-Roman traces are seen mainly in place names, for example Málaga (Phoenician *malka*, "trading factory"), Ibiza (from Carthaginian), Ampurias (Greek *emporion*, "market"), and Ebro (Iberian *Iberus*, whence the patronymic of these people, who may have been a number of unrelated migrant tribes). A few common nouns, like *manteca* ("butter") and *bruja* ("witch"), are also pre-Roman. Castilian has some similarities to the agglutinative non-Indo-European language of the Basques. An important phonological detail is the lack of the Latin *f*-sound in Basque, comparable to the Castilian loss of Latin *f* in some contexts, for example *hablar*, "to speak" (Latin *fabulare*) and *hacer*, "to do, make" (Latin *facere*). Celtic migrations around 900 and 600 BCE left their mark both in place names and in some common nouns: Segovia (Celtic *sego*, "victory") and *cerveza* ("beer"). With the decline of Rome, Germanic tribes (Suevi, Asding and Siling Vandals, and Alans) invaded the peninsula (409), followed (415) by a contingent of romanized Visigoths from Toulouse who were sent as protection against them. As a result about 2500 Spanish place names are traceable to these Germanic settlers (for example, Andalusia, via Arabic *al-Andalus*, from *-andal-*, "Vandal") as are typical personal names—*Fernando*, *Gusmán* ("good man"), *Ramón*, *Bermudo*, *Manrique*, *Rodrigo*, etc. The Moorish invasion of 711 had a telling effect on vocabulary, contributing about 4000 lexical items, with the Arabic in a number of instances replacing the Latin term. Many of these words, especially in science, became part of a common European vocabulary (*alcohol*, *algebra*, *alquimia*, *nadir*, *elixir*, etc.). At various more recent stages Spanish vocabulary has been influenced by French, Italian, and classical Latin (through learned borrowings in the Renaissance and later). The American empire provided a number of Indian words for common products—*tomate*, *chocolate*, *coca*, *maíz*, *patata*, *hamaca*, etc.

With the completion of the reconquest of Andalusia by Ferdinand II in 1492, Castilian was assured the position of dominant dialect, though previously it had been just one of four major forms of Spanish, the other three being Aragonese (in Aragon and Navarre), Leonese (in León), and Mozarabic (the Spanish of those who chose to remain under Moorish rule after 711). NEBRIJA's *Gramática* (1492) was the earliest scientific grammar of any European vernacular language, and the *Tesoro de la lengua castellana o española* (1611) of Sebastián de Covarrubias y Orozco (fl. 1545–72) was the first major Spanish dictionary. The Real Academia Española was founded in Madrid in 1713, one of its primary purposes being the compilation of an authoritative dictionary of the language. Six volumes were subsequently published (1726–37).

## Speed, John (c. 1552–1629) *English cartographer and historian*

Born in Farringdon, Cheshire, Speed began his career as a tailor. Through Fulke GREVILLE's patronage he was allowed to present maps to Queen Elizabeth in 1598. He earned the admiration of the Society of ANTIQUARIES, whose members helped him compile and publish his two most famous works. *The Theatre of the Empire of Great Britain* (1611–12) was an atlas based on existing maps. This work was a prologue to the rather less valuable *Historie of Great Britaine* (1611). These works were often republished and were influential for many years, as was Speed's world atlas, *A Prospect of the Most Famous Parts of the World* (1627).

## Spenser, Edmund (c. 1552–1599) *English poet*

Spenser was born in London and attended the Merchant Taylors' School there before going to Cambridge. At Cambridge he became friends with the scholar Gabriel HARVEY, with whom he corresponded about poetics, but soon made more influential acquaintances in the earl of Leicester's circle (*see* AREOPAGUS). To one of these, Sir Philip SIDNEY, he dedicated his first major publication, the set of 12 eclogues named after the months of the year and entitled *The Shepheardes Calender*. In 1580 he went as secretary to the lord deputy, Lord Grey, to Ireland, where he spent much of the rest of his life. From 1589 to 1598 he lived on his estate at Kilcolman; despite the friendship of RALEIGH and later the earl of ESSEX, he obtained little recognition at court, apart from a £50 pension. When Kilcolman was sacked during Tyrone's revolt (1598), Spenser withdrew to London, where he died.

Spenser probably began work on THE FAERIE QUEENE before his departure for Ireland; only six books and a fragment of a seventh were completed before his death. His other poetic works include *Complaints* (1591), an assortment of original poems and translations; *Colin Clouts Come Home Again* (1595), recording his fruitless journey to court in 1590/91 in search of patronage; "Astrophel" (1595), an elegy on Sidney's death; *Amoretti* (1595) and "Epithalamion," a sonnet sequence and bridal ode commemorating his marriage to Elizabeth Boyle; and *Fowre Hymns* (1596) on Platonic themes of love and beauty. His *View of the Present State of Ireland*, written between 1594 and 1597, was not published until 1633.

**Further reading:** Andrew Hadfield (ed.), *The Cambridge Companion to Spenser* (Cambridge, U.K.: Cambridge University Press, 2001); A. C. Hamilton *The Spenser Encyclopedia* (Toronto, Canada; University of Toronto Press, 1991).

## Sperandio, Savelli (c. 1425–c. 1504) *Italian medalist, goldsmith, and sculptor*

Possibly born in Mantua, Sperandio was the pupil of his father Bartolommeo. He also worked in Ferrara, Milan, and Faenza, and in 1482 completed the terracotta monument to Pope Alexander V in San Francesco, Bologna. In 1496 he moved to Venice. He executed a number of portrait medals, but the strong designs are sometimes marred by careless workmanship.

## Speroni, Sperone (1500–1588) *Italian humanist and literary critic*

Speroni was born at Padua and educated at Bologna under POMPONAZZI, graduating in philosophy and medicine in 1518. His main importance was as a critic and student of literary language. He used the dialogue as a medium for his ideas, his most important work being the dialogue *Delle lingue* (1542) in which he maintained that the Italian language was capable of achieving any of the effects of Latin. He also wrote a tragedy, *Canace* (1542), in an irregular meter later borrowed by TASSO and GUARINI and produced critical works on Dante, Virgil, and Ariosto, which treated vernacular literature as worthy of serious discussion.

## Speyer, Diets of See SPIRES, DIETS OF

## spheres, armillary See ARMILLARY SPHERES

## spheres, celestial See CELESTIAL SPHERES

## Spiegel, Hendrick Laurensz. (1549–1612) *Dutch writer*

He was a native of Amsterdam and a member of the Egelantier chamber of rhetoric, who made himself the center of a distinguished literary circle based at his country estate on the Amstel. He was the main author of the *Twespraack van de Nederduitsche letterkunst* (1584), to which his friend COORNHEERT contributed the preface; it was influential in promoting notions of correctness in the use of the Dutch language. Although brought up as a poet in the *rederijker* tradition (*see* CHAMBERS OF RHETORIC), Spiegel became after 1578 an exponent of Renaissance poetic meters, principally the alexandrine. His major work, *Hertspiegel* (published posthumously in 1614), is a long allegorical poem written in this meter and blending Christian and Platonic philosophy. Spiegel also wrote the play *Numa*, drawn from Plutarch, and a hymn of praise for the defeat of the SPANISH ARMADA.

**Spires, Diets of** (1526, 1529) Assemblies (*Reichstage*) of the Holy Roman Empire at Spires (Speyer) in southern Germany. At the 1526 meeting, on the grounds that Emperor CHARLES V was now at war with the pope, the princes repudiated instructions previously received from Charles to cease innovations and enforce the Edict of WORMS. It was agreed that each prince should determine the established religion of his own territory, and that others should be tolerated. LUTHER agreed to union with Rome, provided that only biblical institutions and ceremonies were regarded as essential and that all others were reserved for decision by a general council of the Church.

At the 1529 assembly there was a large majority of Roman Catholics, and toleration of dissenters in Catholic territories was revoked. Six princes and 14 cities made a formal protest (*Protestatio*) against this decision; this was the origin of the term PROTESTANT.

**Spiritual Exercises** See IGNATIUS LOYOLA, ST; JESUITS

**Spirituali** The name given to a group of Roman Catholic reformers in the early years of the Reformation that included Gasparo CONTARINI and Reginald POLE. They worked for reconciliation with Lutheranism and gave a cautious welcome to his teachings on JUSTIFICATION BY FAITH. The Spirituali circulated a tract entitled *Beneficio di Christo* in the 1540s which turned out to be a paraphrase of part of Calvin's INSTITUTES. Their influence was effectively ended by the failure of the Colloquy of REGENSBURG (1541) to bear fruit.

**Spranger, Bartholomäus** (1546–1611) *Flemish painter*
Born in Antwerp, Spranger studied landscape painting there under Jan Mandijn and Cornelius van Dalem. He then spent some years in Paris, Rome, and other Italian cities (1565–75), where he learnt figure painting from PARMIGIANINO and Federico ZUCCARO. In Rome he met the Flemish painter Carl van MANDER, who later spread Spranger's style through Flanders. In 1575 he was at the court of Emperor Maximilian II in Vienna, and after the emperor's death (1576) Spranger worked for Maximilian's son, Emperor RUDOLF II, in Prague. As Rudolf's taste was for the erotic, expressed through mythological and allegorical themes, Spranger's work consists largely of nudes in formalized scenes from Greek and Roman mythology, such as *Minerva Conquering Ignorance* (c. 1591) and *Hercules and Omphale* (both Vienna). Spranger probably came closest of all German and Dutch artists to the spirit of Italian Mannerism, although his work still retained a northern restlessness. It was extremely popular and influential, and much copied.

*sprezzatura* A term used in *Il cortegiano* (THE COURTIER) by CASTIGLIONE, sometimes translated as "nonchalance." The ideal courtier must be formidably accomplished, but it is essential that he avoid offensive or undignified display. *Sprezzatura* refers to the easy grace and superiority required to "make whatever is done or said to appear to be without effort."

**Squarcialupi, Antonio** (1416–1480) *Italian organist*
The son of a Florentine butcher, Squarcialupi became organist at Orsanmichele in Florence in 1431, and in the next year was appointed organist at the cathedral there, a post he held until his death. Squarcialupi was probably the most famous organist of his day, and is known to have corresponded with Guillaume DUFAY. The Squarcialupi Codex, a famous manuscript containing secular works of the Trecento, belonged to him.

**Squarcione, Francesco** (1397–1468) *Italian painter*
He was born the son of a notary in Padua, and, as a teacher of as many as 157 pupils, he is traditionally described as the founder of the Paduan school, a term associated with painters such as MANTEGNA, Marco ZOPPO, Giorgio Schiavone (1436/7–1504), and Cosimo TURA, who were either taught or influenced by Squarcione. In his youth he traveled in Greece and Italy collecting antique sculpture and paintings, which resulted in the interest in classical architecture and antique works often associated with the Paduan style. His only surviving paintings are a *Madonna* (Staatliche Museen, Berlin) and a damaged polyptych (1449–52; Museo Civico, Padua). These show the influence of the Florentine sculptor DONATELLO, who worked in Padua between 1443 and 1453. Little remains of the frescoes of scenes from the life of St. Francis which Squarcione painted on the exterior of San Francesco at Padua (c. 1452–66) but they would indicate that, among other artists, he spread the early Renaissance style of Florence in his native city.

**Staden, Hans** (fl. mid-16th century) *German soldier*
Almost nothing is known of Staden's life apart from his *Warhaftige Historia* (1557), which tells how he sailed in Portuguese service to Brazil (1547–48), was captured by the cannibalistic Tupinambá Indians (c. 1554), escaped after nine months, and reached France in February 1555. His close personal observation of the Tupinambá during his captivity make his book a pioneering ethnographic text. It had numerous early editions in German and Latin.

**Stampa, Gaspara** (c. 1523–1554) *Italian poet and courtesan*
She was born in Padua but lived in Venice after 1531, cultivating her literary interests, entertaining leading figures in her salon, and becoming known for her poetry, musical ability, and beauty. As "Anassilla" she was a member of the Accademia dei Pellegrini. *Rime* (1554), published posthumously by her sister Cassandra and dedicated to Giovanni DELLA CASA, consists of some 300 Petrarchan lyrics, mostly

sonnets, inspired by her love for Collaltino di Collalto, Count of Treviso, whom she met in 1549 and who eventually deserted her for another woman. Not widely known until rediscovered by 19th-century Romantics, the work is notable for its spontaneity and narrative continuity.

## Stefano da Verona (Stefano da Zevio) (c. 1375–c. 1450) *Italian painter*

The town of Zevio, just east of Verona, was reputedly the painter's birthplace, but his career is associated with Verona itself, where he was a leading exponent of the International Gothic style. The influence of ALTICHIERO can be seen in his work; frescoes by them both appear in several Veronese churches. The *Madonna del Roseto* (Castelvecchio, Verona) is a good example of his style, but his only dated work is the late *Adoration of the Magi* (1435; Brera, Milan).

## Stephanus See ESTIENNE PRESS

## Stevin, Simon (1548–1620) *Belgian mathematician and engineer*

Little is known of Stevin's life other than that he was born at Bruges, started life as a merchant's clerk in Antwerp, and then served as quartermaster-general of the Dutch army. He is best known as the author of *De thiende* (The tenth; 1585; French translation *L'Arithmetique*, 1585) in which he introduced decimal fractions into Western mathematics. Translated into English in 1608, it contains the first English use of the word "decimal." In works on statics and hydrostatics Stevin made a number of mechanical advances, the most important of which was his formulation of the triangle of forces. He was the first Renaissance author to take up and develop the work of the Hellenistic mathematician and engineer Archimedes. Stevin published in 1594 a work on FORTIFICATION which tackled the problem of designing forts capable of withstanding ARTILLERY assaults. His *Castrametatio* (1617) contains interesting details of contemporary army life. A good complete edition of his *Oeuvres Mathematiques* was published by the Elzevier press in 1634.

## stiacciato See SCHIACCIATO

**stilnovismo** Collectively, the practitioners of the poetic style described by DANTE as the DOLCE STIL NUOVO (*Purgatorio* XXIV 57). The names originally mentioned by Dante are Guido Guinizelli, CAVALCANTI, Lapo Gianni, Cino da Pistoia, and himself. They were apparently those poets who shared certain literary ideals, rather than a formally constituted movement. Later scholarship has extended this list by the addition of Gianni Alfani, Dino Frescobaldi, Guido Orlandi, and Guido Novello da Polenta. PETRARCH transmitted the style to the whole of Europe. A number of other Italian poets are categorized as *stilnovisti*,

for example Franceschino degli Albizzi, Sennuccio del Bene, BOCCACCIO, Matteo Frescobaldi, Giovanni Gherardi da Prato, and Cino Rinuccini, and later heirs include Lorenzo de' MEDICI, MICHELANGELO, and Torquato TASSO.

## Stimmer, Tobias (1539–1584) *Swiss artist*

Stimmer was born into a family of artists at Schaffhausen, where he decorated the Haus zum Ritter with frescoes of figures from ancient stories. After 1570 he was active mainly in Strasbourg and painted the case of the astronomical clock in the cathedral there. The portraits of Jakob Schwyzer and his wife (Basle museum) demonstrate his proficiency as a portraitist. Besides these undertakings, the versatile Stimmer was significant as a draftsman, designer of woodcuts and glass paintings, book illustrator, and poet.

## Stoss, Veit (c. 1450–1533) *German woodcarver and sculptor*

Leaving his native Nuremberg in 1476, Stoss went to Cracow where he created the huge and complex altarpiece of the Virgin Mary for the Marienkirche (1477–89). The intensely dramatic and moving central panel depicts the Dormition of the Virgin with the Assumption above; the heads of the mourning apostles are vividly individualized and the intricately folded drapery adds to the richness of effect. Stoss also made the red marble tomb of King Casimir IV Jagellon (died 1492) in Cracow cathedral. In 1496 Stoss returned to Nuremberg where he carried out some major commissions in the city's churches. Among his other carvings, a *St. Roch* in unpainted limewood (1516; SS. Annunziata, Florence) elicited high praise from VASARI; generally, however, Stoss's statues were polychromed in accordance with the prevailing Gothic style.

## Strada, Jacopo (c. 1515–1588) *Italian-born artist, antiquarian, and collector*

Although he was born in Mantua, Strada belonged to a Netherlandish family. At an early age he began collecting antique coins, on the basis of which he published his *De consularibus numismatibus* in the 1550s. In the late 1540s he moved to Augsburg, where he lived in the house of Johann Jakob Fugger (*see* FUGGER FAMILY) before moving on to Paris and Lyons. In France he acquired from SERLIO the manuscript and plates of the seventh book of his great work on architecture; Strada published this in 1575. In 1553 Strada issued a major work on the Roman emperors illustrated from coins, *Epitome thesauri antiquitatum*, and the following year he returned to Rome to enter the papal service. He then moved to Nuremberg, where he worked for the Fuggers as artist and goldsmith.

In Nuremberg Strada attracted the attention of Archduke Ferdinand of Austria (later Emperor FERDINAND I) and from 1557 he was in his employment. Under Ferdinand's successors, MAXIMILIAN II and RUDOLF II, Strada attained the position of court antiquary and was instrumental in obtaining for the emperors all manner of antiquities, books, and *objets d'art*. TITIAN's portrait of Strada (1567/68) shows him holding an antique statuette, with a torso and ancient coins on the table before him. He was also the possessor of a remarkable library, said to have comprised over 3000 volumes in 13 languages. At his death he left numerous manuscripts dealing with antiquities and problems in mechanics; his work on various sorts of mill was published in part by his grandson in 1617. Strada's daughter Katharina was for many years the mistress of Rudolf II and bore him several children.

**Stradano, Giovanni** See STRAET, JAN VAN DER

***stradiotti*** Cavalrymen from various parts of the Balkans, employed by Venice to guard her sea empire. They were usually posted away from their homes because they also performed policing duties. Armed with lances, scimitars, and shields, the *stradiotti* fought bravely and loyally for Venice in various Italian wars during the 16th century and became the republic's main protection. They were much admired by European rulers and were also employed in Germany and France in the 16th century. From the mid-16th century *stradiotti* helped to maintain law and order on the Venetian mainland.

**Straet, Jan van der** (Giovanni Stradano) (1523–1605) *Netherlands painter and designer of tapestries*
Born in Bruges and a pupil of Pieter AERTSEN, van der Straet became a master in 1545. Shortly afterward he traveled via Lyons and Venice to Florence, where he joined VASARI's circle. There he assisted Vasari in the decoration of the Palazzo Vecchio and designed tapestries, the most important of which was a series of hunting scenes for the Medici villa of Poggio a Caiano (1567). Although he was based in Florence, he also visited Rome and Naples and even returned to the Netherlands between 1576 and 1578. His early works reveal the impress of his northern training but his later style was heavily conditioned by that of Vasari.

**Strasbourg** (German **Strassburg**) A French city on the River Rhine, formerly one of the German imperial free cities until seized by Louis XIV in 1681. As Argentorate, Strasbourg was a Roman legionary camp on the site of a Celtic settlement. The Franks took control in the late fifth century and gave it its present name. Prolonged struggles between Strasbourg's citizens and its bishop were eventually settled in the mid-13th century, and its status as an imperial free city was firmly established. It was in Strasbourg that GUTENBERG, who lived in the city for about 18 years from 1430, began his experiments with type; by 1460 there was a printing press there. Humanism reached Strasbourg at the end of the 15th century, when its leading light was Sebastian BRANT. From 1523 it was an important early center of the Reformation, piloted through the upheavals and controversies of the following years by Martin BUCER and Jakob STURM. Katharina ZELL was notable for her work on behalf of the many Protestant refugees who fled there as religious persecution grew in adjacent territories.

**Strigel, Bernhard(in)** (1460–1528) *German painter*
Trained by his father and uncle in his home town of Memmingen, Strigel first worked on their altars for Disentis and Obersaxen. His work of the 1490s reveals the influence of BOUTS and Bartholomäus Zeitblom (1455/60–1518/22) of Ulm. By 1499 he had come into contact with Emperor Maximilian I, whom he painted many times. In Memmingen Strigel held a number of municipal and guild offices and even served as an ambassador. He also continued to paint religious pictures, such as the wings of the Schussenried altarpiece (c. 1515; Berlin). Strigel never entirely outgrew his original late Gothic style, which served him well in profile portraits. His court portraits have an almost heraldic monumentality of form but little psychological intimacy.

**Strigel, Victorinus** (1524–1569) *German evangelical theologian*
Strigel was born at Kaufbeuren, near Kempten, and educated at Fribourg and Wittenberg, where he was influenced by Philipp MELANCHTHON. He taught at Erfurt, and in 1548 was appointed first professor and rector of the secondary school (gymnasium) at Jena. He worked with Justus JONAS, opposed the stricter forms of Lutheranism, and lectured on Melanchthon's *Loci communes*. In 1563 he was appointed professor at Leipzig and in 1567 at Heidelberg. He was the author of a commentary on the Bible and of philological and historical works.

**Striggio, Alessandro** (c. 1540–1592) *Italian composer and lira da gamba player*
Of noble birth, Striggio was a leading composer in the Medici court in Florence in the 1560s, where he collaborated with other composers to provide INTERMEDII for great festivities. His fame spread, as in 1568 his 40-part motet *Ecce beatam lucem* was sung at the marriage of Duke Albrecht IV of Bavaria. The patronage of music at the Medici court declined in the 1570s, and little is known of Striggio's activities at this time. In 1584 he visited the court at Ferrara, and later that year returned to his native Mantua, where he remained until his death, patronized by both the Gonzaga and Medici. Striggio was a virtuoso lira da gamba player, but it is for his madrigals that he is chiefly renowned. Often highly descriptive, they were much admired abroad. His son, Alessandro the younger (1573–1630), also served the Gonzaga and was a friend of MONTEVERDI.

## Strozzi, Ercole (c. 1473–1508) *Italian poet*
Ercole was from the branch of the Strozzi family that had established itself in Ferrara in the early 15th century. Like his father Tito Vespasiano Strozzi (1424–1505) he was famous as a writer of Latin elegies; their works were published together as *Strozzi poetae pater et filius* (1513). A few vernacular sonnets have also survived. His circle of friends included the young ARIOSTO, Pietro BEMBO, and Lucrezia BORGIA. He was murdered in mysterious circumstances and his wife, the renowned beauty Barbara Torelli (1475–1533), is credited with a moving sonnet on his death.

## Strozzi family *Italian bankers.*
A member of a noble Florentine banking family, Filippo I (1428–91) returned to Florence from exile in 1466; he prospered and became Lorenzo de' MEDICI's trusted adviser in foreign affairs. Filippo began (1489) the construction of the magnificent Palazzo Strozzi. His grandson Filippo II (1488–1538), despite his marriage to a Medici, opposed Medici power and was a leader of the rising (1527) that expelled the Medici from Florence. He went into exile when the Medici were restored (1530) but then led a band of republican exiles in an unsuccessful attack on Florence (1537); he was caught and tortured before his death in captivity. The Strozzi clan then moved to France, where several members became valued servants of the French kings.

## Stuart, Lady Arabella (1575–1615) *English noblewoman*
Her great-grandmother was Margaret Tudor, daughter of Henry VII, and in some quarters she was the favored candidate to succeed Elizabeth I, in preference to her cousin, James VI of Scotland, as she was English by birth. Having lived in seclusion at Hardwick Hall, Derbyshire, she was allowed back to court in England after James's accession, but was imprisoned in 1609 when he feared she would gain political support by marrying a foreign prince. On her release she married William Seymour in secret (1610). But, as a descendant of Mary Tudor, sister of Henry VIII, Seymour too was a claimant to throne, and the couple were arrested. Although Seymour escaped and fled to Belgium, Arabella was captured, having escaped house arrest, while attempting to join him. Sent to the Tower of London, she became unhinged and died of self-imposed starvation.

## Stuart style See JACOBEAN STYLE

## Sturm, Johannes (1507–1589) *German educationist*
A native of Schleiden, Sturm underwent the usual humanistic training at Liège and at Louvain, where he started a printing press. He then went to Paris, where under the influence of Martin BUCER he became a Protestant. In 1537 he became professor of rhetoric and dialectic at the Collegium Praedicatorum in Strasbourg, and there in 1538 he founded the first gymnasium in northern Europe. He remained its principal for 43 years. Sturm was a zealous supporter of the Swiss reformers and engaged in lively controversies with the Lutherans. He wrote numerous educational works, in which, as in his school, he promoted his ideal of wise and eloquent piety, produced an edition of CICERO (1557) and a Latin translation of Aristotle's *Rhetoric*, and wrote the biography of Beatus RHENANUS.

## Suarez, Francisco (1548–1617) *Spanish Jesuit theologian and philosopher*
Born in Granada, he became a Jesuit in 1564, was ordained in 1572, and studied canon law, theology, and philosophy at the universities of Ávila, Segovia, Valladolid, Alcalá, Salamanca, and Rome. In 1597 Philip II appointed Suarez professor of philosophy at the university at Coimbra, where he remained until 1615. At Pope Paul V's request, he wrote *De defensione catholicae fidei* (1613) against James I of England and *De immunitate ecclesiastica* against the antipapalism of Venice (1615). He was a prolific writer and his *Opera omnia* (Venice, 1747) totalled 23 volumes. Although a Thomist, he was not a mere echo of St. Thomas Aquinas nor of Aristotle, and he founded a school of thought called Suarism. He represents a late Renaissance resurgence of scholasticism, the more universal success of which was thwarted by the new science, and he is still considered one of the founders of modern international law, mainly by virtue of his summary of the principles of the law in *De legibus* (1612). He died in Lisbon.

## Sublime Porte (French, "High Gate")
The name, often shortened to "Porte," by which the Ottoman seat of government in CONSTANTINOPLE (Istanbul) was known in the West. The French phrase translates the Turkish *Babi Ali*, which suggests not just "physically lofty" but also "honorable". It refers to the gateway in the outer wall of Istanbul's Topkapi Serai that led to the offices and palace of the grand vizier, it being here that much of the official business of the Ottoman empire was conducted and ambassadors from foreign powers were received.

## Sully, Maximilien de Béthune, Duke of (1560–1641) *French Huguenot statesman*
As HENRY IV's most important minister, Sully did much to aid France's recovery from the religious wars, in which he had served with distinction. He encouraged agriculture, improved the posts and roads, and started major canals. An honest man in an age of corruption, Sully, as superintendent of finances (1598–1610), rescued French finances from bankruptcy. He removed the worst abuses of the fiscal system, cut extravagance at the court, and introduced a system of book-keeping to check on tax-farmers and officials. In 1602 he was made governor of the Bastille. In 1606 he was created a duke. He was forced to retire in 1611, the year after Henry IV's assassination, and devoted

most of his remaining years to writing his memoirs, the *Économes royales d'état, domestiques, politiques et militaires* (1638).

**supererogation, works of** In Roman Catholic doctrine, acts of exemplary virtue that go beyond what God explicitly commands. An example would be maintaining a vow of poverty: the believer does not have to be poor, but poverty is held to benefit the soul. Reformers repudiated the doctrine of supererogation, disliking the Church's promotion of practices that were not ordained by God in the Scriptures. The THIRTY-NINE ARTICLES of the Church of England assert that teaching on supererogation involves "arrogancy and impiety."

**Surrey, Henry Howard, Earl of** (1517–1547) *English poet and courtier*
The elder son of Thomas Howard, who became 3rd duke of Norfolk in 1524, Surrey was raised with the duke of Richmond, an illegitimate son of HENRY VIII, and traveled to France (1532) with the royal entourage. He led a tempestuous life at court, alternately distinguishing himself and being in disgrace for various offenses. Although he and his father helped suppress the PILGRIMAGE OF GRACE, it was rumored that they secretly sympathized with the rebels. Early in 1544 he began building, at Mount Surrey near Norwich, what was reputedly the first English house in Italian classical style, but nothing of it survives. In 1545–46 he held military commands in France, but was recalled after losing a skirmish at St.-Étienne and beheaded on several charges of treason.

Although small, Surrey's poetic output is of high quality and shows his awareness of Continental Renaissance trends in verse. He wrote successful versions of Petrarchan sonnets and some other fine lyrics, as well as biblical paraphrases in poulter's measure (couplets of lines of 12 and 14 syllables). His most interesting achievement is his translation of books two and four of VIRGIL's *Aeneid*, the earliest blank verse poem in English. Many of his poems were first published in the anthology *Tottel's Miscellany* in 1557. He wrote a fine elegy for Thomas WYATT ("Wyatt resteth here, that quick could never rest"), with whom his name is often linked as being the first Renaissance poets in England. The earl presents himself as a thoroughly Renaissance figure in his full-length portrait by William (Guillim) Scrots (c. 1546; National Portrait Gallery, London/Arundel Castle), which depicts him, in a design copied from a FONTAINEBLEAU school print, standing in an arched niche embellished with various classical motifs.

**Further reading:** Elizabeth Heale, *Wyatt, Surrey and Early Tudor Poetry* (Harlow, U.K.: Pearson Longman, 1998); William A. Sessions, *Henry Howard: The Poet Earl of Surrey: A Life* (Oxford, U.K. and New York: Oxford University Press, 1999).

**surveying** The skill traditionally involving the ability to determine and represent the height, distance, and direction (azimuth) of an object from a particular reference point. The first book to deal with the subject, Hero of Alexandria's *Dioptra*, dates from about 100 CE. Techniques described were simple. A trough of water to find a level, a plumb line, and a hodometer to measure distance, together with a few instruments to measure angles, constituted the surveyor's stock-in-trade. To these the medieval period added the cross-staff (*see* BACKSTAFFS).

Political and social conditions in the Renaissance—increased wealth, a growing population, the demands of ballistics, and the spread of the enclosure movement—made extra demands on the surveyor, and new techniques and instruments were developed to meet his needs. The most fundamental was the technique of triangulation, first proposed by GEMMA FRISIUS in the early 16th century. With triangulation all distance measurements, apart from the original base line, could be ignored. A high premium was consequently placed on the accuracy of the original measurement and its correct plotting. To this end two 16th-century innovations were crucial: the theodolite and the plane table. The theodolite, initially described by Leonard DIGGES in *Pantometria* (1571), consisted of a horizontal circle divided into 360°, on which an adjustable semicircle had been placed at right angles. The plane table was first described in 1551 by Abel Foullon, a Frenchman at Henry II's court. Once fully developed into workable instruments they permitted a genuinely geometrical form of surveying to emerge before 1600.

**Sustris, Frederik Lambertsz.** (c. 1540–1599) *Italianborn painter of Netherlands descent*
The son of Lambert SUSTRIS, Frederik was born in Venice and was presumably trained by his father during the latter's decade in Padua, which began about 1554. In 1560 Frederik visited Rome and between 1563 and 1567 he lived in Florence, where he assisted VASARI in the decoration of the Palazzo Vecchio and, in 1565, became a member of the Florentine academy of drawing. Anton FUGGER summoned him to Munich in 1568, where he worked beside Antonio Ponzano and Alessandro Paduano on the decoration of the Fugger palace. In 1573 he entered the service of Wilhelm von Landshut, later duke of Bavaria. The latter employed him on numerous important court commissions in Munich, such as the decoration of the Jesuit Michaelkirche (begun 1583) and the layout of the garden and grotto of the ducal Residenz between 1582 and 1586. Sustris also worked beside Pieter de WITTE on the decoration of the Munich Antiquarium. The chief artist and designer at the Bavarian court, Sustris's role was analogous to that of Vasari as court artist of the Medici dukes.

**Sustris, Lambert** (Alberto da Olanda) (c. 1515/20–c. 1584) *Netherlands painter*
Sustris was born in Amsterdam but nothing is known of his training prior to his arrival at TITIAN's Venetian studio in the mid-1540s. There he seems to have specialized in the painting of landscape backgrounds. In 1548 and 1550–51 he accompanied Titian to Augsburg. The portraits which he painted in Germany are a successful synthesis of the northern tradition and the style of Titian. On his return to Italy, Sustris was influenced by the mannerist styles of TINTORETTO and SCHIAVONE, as well as by the prints of PARMIGIANINO. Although thoroughly Italianized, the mature Sustris remained expert in the quintessentially Netherlandish genre of the extensive landscape peopled with numerous little figures. After moving to Padua in 1554, Sustris returned to Venice during the late 1560s. There he superseded Tintoretto as a painter of official portraits, of which the latest known is dated 1584.

**Sweelinck, Jan Pietersz.** (1562–1621) *Dutch composer*
Sweelinck was born in Deventer in the Netherlands and his family moved to Amsterdam two years later. He began his musical education with Jacob Buyck at the Oude Kerk (Old Church) in Amsterdam where he succeeded his father as organist (c. 1580). He remained in this position until his death and led a sedentary life; his only recorded excursion was a visit to Antwerp to purchase a harpsichord.

Sweelinck was not, however, cut off from the musical traditions of Europe. He collected manuscripts of English variations and fantasias, Italian toccatas and canzonas, and keyboard music from Spain. He was especially influenced by the work of CABEZÓN and probably met the exiled English composer John BULL, who wrote a *Fantasia on a Theme of Sweelinck*. He synthesized the techniques and styles from all these different sources to create his own innovative style which, in turn, was disseminated to different parts of Europe, especially Germany. His compositions include secular and sacred choral music, including chansons, madrigals, psalm settings, and a collection of motets, *Cantiones sacrae* (1619). However, it is for his keyboard music that he is now best known, although nothing of it was published during his lifetime. The keyboard works consist mainly of fantasias and toccatas influenced by the Venetian School, in addition to sets of variations on secular melodies.

Sweelinck was an influential and sought-after teacher whose pupils included the oragnist-composers Heinrich Schiedemann (c. 1596–1663) and Samuel Scheidt (1587–1654). Through these members of the north German organ school, Sweelinck had an influence on both J. S. Bach and Handel. He was thus one of the great transitional figures in the development of organ music from Renaissance to BAROQUE compositional styles. He was acclaimed by a contemporary poet as "the Orpheus of Amsterdam."

**Swiss Guard** The special military guardians of the pope and the Vatican Palace since the early 16th century. JULIUS II (pope 1503–13) agreed to pay Swiss cantons for the services of Swiss soldiers, who were excellent fighters and had the advantage of being unlikely to become involved in Roman politics. The Swiss Guard now consists of about 100 men recruited from the Swiss cantons. They wear a distinctive parade uniform, designed by MICHELANGELO, of tunic, breeches, and boldly striped stockings.

**Sylvester, Joshua** (1563–1618) *English poet and translator*
Born in Kent, Sylvester was sent to school in Southampton, where he acquired an excellent knowledge of French. He earned a living in trade, but infinitely preferred poetry, at which he was prolific if undistinguished. His fame rests on his translations of the French poet DU BARTAS; parts of his translation of *La Semaine* appeared from 1592 onward and the first complete version, *Du Bartas his Devine Weekes and Works*, was issued in 1605–06. In 1606 Prince Henry gave him a small pension, but on the prince's death (1612) he obtained a post in the Company of Merchant Venturers (1613) and was sent to Middelburg in Holland, where he died. Sylvester's version of Du Bartas's long poem remained influential in England until the Restoration.

# T

**Tacitus, Cornelius** (c. 55–c. 117) *Roman historian and provincial governor*
His *Histories* cover the reigns of the Roman emperors from Galba to Domitian, partly overlapping his own lifetime, and his *Annals* cover the earlier period from the accession of Tiberius; both are only partially preserved and were virtually unknown in the Middle Ages. BOCCACCIO apparently possessed a manuscript of the *Annals* and *Histories* containing sections of the works unknown before the 14th century, possibly from the monastery of Monte Cassino. Niccolò NICCOLI obtained a codex with minor works of Tacitus from the German library of Fulda. Tacitus's *Germania* was edited by CELTIS (1500) and RHENANUS (1519) as being of particular interest to northern European antiquarians. The history of imperial Rome did not greatly appeal to the 15th-century Italians with their republican ideals, and Tacitus's importance was only fully recognized through the work of LIPSIUS in the late 16th century.

Further reading: Kenneth C. Schellhase, *Tacitus in Renaissance Political Thought* (Chicago, Ill. and London: University of Chicago Press, 1976).

**Taddeo di Bartolo** (c. 1363–c. 1422) *Italian painter*
The last major representative of the Trecento tradition in his native Siena, Taddeo frescoed the chapel of the Palazzo Pubblico there (1407–14) and also executed commissions in the Palazzo Piccolomini and several churches. He also worked in Pisa and is represented by several pictures in the Galleria Nazionale dell'Umbria in Perugia. SASSETTA was one of his closest followers.

**Tafur, Pero** (c. 1410–c. 1484) *Spanish traveler*
Born to a noble family in Cordoba, Tafur traveled extensively in the Mediterranean, the Near East, and Central Europe in the later 1430s. During this period he visited Jerusalem, Egypt, Mount Sinai (where he met Niccolò dei CONTI), Rhodes, Constantinople, Trebizond, and Vienna before returning to Italy in time to see the start of the Council of Ferrara (*see* FLORENCE, COUNCIL OF) in 1438. Moving in exalted social circles, Tafur recorded meetings with contemporary rulers in many places he visited. His travel manuscript (surviving only in an early-18th-century copy at Salamanca) was not published until 1874.

**Taille, Jean de la** See LA TAILLE, JEAN DE

**Tallis, Thomas** (c. 1505–1585) *English composer*
Tallis is first mentioned as organist at Dover priory in 1532. He served at the church of St. Mary-at-Hill, London, in 1537, probably as organist, and in about 1538 moved to Waltham abbey, where he was organist until its dissolution (1540). In 1541–42 he was a lay clerk at Canterbury cathedral, and he probably served as a full-time gentleman of the Chapel Royal from the following year until his death at Greenwich. In 1575 he was granted an exclusive patent to print and publish music with William BYRD. Of his 42 motets, 17 appear in their joint publication of that year, *Cantiones sacrae*.

Tallis was one of the most important English composers whose work spanned the period of the English Reformation. His early, Latin compositions are florid in style, but there is a tendency away from this in the last years of Henry VIII's reign, under the influence of the Protestant Thomas CRANMER. The trend was reversed in the reign of the Catholic Mary I, when Tallis wrote one of his richest compositions, *Gaude gloriosa Dei mater* for six voices. On the abolition of the Sarum rite in 1559, Tallis's Latin settings were probably no longer used liturgically. He was one of the first musicians to compose for the Anglican liturgy of 1547–53; his settings from this period are succinct, with little polyphony and more use of chords. Tallis's music thus embraces several styles largely dictated by the religious upheavals of the time; his 40-part motet, *Spem in alium*, is a curiosity of the mid-Tudor contrapuntal style, while his Anglican anthems tend towards homophony and simplicity. A few keyboard works survive, among which are the earliest datable English plainsong settings.

**Tansillo, Luigi** (1510–1568) *Italian courtier and poet*
From 1535 Tansillo, who was born at Venosa, served in administrative and military posts under the Spanish viceroys of Naples, taking an active part in many campaigns. A prolific author, he was influenced by Giovanni PONTANO and Jacopo SANNAZARO. His work is associated with Mannerism in its style but formally various, ranging from Petrarchan sonnet and eclogue to didactic poetry and religious verse suggestive of the Baroque. *Il vendemmiatore* (*The Grape Harvester*; 1532) gained notoriety for supposedly licentious passages and was put on the Index of forbidden books. To make amends, Tansillo devoted years to his epic *Le lagrime de San Pietro* (*The Tears of St. Peter*; 1585), notable mainly as the model for François de MALHERBE. Numerous lyrics, anthologized in Venice by Gabriele Giolito (1552), achieved wide circulation. The didactic *La balia* (*The Nurse*; 1566) was written to encourage mothers to nurse their own babies.

**tapestry** During the 15th century most European requirements for tapestries were met by workshops in France and Flanders. In Italy small workshops under noble patronage flourished sporadically, only that at Ferrara, founded (c. 1445) by Leonello d'Este, being of much importance. Using Flemish weavers, it executed cartoons by the local painter Cosimo TURA. Throughout the Italian Renaissance tapestry weaving was subordinated to painting, so that for instance the famous *Acts of the Apostles*, commissioned in Brussels by Pope Leo X after cartoons by Raphael, made no concession to the possibilities of tapestry as a medium.

When war brought about the decline of the 15th-century centers of Arras and Tournai, Brussels became the main source for European tapestry (*see also* PANNEMAKER FAMILY). Its characteristic Renaissance style was established by the Flemish painter Bernard van ORLEY. His early work reflects medieval influence but later on that of the Raphael cartoons prevails. In designs based on biblical and historical narrative van Orley attempted to harmonize the Flemish taste for genre and narrative and the Italian preference for monumentality with the artistic potential of tapestry. A famous example of his work is the series the *Hunts of Maximilian I* (c. 1530; Louvre, Paris). Other minor centers in 16th-century Flanders, such as Oudenaarde, produced verdures (tapestries with designs of trees and other vegetation).

In France tapestries were made at FONTAINEBLEAU under the patronage of Francis I from 1538, using Flemish weavers to execute cartoons by the king's Italian painters. These were the first tapestries to imitate paintings in the *trompe l'oeil* manner. In Italy, where the warmer climate made wall-hangings less essential to comfort in drafty palaces, the most important workshop was established (1545) by Duke Cosimo I de' Medici at Florence. Run by Flemish craftsmen, such as Jan Rost (or Rossi; died 1564), who came from Brussels via a sojourn (1536–45) in Ferrara, it worked from cartoons by the leading Florentine mannerists, Pontormo and Bronzino. It also executed some fine tapestries designed by Bachiacca (1490–1557) of grotesques on a yellow ground (Uffizi, Florence).

**Niccolò Tartaglia** A woodcut of the author from the first volume of his *Trattato di numeri et misure* (1556), an encyclopedic work on elementary mathematics.

**Tartaglia, Niccolò** (1499–1557) *Italian mathematician*
Born Niccolò Fontana at Brescia, Lombardy, Tartaglia derived his name "stammerer" from the impediment to his speech caused by the wounds he received at the hands of

the French in 1512. Largely self-educated, Tartaglia began his mathematical career giving private tuition in Verona. He soon, however, established his reputation by claiming to be able to solve any cubic equation of the form $x^3 + qx = r$. The claim was justified publicly in a competition with the Italian mathematician Scipione del Ferro in Venice in 1535. Shortly afterward he was appointed to the chair of mathematics at Venice. Although he refrained from publishing his general solution of cubic equations, he was persuaded to reveal the solution to Girolamo CARDANO who, despite swearing an oath of secrecy, disclosed the result in his *Ars magna* (1545). Tartaglia also worked on the application of mathematics to artillery, publishing his conclusions in *Nova scientia* (1537), and on the geometrical concepts behind military architecture; his book on fortification, *Quesiti, et inventioni diverse* (1546) was dedicated to Henry VIII. He also published and extensively annotated the first Italian translation of Euclid (1543) and composed a major treatise on arithmetic and number theory, the two-volume *Trattato di numeri et misure* (1556–60). The latter is generally considered the most significant Italian mathematical work of the 16th century, combining theory with application and giving insights into everyday life, mercantile practices, and the ongoing efforts to refine arithmetic.

## Tasso, Bernardo (1493–1569) *Italian poet*
Tasso was born into a patrician family from Bergamo and entered the service of Ferrante Sanseverino, prince of Salerno. By his Neapolitan wife Porzia de' Rossi he was the father of Torquato TASSO. In 1552 his patron fell into disfavor with the Spanish rulers of Naples and was exiled; the elder Tasso followed him into exile. In 1557 he moved to the court of Guidobaldo II, Duke of Urbino. He died at Ostiglia to which he had been sent as governor by the duke of Mantua. He wrote poems (*Rime*, 1560) and some interesting letters, but his chief claim to fame is the epic poem *Amadigi di Gaula* (1560) based on the Spanish prose romance *Amadís de Gaula*. It attempts to marry the Aristotelian theory of heroic poetry to the meter and material of ARIOSTO—with longwinded and tedious results.

## Tasso, Torquato (1544–1595) *Italian poet*
Tasso was born at Sorrento and as a boy accompanied his father Bernardo TASSO into political exile, spending a short time at the court of Urbino and studying at the universities of Padua and Bologna. *Rinaldo* (1562), a chivalric romance, demonstrated a youthful poetic competence. In 1565 he joined the retinue of Cardinal Luigi d'Este and in 1572 won the patronage of Duke Alfonso II d'Este and was appointed (like ARIOSTO before him) as court poet of Ferrara. He produced his *Aminta*, one of the outstanding PASTORAL plays of the Renaissance, before the court in the summer of 1573. By 1575 he had completed the first of many versions of his masterpiece, the epic GERUSALEMME LIBERATA.

Soon afterwards Tasso betrayed signs of the mental instability that had a tragic effect on the rest of his life. In 1577, after a violent outburst in the presence of Lucrezia d'Este, Tasso was briefly confined but soon fled to the south. After two years of restless wandering throughout Italy, he returned to Ferrara, but after another episode in which he violently abused the duke in public, he was confined in the hospital of Sant' Anna (1579–86). After his release (authorized by Alfonso), he continued wandering, but now with the protection of prominent men and welcomed by various academies and religious orders. He settled finally at the monastery of Sant' Onofrio in Rome, dying before his coronation as poet laureate, which Pope Clement VIII had intended for him, could take place. His other works include almost 2000 formally composed letters; 28 *Dialoghi* on various subjects; *Discorsi del poema eroico* (1594), a critical study that throws light on his own poetry; the tragedy *Torrismondo* (1587), based on Sophocles' *Oedipus Rex; Rime* (1593), comprising more than 1000 of his shorter poems; and the long hexameral poem in blank verse, *Il mondo creato* (1594).

Tasso's *Aminta*, like GUARINI's *Il pastor fido*, helped shape, and shared to a marked degree in, the fashion for pastoral in the 17th century. An almost complete English version in hexameters was published by Abraham Fraunce in 1591 under the title *The Affectionate Life and Unfortunate Death of Phillis and Amyntas*. There followed *Aminta Englisht* (1628) by Henry Reynolds and later in the 17th century there were two further versions (1660, 1698). Leigh Hunt produced a verse translation in 1820. Grillo's 1924 edition has parallel Italian and English texts, and L. E. Lord published a prose version in 1931. A new translation by Charles Jernigan and Irene Marchegiani Jones appeared in 2000 (New York: Italica). *Gerusalemme liberata* was first partially translated into English in 1594 by Richard Carew, who published five cantos in octaves, with parallel Italian and English texts. The major Renaissance English translation is Edward Fairfax's version in Spenserian stanzas, under the title *Godfrey of Bulloigne* (1600). This was reprinted in 1624 and 1687, and a modern critical edition was published by K. M. Lea and T. M. Gang (Oxford, U.K., 1981).

**Further reading:** Charles P. Brand, *Torquato Tasso: A Study of the Poet and of his Contribution to English Literature* (Cambridge, U.K.: Cambridge University Press, 1965); Valeria Finucci, *Renaissance Transactions: Ariosto and Tasso* (Durham, N.C.: Duke University Press, 1999).

## Tatti, Jacopo See SANSOVINO, JACOPO

## Tausen, Hans (1494–1561) *Danish religious reformer*
The son of a peasant at Birkende, Tausen was converted to Lutheran teachings at Wittenberg (1523). On returning to

Denmark he was imprisoned for spreading heretical ideas, but, undeterred, he soon afterwards established the first Danish Lutheran congregation at Viborg. He was appointed royal chaplain (1526) and his preaching at Copenhagen won support from the Danish national assembly (1529); he then drew up a radical confession of faith for the Danish Church, but this was later rejected in favor of the more conciliatory Confession of AUGSBURG. A firm believer in the use of the vernacular for ecclesiastical purposes. Tausen wrote sermons and hymns and translated sections of the Old Testament. In 1542 he was appointed bishop of Ribe.

**Taverner, John** (c. 1490–1545) *English composer*
Taverner served as a lay clerk at the collegiate church of Tattershall in Lincolnshire in the early 1520s, and in 1525 was invited by the bishop of Lincoln to become the first choirmaster at Cardinal College (now Christ Church), Oxford. He took up the post in 1526, but left four years later when the college began to be run down after WOLSEY's fall from favor. He returned to Lincolnshire and became master of the choristers at the parish church of St. Botolph, Boston. By 1537 he had left the post but remained in Boston, where he died as a highly respected, wealthy local dignitary. Generally regarded as the greatest English composer of the early 16th century, he wrote eight Masses, 28 motets, and three secular pieces. The motets include antiphons, Magnificat settings, and responds; in the last, plainsong *cantus firmi* with equal note values are treated polyphonically. There are three six-voice festal Masses written in an archaic style based on a plainsong material with long melismas and constructional devices; these are the last examples from almost a century of the English festal Mass. Taverner's famous *Western Wynde* Mass is on a smaller scale. It is for four voices and consists of a series of variations on a popular melody.

**Tè, Palazzo del** The palace on the outskirts of Mantua constructed (c. 1525–35) by GIULIO ROMANO for Federico II Gonzaga. Challenging classical principles and combining the elegance and sophistication of Raphael and Michelangelo, Giulio created the structure in brick and terracotta (local stone being unavailable) as one of the earliest masterpieces of mannerist architecture. The most dramatic of the palace's decorative features is the Sala dei Giganti, painted by Giulio from floor to ceiling with frescoes of the fall of the Titans with over-lifesize bodies of tumbling giants and hurtling rocks.

**Teatro Farnese** See THEATERS

**Teatro Olimpico** See THEATERS

**technology** The Renaissance saw a number of major technological innovations, four of which (PRINTING, GUN-POWDER, mechanical CLOCKS, and the mastery of ocean NAVIGATION) brought about fundamental changes in the nature of society and transformed the course of world history. The first of these, printing, dates from the invention of movable type in the period 1440–50. This in turn was only made possible by the introduction of paper, via China and Islam, into early 14th-century Italy. Before 1500 some 20 million INCUNABULA were published, an operation scarcely conceivable without the benefit of printing and paper. Gunpowder, an earlier invention attributed to Roger Bacon in the 13th century, was first seen in its full significance in Europe in the early 14th century. At the same time mechanical clocks began to spread across Europe. A century later improvements in ship design, the development of more efficient sails, and the introduction of CANNON on the main deck gave the merchants of Europe the basic equipment with which to dominate world trade.

Within Renaissance Europe itself, the main sources of power remained wind and water. The windmill first arrived in Europe in the late 12th century in the form of the post-mill, in which a change in wind direction required the whole of the mill's superstructure to be realigned. The less cumbersome tower-mill first appeared in the late 14th century. Although initially used for grinding corn they later came to be used mainly for raising water. More versatile and more ancient were the water wheels that spread extensively throughout Europe; by the beginning of the Industrial Revolution some 600,000 had been constructed. With their aid a range of new industries became possible. Used to drive tilt hammers, mechanical saws, bellows, pumps, and beaters they were partly responsible for the growth of, among others, the paper, iron, tanning, and fulling industries. Before power could be conveniently deployed, however, it was first necessary to convert the rotary motion of the mill into the reciprocating motion of the hammer or saw. It was also necessary to provide efficient and adaptable systems of gears. To this end the Renaissance engineer displayed his ingenuity with the deployment of cranks, compound cranks, flywheels, and cam shafts (see illustration p. 404).

The Renaissance also saw the development of a number of smaller if more specialized industries. In CERAMICS, for example, a growing confidence in the use of glazes allowed 14th-century Italian potters to produce MAJOLICA ware. At about the same time colored GLASS began to be produced in Venice. Both these, and such other industries as distilling, dyeing, and tanning, depended at least partly on the skills of the chemist who began to figure more prominently in the technology of his age. Less successful were the attempts of Renaissance engineers to improve means of inland transport (*see* COMMUNICATIONS). The means and speeds suffered by the 14th-century traveler were precisely those endured by a comparable 18th-century figure. Goods could, thus, take longer to travel a few miles by road than to be shipped scores of miles by water. Significant improvements came only with the development of the steam engine and better road-building methods long after the Renaissance had ended.

**Further reading:** Carlo M. Cipolla, *Guns and Sails in the Early Phase of European Expansion, 1400–1700* (New York: Pantheon Books, 1965); Denis Cosgrove *et al, Water, Engineering and Landscape* (Chichester, U.K.: John Wiley & Sons, 1994); Richard Leslie Hill, *Power From the Wind: A History of Windmill Technology* (Cambridge, U.K.: Cambridge University Press, 1994; repr. 1996); William B. Parsons, *Engineers and Engineering in the Renaissance* (Cambridge, Mass.: MIT Press, 1968); Terry S. Reynolds, *Stronger Than a Hundred Men: A History of the Vertical Water Wheel* (Baltimore, Md.: Johns Hopkins University Press, 1999; repr. 2003); Paolo Rossi, *Philosophy, Technology and the Arts in the Early Modern Era* (New York and London: Harper & Row, 1970).

## Teixeira, Pedro (fl. 1587–1610) *Portuguese traveler and historian of Persia*

Texeira, who may have been a doctor by profession, probably sailed for Goa in 1586. He traveled extensively in Portuguese India, then moved to Hormuz (c. 1593–97), where he became proficient in Persian. From Malacca (1597–1600) he returned home (1600–01) by a route via Acapulco, across Mexico on horseback, then by ship to Cuba, and eventually Seville. Discovering that money he had sent home via the Cape had not arrived, he sailed again for Goa (1602), returning by land through Mesopotamia (1604–05). On his return he settled in Antwerp. His account of his travels was published with his Persian history: *Relaciones ... d'el Origen, Descendencia y Succession de los Reyes de Persia, ...y de un Viage hecho por el mismo Autor dende la India Oriental hasta Italia por tierra* (1610).

## telescopes

Optical instruments for making distant objects appear larger. The first undisputed description of a telescope, in the official Hague records for 1608, attributes the invention to Hans Lippershey (died c. 1619), a spectacle maker of Middelburg, Holland. Details are scarce and the precise nature of the instrument is unknown. The claim was challenged immediately by James Metius of Alkmaar and Zacharias Janssen of Middelburg. It is now known that all three had in fact been anticipated by Thomas HARRIOT. All such instruments were refractive telescopes and operated with a biconvex object lens and biconcave eyepiece. Word of the new invention spread quickly, for in 1609 in Padua a similar refractor capable of magnifying 33 times had been made by GALILEO. Such instruments, known as Dutch telescopes, produced an erect image (which fitted them well for military and naval applications) but presented an unacceptably small field of view. The latter defect was overcome by Johannes KEPLER in 1611, by using two biconvex lenses, though at the price

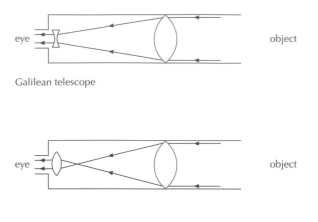

Galilean telescope

Keplerian telescope

**Telescopes** The operation of the two kinds of refractive telescope produced by the early pioneers in the field, Galileo and Kepler.

of producing an inverted image. This was not a serious drawback for astronomers, and Kepler's arrangement became known as the "celestial" telescope—as opposed to the "terrestrial" or Galilean instrument.

More serious faults remained. The images produced were distorted and often surrounded by colored rings. The defects, known respectively as spherical and chromatic aberration, were in fact inherent properties of refracted light. At best they could be minimized by constructing telescopes, the so-called aerials, with very long focal lengths. Instruments 150 feet long were in fact constructed, but proved too impractical. The solution—to construct reflective rather than refractive telescopes—came much later (1672) with Isaac Newton.

**See also:** OPTICS

**Further reading:** Richard Parek, *Seeing and Believing: How the Telescope Opened Our Eyes to the Heavens* (New York: Penguin Viking, 1998).

## Telesio, Bernardino (1509–1588) *Italian natural philosopher*

Telesio was born at Cosenza and was educated by his uncle who taught him Greek, thus enabling him to make direct contact with Greek scientific writings. He studied at Padua where he became disillusioned with contemporary ARISTOTELIANISM, influenced as it was by Arabic interpretations. After he left Padua he spent some years developing his own views, which amount to a return to the authentic opinions of Aristotle. In 1565 he published his first book, *De rerum natura iuxta propria principia*, a work that he continued to expand and that reached its final form in 1586. In 1566 he founded the Academia Telesiana, a scientific society. He died at Cosenza.

Telesio believed that sense is the only basis for speculation about nature. His importance lies in his use of Aristotelian concepts to present an essentially physical explanation of natural phenomena. His system depends on two active natures, heat and cold, and an inert mass on which the two natures react. Telesio also introduced approaches to space and time that in some ways foreshadowed Newtonian physics. He numbered CAMPANELLA and Giordano BRUNO among his followers.

**Téllez, Gabriel** See TIRSO DE MOLINA

**Tempesta, Antonio** (1555–1630) *Italian engraver, painter, and etcher*
Tempesta trained in his native Florence under Jan van der STRAET and also assisted VASARI on the decorative schemes for the Palazzo Vecchio. For much of his life, however, he was based in Rome, where he contributed to the decoration of several palaces, including the Vatican, and of the Villa Farnese at Caprarola. His prints, mainly of hunting and battle scenes, were widely disseminated and copied by other artists.

**Tempio Malatestiano** The "temple" of Sigismondo MALATESTA at Rimini. Conceived by Sigismondo as a temple dedicated to the arts and philosophy and as a monument to himself and his third wife, Isotta degli Atti, the Tempio is a remodeling of the 13th-century Gothic church of San Francesco. The interior was begun in 1450 by Matteo de' PASTI, whose work obliterated earlier frescoes by GIOTTO. Chapels were built for Sigismondo and Isotta, with reliefs, notably, of the Arts and Sciences by AGOSTINO DI DUCCIO and a fresco (1451) by PIERO DELLA FRANCESCA that depicts Sigismondo kneeling before St. Sigismund. The exterior is the work of ALBERTI, who designed a classical shell to encase the earlier building. The structure is based on the motif of the Roman triumphal arch, inspired by the arch of Augustus nearby, and was to be surmounted by a dome. Because of his conflict with Pope Pius II, Sigismondo abandoned work on the Tempio in 1460.

**Templars** See KNIGHTS TEMPLAR

**Ten, Council of** See COUNCIL OF TEN

**Ten of War** (Italian *dieci di libertà et pace*) The Florentine council concerned with the conduct of diplomacy and warfare. It was accountable to the *signoria* but had considerable freedom in the way it arranged embassies and ran the military establishment. MACHIAVELLI was its secretary for 14 years (1498–1512), and his correspondence from this period gives a detailed picture of the Ten's operations.

**Terence** (Publius Terentius Afer) (195/185–159 BCE) *Roman comic playwright*
An African-born slave, Terence was received into the cultivated Roman circle of Scipio Aemilianus, to whose taste his plays catered. The plays number six, with four of them being adaptations from the Greek comedy of Menander. Terence was much admired by later Roman writers for the purity of his style, and he similarly appealed to Renaissance pedagogues who recommended his plays for school reading and acting. Although he used much the same material as PLAUTUS, Terence's sentiments are generally more refined, affording, as Renaissance educationists saw it, moral edification as well as stylistic benefit to students.

**Teresa of Ávila, St.** (Teresa Sánchez de Cepeda y Ahumada) (1515–1582) *Spanish Carmelite reformer and mystic*
She was born near Ávila and, already infused with a heightened religious enthusiasm at the age of seven, set off with her brother Rodrigo for Moorish territory to be beheaded for Christ. Her uncle stopped them. After her mother died she was placed in the Augustinian convent of Sta. Maria de Gracia in 1531. Her spiritual ardour finally compelled her to take up the religious habit and pursue an ascetic life. She entered a Carmelite nunnery in Ávila in 1538 and later fell ill and was paralysed as a result of her self-deprivations. In 1554 she recorded her first visions and ecstatic union with God. She became an ardent reformer and in 1562 founded the Convent of the Incarnation of Discalced Carmelite nuns. In subsequent years she wrote *The Way of Perfection* as a guide for the nuns of her Ávila convent and *Meditations on the Canticle*. In 1567 she and St. JOHN OF THE CROSS began founding other Discalced Carmelite monasteries. Their opponents, the Calced Carmelites, tried to deport her to New Spain but succeeded only in limiting her activities to Toledo. During this difficult time she wrote her most famous work, *The Interior Castle*. She died in Alba shortly after founding yet another Discalced Carmelite house at Burgos. In 1617 the Spanish *cortes* declared her "Patroness of Spain," and she was canonized in 1622, along with IGNATIUS LOYOLA, FRANCIS XAVIER, and PHILIP NERI.

St. Teresa of Ávila represents, along with St. John of the Cross, the most intense mysticism of the COUNTER-REFORMATION. As a woman in 16th-century Spain, she was not educated in a formal sense, and her writings display a rustic style. Although historians commonly say that in her writings her rapturous religious fantasies are mixed with intense sensual and erotic sentiments, this assertion is exaggerated; in this respect her writings are more moderate than those of St. John of the Cross. The mystical enthusiasm of Teresa has been well captured by Gian Lorenzo Bernini's renowned sculpture *St. Teresa in Ecstasy* (1645–52; Sta. Maria della Vittoria, Rome).

**Further reading:** Cathleen Medwick, *Teresa of Avila: The Progress of a Soul* (New York: Knopf, 1999); Carole Slade, *St. Teresa of Avila: Author of a Heroic Life* (Berkeley, Calif. and London: University of California Press, 1995).

**terza rima** A type of rhymed verse introduced by Dante in the DIVINE COMEDY. It consists of triplets of usually 11-syllable lines, the triplets being joined by a *rima incatenata* or linked rhyme having the pattern aba bcb cdc ded … etc. The *chiusa* or conclusion is a single line, e.g. … xyx yzy z. Perhaps derived from Provençal forms (*sirventes*) or from types of sonnet, *terza rima* acquires a powerful and obvious symbolic value in the *Divine Comedy*. It was later adapted to many different uses, including satire. PETRARCH, BOCCACCIO, and in English CHAUCER, WYATT, DANIEL, Lord Byron, and P. B. Shelley all wrote poems in *terza rima*.

**Teutonic Knights** A military religious order founded in the 12th century and originally attached to the German hospital of St. Mary in Jerusalem. In the 13th century they were granted territory in eastern Germany from which to subdue Prussia, and with papal support, rapidly increased in wealth and numbers. From 1308 the order's headquarters was Marienburg on the River Vistula. They protected the merchants of the HANSEATIC LEAGUE, who brought great prosperity to many towns in the Knights' Baltic territories of Prussia and Livonia. Conflict with Poland brought the crushing defeat of the Knights at Tannenberg (1410) from which the order never wholly recovered, and under the peace of Torun (1466) Poland obtained west Prussia, confining the Knights to the east, which they held as a Polish fief. On their eastern frontiers they continued active into the 16th century against Russian encroachments but the growing nationalism of Poland-Lithuania effectively ended their territorial independence.

**theaters** The important Renaissance innovations in theater building occurred in 15th- and 16th-century Italy. Interest in the Roman plays of PLAUTUS and TERENCE led to the rise of the COMMEDIA ERUDITA; accompanying this was an interest in authentic classical staging. In 1414 the discovery at the monastery of St. Gall of VITRUVIUS's *De architectura*, book five of which dealt with theater design, provided the classicizing stimulus to Italian innovators. The manuscript was printed without its illustrations in about 1486, with them in 1511, and in Italian translation in 1521. Vitruvius's principles and his emphasis on symmetry, proportion, and acoustics were eagerly adapted, with varying results. A famous woodcut in an edition of Terence (1493) illustrates the imposition of classical style on earlier traditions of staging. (The *theatrum* (auditorium), placed above a ground storey of arches (*fornices*), had three tiers for spectators who faced a *proscenium* (stage wall), which was divided by columns with curtains between them.) *Periaktoi* (or, later, *telari*), triangular devices at either side of the stage, the faces of which were painted with rudimentary scenes and revolved to indicate scene changes, were also adapted from the classical model and were increased in number and improved by Bastiano SANGALLO. LEONARDO DA VINCI was an early experimenter with painted scenery, producing a *trompe l'oeil* city scene for a performance of Baldassare Taccone's *Danae* in 1496. Knowledge of perspective also vastly improved painted sets, a feature that much impressed CASTIGLIONE at the 1513 staging of BIBBIENA's *La calandria* in Urbino.

By the early 16th century several temporary theaters had been constructed under the auspices of Italian courts from the Vitruvian model. Although Ferrara had led the way in classical performances (Plautus's *Menaechmi* was staged by Duke Ercole d'Este in the palace courtyard in 1486), Vicenza became the center of theater construction. In the 1530s Sebastiano SERLIO built a classically inspired temporary theater for the Vicenzan Accademia Olimpica. He also recorded detailed plans for building a stage and auditorium in a banqueting hall (*Regole generali di architettura*, book 2); the stage sets behind the shallow playing area, were designed with pronounced perspective effects, and comedy, tragedy, and satire each had its own characteristic set—a street of palaces for tragedy, houses for comedy, and woodland for satire. PALLADIO, himself a member of the Accademia Olimpica, was commissioned to build the permanent theater. Based on Daniele BARBARO's commentary on Vitruvius (1556), Palladio's Teatro Olimpico, completed by SCAMOZZI, opened in 1585 with a performance of Sophocles' *Oedipus Rex*. This was the culmination of neoclassical design, although, with its fixed scenery of a piazza and perspective streets, it proved to be dead-end and impractical for performances, even of Roman comedy. A far more flexible arrangement was that of the Teatro Farnese in Parma (1618; destroyed in World War II), built to designs by Giovanni Battista Aleotti (c. 1546–1636); there the proscenium arch and curtained stage made their appearance, with a U-shaped (instead of the previous semicircular) auditorium. Further developments, such as the horseshoe auditorium adopted for opera and ballet, belong to a somewhat later period.

As in other fields, Italian Renaissance experimentation was far in advance of the rest of Europe in responding to classical ideas. However, new theaters having their own national characteristics multiplied in the 16th century. The first permanent theater in Paris was a long narrow structure, the Théâtre de l'Hôtel de Bourgogne, in the rue Mauconseil. It was built in 1548 by the Confrérie de la Passion, a lay society dedicated to performing *mystères*; after 1578 it was occasionally let to professional companies. Spanish and Elizabethan English stages remained open air. In Spain the typical stage was raised on scaffolding in a courtyard and surrounded by spectators on balconies or at windows. The unroofed London theaters, such as the Globe (c. 1599) and Swan (c. 1595), reflected

**Theater** An Elizabethan theater in which spectators either sat in covered galleries or stood in the open pit. The 1996 replica of the original Globe Theatre in London (1598–1642) is virtually identical to this illustration, except that the galleries form a complete circle round the pit.

a similar evolution from the performances of wandering players given in the yards of inns. Although the acting companies also used indoor theaters, such as that at Blackfriars. A famous sketch of the Swan made c. 1596 shows three tiers of galleries enclosing the courtyard at the back of which is the thatched three-story stage building with the stage projecting in front of it. The public playhouses of London were sited on the south bank of the River Thames among other venues for popular entertainment and attracted an audience from all social classes. This was partly because admission was very cheap for "groundlings" (those who were willing to stand in the area in front of and below the stage); those able and prepared to pay more sat in the galleries or even on stools on the stage.

Further reading: John Orrell, *The Human Stage: English Theatre Design 1567–1640* (Cambridge, U.K.: Cambridge University Press, 1988).

**Theatine Order** (**Congregation of Clerks Regular of the Divine Providence**) A religious order founded in 1524 by Gaetano da Thiene (St. Cajetan) and Giampietro Caraffa, Bishop of Chieti (Theate), who later became Pope PAUL IV. Members were bound by vows and lived in common; they held no property, but were not mendicants, and they were distinguished from the secular clergy by their white socks. They engaged in pastoral work to combat heresy, were zealous promoters of the COUNTER-REFORMATION, and sought to remove abuses and to encourage piety in the life of the Church. The order spread from Italy to Spain and central Europe and from 1583 it included some nuns.

**Theotokopoulos, Domenikos** See GRECO, EL

**Thirty-nine Articles** A set of formulations in which the Anglican Church defined its position on various doctrinal questions. Such formulations had been sought from 1536 onward, but eventually it was Archbishop Matthew PARKER's industry that led to a definitive text being established at the 1571 Convocation. Eschewing both Roman Catholicism and Anabaptist or Puritan extremes, the Articles, together with the BOOK OF COMMON PRAYER and the Ordinal, elucidate the Church of England's thinking on the main points that had split Christians during the 16th century. In doing so, they embody Anglicanism's unique compromise between Catholic conservatism and Protestant innovation.

**Tibaldi, Pellegrino** (1527–1596) *Italian painter, sculptor, and architect*
He was born at Puria di Valsolda, near Milan, and following his early training in Emilia, he lived in Rome (1549–53), where he was greatly influenced by DANIELE DA VOLTERRA and even more by MICHELANGELO. This is evident in such works as his *Adoration of the Christ Child* (1549; Galleria Borghese, Rome). He later worked in Bologna, where he built the Palazzo Poggi (now the university), decorating the Sala di Ulisse there (c. 1554) with illusionistic frescoes; he also designed and decorated a chapel in the church of San Giacomo Maggiore (c. 1555). In Milan in the 1560s and 1570s he was mainly involved in architecture, building the Jesuit church of San Fedele (begun 1569) and the round church of San Sebastiano (1576). In 1567 Cardinal (later St) CHARLES BORROMEO put him in charge of architectural and sculptural additions to Milan cathedral; Tibaldi designed several parts of the Duomo including the screen between the choir and ambulatory. In 1588 he went to Madrid to execute sculpture and paintings for Philip II in the ESCORIAL, only returning to Milan shortly before his death. The paintings of the liberal arts on the barrel-vaulted ceiling of the Escorial's library, for instance, are his work. The same mannerist style which is found in his paintings is evident in the huge frescoes in the Escorial, in which he breaks down forms into geometric shapes. He was in part responsible for diffusing MANNERISM outside Rome.

**Tinctoris, Johannes** (c. 1435–c. 1511) *Franco-Flemish music theorist and composer*
Born at Nivelles, he may have known Guillaume DUFAY while a singer at Cambrai in 1460. In 1463 Tinctoris was instructor of the choirboys at Orleans cathedral. Around 1472 he was appointed tutor to the daughter of the king of Naples and maintained connections with the court there for at least the next 15 years. Tinctoris composed some music, but is remembered as one of the most important music theorists of his day; he wrote 12 treatises, two of which were printed. The most important of these is his *Terminorum musicae diffinitorium*, the oldest printed music dictionary, in which 299 musical terms are defined. His other writings treat the aesthetics of music, its educational and therapeutic roles, and its use in religion, as well as composition and improvisation. His writings furnish great insight into the music of the Renaissance.

See also: MUSIC THEORY

**Tintoretto** (Jacopo Robusti) (1518–1594) *Italian painter*
Born in Venice, where he spent most of his life, Tintoretto acquired his nickname (meaning "little dyer") by reference to his father's trade as a dyer (*tintore*). Although few details of his life are known, Tintoretto was briefly (according to his 1642 biographer, Carlo Ridolfi) a pupil of TITIAN, from whom he certainly learnt much about the handling of color. He was also familiar—possibly through prints and engravings—with the works of MICHELANGELO from whom he inherited a deep interest in draftsmanship. Ridolfi is the source for the story that Tintoretto wrote up in his studio as his prescription for painting: "Il disegno di Michelangelo ed il colorito di Tiziano." Tintoretto also apparently used wax and clay models, which he set in a box with a light in order to experiment with different lighting effects. His early paintings are notable for their daring use of color and unconventional groups of figures: among them are his masterly *Last Supper* (1547; San Marcuola) and *St. Mark Reviving a Slave* or *The Miracle of the Slave* (1548; Accademia, Venice), the latter being one of four commissioned by the Scuola di San Marco, the enthusiastic reception of which established Tintoretto's fortunes.

Tintoretto was later influenced by Paolo VERONESE with whom he collaborated on the important commission for the decoration of the interior of the doge's palace in Venice after the fire of 1577; there he executed the massive paintings of *The Siege of Zara* (1584–87) and *Paradise* (1588) and a portrait sequence of 72 doges, among numerous other paintings glorifying Venice. A deeply religious man, Tintoretto often worked for religious institutions, most notably the Scuola di San Rocco, for whom he painted an extensive cycle of wall and ceiling paintings (1565–87), including scenes from the Old and New Testaments, in which he demonstrated his skill in depicting different light effects and experimented with certain illusionistic devices.

Always a prolific artist, he completed the huge *Crucifixion* in the Sala dell' Albergo there in 1565, and the decorative scheme for the Scuola and adjacent church comprise over 50 major paintings. The dramatic swooping flight of the angels and the startled Virgin in the *Annunciation* are just one example of Tintoretto's ability to imbue familiar scenes with drama, and his manipulation of figures and *chiaroscuro* in these paintings mark him out as a leading artist in the mannerist mode. Tintoretto had learnt to paint rapidly as a young man while collaborating with SCHIAVONE on frescoes in the Palazzo Zen. In later years his sons Domenico and Marco and his daughter Marietta worked as his assistants. Other notable works include many portraits and the famous *Susanna Bathing* (c. 1550; Kunsthistorisches Museum, Vienna). The voluptuous Venetian nude exemplified in the figure of Susanna also found a place in several of Tintoretto's paintings on mythological subjects, such as the Dresden *Liberation of Arsinoe* and the London *Origin of the Milky Way*. Tintoretto died of a fever and was buried in the church of the Madonna dell' Orto, for which he had painted three of his greatest pictures, the virtuoso pyramidal composition of *The Presentation of the Virgin*, *The Worship of the Golden Calf*, and *The Last Judgment*.

**Further reading:** Anna Pallucchini, *Tintoretto: The Life and Work of the Artist*, transl. Pearl Sanders (London:

Thames & Hudson, 1969); Carlo Ridolfi, *The Life of Tintoretto and of His Children Domenico and Marietta* (Philadelphia, Pa: Pennsylvania State University Press, new ed. 1984).

**Tirso de Molina** (**Gabriel Téllez**) (1583–1648) *Spanish playwright*
Very little is known for certain of Tirso's early life. It has been argued that he was the illegitimate son of the duke of Osuna but there are serious objections to the theory. He studied at Alcalá, became a Mercedarian friar (1601) and probably lived in Toledo (1605–15), where he may have written the first of some 400 plays, about 86 of which (some of doubtful ascription) are extant. He traveled extensively and after 1625, when he was reprimanded by the council of Castile for too frankly portraying vice on stage, abandoned the theater. He became official chronicler of his order in 1637, producing a recently discovered *Historia general de la orden de Nuestra Señora de las Mercedes*, and died as a prior of a Mercedarian monastery.

Five collections of his plays were published during his lifetime, as well as two miscellanies (1621, 1635) of tales, plays, and poems set in *Decameron*-like frameworks. The most distinguished disciple of Lope de VEGA, Tirso wrote comedies of intrigue and plays on historical and religious themes. A number of these are notable for the prominent roles given to women. His most popular intrigue comedy was *El vergonzoso en palacio* (The shy man in the palace; 1611); but he is now best known for two plays on theological issues of faith, the acceptance or refusal of grace, and salvation: *El condenado por desconfiado* and *El burlador de Sevilla* (both 1620s). The last introduced one of the most memorable of Spanish fictions, the story of the heartless seducer Don Juan Tenorio.

**Tisi, Benvenuto** See GAROFALO, IL

**Titian** (**Tiziano Vecellio**) (c. 1490–1576) *Italian painter*
The old tradition that Titian attained the age of 99 is very doubtful, and his birth date is plausibly given by VASARI as around 1490. Titian was born in Pieve di Cadore and moved south to Venice at age nine to train as a painter. There he was taught by Gentile and Giovanni BELLINI and assisted GIORGIONE, by whom his early work was strongly influenced, with frescoes commissioned for the German merchants' warehouse. He visited Padua in 1511 to paint frescoes in the Scuola del Santo and then returned to Venice where he executed a number of works that show him gradually moving beyond the Giorgionesque idiom. These include some celebrated half-lengths of beautiful women (the so-called *Vanity* in Munich and the Uffizi *Flora* among them), some accomplished portraits, the allegories of *The Three Ages of Man* (Edinburgh, Sutherland loan) and *Sacred and Profane Love* (Galleria Borghese, Rome), and the first of his great mythological pieces, *The*

*Worship of Venus* (Prado, Madrid) and *Bacchus and Ariadne* (National Gallery, London). Also in this period he received his first major public commission: an *Assumption of the Virgin* for the high altar of Sta. Maria dei Frari, Venice (1516–18), a masterpiece of dramatic animation and vivid coloring. He also painted the *Madonna di Ca' Pésaro* (1523) for the same church. Another early altarpiece (1522) is the *Resurrection* triptych, with its notable figure of St. Sebastian, in SS. Nazaro e Celso, Brescia.

In 1516 Titian had obtained the post of official painter to the Venetian Republic but that did not stop him from accepting commissions from Duke Alfonso d'Este of Ferrara (1516), the Gonzagas in Mantua (1523), and the DELLA ROVERE FAMILY in Urbino (1532). He painted fine portraits for all of these, and his portrait (1535–38; Kress Collection, National Gallery, Washington) of Doge Andrea Gritti exemplifies Titian's extraordinary ability to capture both the dignity and pathos of the old age of the powerful. In 1530 Titian was introduced to Emperor CHARLES V at Bologna, and his full-length portrait of the emperor with his hound (1532; Prado) ensured his appointment as court painter, with the title of count palatine (1533). Titian also painted several other portraits of Charles that are now lost, but two that have survived are those painted in Augsburg in 1548: an equestrian portrait commemorating Charles's victory at MÜHLBERG (Prado) and a full-length seated figure in black (Alte Pinakothek, Munich). On a second visit to Augsburg (1550–51), Titian was probably entrusted with the commission for the great devotional picture known as the *Gloria* or *Trinity* (1551–54; Prado), in which the emperor, wrapped in his winding sheet, kneels in adoration. The emperor's sister, MARY OF HUNGARY, regent of the Netherlands, was also an enthusiastic collector of Titian's work.

PHILIP II of Spain continued his father's patronage of Titian. At the end of 1548 the artist traveled to Milan to meet the prince; one fruit of this first encounter may have been the *Venus with Cupid and an Organist* (Berlin), in which the organist appears to be a portrait of Philip. The famous series of erotic poesies (*see* POESY) for Philip was begun in the early 1550s with *Danaë* (Prado). Titian was also invited to paint a *Martyrdom of St. Laurence* (1564–67) for the central altar of the church of the ESCORIAL. *The Allegory of the Battle of Lepanto* (1571–75; Prado) was the last of Titian's works to be sent to Spain and shows how heavily the aged artist was by then relying upon his assistants.

Besides the pictures painted for his Hapsburg patrons and the ducal families of Italy, Titian continued to execute commissions for the Venetian Republic, including the lost *Battle of Cadoro*, completed in 1538, for the Sala del Gran Consiglio. Another of Titian's patrons was Pope PAUL III, the first portrait of whom was painted in Bologna in 1543. In 1545 Titian traveled to Rome, where he met Michelangelo and painted another portrait of the pope, this time with his grandsons (1546; Museo Nazionale, Naples); the group poignantly captures the tension between the frail elderly pope, the scheming Ottavio, and the indifferent Alessandro (*see* FARNESE FAMILY). The charming portrait of two-year-old Clarice Strozzi (1542) shows a very different aspect of Titian's abilities. In the 1550s he also painted several portraits of his daughter Lavinia and a self-portrait now in Berlin.

Although Titian's output of portraits, and religious, mythological, and historical paintings was aided, particularly in his declining years, by numerous assistants in his Venetian studio—Vasari, who visited Titian in 1566, describes their practice—the quantity and quality of the work he produced throughout his long life is astonishing. His last painting was a *Pietà* (1576; Accademia, Venice) intended for his own tomb in the Frari. He left it unfinished and it was completed by PALMA GIOVANE.

**Further reading:** Bruce Cole, *Titian and Venetian Painting, 1450–1590* (Boulder, Colo.: Westview Press, 1999); Rona Goffen, *Titian's Women* (New Haven, Conn.: Yale University Press, 1997); Charles Hope, *Titian* (London: Jupiter Books, 1980); Filippo Pedrocco, *Titian* (Milan, Italy: Rizzoli, 2001).

**Toledo** A city in south central Spain, by the River Tagus. Toledo was a Roman colony (founded 193 BCE), a Visigoth capital, and an important Moorish city (712–1085). After the Christian reconquest (1085) Toledo was a great Castilian city where Arabs, Jews, and Christians met; it was known for its Hebrew studies until the expulsion of the Jews in the late 15th century. Despite its part in the revolt of the COMUNEROS (1520–21) Toledo was a favorite residence of King Charles I of Spain (Emperor CHARLES V). When PHILIP II made Madrid his capital (1560) Toledo's importance declined, but it continued to prosper from its cloth and silk industries and the manufacture of fine steel goods, notably swords.

During the Renaissance the great Catholic reformer, Cardinal XIMÉNES, was archbishop of Toledo and an important patron of scholarship. El GRECO lived in Toledo from 1577 until his death in 1614. Notable buildings include the Moorish quarter, the cathedral (1226–1493), the monastery of San Juan de los Reyes and the Casa de la Santa Hermandad (both built in the late 15th and 16th centuries), and the Alcázar (begun 1531), with its facade by Juan de HERRERA.

**Tolomei, Claudio** (1492–1556) *Italian writer*
Tolomei was born in Siena but was banished in 1526 because of his association with the Medici. He was later recalled and achieved high political office in the city. Tolomei is chiefly known for two dialogues, *Il Polito* (1525) and *Il Cesano* (1555) in which he discusses the phonology of the Tuscan language, the relation between speech and text, and the origins of language. In his poetry

he applied classical metrical forms to vernacular verse (*Versi e regole della nuova poesia toscana*, 1539). His letters were published in seven books (1547).

**Tomkins, Thomas** (1572–1656) *English composer*
Tomkins received his early musical education at St. David's cathedral, Pembrokeshire. He was sent to London in 1594 to study with William BYRD, and in 1596 he was appointed organist and choirmaster of Worcester cathedral, a post he held until 1646 when the Civil War brought an end to choral services there. He graduated in music at Oxford in 1607, and became a Gentleman of the Chapel Royal in 1617 and its organist in 1621. The most important collection of his compositions is the posthumous *Musica Deo Sacra* (1668). He also published a volume of madrigals entitled *Songs* (1622).

**Topsell, Edward** (1572–1625) *English naturalist*
Little is known of Topsell's life other than that he was a clergyman and held a number of livings in southeast England. His interest in zoology appears to have been stimulated by the need to identify the various animals referred to in the Bible. The result of his researches was his *Historie of Four-footed Beastes* (1607) and *Historie of Serpents* (1608). Both works are entirely uncritical and derivative; they are, nonetheless, the first illustrated natural history works to be published in English.

**See also:** ZOOLOGY

**Tordesillas, Treaty of** (June 7, 1494) The agreement between Portugal and Spain intended to settle conflicting claims in the New World and to exclude other rivals. In 1493 Pope ALEXANDER VI established a line of demarcation from pole to pole 100 leagues west of the Cape Verde islands. Portugal was to have the monopoly of exploration to the east of the line and Spain to the west, but neither should occupy territories already under Christian rule. Portugal was understandably dissatisfied; after prolonged negotiations the Portuguese and Spanish ambassadors agreed on the Treaty of Tordesillas, which confirmed the papal idea of demarcation but moved the line 270 leagues further west. This enabled Portugal to claim Brazil when CABRAL landed there (1500). Pope JULIUS II approved the treaty in 1506.

**Torquemada, Tomás de** (1420–1498) *Spanish Dominican inquisitor*
As confessor to the Spanish monarchs FERDINAND (II) AND ISABELLA I, Torquemada, himself born of Jewish descent in Valladolid, encouraged them to attack openly practicing Jews and CONVERSOS. In 1478 the queen persuaded Pope Sixtus IV to unify the inquisitions of Castile and Aragon under Torquemada's control, giving him power to appoint, dismiss, and hear appeals from other inquisitors. He organized the SPANISH INQUISITION under five territorial tri-

bunals, with one supreme appellate council directed by himself. The Ordinances he issued (1484) regulated inquisitorial procedures in Spain for the next 300 years. From 1483 onwards Torquemada used these vast policing and judicial powers to try and punish spiritual offenders on a grand scale: 2000 were executed during his tenure of office, and vast numbers were punished with imprisonment and confiscation of property. Torquemada used an alleged ritual murder of a Christian baby by Jews in La Guardia as a pretext to expel non-*converso* Jews and Muslims from Spain in 1492.

## Torres Naharro, Bartolomé de (c. 1485–c. 1524) *Spanish playwright*
He was born at La Torre de Miguel Sesmero, near Badajoz, and was probably educated at Salamanca. For a time he served as a soldier, was captured by pirates, sold into slavery in Algiers, and later ransomed. He was then ordained a priest and spent his life in Italy, at Rome and Naples, where a number of prelates were his patrons. A collection of comedies together with some poems and a theoretical "Prohemio" on comedy was published in 1517 as *Propalladia*. (Literally, "the first things of Pallas," the title suggests that a further volume of works was to follow, but none was published.) The collection was widely read and reprinted a number of times with additional comedies (ultimately six, after the addition of *Calamita*, 1520, and *Aquilina*, 1524).

In the "Prohemio" Torres Naharro defines comedy as an ingenious arrangement of incidents with a happy ending. He follows the five-act structure and divides comedies into two types: *comedias a noticia*, realistic plays about the lower social orders; and *comedias a fantasía*, imaginative plays. To the latter category of romantic comedy belong *Serafina*, *Himenea*, *Calamita*, and *Aquilina*. *Comedia Himenea*, his best play, owes something to LA CELESTINA and was the earliest *capa y espada* (cape and sword) play on the theme of honor; it introduced such conventional characters as the lover (*galán*), the lady (*dama*), and the comic servant (*gracioso*). His realistic *comedias a noticia* are *Comedia Soldadesca* and *Comedia Trinellaria*. His works were placed on the 1559 INDEX LIBRORUM PROHIBITORUM, but an expurgated edition was allowed in 1573.

## Torrigiano, Pietro d'Antonio (1472–1528) *Italian sculptor*
A native of Florence, Torrigiano is notorious for breaking the nose of MICHELANGELO when they were fellow students, an exploit for which he was vilified by CELLINI, VASARI, and other contemporaries. After wandering about Italy for some time as a soldier, Torrigiano visited Antwerp and in about 1511 reached England, where he executed his finest works. The first representative of the Italian Renaissance in English art, he was commissioned to produce the tombs of Henry VII and his wife Elizabeth of York

(1511–18) in Westminster Abbey, and also that of Henry's mother Lady Margaret BEAUFORT. Other works in England included an altar (1517, destroyed in 1641), a medallion of Sir Thomas Lovell, and the tomb of Dr John Yonge (1516; Public Record Office). Moving to Seville during the 1520s, Torrigiano was imprisoned by the Spanish Inquisition and starved himself to death. Works executed in Seville include two polychromed terracottas, *St. Jerome Kneeling in Penitence* and a *Virgin and Child*.

## Toscanelli, Paolo dal Pozzo (1397–1482) *Italian mathematician and geographer*
Toscanelli was educated at Padua and became an official astrologer at Florence, where he moved in a circle of distinguished humanists. He exerted a notable influence on his contemporaries, particularly with his theories about perspective and the possibility of a sea route westward across the Atlantic to China; despite their inaccuracy, his calculations on the latter issue, which overturned those of the geographers of antiquity, are known to have inspired COLUMBUS.

## Tostado, El See MADRIGAL, ALFONSO DE

## Totentanz See DANCE OF DEATH

## Tournèbe, Adrien (Turnebus) (1512–1565) *French humanist scholar*
He was born at Les Andelys, Normandy, and studied at Paris before becoming professor of belles-lettres at Toulouse. Returning to Paris in 1547 he became *lecteur royal* at the Collège de France and in 1552 succeeded Robert ESTIENNE as director of the royal press. In this role he oversaw the production of major new texts of the Greek playwrights Aeschylus and Sophocles (1552–53) and of Homer's *Iliad* (1557). He was also renowned for his knowledge of ancient Greek philosophy, and his extensive interests were demonstrated in his *Adversaria* (1564–65) and in his complete works, published by his son Étienne in 1600.

## tragedy
In the Middle Ages tragedy, like COMEDY, was understood in literary rather than dramatic terms. It concerned the fall of a prince or other great personage from prosperity to adversity and thus illustrated the mutability of FORTUNE. The remedy, most eloquently stated in the *De consolatione philosophiae* of Boethius (c. 480–524 CE), was faith in divine providence. Attachment to worldly things binds man to the wheel of Fortune; awareness of his true end frees him from its inevitable fluctuations. In this thoroughly Christian context, tragedy in the classical mode was not possible. No action was complete in this life but extended beyond; the ultimate outcome was a matter for comedy, in DANTE's sense. Thus even Adam's sin and the fall of man involved the paradox of the *felix culpa* in that

it led to the Incarnation and the redemption of mankind by Christ. Such conceptions continued into the Renaissance and are found, for example, in works by PETRARCH, BOCCACCIO, and CHAUCER.

Toward the beginning of the 16th century, however, there was a renewed, classically inspired interest in tragedy as drama. SENECA whose closet dramas on Greek models had colored the medieval literary view of tragedy, was translated into Italian in 1497. His influence was a dominant strand in Renaissance tragedy and in Elizabethan England was responsible for the vogue of the revenge play. In Italy an improved Latin translation of Aristotle's *Poetics* was published in 1498 and the Greek text in 1508. At the turn of the century appeared the ALDINE PRESS edition of the Greek tragedians, and ERASMUS's Latin translations of Euripides' *Hecuba* and *Iphigenia* were published in Paris in 1506. Giangiorgio TRISSINO's *Sophonisba* (1515; performed 1562) is the earliest Renaissance tragedy in purely classical style, a direct imitation of Greek models. CINTHIO's *Orbecche* (1541) established the Senecan model (a five-act structure with horrendous carnage and appropriate moralizing). Other notable Italian plays were Giovanni Rucellai's *Rosamunda* (1525), ALAMANNI's *Antigone* (1533), SPERONI's *Canace e Macereo* (1542), Pietro ARETINO's *Orazia* (1546), GROTO's *Dalida* (1572), TASSO's *Torrismondo* (1587), and Federico della Valla's *Reina di Scozia* (1595). The pressure of classical imitation restricted the development of Italian tragedy; it failed to achieve successes equal to the less purist (and more popular) English examples and was soon displaced by the taste for tragicomedy and opera.

Although there are no significant French tragedies before the era of Pierre Corneille and Jean Racine, some 16th-century works of note are: Lazare de Baïf's translation of Sophocles' *Electra* (1537), the Bordeaux-based Scot George BUCHANAN's Latin versions of Euripides (*Medea* and *Alcestis*, written c. 1539) and his own *Baptistes sive calumnia* and *Jephthes sive votum* (written c. 1540 and 1542, respectively), Marc-Antoine MURET's *Julius Caesar tragoedia* (1544), Jean Bochetel's translation of Euripides' *Hecuba* (1544), and the first original French tragedy, Étienne JODELLE's *Cléopâtre captive* (acted 1552).

In Spain Jerónimo Bermúdez (c. 1530–99), Cristóbal de Virués (c. 1550–1614), and Lupercio Leonardo de Argensola (1559–1613) wrote Senecan plays. Juan de la CUEVA produced four tragedies, but CERVANTES' *El cerco de Numancia* is the most distinguished example before Lope de VEGA and the heyday of the Spanish theater. In England publication of the historical chronicles of Edward Hall (1548) and Raphael Holinshead (1577), Jasper Heywood's translations of Seneca (from 1559), and Thomas NORTH's version of Plutarch's *Lives* (1579) all stimulated the making of tragedies. The earliest was *Gorboduc* (1561), a Senecan drama by Thomas Sackville and Thomas Norton, which introduced blank verse to the English stage.

Thomas Preston's clumsy and incoherent *Cambises* (1569) was followed by the great tragedies of MARLOWE, KYD's *Spanish Tragedy*, and SHAKESPEARE's masterpieces.

**Further reading:** Gordon Braden, *Renaissance Tragedy and the Senecan Tradition: Anger's Privilege* (New Haven, Conn.: Yale University Press, 1985); Gillian Jondorf, *French Renaissance Tragedy: The Dramatic Word* (Cambridge, U.K.: Cambridge University Press, 1990); Thomas McAlindon, *English Renaissance Tragedy* (Vancouver, Canada: University of British Columbia, 1986).

**translation** The translation of texts was one of the characteristic activities of the Renaissance, enabling a wider range of people than ever before to profit from contact with the literature of ancient Greece and Rome (*see* TRANSLATIONS OF CLASSICAL AUTHORS) and with the major works written in other European tongues (*see* TRANSLATIONS OF CONTEMPORARY AUTHORS). Similarly, the numerous vernacular versions of the Bible (*see* BIBLE, TRANSLATIONS OF) were both motive and product of the religious ferment of the times.

The principles governing translation had been discussed in antiquity—by CICERO, HORACE, and St. Jerome, among others—and the debate was continued by the early humanists. Leonardo BRUNI, one of the busiest of the early translators, expounded his theory of translation in introductions to his Latin versions of Greek masters, and in his *De interpretatione recta* he castigated the medieval translators while attempting a formal justification of his own method. Translators' "apologies" became a standard feature of translations and often throw interesting light on the contemporary status of the author translated as well as on a whole range of linguistic and literary values. Gavin DOUGLAS, for instance, wrote a 500-line prologue to his Scots *Eneados*, in which he expresses some very characteristic preoccupations: extreme reverence for his author ("Virgillis volume maist excellent"), outrage at earlier botched attempts at translation (in this case CAXTON's 1490 *Eneydos*, taken from a French version), and diffidence about his own ability and that of his native "Scottis" tongue ("my rurall vulgar gros") to do justice to the conception and dignity of VIRGIL's poem.

The point about the insufficiency of the VERNACULAR as a vehicle for the thoughts of the great writers of antiquity was one that vexed most early translators. In the long run their efforts, even if they sometimes stretched the language beyond its limits, had a beneficial effect of raising the level of stylistic awareness and of testing the flexibility of a vernacular in a variety of genres. Douglas regrets that he had to resort on occasions to "Sum bastard Latyn, French or Inglys oys [usage]/Quhar scant was Scottis—I had nane other choys." Such necessity became in many instances a virtue, enlarging and enriching the vocabulary of the vernaculars.

Another question frequently raised by translators was that of fidelity to the words of the original versus fidelity to the spirit. Even those translators who professed the greatest reverence for the original frequently indulged in practices that would be frowned upon by modern purists and scholars; for example, Douglas silently incorporates in his text, at points where he thinks his readers may require it, explanatory material taken from BADIUS's prose paraphrase of the poem. Likewise a modern translator would not adopt the cavalier attitude to cuts and omissions displayed by Sir John HARINGTON in his preface to his English *Orlando furioso* (1591), where he admits that he has left out "matters impertinent to us" and "tediouse flatteries of persons that we never heard of."

The status of translation in this period accords with the humanistic and patriotic high-mindedness of most translators. The desire to be useful to one's fellow-citizens and to improve their cultural environment runs strongly through their accounts of their motives; underpinning this was the theory that it was beneficial to copy a good model (*see* CRITICISM, LITERARY). As Harington observed, it was preferable "to be called rather one of the not worst translators then one of the meaner makers." Certainly in the hands of Jacques AMYOT in France or Philemon HOLLAND in England the translator's profession attained a literary dignity that it has seldom, if ever, attained since.

**translations of classical authors** The earlier Renaissance was preoccupied with the need to make Greek literature accessible to a Latined audience, and the first translations reflected this need. They also reflected the intellectual priorities of the first humanists; prose precedes verse, and philosophy and history precede other types of prose. Leonardo BRUNI translated Aristotle's *Economics* (1419/20), *Ethics* (before 1416), and *Politics* (1437), and by 1480 most of the major Aristotelian works had been made available in Latin from the Greek. Translations of PLATO began in 1414, Bruni again leading the way with the *Apology*, and reached a climax with FICINO's comprehensive rendering, completed in 1477. The Greek historians attracted attention as well as the more historical public speeches of Demosthenes. The chief works here were Lorenzo VALLA's incomplete version of Herodotus (1457) and his complete translation of Thucydides (1452). By 1460 all the important Greek historians were available and the indefatigable Bruni had translated *On the Crown*, the *Olynthiacs*, and *On the False Embassy*, among other public speeches in the Demosthenic corpus. Poetry and purely literary texts were less commonly translated. Homer's *Iliad* was translated into Latin prose as far as book 16 by Valla (1442–44). Some of Lucian's *Dialogues* were translated by Bruni and many more by ERASMUS, who also translated *Hecuba* and *Iphigenia* by Euripides (1506).

As the ideas of the Renaissance began to spread they were diffused to an audience which has no access to the classical languages. The prestige of the classics made more people eager to make contact with ancient literature and the increased affluence of the mercantile classes created a market for vernacular translations to satisfy a public who had neither time nor inclination to submit themselves to the long apprenticeship of learning Latin and Greek. A common feature of vernacular translations is the expressed desire of the translators to benefit their audience either in practical ways or by increasing the general level of cultivation in society. The number of vernacular translations in the period before 1620 was huge, and the quality inevitably varied.

Classical works for translation into the vernacular were selected on different criteria from those used by scholars turning Greek into Latin for the benefit of the learned community. Although improvement of the reader was a prime (expressed) aim, entertainment and relaxation were also important. Fidelity to the original was not high on the list of priorities; rather, the aim was to make the ancient author "live" again in the translator's native tongue. Some highly successful translations were not even taken from the original text but from an intervening translation, as was the case with Plutarch's *Lives* (1579) translated by Thomas NORTH from the French version (1559) of Jacques AMYOT.

**translations of contemporary authors** The perceived inferiority of the VERNACULAR among many Renaissance savants dampened the impulse to translate original works in these tongues into other vernaculars. Proficiency in European tongues other than one's own only gradually gained ground as an educational accomplishment, and then it was ambassadors, merchants, and other travelers, rather than scholars, who were responsible for vernacular to vernacular translations. The automatic respect accorded to ancient Latin and Greek authors (*see* TRANSLATIONS OF CLASSICAL AUTHORS) recommended them to the translators' attention, while a contemporary writer, however esteemed in his own country, might be suspect on religious, political, or moral grounds.

The international organization of the BOOK TRADE enabled books, especially in Latin, to circulate easily throughout Europe, and popular and controversial contemporary texts like Erasmus's *Encomium Moriae* (*see* PRAISE OF FOLLY, THE), More's UTOPIA, and Calvin's INSTITUTES were quickly translated. Sometimes a vernacular work was translated into Latin to increase its readership, as in the case of Sebastian BRANT's *Das Narrenschyff* (1494); Jakob Locher made a free Latin translation (*Stultifera Navis*, 1497), which was again freely interpreted by Alexander Barclay in his *Ship of Fools* (1509). By such processes Renaissance translations sometimes came to bear little resemblance to their purported originals.

Vernacular to vernacular translations were a product both of the international book trade and of fashions in travel. The young Englishmen who visited Italy in the second half of the 16th century, for instance, promoted an interest in the Italian language and literature, which manifested itself in translations of works ranging from bawdy tales to moral tracts. Books on morals and manners seem to have achieved a particularly wide circulation in translation. Castiglione's *Il cortegiano* (1528; *see* COURTIER, THE) progressed quickly into Spanish (1534) and French (1538), then English (1561) and Polish (1566), and a Latin version in 1571. A trilingual (Latin, French, Spanish) version of *Il Galateo* (1558) by DELLA CASA appeared in 1598. Guevara's *Reloj de príncipes* (1539) spawned French, Italian, and English versions within two decades of publication. The admiration accorded to Ariosto's OR-LANDO FURIOSO as the preeminent epic of the early Renaissance is reflected in numerous partial or complete translations: into Spanish (1549), a French prose version (1555), Latin extracts (1588), English (1591; *see* HARING-TON, SIR JOHN), Dutch (1615), and German (1636), among others. Two Spanish prose narratives that attracted the translators and became influential throughout Europe in their respective genres were the pastoral romance LA DIANA (1559) by Jorge de Montemayor and Cervantes's novel DON QUIXOTE.

See also: TRANSLATION

**transport** See COMMUNICATIONS

**transubstantiation** The Roman Catholic doctrine that, at a priest's consecrating words, the deep reality (the "substances") of the bread and wine in the Eucharist becomes the body and blood of Christ, although the appearance (or "accidents") of the elements remains unchanged. The doctrine became a matter of fierce controversy in the 16th century, when it was repudiated as unscriptural and idolatrous by leading reformers. In its place LUTHER taught a relatively conservative doctrine of "consubstantiation," in which the substances of the bread and wine are held to co-exist with the substances of Christ's body and blood. The Swiss Protestant ZWINGLI went much further, insisting that the Eucharistic elements are mere symbols, while Calvinists and most Anglicans held an intermediate position, in which Christ was considered to be spiritually but not physically present (*see* REAL PRESENCE). As the 16th century progressed, the Catholic Church increased its emphasis on the importance of transubstantiation, as it provided a unifying belief, distinguishing Roman faith from Protestant objections. Pius IV underlined papal commitment to transubstantiation in a Bull of 1565.

**travel** Travel during the Renaissance was essentially a serious matter, undertaken with a definite goal in mind and, because of the many perils and discomforts that beset it, never embarked on lightly. The concept of travel for leisure or pleasure-seeking was unheard-of, although there is evidence, increasing toward the end of the period, of a minority for whom the experience of travel itself and the acquisition of knowledge about foreign places and people were the paramount objectives. The Renaissance coincided with the start of the great age of European EX-PLORATION, but of course not all journeys were undertaken as trail-blazing voyages of discovery; travel in more or less known lands—Europe, the Mediterranean basin, the Near East—also played an important part in the fabric of Renaissance experience.

Travelers' narratives of the late Middle Ages and Renaissance are the work of the very small number of people who had both the incentive and the financial means to travel as well as some specific purpose in mind in writing up their experiences. There were four main categories of motive: military, religious, mercantile, and diplomatic. A war or crusade was obviously an occasion that took large numbers of men far from home, but the ordinary illiterate soldier left no written record. PILGRIMAGE was another occasion for travel, and here there are a number of surviving accounts written primarily for the edification of the pious at home but often also containing valuable information on travel conditions en route to the major pilgrim destinations of Rome, Jerusalem, and Santiago de Compostela. Pilgrimage is also significant in that it was almost the only respectable pretext on which a woman could travel. Within Europe and the Near East, trade and commerce were prime motives for travel, as they were for exploration further afield. As far as DIPLOMACY is concerned, papal envoys and other ecclesiastics had always traversed Christendom on Church business, but in the Renaissance they were joined by a growing number of secular legations.

Long-distance land travel in Europe still relied to some degree on the old network of Roman roads, now much decayed. In a feudal society the lack of any centralized body charged with repairing roads meant that the local peasantry had to be coerced into doing the work as a form of forced labor. The generally poor condition of the roads meant that wheeled traffic was a rarity, and most travelers relied on horses to cover any significant distance, while the poorest walked; goods were mainly carried on mules. Rivers were often a major barrier; to cross them the choice lay between narrow wooden bridges or ferries behind which the travelers' horses and pack animals had to swim. Mountains were an even more serious obstacle; the passes of the Alps had a fearsome reputation for avalanches, storms, and robbers, though the plight of travelers was somewhat eased by the building of hospices on major routes such as the St. Gotthard and Great St. Bernard passes. Different countries and localities had different measures of distance, so journey lengths were generally reckoned in hours or days. An official courier on a main route with regular changes of horses could make much better time than an ordinary traveler relying entirely upon his own beast.

Travel by water had its own set of drawbacks. Cramped and unhygienic conditions were unavoidable on the tiny ships, even for those who could afford to buy space in a cabin. Adverse weather conditions could cause lengthy delays and diversions, and the onset of winter generally meant that no commercial shipping left harbor for several months. Shipwreck was an ever-present possibility, and it even spawned a subgenre of Portuguese literature known as *história trágico-marítima* after the title of the collection of 16th-century pamphlets on such disasters published in Lisbon in 1735. During the 16th century pirates operating in the Adriatic and out of the ports of Muslim North Africa became an increasing hazard for Mediterranean mariners.

Arterial rivers such as the Po and Danube had a limited usefulness. Although progress downstream was easy, the return journey against the current was slow and laborious. On some rivers, such as the Rhine, rapids and narrows made matters even worse, and river traffic was also vulnerable to the predations of the bishops and feudal lords whose territories bordered the river, enabling them to set up toll points, particularly at places where chains could be slung from tower to tower across the stream to halt the boats.

Obtaining funds abroad was a problem that was gradually eased as banks and the larger trading companies developed networks of branches and agents across Europe. In the early 14th century, for example, the bank run by the Florentine BARDI FAMILY had branches from Palermo to Bruges and London to Jerusalem. Since carrying a large amount of gold or silver was both impractical and unwise, travelers before setting out had to organize letters of credit that could be presented at places along their route. From the 15th century onward states often insisted that their citizens obtain letters of passport from a competent authority, giving permission to travel abroad, and these could also act as a safe-conduct.

With the advent of printing, local and informal sources of advice for travelers were supplemented by written texts. The market for information in the vernacular on pilgrimage routes is shown by a number of 15th- and 16th-century publications to meet this demand: *Die Walfahrt und Strass zu sant Jacob* (Strasbourg, 1495) on the Santiago de Compostela route and the London printer/publisher Wynkyn de Worde's *Information for Pilgrims into the Holy Land* (1498) are two early examples of this proto-guidebook genre. *La Guide des Chemins de France* (1552–53), a brainchild of Charles ESTIENNE, appeared under varying titles in a number of editions in the second half of the 16th century and into the 17th. The availability of such practical publications by the early 17th century is assumed in BACON's advice in his essay "Of Travel," that the traveler should "carry with him...some card or book describing the country where he travelleth."

More generalized guidance was made available to English travelers in *Certaine briefe and speciall instructions for Gentlemen, merchants, students, Souldiers, marriners ... employed in service abrode or anie way occasioned to converse in the kingdomes and governements of forren Princes* (1589), the translation by clergyman Philip Jones of a Latin tract by Albertus Meierus, and in Sir Robert Dallington's *A Method for Travell: Shewed by Taking the View of France. As it Stoode in ... 1598* (1605). An indication of the growing tendency to regard travel as an educational experience is the "De Ratione cum fructu peregrinandi" (1578) by Justus LIPSIUS, translated and augmented by Sir John Stradling as *A Direction for Travailers* (1592) for the benefit of the young Earl of Bedford who was about to embark on a tour abroad. The sour Elizabethan Puritan comments on young gentlemen who went abroad and came back dandified, their heads filled with affectation or Roman Catholicism, indicate that not all youthful travelers heeded sage advice.

Although there had always been travelers, such as CYRIAC OF ANCONA, who used their journeys on other business to observe matters that interested them, the concept of travel for intellectual stimulus and personal gratification is best exemplified toward the end of the Renaissance period. Expanding horizons had created a readership for travel narratives, and some early 17th-century British travelers, notably Thomas CORYATE, seem to have embarked on their journeys mainly out of a sense of adventure—and the idea that their experiences could be turned into good copy. In his *Totall Discourse of the Rare Adventures and Painfull Peregrinations of Long Nineteene Yeares Travayles from Scotland to the most Famous Kingdomes in Europe, Asia and Affrica* (1632), William Lithgow (1582–1645), another eccentric traveler, claims to have walked 36,000 miles, while the *Itinerary* (1617) of Fynes MORYSON is an entertaining assemblage of observations, anecdotes, and vigorously expressed opinions masquerading as a guidebook.

**Further reading:** Frans C. Amelinckx and Joyce N. Megay (eds), *Travel, Quest, and Pilgrimage as a Literary Theme: Studies in Honor of Reino Virtanen* (Ann Arbor, Mich.: Society of Spanish and Spanish American Studies, 1978); Daniel Carey (ed.), *Asian Travel in the Renaissance* (Oxford, U.K.: Blackwell, 2003); Andrew Hadfield, *Literature, Travel, and Colonial Writing in the English Renaissance* (Oxford, U.K.: Clarendon Press, 1999); Antoni Mączak, *Travel in Early Modern Europe*, transl. Ursula Phillips (Cambridge, U.K.: Polity Press and Cambridge, Mass.: Blackwell, 1995); Christian K. Zacher, *Curiosity and Pilgrimage: The Literature of Discovery in Fourteenth-Century England* (Baltimore, Md: Johns Hopkins University Press, 1976).

**Traversari, Ambrogio** (Fra Ambrogio, Ambrose of Camaldoli) (c. 1386–1439) *Italian humanist*
He entered the Camaldolese Order in 1400, at the monastery of Sta. Maria degli Angioli at Florence. From 1431 he was general of the order. At the Council of FLORENCE he strove to promote the union between the Eastern and Western Churches. A scholar of refined taste and the owner of a renowned collection of Greek patristic manuscripts, he translated many of the Greek Fathers into Latin. He supported the movement within the Roman Catholic Church for the reform of abuses. Although never canonized, he is commemorated on 20 November. His letters and speeches were published in 1759.

**Trecento** (Italian, "three hundred") The period of artistic and cultural development in Italy during the 14th century. This period was a prelude to the Renaissance of the following two centuries and witnessed the gradual transition from Gothic ideals, despite the disruption caused by the Black Death in 1348. Focused upon such cultural centers as Florence, Siena, and Venice, the Trecento saw the emergence of DANTE, the chief literary figure of the time, the dominance of the PISANO family in the field of sculpture, and the influence of DUCCIO, Simone MARTINI, the LORENZETTI brothers, and GIOTTO and his followers over painted art, most profoundly in their emancipation from Byzantine tradition.

**Tremellius, John** (1510–1580) *Hebrew scholar and reformer*
Born a Jew in Ferrara, he converted to Catholicism (1538) under the influence of Cardinal POLE. He then came under the influence of PETER MARTYR and became a Protestant, fleeing to Basle (1542) and then to Strasbourg and England, where he became King's Reader of Hebrew at Cambridge (1549) and made the acquaintance of Matthew PARKER. The accession of the Catholic Mary I (1553) caused Tremellius to return to Europe where, after extensive traveling and a brief period of imprisonment, he settled at Metz. He spent his last years teaching Hebrew at Sedan, where he died. Tremellius's great work was the translation of the Bible from Hebrew and Syriac into Latin (1569–79). Despite its errors, this became the standard Latin translation used by the reformers to replace the Vulgate.

**Trent, Council of** The ecumenical council of the Roman Catholic Church, convened at Trent (Trento) in northern Italy, which met in three sessions (1545–47, 1551–52, 1562–63) and ushered in the COUNTER-REFORMATION. There had long been calls for an ecumenical council to reform abuses in the Church, but early 16th-century popes had been reluctant to call such a council. There were many reasons for this reluctance. Reforming councils in the late 14th and early 15th centuries had ventured to

limit the power of the popes. (They had achieved this by voting in "nations," according to which the "Italian nation" was always outvoted, even though the Italian bishops present outnumbered those from the "French" and "German" "nations.") More immediately, the Protestant revolt made the situation still more difficult. Emperor CHARLES V wanted desperately to settle the religious question in the empire, as the Lutheran heresy there sapped his power. (The Lutheran princes were always interested in limiting the power of the emperor.) Charles was willing to compromise and in fact, in the 1548 Interim of AUGSBURG, he offered such concessions as clerical marriage and Communion in both kinds (bread and wine) to the Protestant negotiators. In a sense, it was in the interest of Rome to call the reforming council, lest the emperor call a German council and settle the religious question in his domains without taking into account the interests of the papacy. Nor did the French king have much interest in backing the papal call for a council, for he feared the collusion of pope and emperor. The Gallican Church always strove to be independent of the papacy, so much so that there was a point in mid-century when the French king almost followed the example of HENRY VIII in breaking with Rome. Rome itself was not overly anxious to compromise with the Protestants, a reluctance that frustrated the emperor.

Finally, however, the council was called, to be held in the small city of Trent. The first session began on December 13, 1545. Few delegates attended this first meeting; there were only 31 bishops and 50 theologians and canonists in attendance. At one time or another during the three sessions of the council, 270 bishops attended. There were 187 Italians, 31 Spaniards, 26 French, and only two German bishops, figures which might lead one to think that the pope could easily have had his way, since voting was by individual bishop rather than by "nation." However, the Milanese and Neapolitan bishops were constrained to some degree by the wishes of their temporal overlord, Charles V, while the Venetian bishops shared the strong antipapal feeling of Venice. In the third session (1562–63), the very orthodox and unbending Spanish bishops strove to work as a disciplined group, even though they were outnumbered. They resisted any doctrinal novelty and they tried to make the episcopate and the council independent of the pope. Their goal was to allow the pope a primacy of honor but not of power, and they intended to shelter the Spanish national Church from direct papal interference. In addition, the 20 or so French bishops, invested with a Gallican spirit, were intent upon safeguarding the independence of their national Church. However, since all these groups conflicted with each other, the pope eventually prevailed.

Notwithstanding these contradictory forces, the Council of Trent was able to accomplish a great deal. While in the second and third decades of the 16th century it had not always been clear what was Protestant doctrine and what Roman Catholic and what clergyman or layman belonged to which confession, the doctrinal decrees of the first two sessions left no doubts on these questions. Henceforth Roman Catholicism could be readily distinguished from Protestantism, as the Tridentine definitions on Scripture, justification, and sacraments indicate. Whereas the Protestant churches claimed there was only one authority—Holy Scripture—Trent declared that there were two: Scripture and the teaching tradition of the Church whose *magisterium* was embodied in the papacy. While Trent did not forbid vernacular editions of the Bible, it did declare the Latin Vulgate to be the only authentic text and stressed the right of the *magisterium* "to judge of the true sense and interpretation of Holy Scripture." On the question of justification, while Protestants claimed that people are justified by faith alone (*see* JUSTIFICATION BY FAITH) without the works of the Mosaic law, the Council of Trent asserted that people are saved by faith in combination with good works. Regarding sacraments, the Protestant churches held that there were only two (baptism and the Eucharist) and that they were not vehicles of grace; Trent reaffirmed the seven sacraments (baptism, penance, the Eucharist, confirmation, holy orders, marriage, and extreme unction) as vehicles of saving grace. Finally, the last session of the council redefined and reaffirmed almost every belief that such humanist scholars as ERASMUS had considered superstitious (and therefore not obligatory for the believer): the making of vows, belief in Purgatory, the invocation of saints, the veneration of relics, and the giving of INDULGENCES. On November 13, 1564 (the year that John Calvin died), the pope summed up the Roman Catholic faith as taught at Trent in the Creed of Pope Pius IV. This was a fitting capstone to the Council, as it was truly a victory for the papacy and a closing off of all possibility of negotiated compromise with Protestantism for the next 400 years.

See also: HYMNODY; LITURGY

Further reading: Robert Birely, *The Refashioning of Catholicism, 1450–1700: A Reassessment of the Counter-Reformation* (Washington, D.C.: Catholic University of America Press, 1999); Hubert Jedin, *Crisis and Closure of the Council of Trent* (London: Sheed & Ward, 1967).

**Tribolo, Niccolò (Niccolo de' Pericoli) (1500–1550)** *Italian sculptor*
He was born in Florence, where much of his work is to be seen. Tribolo was influenced by MICHELANGELO, of whose works he made copies (Bargello). His own most successful genre was fountain statuary, such as the fountain of Hercules and Cacus at the suburban Villa di Castello (Florence), where Tribolo also laid out the gardens (c. 1540).

**Tribunal of Blood** The popular name for the Council of Troubles, established in 1567 by the Spanish governor of the Netherlands, the duke of ALBA, to try the cases of those suspected of treason during the Dutch revolt (*see* NETHERLANDS, REVOLT OF THE). In the next six years it heard some 12,203 cases, producing 9000 convictions and just over 1000 executions. The slaughter has been exaggerated by propaganda, but fear of the tribunal did drive many rebels and Calvinists out of the Netherlands, 60,000 (2% of the population) fleeing during Alba's rule. The tribunal was abolished by his successor, Don Luis de Requesens, in 1573 in an attempt to conciliate the Dutch.

**Tridentine** Of, or relating to, the Council of TRENT.

**trigonometry** The main achievements of Renaissance mathematicians in the field of trigonometry were twofold. Their first task involved the identification and definition of the main trigonometric ratios. Although trigonometry was developed by ancient Greek mathematicians, it was in fact based on quite different presuppositions. The Greeks were interested in establishing tables of chords. Abandoning this approach, Renaissance mathematicians based their work on the assumption that the trigonometric ratios could be expressed as functions of angles. The first modern attempt to develop trigonometry in this way, though restricted to sines and cosines, was made by REGIOMONTANUS in *De triangulis* (1464; published in 1533). The system was extended to the other trigonometric ratios by RHETICUS in his *Canon doctrinae triangulorum* (1551). The success of this program imposed on mathematicians the second task of constructing the appropriate tables. After more than a decade of intense labor Rheticus succeeded in completing detailed tables of all six trigonometric functions. They were published posthumously in his *Opus Palatinum de triangulis* (1596).

**Trissino, Giangiorgio (1478–1550)** *Italian classicist, critic, dramatist, and poet*
Born to a patrician family in Vicenza, Trissino studied Greek in Milan (1506) and went to the court of Ferrara in 1512. He attended meetings of the Orti Oricellari in Florence in 1513 and the following year moved to the court of Pope Leo X in Rome. He was highly regarded by successive popes, who entrusted him with several important diplomatic missions.

*Sophonisba* (1515; first performed 1562), inspired by an episode in the Roman historian Livy, led the way in introducing a vernacular tragedy based directly on Greek models and Aristotelian principles, instead of on SENECA. Written in blank verse, it was also structurally close to Greek tragedy in alternating episode and chorus and in maintaining the unities of action and time. His comedy *I simillimi* (*The Look-Alikes*; 1548) drew on PLAUTUS's *Menaechmi* but also imitated the Old Comedy of Aristophanes in structure. His blank-verse epic in 27 books, *La Italia liberata da' Gotthi* (1547–48), recounting the Byzantine general Belisarius's sixth-century conquest of Italy under Justinian, aimed at a purely Homeric style. Trissino also wrote Pindaric odes, the first imitation of a Horatian ode in Italian, and a number of Petrarchan poems.

Though influential examples of the careful imitation of classical models, Trissino's drama and poetry are perhaps of less interest today than his critical and linguistic works. These include an *Epistola* to Clement VII (1524) on spelling reform; the treatises *Grammatichetta*, *Dubbii grammaticali*, and *Il castellano* (all 1529); and the important critical work, *La poetica* (1529). Trissino also translated Dante's *De vulgari eloquentia* (1529), finding in it support for his own views in the QUESTIONE DELLA LINGUA controversy, in which he took a leading role. With CASTIGLIONE, he favored an eclectic solution to the problem of a national language.

**Trithemius, Johann** (Johann Heidenberg) (1462–1516)
*German reformer and scholar*
He took his Latin name from his native town of Trittenheim. An associate of John Camerarius at Heidelberg, he had heard Erasmus lecture at Cologne and was influenced by the ideas of Christian humanism. In 1485 he became abbot of the Benedictine monastery at Sponheim and in 1506 abbot of St. James, Wurzburg, where he died. Trithemius was a leader of the Catholic reformation advocated by Nicholas CUSANUS. He wrote an ecclesiastical history and planned a history of Germany for which he collected many documents. Unfortunately his historical works are unreliable, though the information in *Catologus illustrium virorum Germaniae* (1491) is more trustworthy. His *Polygraphia* (1518) is a pioneering work on CRYPTOGRAPHY.

**Troubles, Council of** See TRIBUNAL OF BLOOD

**Troy, legend of** The stories connected with the Trojan war, as originally related by HOMER and VIRGIL and expanded by the pseudo-historical medieval authors known as Dares Phrygius and Dictys Cretensis. The latter two purported to have been participants in the events leading to the fall of Troy, and were consequently highly regarded as sources in the Middle Ages. Hints in them were taken up by poets such as Benoît de Ste.-Maure, author of the 12th-century French *Roman de Troie* and the first to treat at any length the love story of Troilus and Cressida. This story was later detached from the cycle and treated as an autonomous narrative by, among others, BOCCACCIO, CHAUCER, the Scots poet Robert Henryson, and SHAKESPEARE. In the 13th century the Italian Guido delle Colonne made a Latin prose version of Benoît's *Roman*, in which form the expanded Troy legend circulated widely in the Renaissance.

The myth that refugees from Troy or their descendants founded kingdoms and dynasties all over Europe was a potent and attractive one for Renaissance writers eager to compliment their patrons by attributing to them a venerable genealogy (*see also* ARTHUR, LEGEND OF; CHARLEMAGNE, LEGEND OF). In France, the imaginary Francus the Trojan had long been claimed as the progenitor of the French race. ARIOSTO traces the lineage of Bradamante, the fictional ancestress of his ESTE patrons, to "The noble blood that came of ancient Troy" (*Orlando furioso* III 18, Harington's translation), and John Lydgate in his *Troy-book* (written 1412–20) was one of numerous English poets to describe a Trojan settlement of Britain under Brutus, the grandson of Virgil's hero Aeneas, founder of Rome. In these stories London is often referred to as "Troynovant" or "New Troy."

**Tudor, house of** The family of Welsh origin that ruled England from 1485 to 1603 and England and Ireland from 1540 to 1603. Owen Tudor (c. 1400–61), who married (c. 1429) Henry V's widow, Catherine of Valois, established the family's fortunes. Their son, Edmund Tudor (c. 1430–56), was created earl of Richmond by his half-brother Henry VI and married (1455) Margaret BEAUFORT, a Lancastrian descendant of Edward III. Their son, later Henry VII, claimed the English throne through his mother, and seized it after invading England and defeating the Yorkist king, Richard III, at Bosworth (1485). Henry VII (reigned 1485–1509) married Elizabeth of York to unite the Yorkist and Lancastrian branches of the royal family. Their son, HENRY VIII, broke with Rome and initiated the English Reformation. During the reign (1547–53) of his young son EDWARD VI, Protestant doctrine was established in England, and despite the attempts of Henry's elder daughter, MARY I (reigned 1553–58), to restore Catholicism to England, the Protestant settlement was concluded by the last Tudor monarch, ELIZABETH I (reigned 1558–1603). The Elizabethan age saw the high point of the English Renaissance, which had begun during Henry VIII's reign. It included the triumphant victory over Catholic Spain and the continuation of the overseas maritime exploration, which led to the development of the British empire.

**Tudor style** The prevalent architectural and decorative style in England in the period 1485–1558. The reign (1485–1509) of the first Tudor monarch, Henry VII, brought the stability that enabled his son and grandchildren to preside over a resurgence of interest in the arts (*see also* ELIZABETHAN STYLE), and Renaissance influences, although often in misunderstood or debased forms, began to percolate across the English Channel during the early 16th century. Foreign workmen produced some notable artefacts in the new style; one example is the Westminster Abbey tomb of Henry VII himself, commissioned from the Florentine TORRIGIANO in 1512. The availability of ornamental prints, courtesy of the Continental printing presses, ensured that new designs from Italy or northern Europe made an increasing impact upon native craftsmen.

Ecclesiastical architecture, which after the 1520s was affected by the turmoil of the Reformation, continued to favor the Perpendicular style, the final phase of English Gothic. Domestic architecture, on the other hand, saw major developments, notably the increasingly widespread use of brick, often in conjunction with timber framing and with the bricks laid in herringbone or other decorative patterns. Great houses no longer needed to be heavily fortified, so attention could be paid to aesthetic considerations in their construction. Battlements reduced to ornaments and large, elaborately decorated chimneys, often formed in a barleysugar twist, were new exterior features, while decorative fireplace surrounds and wooden paneling, carved in the shallow pattern known as linenfold, were innovations inside. The shallow, four-centered arch was the characteristic shape for doorways, and oriel windows grew in size and prominence. Compton Wynyates in Warwickshire and the parts of HAMPTON COURT PALACE built by Cardinal WOLSEY for HENRY VIII are important examples of Tudor buildings. Nothing now survives of the house begun in 1544 for Henry Howard, Earl of SURREY, which is claimed to have been the first in pure Italian classical style in England.

**Further reading:** Maurice Howard, *The Early Tudor Country House: Architecture and Politics 1490–1550* (London: George Philip, 1987).

**Tuileries** A former palace on the right bank of the Seine in Paris. Named after the tile factories (*tuileries*) that existed in the area in the 13th century, the Tuileries palace was commissioned in 1564 by CATHERINE DE' MEDICI and originally designed by the famous architect Philibert DELORME. Jean BULLANT and Jacques DUCERCEAU also worked on the palace, which gradually became recognized as the source of a national style of decoration. As a royal residence the Tuileries became the target of rioters during the French Revolution. In 1871 the palace was burnt down during the Commune of Paris. The site is now occupied by the Tuileries gardens.

**Tunis, battle of** (July 1535) A Christian victory over the Ottoman Turks in North Africa. In 1534 the admiral of the Turkish fleet, the corsair BARBAROSSA, captured Tunis from its Moorish king. This posed a threat to Spanish provinces in Italy, and Emperor CHARLES V, as king of Spain, resolved to meet the danger decisively. Crossing in person to North Africa with a large army, and with Andrea DORIA as admiral of his fleet, he took Tunis by storm and restored its former ruler as his vassal. This was regarded as a great Christian triumph over the infidel, but it failed to check continued growth of Turkish naval power. Tunis was reconquered by the Turks in 1547.

**Tunstall, Cuthbert** (1474–1559) *English bishop and diplomat*
Tunstall was educated at Oxford, Cambridge, and Padua and became a scholar in theology, law, Greek, and Hebrew. His diplomatic career began in the service of Henry VIII as ambassador at Brussels, where he became friends with Thomas MORE and ERASMUS. In 1522 he became bishop of London before succeeding Thomas WOLSEY as bishop of Durham in 1530. Although Tunstall wrote a number of tracts in Latin defending traditional Catholic dogma and opposed the Protestant reforms, he adopted a position of passive obedience toward them. During the reign of Edward VI he was imprisoned and deprived of his bishopric, but he was reinstated in 1554 under the Catholic Mary I. Tunstall refused to take the Oath of Supremacy under Elizabeth I, was deprived of his bishopric, and interned at Lambeth Palace, where he died soon afterward.

**Tura, Cosimo (Il Cosmè)** (1430–1495) *Italian painter*
He was the founder and the first great artist of the school of his native Ferrara. As court painter to the ESTE dukes he is well known for the series of wall paintings depicting the magnificence of court life with which he decorated the Palazzo Schifanoia in Ferrara (1469–70). It is thought he was trained by Francesco SQUARCIONE in Padua and the sculptured style of his figures show this influence, as well as that of MANTEGNA and PIERO DELLA FRANCESCA. His paintings, such as *Primavera* (c. 1460), an allegorical figure from his early period, a *St. Jerome* from his later years (both National Gallery, London), and the *St. George* organ shutters (1469; Museo del Duomo, Ferrara) illustrate the personal style he developed within the tradition of Squarcione. He used careful detail and rich metallic colors to produce what is often described as a mannered and nervous quality.

**Further reading:** Stephen Campbell, *Cosme Tura of Ferrara: Style, Politics, and the Renaissance City, 1450–1495* (New Haven, Conn.: Yale University Press, 1998).

**Turks** See OTTOMAN TURKS

**Turner, William** (1508–1568) *English divine, physician, and naturalist*
His *New Herball*, published in London (1551) and Cologne (1562–68), was written in English for the benefit of ignorant physicians. Its woodcuts, taken from a 1545 edition of FUCHS's herbal, reflect Turner's intention of making known the work of the Continental botanists he met during his exile in Mary I's reign, which had been necessitated by his belligerent Protestantism.

**Tyard, Pontus de** (1521–1605) *French poet*
From the family château in Bissy, his birthplace, Tyard combined the careers of poet, scholar, ecclesiastic, courtier, and epicure. An associate of Maurice SCÈVE's

group of Lyonnaise poets and a member of the PLÉIADE, he produced the first volume of his *Erreurs amoureuses*, containing some of the earliest examples of the French sonnet, in 1549; the influence of RONSARD is discernible in *Le Livre des vers lyriques* (1555). Tyard's prose works, which include a series of treatises on poetry (*Solitaires*), "Discours de la vérité de divination par astrologie," and writings on astronomy and philosophy, were published in the encyclopedic *Discours philosophiques* (1587). In 1578 Tyard was appointed bishop of Chalon-sur-Saône; his defense of the king during the latter years of the Wars of Religion caused him to suffer at the hands of the ultra-Catholic party and he resigned his office in 1594.

**Tychonic system** The cosmological system devised by Tycho BRAHE. In 1543 COPERNICUS had argued that, contrary to the PTOLEMAIC SYSTEM, the earth and all other celestial bodies orbited around the sun. Brahe rejected the crystalline spheres of antiquity on the ground that comets seemed to pass unobstructed through them, but was equally dismissive of the heliocentric system of Copernicus. The earth's supposed solar orbit, Brahe argued, should lead to a detectable displacement (parallax) in the position of a number of stars. Failing to detect any such effect he sought for an alternative system. The resulting geoheliocentric compromise (see illustration) proposed that the planets and the fixed stars did in fact orbit the sun, but that the sun in turn moved around the earth. Brahe's system was first revealed in his *De mundi aetherei recentioribus phaenominis* (1588). The system found little support, receiving its final formulation in the *Almagestum novum* (1651) of G. B. Riccioli (1598–1671).

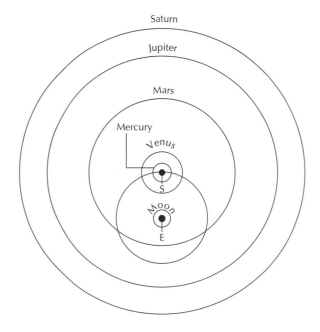

**Tychonic system**

**Tye, Christopher** (c. 1497–1572/3) *English composer*
Little is known of Tye's early life, although he was probably a chorister at Cambridge (1508–1513), where he later received his doctorate in music (1537). He was the choirmaster at Ely cathedral (1541–1561) and was a member of Edward VI's Chapel Royal. He may have been Edward's music teacher and dedicated to him his *Acts of the Apostles* (1553), metrical settings of Bible texts. Tye was ordained in 1560 and in the following year he became Rector of Doddington, Cambridgeshire. After Thomas TALLIS, his contemporary, Tye is the most important contributor to the sacred music of early Reformation England, assimilating Continental structural principles into English music. His most important Latin work is the Mass *Euge bone*, widely regarded as one of the great masterpieces of English Renaissance music. He is credited as the first important early English composer of instrumental chamber music; 31 of his compositions have survived.

**Tyndale, William** (c. 1494–1536) *English translator of the Bible and religious reformer*
Tyndale studied in both Oxford and Cambridge before returning to preach in his native Gloucestershire. Having conceived his project of an English translation of the Bible, and receiving no encouragement from the English ecclesiastical authorities, Tyndale retired abroad, first to Hamburg (1524), and later to Wittenberg, where he met LUTHER. The publication of his New Testament (completed at Worms in 1526) increased the hostility of the English bishops, who made repeated efforts to have him arrested. Tyndale spent most of his remaining years in Antwerp, revising his translation and publishing several other important works, including *The Obedience of a Christian Man* (1528), which is his major constitutional and theological treatise, an attack on Cardinal WOLSEY and the royal divorce (*The Practice of Prelates*, 1530), and a defense against Sir Thomas MORE. He was arrested at Vilvorde near Brussels in 1535 and executed the following year.

> **See also:** BIBLE, TRANSLATIONS OF
>
> **Further reading:** Brian Moynahan, *God's Bestseller: William Tyndale, Thomas More, and the Writing of the English Bible* (New York: St. Martin's Press, 2003).

**typography** The design of metal types for PRINTING at first closely followed prevailing manuscript trends (*see* CALLIGRAPHY). Thus, the first types to be cut for German printers such as GUTENBERG were based on the gothic script that had evolved in northern Europe from the script known as Carolingian minuscule. These types formed the gothic or black-letter family of types. In Italy Renaissance scribes practiced a more rounded variant of Carolingian minuscule, which became the source for the roman family of types. The first successful roman fount was introduced by Nicolas JENSON in Venice in 1470; it was revived in the

USA in 1915 under the name of Centaur. Also in Venice, Aldus MANUTIUS commissioned a highly successful roman face which he used in 1495 to publish a tract by Pietro BEMBO; the 20th-century adaptation of the face, still called Bembo, is much used in modern bookwork. Another beautiful and long-lived Aldine type design, a recutting of the face used in the Bembo tract, is Poliphilus, called after one of Aldus's most famous publications, the HYPNEROTO-MACHIA POLIFILI (1499). The third family of typefaces, the italic, was also an Aldine introduction (1501); with its numerous ligatures, it was an attempt to imitate yet another form of humanist script. A rather different italic fount, with numerous modern descendants, was designed in 1523 by the papal calligrapher Ludovico Arrighi, who derived it from the chancery hand of the papal scribes. After Arrighi's death in the Sack of Rome (1527), the Roman printer Antonio Blado (1490–1567) developed the simpler of Arrighi's designs, which had first appeared in 1526; this face, now called Blado, is still used as the italic counterpart of Poliphilus.

Aldine roman and italic types were greatly admired and imitated with differing degrees of competence all over Italy and France. Typeface usage varied from country to country; in 16th-century Italy, for instance, whole books were often printed in italic, but elsewhere, as in modern practice, italic faces were mainly used as differentiation types. In northern Europe black-letter founts remained the norm for the early years of the 16th century but the greater legibility of roman ensured its ultimate predominance. This came about at different speeds in different countries: in England, for example, works in Latin were often printed in roman, but those in the vernacular were generally in black-letter until the 1580s, after which roman gradually superseded it except in ballads and inexpensive prose items, which continued to be printed in black-letter until the mid-17th century. In Germany black-letter fonts remained the standard throughout the period, although as early as 1467 the Strasbourg printer Adolph Rusch had used his own pure roman type for the first printed edition of Rabanns Maurus's encyclopedia *De universo*.

**Further reading:** Harry Carter, *A View of Early Typography Up To About 1600* (Princeton, N.J.: Princeton Architectural Press, repr. 2002); Daniel Berkeley Updike, *Printing Types: Their History, Forms and Use* (New York: Dover, 1980; repr. Oak Knoll, 2001).

# U

**Uccello, Paolo** (Paolo di Dono) (1397–1475) *Italian painter*

A Florentine by birth, Uccello was praised by Cristoforo LANDINO in 1481 for his skill in foreshortening and for his understanding of the technique of PERSPECTIVE. Uccello's few surviving works demonstrate an interest in the innovations of early Quattrocento artists, especially foreshortening and BRUNELLESCHI's scientific perspective, but united with a strong personal taste for decorative patterns and repeated colors.

Uccello is documented as a youthful assistant to GHIBERTI in the workshop creating the north doors for the Florentine Baptistery; he was admitted as a painter to the Compagnia di San Luca in 1414 and the Arte dei Medici e Speziali in 1415, and worked as a mosaicist at San Marco in Venice in the late 1420s. His stylistic development is exemplified in the *terra verde* Old Testament frescoes of the cloister of Sta. Maria Novella, Florence, which were executed in two campaigns; the earlier paintings (c. 1420s) are still in the International Gothic style, while the later *Flood* (c. 1440s) demonstrates a fascination with Renaissance perspective, foreshortening, and complex drawing problems that threaten to submerge the theme.

In 1436 the supervisors of Florence cathedral commissioned Uccello to execute a frescoed EQUESTRIAN MONUMENT to Sir John Hawkwood (died 1394), the English condottiere who had been employed by the Florentines; Uccello had to repaint his first version, perhaps because it emphasized the foreshortened illusion of the tomb, horse, and rider, as seen from below, at the expense of the portrait. The completed work is ambivalent in viewpoint, but Uccello's subtle surface modeling and his application of geometric shapes to horse and rider alike create a dignified and sculpturesque monument, while the Renaissance interest in the antique is evident in the influence of the horses at San Marco, Venice. For Florence cathedral during the 1440s Uccello undertook two projects: a frescoed clockface with four illusionistic *Heads of Prophets*, and designs for a *Nativity* and *Resurrection* for stained glass rondels in the drum of Brunelleschi's dome in a program that included designs by ANDREA DEL CASTAGNO, DONATELLO, and Ghiberti.

Uccello's *St. George and the Dragon* (c. 1455; National Gallery, London) demonstrates how his interest in certain aspects of Renaissance science and his lively imagination could together produce a charming fantasy (see Plate VIII); it can be related to Landino's praise of Uccello as "a great master of animals and landscape," as can *A Hunt in a Forest* (c. 1460; Ashmolean Museum, Oxford). Uccello's three large panels of the *Battle of San Romano* (before 1456; Uffizi, Florence; National Gallery, London; Louvre, Paris) were painted for the Medici palace, perhaps as decoration for the bedroom of the young Lorenzo de' Medici, who was born in 1449. They honor a victory of 1432 won by a Medici general, Niccolò da Tolentino, but the content is less militaristic than decorative; they offer a delight in patterns of form and color especially appropriate for a secular decoration. Uccello's demonstration of how to represent horses, men, and military equipment in foreshortening is impressive, but the poor state of preservation of the paintings had simplified the once subtle modeling. VASARI reported that Uccello was so enamored of foreshortening that, when his wife called him to bed, she would find him muttering, "Oh what a delightful thing is perspective."

**Further reading:** Franco and Stefano Borsi, *Paolo Uccello* (London: Thames & Hudson, 1994).

**Udall, John** See MARPRELATE CONTROVERSY

**Udall, Nicholas (Nicholas Uvedale) (1505–1556)**
*English schoolmaster and playwright*
Born in Southampton, Udall was educated at Winchester College and Oxford, but was forced to leave the latter (1529), probably on account of his Lutheran tendencies. He was headmaster of Eton College (1534–41) until dismissed on charges of dishonesty, but this did not prevent his obtaining patronage from Queen Catherine PARR and Princess Mary (later Mary I), and he helped the latter translate part of ERASMUS's *Paraphrases* (1548). He also translated Erasmus's *Apophthegmata* (1542) and PETER MARTYR's *Tractatio de sacramento eucharistiae* (c. 1550). Edward VI favored Udall, and he became a canon of Windsor in 1551. In 1555 he was appointed headmaster of Westminster School. His most famous literary production was *Ralph Roister Doister*, published in 1567, but probably written in the early 1550s for a London school. The earliest surviving English comedy, it grafts native comic elements onto a dramatic structure similar to the Latin plays of PLAUTUS and TERENCE.

**Uffizi** A palace in Florence, now housing the world's finest collection of Italian Renaissance works of art. The palace was commissioned in 1560 by COSIMO I DE' MEDICI and designed by VASARI in the mannerist style. Artistic treasures in the Uffizi include works by such Italian masters as CIMABUE, GIOTTO, GENTILE da Fabriano, UCCELLO, Fra ANGELICO, Fra Filippo LIPPI, BOTTICELLI, LEONARDO DA VINCI, MICHELANGELO, RAPHAEL, PARMIGIANINO, TITIAN, and VERONESE. Artists from other countries represented in the Uffizi include DÜRER and ALTDORFER from Germany, Rogier van der WEYDEN and Hugo van der GOES from the Netherlands, and various French artists. Many of these works were passed to the Uffizi from collections assembled by the Medici family. The palace also houses fine collections of antique sculpture and tapestries, as well as prints and drawings.

**Ugo da Carpi (c. 1450–c. 1525)** *Italian artist*
Born at Carpi, near Modena, Ugo was in Venice in 1516, when he requested from the Venetian senate a patent for his technique for making *chiaroscuro* WOODCUTS. As the first Italian practitioner of the technique (his earliest known print dates from 1518), Ugo da Carpi was successful in achieving quite complex effects by the use of three blocks. Among his best products are a *Descent from the Cross* (after Raphael) and *Diogenes* (after Parmigianino).

**Umbrian school** The school of painting associated with the towns of the hilly district of Umbria in central Italy,

particularly Perugia, Todi, and Orvieto. Umbrian art was characterized by qualities described as "softness" and "sweetness." PERUGINO and PINTURICCHIO were its most famous figures and the young RAPHAEL was trained in the Umbrian style.

**universities** The usual medieval term for a university, *studium generale*, implied a teaching center open to all. The word *universitas*, which gradually superseded *studium generale*, applied to any corporate body and is a reminder that the earliest universities were originally groups of scholars and teachers, who formed themselves, like any trade guild, into a body for reasons of self-protection and self-interest. From the 13th century onward many of these bodies put themselves on a more formal footing by obtaining from pope, king, or emperor a license enabling them to confer degrees; degrees themselves were licenses to teach. Later medieval universities were generally founded by papal bull. By 1400 there were 65 of them spread throughout Europe from Oxford to Prague.

In their earliest form universities were specialist institutions intended to enlarge the scope of EDUCATION available through Church schools; thus Salerno was dedicated to medicine, Bologna to law, and Seville to linguistic studies. Paris began as a school for logic but in 1231 gained the right to establish several faculties, of which the theology faculty (the Sorbonne) gained a preeminence that it retained until the Reformation. By the 14th century many universities possessed four faculties: the arts faculty, which offered a preliminary course, and the three higher faculties of theology, medicine, and law. In many places this pattern of studies prevailed throughout the Renaissance period and beyond as universities became centers of conservatism, dedicated to repressing the effects of humanist studies and religious dissent. On the other hand, with Latin as the universal medium of instruction, students and teachers could and did migrate freely across Europe. The cosmopolitan nature of the academic community was reflected in the frequent subdivision of universities into "nations," for example French, Norman, Picard, and English at Paris.

Over 30 new universities were founded during the 15th century, but the rise of HUMANISM in Italy was fueled not so much by them as by individual patrons and by the ACADEMIES. The university of Florence made the temporary appointment of Manuel CHRYSOLORAS as professor of Greek in 1395; a century later GREEK STUDIES had found their way into many academic institutions. HEBREW STUDIES too secured an academic footing in the 15th century, principally because, like Greek, they were adjuncts to theological scholarship. With the advent of printing the universities' traditional role of supervising the production of accurate manuscript texts for the use of their students became obsolete; instead university presses began to be founded, the Sorbonne leading the way in 1470, when three Germans set up their press there for a couple of years.

The Reformation posed a massive challenge to the universities in so far as their authority derived from the Roman Catholic Church. Although the influence of great teachers, such as ERASMUS at Fribourg and Johan REUCHLIN at Tübingen, promoted humanist studies, in many places the teaching of Greek fell under suspicion of encouraging heresy. Institutions such as the Dominican-dominated university of Cologne led the antihumanist, antireformist backlash (*see* EPISTOLAE OBSCURORUM VIRORUM). New colleges and new universities however were founded, more receptive to new ideas. The university of Wittenberg, nursery of the Reformation, was founded in 1502 by imperial decree, although with papal approval. Corpus Christi College, Oxford, founded in 1517, made special provision for Greek instruction in its statutes; feelings in Oxford ran so high over the question of Greek that there were street brawls between the pro-Greek faction and its opponents (dubbed, inevitably, "Trojans").

The first Protestant university was founded at Marburg (1527) by Luther's supporter, PHILIP OF HESSE; it soon attracted students from all over Europe. Other famous Lutheran universities were Königsberg (1544), Jena (1558), and Helmstedt (1575). Calvin's GENEVAN ACADEMY, although a theological college rather than a university, similarly welcomed students from other countries. In Scotland the universities of St. Andrews (founded 1411) and Glasgow (1459) readily embraced Protestantism, the latter being John KNOX's university, while in England Cambridge became a stronghold of Puritanism. Leyden, the first Dutch university to be founded (1575), quickly established an association with ARMINIANISM; in the 17th century it also became famous for its science—a rare phenomenon among universities at the time. During the Renaissance period advances in science were generally made by individuals in the teeth of opposition from the Church and the traditional academic establishment or left to private enterprise, of which the college endowed in London by Sir Thomas GRESHAM is an example.

The universities' potential for assisting the COUNTER-REFORMATION was speedily recognized by the Church, spearheaded by the Jesuits, who had their own university, the GREGORIANA, in Rome. As early as 1556 they established themselves at Ingolstadt, which had long been a bulwark against the reformers. Secular rulers sympathetic to the Counter-Reformation cause might even found a university and hand it over to the Jesuits to run, as Duke Charles III of Lorraine did at Pont-à-Mousson in 1572. Indeed, by 1600 the Jesuits had established a virtual monopoly over higher education in France, with the exception of Paris. The universities of Spain, heartland of Catholic orthodoxy, were renowned in the 16th century for their study of scholastic philosophy, revitalized at Salamanca by Francisco de VITORIA.

**Further reading:** Jonathan Davies, *Florence and Its University during the Early Renaissance* (Leyden, Netherlands: Brill, 1998); Paul F. Grendler, *The Universities of the Italian Renaissance* (Baltimore, Md.: Johns Hopkins University Press, 2002).

**University Wits** The name given by the critic G. E. B. Saintsbury (1845–1933) to a distinct group of educated young men in England who, lacking patrons, made their living by writing for the theaters and bookstalls of the 1580s. Chief among them were Thomas LODGE and George PEELE from Oxford, and Robert GREENE, Christopher MARLOWE, and Thomas NASHE from Cambridge.

**Urbino** A city and former ducal capital in the Marches of central Italy. Umbrians, Etruscans, Celts, Gauls, Romans, and the Church ruled Urbino until it passed to the MONTEFELTRO (1234–1508) and DELLA ROVERE FAMILIES (1508–16, 1521–1631). As the ducal capital (1474–1536) Urbino was an important center of culture and learning, despite the political weakness of the duchy. When the capital was moved to Pesaro (1536) Urbino itself became a minor mercantile center, known mainly for its MAJOLICA ware.

During the reigns (1474–1508) of the two Montefeltro dukes, Federico and Guidobaldo, the city was admired throughout Italy for its humanist learning and cultivated ways. The court was the setting for Castiglione's THE COURTIER, the splendid ducal palace and library were built to house the Montefeltro treasures and manuscripts, the mausoleum of San Bernardino was constructed, and the university was founded in 1506. The 15th-century cathedral was destroyed by earthquake in the 18th century. BRAMANTE and RAPHAEL were born in Urbino, and Luciano LAURANA, PIERO DELLA FRANCESCA, Girolomo GENGA, and (probably) FRANCESCO DI GIORGIO MARTINI were involved in the construction of the Palazzo Ducale. Later Federico BAROCCI was the city's principal artist.

**Urfé, Honoré d'** (1567–1625) *French author*
D'Urfé was born in Marseilles but as an active supporter of the Catholic party, he was forced to leave France after its defeat by Henry IV; he took refuge in the duchy of Savoy, fighting for the duke, with whose family his mother was connected, in the war between Savoy and Genoa. D'Urfé's best-known work is *L'Astrée* (1607–27; translated as *Astrea*, 1657–78), a pastoral romance in five parts set in the fifth century: the plot revolves around the love of the shepherd Céladon for the shepherdess Astrée, their individual adventures, and the lovers' eventual reunion. *L'Astrée* had a considerable influence on 17th-century literature and outshone d'Urfé's earlier writings, which include *Epîtres morales* (1598), inspired by the Platonic theory of love, and the pastoral poem *Sireine* (1604).

**Ursulines** A religious order for women founded at Brescia in 1535 by St. ANGELA MERICI. Its primary purpose was the education of women, and to this end it was intended by the founder that members should live unenclosed. The order was approved by Pope Paul III in 1544 but underwent a radical change in 1572 when communal life was introduced. In 1612 the Ursulines of Paris adopted strict enclosure and solemn vows, following a version of the Augustinian rule.

*Utopia* A social and political satire written in Latin by Sir Thomas MORE, whose friend ERASMUS arranged its publication in Louvain in 1516. Part of *Utopia* was drafted while More was on an embassy in Flanders in 1515, and the book's framework is the narrative of Raphael Hythloday, a fictitious traveler whom More purports to have met in Antwerp. In the first book Hythloday outlines the shortcomings of English society and in the second describes the perfect society of the imaginary island of Utopia (literally, "Nowhere"), which he visited in the New World. The Utopians are ruled by a monarch elected for life, hold all property in common, extend religious toleration to all, operate a system of universal education for men and women, never make war except in self-defense, limit working hours to six a day, and promote cultural activities in the citizens' leisure time. Wrongdoers are enslaved until they amend, an aspect of the system that has been much criticized. Public sanitation, hygiene, and housing are all much in advance of those in 16th-century England.

*Utopia* spawned several later Renaisance imitations, such as CAMPANELLA's *Città del sole*, and has given its name to political philosophies that insist upon the creation of a perfect society. The popularity of the original Louvain edition of *Utopia* was such that other Latin editions quickly followed: Paris (1517), Basle (1518), and Vienna (1519). The Basle editions of 1518 and 1520 have illustrations by HOLBEIN. It was translated into German (1524), Italian (1548), and French (1550) before the issue of the first English version by Raphe Robinson (1551); a Dutch version appeared in 1553. A facsimile of the 1516 Latin edition was issued by the Scolar Press (Leeds, 1966) and a facsimile of the Robinson version of 1551 was issued in Amsterdam in 1969. In 1963 Yale University Press began publication of the *Complete Works of St. Thomas More*, in which *Utopia*, ed. E. Surtz and J. H. Hexter, comprises vol. IV (1965). A handy modern translation is the Penguin Classics version by Paul Turner (Harmondsworth, U.K., 1965).

**Further reading:** John C. Olin (ed.), *Interpreting Thomas More's* Utopia (New York: Fordham University Press, 1990).

**Utrecht, Union of** See NETHERLANDS, REVOLT OF THE

**Uvedale, John** See MARPRELATE CONTROVERSY

**Uvedale, Nicholas** See UDALL, NICHOLAS

# V

**Vaenius** See VEEN, OTTO VAN

**Vair, Guillaume du** See DU VAIR, GUILLAUME

**Valdés, Alfonso de** (c. 1490–1532) *Spanish humanist and writer*
Born like his brother Juan at Cuenca, Valdés, a *converso*, became a Latin secretary (1526) to CHARLES V and left Spain with the imperial court in 1529. Like Juan, he was a disciple of ERASMUS, with whom he carried on a correspondence. His two dialogues, biting satirical attacks on the corruption of the Church, written in an austere, ironic Erasmian style, were published together in 1530 and reprinted several times in the 16th century. Although he was reported to the Inquisition, he died as a Catholic, a victim of the plague in Vienna.

*Diálogo de las cosas acaecidas en Roma* is a defense of the Sack of ROME by the imperial armies in 1527, which is interpreted as a divine punishment of the papal Curia and the clergy in general for their failure to heed the criticisms of such writers as Erasmus. *Diálogo de Mercurio y Carón* continues the justification of Charles V's imperial policy and broadens the anticlerical satire by contrasting *exempla* of corrupt clergy, dedicated to the letter of religion, and good clergy, dedicated to its spirit.

**Valdés, Juan de** (c. 1491–1541) *Spanish humanist and religious writer*
A *converso*, born at Cuenca, he studied classical languages at Alcalá and, like his brother Alfonso, became a committed follower of ERASMUS, with whom he corresponded. *Diálogo de doctrina cristiana* (1529) caused him to be denounced for heresy and he moved to Rome in 1531 to es-

cape the Inquisition. He lived the final years of his life in Naples where he gathered a circle of followers who shared his Protestant, though not strictly Calvinistic or Lutheran, religious views on JUSTIFICATION BY FAITH, biblical exegesis, and dogma.

The theological thought of Valdés is summed up in *Ciento y diez consideraciones divinas* (One hundred and ten religious considerations; 1539), written with his brother. His most important work, however, is *Diálogo de la lengua* (written c. 1535, published 1737), a dialogue in which two Italians and two Spaniards (one called "Valdés") discuss the Spanish language in all aspects of vocabulary, spelling, style, and so on. The work was influenced by Pietro BEMBO's *Prose della volgar lingua* (1525). Valdés recommends an unadorned plain style and mocks the excesses of the chivalric narratives. The Italians are encouraged to improve their Spanish by considering faultlessly chosen literary examples and some 200 proverbs that are models of terseness.

**Further reading:** José C. Nieto, *Juan de Valdés and the Origins of the Spanish and Italian Reformation* (Geneva: Droz, 1970).

**Valencia** A city in eastern Spain, on the River Turia, close to the Mediterranean. It was a Roman settlement in the second century BCE, was taken by the Visigoths (413), and subsequently changed hands between Moors and Christians several times before becoming part of Aragonese territory (1238). It was the site of Spain's first printing press (1474), and its university was founded around 1500. From the late 14th century Valencia had a thriving school of artists, the early ones mainly anonymous, but the later ones including Luis DALMAU and Francisco de RIBALTA. It was also famous for its exported majolica wares, especially in the 15th century.

**Valerianus, Pierius** (**Giovanni Pietro delle Fosse**) (1477–1558) *Italian humanist scholar and poet*
He was born in Belluno and became the protégé of Giulio de' Medici (Pope CLEMENT VII), who employed him as tutor to his wards Ippolito and Alessandro de' Medici in Rome and made him his apostolic protonotary. Among his contemporaries Valerianus had a phenomenal reputation for learning and is primarily remembered for his contribution to EGYPTIAN STUDIES in his *Hieroglyphica* (1556), the first book to ascertain the historical truth about the writing system of ancient Egypt on the basis of the BEMBINE TABLE, inscriptions on Roman obelisks, the *Hieroglyphica* of Horapollo, and hints in other ancient writers. Around 1516 he also wrote an interesting contribution to the QUESTIONE DELLA LINGUA, advocating the use of the *lingua cortigiana* as a basis for literary Italian rather than the local dialect of Florence; this *Dialogo della volgar lingua* was not published until 1620. Besides scholarly works in Latin he also published love poetry, the *Amorum libri* (1549).

**Valla, Lorenzo** (1407–1457) *Italian humanist scholar*
Valla was born at Rome and studied and taught at Pavia before becoming secretary to ALFONSO I of Naples in 1437. Returning to Rome in 1447, he became papal secretary and taught at the university until his death. He wrote a renowned eulogy on classical Latin composition *Elegantiarum linguae Latinae* (1444), of which 59 editions were printed before 1536. He also wrote philosophical treatises on pleasure and free will, *De voluptate* (1431) and *De libero arbitrio* (c. 1440), and his *Dialecticae disputationes* (1439) was a cogent attack on medieval Aristotelianism. His forcefully stated views on both philology and philosophy provoked confrontations with other humanist scholars, including Poggio BRACCIOLINI. His most famous work was his exposure (1440) of the Donation of Constantine as a medieval forgery. This document purported to be a grant from Constantine the Great to the pope, giving the latter authority over the empire. Using philological analysis Valla demonstrated that the language of the Donation was incompatible with the age of Constantine, a discovery that undermined papal claims to supremacy over secular rulers and was useful to his then employer, Alfonso. Valla's reasoning foreshadowed later developments in the attack on Catholic claims by Protestant reformers. Valla also produced influential Latin translations of Thucydides (1452) and Herodotus (1457), whose works became far better known in the Renaissance through Valla's translations than in the original.

**Valladolid** A city on the River Pisuerga in northwest Spain. Valladolid was granted to the Ansurez family in 1074 and passed to the Castilian Crown in 1208. During the late Middle Ages and the Renaissance the city became important as a favored residence of the Castilian and Spanish courts. FERDINAND II of Aragon and Isabella of Castile were married there in 1469. The city was a center of the revolt of the COMUNEROS (1520–21) and of a short-lived movement for religious reform which was crushed by the SPANISH INQUISITION in the late 1550s. Valladolid's university (founded 1346) is one of the oldest in Spain. Notable buildings from the period of the Renaissance include the cathedral, begun by Juan de HERRERA in 1585, the 15th-century Colegio de San Gregorio, and the Colegio de Sta. Cruz (1479–92), built in the PLATERESQUE style. Alonso BERRUGUETE, Juan de JUNI, and Gregório FERNÁNDEZ all worked in Valladolid. Its Plaza Mayor, laid out in the 16th century after a fire had devastated the city, is an early example of this kind of civic space and was much imitated in Spain and the Spanish American colonies.

**Valle, Pietro della** See DELLA VALLE, PIETRO

**Valois, house of** The family that ruled France from 1328 to 1589. Its founder was Charles of Valois, younger son of the Capetian king, Philip III, who awarded Charles the county of Valois in 1285. When the direct Capetian line died out Philip of Valois became Philip VI of France. There was a direct line of succession until the death of Charles VIII (1498) without issue. LOUIS XII, head of a junior branch of the family, the Valois-Orléans, then succeeded to the throne. When Louis also died childless (1515) the throne passed to FRANCIS I, head of another junior branch, the Valois-Angoulême.

Despite the English claim to the French throne and many setbacks in the Hundred Years' War against England, the Valois established their power in France, defeating overmighty feudal lords and unifying the country under their authority. During the late 15th and early 16th centuries Valois claims in Italy led to bitter conflict with the house of HAPSBURG. The Renaissance flourished in France during the reigns of Francis I (1515–47) and HENRY II (1547–59), but the Wars of RELIGION considerably weakened the power of the last Valois monarchs. When HENRY III died without an heir (1589) the throne passed to Henry of Navarre (HENRY IV) and the house of Bourbon.

**Valturio, Roberto** (1405–1475) *Italian military adviser and expert*
After some years of legal work for the papacy Valturio returned to his birthplace of Rimini and the service of the lord of Rimini, Sigismondo MALATESTA. In 1472 he published his 12-book treatise on the art of war (*De re militari*). This included beautifully executed woodcuts of military machines (possibly by Matteo de' PASTI) and many practical comments on contemporary warfare. Some

of the ideas for military devices were impractical, such as the plan for a cart driven by windmills geared to its wheels, but the book was widely influential, appearing in both Italian (1483) and French (1532) versions.

**van Eyck, Hubert** and **Jan** See EYCK, HUBERT VAN AND JAN VAN

**Varchi, Benedetto** (1503–1565) *Italian scholar and critic*
Varchi was born and lived most of his life in Florence, but was influenced in his critical theories by a spell as a student at Padua, where he was imbued with the prevailing Aristotelianism. Believing in the classical ideal of republicanism, he supported the exiling of the MEDICI rulers of Florence in 1527, and was himself exiled on the restoration of the Medici in 1530. Despite taking part in Piero Strozzi's abortive expedition against the Medici (1537), he was recalled in 1543 to the service of Duke COSIMO I DE' MEDICI and provided with a pension to write his *Storia fiorentina*, a history of Florence from 1527 to 1538; notable for its careful documentation, the 16-book history was eventually published in 1721. Varchi also wrote poems (*Sonnetti*, 1555–57), plays, and translations from classical authors. Among his critical works, *L'Ercolano* (1560) supports the use of the vernacular in literature.

**Varthema, Ludovico** (before 1470–1517) *Italian traveler*
Not much is known of his life apart from the autobiographical data in his *Itinerario* (1511). Motivated apparently by mere curiosity and a spirit of adventure, he set out via Egypt and Syria before visiting Mecca disguised as a Mameluke pilgrim. After various adventures he went on to Persia, India, Sri Lanka and as far east as Borneo, Java, and the Moluccas, before getting a passage back to Europe in a Portuguese vessel via the Cape of Good Hope. He gave public lectures in Venice in 1508 on his experiences, and his book became a 16th-century bestseller, with translations into Latin, German, Spanish, Flemish, and English. Despite some tall stories, the *Itinerario* gives valuable geographical and ethnographical insights into the East before the era of sustained contact with Europeans.

**Vasari, Giorgio** (1511–1574) *Italian painter, architect, and art historian*
The son of a potter at Arezzo, Vasari came as a boy to the notice of Cardinal Silvio Passerini, who sent him to Florence to be educated with the young Ippolito and Alessandro de' Medici. Patronage by the MEDICI continued throughout his career. They and other prominent benefactors encouraged his prolific output, but his posthumous artistic reputation has not remained as high as it was among his contemporaries. Examples of his work as a painter (and decorator) are the posthumous portrait of Lorenzo the Magnificent and decorations in various parts of the Palazzo Vecchio in Florence and in the Sala Regia in the Vatican. He was the architect of the UFFIZI in Florence and the modernized Palazzo dei Cavalieri (1562) in Pisa.

It was as the first art historian, the author of *Vite ...* (*Lives of the Most Excellent Painters, Sculptors, and Architects*; 1550, revised 1568), that Vasari has exercised the most profound influence. The biographies were carefully researched and included coverage of technical matters and critical judgments. The book also introduced the idea of a rebirth, or renaissance, of painting and analysed its development in three anthropomorphic stages corresponding to childhood (c. 1250), youth (c. 1400–c. 1500), and maturity (to the death of MICHELANGELO, 1564), citing representative artists for each stage: respectively (GIOTTO; MASACCIO; LEONARDO, RAPHAEL, and Michelangelo). This conception of the Renaissance of art and its progressive development has influenced critical judgments and taste up to the present.

The massive compilation of Vasari's *Vite* was first translated into English in its entirety by Mrs J. Foster between 1850 and 1885. An abridged version of her text appeared in 1960, and it has also been published in a two-volume format (New York, 1967). A revised edition of A. B. Hinds's translation by William Gaunt has appeared in four volumes (London, 1980). An illustrated selection of lives entitled *Artists of the Renaissance* (London, 1978) was made by George Bull, who also translated the extracts in the Penguin Classics volume (Harmondsworth, 1965). A recent translation is that by Julia and Peter Bondanella for Oxford University Press (1998).

**Further reading:** T. S. R. Boase, *Giorgio Vasari: The Man and the Book* (Princeton, N.J.: Princeton University Press, 1979; repr. 1987); Philip Jacks (ed.), *Vasari's Florence: Artists and Literati at the Medicean Court* (Cambridge, U.K.: Cambridge University Press, 1998); Patricia Lee Rubin, *Giorgio Vasari: Art and History* (New Haven, Conn.: Yale University Press, 1995); Leon Satkowski, *Giorgio Vasari, Architect and Courtier* (Princeton, N.J.: Princeton University Press, 1993).

**Vasconcelos, Jorge Ferreira de** (c. 1515–c. 1563) *Portuguese playwright and novelist*
His birthplace is unknown and little else is known of his early life, though his familiarity with Coimbra and his obvious learning suggest that he may have studied there. He was an attendant of Prince Edward at the court of King John III until 1540 and thereafter became secretary of the treasury and secretary of the India House. His three prose comedies are perhaps better classified as dramatic dialogues intended for reading, in the tradition of LA CELESTINA, rather than as plays for stage performance. *Eufrosina* (between 1537 and 1543), in which youthful love happily ends in marriage, is set in the academic city of Coimbra and is obviously indebted to *Celestina*. *Ulisipo* (a learned form of "Lisbon"; c. 1554) attacks the materialism of the Lisbon middle class. *Aulegrafia* (c. 1555) is con-

cerned with courtiers. Vasconcelos's novel, *Memorial da Segunda Távola Redonda* (c. 1554), defends the old values of chivalry; lyrical passages are interspersed in a narrative that involves both the Arthurian knights of the Round Table and deities from classical mythology.

**Vatican Library** (**Bibliotheca Apostolica Vaticana**) The LIBRARY housing the papal collections in the Vatican City, Rome. The Vatican Library developed from a library established in Rome in the 15th century by Pope Nicholas V, who gathered together valuable manuscripts from Germany, England, Greece, and other countries and presented them to the public view, although an inventory (1295) of 443 works survives of an earlier papal collection in the time of Boniface VIII (pope 1294–1303). The present building was erected by Domenico FONTANA at the end of the 16th century and the collection was moved there from the Floreria beneath the Borgia apartments by Sixtus V (pope 1585–90). In later years the library has been enriched by a number of major bequests and now houses about 60,000 manuscripts, 7000 incunabula, and 950,000 other printed books. The present library comprises 12 basic collections, including the Palatini (*see* PALATINA, BIBLIOTHECA), the Reginenses (formerly belonging to Queen Christina of Sweden), the Borghesiani, and the Barberiniani.

**Further reading:** Anthony Grafton (ed), *Rome Reborn: The Vatican Library and Renaissance Culture* (New Haven, Conn.: Yale University Press, 1993).

**Vecchi, Orazio** (1550–1605) *Italian composer*
Born in Modena, Vecchi took holy orders. He is known to have been active in Venice, and became *maestro* at Salò cathedral in 1581. Three years later he was appointed to the same post at Modena. In 1586 he worked for a short period in Reggio Emilia and then became *maestro* at Correggio. He returned to his original post at Modena in 1593, and in 1598 also became *maestro* at the court chapel of Duke Cesare d'Este. In this capacity he was celebrated as a composer of entertainments; though a priest and a composer of sacred works, it is for his madrigals and canzonettes that Vecchi is remembered. His most famous work is his *L'Amfiparnaso* (1597), a madrigal comedy comprising 14 madrigals for five voices setting a COMMEDIA DELL'ARTE text.

**Vecchietta, Lorenzo di Pietro, Il** (c. 1412–1480) *Italian painter, sculptor, and architect*
A native of Siena, Vecchietta was a pupil of Stefano di SASSETTA and was greatly influenced by Florentine art. The influence of DONATELLO is particularly strong upon Vecchietta's masterpiece, the painting *The Assumption of the Virgin* (1461–62; Pienza cathedral), which is distinguished by its linear but naturalistic style. The influence of Donatello is also evident upon his marble and bronze

sculptures, notably the relief *The Resurrection* (1472; Frick Collection, New York). Other works include an illuminated codex of the *Divine Comedy* (British Museum), a ciborium in Siena cathedral (1467–72), the painting *St. Bernardino Preaching* (Liverpool), and frescoes (1441–49) in the Ospedale di Sta. Maria della Scala, Siena. His pupils included MATTEO DI GIOVANNI.

**Veen, Otto van** (**Vaenius**) (1556–1629) *Flemish painter*
Van Veen, who although illegitimate was of patrician birth, studied under Isaac Swanenburgh in his native Leyden before moving briefly to Liège (1573). He then spent time in Italy (1575–80), during which he acquired under Federico ZUCCARO in Rome an Italian mannerist overlay to his original Flemish style. On his return to the Catholic Netherlands, he became court painter (1585–92) to the duke of Parma and later held the equivalent post with the archduke Albert. Between 1596 and 1600 RUBENS did his final training in van Veen's Antwerp studio. Religious, historical, and allegorical subjects feature among van Veen's output, and his self-portrait, showing him at his easel surrounded by his extensive family, is in the Louvre, Paris.

**Veer, Gerrit de** (late 16th century) *Dutch explorer and surgeon*
Veer accompanied Willem BARENTS on his three voyages in search of the NORTHEAST PASSAGE, and his *Waerachtighe beschryvinghe van de drie seylaegien by Noorden* (1598) gives a lively account of these journeys, in particular the winter of 1596/97 passed by Barents's men in their makeshift shelter on the ice of Novaya Zemlya. The book quickly became famous, and was translated into English (1609) and other European languages.

**Vega Carpio, Lope Félix de** (1562–1635) *Spanish dramatist, poet, and novelist*
He attended a Jesuit school in his native Madrid, perhaps studied at Alcalá, and spent a period at Salamanca. He had numerous romantic entanglements throughout most of his life. That with Elena Osorio in the 1580s inspired in part his dialogue novel *La Dorotea* (1632). Shortly after marrying the aristocrat Isabel de Urbina, he sailed with the SPANISH ARMADA (1588), which he survived. In 1590 he became secretary to the duke of ALBA; his pastoral novel, *La Arcadia*, dates from this period. His wife died in 1594, and in 1598 he married Juana de Guardo, while continuing an affair with Micaela de Luján. In 1610 he settled in Madrid. After his second wife died in 1613, he had several other relationships but nevertheless prepared to be ordained as a priest. His final tragic affair was with Marta de Nevares Santoyo, whom he met in 1616. She gradually became blind and then insane, dying in 1632. Though long famous, he himself died poor.

Lope established the form of Spanish comedy in the 17th century. Of more than 1500 theatrical works credited to him by contemporaries, about one third survive, including *entremeses* (farcical interludes) and *autos* (religious plays) as well as *comedias* (published 1604–47 in 25 volumes, with occasional additional volumes since). His three-act verse plays draw on the widest possible range of subject matter (Spanish history, legend, and balladry, mythology, chivalric romance, Italian *novelle*, pastoral, and biblical and religious literature). The plays often have a comic subplot related to the main action, an unforeseen dénouement, and characters not portrayed with deep realism but with speech suited to their class; they are intended as moral instruction as well as entertainment. Lope brought to full development a number of stock characters like the *gracioso* (comic servant). His formula for writing plays was set forth in an ironic poem, *Arte nuevo de hacer comedias* (New art of making comedies; c. 1607). The theme of honor, he noted there, was particularly popular. The *capa y espada* (cape and sword) type, with upper-class characters and appropriate sword-play, forms the largest group of his comedies. To mention but a few, his plays include *El caballero de Olmedo*, *Fuenteovejuna*, *La discreta enamorada*, *El castigo sin venganza*, and *Peribáñez*.

Almost equally prolific as a poet and adept in a number of genres, Lope wrote Petrarchan and religious sonnets, ballads, poems in the elaborate style of GÓNGORA (whom he attacked but imitated), and philosophical works. His lyrics, collected by friends, were published in *La Vega del Parnaso* (1637). He also wrote several epics (*La hermosura de Angélica*, *La Jerusalén conquistada*, *Andromeda*, and *La Dragontea*, the last-named an attack on Sir Francis Drake and the English) and a burlesque battle of cats, *La gatomaquia*.

**Further reading:** Donald R. Larson, *The Honor Plays of Lope de Vega* (Cambridge, Mass.: Harvard University Press, 1978); Melveena McKendrick, *Playing the King: Lope de Vega and the Limits of Conformity* (Boston, Mass. and London: Tamesis, 2002); Robert R. Morrison, *Lope de Vega and the Comedia de Santos* (New York: Peter Lang, 2000).

**Vegio, Maffeo** (1407–1458) *Italian poet and humanist*
Born at Lodi, he studied at Milan and Pavia before publishing (1427) his own 13th book of the *Aeneid* as testimony to his admiration for VIRGIL. This supplement, covering Aeneas's death and deification and the subsequent greatness of Rome, remained an accepted part of the text of the *Aeneid* for about 150 years. This made his reputation and led to his appointment as secretary of briefs and canon of St. Peter's, Rome (1444). He taught poetry at the university of Pavia and produced much Latin verse on a variety of subjects, including mythology (*The Golden Fleece* in four books), as well as epigrams and a poem on the Vatican which gives a picture of the building before it was demolished and reconstructed by Nicholas V. Vegio also wrote the educational treatise *De educatione liberorum* (1445–48).

**Veleslavín, Daniel Adam of** (1546–1599) *Czech humanist, printer, and historian*
Veleslavín lived and worked in Prague, where he was a professor at the Charles University until disqualified from his post by marriage. His father-in-law ran the city's major publishing house, and under Veleslavín's management (from 1580) this press put out some important historical compilations and dictionaries. Several of these were Veleslavín's own work, including *Silva quadrilinguis* (1598), a multilingual dictionary reflecting the international culture of contemporary Prague. Veleslavín's own prose style was much admired and imitated.

**Venetian Academy** See NEAKADEMIA

**Venetian school** During the Renaissance, those painters working in or near Venice whose art evolved in a manner distinct from that of other northern Italian towns in the 15th century. The movement away from the prevailing Byzantine and Gothic modes began with the Bellini family, in particular with Giovanni BELLINI, who had numerous disciples. The prolific VIVARINI workshop at Murano was also significant in establishing the separate identity of Venetian painting, while another Venetian characteristic, the depiction of landscape and townscape, surfaces in the work of CARPACCIO.

With GIORGIONE and TITIAN Venetian painting reached its apogee, and artists even from northern Europe came to Venice to study there. The quality that above all distinguished Venetian art of the Cinquecento was its warmth and richness of color, which these two painters exemplified to an extraordinary degree. Other Venetian masters included PALMA VECCHIO, Paolo VERONESE, and TINTORETTO, while SEBASTIANO DEL PIOMBO, Dosso DOSSI, and Lorenzo LOTTO, although not settled in Venice, retained a Venetian flavor to their works as a result of early influences. In the later 16th century Mannerism, as exemplified by PALMA GIOVANE, prevailed over the characteristically Venetian style and the school lost its identity, which only reemerged in the great 18th-century masters, Canaletto and Francesco Guardi.

**Venice** A northern Italian city and port, built on the islands of an Adriatic lagoon, formerly a city state and ruler of a maritime empire. Venice has long been famous for its waterways; in the 15th century the Grand Canal was described as "the finest street in the world." Venice originated with the arrival of refugees from the Lombard invasions (568); by the ninth century Venice was a city ruled by a popularly elected DOGE and associated with the Byzantine empire. By the late Middle Ages the doge had lost much of his executive power to elected councils and Venice was a great mercantile state competing and trading with Constantinople.

During the 14th and 15th centuries Venice was one of the main political, mercantile, and maritime powers of Europe. It ruled over an eastern Mediterranean empire and obtained great wealth from its trade with the Levant, Mediterranean countries, and northern Europe, while through its Egyptian depots it monopolized the import of spices from the Far East. Its dependence upon the sea for its power and wealth was symbolized in the annual ceremony of the *spozalizio del mar* (see BUCINTORO). Venetian shipbuilding was based on the Arsenale, which employed up to 16,000 workers and at one stage produced a galley every day for 100 days for the war against the Turks. Although great patrician merchant families dominated Venice, its constitution was regarded as a model of cooperation between the monarchical, oligarchic, and democratic elements of society. Greek refugees in the late 15th century made Venice a magnet for European scholars; their activities focused on the NEAKADEMIA of Aldus MANUTIUS, whose ALDINE PRESS placed the city in the forefront of PRINTING in Europe. Equally significant, at the very beginning of the 16th century, Ottaviano PETRUCCI's laborious process for printing polyphony—and the simplified technique evolved by his successor Antonio Gardano—meant that Venice led the rest of Europe in the printing and dissemination of music (see MUSIC PRINTING AND PUBLISHING).

Venice's great power and wealth led it into conflict both with its Italian neighbors and with major European powers. Maritime rivalry resulted in war with Genoa in the 14th century, and Venetian territorial expansion led to war with Milan in the 15th. Venice was so greatly feared that its Italian neighbors, the papacy, Aragon, and France combined against it in the League of CAMBRAI (1508). From the second half of the 15th century Venice also spent many years in wars against the Turks and suffered a number of setbacks. By the 16th century numerous wars, the Portuguese discovery of an alternative route to the rich spice trade of the Far East, and Venice's inability to compete effectively with the new nation states of western Europe led to the beginning of Venice's centuries-long decline.

During the period of the Renaissance Venice was renowned for its banks in the Rialto, the site of Europe's first bank in the 12th century. The wealth of Venice supported the work of the numerous artists of the VENETIAN SCHOOL and the construction of many great palaces and churches. Notable Renaissance constructions include the doge's palace (14th century), the Arsenale (founded in the 12th century), the Rialto bridge (c. 1590), and the Bridge of Sighs (1600).

The Piazza di San Marco, onto which fronts the great medieval basilica of San Marco, is still the heart of the city; it is surrounded by handsome Renaissance buildings with, in the northern corner, Mauro CODUSSI's Torre dell' Orologico (clock-tower) with two bronze figures (the "Mori"), dating from 1497, to strike the hours. Adjacent to the Piazza di San Marco is the Piazzetta with the Libre-ria Sansoviniana housing the Bibliotheca MARCIANA. In the Renaissance period the basilica of San Marco, along with some others of the Venetian churches, was the heart of a thriving musical culture, with musicians of the caliber of Andrea and Giovanni GABRIELI performing and composing music to be performed there.

**Further reading:** William J. Bouwsma, *Venice and the Defense of Republican Liberty: Renaissance Values in the Age of Counter Reformation* (Berkeley, Calif.: University of California Press, 1968); David Chambers, *The Imperial Age of Venice, 1380–1580* (London: Thames & Hudson, 1970); Patricia Fortini Brown, *Art and Life in Renaissance Venice* (Upper Saddle River, N.J.: Prentice Hall, 1997); Paul Hills, *Venetian Color: Marble, Mosaic, Painting and Glass 1250–1550* (New Haven, Conn.: Yale University Press, 1999); Deborah Howard, *Venice and the East: The Impact of the Islamic World on Venetian Architecture 1100–1500* (New Haven, Conn.: Yale University Press, 2000); Norbert Huse and Wolfgang Wolters, *The Art of Renaissance Venice: Architecture, Sculpture and Painting 1460–1590* (Chicago, Ill.: University of Chicago Press, 1990); John McAndrew, *Venetian Architecture of the Early Renaissance* (Cambridge, Mass.: MIT Press, 1980); Brian Pullan, *Rich and Poor in Renaissance Venice: The Social Institutions of a Catholic State, to 1620* (Oxford, U.K.: Blackwell, 1971); David Rosand, *Myths of Venice: The Figuration of a State* (Chapel Hill, N.C.: University of North Carolina, 2001).

**Venus** The Roman goddess of love, beauty, and fertility, frequently identified in classical antiquity, and later, with the Greek goddess Aphrodite. One of the earliest Renaissance paintings to celebrate a pagan subject was BOTTICELLI's *The Birth of Venus*, which recreates the Greek myth telling of Aphrodite's birth from the foam of the sea. The choice of subject was intended to recall one of the most famous works of art of antiquity—Apelles' lost painting known as *Aphrodite Anadyomene* (or *Aphrodite rising from the Sea*).

In the Greek pantheon Aphrodite was married to the lame smith god Hephaestos (Roman Vulcan), but was unfaithful to him and became the mistress of the god of war, Ares (Roman Mars). Depictions of the lovers were a favorite theme in Renaissance art, often presented as an allegory of War subdued and disarmed by Love, but also as erotic art for its own sake; Botticelli, PIERO DI COSIMO, and VERONESE in their different renderings of the subject show little Cupids carrying off and playing with Mars's warlike accouterments (see also CUPID). Another scene that appealed to painters as offering the scope for depicting female nudes in a pastoral landscape was the judgment of Paris, who, according to the story, was appointed as arbiter by the goddesses Aphrodite, Hera, and Athene in their contest to decide which of them was the most beautiful. Besides Cupid or Cupids, Venus is often depicted with roses and myrtles, the plants traditionally associated with her, and with doves, sparrows, or swans, who either carried messages for her or drew her chariot. The frequent inclusion of sea shells in these scenes is a reminder of her marine origin, and occurs, with the birds, in a low-relief panel of the goddess in the TEMPIO MALATESTIANO, possibly by Matteo de' PASTI.

Several antique statues of Venus, mainly Roman copies of Hellenistic originals, were known to the Renaissance, among them the Medici Venus (Uffizi, Florence), discovered in Rome in the 16th century. These inspired some imitations, and the Mars and Venus theme was also taken up by mannerist and baroque sculptors.

**Further reading;** Marina Warner, *Monuments and Maidens: The Allegory of the Female Form* (London: Weidenfeld & Nicolson, 1985; repr. 1996).

**Verdelot, Philippe** (c. 1475–before 1552) *French composer*
Born in northern France, Verdelot presumably went to Italy early in his career. He became *maestro* at the baptistery in Florence (1523–25) and at the cathedral there (1523–27). He is also known to have been in Rome around 1523. Verdelot wrote two Masses, a Magnificat, about 57 motets, and nine volumes of madrigals. Though his church music was popular throughout Europe (his motets were parodied by, among others, LASSUS and PALESTRINA), it is for his madrigals that he is chiefly remembered, as he was one of the earliest exponents of the genre. In some he adopts a syllabic approach to the text and in others he uses more imitation. The madrigals were popular in Verdelot's day and influenced other madrigalists.

**Vergil, Polydore** (c. 1470–1555) *Italian historian*
Born at Urbino and educated in Italy, Vergil was sent to England as deputy to the collector of PETER'S PENCE (1502). He remained in England for the following 50 years, naturalized in 1510, and held a number of positions in the English Church. Before leaving Italy he published a pioneering history of inventions, *De inventoribus rebus* (1499). In England, however, his attention turned to British history. His most important work in this field was his *Anglica historia* (1534). It began by censuring such traditional parts of British history as the Arthurian legends and went on to present an equally traditional view of British history as leading inevitably to the Tudor monarchy. He also published the first scholarly edition of the earliest history of Britain, Gildas's sixth-century *De excidio et conquesta Britanniae* (On the Ruin and Conquest of Britain; 1526).

**Vermeyen, Jan Cornelis** (Jan May) (c. 1500–1559) *Netherlands painter and engraver*
Born at Beverwijk, near Haarlem, Vermeyen may have studied under Jan Gossaert. He held the post of court painter (1525–29) to MARGARET OF AUSTRIA and subse-

quently was attached to the entourage of Emperor CHARLES V, with whom he was a great favorite. He accompanied the emperor on his Tunis campaign (1535) and designed the series of tapestries commemorating it. His style as a painter was influenced by that of his friend Jan van SCOREL. Numerous engravings by him have survived. Vermeyen's nickname "Jan met de Baard" or "Barbalonga" refers to his fine beard, which he wore so long that he sometimes trod on it.

**Vermigli, Pietro Martire** See PETER MARTYR (Pietro Martire Vermigli)

**vernacular** The rise of the vernacular languages of Europe to accepted status as literary media was a phenomenon closely associated with the Renaissance, even if it was not completed during this period. The original lowly status of these languages is indicated by their name, "vernacular" being derived from the Latin word *verna*, a household slave. In medieval Europe culture and education were Latin-based and Church-mediated, which meant in practice that they were accessible only to males destined for an ecclesiastical career or one of its professional offshoots such as the law. Poetry and chivalric romances in the vernacular, some of which are now recognized as being of the very highest quality, were produced for the recreation of certain aristocratic societies, notably by the Provençal troubadours and German Minnesingers; no contemporary claims however were made for their significance as "great" literature entitled to the attention either of posterity or of anyone beyond the immediate cultural circle for which they were produced. The idea of immortalizing a beloved in a sonnet ("So long as men can breathe or eyes can see,/So long lives this, and this gives life to thee," as SHAKESPEARE boasted) arises from self-conscious and self-confident assumptions about the status of vernacular literature alien to the spirit of medieval verse. In practical terms, limited literacy, the vagaries of scribes, the vulnerability of manuscripts, and the condition of the principal languages themselves (fragmented into numerous dialects, lacking any accepted ORTHOGRAPHY) meant that medieval bards were realistic in not setting too much store by posterity or a wider audience.

The ITALIAN LANGUAGE was the first to begin to undergo the evolutionary process that transformed the despised vernacular into a respectable literary medium. In this process the works of the great Florentine writers of the 14th century—DANTE, PETRARCH, and BOCCACCIO—played a key role; later the QUESTIONE DELLA LINGUA debate raised issues of linguistic analysis and the concept of "correctness" that encouraged both interest and pride in the use of the vernacular. A similar route was followed by other languages, and the spread of PRINTING throughout Europe reinforced the tendency towards standardization. Confidence in a vernacular's qualities as a literary medium to replace or at least equal Latin developed at different speeds in different countries, either helped by HUMANISM, as in Italy, where it was promoted by scholars like Leonardo SALVIATI and Sperone SPERONI, or hindered by it, as in Germany (*see* GERMAN LANGUAGE). The process was consolidated once there was a sufficient body of literature in the vernacular of a quality that demanded serious attention from the literary critics (*see* CRITICISM, LITERARY). On the other hand, the use of Latin for serious works on such subjects as law or religion, remained unchallenged until the 17th century and even later in cases where the writer wished to reach an international audience.

TRANSLATION was a major factor in the advance of the vernaculars during the Renaissance (*see also* BIBLE, TRANSLATIONS OF; TRANSLATIONS OF CLASSICAL AUTHORS; TRANSLATIONS OF CONTEMPORARY AUTHORS). Although motives for translating the Bible differed from those for translating the classical Greek and Latin authors, the acknowledged standing of the original texts in both cases compelled their translators to exert themselves to the utmost to find an appropriate style in the vernacular, with generally beneficial results. Translation between vernaculars became an important means of creating a new European secular culture, accessible to women and laymen.

**Verona** A city on the River Adige in the Veneto region of northern Italy. Verona became a Roman colony in 89 BCE; it was later ruled by Ostrogoths and taken by Charlemagne (774). By the 12th century Verona was an independent commune frequently torn apart by factional conflicts; the story of Romeo and Juliet is based on family feuds in Verona at the start of the 14th century. From 1260 the DELLA SCALA FAMILY began to establish its authority over Verona first as *capitani* and from 1300 as hereditary *signori*. In 1387 Verona passed to the VISCONTI FAMILY of Milan and in 1405 to Venice. Venice ruled Verona until 1797, except for when the town was occupied by Emperor MAXIMILIAN I.

During the period of the Renaissance Verona was not only a prosperous center of trade but also an important bastion of humanist studies and artistic output. The artists PISANELLO and VERONESE worked in Verona. Notable buildings include the Castelvecchio (1354), the cathedral (rebuilt in the 15th century), the church of Sant' Anastasia, and the fortifications and triumphal gates designed by the great architect of Verona, Michele SANMICHELI.

**Veronese, Paolo** (Paolo Caliari) (c. 1528–1588) *Italian artist*
Born in Verona, from which he acquired the name by which he is better known, Veronese was apprenticed to the local painter Antonio Badile (1486–1541) at age 14. Badile's influence is strong upon Veronese's earliest known work, the Bevilacqua-Lazise altarpiece (1548). Other early influences include those of GIULIO ROMANO and TITIAN, whose use of color and control of illusionistic devices is reflected in Veronese's frescoes for the Villa Soranza, executed in collaboration with G. B. Zelotti (1532–78) but now largely destroyed. Veronese was also moved by the influence of MICHELANGELO in such paintings as the *Temptation of St. Anthony* (1552), executed for Mantua cathedral.

In about 1553 Veronese arrived in Venice, where he established himself as a leading painter in the mannerist style (*see* MANNERISM). As a prolific artist who specialized in huge paintings on allegorical, biblical, or historical themes, Veronese was in high demand: typical of his early work was his decoration of the church of San Sebastiano, begun in 1555, in which he sought the effective integration of painting with architecture and continued his experiments with foreshortening and light effects. Particularly brilliant in these respects was his decoration of the interior of the Villa Barbaro at Maser (c. 1561), in which Veronese abandoned his mannerist style in order to react freely to PALLADIO's design. Subsequent works included several notable paintings, including the *Marriage at Cana* (1562–63; Louvre, Paris), *The Family of Darius before Alexander* (c. 1570; National Gallery, London), and *The Adoration of the Magi* (1573; National Gallery, London). His famous *Feast in the House of Levi* (1573; Accademia, Venice), caused a considerable stir by its unconventional inclusion of such details as a dog and soldiers in what purported originally to be a version of the Last Supper. Veronese was called before the Inquisition and, despite his spirited defense of the intellectual liberty of the artist, was obliged to change the painting's title to its present form.

Towards the end of his life Veronese received so many commissions that he had to rely heavily on workshop assistance. From 1577 he was involved, with TINTORETTO, in the redecoration of the doge's palace after a serious fire there. His brother, Benedetto Caliari (1538–98), assisted him with this work, which included the magnificent *Apotheosis of Venice* (c. 1585) in the ceiling of the Sala del Maggior Consiglio.

**Further reading:** Richard Cocke, *Veronese* (London: Jupiter, 1980); ~, *Paolo Veronese: Piety and Display in an Age of Religious Reform* (Aldershot, U.K.: Ashgate, 2002); W. R. Rearick, *The Art of Paolo Veronese 1528–1588* (Cambridge, U.K.: Cambridge University Press, 1988).

**Verrazzano, Giovanni da** (died 1528) *Italian explorer*
Born in Florence of a noble family, Verrazzano was sponsored by a group of bankers to find a western route to China. He sailed from Brittany with a crew of 50 in a French ship, *La Dauphine*, in 1524. On reaching America, he mistook Pamlico Sound, North Carolina, for a strait leading to the Pacific and sent home reports which misled explorers and cartographers for 100 years and caused an imaginary Sea of Verrazzano (Mare de Verrazana) to appear on North American maps. The search for a passage to China was Verrazzano's sole objective, and although he did stop in New York Bay, the first European to do so, he

left when he realized it did not lead to a strait. He continued north to Newfoundland before admitting defeat and returning home. Evidence for his later voyages is less certain but it is said that a southerly voyage in 1528 cost Verrazzano his life, when he landed on an island, possibly Guadeloupe, and was killed by cannibals.

## Verrocchio, Andrea del (1436–1488) *Italian goldsmith, sculptor, and painter*

A native of Florence, Verrocchio was probably a pupil of DONATELLO, after whose death he worked at the court of Lorenzo de' Medici. Many artists were trained in Verrocchio's workshop, in its heyday the biggest in Florence; among them were LEONARDO DA VINCI and PERUGINO. Few paintings attributed to Verrocchio survive; one is a *Baptism of Christ* (c. 1474–75; Uffizi, Florence) in which it is possible that the head of one angel was painted by the young Leonardo. Verrocchio's sculptural style illustrates the developing interest of Florentine art in naturalism and movement. In the bronze statue of David (c. 1476; Bargello, Florence) Verrocchio conveyed the arrogance of a young man through expression as well as through the aggressive pose (and incidentally criticizes Donatello's suaver treatment of the same subject). In the bronze *Putto with a Dolphin* (c. 1480; Palazzo Vecchio), designed for a fountain at the Medici villa at Careggi, he successfully presented movement in three dimensions so that the pattern in the work appears to change from each angle. The famous life-size bronze equestrian statue of Bartolommeo COLLEONI (c. 1479–88; Campo San Zanipolo, Venice), completed after his death, shows Verrocchio's interest in another type of figure than that of youth—the strong, dynamic, and ruthless warrior. His most important work in Florence is perhaps the bronze *Christ and St. Thomas* (1467–83), on the outside of Orsanmichele. Examples of his fine portrait busts are those of a noblewoman holding flowers (Bargello, Florence) and of Lorenzo de' Medici (National Gallery, Washington). He is regarded as one of the most influential Florentine artists of his time.

Further reading: Andrew Butterfield, *The Sculptures of Andrea del Verrocchio* (New Haven, Conn.: Yale University Press, 1997); Günter Passavant, *Verrocchio* (London: Phaidon, 1969); Charles Seymour, *The Sculpture of Verrocchio* (London: Studio Vista, 1971).

## Vesalius (Andrea Vesalio) (1514–1564) *Belgian-born anatomist*

The son and grandson of physicians who had practiced at the imperial court, Vesalius, after studying medicine in Paris and Padua, followed the family tradition and served successively Emperor CHARLES V and his son, PHILIP II of Spain. He began his anatomical work with the publication of six detailed plates in his *Tabulae sex* (1538), and completed his program with the most comprehensive and lavishly illustrated of all Renaissance anatomical texts, *De humani corporis fabrica* (On the structure of the human body; 1543). Although Vesalius attempted to base his ANATOMY on human DISSECTION, cadavers were too scarce to allow his program to be realized. Consequently, at several points, he was compelled to fall back reluctantly on the authority of Galen (*see* GALENISM, RENAISSANCE). In 1562, for unknown reasons, Vesalius left the service of Philip II. He died in mysterious circumstances while returning from a pilgrimage to the Holy Land and was buried on the Ionian island of Zakynthos (Zante).

*De humani corporis fabrica libri septem* appeared in a number of editions in several countries within a few years of its initial publication at Basle. The remarkable illustrations by Jan Steven van CALCAR were plagiarized in England as early as 1545 by the engraver Thomas Geminus for an abridged version of Vesalius' work entitled *Compendiosa totius anatomie delineatio*; this abridgment was translated into English by Nicholas UDALL (1553; repr. 1559). A version in modern English is *The Epitome of Andreas Vesalius* by C. R. Lind (Cambridge, Mass., 1969). Publication of the whole work, together with the original illustrations, in a new multivolume translation by William Frank Richardson and John Burd Carman began in 1998 (Novato, Calif.: Norman Publishing).

Further reading: Charles D. O'Malley, *Andreas Vesalius of Brussels, 1514–1564* (Berkeley, Calif: University of California Press, 1964).

## Vespasiano da Bisticci See BISTICCI, VESPASIANO DA

## Vespucci, Amerigo (1454–1512) *Italian explorer*

Born in Florence, Vespucci was introduced to astronomy and geography by an uncle. He studied law at Pisa before entering the service of the Medici family around 1480. From 1494 he worked for them as a shipping agent in Seville. When COLUMBUS's administration of Hispaniola was called in question (1497), Vespucci sailed there with the commission of investigation, thus beginning a career in active exploration. He made several voyages to the New World, although exactly how many and their destinations are unclear. In 1498–99 he sailed with Alonso de Ojeda, exploring the Gulf of Mexico and possibly northern Brazil.

In 1500 Vespucci and Gonzalo Coelho led a three-ship Portuguese expedition down the coast of Brazil. This voyage was extensively documented and charted, and one of Vespucci's letters describing it, *The New World* (*Mundus Novus*), was the first document to define America as a continent separate from Asia. The cartographer Martin Waldseemüller was the first to christen the new land mass America in Vespucci's honor on his world map of 1507, and *The New World* soon appeared in Italian, French, and German editions. Back in Spain Vespucci held the post of pilot major from 1505 until his death.

Further reading: Giancarlo Masini and Iacopo Gori, *How Florence Invented America: Vespucci, Verrazzano, and*

**Vesalius** The title page of his *De humani corporis fabrica* (1543) depicts a dissection in the crowded lecture theater at Padua. The engraving is by Jan Steven van Calcar.
*Mansell/Time Life Pictures/Getty Images*

*Mazzei and Their Contribution to the Conception of the New World* (San Francisco, Calif.: Marin, 1999).

**vestments** The ceremonial garments worn by clergy for religious services. The vestments of the Catholic Church—some, like the alb, cope, and chasuble, developed from classical Roman garments—were often charged with symbolism (for instance, the whiteness of the alb denoting purity). Festal copes and chasubles were often of velvet sumptuously embroidered with figures and scenes from the Bible in colored silks, gold and silver threads, and tiny pearls; the work of medieval English embroiderers in this style (*opus anglicanum*) was particularly prized.

Such magnificent display clashed with the reformers' ideal of a Church that manifested Christ's humility and voluntary poverty to the world, and vestments fell victim to outbreaks of ICONOCLASM throughout the Reformation period. In Germany extremists like Andreas CARLSTADT wanted to do away entirely with the use of vestments, but the more moderate LUTHER believed that some at least should be retained for Eucharistic services. CALVIN on the other hand emphasized preaching and Bible reading over the sacraments and demanded simplicity in public worship, so ministers in churches that followed the Genevan model wore a black loose-fitting gown with a small white ruff. In England vestments long remained a matter of controversy, with the different versions of the BOOK OF COMMON PRAYER charting their periods of favor or disfavor. The more Calvinistic of Elizabeth I's subjects complained bitterly of "popery" when she showed herself inclined to favor traditional vestments and did their best to suppress them; in 1566 Archbishop Matthew PARKER's *Advertisements* ruled that clergy should wear copes on some occasions but that surplices (white, loose-fitting linen tunics) were obligatory at services.

See also: LITURGY

**Vettori, Piero** (Petrus Victorius) (1499–1585) *Italian humanist scholar*
Vettori was born in Florence and attended Pisa university. He then spent some time in Rome before returning to Florence, where he held the university chairs in Greek, Latin, and moral philosophy. A dominant figure in European classical studies of his time, Vettori conducted an extensive correspondence; Pope Julius III, Henry III of France, and Grand Duke Cosimo of Florence were among his admirers. His letters were collected and published in 1577 and 1597.

Vettori's editions and commentaries show the astonishing scope of his Greek scholarship: editions of Euripides, Aeschylus, and Sophocles; commentaries on Aristotle's *Rhetoric*, *Poetics*, *Politics*, and *Nicomachean Ethics*; editions of Porphyry, Dionysius of Halicarnassus, and Clement of Alexandria. Among the Latin authors who attracted his attention were CICERO (his annotations on Cicero's letters (1587) are particularly important), Cato, Varro, and Columella. His other observations on classical writers were collected in 25 books of *Variae lectiones* (1553; subsequently enlarged to 38 books, 1569, 1582).

**Vicente, Gil** (c. 1465–c. 1537) *Portuguese playwright and poet*
Biographical details are few concerning the dramatist sometimes called the father of the Portuguese theater and perhaps the country's greatest poet after CAMÕES. He may have been born at Guimarães and educated at Coimbra. It has also been suggested that he started life as a goldsmith and in this role created the fantastically elaborate gold and enamel Belém monstrance (1506; Lisbon museum) in the Manueline style. He married in 1500 and his two children edited his works (1562). Attached to the courts of Manuel I and John III, he supervised dramatic productions at court. His works, particularly his religious *autos*, were influenced by Juan del ENCINA; they were also indebted to ERASMUS, who compared him to the Roman playwright PLAUTUS.

Virtually all of Vicente's lyric poetry, which draws on the traditional and folk verse of medieval Portugal and Spain, is contained in his plays and reflects the fact that he was a musician as well as a poet. His 44 plays consist of *autos*, tragicomedies for courtly audiences, and comedies and farces for popular audiences. Sixteen of these are in Portuguese, 11 (including many of his best non-religious plays) in Spanish, and 17 in a mixture of the two languages. The tragicomedy *Dom Duardos* (1525) is some-times considered his masterpiece; other examples of his work are *Comédia del Viudo* (1514), *Comédia de Rubena* (1521), *Auto da Feira* (1528), and *Amadís de Gaula* (1533). The opposition of the Inquisition, introduced in Portugal in 1536, the fashion for Italianate verse, and the popularity of Lope de VEGA checked the growth of a Portuguese national theater, which Vicente's work seemed to herald.

**Vicentino, Nicola** (1511–1576) *Italian composer and theorist*
Born in Vicenza, Vicentino studied in Venice under Adrian WILLAERT and took holy orders. He later moved to Ferrara, where he was employed by Cardinal Ippolito d'Este and taught music to the ducal family. Vicentino traveled throughout Italy with his patron, but by 1563 he had become *maestro* at Vicenza cathedral. The following year he left and went to Milan, where he died of the plague. Vicentino wrote motets and madrigals but is principally noted for his theoretical works. In *L'antica musica ridotta alla moderna prattica* (1555) he advances modal theories which encouraged composers towards equal temperament and describes the arcicembalo, an instrument with a 31 note octave.

**Vicenza** A city in the Veneto region of northern Italy, and the heart of a rich agricultural region. During the period of the Renaissance Vicenza prospered from its woolen cloth industry. The city was ruled by Romans, Lombards, by the DELLA SCALA FAMILY of Verona (1311–87), by the VISCONTI FAMILY of Milan (1387–1405), and by Venice from 1405. Vicenza's most famous citizen was the architect PALLADIO, whose work in the city was continued by Vincenzo SCAMOZZI. Palladian structures that survive include the Basilica (1549–1614), the Villa ROTONDA (1553–89), the Loggia del Capitaniato (1571), and the Teatro Olimpico (1580–84). Among other well-known Vicentines are the poet TRISSINO and the navigator PIGAFETTA; the painter Bartolommeo MONTAGNA also spent much of his working life in the city.

**Victoria, Tomás Luis de** (1548–1611) *Spanish composer*
Victoria sang as a boy at the cathedral of his native Ávila, but by 1565 he was enrolled as a singer at the German College, Rome. From 1569 he was employed at the Roman church of Sta. Maria di Monserrato and in 1571 taught music at the German College, being appointed *maestro* in 1573. After taking holy orders (1575) he became chaplain at the church of San Girolamo della Carità in 1578. From 1587 Victoria served Empress Maria, widow of Maximilian II, as chaplain at the monastery of Las Descalzas de Sta. Clara in Madrid, a post he held until his death, although he continued to visit Rome frequently. Victoria is generally regarded as the greatest Spanish composer of the Renaissance. All his compositions are sacred, and they

comprise 20 Masses, 52 motets, and many other liturgical pieces. His works are in a style as sophisticated as PALESTRINA's, whose pupil he may have been, but of an emotional intensity rarely equaled elsewhere. Perhaps best known are his motet *O quam gloriosam* and the Mass that he based upon it.

**Further reading:** Gustave Reese, *The New Grove High Renaissance Masters: Josquin, Palestrina, Lassus, Byrd, Victoria* (London: Macmillan, 1984).

**Victorius, Petrus** See VETTORI, PIERO

**Vida, Marco Girolamo** (c. 1485–1566) *Italian prelate and poet*
Born at Cremona and educated in Mantua, Vida went in 1510 to Rome and the papal court of Leo X, where he became acquainted with CASTIGLIONE, BEMBO, and other eminent literary figures. He was consecrated bishop of Alba in 1535 and took part in the Council of TRENT. His works are important contributions to neo-Latin literature in the Renaissance. His *Christus* or *Christiad* (1535), written in Virgilian hexameters, adapted the epic to Christian matter in presenting Christ as the heroic redeemer. The episode of a council in Hell, borrowed from Boccaccio's *Filocolo*, influenced similar scenes in TASSO's epic and, through Tasso, Milton's *Paradise Lost. De arte poetica* (1527), in the tradition of critical essays that extends from Horace to Alexander Pope, is concerned with epic style and imitation of classical models. Among other works are the didactic poems *Scacchia ludus* (*The Game of Chess*; 1527), which expounds chess in the guise of a mock-heroic account of a match between Apollo and Mercury, and *De bombyce* (*On the Silkworm*; 1527), on the production of silk.

**Vienna** (German **Wien**) The capital city of Austria on the River Danube. Celts and Romans lived on the site, but Vienna's history is continuous only from the early 12th century. The city was granted its charter in 1147 and as the capital of the dukes of Babenberg from 1156 became a center of courtly patronage. When the HAPSBURGS took over in 1278 they made Vienna their capital and from 1558 it became the capital of the Holy Roman Empire, although under Emperor RUDOLF II its primacy was usurped by Prague. It was not only its capital status but also its position on important trade routes that brought prosperity to the city. Vienna was temporarily occupied by the Hungarian monarch in the late 15th century and it heroically resisted the siege by the OTTOMAN TURKS in 1529. Both in 1529 and in 1683 it was the bastion against the Turkish advance into the heart of Europe. Under Hapsburg rule Vienna was a center of the Counter-Reformation in southern and eastern Europe. Vienna possesses a number of fine 14th-century Gothic churches and the cathedral of St. Stephen (1137–1578).

**Viète, François** (1540–1603) *French mathematician*
Although the greatest French mathematician of the century, Viète, who was born at Fontenay-le-Comte, trained initially in law at the university of Poitiers. Much of his early life was spent in politics. He served as a member of the Brittany *parlement*, practiced law in Paris, and in 1580 was appointed an officer of the Paris *parlement*. As Henry IV's cryptographer, he broke an elaborate cipher used by Spanish agents. It is, however, as an algebraist that he is mainly remembered. In his *In artem analyticam isagoge* (1591) Viète introduced such basic algebraic conventions as using letters to represent both known and unknown quantities, while improving the notation for the expression of square and cubic numbers. Further advances in the solutions of cubic and quartic equations were described by Viète in the posthumously published *De aequationum recognitione* (1615).

**Vigarni, Felipe** (**Felipe Biguerny**) (died 1543) *Burgundian-born sculptor*
Vigarni was active chiefly in Spain after 1498. Combining features of northern European art with Italian ideas, Vigarni executed work for Burgos cathedral and the chapel royal at Granada (1520–21) before embarking upon his best-known work at Toledo cathedral. In collaboration with Diego Copin and Cristiano from Holland, Rodrigo the German, Sebastián de Almonacid, and the painter Juan de Borgoñia, Vigarni executed the high wooden altar (1498–1504), designed by Peti Juan. His other works included a number of medals, such as that of Cardinal XIMÉNES DE CISNEROS (before 1517; Madrid university).

**Vigenère, Blaise de** (1523–1596) *French diplomat and cryptographer*
Vigenère, who was born at St.-Pourçain, began his career as a secretary to Francis I in 1540. Shortly afterwards he entered the service of the duke of Nevers with whom, apart from several diplomatic missions, he remained for the rest of his life. He first came into contact with cryptology while in Rome in 1549 on diplomatic business. In 1570 Vigenère retired from the court to write. Of the more than 20 books he published two are still remembered. The first, *Traicté des cometes* (1578), was one of the earliest works to suggest that comets were natural phenomena, bringing no special dangers for monarchs and princes. Many great kings, he pointed out, had died unheralded by any comet. In the second and more important work, *Traicté des chiffres* (1586), Vigenère laid the foundations of modern CRYPTOGRAPHY.

**Vignola, Giacomo Barozzi da** (1507–1573) *Italian architect*
Named after his birthplace of Vignola, near Modena, Vignola worked in the mannerist style and is best known for his highly influential treatise upon VITRUVIUS, the *Regola*

*delle cinque ordini d'architettura* (1562). The ideals expressed in this work, which was translated into most European languages, were reflected in many of Vignola's own designs and were themselves derived from his study of antique models during his training in Bologna and Rome. In 1541 he widened his horizons with work at FONTAINEBLEAU, returning to Italy two years later in order to produce his own designs.

After executing plans for the Palazzo Bocchi at Bologna (1545), Vignola moved to Rome where he was appointed papal architect by Pope Julius III in 1550. In 1551 he began work on the Villa Giulia in collaboration with VASARI and AMMANATI, basing the design closely on classical examples. At about the same time, however, he also began work on the designs for the churches of Sant' Andrea (1550–54) in the Via Flaminia and Anna dei Palafrenieri (begun 1565), which constituted a radical break with the classical tradition and anticipated Baroque architecture. After Michelangelo's death (1564) Vignola led the architectural team working to complete ST. PETER'S.

Vignola's most important building, the church of Il Gesù in Rome, was nonetheless designed in the classical style. Begun in 1568, the church was built for the Jesuits and had a profound influence on later architects, even though it was completed after Vignola's death in a form somewhat different from the original plans. Another highly original building by Vignola was the Villa Farnese at Caprarola, a polygonal structure begun by Antonio da SANGALLO the Younger and PERUZZI, for which Vignola designed (1559) a circular courtyard and magnificent spiral staircase. He also wrote a treatise on perspective, *Le due regole della prospettiva pratica* (1583).

## Villamediana, Don Juan de Tassis y Peralta, Count of (1580–1622) *Spanish poet, satirist, and courtier*

Born at Lisbon, the son of a diplomat, Villamediana was a gambler and libertine, who, on being banished from court in 1608, traveled and fought in Italy. Returning in 1617, he soon made himself so unpopular with his savage lampoons that he was forced to withdraw from Madrid again, but in 1621 he was appointed gentleman-in-waiting to the young Queen Isabel, wife of Philip IV. His attentions to her soon attracted the notice of his many enemies. During the performance of his masque *La Gloria de Niquea* in May 1622 a fire broke out and Villamediana's rescue of the queen caused further scandal. Three months later he was assassinated at the instigation of the king and his minister, the duke of Olivares.

Villamediana was the friend and patron of GÓNGORA, by whose style his own was deeply influenced. His satires combine concentrated venom with polished versification, and he also wrote some fine love poems and poetical fables.

**villanelle** A verse form developed in 16th-century France by the poets Joachim DU BELLAY, Philippe DESPORTES, Jean PASSERAT, and others and revived in the 19th century. The word "villanelle" is derived from *villanella*, a type of Italian rustic song or dance: the content of the villanelle is usually of a pastoral or popular nature. The villanelle consists of a variable number of three-line stanzas (usually five) with the rhyming pattern aba, followed by a four-line stanza with the rhyming pattern abaa. The first and third lines of the first stanza are used alternately as the third lines of the second, third, fourth, and fifth stanzas; both lines reappear as the third and fourth lines of the final stanza.

## Vinci, Leonardo da See LEONARDO DA VINCI

## Vinck(e)boons, David (1576–1632) *Netherlands painter and print designer*

In 1579 Vinckboons's family moved from his birthplace of Malines to Antwerp, where he received his initial training from his father Philip, a watercolorist. After the return of the Spanish army, the family moved on (1591) to Amsterdam, where Vinckboons studied under another Flemish émigré, Gillis (III) van Coninxloo. The latter's influence was decisive upon Vinckboons's many landscapes populated by numerous tiny figures. However, in such works as the *Kermis* (c. 1610; Dresden), the influence of the peasant scenes of Pieter BRUEGHEL the Elder is paramount. Vinckboons was one of the most popular and prolific painters and print designers of his day. His work constitutes a bridge between the Netherlandish genre traditions of the 16th and 17th centuries.

## Virgil (Publius Vergilius Maro) (70–19 BCE) *Roman poet*

Born near Mantua, where he later farmed, Virgil studied philosophy and rhetoric at Rome. There he was accepted into the literary circle surrounding MAECENAS and the future Emperor Augustus. Virgil's three great works—the *Eclogues* (37 BCE), the *Georgics* (30 BCE), and the *Aeneid* (virtually complete at the poet's death)—have had an incomparable influence over subsequent European literature. Known, copied, and studied throughout the Middle Ages, these poems were accorded a veneration that partially offset the dubious reputation acquired by their author as a powerful wizard. On the credit side, however, it was believed that Virgil's Fourth Eclogue was a prophecy of the birth of Christ, and it was the more positive assessment of Virgil in medieval tradition that led Dante to appoint him as his guide in the first two parts of the DIVINE COMEDY.

The *Eclogues* comprise 10 short poems in hexameters, written in imitation of the *Idylls* of the third-century BCE Greek poet Theocritus. From him Virgil adapted such motifs as the incantations used by a country girl to draw back a faithless lover from the town, a singing match between shepherds, and laments for unrequited love; these recur in countless Renaissance imitations in Latin and in the vernaculars. Theocritus, who was virtually rediscovered in the early 15th century, and Virgil together laid the foundations of the PASTORAL.

The *Georgics* are four didactic poems, also in hexameters, on the subject of farming. They deal respectively with the cultivation of crops, the growing of trees, cattle rearing, and beekeeping. The *Georgics* had fewer Renaissance admirers, but among them was Girolamo FRACASTORO, who imitated them in his *Syphilis*. One reason for the comparative lack of enthusiasm for the *Georgics* was Aristotle's strictures on didactic poetry, aired particularly by Lodovico CASTELVETRO.

The *Aeneid* was the virtually unchallenged model for a national EPIC in the Renaissance, greatly preferred to HOMER by, among others, VIDA and Julius Caesar SCALIGER. The text known to the Renaissance was generally supplemented by a 13th book, added in 1427 by Maffeo VEGIO. Finding an adequate meter to reproduce the dignity and power of Virgil's Latin hexameters was one of the major tasks of his translators and imitators.

**Vischer family** A family of sculptors and bronze founders in Nuremberg, Germany. The foundry was started in 1453 by Hermann the Elder (died 1488), whose most important work was the bronze font (1457) in the Stadtkirche, Wittenberg. His son Peter the Elder (c. 1460–1529), the most renowned member of the family, gave the foundry its wide reputation. A gifted sculptor, he made many of the models for his work himself. He worked in the late Gothic naturalistic style with a touch of classicism, which was apparent, for example, in the monument of Archbishop Ernst of Saxony in Magdeburg cathedral (1494–95). To him is attributed the "Bough-Breaker" (1490; Munich), a key work of German bronze sculpture because of its early three-dimensionality and interest in movement. Another important work was the pair of bronze statues of Theodoric and King Arthur for the tomb of Emperor Maximilian I at Innsbruck (1513). Peter's most famous work is the large and impressive reliquary shrine of St. Sebald for the church of St. Sebald in Nuremberg, erected in 1519. Peter was assisted in this by his talented sons who carried on the foundry, Hermann the Younger (c. 1486–1517), Peter the Younger (1487–1528), and Hans (c. 1489–1550). The first two visited Italy (c. 1512–15), and Italian influence is apparent in their work, including the St. Sebald shrine. The design of the whole structure and the main figures of the apostles are still essentially Gothic, but much of the decoration is mannerist, including a profusion of biblical, mythological, and allegorical figures. Hermann cast many funeral monuments, including the tomb of Elisabeth and Hermann VIII of Henneberg at Römhild (probably after 1507). Peter produced medals and plaques in a full-blown Renaissance style, as well as monuments. Hans's work includes reliefs for the Fugger chapel in Augsburg (1537–40). Hans's son Georg (1520–92) was a maker of small decorative items in bronze.

**Visconti family** A family predominant in Milan from the late 13th century. The careers of Ottone Visconti (1207–95; archbishop of Milan, 1262–95), who ousted the rival della Torre family, and his great-nephew Matteo (captain of the people, 1287–1302; imperial vicar, 1311–22) were the basis of the Visconti family fortunes. In 1349 the council of the commune bestowed upon Matteo's heirs the perpetual title of *Signore*. Despite papal opposition, they extended their lands and influence throughout Lombardy and Piedmont. The height of Visconti power came under Giangaleazzo (1351–1402), who succeeded his father Galeazzo II (c. 1321–78) in the western part of the family's lands in 1378 and ousted his uncle, Bernabò (1323–85), from the remainder in 1385. He was made duke of Milan in 1395, and by his death only Florence stood out against Visconti overlordship of northern Italy. Giangaleazzo was succeeded by his weak son Giovanni Maria (1388–1412; duke, 1402–12); after a troubled reign, during which he relied heavily on the support of Facino CANE and his *condottieri*, he was succeeded by his brother, Filippo Maria (1392–1447; duke, 1412–47), who restored Visconti power, but was thwarted in his dreams of wider expansion by Florence and Venice in a war that lasted from 1423 to 1428. Increasing reliance upon *condottieri* in his later years did not prevent his suffering heavy territorial losses, including that of Genoa, which he had seized in 1412. He produced no male heirs and at his death the line was extinguished. Power passed briefly to the AMBROSIAN REPUBLIC, and then (1450) to Filippo Maria's son-in-law, Francesco SFORZA. See family tree overleaf.

**Vitoria, Fray Francisco de** (c. 1483–1546) *Spanish theologian*
He may have been born at Burgos, where, having entered the Dominican Order (c. 1502), he studied at the convent of San Pablo, before going to Paris in 1506. There he was ordained priest (1509), taught arts and philosophy (1512–17), and became a doctor of theology (1523). After lecturing on theology at Valladolid (1523–26), he was appointed to the first chair of theology at Salamanca, where he reformed theological studies by his changes to the curriculum and his insistence upon a humanistic approach to the subject. Melchior CANO was among his pupils. His *Relectiones* (1557, 1565, 1604) covered many of the moral questions of the time, including the conquest of the American Indians (he was critical of Spanish methods) and the concept of a just war (war is only held to be justifiable if undertaken to redress a wrong already inflicted).

**Visconti Family**

Lords of Milan are shown in bold; the first Visconti to hold the title "duke" was Giangaleazzo. The direct male line of Visconti rulers of Milan died out with Duke Filippo Maria, but the dynastic marriages of the previous 80 years had raised Milan to the status of a European power. It was through Valentina's marriage to Louis of Orleans that the French royal house made their claim to Milan.

**Vitruvius Pollio** (active c. 50–26 BCE) *Roman military engineer*

Vitruvius is important as the author of *De architectura*, the only treatise on the subject surviving from the ancient world (*see* ARCHITECTURE). Copies of the work were known in Italy in the Middle Ages, but interest in it only escalated with Poggio BRACCIOLINI's discovery of a superior manuscript of this notoriously problematical text. It was avidly studied by ALBERTI and PALLADIO, among others, and it provided the basis for a theory of architecture in conscious opposition to Gothic practice, as well as providing models for buildings such as THEATERS for which there was no medieval equivalent.

Vitruvius's text, edited by Joannes Sulpitius, was first printed in Rome in an undated edition at the end of the 15th century. The edition by Fra Giovanni GIOCONDO (Venice, 1511) was the first to contain illustrations other than diagrams. The first version in Italian, a translation by Cesare Cesariano, was a magnificently produced edition (Como, 1521) containing, among numerous full-page woodcuts, plans of Milan cathedral that were probably the earliest printed plans representing a Gothic building. However, it was the editions by Daniele BARBARO—his own Italian translation (1556) reprinted along with his edition of the Latin text (1566)—that became the standard versions. The first French edition appeared in 1547 with an appendix on sculpture by Jean GOUJON, and Walter Rivius's *Vitruvius Teutsch* was published the following year, with woodcuts by Virgil SOLIS. A modern English translation is *Ten Books on Architecture*, translated by Ingrid Rowland, with commentary and illustrations by Thomas Noble Howe (Cambridge University Press, 1999).

**Vitry, Philippe de** (1291–1361) *French music theorist, poet, and composer*

Vitry studied at the Sorbonne, was a canon at the cathedrals of Cambrai, Clermont, and Verdun among others, and became bishop of Meaux in 1351. For much of his life he was active in the French court as secretary to Charles IV, Philip VI, and John II. Vitry was recognized in his day as a leading intellectual; his famous treatise, *Ars nova musicae* (c. 1320), is a fundamental source of information on rhythmic notation in which Vitry developed the mensural system of notation (*see* ARS NOVA). Of Vitry's compositions only motets survive; these are often lyrical in quality and demonstrate the use of isorhythm and the hocket.

**Vittoria, Alessandro** (1525–1608) *Italian sculptor*
A native of Trent (Trento) in northern Italy, Vittoria
was active after 1543 chiefly in Venice where he became
the leading sculptor in the city. A friend of TITIAN, TIN-
TORETTO, PALLADIO, and other notable mannerists, Vittoria
was a pupil of Jacopo SANSOVINO and undertook work in
several different media—marble, bronze, and terracotta.
Among his best-known work is the elaborate stucco decoration of the Scala d'Oro (1555–59) in the doge's palace in
Venice, where he also created three statues in the Sala
delle Quattro Porte (1587) and other pieces, both before
and after the fire of 1577. He also produced a number of
important religious works for the church of Sta. Maria de'
Frari and other Venetian churches. Other works included
stucco decorations at Daniele BARBARO's Palladian Villa
Barbaro (now Villa Volpi) at Maser, near Asolo, and several important tombs, numerous portrait busts, and
bronze figurines. His own particular brand of MANNERISM
survived after his death in the styles of several of the
pupils of the school he founded.

**Vittorino da Feltre** (Vittorino de' Rambaldoni) (1378–
1446) *Italian humanist educator*
Vittorino is generally called after his birthplace, Feltre,
north of Treviso. He studied and then taught at Padua university, met GUARINO DA VERONA, and began to evolve the
educational theories that laid the foundation of humanistic pedagogy. In 1423 he was invited to Mantua by Gianfrancesco (I) Gonzaga to establish a school for the
children of the Gonzaga court. For 22 years Vittorino administered every aspect of the intellectual, moral, and
physical development of about 70 pupils, including some
paupers, who were boarded in the Gonzaga villa known as
the Casa Giocosa.

The basis of the curriculum was the teaching of Latin
and Greek grammar, and the classical ideal of the eloquent
and virtuous citizen was held up for the pupils, among
them a number of girls, to emulate. One of Vittorino's star
pupils was Gianfrancesco's daughter, Cecilia (1424–51),
who became so passionate about her studies that she rejected the marriage that had been arranged for her with
the duke of Urbino and opted instead to enter a convent.
Mathematics, music, and philosophy (both Platonic and
Aristotelian) were also taught, but there was a strong emphasis on sound Christian doctrine, and physical education was not neglected.

**Vivarini family** A family of artists in 15th-century
Venice. The founder of the Vivarini workshop at Murano
was Antonio Vivarini (c. 1415–84), also known as
Antonio da Murano. His early commissions included a
number of Madonnas, such as that painted for the
Oratorio dei Filippini in Padua (c. 1440). A prolific artist,
Antonio favored a more naturalistic approach in his later
works, many of which were executed with the col-

laboration of his brother-in-law Giovanni d'Alemagna
(died 1450). The two men together produced several
gilded and elaborate altarpieces for churches in Venice
and also collaborated upon Antonio's masterpiece, the
polyptych *Virgin and Child Enthroned with Saints* (1448;
Pinacoteca Nazionale, Bologna), which also exhibits the
influence of Antonio's younger brother Bartolommeo
(1432–91). From 1447 to 1450 Antonio and Giovanni
d'Alemagna lived in Padua, where they worked alongside
Andrea MANTEGNA and Niccolò Pizzolo upon a fresco
cycle in the Ovetari chapel of the church of the Eremitari
(destroyed in World War II) that reflected the influence of
GENTILE da Fabriano and MASOLINO. Antonio's son Alvise
(1445–1505) was influenced by ANTONELLO DA MESSINA
and Giovanni BELLINI and produced a number of original
works, including *Christ Blessing* (1498; Brera, Milan) and
*St. Anthony of Padua* (undated; Museo Correr, Venice).

**Vivès, Juan Luis** (1492–1540) *Spanish humanist scholar
and educator*
Vivès was born and educated in Valencia and subsequently
studied at Paris (1509–c. 1512), Bruges, and Louvain.
While in Paris (1519) he met ERASMUS, who already knew
of him through Thomas MORE. In 1520 Vivès was appointed lecturer at Louvain, and soon afterwards began
work at Erasmus's request on a commentary on St. Augustine's *City of God* (1522). When HENRY VIII and Catherine
of Aragon visited Bruges (1521), Vivès was presented to
them, and they and Cardinal Wolsey welcomed him when
he moved to England in 1523. He made his home at Oxford, becoming a fellow of the newly founded Corpus
Christi College. His support for Catherine over the royal
divorce proceedings cost him Henry's favor and even led
to his being placed under house arrest for six weeks. He
then withdrew to the Continent, where, between 1528
and 1531 he wrote his famous treatise on education *De
tradendis disciplinis* (1531). This ranks as his major educational work but he also wrote a book on the education
of women, translated into English as *The Instruction of a
Christian Woman* (1540), and *Linguae Latinae exercitatio*
(1539) to provide practice in Latin for schoolchildren. His
educational theories marked an important development in
Christian humanism. In philosophy, his *De causis corrup-
tarum artium* (1531) embodied his opposition to scholasticism and *De anima et vita* (1538) offered a fresh
approach to psychology. He died in Bruges of fever.

**Volterra, Daniele (Ricciarelli) da** See DANIELE (RICCIA-
RELLI) DA VOLTERRA

**Vos, Maarten Pietersz. de** (1532–1603) *Netherlands
painter and print designer*
De Vos was born in Antwerp and trained by his artist father Pieter de Vos and by Frans FLORIS. He seems to have
visited Italy, possibly in the company of Pieter Brueghel.

He is reputed to have worked at Venice in the studio of Tintoretto as an assistant in the painting of landscapes. In 1558 he returned to Antwerp, where he joined the artists' guild and in 1572 became its dean. Having Lutheran sympathies, de Vos became involved with the liberal, reformist circle of the famous geographer Abraham ORTELIUS. These connections did not prove incompatible with his work as a painter of altarpieces, which he produced to replace those which had been destroyed by iconoclastic riots. De Vos also designed illustrations for Christopher PLANTIN and, in 1594, collaborated with Ambrosius Francken on the decorations for the triumphal entry of Archduke Ernest of Austria. As a painter of historical, religious, and mythological scenes, de Vos continued the style of Frans Floris, somewhat modified by a coloristic sense derived from his Venetian experiences.

**Vredeman de Vries, Hans** (1527–c. 1604) *Netherlands architect and designer*
Born at Leeuwarden, Friesland, Vredeman de Vries was a student of Cornelis FLORIS, whose style he plagiarized, primarily in a long series of variations upon the design of Antwerp town hall. Several of these variants are reproduced, together with numerous other architectural fantasies, in his *Varia architecturae formae* (1601). Vredeman de Vries does not appear to have been an architect in the generally accepted sense, in that no known buildings can be securely attributed to him. However, his journeys through the Netherlands and Germany and his books of prints popularized his designs, reflections of which may be seen in the guildhalls of Antwerp and the butchers' hall of Namur. A seminal, rather than an original figure, Vredeman de Vries's influence may be traced well into the 17th century.

**Vriendt, Cornelis de** See FLORIS, CORNELIS

**Vriendt, Frans de** See FLORIS, FRANS

**Vries, Adriaen de** (1546–1626) *Dutch sculptor*
Adriaen de Vries was born in The Hague and became a pupil of GIAMBOLOGNA in Florence. His first major commissions were the Mercury fountain and the Hercules fountain, completed respectively in 1599 and 1602, for Augsburg. Although de Vries designed both works, he did so in Rome; the actual casting and finishing was done, from his models, by other sculptors in Augsburg. As early as 1593 de Vries was already executing commissions for Emperor RUDOLF II, including the famous *Abduction of Psyche by Mercury* in Paris. In 1601 he moved to Prague, where he worked mainly for the emperor on portrait busts and allegorical reliefs, such as *Rudolf II Bringing the Arts and Sciences into Bohemia* (1609; Windsor Castle, England). After the emperor's death in 1612 and the removal of the imperial court to Vienna, de Vries widened his circle of patrons. For Count Ernst of Schaumburg he executed the font in Bückeburg parish church and the count's tomb in Stadthagen, as well as a pair of bronze groups, since lost, for the bridge leading to Bückeburg castle. All of this work was designed and cast in Prague, being subsequently transported to north Germany by road. De Vries collaborated with Hans von AACHEN and Bartholomäns SPRANGER and was influenced by artists as diverse as Raphael and Dürer, but his principal model remained Giambologna. Adriaen de Vries was the last great northern mannerist sculptor and a leading light in the international "hothouse" culture that briefly and spectacularly flourished in imperial Prague at the turn of the 16th and 17th centuries.

# W

**waggoners** Navigational guides containing charts and sailing instructions. The word is an English corruption of the Dutch name "waghenaer." Lucas Jansz. Waghenaer's *Spieghel der Zeevaerdt* (1584–85; translated as *The Mariners Mirrour*, 1588) popularized printed sailing charts, standardized navigational techniques, and brought the best contemporary mathematical and astronomical data within reach of the ordinary mariner.

**warfare** Wars in all their varieties constantly swept Renaissance Europe. The HOLY ROMAN EMPIRE never fully reintegrated itself after local and religious wars; the Hundred Years' War (1337–1453) and the Wars of RELIGION (1562–98) brought France close to collapse; the Hapsburg–Valois conflict raged over Europe for over 60 years; the Turkish army twice threatened Vienna. At the same time as warfare advanced technically and the horrors of FIREARMS became more apparent there was a growing awareness of the brutality of war and correspondingly less emphasis on its romantic glories.

The English longbow was the most effective 14th-century weapon, but the introduction, probably by the English at Crécy (1346), of GUNPOWDER was the most significant development. Warfare became more technical and more expensive; this favored the evolution of royal and national armies and weakened the private feudal armies. Monarchs relied more on skilled MERCENARIES and less on untrained feudal levies. By the 15th century the new CANNON could demolish medieval castle walls, a further blow to the power of feudal lords. The efficacy of gunpowder in artillery and, slightly later, in mining posed new challenges to the military architects and engineers responsible for defensive FORTIFICATION. The arquebus, a firearm that a man could carry, was developed. The first printed edition of the Latin text of *De re militari* by the late Roman military writer Flavius Vegetius appeared in Utrecht in 1473, and it was published in at least four further editions before 1500, in addition to translations into German (Ulm, 1475) and English (published by Caxton, 1489). The study of tactics, artillery, and technique was all part of the more professional approach to warfare, with military experts (such as VALTURIO) and theoreticians (such as MACHIAVELLI) commanding an attentive audience.

In the 16th century pistols and muskets were invented. At the battle of PAVIA (1525) General Fernando de Avalos proved the worth of the musket in the rout of the French cavalry by Spanish musketeers. The 16th century also saw great advances in naval warfare. Admirals, such as Sir Francis DRAKE, Andrea DORIA, and Don JOHN OF AUSTRIA, made effective use of lighter and more maneuverable ships.

**Further reading:** John F. Guilmartin Jr, *Gunpowder and Galleys: Changing Technology and Mediterranean Warfare at Sea in the Sixteenth Century* (London and New York: Cambridge University Press, 1974); John R. Hale, *War and Society in Renaissance Europe 1450–1620* (Leicester, U.K.: Leicester University Press and London: Fontana, 1985); ~, *Artists and Warfare in the Renaissance* (New Haven, Conn. and London: Yale University Press, 1990); Bert S. Hall, *Weapons and Warfare in Renaissance Europe: Gunpowder, Technology, and Tactics* (Baltimore, Md.: Johns Hopkins University Press, 2002); David Kunzle, *From Criminal to Courtier: The Soldier in Netherlandish Art 1550–1672* (Leyden, Netherlands: Brill, 2002).

**Wars of Italy** See ITALY, WARS OF

**Wars of Religion (French)** See RELIGION, (FRENCH) WARS OF

**Wassenhove, Joos van** See JUSTUS OF GHENT

**watches** The first watches appeared shortly before 1500, supposedly the invention of Peter Henlein (c. 1479–1542), a Nuremberg locksmith. More plausibly, they emerged in several centers as a natural development from small table CLOCKS. These, in turn, were made possible by the invention in the late 15th century of the spring-driven escapement. Thereafter no further fundamental advance in watch design and accuracy took place before the invention of the balance spring in 1675. Before this, without minute or second hands, the Renaissance watch was valued more as an item of jewelry or a toy than as an instrument for measuring time. Watches were accordingly expensive, highly decorated luxuries produced mainly to satisfy the whims of the wealthy. Typical of such pieces are, for example, the two very expensive watches bought by Francis I in 1518 to fit into the hilt of his dagger or the miniature timepiece Elizabeth I had made to fit into her ring.

See also: HOROLOGY

**Wechel family** A dynasty of printers based from the 1520s in Paris and from 1572 in Frankfurt and other German towns. The first in the family was Christian (fl. 1520–54), who worked in Paris, where he established the firm's special line in medical books and parallel Greek and Latin texts of the classics. He also produced Cornelius AGRIPPA's *De occulta philosophia* (1531), several editions of the Latin, French, and German texts of Andrea Alciati's EMBLEM book, the earliest in 1534, and the third book of Rabelais's *Pantagruel* (1546). Wechel's son Andreas (died 1581) took over in 1554 and moved for religious reasons to Frankfurt in 1572, where he produced a number of historical and geographical works, both classical and modern. Other members of the family continued printing at Frankfurt, and also at Hanau and Basle, until the outbreak of the Thirty Years' War effectively strangled humanistic publishing enterprise. The international and eclectic scope of the Wechel presses after 1572 is indicated by the variety of their modern authors: SADOLETO, BUCHANAN, DU PLESSIS-MORNAY, FALLOPPIO, FERNEL, Giacomo ZABARELLA, SERLIO, PARACELSUS and his disciples Thomas Moffett and Gerard Dorn, BRUNO, Giambattista DELLA PORTA, DEE, and RAMUS and authors on both sides of the RAMIST CONTROVERSY.

**Weelkes, Thomas** (c. 1576–1623) *English composer*
Nothing is known of Weelkes's early life. In 1598 he was appointed organist at Winchester College, where he probably remained until at least 1601, when he became organist and choirmaster at Chichester cathedral. In 1602 he was awarded the Oxford BMus. degree. Weelkes's employment at Chichester was tempestuous: he was periodically reproved for unruliness, drunkenness, and neglect of duty, and in 1617 he was even dismissed from the post, though he later resumed it. He died in London. Weelkes is important as a composer of both church music and madrigals. He wrote 10 Anglican services and around 40 anthems, of which *When David heard* is perhaps one of the finest. The madrigals are in a less restrained style, often for four, five, and six voices. In his four published collections, Weelkes demonstrated to great effect his intricate style, using fine counterpoint and brilliant imagery. A contemporary of Thomas MORLEY, he contributed to Morley's collection *The Triumphs of Oriana* (1601).

**Weerbeke, Gaspar van** (c. 1445–post-1517) *Franco-Flemish composer*
By 1472 Weerbeke was in the employ of the SFORZA FAMILY in Milan, and around 1481 he joined the papal choir in Rome. He returned to the Sforza court in 1489. From 1495 he was associated with Philip the Handsome, archduke of Austria and duke of Burgundy. He probably returned to Milan in 1498 and then to Rome in 1500, where he again sang in the papal choir. He is last documented as a canon at St. Maria ad Gradus in Mainz. Weerbeke worked with Josquin DES PRÉS at the Sforza court. Some eight Masses, 28 motets, and several other liturgical works survive, including substitution Masses. Five of his Masses were published by Ottaviano PETRUCCI.

**Weiditz, Hans (I)** (Hans Wydyz) (active 1497–1510) *German sculptor*
Weiditz was a wood carver working in a sculptural, three-dimensional style. He settled in Fribourg im Breisgau, and his altarpieces include the Schnewlin altar for a choir chapel in the minster there (c. 1512–14), depicting the *Rest on the Flight into Egypt* (after an etching by DÜRER). He also produced small-scale figures and groups, such as his *Adam and Eve* (c. 1510).

**Weiditz, Hans (II)** (pre-1500–1536) *German illustrator*
Presumed to be the son of Hans (I) Weiditz, he was probably born in Fribourg and worked in Augsburg and later Strasbourg. He is known as the gifted illustrator of numerous humanist, classical, sacred, and scientific books, for which he designed woodcuts. These included Cicero's *De officiis* (1531), which was extremely popular at the time, and Otto BRUNFELS's *Herbarum vivae eicones* (1530–36). His illustrations often satirize particular sections of society, such as the clergy and nobility.

**Weigel, Valentin** (1533–1588) *German mystic*
He was a Lutheran pastor near Chemnitz in the latter part of his life, but his writings show him to have held highly unorthodox ideas on the nature of the universe, some of

Buchenfchell. Backerfraut.

**Hans (II) Weiditz** Weiditz's careful observation of living plants is exemplified in this woodcut of a pasque flower (*Pulsatilla vulgaris*) for Brunfels's *Herbarum vivae eicones*.

which can be traced to the influence of PARACELSUS. He himself influenced Jakob BOEHME. Although his writings, and those ascribed to him, were not published until 20 years after his death, they circulated widely in manuscript during Weigel's lifetime.

## Wert, Giaches de (1535–1596) *Flemish composer*

Wert went to Italy as a child to sing at the court of the marchese della Padulla at Avellino near Naples. By 1558 he was in the employ of Count Alfonso Gonzaga at Novellara. He sang in choirs in Parma and Milan, and from 1565 until his death was *maestro* at the Gonzaga chapel of Sta. Barbara in Mantua. He also traveled to Augsburg and Venice, and is known to have had associations with the Este court in Ferrara in the 1570s and 1580s. Wert was a prolific composer; numerous Masses, motets, and Magnificats survive, but his most celebrated compositions are his MADRIGALS. A strong influence on MONTEVERDI, he published 13 madrigal collections, often with texts of a high quality, declamatory in style and with the three upper voices frequently emphasized; these were written for virtuoso court singers, and in particular the renowned Ferrarese female singers, the *concerto delle donne*.

## Weston, Elizabeth Jane (Westonia) (1582–1612) *English-born poet, linguist, and scholar, who gained a considerable reputation in Continental Europe*

Her family were forced to flee abroad because of her father's debts and settled in Bohemia. After he died in 1597, Elizabeth and her mother appealed to Emperor Rudolf II and other influential figures for assistance. By this time Elizabeth had attracted attention for her scholarship. Fluent, in English, German, Czech, Greek, and Italian, she wrote prose and verse in Latin and translated Aesop's ables. She corresponded with English and European scholars, many of whom rated her work highly and compared it with that of leading neo-Latin poets. In 1602 one of her patrons, at his own expense, published her verse at Frankfurt an der Oder as *Parthenicon Elisabethae Joannae Westoniae, virginis nobilissimae, poetriae florentissimae, linguarum plurimarum peritissimae*; there were several subsequent editions. Around the same time she married a lawyer, Johann Leon. She died in Prague.

## Weyden, Rogier van der (1399/1400–1464) *Netherlands painter*

Rogier is first heard of in 1427 as the student of Robert CAMPIN. In 1432 he entered the guild of his native Tournai but by 1435 had already moved to Brussels where he settled permanently. Rogier attracted commissions from numerous patrons, both within the Netherlands and abroad, and was civic painter of Brussels. None of his paintings is exactly dated and his oeuvre presents numerous attributional problems, as he had many followers. Rogier's earliest surviving work, such as the Louvre *Annunciation*, was strongly influenced by Campin. Later, the Boston *St. Luke Drawing the Virgin* incorporates motifs borrowed from Jan van EYCK. The Madrid *Descent from the Cross* (second half of the 1430s) is probably the artist's greatest work. In this composition, Rogier compressed ten nearly life-size figures within a gilded niche, simulating the appearance of a sculptured altarpiece of polychromed wood.

In 1439–41 Rogier worked on the four panels of his only secular narrative cycle, *The Justice of the Emperor Trajan and Count Herkinbald*, which decorated Brussels town hall until their destruction in 1695. The artist's fame had already spread to Castile by 1445, when King John II donated his altarpiece of the *Virgin* (now in Berlin) to the Charterhouse at Miraflores near Burgos. Rogier painted the enormous *Last Judgment* altarpiece in the hospital founded by Nicholas Rolin at Beaune, near Dijon, during the late 1440s. With its gold background, sculptural associations, and emotional intensity, it is closely comparable with the earlier *Descent from the Cross*. In 1449–51 Rogier was executing commissions for the Este of Ferrara and, in 1450, he visited Rome. Shortly after his return home, he executed two altarpieces for the Medici, the Frankfurt *Madonna and Child with Four Saints* and the Uffizi *Entombment*. Rogier's Braque triptych in Paris reinterprets a

Tuscan format of the Trecento, but is innovative in its juxtaposition of half-length figures against a landscape background—an idea subsequently adopted in the portraits of MEMLING and others. His last work is probably the *St. Columba* altarpiece in Munich, which is remarkable for its formal and coloristic harmony.

In addition to religious works, Rogier painted numerous portraits in which he developed a new mode of aristocratic likeness by subjectively manipulating the appearance of his sitters. Rogier's numerous exported works and his large *atelier*, which even attracted students from Italy, broadcast his style throughout Europe, making him the most influential northern painter of the 15th century.

**Further reading:** Dirk de Vos, *Rogier van der Weyden: The Complete Works* (Antwerp, Belgium: Mercatorfonds, 1999).

**White Mountain, battle of the** (1620) An important Catholic victory early in the Thirty Years' War. Following the election of the Calvinist WINTER KING, Frederick V, Elector Palatine, to the Bohemian throne, Emperor Ferdinand II promised to give Bohemia to Maximilian of Bavaria if he drove out the Calvinists. The Calvinists, led by Christian of Anhalt, met the imperial forces under Maximilian at the White Mountain near Prague. The decisive imperial victory led to Frederick's expulsion from Bohemia (1620) and then from the Palatinate (1623). It was followed by harsh Catholic retribution in Bohemia. The scale of the victory brought a number of Protestant powers into the war against the Hapsburgs.

**Wickram, Jörg** (1505–c. 1560) *German novelist and dramatist*
The illegitimate son of a municipal official, Wickram himself became an official in his native Colmar and later town clerk of Burgheim. Wickram, who was a *Meistersinger*, founded a school of MEISTERGESANG in Colmar in 1549. He was influential in the development of the German novel out of the medieval chivalric romance; the chivalric roots are still clear in, for example, his *Ritter Galmy uss Schottland* ("Sir Galmy from Scotland"; 1539). Gradually, however, the world and values of the knight are replaced by those of peasant and burgher in his work, which becomes increasingly didactic and moralizing, as in *Der Jungen Knaben Spiegel* (1554). Wickram's most popular work was his *Rollwagenbüchlin* ("Stagecoach Booklet"; 1555), a collection of anecdotes and SCHWÄNKE (a popular literary form then), intended as entertainment for travelers and lacking all didacticism. Wickram's plays are largely *Fastnachtspiele* (comic Shrovetide plays) and biblical tragedies, such as *Tobias* (1550).

**Wiericx, Anthonie** (c. 1552–1624), **Hieronymus** (c. 1553–1619), and **Johan** (c. 1549–1615) *Netherlands engravers*
Born in Antwerp and trained by their painter father, also named Anthonie, the brothers were child prodigies, as is indicated by their ages (prefixed *aet*), which appear on their line engravings. Johan's copies of Marcantonio RAIMONDI's *Venus and Cupid* and DÜRER's *Fall of Man* date from when he was, respectively, 14 and 16 years old. Hieronymus executed copies of Dürer's *St. George* and *St. Jerome* when he was, respectively, only 12 and 13. It should be stressed that these copies are, probably, the best in existence, following the originals virtually line for line. Given the remarkable sophistication of Dürer's engraved technique, the quality of the Wiericx brothers' copies reveals astonishing technical virtuosity. The brothers produced more than 2000 prints, many of which were small devotional works of a type popularized by the Jesuits in their campaign against the Protestant reformers. Although the Wiericx workshop also produced the brothers' own designs, the early copies after Dürer may be counted as its finest achievement.

**Wilbye, John** (1574–1638) *English composer*
Born at Diss, Norfolk, Wilbye worked from 1598 for the Kytson family at Hengrave Hall near Bury St. Edmunds, where he remained for 28 years. In 1628, on the death of Lady Elizabeth Kytson, he moved to Colchester. Influenced by Thomas MORLEY and Alfonso FERRABOSCO, Wilbye is one of the finest English madrigalists. He published only two books of madrigals (1597, 1609), but the second is generally regarded as one of the greatest English MADRIGAL collections. It contains arguably the finest of Wilbye's madrigals, "Draw on sweet Night," in which major and minor tonalities are used to depict intense melancholy.

**Willaert, Adrian** (c. 1490–1562) *Flemish composer*
Probably born in Bruges, Willaert studied music with Jean Mouton (c. 1459–1522) in Paris. From 1515 he was employed as a singer in the household of Cardinal Ippolito d'Este in Ferrara, traveling widely with him and spending two years in Hungary. On the cardinal's death (1520) Willaert transferred to the service of Duke Alfonso I d'Este. In 1527 he was appointed *maestro* at St. Mark's, Venice, where he remained until his death. Here he presided over a flourishing musical scene. His pupils included important composers, such as Ciprien de RORE, Nicola VICENTINO, and Andrea GABRIELI, and he is regarded as a major figure in the development of Italian music.

Willaert was a most prolific and versatile composer; he published a great deal of church music, many madrigals, chansons, villanelles, and a few instrumental pieces. His *Salmi spezzati* (1550) contains music for double choirs and set a tradition for polychoral music in St. Mark's. As a madrigalist Willaert paid great attention to the text. His collection of motets and madrigals, *Musica nova* (1559, though probably written much earlier), is arguably his most important work.

## William (I) the Silent (1533–1584) *Prince of Orange (1544–84) and Count of Nassau (1559–84)*

The son of William of Nassau and Juliana of Stolberg, William inherited Orange and substantial territories in Brabant and Franche-Comté from a cousin in 1544. At CHARLES V's insistence William was educated in Orange as a Catholic. He enjoyed the favor of Charles, who made him commander of the army in the Netherlands and governor of Holland, Zeeland, and Utrecht in 1555. William also served PHILIP II of Spain against France and negotiated the preliminaries of the peace of CATEAU-CAMBRÉSIS (1559) between Spain and France.

Despite his concern at the persecution of Dutch Protestants in the early 1560s, William remained loyal to Philip II until the duke of ALBA began his reign of terror in the Netherlands. William then resigned his offices, refused to take the oath of loyalty to Alba, and in 1568 openly declared his Protestant faith. He then embarked on his long struggle to drive the Spanish from the Netherlands. His efforts enjoyed little success until the SEA-BEGGARS seized Brill (1572) and flew the flag of Orange over its walls. Other towns followed, and in 1579 the seven northern states formed the Union of Utrecht. In 1581 they declared their independence and settled the hereditary stadtholdership on William, who was henceforth acclaimed as founder of the Republic of the United Netherlands. His assassination by a Catholic three years later gave the Dutch a martyr and inspired them to continue their struggle for full independence for the Netherlands.

**Further reading:** Koenraad W. Swart, *William the Silent and the Revolt of the Netherlands* (London: Historical Association, 1978).

## William (IV) the Wise (1532–1592) *Landgrave of Hesse-Kassel (1567–92)*

In 1552 William championed the Protestant cause against Emperor CHARLES V, and helped secure the release of his father, PHILIP OF HESSE, from five years' captivity. William succeeded his father as landgrave, but had to share the inheritance with his three brothers. He was an outstanding administrator and organizer with a considerable talent for economics. The survey, Ökonomische Staat, compiled for him in 1585 is a model of administrative statistics. William had a particular interest in astronomy; he constructed astronomical instruments, calculated stellar positions, and was a friend of Tycho BRAHE and patron of Jost BÜRGI.

## Wimpfeling, Jakob (1450–1528) *German humanist and educator*

The son of a saddler at Schlettstadt (now Sélestat, Alsace), Wimpfeling was educated at the universities of Fribourg, Erfurt, and Heidelberg. He also taught at Heidelberg (1471–84, 1498–1500), becoming rector there from 1481 until 1484. In Strasbourg (1501–15) he founded a literary society with Sebastian BRANT and Johannes Geiler. Although a critic of ecclesiastical abuses, as his satirical *Stylpho* (performed in 1480—the first Latin comedy by a German humanist) makes clear, he could never endorse the Reformation. His ideas on education were expressed in two books: *Isidoneus germanicus* ("Guide to the German Youth"), in which he argued for moral teaching in education and also recommended the reading of selected pagan Latin authors (many educators totally rejected their use), and the highly successful *Adolescentia* ("Youth"), a collection of ideas and advice from other authors. The patriotic element of Wimpfeling's humanism (in reaction to Italian cultural domination) is seen in his polemical treatise *Germania* (1501), in which he claimed that Alsace was incontestably German, and in his *Epitome rerum germanicarum* (1505; translated as *A Short History of Germany*), the first attempt at a systematic history of Germany. He died in Schlettstadt, where he had become involved in controversy with younger humanists over their blanket endorsement of the pagan poets.

## Winter King

The sobriquet of Frederick V (1596–1632), Elector Palatine (1610–23), on account of the brevity of his reign as king of Bohemia (1619–20). He married (1613) Elizabeth, daughter of James I of England; she became known as the Winter Queen. As head of the Protestant Union, Frederick accepted the Bohemian throne from nobles in rebellion against the Catholic Hapsburgs, but at the WHITE MOUNTAIN (1620) the imperial forces defeated the Protestants and went on to drive Frederick out of both Bohemia (1620) and the Palatinate (1623).

## witchcraft

A set of practices believed to give its practitioners extraordinary or supernatural power over events and people, generally, but not always, to be used for malign purposes. In the Renaissance period witchcraft was mainly associated with the poor and illiterate, who were considered to be the willing dupes of the Devil and his cohorts. It therefore differed from the scholarly and arcane practice of MAGIC (though a magus could lay himself open to charges of witchcraft and accusations of selling his soul to the Devil—witness the stories of FAUST and of Cornelius AGRIPPA von Nettesheim's familiar spirit in the form of a dog).

Although witchcraft had been attested from ancient times, the text often singled out as sparking off the obsession with it in the Renaissance period is the *Malleus Maleficarum* (1486) of the Dominican inquisitors Jakob

Sprenger and Heinrich Krämer, who had been authorized by papal bull in 1484 to suppress witchcraft in the Rhineland. Witch-hunting, hitherto a local and spasmodic phenomenon, was thus given official backing and legal respectability throughout Christendom, and the learned flocked to take part in the arguments about the nature of witchcraft and the danger it posed. James VI of Scotland, before he became JAMES I of England, took a close interest in several Scottish witch trials and wrote his credulous *Daemonologie* (1597) on his conclusions. In England the Cambridge theologian William Perkins contributed *A Discourse of the Damned Art of Witchcraft* (1608) to the Protestant side in the debate. These are however slight tracts compared with some of the Roman Catholic textbooks published on the Continent, such as the lawyer Nicolas Rémy's *Daemonolatreia* (1595).

Outbreaks of witch mania occurred at different times in different countries and with varying degrees of ferocity from the 15th to the 17th century, but they can broadly be linked to periods of social or religious turmoil. Thus southern Germany and Switzerland remained fertile ground for the witch-hunters as first the Reformation and then the Counter-Reformation swept across the area; Lutherans and Calvinists on the one side and Dominicans and Jesuits on the other strove to outdo each other in the pious zeal with which they pursued suspects. Institutional misogyny in both Church and State meant that the vast majority of the accused were women, as it was agreed among male clergy and lawyers that women's feeble minds and dangerous sexuality rendered them far more susceptible than men to the Devil's wiles. However, even the wealthy and educated and small children could fall foul of the witch-hunters' standard accusations of making a pact with the Devil, harming neighbors, and bizarre sexual practices. With torture routinely employed, confessions were easily extracted and a near 100% conviction rate achieved. In many of the worst-afflicted areas, such as the Rhineland, Savoy, and Switzerland, outbreaks of witch mania saw hundreds of people burnt at the stake—although in some jurisdictions enlightened secular rulers were able to curb the worst excesses of the clergy. In Italy the scepticism of the humanist intelligentsia created a climate of opinion generally unfavorable to witch mania: Andrea ALCIATI, for instance, regarded witches as deluded and therefore as subjects for medication rather than punishment, while Pietro POMPONAZZI considered that ignorant people ascribed to witchcraft natural phenomena that they did not understand. However, even here, in the late 16th century in Friuli, the Inquisition mobilized to conduct some well-documented inquiries into the activities of the *benandanti*, adherents of a rural cult whose practices the inquisitors condemned as witchcraft.

The few courageous sceptics and those who objected to the barbaric methods used by the witch-hunters had to battle against not only the apparatus of the Church and civil authority but also biblical texts such as Exodus 22.18 ("Thou shalt not suffer a witch to live"); they also had to be careful that their arguments against the operations of demons through witchcraft did not slip (or be interpreted as slipping) into the heresy of Sadduceeism, the denial of the existence of spirits. Most influential among the sceptics was Johann Weyer, whose *De praestigiis daemonum* (1563) maintained that the activities to which witches confessed were delusions caused by demons or morbidity. Weyer's book and *The Discoverie of Witchcraft* (1584) by his English follower Reginald Scot were both burnt by civil or ecclesiastical authorities.

**See also:** ANTISEMITISM

**Further reading:** Stuart Clark, *Thinking With Demons: The Idea of Witchcraft in Early Modern Europe* (Oxford, U.K.: Oxford University Press, 1999); Carlo Ginzburg, *The Night Battles: Witchcraft and Agrarian Cults in the Sixteenth and Seventeenth Centuries* (London: Routledge & Kegan Paul and Baltimore, Md: Johns Hopkins Press, 1983; repr. 1992); Christina Larner, *Enemies of God: The Witch-Hunt in Scotland* (London: Chatto & Windus, 1981; repr. Edinburgh: John Donald, 2000); ~, *Witchcraft and Religion: The Politics of Popular Belief* (Oxford, U.K. and New York: Blackwell, 1984); Brian P. Levack, *Witch-Hunt in Early Modern Europe* (New York and London: Longman, 1987); Hugh Trevor-Roper, *The European Witch Craze of the 16th and 17th Centuries* (Harmondsworth, U.K.: Penguin, 1969); Charles Zika, *Exorcising Our Demons: Magic, Witchcraft and Visual Culture in Early Modern Europe* (Leyden, Netherlands: Brill, 2003).

**Witte, Pieter de** (Pietro Candido) (c. 1548–1628)
*Netherlands painter*
Born in Bruges, from about 1570 Witte was active in Florence, Rome, and Volterra (hence the Italian form of his name "Pietro Candido"). In 1586 he arrived in Munich where he worked beside Frederik Sustris on the decoration of the Antiquarium, the first museum of antiquities to be built in modern times, which was itself destroyed during World War II. From 1587 he worked on the decorations of the grotto court, also at the ducal palace. In 1588 he executed a *Martyrdom of St. Ursula* for the Michaelkirche and in 1620 painted the high altarpiece at the Frauenkirche. He also designed series of tapestries of the *Months* and the life of Otto of Wittelsbach. Highly praised by the painter Joachim von Sandrart for his versatility, he incorporated both Venetian and Tuscan elements in his mannerist style and remained dominant in Munich until the arrival of Rubens' style in Bavaria in 1619.

**Wittenberg** A capital city in Saxony, on the River Elbe. First mentioned in the 12th century, Wittenberg was granted its municipal charter in 1293 and became the capital of the Ascanian dukes and electors of Saxony until 1423, when it passed to the house of Wettin. Wittenberg continued to be the capital of Saxony until 1547, when the electorate passed to the Albertine line of the house of Wettin. The University of Wittenberg (founded 1502) was made famous by two of its teachers who were leading religious reformers—LUTHER and MELANCHTHON. The REFORMATION is taken as beginning in Wittenberg in 1517 when Luther posted his Ninety-five Theses on the doors of the church of All Saints. Lucas CRANACH was court painter at Wittenberg from 1505. Notable buildings from this time include the castle (1490–99) and the town hall (1524–40). The Augusteum, erected (1564–83) on the site of the Augustinian monastery associated with Luther, became a Lutheran seminary in the 18th century.

## Witz, Konrad (c. 1400–c. 1445) *German painter*

Witz was probably born near Württemberg or near Baden; little is known of his life, although his father was an artist working for the duke of Burgundy, and Witz probably traveled with him to France and Flanders. His work shows the influence of contemporary Flemish painting. He moved to Basle around 1430, and all his known work was executed in Basle and Geneva. Witz stands at the end of the Gothic artistic tradition, rejecting its patterns and elegant curves for an accurately observed realism, and using light in his paintings in a dramatic and innovatory way. His surviving works are panels from altarpieces, of which the latest, *Christ Walking on the Water and the Miraculous Draught of Fishes* from the St. Peter altarpiece (1444; Geneva), is a remarkable achievement. The figures, the water, the reflections, and the various effects of light are all finely observed, and the landscape around the lake is clearly that of Lake Geneva. This represents one of the earliest depictions in European art of a real, recognizable landscape.

## Wolf, Hieronymus (1516–1580) *German humanist scholar*

Wolf was born in Oettingen and was the pupil of both Philipp MELANCHTHON and Joachim CAMERARIUS. Despite a peripatetic life, he managed to produce editions of the Greek orators Isocrates (1548) and Demosthenes (1549) that formed the basis of a definitive critical edition (1572) unsuperseded for more than 200 years. From 1551 to 1557 he was employed as secretary and librarian to the FUGGER FAMILY in Augsburg. In the latter year he began publication of the works of Byzantine historians, with the object of assembling the complete corpus of Byzantine historiography. Also from that year he was head of the Protestant school in Augsburg, a post which he combined with that of city librarian until his death.

## Wolgemut, Michael (1434–1519) *German artist*

A native of Nuremberg, Wolgemut was apprenticed to his father Valentin. The altarpieces attributed to him at Zwickau in Saxony (1479), Feuchtwangen (1484), and Schwabach (1508) show him painting in a predominantly Netherlandish style. His major importance resides however in his development of the WOODCUT as a medium for BOOK ILLUSTRATION. The blocks for the famous and handsome Nuremberg Chronicle (1493) were a product of Wolgemut's prolific workshop, but most important of all, he was DÜRER's master in the technique of woodcut, and the refinements that Wolgemut had introduced were brought to fruition in the work of the younger artist.

## Wolsey, Thomas (c. 1473–1530) *English cardinal and statesman*

The son of an Ipswich butcher, Wolsey attended Magdalen College, Oxford, of which he was bursar before becoming chaplain to Henry VII (1507). He was appointed almoner under HENRY VIII (1509) and had become a leading councilor by 1513, when his efficient organization of a military expedition to France recommended him to the king. His willingness to manage the routine of government and most affairs of state appealed to the pleasure-loving Henry, and Wolsey virtually governed England from 1515, when he became chancellor, until his fall from favor in 1529, over his failure to secure the annulment of Henry's marriage to CATHERINE OF ARAGON. He died at Leicester, on his way to London to answer charges of treason.

Wolsey's main interest was foreign affairs, in which he strove to maintain England's security in a Europe dominated by the Hapsburg–Valois rivalry, while also preserving his own position as papal legate (from 1518) and indulging Henry VIII's unrealistic desire to revive the glories of the Hundred Years' War. He was not unsuccessful until 1529, when a temporary Hapsburg–Valois *rapprochement* left England isolated. In domestic affairs he was no great innovator but an energetic administrator who kept the government functioning efficiently. His most enduring achievement was the firm establishment of the court of chancery as the court of equity in civil cases. As archbishop of York from 1514 and a cardinal from 1515, he ruled the English Church by virtue of his legatine commission, reducing the archbishop of Canterbury to a cipher. Perhaps his weakest area was finance, as he consistently failed either to obtain sufficient taxes or to cut expenditure.

Wolsey used his position to amass a large personal fortune. Its basis was his collection of ecclesiastical posts: in addition to the archbishopric of York he held other bishoprics in England—Lincoln (from 1514), Bath and Wells (1518–24), Durham (1524–29), and Winchester (1529–30)—and was bishop of Tournai (1513–18) and abbot of St. Albans (from 1521). His annual income was as high as £35,000 (six times that of the richest peer), enabling him to found colleges at Ipswich and Oxford (Cardinal College, 1525; refounded as Christ Church, 1546), build HAMPTON COURT PALACE, and enjoy an ostentatious way of life.

**woodcuts** Woodcut is a relief printing process in which an image is printed from a block of wood onto a sheet of paper, in much the same way as text is printed from movable type. The image is first drawn, in reverse, on the block. Those areas of the block's surface corresponding to those parts of the print which the artist wishes to appear white are then gouged out with special knives. After cutting, the untouched wood which stands out corresponds to the black lines of the resultant print. This remaining surface of the block is then inked and pressed firmly against a sheet of paper, transferring the image from the former to the latter. As the woodblock is less malleable than the plate used in ENGRAVING it is more suitable for printing large editions, such as those required by publishers of illustrated books. However, the technique is less subtle than engraving and less amenable to the printing of fine detail.

The earliest European woodcuts, such as the "Bois Protat," date from about 1400 and may originally have been used for textile printing. The technique was also used from an early date for the printing of playing cards which, for obvious reasons, had to appear as much like one another as possible. Some illustrated books were published from large woodcuts, with text and illustrations cut on the same block. After GUTENBERG's invention of PRINTING with movable metal type in the 1450s, such experiments were abandoned, and the woodcut illustration, together with the metal type, became the two essential components in the printing of illustrated books. At the beginning of the 16th century, the so-called "chiaroscuro woodcut" was developed, initially by Hans BURGKMAIR and Lucas CRANACH in Germany and by UGO DA CARPI in Italy. This technique utilizes a series of blocks, printed one after the other to create color effects. As it was both expensive and complicated, this technique was used for individual prints rather than for books during the Renaissance.

From the earliest times, artists supplied the designs for woodcuts, while the task of cutting the block was entrusted to specialist block cutters, who were actually a kind of highly trained carpenter. During the 15th century, woodcut, like printing itself, was essentially a German art form, which reached its highest expression in deluxe illustrated books, such as the Nuremberg Chronicle (*Liber chronicarum*) of Hartmann Schedel, published by Anton Koberger with numerous woodcuts by Michael WOLGEMUT at Nuremberg in 1493. Initially the Italians lagged somewhat behind, but by 1499 a distinctively Italian aesthetic of woodcut illustration had been created, in such works as the HYPNEROTOMACHIA POLIFILI of Francesco Colonna, published by Aldus MANUTIUS in Venice with numerous unsigned woodcuts of superb quality. Albrecht DÜRER revolutionized the woodcut as an artistic medium by refining its technique to a level of subtlety that had previously only been found in engravings. To achieve this, he

**Woodcut** *The Four Horsemen of the Apocalypse* (1498). This woodcut from Dürer's *Apocalypse* portrays the four scourges of humanity as described in the biblical book of Revelation (6:2–8).
*Mansell/Time Life Pictures/Getty Images*

must necessarily have trained a team of block cutters to his own, uniquely exacting standards.

However, despite this technological leap, there is a gradual falling off in the artistic quality of later woodcuts. HOLBEIN's *Dance of Death* (1523/24) cycle is, arguably, the last great Renaissance masterpiece in this technique. Although later woodcuts were often of outstanding technical virtuosity and of considerable formal and iconographic variety, the technique steadily became less the province of avant-garde artists and more that of publishers and printers (*see* BOOK ILLUSTRATION).

**Worms, Diet of** (1521) An assembly (*Reichstag*) of the estates of the Holy Roman Empire, the most important business of which was the condemnation of Martin LUTHER. The case against Luther, who had already been excommunicated, was stated by the papal legate, Girolamo ALEANDRO, in the presence of Emperor CHARLES V. In a famous act of defiance Luther refused to retract his antipapal writings and was outlawed. At the same diet, the estates agreed to the establishment of a government council (*Reichsregiment*) to function in the absence of the emperor, and Charles made over the government of Austria to his brother FERDINAND (I).

## Wotton, Edward (1492–1555) *English physician and naturalist*

Wotton was educated at his native Oxford and at Padua. On his return to England he practiced medicine in London and held office, including the presidency (1541–43), in the College of Physicians. He was also the author of *De differentiis animalium* (1551) which, though published in Paris, was the first serious work on natural history written by an Englishman. The work itself is derivative and contains little that cannot be found in GESNER.

## Wright, Edward (1558–1615) *English mathematician*

Wright was born in Garveston, Norfolk, and educated at Cambridge. He became aware of the inadequacies of current navigational practice during a voyage in 1589 to the Azores. The conventional plane chart with its parallel lines of latitude and longitude prevented mariners from setting an accurate course directly on the chart; nor were the mathematically sophisticated innovations of MERCATOR much help to the average seaman. Wright worked on the problem, publishing tables in his *Certaine Errors in Navigation* (1599) which allowed mariners to make the necessary adjustments on their charts; for the first time nautical triangles could be plotted, showing the correct relation between direction and distance. After 1614 he lectured on mathematics for the East India Company. Wright's translation into English of John NAPIER's work on logarithms was published in 1616.

## Württemberg Confession (1552)

The Protestant confession of faith drawn up by the Württemberg reformer Johann Brenz (1499–1570) with the specific aim of presenting the Protestant viewpoint at the Council of TRENT. Comprising 35 articles, it is based on the Confession of AUGSBURG, and so is generally Lutheran in its stance, though with some Calvinist elements. Consulted by Archbishop PARKER, the confession played a role in the evolution of the THIRTY-NINE ARTICLES of the Church of England.

## Wyatt, Sir Thomas (c. 1503–1542) *English poet and diplomat*

Educated at Cambridge, he found favor at HENRY VIII's court, where he excelled at tournaments, music, and languages. He was reputed to have been a lover of Anne BOLEYN before she was courted by the king. Wyatt served as high marshal of Calais (1529–30), but in 1536 he was detained in the Tower, probably to give evidence against Anne. In 1537 he was knighted and sent abroad on diplo-matic missions. Wyatt's enemies accused him of involvement in Thomas CROMWELL's treachery; in the Tower again, he confessed to some faults and was pardoned by Henry VIII in 1541. He died suddenly of a fever.

Wyatt's fame rests mainly on his poetry. He was the first to introduce the Petrarchan sonnet form to England. His poems and songs, which convey a strong personal quality, were printed in *Certayne Psalmes…drawn into Englyshe meter* (1549) and *Tottel's Miscellany* (1557). His son, Sir Thomas Wyatt the younger (c. 1521–54), was executed for instigating Wyatt's Rebellion (1554), an abortive protest against Mary I's proposal to marry Philip II of Spain.

**Further reading:** Elizabeth Heale, *Wyatt, Surrey, and Early Tudor Poetry* (Harlow, U.K.: Pearson Longman, 1998); Raymond Southall, *The Courtly Maker: An Essay on the Poetry of Wyatt and his Contemporaries* (Oxford, U.K.: Blackwell, 1964).

## Wyclif, John (John Wycliffe, John Wicliff) (c. 1330–1384) *English philosopher and religious reformer*

A Yorkshireman, Wyclif studied at Oxford and lectured on philosophy there from the mid-1350s. His chief philosophical work, the *Summa de ente* (c. 1365–72), rejects the nominalism then current at Oxford, arguing that universals have a real, substantial existence as ideas in the mind of God. Wyclif first emerged as the scourge of ecclesiastical abuses with two huge treatises on divine and civil authority, *De dominio civi* and *De dominio divino* (1374–76); here he distinguished between the eternal, invisible Church and its visible institutions, arguing that the latter could claim no authority when they departed from God's grace. He also challenged the Church to relinquish its endowments and return to a state of poverty. Although these views attracted fierce censure, Wyclif found a powerful patron in John of Gaunt, King Richard II's uncle, who had his own quarrel with the Church. Under Gaunt's protection, Wyclif's writings of the late 1370s became even more provocative, insisting that the Bible was the sole foundation for Christian belief and that the Scriptures provided little support for papal authority and none for monasticism.

However, in 1381 Wyclif alienated Gaunt and many other supporters by switching his attack from the Church's institutions to its sacraments. In *De eucharista* he argued against TRANSUBSTANTIATION on technical, philosophical grounds and inveighed against what he considered the superstitious abuse of the sacrament. Such ideas were held especially dangerous after the Peasants' Revolt (1381), which was widely, if erroneously, thought to have been inflamed by Wyclif's earlier teaching. In 1382, 24 theses taken from Wyclif's writings were condemned by a special council at Blackfriars, London, and he and his followers banned from preaching and lecturing. Now in poor health, Wyclif retreated to his country parish of Lutterworth, but continued to write, maintaining a stream of invective against his enemies. In these years he also instigated the first translation of the whole Bible into English, a work that would be completed by his followers.

After his death, Wyclif's ideas remained a disruptive influence for another 50 years in the populist form spread by the LOLLARDS. Whether they also had a direct influence on the English Reformation is disputed, but the fact that Wyclif had anticipated almost all the conclusions of the 16th-century reformers from a position based firmly in medieval philosophy remains remarkable.

See also: HUSSITES

Further reading: Joseph Henry Dahmus, *The Prosecution of John Wyclyf* (Hamden, Conn.: Archon Books, 1970); L. J. Daly, *The Political Theory of John Wyclif* (Chicago, Ill.: Loyola University Press, 1962); Anthony Kenny, *Wyclif* (Oxford, U.K. and New York: Oxford University Press, 1985); Stephen E. Lahey, *Philosophy and Politics in the Thought of John Wyclif* (Cambridge, U.K.: Cambridge University Press, 2003); G. H. W. Parker, *The Morning Star: Wycliffe and the Dawn of the Reformation* (Grand Rapids, Mich.: Eerdmans, 1966).

**Wyttenbach, Thomas** (1472–1526) *Swiss reformer*
He was born at Biel and attended university in Tübingen. As a lecturer at Basle he taught Ulrich ZWINGLI, whom he encouraged to study the Bible without reliance upon the scholastic commentaries, and interested himself in the implications of the new humanist approach to literary studies. From 1515 he was pastor in his native town, but eight years later publicly aligned himself with the Reformation and in 1524 lost his post upon his marriage.

# X, Z

**Xavier, St. Francis** See FRANCIS XAVIER, ST

**Ximénes de Cisneros, Cardinal Francisco** (1436–1517) *Spanish churchman, politician, and scholar*
A Castilian by birth, he studied at Alcalá and Salamanca, becoming doctor in both canon and civil law. In 1492 Isabella of Castile chose him as her confessor and in 1495 he became archbishop of Toledo. He was an energetic reformer, seeking a return to more austere standards of Christian life, and he encouraged the conversion of the Moors of Granada. In 1507 Ximénes became cardinal and inquisitor-general. From January 1516 until his death (November 1517) at Valladolid, he was governor of Castile and consolidated the unification of Spain achieved by FERDINAND II AND ISABELLA I. Cardinal Ximénes spent his income lavishly on educational projects and public works; he founded the university of Alcalá (1500) and was its great benefactor. His main monument is the great polyglot Bible known as the COMPLUTENSIAN POLYGLOT (Complutum was the Roman name for Alcalá), which provided for the first time a printed text of the Scriptures in their original languages.

**Zabarella, Cardinal Francesco** (1360–1417) *Italian canonist*
After studying at Bologna, Zabarella taught canon law at Florence (1385–90) and Padua (1390–1410). He attended the Council of CONSTANCE as legate of Pope John XXIII, who created him cardinal in 1411. In 1408 he wrote *De iurisdictione imperiali* in which he insisted that the pope was only the highest servant of the Church to whom executive power was entrusted. An ecumenical council had the power to discipline a pope and he could be deposed if it seemed necessary to such a council. The Council of Constance accepted this doctrine and its corollary of regular ecumenical councils. Had this become established practice, Zabarella would have effected a fundamental change in the government of the Roman Catholic Church.

**Zabarella, Giacomo** (1533–1589) *Italian philosopher*
Zabarella was the leading representative of ARISTOTELIANISM in his native Padua during the 16th century. He engaged in controversy with Francesco Piccolomini over his interpretation of Aristotle's logic, which gained him great notoriety among his contemporaries, but modern students have shown more interest in Zabarella's work on the immortality of the soul. There are close similarities between his solution to this problem and that proposed by Pietro POMPONAZZI: he excluded the notion of a prime mover and insisted on the soul's independent and autonomous nature. Zabarella also published *De rebus naturalibus libri XXX* (1589) in which he discussed the traditional problems of Aristotelian physics.

**Zaluzanský, Adam** (1558–1613) *Czech botanist*
Zaluzanský was a leading figure in Prague intellectual circles during the reign of RUDOLF II and a convinced proponent of Ramism (*see* RAMIST CONTROVERSY). He published on medical and other topics, including university reform, but is mainly remembered as the author of *Methodi herbarii libri tres* (1592), which advocates the systematic study of botany and makes important observations on plant classification.

**Zaragoza (Saragossa)** A city in northeastern Spain on the River Ebro. The major Roman center in the Ebro valley, it was captured in 476 by the Visigoths and in 712 by the Moors. Alfonso I of Aragon (reigned 1104–34) expelled the Moors in 1118. Zaragoza remained the capital of Aragon until the latter part of the 15th century when the court transferred to Valladolid. Zaragoza's stone bridge over the Ebro, the Puente de Piedra, dates from 1447. The older of its two cathedrals, "La Seo" (mainly 14th century), is Gothic-Mudéjar in style with some plateresque additions and an important retable by the German Renaissance sculptor Hans of Swabia. Its university was founded in 1474.

**Zaragoza, Treaty of** (1529) The agreement between Spain and Portugal dividing the Pacific between them, as the Treaty of TORDESILLAS had done with the Atlantic. The demarcation ran along a line cutting through the southwest corner of Japan and the northwest corner of New Guinea. This was intended to prevent conflict over colonial rights in a situation in which the Spanish were sailing west across the Pacific from their American possessions to seek footholds in Asia and the Portuguese were sailing east from India to set up trading posts in Southeast Asia and the Spice Islands, but it did not deter the Spanish from establishing themselves in the Philippines from the 1560s on.

**Zarlino, Gioseffo** (c. 1517–1590) *Italian composer and music theorist*
Born in Chioggia, Zarlino was educated by the Franciscans, whom he joined in 1521. In 1536 he was a singer at Chioggia cathedral. From 1539 he was organist there before moving to Venice in 1541, where he became a pupil of Adrian WILLAERT. In 1565 he was appointed *maestro* at St. Mark's and remained in this post until his death. Zarlino wrote motets and madrigals, but is most significant as a theorist. His major work, *Le istitutioni harmoniche* (1558), caused Willaert's methods of contrapuntal writing to become models of the style. In it he also discusses theories of modes and intervals, as well as looking back to classical models.

See also: MUSIC THEORY

**Zell, Katharina** (c. 1497–1562) *German Protestant and writer*
Katharina Schutz was born into a middle-class family and became an early convert to Lutheran views. In 1527 she caused scandal by marrying Matthias Zell (1477–1548), a priest of Strasbourg cathedral. Although excommunicated, Zell continued to minister in the cathedral and became a recognized leader of the Reformation in Strasbourg. Katharina took an active share in his ministry, becoming well known for her charitable work with prisoners, plague victims, and refugees; she also published hymns and religious polemics. The best known of her writings is probably her lengthy *Letter to the Entire Citi-*

*zenry of the Town of Strasbourg* (1557), in which she passionately defends her right, as a woman, to engage in public controversy. In literary terms, she is significant as one of the first women to make a public impact by writing in German.

**Further reading:** Elsie Anne McKee, *Katharina Schutz Zell* (Leyden, Netherlands: Brill, 1998).

**Zenale, Bernard(in)o** (c. 1450–1526) *Italian painter*
Zenale was born at Treviglio, for the cathedral of which, in collaboration with his fellow-townsman Butinone (c. 1450–c. 1507), he painted the splendid polyptych that is his best-known work. They also worked on frescoes depicting the life of St. Ambrose (1490) in the church of San Pietro in Gessate, Milan. Zenale also wrote a treatise on perspective now apparently lost.

**zoological collections** Animals for both hunting and display had long been kept by kings and other rulers. One such collection of wild animals was established in 1252 by Henry III at the Tower of London. The animals in these menageries were either viewed as curiosities or set to fight against each other or against dogs to provide a gory spectacle for their owners. James I of England, for instance, kept a pack of bull mastiffs that were used to fight the lions housed in the Tower of London. Live exotic animals were acceptable gifts between princes for their menageries. Roelant SAVERY had the advantage of being able to observe the creatures in Emperor Rudolf II's menagerie for his well-known depictions of animals living in harmony in paradisical surroundings—which include the first known portrait of the dodo (the bird had only been discovered in 1598).

Early BOTANIC GARDENS, such as the one at Padua, often made provision for displaying animals, live or dead, alongside their plant collections, and Renaissance noblemen included in their newly created *musei* natural history specimens, along with their antiquities and their art collections. One of the earliest such *musei* was founded by Lorenzo de' Medici (the Magnificent) in Florence in the 15th century. He was soon followed by the Este in Ferrara and the Montefeltro in Urbino. Some 250 such collections were established in 16th-century Italy, one of them by Ulisse ALDROVANDI in Bologna. Scholars also began, on a much smaller scale, to assemble their own more specialized collections. Known as CABINETS, they provided the Renaissance scholar with his basic research material. Konrad GESNER, for example, based his *De omni rerum fossilium genere* (1565) on his own cabinet of fossils. Most commonly, collections of natural history specimens were assembled for their putative value as *materia medica*. Medical education was the purpose underlying the famous collection assembled in the first half of the 17th century by Ole Worm, professor of medicine at Copenhagen, which is illustrated in *Museum Wormianum* (Leyden, 1655) in an engraving showing a shark, armadillo, polar bear, spoonbill, and assorted smaller birds, fish, and reptiles displayed amid minerals and items of anthropological interest.

**Further reading:** Daniel Hahn, *The Tower Menagerie: Being the Amazing True Story of the Royal Collection of Wild and Ferocious Beasts* (New York: Simon & Schuster, 2003).

**zoology** Considerable zoological knowledge was collected by Aristotle and presented in his *Historia animalium* and other works, but the Aristotelian tradition, technical, detailed, and pedestrian, held little appeal for medieval scholars. In its place two more imaginative approaches flourished. One, typified by Solinus (fl. 200 CE) and his *Collecteana rerum memorabilium*, concentrated almost exclusively on such wonders as men with dog's heads or ants as large as lions which guarded the gold of India. An alternative tradition, clearly seen in the medieval bestiaries, looked on nature as a source of moral inspiration; thus the phoenix inevitably is a reminder of Christ, and the fox, because of its skill in entrapping its victims, recalls the devil. Both traditions persisted throughout much of the Renaissance.

Although the leading Renaissance zoologists, Ulisse ALDROVANDI and Konrad GESNER, devoted much less space to moralistic or mythological themes, neither they nor their disciples were entirely free from such preoccupations. Much less gullible than Solinus, they still found space for dragons, unicorns, basilisks, and the phoenix. Nor were their works restricted to specifically zoological data; their encyclopedic scope embraced all facts, whether linguistic, mythological, historical, or gastronomic. Aldrovandi, for example, after devoting a page or two to the various breeds of chicken, went on to present a further 300 pages on folklore about the bird. A clear example of the literary nature of Renaissance zoology is provided by Ermolao Barbaro's *Castigationes Pliniae* (1492) in which he sought to do no more than identify the numerous errors of the Roman author Pliny. When genuinely zoological issues were tackled they tended to be dealt with in an unambitiously Aristotelian manner. Classification at higher levels depended, accordingly, on whether the animals were oviparous or viviparous, and became trivially alphabetical at the level of species.

One area in which zoology did advance was in the field of experimental embryology. Volcher Coiter (1534–c. 1576) made a detailed study of the development of embryonic chickens. Further advances were made by Giralomo FABRICIUS, whose *De formato foetu* (1600), the first modern work on comparative embryology, described the development of man, various domestic animals, the dogfish, and the viper.

The Renaissance also saw the emergence of the zoological monograph. Some, such as the work of Jacob Bondt (1592–1631) on the East Indies, were regional studies, others, such as the *De omni rerum fossilium genere* (1565) of Gesner, were restricted to a single topic. Works of this kind tended to be more singleminded in their pursuit of zoological issues than the better known encyclopedic collections. Missing completely, however, from Renaissance zoology are any of the great theoretical issues that would puzzle scientists of a later period. For the Renaissance zoologist, animals had been created by God as

**Zoology** This illustration of a whale sinking a ship, taken from Gesner's *Historiae animalium*, owes more to the medieval bestiary tradition than to personal observation.

described in Genesis and were linked with man as constituents of the great CHAIN OF BEING. How then, it was asked, did the alpaca and guanaco reach Peru? Were they created there? And, if so, what of Noah? The orthodox answer came from the naturalist and missionary José de ACOSTA. All animals came out of the ark and dispersed over long-since-flooded land bridges to the environments best suited to them. Few voices were heard in dissent before the 18th century.

### Zoppo, Marco (Marco d'Antonio di Ruggero) (1433–1478) *Italian painter and draftsman*

Born near Bologna, Zoppo was probably a pupil of Cosimo TURA and later, at the age of 21, became the adopted son of and assistant to SQUARCIONE in Padua. Zoppo was also active in Venice (1455, 1468–73) and executed further works in Bologna, including a triptych for the Collegio di Spagna. Influenced by MANTEGNA and by Jacopo and Giovanni BELLINI, Zoppo produced paintings in a distinctively harsh and precise style and an album of drawings formerly attributed to Mantegna (British Museum, London).

### Zuccaro, Federico (c. 1540–1609) *Italian painter*

Born at Vado, south of Bologna, Zuccaro began his artistic career as assistant and pupil to his older brother Taddeo. In 1565 he was in Florence, working under VASARI, after which he visited France and the Netherlands (1574) and then England (1575), where he drew (and perhaps painted) full-length portraits of Elizabeth I and the earl of Leicester (British Museum, London). Subsequently he helped in the painting of the dome of Florence cathedral (1575–79) and executed the painting *Barbarossa Making Obeisance to the Pope* (1582), influenced by Tintoretto and Raphael, for the doge's palace in Venice. Summoned to Spain by Philip II, Zuccaro produced several works, chiefly altarpieces, for the ESCORIAL (1585–88), which failed to win the royal approval. He returned to Italy, and in 1593 he established the Accademia di San Luca in his own house in Rome, later becoming the academy's first president. Other works included the *Adoration of the Magi* (1594; Lucca cathedral), paintings in the Sala Regia of the Vatican, a book on aesthetic theory, *L'Idea de' pittori, scultori, et architetti* (1607), and a series of 90 drawings illustrating Dante's *Divine Comedy* (Uffizi, Florence). Through the medium of prints his accomplished mannerist style became widely known in Italy and beyond.

### Zuccaro, Taddeo (1529–1566) *Italian painter*

Born, like his brother and pupil Federico, at Vado, Taddeo Zuccaro became a leading painter in the mannerist style in Rome, where he settled in 1551. He was largely self-trained and was influenced chiefly by the works of CORREGGIO, which he had encountered at Parma. The body of Taddeo Zuccaro's works consisted of decorative frescoes and religious paintings, many of which were later completed by Federico. His most influential work was the series of frescoes and stucco decorations executed (1561–66) for the Villa Farnese at Caprarola, in which elements of northern Italian art and the manner of Michelangelo and Raphael were fused. Other works included a fresco cycle in the Sala Regia of the Vatican and another in the Cappella Frangipane, San Marcello al Corso, Rome, incorporating the altarpiece *The Conversion of St. Paul* (c. 1563).

### Zürich Agreement (1549) The formulation of a common sacramental doctrine agreed at Zürich between J. H. BULLINGER, who represented the Zwinglian churches of German Switzerland, and CALVIN and Guillaume FAREL representing Geneva and the Protestant churches of French Switzerland. ZWINGLI had supported a purely symbolic interpretation of the Eucharist, resulting in a split with LUTHER that led to a rift between the German and Swiss churches (*see* MARBURG, COLLOQUY OF). Calvin's position, midway between the Swiss and the Lutheran, was more acceptable to the Zwinglians, and the Zürich Agreement proved an important milestone on the road to a distinctive form of Swiss Protestantism.

### Zurita, Jerónimo de (1512–1580) *Spanish historian*

The son of a doctor at the court of FERDINAND II of Aragon, Zurita was born at Zaragoza, educated at Alcalá, and became official chronicler of Aragon (1548). *Anales de la corona de Aragón* (six volumes, 1562–80) covered the history of the kingdom from the Moorish invasion to the death of Ferdinand (1516). An index was published in 1604. (The third edition, in seven volumes (1610–21), is considered the best.) Though it lacks literary distinction, Zurita's history is the first in Spanish to be compiled critically and methodically. He took pains to read primary materials, excluded supernatural matter, and took account of conflicting evidence.

### Zwingli, Ulrich (1484–1531) *Swiss reformer*

The son of a well-to-do farmer at Wildhaus, Zwingli studied in Basle and Berne before embarking on a conventional church career. He was ordained in 1506 and from 1506 to 1516 served as parish priest at Glarus. While there he continued his humanistic studies and published his first original work, a verse satire criticizing the involvement of Swiss mercenaries in the dynastic quarrels of the European powers (*De bello Judaico*, 1510). In December 1518 Zwingli was elected a stipendary priest in the minster at Zürich, where his preaching and lectures on the New Testament evoked an enthusiastic response. Zwingli's sermons, in which he moved to an increasingly forthright denunciation of purgatory, monasticism, and other Catholic dogma and practices, paved the way for the Zürich reformation, carried through between 1522 and 1525 under Zwingli's leadership.

By this time too Zwingli had begun to develop his characteristic Eucharistic doctrine, which diverged significantly from that of LUTHER. In rejecting TRANSUBSTANTIATION Zwingli also rejected any sort of REAL PRESENCE, expounding a purely symbolic interpretation of the sacrament. The ensuing conflict between the two men, which a personal meeting (*see* MARBURG, COLLOQUY OF) could not resolve, led to a permanent division between the Swiss and German strands of Protestantism. Zwingli remained until his death the key figure in the Swiss Reformation, and played a leading role in the promotion of Protestantism in the other Swiss cantons.

**Further reading:** Bruce Gordon, *The Swiss Reformation* (Manchester, U.K.: Manchester University Press, 2002); George R. Potter, *Zwingli* (Cambridge, U.K.: Cambridge University Press, 1976).

# CHRONOLOGY

The following table lists key events in European politics, religion, science, and culture during the period 1300–1620. There is, however, no attempt to provide a comprehensive account of European history and civilization during this period. The aim is, rather, to provide a chronological framework that will enable the reader to contextualize events, achievements, and personalities described in the main text.

| Secular Events | Religion | Rulers | Sciences | Arts and Literature |
|---|---|---|---|---|
| **1300** | | | | |
| *1300* Edward I of England invades Scotland | | | | |
| *1301* Dante exiled from Florence | | *1301* Edward I of England creates his son prince of Wales | | |
| *1302* Flemings defeat French at Courtrai | *1302* Papal Bull *Unan Sanctam* declares papal authority supreme | | | |
| | *1305* Clement V pope | | | *c. 1305* Giotto at work on Arena Chapel frescoes (Padua) |
| | | | | *1306* Dante at work on *Divina Commedia* |
| | | *1307* Edward II king of England (→1327) | | |
| | | *1308* Henry VII of Luxembourg becomes emperor (→1313) | | |
| *1309* Emperor recognizes Swiss League; Knights Hospitalers settle in Rhodes | *1309* Papal court moves to Avignon (→1378) | *1309* Robert of Anjou king of Naples (→1343) | | |
| **1310** | | | | |
| *1314* Scots defeat English at Bannockburn | *1312* Council of Vienne | *1314* Louis IV of Bavaria becomes emperor (→1347) | | |
| *1315* Florentines defeated by Pisans at Montecatini | | | | |
| *1319* Sweden and Norway united under Magnus VII | *1316* John XXII pope | | | |
| **1320** | | | | |
| *1320* Peace of Paris (between France and Flanders) | | | | *c. 1320* De Vitry's *Ars nova musicae* published |
| | | *1324* Louis IV excommunicated | | *1321* Death of Dante |
| *1326* Ottoman Turks capture Bursa | | *1327* Edward III king of England (→1377) | | |
| | | *1328* Louis IV crowned emperor in Rome; Philip VI first Valois king of France (→1350) | | |
| *1329* Compact of Pavia | | | | |
| **1330** | | | | |
| *1330* Treaty of Hagenau | | *1333* Casimir III king of Poland (→1370) | | |
| *1336* Van Artevelde revolt in Flanders | *1334* Benedict XII pope | | | |
| *1337* Outbreak of Hundred Years' War between England and France | | | | |
| **1340** | | | | |
| *1340* English defeat French at Sluys | *1342* Clement VI pope | *1342* Louis I king of Hungary (→1382) | | |

| Secular Events | Religion | Rulers | Sciences | Arts and Literature |
|---|---|---|---|---|
| | | *1343* Joanna I queen of Naples (→*1381*) | | |
| *1346* English defeat French at Crécy | | | | |
| *1347* Plague reaches Italy | | *1347* Charles IV of Luxembourg becomes emperor (→*1378*) | | |
| *1348* Black Death in England | *1348* Pope purchases town of Avignon | | | *1348* Boccaccio at work on *Decameron* |
| **1350** | | | | |
| *1351* Zürich joins Swiss League | | *1350* John II king of France (→*1364*) | | |
| | *1352* Innocent VI pope | | | *1353* Petrarch's *Canzoniere* written |
| *1356* English defeat French at Poitiers; Golden Bull issued | | *1355* Charles IV crowned emperor in Rome | | |
| *1357* Turks capture Adrianople (Edirne) | | | | |
| *1358 Jacquerie* (peasants' revolt) in France | | | | |
| **1360** | | | | |
| *1360* Treaty of Brétigny | | | | |
| *1361* Denmark at war with Hanseatic League | *1362* Urban V pope | | | |
| *1363* Austria obtains Tyrol | | *1364* Charles V king of France (→*1380*) | *1364* Dondi's astronomical clock at Pavia completed | |
| | | *1365* Charles IV crowned king of Burgundy at Arles | | |
| *1367* English defeat Castilians at Nájera | | *1369* Henry II first Trastamara king of Castile (→*1379*) | | |
| **1370** | | | | |
| *1370* English sack Limoges | *1370* Gregory XI pope | *1371* Robert II first Stuart king of Scotland (→*1390*) | | |
| *1375* War of the Eight Saints | | *1377* Richard II king of England (→*1399*) | *1375* Catalan Atlas compiled | |
| | *1378* Great Schism begins | *1378* Wenceslas of Luxembourg becomes emperor (→*1400*) | | |
| **1380** | | | | |
| *1380* Norway and Denmark united under Olaf IV | | *1380* Charles VI king of France (→*1422*) | | |
| *1381* Peasants' Revolt in England | | | | |
| *1382* Turks capture Sofia | *1384* Death of Wyclif | | | |
| *1385* Portuguese defeat Castilians at Aljubarrota | | *1385* John I first Avis king of Portugal (→*1433*) | | |
| | | *1386* Ladislas II first Jagellon king of Poland (→*1434*) | | |
| | | | | *1387* Chaucer's *Canterbury Tales* written |

| Secular Events | Religion | Rulers | Sciences | Arts and Literature |
|---|---|---|---|---|
| *1389* Turks defeat Serbs at Kosovo | | | | |

**1390** ───────────────────────────────────

| Secular Events | Religion | Rulers | Sciences | Arts and Literature |
|---|---|---|---|---|
| | | *1393* Niccolò III d'Este created first marquis of Ferrara | | |
| | | *1395* Giangaleazzo Visconti created first duke of Milan | | |
| *1396* Turks complete conquest of Bulgaria | | | | |
| *1397* Union of Kalmar unites Norway, Sweden, and Denmark | | | | |
| | | *1399* Henry IV king of England (→1413) | | |

**1400** ───────────────────────────────────

| Secular Events | Religion | Rulers | Sciences | Arts and Literature |
|---|---|---|---|---|
| | | *1400* Robert of Bavaria becomes emperor (→1410) | | |
| | *1401* First Lollard martyr | | | *1401* Ghiberti wins competition to execute bronze doors for Florentine baptistery |
| | *1409* Council of Pisa | | | |

**1410** ───────────────────────────────────

| Secular Events | Religion | Rulers | Sciences | Arts and Literature |
|---|---|---|---|---|
| *1410* Ladislas II of Poland defeats Teutonic Knights | | *1410* Sigismund of Luxembourg becomes emperor (→1437) | | |
| | | *1413* Henry V king of England (→1422) | | |
| | *1414* Council of Constance convened | *1414* Joanna II queen of Naples (→1435) | | |
| *1415* Portuguese capture Ceuta | *1415* Martyrdom of Huss | | | |
| | *1417* Election of Martin V as pope ends Great Schism | | | |
| *1419* Defenestration of Prague | *1419* Outbreak of Hussite Wars | *1419* Philip the Good duke of Burgundy (→1467) | | |

**1420** ───────────────────────────────────

| Secular Events | Religion | Rulers | Sciences | Arts and Literature |
|---|---|---|---|---|
| *1420* Treaty of Troyes makes Henry V heir to French throne | *1420* Four Articles of Prague | | | |
| | | *1422* Henry VI king of England (→1461) | | |
| *1423* Council of Pavia | | | | |
| *1429* Siege of Orleans lifted | | *1429* Charles VII of France crowned | | *1429* Brunelleschi's Pazzi chapel, Florence, begun |

**1430** ───────────────────────────────────

| Secular Events | Religion | Rulers | Sciences | Arts and Literature |
|---|---|---|---|---|
| *1431* Joan of Arc burned | *1431* Council of Basle; Eugenius IV pope | | | |
| *1432* Portuguese discover Azores | | | | *1432* Van Eyck brothers' *Adoration of the Lamb* altarpiece (Ghent) |
| | *1433* Compacts of Prague | *1433* Sigismund crowned emperor; Gianfrancesco I Gonzaga first marquis of Mantua | | |
| | *1434* Revolt in Rome forces pope to flee to Florence | *1434* Cosimo de' Medici returns to Florence | | |

| Secular Events | Religion | Rulers | Sciences | Arts and Literature |
|---|---|---|---|---|
| *1435* Congress of Arras allies Burgundy with France | | *1435* Rene of Anjou king of Naples *(→1442)* | | *1435* Donatello's *David* |
| | *1438* Pragmatic Sanction of Bourges; Council of Ferrara | *1438* Albert II of Hapsburg becomes emperor *(→1439)*; Afonso V king of Portugal *(→1481)* | | |
| | *1439* Council of Florence | | | |
| **1440** | | | | |
| | | *1440* Frederick III of Hapsburg becomes emperor *(→1493)* | | |
| | *1442* Council of Rome | *1442* Alfonso I (Alfonso V of Aragon) king of Naples *(→1458)* | | |
| | *1443* Papacy returns to Rome | | | |
| *1444* Turks defeat Poles at Varna | | | | *1444* Michelozzo's Palazzo Medici-Riccardi, Florence, begun |
| | | *1446* János Hunyadi elected regent of Hungary | | |
| *1447* Ambrosian Republic in Milan | *1447* Nicholas V pope | *1447* Casimir IV king of Poland *(→1492)* | | |
| *1448* By Concordat of Vienna Emperor Frederick III pledges obedience to papacy | | | *1448* Gutenberg printing at Mainz | |
| *1449* French take Rouen | | | | |
| **1450** | | | | |
| | | *1450* Francesco Sforza first Sforza duke of Milan *(→1466)* | | |
| | *1452* Greek Orthodox–Latin Church union declared | *1452* Frederick III crowned emperor in Rome | | *c. 1452* Piero della Francesco at work on the *Legend of the* True Cross fresco cycle at Arezzo |
| *1453* French victory at Castillon ends Hundred Years' War; Turks capture Constantinople | | | | |
| *1454* Peace of Lodi | | | | |
| *1455* Outbreak of Wars of the Roses in England | *1455* Calixtus III pope | | | *1455* Uccello's *Battle of San Romano* painted |
| *1456* János Hunyadi raises Turkish siege of Belgrade; Cape Verde Islands discovered | | | | |
| *1457* Poles capture Marienburg | *1458* Pius II pope | *1458* Matthias Corvinus king of Hungary *(→1490)*; Ferdinand I king of Naples *(→1494)* | | |
| *1459* Turks overrun Serbia | | | *1459* Camaldolese Chart completed | *1459* Gozzoli commissioned to decorate the Palazzo Medici-Riccardi chapel (Florence); Pienza project begun |
| **1460** | | | | |
| | | *1461* Louis XI king of France *(→1483)*; Edward IV king of England *(→1483)* | | |

| Secular Events | Religion | Rulers | Sciences | Arts and Literature |
|---|---|---|---|---|
| *1462* Castilians capture Gibraltar from Arabs | | | *1462* Death of Henry the Navigator | |
| *1463* Turks overrun Bosnia | *1464* Paul II pope | | *1464* Regiomontanus's *De triangulis*, first modern book on trigonometry, published | |
| *1466* Peace of Torun | | | | |
| | | *1467* Charles the Bold duke of Burgundy *(→1477)* | | |
| | | *1469* Marriage of Isabella of Castile and Ferdinand II of Aragon; Lorenzo the Magnificent head of the Florentine republic *(→1492)* | | |

**1470** ——————————————————————————————————————

| Secular Events | Religion | Rulers | Sciences | Arts and Literature |
|---|---|---|---|---|
| *1471* Portuguese capture Tangier | *1471* Sixtus IV pope; death of Thomas à Kempis | *1471* Ercole I d'Este created first duke of Ferrara | | |
| *1472* Portuguese reach Fernando Po | | *1474* Isabella queen of Castile *(→1504)*; Federico II da Montefeltro created first duke of Urbino | | |
| *1476* Swiss defeat Burgundians at Morat | | | *1476* Caxton printing at Westminster | *c. 1475* Van der Goes's Portinari altarpiece |
| | | *1477* Maximilian, heir to Emperor Frederick III, marries Mary of Burgundy | | |
| *1478* Pazzi conspiracy against the Medici | *1478* Start of Spanish Inquisition | | | *1478* Pulci's *Il Morgante* |
| *1479* Union of Aragon and Castile | | *1479* Ferdinand II king of Aragon *(→1516)* | | *1479* Verrocchio at work on Colleoni statue |

**1480** ——————————————————————————————————————

| Secular Events | Religion | Rulers | Sciences | Arts and Literature |
|---|---|---|---|---|
| | | | | *c. 1480* Botticelli's *Primavera* painted |
| | | *1483* Richard III king of England *(→1485)*; Charles VIII king of France *(→1498)* | | *1483* First two books of Boiardo's *Orlando innamorato* published |
| *1485* Matthias Corvinus takes Vienna from Frederick III | *1484* Innocent VIII pope | *1485* Henry VII, first tudor king of England *(→1509)* | | *1485* Alberti's *De re aedificatoria* published |
| *1487* Diaz rounds Cape of Good Hope | | | | |
| *1489* Cyprus ceded to Venice | | *1488* James IV king of Scotland *(→1513)* | | |

**1490** ——————————————————————————————————————

| Secular Events | Religion | Rulers | Sciences | Arts and Literature |
|---|---|---|---|---|
| *1491* Treaty of Pressburg recognizes Hapsburg rights to Bohemia and Hungary | | | *1491* Froben printing at Basle | |
| *1492* Conquest of Granada completes *Reconquista*; Jews expelled from Spain; Columbus lands in New World | *1492* Alexander VI pope | | | |

| Secular Events | Religion | Rulers | Sciences | Arts and Literature |
|---|---|---|---|---|
| | | *1493* Maximilian I becomes emperor *(→1519)* | | *1493 Nuremberg Chronicle* published |
| *1494* Charles VIII of France invades Italy; Medici expelled from Florence; Treaty of Tordesillas | | | | |
| *1495* Holy League against the French | | *1495* Charles VIII of France crowned king of Naples; Manuel I king of Portugal *(→1521)* | | *1495* Leonardo at work on his *Last Supper* (Milan) |
| | | *1496* Philip the Handsome, heir to Emperor Maximilian I, marries Joanna, heiress of Spain | | |
| *1497* Cabots reach Nova Scotia; Jews expelled from Portugal | | | | |
| *1498* Vasco da Gama reaches India | *1498* Savonarola burned | *1498* Louis XII king of France *(→1515)* | | *1498* Dürer's *Apocalypse* woodcuts |
| *1499* Peace of Basle effectively ensures Swiss independence; Louis XII occupies Milan; *Morisco* revolt in Andalusia | | | | *1499 Hypnerotomachia Polifili* and Rojas' *La Celestina* published; Michelangelo's first *Pietà* (St. Peter's, Rome) |

## 1510

| Secular Events | Religion | Rulers | Sciences | Arts and Literature |
|---|---|---|---|---|
| *1500* Treaty of Granada agrees French/Spanish partition of Italy; Cabral discovers Brazil | | | | *1500* Erasmus's *Adagia* published |
| *1501* Basle joins Swiss League | | *1501* Cesare Borgia created duke of Romagna | | |
| | | | | *1502* Bramante's Tempietto at San Pietro in Montorio, Rome; Pinturicchio at work on fresco cycle in the Piccolomini library, Siena |
| | *1503* Pius III pope; Julius II pope | *1503* Alfonso d'Este duke of Ferrara *(→1534)* | | |
| *1504* France cedes Naples to Spain under treaty of Lyons | | | | *1504* Michelangelo's *David* |
| *1505* Portuguese reach Sri Lanka | | | | |
| | *1507* Indulgence for building of St. Peter's | *1507* Margaret of Austria regent of Netherlands *(→1530)* | | *1506* Bramante commissioned to build new St. Peter's, Rome; Leonardo's *Mona Lisa* |
| *1508* League of Cambrai against Venice | | *1508* Francesco Maria I first della Rovere duke of Urbino | | *1508* Michelangelo begins work on Sistine Chapel ceiling |
| *1509* Venice defeated at Agnadello; Spaniards conquer Oran | | *1509* Henry VIII king of England *(→1547)*; Philip II the Magnanimous landgrave of Hesse *(→1567)* | | *1509* Raphael begins work on the Stanze della Segnatura frescoes (Rome) |

## 1510

| Secular Events | Religion | Rulers | Sciences | Arts and Literature |
|---|---|---|---|---|
| *1510* Portuguese capture Goa | | | | |
| | | | | *1511* Erasmus's *Encomium Moriae* published |

| Secular Events | Religion | Rulers | Sciences | Arts and Literature |
|---|---|---|---|---|
| *1512* Medici restored in Florence | *1512* Fifth Lateran Council | | | |
| *1513* English defeat French at battle of the Spurs and Scots at Flodden; Balboa discovers Pacific Ocean | *1513* Leo X pope | | | |
| | *1514* Tetzel sells indulgences in Germany | | | |
| *1515* French defeat Milanese at Marignano | | | | *1515* *Epistolae obscurorum virorum* published |
| | *1516* Concord of Bologna | | | *1516* More's *Utopia* and first edition of Ariosto's *Orlando furioso* published; Titian official painter to Venetian Republic |
| | *1517* Luther's Ninety-five Theses | | | *1517* Del Sarto's *Madonna of the Harpies* |
| *1519* Magellan sets out on voyage of circumnavigation | *1519* Capuchin rule established | *1519* Charles V becomes emperor (→*1556*) | | |

**1520** ────────────────────────────────────────

| | | | | |
|---|---|---|---|---|
| *1520* Field of the Cloth of Gold; start of Revolt of the Communeros in Spain | *1520* Luther excommunicated | | | |
| *1521* Cortés destroys Tenochtitlan (Mexico City); Turks capture Belgrade | *1521* Diet of Worms; Melanchthon's *Loci communes* published | *1521* Ferdinand (I) regent of Austria | | |
| *1522* Turks expel Knights Hospitalers from Rhodes; del Cano completes circumnavigation | *1522* Adrian VI pope; Complutensian Polyglot Bible published | | | |
| | *1523* Clement VII pope | *1523* Gustavus I Vasa king of Sweden (→*1560*) | | *1523* Michelangelo designs Bibliotheca Laurenziana (Florence) |
| *1524* Peasants' Revolt begins in Germany | *1524* Theatine Order founded | | | |
| *1525* Battle of Pavia; Milan becomes Hapsburg territory | | | | |
| *1526* Treaty of Madrid; League of Cognac; battle of Mohács | *1526* First Diet of Spires | | | *1526* Holbein's first visit to England |
| *1527* Sack of Rome; Medici expelled from Florence | *1527* First Protestant university founded at Marburg | | | |
| *1528* Andrea Doria in power in Genoa | | | | |
| *1529* Peace of Cambrai; Turks besiege Vienna; Treaty of Zaragoza | *1529* Colloquy of Marburg; Articles of Schwabach; second Diet of Spires | | | |

**1530** ────────────────────────────────────────

| | | | | |
|---|---|---|---|---|
| *1530* Charles V gives Malta to Knights Hospitalers; Medici restored in Florence | *1530* Confession of Augsburg | *1530* Charles V crowned emperor; Federico II Gonzaga created first duke of Mantua | | |
| *1531* Pizarro destroys Inca empire | *1531* Schmalkaldic League; death of Zwingli | *1531* Mary of Hungary regent of Netherlands (→*1556*) | | |

| Secular Events | Religion | Rulers | Sciences | Arts and Literature |
|---|---|---|---|---|
| | | | | *1532* Machiavelli's *Il Principe* and the first novel in Rabelais's *Gargantua and Pantagruel* cycle published |
| | *1533* Henry VIII of England excommunicated | *1533* Catherine de' Medici marries the future Henry II of France | | |
| *1534* Barbarossa captures Tunis | *1534* Ignatius Loyola founds Jesuits; Henry VIII supreme head of Church in England; Paul III pope; Anabaptists seize control of Münster; first Confession of Basle | | | |
| *1535* Battle of Tunis | *1535* Ursuline Order founded | | | |
| *1536* French occupy Savoy-Piedmont; Cartier claims Canada for France | *1536* Dissolution of English monasteries begins; first Helvetic Confession; death of Erasmus; Pilgrimage of Grace; Calvin's *Christianae religionis institutio* published | | | *1536* Bibliotheca Marciana, Venice, begun |

**1540** ———————————————————————————————————————

| Secular Events | Religion | Rulers | Sciences | Arts and Literature |
|---|---|---|---|---|
| *1540* Spaniards discover California; Perugian Salt War | | | | |
| | *1541* Colloquy of Regensburg; Calvin's Ecclesiastical Ordinances at Geneva; Xavier begins missionary journey to East | | | *1541* Michelangelo's *Last Judgment* in Sistine Chapel |
| *1542* English defeat Scots at Solway Moss | *1542* Roman Inquisition reestablished | *1542* Accession of infant Mary, Queen of Scots | *1543* Vesalius's *De humani corporis fabrica* and Copernicus's *De revolutionibus* published; first botanic garden founded (Pisa) | |
| *1544* English capture Boulogne | | *1544* William I the Silent prince of Orange (→1584) | *1544* Münster's *Cosmographia universalis* published | |
| | *1545* First session of the Council of Trent | *1545* Pierluigi Farnese created first duke of Parma | | *1545* Cellini's *Perseus and Medusa* begun |
| *1547* Battle of Mühlberg | *1546* Death of Luther | *1547* Edward VI king of England (→1553); Henry II king of France (→1559) | *1546* Fracastoro's *De contagione* published | *1546* Lescot designs Louvre, Paris |
| | *1548* Interim of Augsburg; Ignatius Loyola's *Ejercicios espirituales* published | | | |
| | *1549* Zürich Agreement; first Book of Common Prayer | | | |

**1550** ———————————————————————————————————————

| Secular Events | Religion | Rulers | Sciences | Arts and Literature |
|---|---|---|---|---|
| *1550* Peace of Boulogne between England, France, and Scotland | *1550* Julius III pope | | *1550* Ramusio's *Delle navigationi et viaggi* published | *1550* First edition of Vasari's *Vite* published |

| Secular Events | Religion | Rulers | Sciences | Arts and Literature |
|---|---|---|---|---|
| | *1551* Council of Trent reconvoked; Jesuit college (later Gregoriana) founded at Rome | | *1551* Reinhold's Prutenic Tables published | |
| | *1552* Second Book of Common Prayer; Württemberg Confession | | | |
| | *1553* England reconciled with papacy; Servetus burned at Geneva | *1553* Mary I queen of England *(→1558)* | | |
| | | *1554* Philip, heir to Emperor Charles V, marries Mary I of England | | *1554 Lazarillo de Tormes* published |
| *1555* Spaniards capture Siena; Muscovy Company granted royal charter | *1555* Peace of Augsburg; Protestants persecuted in England; Marcellus II pope; Paul IV pope | | | *1555* Ramus's *Dialectique* published |
| | | *1556* Emperor Charles V abdicates; Ferdinand I emperor *(→1564)*; Philip II king of Spain *(→1598)* | | |
| *1557* Battle of St. Quentin | *1557* First Index Librorum Prohibitorum issued | | | |
| *1558* French recover Calais from English | | *1558* Elizabeth I queen of England *(→1603)* | | |
| *1559* Peace of Cateau-Cambrésis | *1559* Protestantism reestablished in England; Pius IV pope; Gallican Confession | *1559* Francis II king of France *(→1560)*; Margaret of Parma regent of Netherlands *(→1567)* | | *1559* Montemayor's *La Diana* published |

## 1560

| | | | | |
|---|---|---|---|---|
| | *1560* Church in Scotland set up on presbyterian principles | *1560* Charles IX king of France *(→1574)* with Catherine de' Medici as regent | | |
| | *1561* Colloquy of Poissy attempts reconciliation of French Catholics and Huguenots; Belgic Confession; Naumburg Convention | | | |
| *1562* Outbreak of Wars of Religion in France | *1562* Edict of St. Germain; Council of Trent reconvoked for final sessions; Heidelberg Catechism; Enclosed community of Carmelite nuns founded at Ávila by future St. Teresa | | | *1562* Escorial begun |
| | *1564* Death of Calvin | *1564* Maximilian II *(→1576)* | | *1564* Tuileries palace, Paris, commissioned by Catherine de' Medici |
| *1565* Turks besiege Malta | | | | *1565* Tintoretto at work on Scuola di San Rocco, Venice |
| *1566* Compromise of Breda | *1566* Pius V pope; second Helvetic Confession; "Iconoclastic Fury" in Netherlands | | | |
| *1567* Duke of Alba sent to Netherlands | *1567* Conspiracy of Meaux | *1567* Mary, Queen of Scots, compelled to abdicate; James VI king of Scotland *(→1625)*; William the Wise landgrave of Hesse-Kassel *(→1592)* | | |

| Secular Events | Religion | Rulers | Sciences | Arts and Literature |
|---|---|---|---|---|
| *1568* Tribunal of Blood | *1568* Antwerp Polyglot Bible begins publication; St. John of the Cross founds community of reformed Carmelite friars | | | |
| *1569* Union of Lublin unites Poland and Lithuania | *1569* Northern Rebellion in England | *1569* Cosimo I of Florence created grand duke of Tuscany | *1569* Mercator projection used in Mercator's world chart | |
| **1570** | | | | |
| | *1570* Elizabeth I of England excommunicated; Peace of St. Germain | | | *1570* Palladio's *Quattro libri dell' architettura* published |
| *1571* Battle of Lepanto | *1571* Synod of Emden | | *1571* Ortelius's *Theatrum orbis terrarum* published | *1571* Bibiotheca Laurenziana opened to public |
| *1572* Sea-beggars seize Brill and Flushing, marking start of the Revolt of the Netherlands | *1572* Massacre of St. Bartholomew; Gregory XIII pope | *1572* Sigismund II, last Jagellon king of Poland, dies | *1572* New star discovered by Tycho Brahe | *1572* Camões' *Os Lusíadas* published |
| | | | | *1573* Veronese's *Feast in the House of Levi* |
| *1574* Relief of Leyden by sea-beggars | *1575* English College at Rome founded; Bohemian Confession | *1574* Henry III king of France *(→1589)* | | |
| *1576* "Spanish Fury" at Antwerp | | *1576* Rudolf II becomes emperor *(→1612)* | *1576* Tycho Brahe begins to build his observatory on Hven | |
| | *1577* Formula of Concord | | | *1577* El Greco moves to Spain |
| | *1578* Matteo Ricci begins missionary journeys in the East | *1578* Alessandro Farnese appointed governor of Netherlands | | |
| *1579* Union of Utrecht; peace of Arras | | | | *c 1579* Palladio commissioned to build Teatro Olimpico (Vicenza) |
| **1580** | | | | |
| *1580* Drake completes circumnavigation; Philip II of Spain occupies Portugal | *1580* Lutheran Book of Concord published | *1580* Carol Emmanuele I duke of Savoy *(→1630)* | | *1580* First two books of Montaigne's *Essais* published |
| | | | | *1581* Tasso's *Gerusalemme liberata* published |
| | | | *1582* Gregorian calendar reform | |
| *1583* Gilbert claims Newfoundland for England; Linschoten sails for India | | *1583* Emperor Rudolf II moves his capital to Prague | | |
| | | *1584* Assassination of William I the Silent of Orange | | |
| *1585* Drake raids Spanish possessions in New World; first attempt to found colony in Virginia; Spanish under Farnese capture Antwerp | *1585* Sixtus V pope | | *1585* First part of Mercator's *Atlas* published; Stevin's *De tiende* published | |
| *1586* Battle of Zutphen | | | | |
| *1587* Drake's raid on Cádiz | | *1587* Execution of Mary, Queen of Scots | | *1587* Marlowe's *Tamburlaine* acted |
| *1588* Spanish Armada; assassination of duke of Guise; Journée des Barricades (Paris); Cavendish completes circumnavigation | *1588* Start of Marprelate controversy | | | |

| Secular Events | Religion | Rulers | Sciences | Arts and Literature |
|---|---|---|---|---|
| | | *1589* Death of Catherine de' Medici; Henry of Navarre (Henry IV) first Bourbon king of France (→*1610*) | *1589* First edition of Hakluyt's compilation of voyages published | *1589* Guarini's *Il pastor fido* published |
| **1590** | | | | |
| *1590* Henry IV defeats Catholic forces at Ivry; Paris besieged | *1590* Urban VII pope; Gregory XIV pope | | | *1590* Sidney's *The Countesse of Pembroke's Arcadia* and first three books of Spenser's *Faerie Queene* published |
| | *1591* Innocent IX pope | | | |
| | *1592* Clement VIII pope | | | |
| | *1593* Henry IV of France converts to Catholicism; Swedes accept Lutheran catechism | | | *1593* Louis Elzevir publishing at Leyden |
| *1594* Philip II of Spain closes port of Lisbon to Dutch ships | *1594* First four books of Hooker's *Lawes of Ecclesiasticall Politie* published | | *c. 1594* Davis invents backstaff | |
| *1595* O'Neill's revolt in Ireland; Houtman explores trade routes to Asia; Raleigh explores Guiana | | | | |
| *1596* Sack of Cádiz; Barents overwinters in Arctic | | | | |
| *1598* Ferrara passes to papacy; southern Netherlands handed over to Archdukes Albert and Isabella | *1598* Edict of Nantes | *1598* Philip III king of Spain (→*1621*) | | |
| | | | *1599* Tycho Brahe settles in Prague | *1599* First part of Alemán's *Guzmán de Alfarache* published |
| **1600** | | | | |
| *1600* English East India Company granted charter | | *1600* Henry IV of France marries Marie de' Medici | | |
| *1602* Dutch East India Company granted charter | *1602* Piarists founded | | | |
| | | *1603* James I (VI of Scotland) first Stuart king of England (→*1625*) | | |
| | *1604* Hampton Court Conference | | | *1604* Van Mander's *Het Schilderboeck* published |
| *1605* Gunpowder Plot | *1605* Leo XI pope; Paul V pope | | *1605* Bacon's *The Advancement of Learning* published | *1605* First part of Cervantes' *Don Quixote* published |
| | | | | *1607* Monteverdi's *Orfeo* performed |
| | | *1608* Emperor Rudolf II forced to cede Hungary to Matthias | *1608* First mention of telescope | |
| *1609* Twelve-year truce agreed between Netherlands and Spain | *1609* Rudolf II grants concessions to Bohemia Protestants under Letter of Majesty | | *1609* Kepler's *Astronomia Nova* published; Galileo constructs astronomical telescope | |
| **1610** | | | | |
| | *1610* Arminian Remonstrance | *1610* Louis XIII king of France (→*1643*) with Marie de' Medici as regent | *1610* Galileo's *Sidereus nuncius* published | *1610* Rubens's *The Raising of the Cross* painted |

| Secular Events | Religion | Rulers | Sciences | Arts and Literature |
|---|---|---|---|---|
| *1611* War of Kalmar between Denmark and Sweden | *1611* Authorized Version of the Bible in English published | *1611* Gustavus II Adolphus king of Sweden (→1632) | *1611* Maurolico's *Photismi* (on lenses) published; Kepler invents celestial telescope | *1611* Shakespeare's last play, *The Tempest* |
| | | *1612* Matthias becomes emperor (→1619) | | |
| | | *1613* Michael first Romanov tsar of Russia (→1645) | *1614* Napier's book on logarithms published | |
| *1617* War between Sweden and Poland | *1618* Synod of Dort | *1617* Ferdinand of Styria elected king of Bohemia | | *1617* Duytsche Academie founded |
| *1618* Defenestration of Prague | *1619* Capuchins recognized as independent order | *1619* Ferdinand of Styria becomes emperor as Ferdinand II (→1637) | *1619* Kepler's *Harmonices mundi* published | |
| *1619* Execution of Oldenbarneveldt | | | | |

**1620** ————————————————————————————————————————————

| Secular Events | Religion | Rulers | Sciences | Arts and Literature |
|---|---|---|---|---|
| *1620* Battle of the White Mountain, first major engagement of Thirty Years' War | *1620* Pilgrim Fathers sail for America | | *1620* Bacon's *Novum organum* and Bürgi's work on logarithms published | |

# BIBLIOGRAPHY

The following is a list (necessarily highly selective) of accessible, English-language texts that take a general or panoramic view of the period in one or more of its major aspects. For works on individual figures, or more specific topics, the reader is referred to the Further Reading lists that accompany the relevant entries in the Encyclopedia. For reasons explained in the Preface, primary sources are generally discussed within the entries themselves. Although a number of older works such as the landmark studies by Berenson, Burckhart, and Cassirer, have been included here, the main emphasis is on recent texts reflecting the latest scholarship in the field.

Francis Ames-Lewis, *The Intellectual Life of the Early Renaissance Artist* (New Haven, Conn.: Yale University Press, 2000)

Frederic J. Baumgartner, *France in the Sixteenth Century* (New York and London: Palgrave Macmillan, 1995)

Michael Baxandall, *Painting and Experience in Fifteenth Century Italy: A Primer in the Social History of Pictorial Style* (Oxford, U.K.: Oxford University Press, 2nd ed. 1988)

Bernhard Berenson, *The Italian Painters of the Renaissance* (1952; new ed. New York: Ursus, 1998)

Sergio Bertelli, Franco Cardini, and Elvira Garberzorz, *The Courts of the Italian Renaissance* (New York: Facts on File, 1986)

Robert Birely, *The Refashioning of Catholicism, 1450–1700: A Reassessment of the Counter-Reformation* (Oxford, U.K.: Blackwell, 1987)

Robert Black (ed.), *Renaissance Thought: A Reader* (London: Routledge, 2001)

Anthony Blunt, *Art and Architecture in France 1500–1700* (London: Penguin, 1953; 5th ed. New Haven, Conn. and London: Yale University Press, 2001)

William James Bouwsma, *The Waning of the Renaissance 1550–1640* (New Haven, Conn.: Yale University Press, 2001; repr. 2002)

Fernand Braudel, *The Mediterranean and the Mediterranean World in the Age of Philip II*, 2 vols, transl. Sian Reynolds (New York: Harpers & Row, 1972, 73; concise ed. HarperCollins, 1992)

——, *Civilization and Capitalism, 15th–18th Century*, 3 vols, transl. Sian Reynolds (New York: Harpers & Row, 1983–86)

Jerry Brotton, *The Renaissance Bazaar: From the Silk Road to Michelangelo* (Oxford, U.K.: Oxford University Press, 2002)

Gene A. Brucker, *Renaissance Florence* (New York: Wiley, 1969; new ed. Berkeley, Calif.: University of California Press, 1983)

David Buisseret, *The Mapmakers' Quest: Depicting New Worlds in Renaissance Europe* (Oxford, U.K.: Oxford University Press, 2003)

Jacob Burckhart, *The Civilization of the Renaissance in Italy* (1860; new ed. New York: Penguin USA, 1990)

Peter Burke, *The Italian Renaissance* (Princeton, N.J.: Princeton University Press, 1987; 2nd ed. 1999)

——, *The European Renaissance: Centres and Peripheries* (Oxford, U.K.: Blackwell, 1998)

Gordon Campbell (ed.), *The Oxford Dictionary of the Renaissance* (Oxford, U.K. and New York: Oxford University Press, 2003)

Franco Cardini, *Europe 1492: Portrait of a Continent Five Hundred Years Ago* (New York: Facts on File, 1989)

Ernst Cassirer, *The Individual and the Cosmos in Renaissance Philosophy* (Oxford, U.K.: Blackwell, 1963: repr. New York: Dover, 2000)

Ernst Cassirer, Paul Oskar Kristeller, and John H. Randall, *The Renaissance Philosophy of Man: Petrarca, Valla, Ficino, Pico, Pomponazzi, Vives* (Chicago, Ill.: University of Chicago Press, 1948; repr. 1956)

Owen Chadwick, *The Early Reformation on the Continent* (Oxford, U.K.: Oxford University Press, 2001)

E. R. Chamberlin, *Everyday Life in Renaissance Times* (New York: Putnam, 1966; repr. 1980)

David Chambers, *The Imperial Age of Venice, 1380–1580* (London: Thames & Hudson, 1970)

Eric W. Cochrane, *Historians and Historiography in the Italian Renaissance* (Chicago, Ill.: and London: University of Chicago Press, 1981; repr. 1985)

Elizabeth S. and Thomas V. Cohen, *Daily Life in Renaissance Italy* (Westport, Conn.: Greenwood, 2001)

Bruce Cole, *Italian Art 1250–1550: The Relationship of Renaissance Art to Life and Society* (New York and London: Harper & Row, 1987)

Patricia Crawford and Sara Mendelson (eds), *Women in Early Modern Europe 1550–1720* (Oxford, U.K.: Clarendon Press, 1998; repr. Oxford University Press, 1999)

Brian Cummings, *The Literary Culture of the Reformation: Grammar and Grace* (Oxford, U.K.: Oxford University Press, 2002)

Nicholas S. Davidson, *The Counter-Reformation* (Oxford, U.K.: Blackwell, 1987)

Dirk De Vos, *The Flemish Primitives* (Princeton, N.J.: Princeton University Press and Amsterdam, Netherlands: Amsterdam University Press, 2003)

Arthur G. Dickens, *The Age of Humanism and Reformation: Europe in the Fourteenth, Fifteenth, and Sixteenth Centuries* (Eaglewood Cliffs, N.J.: Prentice Hall, 1972)

——, *The German Nation and Martin Luther* (London: Edwin Arnold, 1974)

C. Scott Dixon, *The Reformation in Germany* (Oxford, U.K.: Blackwell, 2002)

Samuel Dresden, *Humanism in the Renaissance* (London: Weidenfeld & Nicolson, 1968)

Eamon Duffy, *The Stripping of the Altars: Traditional Religion in England c. 1400–c. 1580* (New Haven, Conn. and London: Yale University Press, 1992)

Richard S. Dunn, *The Age of Religious Wars 1559–1715* (New York: W. W. Norton, 2nd ed. 1980)

Will Durant, *The Renaissance: A History of Civilization in Italy from 1304–1576* (New York: Simon & Schuster, 1955; repr. Fine Communications, 1997)

Elizabeth Eisenstein, *The Printing Press as an Agent of Change: Communications and Cultural Transformations in Early Modern Europe*, 2 vols (Cambridge, U.K.: Cambridge University Press, 1979; concise ed. 1993)

J. V. Field and Frank A. J. L. James (eds), *Renaissance and Revolution: Humanists, Scholars, Craftsmen, and Natural Philosophers in Early Modern Europe* (Cambridge, U.K.: Cambridge University Press, 1994; repr. 1998)

Paula Findlen (ed), *The Italian Renaissance: The Essential Readings* (Oxford, U.K.: Blackwell, 2003)

Patricia Fortini Brown, *Art and Life in Renaissance Venice, 1380–1580* (London: Thames & Hudson, 1970)

Richard Fremantle, *God and Money: Florence and the Medici in the Renaissance* (Florence, Italy: Olschki, 1992)

E. B. Fryde, *Humanism and Renaissance Historiography* (London: Hambledon, 1983)

Owen Gingerich, *The Eye of Heaven: Ptolemy, Copernicus, Kepler* (Berlin: Springer Verlag, 1993)

Joscelyn Godwin, *The Pagan Dream of the Renaissance* (Grand Rapids, Mich.: Phanes, 2002)

Kenneth Gouwens, *The Italian Renaissance: The Essential Sources* (Oxford, U.K.: Blackwell, 2003)

Anthony Grafton, *New Worlds, Ancient Texts: The Power of Tradition and the Shock of Discovery* (Cambridge, Mass.: Belknap Press of Harvard University Press, 1992; repr. 1995)

——, *Bring Out Your Dead: The Past as Revelation* (Cambridge, Mass.: Harvard University Press, 2002)

Stephen J. Greenblatt, *Marvelous Possessions: The Wonder of the New World* (Chicago, Ill.: University of Chicago Press and Oxford, U.K.: Clarendon Press, 1991)

John Guy, *Tudor England* (Oxford, U.K.: Oxford University Press, 1990; repr. 1997)

James Haar, *The Science and Art of Renaissance Music* (Princeton, N.J.: Princeton University Press, 1998)

John R. Hale, *Renaissance Exploration* (New York: W. W. Norton, 1972)

——, *A Concise Encyclopedia of the Italian Renaissance* (New York: W. W. Norton, 1981), illustrated ed. *The*

*Thames and Hudson Dictionary of the Italian Renaissance* (London: Thames & Hudson, 1985)

——, *War and Society in Renaissance Europe 1450–1620* (Leicester, U.K.: Leicester University Press and London: Fontana, 1985)

——, *The Civilization of Europe in the Renaissance* (New York: Scribner, 1994; repr. 1995)

James Hankins, *Plato in the Italian Renaissance*, 2 vols (Leyden, Netherlands: Brill, 1990; 3rd ed. 1994)

Ludwig H. Heydenrich and Wolfgang Lotz, *Architecture in Italy: 1400–1600* (London: Penguin, rev. ed. 1995)

Christopher Hibbert, *The House of Medici: Its Rise and Fall* (Harmondsworth, U.K.: Penguin, 1974; repr. Perennial, 1999)

Gerhart Hoffmeister, *The Renaissance and Reformation in Germany: An Introduction* (New York: Ungar, 1977)

Mary Hollingsworth, *Patronage in Renaissance Italy: From 1400 to the Early Sixteenth Century* (Baltimore, Md.: Johns Hopkins University Press, 1996)

George Holmes, *The Florentine Enlightenment, 1400–1450* (London: Weidenfeld & Nicolson, 1969; rev. ed. 1992)

——, *Florence, Rome and the Origins of the Renaissance* (Oxford, U.K.: Clarendon Press, 1986)

——, *Renaissance* (New York: St. Martin's Press, 1997)

Andrew Hopkins, *Italian Architecture: From Michelangelo to Borromini* (London: Thames & Hudson, 2002)

Johann Huizinga, *The Waning of the Middle Ages* (New York: Doubleday, 1954; new ed. Dover, 1999)

Norbert Huse and Wolfgang Wolters, *The Art of Renaissance Venice: Architecture, Sculpture and Painting 1460–1590* (Chicago, Ill.: University of Chicago Press, 1990)

Lorna Hutson (ed.), *Feminism and Renaissance Studies* (Oxford, U.K.: Oxford University Press, 1999)

James R. Jacob, *The Scientific Revolution: Aspirations and Achievements, 1500–1700* (Amherst, N.Y.: Humanity, 1998)

Lisa Jardine, *Worldly Goods: A New History of the Renaissance* (New York: W. W. Norton, 1998)

Lisa Jardine and Jerry Brotton, *Global Interests: Renaissance Art Between East and West* (Ithaca, N.Y.: Cornell University Press, 2000)

Martin D. W. Jones, *Clash of Empires: Europe 1498–1560* (Cambridge, U.K.: Cambridge University Press, 2001)

Norman Jones, *The English Reformation: Religion and Cultural Adaptation* (Oxford, U.K.: Blackwell, 2001)

H. A. F. Kamen, *The Spanish Inquisition: An Historical Revision* (London: Weidenfeld & Nicolson, 1965; new ed. Phoenix, 2000)

——, *Spain 1469–1714: Society of Conflict* (Reading, Mass.: Addison–Wesley, rev. ed. 1995)

David I. Kertzer and Marzio Barbagli (eds), *Family Life in Early Modern Times, 1500–1789* (New Haven, Conn.: Yale University Press, 2001)

Margaret L. King and Catharine R. Stimpson (eds), *Women of the Renaissance* (Chicago, Ill.: University of Chicago Press, 1991)

Christine Klapisch-Zuber, *Women, Family and Ritual in Renaissance Italy* (Chicago, Ill. and London: University of Chicago Press, 1985)

Angus Knostam, *A Historical Atlas of Exploration* (New York: Checkmark, 2000)

Jill Kraye (ed.), *The Cambridge Companion to Renaissance Humanism* (Cambridge, U.K.: Cambridge University Press, 1996)

Paul Oskar Kristeller, *Renaissance Thought and Its Sources* (New York: Columbia University Press, 1979; repr. 1981)

——, *Renaissance Thought and the Arts* (Princeton, N.J.: Princeton University Press, expanded ed. 1980; repr. 1990)

Thomas S. Kuhn, *The Copernican Revolution* (Cambridge, Mass.: Harvard University Press, 1966)

Michael Levey, *Florence: A Portrait* (London: Cape, 1996)

Bernard Lewis, *Cultures in Conflict: Christians, Muslims, and Jews in the Age of Discovery* (New York and Oxford, U.K.: Oxford University Press, 1994; repr. 1996)

Carter Lindberg, *The European Reformations* (Oxford, U.K.: Blackwell, 1996)

Wolfgang Lotz, *Studies in Italian Renaissance Architecture* (Cambridge, Mass. and London: MIT Press, 1977)

Guy F. Lytle and Stephen Orgel (eds), *Patronage in the Renaissance* (Princeton, N.J.: Princeton University Press, 1981)

Diarmuid MacCulloch, *Reformation: Europe's House Divided 1490–1700* (London: Allen Lane, 2003), as *The Reformation: A History* (New York: Penguin V. King, 2004)

Jo McMurtry, *Understanding Shakespeare's England: A Companion for the American Reader* (Hamden, Conn.: Archon, 1989)

Michael Mallett, *The Borgias: The Rise and Fall of a Renaissance Dynasty* (London: Bodley Head, 1969; new ed. Academy Chicago, 1987)

Robert L. R. Mandrou, *From Humanism to Science, 1480 to 1700*, transl. Brian Pearce (Harmondsworth, U.K.: Penguin, 1978)

Howard Margolis, *It Started With Copernicus: How Turning the World Inside Out Led to the Scientific Revolution* (New York: McGraw-Hill, 2002)

Lauro Martines, *Power and Imagination: City-States in Renaissance Italy* (New York: Random House, 1979; repr. Baltimore, Md.: Johns Hopkins University Press, 1988)

Ingrid Merkel and Alan G. Debus, *Hermeticism and the Renaissance: Intellectual History and the Occult in Early Modern Europe* (New York: Folger, 1988)

Samuel Eliot Morison, *The European Discovery of America*, 2 vols (New York: Oxford University Press, 1971, 74)

Richard A. Muller, *After Calvin: Studies in the Development of a Theological Tradition* (New York: Oxford University Press, 2003)

Michael Mullett, *The Catholic Reformation* (London: Routledge, 1999)

Peter Murray, *The Architecture of the Italian Renaissance* (New York: Schocken, 1986)

——, *Renaissance Architecture* (London: Faber, 1986)

Charles G. Nauert Jr, *Humanism and the Culture of Renaissance Europe* (Cambridge, U.K.: Cambridge University Press, 1995)

Kenneth Nebenzahl, *Atlas of Columbus and the Great Discoveries* (Chicago, Ill.: Rand McNally, 1990)

*The New Cambridge Modern History*: Vol. I *The Renaissance, 1493–1520*, ed. G. R. Potter (Cambridge, U.K.: Cambridge University Press, 1957)

——, Vol. II *The Reformation 1520–59*, ed. G. R. Elton (Cambridge, U.K.: Cambridge University Press, 1958)

——, Vol. III *The Counter-Reformation and Price Revolution, 1559–1610*, ed. R. B. Wernham (Cambridge, U.K.: Cambridge University Press, 1968)

*The New Oxford History of Music*: Vol. III *Ars Nova and the Renaissance, 1300–1540*, eds Anselm Hughes and Gerald Abraham (London: Oxford University Press, 1960)

——, Vol. IV *The Age of Humanism, 1540–1630*, ed. Gerald Abraham (London: Oxford University Press, 1968)

Bodo Nischan, *Lutherans and Calvinists in the Age of Confessionalism* (Aldershot, U.K.: Ashgate, 1999)

Steven Ozment, *The Age of Reform 1250–1550: An Intellectual and Religious History of Late Medieval and Restoration Europe* (New Haven, Conn.: Yale University Press, 1981; repr. 1986)

Peter Partner, *Renaissance Rome, 1500–1559: A Portrait of a Society* (Berkeley, Calif.: University of California Press, 1976)

J. H. Plumb, *The Italian Renaissance* (1961; repr. New York: American Heritage, 1986; expanded ed. Houghton Mifflin, 2001)

John Pope-Hennessy, *Italian Renaissance Sculpture* (1958; 3rd ed. Oxford, U.K.: Phaidon, 1986)

——, *Italian High Renaissance and Baroque Sculpture* (1963; new ed. Oxford, U.K.: Phaidon, 1986)

M. Prestwich, *International Calvinism, 1541–1715* (Oxford, U.K.: Clarendon Press and New York: Oxford University Press, 1986)

Eugene F. Rice Jr and Anthony Grafton, *The Foundations of Early Modern Europe 1460–1559* (New York: W. W. Norton, 2nd ed. 1994)

Ingrid D. Rowland, *The Culture of the High Renaissance: Ancients and Moderns in Sixteenth-Century Rome* (Cambridge, U.K.: Cambridge University Press, 1998)

Robert W. Scribner, *The German Reformation* (London: Macmillan, 1986; 2nd ed. Basingstoke, U.K.: Palgrave Macmillan, 2003)

Moses A. Shulvas, *The Jews in the World of the Renaissance*, transl. Elvin I. Kose (Leyden, Netherlands: Brill and Spartus College of Judaica Press, 1973)

Christine Smith, *Architecture in the Culture of Early Humanism: Ethics, Aesthetics and Eloquence, 1400–1470* (Oxford, U.K.: Oxford University Press, 1992)

James Snyder, *Northern Renaissance Art: Painting, Sculpture, the Graphic Arts from 1350 to 1575* (New York: Harry N. Abrams and New Jersey: Prentice Hall, 1985)

Roy Strong, *Splendor at Court: Renaissance Spectacle and the Theater of Power* (Boston, Mass.: Houghton Mifflin, 1973)

Margo Todd, *Christian Humanism and the Puritan Social Order* (Cambridge, U.K.: Cambridge University Press, 1988)

Rolf Toman and Achim Bednorz, *The Baroque: Architecture, Sculpture, Painting* (Cologne, Germany and New York: Konemann, 1998)

Hugh Trevor-Roper, *The European Witch Craze of the 16th and 17th Centuries* (Harmondsworth, U.K.: Penguin, 1969)

——, *Renaissance Essays* (Chicago, Ill.: University of Chicago Press, 1989)

Charles E. Trinkhaus, *In Our Image and Likeness: Humanity and Divinity in Italian Humanist Thought*, 2 vols (Chicago, Ill.: Chicago University Press and London: Constable, 1970; new ed. University of Notre Dame Press, 1995)

——, *The Scope of Renaissance Humanism* (Ann Arbor, Mich.: University of Michigan Press, 1983)

Brian Vickers (ed), *Occult and Scientific Mentalities in the Renaissance* (Cambridge, U.K.: Cambridge University Press, 1984)

Kim Walker, *Women Writers of the English Renaissance* (New York: Twayne, 1996)

Charles Webster, *From Paracelsus to Newton: Magic and the Making of Modern Science* (Cambridge, U.K.: Cambridge University Press, 1982)

Evelyn S. Welch, *Art and Society in Italy 1350–1500* (New York and Oxford, U.K.: Oxford University Press, 1997)

Peter H. Wilson, *The Holy Roman Empire 1495–1806* (New York and London: Palgrave Macmillan, 1999)

Rudolf Wittkower, *Architectural Principles in the Age of Humanism* (Chichester, U.K.: Academy Editions, 5th ed. 1998)

Charles Zika, *Exorcising Our Demons: Magic, Witchcraft and Visual Culture in Early Modern Europe* (Leyden, Netherlands: Brill, 2003)

# INDEX

Although the alphabetical arrangement and copious cross-references in the main Encyclopedia text make it largely self-indexing, the following index of historical figures provides an additional resource. Page numbers in slightly larger **bold type** indicate main entries; those in *italic* refer to illustrations (including family trees) and their associated captions. The symbol ❖, followed by a roman numeral, refers to the section of color plates at the center of the book.